23rd Iberoamerican Conference on Software Engineering (CIbSE 2020)

Online
6 – 9 May 2020

ISBN: 978-1-7138-1853-3

Printed from e-media with permission by:

Curran Associates, Inc.
57 Morehouse Lane
Red Hook, NY 12571

Some format issues inherent in the e-media version may also appear in this print version.

Printed with permission by Curran Associates, Inc. (2020)

For permission requests, please contact CIbSE - IberoAmerican Conference on Software Engineering at the address below.

CIbSE - IberoAmerican Conference on Software Engineering
c/o Luca Cernuzzi
Universidad Católica "Nuestra Seóra de la Asunción",
Campus Universitario, Asunción
Barrio Santa Ana, C.C.1683, C.P. 1364
Asunción - Paraguay

Phone: +595 21 334650
Fax: +595 21 310587

lcernuzz@uca.edu.py

Additional copies of this publication are available from:

Curran Associates, Inc.
57 Morehouse Lane
Red Hook, NY 12571 USA
Phone: 845-758-0400
Fax: 845-758-2633
Email: curran@proceedings.com
Web: www.proceedings.com

Session 1: Software Quality

Herramientas para pruebas automatizadas de seguridad en aplicaciones Web: Un mapeo sistemático de la literature 1

Elizabeth Gamboa (Universidad de Costa Rica, Costa Rica)

Christian Quesada-López (Universidad de Costa Rica, Costa Rica)

Alexandra Martínez (Universidad de Costa Rica, Costa Rica)

Marcelo Jenkins (Universidad de Costa Rica, Costa Rica)

Identification of quality characteristics in mobile applications 15

Vitor Carneiro Maia (Universidade Federal do Rio de Janeiro/UFRJ - COPPE, Brasil)

Ana Regina Cavalcanti da Rocha (Universidade Federal do Rio de Janeiro/UFRJ - COPPE, Brasil)

Taisa Guidini Gonçalves (Universidade Federal do Rio de Janeiro/UFRJ - COPPE, Brasil)

La representación del diseño detallado utilizando plantillas y sus efectos en la calidad del software 29

Silvana Moreno (Universidad de la República, Uruguay)

Vanessa Casella (Universidad de la República, Uruguay)

Martín Solari (Universidad de la República, Uruguay)

Diego Vallespir (Universidad de la República, Uruguay)

Session 2: Software Architecture and Microservices

Selection Methods for Criticality in Microservices Architectures: A Systematic Mapping 43

Eduardo F. Mioto de Oliveira dos Santos (Universidade Federal do Rio de Janeiro/UFRJ - COPPE, Brasil)

Claudia Maria Lima Werner (Universidade Federal do Rio de Janeiro/UFRJ - COPPE, Brasil)

Marcelo de França Costa (Universidade Federal do Rio de Janeiro/UFRJ - COPPE, Brasil)

Frameworks and High-Availability in Microservices: An Industrial Survey 57

Gastón Márquez (Universidad Técnica Federico Santa María, Chile)

Jacopo Soldani (Università di Pisa, Italy)

Francisco Ponce (Universidad Técnica Federico Santa María, Chile)

Hernán Astudillo (Universidad Técnica Federico Santa María, Chile)

Approaches for Describing Reference Architectures: A Systematic Mapping Study 71

Pedro Henrique Dias Valle (University of São Paulo - ICMC-USP, Brazil)

Lina Garcés (University of São Paulo - ICMC-USP, Brazil)

Milena Guessi (University of São Paulo - ICMC-USP, Brazil)

Silverio Martínez-Fernández (Universitat Politècnica de Catalunya, Spain)

Elisa Yumi Nakagawa (University of São Paulo - ICMC-USP, Brazil)

Session 3: IoT

Managing Evolution of API-driven IoT Devices through Adaptation Chains 85

Rafael Bustamante (Department of Systems and Computing Engineering, Universidad de los Andes, Colombia)

Kelly Garcés (Department of Systems and Computing Engineering, Universidad de los Andes, Colombia)

Performance Evaluation of Kubernetes as Deployment Platform for IoT Devices 96

Alessandro Caetano Beltrão (Universidade Federal do Rio de Janeiro/UFRJ - COPPE, Brasil)

Breno Bernard Nicolau de França (University of Campinas, UNICAMP, Brazil)

Guilherme Horta Travassos (Universidade Federal do Rio de Janeiro/UFRJ - COPPE, Brasil)

Session 4: Configuration Management

Commit Classification using Natural Language Processing: Experiments over Labeled Datasets 110

Geanderson E. dos Santos (Federal University of Minas Gerais, Brazil)

Eduardo Figueiredo (Federal University of Minas Gerais, Brazil)

STONE: A Software Configuration Management Process for Academic Projects 124

Rebeca M. Pontes (Universidade Federal do Ceará, Russas, Brasil)

Valéria Lelli (Universidade Federal do Ceará, Fortaleza, Brasil)

Software system deployment process: A systematic mapping study 138

Marisa Panizzi (National University of La Plata, La Plata, Argentina)

Marcela Genero (University of Castilla-La Mancha, Ciudad Real, Spain)

Rodolfo Bertone (National University of La Plata, La Plata, Argentina)

Session 5: Software Process and Product Lines

Prevenção de Anomalias Arquiteturais na Otimização de Projeto de Linha de Produto 152

Tiago Tadeu Madrigar (Universidade Estadual do Maringá, Brasil)

Thelma Elita Colanzi (Universidade Estadual do Maringá, Brasil)

Willian Oizumi (PUC-Rio - Rio de Janeiro, RJ, Brasil)

Alessandro Garcia (PUC-Rio - Rio de Janeiro, RJ, Brasil)

Empirical Study on Product Configuration and Traceability in UML-based Product-Lines 166

Thais Nepomuceno (State University of Maringá, Brazil)

Edson OliveiraJr (State University of Maringá, Brazil)

Raqueline Penteado (State University of Maringá, Brazil)

Marco A. Graciotto Silva (Federal University of Technology, Campo Mourão, Brazil)

Avelino F. Zorzo (Pontifical Catholic University of Rio Grande do Sul, PUCRS, Brazil)

Evaluating the Usefulness and Ease of Use of a Software Process Line Tool 180

Diogo Matheus Costa (Universidade Federal do Rio de Janeiro/UFRJ - COPPE, Brasil)

Eldânae Nogueira Teixeira (Universidade Federal do Rio de Janeiro/UFRJ - COPPE, Brasil)

Cláudia Maria Lima Werner (Universidade Federal do Rio de Janeiro/UFRJ - COPPE, Brasil)

Session 6: Agile Methods

Elicitação de Requisitos em Metodologias Ágeis: Um Mapeamento Sistemático da Literatura 194

Ramon Fonseca (Federal University of Rio Grande do Norte, Brazil)

João Carlos Epifânio (Federal University of Rio Grande do Norte, Brazil)

Luana Souza (Federal University of Rio Grande do Norte, Brazil)

Marcia Lucena (Federal University of Rio Grande do Norte, Brazil)

A comparative study on measuring software functional size to support effort estimation in agile 208

Fabián Ugalde (University of Costa Rica, San Pedro, Costa Rica)

Christian Quesada-López (University of Costa Rica, San Pedro, Costa Rica)

Alexandra Martínez (University of Costa Rica, San Pedro, Costa Rica)

Marcelo Jenkins (University of Costa Rica, San Pedro, Costa Rica)

Ciencia de datos y Agilidad: una revisión de la literature 222

Paula B. Lima (CInApTIC, UTN Facultad Regional Resistencia, Chaco, Argentina)

Gabriel E. Giana (CInApTIC, UTN Facultad Regional Resistencia, Chaco, Argentina)

Verónica Andrea Bollati (CONICET - CInApTIC, UTN Facultad Regional Resistencia, Chaco, Argentina)

Liliana Cuenca Pletsch (CInApTIC, UTN Facultad Regional Resistencia, Chaco, Argentina)

Session 7: Requirements Engineering

Recomendações de técnicas complementares de elicitação de requisitos em um guia facetado 236

Nathália Liz de Brito (Universidade Federal de Santa Catarina, Brasil)

Fabiane Barreto Vavassori Benitti (Universidade Federal de Santa Catarina, Brasil)

Avaliando o processo de derivação de casos de uso a partir de i* e BPMN e suporte computacional 250

Gustavo Cesar Lopes Geraldino (Universidade Estadual do Oeste do Parana, Brasil)

Rafael Gomes da Silva (Universidade Estadual do Oeste do Parana, Brasil)

Victor Francisco Araya Santander (Universidade Estadual do Oeste do Parana, Brasil)

Avaliação de Abordagem Centrada em Modelos Conceituais em OntoUML para Apoiar a Derivação de Requisitos Funcionais 264

Joselaine Valaski (Pontifícia Universidade Católica do Paraná - PUCPR, Brasil)

Sheila Reinehr (Pontifícia Universidade Católica do Paraná - PUCPR, Brasil)

Andreia Malucelli (Pontifícia Universidade Católica do Paraná - PUCPR, Brasil)

Session 8: Runtime Analysis

Técnicas de aprendizaje automático para mejorar el rendimiento de aplicaciones web: un mapeo sistemático de literature 278

Jean Carlo Zúñiga-Madrigal (Universidad de Costa Rica, San Pedro, Costa Rica)

Christian Quesada-López (Universidad de Costa Rica, San Pedro, Costa Rica)

Marcelo Jenkins (Universidad de Costa Rica, San Pedro, Costa Rica)

Alexandra Martínez (Universidad de Costa Rica, San Pedro, Costa Rica)

Perfil Operacional do Software: investigando aplicabilidades específicas 292

Luiz Cavamura Júnior (Universidade Federal de São Carlos, UFSCar, Brasil)

Sandra Fabbri (Universidade Federal de São Carlos, UFSCar, Brasil)

Auri M. R. Vincenzi (Universidade Federal de São Carlos, UFSCar, Brasil)

How Difficult and Effective is Writing Assertions for Observing Bugs at Runtime? 306

Fischer Ferreira (Federal University of Minas Gerais, UFMG, Brazil)

Eduardo Fernandes (Pontifical Catholic University of Rio de Janeiro, PUC-Rio, Brazil)

Johnatan Oliveira (Federal University of Minas Gerais, UFMG, Brazil)

Maurício Souza (Federal University of Lavras, UFLA, Brazil)

Eduardo Figueiredo (Federal University of Minas Gerais, UFMG, Brazil)

Session 9: New Generation of Requirements Engineering Approaches

Design Thinking in Software Requirements: What Techniques to Use? A Proposal for a Recommendation Tool 320

Rafael Parizi (Pontifícia Universidade do Rio Grande do Sul, PUCRS, Brasil)

Marina Moreira da Silva (Pontifícia Universidade do Rio Grande do Sul, PUCRS, Brasil)

Igor Couto (Pontifícia Universidade do Rio Grande do Sul, PUCRS, Brasil)

Kendra Trindade (Pontifícia Universidade do Rio Grande do Sul, PUCRS, Brasil)

Matheus Plautz (Pontifícia Universidade do Rio Grande do Sul, PUCRS, Brasil)

Sabrina Marczak (Pontifícia Universidade do Rio Grande do Sul, PUCRS, Brasil)

Tayana Conte (Universidade Federal do Amazonas, UFAM, Manaus, Brasil)

Heloisa Candello (Conversation Intelligence group – IBM Research Lab, São Paulo, Brasil)

Handling Nonfunctional Requirements for Smart Cities 334

Isabel Sofia Brito (Polytechnic Institute of Beja, Portugal)

Ana Moreira (Universidade NOVA de Lisboa, Portugal)

João Araújo (Universidade NOVA de Lisboa, Portugal)

Uma Tecnologia para Apoiar a Engenharia de Requisitos de Sistemas de Software IoT 342

Danyllo Valente da Silva (Universidade Federal do Rio de Janeiro/UFRJ - COPPE, Brasil)

Bruno Pedraça de Souza (Universidade Federal do Rio de Janeiro/UFRJ - COPPE, Brasil)

Taisa Guidini Gonçalves (Universidade Federal do Rio de Janeiro/UFRJ - COPPE, Brasil)

Guilherme Horta Travassos (Universidade Federal do Rio de Janeiro/UFRJ - COPPE, Brasil)

Session 10: Software Testing

Towards Supporting the Specification of Context-Aware Software System Test Cases 356

Andréa Cristina de Souza Doreste (Universidade Federal do Rio de Janeiro/UFRJ - COPPE, Brasil)

Guilherme Horta Travassos (Universidade Federal do Rio de Janeiro/UFRJ - COPPE, Brasil)

TestTDO: A Top-Domain Software Testing Ontology 364

Guido Tebes (Facultad de Ingeniería, UNLPam, Argentina)

Luis Olsina (Facultad de Ingeniería, UNLPam, Argentina)

Denis Peppino (Facultad de Ingeniería, UNLPam, Argentina)

Pablo Becker (Facultad de Ingeniería, UNLPam, Argentina)

Specifying the Design Science Research Process: An Applied Case of Building a Software Testing Ontology 378

Guido Tebes (Facultad de Ingeniería, UNLPam, Argentina)

Belen Rivera (Facultad de Ingeniería, UNLPam, Argentina)

Pablo Becker (Facultad de Ingeniería, UNLPam, Argentina)

Maria Fernanda Papa (Facultad de Ingeniería, UNLPam, Argentina)

Denis Peppino (Facultad de Ingeniería, UNLPam, Argentina)

Luis Olsina (Facultad de Ingeniería, UNLPam, Argentina)

Session 11: Knowledge and Project Management

Knowledge Management in Human-Computer Interaction Design: A Mapping Study 392

Murillo Vasconcelos H. B. Castro (Federal University of Espírito Santo, UFES, Brazil)

Simone Dornelas Costa (Federal University of Espírito Santo, UFES, Brazil)

Monalessa P. Barcellos (Federal University of Espírito Santo, UFES, Brazil)

Ricardo de A. Falbo (Federal University of Espírito Santo, UFES, Brazil)

Extraction of Useful Information from Unstructured Data in Software Engineering: A Systematic Mapping 406

Patrick R. Silva (Federal University of Technology - Paraná, UTFPR, Cornélio Procópio - Brazil)

Vinicius dos Santos (Universidade de São Paulo, São Carlos - Brazil)

Érica F. Souza (Federal University of Technology - Paraná, UTFPR, Cornélio Procópio - Brazil)

Giovani V. Meinerz (Federal University of Technology - Paraná, UTFPR, Cornélio Procópio - Brazil)

Katia R. Felizardo (Federal University of Technology - Paraná, UTFPR, Cornélio Procópio - Brazil)

Nandamudi L. Vijaykumar (National Institute for Space Research, Brazil)

Método Multicritério Aplicado à Priorização dos Desafios da Gerência de Projetos em Desenvolvimento Distribuído de Software 420

Maycon Amorim dos Santos (State University of Maringá, Brazil)

Douglas Rorie Tanno State University of Maringá, Brazil)

Renato Balancieri (State University of Paraná, Brazil)

Gislaine Camila Lapasini Leal (State University of Maringá, Brazil)

Edwin Vladimir Cardoza Galdamez (State University of Maringá, Brazil)

Session 12: Bad Smells and Defects

Revisiting the Bad Smell and Refactoring Relationship: A Systematic Literature Review 434

Cleiton Silva (Federal University of Minas Gerais, Brazil)

Amanda Santana (Federal University of Minas Gerais, Brazil)

Eduardo Figueiredo (Federal University of Minas Gerais, Brazil)

Mariza A. S. Bigonha (Federal University of Minas Gerais, Brazil)

Predicción de Defectos Usando Métricas Estáticas y de Cambio: un caso de estudio en un Lenguaje Dinámicamente Tipado 448

Mauro Gullino (Universidad Tecnológica Nacional, Buenos Aires, Argentina)

Gabriela Robiolo (Universidad Austral, Pilar, Argentina)

A survey on test practitioners' awareness of test smells 462

Nildo Silva Junior (Federal University of Bahia - UFBA, Brazil)

Larissa Rocha (Federal University of Bahia - UFBA, Brazil)

Luana Almeida Martins (Federal University of Bahia - UFBA, Brazil)

Ivan Machado (Federal University of Bahia - UFBA, Brazil)

Session 13: Human Aspects and Software Transparency

Technical knowledge and soft skills in the founding teams of software startups 476

Gerardo Matturro (Universidad ORT Uruguay, Montevideo, Uruguay)

Martín Solari (Universidad ORT Uruguay, Montevideo, Uruguay)

Angélica Buffa (Universidad ORT Uruguay, Montevideo, Uruguay)

Diego Febbles (Universidad ORT Uruguay, Montevideo, Uruguay)

Análise Comparativa das Características e Impactos de Conflitos Interpessoais no Contexto da Engenharia de Requisitos 490

Gustavo Dias Alexandre (Universidade de Pernambuco, Recife, Brasil)

Maria Lencastre (Universidade de Pernambuco, Recife, Brasil)

Mapeamento de Critérios de Aceitação de Transparência de Software para Testes Automatizados 504

Bruno Luiz Gonçalves (Universidade Federal de Santa Catarina, Brasil)

Ernani César Dos Santos (Universidade Federal de Santa Catarina, Brasil)

Patrícia Vilain (Universidade Federal de Santa Catarina, Brasil)

Session 14: Software Engineering Education and Training

Systematic mapping on the use of games for software engineering education 512

Diego Castro (Federal University of Rio de Janeiro, Brazil)

Diogo Matheus Costa (Federal University of Rio de Janeiro, Brazil)

Cláudia Maria Lima Werner (Federal University of Rio de Janeiro, Brazil)

Evaluating the Students' Experience with a requirements elicitation and communication game 526

Jéssyka Vilela (Universidade Federal de Pernambuco, Brasil)

Jonas Lopes (Universidade Federal do Ceará, Brasil)

Teaching Scrum Practices with the Support of Brazilian Startups: an Initiative in Software Engineering Course 540

Leo Natan Paschoal (Institute of Mathematics and Computer Sciences – University of São Paulo, Brazil)

Simone R. S. Souza (Institute of Mathematics and Computer Sciences – University of São Paulo, Brazil)

Session 15: Agility and Testing

Combining Design Thinking and Scrum to enhance Test Suite during innovative software development 554

Flávia Lobato de Morais (SIDIA - Institute of Science and Technology, Manaus, Brazil)

Awdren Fontão (FACOM - Federal University of Mato Grosso do Sul, Brasil)

Sergio Cleger Tamayo (SIDIA - Institute of Science and Technology, Manaus, Brazil)

Model-Based Testing in Agile Projects: An Approach Based on Domain-Specific Languages 568

Aline Zanin (PUCRS - Porto Alegre, Brazil)

Avelino Fracisco Zorzo (PUCRS - Porto Alegre, Brazil)

Henry Cabral Nunes (PUCRS - Porto Alegre, Brazil)

Posters

iStar4G: Estendendo a linguagem iStar 2.0 para modelagem de jogos digitais 582

Sanderson de Paula Barbosa (Departamento de Computação, UFRRJ, Seropédica, Brasil)

André Luiz de Castro Leal (Departamento de Computação, UFRRJ, Seropédica, Brasil)

Quality-based Methodology for Assessing the Applicability of Microservices Architecture 590

Andrés Nebel (Universidad de la República, Montevideo, Uruguay)

Laura González (Universidad de la República, Montevideo, Uruguay)

Uso de experimentação contínua para a instrumentação e o empacotamento do coorte PIPA UFRJ 598

Luciana Nascimento (PESC/COPPE-UFRJ, Brasil)

Cecilia Apa (Fing/UdelaR, Uruguay)

Diego Cerqueira (PESC/COPPE-UFRJ, Brasil)

Michael Rassu (Avignon Université, França)

Vladimir Erthal (PESC/COPPE-UFRJ, Brasil)

Vitor Maia (PESC/COPPE-UFRJ, Brasil)

Thatiana Fernandes (IESC-UFRJ, Brasil)

Guilherme Horta Travassos (PESC/COPPE-UFRJ, Brasil)

SmartMoving: una aplicación para peatones con movilidad reducida 606

Mónica Fatecha (Universidad Católica Nuestra Señora de la Asunción, Paraguay)

Patricia Fauvety (Universidad Católica Nuestra Señora de la Asunción, Paraguay)

Nathalie Aquino (Universidad Católica Nuestra Señora de la Asunción, Paraguay)

Magalí Gonzáalez (Universidad Católica Nuestra Señora de la Asunción, Paraguay)

Daniel Romero (Universidad Católica Nuestra Señora de la Asunción, Paraguay)

Luca Cernuzzi (Universidad Católica Nuestra Señora de la Asunción, Paraguay)

Javier Paniagua (Universidad de Trento, Italy)

Ronald Chenú-Abente (Universidad de Trento, Italy)

Descripción de code smells: Enfoque ontológico 614

Ivian Laobel Castellano Betancourt (Universidad de las Ciencias Informáticas, Habana, Cuba)

Nemury Silega Martínez (Universidad de las Ciencias Informáticas, Habana, Cuba)

Katya Martha Faggioni Colombo (Universidad de Guayaquil, Guayaquil, Ecuador)

Gilberto F. Castro (Universidad de Guayaquil, Guayaquil, Ecuador)

Doctoral Symposium

A Framework to support the Experimental Evaluation Process of the Pedagogical Conversational Systems 622

Leo Natan Paschoal (Institute of Mathematics and Computer Sciences – University of São Paulo, Brazil)

Software Deployment and Self-adaptation of IoT Systems 630

Iván Alfonso (Universidad de los Andes, Bogotá, Colombia)

A Test Strategy for Configurable Software Systems Using Machine Learning 638

Fischer Ferreira (Federal University of Minas Gerais, Brazil)

Preface

On behalf of the CIbSE Organizing Committee, we are proud to present the proceedings of the 23rd Iberoamerican Conference on Software Engineering (CIbSE 2020), originally planned to be held in Curitiba, Brazil. The hosting institution is the Pontifícia Universidade Católica of Paraná.

CIbSE is the leading research forum on Software Engineering (SE) in Ibero-America. Its primary objective is to promote high-quality scientific research in Ibero-American countries and, thus, support the researchers in this community in publishing and discussing their work. In addition, the conference fosters collaboration and cross-fertilization among academics, students, and practitioners from the industry. CIbSE has distinct characteristics as it welcomes contributions in three languages: Portuguese, Spanish, or English. It is backed by 22 previous conferences held in various countries:

Torres, Brazil (IDEAS'98)
San José, Costa Rica (IDEAS'99)
Cancun, Mexico (IDEAS'00)
Heredia, Costa Rica (IDEAS'01)
Habana, Cuba (IDEAS'02)
Asunción, Paraguay (IDEAS'03)
Arequipa, Peru (IDEAS'04)
Valparaiso, Chile (IDEAS'05)
La Plata, Argentina (IDEAS'06)
Isla Margarita, Venezuela (IDEAS'07)
Recife, Brazil (IDEAS'08)
Medellín, Colombia (IDEAS'09)
Cuenca, Ecuador (CIbSE'10)
Rio de Janeiro, Brazil (CIbSE'11)
Buenos Aires, Argentina (CIbSE'12)
Montevideo, Uruguay (CIbSE'13)
Pucón, Chile (CIbSE'14)
Lima, Peru (CIbSE'15)
Quito, Ecuador (CIbSE'16)
Buenos Aires, Argentina (CIbSE'17)
Bogotá, Colombia (CIbSE'18)
La Habana, Cuba (CIbSE'19).

CIbSE is an evolution of the successful Iberoamerican Workshop on Environments and Software Requirements Engineering (IDEAS), which began in 1998. It was strengthened with the integration of two specialized events: the Workshop on Requirements Engineering (WER) in 2010 and the Experimental Software Engineering Latin American Workshop (ESELAW) in 2011. As a result, nowadays CIbSE consists of three tracks. The issues related to Requirements Engineering are discussed under the RET track, while

Experimental Software Engineering topics are handled by ESELAW track. All remaining Software Engineering themes are discussed under the SET Track. In addition, CIbSE hosts a Doctoral Symposium (DS), aiming at bringing together doctoral students working on foundations, techniques, tools, and applications of SE and giving them the opportunity to present and discuss their research in a constructive and international atmosphere.

CIbSE has also hosted the Advanced Ibero-American School on Software Engineering (EIbAIS) and the Industry Talks. EIbAIS aims at promoting a forum for discussions regarding SE and its related technologies and theoretical foundations, allowing the participation of practitioners, undergraduate and graduate students, and researchers in the conference's activities. Industry Talks aim at providing the industry and practitioners means to discuss and work together in exploring how SE processes, methods, techniques, and tools can provide the industry with better solutions. Furthermore, partnering with the Journal of Software Engineering Research and Development (JSERD), this edition of CIbSE incorporates a Journal First paper presentation into the CIbSE main tracks.

A Program Committee formed by leading experts in the topics of the corresponding tracks selected the technical program. This year, 128 papers were submitted. Each submission was reviewed by at least three members of the Program Committee. After thorough discussions based on the reviews and overall assessments, 49 papers were finally selected in all tracks (38% acceptance rate).

In line with CIbSE's spirit, a plural program was prepared. The keynote speakers were among the main conference highlights. Margaret Burnett (Oregon State University, USA and ACM Distinguished Speaker) addresses gender inclusiveness in software companies, a relevant aspect in today's society. Oscar Pastor (Universidad Politécnica de Valencia, Spain) discusses the application of advanced conceptual models and data science technologies to understand the secrets of life that the genome code hides. Guilherme Travassos (COPPE/UFRJ, Brazil) provides an insightful discussion on the challenges of SE for contemporary software systems. In addition, four contemporary tutorials on the subjects of process mining, design thinking, continuous software engineering, and gender management are offered by relevant researchers in the SE community: Edson Scalabrin, Frederick van Amstel, Breno de França, and Margaret Burnett, respectively.

We are thankful for the opportunity of serving as chairs for this conference. The Program Committee members and reviewers provided excellent support in selecting the papers. We are also grateful to all authors of submitted manuscripts, presenters, and session chairs for their time and effort in making CIbSE 2020 a success. We would also like to thank the CIbSE Steering Committee members for the guidance and support in the organization process as well as the track chairs that did a great job in their corresponding tracks.

Furthermore, this year, humanity has experienced turbulent changes due to the emergence of COVID-19 in most countries and has had to adapt to exceptional situations. In this context, CIbSE was first postponed from its original dates in May to November. Then, we opted to run CIbSE in a virtual format, free of charges for authors and participants. We thank all the keynotes, tutorialist, authors, and participants for their willingness to adapt to the situation and our special recognition to everyone in the organization team for making CIbSE 2020 possible. Its experience will live in the participants' memory for years to come.

Claudia Ayala
Leonardo Murta

PC-General Chairs

Andreia Malucelli
Sheila Reinehr

General Organizing Chairs

Organizing Committee

General Chair

Andreia Malucelli (PUCPR, Brazil)

Sheila Reinehr (PUCPR, Brazil)

General Program Co-Chairs

Claudia Ayala (UPC, Spain)

Leonardo Murta (UFF, Brazil)

Software Engineering Track (SET) Chairs

Daniela Soares Cruzes (SINTEF, Norway)

Eduardo Figueiredo (UFMG, Brazil)

Requirements Engineering Track (RET) Chairs

Carla Silva (UFPE, Brazil)

Jose Luis de la Vara (UCLM, Spain)

Empirical Software Engineering Track (ESELAW) Chairs

Breno França (UNICAMP, Brazil)

Martin Solari (ORT, Uruguay)

Ibero-American School on Software Engineering (EIbAIS) Chairs

Luca Cernuzzi (UC, Paraguay)

Monalessa Perini Barcellos (UFES, Brazil)

Doctoral Symposium (DS) Chairs

Guilherme Horta Travassos (COPPE/UFRJ, Brazil)

Oscar Pastor (UPV, Spain)

Industry Talks Chairs

Marco Paludo (PUCPR, Brazil)

Rafael Prikladnicki (PUC-RS, Brazil)

Publicity Chairs

Marcela Genero (University of Castilla-La Mancha, Spain)

Tayana Uchôa Conte (UFAM, Brazil)

Proceedings Chair

Ivan Machado (UFBA, Brazil)

Webmaster

Luan Melo (PUCPR, Brazil)

SET Preface

Welcome to the Software Engineering Track (SET) at the 23rd Ibero-American Conference on Software Engineering (CIbSE 2020), originally planned to be held in Curitiba, Brazil. SET is a forum where researchers and practitioners from the Ibero-American community may report and discuss new research results in all areas of Software Engineering, except for topics in requirements engineering and empirical software engineering, which are discussed in the corresponding specialized tracks.

Of course, a conference would not be a success without the hard work of the many researchers and practitioners who submitted their papers for review. We received submissions in many different topics in Software Engineering. This year we have updated the topics to accommodate topics related to software engineering in emerging practices (e.g., cloud computing, big data applications, IoT, cyber-physical systems, socio-technical systems, block chains, etc.).

This year, the SET track received 72 submissions. After a careful peer-review process, the conference accepted 25 papers yielding an acceptance rate of 34,72%. In addition, 3 papers will be presented as posters at CIbSE 2020. Each paper received 3 reviews from members of the program committee, and was individually discussed before the final decision. We would like to thank the time and effort of the 67 members of the program committee, who were globally distributed across 18 countries, for helping to select such a high quality program.

We would like to gratefully acknowledge the hard work of the organizing committee that has done a great work on leading the work in each step of the process.

Once again, we welcome you to the SET- CIbSE 2020 and are excited about the wonderful conference program that so many have contributed to in so many ways.

Daniela Soares Cruzes, Eduardo Figueiredo
CIbSE 2020- SET Track Chairs

Program Committee – SET Track

Alejandra Garrido (Universidad Nacional de la Plata, Argentina)
Alejandro Catala (University of Santiago de Compostela, Spain)
Alexandre Bergel (University of Chile, Chile)
Ana Paiva (University of Porto, Portugal)
Andre Cavalcante Hora (Universidade Federal de Minas Gerais, Brazil)
Antonio Brogi (Universita di Pisa, Italy)
Antonio Rito Silva (Universidade de Lisboa, Portugal)
Beatriz Marin (Universidad Diego Portales, Chile)
Brenda Leticia Flores (Universidad Autonoma de Baja California, Mexico)
Carlos Cetina (Universidad San Jorge, Spain)
Claudia Pons (Universidad Nacional de La Plata, Argentina)
Claudio Sant'Anna (Universidade Federal da Bahia, Brazil)
Daniel Romero (Universidad Nacional de Asuncion, Paraguay)
Daniela Cruzes (SINTEF, Norway)
Daniela Godoy (Universidad Nacional del Centro de la Provincia de Buenos Aires, Argentina)
Davi Viana (Universidade Federal do Maranhao, Brazil)
David Benavides (Universidad de Sevilla, Spain)
Diego Vallespir (Universidad de la Republica, Uruguay)
Dolors Costal (Universitat Politecnica de Catalunya, Spain)
Eduardo Figueiredo (Universidade Federal de Minas Gerais, Brazil)
Elena Navarro (Universidad de Castilla-La Mancha, Spain)
Ernest Teniente (Universitat Politecnica de Catalunya, Spain)
Ernesto Pimentel (Universidad de Malaga, Spain)
Eugenio Scalise (Universidad Central de Venezuela, Venezuela)
Fabio Costa (Universidade Federal de Goias, Brazil)
Fernando Brito e Abreu (Instituto Universitário de Lisboa, Portugal)
Gerardo Matturro (Universidad ORT, Uruguay)
Gustavo Rossi (Universidad Nacional de La Plata, Argentina)
Hernan Astudillo (Universidad Tecnica Federico Santa Maria, Chile)
Ivan Machado (Universidade Federal da Bahia, Brazil)
Jacome Cunha (Universidade Nova de Lisboa, Portugal)
Jeny Ruiz (Universidad de Holguin, Cuba)
João Paulo Fernandes (Universidade de Coimbra, Portugal)
John W. Castro (Universidad de Atacama, Chile)
Jose Ignacio Panach (Universitat de Valencia, Spain)
Jose Raul Romero (Universidad de Cordoba, Spain)
Juan de Lara (Universidad Autonoma de Madrid, Spain)
Juan Pablo Carvallo (Universidad del Azuay, Ecuador)
Juliana Alves Pereira (University of Rennes, France)

Kelly Garces Pernett (Universidad de los Andes, Colombia)
Kleinner Farias (University of Vale do Rio dos Sinos, Brazil)
Lourdes Moreno (Universidad Carlos III de Madrid, Spain)
Luca Cernuzzi (Universidad Catolica, Paraguay)
Luciano Baresi (Politecnico di Milano, Italy)
Luis Olsina (Universidad Nacional de La Pampa, Argentina)
Marcela Ruiz (Utrecht University, Netherlands)
Marcelo Jenkins (University of Costa Rica, Costa Rica)
Maria Cecilia Bastarrica (Universidad de Chile, Chile)
Mauricio Aniche (TU Delft, Netherlands)
Mauricio Souza (Universidade Federal de Lavras, Brazil)
Miguel Monteiro (Universidade Nova de Lisboa, Portugal)
Miguel Morales-Trujillo (Universidad Nacional Autonoma de Mexico, Mexico)
Nelly Condori-Fernandez (VU University of Amsterdam, Netherlands)
Nestor Garay-Vitoria (Universidad del Pais Vasco, Spain)
Oscar Pastor (Universitat Politecnica de Valencia, Spain)
Pablo Becker (Universidad Nacional de La Pampa, Argentina)
Pablo Villarreal (Universidad Tecnologica Nacional, Argentina)
Paulo Alencar (University of Waterloo, Canada)
Rafael Prikladnicki (Pontificia Universidade Catolica do Rio Grande do Sul, Brazil)
Regina Maria Maciel Braga Villela (Universidade Federal de Juiz de Fora, Brazil)
Rosana Braga (University of Sao Paulo, Brazil)
Sheila Reinehr (Universidade Catolica do Parana, Brazil)
Silverio Martinez_Fernandez (Universitat Politecnica de Catalunya, Spain)
Silvia T. Acuña (Universidad Autonoma de Madrid, Spain)
Toacy Oliveira (Universidade Federal do Rio de Janeiro, Brazil)
Veronica Andrea Bollati (Universidad Tecnologica Nacional, Argentina)
Victor Santander (Universidad Estadual do Oeste do Parana, Brazil)
Vitor E. Silva Souza (Universidade Federal do Espirito Santo, Brazil)

RET Preface

Welcome to the Requirements Engineering Track (RET) of the 23rd edition of the Ibero-American Conference on Software Engineering (CIbSE 2020), originally planned to be held in Curitiba, Brasil, from May 6th to 9th, 2020.

Requirements Engineering can be roughly defined as the software engineering area concerned with the discovery and documentation of the purpose of a system. The goal of RET is to explore and discuss relevant advances and contributions to the Requirements Engineering field and its relation with different domains of applications, through integrated and robust solutions proposed by researchers and practitioners. RET provides a stimulating forum where researchers and practitioners can present and discuss recent research results on a wide range of topics related to Requirements Engineering, in addition to exchanging ideas, experiences, and challenging problems.

The international program committee of RET consisted of 41 experts from academia and industry from nine countries (Argentina, Brazil, Canada, Chile, Luxembourg, Paraguay, Portugal, Spain, and Venezuela). We received 29 abstract submissions, which were finally materialized in 20 valid submissions from eight countries. Each paper was reviewed by at least three members of the program committee and, after some online discussions, 9 papers were accepted for presentation at the Track. The accepted papers present advances in the field, covering topics such as new generation of Requirements Engineering approaches, requirements elicitation, requirements analysis, human aspects, and education & training, among others.

We would like to thank the authors of the submitted papers, the members of the program committee, and the additional reviewers for their invaluable contribution towards realizing RET. We also thank the other members of the CIbSE 2020 organization committee for their constant support, the Pontifical Catholic University of Paraná for hosting the conference, and the sponsors for financially supporting CIbSE.

Last but not least, we hope that you enjoy the Requirements Engineering Track.

Carla Silva and Jose Luis de la Vara
CIbSE-2020 RET Track Chairs

Program Committee – RET Track

Camilo Almendra, Universidade Federal de Pernambuco, Brazil
Carlos Cares, Universidad de La Frontera, Chile
Carme Quer, Universitat Politècnica de Catalunya, Spain
Clara Ayora, Tree Technology, Spain
Cristina Palomares, Universitat Politècnica de Catalunya, Spain
Denis Silveira, Universidade Federal de Pernambuco, Brazil
Enyo Gonçalves, Universidade Federal do Ceará, Brazil
Eugenio Parra, Universidad Carlos III de Madrid, Spain
Fernanda Alencar, Universidade Federal de Pernambuco, Brazil
Giovanni Giachetti, Universidad Tecnológica de Chile, Chile
Gladys Kaplan, Universidad Nacional de La Matanza, Argentina
Gonzalo Génova, Universidad Carlos III de Madrid, Spain
Graciela Hadad, Universidad Nacional del Oeste, Argentina
Isabel Sofia Brito, Instituto Politécnico de Beja, Portugal
Jéssyka Vilela, Universidade Federal de Pernambuco, Brazil
João Araujo, Universidade Nova de Lisboa, Portugal
João Pimentel, Universidade Federal Rural de Pernambuco, Brazil
Jorge Barreiros, Universidade Nova de Lisboa, Portugal
Juan Sánchez, Universitat Politècnica de València, Spain
Judith Barrios, Universidad de los Andes, Venezuela
Leandro Antonelli, Universidad Nacional de La Plata, Argentina
Lidia Lopez, Universitat Politècnica de Catalunya, Spain
Luiz Martins, Universidade Federal de São Paulo, Brazil
Luiz Marcio Cysneiros, York University, Canada
Marcela Ridao, Universidad Nacional del Centro de la Provincia de Buenos Aires, Argentina
Márcia Lucena, Universidade Federal do Rio Grande do Norte, Brazil
Maria Lencastre, Universidade de Pernambuco, Brazil
Maria Pinto-Albuquerque, Instituto Universitário de Lisboa, Portugal
Mauricio Alferez, University of Luxembourg, Luxembourg
Nathalie Aquino, Universidad Católica Nuestra Señora de la Asunción, Paraguay
Pedro Valderas, Universitat Politècnica de València, Spain
Rafael Prikladnicki, Pontifícia Universidade Católica do Rio Grande do Sul, Brazil
Raúl Lapeña, Universidad San Jorge, Spain
Renata Guizzardi, Universidade Federal do Espírito Santo, Brazil
Roberto Avila Paldes, Centro Universitário de Brasília, Brazil
Sabrina Marczak, Pontifícia Universidade Católica do Rio Grande do Sul, Brazil
Vera Werneck, Universidade do Estado do Rio de Janeiro, Brazil
Victoria Torre, Universitat Politècnica de València, Spain
Wilkerson Andrade, Universidade Federal de Campina Grande, Brazil

ESELAW Preface

Welcome to the Experimental Software Engineering Track (ESELAW) of the 23rd Iberoamerican Conference on Software Engineering (CIbSE 2020). This year, the event was originally planned to be held at Curitiba (Brazil) and organized by the Pontifícia Universidade Católica do Paraná (PUCPR).

Since 2004, the former ESELAW workshop has become an important forum for researchers and practitioners to report on and discuss new research results in Experimental Software Engineering, bringing together Latin America's academic and industrial communities. It encourages the exchange of ideas to understand the strengths and weaknesses of software engineering technologies, focusing on the entire process for conducting field studies, as well as focusing on specific activities.

To strengthen its goal of becoming a landmark event on Software Engineering in Iberoamerica, since 2011, ESELAW has been held into the context of CIbSE – the leading research forum on Software Engineering in Ibero-America. This year's program has been structured in mixed technical sessions, involving papers from the different CIbSE tracks.

ESELAW 2020 received a total of 28 complete submissions from 12 different countries written in any of three official languages of the conference (Spanish, Portuguese and English). The papers were peer reviewed by 3-4 members of the Program Committee, composed of prominent researchers from the community. After a tough revision process, 9 full high-quality scientific works addressing issues on experimentation in software engineering under different perspectives were accepted. It results in an acceptance rate of 32.1%, which shows the rigour of the process. In addition, 1 paper was published as a poster. The effort and dedication of the Program Committee and the additional reviewers who collaborated in the revision process were outstanding and deserve recognition.

We would like to acknowledge all people that have made possible the organization of CIbSE-ESELAW 2020: the authors who submitted their papers; the Program Committee members and the additional reviewers who made possible the conference program; and the organizing committee members who handled all the complexity of arranging an event such as CIbSE 2020.

Finally, we want to offer a warm welcome to all speakers, authors, students and general audience who attend ESELAW 2020. We hope you enjoy the event.

Breno Bernard Nicolau de França and Martin Solari
CIbSE 2020 - ESELAW Track Chairs

Program Committee – ESELAW Track

Andreia Malucelli, PUCPR
Arilo Claudio Dias-Neto, UFAM
Bruno Cartaxo, IFPE
César França, UFRPE
Claudia P. Ayala, Universitat Politècnica de Catalunya
Clemente Izurieta, Montana State University
Davi Viana, UFMA
Efraín R. Fonseca C., Universidad de las Fuerzas Armadas
Ellen Barbosa, ICMC-USP
Emilia Mendes, Blekinge Institute of Technology and Oulu University
Fáber Danilo Giraldo Velásquez, University of Quindío
George Valença, UFPE
Gerardo Matturro, Universidad ORT Uruguay
Gleison Santos, UNIRIO
Guilherme Horta Travassos, COPPE-UFRJ
Jose Antonio Cruz-Lemus, University of Castilla-La Mancha
José Carlos Maldonado, ICMC-USP
Juan Pablo Ucán Pech, UADY
Katia Felizardo, UTFPR
Luis Jorge Enrique Rivero Cabrejos, UFAM
Marcela Genero, University of Castilla-La Mancha
Marcelo Marinho, UFPE
Marco Antônio Araujo, IF Sudeste MG
Marcos Kalinowski, Pontifical Catholic University of Rio de Janeiro (PUC-Rio)
Miguel Goulão, Universidade Nova de Lisboa
Monalessa Barcellos, UFES
Natasha Malveira Costa Valentim, UFPR
Nauman Bin Ali, Blekinge Institute of Technology
Omar S. Gómez, Technical School of Chimborazo
Oscar Dieste, Universidad Politécnica de Madrid
Paulo Sérgio Santos, UNIRIO
Rafael Prikladnicki, PUCRS
Raúl Antonio Aguilar Vera, Universidad Autónoma de Yucatán
Raul Wazlawick, UFSC
Rodrigo Santos, UNIRIO

Additional Reviewers

Doctoral Symposium Preface

One more year, CIbSE is organizing a Doctoral Symposium (DS), under the firm conviction that a DS provides a valuable forum to give PhD students a chance to present and discuss their research work while it is in a full development process. In the natural iberoamerican working context of CIbSE, this dissemination of such a relevant research-in-progress conducted by novice researchers is fully aligned with the CIbSE spirit of pushing iberoamerican research of high quality. This doctoral event counts with the support of a board of experts that will discuss face-to-face with the researchers of the selected works, in order to suggest new perspectives and improvements to the corresponding Ph.D. thesis.

With this important goal in mind, a call for doctoral contributions was issued. The submissions were invited to address any of the CIbSE 2020 research topics, with the explicit recommendation of presenting a research that is at least in an intermediate stage (~ 2nd year) so that experts' suggestions could be included in the Ph.D. work.

Up to 6 submissions were submitted. All of them had a significant quality level that required a careful selection process. The works were reviewed by at least 2 experts from the Program Committee formed by 12 members whose excellent and professional reviewing work we strongly appreciate. From this set of 6 submissions, 3 were finally accepted to conform the central DS session, that will be complemented with a practical tutorial on Design Science for PhD students, open to a larger community of interested students and researchers at the conference site.

We are firmly convinced about the relevance of having such an attractive event in CIbSE, and we invite all the participants to share it with us. We specially thank the panel of experts that will evaluate and make recommendations to the selected PhD students, and that beyond us –Guilherme Travassos and Oscar Pastor, the DS Chairs-, will be constituted by Professors Luca Cernuzzi, Luis Olsina and Ernesto Pimentel.

Finally, we want to recognize the excellent work of the Organizing Committee that is working hard to make the Conference become a big success in this complex times.

Guilherme Travassos, Oscar Pastor
CIbSE 2020 DS Chairs

EIbAIS Preface

Welcome to the Advanced Ibero-American School on Software Engineering (EIbAIS) 2020! EIbAIS represents the CIbSE initiative to disseminate Software Engineering knowledge in Ibero-America. It aims to promote a forum for discussions regarding Software Engineering, its related technologies and theoretical foundations, allowing the participation of practitioners, undergraduate and graduate students, and researchers.

EIbAIS offers tutorials that discuss aspects related to Software Engineering state-of-the-practice and state-of-the-art. Concerning state-of-the-practice, tutorials explore topics of general interest, providing to the participants improvement of Software Engineering applied knowledge and practices. As for state-of-the-art, tutorials discuss topics of prospective interest of the Software Engineering community, providing information on breakthroughs in Software Engineering technologies.

This year, EIbAIS presents four tutorials to provide to the participants a wide spectrum of theoretical and practical knowledge, covering Human-Computer Interaction, Continuous Software Engineering, Design Thinking, and Process Mining subjects. The tutorials are presented by professors from Brazilian and USA universities, with solid backgrounds and practical experience that promote a favorable environment to the participants learn by doing. The tutorials are covering the following topics:

- How to use the GenderMag Method to find gender-inclusiveness issues in software: In this tutorial, professor Margaret Burnett (Oregon State University) explores Human-Computer Interaction (HCI) aspects presenting GenderMag, a method that helps software developers and usability professionals find and fix software features with gender-inclusiveness "bugs".
- Continuous Software Engineering: Continuous Software Engineering (CSE) refers to a recent stem from Software Engineering, and its principles are rooted in Agile and Lean Software Development. In this tutorial, professor Breno França (UNICAMP) addresses the principles and practices in the context of CSE, as well as the need for empirical and experimental studies regarding business strategy, development, and operations practices from a holistic view.
- Thinking (and doing) software with Design Thinking: Design Thinking is a contemporary approach to innovation that takes the way of thinking from the Design discipline to other areas of expertise, such as Software Engineering. In this tutorial, professor Frederick van Amstel (UFTPR) points out the importance of creative

processes and spaces in software development and describes how to relate, in practice, Design Thinking and Software Engineering.

- Process Mining in Software Engineering: Process mining is an analytical discipline that provides computational tools to discover, monitor and improve real processes, extracting knowledge from event logs available in information systems. Process mining allows to obtain objective factual information that helps audit, analyze, assess compliance and performance, and improve existing processes. In this tutorial, professor Edson Scalabrin (PUCPR) aims to show, in practice, how to automatically discover process instance models, verify compliance and generate operational support information to software organizations.

Many people contributed to make EIbAIS possible. We acknowledge them all, particularly the speakers, the general program chairs and the organizing committee members who organized CIbSE 2020.

Finally, we offer a warm welcome to all speakers, students, researchers, practitioners and general audience who attend EIbAIS 2020. We hope you enjoy the event.

Luca Cernuzzi and Monalessa Perini Barcellos
CIbSE 2020 - EIbAIS Chairs

Prefácio das Palestras da Indústria

Sejam bem-vindos à edição de 2020 da trilha de Palestras da Indústria (Industry Talk) do XXIII Congresso Ibero-Americano em Engenharia de Software. Esta trilha visa oferecer meios para profissionais da indústria apresentarem e discutirem trabalhos que ataquem problemas cotidianos de Engenharia de Software.

O objetivo é que pesquisadores e profissionais trabalhem em conjunto, para aproximar os pesquisadores da realidade do dia a dia dos praticantes, assim como viabilizar que as práticas sejam aprimoradas por meio da discussão e colaboração que a academia pode prover.

Serão abordados desafios e temas emergentes da Engenharia de Software, com assuntos relacionados a processos, métodos e técnicas, capital humano na área de Tecnologia da Informação, dentre outros. Este ano recebemos oito submissões de dois países e várias regiões, sendo seis deles aceitos para apresentação. Os temas que foram selecionados e que serão objeto das discussões dos participantes são:

- Modelo para mensuração de produtividade para equipes de Tecnologia da Informação
- Desenvolvimento de competências em times de Tecnologia da Informação
- Modelo colaborativo para elicitação de requisitos em ambientes ágeis
- Impactos da LGPD na indústria e Privacy by Design
- Machine translation summary e agentes inteligentes de aprendizagem na educação
- O novo modelo MPS.BR - Melhoria de Processo do Software Brasileiro

A última sessão da trilha será composta por um painel, onde empresas de impacto significativo na região irão debater as melhores práticas e processos de inovação que estão empregando atualmente, assim como discutirão as perspectivas futuras da Engenharia de Software em suas organizações e na indústria.

Gostaríamos de agradecer a todos os autores e organizações que submeteram propostas de palestras que irão viabilizar excelentes discussões. Esta trilha irá alavancar sobremaneira o alinhamento entre a academia e a indústria e seus participantes poderão contribuir ativamente para a evolução da Engenharia de Software. Também agradecemos ao Comitê de Programa por todo o suporte para viabilizar a Trilha de Palestras da Indústria como parte do CIbSE 2020.

Marco Paludo, Rafael Prikladnicki

Coordenadores das Palestras da Indústria do CIbSE 2020

Keynote "Gender-Inclusive Software" (in English)

Margaret Burnett – Oregon State University, United States

Bio: Margaret Burnett is a Distinguished Professor at Oregon State University. She began her career in industry, where she was the first woman software developer ever hired at Procter & Gamble Ivorydale. A few degrees and start-ups later, she joined academia, with a research focus on people who are engaged in some form of software development. She was the principal architect of the Forms/3 and FAR visual programming languages, and co-founded the area of end-user software engineering, which aims to improve software for computer users that are not trained in programming. She pioneered the use of information foraging theory in the domain of software debugging, and leads the team that created GenderMag, a software inspection process that uncovers gender inclusiveness issues in software from spreadsheets to programming environments. Burnett is an ACM Fellow, a member of the ACM CHI Academy, and an award-winning mentor. She has served in over 50 conference organization and program committee roles. She is also on the Academic Alliance Advisory Board of the National Center for Women & IT (NCWIT).

Abstract: Gender inclusiveness in software companies is receiving a lot of attention these days, but it overlooks a potentially critical factor: software itself. But how can software professionals assess whether their software supports diverse users? And if they find problems, how can they fix them? To help fill this gap, we developed GenderMag, a systematic method for software professionals to find and fix "gender inclusivity bugs" in software interfaces and workflows. At the core of the method are 5 cognitive facets drawn from a large body of foundational work on gender differences from computer science, psychology, education, communications, and women's studies. We present GenderMag and its foundations, present results of software professionals' experiences finding and fixing inclusivity bugs in their software, and then introduce a new generalization of GenderMag called InclusiveMag along with our early experiences with it.

Keynote "Até que sou sensível, mas ainda não tenho como te garantir... São tantas coisas envolvidas em meu ciclo de vida que preciso de sua ajuda para resolver..." (in Portuguese)

Guilherme Travassos – COPPE/UFRJ, Brazil

Bio: Engenheiro Eletricista (UFJF, 1985), Mestre (1990) e Doutor (1994) em Engenharia de Sistemas e Computação pela COPPE/UFRJ. Realizou estágio de Pós-Doutorado na UMDCP juntamente com o SEL/NASA (USA - 98/00), tendo como focos principais experimentação aplicada na Engenharia de Software e linha de produto de software. Atualmente é professor titular e coordenador do Programa de Engenharia de Sistemas e Computação (PESC) da COPPE/UFRJ. Seus interesses de pesquisa estão inseridos no contexto da Engenharia de Software Experimental e na Engenharia de Sistemas de Software Contemporâneos, atuando principalmente nos seguintes temas: qualidade de software (VV&T), sistemas ubíquos e sensíveis ao contexto, Internet das Coisas, simulação em engenharia de software, ambientes e ferramentas para apoiar o desenvolvimento e experimentação em software. Lidera o grupo de Engenharia de Software Experimental da COPPE/UFRJ e faz parte da ISERN. É membro da SBC e membro profissional da ACM. É editor associado do periódico Elsevier- IST e compõem o corpo editorial dos periódicos SBC/JSERD, World Scientific/IJSEKE e e-Informatica Software Engineering Journal (eISEJ).Colabora com a indústria de software através dos projetos de pesquisa & desenvolvimento desenvolvidos pela COPPE/UFRJ. Informações complementares podem ser obtidas em www.cos.ufrj.br/~ght.

Abstract: Assistimos ao longo dos anos a evolução sistêmica e a "invasão" do software no dia a dia da sociedade. As soluções inicialmente construídas de forma monolítica e isoladas deixaram de ser, atualmente, o elemento central da inovação em software. É verdade que aprendemos e evoluímos bastante na engenharia desses sistemas. Entretanto, sistemas de software contemporâneos (sensíveis ao contexto, Internet das Coisas, Indústria 4.0, sistemas ciber-físicos, dentre outros) tem dominado o cenário tecnológico e se tornado cada vez mais presentes e influentes nas atividades da sociedade. Entretanto, a engenharia desses sistemas de software contemporâneos tem revelado preocupações e propriedades intrínsecas e multidisciplinares, para as quais as tecnologias de software convencionais não são apropriadas. Nesse sentido, os riscos associados ao uso de sistemas de software contemporâneos que têm sido diariamente disponibilizados para a sociedade ainda são altos, com alguns sistemas provocando perdas humanas. Essa palestra tem a intenção de apresentar alguns desses desafios e chamar atenção da comunidade para a engenharia de sistemas de software contemporâneos.

Keynote "Genome Data Science-based Solutions for Personalized Health Care" (in Spanish)

Óscar Pastor – Universitat Politècnica de València, Spain

Bio: Full Professor and Director of the Research Center on "Métodos de Producción de Software (PROS)" at the Universidad Politécnica de Valencia (Spain). He received his Ph.D. in 1992. He was a researcher at HP Labs, Bristol, UK. He has published more than four hundred research papers in conference proceedings, journals and books, received numerous research grants from public institutions and private industry, and been keynote speaker at several conferences and workshops. Chair of the ER Steering Committee, and member of the SC of conferences as CAiSE, ESEM, ICWE, CIbSE or RCIS, his research activities focus on conceptual modeling, web engineering, requirements engineering, information systems, and model-based software production. He created the object-oriented, formal specification language OASIS and the corresponding software production method OO-METHOD. He led the research and development underlying CARE Technologies that was formed in 1996. CARE Technologies has created an advanced MDA-based Conceptual Model Compiler called IntegraNova, a tool that produces a final software product starting from a conceptual schema that represents system requirements. He is an internationally recognized researcher in the domain of Conceptual Modeling, being ER Fellow since 2010 and having being awarded with the Peter C. Chen in 2017. He is currently leading a multidisciplinary project linking Information Systems and Bioinformatics notions.

Abstract: Everybody accepts that understanding the Human Genome is a big challenge for the humanity. It will take at the very least decades to achieve such a goal reasonably well. But new advances that are showing promising results come continuously. Day after day new data are is provided and new information is derived from them. As DNA sequencing technologies improve and evolve, it is an evidence that the rate of data generation at a local level is increasing dramatically. In this scenario, assuring the interoperability and consistence of data at the global level becomes both a challenge and a need. To face these problems adequately, the most advanced Data Science technologies are strongly required, with a particular emphasis on how relevant Conceptual Modeling must be in order to understand the ontological ground of relevant genomic concepts. By Genome Data Science we refer to the set of methods and techniques to be applied to cover the needs of better data capture, organization and storage, improved data analysis and interoperability, and more efficient data standardization with the support of foundational ontologies. This idea is in the "Genome" of this keynote. Using Advanced Conceptual Model and Data Science Technologies, there is an opportunity to understand the secrets of life that the Genome Code hides. More and more data that relate genotype and phenotype are available, with especially attractive clinical applications. These ideas will be approached in the keynote, showing that the challenge of understanding the human genome can suppose a conceptual revolution: understanding the genome could allow to improve human being features, something that has never in our hands as humans.

Herramientas para pruebas automatizadas de seguridad en aplicaciones Web: Un mapeo sistemático de la literatura

Elizabeth Gamboa, Christian Quesada-López, Alexandra Martínez, Marcelo Jenkins

Universidad de Costa Rica, San Pedro, Costa Rica
{elizabeth.gamboa, cristian.quesadalopez, alexandra.martinez, marcelo.jenkins}@ucr.ac.cr

Resumen Las herramientas utilizadas para automatizar las pruebas de seguridad en aplicaciones Web son esenciales para detectar vulnerabilidades y prevenir ataques cibernéticos. En este estudio identificamos herramientas reportadas entre el 2006 y el 2019 para probar la seguridad de aplicaciones Web. Cada una de las herramientas es clasificada en términos de los tipos de vulnerabilidades que prueban. Para ello, realizamos un mapeo sistemático de la literatura en el que se analizaron 63 estudios primarios, de los cuales identificamos 66 herramientas utilizadas para realizar pruebas automatizadas de seguridad. Las herramientas se clasificaron según los tipos de la metodología de pruebas de seguridad para determinar vulnerabilidades del proyecto abierto de seguridad en aplicaciones Web *(OWASP)*. La categoría de pruebas para detectar vulnerabilidades más común fue la de *Input Validation Testing (4.8)* con 55 herramientas, seguido de las pruebas de *Configuration and Deployment Management Testing (4.3)*, *Session Management Testing (4.7)*, y *Client Side Testing (4.12)* con 15 herramientas utilizadas cada una. Los tipos de pruebas más reportados fueron los de la categoría *Input Validation Testing (4.8)*. En este caso *SQL Injection (4.8.5)* con 40 herramientas, *Cross-Site Scripting (4.8.2)* con 30 herramientas, y *Testing for HTTP Incoming Requests (4.8.17)* con 19 herramientas utilizadas.

Palabras clave: Pruebas de seguridad, herramientas, aplicaciones Web, vulnerabilidades, OWASP, mapeo sistemático.

1. Introducción

Las pruebas de seguridad para aplicaciones Web son esenciales para prevenir la explotación de vulnerabilidades que generalmente buscan comprometer o dañar un sistema y la información que este administra. Se estima que más del 90 % de las aplicaciones Web son vulnerables, con una media de más de 10 vulnerabilidades por aplicación [1]. Una prueba de seguridad es un método para evaluar la seguridad de un sistema Web mediante la validación y verificación metódica de la efectividad de los controles de seguridad de la aplicación [2]. Una prueba de seguridad Web se centra en evaluar la seguridad de una aplicación

Web, cuyo proceso implica un análisis activo de dicha aplicación en busca de debilidades, fallas técnicas o vulnerabilidades [2]. Para proteger las aplicaciones Web es necesario identificar y eliminar las vulnerabilidades que estas presentan. Una vulnerabilidad es una falla o debilidad en el diseño, implementación, operación o administración de un sistema que podría explotarse para comprometer dicho sistema [2]. Las herramientas de pruebas automatizadas pueden complementar los procesos de pruebas manuales para brindar mayor confiabilidad en la cobertura y para reducir el tiempo de ejecución de los casos de prueba de seguridad. Asimismo, pueden apoyar a los equipos de desarrolladores en la ejecución de estos tipos de pruebas. Por otro lado, estas herramientas aun cuentan con algunas limitantes y retos asociados que deben ser estudiados para así poder incrementar el valor agregado que pueden ofrecer a los equipos de calidad [3,4].

El proyecto abierto de seguridad de aplicaciones Web *(OWASP)* se dedica a promocionar el desarrollo de aplicaciones confiables. Este provee recursos abiertos sobre herramientas, documentos y capítulos para cualquier interesado en mejorar la seguridad de las aplicaciones [5]. El *OWASP* detalla los lineamientos para pruebas de seguridad en el cual lista las vulnerabilidades que las pruebas de seguridad Web deben evaluar [5].

En los últimos años, múltiples estudios sobre el uso de herramientas que permiten generar y ejecutar pruebas automatizadas para evaluar la seguridad de las aplicaciones Web han sido reportadas en la literatura [6]. Estas herramientas permiten conocer las vulnerabilidades que sufren las aplicaciones Web para la protección de los datos que administran. El objetivo de las herramientas es habilitar mecanismos para mejorar la confiabilidad y la seguridad de las aplicaciones que prueban.

El objetivo de esta investigación es identificar las herramientas que han sido utilizadas para probar de forma automatizada la seguridad de aplicaciones Web. Las herramientas se clasificaron según los tipos de la metodología de pruebas de seguridad para determinar vulnerabilidades del proyecto abierto de seguridad en aplicaciones Web [5]. Para lograr el objetivo realizamos un mapeo sistemático de la literatura en el que se analizaron 63 estudios primarios, de los cuales identificamos 66 herramientas utilizadas para realizar pruebas automatizadas de seguridad.

El resto del artículo se estructura de la siguiente manera. La sección 2 menciona las vulnerabilidades de las aplicaciones Web. La sección 3 presenta los trabajos relacionados. La sección 4 explica la metodología del mapeo de literatura. La sección 5 analiza los resultados. La sección 6 presenta las discusiones de este estudio. Finalmente, la sección 7 presenta las conclusiones.

2. Marco Teórico

El proyecto abierto de seguridad de aplicaciones Web *(OWASP)* [7] provee información sobre la seguridad de las aplicaciones Web y periódicamente actualiza listas de los ataques de seguridad más comunes. Asimismo, proporciona documentación técnica sobre estas vulnerabilidades que permite implementar mecanismos de seguridad que prevengan ataques que exploten dichas vulnerabilidades. En el 2017, el *OWASP* reportó los 10 riesgos más críticos para las aplicaciones Web [8] los cuales indicaron que las fallas de inyección (A1:2017), como SQL, NoSQL, OS o LDAP es la principal vulnerabilidad. Los siguientes riesgos fueron la pérdida de autenticación en las funciones de la aplicación relacionadas a autenticación y gestión de sesiones (A2:2017), la exposición de datos sensibles en las aplicaciones Web y APIs que no los protegen adecuadamente (A3:201), las entidades externas XML (XXE) donde los procesadores XML antiguos o mal configurados evalúan referencias a entidades externas en documentos XML (A4:2017), la pérdida de control de acceso y las restricciones sobre lo que los usuarios autenticados pueden hacer (A5:2017), la configuración de seguridad incorrecta (*ad hoc* o por omisión) (A6:2017), la secuencia de comandos en sitios cruzados (XSS) con datos no confiables enviados al navegador Web sin una validación y codificación apropiada (A7:2017), la deserialización insegura cuando una aplicación recibe objetos serializados dañinos que son manipulados o borrados por el atacante (A8:2017), los componentes con vulnerabilidades conocidas que se ejecutan con los mismos privilegios que la aplicación (A9:2017), y finalmente el registro y monitoreo insuficientes con la falta de respuesta ante incidentes (A10:2017).

OWASP mantiene una metodología de pruebas de seguridad para determinar vulnerabilidades de seguridad en aplicaciones Web [5]. Esta metodología en su sección 4 detalla 11 categorías donde para cada una lista el conjunto de vulnerabilidades asociadas que se deben evaluar en las aplicaciones Web: *Information Gathering (4.2)* que detalla 10 tipos de vulnerabilidades, *Configuration and Deployment Management Testing (4.3)* que detalla 9 tipos de vulnerabilidades, *Identity Management Testing (4.4)* que detalla 5 tipos de vulnerabilidades, *Authenticaion Testing (4.5)* que detalla 10 tipos de vulnerabilidades, *Authorization Testing (4.6)* que detalla 4 tipos de vulnerabilidades, *Session Management Testing (4.7)* que detalla 8 tipos de vulnerabilidades, *Input Validation Testing (4.8)* que detalla 17 tipos de vulnerabilidades, *Error Handling (4.9)* que detalla 2 tipos de vulnerabilidades, *Weak Cryptography (4.10)* que detalla 4 tipos de vulnerabilidades, *Business Logic Testing (4.11)* que detalla 9 tipos de vulnerabilidades, *Client Side Testing (4.12)* que detalla 12 tipos de vulnerabilidades. A partir de estas categorías, la clasificación de vulnerabilidades para las aplicaciones Web permite enfocar esfuerzos para estudiar herramientas y pruebas que permitan automatizar la identificación de dichas vulnerabilidades.

3. Trabajo Relacionado

Distintos estudios han discutido la seguridad del software en la literatura. En el 2003, Thompson [9] estudió por qué las pruebas de seguridad son difíciles. El autor planteó que no se puede cubrir el cien por ciento del software y que es importante contar con herramientas para pruebas de seguridad automatizadas que mejoren la eficiencia con respecto a la ejecución de pruebas manuales.

Por su parte en el 2006, Curphey y Arawo [10] listaron un conjunto de herramientas para pruebas de aplicaciones Web e indicaron que no existen herramientas que evalúen todas las vulnerabilidades. Los autores indicaron la importancia de contar con diferentes herramientas para evaluar la seguridad, cada una enfocada en distintas fases del ciclo de vida de desarrollo y para distintos tipos de pruebas tales como pruebas de base de datos, de los *web services*, en *runtime*, de *proxy*, para análisis de código, entre otras.

En el 2010, Pfleeger y Cunningham [11] estudiaron la dificultad de medir la seguridad de las aplicaciones y las estrategias para lograr medir los objetivos de seguridad. Los autores indican que la dificultad es determinar métricas efectivas que permitan una rigurosa y práctica medición de la seguridad.

En el 2015, Rafique et al. [6] identificaron soluciones disponibles para las vulnerabilidades de las aplicaciones Web mediante un mapeo de literatura. Para esto clasificaron las soluciones de acuerdo con la lista de los 10 tipos de vulnerabilidades reportadas por *OWASP* en el 2013. Asimismo, identificaron la fase del ciclo de vida de desarrollo en las que propone una solución para las vulnerabilidades.

Mohammed et al. [12] identificaron 54 enfoques de pruebas de seguridad utilizadas en las fases del ciclo de vida de desarrollo del software (SDLC) mediante un mapeo de literatura en el 2017. Estos enfoques se basan principalmente en análisis estático y análisis dinámico de los artefactos de software. En el 2018, Jafari y Rasoolzadegan [13] exploraron estudios que realizan la definición de patrones de seguridad para las aplicaciones de software. Los autores determinaron que la utilización de los patrones de seguridad ha ido creciendo en las nuevas metodologías de desarrollo o la mejora de las existentes. Este estudio complementó estudios secundarios previos sobre patrones de seguridad [14,15].

En nuestro trabajo realizamos una clasificación de herramientas según los tipos de la metodología de pruebas de seguridad para determinar vulnerabilidades del proyecto abierto de seguridad en aplicaciones Web [5] y cuantificamos las vulnerabilidades más reportadas por los estudios identificados. Realizamos un mapeo de las herramientas desde el 2006 hasta el 2019, lo que proporciona una lista de herramientas actualizada que complementa los estudios previos.

4. Metodología

El mapeo sistemático de la literatura se realizó siguiendo los lineamientos establecidos por Petersen, Vakkalanka y Kuzniarz [16] y las recomendaciones de Kitchenham y Charters [17].

El objetivo de este estudio, formulado con el modelo *Goal Question Metric (GQM)* [18] fue *analizar* las herramientas utilizadas para realizar pruebas automatizadas de seguridad *con el propósito de* caracterizarlas *con respecto a* las vulnerabilidades de seguridad que prueban *desde el punto de vista de* los investigadores *en el contexto* de aplicaciones Web. Para guiar este estudio, se definió la siguiente pregunta de investigación: (RQ) ¿Cuáles herramientas se han utilizado para automatizar las pruebas de seguridad de aplicaciones Web?

4.1. Estrategia de búsqueda y proceso de selección de estudios

Primero se realizó una búsqueda exploratoria para identificar estudios relevantes, que fueron usados como artículos de control. Los artículos de control seleccionados [S01, S02, S03] fueron usados como base en la definición y validación del protocolo de investigación. Estos artículos presentan herramientas para la detección de vulnerabilidades en aplicaciones Web y se seleccionaron por contar con la información necesaria para responder la pregunta de investigación.

A partir del objetivo planteado, las preguntas de investigación, y los términos clave extraídos del título y del resumen de los artículos de control, se construyó la versión inicial de la cadena de búsqueda. Para esto se utilizó el modelo PICO (Población, Intervención, Comparación, Salidas) en el proceso de construcción. La cadena final, que se muestra a continuación, fue producto de un proceso de refinamiento que incluyó varias pruebas piloto para reducir el ruido.

("automat*" OR "tool") AND ("secur* test*") AND ("web*")

Las búsquedas automatizadas se realizaron en las bases de datos *SCOPUS*, *IEEE Xplore*, y *Web of Science*. Se realizó la búsqueda en el título, el resumen y las palabras clave de los artículos. El protocolo del mapeo se desarrolló de Marzo a Mayo del 2019, y la búsqueda automatizada se realizó en Junio del 2019. Los estudios se analizaron entre Junio y Diciembre del 2019.

El número de estudios recuperado para cada base de datos fue de 159 artículos en *SCOPUS*, 81 artículos en *IEEE Xplore*, y 20 artículos en *Web of Science*.

En total se obtuvieron 260 artículos de los cuales 75 eran duplicados, tal como se presenta en la Figura 1.

Los artículos fueron tabulados en MS Excel para los procesos de selección, evaluación y extracción de datos. Se eliminaron los duplicados, se aplicaron los criterios de inclusión y exclusión (I/E) y finalmente se hizo la extracción y el análisis de los resultados. Tras la eliminación de duplicados, se obtuvo un conjunto de 185 estudios.

El proceso de I/E se hizo con base en el título y el resumen de los artículos (cuando hubo duda, se hizo lectura completa del artículo). Se excluyeron publicaciones donde no se encontraba disponible el texto completo (E1) y los artículos secundarios y terciarios (E2). Se incluyeron publicaciones de artículos que trataran sobre herramientas utilizadas para pruebas de seguridad en aplicaciones Web (I1) y solo los artículos en idioma inglés (I2).

A partir de la estrategia de búsqueda y el proceso de selección, se obtuvo un total de 63 artículos. En la Figura 1 detallamos el resultado del proceso de búsqueda y selección de artículos.

La lista completa de los estudios relevantes identificados puede consultarse en el enlace: `https://tinyurl.com/w9e48g3`. Adicional a la información de los artículos y su clasificación de acuerdo a las vulnerabilidades para aplicaciones Web, en este enlace se encuentran los detalles de las herramientas (nombre de la herramienta, lenguaje de programación, entre otros), el grado de automatización de las pruebas de seguridad (automatizadas, semi-automatizadas o manuales), y los tipos de pruebas que realiza cada herramienta. Finalmente, se encuentran los detalles de la evaluación de calidad por artículo, el cual describimos a continuación.

4.2. Evaluación de calidad

La evaluación de la calidad de los estudios se realizó para determinar el nivel de detalle ofrecido sobre los aspectos de interés del análisis y basado en la pregunta de investigación. Estos permiten obtener un *ranking* de la completitud de

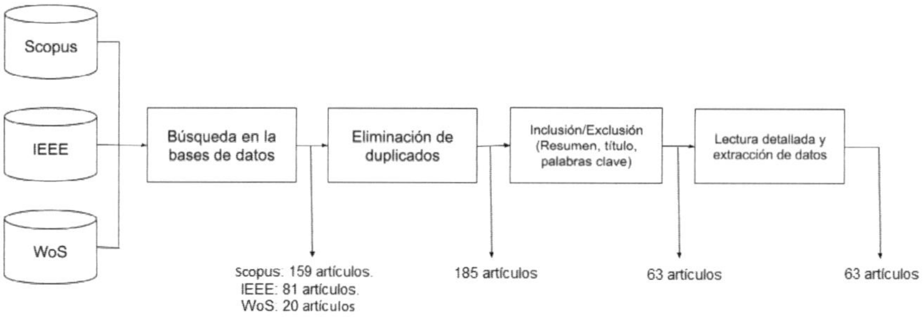

Figura 1: Proceso de búsqueda y selección de artículos

las publicaciones para responder la pregunta de investigación. Los criterios de calidad establecidos para la evaluación de los artículos fueron los siguientes: (Q1) El artículo describe la construcción y la funcionalidad de la herramienta para realizar las pruebas de seguridad. (Q2) El artículo describe cómo se ejecutan las pruebas automatizadas de seguridad utilizando la herramienta. (Q3) El artículo detalla el procedimiento de evaluación de la efectividad de la herramienta utilizada y sus resultados. El puntaje se otorga en una escala de 0 a 2, donde 0 = No en lo absoluto, 1 = Parcialmente y 2= Totalmente.

Los valores de calidad obtenidos por los estudios variaron entre 0 y 6, con una mediana de 4 y un promedio de 3.70, lo que refleja que los estudios tienen un nivel de detalle aceptable. El detalle de la evaluación de calidad por artículo se encuentra disponible en el enlace: `https://tinyurl.com/w9e48g3`.

4.3. Extracción y análisis de los datos

Para la extracción de la información de los 63 artículos se elaboró una tabla con los elementos que permitían responder la pregunta de investigación. Para la pregunta de investigación (RQ) se extrajo la herramienta utilizada y su descripción, el contexto donde se ejecuta la herramienta, la información de las pruebas que realiza para detectar las vulnerabilidades de las aplicaciones Web. Una vez que se contó con la información tabulada se procedió con el análisis de las frecuencias de vulnerabilidades por herramientas y la identificación de las evaluaciones de efectividad de las herramientas. Del mismo modo, el formularios de extracción se encuentra disponible en el enlace: `https://tinyurl.com/w9e48g3`.

4.4. Amenazas a la validez

A continuación se discuten algunas de las limitaciones del estudio. La cadena de búsqueda fue definida a partir de una búsqueda exploratoria en bases de datos y un conjunto de artículos de control. Además fue refinada mediante un conjunto de pruebas piloto. Las bases de datos seleccionadas son reconocidas por tener una buena cobertura de información en el campo de ingeniería de software. Durante el proceso de inclusión o exclusión, si existían dudas sobre un artículo específico, se procedió a su lectura completa.

Las clasificaciones presentadas en este estudio, así como la interpretación de los resultados, se realizaron usando el criterio de la investigadora principal y con la validación de los demás investigadores. Además, la aplicación de los criterios de calidad fue realizada por una sola investigadora. Para la clasificación de las herramientas, se utilizó la metodología de pruebas para aplicaciones Web de *OWASP*. En la mayoría de los casos la clasificación fue extraída de manera explícita de los artículos; sin embargo, para algunos casos la selección de la vulnerabilidad se realizó de manera implícita a partir de los datos reportados. Todo el proceso se reportó de forma detallada para facilitar su análisis y utilización en estudios posteriores.

5. Resultados

A continuación se presentan los resultados del mapeo sistemático de la literatura que identifican las herramientas utilizadas para la automatización de pruebas de seguridad de aplicaciones Web.

En total identificamos 66 propuestas de herramientas utilizadas para realizar pruebas automatizadas de seguridad. Las herramientas se clasificaron según las 11 categorías de la Sección 4 de la metodología de pruebas de seguridad para determinar vulnerabilidades del proyecto abierto de seguridad en aplicaciones Web de *OWASP* (basado en el primer nivel de la clasificación) [5].

El Cuadro 1 agrupa las herramientas para cada una de las categorías de vulnerabilidades del primer nivel de la clasificación de *OWASP*. Las categorías para las cuales se identificaron herramientas fueron: *Configuration and Deployment Management Testing (4.3)*, *Identity Management Testing (4.4)*, *Authenticaion Testing (4.5)*, *Authorization Testing (4.6)*, *Session Management Testing (4.7)*, *Input Validation Testing (4.8)*, *Error Handling (4.9)*, *Weak Cryptography (4.10)* y *Client Side Testing (4.12)*.

Para cada categoría (Id) se presenta la lista de herramientas, referencias de los artículos que la evaluaron, y la cantidad de herramientas (Q). Los resultados indican que la categoría de pruebas para detectar vulnerabilidades más común fue *Input Validation Testing (4.8)* con 55 herramientas, seguido de las pruebas de *Configuration and Deployment Management Testing (4.3)*, *Session Management Testing (4.7)* y *Client Side Testing (4.12)* con 15 herramientas utilizadas cada una.

Para el Cuadro 1 se cuantificó la cantidad de artículos que trabajaron cada categoría de vulnerabilidad y el total de ocurrencias de las vulnerabilidades de una categoría en los artículos. Los resultados muestran una tendencia similar a las de las herramientas donde la categoría de pruebas para detectar vulnerabilidades con más artículos fue la *(4.8)* con 52 artículos y 113 vulnerabilidades evaluadas. En el caso de las pruebas de *(4.3)* la cantidad de artículos y vulnerabilidades evaluadas fue 15. Finalmente, las categorías *(4.7) y (4.12)* fueron reportadas en 12 artículos y en el caso de la categoría *(4.7)* evaluó 12 vulnerabilidades y en la categoría *(4.12)* evaluó 17 vulnerabilidades.

Las herramientas *ZAP* [S58, S37, S42], *ISTA* [S05, S48], *SPaciTE* [S12, S63] y *Volcano* [S49, S52] fueron las únicas reportados por dos o más artículos. Esto

Cuadro 1: Herramientas por categoría de *OWASP* (primer nivel)

Id	Herramientas y referencias	Q
4.3	ISTA [S48], AppScan [S34], Urls black box tests on the Web pages [S32], Fuzz testing tool [S65], HJ2IF [S28], IPT-WS [S54], MobSTer [S04], SAML-based SSO IdP by Google [S64], SECEVAL [S46], WS-Attacker [S33], WSFAgressor [S61], WSInject [S59], WSSecTool [S66], WSAttaker [S57], WSVTS [S58]	15
4.4	SPaCiTE [S12, S63], AppScan [S34]	2
4.5	ZAP [S07, S37], DAST [S37], Fortify [S10], IMAATT [S45], JBroFuzz [S10], OAuthTester [S55], Paros [S10], PBST [S36], Selenium IDE [S20], WebScarab [S10]	10
4.6	ISTA [S05], OAuthTester [S55], SPaCIoS [S19]	3
4.7	ZAP [S07], ISTA [S05], CodePulse [S26], Magento [S14], MobsTer [S04], PBST [S36], SAMATE [S16], Selenium IDE [S20], AOP [S39], Urls black box tests [S32], Deemon [S38], Fortify [S10], JBroFuzz [S10], Paros [S10], WebScarab [S10]	15
4.8	ZAP [S07, S37, S42], ISTA [S05], SPaCiTE [S12, S63], Volcano [S49, S52], AOP [S39], Sign-WS [S54], ATUSA [S51], BIOFUZZ [S43], BurpTool [S42], CRAXweb [S17], Circe [S21], CodePulse [S26], DAST [S37], Deemon [S38], XSS, black box and SQLI injection point [S30], Eclipse IDE [S62], Eclipse IDE test cases [S50], Urls black box tests on the Web pages [S32], Fortify [S10], IAAT [S22], IMATT [S45], JBroFuzz [S10], JWebUnit [S23], JWAST [S40], KamaleonFuzz [S47], Magento [S14], MobSTer [S04], MBT [S41], Noncespace [S06], PHP2XMI [S08], PURITY [S09], Paros [S10], RBVT [S44], RAD-WS [S54], SAFELI [S35], SAMATE [S16], SAML [S64], SAP HANA XS Applications [S56], SECEVAL [S46], SSES [S15], SPaCIoS [S19], SQLIVDT [S18], SQLMAP [S13], Selenium IDE [S20], IDS [S53], Signature evaluation [S24], Tamper data [S60], Tool-prototype [S11], WAP [S35], WSFAgressor [S61], WSInject [S59], WSVTS [S58], WebScarab [S10], XSSINJECTOR [S27], XSS and SQLI [S25]	55
4.9	ZAP [S07]	1
4.10	ISTA [S05], Fortify [S10], JBroFuzz [S10], Paros [S10], SAML-based SSO IdP service provided by Google [S64], WebScarab [S10]	6
4.12	ZAP [S37], ISTA [S52], AOP [S39], ATUSA [S51], Code Pulse [S26], DAST [S37], Fortify [S10], JBroFuzz [S10], JWAST [S40], KITE [S31], Paros [S10], SAP HANA XS Applications [S56], SQTL [S29], WebScarab [S10], XSSINJECTOR [S27]	15

indica la necesidad de que los investigadores realicen replicaciones utilizando propuestas de herramientas existentes.

En la Figura 2 se presenta la tendencia de vulnerabilidades evaluadas por categoría de *OWASP* del primer nivel por cada año desde el 2006 hasta el 2019. Los resultados confirman que la categoría de vulnerabilidad *Input Validation Testing (4.8)* es la más evaluada por las herramientas entre los años 2007 al 2019, siendo el año 2014 y 2018 el más evaluado con 21 y 17 ocurrencias respectivamente.

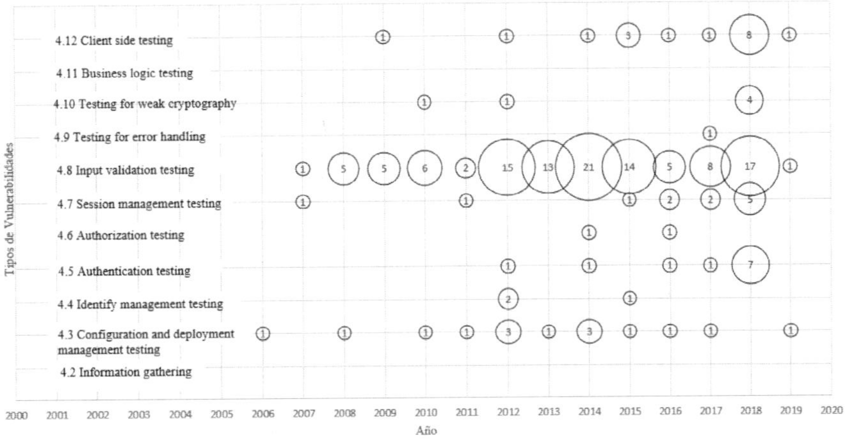

Figura 2: Tendencia de vulnerabilidades del primer nivel de *OWASP* por año

El Cuadro 2 presenta las vulnerabilidades del segundo nivel de *OWASP* para las categorías en que se identificaron herramientas. Las vulnerabilidades para las cuales se identificaron herramientas fueron: *Testing for Privilege Escalation (4.6.3)*, *Testing for Insecure Direct Object References (4.6.4)*, *Testing for Cookies attributes (4.7.2)*, *Testing for Cross Site Request Forgery (CSRF) (4.7.5)*, *Testing for Reflected Cross Site Scripting (4.8.1)*, *Testing for Stored Cross Site Scripting (4.8.2)*, *Testing for SQL Injection (4.8.5)*, *Testing for LDAP Injection (4.8.6) Testing for XML Injection (4.8.8) Testing for XML injection (4.8.9) Testing for XPath Injection (4.8.10) Testing for Command Injection (4.8.13) Testing for HTTP Incoming Requests (4.8.17) Testing for DOM based Cross Site Scripting (4.12.1) Testing for JavaScript Execution (4.12.2) Testing for HTML Injection (4.12.3).*

Para cada vulnerabilidad (Id) se presenta la lista de herramientas y referencias de los artículos que la evaluaron, y la cantidad de herramientas (Q). Los tipos de pruebas más reportadas fueron los de la categoría *Input Validation Testing (4.8)* en la que se encontraron las vulnerabilidades más reportadas. Las vulnerabilidades más comúnmente evaluadas fueron la *SQL Injection (4.8.5)* con 40 herramientas, *Cross-Site Scripting (4.8.2)* con 30 herramientas, y *Testing for HTTP Incoming Requests (4.8.17)* con 19 herramientas utilizadas.

En la Figura 3 se presenta la tendencia de vulnerabilidades evaluadas del segundo nivel de *OWASP* por cada año desde el 2007 hasta el 2019. Los resultados confirman que las vulnerabilidades *Testing for SQL Injection (4.8.5)* y *Cross-Site Scripting (4.8.2)* son las más evaluadas por las herramientas.

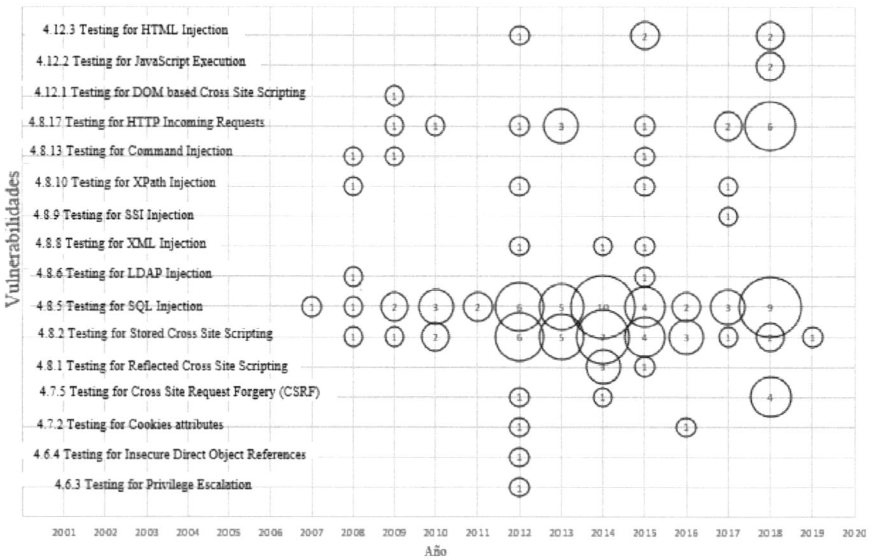

Figura 3: Tendencia de vulnerabilidades del segundo nivel de *OWASP* por año

6. Discusión

La clasificación de las distintas herramientas disponibles para evaluar cada una de las vulnerabilidades de las aplicaciones Web puede apoyar a los profesionales en la selección de potenciales herramientas para sus procesos de pruebas de seguridad. Estas herramientas pueden apoyar la evaluación de la seguridad de las aplicaciones Web de forma automatizada en distintas fases del ciclo de vida de desarrollo de las aplicaciones Web o inclusive cuando se encuentra en producción.

Se identificó gran variedad de herramientas que se utilizan para automatizar distintas pruebas de seguridad de acuerdo con las distintas vulnerabilidades que existen en la actualidad. Para evaluar la seguridad de las aplicaciones Web, las herramientas deben de contar con pruebas actualizadas de acuerdo con las vulnerabilidades y ataques cibernéticos actuales. La identificación de herramientas demostró que se mantiene la tendencia de realizar pruebas para la *SQL Injection* y *Cross-Site Scripting*. Sin embargo, no se encontraron herramientas para algunos de los escenarios reportados como los 10 ataques con más riesgosos y frecuentes por *OWASP*, tales como: *Insecure Deserialization, Using Components with known vulnerabilities* e *Insufficient Logging & Monitoring*.

Por otro lado, de las 66 propuestas de herramientas utilizadas para realizar pruebas automatizadas de seguridad solo 41 reportaron una evaluación de la efectividad. De las 41 herramientas, 16 fueron evaluadas a partir de criterios de

Cuadro 2: Herramientas por vulnerabilidad de *OWASP* (segundo nivel)

Id	Herramientas y referencias	Q
4.6.3	ISTA [S48]	1
4.6.4	ISTA [S48]	1
4.7.2	AOP [S39], Urls and performing black box tests on the Web pages [S32]	2
4.7.5	ISTA [S05], Deemon [S38], Fortify [S10], JBroFuzz [S10], Paros [S10], WebScarab [S10]	6
4.8.1	ZAP [S07], BurpTool [S42], MBT [S41], SPaCIoS [S19]	4
4.8.2	ZAP [S07, S37, S42], ISTA [S05], SPaCiTE [S12, S63], AOP [S39], BurpTool [S42], CRAXweb [S17], Circe [S21], CodePulse [S26], DAST [S37], XSS, black box and SQLI based on injection point [S30], IAAT [S22], IMAATT [S45], JwebUnit [S10], JWAST [S40], KamaleonFuzz [S47], MobSTer [S04], MBT [S04], Noncespaces [S06], PHP2XMI [S08], PURITY [S09], RBVT [S44], SSES [S15], SPaCIoS [S19], SQLIVDT [S18], Selenium IDE [S20], Tamper data [S60], Tool-prototye [S11], WSInject [S59], XSSINJECTOR [S27], XSS and SQLI evaluation [S25]	30
4.8.5	ZAP [S07,S37], ISTA [S05], SPaCiTE [S12, S63], Volcano [S49, S52], AOP [S39], BIOFUZZ [S43], CRAXweb [S17], Circe [S21], CodePulse [S26], DAST [S37], XSS, black box and SQLI based on injection point [S30], Eclipse IDE [S62], Fortify [S10], IAAT [S22], IMAATT [S45], JBroFuzz [S10], JWAST [S40], Magento [S14], MobSTer [S04], PHP2XMI [S08], PURITY [S09], Paros [S10], RBVT [S44], RAD-WS [S54], Eclipse IDE test cases execution [S50], SAFELI [S35], SAMATE [S16], SAP HANA XS Applications [S56], SSES [S15], SPaCIoS [S19], SQLIVDT [S18], SQLMap [S13], Selenium IDE [S20], IDS [S53], Signature evaluation [S24], Tamper data [S60], Tool-prototype [S11], WAP [S35], WebScarab [S10], XSS and SQLI security evaluation [S25]	40
4.8.6	JWAST [S40], SSES [S15]	2
4.8.8	Eclipse IDE [S62], JWAST [S40], SPaCioS [S19]	3
4.8.9	Sign-WS [S54]	1
4.8.10	Eclipse IDE [S62], JWAST [S40], RAD-WS [S54], SSES [S15]	4
4.8.13	JWAST [S40], SSES [S15]	2
4.8.17	ZAP [S07, S37, S42], ATUSa [S51], BurpTool [S42], CRAXweb [S17], DAST [S37], Deemon [S38], XSS, black box and SQLI based on injection point [S30], Urls and performing black box tests on the Web pages [S32], Fortify [S10], JBroFuzz [S10], JWAST [S40], Paros [S10], SAML-based SSO IdP service by Google [S64], SECEVAL [S46], SPaCIoS [S19], Tamper data [S60], WSFAgressor [S61], WSVTS [S58], WebScarab [S10]	19
4.12.1	ATUSA [S51]	1
4.12.2	ZAP [S37], DAST [S37], JWAST [S40], SAP HANA XS Applications [S56]	4
4.12.3	ZAP [S37], ISTA [S05], DAST [S37]	3

eficiencia, 13 a partir de criterios de eficacia y 12 fueron evaluadas a partir de ambos criterios. Las herramientas fueron evaluadas para determinar el tiempo que toma la ejecución de las pruebas (por ejemplo: [S07, S13, S34, S54, S61]), comparar la efectividad entre herramientas (por ejemplo: [S04, S30, S58]), y determinar la relación entre eficiencia y efectividad (cantidad de pruebas ejecutadas y tiempo que tomó la ejecución de las pruebas, por ejemplo: [S11, S41, S24, S30, S32, S38, S43, S51]). Por ejemplo, las herramientas [S35, S36, S47, S54, S59, S61, S04, S51] evaluaron la cantidad de falsos positivos en los resultados de ejecución de las pruebas y la herramienta [S10] comparó los resultados obtenidos al ejecutar pruebas automatizadas contra la ejecución de pruebas manual para comparar los resultados obtenidos. En muchas de las evaluaciones se validó el éxito de la ejecución de pruebas a partir de la cantidad de vulnerabilidades encontradas (por ejemplo: [S09, S18, S19, S20, S21, S23, S25, S31, S10, S30, S32, S43, S58, S42]). Otras evaluaciones se limitaron a verificar la funcionalidad implementada por la herramienta (por ejemplo: [S22, S05, S24, S38, S51, S49]).

Del total de herramientas, 29 herramientas reportaron algunos de los retos que enfrentaron durante la ejecución de las pruebas. Diez herramientas plantean la necesidad de actualizar y cambiar sus tipos de pruebas para mejorar el desempeño, la efectividad y la escalabilidad [S05, S18, S41, S47, S52, S58, S59, S60, S62]. Ocho herramientas plantean la necesidad de crear nuevos casos de pruebas para detectar otros tipos de vulnerabilidades [S04, S08, S13, S14, S23, S30, S36, S51, S57]. Una propuesta plantea la necesidad de mejorar la configuración de la herramienta [S09], otra la mejora en la priorización de las pruebas para utilizarlas en pruebas de regresión [S20], cuatro indican la necesidad de optimizar el código, los métodos y las funcionalidades de la herramienta [S34, S38, S45, S46], así como también la mejora en la detección de los falsos positivos en los resultados [S37]. Finalmente, 3 herramientas plantean la necesidad de mejorar el soporte para distintas [S11, S26, S33].

7. Conclusiones

Este estudio reportó los resultados de un mapeo sistemático de la literatura sobre herramientas utilizadas para probar la seguridad de aplicaciones Web. Se identificaron 63 estudios primarios que reportaron 66 propuestas de herramientas utilizadas para realizar pruebas automatizadas de seguridad. Las herramientas se clasificaron según los tipos de la metodología de pruebas de seguridad para determinar vulnerabilidades del proyecto abierto de seguridad en aplicaciones Web.

Los resultados demuestran que se mantiene la tendencia de realizar pruebas para la *SQL Injection* y *Cross-Site Scripting*. Sin embargo, los casos de prueba que realizan las herramientas identificadas solo evalúan algunos de los escenarios reportados como los 10 ataques más riesgosos y frecuentes por *OWASP*. Además, aunque se identificó gran variedad de herramientas que realizan distintos tipos de pruebas de seguridad, solo pocas herramientas se encuentran en la lista de herramientas recomendadas por *OWASP*, lo que denota la necesidad de contar con evaluaciones empíricas de herramientas existentes en el área.

Como trabajo futuro, se desea seleccionar un conjunto de herramientas de pruebas de seguridad que permitan verificar las principales vulnerabilidades reportadas para las aplicaciones Web y evaluar su efectividad con el fin de generar evidencia para la industria. Asimismo, como trabajo futuro se desea identificar las clasificaciones de vulnerabilidades brindadas por *OWASP* que no fueron cubiertas por ninguna herramienta del mapeo y realizar un estudio de la razón por la cual las actuales herramientas no evalúan estas vulnerabilidades y la importancia de que las herramientas ejecute pruebas para estas vulnerabilidades.

Referencias

1. P. Zech, M. Felderer, and R. Breu, "Knowledge-based security testing of web applications by logic programming," *International Journal on Software Tools for Technology Transfer*, vol. 21, no. 2, pp. 221–246, 2019.
2. OWASP, "Testing: Introduction and objectives," *The Open Web Application Security Project*, 2019.
3. S. De Vries, "Security testing web applications throughout automated software tests," *Corsaire Ltd*, vol. 3, 2006.
4. Y. Stefinko, A. Piskozub, and R. Banakh, "Manual and automated penetration testing. benefits and drawbacks. modern tendency," in *2016 13th International Conference on Modern Problems of Radio Engineering, Telecommunications and Computer Science (TCSET)*. IEEE, 2016, pp. 488–491.
5. OWASP, "Testing guide v4, web application security testing," *The Open Web Application Security Project*, 2019.
6. S. Rafique, M. Humayun, B. Hamid, A. Abbas, M. Akhtar, and K. Iqbal, "Web application security vulnerabilities detection approaches: A systematic mapping study," in *2015 IEEE/ACIS 16th International Conference on Software Engineering, Artificial Intelligence, Networking and Parallel/Distributed Computing (SNPD)*. IEEE, 2015, pp. 1–6.
7. OWASP, "The open web application security project," *The Open Web Application Security Project*, 2019.
8. ——, "Top 10–2017–the ten most critical web application security risks," *The Open Web Application Security Project*, 2017.
9. H. H. Thompson, "Why security testing is hard," *IEEE Security Privacy*, vol. 1, no. 4, pp. 83–86, July 2003.
10. M. Curphey and R. Arawo, "Web application security assessment tools," *IEEE Security & Privacy*, vol. 4, no. 4, pp. 32–41, 2006.
11. S. Pfleeger and R. Cunningham, "Why measuring security is hard," *IEEE Security Privacy*, vol. 8, no. 4, pp. 46–54, July 2010.
12. N. M. Mohammed, M. Niazi, M. Alshayeb, and S. Mahmood, "Exploring software security approaches in software development lifecycle: A systematic mapping study," *Computer Standards & Interfaces*, vol. 50, pp. 107–115, 2017.
13. A. J. Jafari and A. Rasoolzadegan, "Security patterns: A systematic mapping study," *arXiv preprint arXiv:1811.12715*, 2018.
14. M. Bunke, "Software-security patterns: degree of maturity," in *Proceedings of the 20th European Conference on Pattern Languages of Programs*. ACM, 2015, p. 42.
15. Y. Ito, H. Washizaki, M. Yoshizawa, Y. Fukazawa, T. Okubo, H. Kaiya, A. Hazeyama, N. Yoshioka, and E. B. Fernandez, "Systematic mapping of security patterns research," in *Proceedings of the 22nd Conference on Pattern Languages of Programs*. The Hillside Group, 2015, p. 14.

16. K. Petersen, S. Vakkalanka, and L. Kuzniarz, "Guidelines for conducting systematic mapping studies in software engineering: An update," vol. 64. Elsevier, 2015, pp. 1–18.
17. B. Kitchenham and S. Charters, "Guidelines for performing systematic literature reviews in software engineering," *Technical report, EBSE Technical Report EBSE-2007-01*, pp. 1–57, 2007.
18. V. Basili, C. Gianluigi, and D. Rombach, "The goal question metric approach," *Encyclopedia of software engineering*, pp. 528–532, 1994.

Identification of quality characteristics in mobile applications

Vitor Carneiro Maia[0000-0001-9999-0195], Ana Regina Cavalcanti da Rocha[0000-0003-2269-5619] e Taisa Guidini Gonçalves[0000-0002-7108-1763]

Federal University of Rio de Janeiro – PESC/COPPE, Rio de Janeiro, Brazil
vcm@ufrj.br, darocha.anaregina@gmail.com, taisa@cos.ufrj.br

Abstract. Mobile devices and their applications became popular since the creation of the app stores' distribution model. There is a great variety of apps available and we are inclined to use the best ones, what make it essential to develop apps of distinctive quality. To identify pertinent quality characteristics of mobile applications based on available literature, we conducted a systematic mapping study regarding the quality of mobile applications. It was executed in five search engines: Scopus, IEEE, Web of Science, Engineering Village and ACM. The resulting papers were analyzed in search of occurrences of quality characteristics of mobile applications. At all, 53 papers were analyzed. From the quality characteristics present in ISO/IEC 25010 models, the most cited were usability, performance efficiency, functional suitability, reliability, and context coverage. Fifteen extra quality characteristics were also found. The systematic mapping study permitted the formulation of an initial list of quality characteristics, which may be the most pertinent in the context of mobile applications.

Keywords: Systematic mapping study, Software engineering, Quality characteristics, ISO/IEC 25010, Mobile applications.

1 Introduction

Mobile devices and applications became especially popular after the creation of the app stores' distribution model [1]. Since then, the quantity of available mobile applications (apps) has increased significantly every year. There is a great variety of apps available and we are inclined to use the best ones.

Generally, if apps are not developed with distinctive quality, users will naturally find and install better competing apps with the same functionalities. Although the app stores contain publication guidelines, they are not broad enough to prevent the submission of mobile applications not in conformity with the users' expectations.

Given the flaws of the stores' publication guidelines, App Quality Alliance (AQuA) [2] provides documents with best practices guidelines regarding mobile applications. Although, these guidelines are not frequently updated and are not in conformity with international software quality standards.

The ISO/IEC 25000 series defines quality models, measures and requirements for a diversity of generic software quality characteristics [3]. Quality models are general-purpose and made to be applied to any kind of software product. However, not every quality characteristic is appropriate in all cases and some may be more relevant depending on context and stakeholders. This generality makes it necessary to identify which characteristics are more relevant for a certain kind of application.

This paper describes a Systematic Mapping Study (SMS) about the identification of quality characteristics in the context of mobile applications. The results provide a list of quality characteristics to support development and quality evaluation of apps.

The remainder of the paper is structured as follows: Section 2 presents the background. Section 3 explains the research methodology and the results. Section 4 presents a discussion about the results. Section 5 presents the threats to validity. Finally, section 6 concludes the paper.

2 Background and related work

In this section, we discuss some concepts related to software quality.

The ISO/IEC 25000, also known as SQuaRE, contains a set of standards relative to software quality. These standards define management guidelines, quality models, measures, requirements and software evaluation processes. ISO/IEC 25010 [3] defines two quality models: **Quality in Use**, with quality characteristics (Effectiveness, Efficiency, Satisfaction, Freedom from risk, and Context coverage) related to the outcome of interaction when a product is used in a context of use; and **Product Quality**, with characteristics (Functional suitability, Performance efficiency, Compatibility, Usability, Reliability, Security, Maintainability, Portability) related to static and dynamic properties of software. This standard defines the quality of a system as the degree to which the system satisfies the stated and implied needs of its various stakeholders, and thus provides value.

The software quality models may not be entirely used to evaluate a product. Every kind of software has its own specific features, stakeholders, hardware and so on. It becomes necessary to particularize quality models in view of these peculiarities.

Barney & Wohlin [4] reports a case study in which a questionnaire was elaborated with the quality characteristics in ISO/IEC 9126 and some other models found in literature. Several employees from Ericsson with different functions and involved in different projects were requested to distribute 1000 points among the characteristics they considered the most important. The objective of the study was to identify different points of view of stakeholders.

A survey was carried out in Haigh [5], with the purpose of identifying opinions about the importance of quality characteristics. The respondents were students and ex-students from an unnamed MBA program in the USA, each performing different roles in software projects. Users prioritized integrity, portability and usability. Developers prioritized maintainability and testability. Managers prioritized accuracy.

A study with the purpose of determining a quality model for IoT based on ISO/IEC 9126 and ISO/IEC 25010 is described in Kim et al. [6]. The study lists general characteristics of IoT applications. As a conclusion, metrics were developed for five quality characteristics: Functionality, Reliability, Efficiency, Portability and Security.

The studies described above are some examples of surveys or particularization studies, which reiterates the importance of identifying specific quality characteristics for different types of software.

3 Research methodology and protocol

This systematic mapping study (SMS) aims to characterize the current state of research into the quality of mobile applications. To conduct this SMS, we followed Biolchini et al. [7] process, which consists of four phases, as showed in Fig. 1.

Fig. 1. Summary of the Systematic Review Process [7]

In the first phase (Planning) we defined the research goal, research questions and methods for the execution and analysis phases. We also defined the search string, the search engines and the inclusion and exclusion criteria. Next, in the Execution phase we executed the search string to obtain the set of papers. The previously defined set of inclusion and exclusion criteria are applied to the resulting papers.

In the third phase (Result analysis) we read the papers and extract their relevant data to an extraction form, according to the research questions. Then, the extracted data are assembled and interpreted to answer the questions. The Packaging phase was executed throughout the whole process, keeping documented all the decisions and information.

Kitchenham and Charters [8] also describe the Reporting phase, in which the produced results and documentation are made available to potential stakeholders. Given that this SMS documents the results but does not report them to potential stakeholders, this approach was not followed. Thus Biolchini's approach is similar to Kitchenham's.

3.1 Research Goal

The main objective of this SMS is to identify which quality characteristics are relevant in the context of mobile applications. Table 1 presents the aim of this study, using the GQM paradigm [9].

Table 1. Research goal, according to GQM paradigm

Analyze	Quality characteristics
For the purpose of	Characterizing
With respect to	Pertinence
From the point of view of	Software engineering researchers
In the context of	Mobile applications

3.2 Research questions

The original objective of the research was to list pertinent quality characteristics of mobile applications independently of existing quality models, but it seemed clear that the result would contain many occurrences of quality characteristics from the two models in ISO/IEC 25010. Due to this observation, two research questions were developed. They are present in Table 2.

Table 2. Research Questions

Research Question		Rationale
RQ1	**Which quality characteristics from ISO/IEC 25010 are identified as pertinent in the context of mobile applications?**	The answer indicates the ISO/IEC 25010 characteristics considered pertinent in several researches about quality of mobile applications present in literature.
RQ2	**Which quality characteristics are not present in ISO/IEC 25010, but are identified as pertinent in the context of mobile applications?**	The answer indicates the characteristics considered pertinent in several researches about quality of mobile applications present in the literature, but not covered by ISO/IEC 25010.

3.3 Search string and search engines

The selection of papers was carried out through a search string, applied in several search engines. The string followed the PICO process [10]. The subject of the research should be decomposed in four parts: population, intervention, comparison and outcome. There is no comparison in the scope of this work. Our search string is composed by the keywords: Population = mobile applications; Intervention = software quality models, quality in use, quality requirements; and Outcome = characteristics, metrics, measures, evaluation criteria, attributes. The terms in both intervention and outcome are common in the context of the ISO/IEC 25000 standards.

The "quality requirements" intervention was not considered in the first version of the string, although they could be helpful to infer implied qualities of a software product. So, the string was modified once to include it. The final search string was: **(("mobile app*") AND ("software quality" OR "quality model" OR "quality in use" OR "quality requirement") AND ("characteristic" OR "metric" OR "measure" OR "evaluation criteria" OR "attribute")).**

It was executed in five search engines: Scopus, IEEE, Web of Science, Engineering Village and ACM. The first execution occurred in May 2018 and the last (and second) in September 2018.

3.4 Inclusion and exclusion criteria

The execution of the search string in the search engines returned several papers, but not all of them might be suitable for the purpose of this study. Therefore, inclusion and exclusion criteria were developed to refine the initial list of papers. Exclusion criteria are in Table 3. The inclusion criteria are the opposite of exclusion criteria (E1 to E4).

Table 3. Exclusion Criteria

E1	The paper was not published in conferences or journals.
E2	The paper is not available in the internet.
E3	The paper is not in English.
E4	The paper is not about quality in mobile applications.
E5	The paper is similar to another paper by the same authors.
E6	The paper is about design patterns, source code or quality of services.

3.5 Execution

The exclusion criteria E1 to E3, which are not dependent on the reading of the papers, were applied to the initial set of papers. The application of the other exclusion criteria depended on further interpretation, so the authors read the abstracts of the remaining papers, then decided together on more exclusion, based on criteria E4 to E6. Some papers could only be safely excluded after the full text was read. Table 4 shows the number of results before and after the application of exclusion criteria. E6, which comprises qualities of code and services, was also considered because this research analyses specifically app quality from the viewpoint of software products.

Table 4. Search Results

Search Engine	Initial Set	After E1, E2 & E3	After E4, E5 & E6
Scopus	57	45	29
IEEE	27	26	13
Engineering Village	27	19	13
Web of Science	30	23	13
ACM	7	7	3

Most of the papers were found in more than one search engine. In total, 35 papers were selected using the search string. In addition, from the included papers' references, 18 other papers were manually selected based on their titles (snowballing). Thus, we have 53 papers selected. At all, 28 papers were excluded, based on Exclusion Criteria. Table 5 shows the papers included via search string and via snowballing.

E4 also considered papers concerning specific types of apps. e.g., papers regarding medical apps would not be excluded. We were aware of the possibility of bias due to a quality characteristic being pertinent just in the context of a specific type of app. In order to reduce the bias, these papers were cautiously read and the occurrences of characteristics which seemed only related to the specific topic were not accounted.

The 53 selected papers were analyzed by means of the two research questions. The extracted data, which answers these questions, were collected with the assistance of a form. As far as possible, the research questions must be objectively answered by the reading and interpretation of each paper. These data would subsequently be merged and analyzed to answer the research questions.

To answer RQ1, the form contains tables to store information on quality characteristics and sub-characteristics of both quality models from ISO/IEC 25010, which might be described as relevant in the paper. To answer RQ2, the form contains a table to retain information on characteristics apparently not related to those proposed by ISO/IEC 25010. The form also contains tables for measures, requirements and device limitations, which might be important to relate, characterize and interpret the quality characteristics present in each paper. Other information such as the authors, the year of publication, the search engines, the software quality standard, and the definition of mobile application (if present) are included in the form.

Table 5. Papers included via search string and snowballing

ID	Papers (search string)	ID	Papers (search string)	ID	Papers (snowballing)
M1	Fauzia et al. [11]	**M19**	Lew and Olsina [12]	**M36**	Cortimiglia et al. (2011)
M2	Idri et al. [13]	**M20**	Zhenyu et al. [14]	**M37**	Dantas et al. (2009)
M3	Mohsin et al. [15]	**M21**	Karima and Idri [16]	**M38**	Spriestersbach and Springer (2004)
M4	Barnett et al. [17]	**M22**	Lizhi et al [18]	**M39**	Sá and Carriço (2008)
M5	Idri et al. [19]	**M23**	Kolski et al. [20]	**M40**	Huang (2009)
M6	Franke et al. [21]	**M24**	Moumane et al. [22]	**M41**	Harrison et al. (2013)
M7	Baloh et al [23]	**M25**	Corral [24]	**M42**	Lai (2015)
M8	Yildiz et al. [25]	**M26**	Holl and Vieira [26]	**M43**	Lim et al. (2015)
M9	Alaa et al. [27]	**M27**	Nayebi et al. [28]	**M44**	La et al (2011)
M10	Kabir et al. [29]	**M28**	Ryan and Rossi [30]	**M45**	Gafni (2009)
M11	Idri et al. [31]	**M29**	Corral et al [32]	**M46**	Holl and Elberzhager (2014)
M12	Souza and Aquino [33]	**M30**	Khalid et al. [34]	**M47**	Holzinger et al. (2012)
M13	Fang et al. [35]	**M31**	Olsina and Lew [36]	**M48**	Wasserman (2010)
M14	Pretel and Vilarino [37]	**M32**	Peischl et al. [38]	**M49**	Kim et al. (2011)
M15	Franke and Weise [39]	**M33**	Khalid et al. [40]	**M50**	Balagtas-Fernandez and Hussmann (2009)
M16	Hess et al. [41]	**M34**	Grano et al. [42]	**M51**	Zahra et al. (2013)
M17	Soad and Duarte Filho [43]	**M35**	Abusair [44]	**M52**	Hussain et al. (2009)
M18	Marinho and Resende [45]			**M53**	Savio and Braiterman (2007)

3.6 Publication Frequency

Fig. 2 contains a chart regarding the frequency of publications found in this study.

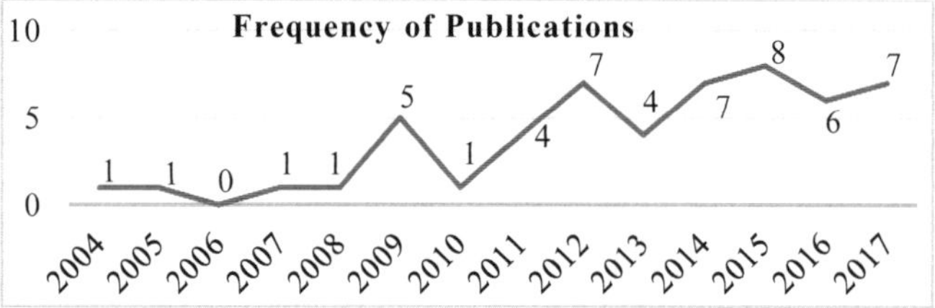

Fig. 2. Frequency of publications over the years

Only a few papers are earlier than 2009. Android and iOS technologies emerged in 2007 and popularized the distribution model of the app stores [1]. From this point onwards, it became easier to develop and download applications. It may be the reason for the sudden interest in this research area after 2009, which remains relatively unchanged ever since. By the moment of the SMS' last execution there existed papers from 2018 in the resulting set, but curiously none of them entered the group of included papers.

3.7 Research Question 1

The ISO/IEC 25000 series identify 8 product quality characteristics and link them to 30 sub-characteristics. It also identify 5 quality in use characteristics and link them to 9 sub-characteristics [3]. A process was followed in order to identify characteristics in the included papers:

- Identify quality characteristics and sub-characteristics, both in use or product quality, associated with mobile applications, where authors explicitly reference ISO/IEC 25000.
- Identify quality characteristics and sub-characteristics, both in use or product quality, associated with mobile applications, where authors explicitly reference ISO/IEC 9126 [46], predecessor of ISO/IEC 25010. Both standards were combined using a comparative table in ISO/IEC 25010's annex A [3].
- Identify quality characteristics and sub-characteristics, both in use or product quality, associated with mobile applications, where authors do not explicitly reference SQuaRE standards nor its predecessor ISO/IEC 9126. In this case, there are two possible situations: (1) there is an equivalent and similar definition to those in the standards; or (2) the paper does not contain a definition, but the context permits the association.
- Identify attributes associated with mobile applications equivalent to characteristics and sub-characteristics, both in use or product quality by similarity. In this case it was considered a synonym (e.g. Functional Suitability, Functionality and Functional Quality), following the proposal of Marinho & Resende [45].
- Still following the proposal of Marinho & Resende [45], characteristics and sub-characteristics were added when the paper defines problems or restrictions to the use, suggesting the necessity of a characteristic or sub characteristic (e.g. "abandoning the use of the application due to faults" suggests the necessity of the characteristic Reliability).

Marinho & Resende's methodology was followed as a basis due to its similarity with the current study. As well as us, they also needed to group occurrences of quality characteristics by synonyms. Table 6 and Table 7 contain some characteristics and sub-characteristics from the ISO/IEC 25010 product quality and quality in use models, respectively. Only the characteristics whose sub-characteristics occurred from 5 to 7 times were listed. The characteristics' occurrences were also presented. The complete list can be found in https://maia.mobi/arq/tech_report_mapping.pdf.

In order to achieve the results, described in Table 8 and Table 9, we followed the same previously explained steps. Table 8 presents the product quality characteristics and sub-characteristics do not present in ISO/IEC 25010. Table 9 presents the quality in use characteristics and sub-characteristics not present in ISO/IEC 25010.

Table 6. Occurrences of ISO/IEC 25010 product quality characteristics and sub-characteristics

Characteristics & Sub-Characteristics		Occurrences
Functional Suitability		-
Sub-characteristic	**Functional correctness**	[M8] [M17] [M19] [M22] [M29] [M31] *Subtotal: 6*
Compatibility		-
Sub-characteristic	**Interoperability**	[M22] [M29] [M47] [M48] [M53] *Subtotal*: 5
Usability		-
Sub-characteristics	**Appropriateness Recognisability**	[M11] [M19] [M22] [M29] [M31] [M38] [M45] *Subtotal*: 7
	User error protection	[M19] [M31] [M37] [M41] [M50] *Subtotal:* 5
	User interface aesthetics	[M11] [M13] [M22] [M29] [M37] [M45] [M52] *Subtotal:* 7
	Accessibility	[M7] [M11] [M29] [M39] [M37] [M52] *Subtotal:* 6
Reliability		-
Sub-characteristic	**Fault tolerance**	[M3] [M8] [M9] [M11] [M22] *Subtotal:* 5
Security		-
Sub-characteristic	**Confidentiality**	[M20] [M29] [M31] [M33] [M37] [M38] [M51] *Subtotal:* 7

Table 7. Occurrences of ISO/IEC 25010 quality in use characteristics and sub-characteristics

Characteristics & Sub-Characteristics		Occurrences
Satisfaction		-
Sub-characteristics	**Usefulness**	[M19] [M29] [M37] [M42] [M49] *Subtotal:* 5
	Pleasure	[M19] [M27] [M29] [M40] [M42] [M49] *Subtotal:* 6

3.8 Research Question 2

This question aims to identify other quality attributes, which authors identified as necessary for mobile applications and which are not present in ISO/IEC 25010.

We tried to identify new quality attributes in the included papers. Initially 90 attributes were identified. Similarities were observed in an in-depth analysis of them. A final list was drawn-up following the proposal of Marinho & Resende [45]:

- Identify attributes listed as important in the included papers, which are not synonyms with ISO/IEC 25010 quality characteristics.
- Group synonyms or similar attributes according to their definitions.
- Add an attribute when the included paper defines problems or restrictions to the use, suggesting the necessity of a quality attribute.

- Select the most suitable definition for the attribute. A definition must be manually composed if the attribute is explained but not defined in the papers.

Table 8. Product quality characteristics not present in ISO/IEC 25010

Characteristics & Sub Characteristics		Occurrences
Information Quality		[M19] [M31] *Subtotal*: 2
Sub-characteristics	**Information Correctness**	[M31] *Subtotal*: 1
	Information Credibility	[M31] *Subtotal*: 1
	Information Conciseness	[M19] *Subtotal*: 1
Usability (ISO/IEC 25010)		-
Sub-characteristics	**Navigation**	[M19] [M40] *Subtotal*: 2
	Visibility	[M19] *Subtotal*: 1
Use of Clear Forms		[M19] *Subtotal*: 1
Use of Minimized Forms		[M4] *Subtotal*: 1
Use of Hierarchical Menus		[M19] [M40] *Subtotal*: 2
Data Persistence		[M4] [M6] [M15] [M51] *Subtotal*: 4

Table 9. Quality in use characteristics not present in ISO/IEC 25010

Characteristics & Sub Characteristics		Occurrences
Sense of Community		[M10] [M19] *Subtotal*: 2
Usability in Use		[M19] *Subtotal*: 1
Sub-characteristics	**Learnability in Use**	[M19] [M41] [M53] *Subtotal*: 3
	Continuous Communication	[M19] *Subtotal*: 1
	Memorability	[M41] *Subtotal*: 1

3.9 Software Quality Standards

The preliminary execution of the search string returned plenty of papers about the quality of mobile applications basing their results in ISO/IEC 9126 or ISO/IEC 25010. Given the degree of formality found in the literature, from this point the research questions were updated to separate the quality characteristics by origin. At all, 25 papers used standards, nearly half of them; 24% used ISO/IEC 9126; 23% used ISO/IEC 25010; and 53% did not reference quality models.

3.10 Search Engines

At all, five search engines were selected for the execution of the search string. Out of curiosity, the ones included via snowballing were also manually searched in each engine. A closer look at these tables reveals that almost every paper was found in Scopus. For those included by the execution of the search string, only six were found elsewhere, and for the snowballing papers, six were not found in Scopus nor in any of the other engines and one was only found in Web of Science. It represents a coverage of 75.5% of the results by Scopus.

Scopus indexes the content of several other engines. The papers (M26, M27, M28, M33, M34, and M35) originally not found in Scopus by the execution of the string were manually searched and found in Scopus. The reason for not being returned before lies on the different indexing of the papers in each engine. A better calibration of the search string could possibly have returned all the included papers in one go.

4 Discussion

The selected papers explore a range of points of view: quality of specific categories of apps, researches into device limitations, researches into the importance of a single quality characteristic, proposal of quality models, guidelines, measures, requirements, among others. This variety positively influenced the study and diversified the conclusions about the pertinence of quality characteristics in the context of apps.

The results of the first research question indicate that **usability** is the most addressed product quality characteristic, followed by **performance efficiency**, **functional suitability** and **reliability**. As for quality in use, **efficiency**, **satisfaction** and **context coverage** are the most addressed quality characteristics. Regarding the sub-characteristics of both quality models, the most frequent ones are consequently related to **usability**, **performance efficiency** and **satisfaction**. The results for the second research question indicate the importance of additional quality characteristics strongly related to usability, thereby reinforcing the results obtained from the previous question. Some of the proposed new quality characteristics are **information quality**, **data persistence** and **sense of community**.

Some papers briefly discuss inherent characteristics and limitations of mobile devices and their impact on the quality of the applications. Common limitations such as battery consumption, CPU usage and low memory directly affect the performance efficiency. Limited screen size, few resolutions and limited input directly affect usability. A frequently mentioned limitation concerns the instability of internet connections, due to the mobility of devices, which restricts the use of wireless network. It might outline the importance of reliability and context coverage. Other frequently mentioned limitation is the occurrence of unexpected interruptions (e.g. receiving a call), which outlines the importance of the proposed quality characteristic data persistence.

5 Threats to Validity

Threats classification presented by Petersen et al. [47] were followed.

Descriptive validity is the extent to which observations are described accurately and objectively. The extraction form objectively kept relevant information present in each paper regarding the research questions. However, the extraction may not guarantee the correctness of the results. In general, a quality characteristic was included if the paper presented a description and an adequate reason for considering it pertinent. Furthermore, some papers provided quality characteristics with differing definitions from ISO/IEC 25010, which demanded a deep interpretation of what the authors meant.

Theoretical validity is determined by our ability to be able to capture what we intend to capture. The search string may not have captured many other relevant papers. As stated in section 3.10, most of the 53 included papers were present in Scopus, but the search string did not return most of them there. The same way, other important papers might not have been found. In addition, the interpretation of abstracts and the manual selection of papers via snowballing may have biased the results. To reduce the bias, inclusion and extraction of papers were reviewed many times by two researcher.

Interpretive validity is achieved when the conclusions drawn are reasonable given the data, and hence maps to conclusion validity. The research questions were subjective and demanded effort to both understand what to be extracted and how to interpret the extracted data. To reduce bias, the results were debated over several meetings until a consensus was reached.

Finally, considering the generalizability, the quantity of papers may have been relatively small, possibly due to a too restrictive search string. However, the search engines provided good coverage of the topic, especially Scopus.

6 Conclusion

This study investigated quality characteristics pertinent to the context of mobile applications. A systematic mapping study was designed in order to achieve this objective. The research questions were based on ISO/IEC 25010, which was particularized to the context of mobile applications. It was necessary because quality models are general-purpose, made to be applied to any kind of software product.

Occurrences of quality characteristics were accounted when present in the resulting papers of the mapping. It was possible to identify the most cited quality characteristics from ISO/IEC 25010: Usability, Functional Suitability, Efficiency, Reliability and Context Coverage. It was also possible to identify 15 quality characteristics, which were not previewed by the used quality models. It is expected that the results of this study will improve the development and the quality of mobile applications.

Acknowledgments. This work was greatly assisted by Guilherme Horta Travassos.

References

1. Cortimiglia, M.N., Ghezzi, A., Renga, F.: Mobile Applications and Their Delivery Platforms. IT Professional. vol 13, issue 5, 51–56 (2011). https://doi.org/10.1109/MITP.2011.84.
2. AQuA Quality Alliance - Best Practices Guidelines for Developing Quality Mobile Apps, https://www.appqualityalliance.org/AQuA-best-practice-guidelines.
3. ISO/IEC 25010:2011: Systems and software engineering - Systems and software Quality Requirements and Evaluation (SQuaRE) - System and software quality models, (2011).
4. Barney, S., Wohlin, C.: Software Product Quality: Ensuring a Common Goal. In: Wang, Q., Garousi, V., Madachy, R., and Pfahl, D. (eds.) Trustworthy Software Development Processes. pp. 256–267. Springer Berlin Heidelberg, Berlin, Heidelberg (2009).
5. Haigh, M.: Software quality, non-functional software requirements and IT-business alignment. Software Qual J. vol 18, issue 3, 361–385 (2010). https://doi.org/10.1007/s11219-010-9098-3.

6. Kim, M., Park, J.H., Lee, N.Y.: A Quality Model for IoT Service. In: Park, J.J. (Jong H., Pan, Y., Yi, G., and Loia, V. (eds.) Advances in Computer Science and Ubiquitous Computing. pp. 497–504. Springer Singapore, Singapore (2017).
7. Biolchini, J., Mian, P.G., Natali, A.C., Travassos, G.H.: Systematic Review in Software Engineering: Relevance and Utility. PESC/COPPE/UFRJ, Brazil (2005).
8. Kitchenham, B., Charters, S.: Guidelines for performing systematic literature reviews in software engineering. Keele University and Durham University (2007).
9. Basili, V.R., Caldiera, G., Rombach, D.H.: The Goal Question Metric Approach. In: Encyclopedia of Software Engineering. pp. 528–532. John Wiley & Sons (1994).
10. Pai, M., McCulloch, M., Gorman, J.D., Pai, N., Enanoria, W., Kennedy, G., Tharyan, P., Colford, J.M.: Systematic reviews and meta-analyses: an illustrated, step-by-step guide. The National Medical Journal of India. vol 17, issue 2, 86–95 (2004).
11. Fauzia, H., Laksmiwati, Ir.H., Hendradjaya, B.: A quality model for mobile thick client that utilizes web API. In: 2014 International Conference on Data and Software Engineering (ICODSE). pp. 1–6. IEEE, Bandung, Indonesia (2014). https://doi.org/10.1109/ICODSE.2014.7062681.
12. Lew, P., Olsina, L.: Relating User Experience with MobileApp Quality Evaluation and Design. In: Sheng, Q.Z. and Kjeldskov, J. (eds.) Current Trends in Web Engineering. pp. 253–268. Springer International Publishing, Cham (2013). https://doi.org/10.1007/978-3-319-04244-2_23.
13. Idri, A., Bachiri, M., Fernandez-Aleman, J.L., Toval, A.: ISO/IEC 25010 Based Evaluation of Free Mobile Personal Health Records for Pregnancy Monitoring. In: 2017 IEEE 41st Annual Computer Software and Applications Conference (COMPSAC). pp. 262–267. IEEE, Turin (2017). https://doi.org/10.1109/COMPSAC.2017.159.
14. Zhenyu Liu, Yun Hu, Lizhi Cai: Research on software security and compatibility test for mobile application. In: Fourth edition of the International Conference on the Innovative Computing Technology (INTECH 2014). pp. 140–145. IEEE, Luton, UK (2014). https://doi.org/10.1109/INTECH.2014.6927764.
15. Mohsin, A., Naqvi, S.I.R., Khan, A.U., Naeem, T., AsadUllah, M.A.: A comprehensive framework to quantify fault tolerance metrics of web centric mobile applications. In: 2017 International Conference on Communication Technologies (ComTech). pp. 65–71. IEEE, Rawalpindi, Pakistan (2017). https://doi.org/10.1109/COMTECH.2017.8065752.
16. Idri, A., Moumane, K., Abran, A.: On the Use of Software Quality Standard ISO/IEC9126 in Mobile Environments. In: 2013 20th Asia-Pacific Software Engineering Conference (APSEC). pp. 1–8. IEEE, Bangkok (2013). https://doi.org/10.1109/APSEC.2013.12.
17. Barnett, S., Vasa, R., Tang, A.: A Conceptual Model for Architecting Mobile Applications. In: 2015 12th Working IEEE/IFIP Conference on Software Architecture. pp. 105–114. IEEE, Montreal, QC, Canada (2015). https://doi.org/10.1109/WICSA.2015.28.
18. Liu, Z., Hu, Y., Cai, L.: Software Quality Testing Model for Mobile Application. In: Awan, I., Younas, M., Franch, X., and Quer, C. (eds.) Mobile Web Information Systems. pp. 192–204. Springer International Publishing, Cham (2014). https://doi.org/10.1007/978-3-319-10359-4_16.
19. Idri, A., Bachiri, M., Fernández-Alemán, J.L.: A Framework for Evaluating the Software Product Quality of Pregnancy Monitoring Mobile Personal Health Records. J Med Syst. vol 40, issue 3, paper 50 (2016). https://doi.org/10.1007/s10916-015-0415-z.
20. Ben Ayed, E., Kolski, C., Magdich, R., Ezzedine, H.: Towards a context based Evaluation Support System for Quality in Use assessment of mobile systems. In: 2016 IEEE International Conference on Systems, Man, and Cybernetics (SMC). pp. 004350–004355. IEEE, Budapest, Hungary (2016). https://doi.org/10.1109/SMC.2016.7844915.
21. Franke, D., Kowalewski, S., Weise, C.: A Mobile Software Quality Model. In: 2012 12th International Conference on Quality Software. pp. 154–157. IEEE, Xi'an, Shaanxi, China (2012). https://doi.org/10.1109/QSIC.2012.49.

22. Moumane, K., Idri, A.: Software quality in mobile environments: A comparative study. In: 2017 4th International Conference on Control, Decision and Information Technologies (CoDIT). pp. 1123–1128. IEEE, Barcelona (2017). https://doi.org/10.1109/CoDIT.2017.8102750.
23. Baloh, M., Zupanc, K., Kosir, D., Bosnic, Z., Scepanovic, S.: A quality evaluation framework for mobile learning applications. In: 2015 4th Mediterranean Conference on Embedded Computing (MECO). pp. 280–283. IEEE, Budva, Montenegro (2015). https://doi.org/10.1109/MECO.2015.7181923.
24. Corral, L.: Using software quality standards to assure the quality of the mobile software product. In: Proceedings of the 3rd annual conference on Systems, programming, and applications: software for humanity - SPLASH '12. p. 37. ACM Press, Tucson, Arizona, USA (2012). https://doi.org/10.1145/2384716.2384734.
25. Yildiz, E., Bilgen, S., Tokdemir, G., Cagiltay, N.E., Erturan, Y.N.: Analysis of B2C Mobile Application Characteristics and Quality Factors Based on ISO 25010 Quality Model. In: Awan, I., Younas, M., Franch, X., and Quer, C. (eds.) Mobile Web Information Systems. pp. 261–274. Springer International Publishing, Cham (2014). https://doi.org/10.1007/978-3-319-10359-4_21.
26. Holl, K., Vieira, V.: Focused Quality Assurance of Mobile Applications: Evaluation of a Failure Pattern Classification. In: 2015 41st Euromicro Conference on Software Engineering and Advanced Applications. pp. 349–356. IEEE, Madeira, Portugal (2015). https://doi.org/10.1109/SEAA.2015.36.
27. Alaa, G., Menshawi, M., Saeed, M.: Design criteria and software metrics for efficient and effective web-enabled mobile applications. In: 2013 8th International Conference on Computer Engineering & Systems (ICCES). pp. 295–300. IEEE, Cairo, Egypt (2013). https://doi.org/10.1109/ICCES.2013.6707222.
28. Nayebi, F., Desharnais, J.-M., Abran, A.: The state of the art of mobile application usability evaluation. In: 2012 25th IEEE Canadian Conference on Electrical and Computer Engineering (CCECE). pp. 1–4. IEEE, Montreal, QC (2012). https://doi.org/10.1109/CCECE.2012.6334930.
29. Kabir, M.A., Han, J., Colman, A., Aljohani, N.R., Basheri, M., Xing, Z., Lin, S.-W.: Engineering Socially-Aware Systems and Applications. In: 2016 21st International Conference on Engineering of Complex Computer Systems (ICECCS). pp. 81–90. IEEE, Dubai, United Arab Emirates (2016). https://doi.org/10.1109/ICECCS.2016.019.
30. Ryan, C., Rossi, P.: Software, Performance and Resource Utilisation Metrics for Context-Aware Mobile Applications. In: 11th IEEE International Software Metrics Symposium (METRICS'05). pp. 12–12. IEEE, Como, Italy (2005). https://doi.org/10.1109/METRICS.2005.44.
31. Idri, A., Bachiri, M., Fernandez-Aleman, J.L., Toval, A.: Experiment design of free pregnancy monitoring mobile personal health records quality evaluation. In: 2016 IEEE 18th International Conference on e-Health Networking, Applications and Services (Healthcom). pp. 1–6. IEEE, Munich, Germany (2016). https://doi.org/10.1109/HealthCom.2016.7749501.
32. Corral, L., Sillitti, A., Succi, G.: Defining Relevant Software Quality Characteristics from Publishing Policies of Mobile App Stores. In: Awan, I., Younas, M., Franch, X., and Quer, C. (eds.) Mobile Web Information Systems. pp. 205–217. Springer International Publishing, Cham (2014). https://doi.org/10.1007/978-3-319-10359-4_17.
33. de Souza, L.S., de Aquino, G.S.: Mobile Application Estimate the Design Phase. In: Maciaszek, L.A. and Filipe, J. (eds.) Evaluation of Novel Approaches to Software Engineering. pp. 155–167. Springer International Publishing, Cham (2015). https://doi.org/10.1007/978-3-319-27218-4_11.

34. Khalid, H., Nagappan, M., Hassan, A.E.: Examining the Relationship between FindBugs Warnings and App Ratings. IEEE Softw. 33, 34–39 (2016). https://doi.org/10.1109/MS.2015.29.
35. Fang, J., Li, J., Wang, R.: Mobile Travel Apps' Adoption: Integrating Perceived Characteristics of Innovation and Software Quality. In: Proceedings of the 2017 International Conference on Software and e-Business (ICSEB 2017). pp. 38–42. ACM Press, Hong Kong, Hong Kong (2017). https://doi.org/10.1145/3178212.3178213.
36. Olsina, L., Lew, P.: Specifying mobileapp quality characteristics that may influence trust. In: Proceedings of the 13th Central & Eastern European Software Engineering Conference in Russia on (CEE-SECR '17). pp. 1–9. ACM Press, St. Petersburg, Russia (2017). https://doi.org/10.1145/3166094.3166097.
37. Pretel, I., Lago, A.B.: Mobile-Human Interaction Monitoring System. In: Del Ser, J., Jorswieck, E.A., Miguez, J., Matinmikko, M., Palomar, D.P., Salcedo-Sanz, S., and Gil-Lopez, S. (eds.) Mobile Lightweight Wireless Systems. pp. 198–205. Springer Berlin Heidelberg, Berlin, Heidelberg (2012). https://doi.org/10.1007/978-3-642-29479-2_15.
38. Peischl, B., Ferk, M., Holzinger, A.: The fine art of user-centered software development. Software Qual J. 23, 509–536 (2015). https://doi.org/10.1007/s11219-014-9239-1.
39. Franke, D., Kowalewski, S., Weise, C., Prakobkosol, N.: Testing Conformance of Life Cycle Dependent Properties of Mobile Applications. In: 2012 IEEE Fifth International Conference on Software Testing, Verification and Validation. pp. 241–250. IEEE, Montreal, QC, Canada (2012). https://doi.org/10.1109/ICST.2012.104.
40. Khalid, H., Shihab, E., Nagappan, M., Hassan, A.E.: What Do Mobile App Users Complain About? IEEE Softw. vol 32, issue 3, 70–77 (2015). https://doi.org/10.1109/MS.2014.50.
41. Hess, S., Kiefer, F., Carbon, R.: Quality by Construction Through mConcAppt: Towards Using UI-construction as Driver for High Quality Mobile App Engineering. In: 2012 Eighth International Conference on the Quality of Information and Communications Technology. pp. 313–318. IEEE, Lisbon, TBD, Portugal (2012). https://doi.org/10.1109/QUATIC.2012.48.
42. Grano, G., Di Sorbo, A., Mercaldo, F., Visaggio, C.A., Canfora, G., Panichella, S.: Android apps and user feedback: a dataset for software evolution and quality improvement. In: Proceedings of the 2nd ACM SIGSOFT International Workshop on App Market Analytics (WAMA 2017). pp. 8–11. ACM Press, Paderborn, Germany (2017). https://doi.org/10.1145/3121264.3121266.
43. Soad, G.W., Filho, N.F.D., Barbosa, E.F.: Quality evaluation of mobile learning applications. In: 2016 IEEE Frontiers in Education Conference (FIE). pp. 1–8. IEEE, Erie, PA, USA (2016). https://doi.org/10.1109/FIE.2016.7757540.
44. Abusair, M.: User- and analysis-driven context aware software development in mobile computing. In: Proceedings of the 2017 11th Joint Meeting on Foundations of Software Engineering (ESEC/FSE 2017). pp. 1022–1025. ACM Press, Paderborn, Germany (2017). https://doi.org/10.1145/3106237.3119873.
45. Marinho, E.H., Resende, R.F.: Quality Factors in Development Best Practices for Mobile Applications. In: Murgante, B., Gervasi, O., Misra, S., Nedjah, N., Rocha, A.M.A.C., Taniar, D., and Apduhan, B.O. (eds.) Computational Science and Its Applications – ICCSA 2012. pp. 632–645. Springer Berlin Heidelberg, Berlin, Heidelberg (2012). https://doi.org/10.1007/978-3-642-31128-4_47.
46. ISO/IEC 9126-1:2001: Software engineering – Product quality – Part 1: Quality model, (2001).
47. Petersen, K., Vakkalanka, S., Kuzniarz, L.: Guidelines for conducting systematic mapping studies in software engineering: An update. Information and Software Technology. 64, 1–18 (2015). https://doi.org/10.1016/j.infsof.2015.03.007.

La representación del diseño detallado utilizando plantillas y sus efectos en la calidad del software

Silvana Moreno[1], Vanessa Casella[1], Martín Solari[2], and Diego Vallespir[1]

[1] Universidad de la República, Uruguay
{smoreno,vcasella,dvallesp}@fing.edu.uy
[2] Universidad ORT Uruguay
{martin.solari}@ort.edu.uy

Resumen El diseño de software es una práctica que busca contribuir en la construcción de software de calidad. Durante el diseño se traducen los requisitos en una representación del software cuya calidad puede ser evaluada. Para los estudiantes de pregrado, el diseño es difícil de entender y realizar. De hecho, construir un buen diseño parece requerir de un cierto nivel de desarrollo cognitivo que pocos estudiantes alcanzan. El objetivo de este trabajo es conocer el efecto en la calidad del software cuando estudiantes de pregrado utilizan plantillas para representar el diseño detallado. Conducimos un estudio empírico donde los estudiantes desarrollan 8 proyectos siguiendo un proceso definido y registrando datos de la ejecución del mismo en una herramienta. Encontramos que el uso de plantillas de diseño no mejoró la calidad del código medido como la densidad de defectos en la fase de prueba unitaria. Tampoco el uso de plantillas logró reducir la cantidad de *code smells* presentes en el código analizado.

Palabras claves: diseño detallado · calidad de diseño · estudiantes

1 Introducción

El diseño de software es uno de los componentes más importantes para asegurar el éxito de un sistema de software [13]. Este contiene dos actividades entre el análisis de requisitos y la construcción del software: el diseño arquitectónico y el diseño detallado. Durante el diseño arquitectónico se estructuran e identifican los componentes de alto nivel. Durante el diseño detallado se especifica cada componente en detalle [3]. Este trabajo está enfocado en el diseño detallado.

El diseño es una disciplina difícil de comprender para los estudiantes de pregrado, y el éxito (i.e. construir un buen diseño) parece requerir un cierto nivel de desarrollo cognitivo que pocos estudiantes alcanzan [6, 13, 19]. La capacidad de los estudiantes para construir un buen diseño está relacionada con la capacidad de abtracción, comprensión, razonamiento y procesamiento de la información [17, 18, 26].

Construir software de calidad es cada vez más importante. Dependemos del software en nuestra vida diaria y, cada vez más, dependemos de su correcto funcionamiento. Un diseño de software de calidad permite construir software de calidad; con menos defectos y más mantenible. Los profesionales de la industria son conscientes de la importancia de la calidad del diseño de software y, entre otros, utilizan prácticas de *clean code* (código limpio), revisiones y herramientas para contribuir en este sentido [4, 11, 29].

Conocer cómo diseñan los estudiantes de pregrado es de interés de varios autores [7–9, 20, 30]. La mayoría de sus estudios encontraron que los estudiantes no logran producir un buen diseño de software. Algunos de los problemas detectados son la falta de consistencia entre los artefactos de diseño y el código, diseños incompletos y la falta de entendimiento de qué tipo de información incluir al diseñar software [8, 9, 20].

En este trabajo estudiamos la práctica del diseño de software en estudiantes de pregrado, que ya han aprobado cursos de programación y diseño. Conducimos un experimento en el contexto de cursos con el objetivo de estudiar el efecto en la calidad del software que tiene la representación del diseño utilizando plantillas específicas.

El documento se estructura así: la sección 2 plantea los trabajos relacionados; las secciones 3 y 4 presentan el método experimental; la sección 5 presenta los resultados y en la 6 se realiza su discusión; las amenazas a la validez se mencionan en la sección 7; y la sección 8 presenta las conclusiones y trabajo a futuro.

2 Trabajos relacionados

El diseño de software es una actividad importante para garantizar la calidad de un sistema de software [13, 24]. Implica identificar y describir de forma abstracta el sistema de software y sus relaciones. Buenos diseños ayudan al desarrollo de software robusto, mantenible y con pocos errores [23, 28]. El diseño detallado de software es una actividad creativa, que puede realizarse de distintas formas: en la mente del desarrollador de software, en un bosquejo en papel, mediante diagramas, utilizando lenguajes o herramientas tanto formales como informales. El estándar internacional ISO 9126 propone un modelo con métricas de calidad de software internas y externas. Las internas son aquellas que no dependen de la ejecución del software (medidas estáticas), mientras que las externas son aquellas aplicables al software en ejecución [15].

En los últimos años, el uso de prácticas de *clean code* y de herramientas ha contribuido en la mejora de la calidad del diseño [29]. Los *code smells, anti patterns* y *design flaws* son algunos de los indicadores utilizados actualmente para medir la calidad del diseño [4, 11]. SonarQube [5] y FindBugs [2] son algunas de las herramientas utilizadas para medir la calidad del código a través de la detección de "*bad smells*".

Las prácticas actuales de la industria hacen necesario que los graduados tengan la capacidad de entender y de construir diseños de software. Sin embargo, los estudiantes de pregrado tienen dificultades para diseñar. Construir un buen diseño requiere un cierto nivel de desarrollo cognitivo que pocos estudiantes alcanzan [6, 13, 19]. Estos desarrollos cognitivos tienen que ver con la capacidad para lograr dimensionar el software, la capacidad de reconocer patrones de diseño, estilos y datos relacionados, así como la capacidad lógica y deductiva para descomponer el sistema en subsistemas y componentes [13].

De hecho, para los estudiantes aprender a diseñar es más difícil que aprender a programar. Esta dificultad ocurre porque para la mayoría de los lenguajes de programación, los estudiantes obtienen retroalimentación del compilador y errores en tiempo de ejecución. Sin embargo, esto no ocurre con el diseño [16].

El diseño orientado a objetos (OO) es uno de los enfoques de diseño más utilizados en la industria y uno de los temas que normalmente se enseña en las universidades [10]. Los diagramas y lenguajes de modelado OO permiten modelar aspectos estáticos y dinámicos del sistema. Varios estudios empíricos analizan la comprensión y los beneficios del uso de diagramas utilizando el lenguaje de modelado UML [1, 12, 31]. Los diagramas UML ayudan a entender el diseño y a mantener el código fuente.

Sin embargo, en varios estudios, los estudiantes de pregrado no logran obtener beneficios en el diseño utilizando estos diagramas [12, 31]. Gravino encuentra que los estudiantes que utilizan diagramas UML para diseñar no logran mejoras significativas en tareas de comprensión de código fuente comparado con los estudiantes que no lo utilizan. Además, los estudiantes que utilizan diagramas usan el doble del tiempo en la misma tarea de comprensión de código fuente respecto a los estudiantes que no los utilizan. Al analizar el factor experiencia, encuentra que los estudiantes mas experimentados logran una mejora en la comprensión del código fuente [12, 27].

Para los profesionales de la industria el uso de UML continúa siendo una resistencia [29]. Una encuesta realizada a 50 profesionales del software indica que aunque la calidad del software es un aspecto importante, el uso de UML es selectivo (informal, sólo por un tiempo, luego se descarta) y con baja frecuencia [22].

Las habilidades de diseño que tienen los estudiantes de pregrado son reportadas por un conjunto de estudios que examinan los artefactos producidos por estos para conocer cómo diseñan software [7–9, 20, 30]. Estos estudios utilizan la misma especificación de requerimientos con diferentes enfoques: diseños producidos de forma individual, diseños realizados de forma grupal y diseños producidos en diferentes niveles de formación. En general, los autores coinciden en que los estudiantes de pregrado no son capaces de diseñar un sistema de software. La falta de consistencia entre los artefactos de diseño y el código, los diseños incompletos y la falta de entendimiento de qué tipo de información incluir al diseñar software son algunas de las dificultades reportadas [8, 9, 20].

En un trabajo anterior [21], estudiamos cuánto esfuerzo dedican los estudiantes al diseño de software y cuál es su percepción respecto al diseño y a la enseñanza de esta disciplina durante la carrera de grado en computación de la Universidad de la República. El análisis realizado muestra que los estudiantes dedican al menos 4 veces más de tiempo a la codificación que al diseño de software. Además, pocos estudiantes se dan cuenta que no dedican el tiempo suficiente en etapas tempranas del desarrollo.

Creemos, al igual que Loftus et al. [20], que los estudiantes no saben qué hacer cuando tienen que diseñar software. Además, varios autores analizaron los artefactos producidos y coinciden en que los estudiantes no saben diseñar [7–9, 20, 30]. Esto motivó el trabajo presentado aquí; que propone brindar a los estudiantes plantillas de diseño como herramienta de apoyo a la representación del diseño. A diferencia de Gravino y Torchiano que analizan los beneficios del uso de diagramas en la comprensión del código [12, 31], nuestro enfoque analiza el efecto del uso de plantillas en la calidad del software. Analizamos la calidad desde el punto de vista de los defectos y de los *code smells* en el código. El foco de nuestra investigación es el diseño orientado a objetos y detallado (a nivel de clase y componente).

3 Método

Nos interesa conocer el efecto del diseño en la calidad del software cuando se exige a los estudiantes de pregrado la representación del diseño utilizando un conjunto específico de plantillas. Para ello, llevamos adelante tres experimentos en el contexto de un curso de la carrera de grado en computación de la Universidad de la República, durante los años 2015, 2016 y 2017. En los experimentos participaron estudiantes avanzados de la carrera de grado de informática de la Facultad de Ingeniería, que ya tenían aprobados los cursos donde se enseña diseño detallado de software: principios de diseño, artefactos y diagramas de diseño, UML, patrones de diseño, etc.

3.1 Contexto del curso

El curso tiene todos los años el mismo formato. Comienza con dos clases teóricas donde se enseña el proceso de desarrollo que van a utilizar en el curso (que denominamos proceso base) y se explica la dinámica del trabajo práctico. El proceso base es un proceso definido y disciplinado que ayuda a realizar mejor el trabajo. El trabajo práctico consiste en que cada estudiante desarrolle 8 proyectos siguiendo el proceso base y registrando datos de la ejecución del proceso en una herramienta. Los estudiantes realizan los proyectos de forma individual y consecutiva.

Los proyectos son asignados semanalmente a los estudiantes por parte de un docente tutor. La asignación consiste en el envío de los requerimientos del proyecto. La entrega de cada estudiante consiste en el código que resuelve el problema, los casos de pruebas ejecutados y los datos registrados en la herramienta. Los estudiantes realizan los proyectos en sus casas y tienen un docente asignado que será el responsable de asignar, corregir y evacuar de cada proyecto. Antes de comenzar el primer proyecto cada estudiante debe elegir el lenguaje de programación a utilizar a lo largo del curso. Nuestro interés es recolectar datos de la ejecución del proceso de desarrollo con el uso de un lenguaje que el estudiante domina y no datos del aprendizaje de un lenguaje.

Las fases del proceso, los scripts y el registro de datos (logs) se presentan en la figura 1. El proceso base consiste de las siguientes fases: planificación, diseño, codificación, compilación, pruebas unitarias (PU) y postmortem. Para seguir el proceso base se brinda un conjunto de scripts. Los scripts son una guía que establece las entradas, salidas y actividades a realizar en cada fase. Los scripts ayudan al estudiante a encaminar las actividades del desarrollo pero sin exigir cómo deben realizarse. Por ejemplo, el script para la fase de diseño, tiene como entrada los requerimientos y establece como actividad central producir un diseño que satisfaga los mismos (no se establece cómo debe producirse ni cómo debe representarse dicho diseño). Los datos que se registran son el tiempo dedicado a cada fase del proceso, los defectos detectados y removidos en cada fase y el tamaño en locs del programa construido.

Figura 1. Proceso base, scripts y logs

Los proyectos son todos de naturaleza matemática, de baja y similar complejidad. Los percentiles 5 y 95 de los datos recolectados para todos los estudiantes a lo largo de los 8 proyectos son 26 locs y 242 locs respectivamente. La fase de diseño se refiere al diseño detallado; i.e. identificar clases, atributos, operaciones, escenarios del programa (o componente), cambios de estado y/o pseudo-código. Cada experimento se corresponde con una instancia del curso y los estudiantes que participan de una instancia no vuelven a participar de una instancia posterior.

3.2 Objetivos y diseño experimental

Los experimentos tienen como objetivo conocer el efecto en la calidad del software cuando los estudiantes representan su diseño utilizando un conjunto específico de plantillas de diseño. La completitud de las cuatro plantillas (Operacional, Funcional, Lógica, Estado) permiten describir el diseño de forma completa y precisa [14]. Las plantillas son documentos con una estructura predefinida en las cuales los estudiantes deben representar el diseño realizado.

Las plantillas permiten describir desde la operación del sistema (Operacional) hasta el seudocódigo de cada método (Lógica). A continuación se presenta una breve descripción de cada una.

- Plantilla operacional: especifica la interacción del sistema y los usuarios. El contenido puede verse como similar a los casos de uso.

- Plantilla funcional: se especifica el comportamiento de las invocaciones y retornos del programa (variables, funciones, clases y métodos). La figura 2 presenta un ejemplo de uso de esta plantilla para una clase del proyecto 6.
- Plantilla lógica: en esta plantilla se registra el seudocódigo de cada método que aparece en las plantillas funcionales.
- Plantilla de estado: define las transiciones y las condiciones de los estados internos del programa. El contenido es similar a los diagramas de máquinas de estado.

Student	Student X	**Date**	07/05/17
Program	Problema 6	**Program #**	
Instructor	Instructor Y	**Language**	Java

Class Name	CalculoValorX
Parent Class	

Attributes

Declaration	**Description**
P:double	Valor de la integral.
Dof:int	Grados de libertad.
XIni: double	X inicial a probar(se toma 1,0)
DebeAjustar:boolean	Dice si se debe ajustar el valor de d
EsMenor:boolean	Dice si el valor de la integral calculada con el nuevo x es menor al valor de p.
Xprueba:double	Valor de x a probar.

Items

Declaration	**Description**
calcularX(p:double, dof:int, xIni:double)	Se encarga de calcular el valor de x, la primera vez usando Simpson y en caso que esta primera vez no sea la correcta usando el método recursivo recalcularX
ajustarD(debeAjustar:boolean, esMenor:boolean)	Ajusta el valor de d. Si es menor true entonces el valor retornado es positivo, en caso contrario es negativo. Si debeAjustar, entonces d = 0,5/2, de lo contrario es 0,5
recalcularX(p:double, dof:int, xPrueba:double, esMenor:boolean)	Se encarga de realizar el cálculo de x recursivamente hasta encontrar el valor correcto.

Figura 2. Plantilla Funcional

El diseño de este experimento es de medidas repetidas y de un factor (la representación del diseño de software) con dos alternativas: utilizando plantillas y sin utilizar plantillas. Las variables de respuesta consideradas en este experimento son la calidad interna y externa del software. Para evaluar la calidad externa consideramos la densidad de defectos en la fase de pruebas unitarias del proceso base. Es decir, se cuentan la cantidad de defectos encontrados en dicha fase y se divide entre las locs del proyecto. Conocer la densidad de defectos en esta fase del proceso de desarrollo da una idea de los defectos remanentes en el software[25]. Para evaluar la calidad interna analizamos los *code smells* en los que incurren los estudiantes. Conocer la cantidad de *code smells* presentes en el código fuente del producto nos da una idea de los costos de mantenibilidad a futuro [11].

4 Operación

Los experimentos se ejecutaron en 2015, 2016 y 2017 y participaron 25, 17 y 19 estudiantes respectivamente. Todos los estudiantes aplican el proceso base en los primeros cuatro proyectos y registran sus datos en la herramienta. Durante los primeros cuatro proyectos la fase de diseño no exige la entrega de la representación del diseño. Una vez finalizado el proyecto 4 se divide a los estudiantes en dos grupos mediante un sorteo; denominamos los grupos como "con representación de diseño utilizando plantillas" (*conPRD*) y "sin plantillas para la representación de diseño" (*sinPRD*). El cuadro 1 presenta el diseño del experimento.

Cuadro 1. Diseño experimento

Grupo	**proyecto 1 to 4**	**proyecto 5 to 8**
conPRD	proceso base	proceso base + rep. diseño con plantillas
sinPRD	proceso base	proceso base

El grupo *sinPRD* es el grupo de control, que continúa aplicando el proceso base a lo largo de los proyectos 5 al 8. El grupo *conPRD* asiste a una clase donde se presentan las cuatro plantillas que permiten representar el diseño; que deben utilizar para representar su diseño a partir del ejercicio 5 y hasta el 8. La entrega de la representación del diseño utilizando plantillas es obligatoria (salvo la plantilla de estado que es opcional). Cuando el estudiante entrega el proyecto, el docente asignado chequea (entre otras cosas) que las plantillas sean consistentes con el código. De esta forma se mitiga que el estudiante diseñe una solución y luego codifique otra. Sin embargo, no se controla que el diseño sea completo y verificable.

5 Resultados y Análisis

Con el objetivo de estudiar el efecto de la representación del diseño con plantillas en la calidad analizamos la calidad desde los puntos de vista externo e interno.

5.1 Calidad Externa

Para analizar la calidad externa definimos las siguientes hipótesis nula y alternativa:

H0: El uso de plantillas de diseño no modifica la densidad de defectos en la fase de pruebas del proceso base.

H1: El uso de plantillas de diseño modifica la densidad de defectos en la fase de pruebas del proceso base.

Proponemos analizar la calidad externa de dos formas: intra grupo y entre grupos. Entre grupos se refiere a conocer si existe una diferencia significativa en la calidad del software entre el grupo *conPRD* y el grupo *sinPRD*. Es decir, conocer si hay una diferencia en la calidad entre el grupo que utiliza las plantillas y el grupo que no. Para este análisis, plantemos las siguientes hipótesis de investigación:

H0: Mediana(Densidad def. PU i) = Mediana (Densidad def. PU j)
H1: Mediana(Densidad def. PU i) > Mediana (Densidad def. PU j)
siendo i, j los estudiantes de los grupos conPRD y sinPRD respectivamente.

Cada muestra corresponde a la densidad de defectos en PU de cada estudiante considerando los programas 5 a 8. Se calcula de la siguiente manera:

$$\frac{1000 * \sum_{n=5}^{8} \#defectosPU_n}{\sum_{n=5}^{8} \#LOC_n} \tag{1}$$

Las muestras son independientes porque se corresponden a estudiantes diferentes, por lo que aplicamos la prueba de Mann-Whitney. Los resultados indican un valor de W = 354, p-value = 0.1656, con lo cual no podemos rechazar la hipótesis nula (significancia = 0.05). Por lo tanto, no podemos afirmar que los estudiantes que utilizaron las plantillas logran desarrollar productos con menos defectos que los estudiantes que no utilizaron los mismos.

El resultado anterior indica que no hay una diferencia estadística entre los estudiantes que usaron las plantillas de los que no. Sin embargo, también queremos conocer si los estudiantes que utilizaron plantillas mejoraron la calidad del software desarrollado. Para conocer esto analizamos la densidad de defectos en PU en los proyectos 1 al 4 y en los proyectos 5 al 8 para el grupo *conPRD*. Estudiar el comportamiento del mismo grupo nos permite conocer si hay un cambio en la calidad del software a partir del proyecto 5 (que es cuando se introducen las plantillas).

Debido a la complejidad del proyecto 2 respecto al resto de los proyectos decidimos no incluir los datos de este proyecto en el análisis. La naturaleza del proyecto 2 y los análisis reportados en nuestro estudio anterior [21] muestran que es un proyecto con una dificultad superior al resto y por lo tanto no comparable. Planteamos las siguientes hipótesis de investigación:

H0: Mediana(Densidad def. PU i) = Mediana (Densidad def. PU j)
H1: Mediana(Densidad def. PU i) > Mediana (Densidad def. PU j)
siendo i los estudiantes del grupo *conPRD* durante los proyectos 1, 3 y 4; y j los mismos estudiantes del grupo *conPRD* durante los proyectos 5 al 8.

En este caso las muestras están apareadas, por lo que aplicamos la prueba de Wilcoxon (*signed rank test*) para muestras apareadas. Los resultados indican un valor de V = 138 y p-value = 0.1438. Dado que el p-value es mayor a 0.05 (valor de la significancia) no es posible rechazar la hipótesis nula. Esto indica que no podemos afirmar que los estudiantes mejoran la calidad del software que producen al utilizar plantillas de diseño.

5.2 Calidad Interna

Para evaluar la calidad interna realizamos un análisis de los *code smells* en los que incurren los estudiantes al desarrollar los proyectos del curso. La intención de este análisis es conocer si el uso de plantillas de diseño evita que los estudiantes cometan ciertos *code smells*.

Los tipos de *code smell* dependen del lenguaje de programación. Dado que los estudiantes pueden elegir el lenguaje en el cual desarrollar los proyectos, hay que realizar este análisis teniendo en cuenta los distintos lenguajes utilizados. Con el objetivo de realizar un análisis inicial, y que aportara valor a nuestro estudio, se seleccionaron los estudiantes que desarrollaron los proyectos con los lenguajes Java, C#, C, C++ y Ruby; descartándose los desarrollados con PHP y Python. Agregar Python y PHP reducía mucho la cantidad de *code smells* comunes con los otros lenguajes, por ende, se descartaron ambos lenguajes para este análisis inicial. Esto dejó para el análisis un total de 45 estudiantes, 19 del año 2015, 14 del 2016 y 12 del 2017.

Para detectar los *code smell* se utilizó la herramienta SonarQube[1], ya que es una herramienta de software libre para una gran variedad de lenguajes de programación, que presenta actualizaciones constantes por la comunidad y una documentación muy amplia, entre otros.

Seleccionamos 16 *code smells* para el análisis. Estos cumplen que son comunes para los lenguajes de programación que seleccionamos y que son detectables por SonarQube. Los *code smells* son: 1) Las declaraciones "if ... else if" deben terminar con la cláusula "else", 2) Las declaraciones "switch"/"case" no deben estar anidadas, 3) Las declaraciones "switch"/"case" no deben tener demasiadas cláusulas "case"/"when", 4) La complejidad cognitiva de las funciones o métodos no debe ser demasiado alta, 5) Las declaraciones colapsables "if" deben fusionarse, 6) Las declaraciones de flujo de control "if", "for", "while", "switch" y "try" no deben anidarse demasiado, 7) Las expresiones no deben ser demasiado complejas, 8) Los archivos no deben tener demasiadas líneas de código, 9) Las funciones o métodos no deben tener demasiadas líneas de código, 10) Las funciones o métodos no deben tener demasiados parámetros, 11) Las líneas de código no deben ser demasiado largas, 12) Las funciones o métodos no deben ser vacíos, 13) Las declaraciones deben estar en líneas separadas, 14) Dos ramas en una estructura condicional no deben tener exactamente la misma implementación, 15) Los parámetros de una función o método no utilizados deben

[1] http://www.sonarqube.org

eliminarse, 16) Las variables locales no utilizadas deben eliminarse. Por motivos de espacio del artículo no se brinda una descripción más detallada de cada uno.

El Cuadro 2 presenta el porcentaje de estudiantes que al menos incurrió en un *code smell*, segmentado por proyecto (del 1 al 8) y por grupo (*sinPRD* y *conPRD*). Los *code smell* 3, 8 y 12 no están presentes en ninguno de los proyectos analizados.

Cuadro 2. Porcentaje de estudiantes que incurren en al menos un code smell por tipo de code smell y grupo.

Code smell	**Grupo**	Proyecto							
		1	**2**	**3**	**4**	**5**	**6**	**7**	**8**
1	*sinPRD*	4%	29%	0%	4%	13%	13%	4%	13%
	conPRD	19%	19%	10%	0%	5%	5%	5%	5%
2	*sinPRD*	0%	0%	0%	0%	0%	0%	0%	0%
	conPRD	0%	0%	0%	0%	0%	0%	0%	5%
4	*sinPRD*	8%	58%	0%	13%	30%	46%	29%	50%
	conPRD	24%	43%	5%	10%	10%	43%	24%	95%
5	*sinPRD*	4%	21%	0%	0%	0%	0%	0%	0%
	conPRD	0%	24%	10%	0%	0%	5%	0%	5%
6	*sinPRD*	13%	63%	8%	29%	30%	38%	13%	42%
	conPRD	38%	67%	29%	29%	33%	52%	57%	62%
7	*sinPRD*	0%	25%	0%	0%	0%	4%	8%	0%
	conPRD	0%	19%	0%	0%	0%	5%	0%	5%
9	*sinPRD*	0%	4%	8%	17%	10%	21%	21%	67%
	conPRD	0%	10%	19%	14%	10%	29%	38%	71%
10	*sinPRD*	0%	0%	0%	0%	0%	0%	8%	54%
	conPRD	0%	0%	5%	0%	0%	0%	19%	38%
11	*sinPRD*	4%	46%	42%	8%	40%	4%	46%	75%
	conPRD	0%	29%	29%	0%	14%	5%	24%	62%
13	*sinPRD*	0%	0%	0%	0%	10%	0%	0%	4%
	conPRD	5%	0%	5%	0%	0%	0%	5%	19%
14	*sinPRD*	0%	8%	0%	0%	10%	0%	0%	0%
	conPRD	0%	0%	0%	0%	0%	0%	0%	0%
15	*sinPRD*	0%	0%	8%	4%	20%	0%	13%	17%
	conPRD	0%	0%	0%	0%	5%	0%	0%	0%
16	*sinPRD*	8%	13%	8%	8%	40%	8%	17%	29%
	conPRD	5%	5%	10%	10%	0%	0%	10%	10%

Al analizar el cuadro entre los grupos *sinPRD* y *conPRD* a partir del programa 5 (a partir del uso de plantillas) se desprende una gran variabilidad, tanto si se mira por proyecto como si se mira por *code smell*.

Para los code smell 4, 7, 10 y 13 se observa que para ciertos proyectos un grupo está mejor y para ciertos otros proyectos está mejor el otro grupo. Para los *code smell* 1, 2, 5, 6, 9 y 14 sucede que la diferencia es muy chica entre los grupos. En definitiva, para ninguno de estos *code smells* se observan cambios al usar las plantillas.

Para el caso del *code smell* 11 se observa un porcentaje muy menor en los proyectos 5 y 7 y menor en el proyecto 8 por parte del grupo que utiliza las plantillas. En el proyecto 6 ambos grupos se comportan casi igual. Desde el punto de vista de las plantillas quizás sea la plantilla de seudocódigo la que esté ayudando a los estudiantes a disminuir la introducción de este *code smell*.

Los *code smell* 15 y 16 tienen un comportamiento similar. Para ambos casos el grupo *conPRD* casi no incurre en ellos mientras que el grupo *sinPRD* incurre y a veces en un alto porcentaje. El 15 refiere a parámetros no utilizados en los métodos y el 16 a variables locales no utilizadas. Claramente estos tipos de *code smells* pueden ser evitados con buenos diseños de software. Desde el punto de vista del uso de las plantillas, quizás el desarrollo de seudocódigo (plantilla Lógica) y la plantilla Funcional estén evitando que los estudiantes del grupo *conPRD* incurran en estos *code smells*. De todas formas, es necesario analizar manualmente las plantillas entregadas por los estudiantes y tener entrevistas con ellos para conocer mejor si esto puede estar sucediendo por los motivos descritos. Esto aún no se ha realizado.

Sin embargo, al analizar el cuadro, pero solamente considerando los datos del grupo *conPRD* a lo largo de los 8 proyectos, no vemos que el uso de plantillas mejore la calidad interna.

Vale la pena notar que este grupo normalmente no incurrió (o lo hizo en muy bajo porcentaje) en los *code smells* 15 y 16. Observando los proyectos 1 a 4 y 5 a 8 por separado, no vemos una diferencia entre ellos. Es decir, el comportamiento de este grupo antes de usar plantillas y durante su uso no cambia para estos *code smells*. Entonces, la diferencia presentada en el análisis anterior entre los grupos *conPRD* y *sinPRD* no responde al uso de las plantillas.

Algo similar sucede con el *code smell* 11. Los resultados no presentan una disminución de este *code smell* al utilizarse las plantillas.

Se puede observar que en el proyecto 8 aumenta significativamente el porcentaje de ocurrencia de los *code smells* 4, 9 y 10 para ambos grupos. Este aumento hace pensar que el proyecto 8 resulta mas complejo para los estudiantes. Estos tres *code smells* indican que el código desarrollado es demasiado complejo y largo para su comprensión. Es decir, el uso de las plantillas no ayudó a los estudiantes a elaborar un diseño menos complejo y entendible.

Juntando ambos análisis se desprende que el uso de las plantillas no mejora la calidad interna. En particular, el uso de las plantillas no tiene un efecto en los *code smells* en los que incurren los estudiantes al desarrollar software.

6 Discusión

En el contexto de nuestro experimento encontramos que la representación del diseño utilizando plantillas no ayudó a desarrollar productos de software de mayor calidad. Los resultados arrojan que el uso de plantillas no mejoró en la cantidad de defectos que contiene el código desarrollado (medido como densidad de defectos en PU) ni mejoró la calidad interna (medido como *code smells* en el código). Estos resultados se relacionan con los reportados por Gravino [12], donde el uso de diagramas UML no logró mejoras en la comprensión de código fuente respecto al no uso de los mismos.

El uso de plantillas para representar el diseño no tuvo un efecto positivo en la calidad. Los estudiantes que las usaron no mejoraron la misma. Esto puede deberse a varios factores que deberemos analizar en el futuro. Podría ser, entre otros motivos, que no están habituados a estas plantillas y por ende no se obtuvo el beneficio esperado, podría ser que simplemente completaron las plantillas pero no se preocuparon en ese momento por pensar y desarrollar un diseño de calidad o podría ser que los estudiantes no saben qué y cómo diseñar.

Si bien falta más análisis, nosotros coincidimos con varios autores en que los estudiantes de pregrado tienen dificultades para diseñar y no parecen entender qué tipo de información incluir para diseñar software [8, 9, 20].

7 Amenazas a la validez

La mayoría de los estudios empíricos se ven amenazados por la forma en que la investigación se lleva a cabo. En esta sección se describen las amenazas a la validez que hemos detectado.

Investigar con estudiantes implica varias amenazas. Por un lado, el hecho que el contexto del experimento sea un curso implica que el estudiante se desenvuelva de forma distinta al contexto profesional. Intentamos minimizar esta amenaza con un curso sin calificación, es decir el estudiante aprueba o reprueba. Además hacemos hincapié en la importancia de seguir y registrar el proceso tal cual fue y dejando claro que no se evaluará por los resultados, defectos encontrados o esfuerzos dedicados. Además, para el análisis realizamos una agregación de los datos de los tres cursos; sabiendo que distintos cursos pueden influir en los datos recolectados por ser un modelo jerárquico. Intentamos disminuir esta amenaza mediante el uso de un proceso definido y disciplinado que siguen los estudiantes y manteniendo el mismo material y los mismos docentes a lo largo de los 3 cursos.

Por otro lado, los estudiantes realizan los proyectos desde sus casas lo que provoca un control limitado por parte de los investigadores. Intentamos reducir esta amenaza asignando un tutor a cada estudiante de forma de supervisar y atender las consultas durante la realización de proyectos. Además, el tutor revisa cada proyecto una vez finalizado y envía feedback correcciones a sus estudiantes.

Por último, la cantidad de estudiantes en el estudio constituye una amenaza a la conclusión estadística. Participaron 61 estudiantes durante las 3 ejecuciones. Esto provoca la realización del análisis estadístico utilizando test no paramétricos cuya potencia estadística es menor a los test paramétricos.

8 Conclusiones

Este trabajo es un paso más hacia la comprensión de la práctica del diseño de software. Los resultados de nuestro experimento muestran que los estudiantes de pregrado no mejoran la calidad del software cuando utilizan plantillas para representar el diseño. Analizamos la calidad del software desde los puntos de vista interno y externo. Por un lado, comprobamos estadísticamente que el uso de plantillas para representar el diseño no mejora la calidad externa del software medida como la densidad de defectos en las pruebas unitarias. Desde el punto de la calidad interna, el uso de las plantillas no tiene un efecto positivo significativo en los *code smells* en los que incurren los estudiantes al desarrollar software.

Estos resultados, sumados al reportado previamente (los estudiantes dedican cuatro veces menos esfuerzo al diseño que a la codificación) [21], nos generan nuevas interrogantes sobre la práctica del diseño de software: ¿Qué diseñan habitualmente los estudiantes?, ¿Qué tipo de información incluyen al diseñar?, ¿Es posible que realicen sus diseños mentalmente sin representarlos?, ¿Conocen el efecto de un buen diseño en la calidad del software? Como trabajo a futuro proponemos analizar los diseños realizados en las plantillas para conocer qué diseñan, y poder detectar problemas. Por otro lado, nos interesa ejecutar un nuevo experimento que nos permita analizar qué diseñan los estudiantes sin la exigencia de entregar una representación definida por los investigadores. Estudiar el comportamiento habitual del estudiante al diseñar software nos permitirá detectar posibles problemas en las prácticas de diseño y proponer mejoras en la enseñanza que permitan la construcción de software de calidad.

Referencias

1. Arisholm, E., Briand, L.C., Hove, S.E., Labiche, Y.: The impact of uml documentation on software maintenance: an experimental evaluation. IEEE Transactions on Software Engineering **32**(6) (2006)
2. Ayewah, N., Pugh, W., Hovemeyer, D., Morgenthaler, J.D., Penix, J.: Using static analysis to find bugs. IEEE software **25**(5) (2008)
3. Bourque, P., Fairley, R.E.: Guide to the Software Engineering Body of Knowledge - SWEBOK v3.0. IEEE CS, 2014 version edn. (2014)
4. Brown, W.H., Malveau, R.C., McCormick, H.W., Mowbray, T.J.: AntiPatterns: refactoring software, architectures, and projects in crisis. John Wiley & Sons, Inc. (1998)
5. Campbell, G.A., Papapetrou, P.P.: SonarQube in Action. Manning Publications Co, 2013 version edn. (2013)
6. Carrington, D., K Kim, S.: Teaching software design with open source software. In: 33rd Annual Frontiers in Education, 2003. FIE 2003. (2003)
7. Chen, T.Y., Cooper, S., McCartney, R., Schwartzman, L.: The (relative) importance of software design criteria. In: ITiCSE (2005)
8. Eckerdal, A., McCartney, R., Moström, J.E., Ratcliffe, M., Zander, C.: Can graduating students design software systems? In: SIGCSE'06. ACM (2006)
9. Eckerdal, A., McCartney, R., Moström, J.E., Ratcliffe, M., Zander, C.: Categorizing student software designs: Methods, results, and implications. Computer science education **16**(3) (2006)
10. Flores, P., Medinilla, N.: Conceptions of the students around object-oriented design: A case study. In: XII Jornadas Iberoamericanas de Ingenieria de Software e Ingeniería del Conocimiento (2017)

11. Fowler, M.: Refactoring: improving the design of existing code. Addison-Wesley Professional (2018)
12. Gravino, C., Scanniello, G., Tortora, G.: Source-code comprehension tasks supported by uml design models: Results from a controlled experiment and a differentiated replication. Journal of Visual Languages & Computing **28** (2015)
13. Hu, C.: The nature of software design and its teaching: an exposition. ACM Inroads **4**(2) (2013)
14. Humphrey, W.S.: A discipline for software engineering. Addison-Wesley Longman Publishing Co., Inc. (1995)
15. ISO/IEC: ISO/IEC 9126. Software engineering – Product quality. ISO/IEC (2008)
16. Karasneh, B., Jolak, R., Chaudron, M.R.V.: Using examples for teaching software design: An experiment using a repository of uml class diagrams. In: 2015 Asia-Pacific Software Engineering Conference (APSEC) (2015)
17. Kramer, J.: Is abstraction the key to computing? Commun. ACM **50** (2007)
18. Leung, F., Bolloju, N.: Analyzing the quality of domain models developed by novice systems analysts. In: 38th Hawaii International Conference on System Sciences (2005)
19. Linder, S.P., Abbott, D., Fromberger, M.J.: An instructional scaffolding approach to teaching software design. Journal of Computing Sciences in Colleges **21** (2006)
20. Loftus, C., Thomas, L., Zander, C.: Can graduating students design: revisited. In: Proceedings of the 42nd ACM technical symposium on Computer science education. ACM (2011)
21. Moreno Silvana, V.D.: ¿los estudiantes de pregrado son capaces de diseñar software? estudio de la relación entre el tiempo de codificación y el tiempo de diseño en el desarrollo de software. In: Conferencia Iberoamericana de Ingeniería de Software 2018 (2018)
22. Petre, M.: Uml in practice. International Conference on Software Engineeringn **35** (2013)
23. Pierce, K., Deneen, L., Shute, G.: Teaching software design in the freshman year. In: Software Engineering Education. Springer Berlin Heidelberg (1991)
24. Richard N. Taylor: Proc. 33rd International Conference on Software Engineering (ICSE 2011). ACM (2011)
25. Schneidewind, N.F., Keller, T.W.: Applying reliability models to the space shuttle. IEEE Software **9**(4) (1992)
26. Siau, K., Tan, X.: Improving the quality of conceptual modeling using cognitive mapping techniques. Data & Knowledge Engineering **55**(3) (2005), quality in conceptual modeling
27. Soh, Z., Sharafi, Z., Van den Plas, B., Cepeda Porras, G., Guéhéneuc, Y.G., Antoniol, G.: Professional status and expertise for uml class diagram comprehension: An empirical study. In: IEEE International Conference on Program Comprehension (2012)
28. Sommerville, I.: Software Engineering. Pearson (2016)
29. Stevenson, J., Wood, M.: Recognising object-oriented software design quality: a practitioner-based questionnaire survey. Software Quality Journal **26** (2018)
30. Tenenberg, J.: Students designing software: a multi-national, multi-institutional study. Informatics in Education **4** (2005)
31. Torchiano, M., Scanniello, G., Ricca, F., Reggio, G., Leotta, M.: Do uml object diagrams affect design comprehensibility? results from a family of four controlled experiments. Journal of Visual Languages & Computing **41** (2017)

Selection Methods for Criticality in Microservices Architectures: A Systematic Mapping

Eduardo F. Mioto de Oliveira dos Santos[1], Claudia Maria Lima Werner[2], Marcelo de França Costa[3]

Universidade Federal do Rio de Janeiro, Rio de Janeiro RJ 08544, Brazil
{mioto[1], werner[2]}@cos.ufrj.br, aluno@franca.pro.br[3]

Abstract. The selection method for criticality associated with Microservices Architecture (MSA) has great importance associated with system reliability. Since MSA is a new research area, the need for a systematic literature review is crucial in order to elucidate the possible ways to identify consolidated criticality methods. The proposal of this systematic mapping is to identify the gaps and approaches used on previous similar situations on studies related to MSA, also including SOA and components, considering these being part of microservices background and evolution. Thus this study focuses on identifying methods to evaluate a decision focused on highlighting the most critical component, service or MSA. In this paper, 68 primary studies about this topic published from 2012 to 2019 were selected. Results indicate that the software engineering community has increasingly invested effort in studying criticality evaluation. Nevertheless, it is still an immature area when focused on MSA.

Keywords: Microservices, SOA, Components, Selection, Multiple Criteria, Criticality, Systematic Review

1 Introduction

According to Haselböck, Weinreich, and Buchgeher [7], introducing a Microservice Architecture (MSA) is not an effortless journey, a company undertaking such an endeavor needs to make a variety of decisions considering a wide range of development practices, technology, and infrastructure to handle the additional challenges and complexity that accompany this architectural style.

MSA arises from the broader area of Service Oriented Architecture (SOA) and focuses on specific aspects, such as componentization of small services, application of agile practices for development, deployment, and testing of services [18]. According to Montesi and Weber [16], the key difference between MSA and SOA lies in granularity. Gabbrielli et al. [17] also mention that scaling a microservice architecture does not imply duplication of all its components and developers can conveniently deploy or dispose of instances of services in accordance with their load.

MSA development is an architectural model to be followed to designing software applications as independent service groups. These applications are cohesive and small in size, and can be easily integrated with reduced creation, validation and deployment time. Microservices can be updated and sized individually, leading to greater architectural stability and greater resilience [22].

The need to know the most critical microservices comes from the complexity in decision making regarding the maintenance and evolution of architectures based on this architectural model. After a microservice oriented architecture deployment, the architecture maintenance process tends to be complex, considering the multiple services to be observed.

Francesco, Malavolta and Lago [13] mention that the need to understand the current state of the art on architecting microservices is confirmed by the fact that three different mapping studies [13, 14, 15] have been published recently and are providing important characterization to the field, although, none of them associated with criticality to MSA.

This paper contextualizes the use of decision models to support the establishment of an MSA considering the criticality evaluation methods. Decision models represent a well-known approach for exploring the design space, making decisions, documentation, and reuse in software architecture [7, 8, 9].

Since MSA is an architectural style, the objective of this study is to explore how previous research has supported microservices through architectural approaches. The aim of the study is to focus on the research questions exposed on the Section (2.1), closely link and correlate the research questions to the review study results and provide quantified evidence from the available publications.

The contribution of this paper is a comprehensive overview of existing approaches on selection methods for criticality in MSA developed over the last years and their focus in terms of the different activities. The criticality analysis is a process through which artifacts are evaluated in terms of potential risk of degradation, partial failure or total failure [20]. On software context, performing a criticality analysis helps to clarify the available methods to reduce the risk associated with each software asset.

Three main aspects distinguish this work from previous, similar work is this area. First, approaches for components and SOA based on published studies were identified, by aggregating related studies that considered the same approach or variations. Second, for each approach, the focus of the performed research was determined. Finally, the provided evidence in terms of associated studies not related to general approach was identified.

The remainder of this paper is structured as follows. Section 2 presents the research method, elucidating the research questions, the search process, and the inclusion and exclusion criteria, also exposing the search string, as well as detailing the quality assessment and data collection. In Section 3, the results and their implications are detailed, also considering the data extraction and research questions answering, as well as the threats to the validity and study limitations. In Section 4 the related works are listed. The paper is concluded in Section 5, which presents the conclusion and future researches.

2 Research Method

Based on the methodology of systematic literature reviews (SLR) [1, 2, 3, 4, 5], a scheme was developed for the review, selection and extraction of information in the following phases: (i) Planning the Review, (ii) Conducting the Review and (iii) Reporting the Review.

According to the Australian National Health and Medical Research Council [1], an SLR is a means of identifying, evaluating and interpreting all available research relevant to a particular research question, topic area, or phenomenon of interest. Individual studies contributing to an SLR are called primary studies; an SLR is a form of a secondary study. This paper intends to identify gaps in the current state of the art in order to suggest areas for further investigation.

Systematic literature reviews (SLRs) are considered comprehensive and rigorous reviews of specific research questions in an area or a topic, which aim to identify the gaps in the literature and identify where new or better primary studies are needed to be put in place [18]. Systematic mapping is a secondary study method based on a structured and repeatable process or protocol that explores studies and provides a result in the form of an overview of a particular subject [23].

2.1 Research Questions

The overall goal of this systematic mapping is to identify existing MSA, SOA and components approaches and to determine their support for architecture decisions associated with criticality. Accordingly, the following three research questions (RQs) were formulated:

RQ1 - What are the established selection models for MSA, SOA, and components? In RQ1, the approaches and families of approaches to MSA, SOA, and components associated with selection models will be identified by combining related studies obtained from the literature.

RQ2 - What are the multiple criteria evaluation approaches for MSA, SOA, and components? The information from RQ2 intends to determine which microservices, SOA and components activities related to multiple criteria evaluation are well supported by current researches on literature. Therefore, gaps in current approaches and needs for future research with respect to support for MSA, SOA and components activities can be identified.

RQ3 - What are the established criticality methods in MSA, SOA, and components? With RQ3, it is desired to gain better insights into how well existing approaches have been validated both with respect to academic and industrial studies. The evidence provided for existing approaches is rated with respect to how they support the MSA, SOA and components activities related to criticality.

2.2 Search Process

Initially, a set of research questions were drafted for investigation during the study. The motivation behind each research question was reviewed and refined. Subsequently, selected papers were assessed against quality criteria and a classification scheme was iteratively developed following a synthesis method.

2.3 Inclusion and exclusion criteria

It was defined a number of criteria on the basis of which papers were included in the review or excluded from the review. The defined inclusion (I1-I3) and exclusion (E1-E7) criteria are exposed in Table (1).

Table 1. Inclusion and Exclusion criteria

Criteria Type	*Criteria Description*
Inclusion (I1)	The paper is related to microservices selection, decision making or criticality
Inclusion (I2)	The paper is related to SOA services selection, decision making or criticality
Inclusion (I3)	The paper is related to components selection, decision making or criticality
Exclusion (E1)	The paper is not related to MSA, SOA or components
Exclusion (E2)	The paper is not related to selection, decision support or criticality
Exclusion (E3)	The paper is based on Gray Literature
Exclusion (E4)	The paper was not found.
Exclusion (E5)	The paper was not found without cost.
Exclusion (E6)	The paper is not written in English.
Exclusion (E7)	The paper does not represent a primary study

During the study selection phase, some filtering information was also considered to be able to get just the most updated information regarding the research area. These filters were:

- Qualitative studies will be considered.
- Language: English only
- Years: Between 2012 and 2019
- Document Types: All types of articles except gray literature.
- Outcome Measure: Number of identified methods
- Keywords: microservices, SOA, components, architecture, criticality, AHP, MDS
- Search Engines: Scopus, IEEE, Web of Science, Springer and Science Direct
- Experimental Design: there will not be applied to statistical methods

During the evaluation of the qualitative studies, it was also considered a duplicity filter. Thus after adapting the search criteria to the filters mentioned above, having run the inclusion and exclusion criteria, all studies returned by the search that are not duplicitous were accepted. At the end of the bibliographical survey, it is expected to identify the state of the art of criticality treatment models in microservices oriented architectures.

2.4 Conducting the Systematic Mapping

In this phase, the process specified in the protocol previously described was carried out. The main steps were: (i) Identification of Research, (ii) Selection of Primary Studies, (iii) Data Extraction, and (iv) Data Analysis based on the method used by Khan et al [4]. On digital libraries, the search string shall be adapted to each engine in order to obtain suitable results.

Table 2. Search String

Search String: *"prioritize and microservices"* **OR** *"ahp and microservices"* **OR** *"mds and microservices"* **OR** *"multidimensional and microservices"* **OR** *"multicriteria and microservices"* **OR** *"decision and microservices"* **OR** *"selection and microservices"* **OR** *"ahp and architectures"* **OR** *"mds and architectures"* **OR** *"multidimensional and architectures"* **OR** *"multicriteria and architectures"* **OR** *"decision and architectures"* **OR** *"selection and architectures"* **OR** *"criticity and microservices"* **OR** *"criticality and microservices"*

Selection of Primary Studies: In the first filter, the title, abstract, keywords of the papers were read. Based on this information, the inclusion and exclusion criteria were applied. After this step, 16 papers were classified as duplicated, 451 were rejected and 140 were accepted.

During the second filter, named as the extraction phase and detailed in Section (3), 140 accepted studies were analyzed considering the entire paper content. At the end, a total of 68 studies were accepted, a total of 523 studies were rejected, and 16 studies were considered duplicated.

2.5 Quality Assessment

The authors Kitchenham et al. [6] propose four quality questions for evaluating SLR. These are presented in the following, along with an evaluation of this study against these questions:

QA1: Are the reviews inclusion and exclusion criteria described and appropriate? It was explicitly defined and discussed the inclusion and exclusion criteria used in Section (2.3), so this quality criterion is met.

QA2: Is the literature search likely to have covered all the relevant studies? According to Kitchenham et al. [6], this criterion is met if four or more digital libraries have been searched and additional search strategies have been included. This quality criterion is

met, as it was performed an automatic search in five scientific databases (Scopus, IEEE, Web of Science, Springer and Science Direct).
QA3: Did the reviewers assess the quality/validity of the included studies? It was explicitly assessed the quality of each primary study according to the defined quality criteria. As part of the data synthesis, it was explicitly validated the level of evidence presented for each approach with respect to the MSA, SOA and components activities each supported.

QA4: Were the basic data/studies adequately described? This quality criterion was considered met since a detailed data collection form was used for each study. The results of merging papers to approaches, their focus, and support in terms of the different MSA, SOA, and components activities were also grouped for summarizing.

2.6 Data Collection

To answer the proposed research questions, each publication from the final set of papers was read in detail, extracting specific data about the presented approach or concept. In addition to general information about the selected paper, data regarding the underlying microservices, SOA and components model in the decision-making process were extracted.

To systematically search for scientific sources, population, intervention, comparison, and outcome (PICO) criteria to define the terms for the database search were used. The population in this paper is represented by components, SOA and MSA papers because it is only interested in criticality approaches applicable to these areas. The intervention is architectural knowledge and any synonyms thereof. Comparison is not applicable in this case, as this paper did not take a comparative approach. The search source was selected based on the capability to research reproducibility and indexing of the main periodicals and publications of the area.

3 Results and Discussion

In this section, the answers to the research questions are discussed, considering the broad-spectrum of approaches.

3.1 Search Results

This section presents the results of search and selection. Table (3) exposes the paper selection status separated by the search engine. After the extraction phase mentioned in Section (2.4), the studies were classified by publication year and publishing vehicle. In total, 68 selected studies were included, 8 being published in journals and 60 published in conference proceedings.

Table 3. Papers selection status per search engine

Engine	Articles			
	Total	***Accepted***	***Rejected***	***Duplicated***
Scopus	101	19	81	1
IEEE	164	24	126	14
Web of Science	75	7	68	0
Springer	258	13	245	0
Science Direct	9	5	3	1

It was obtained a total of 607 articles after search phase and accepted a total of 68 articles

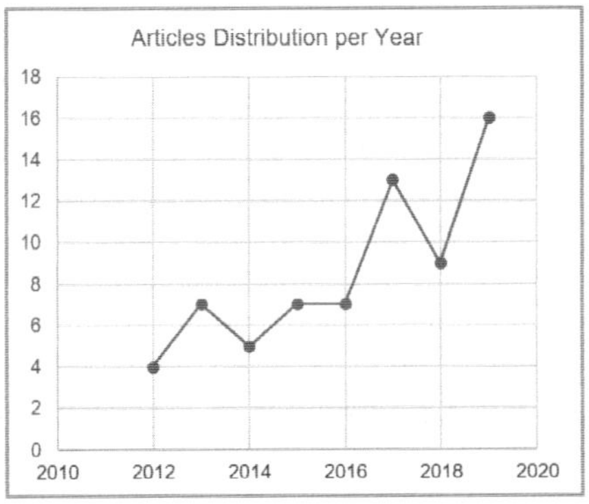

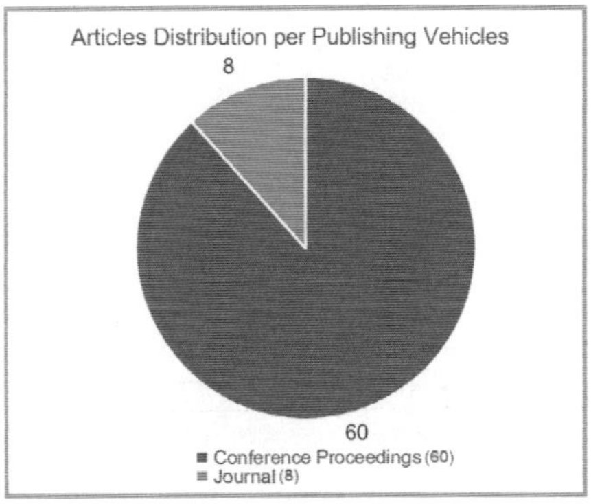

Figure 1. Papers by Year and Type of Publishing Vehicles

Figure (1) shows the distribution of studies included in this paper. The distribution of studies over the years, from 2012 to 2019. This figure shows a trend of increasing publications on MSA, SOA and components approach between 2017 and 2019, in which publications on MSA, SOA, and components approaches are published with a slight variation in 2018, but with an increasing tendency.

Other studies on similar topics also show that MSA, SOA and components and related topics such as design decisions and documentation are still an active research discipline in general. All of them show a similar increase after 2015 with slight increases and decreases in the following years. A full list containing the selected articles is available on-line (http://www.eduardomioto.com/review/cibse2020.htm).

3.2 Selection Methods for MSA, SOA, and Components (RQ1)

As regards to selection methods, 18 papers did not propose any selection method. Considering the approaches to MSA, SOA, and components that have been used by the research community over the years between 2012 and 2019, 15 different selection methods to MSA, SOA and components were identified as shown on Figure (2).

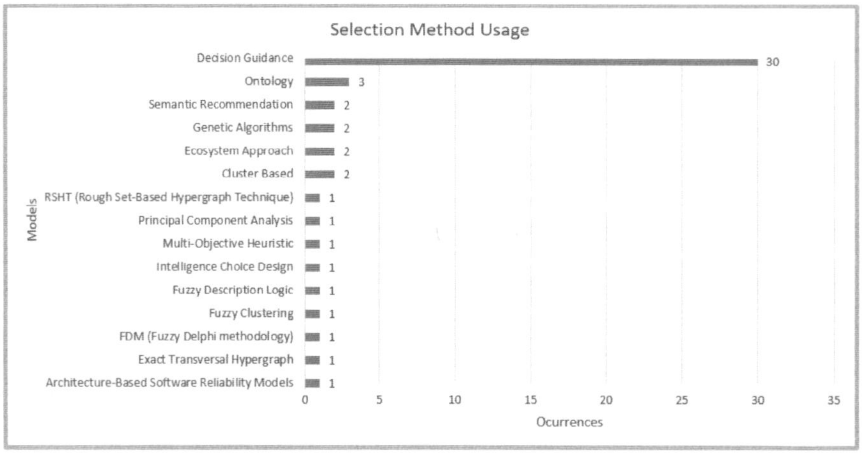

Figure 2. Number of papers per selection method

Based on these data, it was concluded that "Decision Guidance" is the most used method for selection, being used by 30 papers (44.11%) from a total of 68. The second most used selection method was "Ontology" with 3 papers, followed by "Semantic Recommendation", "Genetic Algorithms", "Ecosystem Approach" and "Cluster-Based" each of them used by 2 papers (2.94%) from the total of 68 (4.41%). All other selection models used were found in one study each (1.47% each one).

3.3 Multiple Criteria Evaluation Model (RQ2)

As regards to criticality based evaluation models, 29 papers (42.64%) did not propose any multiple criteria evaluation model. Considering the approaches to MSA, SOA, and components that have been used between 2012 and 2019, 16 different multiple criteria approaches to MSA, SOA and components were identified as shown on Figure (3).

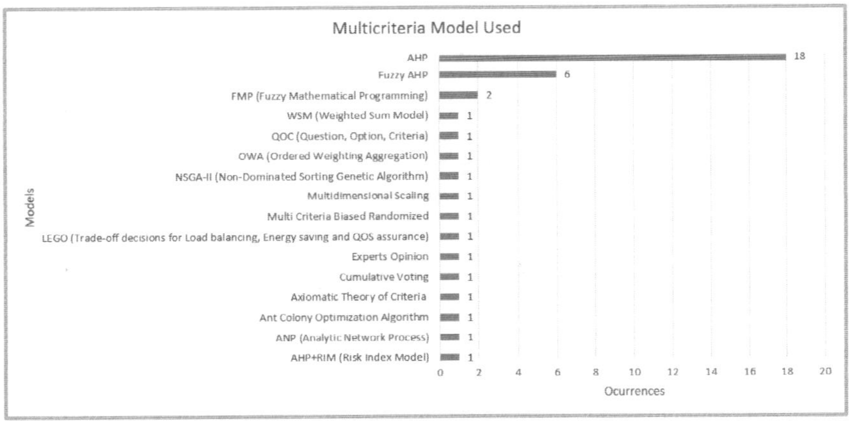

Figure 3. Number of papers per multiple criteria method

Analytic Hierarchy Process (AHP) model was used in 18 studies from a total of 68 studies (26.47%), Fuzzy AHP model was used in 6 studies (8.82%), followed by Fuzzy Mathematical Programming used in 2 studies (2.94%). All other multiple criteria models used were found in one study each (1.47% each one).

It was possible to conclude that there is a common acceptance regarding the usage of AHP as a multiple criteria approach, also considering its adaptation variations to the user requirements, as observed with Fuzzy AHP.

3.4 Criticality Based Evaluation Model (RQ3)

As regards to criticality based evaluation models, 63 papers (92.64%) did not propose any criticality evaluation model from a total of 68 selected papers. Considering the approaches to MSA, SOA and components that have been developed by the research community over the last years between 2012 and 2019, 5 different criticality based evaluation models to MSA, SOA and components were identified.

As regards to criticality based evaluation models, all occurrences were found at the same proportion, as shown in Figure (4). The model "Quality Attributes on Architecture Trade-Off Centered Analysis" was found in 1 study (1.47%) from a total of 68 studies; as well as "Dynamic Weights", "Architecture-based Software Reliability Models", "Components Reliability based on Defect" and "Failure Mode Effect and Analysis.

This variety of models highlights that there is not a consensus regarding the most relevant criticality evaluation model and most of them (4 out of 5) focused on components and just the minority part (1 out of 5) focused on MSA.

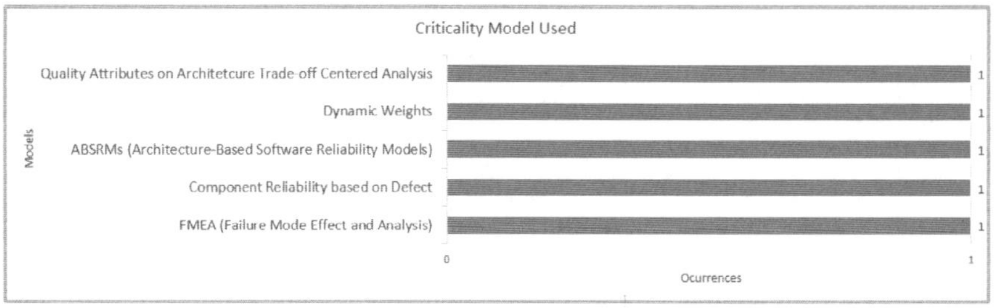

Figure 4. Number of papers per criticality method

Related to the single paper that treats the criticality focused on microservices [21], a criticality evaluation approach called ACISM was used to analyze the quality of services. The ACISM approach uses the dynamically acquired weight information to obtain the result and uses the result to select instances of microservices. According to the authors, the proposed method can weaken the decisiveness of user's subjective selection by using the dynamical weight information. The method balances the influence of subjective and objective factors and can improve the accuracy of microservice instances selection and shorten the response time.

Based on the results obtained, it was possible to conclude that there is no standardized nomenclature and semantic of concepts, which may hinder the understanding and comparison. This may be a sign of a lack of maturity in the microservices criticality research area.

3.5 Threats to Validity

In order to analyze threats to validity related to this systematic mapping, relevant concerns are described separately as follows:

Discovering the primary studies: considering the focus on the discovery of the primary study considering multiple search criteria, the search string was developed associating to synonyms and was reviewed by the second and third authors. In addition, they contain synonyms and both singular and plural forms of the main terms. However, the number of digital libraries would not consider all the content available. Finally, only papers written in English were read. Therefore, this paper may have ignored some potentially relevant primary studies.

Increasing transparency and repeatability: are improved by documenting and disseminating the research questions, search strings, inclusion and exclusion criteria, digital libraries used, and the process was undertaken. However, full transparency is not possible as some information cannot be presented in this paper, motivated by the space needed.

Conducting the search: The digital databases do not have compatible search rules, so different search string were used, but considering some keywords. It was considered to reduce any possible bias in the manner of conducting the review, avoiding to include or exclude studies without considering the inclusion and exclusion criteria. However, when it comes to the data analysis, there might still have been the possibility of incomplete findings or conclusions based on personal interest or opinions.

Avoiding misclassification of primary studies: as a measure to mitigate the risk of erroneous classification, it also validated the conferences and journals in which the papers were published, when applicable, as well as the references of each one, however, some misclassification may be occurred and it is not guaranteed that the outcome of the extraction made by other researches would be identical to those presented in this paper.

3.6 Study Limitations

Even considering English as being the most accepted language on academic publication, a diversity of studies not being published on this language can be observed, therefore not being considered in this systematic mapping.

The years considered as primary filter were between 2012 and 2019, however relevant studies associated with SOA and components could have been published before these years and were not considered on this systematic mapping.

4 Related Work

The authors Badampudi, Wohlin, and Petersen [10] conducted an SRL related to component-based software systems, which in accordance with them, requires decisions on component origins for acquiring components that are an alternative of where to get a component from. The SLR conducted by Badampudi, Wohlin, and Petersen [10] is similar to this present paper in terms of multiple criteria approach investigation, however, their paper did not include the MSA perspective or even the criticality aspect.

The authors [10] identified factors that could influence the decision to choose among different component origins and solutions for decision-making in the literature. In total was included twenty-four primary studies. The component origins compared were mainly focused on in-house compared with COTS (Components off-the-shelf) and COTS compared with OSS (Open Source Software). The authors identified eleven factors affecting or influencing the decision to select a component origin. Most of the solutions were proposed for in-house vs. COTS selection and time, cost and reliability were the most considered factors in the solutions.

Another SLR, conducted by Breivold, Crnkovic, and Larsson [11], evaluate the software evolution capability in the architecture perspective, intending to obtain an overview of the existing approaches in analyzing and improving software evolution capability at an architectural level, and investigate impacts on research and practice. The SLR conducted by Breivold, Crnkovic, and Larsson [11] is similar to this present paper in terms of the architectural perspective investigation, however, it did not include the criticality aspect.

In accordance with Breivold, Crnkovic, and Larsson [11], the software evolution capability describes a software system's ability to easily accommodate future changes, being a fundamental characteristic for making strategic decisions, and increasing economic value of software. For long-lived systems, there is a need to address evolution capability explicitly during the entire software lifecycle in order to prolong the productive lifetime of software systems. The authors identified five main categories of research topics, (i) techniques supporting quality consideration during software architecture design, (ii) architectural quality evaluation, (iii) economic valuation, (iv) architectural knowledge management, and (v) modeling techniques.

The findings of Breivold, Crnkovic, and Larsson's [11] review reveals that it is necessary to establish a theoretical foundation for software evolution research due to the fact that the expertise in this area is still built on the basis of case studies instead of generalized knowledge; as well as it is necessary to combine appropriate techniques to address the multifaceted perspectives of software evolution capability due to the fact that each technique has its specific focus and context for which it is appropriate in the entire software lifecycle.

The SLR conducted by Yingkui and Jing [12] evaluates the reliability analysis considering multiple possible states, which is known as multi-state (MS) reliability analysis. Multi-state reliability models provide more realistic and more precise representations of engineering systems, being more complex and present major difficulties in system definition and performance evaluation. This SRL present by presents Yingkui and Jing [12] is about the latest studies and advances about multi-state system reliability evaluation, multi-state systems optimization and multi-state systems maintenance, however, it's not associated with software architecture or MSA. This review is similar to this paper in terms of criticality associated.

There is still no general agreement for addressing the problem of criticality suggestions associated with MSA on literature. The analysis also reveals a broad spectrum of approaches supporting decision-making [10], architecture evaluation and review [11], and criticality [12], however, it was not possible to locate an SLR associated with all aspects that involve the selection methods for criticality in MSA.

5 Conclusions

This paper presented the process followed to perform an systematic mapping aiming to get an overview of existing researches on criticality suggestions related to MSA.

The research questions on this systematic mapping were intrinsically associated, considering that established selection models' question intends to identify models focused on helping the selection process associated to MSA, SOA and components in order to promote a base to decision making process.

The first research questions (RQ1) is directly associated with the multiple criteria evaluation approach question (RQ2), that aggregated with the criticality scope (RQ3), seeks to compose a well-grounded foundation of the most used criticality methods on the MSA perspective.

The results show an increasing interest in criticality research. They also suggest the immaturity of the area associated with MSA, since there is not an established guideline or proposal that focus on suggesting the critical microservices, differently from SOA and components that already have a diversity of studies around these areas.

Another weakness is the low number of works that performed comparative studies to highlight the advantages and disadvantages of their approaches and related work. However, this area has been showing signs of an increase in maturity since the numbers of published papers are increasing and MSA has been applied in practice.

A research trend was identified since the increasing number of experience reports in industry and academy showing evidence that the criticality approaches are feasible and beneficial to be applied in a real context. Nevertheless, further researches with more rigorous methods, including a case study for this purpose, would indicate new findings. Researchers intending to conduct researches related to criticality applied to MSA would use the results obtained by this paper to serve as a base to produce subsequent analysis in order to promote the maturity of this area. To address the lack of literature associated to criticality method related to MSA, the authors are conducting a research to propose a multiple criteria criticality method focused on MSA [19].

References

1. Australian National Health and Medical Research Council. How to review the evidence: systematic identification and review of the scientific literature, 2000. ISBN 186-4960329.
2. Australian National Health and Medical Research Council. How to use the evidence: assessment and application of scientific evidence. February 2000, ISBN 0 642 43295 2.
3. Cochrane Collaboration. Cochrane Reviewers' Handbook. Version 4.2.1. December 2003
4. Khan, Khalid, S., ter Riet, Gerben., Glanville, Julia., Sowden, Amanda, J. and Kleijnen, Jo. (eds) Undertaking Systematic Review of Research on Effectiveness. CRD's Guidance for those Carrying Out or Commissioning Reviews. CRD Report Number 4 (2nd Edition), NHS Centre for Reviews and Dissemination, University of York, IBSN 1 900640 20 1, March 2001.
5. D. D. de Carvalho, L. F. Chagas, A. M. Lima, and C. A. L. Reis, "Software process lines: A systematic literature review", in *International Conference on Software Process Improvement and Capability Determination*, Vilnius, Lithuania, 2014, p. 118–130.
6. O.P. Brereton, B.A. Kitchenham, D. Turner Budgen, M. Khalil, "Lessons from applying the systematic literature review process within the software engineering domain", Journal of Systems and Software Volume 80, Issue 4, April 2007, Pages 571-583
7. S. Haselböck, R. Weinreich, and G. Buchgeher, "Decision Models for Microservices: Design Areas, Stakeholders, Use Cases, and Requirements", in Software Architecture, ECSA 2017, Canterbury, UK, 2017, p. 155–170.
8. Lytra, I., Tran, H., Zdun, U.: "Supporting consistency between architectural design decisions and component models through reusable architectural knowledge transformations". In: Drira, K. (ed.) ECSA 2013, Montpellier, France, 2013. LNCS, vol. 7957, pp. 224–239. Springer, Heidelberg (2013). doi:10.1007/978-3-642-39031-9 20
9. Capilla, R., Jansen, A., Tang, A., Avgeriou, P., Babar, M.A.: "10 years of software architecture knowledge management: practice and future". Journal of Systems and Software Volume 116, June 2016, p. 191-205 (2015)

10. D. Badampudi, C. Wohlin, and K. Petersen, "Software component decision-making: In-house, OSS, COTS or outsourcing-A systematic literature review", *Journal of Systems and Software*, vol. 121, p. 105–124, 2016.
11. H. P. Breivold, I. Crnkovic, and M. Larsson, "A systematic review of software architecture evolution research," *Information and Software Technology*, vol. 54, no. 1, pp. 16–40, 2012.
12. G. Yingkui and L. Jing, "Multi-state system reliability: A new and systematic review," *Procedia engineering*, vol. 29, pp. 531–536, 2012.
13. P. D. Francesco, I. Malavolta, and P. Lago, "Research on Architecting Microservices: Trends, Focus, and Potential for Industrial Adoption," in 2017 IEEE International Conference on Software Architecture (ICSA), 2017, pp. 21–30.
14. N. Alshuqayran, N. Ali, and R. Evans, "A Systematic Mapping Study in Microservice Architecture," in 2016 IEEE 9th International Conference on Service-Oriented Computing and Applications (SOCA), Macau, China, 2016, pp. 44–51.
15. C. Pahl and P. Jamshidi. Microservices: A Systematic Mapping Study. In Proceedings of the 6th International Conference on Cloud Computing and Services Science, Rome, Italy, pages 137–146, 2016
16. F. Montesi and J. Weber, "Circuit Breakers, Discovery, and API Gateways in Microservices," *CoRR*, vol. abs/1609.05830, 2016.
17. M. Gabbrielli, S. Giallorenzo, C. Guidi, J. Mauro, and F. Montesi, "Self-reconfiguring microservices," in *Theory and Practice of Formal Methods*, Springer, 2016, pp. 194–210.
18. N. Dragoni et al., "Microservices: yesterday, today, and tomorrow," CoRR, vol. abs/1606.04036, 2016.
19. E. F. M. de O. dos Santos and C. M. L. Werner, "A Survey on Microservices Criticality Attributes on Established Architectures," in 2019 International Conference on Information Systems and Software Technologies, Quito, Equador, 2019, pp. 149–155
20. A. S. Agarwala, "Shortcomings in MIL-STD-1629A guidelines for criticality analysis," in *Annual Proceedings on Reliability and Maintainability Symposium*, Los Angeles, CA, 1990, pp. 494–496.
21. J. Shao, X. Zhang, and Z. Cao, "Research on Context-based Instances Selection of Microservice," in *Proceedings of the 2nd International Conference on Computer Science and Application Engineering*, Hohhot, China, 2018, pp. 1–5
22. J. Stubbs, W. Moreira, and R. Dooley, "Distributed Systems of Microservices Using Docker and Serfnode," in *2015 7th International Workshop on Science Gateways*, Budapest, Hungary, 2015, pp. 34–39, doi: 10.1109/IWSG.2015.16.
23. I. Steinmacher, A. P. Chaves, and M. A. Gerosa, "Awareness support in distributed software development: A systematic review and mapping of the literature," Computer Supported Cooperative Work (CSCW), vol. 22, no. 2-3, 2013, pp. 113–158.

Frameworks and High-Availability in Microservices: An Industrial Survey

Gastón Márquez[1], Jacopo Soldani[2], Francisco Ponce[1], and Hernán Astudillo[1]

[1] *Toeska Research Group*
Universidad Técnica Federico Santa María,
Avenida España 1680, Valparaíso, Chile
gaston.marquez@sansano.usm.cl, francisco.ponceme@usm.cl,
hernan@inf.utfsm.cl
[2] Dipartimento di Informatica, Università di Pisa, Pisa, Italy
soldani@di.unipi.it

Abstract. While building microservice-based applications, architects need to choose among different frameworks to provide generic functionalities to address quality attribute concerns, such as high-availability. Although using frameworks brings various benefits, it is not clear how they actually impact on the properties characterising the high-availability of microservices. To this end, this article reports the level of agreement among practitioners on the positive and negative impact of frameworks on the high-availability of microservices. More precisely, we first systematically identify 12 properties characterising the high-availability of microservices. We then present the outcomes of an industrial study showing how existing open-source frameworks positively/negatively impact on the 12 properties characterising high-availability of microservices. Results indicate that practitioners agree on the fact that frameworks do positively/negatively impact on high-availability of microservices, and provide a first body of knowledge for suitably selecting frameworks while developing and deploying microservices.

Keywords: Microservices · High-availability · Frameworks · Survey

1 Introduction

Microservices are gaining momentum in enterprise IT, with core businesses of major IT players (e.g., Amazon, Netflix, Spotify and Twitter) already being delivered through microservice-based solutions [23]. This is because microservices (if properly setup) can help ensuring quality attributes of applications, e.g., availability, portability, scalability [19].

A key question is hence how to properly setup microservices to ensure quality attributes, and (as for the scope of this paper) to ensure their high-availability. While developing and deploying microservice-based applications, various decisions must indeed be tackled to make them truly featuring high availability properties. Such decisions include suitably selecting *frameworks* for implementing their components and deployment infrastructure [17, 21]. We hereafter refer to frameworks as collections of reusable software elements providing generic functionalities to address recurring domain and quality attributes [13]. In this same concept, we also include *technological tools* that use sets of frameworks to provide their respective functionalities (such as Kubernetes, MongoDB, among others).

Although there exist frameworks geared towards ensuring high-availability in microservices-based applications [16], to the best of our knowledge, there is currently no body of knowledge recapping the actual impact of frameworks on the high-availability of microservices, from the industrial practitioners' viewpoint. Different frameworks indeed target different properties characterising both high-availability and other quality attributes, and the lack of the above mentioned body of knowledge makes it not clear which of the properties characterising high-availability are positively or negatively affected by a particular framework. This may result in incorrect selections of frameworks, with application administrators that may select frameworks not negatively impacting on one of the properties characterising the high-availability of microservices, which they consider crucial.

A support for suitably selecting frameworks is hence needed, and this paper tries to make a first step in this direction by focusing the following question: *Is a framework positively or negatively impacting on the properties defining high-availability of the microservices forming an application?*

To answer the above question, we first identified the properties characterising the high-availability of microservices with a systematic multivocal review. We then considered the microservice-related frameworks identified in [16], and we systematically elicited their positive and negative impact on the identified high-availability properties by analysing the issues and comments raised within the repositories of 18 open-source microservice-based projects. Finally, to evaluate our findings, we conducted a survey targeting 40 practitioners daily working with microservices, aimed at analyzing their level of agreement on the elicited positive and negative impacts of frameworks on the properties characterising high-availability of microservices.

The main contributions of this paper are hence (i) a list of properties characterising the high-availability of microservices, and (ii) a two-stage exploratory study illustrating positive and negative impacts of existing frameworks on such properties. Our contributions provide a first body of knowledge on the actual impact of framewoks on the properties characterising the high-availability of microservices, and confirm that selecting different frameworks differently impacts on the different properties.

The rest of this article is structured as follow: Section 2 sets the stage of our study by listing the open-source frameworks known to relate to the high-availability of microservices; Section 3 elicits the properties characterising the high-availability of microservices, and Section 4 analyses the impact of frameworks on such properties; Section 5 describes and discusses the results of our study; Section 6 and 7 discuss threats to validity and related work, respectively; Section 8 draws some concluding remarks.

2 Setting the stage

In our previous study [16], we conducted an empirical study aiming at identifying frameworks used to develop microservices-based systems, and their relation with microservice patterns and quality attributes. Figure 1 recaps the process we conducted to obtain frameworks.

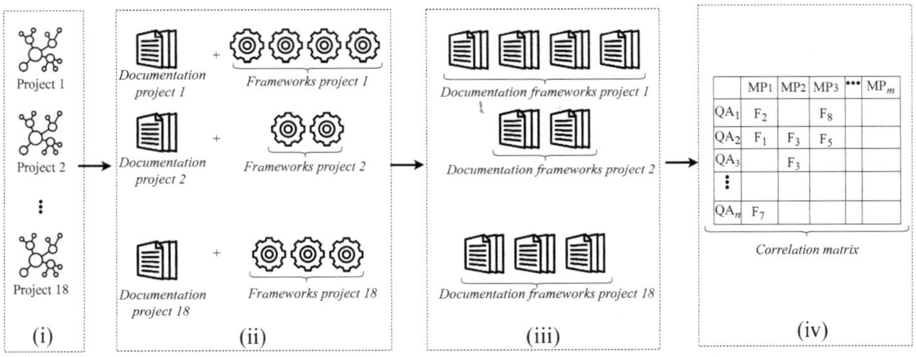

Fig. 1. Process to obtain frameworks. "QA", "MP", and "F" represents quality attributes, microservices patterns, and frameworks, respectively.

We firstly (i) explored 18 open-source microservices projects chosen using the benchmark requirements for microservices research proposed in [1]. We then (ii) analysed documentation and configuration files of each project into elicit the frameworks used in such projects used, and we (iii) analysed the documentation of each framework to identify which microservice patterns are implemented by each framework and which quality attributes are addressed by such framework. Finally, we (iv) created a correlation matrix recapping the results of our analysis by relating framework to quality attributes and microservices patterns.

The outcome of our previous study [16] is a mapping of 23 open-source frameworks to 17 microservice patterns and 6 quality attributes. Such a mapping sets the stage for the study presented in this paper, as it allows to focus on the open-source frameworks known to be related to the high-availability of microservices. Such frameworks are listed in Table 1. We selected these frameworks because, according to their documentation, the main functionalities they address are associated with high availability features.

3 Eliciting high-availability properties

The first activity in our study was to identify the properties characterising the high-availability of microservices (hereafter called *high-availability properties*, for brevity reasons). The activity consisted in conducting a systematic multivocal review, which (due to space limitations) we briefly present hereafter.

Table 1. Open-source frameworks related to the high-availability of microservice.

Framework	Description
RabbitMQ	Open-source message-broker application framework
Apache Zookeper	A service for distributed systems offering several functionalities
Docker	A set of platform as a service (PaaS) products
Apache Cassandra	Distributed NoSQL database management system
Netlifx Eureka	Service registry for resilient mid-tier load balancing and failover
Kubernetes	Container-orchestration system
MongoDB	Cross-platform document-oriented MoSQL database application

The search in our systematic review was driven by availability checklist described in [3]. The checklist provides guidelines for designing and analysing the availability of system, organised among the following categories: allocation of responsibilities, coordination model, data model, mapping among architectural elements, resource management, binding time, and choice of technology. For each category, there is a further checklist to be analyzed when availability requirements or properties should be satisfied.

We exploited the checklist for searching for white literature (i.e., peer-reviewed academic research papers) and grey literature (i.e., industiral white paper and blog posts) discussing properties related to the element of the checklist. The search for white literature was done on well-known indexing sources, i.e., Google Scholar (primary), ACM Digital Library, IEEE Xplore and Scopus. The search for grey literature was instead run on Google (with analogous stopping criteria to those in [19]) and on renowned blogs, i.e., InfoQ (`https://www.infoq.com`) and Dzone (`https://dzone.com`).

Finally, we conducted inter-rater reliability assessment and brainstorming sessions to refine the list of identified high-availability properties. To this end, we held (virtual) meetings to identify and describe the properties. Each property was discussed and negotiated until all research team members agreed on the property. As a final result, we elicited 12 high-availability properties, which are listed and described in Table 2.

4 Analysing the impact of frameworks on high-availability

We hereafter illustrate our approach to analyse the impact of frameworks on high-availability properties. We first illustrate how we elicited the impact of frameworks from existing open-source microservice-based projects (Sect. 4.1). We then show how we evaluated the actual perception of industrial practioners of such impact, based on an online survey (Sect. 4.2).

4.1 Eliciting the impact of frameworks on high-availability, from existing projects

We analysed the impact of frameworks on high-availability properties by starting from 18 existing open-source microservice-based project, and by collecting the

Table 2. High-availability properties in microservices-based systems

Id	Name	Description
P1	*High detection of failed host*	This property defines the capability of detect failed hosts in order to a load balancer can stop requests to them.
P2	*Intermittently asynchronous data transmission*	Communication property where a message sender does not wait for a response.
P3	*Regular snapshots*	Property related to recovering the system from planned host maintenance owing to hardware upgrade, soft reboot, etc.
P4	*Efficient duration of timeouts periods*	Property that prevents remote procedure calls from waiting indefinitely for a response.
P5	*High isolation*	The property where each microservices is its own encapsulated application.
P6	*Effective load balancing*	Efficiently distributing incoming network traffic among groups of backend servers.
P7	*Quick broken state recovery*	Capability to restart states when they are broken for a more extended period.
P8	*High control of failure propagation*	Property which indicates the capability of isolate failures through a good definition of service boundaries.
P9	*High service monitoring visibility*	Property that allows visibility into the health of the microservice architecture.
P10	*Periodic heartbeat signal*	Property related to the periodic signal to check the status of services.
P11	*Low application restarting*	This property refers to the low rate of restart services when a failure occurs.
P12	*Efficient resources consumption*	Property related to the impact on the resources consumption (hardware/software) of a system.

(*positive* and *negative*) issues and comments on developers on frameworks and high-availability. We used the following inclusion and exclusion criteria to select the 18 open-source projects we considered:

- *Inclusion criteria*: Benchmark requirements for microservices projects proposed in [1], and projects with source code available.
- *Exclusion criteria*: Projects with no robust information (basic examples, projects in process, others), tools to build microservices (instead of frameworks), component-based projects to build microservices (e.g., projects just for gateway components to microservices), and projects used as an example for lectures or talks.

To collect and organise the issues and comments on high-availability of microservices (hereafter simply called *high-availability issues*), we followed the process shown in Figure 2. For each project, we explored open and closed issues to identify, collect and organise high-availability issues reported by developers and related to the at least one of the microservices frameworks listed in Table 1

From a total of 4,188 candidate high-availability issues, we filtered out all such issues where developers were not describing the rationale for selecting frame-

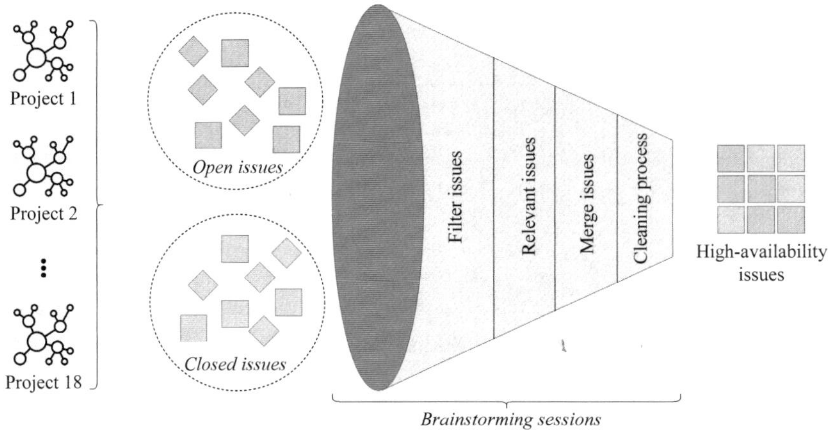

Fig. 2. Process to obtain high-availability issues

works, reducing the scope to 958 ($\approx$ 22.8%) candidate issues. We further refined the scope by restricting to those issues where we found posts explicitly relating one of the frameworks in Table 1 to one of the high-availability properties in Table 2. This allowed us to restrict the scope to 87 high-availability issues, examples of which (concerning RabbitMQ) are reported below:

- Positive issue: "*the Event bus is based on async communication based on RabbitMQ [...] It is used for integration events derived from transactions that happened in any of the microservices and when other microservices need to be aware of those events*".
- Negative issue: "*If RabbitMQ is unreachable when the service tenant starts up, the existing connection is lost for whatever reason, it won't reconnect*"

Afterwards, we proceed by identifying and merging similar/analogous candidate high-availability issues. We clustered issued based on the frameworks they correspond to and we analysed clusters to elicit positive and negative high-availability issues. This allowed us to obtain 8 merged high-availability issues, an example of which is the following: "*RabbitMQ permits implementing asynchronous communication among microservices. But, if a connection is lost, RabbitMQ can affect the number of long-lived connections.*"

From the obtained high-availability issues, we extracted 17 statements concerning the impact of frameworks on high-availability properties. Such statements are listed in Table 3. The table also indicates whether a statement denotes a postive or negative impact over corresponding high-availability properties.

4.2 Evaluating high-availablity issues, based on a survey

To evaluate the actual recognition of the statements in Table 3 among industrial practitioners, we conducted an online survey (following the guidelines described

Table 3. Statements on the positive/negative impact of open-source frameworks on high-availability properties.

Statement	Impact	Prop.
S1: RabbitMQ permits implementing asynchronous communication among microservices	Positive	P2
S2: RabbitMQ can affect the number of long-lived connections if a connection is lost	Negative	P1
S3: Apache Zookeeper supports session timeouts	Positive	P4
S4: Apache Zookeeper can significantly impact on the resources consumption (hardware/software) of a system	Negative	P12
S5: Docker is a good solution for packaging and isolating microservices into containers	Positive	P5
S6: Docker can significantly impact on the resources consumption (hardware/software) of a system.	Negative	P12
S7: Docker can hamper the heartbeat-based monitoring	Negative	P10
S8: Kubernetes supports services monitoring	Positive	P9
S9: Kubernetes can significantly impact on the resources consumption (hardware/software) of a system	Negative	P12
S10: Apache Cassandra supports database service replication	Positive	P6
S11: Apache Cassandra can significantly impact on the resources consumption (hardware/software) of a system	Negative	P12
S12: Netflix Eureka helps monitoring microservices, by allowing to locate them and their logs	Positive	P9
S13: Netflix Eureka can significantly impact on the resources consumption (hardware/software) of a system	Negative	P12
S14: MongoDB supports the isolation of database services	Positive	P5
S15: MongoDB can hamper the heartbeat-based monitoring of database services	Negative	P10
S16: MongoDB automatically routes requests to the appropriate databases	Positive	P2
S17: MongoDB does not support fanning simple transactions out to different database partitions	Negative	P8

in [14, 15]). We hereafter present the survey setting, while its results are discussed in Sect. 5.

Scope and target audience The scope of the survey falls within the IT industry, and in particular that regarding the usage of microservices to deliver core businesses. Within such scope, the focus was on the usage of open-source frameworks to develop and deploy microservices.

The target audience hence entailed industrial practitioners daily working with microservices, either directly part of the authors' relationship networks or reachable through professional networks, frameworks-oriented social networks and technology-related portals. Furthermore, practitioners were also reached by exploiting the snowballing sampling approach [15]. The target audience was given the possibility to participate in the survey in the period lasting from the 1st of March 2019 to the 31st of October 2019.

Goal and research questions The goal of the survey was to evaluate the impact of open-source frameworks on the high-availability of microservices, as per its actual perceiving by industrial practitioners daily working with microservices. In particular, we aimed at evaluatiing their level of agreement with the statements we elicited in Table 3. To this end, we established the following research questions:

- **RQ1**: *Which is the level of agreement of respondents concerning positive contributions related to specific frameworks and high-availability properties?* By answering this research question, we aimed at identifying to which level frameworks are considered to positively impact on high-availability properties.
- **RQ2**: *Which is the level of agreement of respondents concerning negative contributions related to specific frameworks and high-availability properties?* As for RQ1, the goal of this research question was to understand to which level frameworks are considered to negatively impact on high-availability properties.

Survey questions and response format The survey questions were built by directly submitting the statements in Table 3. Respondents were then given the possibility to make their level of agreement with such statements by marking one of the following 3 Likert-scale responses: *Strongly agree*, *Agree*, *Not agree*. We selected this type of scale to obtain more concise answers and, in turn, to facilitate the analysis of the respondents [12].

We used an online questionnaire as survey methodology since we intend to ask precise questions in the context of availability. Furthermore, such a methodology is known to allow to search and explore widespread opinions on a specific topic. For specific domains (including that considered by our study), online questionnaires offer several other advantages, e.g., the effort to handle the questionnaire is reduced (for the participants), it is possible to navigate easily through the questionnaire [18].

Data analysis For each response, we proceed to perform a descriptive analysis based on the frequency of responses in order to better understanding of results. In addition, with the aim of further elaborating the key findings regarding the survey, we performed a series of brainstorming sessions. Obtained results are presented and discussed in the following section.

5 Results and discussion

We hereby illustrate the outcomes of our survey. More precisely, we first show the data about the recognised positive and negative impacts of frameworks (Section 5.1), and we then discuss the outcomes of the study (Section 5.2).

In doing so, we shall establish the agreement on a statement by defining a threshold based on the absolute majority of respondents (as in [7]). The latter means that a candidate statement must obtain over a half of the votes to get agreed, i.e., given n the total amount of respondents, it must get $(n+1)/2$ votes if n is odd, or $(n+2)/2$ votes if n is even. As a total of 40 practitioners participated to our survey, this means that a candidate statement is agreed if at least 21 respondents agree with it.

5.1 Practitioners' recognition on considered impact of framewors

Figures 3 and 4 plot the frequencies of answers on the statements concerning the impact of frameworks on high-availability properties. In both cases, we can

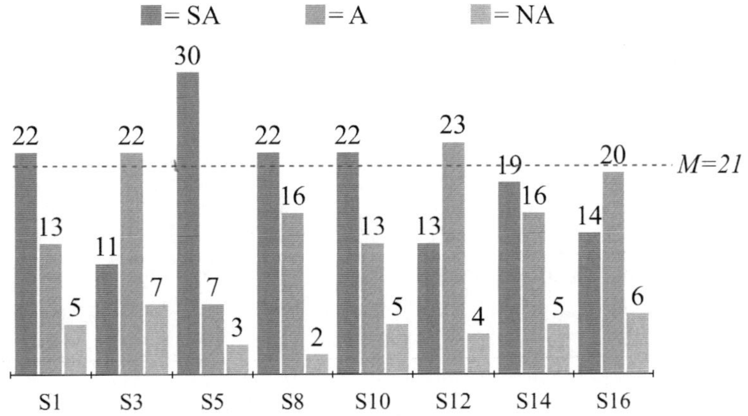

Fig. 3. Survey results regarding positive contribution of frameworks. "SA" correspond to *Strongly agree*, "A" to *Agree*, "NA" to *Not agree*, and "M" to the absolute majority

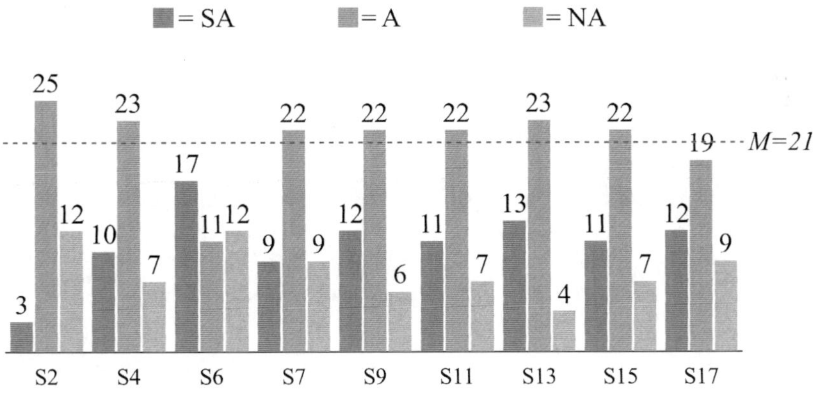

Fig. 4. Survey results regarding negative contribution of frameworks. "SA" correspond to *Strongly agree*, "A" to *Agree*, "NA" to *Not agree*, and "M" to the absolute majority

observe that the vast majority of respondents agrees on the proposed statements (if we considers the sums of *Strongly Agree* and *Agree* answers), hence confirming that our statements on the impact of frameworks on high-availability properties are reflected by the community.

Focusing on Figure 3, we observe that, according to the responses, there is a "strong agreement" on statements S1, S5, S8, S10 and S14, and an "agreement" on statements S3 and S12. Statements S14 and S16 instead do not have a majority of *Strongly Agree* or *Agree* answers, but their sum fairly outgoes the threshold.

Concerning Figure 4, we observe that respondents where lighter in agreeing with statements, as their majority "agree" (not strongly) on all statements but S6 and S17. However, if we consider the sum of *Strongly agree* and *Agree* answers, we observe an overall agreement on all statements.

5.2 Discussion

On the positive compensations side, the survey results indicate that RabbitMQ, Docker, Kubernetes, and Apache Cassandra positively satisfy (*Strongly agree* selection) properties P2, P5, P9, and P6, respectively. Regarding Apache Zookeeper and Netflix Eureka, although respondents indicate that these frameworks are a positive contribution to properties P4 and P9, results indicate that there is no unanimous agreement (*Agree* selection) regarding the positive effect of these frameworks for the P4 and P9.

About negative compensations, the most affected property is P12. This indicates that Apache Zookeeper, Docker, Kubernetes, Apache Cassandra, and Netflix Eureka compromise resource consumption. However, the level of agreement illustrates that the respondents are not categorical with this situation since everyone selected the *Agree* option. This is because, according to what we could investigate, property P12 will be affected depending on the size of the microservices project. For properties P1 and P10, the same situation occurs.

According to the results described in Figures 3 and 4, in the statement S6, S14, S16, and S17 it is not possible to identify the level of agreement. 3 of the 4 statements correspond to MongoDB and 1 to Docker. In order to investigate why there is no agreement in these statements, we conducted a rapid review [4] to establish the final decision regarding which level of agreement should be assigned for these statements.

Regarding statements of MongoDB, Ueda et al. [24] conducted an empirical study with attention to understand the characteristics to design an infrastructure optimized for microservices. The authors mention that, since MongoDB implements a transactional ACID model(Atomicity, Consistency, Isolation, and Durability) on different documents, the way on how the model reference documents to ensure integrity is done by nesting documents, promoting the isolation of the data. Likewise, the same authors describe that one of the significant disadvantages of MongoDB is that it does not support transactions at the moment of updating more than one document or collection. Gadea et al. [8] also mention this observation in the conclusions of his experience of using microservices architecture in a collaborative document editing system. Nevertheless, new MongoDB releases (such as 4.0[3]) provide the ability to perform multi-document transactions against replica sets.

[3] https://docs.mongodb.com/manual/release-notes/4.0/#multi-document-transactions

Other empirical studies, such as [26], mention that MongoDB has the capability to aggregate, route and indexes the unique document ID automatically, improving the performance and scalability in queries against indexed and non-indexed collections, for various (virtual) server hardware configurations [9].

About the Docker resource consumption statement, although some authors (such as [2] and [20]) describe that this situation depends on the project's characteristics, Casalicchio et al. [5] provide an extensive empirical study related to docker performance. One of the conclusions emerged from the authors' experiments is related to the tendency of Docker to use high disk I/O overhead. The authors mentioned that Docker heavily penalizes the execution time when the number of container increase.

Therefore, the studies' results corroborate the answers of sentences S6, S14, S16, and S17. This means that we could take into account the answers with the highest tendency for these sentences (S6→SA, S14→SA, S16→A, and S17→A) in the first instance. Nevertheless, although the studies provide significant research related to the statements' frameworks, there is not sufficient data and evidence to conclude irrefutably the level of agreement of the aforementioned sentences. As future work, we plan to further investigate this finding in order to establish a level of agreement to these sentences.

Finally, we find contributions in 9 of 12 high-availability properties. The properties where we do not find evidence are P3, P7, and P11. The three aforementioned properties are related to specific scenarios of fault recovery. To best of our knowledge, *how to recover microservices-based applications from failures* is one of the research challenges regarding availability in microservices (as also discussed in [19]).

6 Threats to validity

We hereby discuss potential threats to the validity of our study, following the taxonomy in [27]. *Threats to internal validity* describe factors that could affect the results obtained from the study. To mitigate these threats, the participation in the survey was voluntary and anonymous to ensure that answers were as honest as possible. Given that the availability issues are associated with specific technologies, the survey was promoted (i) in communities related to such technologies and (ii) among developers of microservice-based applications. Furthermore, we reinforced the results through interviews with practitioners with microservices-based projects development experience.

Construct validity refers to the extent to which operationalizations of a construct do actually measure what the theory says they do. The threats related to the construct validity were mitigated by careful questionnaire design. Moreover, we piloted the questionnaire internally several times in order to refine the vocabulary and make it as simple possible.

Threats to external validity are conditions that limit our ability to generalize the results. In this context, the survey participants may not represent the entire population of microservices practitioners. To mitigate this risk, we promoted the survey in different communities to include practitioners from different software domains. Furthermore, we decided to interview practitioners (with experience in the development of microservices-based applications) and discuss with them our findings in brainstorming sessions.

7 Related work

Usman et al. [25] presented DRSR, a highly available and fault-tolerant data replication strategy for service registry in a microservice architecture. Similarly, Wu et al. [28] proposed an extensible fault tolerance testing framework for microservice-based applications based on the non-intrusive fault injection.

Tang et al. [22] proposed a distributed service discovery mechanism, which improves the Raft algorithm according to the characteristics of the data, ensures the strong consistency of data between cluster nodes, and improves the availability of service discovery. Heinrich et al. [11] argued why new solutions to performance engineering for microservices are needed. Furthermore, the authors identified open issues with regard to performance aware testing, monitoring, and modeling of microservices.

Despite the significant contribution of previous studies, our study differs from the previous ones in the discussion of positive and negative compensations in high-availability properties related to microservices-based systems. It also differs from other existing industry-driven studies on microservices, such as [19], [21], [6], [10] and [17]. Such studies indeed focus on identifying and discussing advantages and disadvantages of microservices, and/or on distilling best practices. We instead focus on identifying and distilling the positive and negative impact of frameworks on the high-availability of microservices.

8 Conclusions

Our main contributions in this paper are (i) 12 properties characterising the high-availability of microservices (obtained by means of a systematic multivocal review), and (ii) an exploratory study to understand how the usage of existing open-source frameworks positively/negatively impacts on such properties. The exploratory study consisted in a systematically analysing the issues and comments in the repositories of 18 open-source microservice-based projects, which we exploited to extract 17 statements indicating how existing open-source framework impact on the high-availability of microservices. We also conducted an online survey involving practitioners daily working on microservices, whose vast majority agrees with the statements we identified, hence confirming that the impact indicated by such stamements is recognised by the community.

In addition, we provide a first body of knowledge on the actual impact of framewoks on the properties characterising the high-availability of microservices, and confirm that selecting different frameworks differently impacts on the different properties. We plan to work towards extending such a body of knowledge, by including other quality attributes peculiar to microservices, e.g., scalability and technology freedom. We also plan to exploit such a body of knowledge to devise a decision support system, aimed at helping researchers and practitioners finding suitable trade-offs for such quality attributes when designing and developing microservice-based applications.

Acknowledgments. This work was partly supported by the following CONICYT PCHA/Doctorado Nacional through grants 2016-21161005 and 2019-21191132; by CONICYT PIA (Basal FB0821 CCTVal); and by the projects *AMaCA* (POR-FSE, Regione Toscana) and *DECLware* (PRA_2018_66, University of Pisa).

References

1. Aderaldo, M., Mendonça, C., Pahl, C., Pooyan, J.: Benchmark requirements for microservices architecture research. In Proceedings of the 1st International Workshop on Establishing the Community-Wide Infrastructure for Architecture-Based Software Engineering (ECASE'17) pp. 8–13 (2017)
2. Anderson, C.: Docker [software engineering]. IEEE Software **32**(3), 102–c3 (2015)
3. Bass, L., Clements, P., Kazman, R.: Software Architecture in Practice (3rd Edition). SEI Series in Software Engineering (2013)
4. Cartaxo, B., Pinto, G., Soares, S.: The role of rapid reviews in supporting decision-making in software engineering practice. EASE pp. 24–34 (2018)
5. Casalicchio, E., Perciballi, V.: Measuring docker performance: What a mess!!! Proceedings of the 8th ACM/SPEC on International Conference on Performance Engineering Companion pp. 11–16 (2017)
6. Di Francesco, P., Lago, P., Malavolta, I.: Migrating towards microservice architectures: An industrial survey. In: 2018 IEEE Int. Conf. on Software Architecture (ICSA). pp. 29–38 (2018)
7. Dougherty, K.L., Edward, J.: The properties of simple vs. absolute majority rule: cases where absences and abstentions are important. Journal of Theoretical Politics **22**(1), 85–122 (2010)
8. Gadea, C., Trifan, M., Ionescu, D., Cordea, M., Ionescu, B.: A microservices architecture for collaborative document editing enhanced with face recognition. EEE 11th International Symposium on Applied Computational Intelligence and Informatics (SACI) pp. 441–446 (2016)
9. Gan, Y., Delimitrou, C.: The architectural implications of cloud microservices. IEEE Computer Architecture Letters **17**(2), 155–158 (2018)
10. Ghofrani, J., Lübke, D.: Challenges of microservices architecture: A survey on the state of the practice. In: Proc. of the 10th Workshop on Services and their Composition (ZEUS 2018). pp. 1–8. CEUR-WS.org (2018)
11. Heinrich, R., van Hoorn, A., Knoche, H., Li, F., Lwakatare, L.E., Pahl, C., S., S., Wettinger, J.: Performance engineering for microservices: Research challenges and directions. Proceedings of the 8th ACM/SPEC on International Conference on Performance Engineering Companion pp. 223–226 (2017)
12. Joshi, A., Kale, S., Chandel, S., Pal, D.K.: Likert scale: Explored and explained. British Journal of Applied Science & Technology **7**(4), 396 (2015)
13. Kazman, R.: Rapid software composition by assessing untrusted components,. SEI (2018), `https://insights.sei.cmu.edu/sei\_blog/2018/11/rapid-software-composition-by-assessing-untrusted-components.html`
14. Kitchenham, B., Pfleeger, S.L.: Principles of survey research part 4: questionnaire evaluation. ACM SIGSOFT Software Engineering Notes **27**(3), 20–23 (2002)

15. Kitchenham, B., Pfleeger, S.L.: Principles of survey research: part 5: populations and samples. ACM SIGSOFT Software Engineering Notes **27**(5), 17–20 (2002)
16. Márquez, G., Astudillo, H.: Actual use of architecture patterns in microservices-based open source projects. 25th Asia-Pacific Software Engineering Conference (APSEC) pp. 31–40 (2018)
17. Neri, D., Soldani, J., Zimmermann, O., Brogi, A.: Design principles, architectural smells and refactorings for microservices: a multivocal review. SICS Software-Intensive Cyber-Physical Systems (2019), *[In press]*
18. Punter, T., Ciolkowski, M., Freimut, B., John, I.: Conducting on-line surveys in software engineering. International Symposium on Empirical Software Engineering pp. 80–88 (2003)
19. Soldani, J., Tamburri, D.A., Heuvel, W.J.V.D.: The pains and gains of microservices: A systematic grey literature review. Journal of Systems and Software **146**, 215 – 232 (2018)
20. Stubbs, J., Moreira, W., Dooley, R.: Distributed systems of microservices using docker and serfnode. 7th International Workshop on Science Gateways pp. 34–39 (2015)
21. Taibi, D., Lenarduzzi, V.: On the definition of microservice bad smells. IEEE Software **35**(3), 56–62 (2018)
22. Tang, W., Wang, L., Xue, G.: Design of high availability service discovery for microservices architecture. In: Proceedings of the 2019 3rd International Conference on Management Engineering, Software Engineering and Service Sciences. pp. 253–257. ICMSS 2019, ACM, New York, NY, USA (2019)
23. Thönes, J.: Microservices. IEEE Software **32**(1), 113–116 (2015)
24. Ueda, T., Nakaike, T., Ohara, M.: Workload characterization for microservices. IEEE international symposium on workload characterization (IISWC) pp. 1–10 (2016)
25. Usman, A., Zhang, P., Theel, O.: A highly available replicated service registry for service discovery in a highly dynamic deployment infrastructure. In: 2018 IEEE International Conference on Services Computing (SCC). pp. 265–268 (July 2018)
26. Viennot, N., Lecuyer, M., Bell, J., Geambasu, R., Nieh, J.: Synapse: a microservices architecture for heterogeneous-database web applications. Proceedings of the Tenth European Conference on Computer Systems p. 21 (2015)
27. Wohlin, C., Runeson, P., Höst, M., Ohlsson, M.C., Regnell, B., Wesslén, A.: Experimentation in software engineering. Springer Science and Business Media (2012)
28. Wu, N., Zuo, D., Zhang, Z.: An extensible fault tolerance testing framework for microservice-based cloud applications. In: Proceedings of the 4th International Conference on Communication and Information Processing. pp. 38–42. ICCIP '18, ACM, New York, NY, USA (2018)

Approaches for Describing Reference Architectures: A Systematic Mapping Study

Pedro Henrique Dias Valle[1], Lina Garcés[1], Milena Guessi[1], Silverio Martínez-Fernández[2], and Elisa Yumi Nakagawa[1]

[1] Institute of Mathematical and Computer Sciences,
University of São Paulo (ICMC-USP),
São Carlos, SP, Brazil
[2] Universitat Politècnica de Catalunya, BarcelonaTech
Barcelona, Spain
pedrohenriquevalle@usp.br, linamgr@icmc.usp.br, milena@icmc.usp.br,
smartinez@essi.upc.edu, elisa@icmc.usp.br

Abstract. Reference architectures have emerged as an important artifact of software engineering, since they provide knowledge and experience about how to design architectures of software systems in a specific domain, favoring their reuse, and standardization. Describing reference architectures still is a great challenge, since knowledge about the domain and the concrete architectures should be described and documented in a coherent, cohesive, unambiguous, and complete way. However, reference architectures practical use is difficult due mainly to problems in their descriptions. The main goal is evaluate existing approaches for describing RAs, analyzing six key aspects while describing RAs: type, adherence to ISO/IEC 42010, applicability, maturity, interoperability, and dynamism. For this, we conducted a systematic mapping and identified 21 primary studies with approaches to describe reference architectures. We evaluated 21 approaches to describe RAs, of which four approaches (S4, S7, S16, S17) adhered to at least half of the ISO/IEC standard, six (S3, S4, S5, S7, S8, and S19) achieved a medium technological readiness level, one (S4) adopted a standard to achieve interoperability among systems, and only one (S8) considered the dynamism in the description of RA. We highlight the need to propose methods for describing RAs, considering the guides and tools to support the description of RAs.

Keywords: Reference Architecture, Architecture Description, Software Engineering, Systematic Mapping, Secondary Study

1 Introduction

In the last years, the size and complexity of software systems have increased, and consequently, the design, specification, and analysis of overall system structures have become a critical issue [1]. Software architectures have contributed to software systems design, playing a fundamental role in determining the quality of systems, because they considered several characteristics of quality as interoperability, performance, portability, adaptability, and maintainability. According to Bass [2], a software architecture *"is the structure or structures of the system, which is composed of software components, the externally visible properties of those components, and the relationships between them"*.

The Reference Architecture (RA) concept has emerged as an important type of software architecture [2]. A RA is defined as an architecture that aggregates knowledge about how to design software architectures of systems in a specific application or technical domain [2]. A RA is a more generic and abstract type of architecture that includes business rules, standards and legislations, domain knowledge, software and hardware elements, architectural styles and patterns, and best practices of software development, among others artifacts [3, 4]. Reference architectures provide templates and guidelines for designing software systems in a particular domain [5]. Therefore, the purpose of a RA is to guide the development, standardization, and evolution of systems [6], at the same that enhances reuse and reduces time spent during software activities. RAs have successfully supported the development of critical systems in industry in domains as automotive, healthcare, industry 4.0, agriculture, among others [7]. A RA can be established for *standardization* of concrete architectures or *facilitation* of the design of such architectures [3]. In this sense, a RA must be described to communicate reliably the knowledge it contains. Architecture descriptions are used to improve communication and co-operation of software teams, enabling them to work in an integrated and coherent fashion, and improve software development through reuse and standardization [4].

The information contained in the architecture description should be accessible to a wide range of stakeholders. The standard ISO/IEC 42010 provides a core ontology for the description of architectures [8] and defines that the architecture description can be used for the following purposes: (i) as basis for system design and development activities; (ii) as basis to analyze and evaluate alternative implementations of an architecture; (iii) as development and maintenance documentation; (iv) for documenting the characteristics, features and design of a system for potential clients, acquirers, owners, operators and integrators; and (v) for sharing lessons learned and reusing architectural knowledge through viewpoints, patterns, and styles. Some studies have been conducted to investigate what approaches have been used for describing software architectures [9] and [10]. However, they are focused on the overall scope of software architecture and do not present specificities of RAs description considering the impact that good descriptions have on the quality and value of RAs in practice.

In this paper, we present an overview of existing approaches for describing RAs. We analyzed their adherence to the standard ISO/IEC 42010, as well as their applicability and maturity. We also analyzed whether such approaches support the description of interoperability and dynamism in RAs, since these quality characteristics are now than ever considered as important for modern systems as those based on microservices architectures, IoT (Internet of Things), software ecosystems, big data, and Systems-of-Systems (SoS). This paper is organized as follows: Section 2 presents the protocol of the SMS conducted in this work. Section 3 describes the results of analyzing the existing approaches for RAs description. Section 4 discusses the important findings of our study. Section 5 states the main threats to the validity of this work. Finally, Section 6 presents the main conclusions and future work.

2 Systematic Mapping Study (SMS)

This SMS was conducted following the guidelines proposed by Petersen *et al.*, [11] and Kitchenham and Charters [12]. In this section, we present the protocol of this systematic mapping, showing the objective research questions and metrics, and strategies for selection criteria, and data extraction and analysis.

Objective: The main objective of this paper is to evaluate the approaches identified for describing RAs regarding their completeness, applicability, maturity, and analyze how interoperability and dynamism have been addressed by such approaches in the description of RAs.

Research Questions: In order to obtain evidence for addressing our objective, we defined six Research Questions (RQs). For each RQ, we established some metrics that were used to support the analysis of the results, as presented following:

RQ_1: *Which approaches have been proposed to describe RAs?*

RQ_2: *Which is the adherence level of approaches to describe RAs to the standard ISO/IEC 42010?*

RQ_3: *How the approaches support the description of RAs?*

RQ_4: *Which is the level of maturity of the approaches to describe RAs?*

RQ_5: *How the approaches address interoperability and dynamism in the description of RAs?*

Search Strategy: We selected the search terms, the most suitable words, synonyms, acronyms or alternative spelling within the research field for composed our search string. In the context of our study, we wanted to identify all studies that proposed any approaches for describing references architectures. In this sense, we identified the related terms, considering the plural form of all keywords and related terms. Following, we present our search string:

(*"reference architecture?"*) ***AND*** (*"software architecture?" or "software structure?" or "software design?" or "system architecture?" or "systems structure?" or "system design?"*)

We executed the search string in the following digital libraries: Scopus, IEEE Xplore, ACM Digital Library, ScienceDirect, and SpringerLink. For complementary the set of studies, we perform manual searches in relevant conferences in the software architecture area.

Selection Criteria: We established one inclusion criteria and three exclusion criteria for selected the studies that were used to answer our RQs. *Inclusion Criteria*

(IC): (i) the work is mainly focused on an approach to support the description of RAs. *Exclusion Criteria (EC):* (i) the topic of the paper is not focused on a RA for software systems, but in other areas (e.g., enterprise architecture, or hardware architectures); (ii) the work only claims to present an approach to support RAs engineering, but it is not mainly focused on architecture description; and (iii) the work was not peer-reviewed.

Data Extraction and Analysis

We use an online data extraction form[3] for extracting data from each considered study. This form contains information related to each research question and metric. The dataset gathered from these forms supported the synthesis of the results. Data of each study were extracted by one researcher involved in this study, during the data extraction. When there was a case of doubt, discussions with other researchers were conducted. To draw conclusions and answer our research questions, we performed qualitative and qualitative analysis.

3 Results

This study was conducted by researchers with experience in RA, software architecture, software engineering, and systematic literature review. This study was conducted between January 2018 and August 2018. In order to conduct this SMS, we executed the following steps: (i) *perform search string in data libraries.* In this step, we obtained a total of 989 studies; (ii) *removing of duplicate studies.* In this step, we removed 400 duplicated studies, therefore, 589 studies remained for the next step; (iii) *first selection activity,* analyzing the title, abstract, and keywords and apply the selection criteria, 323 studies were excluded, and 266 studies were selected for detailed inspection; (iv) *second selection,* the full text of each study was read and the selection criteria were again applied. As a result, 17 primary studies were selected to be included in this SMS; and (v) *perform snowballing inspection in the related works.* We included 4 relevant works after performed the snowballing inspection. We manual search in the following conferences: IEEE International Conference on Software Architecture (ICSA), European Conference on Software Architecture (ECSA 2020), Brazilian Symposium on Components, Architectures and Software Reuse (SBCARS), and International Conference on Software Engineering (ICSE).

Therefore, we selected a final list with *21 studies*[4] as presented in Table 1. The first column shows the ID for each study, the second column contains the title of studies, the third column shows the distribution of these studies over the years, the fourth column presents the orientation of the approaches. Still on this table, the fifth column presents the types of approaches (i.e., process, method, model, framework, among others) identified, and finally, the sixth column shows the TRL for each analyzed approach.

Overview of approaches for describing RAs

[3] Available on: https://forms.gle/RFnaXExvEyASuNVB7

[4] References of included studies are available on: `https://bit.ly/2kzZ35J`

Table 1. Approaches for describing reference architectures

ID	Title	Year	Orientation	Type of Approaches	TRL	Conformance with ISO/IEC 42010
S1	A reference architecture for control of mechanical systems	1994	Academy	Process	TRL 2	No
S2	NSA's MISSI reference architecture - Moving from prose to precise specifications	1998	Academy	ADL	TRL 3	ADL (H)
S3	PuLSE-DSSA—a method for the development of software RAs	1998	Industry	Method	TRL 4	Model Kind (M)
S4	Describing, instantiating and evaluating a reference architecture: A case study	2003	Academy	Method	TRL 5	View (H), Viewpoint (H), Model Kind (M), Stakeholder (H), Concern(H)
S5	Definition of RAs based on existing systems	2004	Industry	Process	TRL 6	View (M), Viewpoint (L), Model Kind (H)
S6	An Approach to Reference Architecture Design for Different Domains of Embedded Systems	2008	Academy	Method	TRL 2	Model Kind (M)
S7	Architectural Knowledge in an SOA Infrastructure Reference Architecture	2009	Industry	Method	TRL 4	Viewpoint (M), Model Kind (L), Concern (L), Decisions (L), Rationale (L)
S8	Formal modelling and analysis of HLA architectural style	2010	Academy	Architectural Style	TRL 4	ADL (H)
S9	A Methodology for Developing an Agent Systems Reference Architecture	2011	Academy	Process	TRL 2	View (M), Model Kind (L), Stakeholder (L)
S10	A reference architecture for integrated EHR in Colombia	2011	Academy	Process	TRL 2	View (L), Viewpoint (L)
S11	Empirically-grounded RAs: A proposal	2011	Academy	Process	TRL 2	View (L), Stakeholder (L)
S12	A knowledge-based framework for RAs	2012	Academy	Framework	TRL 2	No
S13	A reference architecture template for software-intensive embedded systems	2012	Academy	Document Template	TRL 3	View (L), Stakeholder (M)
S14	RAModel: A Reference Model for RAs	2012	Academy	Model	TRL 3	No
S15	Towards a bottom-up development of RAs for smart energy systems	2013	Industry	Process	TRL 4	View (L)
S16	An approach for capturing and documenting architectural decisions of RAs	2014	Academy	Method	TRL 3	Viewpoint (M), Model Kind (L), Stakeholder (L), Decisions (M), Rationale (M)
S17	Development and Specification of a Reference Architecture for Agent-Based Systems	2014	Academy	Process	TRL 5	View (H), Model Kind (M), Stakeholder (M), Decisions (L)
S18	Modeling and reusing robotic software architectures: The HyperFlex toolchain	2014	Academy	Process	TRL 3	No
S19	Variability viewpoint to describe RAs	2014	Academy	Viewpoint	TRL 4	Viewpoint (H), Model Kind (L), Stakeholder (M)
S20	Design and Evaluation of a Customizable Multi-domain Reference Architecture on Top of Product Lines of Self-driving Heavy Vehicles: An Industrial Case Study	2015	Academy	Process	TRL 4	Model Kind (L), Stakeholder (L)
S21	Quality-based heuristic for optimal product derivation in Software Product Lines	2015	Academy	Process	TRL 4	View (L), Stakeholder (L)

Results presented in this section correspond to RQ_1. We observed that the first studies on RA description began to be investigated in the early 1990s and that the community has had a greater interest in this research topic in the last decade. It is worth to highlight that until the conduction of this mapping study (August 2018), the most recent approach was published in 2015. Regarding the venue of publication, 52% (S6, S8, S11, S12, S13, S14, S16, S18, S19, S20, and S21) of papers were published in conferences, while 24% (S1, S2, S3, S9, and S15) of papers were published in workshops. Only 10% (S10, and S17) of papers were published in the journal. Finally, 10% of papers (S4, and S5) were published as technical reports, and only 5% (S7) published as a book chapter.

Approaches orientation: we also checked whether the approaches were proposed in the academic or industry context. For this, we analyzed the authors' affiliation and how was performed the development and evaluation of such approaches. As a result, we found that 19% (S3, S5, S7, and S15) of papers were proposed in the industry. 81% (S1, S2, S4, S6, S8, S9, S10, S11, S12, S13, S14, S15, S16, S18, S19, S20, and S21) of papers were proposed and validated in the academic context.

Approaches domains: we analyzed whether the approaches for describing RAs were proposed for some specific domain or general-purpose. In short, 7 approaches were proposed for a specific domain, while 14 studies were proposed for general purpose. S1 was proposed for mechanical systems, S9 and S18 were proposed for agent-based systems domain, while S10 developed an approach for health domain. In S13, the authors proposed an approach for embedded systems domain, S15 was proposed for the robotic domain, and S20 proposed an approach for the automotive domain. It is worth highlighting that all the studies that were created for help describing RAs for a specific domain were proposed in the academic context.

Approaches types: we identified 8 approaches types that proposed some mechanism to support the description of RAs, namely, processes, methods, architecture description language (ADL), architectural style, framework, model, viewpoint, and document template. Process and methods were the most recurrent approaches found in our study.

Process ($\approx$ 48%): it defines *what* is required to be done, without specifying *how* each task must be performed. We identified 10 processes (S1, S5, S9, S10, S11, S15, S17, S18, S20, and S21) to support the description of RAs. S5 defined a RA using the experience of existing systems, while S15 proposed an incremental development of RA for smart energy systems. In the academic context, S1 built and assessed a RA for control of mechanical systems. S9 presented a process for developing a RA that documents agent-based systems from different system viewpoints, while S10 presented a process for developing a RA for the implementation of an integrated EHR (Electronic Health Record), S11 proposed a six-steps process which helps to systematically design RA. S17 proposed a process for developing agent systems RA, using an approach based on software engineering techniques adapted to study agent frameworks. S18 defined how RA can be exploited for building robotic applications. S20 presented a systematic way to design of RA involving all relevant external and internal stakeholders, development documents, low-level artifacts, and literature. Finally, S21 proposed a process to support architectural decisions in the derivation of specific products of a software product line (SPL) family according to customer requirements, from an optimal feasible solution among a set of feasible solutions.

Method ($\approx 24\%$): we identified 5 studies that proposed methods for supporting the description of RAs. It is important to note that S3 and S7 proposed methods in the industry context. In short, S3 proposed the systematic and iterative development of RAs for SPL, while S7 presented how to harvest architectural knowledge from industry projects to create RA. S4 proposed to describe a RA instantiating it into a software architecture by making implementation decisions and evaluating it for quality attributes. S6 proposed a service-based method for design in RAs. Finally, S16 presented a systematic method for capturing and documenting architectural decisions of RAs. The authors carried out a case study showing how their approach can be used for enhancing the architecture description of RAs.

ADL ($\approx 4\%$): S2 discussed the definition and modeling of RA and the notion of conformance. The authors demonstrated that Rapide ADL can specify interfaces, connections and operational constraints, and also to specify how it is related (or conforms) with other architectures or to implementations.

Architectural Style ($\approx 4\%$): it provides a way to reuse the design decisions and constraints that are applied to an architecture to induce chosen desirable qualities. S8 was the only study in this line proposing a formal model for HLA (High Level Architectural) style.

Framework ($\approx 4\%$): it is a real or conceptual structure intended to serve as a support or guide for the building of something that expands the structure into something useful. S12 is the only study that presented a framework, named KRAF (knowledge-based Reference Architecture Framework), for providing a better understanding of the contents of RAs, enabling the development of more complete, efficient RAs.

Model ($\approx 4\%$): S14 presented a reference model for RA, named RAModel (Reference Architecture Model), that intends to improve the understanding about what RAs are, as well as their components and relationships, assisting the establishment, use, and evolution of such architectures.

Viewpoint ($\approx 4\%$): it is a representation of one or more aspects of an architecture that illustrates how the architecture addresses the concerns held by one or more of its stakeholders [13]. S19 proposed an architecture viewpoint to represent variability in RA. The authors described how they created such a viewpoint.

Document template ($\approx 4\%$): S13 presented a document template for RAs for the domain of software-intensive embedded systems. The template addresses the somewhat conflicting needs when documenting a RA.

Architectural views and viewpoints: an architecture view expresses the architecture of a system from the perspective of specific system concern. An architecture viewpoint establishes the conventions for the construction, interpretation, and use of architecture views to frame specific system concerns [8]. In our analysis, we selected the *views* that were proposed or used in studies, or only cited by them throughout the paper. We identified 24 views: functional logical view (S4, S5, S11, S17, and S21), process view (S5, S9, S10, and S17), components view (studies S5, S10, and S15), implementation view (studies S9, S10, and S17), scenario view (studies S5, S9, and S17), platform view (studies S5, and S10), technical view (S11), physical view (S5), view (S11), deployment view (S4), model view (S9), context view (S5), informal view (S13), information models view (S10), domain view (S5), New view, interface view (S5), code view (S5), module view (S5), execution view (S5), conceptual view (S5), execution view (S5), new view (S5), filtered view (S5), and augmented view (S5).

Adherence of the approaches with the standard ISO/IEC 42010

The RQ_2 is related to analyze the adherence level of the approaches with the architectural description standard ISO/IEC 42010 [8]. To answer RQ_2, we analyzed the studies to know whether they addressed the proposed elements by the standard (i.e., *views*, *viewpoint*, *model kind*, *stakeholder*, *concern*, *architectural decisions*, *rationale*, and *ADL*). For each element, we consider the level of details, that are: N (no details), L (low level of details), M (medium level of details), and H (high level of details), that were addressed by each approach. A summary of this analysis is shown in Table 1.

In general, the studies considered only a few set of elements (i.e., views, viewpoints, and model kind) proposed by the standard ISO/IEC 42010. It is important to note that, 42% of the approaches (S1, S6, S10, S11, S9, S12, S15, S18, and S20) were described in a high-level abstraction. Regarding the adherence with the standard, only two studies (S11 and S18) followed the recommendations proposed by this standard. Nevertheless, these studies did not provide details on how to establish the artifacts that are part of the architectural description. A discussion for each element is presented as follows.

We identified some viewpoints, and selected the ones that were proposed, used or cited by the authors throughout the paper. We found 25 *viewpoints* to represent and describe RAs. In S3, five viewpoints that were used to represent the RAs: use-case viewpoint, logical viewpoint, deployment viewpoint, implementation viewpoint, and data viewpoint. S5 presents a set of viewpoints, as build-time viewpoint, behavioral viewpoint, execution architecture viewpoint, code architecture viewpoint, module architecture viewpoint, conceptual architecture viewpoint, and feature viewpoint. S7 used three viewpoints, that are: physical viewpoint, scenario viewpoint, decision viewpoint. S10 proposed a process that established five system's perspectives, such as enterprise viewpoint, information viewpoint, computational viewpoint, engineering viewpoint, and technology viewpoint. S16 used four viewpoints: decision detail viewpoint, decision relationship viewpoint, decision chronology viewpoint, and decision stakeholder viewpoint. Finally, S19 proposed a viewpoint to represent the variability in RA. S5 presents a set of viewpoints, as build-time viewpoint, behavioral viewpoint, execution architecture viewpoint, code architecture viewpoint, module architecture viewpoint, conceptual architecture viewpoint, and feature viewpoint. S7 used three viewpoints, that are: physical viewpoint, scenario viewpoint, decision viewpoint. S10 proposed a process that established five system's perspectives, as enterprise viewpoint, information viewpoint, computational viewpoint, engineering viewpoint, and technology viewpoint. S16 used four viewpoints: decision detail viewpoint, decision relationship viewpoint, decision chronology viewpoint, and decision stakeholder. Finally, S19 proposed a viewpoint to represent the variability in RA.

We also identified *models* to model and represent RAs. An architecture model can be a part of more than one architecture view [8]. In particular, S16 used the activity diagram, requirements diagram, parametric diagram, state machine diagram, and use case diagram to represent viewpoints and show the flow of activities for architectural decision-making. S3, S4, S5, S7, and S9 used UML diagrams to represent views and viewpoints, that are: use-case diagram, component diagram, activity diagram, package diagram, workflow diagrams, sequence diagram, state diagram, collaboration diagram, class diagram, and message sequence charts. S6 used the feature model to manage the variability and product derivation, while S19 used the internal block diagram (SysML) to model the variability viewpoint. Finally, S20 used the use case diagram to represent the stakeholders and model the RA. Finally, the studies S8 used the π-ADL to model the HLA architectural style in a formal way, while S2 proposed the Rapide ADL that is a formal language to simulate the behavior of system architectures.

We identified several stakeholders that could be considered for the description of RA. It can be an individual, team, or organization that have an interest in a system [8]. The stakeholders that identified were: architects, system designers, attribute leaders, component designers, project managers, suppliers, developers, domain experts, business-persons, customers, system users, and engineers. The most common stakeholders of these approaches are architects, project managers, and developers. In general, the studies only presented who are the important stakeholders for the architecture description activity, and did not show how to represent and manage these stakeholders. We also found a description of the rationale records explanation, justification or reasoning about architecture decisions that have been made. The rationale for a decision can include the basis for a decision, alternatives, and trade-offs considered, potential consequences of the decision. In this context, we analyzed the architecture decisions on RAs. Only 14% of studies addressed this element. Specifically, S7 represented the architectural decisions in a semi-formal way using architectural patterns, and a meta-model to represent them, while S16, S17 represented these decisions an informal way through text description. S7 addressed the rationale for architectural decision-making through a table using a textual description with the reasons to choose an alternative, while S16 used a meta-model and the textual description to show which are the reasons for choosing an architectural solution.

Applicability of approaches for describing RAs

The RQ_3 aims to analyze how much the approaches are easy to use for the development of RAs description. For this, we analyzed the level of the details of the approaches, the tools suggested by these approaches to facilitating the building of the description of RAs, and the guidelines available to help on the use of these approaches. We classified the level of description of the approaches into four categories: *N* (no details), *L* (low level of details), *M* (medium level of details), and *H* (high level of details), as shown in Table 1. In general, the approaches are described with a high-level of abstraction and they do not present details on how to use the approaches to create an architectural description, and neither steps/tasks that are necessary to the building of such descriptions.

The studies S1, S2, S6, S9, S10, S11, S12, S15, S18, and S20 were classified in the category *L* (low level of details) because these studies proposed generic activities/tasks for the building of description of RAs, without showing *what* and *how* to build the artifacts that are part of an architectural description. In category *M* (medium level of details) the studies S2, S5, S7, S8, S14, S16, S19, S21 were classified because they presented with more details, the views, viewpoints, and models that could be used to build a description of RAs, S4, and S17 were classified as *H* (high level of details), since they offered more information about the views, viewpoints, models, architectural patterns, and examples that could support RAs description. None approaches providing guidelines to facilitate their application were identified, neither we do not find extra material to support their use. We also analyzed whether the approaches suggested tools to facilitate their application in practice. Only S18 suggested HyperFlex toolchain an open-source tool for supporting the design and the reuse of RAs. Therefore, this area still needs to be better explored in a further research tool.

Maturity of the approaches for describing RA

The RQ_4 aims to analyze what is the approaches level of maturity. For this, we used the TRL (*Technological Readiness Level*), which is a type of measurement used to assess the maturity level of a particular technology [14]. There are nine technology readiness levels.

TRL 1 is the lowest maturity level and TRL 9 is the highest one. S1, S6, S9, S10, S11, and S12 were classified as TRL 2. At this level, the approach is in the beginning. Only basic principles are observed the applications are speculative, and there may be no proof or detailed analysis to support the assumptions. S2, S13, S14, S16, and S18 were classified as TRL 3 since they include analytical and laboratory studies to physically validate the analytical predictions of separate elements of the technology. We classified S3, S7, S8, S15, S19, S20, and 21 as TRL 4 because their validation was carried out in the laboratory, and basic technological components were integrated to establish that they will work together, S4 and S17 were classified as TRL 5, because their basic technological components were integrated for testing in a simulated environment. Finally, only S5 was classified as TRL 6, because at this level a model or prototype was developed, representing a nearly desired configuration. Activities include testing in a simulated operational environment or laboratory. In this paper, we considered the studies that had TRL greater or equal than level 4 as a good level of maturity. In this sense, we observed that all the studies that were proposed in the industrial context obtained a good level of maturity, and the most of them (S3, S4, S5, S7, S8, and S19) were proposed for general purpose, as shown in Table 1. It is worth highlighting that no studies were classified with TRL greater than level 6.

Interoperability and Dynamism

The RQ_5 aims to analyze how the approaches have addressed interoperability and dynamism concerns in the description of RAs. We analyzed the level of interoperability (i.e., technical, syntactic, semantic, and organizational) that the approaches considered in the architectural description, and the strategies used to provide the interoperability. In short, few studies addressed the interoperability indeed, since most of them only commented on the text that RAs help to achieve the interoperability in systems, but no evidence to support this was found. In S1, the authors suggested that interoperability among different systems can be achieved through the use of protocols. The only study with concrete action about interoperability is S4, the authors adopted International Learning Technology standards, to achieve interoperability among different systems, which is currently a major issue in the domain of LMS (Learning Management System).

Regarding to dynamism we investigate whether the types of dynamism (i.e., description programmed, self-manageable, and ad-hoc) were considered by approaches and the strategies used to represent the dynamism in such architectures. In this sense, only S8 considered the dynamism in the description of RA proposing a formal model for HLA architectural style using the π-ADL, which is aimed at the description of architecture dynamic evolution. The type of dynamism considered in this study was programmed.

4 Discussion of results

This study aimed to present an overview of how to RAs have been described and represented, showing the main existing approaches for building the description of such architectures. However, we did not find approaches that fully adhered to the ISO/IEC 42010 standard. In this sense, we identified research gaps that could be explored in future work.

The ISO/IEC 42010 specifies how architecture descriptions of systems are organized and expressed, presenting the architecture viewpoints, architecture frameworks, and architectures languages for use in architecture description. In this sense, **adherence to standards** could be considered as a research gap in RAs description. As shown in Table 1, few approaches adhered with this standard as a base for supporting the building the architecture descriptions. The few studies that considered the elements proposed by ISO/IEC 42010, described and represented these elements with few details, and with a high level of abstraction. This scenario makes difficult the building of RAs descriptions of systems, besides difficulties in the standardization of RAs. Therefore, it is interesting to consider the standard ISO/IEC 42010 to propose approaches for RAs description because it is the well-known standard used for representation and documenting software architectures, and we believe RAs could benefit from this. The approaches identified in this work were proposed superficially without giving details on what tasks/activities are needed for building a suitable architecture description. The activities proposed indicate only that something must be done, but they do not indicate how this should be done. In this sense, there is a need to improve or propose new approaches to describe RAs that should be described in detail way, showing for architects what tasks/activities should be performed.

Guidelines and tools also considered as a research gap. When approaches are made available to the scientific community, different stakeholders may use them to describe RAs. It is important to highlight that when these approaches are used for the building of architecture descriptions without support materials (as usage guidelines) this may lead to erroneous interpretations and consequently affect the quality of description of RAs because such guidelines may help understanding better how to use these approaches. Tools can automate some tasks/activities to describe RA, as well as, made easy the representation of such architectures. Despite the importance of the guidelines and tools, only one study proposed a support tool and no approach provided supporting guidelines. In this sense, we note that there is a lack of approaches that provide guidelines and tools to support the description of RAs suitably.

Characteristics of complex systems have been calling the attention of researchers in recent years, since the size and complexity of modern software systems. It is expected that new RAs are proposed for these systems in a short time. Such architectures should consider different characteristics that concern to complex systems, such as **interoperability** and **dynamism**. From the result of this paper, we observed that few approaches address the interoperability and dynamism in current systems. Therefore, we expect that new initiatives will be proposed to support the dynamism and interoperability description in RAs.

We analyzed the validation of the approaches using the TRL. Most studies were classified with a low maturity level because few approaches have been evaluated using real case studies. Therefore, **validation of approaches** should be conducted to evaluate the approaches to describe RAs to apply these approaches in the industry in real situations so that will be analyzed the effectiveness of the approaches to support the architecture descriptions. Regarding the identified studies in partnership with the industry, we found only four approaches that were proposed and/or validated by the industry. We believe that studies with **contribution for the industry** should be conducted since our analysis shows a lack of studies that investigate how the industry has described and represented RAs. Therefore, the academy may be performing research that does not meet the real needs of the software industry. It is also necessary to understand how the software industry represents currently such architectures.

5 Threats to Validity

In order to minimize biases of our study, we discuss some actions that we performed to mitigate threats to construct, internal, external, and conclusion validity [15, 16]:

Construct validity: we applied a mapping study protocol with relevant details (i.e., RA description concepts, research questions, search method, study selection, data extraction, analysis), which was reviewed by researchers. This helped mitigating an imprecise description of the mapping study setting.

Internal validity: a threat to internal validity comes from study selection bias. We piloted the inclusion/exclusion criteria with three researchers to mitigate this threat. This helped to clarify differences and build a common understanding of the inclusion/exclusion criteria. Additionally, we performed researcher triangulation in order to minimize researcher bias when selecting the primary studies.

External validity: the amount and relevance of included studies may be considered as a threat to validity to the generalization of the results.

Conclusion validity: during data extraction, not all the information were obvious to answer the research questions and some data was interpreted (e.g., some elements proposed by ISO/IEC 42010). Therefore, in the event of a disagreement among authors, discussions among the participants were conducted.

6 Conclusion and future work

The current systems have become increasingly complex and larger. Consequently, developing and maintaining such systems have become a critical issue. In response to this scenario, RAs can provide a set of knowledge and experience about how to architect a set of software systems to a specific domain. In this perspective, this secondary study aimed to evaluate the existing approaches to describe RAs, analyzing their adherence to ISO/IEC 42010, applicability, maturity, and checking how the interoperability and dynamism have been addressed in the description of RAs. For this analysis, we identified and selected 21 approaches to describe RAs.

As main results, we identified works to describe RAs. Two approaches (S4, S17) were classified as TRL 5, adhering three elements of the ISO/IEC 42010 (view, model kind, and stakeholders). One approach (S5) was classified as TRL 6, also addressing three elements of the ISO/IEC 42010 (view, viewpoint, and model kind). These approaches were considered the most complete to describe RAs. Other approaches also could contribute to describe RAs as S7, S16 that adhere to at least half the ISO/IEC standard, S3, S8, and S19 achieve a medium TRL, and S8 that considered the dynamism in the description of RA.

As future work, we intend to establish a method for describing RAs considering the elements proposed by standard ISO/IEC 42010, and the concerns of modern software systems. This method will be composed of guides and tools to support the description of such architectures.

Acknowledgment

This work was supported in part by CNPq (Grant: 141602/2017-1, 312634/2018-8), FAPESP (Grant: 2018/07437-9, 2018/24173-5, 2017/22107-2, 2017/06195-9), and CoSmart Spanish project (contract TIN2017-83964-R).

References

1. Garcés, L., Oquendo, F., Nakagawa, E.Y.: Software mediators as first-class entities of systems-of-systems software architectures. Journal of the Brazilian Computer Society **25** (2019) 8
2. Bass, L.: Software architecture in practice. 3rd edn. Addison-Wesley (2013)
3. Angelov, S., Grefen, P., Greefhorst, D.: A classification of software reference architectures: Analyzing their success and effectiveness. In: WICSA/ECSA Joint Working IEEE/IFIP Conference on Software Architecture & European Conference on Software Architecture, Cambridge, UK, IEEE (2009) 141–150
4. Martinez-Fernandez, S., Ayala, C.P., Franch, X., Marques, H.M.: Benefits and drawbacks of software reference architectures: A case study. Information and Software Technology **88** (2017) 37 – 52
5. Galster, M., Angelov, S., Martínez-Fernández, S., Tofan, D.: Reference architectures and scrum: Friends or foes? In: Proceedings of the 2017 11th Joint Meeting on Foundations of Software Engineering (ESEC/FSE 2017), Paderborn, Germany, ACM (2017) 896–901
6. Martínez-Fernández, S., Ayala, C.P., Franch, X., Martins Marques, H., Ameller, D.: Towards Guidelines for Building a Business Case and Gathering Evidence of Software Reference Architectures in Industry. Journal of Software Engineering Research and Development (JSERD) **2** (2014)
7. Nakagawa, E.Y., Oquendo, F., Avgeriou, P., Cuesta, C.E., Drira, K., Maldonado, J.C., Zisman, A.: Foreword: towards reference architectures for systems-of-systems. In: International Workshop on Software Engineering for Systems-of-Systems (SESoS), Florence, Italy, IEEE Press (2015) 1–4
8. ISO, I.: Iso/iec/ieee 42010: Systems and software engineering–architecture description. Technical report (2011)
9. Guessi, M., Nakagawa, E.Y., Oquendo, F., Maldonado, J.C.: Architectural description of embedded systems: A systematic review. In: Proceedings of the 3rd international ACM SIGSOFT symposium on Architecting Critical Systems, ACM (2012) 31–40
10. Guessi, M., Neto, V.V.G., Bianchi, T., Felizardo, K.R., Oquendo, F., Nakagawa, E.Y.: A systematic literature review on the description of software architectures for systems of systems. In: Proceedings of the 30th Annual ACM Symposium on Applied Computing, ACM (2015)
11. Petersen, K., Vakkalanka, S., Kuzniarz, L.: Guidelines for conducting systematic mapping studies in software engineering: An update. Information and Software Technology **64** (2015) 1 – 18
12. Kitchenham, B., Brereton, O.P., Budgen, D., Turner, M., Bailey, J., Linkman, S.: Systematic literature reviews in software engineering - a systematic literature review. Information and Software Technology **51** (2009)
13. Guessi, M., Oquendo, F., Nakagawa, E.Y.: Variability viewpoint to describe reference architectures. In: Proceedings of the Working IEEE/IFIP Conference on Software Architecture, Sydney, Australia, ACM (2014)
14. Mankins, J.C.: Technology readiness levels. White Paper, April **6** (1995) 1995
15. Wohlin, C., Runeson, P., Höst, M., Ohlsson, M.C., Regnell, B., Wesslén, A.: Experimentation in software engineering. Springer Science & Business Media (2012)
16. Zhou, X., Jin, Y., Zhang, H., Li, S., Huang, X.: A map of threats to validity of systematic literature reviews in software engineering. In: 23rd Asia-Pacific Software Engineering Conference (APSEC). (2016) 153–160

Managing Evolution of API-driven IoT Devices through Adaptation Chains

Rafael Bustamante, Kelly Garcés

Department of Systems and Computing Engineering, Universidad de los Andes (CO)
{r.bustamante32,kj.garces971}@uniandes.edu.co

Abstract. Technological advancements, updates to legal regulations, and emerging industry standards have immersed the IT industry in a never-ending cycle were RESTFul APIs are required to keep up with the latest trends. IoT developers often hard-code the API invocation in the clients (i.e., IoT devices); this makes the continuous upgrade/delivery of new API versions laborious or even impossible. In this article, we introduce an API Adaptation approach that addresses the problem by transforming messages exchanged between devices and the API server. In our approach, compatibility is achieved by adjusting the information after it leaves the source and before it reaches the target destination. The evaluation over a large/real API offers initial insights into the feasibility of our approach.

Keywords: API; Changes; Software Defined Networking; Middleware; Internet of Things.

1 Introduction

With the latest technological advancements and the ever increasing number of devices connected to the Internet, humanity has been able to gather data and integrate electronic devices with the physical world like never before. All of this has enabled a technological trend known as the *Internet of Things* (IoT). The Internet of Things is based on machine to machine communication, cloud computing and networks of sensors [2]. This integration of systems has the possibility of making every device smart by combining all gathered data with the power of cloud computing and machine learning.

An IoT architecture consists of three tiers[1]: IoT devices, connectivity, and services. The connectivity tier typically has gateway devices responsible for interfacing directly with the services and providing an API (Application Program Interface) (e.g., RESTFul) to IoT devices. As developers modify services' APIs, these may become unresponsive as the data sent from the IoT devices may no longer be consumable. This challenge can be expressed as the need of maintaining compatibility between constantly developed and improved APIs and their continuously increasing number of clients.

Keeping new and legacy API Clients compatible with the latest changes of an API is a complex process. The evolution and adaptation of APIs for Web-based software have been studied in recent years [15] and some solutions have been proposed, e.g., Software Defined Networks (SDN). However, when it comes to evolution of APIs for IoT systems, such solutions may not be fully applicable because client devices may: (1) have very few resources which constrain their ability to properly adapt to changes in the API or (2) either be hard-coded or hard to access, which makes continuous upgrade/delivery laborious or even impossible.

These factors represent a challenge that deserves attention and research. To reach a more appropriate solution, adhesion to modern trends in software engineering such as continuous integration and DevOps is required. In this paper, we propose an approach in early stages of research that suggests a revisited perspective of SDN applicable to IoT. This work is aligned with the H2020 2018-2020 work package; specifically with the activities ICT-15-2019-2020 [5] about engineering methods for cyber-physical systems of systems (CPSoS) and ICT-16-2018 about software engineering methods and tools applicable across domains such as IoT and Cloud[6]. This work contributes initial insights to the feasibility of software engineering practices that result in improvements in maintenance for API-driven IoT devices.

Our approach (see Section 4) focuses on addressing compatibility between an API and its clients[1] by adapting messages as they leave the source to make them understandable by the target destination by applying successive transformations to the exchanged data. The approach can handle input and output interface changes of individual APIs, that correspond to syntactic changes, thus changes in the semantics of the APIs are out of the scope of this paper. We adapt existing strategies in the IoT research landscape. The rest of this document is organized as follows: Section 2 presents related work. Section 3 describes an API evolution scenario to provide more context for the work presented here. Section 5 summarizes the results obtained after testing the proposed strategy over a real API in production environment. Section 6 contains thoughts and further considerations for the adaptation approach outlined in this document.

2 Related Work

There are several papers in the areas of API adaptation (e.g., [16, 13, 12, 10, 18]), business process adaptation (e.g., [17]), web service composition adaptation for changing workflow/business processes (e.g., [9, 4]). In this paper, we took inspiration from the algorithms found in those works and adapt them for APIs in the IoT domain. Whereas most of the approaches found in the literature tackle the challenge of adapting Web/mobile/third party systems to evolving software artifacts, we found only two approaches addressing the API compatibility issues for IoT clients. The next paragraphs briefly describe these two approaches and their limitations, and a comparison ends the section.

[1] API clients and IoT devices will be used as interchangeable names in the remaining sections

Software Defined Networking (SDN) [15]: This approach proposes a segmentation of concerns between *how the API is navigated* and *what data is passed between calls to the API.* In the same manner, the API is configured by setting available navigation paths in a programmatic sense instead of the traditional resource path in a REST API [14]. Under this approach, a software Petri Net is configured with the API Paths (represented as nodes) and the client is redirected across them as required. To do this, the client incorporates two software components: a Client Oracle that knows how the API is traversed and a Client Agent that knows what data is to be passed to the current node indicated by the navigation. In this way the evolution of the API is managed by sharing navigation and API data changes with the client, which in turn updates the definitions of its Oracle and Agent. Although this approach offers flexibility and guarantees that clients are updated with the changes deployed in the API, it represents a major shift away from the RESTful API standard. Also, this approach means that existing clients should be modified to include the Oracle and Agent, which is difficult or even impossible in constrained IoT devices.

Multi-Versioning [8]: This approach focuses on keeping multiple versions of the same API published and available at the same time. This way, compatibility between all clients with the API is guaranteed as each client will be able to consume their corresponding version. However, this approach does represent major challenges in terms of proper resource allocation as it requires additional servers and platform resources for each deployed API version. Additionally, this approach also implies that corrections and upgrades to any API likely need to be propagated to other versions, meaning that additional maintenance costs would be incurred.

The improvements on maintainability offered by SDN-based approaches (including our own) cause a degradation on performance. In multi-versioning approaches is the other way around. In certain contexts (e.g., safety-critical systems) this degradation cannot be tolerated. Therefore, both approaches are valid and can be seen as complementary to satisfy the requirements from a broad variety of IoT devices. All the other approaches focus on helping the developers change their source code to make applications compatible with a new version of an API, which in the context of IoT where the code that makes use of the API is on a device, changing that source code is something difficult or in some cases impossible to achieve.

3 Case Study

The case study consists of a residential smart-home system that monitors and alerts house residents about fire situations. The system works by continuously reading data from a fire detection device, detecting anomalous measurements, and warning stakeholders of possibly dangerous situations.

The fire alarm device is composed of a temperature sensor and a flame sensor. The main purpose is to monitor the room temperature and detect the presence of flames. The temperature and flame sensors monitor their associated physical variables. A detection of fire sends an alert to the corresponding authorities through a fire alarm service. In addition to this notification, the fire alarm service also announces the event locally with a visual or sound alarm depending on the location and activities of the residents. The target API is assumed to be Open API 3.0.0 compliant.

The case study API is composed of a single fire report resource published on an HTTP server. This resource represents the interface with the fire department service and exposes two operations: a GET and a POST request. The GET operation returns an array of JSON objects representing a fire report. The POST operation is used to deliver a JSON object that represents a fire sensor data report and receives, as response, a JSON object that describes the fire department that will attend the emergency and their estimated time of arrival to the house. The object diagram in Fig. 1 depicts two overlapped versions of the fire alarm service's API. This case study is introduced to add additional context to the proposal discussed in the following section.

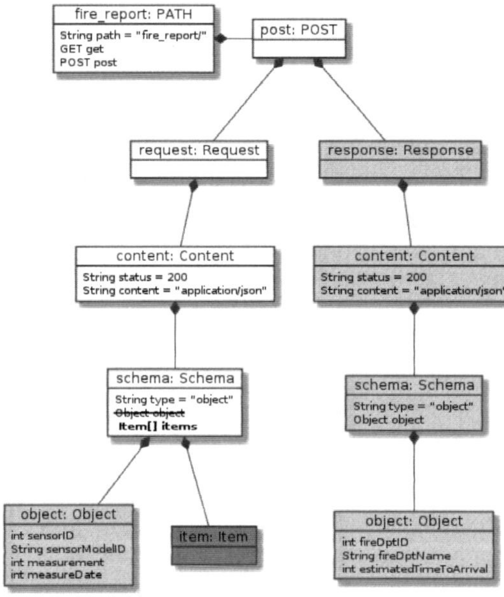

Fig. 1. Object diagram representing an excerpt of the fire alarm service API

4 The API Adapter

Keeping in mind the reasons for continuous/mandatory API evolution and the hurdles that hinder compatibility between APIs and clients, the API Adaptation approach was designed with the following considerations as guidelines: (1)

Since the technological gap between legacy and modern API clients will broaden throughout the upcoming years, the solution should cover the widest range of devices consuming the target RESTful API. (2) Despite the latest advances, IoT devices still have a low amount of resources when compared to those of API servers, thus being constrained devices. The solution should compromise as little resources as possible from API clients. Hence, the solution is designed as an independent component with no ties to any of the IoT devices. (3) The solution should keep the API version management as simple as possible without additional complexity. Therefore, only the newest version of the target API should be required.

The solution incorporates a middleware, which will be referred to as *API Adapter*, focused on keeping all client interactions compatible with the most recent version of the published API, as well as all responses delivered by the API compatible with the clients' expectations. The overall strategy by which compatibility between different versions of the API is obtained is divided into two phases: The *Conflict Identification Phase* and the *Message Adaptation Phase.*

The *Conflict Identification Phase* takes place whenever a new API version is deployed. This phase identifies the differences between the source version of the API and the new target version; it creates the message adaptation transformations required to make both versions (source and target) compatible. This part of the strategy is summarized in the following steps: (1) Load source and target API definitions. (2) Compare the source API version against the target and distill all differences as atomic differentials. (3) Process each API differential and map it against its corresponding category within a previously established taxonomy. The category indicates which service performs the adaptation. (4) Format this information as a request to an Adaptation Service.

The second phase is the *Message Adaptation Phase* and it occurs whenever a message is dispatched from an API client to consume a resource in the API server. This side of the approach is briefly described in the list up next: (1) Receive a request message from any API client. (2) Find the client's expected API version. (3) Apply successive transformations to the messages to make the request from the client compatible with the newest API version. (4) Transform the response from the API server back into the client's expected API version via successive calls to Adaptation Services. The architecture of the *API Adapter* is depicted in Fig. 2. A description of its components follows.

4.1 API Version Manager

This component ensures compatibility of any supplied API with the OpenApi 3.0.0 specification [11]. Once a new API version has been validated as compliant with the standard, it is submitted to the *Differential Comparator* to evaluate the changes in relation with the former API version.

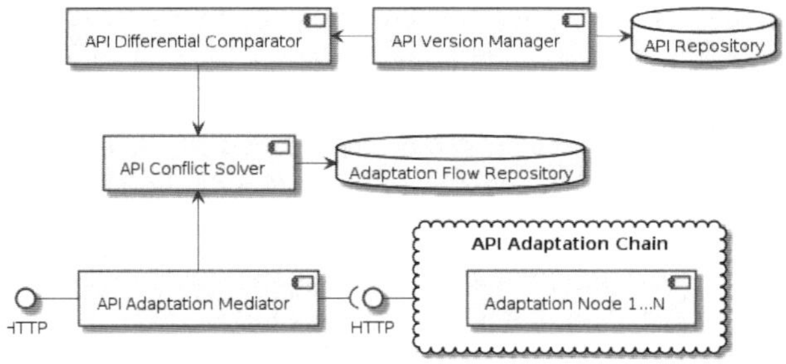

Fig. 2. Component diagram of the API Adapter

4.2 API Differential Comparator

This component compares two different version specifications of the same API. Any differences found are expressed as a set of small differentials, describing whether the changes are modifications to existing elements, additions of new elements, or deletions of existing elements.

The following list describes the steps and considerations followed by the *Differential Comparator* to evaluate two versions of the API. (1) Each API version is loaded into its own *Abstract Syntax Tree* (AST) structure [3].(2) The two ASTs are compared against each other in search of mismatching branches. (3) Each mismatching branch is expressed as an *API Differential* and is described with the following fields: *Element Path:* This is the section of the AST branch where both versions of the API are similar. *API Element:* This is the last node in the Element Path, which is the one undergoing the change. *Differential Type:* This field defines whether the new version of the API is either a *modification* of existing data, an *addition* of new data, or a *deletion* of data. *Differential Phase:* This field defines whether the new version of the API is modifying the API's server *request* or its *response*. *Source Element Value:* This is a representation of the data stored in the nodes directly below the *Element Path* in the tree of the source API. (f)*New Element Value:* This is a representation of the data stored in the nodes directly below the *Element Path* in the tree of the target API.

To further illustrate how differentials are processed, suppose that a change in the new version of the case study API is introduced. In this example, the schema for the POST request is changed from a JSON object to an array of items with no specific structure. In Fig. 1 the two versions are overlapped; the common elements between APIs are colored in white, elements from the source API are colored light gray and the elements from the target API are colored dark gray. White colored objects represent the **Element Path**. As seen in the figure, the change takes place under the *request* node, which is the **API Differential Phase**. This means that the adaptation should take place when the client's request is received in the system. The lowest node in the **Element Path** represents the **API Element** of the path up to which the two APIs are similar. The light gray colored element represents the **Source Element Value** in the source API. The dark gray colored element represents the **New Element Value** in the target API. The striked line over the property *object* in the schema represents the **Differential Type**, which is a modification.

4.3 API Conflict Solver

This component is responsible for processing API Differentials delivered by the *Differential Comparator* and mapping them into properly structured adaptation requests to services in the *Adaptation Chain* (see Section 4.5).

In order to match API Differentials against Adaptation Services, the *Conflict Solver* relies on a *Taxonomy of Changes* [19]. Table 1 summarizes the taxonomy. Each change has a type, an element undergoing the change and an Adaptation Service. The latter transforms the changed element into compatible data.

Table 1. Differential Taxonomy

Name	Adaptation Service
Modify Property Type	Caster
Modify Property Name	Property. Mapper
Add Property	Property Mapper
Remove Property	Property Mapper
Modify Schema Type	Schema Parser
Modify Content Type	Content Mapper
Modify Status Code	Status Mapper
Add Status Code	Status Mapper
Remove Status Code	Status Mapper

The process by which an API Differential is mapped into an Adaptation Service request is summarized in the following steps. (1) Match the incoming *API Element Type* against the taxonomy Element. (2) Match the incoming *API Differential Type* against the taxonomy Differential Type. (3) Match the incoming *API Differential Phase* against the taxonomy Differential Phase. (4) With all the elements matches, find the proper *Adaptation Service* and register the proper call to it as a link of the adaptation chain.

4.4 API Adaptation Mediator

This component is the interface between the API and all its clients. It is responsible for receiving all incoming API client requests, orchestrating calls to Adaptation Services and exchanging the transformed messages between API clients and API servers.

4.5 API Adaptation Chain

This component is responsible for supplying the Adaptation Services for the *API Adaptation Mediator* with the purpose of applying successive transformations to messages exchanged between the API Server and its clients.

Each *Adaptation Service* is focused on providing a specialized transformation which is determined by how an *API Differential* is matched against a taxonomy item by the *Conflict Solver*. Since each API Differential is conceived as the smallest, most representative change applied to an API Element from an API Version to the next, the Adaptation Services are designed to be consumed following a Chain of Responsibility pattern [7] similar to the behavior described in Fig. 3, where the *Adaptation Mediator* calls a Caster Adaptation service. This adaptation should take place before calling the POST method since the incoming JSON object has to be transformed into an array of items. The latter may require casting of data types.

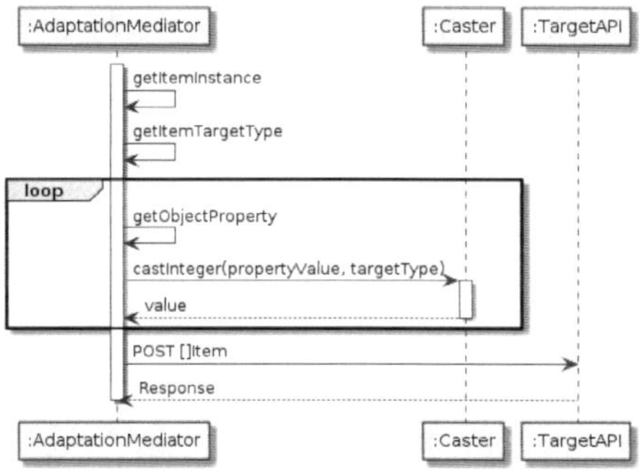

Fig. 3. Sequence diagram representing an adaptation flow for the case study

5 Preliminary Results

The purpose was to test the accuracy of the API Adapter at identifying changes between API's versions. First, we built a prototype of the API Adapter. We provided the API Adapter with two versions of a large API, where the last version included at least three occurrences of each type of change reported in our Change Taxonomy. Then, we manually compared the output from the API Adapter against a table of expected results.

Some characteristics of the API under evaluation are: 23 Resources, 1-4 HTTP Verbs per Resource, 2-4 Status Codes per Response, 1 Application Content, 0-2 Nested Objects, 1-14 Properties per Object. Further elements that describe the complexity of the API follow: Each of the 23 resources exposes on average 2.5 http verbs (GET, POST, PUT, DELETE). Each operation available in a resource has on average 2.5 status codes (200, 400, 401, 403, 500). Only the *application/json* content is considered throughout the API. A resource's schema may have a nested object definition which, in turn, may wrap up to one object as a property. Resource schema objects have on average 6 properties; meaning that some may have a minimum of 1 property and a maximum of 14.

The API adapter is 100% accurate when it comes to determining whether a new element was added or an existing element was removed. Whilst the API comparison is always able to identify element modifications in leafs of an API AST representation, it is only 66.66% accurate when identifying modifications in non-leaf nodes. The reason for this lack of precision is explained by an unexpected behavior in the differential comparator. In order to speed up the process, the current implementation navigates in depth the branches of the AST until a change is detected. As a consequence, operations like modifying the property *name* of elements are not always identified as such; being incorrectly marked as an addition of a new element or a removal of an existing one. To work around this issue, before marking a source element as changed, the algorithm should compare the tree nodes hanging under such an element with those of the target element. If the tree nodes are equal, we are facing an element whose internal properties have been altered (e.g., property renaming). Otherwise, we deal with an element whose pendent elements have underwent a set of modifications. Hence, we can decrease the risk of wrongly identifying additions and deletions when, actually, a modification takes place.

6 Conclusions and Future Work

Throughout the course of this research we identified that our API Adaptation approach relies heavily on determining the spots where changes took place in order to properly apply all required adaptations. Future efforts will be focused on adding efficient recursive calls to the existing algorithm to improve its accuracy.

The use of an API Change Taxonomy proved to be a valuable guideline to set out the scope of the adaptation strategy. Further work around this should extend the Change Taxonomy to include all elements of an Open API specification that may undergo changes.

Since the API Adapter is an additional layer between the IoT devices and the API server, an additional processing overhead appears; this increases based on the subsequent adaptations applied to the message. Parallelism and caching strategies can be evaluated to reduce this overhead. In addition, one could integrate SDN-based approaches and multi-versioning in the same solution along with a smart mechanism to choose the most appropriate option to precisely meet the needs of a given IoT device.

Furthermore, as future work, there needs to be an experimentation that determines the cost of maintaining this adaptation service for a prolonged period of time. We must also compare the approach to find advantages and disadvantages with other approaches, like pushing firmware updates to the IoT devices.

Finally, during the evaluation, we observed that a large amount of adaptations are registered in the system every time the process is executed, some of these adaptations even being redundant. Because of this, future work should include an additional process that compares the target API against all previous registered versions to reduce the amount of adaptations each previous API version would need to match the target.

References

1. Bassi, A., Bauer, M., Fiedler, M., Kramp, T., van Kranenburg, R., Lange, S., Meissner, S.: Enabling Things to Talk: Designing IoT Solutions with the IoT Architectural Reference Model. Springer (2016)
2. Burrus, D.: The internet of things is far bigger than anyone realizes (11 2014), https://www.wired.com/insights/2014/11/the-internet-of-things-bigger/
3. Carnie, A.: Syntax: A Generative Introduction. Wiley-Blackwell (2013)
4. Chafle, G., Dasgupta, K., Kumar, A., Mittal, S., Srivastava, B.: Adaptation in web service composition and execution. In: 2006 IEEE International Conference on Web Services (ICWS'06). pp. 549–557. IEEE (2006)
5. Commission, E.: ICT-15-2019-2020. http://ec.europa.eu/research/participants/portal/desktop/en/opportunities/h2020/topics/ict-15-2019-2020.html, accessed June 11, 2018
6. Commission, E.: ICT-16-2018. http://ec.europa.eu/research/participants/portal/desktop/en/opportunities/h2020/topics/ict-16-2018.html, accessed June 11, 2018
7. Gamma, E.: Design Patterns: Elements of Reusable Object-Oriented Software. Addison-Wesley Professional Computing Series, Addison-Wesley (1994)
8. H. T. Tran, H.B., Kuppili, R.: A notification management architecture for service co-evolution in the internet of things. IEEE 10th International Symposium on the Maintenance and Evolution of Service Oriented and Cloud-Based Environments pp. 9–15 (2016)
9. He, Q., Yan, J., Jin, H., Yang, Y.: Adaptation of web service composition based on workflow patterns. In: International Conference on Service-Oriented Computing. pp. 22–37. Springer (2008)
10. Henkel, J., Diwan, A.: Catchup! capturing and replaying refactorings to support api evolution. Proceedings of the 27th International Conference on Software Engineering **27**, 274 – 283 (2005)
11. Initiative, O.A.: Open api (6 2001), https://www.openapis.org/
12. Kim, M., Notkin, D.: Discovering and representing systematic code changes. In: 2009 IEEE 31st International Conference on Software Engineering. pp. 309–319. IEEE (2009)
13. Kim, M., Notkin, D., Grossman, D.: Automatic inference of structural changes for matching across program versions. In: 29th International Conference on Software Engineering (ICSE'07). pp. 333–343. IEEE (2007)
14. L. Li, W. Chou, W.Z.: Design patterns and extensibility of rest api for networking applications. IEEE Transactions On Network And Service Management **13**(1), 154–167 (5 2016)
15. L. Li L., W.C.: Compatibility checking of rest api based on coloured petri net. Lecture Notes in Business Information Processing (246), 25–43 (3 2016)
16. Nguyen, H.A., Nguyen, T.T., Wilson Jr, G., Nguyen, A.T., Kim, M., Nguyen, T.N.: A graph-based approach to api usage adaptation. ACM Sigplan Notices **45**(10), 302–321 (2010)

17. Oberhauser, R.: A hypermedia-driven approach for adapting processes via adaptation processes. In: 2015 8th International Conference on Advanced Software Engineering & Its Applications (ASEA). pp. 73–80. IEEE (2015)
18. Perkins, J.: Automatically generating refactorings to support api evolution. ACM SIGSOFT Software Engineering Notes **31**, 111 – 114 (2006)
19. Sanctis, M.D., Geihs, K.: Distributed service co-evolution based on domain objects. Lecture Notes in Computer Science **9586**, 48–63 (2016)

Performance Evaluation of Kubernetes as Deployment Platform for IoT Devices

Alessandro Caetano Beltrão[1], Breno Bernard Nicolau de França[2], and Guilherme Horta Travassos[3]

[1,3] Universidade Federal do Rio de Janeiro, COPPE, Rio de Janeiro, Brasil
[2] University of Campinas, UNICAMP, Campinas, Brazil
{alessandrocb,ght}@cos.ufrj.br,
breno@ic.unicamp.br

Abstract. With the advent of the Internet of Things paradigm, more and more devices and sensors are physically distributed to accomplish many tasks in our daily lives. Edge computing has emerged as a way to migrate part of the storage, data processing, and computation capabilities to the edge devices. Such a migration aims at addressing the challenges regarding communication between IoT devices, pressure on the cloud infrastructure generated by a large amount of data, network complexity, and scalability. As these applications migrate to this new paradigm, issues already addressed on developing traditional software begin to emerge as new challenges. One of these challenges is the deployment process of applications on the edge devices since, in a real scenario, the scale of an IoT platform can be tremendous. In this paper, we discuss the usage of Kubernetes as a platform to enable deployments from the cloud to IoT gateways and conduct a performance evaluation of Kubernetes on two common IoT scenarios. The preliminary results show the potential and feasibility of Kubernetes as a platform for deploying applications on edge devices.

Keywords: Internet of Things, Edge Computing, Performance Evaluation, Continuous Deployment

1 Introduction

Recently the Internet of Things (IoT) paradigm has changed the way applications, people, and devices interact with each other [1]. More and more devices are getting integrated into our personal lives and activities to accomplish this new level of interaction with the end-user. They may collect data, act as hubs for communication between other devices, and work collaboratively. As IoT becomes widespread, challenges regarding security, scalability, communication, networking also surfaces, creating a favorable scenario for more investigation and research.

To deal with some of these challenges, one of the approaches that have surfaced is the concept of *edge computing* [2]. It refers to the enablement of edge devices and technologies to perform computation at the edge of a network [2][3][4]. That approach differs from the already established *cloud computing* approach where the cloud is responsible for all the data processing that comes from devices. *Edge computing* also potentially provides some benefits over conventional *cloud computing*. Yi *et al.* described in [5] indicate that a platform for face-recognition had its response time reduced from *900ms* to *169ms* by moving the computation to the edge. Studies [6] and [7] also show positive results regarding response times, energy-consumption by applying concepts of partitioning, merging, migration, and on-demand instantiation from cloud to edge devices.

In IoT or even edge systems, a common challenge is the provisioning and deployments of the application on the devices. In a toy application, it is relatively easy to provision the devices manually. However, in a real-world application, the number and the geographical distribution of the devices can turn this task arduous and complicated. Moreover, to perform such deployments continuously [8], i.e., on a regular and frequent basis, is an even harder activity in the IoT context. Some studies as Rufino *et al.* [9], Morabito [10], Lwakatare *et al.* [11], and Moore *et al.* [12] explore the possibility of utilizing *Linux* container technologies, especially *Docker*, as a way to enable scalable deployments on edge devices, since *Docker*, and containers, generally speaking, are widely used for deployments of microservices into the cloud.

Lwakatare *et al.* [11] collected evidence on the usage of *DevOps* practices on the embedded systems domain, by identifying the challenges as hardware dependency and compatibility with software versions and the lack of the technology to automatically, reliably and repeatedly deploy new features in customer-specific environments among others [11]. Morabito conducted performance testing of virtualization technologies, including *Docker* on boards from different vendors, as *Raspberry* and *ODROID* [10]. The work by Moore *et al.* focuses on the creation of a proof of concept application that uses *Docker* to bootstrap applications on IoT devices [12]. At last, Rufino *et al.* use a proof of concept to propose the usage of *Docker* as an enabler for deployments on Edge Gateways [9].

Our approach differs from the ones stated as it focuses on the performance evaluation of the container orchestration tool *Kubernetes* on the scenario of *Edge Computing*. To evaluate *Kubernetes,* we created a synchronous and asynchronous communication scenario that aimed to reflect the usage of this technology as a means to deploy, schedule, and maintain containers on Edge Gateway nodes. Using those scenarios, we then proceeded to perform a group of performance tests to evaluate the limits of a *Raspberry PI* as a worker node in an architecture where the workers act as Gateways for other devices.

In this paper, we explore the possibility of using *Kubernetes*, a container cluster technology, to enable deployments of IoT-relevant components. To determine the feasibility of our approach, we set up a *Kubernetes* cluster on a group of *Raspberry PI* devices, general-purpose hardware widely available on the market. Then, we executed performance tests on two common IoT scenarios, using both the HTTP and AMQP protocols for synchronous and asynchronous scenarios, respectively. We used the performance tests to determine whether the cluster could keep the IoT components healthy even in a demanding scenario having the *Raspberry PIs* as gateways for other devices like sensors and actuators. The preliminary results for the tests show that while there are still challenges to overcome in the usage of container technologies on Edge Gateways. However, these technologies may be used for specific scenarios considering a determined number of worker nodes. The main contribution of this paper is the evaluation of the performance of Kubernetes in the IoT context. Nonetheless, it is not within our scope to compare this solution to other already established solutions in the market as KubeEdge, Amazon IoT Core, or K3S as this comparison can be explored in other studies.

Besides this introduction, this paper has six more sections. Section 2 aims to familiarize the reader with concepts related to *Edge Computing*, *DevOps,* and the relevance of containers and Kubernetes in this context. Section 3 presents our evaluation method; it shows how we set up the cluster architecture and test parametrization for each scenario. Section 4 presents the preliminary results of the tests and all the discussion related to these results. In Section 5, we discuss the threats to validity for our study, and finally, in Section 6, we give our final remarks regarding our approach.

2 Related Concepts

Usually, devices used on IoT environments are considered *resource-constrained*, a term that, according to Pisani *et al.* [14], is used to describe devices that are limited in terms of memory, power, energy, and processing capabilities. These devices are often equipped with sensors and actuators that allow them to interact with the real world. They may process and parse data streams coming from sensors, and sometimes act accordingly through actuators. However, the amount of data and the transformations required in specific scenarios may become an overhead for the limited resources of IoT devices.

In a typical *client-server* application, the cloud is in charge of processing data generated from the less capable clients. Nevertheless, in an IoT scenario, processing all the data in the cloud may not be feasible because of the order of the magnitude of the data and latency of requests. *Edge computing* aims to bring computing capable devices closer to the end-user as a means to address challenges regarding latency, data processing, and quality of service (QoS). Yu et al. [2] define the structure of *edge computing* into three aspects (Figure 1): *front-end*, *near-end*, and *far-end*.

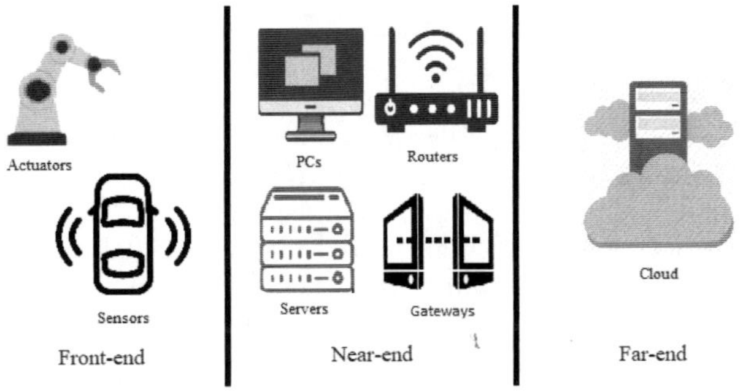

Fig. 1. A typical architecture for *edge computing* networks (adapted from [2]).

In this architecture, the *front-end* devices are usually sensors and actuators. They provide the necessary interaction with the user most of the time using the processing power and capacity from devices nearby and receiving and pushing information from and to IoT gateways, located in the *near-end*. These gateways usually support the flow of information, perform pre-processing, cache data, and perform the offloading, reducing the number of requests made to the cloud servers. The *far-end* devices are cloud servers, proving the necessary computing power and storage for post-processing, data mining, and machine learning [2].

One of the concerns on IoT discussions is the provisioning and deployment of applications into the edge of networks. As the number of devices grows, the number of supporting gateways also increases, and the complexity of deploying and maintaining applications on the devices becomes more and more challenging. Applying *DevOps* practices can help with that task. However, the intrinsic characteristics of IoT devices and applications may not be suitable for all modern *DevOps* solutions.

Studies, as the ones conducted by Rufino *et al.* [9], Morabito [10], Lwakatare *et al.* [11], and Moore *et al.* [12] propose to tackle these challenges using *Linux* Containers, a lightweight form of virtualization, to provide the rapid deployment of microservices into different devices on the *near-end* and *far-end*. Containers allow developers and practitioners to create separate user spaces capable of isolating processes and hardware resources into the same operating system. They started in *Unix* development, in 1979 with the implementation of a group of functionalities that would later be merged into a *system call* named *chroot* [15]. Today, there are many container technologies available for general use; some examples are *LxC*, *Docker*, and *runC*.

However, none of these studies explores the use of container orchestration tools for deployment on an IoT scenario. These tools can help by allowing practitioners to deploy, monitor, and schedule containers across a group of devices that, in most cases, is a server. Although practitioners already use these tools on a conventional software development process, their usage of IoT is still limited and cares for more research.

One of the most used container orchestration tools is *Kubernetes*; it provides a set of functionalities that can be useful to an IoT scenario. *Kubernetes* allows the fast deployment of services by assigning containers to devices in the cluster. It helps by managing node and container communications, providing high availability by migrating failing services into backup nodes, and taking care of updating the nodes in a controlled way.

The usage of Kubernetes as a driving technology for IoT is an idea that is already being explored on the market. Technologies such as *K3S* and *KubeEdge* are being developed to adapt this technology to IoT. *K3S* specifically tries to optimize *Kubernetes* binaries for the *ARM64* and *ARMv7* architecture while also providing optimizations as an *SQLite* as a replacer for the default *etcd* datastore [20]. *KubeEdge* extends *Kubernetes* default controllers to create a device synchronization mechanism while also using *SQLite* as a lightweight database instead of the default, *etcd,* on the edge devices [21].

Some cloud providers, such as Amazon AWS and Azure, are also providing services for the IoT in the cloud. *Amazon IoT Core* aims to provide communication and synchronization between the devices and the cloud, while also adding compatibility with other common AWS infrastructures, such as *S3*, *EC2,* and *SageMaker* [22]. Azure is providing a similar service, called *Azure IoT Hub*, that aims to provide infrastructure to IoT devices on the Edge [23].

3 Evaluation Method

As the research on the usage of *Kubernetes* in the context of IoT is still incipient, we felt the need to evaluate whether this technology could be used in this context. To do that, we started by assessing the performance of *Kubernetes* worker nodes deployed into *Raspberry PIs*. The tests had two main objectives, and the first is to check whether an ARM-based device (as a *Raspberry PI*) with low resources could fulfill the requirements to act as a worker node. The second objective is to evaluate the performance of such nodes in two common IoT scenarios and determine the limits of the container technologies into these nodes.

To execute the performance tests, the first issue was to set up a *Kubernetes* cluster using the *Raspberry PIs* as worker nodes. Using the available *Raspberry PIs*, we provisioned a four-node cluster, with one master and three workers, the master being a workstation computer with four cores and eight threads *x64* Intel processor and 16 gigabytes of *DDR4* ram. We used this setting because the *Raspberry PI* cannot handle all the components of the *Kubernetes* master. The workers were composed of *Raspberry PI Model 3 B+*, which until the time of the test, were the latest ones. Figure 2 represents the architecture of scenario 1. We also put them under a Demilitarized Zone on a router. The use of *Docker* as Container Runtime Environment (CRE) led to disabling the bridge that *Docker* uses to map ports from containers to the device network interface. The usage of the bridge could represent another confounding factor in the test, as the study conducted by Felter *et al.* confirmed that using *Docker NAT* and port mapping represents a loss on performance regarding *Network IO* while Docker without those configurations has the approximated performance of bare-metal applications [17]. We implemented each test using Apache JMeter, a tool for load testing and measuring the performance of applications and servers. Moreover, after each test, the deployment of the application under test was destroyed and recreated.

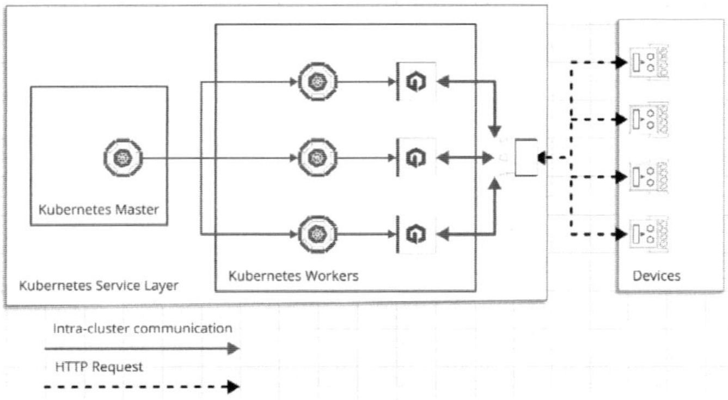

Fig. 2. Cluster Topology for the Synchronous Scenario

The first scenario represents the synchronous communication from IoT Devices (like sensors and actuators) with the IoT Gateway (deployed as Kubernetes Workers), implemented as a simple *HTTP* request that should return response code 200. We set this test up using the official *NGINX*, a widely used application server, and reverse-proxy, Image from *DockerHub*[1]. On this test, the *Raspberry PI* worker node runs a pod with one container that should be able to respond to requests from a client. Each request sent has 114 bytes in data and should get as a response a web page with 850 bytes, being 238 for Header and 612 for Body.

To evaluate this scenario, we designed nine test cases establishing maximum response times of the application being *100ms*, *1000ms,* and *10000ms* based on the work published by Jakob Nielsen in [13]. These times represent thresholds for the attention span of a user in web applications, being *100ms* perceived as real-time, *1000ms* the limit for a user flow of thought, and *10000ms* the limit for keeping user attention. We also established the number of requests per second (RPS) as being powers of 10, as the goal is to stress the cluster to maximum, so the RPS values

[1] https://hub.docker.com/_/nginx

used are 10^1, 10^2 and 10^3, these requests are applied to the system, and not just to each of the nodes. Using the values for max response time and RPS, we applied them into Equation 1 [16] to calculate the total number of threads needed for each test. Table 1 describes each one of the test scenarios, and below, we present the equation used to calculate the thread number used in each execution.

$$\frac{RPS \times Max\ Response\ Time}{1000} = Thread\ Number\ (1)$$

Test ID	RPS	Max Response Time (*ms*)	Thread Number
0	10	100	1
1	10	1000	10
2	10	10000	100
3	100	100	10
4	100	1000	100
5	100	10000	1000
6	1000	100	100
7	1000	1000	1000
8	1000	10000	10000

Table 1. Test Execution Parameters for HTTP Protocol Scenario

The second scenario aimed to represent an asynchronous communication (like a publisher-subscriber architecture) using *RabbitMQ*[2] as a broker, and the *AMQP* protocol, in an IoT application, as shown in Figure 3. The AMQP protocol was chosen because it can be used over mobile and unstable networks and is more robust than the MQTT [19]. In this scenario, we set up the tests to allow the *Raspberry PI* to work as an IoT Gateway. This way, we could simulate tests in which publishers sent data to the gateway; a small number of subscribers took that data to perform another action. Using *JMeter* and *Apache AMQP Client*, we set up two different test configurations (Table 2). For each test, the publishers have to deliver a message that has a hexadecimal body of 850 bytes. The delivery of the message is considered a success when an ACK signal is received. On *RabbitMQ*, an exchange is configured to broadcast all messages to queues, as each test is composed of only one queue.

---

[2] https://hub.docker.com/_/rabbitmq

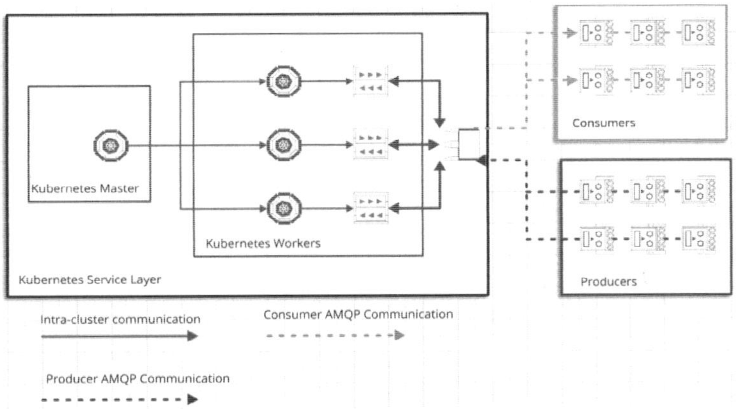

Fig. 3. Cluster Topology for the Asynchronous Scenario

Test ID	Subscribers	Publishers	RPS Limit on Publishers
0	1	10	100
1	10	100	1000

Table 2. Test Execution Parameters for the AMQP Protocol Scenario

Similarly, as in the *HTTP* scenario, on the *AMQP* tests, we also scaled the subscribers and publishers by powers of ten from one test to another. Typically, in an Edge Computing scenario, the number of publishers tends to be higher than the number of subscribers. As the number of devices on the *Front-End*, the sensors and actuators are, in general, higher than the number of devices in the *Near-End*. In a real publisher scenario, each publisher sends messages from time to time, and, to simulate that behavior, we established a limit on the number of requests per second the publishers can make. In both scenarios, the cluster had to support the load of the tests for three minutes and twenty seconds, in which the ten starting seconds is ramp-up, and the last ten is ramp-down time. We consider that the time given for each test scenario was sufficient to show the shortcomings of the architecture and the *Raspberry Pi 3B+* as the number of requests on each test was high and already capable of disrupting the cluster in some scenarios.

4 Preliminary Results

After setting up the cluster and creating the test execution scripts using *JMeter*, we executed the scenarios. The first tests performed are from the *HTTP* scenario. As expected, the cluster could easily handle all the requests from the first five tests with a low standard deviation from the mean response time (Table 3). Test 5 and 6 show that the standard deviation for the response time started to grow exponential-ly along with the number of threads. Still, the number of failures reported by *JMeter* on tests 0 to 5 were mostly insignificant, as to consider the sample failure, the server had to respond with any other status code than 200, and the request-response time should be higher than the max response time defined in the test execution plan. Table 3 shows the results of the tests for all the HTTP test scenarios.

Test ID	Samples	Mean (*ms*)	Min (*ms*)	Max (*ms*)	SD (*ms*)	Error %	Throughput
0	1824	26	13	188	12,93	0,66%	9,6/sec
1	1663	34	14	364	25,23	0,00%	8,3/sec
2	1387	33	13	265	20,43	0,00%	6,9/sec
3	18926	25	12	230	19,60	1,87%	95,1/sec
4	18873	25	11	203	19,03	0,00%	94,4/sec
5	17715	32	12	1028	41,08	0,00%	88,9/sec
6	53701	350	8	21025	785,43	63,30%	263,0/sec
7	54242	3496	8	70138	4359,41	83,42%	253,0/sec
8	78340	23887	0	198230	37907,06	51,80%	371,8/sec

Table 3. Test Execution Results from the *HTTP* Scenario

Table 3 shows that the cluster operated well until the number of threads reached close to one hundred, and the number of requests per second was close to one thousand. The pod could not serve all the static files promptly as *NGINX* started creating new threads to serve requests. Some of the threads needed to wait until it could be processed, creating a queue that generated high response times. On Test 6, 7, and 8, the major problem was the limited number of resources from the *Raspberry PI* Worker node to process all the requests simultaneously. This phenomenon can be observed by looking at the maximum throughput generated, and the *RPM* expected from the tests.

Regarding the results of the tests from the synchronous scenarios, the results show that the maximum throughput that *NGINX* from one pod with only one replica is 371,8/sec. The *Kubernetes* documentation points out ways to achieve higher throughput by horizontally escalating the architecture and allowing more replicas to coexist. Another way to improve the performance of the pods is fine-tuning the resources allocated per pod, as *Kubernetes* enables users to control the number of allocated *CPU shares* and memory. The usage of monitoring tools, together with Kubernetes, also may be useful to detect eviction signals sent by Kubernetes controllers on the *Worker Nodes* [18].

In the second scenario, the use of a more lightweight protocol like *AMQP* greatly favors the *Raspberry PI* Worker nodes. In both executed tests, the results were significantly better. The first test shows that a *Raspberry PI*, as an IoT Gateway, is perfectly capable of handling ten other devices publishing messages at a rate of

100 *m/s*. Also, it could still keep the broker healthy without any failure, as it is possible to see in Figure 4.

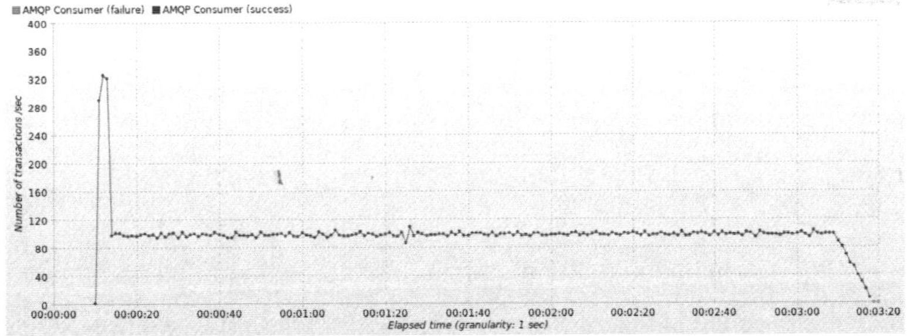

Fig. 4. Subscriber Transactions for Test 0 on the AMQP Scenario

On the second test of the publisher-subscriber scenario, the limits of the *Raspberry PI* as a platform is more apparent. During the test execution, *RabbitMQ* reported that the cluster reached the Memory High Watermark, a configuration that starts to block publishers' queues until the messages are clear and the memory usage lowers. On the cluster, the flag Memory High Watermark was set to be 40% of the node total memory. On the curve generated by the publisher's transactions, we can observe these effects by analyzing the dips in Figure 5. Besides, the green line on the bottom of the graph represents the requests that received a *NACK* from the broker.

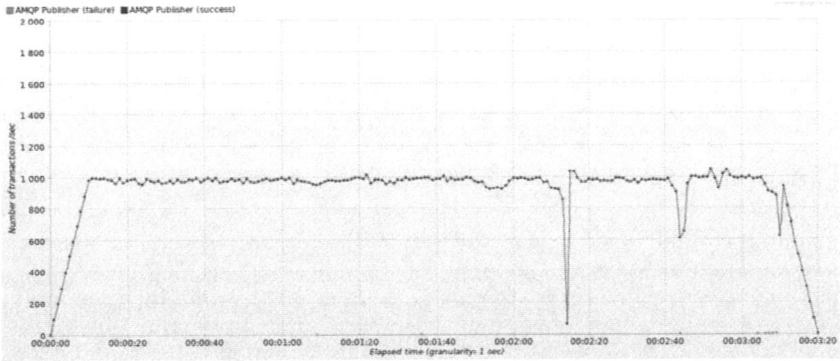

Fig. 5. Publisher Transactions for Test 1 on the *AMQP* Scenario

However, even activating the memory limits, the number of simultaneous publishers connections on a pod got too high. The large connection pool ended up causing the *RabbitMQ* to stop broadcasting messages for the subscriber, as we can see in Figure 6. The graph shows that *RabbitMQ* was prioritizing publisher threads, as they were in a proportion of 10:1 from subscribers. The high peaks characterize that when a subscriber thread could finally be served, it consumed a high number of messages simultaneously and then stopped to consume. At the end of this test, the subscribers left a total of 118,086 messages hanging in the queue.

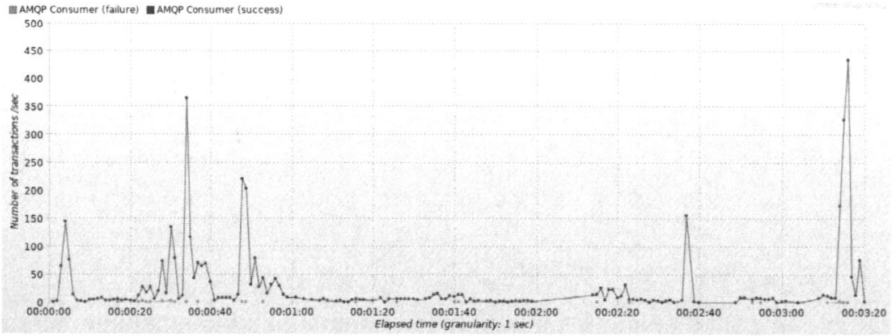

Fig. 6. Subscriber Transactions for Test 1 on the *AMQP* Scenario

In this test, we can see that scaling the publishers and subscribers by powers of ten was not the ideal. The relation between the number of publishers and subscribers also needs a proper tuning as a way to avoid publishers from clogging the broker, a vulnerability for this architecture that can be explored in future research.

5 Limitations and Threats to Validity

Regarding external validity, we acknowledge that our tests are still limited to a small set of devices and technologies, imposing barriers to a broader generalization regarding the applicability of *Kubernetes* on IoT. However, the need to understand the limits of this technology and the particularities of *Edge Computing* sustain the need for further research. Currently, the usage of *Kubernetes* is heavily limited by the processor architecture and nodes resources. However, we believe that as time goes on, the trend is that embedded devices get more powerful resources.

On internal validity, we consider that all the executed tests were adequately set up to reduce noise and interference from any other factor. The environment where the tests executed was a clean *Raspbian Linux* operating system, with a newly instantiated *Kubernetes* cluster and disabling any network configuration made by *Docker*. After each test, the environment was destroyed and recreated automatically. Therefore, any execution of one test could not influence another.

To deal with construct validity, we tried to set up the cluster as close to what a real production environment would be. All the configurations were done by following the official *Kubernetes* documentation [18] and each of the respective documentations for the container images. We executed all the tests from an isolated environment, and they were also parametrized to reflect the usage intensity of a real IoT scenario.

About the evaluation process, we consider that the automated tests generated alongside the configuration files necessary to set-up the cluster should enable any person to execute the tests at any time. Our implementation source code (including cluster setup configurations, compiled binaries for *Kubernetes* on *armv6l* platform, test scripts, and tutorials) are available on an instance of Gitlab[3] and can be accessed by anyone. However, as we did not conduct any statistical tests of the results, this represents a conclusion validity threat to our study.

6 Final Remarks

In this paper, we presented the application of the *Kubernetes* Engine as a deployment platform for IoT devices.

The results shown in this paper presents the applicability of *Kubernetes* for at least two scenarios, one using synchronous (*HTTP*) and one using asynchronous (*AMQP*) protocols. During the tests, the cluster kept the applications alive and handled the high load in the *Raspberry PI*. Furthermore, we believe that container-based technologies may prove as a way to enable deployments on highly distributed environments as envisioned by the IoT paradigm.

The adoption of the *Kubernetes* Engine as a platform for IoT still needs more research, as it still imposes barriers regarding the requirements of the cluster worker and master nodes. The cluster implementation may not be suitable for all constrained devices built for IoT purposes in the market. Nevertheless, on platforms that are capable of handling a *Kubernetes* cluster, the gain from being able to deploy and maintaining those applications can outweigh the complexity and overhead of bootstrapping the cluster on those environments.

As future works, we envision improving our tests by making use of simulations to evaluate how *Kubernetes* would perform in a large-scale scenario. For that, we aim to make use of Smart City simulations tools and specify a configuration that should enable *Kubernetes* to provision IoT Gateways on-demand.

Acknowledgments

The CNPq (Brazilian National Council for Scientific and Technological Development) and CAPES support this research. Prof. Guilherme Horta Travassos is a CNPq researcher (304234/2018-4).

---

[3] https://www.mrdevops-gitlab.com/plataforma-de-desenvolvimento-continuo-para-iot

7 References

1. Atzori L, Iera A, Morabito G (2010). The Internet of Things: A survey. Computer Networks 54:2787–2805. https://doi.org/10.1016/j.comnet.2010.05.010
2. Yu W, Liang F, He X, et al. (2018). A Survey on the Edge Computing for the Internet of Things. IEEE Access 6:6900–6919. https://doi.org/10.1109/ACCESS.2017.2778504
3. Varghese B, Wang N, Barbhuiya S, et al. (2016). Challenges and Opportunities in Edge Computing. In: 2016 IEEE International Conference on Smart Cloud (SmartCloud). IEEE, New York, NY, USA, pp 20–26
4. Shi W, Cao J, Zhang Q, et al. (2016). Edge Computing: Vision and Challenges. IEEE Internet Things J 3:637–646. https://doi.org/10.1109/JIOT.2016.2579198
5. Yi S, Hao Z, Qin Z, Li Q (2015). Fog Computing: Platform and Applications. In: 2015 Third IEEE Workshop on Hot Topics in Web Systems and Technologies (HotWeb). IEEE, Washington DC, DC, USA, pp 73–78
6. Ha K, Chen Z, Hu W, et al. (2014). Towards wearable cognitive assistance. In: Proceedings of the 12th annual international conference on Mobile systems, applications, and services - MobiSys '14. ACM Press, Bretton Woods, New Hampshire, USA, pp 68–81
7. Chun B-G, Ihm S, Maniatis P, et al. (2011). CloneCloud: elastic execution between mobile devices and cloud. In: Proceedings of the sixth conference on Computer systems - EuroSys '11. ACM Press, Salzburg, Austria, p 301
8. Humble, J., Farley, D., 2010. Continuous Delivery: Reliable Software Releases through Build, Test, and Deployment Automation, Addison-Wesley Signature Series (Fowler). Pearson Education.
9. Rufino J, Alam M, Ferreira J, et al. (2017). Orchestration of containerized microservices for IIoT using Docker. In: 2017 IEEE International Conference on Industrial Technology (ICIT). IEEE, Toronto, ON, pp 1532–1536
10. Morabito, R (2017). Virtualization on Internet of Things Edge Devices With Container Technologies: A Performance Evaluation. IEEE Access 5:8835–8850. https://doi.org/10.1109/ACCESS.2017.2704444
11. Lwakatare LE, Karvonen T, Sauvola T, et al. (2016). Towards DevOps in the Embedded Systems Domain: Why is It So Hard? In: 2016 49th Hawaii International Conference on System Sciences (HICSS). IEEE, Koloa, HI, pp 5437–5446
12. Moore J, Kortuem G, Smith A, et al. (2016). DevOps for the Urban IoT. In: Proceedings of the Second International Conference on IoT in Urban Space - Urb-IoT '16. ACM Press, Tokyo, Japan, pp 78–81
13. NIELSEN J (1993). Chapter 5 - Usability Heuristics. In: NIELSEN J (ed) Usability Engineering. Morgan Kaufmann, San Diego, pp 115–163
14. Pisani F, Immich R, Bittencourt LF, Borin E (2019). Fog Computing on Constrained Devices: Paving the Way for the Future IoT. 37
15. Cheswick, B., n.d. An Evening with Berferd In Which a Cracker is Lured, Endured, and Studied 11.
16. JMeter Throughput Shaping Timer, https://jmeter-plugins.org/wiki/ThroughputShapingTimer/, Last accessed 2019/11/12
17. Felter W, Ferreira A, Rajamony R, Rubio J (2015) An updated performance comparison of virtual machines and Linux containers. In: 2015 IEEE International Symposium on Performance Analysis of Systems and Software (ISPASS). pp 171–172
18. Kubernetes Docs, https://kubernetes.io/docs, Last accessed 2019/12/13

19. J. Luzuriaga, P. Boronat, M. Perez, C. Calafate, J.-C. Cano, e P. Manzoni, “A comparative evaluation of AMQP and MQTT protocols over unstable and mobile networks,” 2015, doi: 10.1109/CCNC.2015.7158101.
20. K3s - 5 less than K8s, https://rancher.com/docs/k3s/latest/en/, last accessed 2020/02/26.
21. What is KubeEdge — KubeEdge Documentation 0.1 documentation, http://docs.kubeedge.io/en/latest/modules/kubeedge.html#advantages, last accessed 2020/02/26.
22. Visão geral do AWS IoT Core – Amazon Web Services, https://aws.amazon.com/pt/iot-core/, last accessed 2020/02/26.
23. Hub IoT | Microsoft Azure, https://azure.microsoft.com/pt-br/services/iot-hub/, last accessed 2020/02/26.

Commit Classification using Natural Language Processing: Experiments over Labeled Datasets

Geanderson E. dos Santos[0000-0002-7571-6578] and
Eduardo Figueiredo[0000-0002-6004-2718]

Federal University of Minas Gerais, Belo Horizonte MG 31270-901, Brazil

Abstract. Software commits play an important role in collaborative software development. A commit allows developers to collaboratively contribute to open-source software projects. Previous studies show that developers spend a lot of time in identifying and prioritizing critical issues and respective commits. For this reason, understanding what a software commit is trying to solve in the project is very important. In this context, commit classification could help managers to plan and allocate resources in advance for the software project. Despite its relevance, we still lack accurate models to support automated classification of commits into relevant categories. In this work, we conduct an empirical study to evaluate commit classification techniques using the commit message given by developers as input. After an ad-hoc literature review, we created a dataset based on labeled data from different works found in the literature. Second, we compared five Machine Learning (ML) state-or-art algorithms seeking a reliable baseline model. Finally, we applied Natural Language Processing (NLP) to a novel ML model aiming at improving results compared to the baseline models. Our findings show that the new NLP-based model outperforms the random baseline models by a relevant rate, achieving 91% of F-measure for the commit classification task.

Keywords: software commit classification · natural language processing · machine learning.

1 Introduction

Software commits play an important role in the Version Control System (VCS) allowing practitioners to create collaborative source code repositories [7, 9, 22, 23]. These repositories can be shared with the software community, and many developers around the world contribute to important open source projects. The main representative of these VCS platforms is the well known GitHub[1] Web system, which is responsible for storing millions of projects from companies, research groups, and independent developers. The contributors to these systems have an easy-to-use architecture for introducing new features, fixing bugs, testing existing code, and many other capabilities [7, 8]. On the other hand, dealing with online repositories may introduce serious bugs that may not have been properly

[1] https://github.com/

tested [7, 13, 15, 16]. One approach to deal with the probability of introducing bugs into the project is, for instance, to understand what the commit is doing in the source code. Commit classification can, therefore, support the estimation and planning of bug fixes [5, 10, 20] among other uses. In fact, different approaches for commit classification have been studied in the literature [2, 7, 10, 16, 20].

In this paper, we first evaluate five Machine Learning (ML) algorithms used for commit classification aiming to predict the nature of changes. These ML algorithms are used as baseline models and rely on the text provided by the developer who committed the code. One of the advantages of classifying software commits is that it may help practitioners to plan and allocate resources to the project issues. Therefore, planning the software may reduce uncertainty and improve the cost-effectiveness of tasks related to the project development. To classify a software commit, it is necessary to look at the possible inputs a developer may provide in the commit log.

There is no consensus regarding the different types of classification to which a commit refers. Therefore, after an ad-hoc literature review, we collected labeled datasets and created a unified dataset by classifying commits into five categories: corrective, features, non-functional, perfective and unknown. We adopted the definition of Levin and Yehudai [13] for three of the categories: corrective related to fault fixing, perfective based on system improvements, and adaptive corresponding to new features introduction. We also used the definition of Hindle et al. [9], where non-functional is associated with documents and non-functional requirements. In addition, the category unknown is able to aggregate files that are created by VSC systems. For instance, when a merge is executed automatically in GitHub, some files are committed with generic descriptions. Finally, we propose a novel model able to classify commits. Therefore, the final goal of this paper can be stated as follows.

> Propose and evaluate a model based on Natural Language Processing (NLP) to classify software commits.

To provide a mean for comparison between the novel NLP model and baseline models from the literature, we apply all models to a unified dataset of labeled commits. Other works are available for comparison [2, 10]. However, state-of-art work has different categories for software commit classification. For instance, there is a classification of commits in only three categories related to maintenance activities: corrective, adaptive, and perfective [14]. In such work, the authors were able to achieve an accuracy of around 76% with three categories [14]. These labels are very limited for our purpose. So, we opt for a more deep study of the categories, where five classes of commits are taken into account [8]. Using the same five labels adopted for the commit classification, previous work was able to achieve approximately 65% of accuracy from different models [8]. The NLP model we propose, however, was able to achieve expressive results in the labeled dataset, achieving 91% of F-measure for the commit classification problem.

This paper is organized as follows. Section 2 presents the related work. The experimental design and its main phases are discussed in Section 3. The study is divided into 4 steps (i) ad-hoc literature review, (ii) collecting data from labeled datasets, (iii) experiments with the baseline algorithms, and (iv) experiments with a new NLP model to classify software commits. In Section 4, we discuss the main results of this paper. Finally, Section 5 details the threats to validity involved in this research, and Section 6 concludes this paper with insights for future explorations on software commit classification.

2 Background and Related Work

In this section, we present literature work related to the task of software commit classification. The section is divided as follows. We introduce the problem of commit classification (Section 2.1). Next, we discuss in Section 2.2 the tools and algorithms proposed in the literature.

2.1 Commit Classification

The simplest kind of classification is to identify some unknown object as a member of a known class of objects. Classification is a computationally hard problem, and it is the subject of study in different Computer Science areas. One of the many forms of classifying software commits is through labels. The central idea of the labeling mechanism allows users to decide which labels they think are more applicable to the context of their content, in contrast to other classification mechanisms. Many authors have studied how labels are used in these systems [3, 6]. The use of labels has also been extended to Web-based code hosting platforms where tools like issue-trackers (as the popular Bugzilla) offer this functionality.

Previous studies have attempted to propose accurate models to classify software commits. Most works are based on the commit messages, using text analysis, such as word frequency approaches to find specific keywords [8, 9, 13, 17, 22]. For instance, Mockus and Votta [17] have proposed a commit comment based model to classify a software commit. The authors reported an average accuracy of approximately 60% within the scope of a single project (a very large software system known as Firefox with millions of lines of code). In a similar approach, Hindle and colleagues [9] proposed to classify software commits by training Machine Learners on features extracted from the commit metadata, such as the word distribution of a commit message, commit author, and modules modified by the developers. The authors validated the model through 10-fold cross-validation and reported accuracies above 50%. They also pointed out that the identity of the author of a commit provided a lot of information about the subject of a commit, almost as much as the words of the commit message. Furthermore, the authors propose the identification of six categories for commit classification: "perfective", "merge", "adaptive", "feature addition", "non functional", and "preventive" [20]. Compared to previous work, our proposed model achieved higher accuracy than these projects in a unified labeled dataset and we used several random models as baselines for comparison.

2.2 Tools and Algorithms for Commit Classification

Rosen and colleagues [20] developed a platform to automatically identifies risky (i.e., bug-inducing) commits and built a prediction model to assess the likelihood of a recent commit introducing a bug in future. The platform is known as *Commit Guru* and allows users to download the data for any project that is processed by the system. Several large open source projects have been successfully processed using *Commit Guru*. Besides this tool, other authors [10] present a platform that generates a set of visualizations to facilitate the analysis of issues in a project depending on their label-based categorization. The tool is named GitHub label analyzer (*GiLa*). They argue the visualizations are useful to see the most popular labels and their respective relationships in a project. The tool also allows identifying the most active community members for those labels and a comparison of the typical issue evolution for each label category. In a different work, Levin and Yehudai [13] built a designated repository mining tool that was used to create a metric dataset. The tool is responsible for processing nearly 1,000 highly popular open-source GitHub repositories, consisting of 147 million lines of code and maintained by over 30,000 developers. The computed metrics were then employed to predict the maintenance activity profiles identified in previous works. The authors show how their results may help project managers to detect anomalies in the software development process and to build better development teams.

A previous work [5] discussed the problem of identifying particular changes that occur across several versions of a program. The authors present a plugin known as *Change Distilling*, a tree differentiation algorithm for fine-grained source code change extraction. Similarly, Casalnuovo and others [2] proposed a tool known as *GitcProc*, a lightweight tool based on regular expressions and source code blocks, which downloads projects and extracts their project history including fine-grained source code information and development time bug fixes. These systems present interesting features for the software commit classification. However, both *Commit Guru* and *GiLa* seem to be in maintenance stage or have been closed by their authors [10, 20]. While *Change Distilling* and *GitcProc* are still available, *Change Distilling* is limited to Java IDE Eclipse. As we do not want to face the same availability problem, we have created a replication repository with all our data and tooling publicly available on GitHub[2].

3 Study Setup

In this section, we present the research questions that guided our study (Section 3.1). Section 3.2 presents the study phases we followed in this work. Section 3.3 presents the dataset used to evaluate all models for the software commit classification problem. Finally, we discuss in Section 3.4 the baselines models applied in this research.

[2] https://github.com/gesteves91/fasttext-commit-classification

3.1 Research Questions

Our experiments aim to answer the following research questions concerning the software commit classification problem using a unified labeled dataset.

RQ1: Are random models effective in the commit classification task?

RQ2: Can we improve the effectiveness of random models for the commit classification task by using natural language processing?

3.2 Study Phases

To answer RQ1 and RQ2, we designed and conducted an empirical study composed of four phases. These phases aim to achieve the final goal of proposing and evaluating a model based on the Natural Language Processing (NLP) to classify commit activities. The phases are described as follows.

Phase 1 Literature Review - An ad-hoc literature review was performed to find related work about software commit classification and identify the state-of-art on labeled datasets, whose features are replicated in this work. Other research projects and tools were analyzed to explore the many possibilities that the software commit classification problem had to offer for our study. At the end of this phase, we were able not only to find important research projects about the subject, but also to set the target in terms of the objective of the study and the datasets used in the experimental phase of this research.

Phase 2 Collecting Data from Labeled Datasets - During the literature review, a search was conducted to find labeled datasets publicly available on the internet for researches to freely test and explore new approaches for software commit classification. We aim to test these datasets against a Natural Language Processing (NLP) algorithm in order to investigate its effectiveness for the target problem. This phase was also responsible for joining the many different datasets into one unified dataset to be used in the experimentation phase.

Phase 3 Experiments with the Baseline Models - In this phase, the experiments and their respective analyses were performed in terms of the selected baseline models. Then, for each algorithm, a cross-validation method was used to test the models [12]. The training dataset was evaluated using repeated 5-fold cross-validation with 5 repetitions, i.e., the 5-fold cross-validation was performed 5 times and the average F-measure metric was reported. Note that the test dataset did not take part in the training process, which provides a more realistic evaluation of the problem. It also prevents the study for overfitting and leading us to incorrect conclusions about the data distribution. All models and their evaluations were implemented in the Python language, with the support of the largely used Scikit-learn package [18]. This phase aims to answer our first research question (RQ1).

Phase 4 Experiments with a new NLP Model - In this last phase, the experiments were performed with a novel NLP model. The average F-measure is reported after a grid search of the hyper-parameters. This phase aimed at comparing results from the proposed NLP model against the baseline models in terms of the target evaluation metric (F-measure). This last phase targets our second research question (RQ2).

To exemplify the experiments described in Phases 3 and 4. Figure 1 illustrates three stages applied to generate the baseline and the NLP model. In Stage 1, we vectorize the words contained in the commit messages using the TF-IDF algorithm. Then, in Stage 2, we tested the performance of five baseline models to classify software commits. Finally, in the last stage, we build a new NLP model based on the fastText algorithm [1] to classify software commit expecting better results than the baseline models and the current literature.

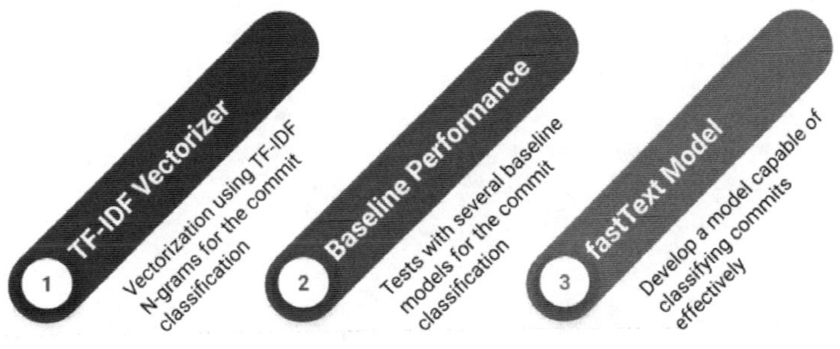

Fig. 1. Phases to create the NLP model to classify software commits.

3.3 Dataset

The dataset collection was gathered from three different sources. These sources are publicly available on the Web under their respective publications [14, 16, 21]. All the provided data were properly labeled using the expertise of experienced developers [14, 16, 21]. Furthermore, the respective authors asked the developers to label their own commits in order to avoid imprecise labels. In total, 5,631 commits were manually classified and unified in our final dataset. The commits are classified following the maintenance activities [14] and the respective authors have applied other methods, such as classifying the similar commits [9].

In order to keep a common version between the datasets and maintaining the nature of the changes, we opted for relabeling the "adaptive" label as "features" since the literature do not agree in this category [9, 14]. Then, the labels we used are "corrective", "features", "non functional", "perfective", and "unknown". Note that even though two of the datasets followed the same classification we used [9], they also classify commits in terms of "merge" and "preventive" labels. Ignoring these classifications, such as "merge" label [11], is common in the literature. In fact, Version Control Systems (VCS) often provide automatic commit messages for merges, such as "merge commits X and Y", which makes their classification pointless.

Figure 2 shows the distribution of labels in the final dataset. The classes (i.e., labels) are imbalanced in the unified dataset. The "corrective" label is significantly more common than the remaining labels. Nevertheless, the "unknown" label has the lowest rate compared to the other classes. The imbalanced classes are not necessarily a problem for this study as it is discussed in the following sections. Evaluating the F-measure and the correct application of the cross-validation process is enough to deal with the imbalanced data [4].

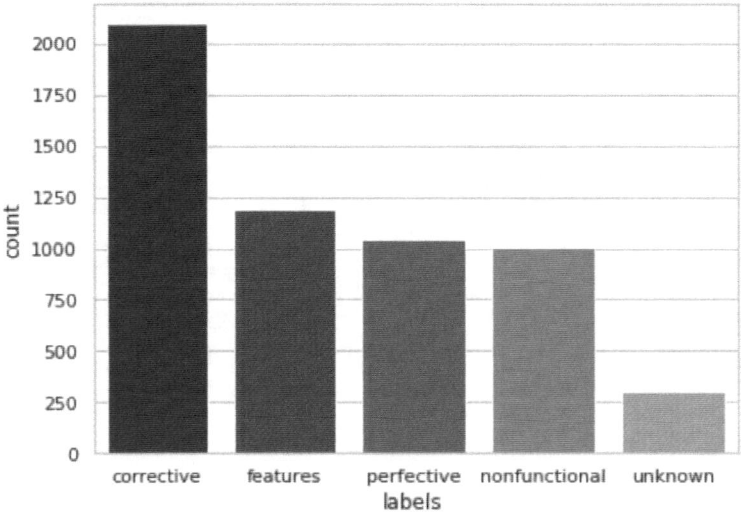

Fig. 2. Distribution of labels x commit messages.

3.4 Baseline and Measures

We considered five machine learning algorithms that are often used for text classification prediction to provide baseline for the comparison [14, 21]: Random Forest (RF), Linear SVC, Multinomial Naive Bayes (NB), Logistic Regression (LR) and Decision Tree (CART). We then evaluate the effectiveness of the considered models using standard F-measure [4].

F-measure is highly necessary for the commit classification problem because, as observed in Figure 2, the labels are not equally distributed in the dataset. In other words, the dataset is fundamentally imbalanced and, then, considering only the accuracy would give imprecise conclusions about the models. F-measure, however, is defined as the weighted harmonic mean of the precision and recall of the test. Therefore, it considers both precision and recall in its fundamental calculation.

4 Results and Discussion

This section presents our results and discusses the main findings of this study, by answering our two research questions (RQ1 and RQ2).

4.1 Random Models for Commit Classification

The first study we conducted is devoted to answering research question RQ1: "Are random models effective in the commit classification task?". To answer this question, we first create a word vector to represent the sentences in the commit message. The commit message is represented as a string when we access the raw dataset. The word vector representation is responsible for creating the matrix that serves as input for the baseline models. To create the word representation, we opt for the technique known as Term Frequency - Inverse Document Frequency (TF-IDF) [19, 24]. This method calculates values for each word in a document through an inverse proportion of the frequency of the word in a particular document to the percentage of documents the word appears in. For this reason, words with high TF-IDF numbers imply a strong relationship with the document they appear in, suggesting that if a word appears in the query, the document could be of interest to the user. This technique seemed to be a reasonable option to generate the word vectors as discussed in the literature [19, 24].

TF-IDF algorithm can output the N-gram relationship between the words in the corpus. For instance, if the commit message is "my code has a bug", the unigram (or 1-gram where N=1) is "my", "code", "has', "a", "bug". On the other hand, the bigram (or 2-gram where N=2) outputs the following result for the same sentence: "my code", "code has", "has a', "a bug" [19]. Table 1 shows the most frequent unigram and bigram outputted by TF-IDF based on the dataset described in Section 3.3. The results generated by TF-IDF unigrams and bigrams are used for all baseline models of this research. As an example in Table 1, the TF-IDF algorithm found out that the most correlated words to the "corrective" label are "bug" and "fix" for the unigram and "new ui" and "fix bug" for the bigrams. The same structure is followed to output the most correlated words for the remaining labels. The algorithm seemed to find good relationships between the labels and the words. Therefore, the TF-IDF vectors were used as input for the machine learning algorithms.

After generating the word vector representation of the commit messages, we applied random models to test their effectiveness in classifying commits. As explained in Section 3.4, we choose five ML algorithms for this task: Random Forest, Linear SVC, Multinomial Naive Bayes, Logistic Regression (LR) and Decision Tree (CART) [16, 14]. To select a metric to evaluate effectiveness of models

Table 1. Most related 2 words Unigrams and Bigrams.

Label	Unigram	Bigram
Corrrective	bug	new ui
	fix	fix bug
Features	features	new features
	feature	add support
Perfective	design	package structure
	structure	structure refactoring
Non-Functional	improve	improve performance
	performance	improved performance
Unknown	duplicated	duplicate code
	duplicate	remove duplicate

for commit classification, we examined several options, such as F-measure, Accuracy, precision, and recall. Not all metrics would deal well with the imbalanced nature of our dataset. Hence, we opted for the F-measure as the standard metric, as it is the harmonic mean of both precision and recall. Thus, the recall and precision are represented under the F-measure values.

Figure 3 shows F-measure numbers for the five baseline models in the commit dataset. Four of the baseline algorithms have perform relatively well for the task of commit classification (Linear SVC, Decision Tree, LR and Multinomial NB). Only Random Forest does not perform well for the task. The F-measure values for Random Forest achieved only around 20%. The other four algorithms performed relatively well: Multinomial NB (around 73%), Decision Tree (74%), Linear SVC (around 75%), and LR on average 76%. Since LR achieved the best results among the baseline models, it was selected as a representative model in our next study about the effectiveness of commit classification (Section 4.2). Thus, we can conclude that random models have not achieved a great performance for the commit classification problem, as the best algorithm (LR) achieved 76% of F-measure.

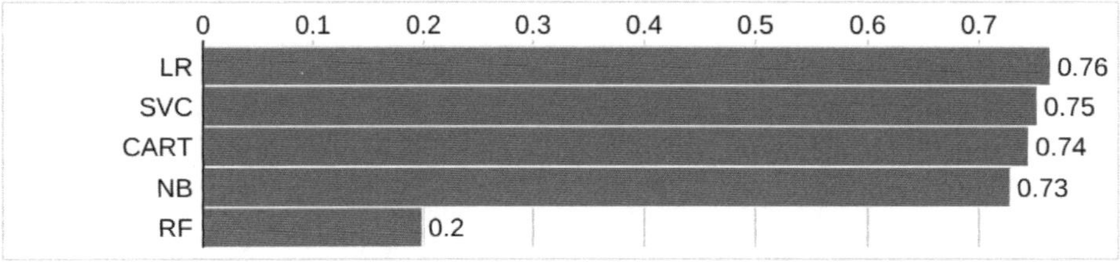

Fig. 3. Baseline ML Models F-measures.

To further support our analysis focusing on LR, we have generated the confusion matrix from the LR execution. Figure 4 exemplifies the errors the LR model has committed. In the left of Figure 4, we have the actual labels from the unified dataset; in the bottom, we represent the predicted label by the LR algorithm. The total commits correctly classified is represented in the diagonal, where the actual and predicted labels for each commit are situated. As we can see, despite most of the labels are classified correctly (as around 76% where correctly classified), there are commits classified wrongly, especially in the "corrective" label (middle column of the figure). It is important to note that the confusion matrix was tested in 20% of the dataset randomly selected from the entire set.

From the findings presented in this section, we may conclude the following answer to RQ1.

> **RQ1**: Random models are reasonably effective for the commit classification task, since the best models achieved a F-measure of around 75%.

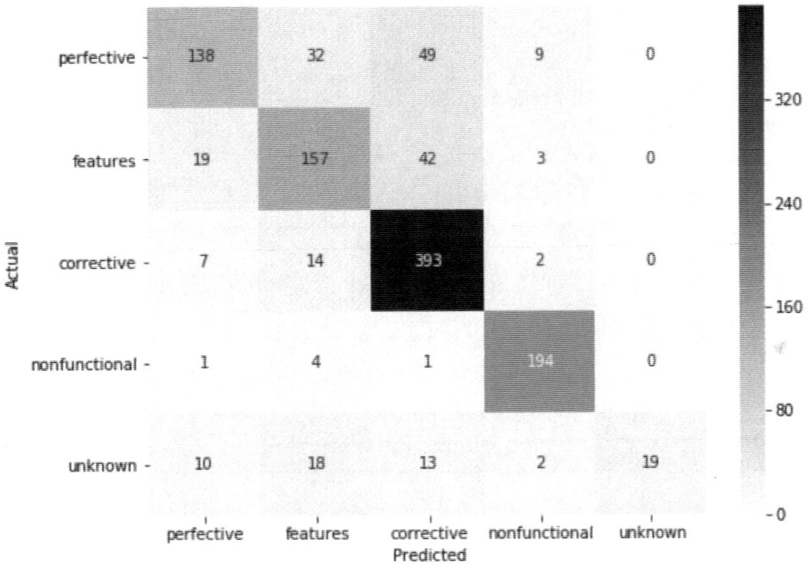

Fig. 4. Confusion Matrix of Actual and Predicted Labels for Logistic Regression.

4.2 Commit Classification using Natural Language Processing

The second experiment is devoted to answering our research question RQ2: "Can we improve the effectiveness of random models for the commit classification task by using natural language processing?". After generating the results shown in the last section, we noticed that Logistic Regression achieved a reasonably acceptable

F-measure for the task of commit classification. However, we also observed an opportunity to improve the results by applying a state-of-the-art NLP algorithm proposed by the Facebook Artificial Intelligence Research [1], named fastText. fastText relies on the skip-gram model, where each word is represented as a bag of character n-grams. Then, the vector representation is associated with each character n-gram, and these words are basically the sum of these representations. It allows the model to compute representations for words that did not appear in the training data. Furthermore, the proponents of fastText also discussed how this approach has made the model execute faster than other algorithms presented in the literature [1]. The fact that fastText algorithm considers words that do not appear on the vocabulary seems important for the commit classification problem because developers are sometimes careless about the commit messages [16]. In other words, it is likely for commit messages to include typos and misspelling words.

Based on this opportunity, we propose the use of fastText to enhance the commit classification task. We evaluated this proposal by replicating our study presented and discussed in Section 4.1 under the same structure and for the same dataset. We have also created a grid search structure for testing the model against different configurations of hyper-parameters. For example, we tested variations of the learning rate and a number of epochs. The best-achieved result is outputted by a learning rate of 0.1 with 25 epochs, where expressively **91%** of F-measure was achieved for the problem of commit classification. We believe the results are high due to fastText nature of dealing well with imbalanced classes [1]. Then, we conclude that fastText was very efficient in the task of commit classification.

Then, we may draw from this experiment the following answer to RQ2.

> **RQ2**: It is possible to more effectively predict software commit by using natural language processing. To do so, we developed a model based on fastText able to achieve 91% of F-measure.

5 Threats to Validity

The study presented in this paper has some limitations that could potentially threaten our results, as we discuss next. The first threat refers to the chosen datasets, the datasets are related to other research projects, and despite they have been labeled for the same purpose of classifying commits into software activities, they do not follow the same fundamental labels. For example, in the maintenance activities dataset, the authors focused on the definition of labels of Levin and Yehudai [14], while in Hindle et al. [9], the authors focused on the definition of commits proposed by the main author. We may not affirm surely in which significance it may interfere in this study results. However, in an ideal circumstance, all the datasets would have the same labels for classification.

Furthermore, we believe the different definitions used by the authors may have impacted in the imbalanced classes of the unified dataset.

Another threat to the validity of our research is related to the features adopted to predict the output using the fastText model. The datasets found in the literature have not considered, for instance, the "preventive" and "merge" labels discussed by Hindle et al. [9]. We could not determine in which extend it may interfere in our results either. However, it is certainly true that our model generated using fastText would not be able to classify commits related to the preventive and merge classes properly. Again, there is no consensus of these labels in the literature. For this reason, it is very difficult to confirm the relevance of these labels to any classification model adopted in further research approaches.

6 Conclusion and Future Work

Software commit classification is extremely relevant for software projects as it allows understanding of whole software life cycle and management. The incorrect introduction of faulty commits is shown to consume most of the project budget. Therefore, understanding how these tasks may be classified is useful for practitioners/managers so that they can plan and allocate resources in advance. State-of-art techniques to classify commits are very limited using a few labels to classify the commits.

In this work, we presented an empirical study to investigate the commit classification based on the commit messages. To do so, we applied a natural language processing approach, considering more labels than the current state-of-art literature about this problem. In this paper, the datasets used from other research projects have five categories: features, corrective, perfective, non-functional, and unknown. In order to compare the baseline models with the natural language processing algorithm, we carried out experiments to evaluate effectiveness of both approaches. First, a hyper-parameter grid was evaluated through repeated 5-fold cross-validation analysis for each algorithm. Then, we evaluated the models in a test dataset, which did not take part in the training phase. We achieved 76% of F-measure by Logistic Regression, which was the best performing baseline model. Moreover, the text representation algorithm (i.e., fastText) was able to reach a high F-measure (approximately 91%). F-measure was chosen for this study because the dataset is imbalanced. Thus, this approach was able to outperform the baseline best performing model; i.e., 76% vs. 91% of F-measure.

As future work, we want to apply the model generated by fastText to other datasets from GitHub or similar tools. Also, the fastText model could eventually be improved with more labeled data from other datasets, or with a practical study to manually labeled data from practitioners. This approach would be similar to the one applied in previous work [14, 16], where the researchers have asked developers to classify their own commits. Furthermore, using our own classified dataset, we could adapt the labels to use all the proposed labels from others [9]; e.g., the preventive and merge labels that were not used in the unified datasets of this research paper. Another possible approach would be the application of the fastText model to classify commits from participants in a controlled experiment. Then, these participants could classify their commits manually allowing the comparison between our model with a human classification.

Finally, our model could be tested against Deep Learning approaches in order to further expand the results reported in this paper. For instance, we could apply both CNN (Convolutional Neural Network) and LSTM (Long Short-Term Memory) models to analyze the results reported by fastText. This is certainly an interesting path that we may take in the next step of this research as we progress with the studies about the commit classification task. We are also already working in an approach to predict software health based on the commit classification generated from this work.

Acknowledgements. This research was partially supported by Brazilian funding agencies: CAPES, CNPq (grant 424340/2016-0), and FAPEMIG (grant PPM-00651-17).

References

1. Bojanowski, P., Grave, E., Joulin, A., Mikolov, T.: Enriching word vectors with subword information. TACL **5**, 135–146 (2017)
2. Casalnuovo, C., Suchak, Y., Ray, B., Rubio-González, C.: Gitcproc: A tool for processing and classifying github commits. In: Proc. of the 26th ACM SIGSOFT Int'l Symposium on Software Testing and Analysis (ISSTA). pp. 396–399 (2017)
3. Crandall, D.J., Backstrom, L., Huttenlocher, D., Kleinberg, J.: Mapping the world's photos. In: Proceedings of the 18th International Conference on World Wide Web (WWW). pp. 761–770 (2009)
4. Davis, J., Goadrich, M.: The relationship between precision-recall and roc curves. In: Proceedings of the 23rd International Conference on Machine Learning. pp. 233–240. ICML '06, ACM, New York, NY, USA (2006). https://doi.org/10.1145/1143844.1143874
5. Fluri, B., Wuersch, M., PInzger, M., Gall, H.: Change distilling:tree differencing for fine-grained source code change extraction. IEEE Transactions on Software Engineering **33**(11), 725–743 (Nov 2007). https://doi.org/10.1109/TSE.2007.70731
6. Golder, S.A., Huberman, B.A.: Usage patterns of collaborative tagging systems. J. Inf. Sci. **32**(2), 198–208 (Apr 2006). https://doi.org/10.1177/0165551506062337
7. Hattori, L.P., Lanza, M.: On the nature of commits. In: Proceedings of the 23rd IEEE/ACM International Conference on Automated Software Engineering. pp. III–63–III–71. ASE'08, IEEE Press, Piscataway, NJ, USA (2008). https://doi.org/10.1109/ASEW.2008.4686322
8. Hindle, A., German, D.M., Godfrey, M.W., Holt, R.C.: Automatic classification of large changes into maintenance categories. In: 2009 IEEE 17th International Conference on Program Comprehension. pp. 30–39 (May 2009)
9. Hindle, A., German, D.M., Holt, R.: What do large commits tell us?: A taxonomical study of large commits. In: Proceedings of the 2008 International Working Conference on Mining Software Repositories. pp. 99–108. MSR '08, ACM, New York, NY, USA (2008)
10. Izquierdo, J.L.C., Cosentino, V., Rolandi, B., Bergel, A., Cabot, J.: Gila: Github label analyzer. In: 2015 IEEE 22nd International Conference on Software Analysis, Evolution, and Reengineering (SANER). pp. 479–483 (March 2015)

11. Jiang, S., McMillan, C.: Towards automatic generation of short summaries of commits. In: 2017 IEEE/ACM 25th International Conference on Program Comprehension (ICPC). pp. 320–323 (May 2017). https://doi.org/10.1109/ICPC.2017.12
12. Kohavi, R.: A study of cross-validation and bootstrap for accuracy estimation and model selection. In: Proceedings of the 14th International Joint Conference on Artificial Intelligence - Volume 2. pp. 1137–1143. IJCAI'95, Morgan Kaufmann Publishers Inc., San Francisco, CA, USA (1995)
13. Levin, S., Yehudai, A.: Using temporal and semantic developer-level information to predict maintenance activity profiles. In: 2016 IEEE International Conference on Software Maintenance and Evolution (ICSME). pp. 463–467 (Oct 2016). https://doi.org/10.1109/ICSME.2016.21
14. Levin, S., Yehudai, A.: Boosting automatic commit classification into maintenance activities by utilizing source code changes. In: Proceedings of the 13th International Conference on Predictive Models and Data Analytics in Software Engineering. pp. 97–106. PROMISE, ACM, New York, NY, USA (2017). https://doi.org/10.1145/3127005.3127016
15. Lientz, B.P., Swanson, E.B., Tompkins, G.E.: Characteristics of application software maintenance. Commun. ACM **21**(6), 466–471 (Jun 1978). https://doi.org/10.1145/359511.359522
16. Mauczka, A., Brosch, F., Schanes, C., Grechenig, T.: Dataset of developer-labeled commit messages. In: 2015 IEEE/ACM 12th Working Conference on Mining Software Repositories. pp. 490–493 (May 2015). https://doi.org/10.1109/MSR.2015.71
17. Mockus, A., Votta, L.G.: Identifying reasons for software changes using historic databases. In: Proceedings of the International Conference on Software Maintenance (ICSM'00). pp. 120–. ICSM '00, IEEE Computer Society, Washington, DC, USA (2000)
18. Pedregosa, F., Varoquaux, G., Gramfort, A., Michel, V., Thirion, B., Grisel, O., Blondel, M., Prettenhofer, P., Weiss, R., Dubourg, V., Vanderplas, J., Passos, A., Cournapeau, D., Brucher, M., Perrot, M., Duchesnay, E.: Scikit-learn: Machine learning in python. J. Mach. Learn. Res. **12**, 2825–2830 (Nov 2011)
19. Ramos, J.: Using tf-idf to determine word relevance in document queries (1999)
20. Rosen, C., Grawi, B., Shihab, E.: Commit guru: Analytics and risk prediction of software commits. In: Proceedings of the 2015 10th Joint Meeting on Foundations of Software Engineering. pp. 966–969. ESEC/FSE 2015, ACM, New York, NY, USA (2015). https://doi.org/10.1145/2786805.2803183
21. Safdari, N.: Project title. https://github.com/nxs5899/Multi-Class-Text-Classification—-Random-Forest (2018)
22. Śliwerski, J., Zimmermann, T., Zeller, A.: When do changes induce fixes? In: Proceedings of the 2005 International Workshop on Mining Software Repositories. pp. 1–5. MSR '05, ACM, New York, NY, USA (2005). https://doi.org/10.1145/1082983.1083147
23. Viggiato, M., Oliveira, J., Figueiredo, E., Jamshidi, P., Kastner, C.: How do code changes evolve in different platforms? a mining-based investigation. In: 35th IEEE International Conference on Software Maintenance and Evolution (ICSME). pp. 218–222 (2019)
24. Wu, H.C., Luk, R.W.P., Wong, K.F., Kwok, K.L.: Interpreting tf-idf term weights as making relevance decisions. ACM Trans. Inf. Syst. **26**(3), 13:1–13:37 (Jun 2008). https://doi.org/10.1145/1361684.1361686

STONE: A Software Configuration Management Process for Academic Projects

Rebeca M. Pontes[1] and Valéria Lelli[2]

[1] Universidade Federal do Ceará (UFC), Campus Russas, Russas, Brasil
rebeca.maia@alu.ufc.br
[2] Universidade Federal do Ceará (UFC), Fortaleza, Brasil
Grupo de Redes de Computadores, Engenharia de Software e Sistemas (GREat)
valerialelli@ufc.br

Abstract. The Software Configuration Management (SCM) is essential to control the changes that occur within a project. Although its application has many benefits, its use isn't encouraged in projects developed by students during their undergraduate course. With a lack of a SCM process that meets the student's needs, their projects do not follow rules to incorporate changes and their artifacts could become inconsistent. In this context, this paper proposes the STONE process for SCM of academic projects. To define the process, a survey was conducted with 67 undergraduate students from the Computer Science course and related areas, through a questionnaire to identify how students dealt with SCM within the projects in which they have participated. The process was applied to an undergraduate class, where the process flow of activities was exemplified using a game. The results showed that the process helped students to manage the changes in their academic projects and the templates provided to generate the process artifacts were essentials to facilitate the execution of the process.

Keywords: Configuration Management, Academic Projects, Software Process.

1 Introdução

A Gerência de Configuração de Software (GCS) desempenha um papel fundamental no processo de desenvolvimento, pois ela se preocupa em realizar todas as atividades que envolvem o controle de mudanças que ocorrem dentro de um projeto de software. Na GCS mantém-se não somente o artefato, mas o que foi modificado, quando e como foi modificado, quem modificou, quanto tempo levou a modificação, qual o impacto da mudança, dentre outras informações [13].

O ensino de Engenharia de Software (ES) e de cursos de áreas afins da Computação estabelece que os alunos devem ter alguma experiência prática nas disciplinas que cursam. Para que os alunos adquiram essa experiência, eles geralmente desenvolvem sistemas ao longo das disciplinas do curso com o intuito de consolidar o conhecimento acerca de determinado tópico [1]. Nesses projetos, à medida que os artefatos de software são desenvolvidos, mudanças naturalmente ocorrem seja pelo amadurecimento do conhecimento do aluno ou por solicitação do professor/tutor. O uso de GCS nesses projetos é feito de maneira bem informal e limitada, pois quando a disciplina de GCS faz parte da matriz curricular do curso, ela é optativa e/ou ofertada nos semestres mais avançados do curso. Dessa forma, quando aquelas mudanças que ocorrem não são gerenciadas corretamente pelos alunos, acarretando em vários problemas, por exemplo, os artefatos são entregues fora do prazo estabelecido pelo professor ou não atendem os requisitos ou falta consistência entre eles. Esses problemas evidenciam a dificuldade dos alunos em lidar com a capacidade de mutabilidade inerente a todos os projetos de desenvolvimento de software, uma característica essencial entre os profissionais da área de Tecnologia da Informação.

Para lidar com os problemas mencionados, alguns estudos de GCS com foco em projetos acadêmicos [2][5][12][16] se preocupam apenas com a fase de codificação e controle de versão do código, negligenciando as outras atividades desenvolvidas pelos alunos, como a documentação dos requisitos do sistema, a modelagem do projeto como a elaboração de diagramas, dentre outras.

Até o presente momento, não foram identificados na literatura estudos que abordassem as principais atividades de GCS - como 'Identificação dos Itens de Configuração', 'Planejamento da Configuração', 'Controle de Mudança' - para auxiliar sua aderência nos projetos desenvolvidos pelos alunos durante seu período na universidade. Portanto, o objetivo deste trabalho é propor um processo de GCS voltado especificamente para projetos acadêmicos com o intuito de auxiliar os alunos a gerenciar as mudanças dos artefatos produzidos nas disciplinas, podendo utilizá-lo nos semestres iniciais do curso, além de familiarizá-los com as técnicas e procedimentos de GCS.

Este trabalho está organizado da seguinte forma: na Seção 2, os principais conceitos abordados na pesquisa são apresentados. Na Seção 3 é apresentada a metodologia utilizada para a definição do processo proposto. Na Seção 4, os resultados do questionário são apresentados. Na Seção 5 é feita a descrição do processo de GCS proposto. Na Seção 6 é apresentado os resultados da aplicação do processo STONE. Na Seção 7 é descrito alguns dos trabalhos relacionados e, por fim, na Seção 8, são apresentadas as considerações finais deste trabalho.

2 Fundamentação Teórica

A GCS é uma subárea da Engenharia de Software que se refere ao processo pelo qual todos os artefatos relevantes para o projeto e os seus relacionamentos são armazenados, recuperados, identificados exclusivamente e modificados [7]. Cada artefato que precisa ser mantido sob o controle de mudanças é denominado um item de configuração (IC) [13]. Dessa forma, conforme os itens de configuração são produzidos, é necessário mantê-los em um repositório. O repositório é uma coleção de todos o os artefatos de software pertencentes a um sistema e a localização/formato na qual tal coleção é armazenada [10]. O propósito deste armazenamento é garantir que o IC não desaparecerá ou será danificado, de maneira que este possa ser encontrado a qualquer momento e entregue nas condições que se deseja encontrar.

A cada alteração que um IC for submetido, é preciso criar uma nova versão para este IC. A versão de um item de software é uma instância identificada de um item.

Pode ser visto como o estado de um item em evolução [8]. Comumente, um projeto de software possui inúmeros ICs e cada um desses precisam ter suas versões controladas.

Uma das tarefas que compõem a elaboração do PGC, é a definição da baseline. No contexto de ES, definimos uma baseline como um conjunto de itens de configuração que devem ser entregues em um determinado momento do projeto.

Quando um IC é liberado ao cliente, ele passa a ser denominado de *release*. Segundo a ISO/IEC 24765 [10], um *release* "é uma versão entregável de uma aplicação que pode incluir toda ou parte de uma aplicação, uma coleção de ICs novos e/ou alterados que foram testados e introduzidos em um ambiente". Dependendo do projeto, essas entregas podem ser feitas feitas incrementalmente. Quando um ou mais ICs são entregues pode-se definir um *baseline* como um marco de referência do desenvolvimento do software.

Todas as atividades de gerenciamento de configuração são guiadas pelo Plano de GCS que é um documento que descreve a abordagem de GCS usada bem como os procedimentos, políticas, responsabilidades, dentre outros.

3 Metodologia

Para a concepção do processo, inicialmente foi feita uma pesquisa bibliográfica para identificar os trabalhos existentes na literatura da área de GCS. Para essa pesquisa foi definida a seguinte string de busca:

(("configuration management" OR "change management" OR "version control" OR "versioning management" OR "version management" OR "code version" OR "release management") AND (process OR approach OR method OR technique OR tool OR pattern) AND ("small project" OR "student project" OR capstone OR short OR academic OR academia) AND ("software development" OR "application development" OR "system development"))

Vale ressaltar que para essa pesquisa não foi feito um mapeamento ou revisão sistemática. Dessa forma, a string de busca foi aplicada apenas em duas bases acadêmicas: ACM e IEEE. Para filtrar os artigos relevantes ao tema, foi feita a leitura dos seus resumos, e aqueles mais relacionados ao tema foram lidos por completo e catalogados através de um fichamento. Esse fichamento registrou o objetivo de cada trabalho e quais informações importantes poderiam ser incorporadas no processo. Na base da IEEE, 307 artigos foram retornados, dos quais 14 foram selecionados. Na ACM, 133 estudos foram extraídos, sendo que 11 foram selecionados, totalizando 25 artigos para esta pesquisa.

Em paralelo, também foi conduzido um estudo dos processos propostos por modelos de qualidade e normas técnicas que tratam GCS, tais como o SWEBOK [8], o Guia de Implementação do MPS-BR [15] e as normas técnicas IEEE 1042 [9] e ISO 10007 [3].

A partir dos dados levantados da pesquisa da literatura e do estudo dos modelos de qualidade, foi proposta a primeira versão do processo de GCS. Em seguida, foi realizada uma pesquisa de opinião através de um questionário para identificar as necessidades dos alunos em relação a GCS em projetos acadêmicos. Com base nos resultados obtidos, foram definidos templates para facilitar a elaboração dos artefatos de GCS. Além disso, um jogo foi criado para que os alunos pudessem compreender melhor os conceitos de GCS e as atividades do processo previamente definido.

O processo foi utilizado em uma disciplina de graduação e seu uso foi avaliado através de um questionário aplicado aos alunos e dos artefatos de GCS que eles produziram. Também foram avaliadas duas ferramentas para o "Controle de Mudanças" sugeridas no processo.

4 Questionário

A pesquisa foi realizada através da aplicação de um questionário online[1] em turmas do curso de Computação e cursos afins da Universidade Federal do Ceará (UFC), obtendo-se um total de 67 participantes. O objetivo do questionário é identificar como os alunos lidavam com a GCS dentro dos projetos em que eles participavam, bem como ressaltar as necessidades que os alunos tinham em relação a GCS.

Sobre o perfil dos alunos, 34 são do curso de Engenharia de Software (ES), seguido pelos cursos de Ciência da Computação (CC) (24), Engenharia da Computação (EngComp) (8) e Sistemas e Mídias Digitais (SMD) (1). A maioria dos alunos (61) já cursaram mais da metade do curso.

Em relação ao conhecimento de GCS, 66 alunos afirmaram que já cursaram uma ou mais disciplinas que introduziram conceitos de GCS. Conforme é ilustrado na Fig. 1, a mais citadas forma Engenharia de Software (32 alunos), Processos de Software (27 alunos) e Qualidade de Software (24 alunos) para os alunos do curso de ES, e a disciplina de Engenharia de Software para os participantes do curso de CC, EngComp e SMD com 25, 7 e 1 respondentes, respectivamente. Na matriz curricular desses cursos, observa-se que essas disciplinas são ofertadas a partir do 5º semestre. Porém, teve 1 aluno do CC que apesar de estar no 6º semestre respondeu que não tinha cursado nenhuma disciplina que abordasse GCS.

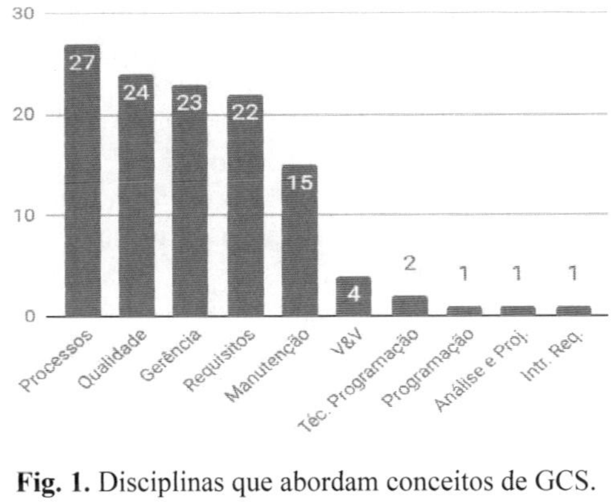

Fig. 1. Disciplinas que abordam conceitos de GCS.

[1] https://forms.gle/yN6DvCsZR5YX1XDK6

Dentre os produtos de trabalho mais produzidos pelos participantes nas disciplinas são: documento de requisitos (52 alunos), cronograma de atividades de projeto (42 alunos), descrição dos papéis e responsabilidades da equipe (41 alunos), código-fonte (34 alunos), plano arquitetural (21 alunos) e plano de teste (4 alunos). Outros artefatos como Termo de Abertura do Projeto (2 alunos), Plano de Projeto (2 alunos) e Relatório de Viabilidade (1 aluno) são produzidos em menor escala. Embora alguns dos produtos de trabalho mencionados, como o cronograma de atividades e a descrição das responsabilidades da equipe, não sejam comumente elaborados separadamente de outros artefatos de ES, observa-se que os alunos costumam elaborá-los para planejar a execução das atividades de seus projetos. Também, observou-se que a maioria desses produtos são entregues ao professor pelos alunos de forma incremental (42), enquanto em outros projetos de disciplinas é realizada apenas uma entrega (25 alunos). Vale ressaltar que nas entregas incrementais a quantidade de artefatos produzidos e entregues tendem a ser maior, o que implica em mais releases, mais relatórios de solicitação de mudança, mais alterações no Plano de Gerência de Configuração, dentre outros. Por outro lado, quando o projeto se baseia em uma única entrega, os alunos costumam fazer as atividades de GCS só no final do projeto, como versionamento e armazenamento dos artefatos.

No que diz respeito ao controle de mudanças, 44 alunos apontaram que a "Política de controle de versões" é essencial para ajudar no controle de mudanças dos artefatos produzidos nas disciplinas, seguido pela "Definição de ferramentas para controle de mudanças" (32), pela "Descrição das solicitações de mudança" (23), pelos "Metadados dos artefatos produzidos" (16) e, pela "Distinção da urgência da mudança" (9). Embora a maioria tenha mencionado a política de controle de versões como principal informação para a aplicação da GCS, a frequência com que eles realizam as atividades de controle de versão ainda deixa a desejar. Embora 32 alunos façam corretamente o controle de versão, *i.e.*, a cada alteração feita no artefato, 18 alunos apenas fazem o controle nas versões entregue ao professor, 7 alunos fazem o controle a cada marco no projeto, 7 não fazem controle de versão, 1 faz versionamento somente em código-fonte e 1 faz controle de versão de acordo com o decorrer do desenvolvimento. Isso indica que a maioria (34) dos alunos têm negligenciado essa atividade fundamental para o processo de GCS, ocasionando problemas na manutenção das versões corretas dos artefatos.

Uma das perguntas aborda sobre quem geralmente valida as alterações nos artefatos, e grande parte (50) são os próprios alunos, membros de equipe, sendo que o restante (17 alunos) respondeu que quem valida é o próprio professor. Esse resultado aponta que os alunos fazem várias alterações antes de entregar o artefato requerido ao professor. Nesse caso, é importante que os alunos saibam gerenciar as alterações para que não ocasione inconsistências nos artefatos.

No que diz respeito ao planejamento das atividades, 53 alunos realizam um planejamento prévio, enquanto o restante (14 alunos) não realiza. Dentre as ferramentas mencionadas, a mais utilizada é o Trello (42) e o Kanban (5) conforme ilustra a Fig. 2. Por outro lado, em relação à ferramenta de controle de versão 51 alunos responderam que utilizam o Git, e apenas um utiliza o mecanismo do Google Drive para manter as versões dos artefatos (e.g., histórico de versões do Google Docs). 15 alunos responderam que não utilizam nenhuma ferramenta para planejamento das atividades e, similarmente, 15 não utilizam ferramentas para o controle de versões.

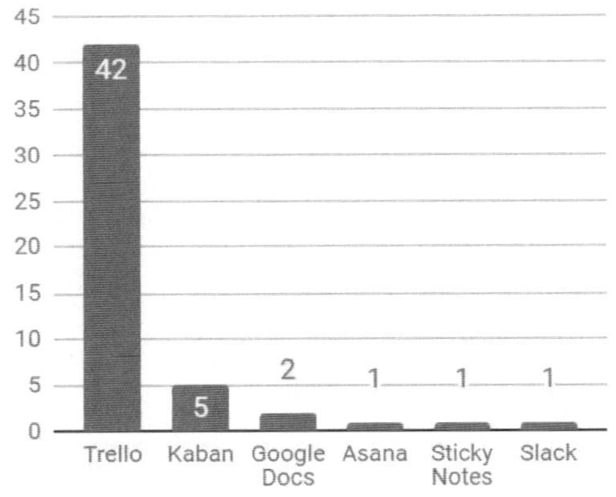

Fig. 2. Ferramentas utilizadas no Planejamento.

Sobre o histórico de alterações, 38 alunos costumam utilizar dentro dos seus documentos (e.g., histórico de revisões), mas o restante (29 alunos) não utiliza. Dos 38 alunos que usam o histórico de alterações, 35 apontam que é essencial incluir quem alterou o artefato, seguida pela data de modificação (35 alunos), o que foi alterado (32 alunos), o motivo da mudança (23 alunos) e o número da versão (21 alunos). O histórico de alterações é útil principalmente para o aluno que não utiliza nenhuma ferramenta para controle de versões e tem o propósito de apontar o que mudou no artefato, quem mudou, a data da modificação e a última versão do artefato.

Em relação ao problemas enfrentados pelos alunos devido à inconsistência entre os artefatos e suas versões, as causas mais apontadas foram: falta de manutenção no histórico de versões (17); alteração de artefato sem o conhecimento da equipe (11); não utilização de ferramentas para controle de mudanças (9); não utilização de um repositório para manter os artefatos (8); entrega de uma versão incorreta de artefato (7); e perda de versões de artefato (3 alunos). Para solucionar os problemas mencionados 30 alunos corrigiram a inconsistência manualmente, 3 alunos optaram por ignorar o problema e 2 fizeram uso de uma ferramenta para corrigir a inconsistência.

Sobre o uso de repositórios para manter os artefatos produzidos, 61 alunos afirmam que utilizam, mas 6 não utilizam. Conforme ilustra a Fig. 3, 45 utilizam o repositório do Google Drive. Outras ferramentas apontadas foram o Github (35), que é voltado para código-fonte, Dropbox (9), Bitbucket (1), Overleaf (1) e Gitlab (1). Dos 6 alunos que não utilizam repositório, todos afirmam que usam o computador pessoal como repositório.

Com o intuito de saber a opinião dos alunos se é melhor delegar a responsabilidade da GCS a uma única pessoa ou à equipe toda, 52 alunos concordaram que é melhor ter um membro do projeto que seja responsável pela aplicação do processo de GCS por motivos de organização. Com uma pessoa coordenando fica mais fácil de executar as atividades previstas. Porém, 11 alunos afirmam que todos da equipe devem ser responsáveis pela execução do processo de GCS e não tem necessidade de apenas uma pessoa assumir toda a responsabilidade.

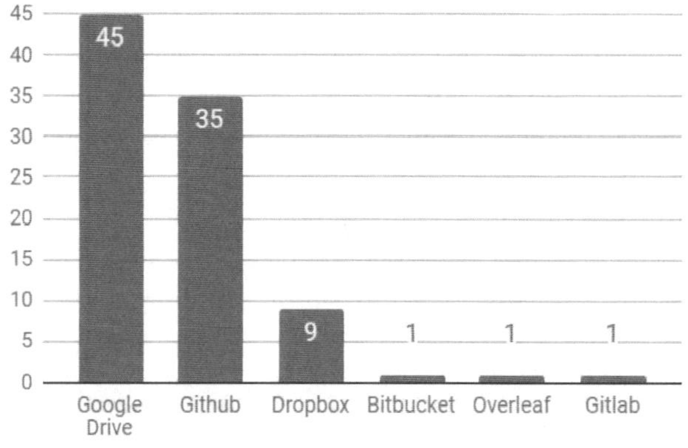

Fig. 3. Repositórios utilizados pelos alunos.

5 Processo STONE

Nesta seção é apresentado o processo STONE (SofTware cOnfiguration maNagemEnt for academic projects) e como este foi definido.

5.1 Concepção do Processo

O processo proposto foi embasado em normas técnicas [3][9], modelos de qualidade [15] e boas práticas de Engenharia de Software [7] que tratam de GCS. A norma técnica IEEE 1042 [9], que fornece orientação às práticas de planejamento de GCS, serviu como base para a definição das fases do processo STONE. Por outro lado, a norma ISO 10007 [3] que provê diretrizes de GCS com o intuito de prover visibilidade e controle das características funcionais do produto de software serviu para definir algumas atividades do processo. Por exemplo, a atividade "Identificar a Configuração" da fase de "Planejamento" foi adaptada dessa norma para se adequar ao escopo do processo, levando-se em consideração o tamanho, a complexidade e a natureza do trabalho.

O SWEBOK [8] serviu como base para a definição das atividades de planejamento da GCS, pois este guia apresenta uma visão de GCS que se relaciona com Garantia de Qualidade de Software (SQA). No SWEBOK, a fase de "Gerenciamento do processo de GCS" contém a atividade de "Planejamento da GCS", que no processo proposto foi adaptada para a atividade "Elaborar Plano de GCS" da fase de Planejamento.

Para a definição das atividades da fase de "Controle de Mudanças" utilizou-se como base o resultado esperado "Modificações em itens de configuração são controladas" da área de conhecimento de GCS do Guia de Implementação do MPS-BR [15]. Já as atividades das fases de "Controle de Versão" e "Gerenciamento de *Releases*" do processo STONE se baseiam em atividades propostas pelo modelo de processo Rugby, proposto por Krusche et al. [11].

Além das normas e modelos supracitados, algumas atividades foram definidas para se adequar ao processo, tais como "Preparar o Ambiente de Configuração" e "Armazenar itens de configuração produzidos".

5.2 Descrição das atividades do Processo STONE

O processo, ilustrado na Fig. 4, é dividido em 4 fases: Planejamento; Controle de Mudanças; Controle de Versão; e Gerenciamento de Releases. Para cada fase foi definido um conjunto de atividades, que por sua vez, possui tarefas a serem realizadas. As atividades têm como saída um novo artefato ou a atualização de um artefato já produzido anteriormente em alguma atividade. Na Figura 4 é apresentada uma visão geral do processo com as suas atividades organizadas de acordo com as fases, o fluxo dessas atividades e os seus artefatos de entrada e saída.

A fase inicial do processo STONE é o "Planejamento". Nessa fase os artefatos do projeto que devem ficar sob o controle de mudanças são identificados e são definidas atividades para elaboração do Plano de Gerência de Configuração (PGC), o principal artefato do processo. As seguintes atividades fazem parte dessa fase:

1. Identificar a configuração: os itens de configuração (ICs) são selecionados e documentados. À medida que novos artefatos são produzidos durante o projeto, é necessário atualizar o PGC.
2. Preparar ambiente de configuração: é definido o ambiente de configuração necessário para a implementação do processo de acordo com os ICs identificados no PGC.
3. Elaborar Plano de Gerência de Configuração: o plano contém a descrição dos papéis e responsabilidades dos membros do projeto, as ferramentas selecionadas para apoiar a execução do processo, a rastreabilidade entre os ICs e a definição dos marcos do projeto.

Na fase de "Controle de Mudanças", os ICs que sofrerem alterações passarão por uma sequência de atividades a fim de controlar as mudanças e manter a consistência entre os demais artefatos do projeto. Ao contrário das outras fases, esta poderá ser iniciada a qualquer momento durante o projeto desde que as atividades da fase de Planejamento tenham sido executadas. As atividades dessa fase são:

1. Solicitar mudança: para cada IC que precisa de alteração, deve ser feito o registro da solicitação através do formulário de solicitação de mudança.
2. Analisar impacto da mudança: após o registro da solicitação da mudança ter sido feito e os demais membros da equipe terem sido notificados sobre esta solicitação, é necessário analisar o impacto da mudança nos ICs que serão afetados.
3. Implementar mudança: caso seja aprovada a implementação da mudança, o IC que será alterado é encaminhado a um membro da equipe que tem conhecimentos para implementá-la e deve ser gerado um relatório de mudança.

Na fase de "Controle de Versão", os ICs que foram alterados na fase de "Controle de Mudanças" devem ter suas versões atualizadas e, caso se aplique, estas devem ser validadas para verificar se a mudança no IC foi implementada corretamente. As seguintes atividades fazem parte dessa fase:

1. Versionar item de configuração que sofreu mudança: após alterado, o IC deve ter sua versão atualizada de acordo com as regras definidas no PGC.
2. Validar IC alterado (optativa): após a alteração, pode ser necessário validar o IC. Porém, essa atividade é optativa e para ser executada dependerá do escopo do projeto.

Na fase de "Gerenciamento de Releases" os ICs que tiveram alguma mudança são entregues ao solicitante, no caso, das disciplinas, o professor ou tutor. As seguintes atividades são executadas:

1. Entregar item de configuração: se o IC precisar ser formalmente entregue ao solicitante, este será encaminhado pelo canal de comunicação definido no PGC.
2. Registrar feedback: após o IC ter sido entregue, o feedback do solicitante deverá ser registrado e armazenado. Se necessitar de uma nova alteração, esta deverá ser encaminhada para a fase de "Controle de Mudanças".

Ao final de cada fase, na atividade "Armazenar itens de configuração produzidos", os ICs que são alterados e os artefatos gerados são armazenados. Quando todos os artefatos do projeto são entregues ao professor, e nenhuma alteração é requerida, o processo é finalizado. Os templates dos artefatos de GCS são fornecidos aos alunos, eles foram elaborados a partir de outros trabalhos na literatura [9] [3] e adaptados ao contexto dos projetos acadêmicos.

Para a execução das atividades apresentadas do processo STONE foi definido dois papéis: aluno e professor e/ou tutor. Cada papel corresponde a um papel funcional no projeto. Por exemplo, o professor ou tutor assume o papel funcional de "Cliente", o qual solicita o software a ser desenvolvido e também pode demandar qualquer alteração nos ICs. Por outro lado, as equipes, que são formadas pelos os alunos, podem assumir diferentes papéis funcionais que podem ser engenheiros de requisitos, desenvolvedores, dentre outros. A escolha dos papéis funcionais dependerá do escopo da disciplina do curso que pode ser voltado para o desenvolvimento do software como um todo (e.g., trabalhos da disciplina de ES) ou apenas focado em uma determinada fase do ciclo de vida do software (e.g., trabalhos da disciplina Verificação e Validação de Software). Tanto o aluno quanto o professor podem solicitar mudanças nos itens de configuração desenvolvidos ao longo do projeto.

Para viabilizar a produção e armazenamentos dos itens de configuração e facilitar a comunicação entre os membros do projeto algumas ferramentas são sugeridas no processo. Por exemplo, o editor de planilhas e de textos (e.g., Google Docs e Sheets, Word) podem ser utilizados para elaborar o formulário de solicitação de mudança, o relatório de mudanças, o PGC, dentre outros.

Para armazenar os itens e artefatos de configuração são sugeridos repositórios, tais como Google Drive, DropBox, dentre outros. Para o controle de mudanças e de versões dos ICs são sugeridos softwares como Mantis para o planejamento de atividades e o Git para versionamento de código.

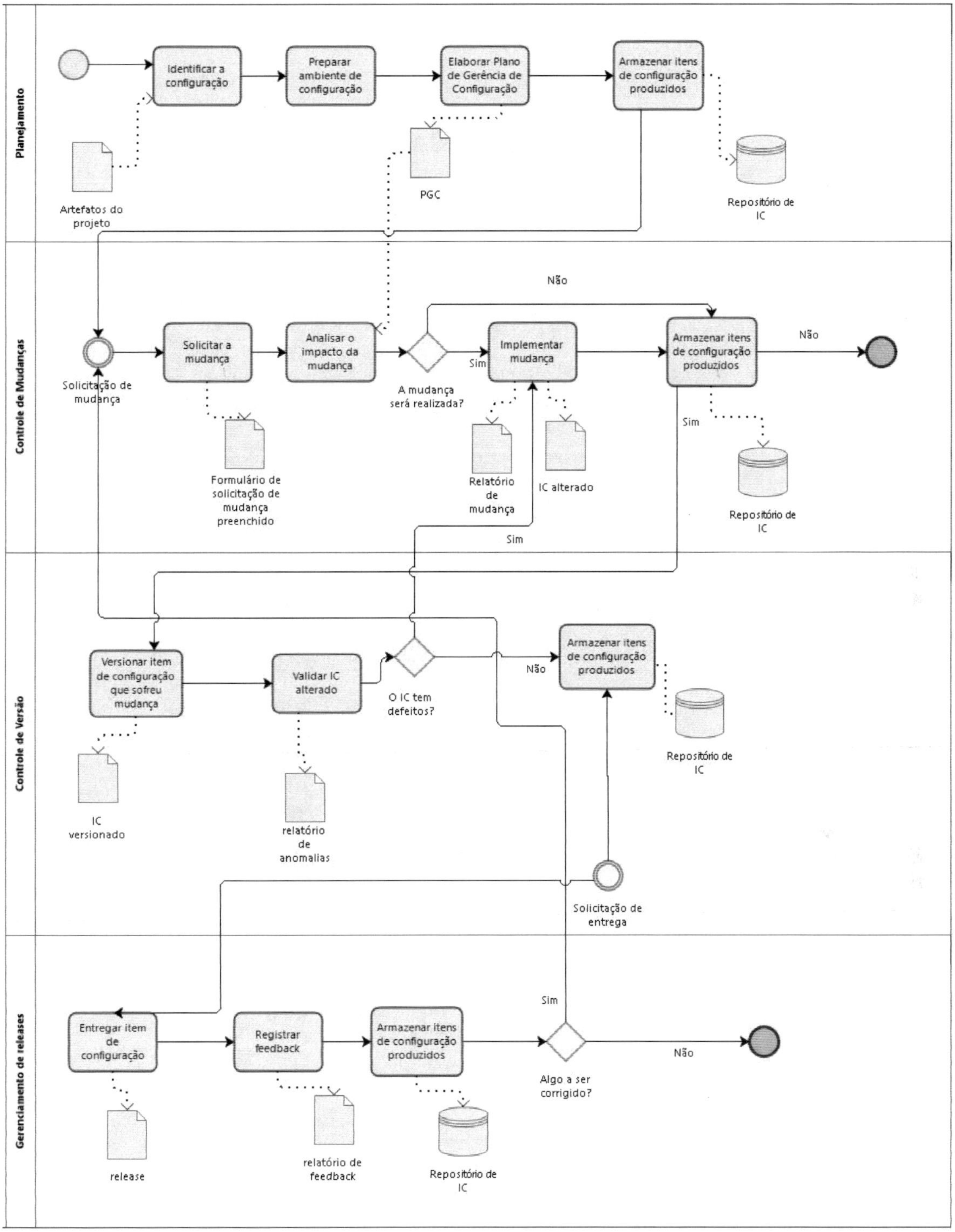

Fig. 4. Processo STONE

6 Aplicação do Processo STONE

Com base nos resultados obtidos no questionário, constatou-se a necessidade de elaborar um jogo de cartas para que os alunos pudessem compreender melhor os conceitos de GCS e as atividades do processo STONE. Dessa forma, o jogo foi aplicado na disciplina optativa de Verificação, Validação e Teste de Software, ofertada para os cursos de CC, EngComp, dentre outros da Universidade Federal do Ceará. A dinâmica do jogo inicialmente consistiu na escolha dos alunos para assumir os papéis do processo STONE. O aluno que assumiu o papel de Gerente de Configuração sorteou uma carta de projeto e a partir dela foram selecionados os artefatos de entrada do processo. O jogo foi dividido pelas fases do processo. Em cada fase um jogador executa as atividades de acordo com o processo, selecionando os artefatos de entrada e saída e as ferramentas necessárias para cada atividade. Ao final da fase de Planejamento, é sorteada uma carta de evento que corresponde a uma solicitação de mudança no projeto. A partir dessa solicitação de mudança, os artefatos de controle de mudanças foram posicionados pelos jogadores, repetindo esse fluxo até a última fase Gerenciamento de Releases. No final do jogo, ganha o jogador que tiver a maior taxa de acerto no posicionamento correto dos artefatos de entrada e saída do processo.

Após o jogo, os alunos, em equipes, utilizaram o processo em artefatos da disciplina que sofreram alterações e, com base nesses artefatos, foram feitas as modificações usando o processo proposto. Os alunos produziram os artefatos iniciais do processo que foram o Plano de GCS, o Formulário de Solicitação de Mudança e o Relatório de Mudanças. Para cada um desses artefatos foram fornecidos templates e guidelines de como utilizá-los.

Para avaliar a utilidade do processo e do jogo os alunos responderam um questionário online. Os alunos apontaram que o processo auxiliou na GCS dos artefatos produzidos e que apesar dos templates fornecidos facilitarem sua execução, necessitavam de melhorias, pois alguns campos ficaram ambíguos, tais como a "necessidade da mudança" e "justificativa de mudança", presentes no "Formulário de Solicitação de Mudança". Os alunos também reportaram que o layout das tabelas fornecido no Formulário e no Relatório de Mudança dificultou a leitura do documento.

Além dos resultados do questionário, os artefatos que os alunos produziram referentes ao processo STONE foram avaliados e alguns problemas foram encontrados. Foram detectadas inconsistências na identificação dos itens de configuração, os alunos tiveram dificuldade de gerar um identificador único para cada versão do artefato. Também foram detectadas múltiplas solicitações de mudança agrupadas como se fossem uma só, o que deveria ser evitado. A recomendação é que cada alteração no artefato deveria ser discriminada em diferentes solicitações de mudança para facilitar a identificação e reparação dos problemas encontrados.

Apesar dos problemas reportados no questionário e na validação dos artefatos de GCS produzidos, observou-se que todos os alunos compreenderam o objetivo dos artefatos para o processo. Também foram apontados pelos alunos como pontos positivos do processo que a elaboração dos artefatos ajudou a manter e controlar as mudanças nos artefatos produzidos durante a disciplina.

À respeito do jogo, os alunos apontaram que a dinâmica foi desafiadora e animada, no entanto, foi um pouco confusa, já que as regras do jogo e os papéis dos jogadores não ficaram muito claros. Também foi mencionado que o jogo despertou o interesse do aprendizado ao processo STONE, pois a explicação do processo somente através da aula expositiva não é tão atrativa. Uma sugestão dos alunos foi a elaboração de um manual para explicar mais detalhadamente a dinâmica do jogo. Outra sugestão foi melhorar sua jogabilidade, já que a execução das etapas não foi tão intuitiva.

A seguir são listadas algumas lições aprendidas em relação ao uso do processo STONE.

LA01: O jogo foi um facilitador para o entendimento do processo, além de estimular o interesse dos alunos nas atividades de GCS. Os alunos mostraram bastante interesse durante o jogo para entender as suas regras e os conceitos de GCS relacionados. Porém, observou-se durante a dinâmica a necessidade de melhorar a jogabilidade e o fornecimento de um manual para que os alunos pudessem entender melhor a dinamicidade do jogo.

LA02: O fornecimento de templates de GCS e exemplos facilitaram a execução das atividades do processo. Contudo, os templates precisam ser refinados, pois a avaliação mostrou que eles não foram claros o suficiente para os alunos e podem ter induzido-os à erros no preenchimento.

LA03: A definição de papéis e a sugestão de recursos/ ferramentas livres foram importantes para o uso do processo. A maioria dos alunos não têm conhecimento das ferramentas de GCS principalmente as que dão apoio às atividades de planejamento. Além disso, a definição de papéis entre os alunos foi essencial para distribuir as atividades de GCS. Por exemplo, um responsável para implementar a mudança e armazenar os IC alterado no repositório, este definido no Plano de GCS. Outro responsável por averiguar se a mudança foi implementada conforme o Formulário de Solicitação de Mudanças.

Em relação às ferramentas sugeridas, foi feita uma avaliação em uma disciplina optativa de "Tópicos Avançados em Engenharia de Software" com 4 alunos das ferramentas Mantis e GitLab. O objetivo era analisar o uso dessas ferramentas nas atividades da fase de "Controle de Mudanças". Inicialmente, foi conduzido um tutorial das ferramentas e foi fornecido um cenário no qual os alunos desempenharam atividades usando ambas as ferramentas. A avaliação do uso das ferramentas foi feita através de um questionário. Os resultados mostraram que os participantes concordaram totalmente (2 alunos) ou parcialmente (2 alunos) que ferramenta GitLab melhorava o desempenho bem como a produtividade das atividades realizadas. Em relação à facilidade e experiência de uso, a maioria dos participantes também apontaram o GitLab em vez do Mantis.

6.1 Ameaças à Validade

Dentre as atividades do processo e a sua aplicação uma limitação diz respeito à definição do processo para atender às necessidades dos alunos no âmbito acadêmico. Para minimizar essa ameaça foi feito um estudo nas normas técnicas e modelos de qualidade que tratavam GCS para que as atividades básicas fossem contempladas no processo, porém, adaptadas aos projetos acadêmicos. Além disso, foi feita uma pesquisa através de um questionário aplicado aos alunos do curso de CC e áreas afins para que as suas necessidades fossem realmente identificadas. Embora, a quantidade de participantes possa não ter sido expressiva (67 alunos), os alunos eram de cursos, de semestres e de campi diferentes da universidade. Outra limitação refere-se à utilização do processo em apenas uma disciplina. Para minimizar essa ameaça, foi selecionada uma turma de graduação de uma disciplina optativa em que os alunos apresentam um maior interesse nas atividades extraclasse. Dessa forma, houve adesão da maioria da turma no uso do processo bem como na elaboração dos artefatos requeridos.

7 Trabalhos Relacionados

Na literatura, diversos trabalhos são propostos para a GCS, e dentre estes foram analisados os trabalhos que apresentavam soluções de GCS em contexto acadêmico [2][4][5][6][12][14][16]. Alguns desses trabalhos são detalhados a seguir.

Conn [4] propõe um processo de Engenharia de Software direcionado para projetos acadêmicos com o intuito de assegurar a qualidade de diferentes artefatos, tais como código, especificações, plano de GCS. Dentre as atividades do projeto, o autor sugere o "Controle de Configuração", na qual o gerente de suporte mantém todos produtos criados ou modificados sob controle de configuração. Porém, o passo a passo para atingir este resultado não é apresentado. Diferente de Conn, este trabalho define atividades de GCS de forma detalhada mostrando o passo a passo para a execução bem com os recursos envolvidos.

Haley et al. [6] propõem a documentação de mudanças em projetos de software acadêmicos através de *wikis* com o intuito de promover uma plataforma de aprendizagem cooperativa entre os participantes. Embora os autores tratem de gerenciamento de mudanças em projetos de software nenhum processo é apresentado.

Ríos et al. [14] definem uma metodologia baseada em plataformas de desenvolvimento colaborativo e sistemas de controle de versão, como o GitLab, para auxiliar os alunos a resolverem tarefas. Diferente dos trabalhos de [4] e [6], os autores dão ênfase em controle de versão e integração contínua aplicados a projetos desenvolvidos na academia, contudo os autores não abordam a GCS nas fases de planejamento e controle de mudanças como é proposto neste artigo.

Outros trabalhos de GCS no âmbito acadêmico [2][5][12][16] dão ênfase no uso de ferramentas (Git) e repositórios (GitHub) para controle de versão de código, não abrangendo as atividades relacionadas ao planejamento e controle de mudanças.

8 Conclusão e Trabalhos Futuros

Neste artigo foi proposto um processo de GCS para auxiliar os alunos em seus projetos acadêmicos. A metodologia consistiu em identificar as necessidades dos alunos em relação à GCS e suas atividades, bem como investigar como a GCS era aplicada pelos alunos em seus projetos acadêmicos. A primeira versão do processo foi definida com base na pesquisa da literatura e na pesquisa (*survey*) realizada com os 67 alunos.

A avaliação do processo foi conduzida em uma turma de graduação do curso de CC, e suas atividades e artefatos foram exemplificados através de um jogo com o intuito de facilitar o entendimento dos alunos à respeito de como utilizar o processo. Após a aplicação do jogo, os alunos utilizaram o processo para modificar as alterações nos seus projetos de disciplina. Os resultados iniciais foram satisfatórios em relação ao uso do jogo, das atividades do processo, dos templates e dos recursos fornecidos. No entanto, os alunos sugeriram melhorias tanto para o processo quanto para o jogo. Como trabalhos futuros, pretende-se aplicar o processo em outras turmas de graduação e, com base nas lições aprendidas, pretende-se refinar o processo e melhorar a dinâmica do jogo para que este possa facilitar a sua aplicação. Além disso, pretende-se automatizar alguns passos do processo para que os alunos possam utilizá-lo de maneira mais eficiente.

Referências

1. Andrade, R. M., Marinho, F. G., Leitão, V. L., & Rocha, L. S. (2008). Uma Proposta de Metodologia para o Ensino de Engenharia de Software. Fórum de Educação em Engenharia de Software (FEES).
2. Arora, R., Goel, S., & Mittal, R. K. (2017, August). Supporting collaborative software development in academic learning environment: A collaborative pair and quadruple programming based approach. In 2017 Tenth International Conference on Contemporary Computing (IC3) (pp. 1-7). IEEE.
3. Comissão de Estudo de Gestão de Configuração. NBR ISO 10007: Gestão da qualidade - Diretrizes para a gestão de configuração. Rio de Janeiro, 1996.
4. Conn, R. (2004, March). A reusable, academic-strength, metrics-based software engineering process for capstone courses and projects. In ACM SIGCSE Bulletin (Vol. 36, No. 1, pp. 492-496). ACM.
5. Feliciano, J., Storey, M. A., & Zagalsky, A. (2016, May). Student experiences using GitHub in software engineering courses: a case study. In Proceedings of the 38th International Conference on Software Engineering Companion (pp. 422-431). ACM.
6. Haley, Elise R.; Collins, Galen B.; Coe, David J. The wonderful world of wiki benefits students and instructors. IEEE Potentials, v. 27, n. 2, 2008.
7. Humble, J., & Farley, D. (2010). Continuous Delivery: Reliable Software Releases through Build, Test, and Deployment Automation (Adobe Reader). Pearson Education.
8. IEEE Computer Society. 2001. Guide to Software Engineering Body of Knowledge (SWEBOK). Los Alamitos: CS Press.
9. IEEE Std. 1042. Guide to Software Configuration Management: An American National Standard. IEEE, 1988.
10. ISO/IEC/IEEE 24765:2009, Systems and Software Engineering–Vocabulary.
11. Krusche, S., Alperowitz, L., Bruegge, B., & Wagner, M. O. (2014). Rugby: an agile process model based on continuous delivery. RCoSE, 14, 42-50.
12. Mäkiaho, P., Poranen, T., & Seppi, A. (2014, June). Version control usage in students' software development projects. In Proceedings of the 15th International Conference on Computer Systems and Technologies (pp. 452-459). ACM.
13. Molinari, L. (2007). Gerência de Configuração-Técnicas e Práticas no Desenvolvimento do Software. Florianópolis: Visual Book.
14. Ríos, Julio César Cortés et al. A methodology for using GitLab for software engineering learning analytics. In: Proceedings of the 12th International Workshop on Cooperative and Human Aspects of Software Engineering. IEEE Press, 2019. p. 3-6.
15. SOFTEX. MR-MPS-SV – Guia de Implementação – Parte 2:2013.
16. Tirkey, A., & Gary, K. A.. Curricular change management with Git and Drupal: A tool to support flexible curricular development workflows. In 2017 IEEE 15th International Conference on Software Engineering Research, Management and Applications (SERA) (pp. 247-253). IEEE.

Software system deployment process: A systematic mapping study

Marisa Panizzi[1,2,3 *], Marcela Genero[4], Rodolfo Bertone[1]

[1] School of Computer Science, Computer Science Research Institute LIDI (III-LIDI), National University of La Plata, La Plata, Argentina
marisapanizzi@outlook.com
pbertone@lidi.info.unlp.edu.ar
[2] Department of Engineering Information Systems, Technological National University at Buenos Aires, Argentina
[3] Institute of Technology and Engineering, National University og Hurlingham, Hurlingham, Argentina
[4] Department of Technologies and Information Systems, University of Castilla-La Mancha, Ciudad Real, Spain
marcela.genero@uclm.es

Abstract. Software system deployment is the process in the software development life cycle during which the software is transferred to the customer. Small and Medium Enterprises (SMEs) need to improve their processes and working methods, but they lack the knowledge and resources to do this. If their deployment process is not carried out properly, then the customer will not accept the software product; the costs and time in the maintenance phase will increase, thus causing the project to fail. We therefore decided to carry out a systematic mapping study in order to analyze the state of the art, aiming to discover whether there are models, methodologies or methods that would serve as a guide for SMEs when they set about deploying software systems, also looking at tools, practices, artifacts and techniques. The search was carried out in Scopus, IEEE Xplore and ACM from 2010 to October 2019. Of the 3,483 papers initially found, 16 primary studies were selected for analysis. 63% of the studies present solutions for the installation activity, of which half are tools that address the automation of these in the quest to reduce time and costs. Only two studies propose models for the deployment process.These models delegate decisions on aspects such as tasks, artefacts, techniques, and practices, to those who apply them; this makes the models more difficult to apply in SMEs This situation shows that it is necessary to have a holistic deployment process providing SMEs a detailed guidance on the phases, activities, tasks, templates and roles for systematizing the deployment of the enterprise software systems.

Keywords: Software processes, Software system deployment process, Systematic mapping study.

1 Introduction

Small and Medium Enterprises (SMEs) make up a large portion of the software industry in many countries around the world [1]. It has also been observed that in

* Corresponding author: Marisa Panizzi

recent years software SMEs have emerged very swiftly, and in most developing economies the sector is dominated by small, young enterprises [2]. These organizations have realized that it is crucial for their business to improve their processes and working methods, but they lack the knowledge and resources to do this. The only way to contribute to the success of projects, therefore, is to define, implement and stabilize the development processes [3]. Deployment is a crucial process of the software development life cycle, in which users frequently report errors while the software system is being deployed [4,5]. Some enterprise software may take months, if not years, to deploy completely, there is an absence of automatized activities, and the execution time for the process is lengthy in this type of enterprises [4]. The above problems present themselves once the deployment is completed, at the same time as the software system is being used, and the issues that arise must thus be resolved in the maintenance phase; this leads to unnecessary effort in terms of economic and human resources [4,5].

At the present time, the most important application of automation in software processes is to support the final phases of software development [6]. Although it is true that there are new techniques/practices such as DevOps [7,8] and Continuous Deployment [9] in the context of agile methodologies, which aim to make deployment more agile and automatised, these techniques are used mainly by large companies, such as Flickr, Netflix, Easy and Amazon, amongst others [6,7] which have both the human resources and the infrastructure to use them successfully. But there are a large number of SMEs which have developed enterprise systems that do not use agile methodologies, and they do not have the resources to use these emerging techniques. Yet the hard fact is that SMEs really need to improve their software development processe if they are to achieve a greater degree of competetiveness. We therefore believe that a model for software deployment process that guides SMEs in a holistic way would make it possible to correct problems that occur in the deployment.

All of the above considerations led us to define the objective of our long-term research, which is to propose a software system deployment process model to help SMEs execute the deploymemt process of enterprise systems. Before starting to define a model, we decided to analyze the existing literature on this topic by means of a systematic mapping study (SMS) [10,11].

The paper is organized as follows: Section 2 gives a description of the planning of the SMS, while Section 3 describes the execution. The results obtained are presented in Section 4. A discussion of the threats to validity is presented in Section 5, and finally, our conclusions and outlines of future work are set out in Section 6.

2 Planning of the SMS

In this section, we present the definition of the protocol of the SMS: research questions, search strategy, study selection criteria and process; data extraction form and data synthesis procedure.

The objective of this SMS was to answer the following main research question (RQ): *What is the state of the art as regards the software system deployment process?*. This question was simultaneously broken down into several other questions (RQ1-4) (see Table 1).

Table 1. Research questions.

	Question	Motivation
RQ1:	What contributions have been made with regard to the software system deployment process?	To find and understand what contributions there are with respect to software system deployment.
RQ2:	In what activities or tasks of the software system deployment process are the contributions made?	To discover what activities or tasks in the deployment process have been researched in relation to the tasks and activities defined in the ISO/IEC/IEEE 12207 standard [12].
RQ3:	In what other technical processes and technical management processes related to the deployment process are the contributions made?	To determine what other technical processes and technical management processes have been researched in relation to the technical management processes defined in the ISO/IEC/IEEE 12207 standard [12].
RQ4:	What types of research are used?	To classify the primary studies according to Wieringa´s classification [13] of types of research, as is recommended in [11],[14].

The search string was built by choosing three major search terms: *"Deployment"*, *"Process"* and *"Software"*. We considered the fisrt major term from RUP [15] and alternative term employed in one internationally-recognized standard: the term 'transition'', from the ISO/IEC/IEEE 12207 standard [12]. In the case of the second major term, we also considered the terms "model" "method", "guide" and "guidelines". Although we recognize that their reach is different, all of them help carry out the software system deployment process in software organizations. In the case of the third major term, we considered "computer system" and "application" from ISO/IEC/IEEE 24765 standard [16]. Finally, the search string was:

TITLE((transition OR deployment) AND (process OR model OR method OR guide OR guidelines) AND (software OR "computer system" OR application))

We decided to perform an automatic search in three digital libraries which are the ones most widely-used in Software Engineering research, namely Scopus, IEEE Xplore and ACM digital library, considering only journal and conference papers, from 2010 to October 19, 2019. We recognize that prior to 2010, standards and methodologies were proposed that consider the software deployment process [15], [17] and earlier versions of ISO/IEC/IEEE 12207 standard [12].

We decided that 2010 was a significant year to use as the starting date for our search, given that there were certain trends and challenges at that time that made an impact on software processes. Among these, we can mention Global Software Development, the Internet as a development environment, which implies a change in the processes of software construction and in the mode of operation of software systems, with the appearance of mobile software [6].

The inclusion and exclusion criteria used in the process of paper selection are shown in Table 2.

Table 2. Inclusion and exclusion criteria.

Inclusion criteria
I1.Papers that answer our research questions.
I2. Duplicate studies. When several papers are written by the same authors describing the same topic or a similar one, the most complete one will be considered.
I3. Papers published from 2010 to October 2019.
I4. Papers written in English.
Exclusion criteria
E1. The paper addresses software that is not considered to be a software system, such as embedded software, operating system, software middleware, services and web services, servers and data servers, software for optimizing communication networks, among others.
E2. Papers available only in the form of abstracts, PowerPoint presentations, PhD theses, books.
E3. The full paper is not written in English.

We decided to perform the search on the title, given that we carried out a pilot search considering title, abstract and keywords in Scopus and found a large number of papers (20,069) that were not relevant to our objective.

The study selection process consisted of the following steps: 1) carry out a search in the three sources using the search string in the title, 2) remove duplicate papers, 3) apply the inclusion and exclusion criteria to the title, abstract and keywords 4) apply the inclusion and exclusion criteria to the full text. This process allowed us to select the primary studies that will be analysed to provide answers to the RQs that were formulated.

The data extraction form (see Table 3) consists of two parts: the first concerning the metadata of each primary study, and the second related to each of the RQs. To help to answer each RQ we defined a classification scheme (see Table 3). Some of the categories of this scheme were defined in the planning of the SMS, but others were extracted from reading the full text. The description of the categories used in the classification scheme is presented in the Appendix [18].

Table 3. Data extraction form.

Metadata	Paper ID, year, title, authors, publication type (journal or conference), country, keywords.
RQ/Dimension	Categories
RQ1/Contribution	Tool, model, method, methodology, artifact, practices,

	techniques, no contribution.
RQ2/ Deployment - Activities and tasks	Install the software system, prepare the environment, migrate the data, initial data load, test procedures, training system (user and operator), prepare documentation, acceptance test, and others . We consider the activities and tasks in the transition process from the ISO/IEC/IEEE12207 standard [12].
RQ3/ Others; technical processes and technical management processes	Validation, verification, risk management, configuration management, planning, others. We consider the processes from the ISO/IEC/IEEE 12207 standard [12].
RQ4/ Types of research	Evaluation research, philosophical paper, solution proposal, validation research, experience report, opinion paper. We used Wieringa´s classification of types of research [13].

In our effort to answer each research question we planned to do a thematic synthesis based on the classification scheme that had been defined, showing the results by means of graphs and tables.

3 Conducting the SMS

By applying the search string to ACM DL, Scopus and IEEE Xplore we retrieved 3,483 papers. Some adaptations of the search string were made for each digital library, as is shown in the Appendix [18]. The first author then made the selection of the primary papers by applying the process of paper selection defined in the protocol. In parallel, the second author replicated the selection process and obtained a set of primary papers. The two sets of primary papers were checked by all authors. Discrepancies were discussed in order to determine whether it was appropriate to include a particular paper or not.

After the selection process, 16 primary studies were selected for analysis in the effort to answer the RQs that had been formulated. The complete list of the primary studies selected is shown in [18].

We should point out that the "snowballing" method was conducted, following the model described by Wohlin in [19]. That is, once a primary study had been identified in one of the data sources, the references in that primary study were explored recursively by following the same search criteria. Finally, the snowballing process did not produce any new paper which we had not already included.

4 Results

We present the results obtained by analyzing the data recorded in the data extraction form defined in Table 3, aiming to answer the RQs formulated previously after analyzing the selected primary studies, which are listed in [18]. A synthesis of the results is presented in Table 4.

Table 4. Results per research question.

Referen ce	Results for each RQ			
	Contributi on (RQ1)	Deployment activities and tasks (RQ2)	Other technical processes and technical management processes (RQ3)	Types of research (RQ4)
[PS1]	Tool	Installation		Validation
[PS2]	Model	Installation Prepare environment Migrate data Initial data load Test procedures Training system Prepare documentation Acceptance test	Verification	Evaluation
[PS3]	Method	Installation		Validation
[PS4]	Practices	Installation		Validation
[PS5]	No contributi on	Installation Prepare environment Migrate data Initial data load Test procedures Training system Prepare documentation Acceptance test		Personal experience
[PS6]	Methodol ogy	Installation Prepare environment Migrate data Initial data load Test procedures Training system Prepare documentation Acceptance test Others	Validation Verification Risk Management Configuration management Planning Others	Evaluation
[PS7]	No contributi on			Evaluation
[PS8]	Tool	Installation		Evaluation
[PS9]	Model	Installation		Evaluation
[PS10]	Model	Installation		Evaluation
[PS11]	Method	Installation		Validation
[PS12]	Tool	Prepare documentation		Evaluation

[PS13]	Model	Installation Prepare environment Migrate data Initial data load Test procedures Training system Prepare documentation Acceptance test	Validation Verification Risk Management Configuration management Planning Others	Evaluation
[PS14]	Tool	Installation		Evaluation
[PS15]	Method	Installation		Evaluation
[PS16]	Tool	Installation		Evaluation

RQ1: What contributions have been made with regard to the software system deployment process?

We included five papers that proposed tools. Asmaa et al., [PS1] proposed an automatic deployment tool which simplifies the deployment process for non-advanced users in the cloud. The purpose of the author's work is to put forward a deployment method and then implement it to automate the process of deploying applications in a cloud environment based on model-driven engineering. Song et al. [PS8] presented the CONSOLAS (CONstraint SOLving for Architecture Setup) tool for model-based, automatic configuration and deployment of cloud applications. CONSOLAS assists application operators in configuring and deploying the application automatically. Operators only need to provide simple hints on how they want to configure the application; the tool generates a complete and valid configuration and deploys it. Fein et al. [PS12], presented a CASE Tool called MATCON (Method and Tool for CONsultants) that guides consultants in structuring documents, templates, and work products into reusable objects; the tool enables them to be cataloged and indexed so that these objects can be easily found and reused on subsequent projects to adapt pre-packaged applications, such as Oracle or SAP, to an organization's needs. García-Galán et al. [PS14] presented a tool called ISA Packager, a generic tool for packaging and deploying SPLs (Software Product Line). The major contribution of ISA Packager is its support for product evolution by updating existing products, thanks to the links established between features and de/installation commands. The contribution made by Günalp et al. [PS16] is Rondo, a tool suite that enables continuous deployment for dynamic, service-oriented applications; as a deployment manager Rondo implements this process, and is capable of conducting deployment and of continuously adapting applications according to the changes in the current target platform.

We also found several models and methods. Subramanian [PS2] proposed a model deployment process that can be broken down into eight steps: verification, negotiation, procurement, installation, initialization, configuration, user acceptance testing (UAT), and production use.

Tian et al. [PS3] contributed with a new method with which to deploy software automatically in large-scale clusters in an effort to improve the traditional deployment method that is based on an installation package.

Tyndall [PS4] presented best practices for building a phased installation software deployment paradigm. When combined with thick image techniques, software installations in both academic and administrative machines become more organized, flexible, and discreet.

Toufaili et al. [PS5] explored the criteria concerning the departments, basic activities and roles involved in the transition process, and researched the ways in which they are implemented in four large software organizations. This paper was, however, included in the no contribution category because, taking into account the classification shown in Table 3, nothing was built.

Carrizo et al. [PS7] presented a methodological guideline for the deployment of any software system; its foundations lie in an adaptation of an ASAP-based methodological guideline.

Paredes et al. [PS6] presented a conceptual framework for understanding the problems that affect the deployment of Enterprise applications in small and medium enterprises (SMEs); this was achieved by conducting a literature review. In addition, by carrying out interviews with companies that used ERP (Enterprise Resource Planning), it was possible to build a summary of influence factors for the deployment of IT enterprise applications; three contexts were considered: Technological, Organizational and Environmental. This paper was, however, included in the no contribution category because, according to the classification shown in Table 3, nothing was built.

Dubois et al. [PS9], presented a model for optimizing the costs of running cloud-based applications. The authors define an approach for refactoring a cloud application in such a way that, when it is deployed, it requires less computational capacity and therefore fewer resources.

Falazi et al. [PS10] proposed a decentralized deployment modeling approach that achieves accountability by using public blockchains and a decentralized storage system to store intermediate states of the collaborative deployment model. This research work focuses on the automation of application deployment.

Saatkamp et al. [PS11] presented a method for automating the deployment of applications in cloud environments. The goal of this method is to reduce the information and APIs which have to be exposed to the outside.

Reascos et al. [PS13] proposed a model that serves as a reference for the deployment of IT applications in public institutions; this model is carried out in 5 stages: initiating, planning, executing, monitoring & controlling, and closing, in compliance with the PMI guidelines. In addition, the model identifies four cross-cutting areas of concern: leadership, communication, change management and project management; these make it possible to balance and control the process of deployment of the IT application.

Deshmukh et al. [PS15], for their part, put forward an innovative method for installing and configuring the application in different environments. It uses the SaltStack tool to deploy the application on different servers. A pillar method is employed to ensure data security and easy data flow.

Of all the contributions, only two [PS2,PS13] propose an activity model that could serve as a guideline for software companies when carrying out the entire deployment process in a systemized manner. In [PS6] we are introduced to a method that serves as a guide for the deployment of any computer system. [PS1,PS8,PS16] propose tools for the automization of the installation activity, and in [PS12] a tool is presented that prepares documentation for the deployment process. In [PS14], ISA Packager provides a way to package SPL assets into an installer, as well as to deploy and update products.

While [PS4] puts forward a set of practices that allow the categorization of software packages into baselines, thus enabling system administrators to organize installers, the authors of [PS5,PS7] do not, according to our proposed classification, make a specific contribution. In [PS3,PS11,PS15] the researchers present a method that enables software to be deployed automatically. The authors of [PS9] define a model for refactoring a cloud application in such a way that, when it is deployed, it requires less computational capacity and therefore fewer resources. Only one contribution [PS10] proposes a decentralized deployment modeling approach.

RQ2: In what activities or tasks of the software system deployment process are the contributions made?

Asmaa et al. [PS1] proposed a tool to automate the installation of applications, in an attempt to reduce the developer's work as regards the cost of installation at the "time and effort" level.

Subramanian's model [PS2] considers all the activities that we have defined for this dimension, and takes into account the transition process activities from the ISO/IEC/IEEE 12207 standard [14].

The proposals of Tian et al. [PS3], Tyndall [PS4], Song et al. [PS8], Dubois et al. [PS19], Falazi et al. [PS10], Saatkamp et al. [PS11], García-Galán et al.[PS14], Deshmukh et al.[PS15] and Günalp et al. [PS16], cover only the activity of installing the software sytem deployment process.

In their study on benchmarking, Toufaili et al. [PS5] consider the following activities: installation, preparing the environment, test procedures, migrate data, initial data load, training system, preparing the documentation, and an acceptance test.

The proposal put forward by Carrizo et al. [PS6] considers all activities that we have defined for this dimension in Table 3.

Paredes et al. [PS7], do not cover any of the activities of the software system deployment process in their work.

Fein et al. [PS12] consider the activity of preparation of the documentation for the deployment process.

In Reascos et al. [PS13], the authors present a model that takes into account all the activities defined in the classification scheme shown in Table 3.

Despite the fact that there are few primary studies, ten of them focus on providing solutions to the installation activity in the software system deployment process.

RQ3: In what other technical processes and technical management processes related to the deployment process are the contributions made?

Only two papers mentioned technical management processes. Subramanian [PS2] considered a verification process in his model, to assist in understanding software requirements and in obtaining sizing estimates. He also identified risks to the organization's information security that may be caused by the deployment of the software. Reascos et al. [PS13] address the whole management process with reference to the processes defined in the ISO/IEC/IEEE 12207 standard [12]. Carrizo et al.´s methodological guide [PS6] considers the entire management process in relation to the activities defined in the classification scheme shown in Table 3.

RQ4: What types of research are used?

Of the primary studies analyzed, eleven of them correspond to "evaluation research" [PS2,PS6,PS7,PS8,PS9,PS10,PS12,PS13,PS14,PS16], four to the "validation type research" [PS1,PS3,PS4,PS11] and one corresponds to a "personal experience" [PS5].

In [PS2] applied the generic deployment model to the deployment of three common types of software: web applications, SaaS, and mobile applications, to attempt to understand the extent of this model's applicability in the real context.

In [PS6] to justify the adoption of their methodology, the authors conducted two types of *ex post* evaluations of deployments of systems in the University of Atacama:
a) a validation list, the purpose of which was to compare the deployment carried out with three software systems against their methodology, and b) a survey carried out on the deployers of another two software systems. .

In [PS7] a case study was carried out at a vehicle sales company in northern Ecuador, aiming to understand how small and medium enterprises implement new software applications in their organizations. In the case study only a set of three interviews was codified and processed, the purpose being to fine-tune future interviews. The authors considered that for their study to be complete, it would be necessary to conduct interviews with other actors in the company. In this research in progress, the authors were able to study in depth only the problem of the deployment of IT enterprise applications.

[PS8] proposes an automatic tool for the configuration and deployment of software applications in the cloud. A case study is presented in which a cloud application is used to show how developers use the tool to specify their applications, as well as to demonstrate how operators use the application to configure and deploy the applications automatically.

In [PS9] the authors' model is evaluated under different scenarios inspired by a real system; the results show that their model-driven application refactoring reduces deployment costs by up to 60% when compared to the results produced by the same approach but without their model's being employed.

In [PS10] deployment models were introduced and the prototype was assessed in real-world use cases by evaluating the costs and additional execution times incurred when using it.

The tool presented in [PS12] demostrates a significant saving in training costs, a 20–30% improvement in productivity, and positive results in large Oracle and SAP implementations.

The model proposed in [PS13] is grounded on the findings of a case study carried out in a medium-sized town that had recently gone through the deployment process of an ERP IT application. The study allowed critical features to be identified in different phases of the deployment process. The study mainly involved interviews with key participants in the process. The model proposed emerged during this study, accounting for the particular issues and concerns identified.

García-Galán et al. [PS14] present a real-world experience through ISA Packager, a generic tool to package and deploy SPLs (Software Product Lines); the case study presented was a local software company which specializes in building Supervisory Control And Data Acquisition (SCADA) system.

In [PS15] a case study is used to demostrate the validity of the installation method presented.

Günalp et al. [PS16] present their approach, validated in multiple projects. Results show the ability of their model to handle the initial provisioning, as well as the continuous adaptations of applications coming from different repositories such as application stores.

In [PS1] with the tool proposed for the automation of the installation of an application, the researchers have experimented with only two basic web applications, since this domain is easily manageable. Knowledge is still lacking as regards how to extend the use of the tool to other types of applications (IoT applications, mobile applications, etc.).

In [PS3] the authors proposed a new method to implement software automatically on a large scale, developing a prototype SDS software: Software Deployment System, to verify and test the method in a laboratory context.

In [PS4] best practices for software installation activity are presented; the examples are implemented using IBM Tivoli Endpoint Manager and Active Directory/Group Policy in the Pennsylvania State University.

The researchers in [PS11] presented a method to facilitate the redistribution of application components and thus reflect strategic decisions on the technical deployment layer, while also validating the practical feasibility by means of a prototype.

In [PS5] four companies are selected for the benchmarking study; one of them manufactures innovative and complicated systems that serve as a backbone for the IT sector, the second one provides the routing infrastructure, the third one manufactures software for automobiles and finally, the last one was a company developing a range of telecom products.

5 Threats to validity

In this section, we analyze the potential threats to the validity that could affect our study, with respect to the four categories suggested by Wohlin et al.[20].

Construct validity. In this SMS, in order to mitigate these threats, we described the meaning that we have given to the software system deployment process, based on internationally-recognized standards and methodologies [12],[15],[17].

Internal validity. To mitigate the internal validity concerns, a review protocol was created by the first author as part of the research of her doctoral thesis, and this was reviewed by the other two authors.

External validity. We decided to use only three search engines in our search of the journals and conference proceedings that are relevant and recommended for the software engineering field. We did not consider grey literature, such as papers available only in the form of abstracts, PowerPoint presentations, PhD theses, or books, because including these might have affected the validity of our results.

Reliability. We attempted to mitigate the publication bias by carefully defining (a) our inclusion and exclusion criteria so as to be able to select primary studies and (b) our exclusion criteria, endeavouring to select rules in this work, based on our predefined research questions. To increase reliability, the first author was responsible for applying these criteria, with the help of the other authors whenever there was any disagreement regarding the inclusion or exclusion of a rule. The entire systematic procedure was performed by the first author. In parallel, the second author replicated the selection process and obtained a set of primary papers. The two sets of primary papers were checked by all authors; discrepancies between them were discussed, the purpose being to determine whether it was appropriate to include a particular paper or not, and the final list was thereby obtained. Moreover, we created a data spread sheet and mapped research questions with the data extraction properties in order to comply with the objectives of this study. We believe that the potential effect of this bias has less importance in mapping studies than in Systematic Literature Reviews. To further substantiate the search process, the snowballing method was applied, but unfortunately it did not allow us to find more primary studies than those found in the initial search.

6 Conclusions and future work

This paper presents the results of an SMS we carried out to discover the state of the art of software system deployment processes. We selected 16 relevant primary studies from an initial set of 3,483 papers, searching in Scopus, IEEE Xplore and the ACM digital library from 2010 until October 2019. After analyzing these primary studies, we can conclude that:

- The tools proposed deal only with aspects of the installation, in an attempt to automate this activity in the process and thereby reduce costs and time.
- 38% (6 studies) of the studies found propose methods, models and practices that cover only the automation of the installation activity.
- Only 25% (4 studies) of the primary studies found contemplate activities and tasks for the deployment of the software system, and only 19% (3 studies) consider technical management processes for the deployment of the software system.
- Of the primary studies analyzed, 69% (11 studies) correspond to the type of research known as "evaluation research"; this evaluation was carried out in the real context through case studies, surveys, and experiments with prototypes. In the "personal experience" research type, two significant points are highlighted. The

first refers to the fact that the software system deployment process is a life cycle process that is not studied as often as the others, while the second refers to the need to create a model for the execution of the process so that both the process and the roles that are specific to it can be systematized, given the diversity of the roles that participate in the processes of the companies studied.

- We discovered two process models that could serve as a guideline for software companies when carrying out the entire deployment process. These models have a certain limitation, which is that they delegate to the organisations that apply them the responsability for making decisions on a series of aspects linked to their deployment. These include tasks, artefacts, techniques, methods, tools and the definition of roles.This delegated responsability makes the application of these models in SMEs potentially more difficult, as these kinds of organisations need processes that are more detailed or more descriptive, and thus easier-to-apply.

Having analysed the existing literature, our long-term research work will consist in defining a software system deployment process model for deploying enterprise systems. This model can be coupled to the software development methodologies that these SMEs use, and will provide detailed guidance on the phases, activities, tasks, templates and roles for systematizing the deployment of the enterprise's software systems. In addition, we plan to validate the proposed model through case studies in Argentine software development companies.

Acknowledgements. The research work presented in this paper has been developed within the following projects: GEMA ("*Consejería de Educación, Cultura y Deporte de la Dirección General de Universidades, Investigación e Innovación de la JCCM*", SBPLY/17/180501/000293, Spain) ECLIPSE ("*Ministerio de Ciencia, Innovación y Universidades, y Fondo Europeo de Desarrollo Regional FEDER*", RTI2018-094283-B-C31, Spain).

References

1. Hisham M. Abushama. PAM-SMEs: process assessment method for small to mediumenterprises. Software: Evolution and Process, 28, pp. 689 –711 (2016).
2. Sharma P., Sangal A.L. Building a hierachical structure model of enablers that affect software process improvement in software SMEs-A mixed method approach. Computer Standards & Interfaces, 66, pp. 1–23 (2019).
3. Ianzen A., Mauda E.C., Paludo M.A., Reinehr S., Malucelli A. Software process improvement in a financial organization: an action research approach. Computer Standard & Interfaces, 36, pp 54–65 (2013).
4. Subramanian N. The software deployment process and automation. CrossTalk, 30(2), pp. 28-34 (2017).
5. Carrizo D., Sanchez L. Benchmarking to Adopt an Asap-Based Methodological. Guideline for Software Systems Deployment. In: Proceedings of the 30th International Business Information Management Association Conference, (IBIMA '17): Sustainable Economic development, Innovation Management, and Global Growth, pp. 183-193 (2017).
6. Fuggetta A., Di Nitto, E. Software Process. In: Proceedings of the 36th International Conference on Software Engineering - Future of Software Engineering (FOSE'14), pp. 1-12 (2014).

7. Erich F.M.A., Amrit C., Daneva M. “A Qualitative Study of DevOps Usage in Practice”. Software: Evolution and Process, 29, pp. 1-20(2017).
8. Bass L., Weber I., Zhu L. DevOps: A Software Architect's Perspective (2015).
9. Agile Alliance. Agile Glosarry. https://www.agilealliance.org. Last accessed 2020/02/25.
10. Kitchenham B., Budgen D., Brereton P. Evidence-Based Software Engineering and Systematic Reviews, Chapman and Hall 1 st.Editon. Chapman and Hall/CRC. USA (2015).
11. Petersen K., Feldt R., Mujtaba S., Mattsson M. Systematic mapping studies in software engineering, In: Proceedings of the 12th International Conference on Evaluation and Assessment in Software Engineering, pp. 68–77 (2008).
12. IEEE ISO/IEC/IEEE 12207:2017(E). Systems and software engineering — Software life cycle processes (2017).
13. Wieringa R., Maiden N., Mead N., Rolland C. Requirements engineering paper classification and evaluation criteria: A proposal and a discussion. Requirements Engineering, 11, pp. 102–107 (2005).
14. Petersen K., Vakkalanka S., Kuzniarz L. Guidelines for Conducting Systematic Mapping Studies in Software Engineering: An Update. Information and Software Technology, 64, pp. 1-18 (2015).
15. Jacobson I, Booch G., Rumbaugh J.The Unified Software Development Process. 1 st Edition. Addison Wesley, USA (1999).
16. IEEE ISO/IEC/IEEE 2475:2010(E). Systems and software engineering - Vocabulary (2010).
17. Agile Business Consortium. The DSDM Agile Project Framework (2014 Onwards). https://www.agilebusiness.org/resources/dsdm-handbooks, last accessed 2019/05/29.
18. Panizzi M., Genero M., Bertone R. Appendix - Software system deployment process: A systematic mapping study. https://doi.org/10.6084/m9.figshare.11922165.v1
19. Wohlin C. Guidelines for snowballing in systematic literature studies and a replication in software engineering, In: Proceedings of the 18th International Conference on Evaluation and Assessment in Software Engineering, pp. 1–10 (2014).
20. Wohlin C., Runeson P., Hst M., Ohlsson M.C., Regnell B., Wessln A. Experimentation in Software Engineering. Springer Publishing Company (2012).

Prevenção de Anomalias Arquiteturais na Otimização de Projeto de Linha de Produto

Tiago Tadeu Madrigar[1], Thelma Elita Colanzi[1], Willian Oizumi[2], and Alessandro Garcia[2]

[1] UEM - Universidade Estadual do Maringá - Maringá, PR, Brasil
tiago@madrigar.com.br, thelma@din.uem.br
[2] PUC-Rio - Rio de Janeiro, RJ, Brasil
woizumi@inf.puc-rio.br, afgarcia@inf.puc-rio.br

Resumo O uso de algoritmos de busca tem sido explorado com sucesso na otimização de projeto de Arquitetura de Linha de Produto de Software (PLA) na abordagem seminal chamada *Multi-Objective Approach for Product-Line Architecture Design* (MOA4PLA). Tal abordagem produz um conjunto de alternativas de projeto de PLA que melhora os diferentes fatores otimizados. Além da otimização desses fatores, os projetos de PLA obtidos deveriam idealmente ser livres de anomalias arquiteturais. Uma anomalia arquitetural pode impactar negativamente tanto a variabilidade e a extensibilidade da PLA como outros atributos não funcionais. No entanto, abordagens baseadas em busca, tais como a MOA4PLA, adversamente introduzem anomalias arquiteturais nas soluções geradas automaticamente. Portanto, no presente trabalho, apresentamos a ferramenta OPLA-Tool-ASP, que implementa diretrizes para prevenir as anomalias *Unused Interface, Unused Brick* e *Concern Overload* no contexto da MOA4PLA. Além disso, investigamos a prevenção da anomalia *Link Overload*. Um estudo envolvendo dois experimentos foi conduzido a fim de analisar a eficiência dessas diretrizes. Os resultados deste estudo mostram que a prevenção das anomalias arquiteturais estudadas é viável e que existem pontos de melhoria com relação à diretriz de prevenção da anomalia *Link Overload*.

Keywords: Software Product Line, Architectural Smell, Search-based Software Engineering

1 Introdução

A aplicação de algoritmos de busca tem alcançado resultados satisfatórios para problemas complexos da Engenharia de Software no campo de pesquisa denominado *Search Based Software Engineering* (SBSE) [8]. Dentre os problemas beneficiados estão alguns relacionados à abordagem de Linha de Produto de Software (LPS). Tal abordagem tem como alvo o desenvolvimento de uma família de produtos de software para um determinado domínio, reutilizando os artefatos gerados [9]. Um dos principais artefatos de uma LPS é a Arquitetura de Linha de Produto (PLA) que contém o projeto comum a todos os produtos deriváveis da LPS [9]. O projeto de PLA é uma atividade que exige grande esforço do arquiteto e para o qual não há uma única solução possível devido aos fatores envolvidos, que vão desde a variabilidade e extensibilidade da PLA até a modularização de características comuns e variáveis.

Nesse contexto, Colanzi et al. [2] propuseram uma abordagem que usa algoritmos de busca para avaliar e melhorar projetos de PLA denominada MOA4PLA (*Multi-Objective Approach for Product-Line Architecture Design)* a fim de facilitar o trabalho do arquiteto. A aplicação desta abordagem foi automatizada por meio da ferramenta OPLA-Tool [4] que gera novas soluções a partir de uma solução inicial dada (o projeto original da PLA). Entretanto, a OPLA-Tool não é capaz de identificar e remover anomalias arquiteturais nos projetos gerados. Anomalias arquiteturais (do inglês *Architectural Smells* ou *Architectural Bad Smells*) são problemas decorrentes de decisões de projeto de arquitetura, intencionais ou não, que afetam negativamente a qualidade do sistema [7]. Em um estudo prévio [10], várias soluções arquiteturais geradas pela OPLA-Tool foram estudadas a fim de identificar as anomalias arquiteturais mais frequentes nas soluções. Uma das principais contribuições desse estudo foi a proposta de diretrizes para detecção e prevenção das anomalias arquiteturais mais frequentes. Porém, tais diretrizes ainda não foram implementadas nem validadas.

A identificação de anomalias arquiteturais em tempo de projeto da PLA: (i) evitaria que os problemas congênitos fossem propagados para a implementação da LPS e (ii) maximizaria atributos não-funcionais de qualidade desde a concepção da PLA. Em particular, certos atributos de qualidade – e.g., reusabilidade e manutenibilidade – são de extrema importância para a engenharia de qualquer LPS [9]. Porém, ainda não existem abordagens para a identificação de anomalias arquiteturais nem para a prevenção da introdução de anomalias em projetos de PLA otimizados por técnicas de SBSE [10].

Diante desse contexto, nosso principal objetivo é contribuir para a evolução da otimização de projeto de PLA por meio de uma ferramenta capaz de detectar e prevenir a introdução de anomalias arquiteturais durante a otimização de projeto de PLA. Para isso, no presente trabalho foi desenvolvida uma evolução da OPLA-Tool, denominada OPLA-Tool-ASP, a qual incorpora as diretrizes propostas por Perissato et al. [10] a fim de prevenir a presença de anomalias arquiteturais nos projetos de PLA gerados automaticamente (Seção 3). A OPLA-Tool-ASP tem o objetivo de prevenir as 3 anomalias mais frequentes no estudo prévio: *Unused Interface* [6], *Unused Brick* [6] e *Concern Overload* [6]. Um estudo experimental foi realizado utilizando a OPLA-Tool-ASP e a versão original da OPLA-Tool, a fim de responder a seguinte questão de pesquisa: ***QP1*** *- Qual é a efetividade da OPLA-Tool-ASP na detecção e prevenção das anomalias Unused Interface, Unused Brick e Concern Overload?* (Seções 4 e 5).

Segundo Perissato et al. [10], *Link Overload* [6] é a quarta anomalia mais frequente nos projetos analisados em seu estudo. Porém, eles perceberam que o cálculo do *threshold* precisa ser adaptado para o contexto de LPS antes de aplicar a diretriz proposta, pois foram identificados vários falsos positivos. Esse fato nos motivou a investigar seguinte questão de pesquisa antes da implementação da diretriz de prevenção de *Link Overload* na OPLA-Tool-ASP: ***QP2*** *- A estratégia utilizada em [10] para identificar a anomalia Link Overload é viável no contexto de LPS?* Nesse sentido, os resultados do nosso estudo experimental foram utilizados para analisar essa questão (Seção 5.3).

Dentre as principais contribuições deste trabalho está um incremento no estado da arte ao oferecer uma ferramenta para detectar e prevenir a geração de alternativas de projeto de PLA que contenham as anomalias arquiteturais *Unused Interface*, *Unused Brick* e *Concern Overload*. Outra contribuição é a adaptação do cálculo do *threshold* para anomalia *Link Overload* visto que o cálculo utilizado atualmente pelo estado da arte não é específico para LPS. Os principais conceitos envolvidos no presente trabalho são apresentados a seguir.

2 Referencial Teórico

2.1 SBSE

No campo de SBSE [8], problemas de Engenharia de Software são formulados como problemas de otimização, onde o objetivo é minimizar ou maximizar uma função ou grupo de fatores por meio de técnicas de busca e assim obter soluções (quasi-)ótimas automaticamente. A essas técnicas geralmente estão associados dois aspectos: um espaço de busca, que contém todas as possíveis soluções para o problema; e uma função de *fitness* que avalia a qualidade das soluções [8].

Dentre as técnicas de busca mais utilizadas em SBSE estão os algoritmos genéticos. Um Algoritmo Genético (AG) [1] é uma metaheurística inspirada na teoria da seleção natural e da evolução genética. A partir de uma população inicial (alternativas de projeto de PLA), operadores de busca são aplicados para evoluir tal população, geração por geração. O operador de seleção seleciona indivíduos com os melhores valores de função de *fitness* para serem pais. Assim, os melhores indivíduos sobreviverão na próxima geração. O operador de cruzamento combina partes de duas soluções pai para criar uma nova. O operador de mutação modifica aleatoriamente uma solução. A população de descendentes criada a partir da seleção, cruzamento e mutação substitui a população pai.

Alguns AGs foram adaptados para resolver problemas multiobjetivos. Tal tipo de algoritmo é chamado de Algoritmo Evolutivo Multiobjetivo (MOEA). O MOEA mais conhecido e amplamente utilizado para resolver problemas multiobjetivos é o *Non-dominated Sorting Genetic Algorithm* (NSGA-II) [3]. Um problema multiobjetivo depende de diversos fatores (objetivos) que estão em conflito e, em geral, não há uma única solução. Assim, existem diversas boas soluções que representam o *trade-off* entre os objetivos definidos. Estas soluções são chamadas de não-dominadas e formam a fronteira de Pareto.

2.2 Otimização de Projeto de PLA

Colanzi et al. [2] propuseram a abordagem MOA4PLA com a finalidade de automatizar a busca por melhores projetos de PLA utilizando MOEAs. A MOA4PLA recebe como entrada um projeto de PLA modelado em um diagrama de classes UML contendo todos os elementos arquiteturais comuns e variáveis. Estereótipos são utilizados para associar cada elemento às características que eles realizam. O arquiteto de LPS deve então escolher qual MOEA deve ser utilizado no processo de otimização assim como os parâmetros de execução. O projeto recebido como entrada é otimizado por meio dos operadores de busca definidos pela abordagem. Esses operadores realizam movimentos básicos dos AGs sendo: operadores de cruzamento de indivíduos e operadores de mutação dos novos indivíduos gerados. A abordagem inclui operadores de mutação específicos para projeto de PLA. Eles são: *Move Method, Move Attribute, Add Class, Move Operation, Add Component* e *Feature-Driven Operator* [2]. Este último visa melhorar a modularização de características entrelaçadas e espalhadas nos elementos arquiteturais.

A MOA4PLA usa um modelo de avaliação proposto para projeto de PLA [12]. Esse modelo fornece um conjunto de funções objetivo baseado em métricas de software, relacionadas a várias propriedades arquiteturais, dentre elas modularização de características, extensibilidade de LPS, variabilidade, coesão e acoplamento [12]. O arquiteto deve selecionar o subconjunto de funções objetivo que ele deseja otimizar. O valor das funções objetivo define o *fitness* de cada alternativa de projeto obtida durante o processo de otimização. A qualidade de cada alternativa de projeto é avaliada conforme seu *fitness*, que está diretamente relacionado aos objetivos selecionados pelo arquiteto a partir do modelo de avaliação. Após o processo de busca, a abordagem retorna um conjunto com as alternativas de projeto de melhor *trade-off* entre os objetivos otimizados. O arquiteto deve escolher uma das soluções obtidas de acordo com suas prioridades para adotar como PLA da LPS em desenvolvimento.

A ferramenta OPLA-Tool [4] automatiza a aplicação da MOA4PLA, permitindo a escolha de funções objetivo, MOEA e operadores de busca a serem utilizados, bem como a visualização das soluções (alternativas de projeto). Dentre os MOEAs disponíveis na OPLA-Tool está o NSGA-II. Como o principal objetivo da MOA4PLA é a otimização de projetos de PLA visando maximizar atributos de qualidade como reusabilidade, extensibilidade e manutenibilidade, é desejável que as soluções de projeto geradas pela abordagem sejam livres de problemas arquiteturais, os quais podem afetar diretamente os atributos mencionados. Porém, a versão atual da ferramenta não previne anomalias arquiteturais.

2.3 Identificação de Anomalias Arquiteturais em projeto de PLA

Anomalias arquiteturais são problemas decorrentes de decisões de projeto de arquitetura, intencionais ou não, que afetam negativamente a qualidade do sistema [7]. A existência de anomalias arquiteturais pode impactar negativamente nos aspectos que afetam as propriedades e estrutura interna do sistema como a capacidade de compreensão, capacidade de teste, extensibilidade e capacidade de reutilização [5] [6]. Após realizarmos um mapeamento sistemático da literatura identificamos que não existem ferramentas para a prevenção de anomalias arquiteturais em projetos de PLA otimizados por técnicas de SBSE.

As quatro anomalias arquiteturais alvo de estudo no presente trabalho estão descritas na Tabela 1. Neste trabalho, foram consideradas as anomalias *Unused Interface, Unused Brick, Concern Overload* e *Link Overload* porque elas foram identificadas como as mais frequentes nas 24 instâncias de projeto de PLA geradas pela OPLA-Tool analisadas em [10]. Na Tabela 1 também são apresentadas as estratégias de identificação utilizadas no estudo prévio bem como as diretrizes propostas para a prevenção de tais anomalias nas soluções obtidas pela OPLA-Tool. No entanto, nenhuma das diretrizes propostas foi implementada.

No estudo prévio [10] a proposta para a prevenção de *Unused Interface* e *Unused Brick* foi descartar as soluções que contivessem tais anomalias de modo a prevenir sua propagação entre as soluções geradas durante o processo de otimização. Para a anomalia *Concern Overload* foi proposta a aplicação do operador de mutação *Feature-Driven Operator* da MOA4PLA, que propicia a modularização de alguma das características associadas à classe/interface anômala, com o intuito de resolver ou amenizar a manifestação da anomalia.

Vários falsos positivos foram identificados ao aplicar o cálculo de *threshold* proposto em [6] porque relacionamentos de herança, normalmente utilizados para resolver variabilidades da LPS, são computados impactando na identificação da anomalia *Link Overload* [10]. Sugeriu-se alterar a estratégia de identificação para não contar este tipo de relacionamento e apontaram a aplicação de uma penalidade ao *fitness* da solução como diretriz para prevenção desta anomalia [10].

3 OPLA-Tool-ASP

Além das funcionalidades da versão original da OPLA-Tool em termos de otimização de projeto de PLA, a primeira versão da OPLA-Tool-ASP implementa as diretrizes para a detecção e a prevenção das anomalias *Unused Interface*, *Unused Brick* e *Concern Overload* propostas em [10]. As próximas subseções apresentam os aspectos de implementação de tais diretrizes na OPLA-Tool-ASP [3].

3.1 Prevenção das anomalias *Unused Interface* e *Unused Brick*

Considerando que a anomalia *Unused Brick* é gerada devido à existência de *Unused Interface*, resolvendo a primeira anomalia, a segunda é resolvida automaticamente. Seguindo a estratégia de identificação de ambas as anomalias (Tabela 1), foi adicionada uma restrição na ferramenta para considerar inválida qualquer solução que contenha interfaces ou classes sem qualquer relacionamento com outros elementos arquiteturais. Para isso foi criado um método chamado *isValidSolution* que é executado sempre que uma nova solução é criada e retorna false quando uma interface/classe isolada for identificada.

O método *isValidSolution* é chamado no laço de repetição em que os operadores de cruzamento e de mutação são aplicados, a fim de gerar populações descendentes como mostrado nas linhas 8 e 11 do Algoritmo 1. Este método também é chamado durante a formação da população inicial. Assim, nenhuma das populações geradas durante o processo de busca conterá soluções com ocorrência das anomalias *Unused Interface* e *Unused Brick*, pois soluções inválidas não são adicionadas às novas populações.

[3] O pacote experimental está disponível em https://github.com/otimizes/opla-tool-asp.

Algorithm 1: GERAÇÃO DA POPULAÇÃO FILHO NO NSGA-II

```
for int i = 0 ; i < (populationSize / 2); i++ do
    if (evaluations < maxEvaluations) then
        parents[0]=(Solution)selectionOperator.execute (population);
        parents[1]=(Solution)selectionOperator.execute (population);
        Object execute=crossoverOperator.execute (parents);
        if (execute instanceof Solution) then
            Solution offSpring=(Solution) crossoverOperator.execute(parents);
            if (isValidSolution((Architecture) offSpring.getDecisionVariables()[0]))
             then
                problem_.evaluateConstraints(offSpring);
                mutationOperator.execute(offSpring);
                if (isValidSolution((Architecture) offSpring.getDecisionVariables()[0]))
                 then
                    problem_.evaluateConstraints(offSpring);
                    problem_.evaluate(offSpring);
                    offspringPopulation.add(offSpring);
```

3.2 Prevenção da anomalia *Concern Overload*

Para a identificação da anomalia *Concern Overload* foi implementado um método chamado *detectCO* (Algoritmo 2). Conforme sugerido na estratégia de identificação (Tabela 1), todas as características associadas às classes e interfaces da PLA são consideradas como *concerns* e são computadas.

Tabela 1: Catálogo de anomalias arquiteturais identificadas na MO4PLA

Tipo	Definição
Unused Interface	**Descrição**: Uma interface de componente é dita não utilizada quando não está ligada a nenhum componente, adicionando, portanto, uma complexidade desnecessária ao sistema e dificultando sua manutenção [6]. **Identificação**: foram consideradas para esta anomalia as interfaces e classes isoladas, ou seja, que não possuíam nenhum relacionamento. **Diretriz**: Considerar inválida a solução que contenha essas anomalias e então descartá-la.
Unused Brick	**Descrição**: Ocorre quando todas as interfaces de um componente apresentam a anomalia Unused Interface, ou seja, quando nenhuma de suas interfaces possui ligação a outro componente [6]. **Identificação**: foram considerados os pacotes em que nenhuma interface ou classe possuía relacionamentos. **Diretriz**: Considerar inválida a solução que contenha essas anomalias e então descartá-la.
Concern Overload	**Descrição**: Um componente que realiza um número excessivo de características, quebrando o princípio da responsabilidade única [6]. **Identificação**: Considerar as características de cada LPS como sendo os *concerns* do projeto de PLA. Utilizar o algoritmo proposto por Garcia [6] para calcular o *threshold* (valor limite) e contar as características associadas às classes e interfaces do projeto. **Diretriz**: Aplicar o operador de mutação *Feature-Driven Operator* para modularizar alguma das características associadas à classe/interface anômala.
Link Overload	**Descrição**: Um componente que possui excessiva dependência de outros componentes, prejudicando assim a separação das funcionalidades e o isolamento das mudanças. Essas dependências podem se manifestar como *links* de entrada, de saída, ou ambos [6]. **Identificação**: o algoritmo proposto em [6] foi utilizado para definir o valor limite para cada tipo de *link*. Relacionamentos de dependência, realização, herança, etc. foram considerados *links*, bem como uma classe possuir um atributo que é do tipo de outra classe. O *threshold* foi calculado para cada direcionalidade: entrada, saída e bidirecional, arredondando valores fracionários. Depois, fez-se a contagem em todas classes e interfaces. **Diretriz**: Penalizar o *fitness* da solução, de modo que ela seja pior avaliada no processo de seleção dos melhores projetos para permanecerem no processo de otimização.

Algorithm 2: DETECÇÃO DA ANOMALIA CONCERN OVERLOAD

```
1  public boolean detectCO(Solution solution) throws JMException {
2  final Architecture arch = ((Architecture) solution.getDecisionVariables()[0]);
3  final List < Package > allPackage = new ArrayList < Package > (arch.getAllPackages());
4  if (!allPackage.isEmpty()) then
5      for (Package selectedPackage: allPackage) do
6          List < Class > lstClass = new ArrayList < >(selectedPackage.getAllClasses());
7          for (Class selectedClass: lstClass) do
8              List < Concern > lstConcern = new ArrayList <
                >(selectedClass.getOwnConcerns());
9              if (lstConcern.size() > threshold) then
10                 return true;
11             end
12         end
13         List < Interface > lstInterface = new ArrayList <
            >(selectedPackage.getAllInterfaces());
14         for (Interface selectedInterface: lstInterface) do
15             List < Concern > lstConcern = new ArrayList <
                >(selectedInterface.getOwnConcerns());
16             if (lstConcern.size() > threshold) then
17                 return true;
```

O método *detectCO* também calcula o *threshold* que é utilizado para identificar se a classe/interface é anômala. O *threshold* é a média do número de *concerns* somada ao desvio padrão [6]. Este trecho foi omitido por falta de espaço.

Nas linhas 6-11 do algoritmo detecta-se a presença de *Concern Overload* nas classes do projeto. Para isso, nesse *loop* verifica-se se o número de características associadas a uma determinada classe é maior do que o *threshold*, retornando *true* quando a condição é verdadeira. O mesmo procedimento é realizado para as interfaces entre as linhas 12 e 17.

O método *detectCO* foi implementado na classe *PLAFeatureMutation*, responsável por implementar os operadores de mutação da MOA4PLA, incluindo o operador *Feature-driven Operator*, que propicia a modularização de características e como consequência, pode diminuir a ocorrência de *Concern Overload*.

Na OPLA-Tool-ASP, conforme sugerido em [10], o método *detectCO* é executado antes de selecionar qual operador de mutação será aplicado. Caso seja detectada a presença da anomalia *Concern Overload*, o operador *Feature-driven Operator* é selecionado para aplicação, caso contrário, o código retorna a seu fluxo normal, sorteando aleatoriamente qualquer operador de mutação.

4 Projeto do Estudo Experimental

Neste trabalho foram conduzidos dois experimentos com intuito de avaliar a efetividade da OPLA-Tool-ASP em prevenir as anomalias *Unused Interface*, *Unused Brick* e *Concern Overload*, além de analisar a estratégia de identificação da anomalia *Link Overload* proposta em [10] no contexto de LPS. O experimento denominado OPLA-Tool foi utilizado como controle, pois trata-se da versão original desta ferramenta. O experimento OPLA-Tool-ASP se refere à versão da ferramenta que contém as diretrizes para detecção e prevenção das anomalias.

Os projetos de PLA utilizados nos dois experimentos são *Arcade Game Maker* (AGM) e *Mobile Media* (MM). A AGM [11] é uma LPS que engloba um conjunto de jogos arcade (Brickles, Bowling e Pong). A LPS MM [13] oferece recursos que lidam com música, vídeos e fotos para dispositivos portáteis.

Para os dois experimentos (OPLA-Tool e OPLA-Tool-ASP) foram utilizadas as seguintes configurações: todos os operadores de mutação da MOA4PLA com probabilidade de mutação igual a 0.9; população com 100 indivíduos; número de avaliações de *fitness* igual a 30.000 (300 gerações); funções objetivo: *Relational Cohesion* (COE), *Class Coupling* (ACLASS) e *Feature Modularization* (FM). As funções COE, ACLASS e FM referem-se à coesão relacional, acoplamento de classes e modularização de características [12]. Em cada experimento foram realizadas 30 execuções independentes para cada PLA. Essas mesmas configurações foram utilizadas em estudos anteriores [2] [12].

Dentre todas as soluções geradas nos dois experimentos, foram coletadas as 36 soluções não-dominadas geradas pelas duas ferramentas após as 30 execuções. A identificação das anomalias foi realizada manualmente por um dos autores e revisada por outro autor. Para cada anomalia arquitetural avaliada neste trabalho, utilizou-se a estratégia de identificação apresentada na Tabela 1. Os valores do *threshold* de *Concern Overload* são AGM = 4 e MM = 5. Devido à formula resultar em valores fracionários, os valores foram arredondados para cima.

5 Resultados

Nesta seção são apresentados os resultados encontrados no estudo experimental realizado. A OPLA-Tool-ASP encontrou 7 soluções para a AGM e 7 soluções para a MM enquanto a versão original da OPLA-Tool encontrou 13 soluções para a AGM e 9 soluções para a MM.

A Figura 1 apresenta as soluções encontradas para AGM dispersas no espaço de soluções. Nos dois gráficos, a curva azul apresenta as soluções encontradas pela OPLA-Tool. A curva em vermelho apresenta as soluções obtidas pela OPLA-Tool-ASP. E a solução original é apresentada em verde. Os valores de *fitness* da função objetivo FM estão apresentados no eixo Y dos dois gráficos e a função COE é apresentada no eixo X do gráfico da esquerda enquanto a função ACLASS está no eixo X do gráfico da direita.

A Figura 2 apresenta a dispersão das soluções encontradas para MM. Nos dois gráficos, o projeto original e as soluções encontradas pela OPLA-Tool e pela OPLA-Tool-ASP são apresentadas em verde, azul e vermelho, respectivamente.

Por meio dos gráficos apresentados, pode-se comparar os valores de *fitness* das soluções encontradas pelos dois experimentos com o *fitness* da PLA original. Considerando que quanto menor o valor das três funções, melhor é o resultado, é possível perceber que ambos experimentos conseguiram melhorar os valores de *fitness* originais das funções objetivo FM e ACLASS tanto para a AGM como para a MM. No caso da AGM, todas as soluções obtidas pela OPLA-Tool-ASP têm melhor valor da função objetivo COE e pior valor da função ACLASS do que a PLA original. Em todos os outros casos o valor da coesão relacional (função objetivo COE) foi pior do que o valor original, mostrando que ao melhorar o acoplamento (ACLASS) , a coesão tende a piorar.

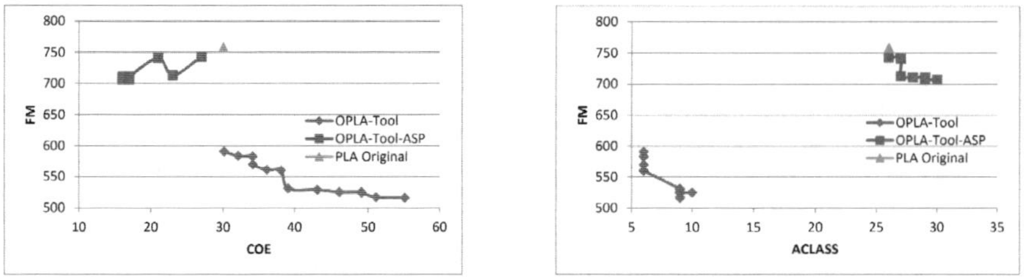

Figura 1: Soluções encontradas para a AGM

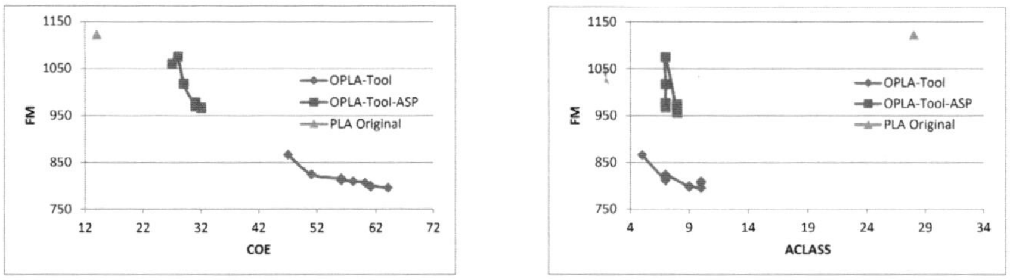

Figura 2: Soluções encontradas para a MM

Tabela 2: Total de anomalias detectadas nas soluções geradas

Anomalia	Original	OPLA-Tool													OPLA-Tool-ASP						
		S1	S2	S3	S4	S5	S6	S7	S8	S9	S10	S11	S12	S13	S1	S2	S3	S4	S5	S6	S7
Arcade Game Maker																					
Unused Interface	0	5	4	4	4	5	1	3	2	4	1	6	3	3	0	0	0	0	0	0	0
Unused Brick	0	11	8	8	8	6	9	6	8	9	9	6	6	8	0	0	0	0	0	0	0
Concern Overload	2	2	2	2	2	2	2	2	2	2	2	2	2	2	2	2	2	2	2	2	2
Mobile Media																					
Unused Interface	0	9	8	6	5	15	7	6	8	15					0	0	0	0	0	0	0
Unused Brick	0	4	3	1	2	2	2	1	2	3					0	0	0	0	0	0	0
Concern Overload	2	1	1	2	1	1	2	2	2	1					1	3	3	1	2	2	1

Comparando as soluções obtidas pelos 2 experimentos (OPLA-Tool-ASP e OPLA-Tool), percebe-se que as soluções obtidas pela OPLA-Tool têm melhores valores da função objetivo FM para as 2 PLAs, o que pode indicar que a soluções obtidas pela OPLA-Tool-ASP têm pior modularização das características. Por outro lado, OPLA-Tool-ASP conseguiu soluções mais coesas (função COE) do que a OPLA-Tool para as 2 PLAs.

Tão importante quanto o *fitness* das soluções é a existência de anomalias arquiteturais nas soluções de projetos obtidas automaticamente. Nesse sentido, a Tabela 2 apresenta o número de ocorrências de cada tipo de anomalia arquitetural em cada solução obtida nos dois experimentos para as PLAs AGM e MM. As soluções obtidas pelos experimentos são identificadas como S[n], onde n representa o número da solução. A quantidade de anomalias observadas nas PLAs originais é apresentada na coluna rotulada como Original.

5.1 *Unused Interface* e *Unused Brick*

As anomalias *Unused Interface* e *Unused Brick* não estão presentes nos projetos originais. Observando a Tabela 2 é possível perceber que nos experimentos conduzidos com a OPLA-Tool, estas anomalias aparecem em todas as soluções obtidas. Já as soluções obtidas com a ferramenta OPLA-Tool-ASP não apresentaram a existência destas anomalias. Devido ao método *isValidSolution* (Seção 3), qualquer solução contendo classes ou interfaces que não possuíam ligação com os demais elementos arquiteturais foi descartava, por ser considerada inválida. Desse modo, todas as populações de soluções geradas durante o processo de busca estava livre das anomalias *Unused Interface* e *Unused Brick*. A implementação da diretriz de prevenção dessas anomalias se mostrou eficaz.

No caso das soluções geradas pela OPLA-Tool onde há ocorrência destas anomalias, percebeu-se que os elementos anômalos são, em geral, novos pacotes que foram criados por operadores de mutação, os quais contêm interfaces que não estão conectadas a nenhum outro elemento arquitetural. Esses novos pacotes geralmente contêm elementos arquiteturais para realizar uma única característica o que impacta beneficamente nos valores de *fitness* da função objetivo FM, por outro lado manifestam ao menos uma das anomalias *Unused Interface* e *Unused Brick*. Por outro lado, as soluções obtidas pela OPLA-Tool-ASP não têm valores de *fitness* da função objetivo FM tão baixos como as soluções da OPLA-Tool, mas não apresentam as anomalias supracitadas. Portanto, por meio dos resultados obtidos pela OPLA-Tool-ASP, observou-se que é pertinente otimizar menos e obter soluções sem tais anomalias arquiteturais.

> ***QP1:*** *A OPLA-Tool-ASP é efetiva para detectar e prevenir as anomalias Unused Interface e Unused Brick.*

5.2 *Concern Overload*

A Tabela 2 mostra que todas as soluções obtidas pela OPLA-Tool-ASP e pela OPLA-Tool contêm a anomalia *Concern Overload*. Nota-se também a existência desta anomalia nas PLAs originais.

No caso da AGM, percebe-se que o número de ocorrências desta anomalia permaneceu constante para todas as soluções obtidas nos dois experimentos. A AGM tem classes associadas a várias características o que dificulta a modularização das características durante o processo de busca. Apesar de os experimentos terem obtido soluções com valor de *fitness* da função objetivo FM melhor do que o valor original (FM=758.0), o número de ocorrências da anomalia não abaixou. As duas classes da AGM que se mantiveram anômalas em todas as soluções geradas são as classes *Puck* (mostrada na Figura 3a) e *Sprite*. Nota-se pelos estereótipos da classe *Puck* que ela tem atributos e métodos que auxiliam na realização de 7 diferentes características («play», «save», «movement», «collision», «bowling», «brickles» e «pong»).

A Tabela 3 apresenta os resultados do experimento OPLA-Tool-ASP para a anomalia *Concern Overload* para alguns elementos arquiteturais (classes ou interfaces) associados a várias características. O número de características associadas ao elemento no projeto original é mostrado nas colunas rotuladas como **O**. Pode-se observar que em alguns elementos o número de características sofreu uma leve redução, como por exemplo a classe *GameBoard* da AGM que na solução original estava associada a 3 *concerns* e foi reduzido para 2 na solução S7 e a interface *ICheckScore* que na solução original estava associada a 2 *concerns*, mas está associada a 1 *concern* nas soluções S4 e S7. O *fitness* da PLA original é (COE=30, ACLASS=26, FM=758), enquanto os *fitness* de S4 e S7 são S4:(COE=17, ACLASS=28, FM=711) e S7:(COE=21, ACLASS=27, FM=741). Logo, nota-se que a modularização das características impacta no valor de FM e que esta função é um bom indicador para o controle de *Concern Overload*.

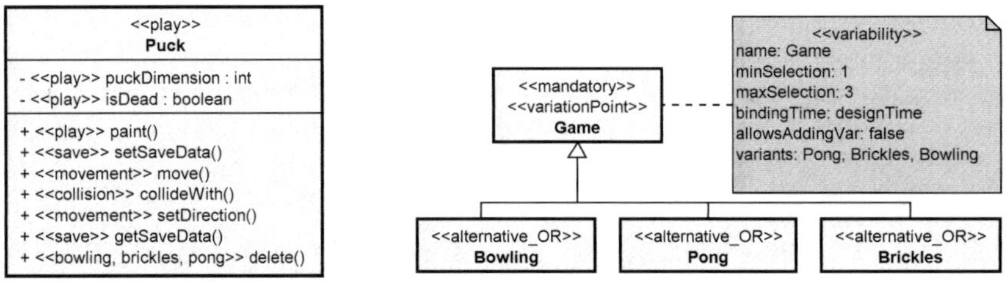

(a) Classe Puck (b) Uso de generalização em ponto de variação

Figura 3: Exemplos de Classes da AGM

Tabela 3: Anomalia *Concern Overload* nas soluções da OPLA-Tool-ASP

Arcade Game Maker									**Mobile Media**								
Classe/Interface	**O**	**S1**	**S2**	**S3**	**S4**	**S5**	**S6**	**S7**	**Classe/Interface**	**O**	**S1**	**S2**	**S3**	**S4**	**S5**	**S6**	**S7**
GameBoard	3	3	3	3	3	3	3	2	IMediaMgt	8	7	6	6	6	7	6	6
ICheckScore	2	2	2	2	1	2	2	1	MediaMgr	8	4	7	6	4	5	4	4
Score	2	2	2	2	1	2	2	1	MediaCtrl	7	5	6	6	3	6	6	5

No caso da MM, houve comportamento semelhante. A classe *MediaMgr*, que na solução original realizava 8 *concerns*, está associada a 5 e 4 *concerns* em várias soluções, deixando de ser anômala, pois o *threshold* foi definido como 5. As alterações no número de características realizadas pelos elementos arquiteturais se devem à aplicação do operador de mutação *Feature-driven Operator*, que tem como objetivo modularizar características que estejam entrelaçadas com outras nos componentes do projeto. Na maioria das soluções, foram criados novos componentes para modularizar características impactando diretamente no número de elementos anômalos.

Tanto para a MM como para a AGM, o número de componentes criados para modularizar características foi maior nas soluções da OPLA-Tool-ASP. Isto se deve ao fato de que na versão original da OPLA-Tool, os operadores de mutação são selecionados aleatoriamente enquanto na OPLA-Tool-ASP o *Feature-driven Operator* sempre é aplicado quando há ocorrência de *Concern Overload*.

Conclui-se que como o número de *concerns* diminuiu em certos elementos (classes/interfaces) e alguns deixaram de ser anômalos, a OPLA-Tool-ASP apresentou resultados satisfatórios em relação a *Concern Overload*. Esses resultados nos permitem supor que o algoritmo de busca precisaria de mais gerações para otimizar ainda mais o valor da função objetivo FM e, assim, obter a soluções sem a ocorrência desta anomalia.

***QP1:** A diretriz implementada na OPLA-Tool-ASP contribui para prevenir a anomalia Concern Overload.*

5.3 *Link Overload*

Em relação a anomalia *Link Overload*, no estudo realizado por Perissato et al. [10], a estratégia de identificação utilizada seguiu o algoritmo definido em [6], no qual todos os relacionamentos são computados para o cálculo do *threshold*. O cálculo consiste na média do número de relacionamentos somada ao desvio padrão. Deve-se calcular o *threshold* para os 3 tipos de direcionalidades dos relacionamentos: entrada, saída e ambos[6]. Seguindo esse cálculo, os *thresholds* de *Link Overload* seriam AGM = (entrada: 2, saída: 2, ambos: 1) e MM = (entrada: 2, saída: 3, ambos: 0).

No entanto, apesar de tal cálculo ser apropriado para projeto arquitetural, ele não é específico para o contexto de LPS gerando falsos positivos. Desse modo, umas das propostas de Perissato et al. foi adaptar o cálculo de *threshold* desconsiderando os relacionamentos de herança, a fim de aumentar a acurácia da estratégia de identificação. No contexto de LPS é habitual utilizar generalização para definir os pontos de variação e seus variantes como ilustrado na Figura 3b, na qual a superclasse *Game* é o ponto de variação e as classes *BowlingGame, PongGame* e *BricklesGame* são os variantes.

A Figura 4 ilustra como seria a avaliação do *threshold* para as LPSs AGM e MM com o *threshold* original (cálculo definido em [6]) e o cálculo do *threshold* proposto (sem considerar as generalizações). Percebe-se que o *threshold* proposto detectaria um número menor de ocorrências dessa anomalia, já que o limiar seria menor, indicando um menor número de prováveis falsos positivos.

A título de ilustração, se não contarmos as generalizações, a classe *Game* (Figura 3b) possui nenhum relacionamento de entrada e de saída e 1 relacionamento bidirecional, logo os valores não excedem o *threshold*. Se as generalizações forem contadas, *Game* seria considerada uma classe anômala,o que constitui um falso positivo. Comportamentos similares ocorreriam com outras classes das duas LPS utilizadas no nosso estudo, como por exemplo, *StationarySprite* da AGM e *Game* da MM. Portanto, conclui-se que a adaptação do cálculo do *threshold* de *Link Overload* é apropriada para o contexto de LPS e será utilizada na implementação da diretriz desta anomalia na OPLA-Tool-ASP.

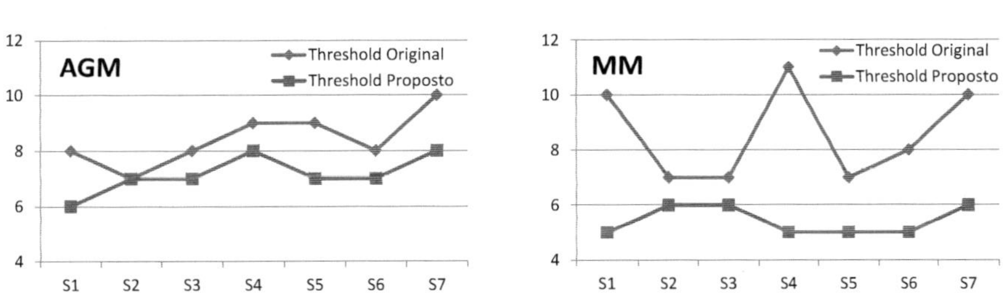

Figura 4: Total de ocorrências de *Link Overload* nas soluções da OPLA-Tool-ASP

Outra análise realizada diz respeito ao número de ocorrências desta anomalia nas soluções obtidas nos experimentos. Nas PLAs originais da AGM e da MM o número de elementos que continham *Link Overload* era 3. Porém, na Figura 4 os números são maiores que 3, independentemente do cálculo de *threshold* utilizado. Além do impacto causado pelos operadores de busca que movimentam elementos arquiteturais no projeto aumentando as ocorrências de *Link Overload* [10], nós percebemos uma outra necessidade de adaptação no cômputo do *threshold* dessa anomalia no que se refere às novas classes/interfaces criadas.

Considerando todas as soluções obtidas para a MM, 10 classes/interfaces foram criadas e seus relacionamentos são bidirecionais. Como o *threshold* para a direcionalidade ambos é 0 para a MM, as novas classes/interfaces, criadas pelo operador *Feature-driven Operator* para modularizar características entrelaçadas, passam a ser consideradas anômalas ainda que tenham somente 1 relacionamento, o que se constitui um falso positivo, já que pressupõe-se ao menos um relacionamento para garantir a visibilidade entre os elementos arquiteturais.

> ***QP2:*** *Para o contexto de LPS é apropriado não contar os generalizações no cálculo do threshold da anomalia Link Overload e classes/interfaces com somente 1 relacionamento não devem ser consideradas anômalas independentemente do valor do threshold.*

5.4 Ameaças à validade

A validade interna e externa estão relacionadas ao conjunto de projetos de PLA utilizados neste estudo. Apesar das soluções analisadas terem sido obtidas a partir de LPS acadêmicas, MM e AGM, foi possível identificar a existência das anomalias arquiteturais investigadas no presente trabalho.

A validade de construção está relacionada à configuração do estudo. Com relação às estratégias de identificação de anomalias utilizadas, buscou-se sempre que possível utilizar critérios objetivos baseados na literatura. Um dos pesquisadores envolvidos nesta pesquisa realizou uma análise por inspeção visual nos 36 projetos de PLA gerados pelas ferramentas. Para mitigar esta ameaça, um especialista realizou uma validação das anomalias identificadas.

A principal ameaça à validade das conclusões é o número de LPSs (2) e projetos de PLA (36) avaliados. Apesar de se tratar de um estudo cujo resultado não pode ser generalizado, foi possível identificar diferenças em relação aos projetos originais que geraram soluções diferentes entre si e que permitiram tanto avaliar o efeito da OPLA-Tool-ASP na prevenção de anomalias no contexto da AGM e da MM, como identificar pontos de adaptação para o cálculo do *threshold* da anomalia *Link Overload.*

6 Conclusão

Neste trabalho apresentamos a ferramenta OPLA-Tool-ASP, que tem como alvo gerar automaticamente projetos de PLA que otimizam os objetivos selecionados pelo engenheiro de software, além de prevenir anomalias arquiteturais nas soluções de projeto geradas. A primeira versão da ferramenta inclui diretrizes para prevenir as anomalias *Unused Interface, Unused Brick* e *Concern Overload.*

As principais contribuições deste trabalho envolvem: (a) o avanço do estado da arte na otimização de projeto de PLA prevenindo a ocorrência de algumas anomalias arquiteturais; (b) os resultados experimentais que indicam a efetividade da OPLA-Tool-ASP para prevenir as anomalias supracitadas e (c) descobertas a respeito da necessidade de adaptação do cálculo do *threshold* para a identificação da anomalia *Link Overload* no contexto de LPS.

Atualmente estamos implementando a prevenção de *Link Overload* na ferramenta. Pretendemos executar novos estudos com maior número de gerações para reavaliar a ocorrência de *Concern Overload* e realizar uma avaliação qualitativa das soluções geradas com especialistas. Na sequência, outras anomalias estudadas em [10] devem ser incluídas na OPLA-Tool-ASP e devidamente validadas por meio de estudos experimentais.

Referências

1. Coello, C.A.C., Lamont, G.B., Van Veldhuizen, D.A., et al.: Evolutionary algorithms for solving multi-objective problems, vol. 5. Springer (2007)
2. Colanzi, T.E., Vergilio, S.R., Gimenes, I., Oizumi, W.N.: A search-based approach for software product line design. In: Proc. of the 18th International Software Product Line Conference-Volume 1. pp. 237–241. ACM (2014)
3. Deb, K., Pratap, A., Agarwal, S., Meyarivan, T.: A fast and elitist multiobjective genetic algorithm: Nsga-ii. IEEE Trans. Evolutionary Comp. **6**(2), 182–197 (2002)
4. Fèderle, É.L., do Nascimento Ferreira, T., Colanzi, T.E., Vergilio, S.R.: Opla-tool: a support tool for s9earch-based product line architecture design. In: Proc. of the 19th International Conference on Software Product Line. pp. 370–373. ACM (2015)
5. Fowler, M.: Patterns of enterprise application architecture. Addison-Wesley Longman Publishing Co., Inc. (2002)
6. Garcia, J.: A unified framework for studying architectural decay of software systems. University of Southern California (2014)
7. Garcia, J., Popescu, D., Edwards, G., Medvidovic, N.: Identifying architectural bad smells. In: 2009 13th European Conf. on Software Maintenance and Reengineering. pp. 255–258. IEEE (2009)
8. Harman, M., Mansouri, S.A., Zhang, Y.: Search-based software engineering: Trends, techniques and applications. ACM Computing Surveys **45**(1), 11 (2012)
9. Linden, F.J., Schmid, K., Rommes, E.: Software product lines in action: the best industrial practice in product line engineering. Springer Science & Bus.Media (2007)
10. Perissato, E.G., Neto, J.C., Colanzi, T.E., Oizumi, W., Garcia, A.: On identifying architectural smells in search-based product line designs. In: VII Brazilian Symposium on Software Components, Architectures, and Reuse. pp. 13–22 (2018)
11. Software Engineering Institute: Arcade game maker: Pedagogical product line `http://www.sei.cmu.edu/productlines/ppl`
12. Verdecia, Y.D., Colanzi, T.E., Vergilio, S.R., Santos, M.C.B.: An enhanced evaluation model for search-based product line architecture design. In: XX Ibero-American Conf. on Software Engineering (CIbSE2017). Buenos Aires (2017)
13. Young, T.J.: Using aspectj to build a software product line for mobile devices. Ph.D. thesis, University of British Columbia (2005)

Empirical Study on Product Configuration and Traceability in UML-based Product-Lines

Thais Nepomuceno[1], Edson OliveiraJr[1], Raqueline Penteado[1], Marco A. Graciotto Silva[2], and Avelino F. Zorzo[3]

[1] State University of Maringá, Maringá-PR, Brazil
thais.nepomuceno1@gmail.com, {edson,raque}@din.uem.br
[2] Federal University of Technology - Paraná, Campo Mourão-PR, Brazil
magsilva@utfpr.edu.br
[3] Pontifical Catholic University of Rio Grande do Sul, Porto Alegre-RS, Brazil
avelino.zorzo@pucrs.br

Abstract. Software Product Line (SPL) can be defined as a set of systems that share common and variable parts. The elements that vary are those that allow the differentiation among products of this family, thus managing the variabilities is an important part of the SPL engineering. In the literature there is a lack of experiments that evaluate and compare approaches for SPL variability management. In this work, two of the existing approaches based on UML, SMarty and PLUS, are compared to verify: (i) the effectiveness of configuring products from use case diagrams and class diagrams; (ii) the influence the knowledge level of participants has when using each approach; (iii) the amount of consultations in the material needed for those using SMarty and PLUS; and (iv) the effectiveness in tracing variable elements from different diagrams. For this, we chose an experimental 1x2 factorial design. Although the overall results do not provide evidence of significant difference between the approaches, assumptions and improvements are discussed for future experiments.

Keywords: Empirical Study · Product Configuration · Software Product Lines · Traceability · UML.

1 Introduction

Software Product Line (SPL) is a steadily increasing approach as it brings several advantages to companies [9]. In SPL, software development targets a family of products and not individual products. To do so, there is an analysis of which characteristics of the software family are common and which are variable [3].

Elements which differentiate SPL products have associated variabilities, which is the ability to change or customize a system [3]. The importance of variability for an SPL makes its management an essential activity as its incorrect application can compromise the degree of SPL reuse [3]. There are several approaches based on feature models [2] and UML [8,19,16]: the former yields problem space, whereas the latter focuses on solution space. Morever, UML-based approaches can be used with current UML tools and builds upon known modeling concepts. Thus, in this study we address approaches on the solution space based on UML.

Despite the existence of several variability management approaches in the literature, they have not been properly evaluated using rigorous scientific methods [4,7]. In a tertiary study conducted by Raatikainen et al. [17], results showed that much of the empirical assessments of SPLs have not been adequately planned or reported.

Motivated by this scenario, we evaluated the management of variability, considering configurability and traceability, of two approaches: Product Line UML-based Software Engineering (PLUS) method [8], and SMarty approach [16].

PLUS is a widely referenced method in the literature and is an important example of a method for managing variabilities based on UML (use cases and classes), using stereotypes to represent these variabilities. Similarly, SMarty defines an UML profile and uses stereotypes and tagged values, supporting also rastreability. This paper answers the following research question: "Can we have more effectiveness and efficiency, at configuring SPL products, and provide traceability using SMarty compared to the PLUS method for use case and class diagrams?".

This study is part of a larger project of experimental evaluation of the SMarty approach throughout Continuous Experimentation, a process of systematic experimentation that has been studied in several aspects such as variability representation capability, product configuration, and traceability. Therefore, the results obtained by Marcolino et al.'s [10,11,12,14,13] and Nepomuceno and OliveiraJr [15] contributed significantly to the experimentation/learning process, proposed by Wohlin et al. [18], by allowing the overall evolution of SMarty. The main idea is that SMarty can be evaluated continuously, based on all SMarty supporting paired diagrams (use case, class, component, sequence, and activity), thus evolving from the results of the experiments. In this study, we considered use case and class diagrams for Mobile Media SPL [6] in the academic setting. Further studies are being prepared to address other UML diagrams and more complex SPL, resembling industrial context.

2 Background and Related Work

This section presents fundamentals on the PLUS method [8] and the SMarty approach [16], as well as related work.

2.1 Product Line UML-based Software Engineering (PLUS)

The PLUS method [8] was conceived for developing SPLs based on UML artifacts. PLUS encompasses the following phases: Inception, which determines whether an SPL is feasible based on its context, functionalities, degree of similarity and variability; Elaboration, in which use case model and features are reviewed and elaborated in greater detail, identifying their variation points and the SPL architecture is expanded including optional and variant components;

Construction, in which components are developed and tested; and Transition, in which components are integrated and made available for users to test.

PLUS allows the identification of variant components through the use of UML stereotypes to represent variability: «kernel» used in mandatory use case and class diagram elements; «optional» applied to use case and class diagram elements that might be present in a specific SPL product; and «alternative» used only for use case mutually exclusive elements. The PLUS method does not provide any kind of support in traceability of elements among different diagrams.

2.2 Stereotype-based Management of Variability (SMarty)

SMarty [16] is a variability management approach composed of an UML profile, the SMartyProfile, and a process for guiding users on how to identify and represent variabilities, the SMartyProcess.

The SMartyProfile encompasses a set of stereotypes and tagged-values for representing variability, variation points and variants in use case, class, component, sequence, and activity diagrams [16]. Such stereotypes are: «variability» represents the concept of variability; «variationPoint» represents a variation point; «mandatory» applied to variants present in every product;«optional» represents a variant which might be present in a product; «alternative_OR» applied to variants of an inclusive group; «alternative_XOR» applied to variants of an exclusive group. The SMartyProcess [16] guides users on identifying, representing, and tracing variabilities by means of a systematic process.

In the SMarty approach, traceability is performed based on the tagged-values of the «variability» stereotype: `realizes+` and `realizes-`. An example of traceability is depicted in Figure 1.

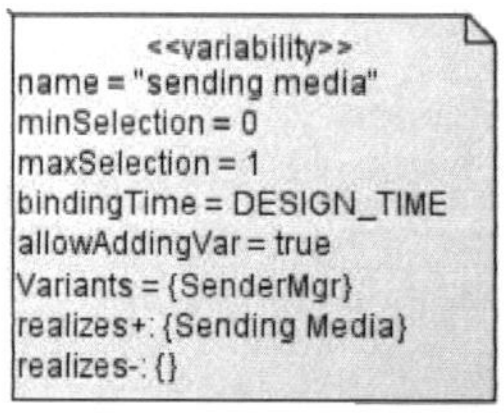

Fig. 1. Tracing elements in the SMarty «variability» tagged-values.

For the identification of traceable elements in a higher level of abstraction, we use the "+" symbol. For lower level of abstraction, we use the "-" symbol. In Figure 1 `realizes+` is a collection of variability names of a high-level element, in this case a variability named "Sending Media" in the use case diagram. Therefore, traceability of elements is facilitated, thus providing round trip course.

2.3 Related Work

Based on non-systematic searches and on the works of Ahnassay et al. [1], Chen and Babar [4] and Galster et al. [7], no work in the literature is directly related to the comparative experimental evaluation between SMarty and PLUS for generating product configurations and traceability based on use case diagrams and class diagrams. However, our research group has been developing several experiments that aim to show the effectiveness of SMarty. Several studies were conducted for identification and resolution of variabilities, and product configuration, while this is the first one aiming at analyzing traceability.

In 2013, Marcolino et al. [12] compared SMarty with PLUS in relation to identification and resolution of variabilities in use case diagrams. In such experiment, SMarty showed to be more effective than PLUS.

In 2014, Marcolino et al. [11] compared SMarty and PLUS to identify and solve variabilities in class diagrams. In such experiment, the PLUS method showed to be more effective. In 2017, two other experiments were conducted by Marcolino et al. [14] and Marcolino and OliveiraJr [13] comparing SMarty and PLUS in class diagrams. In the first experiment, there was no statistical difference between the effectiveness in relation to the ability to interpret and configure products. In the second experiment, PLUS evidenced to be more effective for identification and resolution of variabilities.

In 2018, Nepomuceno and OliveiraJr [15] evaluated the SMarty and PLUS approaches to the effectiveness of configuring correct products using the SPL AGM in use case diagrams. The results showed no advantage from one approach to another.

3 The Empirical Study

This section presents an experimental evaluation to compare the effectiveness of the SMarty approach and the PLUS based on the Wohlin et al.'s template [18].

3.1 Goal and Research Questions

The goal of this experiment is to **compare PLUS and SMarty**, **with the purpose of** identifying which one is more effective, **with respect to** configuration of specific products and tracing elements in use case diagrams and class diagrams, **from the point of view of** researchers in the role of SPL architects, **in the context of** undergraduate students from the State University of Maringá and the Federal University of Technology - Paraná, Campo Mourão campus.

To do so, we defined the following research questions:

RQ.1: Which approach is more effective at deriving SPL product configurations from use case diagrams and class diagrams?

RQ.2: Which approach requires less consultations to the instructional materials for configuring SPL products from use case diagrams and class diagrams?

RQ.3: Is there any influence of the knowledge level of participants on UML and SPL/variability for generating SPL products from use case and class diagrams?

RQ.4: Which approach is more effective in tracing elements in use case and class diagrams?

3.2 Planning

Context Selection This experiment is characterized as off-line. We carried out it in two days: one day at the State University of Maringá (UEM) and one day at the Federal University of Technology - Paraná (UFTPR-CM)

Hypotheses Formulation We formulated the following hypotheses (replace "eff" with "effectiveness" or "number of consultations", "act" with "product configuration" or "traceability", and "diag" with "use case diagram" or "class diagram"):

- Null Hypothesis ($H0_{eff\_act\_diag}$): there is no significant difference in the effectiveness or number of consultations of PLUS and SMarty in configuring products or traceability for use case diagrams or class diagram.
  $\mathbf{H0}_{eff\_act\_diag}$**:** μ**(SMarty)** $=$ μ**(PLUS)**

- ($H1_{eff\_act\_diag}$): there is a significant difference in the effectiveness of PLUS and SMarty in configuring products or traceability for use case diagrams or class diagram.
  $\mathbf{H1}_{eff\_act\_diag}$**:** μ**(SMarty)** $\neq$ μ**(PLUS)**

Variables and Metrics Selection We selected the following variables:

- **Independent variables:** approach being analyzed, which is a factor with two treatments: the PLUS method and the SMarty approach; pre-fixed variable for SPL, the Mobile Media, which was chosen since it has several types of variabilities and possibilities for product configuration, yet with diagrams simple enough to be used for an study without tool support.
- **Dependent variables:** effectiveness of configuring products, number of consultations to instructional material, influence of participant's knowledge on UML and SPL/variability, and effectiveness at traceability.

To calculate effectiveness we used the following equation:

Effectiveness (z,d) = nCorrElem/TotalElem

where:

- z = PLUS or SMarty;
- d = use case diagram or class diagram;

- nCorrElem = number of correct resolved/traced variability elements of a given diagram d using the z approach; and
- TotalElem = total number of variability elements of a given diagram d using the z approach.

Note that effectiveness will always be a value between 0.0 and 1.0. The number of consultation in the material is a discrete positive number. The influence of the participants knowledge is represented by a Likert scale with five options: none, only reading, basic, moderated, advanced. Such influence will be calculated as a correlation between the Likert scale options and the effectiveness at configuring products.

Selection of Subjects Participants were selected in a non-probabilistic manner. All participants from the two universities are undergraduate students enrolled in Computer Science programs.

Choice of Design Type We chose a 1x2 independent factorial experimental design type as treatment, and control has neither interactions nor relationships.

Instrumentation The following materials compose our instrumentation: Informed Consent Term (ICT): contains main information on the experiment to be applied, such as, confidentiality, procedures and benefits; characterization questionnaire, applied to participants to analyze the level of knowledge and experience on UML and SPL/variability; instructional material, with three parts, the first with main concepts of SPL, the second with general description of SPL Mobile Media, and the third with specific concepts for PLUS and SMarty; two use case diagrams of the SPL Mobile Media, one modeled using SMarty and another according to PLUS; two class diagrams of the SPL Mobile Media, one modeled according to SMarty and another according to PLUS; two documents with questions on product configuration and traceability for PLUS and SMarty.

3.3 Operation

The experiment period was one day for each university. For each period, there was a training on general concepts on SPL and, then, for each group, training specific for the given SPL technique and, finally, the experiment tasks.

Training We trained all participants in SPL and variability modeling, configuration of products and traceability. In addition, we trained half of participants using SMarty and the other half using PLUS. Training lasted 35 minutes at both universities. During training, participants received three documents: the ICT, the characterization questionnaire, and the instructional material. Training was based on excerpts of hypothetical SPL use case and class diagrams. Participants were allowed to ask questions at any time during training sessions.

Operation Procedures The following steps were taken in this experiment: experimenter divided participants into two groups balancing them according to their knowledge on UML and SPL/variability; experimenter informed participants they were allowed to use the instructional material during the experiment tasks; experimenter randomly distributed to participants an use case diagram and a class diagram according to PLUS or SMarty, and respective document with questions and tasks to be performed; experimenter asked participants to take notes on how many times they consult the instructional material during tasks; participants configured one specific instance (product) based on both use case and class diagrams from the Mobile Media SPL; participants answered questions on product configuration and traceability by analyzing whether the approach allows identifying variability from one level to another (use case to class diagram traceability) and vice-versa. Participants responded to a couple open questions on improvements and difficulties faced in the experiment; participants gave instruments to experimenter and finished their tasks in the experiment.

3.4 Analysis and Interpretation

Fourty-six (46) participants attended the experiment, 26 participants used the PLUS method and 26 the SMarty approach. All participants had at least basic knowledge of UML, and the median knowledge level was moderate. Regarding SPL/variability, the median knowledge level was low, with 31 with no knowledge on SPL and 15 that could read or had basic knowledge. The average experience was of 33.8 months (median of 36, minimum of 8 and maximum of 48 months of experience). There was no significant difference for knowledge level or experience between participants in control and intervention groups.

Data collected from products derivation are shown in Tables 1 and 2, which refer to PLUS and SMarty, respectively. In such tables there are information on: the number of correct elements (`Correct`), the number of total elements (`Total`) and the effectiveness of the approach (`Effect.`) for each product, the traceability effectiveness from use cases to classes and vice-versa, and the number of consultations on the material. We also inform means, standard deviation and median of such values.

In Table 2, for the SMarty approach, we discarded data from three participants as they either did not complete the tasks requested in the document or due to deviations in the performed experimental tasks. The interpretation of the results were performed to all other participants. Mean, standard deviation and median on Table 2 do not take into account data from excluded participants. All analysis was performed using the R environment.

Effectiveness on Configuring Products (RQ.1) This section presents analysis on the effectiveness of each approach at configuring products.

Normality Test We tested normality of our obtained effectiveness samples with Shapiro-Wilk test. All samples were considered non-normal as p-value < 0.05.

Table 1. Observed values for PLUS.

	Product #1 (use case)			Product #2 (class)			Traceability effectiveness from use cases to classes	Traceability effectiveness from classes to use cases	Number of material consultations
	Correct	Total	Effect.	Correct	Total	Effect.			
Mean	9.47	10	0.94	9.39	10	0.93	0.67	0.23	0.78
St. Dev.	0.99	0.00	0.09	0.59	0.00	0.19	0.46	0.36	2.02
Median	10	10	1.0	10	10	1.0	1.0	0.0	0

Table 2. Observed values for SMarty.

	Product #1 (use case)			Product #2 (class)			Traceability effectiveness from use cases to classes	Traceability effectiveness from classes to use cases	Number of material consultations
	Correct	Total	Effect.	Correct	Total	Effect.			
Mean	8.9	10	0.89	7.35	10	0.73	0.57	0.40	**0.30**
St. Dev	3.05	0.00	0.30	3.80	0.00	0.38	0.43	0.47	0.80
Median	10	10	1.0	9	10	0.90	0.50	0.0	0

Hypothesis Test We chose Mann-Whitney-Wilcoxon as a non-parametric hypothesis test for configuring products as follows:

- Use Case Diagram:
  - the calculated p-value was $p = 0.1898$, which is greater than $\alpha = 0.05$;
  - the Cohen effect size test was applied to samples, thus we obtained $d = -0.4844$, which indicates a small difference in samples observed values;
  - the null hypothesis cannot be rejected, thus there is no significant difference between samples of PLUS and SMarty for use cases.
- Class Diagram:
  - the calculated p-value was $p = 0.02797$, which is less than $\alpha = 0.05$;
  - the Cohen effect size test was applied to samples, thus we obtained $d = 0.5168$, which indicates a medium difference in samples observed values;
  - the null hypothesis can be rejected, thus alternative hypothesis should be accepted. Therefore, PLUS obtained better results than SMarty for configuring products based on classes.

Number of Consultations to Materials (RQ.2) This section presents analysis of results on the number of times a participant consulted the provided instructional material. We intend to demonstrate how such material influences the effectiveness of configuring products for PLUS and SMarty.

Normality Test All samples were considered non-normal as p-value < 0.05.

Hypothesis Test We chose Mann-Whitney-Wilcoxon as a non-parametric hypothesis test for consulting materials on both use case and class diagrams as follows:

- the calculated p-value was $p = 0.6349$, which is greater than $\alpha = 0.05$;

- the Cohen effect size test was applied to samples, thus we obtained $d = 0.277$, which indicates a small difference in samples observed values;
- the null hypothesis cannot be rejected, thus we cannot claim the number of consultations on the material has influenced more one approach over another.

Participants Knowledge Influence (RQ.3) To analyze whether the participants knowledge has influenced more one approach over another, we performed correlations for each diagram. To do so, we converted each Likert scale option to a natural number from 1 to 5. We chose the Spearman correlation technique, as follows:

- Use Case Diagram:
  - for the PLUS method we obtained $\rho = 0.32$ which means a weak positive correlation; and
  - for the SMarty approach we obtained $\rho = 0.16$ which means a weak positive correlation.
- Class Diagram:
  - for the PLUS method we obtained $\rho = 0.24$ which means a weak positive correlation; and
  - for the SMarty approach we obtained $\rho = 0.41$ which means a weak positive correlation.

As we could observe, all correlations are positive and weak. It means: (i) there was no influence on the participants knowledge over the obtained effectiveness at configuring products in both use case and class diagrams; and (ii) PLUS and SMarty comprehensibility seems not dependent on knowledge, as undergraduate students could perform valid configurations on both PLUS and SMarty.

Effectiveness on Tracing Elements (RQ.4) This section presents analysis on the effectiveness on tracing elements from use cases to classes and vice-versa.

Normality Test All samples were considered non-normal as p-value < 0.05.

Hypothesis Test We chose Mann-Whitney-Wilcoxon as a non-parametric hypothesis test for the effectiveness on tracing elements as follows:

- From Use Cases to Classes:
  - the calculated p-value was 0.6442, which is greater than $\alpha = 0.05$;
  - the Cohen effect size test was applied to samples, thus we obtained $d = 0.078$, which indicates an insignificant difference in the observed values;
  - the null hypothesis cannot be rejected, thus there is no significant difference between samples from traceability from use case to class diagrams.
- From Classes to Use Cases:
  - the calculated p-value was 0.176, which is greater than $\alpha = 0.05$
  - the Cohen effect size test was applied to samples, thus we obtained $d = -0.488$, which indicates a small difference in samples observed values;
  - the null hypothesis cannot be rejected, thus there is no significant difference between samples from traceability from class do use case diagrams.

3.5 Validity Evaluation

We identified the following threats and tried to mitigate them. Regarding **internal validity**, all participants are undergraduate with no significant difference in the students skills, thus providing some kind of homogeneity in samples. We tried to mitigate it by inviting students from two different universities. We tried to mitigate lacking of knowledge in SPL/variability by leveling participants in training sessions. We provided them with at least same contents and materials. Therefore, we understand their answers are valid and significant. We avoided communication among participants with a human observer during the experiment tasks all the time.

External Validity: we understand the most external threat to this experiment was the instrumentation with regard to use case diagrams and class diagrams. As they do not come from a commercial and actual SPL, we tried to mitigate it using a well-known SPL in the academic environment, the Mobile Media. The knowledge level of participants might be a threat as they have different experiences in UML and SPL/variability from each university. We tried to mitigate it by performing training sessions and taking Falessi et al. [5] recommendations for granted in this experiment. Accordingly to such authors, populations should not be considered better than other.

Construct Validity: study instrumentation and its validity are major potential construct threats to this experiment. To mitigate it, we performed a pilot project with four master's students from UEM with grounded knowledge in SPL/variability aiming at evaluation of such instrumentation and potential improvements.

Conclusion Validity: the main conclusion validity of this experiment is related to: (i) environment, as only two universities were chosen; (ii) only 41 (46 minus 5 excluded) students took part of the experiment, lowering the behavioral statistical accuracy; and (iii) participant experiences should be more explored towards experts.

4 Discussion on Results

We discuss results in various perspectives in the next sections.

Configuration of Products (RQ.1) We have verified there is evidence that the SMarty approach, in its current version, does not stand out in relation to the PLUS method in the effectiveness of configuration of products based on use case diagrams of the Mobile Media SPL. Such lack of difference is corroborated by a very low effectiveness size value. As for the class diagram, we realized the participants who made use of the PLUS method had more effective product configurations than those who used the SMarty approach, corroborated by a high effectiveness size value.

Although using a more complex SPL compared to that used by Nepomuceno and OliveiraJr [15], our assumption is that the use case diagram of Mobile Media still has few use cases and is relatively simple to understand and configure. In this way, solving the variabilities and configuring specific products was not a complex task, even with the PLUS method that has no guidelines and a support process as the SMarty approach.

Another assumption that arises is the relative simplicity of configuration of products with PLUS, since their diagrams are modeled with only three stereotypes. This may have led to a greater effectiveness in configuring products by the participants based on the medians and standard deviations of each approach.

Usage of Instructional Material (RQ.2) As we observed, the number of consultations to the instructional material did not significantly influenced the effectiveness at configuring SPL products in both use case and class diagrams of one approach over another. Such claim is corroborated by a small effect size value.

With few consultations to materials, the following assumptions rise: training might provide enough basis on PLUS and SMarty for participants performing their tasks; the used diagrams from Mobile Media have few stereotypes representing variability aspects, thus there is no such difficult at syntactically and semantically comprehending them; as discussed in external validity, this might have occurred due to certain participants do not accurately inform the exact number of consultations.

Influence of Participants Knowledge (RQ.3) We verified there is no significant influence of participants knowledge at configuring products with PLUS and SMarty, corroborated with small values of correlations.

On the one hand, we noticed that for the configuration of a product using use case diagram, the knowledge of the participants who used the PLUS method had greater influence than SMarty. On the other hand, when configuring products from the class diagram, less qualified participants were more effective with PLUS than with SMarty.

In the case of configuration of products with use case diagrams, our assumption is that the UML note of the «variability» stereotype might have positively influenced participants using SMarty, which facilitates the resolution of variation points and respective variants.

For configuring products from class diagrams we identified three potential assumptions: (i) PLUS has only two stereotypes, which might justify its simplicity in comprehending such diagrams and, consequently, valid configurations; (ii) the simplicity of Mobile Media class diagrams might also have influenced valid configurations; and (iii) both assumptions (i) and (ii) might make sense.

Traceability (RQ.4) The initial evidence for a better result of SMarty over PLUS was with respect to tracing elements between UML diagrams, especially from the class diagram to the use case diagram.

The PLUS method, unlike the SMarty approach, does not provide any kind of support for tracing elements between UML diagrams. Then, our main assumption is the SMarty UML note for variability, with tagged values `realizes+` and `realizes`- might help participants to obtain better results at tracing elements from class diagrams to use case diagrams.

Results might get some influence due to the lack of an actual SPL and relatively low complexity diagrams, especially with few variation points and variants among use cases and classes levels. This currently led us to plan and conduct a replication of this experiment with a more complex SPL.

SMarty Prospective Improvements and Lessons Learned. With the results of this experiment and participants feedback on open questions, SMarty should be improved.

Guidelines will serve as guidance for providing users specific scenarios according to the type of variability of each diagram, as well as to ease the traceability among elements from different diagrams at different abstraction levels, including navigability of such diagrams.

Another improvement will be an optional feature to use icons rather than stereotypes to represent variability, which might graphically ease the comprehension of modeled variabilities. Icons are very common instruments used by different UML profiles, thus it will not impact the UML metamodel in any way.

We are also currently working on an automated tool to support UML-based SPLs as there is no specific tool for such. The advantage of having this tool is its support to every SPL modeled with Meta Object Facility (MOF) based[4] languages.

Configuring a valid product is not a trivial task, even using a simple SPL. Although we provided training for participants as well as documentation for consultation, they still faced difficulties to correctly set up products in both approaches. Thus, we understand that an automated tool will mitigate such issue. We are currently developing an automated environment to support the whole lifecycle of SMarty-based SPLs.

Although SMarty has support for traceability of variabilities, participants complained on the lack of a guide to do so. Therefore, we believe a set of guidelines should aid to execute this activity.

We tried to increase complexity of adopted SPL moving from the SEI's SPL to Mobile Media. To mitigate this issue, we understand more complex Mobile Media elements are needed for prospective experiments.

5 Conclusion

This paper presented an experiment conducted to compare PLUS and SMarty variability management approaches with relation to four research questions. All instrumentation and data of this experiment is available at `https://doi.org/10.5281/zenodo.3569422`.

With respect to the first research question, the results showed a slight advantage of the PLUS method in relation to the SMarty approach in the configuration

[4] `https://www.omg.org/mof/`

of products from class diagrams. For the use case diagram there was no evidence benefiting one over another.

The number of consultations to the instructional material of each approach did not influence the calculated value of respective effectiveness. This is a great result as we expected participants to understand the approaches comprehensibility in a short period of time.

There is evidence the participant's previous knowledge level in SPL/variability and UML may be related to better results on the use of the approaches for configuring products, especially with regard to the SMarty approach. Thus, less experienced participants were able to configure products with greater effectiveness with SMarty.

It is understood that the SMarty approach provides more subsidies for element tracing between the diagrams, however this aspect still needs to be further experienced in more complex SPLs.

We understand the results of this experiment together with those of the previous experiment for class and use case diagrams provided further subsidies for investing in an SPL approach that focuses on UML diagrams and consequently produces tooling support for UML-based SPL life cycle.

Our next planned experiments, using sequence, activity, and component diagrams, will consider assumptions discussed in this experiment as a way to evolve the SMarty approach, since the purpose is that it is more effective in the identification of variabilities, in the configuration of products and in the tracing of elements among diagrams in relation to the other existing approaches. We shall consider SPLs with more complexity at configuring products.

References

1. Ahnassay, A., Bagheri, D., D, G.: Empirical evaualtion in sofware product line engineering. Tech. rep., Ryerson University (2013), `http://ls3.rnet.ryerson.ca/wp-content/uploads/2013/08/TR-LS3130084R4T.pdf`, tR-LS3-130084R4T
2. Apel, S., Batory, D., Kästner, C., Saake, G.: Feature-Oriented Software Product Lines: Concepts and Implementation. Springer Publishing Company, Incorporated, 1st edn. (2016)
3. Capilla, R., Bosch, J., Kang, K.C.: Systems and Software Variability Management: Concepts, Tools and Experiences. Springer, USA (2013)
4. Chen, L., Ali Babar, M.: A systematic review of evaluation of variability management approaches in software product lines. Inf. Softw. Technol. **53**(4), 344–362 (Apr 2011)
5. Falessi, D., Juristo, N., Wohlin, C., Turhan, B., Münch, J., Jedlitschka, A., Oivo, M.: Empirical software engineering experts on the use of students and professionals in experiments. Empirical Software Engineering **1**(23), 452–489 (06 2017)
6. Figueiredo, E., Cacho, N., Sant'Anna, C., Monteiro, M., Kulesza, U., Garcia, A., Soares, S., Ferrari, F., Khan, S., Castor Filho, F., Dantas, F.: Evolving software product lines with aspects. In: 2008 ACM/IEEE 30th International Conference on Software Engineering. pp. 261–270 (May 2008). https://doi.org/10.1145/1368088.1368124

7. Galster, M., Weyns, D., Tofan, D., Michalik, B., Avgeriou, P.: Variability in software systems—a systematic literature review. IEEE Transactions on Software Engineering **40**(3), 282–306 (March 2014)
8. Gomaa, H.: Designing Software Product Lines with UML: From Use Cases to Pattern-Based Software Architectures. Addison Wesley Longman, Redwood City, CA, USA (2004)
9. Linden, F.J.v.d., Schmid, K., Rommes, E.: Software Product Lines in Action: The Best Industrial Practice in Product Line Engineering. Springer, Berlin (2007)
10. Marcolino, A., OliveiraJr, E., Gimenes, I.: Variability identification and representation in software product line uml sequence diagrams: Proposal and empirical study. In: SBES. pp. 141–150 (2014). https://doi.org/10.1109/SBES.2014.11
11. Marcolino, A., OliveiraJr, E., Gimenes, I., Barbosa, E.F.: Empirically based evolution of a variability management approach at uml class level. In: COMPSAC. pp. 354–363 (2014)
12. Marcolino, A., OliveiraJr, E., Gimenes, I.M.S., Maldonado, J.C.: Towards the effectiveness of a variability management approach at use case level. In: SEKE. pp. 214–219. KSI Institute (2013)
13. Marcolino, A.S., OliveiraJr, E.: Comparing smarty and plus for variability identification and representation at product-line uml class level: A controlled quasi-experiment. Journal of Computer Science **13**(11), 617–632 (2017). https://doi.org/10.3844/jcssp.2017.617.632
14. Marcolino, A.S., OliveiraJr, E., Gimenes, I.M., Barbosa, E.F.: Variability resolution and product configuration with smarty: An experimental study on uml class diagrams. Journal of Computer Science **13**, 307–319 (2017). https://doi.org/10.3844/jcssp.2017.307.319
15. Nepomuceno, T.S., OliveiraJr, E.: Configuring software product line specific products with smarty and plus: An experimental study on use case diagrams. In: SBQS. pp. 81–90. ACM (2018). https://doi.org/10.1145/3275245.3275254
16. OliveiraJr, E., Gimenes, I.M.S., Maldonado, J.C.: Systematic management of variability in uml-based software product lines. Journal of Universal Computer Science (JUCS) **16**(17), 2374–2393 (sep 2010)
17. Raatikainen, M., Tiihonen, J., Männistö, T.: Software product lines and variability modeling: A tertiary study. Journal of Systems and Software **149**, 485 – 510 (2019)
18. Wohlin, C., Runeson, P., Hst, M., Ohlsson, M.C., Regnell, B., Wessln, A.: Experimentation in Software Engineering. Springer, USA (2012)
19. Ziadi, T., Jezequel, J.M.: Software product line engineering with the uml: Deriving products. In: Käköla, T., Duenas, J.C. (eds.) Software Product Lines, pp. 557–588. Springer, Berlin (2006)

Evaluating the Usefulness and Ease of Use of a Software Process Line Tool

Diogo Matheus Costa[1], Eldânae Nogueira Teixeira[1] and Cláudia Maria Lima Werner[1]

[1] Universidade Federal do Rio de Janeiro/UFRJ - COPPE, Rio de Janeiro/RJ, Brasil
{dmc, danny, werner}@cos.ufrj.br

Abstract. Software Process Line (SPrL) provides a systematic way to support software process reuse. However, adopting SPrL approaches without supporting tools may be a very difficult task. Although SPrL supporting tools are becoming more practical, integrated tools are still needed to support all reuse stages. Hence, aiming to support SPrL activities, the Odyssey tool, which provides a software reuse environment, has been improved. Since every proposed technology should be evaluated before being available for use, this paper aims to characterize Odyssey acceptance through its usefulness and ease of use under the perspective of Brazilian software process experts during software process definition using SPrL. This study was designed using Technology Acceptance Model (TAM) and Goal, Question, Metric (GQM) paradigm with a predefined interpretation model. It was performed with seven experts and the collected data provides insights that Odyssey indeed helps the software process definition using SPrL. Although the results are positive, the identified threats highlight the study limitations. Finally, a set of improvements was identified based on the collected data, participants' comments, as well as researchers' notes. These improvements are being implemented.

Keywords: Software Process Line, Supporting Tool, Evaluation.

1 Introduction

Considering the fact that the process by which software is developed influences the final product quality [19, 10], companies are concerned with their process definitions. However, it is considered a complex activity that requires experience and knowledge from a variety of Software Engineering disciplines [1, 2]. Besides that, defining a software process from scratch is risky and requires much time and effort [26, 28].

In this scenario, the Software Process Line (SPrL) technique provides a systematic way to reuse software processes, identifying their similarity and variability. SPrL represents a set of processes in a particular area, or for a specific purpose, that shares characteristics, being built upon reusable process assets [26]. Some of SPrL's expected benefits are: (i) increase of the reuse potential; (ii) risk reduction; and (iii) increase of the processes quality and suitability [20, 12].

However, adopting SPrL approaches without supporting tools may be a very difficult task [3]. The definition of supporting tools can enable the practical use of process reuse approaches, providing a major possibility of their application in real scenarios [25]. Although SPrL supporting tools are becoming more practical, integrated tools are still needed to support all reuse stages [5, 25].

Although there are other tools [1, 3, 14, 15, 22], this work investigates the Odyssey tool [18], which provides a software reuse environment. Odyssey was chosen because of its availability, as well as the improvements made over the past few years to provide integrated support to SPrL concepts and engineering stages [24, 6].

This paper aims to characterize Odyssey acceptance through its usefulness and ease of use under the perspective of Brazilian software process experts during software process definition using SPrL. To achieve this goal an evaluation was designed and performed using Technology Acceptance Model (TAM) [8] and Goal, Question, Metric (GQM) [23].

The remainder of the paper is structured as follows: Section 2 provides some background on SPrL engineering and TAM; Section 3 briefly describes the Odyssey tool; Section 4 details the study design and presents the evaluation results; and Section 5 presents the final considerations, as well as proposals for future work.

2 Theoretical Background

2.1 SPrL Engineering

In its engineering viewpoint, SPrL is divided into two stages [20]: I. Software Process Domain Engineering (SPDE); and II. Project-Specific Process Engineering (PSPE).

In the SPDE stage, development *for* reuse, process engineers define the SPrL reusable artifacts. SPDE activities are focused on understanding the domain, generating a set of models, such as: a) feature model, used to represent the domain knowledge, identifying similarity and variability; and b) context model, used to characterize entities, information and context situations that support the selection of reusable process elements.

In the PSPE stage, development *by* reuse, reusable process elements are selected for a project-specific software process considering the process definition context (e.g., information related to customer, organization, product). PSPE activities are focused on software process definition using SPrL. These activities are: 1) project characterization, identifying its requirements; 2) reusable process elements selection, solving configuration points (i.e., variability); and 3) remaining software process adaptation, to meet specific needs that may not be contemplated in the process domain. The result is a project-specific software process defined with all the elements that should compose its execution.

2.2 Technology Acceptance Model (TAM)

Proposed by Fred Davis [7], Technology Acceptance Model (TAM) was idealized based on Theory of Reasoned Action (TRA), a psychological theory that seeks to explain behavior [9]. Davis concludes that the concepts of perceived usefulness and perceived ease of use influence people's decision to use or not an information system

[7]. In this context, a positive perception of these concepts provides insights of use intent. These concepts are described below:

- **Perceived Usefulness:** The degree to which an individual believes that using a particular system would increase his or her job performance;
- **Perceived Ease of Use:** The degree to which an individual believes that the use of a particular system would be free of physical and mental effort.

3 Odyssey Tool

Odyssey (Fig. 1) is an infrastructure based on domain models, which provides support to development *for* reuse and development *by* reuse [17]. Although this work focuses on the SPrL support, Odyssey also supports other scenarios (e.g., Software Product Line).

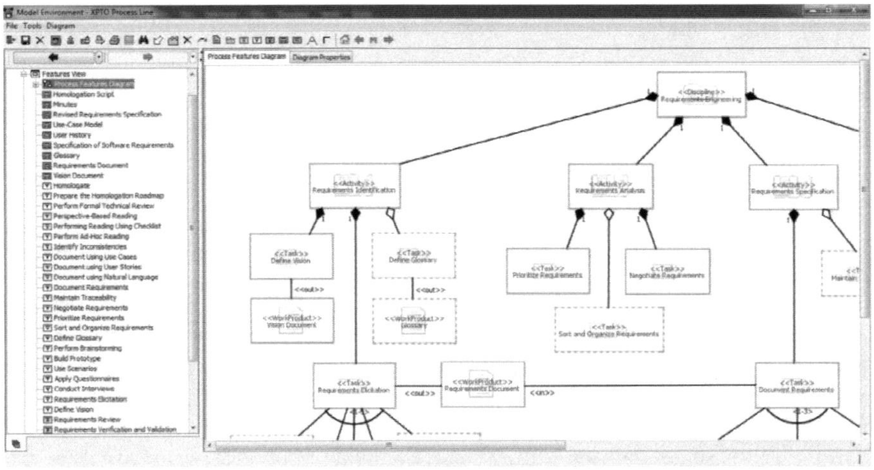

Fig. 1. Odyssey modeling interface.

In the software process context, Odyssey provides support to SPrL engineering activities. Over the past few years, Odyssey has been improved mainly focused on SPDE stage [24]. However, the most recent contributions have focused on PSPE stage support and its integration with SPDE stage [6].

The evaluation presented in this paper focuses on the software process definition using SPrL. In this scenario, Odyssey provides three supporting mechanisms:

- **Slicing Mechanism:** In this mechanism (Fig. 2), the user is supported during the manual selection of process elements through variability and optionality resolution checks, as well as composition rules (i.e., constraints). In this scenario, only the mandatory process elements are pre-selected. During the feature model slicing, selections verifications are conducted and composition rules are analyzed (i.e., Rule-Based System technique) to influence the reusable process elements selection through the defined constraints. If adopted alone, this mechanism provides limited decision-making support. The similarity search mechanism functionalities are available aiming to support the remaining SPrL variability resolution.

- **Context Recognition Mechanism:** In this mechanism, the user describes the software project context by assigning specific values to the context information of the SPrL context model. The support occurs through context rules (i.e., Rule-Based System technique) specified in the SPrL context model based on expected context situations (i.e., actions for expected context definitions). As a result process elements are suggested (i.e., pre-selected) to support the SPrL variability resolution. The functionalities of the slicing mechanism are available, as well as the similarity search mechanism functionalities aiming to support the remaining SPrL variability resolution.
- **Similarity Search Mechanism:** In this mechanism, the user describes the software project context through context entities and information. Based on this characterization, a similarity analysis (i.e., Case-Based Reasoning technique) is performed on the software processes related to the SPrL. The result of this similarity analysis is a list of software processes defined in a similar context, their basic information, representation model and context information.

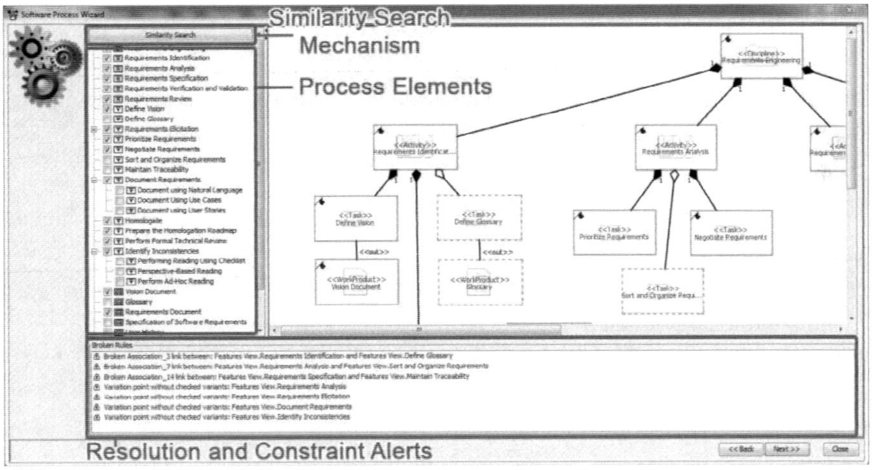

Fig. 2. Odyssey slicing mechanism interface.

The use of the similarity search mechanism alone aims at the full project-specific software process reuse. The goal of full reuse is to adopt a software process defined in a similar context as a starting point to define a project-specific software process. On the other hand, the use of the similarity search mechanism through other mechanisms (slicing mechanism and context recognition mechanism) aims at the partial project-specific software process reuse. The goal of partial reuse is to analyze the decisions taken in software processes defined in a similar context to support the variability resolution.

The Odyssey's software process definition mechanisms are presented in [6], through a usage scenario with illustrations.

4 Evaluation

As mentioned before, Odyssey has evolved over the past few years to support SPrL engineering activities. However, any body of knowledge must be evaluated to be considered scientific [13]. In addition, according to BASILI et al. [4], all proposed technology (e.g., tool, method) must be evaluated before being available for use.

Thus, this evaluation aims to characterize Odyssey acceptance. Besides that, this work can be classified as an observation study, where the participant performs tasks while being observed by an experimenter [21].

In this scenario, a plan was defined based on TAM. In addition, the GQM paradigm was used and the items proposed by DAVIS [8], focused on perceived usefulness and perceived ease of use are applied as questions to characterize acceptance and predict systems usage. Finally, to capture the participant answer and assess each question, the Likert psychometric scale [16] was used to determine the participants' level of agreement or disagreement.

4.1 Planning and Definition

Objective. *Analyze* the Odyssey tool; *with the purpose of* characterizing its acceptance; *with respect to* the perceived usefulness and perceived ease of use; *from the point of view of* Brazilian software process experts; *in the context of* software process definition using SPrL's artifacts defined by the researcher.

This objective does not involve any kind of comparison with other tools. In addition, this work is not intended to answer any performance-related questions to evaluate which is the best software process definition mechanism (Section 3).

Goals, Questions and Metrics. A model was built based on the GQM paradigm, composed of five specific goals, fifteen questions and five metrics. The specific goals are presented in Table 1.

Table 1. Evaluation specific goals.

Goal	Description
G1	Evaluate the training material appropriateness.
G2	Evaluate the similarity search mechanism support to the concept of full project-specific software process reuse.
G3	Evaluate the similarity search mechanism support to the concept of partial project-specific software process reuse.
G4	Evaluate the perceived usefulness of the Odyssey tool.
G5	Evaluate the perceived ease of use of the Odyssey tool.

The G1 goal is focused on the training material, G2-G3 are focused on the support offered by the similarity search mechanism, because it is the Odyssey most recent contribution, and G4-G5 represent TAM's goals (i.e., perceived usefulness and perceived ease of use).

To analyze these specific goals (Table 1), fifteen questions were defined, which are presented in Table 2. As mentioned before, the items proposed by DAVIS [8], focused on perceived usefulness and perceived ease of use, are applied as questions (Q4-Q15), representing the evaluation main questions.

Table 2. Questions applied to analyze the specific goals.

Goal	Question	Description
G1	Q1	The training material applied was sufficient to perform the tasks.
G2	Q2	The similarity search mechanism provides satisfactory support to reuse software processes defined in a similar context as a starting point to adapt them aiming at the project-specific software process definition.
G3	Q3	The similarity search mechanism provides satisfactory support to visualize the decisions made in software processes defined in a similar context aiming at the SPrL variability resolution support during project-specific software process definition using the slicing mechanism.
G4	Q4	Using Odyssey in my job would enable me to accomplish tasks more quickly.
G4	Q5	Using Odyssey would improve my job performance.
G4	Q6	Using Odyssey in my job would increase my productivity.
G4	Q7	Using Odyssey would enhance my effectiveness on the job.
G4	Q8	Using Odyssey would make it easier to do my job.
G4	Q9	I would find Odyssey useful in my job.
G5	Q10	Learning to operate Odyssey would be easy for me.
G5	Q11	I would find it easy to get Odyssey to do what I want to do.
G5	Q12	My interaction with Odyssey would be clear and understandable.
G5	Q13	I would find Odyssey flexible to interact with.
G5	Q14	It would be easy for me to become skillful at using Odyssey.
G5	Q15	I would find Odyssey easy to use.

Finally, each question is answered using a Likert scale composed of five alternatives (i.e., five points) and is assessed by the metrics presented in Table 3.

Table 3. Metrics applied to assess the questions.

Metric	Description
M1	Number of participants who chose "Strongly Disagree".
M2	Number of participants who chose "Partially Disagree".
M3	Number of participants who chose "Indifferent".
M4	Number of participants who chose "Partially Agree".
M5	Number of participants who chose "Strongly Agree".

Interpretation Model. To analyze the collected data, an interpretation model was defined based on the specific goals, its questions and metrics. The model is presented in Table 4 and it should be interpreted by checking each expression to confirm its veracity, following the format "IF *expression*, THEN *interpretation*". In this scenario, the interpretation model was defined based on the evaluation conducted in the work of HERNANDES et al. [11].

Table 4. Data interpretation model.

Nº	Question	Expression	Interpretation
1	Q1	M5+M4+M3 >= M2+M1	The provided training material was sufficient to conduct the evaluation.
2	Q1	M5+M4+M3 < M2+M1	The provided training material was insufficient and may have influenced the result.
3	Q2	M5+M4 >= M3+M2+M1	The similarity search mechanism support was sufficient to meet the concept of full reuse.
4	Q2	M5+M4 < M3+M2+M1	The similarity search mechanism support was insufficient to meet the concept of full reuse. Therefore, participants' comments should be analyzed to identify improvements.
5	Q3	M5+M4 >= M3+M2+M1	The similarity search mechanism support was sufficient to meet the concept of partial reuse.
6	Q3	M5+M4 < M3+M2+M1	The similarity search mechanism support was insufficient to meet the concept of partial reuse. Therefore, participants' comments should be analyzed to identify improvements.
7	Qi, i=4 to 9	M5+M4 >= M3+M2+M1	Odyssey is useful and the next step is to perform an experimental study in real projects (i.e., industry).
8	Qi, i=4 to 9	M5+M4+M3 >= M2+M1	Odyssey is useful, but the next step is to analyze the participants' comments to identify and implement improvements before conducting an experimental study in real projects (i.e., industry).
9	Qi, i=4 to 9	M5+M4+M3 < M2+M1	Odyssey did not show evidence of usefulness. The next step is to review the tool features, as well as analyze the participants feedback to identify and implement improvements before conducting an experimental study in real projects (i.e., industry).
10	Qi, i=10 to 15	M5+M4 >= M3+M2+M1	Odyssey is easy to use and the next step is to perform an experimental study in real projects (i.e., industry).
11	Qi, i=10 to 15	M5+M4+M3 >= M2+M1	Odyssey is easy to use, but the next step is to analyze the participants' comments to identify and implement improvements before conducting an experimental study in real projects (i.e., industry).
12	Qi, i=10 to 15	M5+M4+M3 < M2+M1	Odyssey did not show evidence of ease of use. The next step is to search for usability standards, as well as analyze the participants' feedback to identify and implement improvements before conducting an experimental study in real projects (i.e., industry).

Expectations. It is expected that the collected data present insights that the training material was sufficient to conduct the evaluation, as well as that the similarity search mechanism meets the concepts of full and partial project-specific software process reuse. Finally, it is expected that the collected data present insights that Odyssey indeed helps the software process definition using SPrL.

Research Plan Analysis. In order to check the research plan and its artifacts, an evaluation step was applied. This step occurred iteratively involving three researchers. In this scenario, improvements have been made to mitigate the threats to validity, as well as reduce the time and effort required to accomplish the predefined tasks.

A lab package is available at https://doi.org/10.6084/m9.figshare.11893869. This package contains the participant characterization questionnaire, tasks document (two versions), evaluation questionnaire and the participants' analysis (full version).

4.2 Execution

Pilot. In order to analyze the plan feasibility, a pilot execution was conducted in early November 2018. It was performed by one participant (i.e., software process expert), a D.Sc. member of the Software Reuse Research Group (COPPE/UFRJ). The collected data of this pilot were not considered in the final data analysis.

Based on this pilot execution, some improvements were made: a) high-level tasks were divided into subtasks; b) complex tasks were simplified to specific tasks; and c) one observed defect was solved to avoid a possible impact.

Observation Study. After the pilot execution, the evaluation was conducted with seven software process experts (i.e., with knowledge in software process, as well as SPrL concepts) in December 2018, as described below.

Table 5 partially presents the participants' characterization (full characterization available in the lab package). These data were collected through the participant characterization questionnaire. The participants' experience in related activities was also collected.

Table 5. Participants' characterization.

Item	P1	P2	P3	P4	P5	P6	P7
Group Relationship	External	External	External	Former Member	External	Former Member	External
Academic degree	M.Sc.	M.Sc.	D.Sc.	PostDoc	PostDoc	D.Sc.	D.Sc.
Occupation	D.Sc. Student	Professor	PostDoc Student	Professor	Professor	Systems Analyst	Professor

The evaluation was performed based on steps specified in the planning phase, using communication templates (i.e., email), as well as predefined documents.

Initially, software process experts were mapped by convenience; fifteen experts were invited; seven experts scheduled a date to perform the evaluation; before the scheduled date, the experts received a training material; on the scheduled date, the expert received a consent form, participant characterization questionnaire and a training video focused on the supporting tool; after filling out these documents and watching the training video, the expert received the tasks document and remote access information; finally, at the end of the tasks, the expert received an evaluation questionnaire, which was sent to the researchers to finish the study.

4.3 Data Analysis and Results

Based on the interpretation model, the collected data were interpreted through the expressions aiming to analyze the results. Each specific goal is discussed below.

Goal Analysis (G1). This goal aims to evaluate the training material appropriateness.

Based on the collected data, two participants partially agree, four strongly agree and only one partially disagree. This can be interpreted as described in item 1 of Table 4 (M5 + M4 + M3 >= M2 + M1), indicating a positive result for the provided training material, where it has been considered sufficient to conduct the evaluation.

In this scenario, participant P6 highlighted concern about the participants' profile, selecting "partially disagree". In the participant's opinion, the material may not be sufficient for those who do not have experience in software process variability. However, only software process experts were invited, all with experience in software process variability. In addition, despite having selected "strongly agree", participant P4 indicated that the material could be simplified by reducing the training video duration.

Goal Analysis (G2). This goal aims to evaluate the similarity search mechanism support to the concept of full project-specific software process reuse.

Based on the collected data, four participants partially agree and three strongly agree. This can be interpreted as described in item 3 of Table 4 (M5 + M4 >= M3 + M2 + M1), indicating a positive result for the similarity research mechanism support, where it has been considered sufficient to meet the concept of full reuse.

In this scenario, according to participant P1 the similarity search mechanism support is relevant. However, the participant expressed concern about the use of the mechanism in real scenario (i.e., industry), with multiple disciplines and large amount of process elements.

In addition, participant P5 suggested allowing the user to select the context information that would be considered in the similarity calculation (i.e., subset). P6 participant recommended adding an explanation about how the similarity calculation works. Finally, participants P4 and P7 pointed out that the software process analysis and context comparison functionalities are very useful and informative.

Goal Analysis (G3). This goal aims to evaluate the similarity search mechanism support to the concept of partial project-specific software process reuse.

Based on the collected data, three participants partially agree, three strongly agree and only one partially disagree. This can be interpreted as described in item 5 of Table 4 (M5 + M4 >= M3 + M2 + M1), indicating a positive result for the similarity research mechanism support, where it has been considered sufficient to meet the concept of partial reuse.

In this scenario, although participant P3 selected "partially disagree", no comments were provided in the questionnaire. The participant also showed no interest in analyzing decisions made in processes defined in a similar context, choosing to make his own decisions.

In addition, participants P1 and P7 expressed concern about the use of this mechanism in a real scenario (i.e., industry), with multiple disciplines and a large amount of process elements. Participant P5 suggested allowing the comparison of multiple cases (i.e., software processes) through a facilitating interface.

Finally, participant P4 highlighted that it is very positive to observe the choices (i.e., decisions made) in processes defined in a similar context, indicating that this kind of functionality can make the project manager more confident about his/her decisions.

Goal Analysis (G4). This goal aims to evaluate the perceived usefulness of the Odyssey tool. Fig. 3 presents the collected data focusing on the related questions (Q4-Q9) of this goal.

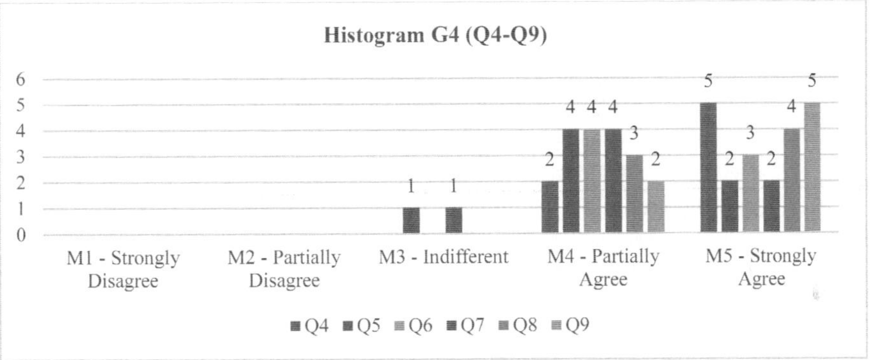

Fig. 3. Participants number X Selected option (G4).

Based on the data observed in Fig. 3, G4 goal can be interpreted as described in item 7 of Table 4 (M5 + M4 >= M3 + M2 + M1), where 21 + 19 >= 2 + 0 + 0 is true. Thus, these data present insights that: "Odyssey is useful and the next step is to perform an experimental study in real projects (i.e., industry)".

In this scenario, participant P4 highlighted the usefulness of comparing context information in the similarity search mechanism. Finally, participant P6 pointed out that consulting similar cases is indeed useful.

Goal Analysis (G5). This goal aims to evaluate the perceived ease of use of the Odyssey tool. Fig. 4 presents the collected data focusing on the related questions (Q10-Q15) of this goal.

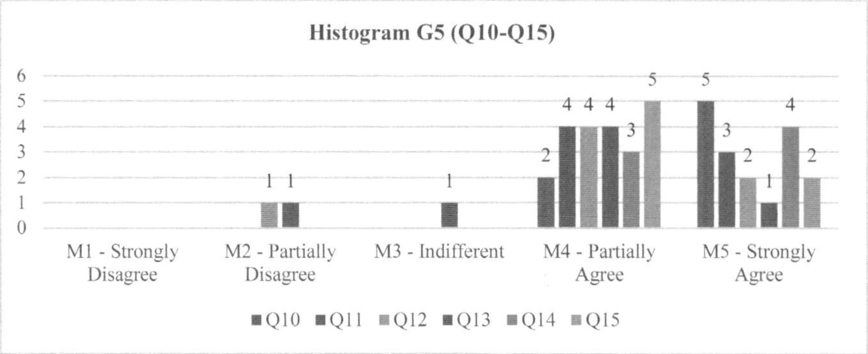

Fig. 4. Participants number X Selected option (G5).

Based on the data observed in Fig. 4, G5 goal can be interpreted as described in item 10 of Table 4 (M5 + M4 >= M3 + M2 + M1), where 17 + 22 >= 1 + 2 + 0 is true. Thus, these data present insights that: "Odyssey is easy to use and the next step is to perform an experimental study in real projects (i.e., industry)".

In this scenario, participant P1 pointed out that Odyssey main menu could be more flexible. Participant P5 suggested adding tutorials to guide the user during tasks. Finally, participant P7 emphasized the simplicity and objectivity of the tool, indicating that an industry study could help identifying tool improvements.

Improvements Identification. Although the collected data present insights of Odyssey's acceptance, an analysis was performed to find improvement opportunities. Thus, ten improvements were identified, which are presented in Table 6.

Table 6. Identified improvements.

Item	Description
1	Add custom menu on Odyssey main screen to offer specific options according to the selected item in the domain tree.
2	Customize the slicing mechanism to make possible to display of process elements specific information from the feature model.
3	Add confirmation message when populating context information if context information without assigned value exists.
4	Keep in memory the information context values in similarity search mechanism when used through other mechanisms.
5	Uncouple the similarity search mechanism when used through other mechanisms, in order to enable similar case analysis while doing a parallel task (e.g., select process elements).
6	Add explanation of how similarity calculation is performed in the similarity search mechanism.
7	Add an option to customize the weights of each similarity search mechanism's context information, as well as filter information by selecting a relevant subset for analysis.
8	Add complementary resources to assist in the visualization of similar case decision-making (e.g., simultaneous analysis of multiple cases).
9	Add tutorials to teach specific activity steps (e.g., software process definition).
10	Evaluate the adopted context information to better understand their different weights to support decision-making in the software process definition activity.

4.4 Threats to Validity

This evaluation was performed to characterize Odyssey acceptance. However, it is common that there are issues that may affect or limit the validity of the observed results. These issues are known as threats to validity [27]. Thus, in this section the threats to validity related to this work are presented.

- **Internal Validity:** The research plan proposes the use of software process experts, assuming that they represent a valuable profile. Besides that, the selection by convenience of the participants represents a threat, but to mitigate this threat, experts from different Brazilian states were invited to participate.
- **External Validity:** The low number, as well as the academic bias of the participants, limit the generalization power of the observed results. In addition, the predefined tasks focused on software process definition using SPrL delimit the study observations to this context (i.e., PSPE stage). In this scenario, only two mechanisms (i.e., slicing and similarity search) were used (Section 3). This delimitation was necessary to make the execution feasible. Besides that, the PSPE support represents the latest contributions to the Odyssey tool.
- ***Constructo* Validity:** The artifacts specified by the researchers (e.g., feature model, context characterization) represents another threat. Besides that, the use of the TeamViewer software to enable experts from different Brazilian states to participate through remote access also represents a threat, because of the risk of impact on the experts' perception.
- **Conclusion Validity:** The data analysis step did not use statistical methods, mainly due to the low number of participants, as well as the use of the Likert scale. In this scenario, to mitigate this threat, an interpretation model was specified in the planning phase to support the data analysis.

5 Conclusions and Future Works

This paper briefly describes a tool, called Odyssey, a software reuse environment. Besides that, an evaluation is presented, focused on characterizing Odyssey acceptance through its usefulness and ease of use by seven software process experts' analyses. In this scenario, the shared lab package can contribute to support future investigations of SPrL tools.

The collected data present insights of Odyssey's acceptance, meeting the study expectations. However, it is not possible to generalize these results based on the identified threats (Section 4.4).

A set of improvements was identified to enhance the support to SPrL engineering concepts based on participants' comments, as well as researchers' notes (Section 4.3) and are being implemented.

As future work, a study will be conducted in industry with the objective of verifying the benefits of Odyssey in real scenario, during SPDE and PSPE's activities, with participants of varied profiles and academic backgrounds. In addition, to increase Odyssey support to PSPE activities, other software process definition mechanisms will be proposed. Finally, SPrL evolution challenges can be investigated to propose a set of practices to assist SPrL artifacts modification.

Although the Odyssey tool is available as an academic project on the Software Reuse Research Group website[1], a release with the SPrL engineering support is still being prepared and is expected to be available by the end of the first semester of 2020.

Acknowledgment. The authors would like to thank CAPES, FAPERJ and CNPq for their financial support.

References

1. ALEIXO, F. A., FREIRE, M. A. SANTOS, W. C., et al., "A Model-driven Approach to Managing and Customizing Software Process Variabilities". In: *Proceedings of the 12th International Conference on Enterprise Information Systems* (ICEIS), v. 3, pp. 92-100, Madeira, Portugal, 2010.
2. BARRETO, A., DUARTE, E., ROCHA, A. R., et al., "Supporting the definition of software processes at consulting organizations via software process lines". In: *Proceedings of the Seventh International Conference on the Quality of Information and Communications Technology* (QUATIC), pp. 15-24, Porto, Portugal, 2010.
3. BARRETO, A., MURTA, L. G. P., ROCHA, A. R. C., 2011, "Software process definition: a reuse-based approach", *Journal of Universal Computer Science*, v. 17, n. 13, pp. 1765–1799.
4. BASILI, V., GREEN, S., LAITENBERGER, O., et al. "Packaging researcher experience to assist replication of experiments". In: *Proceedings of the ISERN Meeting*, pp. 3-6, Sydney, Australia, 1996.
5. COSTA, D. M., TEIXEIRA, E. N., WERNER, C. M. L., "Software Process Definition using Process Lines: A Systematic Literature Review". In: *Proceedings of the XLIV Latin American Computing Conference* (CLEI), São Paulo, Brazil. 2018.
6. COSTA, D. M., TEIXEIRA, E. N., WERNER, C. M. L., "Odyssey-ProcessCase: A Case-Based Software Process Line Approach". In: *Proceedings of the 17th Brazilian Symposium on Software Quality* (SBQS), Curitiba, Brazil. 2018.
7. DAVIS, F., 1985, *A technology acceptance model for empirically testing new end-user information systems: theory and results*. Doctoral Thesis, MIT Sloan School of Management, Cambridge, MA. USA.
8. DAVIS, F., 1989, "Perceived usefulness, perceived ease of use, and user acceptance of information technology", *MIS Quarterly*, v. 13, n. 3, pp. 319-340.
9. FISHBEIN, M., AJZEN, I., *Belief, attitude, intention and behavior: An introduction to theory and research*. 1 ed. California, Addison-Wesley. 1975.
10. FUGGETTA, A. "Software process: a roadmap". In: *Proceedings of the Conference on The Future of Software Engineering*, pp. 25-34, Limerick, Ireland, 2000.
11. HERNANDES, E., ZAMBONI, A., FABBRI, S., et al., 2012, "Using GQM and TAM to evaluate StArt - a tool that supports Systematic Review". *CLEI Electronic Journal*, v. 15, n. 1, pp. 13-25.

[1] http://reuse.cos.ufrj.br/

12. JAUFMAN, I., MÜNCH, J. "Acquisition of a Project-Specific Process". In: *Proceedings of the International Conference on Product Focused Software Process Improvement* (PROFES), pp 328-342, Oulu, Finland, 2005.
13. JURISTO, N., MORENO, A. M., 2001, *Basics of Software Engineering Experimentation*. 1 ed. Springer.
14. LORENZ, W. G., BRASIL, M. B., FONTOURA, L. M., et al., 2014, "Activity-based software process lines tailoring". *International Journal of Software Engineering and Knowledge Engineering* (SEKE), v. 24, n. 09, pp. 1357-1381.
15. MAGDALENO, A. M., BARROS, M. O., WERNER, C. M. L., et al., 2015, "Collaboration optimization in software process composition". *Journal of Systems and Software*, v. 103, pp. 452-466.
16. MCIVER, J., CARMINES, E. G., *Unidimensional scaling*. London, UK, SAGE. 1981.
17. MURTA, L., BLOIS, A., LOPES, M., et al. "Run-Time Variability through Component Dynamic Loading". In: *Tools Notes of the 18th Brazilian Symposium on Software Engineering* (SBES), pp. 67-72. 2004.
18. ODYSSEY, 2019, "Project Odyssey", In: *http://reuse.cos.ufrj.br/projetos/*.
19. OSTERWEIL, L. J., "Software processes are software too". In: *Proceedings of the 9th International Conference on Software Engineering* (ICSE), pp. 2–13, 1987.
20. ROMBACH, D. "Integrated Software Process and Product Lines". In: *Unifying the Software Process Spectrum*, v. 3840, pp. 83-90, 2005.
21. SHULL, F., CARVER, J., TRAVASSOS, G. H., 2001, "An Empirical Methodology for Introducing Software Processes", *ACM SIGSOFT Software Engineering Notes*, v. 26, n. 5, pp. 288-296.
22. SIMMONDS, J., PEROVICH, D., BASTARRICA, M. C., et al., "A megamodel for Software Process Line modeling and evolution". In: *Proceedings of the 18th International Conference on Model Driven Engineering Languages and Systems* (MoDELS), pp. 406-415, Ottawa, Canada, 2015.
23. SOLIGEN, R., BERGHOUT, E. *The Goal/Question/Metric Method: a practical guide for quality improvement of software development*. 1 ed. London, UK, McGraw-Hill Education, 1998.
24. TEIXEIRA, E. N., VASCONCELOS, A., & WERNER, C. M. L., "OdysseyProcessReuse - A Component-based Software Process Line Approach". In: *Proceedings of the 20th International Conference on Enterprise Information Systems* (ICEIS), v. 2, pp. 231-238, 2018.
25. TEIXEIRA, E. N., ALEIXO, F. A., SOUSA, F. D., et al., 2019, "Software process line as an approach to support software process reuse: A systematic literature review". *Information and Software Technology*, v. 116.
26. WASHIZAKI, H., 2006, "Building software process line architectures from bottom up". *Product Focused Software Process Improvement*, v. 4034, pp. 415-421.
27. WOHLIN, C., RUNESON, P., HÖST, M., et al. *Experimentation in Software Engineering: An Introduction*. 1 ed. Springer. 2000.
28. XU, P., RAMESH, B., 2008, "Using Process Tailoring to Manage Software Development Challenges", *IT Professional*, v. 10, n. 4, pp. 39-45.

Elicitação de Requisitos em Metodologias Ágeis: Um Mapeamento Sistemático da Literatura

Ramon Fonseca, João Carlos Epifânio, Luana Souza, and Marcia Lucena

Federal University of Rio Grande do Norte, Natal, Brazil.
raamon.williams@gmail.com,j.carlos.ico@gmail.com, luana.tms@gmail.com
marcia.lucena@gmail.com

Abstract. Requirements Engineering is seen as an indispensable factor to ensure the success of a software product since it aids in understanding its contexts and particularities. In the RE process, requirement elicitation is the phase during which all user needs are raised and analyzed, considering organizational, social and technical restrictions. In the development process currently employed by the industry, agile methodologies are widely used, as they welcome change during the life cycle of software and focus on fast product delivery. However, requirement elicitation happens in a non-systematic and informal manner. Informal practices may cause issues regarding the conception and understanding of the software to be developed. This work presents a systematic mapping that aims to understand how requirement elicitation, when associated with agile methodologies, has been approached by the industry. The systematic mapping analyzed and extracted data from 14 works related to the subject matter. Through data analysis, it was possible to identify how requirement elicitation happens in the industry as well as its methods, difficulties and shortcomings. Finally, the data revealed that communication with stakeholders is still an industry challenge, causing delays and increases in time and cost.

Keywords: Requirements Engineering · Requirements Elicitation · Agile Methodologies.

1 Introdução

Nos últimos anos, a indústria de software tem vivenciado um contexto dinâmico. Os artefatos são modificados rapidamente, e esse fato impossibilita requisitos estáticos durante seu desenvolvimento, uma vez que as necessidades são alteradas com frequência [8]. A literatura atual sugere que os requisitos sejam vistos como um ponto de partida para construção do software, devido a sua importância no processo de obtenção das necessidades do cliente, bem como seu refinamento.

A Engenharia de Requisitos dispõe de um conjunto de técnicas e métodos que são utilizados principalmente nas fases iniciais do projeto [7]. Quando o processo de Engenharia de Requisitos é realizado de forma inconsistente, alguns problemas podem surgir, durante o projeto de um sistema da indústria, que afetam seus custos e prazos [6]. Além desses problemas, a falta de tratamento de um requisito, de forma precisa, pode ocasionar falhar e ocasionar a própria inutilização do artefato.

Para apoiar o processo da Engenharia de Requisitos em projetos na indústria, algumas fases são adotadas: elicitação, análise, especificação, validação e gestão de requisitos. Nesse contexto, a elicitação é uma das fases mais fundamentais para a concepção de uma aplicação [9]. Nessa fase, as demandas dos usuários são analisadas e os requisitos de software são listadas, considerando restrições técnicas, sociais e organizacionais.

Outro recurso bastante utilizado e efetivo, durante a elaboração de sistemas em um contexto dinâmico, são as metodologias ágeis. Essa abordagem de desenvolvimento oferece eficiência e informações mais precisas sobre o avanço do projeto, uma vez que não abandona a documentação e reconhece que existem fatores com prioridade secundária em relação ao software quando considerado funcional [11].

A literatura atual relata a existência de pesquisas relacionadas a elicitação de requisitos no contexto ágil, porém existem lacunas no que se diz respeito ao estudo voltado propriamente para indústria. Além disso, não foram encontrados mapeamentos sistemáticos que tratam desse assunto nos últimos quatro anos, o que nos leva ao questionamento de mudanças na indústria de software nesse período.

Para entender como a elicitação de requisitos vem sendo adotada em desenvolvimentos de software que utilizam de metodologias ágeis, um mapeamento sistemático foi executado. Através da análise de papers será possível identificar os principais desafios e limitações encontradas no uso de técnicas de elicitação em ambientes ageis.

O restante deste estudo está estruturado da seguinte forma: Seção 2,a fundamentação teórica, discorrendo sobre a Engenharia de Requisitos relacionada com as métodos ágeis, bem como os trabalhos relacionados; Seção 3 ,apresentada a metodologia da pesquisa, descrevendo também as fases percorridas com base no protocolo criado; Seção 4, são apresentados os resultados e discussões gerados de acordo com as questões de pesquisa proposta, como também é apresentado as ameaças a validade do estudo; Seção 5, são apresentados os resultados e discussões gerados de acordo com as questões; e Seção 6, são expostas as ideias conclusivas para o trabalho.

2 Mapeamento Sistemático

Uma mapeamento sistemática da literatura assim como outros tipos de estudo experimental, tem como objetivo investigar de forma holística um determinado tema. Em seu processo de desenvolvimento deve ser aplicada uma avaliação e interpretação a partir de métodos precisos e estruturados de busca [13]. Para Petersen (2008) [14] a utilização de um mapeamento sistemático pode ser útil quando houver os seguintes objetivo:

- Para identificar lacunas de pesquisa e tendências para comissionar novas pesquisas;
- Para ter uma visão geral sobre um determinado tema;
- Para investigar questões de pesquisa mais amplas.

De acordo com Budgen (2008) [13] o processo de um mapeamento sistemático normalmente pode ser dividido em três fases, em que cada etapa detém de atividades específicas, a Figura 1 detalha esse processo.

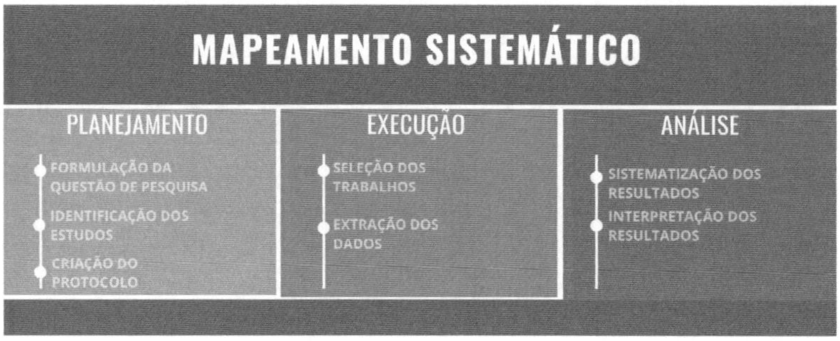

Fig. 1. Processo de Mapeamento Sistemático adaptado de Petersen (2015) [15]

1. Planejamento: Fase construída para delimitar o estudo desenvolvendo um plano formal ou um protocolo de estudo, contendo as questões de pesquisa, seleção de fontes e a estratégia da pesquisa. Além disso, neste documento deve conter os critérios de inclusão e exclusão, bem como identificar as estratégias de extração de dados. Ao final da realização do protocolo, deve-se fazer a execução de um piloto para verificar o encontro de um conjunto de estudos relevantes para a pesquisa.
2. Execução: Nesta etapa são executadas as atividades descritas na fase anterior por meio do protocolo. Ou seja, é nesta fase em que são procuradas evidências para responder às questões de pesquisa do estudo.
3. Análise: Após a fase anterior, com a consolidação dos dados, em seguida, é gerar um documento que reporte as contribuições, entraves e trabalhos futuros do mapeamento sistemático.

3 Trabalhos Relacionados

VILLAMIZAR et al. (2018) [10] apresentam um mapeamento sistemático com um objetivo de pesquisa diferente, o de caracterizar o cenário de publicação de abordagens que lidam com requisitos de segurança em projetos de software ágeis. Ou seja, apesar de analisar 21 trabalhos entre 2005 e 2017 sua pesquisa se limita às questões de segurança em contextos ágeis. Como conclusão deste estudo foi discutido a necessidade de continuação de pesquisas nessa área principalmente no que diz respeito a avaliações empíricas das abordagens existentes.

DE MEDEIROS et al. (2015) [5] realizaram uma revisão sistemática com a intenção de investigar como a Engenharia de Requisitos e as metodologias ágeis vêm sendo utilizadas em projetos de desenvolvimento de software aplicados na indústria. O objetivo da revisão sistemática realizada pelos autores é bastante similar a proposta deste estudo, porém De Medeiros et al. levantam o estado da arte até o ano de 2015, o que faz questionarmos se algo tem mudado nesses quatro anos. Além disso, é importante ressaltar que apesar da revisão sistemática realizada pela autora ter a Engenharia de Requisitos como foco, é importante construirmos um novo estudo na área com uma visão diferente, neste caso, mais focada para elicitação de requisitos. No estudo, os autores focam sua pesquisa principalmente na evolução das técnicas utilizadas na Engenharia de Requisitos. Já o desenvolvimento deste mapeamento sistemático tem o objetivo de questionar como, mais especificamente, a elicitação de requisitos tem sido trabalhada nos últimos quatro anos, relatando seu processo, as técnicas utilizadas, o tempo utilizado, bem como suas dificuldades e limitações.

4 Metodologia

Este estudo seguiu as orientações sugeridas por Kitchenham (2007) [1] e Travassos (2007) [2], com o intuito de identificar e classificar trabalhos de pesquisa de forma sistemática e confiável para possibilitar a reprodução do estudo.

O intuito da realização deste mapeamento sistemático foi segui-lo pela vertente qualitativa dos dados, porém ainda assim alguns resultados desta pesquisa são quantitativos. O paradigma qualitativo é descrito por Rallis e Rossman (1998) [3] que, por essência trabalha com a vertente interpretativa, fornecendo análises mais detalhadas sobre as investigações. Assim, os dados coletados serão interpretados para posteriormente apresentar as conclusões do que se foi analisado.

Já no que se diz respeito a pesquisa quantitativa, de acordo com Creswell (2010) [4], é fundamental para descrever dados quantitativos de forma numérica de tendências, atitudes ou opiniões. Um resumo do protocolo do mapeamento sistemático é apresentado nas próximas seções

4.1 Questões de Pesquisa

Para alcançar os objetivos propostos pela pesquisa foram criadas as seguintes questões de pesquisa:

QP1 Como a elicitação de requisitos tem sido abordada em projetos, na indústria, que incorporam as metodologias ágeis em seu desenvolvimento?

QP2 Quais as técnicas mais utilizadas para elicitar requisitos no contexto ágil da indústria?

QP3 Quais as dificuldades e limitações no processo de elicitação de requisitos em projetos que adotam as metodologias ágeis na indústria?

QP4 Qual o tempo consumido na elicitação de requisitos em projetos realizados pela indústria?

4.2 Estratégias de Busca e Idiomas

De acordo com o objetivo discutido anteriormente, o estudo a ser desenvolvido tem como palavras chaves: 'Engenharia de Requisitos' e 'Metodologias Ágeis'. A partir daí foi criada uma string de busca, derivada das palavras chaves, para auxiliar a busca automática dos estudos. Com auxílio dos conectivos "AND" e "OR" foi criada uma string genérica para retornar o máximo de estudos possíveis, apresentada a seguir:

(("requirements") AND ("agile" OR "agility") AND ("elicitation"))

Os estudos relacionados ao tema encontrados posteriormente por especialistas e que não foram retornados pela string de busca por algum motivo, serão adicionados manualmente para análise. Além disso, serão lidos e analisados os estudos em inglês, espanhol e português.

4.3 Fontes de Dados

Para a seleção dos estudos, as fontes utilizadas para a busca automatizada foram IEEExplore, ACM e Scopus. Além do fator no que diz respeito a relevância dessas bases de dados, a escolha de tais repositórios também justifica-se pela capacidade de indexação de outros estudos pertencentes a outras bibliotecas digitais. Outro fator levado em consideração foi quanto ao acesso institucional permitido para a Universidade Federal do Rio Grande do Norte via Portal de Periódicos da CAPES (Coordenação de Aperfeiçoamento de Pessoal de Nível Superior).

4.4 Critérios de Inclusão e Exclusão

Para fomentar a qualidade da análise do estudo foram criados os critérios de inclusão e exclusão. A realização dessa atividade permite que o resultado da busca nos repositórios digitais sejam mais efetivos, retornando apenas pesquisas capazes de responder às questões da pesquisa. Dessa forma, um estudo a ser incluídos tinha que preencher pelo menos um critérios de inclusão. Já um artigo para ser excluído tinha que pelo menos satisfazer um dos critérios de exclusão. A Tabela 1 apresenta os critérios de inclusão e exclusão instituídos.

4.5 Processo de Seleção dos Estudos

Inicialmente a seleção dos estudos foi feita com base na identificação dos títulos, resumos e palavras-chaves, em seguida foram aplicados os critérios de inclusão e exclusão. Em caso de dúvida, com relação à importância do estudo para o mapeamento sistemático, o artigo foi mantido para análise posterior. A segunda etapa teve como intuito buscar, entre os artigos selecionados na etapa anterior, quais apresentam o estudo de elicitação de requisitos considerando metodologias ágeis no contexto industrial.

Inclusão	Exclusão
Artigos que tem como estudos que tratem da elicitação de requisitos considerando metodologias ágeis na indústria.	Estar fora do intervalo de tempo escolhido para a análise (2015-2019); Artigos que não tratam da elicitação de requisitos no contexto ágil; Artigos incompletos, rascunhos, slides ou resumos; Artigos que não apresentam nenhum tipo de validação prática ; Artigos que não estejam disponíveis para download no ambiente institucional da UFRN.

Table 1. Critérios de Inclusão e Exclusão de Artigos.

4.6 Estratégia de Extração dos Dados

Para extração dos dados, foi criado uma planilha, com o objetivo de realizar uma análise estruturada. Para isso, os seguintes metadados foram considerados:

a) Título;
b) Autores;
c) Ano da publicação;
d) Fonte de publicação;
e) Abordagem da elicitação de requisitos em projetos ágeis da indústria;
f) Técnicas utilizadas;
g) Dificuldades e limitações;
h) Tempo gasto.

4.7 Procedimentos para Síntese dos Dados

A síntese e análise dos dados foi realizada de forma qualitativa para abstrair de forma resumida os estudos coletados que norteiam a pesquisa. Esta atividade foi realizada por um pesquisador e depois revisada por outro pesquisador.

5 Resultados e Discussão

5.1 Visão Geral dos Estudos

Ao iniciar a fase de execução do mapeamento sistemático foram retornados 105 estudos com a utilização da string de busca. Após a eliminação dos duplicados foram considerados 92 trabalhos para analisar título, resumo e palavras-chaves. Nesta etapa foram eliminados 35 estudos que não condizem com a proposta do mapeamento. Em seguida, foram lidos um total de 57 artigos na íntegra, porém foi observado uma má estruturação de resumos em alguns estudos, com ambiguidade e falta de clareza ao descrever seus objetivos, acarretando na exclusão posterior dos mesmo por não satisfazer o objetivo deste mapeamento sistemático. Como resultado, apenas 14 artigos conseguiram responder satisfatoriamente às questões de pesquisas propostas para extração dos dados, apresentados na Tabela 2.

Ademais, como observado na Figura 2, nos últimos quatro anos houve um crescimento de estudos tratando da Engenharia de Requisitos, com enfoque na elicitação.

ID	Autor	Título	Source
ER01	(MATTEN et. al, 2017)	Robust approaches, techniques and tools for requirement engineering in agile development	IEEE Library
ER02	(MAGÜES et. al, 2016)	HCI usability techniques in agile development	IEEE Library
ER03	(SABARIAH et. al, 2019)	Requirement Elicitation Framework for Child Learning Application - A Research Plan	ACM Digital Library
ER04	(RODRIGUES et. al, 2018)	Empirical Evaluation of Formal Method for Requirements Specification in Agile Approaches	ACM Digital Library
ER05	(ALSAQAF et. al, 2019)	Quality requirements challenges in the context of large-scale distributed agile: An empirical study	Scopus
ER06	(MELEGATI et. al, 2019)	A model of requirements engineering in software startups	Scopus
ER07	(CAHILL et. al, 2019)	IoT/sensor-based infrastructures promoting a sense of home, independent living, comfort and wellness	Scopus
ER08	(ALEXA and AVASILCAI, 2018)	The requirement elicitation process of designing a collaborative environment - The CRE@TIVE.BIZ case	Scopus
ER09	(CURCIO et. al, 2018)	Requirements engineering: A systematic mapping study in agile software development	Scopus
ER10	(CARRIZO and QUINTANILLA, 2018)	Prototyping use as a software requirements elicitation technique: A case study	Scopus
ER11	(PASTRANA et. al, 2017)	Requirements elicitation based on inception deck and business processes models in scrum	Scopus
ER12	(TAIBI et. al, 2017)	Comparing requirements decomposition within the Scrum, Scrum with Kanban, XP, and Banana development processes	Scopus
ER13	(HODA and MURUGESAN, 2016)	Multi-level agile project management challenges: A self-organizing team perspective	Scopus
ER14	(ORDÓÑEZ, 2015)	An impact study of business process models for requirements elicitation in XP	Scopus

Table 2. Trabalhos selecionados.

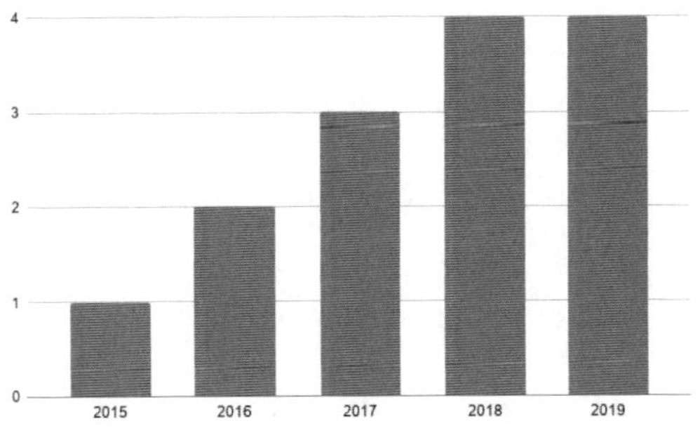

Fig. 2. Artigos por ano de publicação.

5.2 Mapeando Evidências

Nesta subseção serão apresentadas as evidências observadas a partir dos trabalhos lidos por questões de pesquisa.

QP1 Como a elicitação de requisitos tem sido abordada em projetos, na indústria, que incorporam as metodologias ágeis em seu desenvolvimento? Na leitura dos artigos selecionados, buscamos informações sobre o processo de desenvolvimento da elicitação de requisitos considerando os aspectos ágeis. Com isso, verificamos se o processo da elicitação tem sido respeitado e feito de forma concisa.

Ao analisar os trabalhos, podemos observar que a maioria dos autores que relatam sobre o processo de elicitação de requisitos (ER02, ER03, ER05, ER07, ER08, ER10, ER11, ER12, ER13, ER14) compreendem sobre a importância desse processo para aumentar a quantidade e/ou a qualidade dos requisitos. Porém, é perceptível a diferença de efeito quando se há um processo de elicitação conciso em comparação a um realizado com uma má qualidade. Nos estudos ER02, ER14 foram obtidos resultados satisfatórios ao final da pesquisa. Já os resultados publicados pelos estudos ER03 e ER13 observa-se como conclusão uma série de desafios e limitações. A partir da leitura desses estudos é possível evidenciar que uma elicitação bem estruturada auxilia no alcance de bons resultados. Além disso, como mencionado no trabalho de ER12, realizar a elicitação de forma estruturada afeta diretamente a eficiência do processo de desenvolvimento.

Dessa forma, a partir da leitura dos artigos, para uma elicitação de requisitos estruturada é recomendado a aplicação de cinco fases em seu processo:

1. Contextualização: fase em que deve-se apresentar o domínio da aplicação.
2. Identificação da Requisição: etapa idealizada para identificar as fontes dos requisitos, para assim, coleta-los.
3. Análise das Partes Interessadas e Usuários: fase cujo objetivo é identificar e mapear os riscos e demandas geradas na construção de um projeto.

4. Seleção das Técnicas: A partir do cumprimento das fases anteriores deve-se escolher a melhor técnica que se adéqua à construção do software.
5. Aplicação das Abordagens e Ferramentas: fase de execução das técnicas e desenvolvimento do produto.

Além disso, há indícios que a participação direta do usuário no processo de elicitação de requisitos pode ajudar a reduzir problemas na construção de um sistema, reduzindo a má experiencia do usuário. Os trabalhos que relataram negligenciar a estruturação da elicitação de requisitos, bem como a inserção do usuário em seu processo de desenvolvimento relata um resultado com falta de requisitos e, por sua vez, aumentando o custo do projeto.

QP2 Quais as técnicas mais utilizadas para elicitar requisitos no contexto ágil da indústria? Para elencar requisitos com qualidade não podemos tratar esse processo como um problema de dimensão tecnológica, uma vez que, nesta atividade, o contexto social é mais crítico do que na fase de programação, especificação e projeto. Dessa forma, para haver uma elicitação bem executada, são utilizadas técnicas que ajudam a melhorar a comunicação e resolver eventuais problemas de forma rápida e precisa.

Conforme apresentado na Tabela 3 apenas dez trabalhos, dentre os quatorze selecionados, mencionaram técnicas utilizadas para elicitar requisitos. User Story foi a técnica mais utilizada dentre os artigos analisados, seguido das entrevistas e protótipos.

	ER01	ER02	ER06	ER07	ER08	ER09	ER10	ER11	ER12	ER14
UserStory	X	-	-	-	-	-	-	X	X	X
JAD	X	-	-	-	-	-	-	-	-	-
BPMN	-	-	-	-	-	-	-	-	-	X
Personas	-	X	-	-	-	-	-	-	-	-
Entrevista	-	-	X	X	-	-	X	-	-	-
Protótipos	-	-	X	-	X	-	X	-	-	-
Observação	-	-	-	X	-	-	-	-	-	-
Questionário	-	-	-	-	X	-	-	-	-	-
Brainstorming	-	-	X	-	-	-	-	-	-	-
Debate	-	-	-	-	X	-	-	-	-	-
Oficinas de Requisitos	-	-	-	-	X	-	-	-	-	-
Snap Shots	-	X	-	-	-	-	-	-	-	-
Investigação Conceitual	-	X	-	-	-	-	-	-	-	-
Incepcion Deck	-	-	-	-	-	-	-	X	-	-
SleepMind	X	-	-	-	-	-	-	-	-	-
Flex REQ Model	X	-	-	-	-	-	-	-	-	-
Analíse de Tarefas / Dominios	-	-	-	-	X	-	-	-	-	-
ARAM Model	X	-	-	-	-	-		-	-	-
DICOT Model	X	-	-	-	-	-	-	-	-	-

Table 3. Técnicas de elicitação por artigo.

QP3 Quais as dificuldades e limitações no processo de elicitação de requisitos em projetos que adotam as metodologias ágeis na indústria? A busca por softwares está cada vez mais intensa, atrelada também aos fatores externos como prazos reduzidos, mudanças de mercado e tecnologias. Dessa forma, é esperado que o desenvolvimento de sistemas responda com flexibilidade e eficiência as mudanças dos requisitos. É importante observar também quais as dificuldades e limitações que os estudos destacam no que diz respeito ao levantamento de requisitos.

Um total de oito trabalhos responderam a questão de pesquisa (ER01 ER05, ER06, ER07, ER09, ER12, ER13, ER14). Os autores dos estudos ER01 e ER09 mencionam que organizações que trabalham em projetos ágeis comumente encontram problemas de arquitetura na Engenharia de Requisitos devido a especificações não claras de atividades e técnicas, afetando diretamente nas decisões dos projetos. Com isso, podemos observar que na fase da Engenharia de Requisitos é imprescindível observar o contexto do estudo, o tipo do projeto e os recursos disponíveis, para só então escolher as técnicas e métodos que devem ser aplicados. É possível embasar ainda mais esse pressuposto ao relato dos estudos ER12 e ER07, em que foi possível observar que a execução e análise da elicitação não depende apenas da equipe, mas também do processo e técnicas adotadas.

Já o estudo ER05 apresenta uma série de processos que, se adicionados na fase de elicitação de requisitos, possibilita uma otimização de custos e tempo no desenvolvimento de uma aplicação. Entre esses processos são apresentados a documentação mínima de requisitos, limitação observada também pelo estudo ER09, bem como a documentação de requisitos de qualidade de maneira a expor suas dependências. A importância de utilizar esses processos é também garantir a rastreabilidade entre os requisitos, dificuldade também apresentada pelo estudo ER06. Outra dificuldade encontrada no desenvolvimento de sistemas no estudo ER05 foi trabalhar com metodologia ágil, mas com uma mentalidade em cascata, em que os requisitos não conseguiam evoluir. Esse problema atrelado a não identificação de partes interessadas com cautela, levou à falta de requisitos e, por sua vez, aumento de custo do projeto.

No estudo ER09 foi possível identificar obstáculos relacionados ao que se diz respeito da comunicação ambígua entre desenvolvedores e usuários, deficiência apresentada também pelo estudo ER14, bem como obstáculos relacionados às pessoas, como algumas habilidades especializadas, questões de motivação. Já no que se diz respeito aos clientes, é possível perceber limitações na questão da disponibilidade e muitas vezes incapacidade de acordo.

Já no estudo ER13, o desafio apresentado foi com relação a atrasos e alteração de requisitos que foram mal elicitados, dificultando as negociações com o cliente e definição do escopo de projetos. Porém vale salientar que como descrito em seu trabalho, o processo de Engenharia de Requisitos foi realizada de forma concisa, uma vez que é relatado que alguns requisitos foram adiados até chegar ao ponto que as equipes não podiam prosseguir sem os mesmos.

QP4 Qual o tempo consumido na elicitação de requisitos em projetos realizados pela indústria? Existem uma série de pontos a ser atingidos durante o processo de desenvolvimento de um sistema, independente do objetivo do artefato, como redução de custos, otimização de recursos, maior qualidade e etc. Ao final do desenvolvimento é feito um balanço para entender se todos as metas esperadas foram atingidos. Por isso, é fundamental analisar o processo e o tempo gasto na elicitação de requisitos, uma vez que, a mesma pode garantir o sucesso ou insucesso de um software.

Dentre os estudos analisados, apenas ER04, ER05, ER07, ER10 e ER11 dimensionam a temporalidade de algumas fases do seu processo. No entanto, não há como afirmar a estimativa de tempo ideal para se fazer uma elicitação de requisitos de qualidade, uma vez que cada projeto tem suas particularidades, como afirma o estudo ER04, em que o tempo de esforço é relativo também ao conhecimento profissional e pode haver uma curva de redução de trabalho ao longo do tempo. Já no estudo ER05, uma limitação apresentada foi trabalhar com ágil, mas com uma mentalidade em cascata. Ou seja, o tempo gasto no levantamento de requisitos se dá apenas na fase inicial do projeto, sendo dificultada a evolução dos requisitos.

Nos estudos ER07, ER10 e ER11 não é apresentada uma ideia total da fase de elicitação de requisitos. Porém, mencionaram o tempo gasto em algumas de suas técnicas por exemplo, o estudo ER07, para realizar seu projeto, necessitou ao todo de 61h gastas em entrevistas. Já no estudo ER10, para a sessão de elicitação por prototipagem, foram planejadas com duração de 1h. O estudo ER11 menciona brevemente que o tempo de elicitação foi aumentado devido a utilização de BPMN, porém resultou em menos mudanças nas exigências e menos inconformidades.

Portanto, existem indícios que o tempo utilizado na elicitação de requisitos varia de projeto para projeto, uma vez que cada um contém suas restrições, contextos e limitações específicas. Porém, ao identificar esses pontos fazer um levantamento de requisitos eficiente resulta em grandes benefícios como redução de ambiguidades, e aumento da qualidade do produto.

5.3 Ameaças à Validade

Para sistematizar o estudo, foi feito um protocolo para estruturação do estudo e para tentar minimizar a ocorrência de falhas e erros. Além disso, antes de iniciar a extração dos dados foram feitos testes-piloto com o objetivo de "calibrar" a string de busca automática. Para minimizar o viés esta fase foi realizada em dupla. O desenvolvimento e execução deste protocolo foi guiado pelas orientações difundidas por Petersen (2008) [14] e Kitchenham (2007) [1]. Entretanto, ainda assim ameaças à validade podem afetar os resultados obtidos. Nesta seção, discutiremos algumas destas limitações e como tentamos minimizá-los.

Validade externa. Esta ameaça está relacionada a incompletude de estudos relevantes que podem ter sido perdidas, seja por limitações técnicas dos motores de busca automatizados próprios ou seja pelos bancos de dados selecionados que não apresentaram uma lista exaustiva de fontes de publicação, permitindo que outros bancos de dados também pudessem ser indexados. Para tentar minimizar essa ameaça durante o processo do mapeamento sistemático foi possível contar com a ajuda de especialistas no assunto da pesquisa permitindo incluir novos trabalhos.

Validade interna. Foram realizadas reuniões e testes pilotos no decorrer do mapeamento sistemático, com o objetivo de minimizar viés na seleção dos estudos.

Validade de construção. Para reduzir as ameaças referentes a construção do trabalho, foi criado um protocolo bem estruturado, que norteou todas as fases realizadas neste estudo.

6 Conclusão

A construção deste trabalho objetivou investigar como a Engenharia de Requisitos vem sendo adotada em projetos que adotam metodologias ágeis na indústria. Após a execução de um protocolo de mapeamento sistemático foram retornados 14 trabalhos relacionados ao tema de pesquisa publicados nos últimos quatro anos.

De acordo com os estudos analisados, podemos afirmar que a elicitação é uma atividade da Engenharia de Requisitos indispensável, mas que ainda enfrenta algumas dificuldades de execução em em organizações, provocando insucessos como aumento da tempo de desenvolvimento de um artefato podendo atingir até mesmo sua qualidade.

Com a realização deste trabalho ainda foi possível observar de forma geral as técnicas mais utilizadas durante a elicitação de requisitos. A User Story foi a técnica mais utilizada, seguido das entrevistas e protótipos.

Além disso, foi possível criar um panorama entre os trabalhos que tratam do tema de pesquisa com relação às dificuldades no processo de elicitação. A comunicação entre stakeholders é apresentada como uma limitação recorrente entre os trabalhos coletados, ocasionando em problemas arquiteturais, tomada de decisão e aumento de custos. Outro fator que pesa negativamente no levantamento de requisitos é a não identificação correta das partes interessadas no projeto dificultando o fechamento do escopo do projeto.

Já com relação ao tempo gasto na fase de elicitação de requisitos não foi possível coletar com exatidão a duração dessa atividade nos trabalhos retornados pelo mapeamento sistemático, bem como o ciclo realizado em cada projeto. Entretanto, é possível observar que os trabalhos que apresentaram uma boa estruturação no levantamento de requisitos identificaram uma quantidade menor de limitações em seu resultado em comparação aos trabalhos que não estruturaram bem o levantamento de requisitos.

A elaboração desse estudo possibilitou afirmar que a elicitação de requisitos não deve ser entendida unicamente como um problema de dimensão tecnológica, posto que nesta fase a circunstância social é mais crítica em relação a fase de programação, especificação e projeto.

Diante disso, acreditamos que o mapeamento sistemático alcançou os objetivos previstos no início desse estudo, uma vez que foi apresentando limitações da indústria no que se diz respeito a elicitação de requisitos no contexto ágil.

6.1 Direções para pesquisa Futura

No decorrer do desenvolvimento desta pesquisa foram percebidos tópicos que permitirão realizar outros trabalhos, ampliando a concepção deste. Alguns destes tópicos serão descritos a seguir.

Considerando o resultado obtido diante dos artigos selecionados considera-se importante estudar estratégias que auxiliem na melhora da comunicação entre stakeholders, para tentar mitigar a ocorrência de insucessos no desenvolvimento de softwares na indústria. Além disso, como visto anteriormente nos últimos quatro anos houve uma crescente na publicação de trabalhos relacionados ao tema. Dessa forma, aplicar futuramente a atualização desse mapeamento sistemático para saber se algo mudou no cenário trabalhado é uma alternativa de contribuir com a resolução de novas limitações e fazer um comparativo de evolução do cenário estudado.

AGRADECIMENTOS

O presente trabalho foi realizado com apoio da Coordenação de Aperfeiçoamento de Pessoal de Nível Superior - Brasil (CAPES).

References

1. KITCHENHAM, B. A.; CHARTERS, S. Guidelines for performing Systematic Literature Reviews in Software Engineering: Version 2.3. EBSE Technical Report. Keele, UK: Keele University, 2007.
2. TRAVASSOS, G.; BIOLCHINI, J. Revisões Sistemáticas Aplicadas a Engenharia de Software. In: BRAZILIAN SYMPOSIUM ON SOFTWARE ENGINEERING, 21., 2007, João Pessoa, PB. Anais... João Pessoa, PB: SBC, 2007
3. RALLIS, S. F.; ROSSMAN, G. B. Learning in the eld: An introduction to qualitative research. Learning in the eld: an introduction to qualitative research, Sage Thousand Oaks, 1998.
4. CRESWELL, J. W. Projeto de pesquisa métodos qualitativo, quantitativo e misto. In: Projeto de pesquisa métodos qualitativo, quantitativo e misto. [S.l.]: Artmed, 2010.
5. DE MEDEIROS, Juliana Dantas Ribeiro Viana et al. Engenharia de requisitos em projetos ágeis: uma revisão sistemática da literatura, 2015.
6. SOMMERVILLE, IAN; Engenharia de Software; tradução Ivan Bosnic e Kalink G. de O. Gonçalves; revisão técnica Kechi Hirama. – 9.ed. – São Paulo: Pearson Prentice Hall, 2011. Título Original: Software Engineering.
7. VIEIRA, Sérgio Roberto Costa et al. Remo: uma técnica de elicitação de requisitos orientada pela modelagem de processos de negócios. 2012.
8. LAUDON, K. C., LAUDON, J. P., (2011). Sistemas de Informação Gerenciais, Pearson Education; 9ª Edição.

9. ZOWGHI, Didar. Does global software development need a different requirements engineering process. In: Proceedings of International Workshop on Global Software Development. 2002.
10. VILLAMIZAR, Hugo et al. A Systematic Mapping Study on Security in Agile Requirements Engineering. In: 2018 44th Euromicro Conference on Software Engineering and Advanced Applications (SEAA). IEEE, 2018. p. 454-461
11. ELGHARIANI, Kaiss; KAMA, Nazri. Review on Agile requirements engineering challenges. In: 2016 3rd International conference on computer and information sciences (ICCOINS). IEEE, 2016. p. 507-512.
12. BUDGEN, David et al. Using Mapping Studies in Software Engineering. In: PPIG. 2008. p. 195-204.
13. BUDGEN, David et al. Using Mapping Studies in Software Engineering. In: PPIG. 2008. p. 195-204.
14. PETERSEN, Kai et al. Systematic mapping studies in software engineering. In: Ease. 2008. p. 68-77.
15. PETERSEN, Kai; VAKKALANKA, Sairam; KUZNIARZ, Ludwik. Guidelines for conducting systematic mapping studies in software engineering: An update. Information and Software Technology, v. 64, p. 1-18, 2015.
16. DINGSØYR, Torgeir et al. A decade of agile methodologies: Towards explaining agile software development. 2012.
17. BECK, Kent. Extreme programming explained: embrace change. addison-wesley professional, 2000.

A comparative study on measuring software functional size to support effort estimation in agile

Fabián Ugalde, Christian Quesada-López, Alexandra Martínez, and Marcelo Jenkins

University of Costa Rica, San Pedro, Costa Rica
{fabian.ugalde, cristian.quesadalopez, alexandra.martinez, marcelo.jenkins}@ucr.ac.cr

Abstract. Software effort estimation models based on functional size allow software organizations to plan their development projects. A large number of organizations have adopted agile processes, but there is little evidence on the adoption of functional sizing methods to support software effort estimation in agile contexts. In this study, we compare four functional size estimation methods as the basis for effort estimation in the context of a startup company that develops mobile applications using an agile methodology. Measurements of software size, expressed in User Story Points (USP), Use Case Points (UCP), IFPUG Function Points (UFP), and COSMIC Function Points (CFP), were taken for a set of requirements from one project in the company. Effort estimation models were then derived from these measurements, using regression, and their accuracy was determined by the Mean Magnitude of Relative Error (MMRE) and Mean Balanced Relative Error (MBRE). We obtained the following MMRE results for each functional sizing method: 0,86 for UCP, 0,36 for USP, 0,36 for UFP and 0,22 for CFP, and the following MBRE results: 0,98 for UCP, 0,45 for USP, 0,53 for UFP and 0,35 for CFP. The effort estimation model based on COSMIC function points turned out to be the most accurate in the context of the software organization under study. Additionally, convertibility models between sizing measurements were generated to allow the organization to convert its historical measurements into any other software size measure, without having to perform the counting process of the target method.

Keywords: Functional size, software effort estimation, function points, IFPUG FPA, COSMIC FFP, empirical study.

1 Introduction

The use of effort estimation models can help software companies plan, monitor, and control their efforts in terms of costs and development processes [8]. Therefore, having realistic estimates at an early stage of the project life cycle, allows managers to control resources effectively [10]. In agile projects, effort estimations based on functional size are being incorporated to provide more accurate estimates [18]. However, more empirical evidence is needed on the use of functional size measurements to support software effort estimation in agile contexts. According to Lavazza et al [8], the accuracy of effort estimation must be carefully evaluated before its use in a real life environment.

Hence, our study aims to provide empirical evidence on the accuracy of effort estimation based on functional size measurements in an agile context. It also provides enough details of the methods used –as adviced by Kitchenham et al. [6] – so that other researchers can replicate the study in different contexts, thus widening the body of evidence.

In this study, we investigated whether the choice of functional size measurements has an effect on the accuracy of effort estimation models in the context of an agile organization. This organizacion is a startup company that develops mobile applications aimed at promoting healthy lifestyles, through the application of the social network approach to nutritional concepts.

The purpose of our case study is to compare the accuracy of effort estimation models built upon four different functional size measurements: Use Case Points (UCP), COSMIC Function Points (CFP), IFPUG Function Points (UFP), and User Story Points (USP). The four functional size estimation methods were applied to the same set of requirements from a mobile application project within the organization. Regression methods were then used to derive effort estimation models from the four size measurements. The Mean Magnitude of Relative Error (MMRE) and Mean Balanced Relative Error (MBRE) were used to determine which model was more accurate for predicting effort. Criteria set out by [6, 8] were considered to mitigate some threats to validity. To guide this study, two research questions were defined:

RQ1: Which functional size-based effort estimation model yields the most accurate estimates in the context of the organization under study?

RQ2: Can convertibility models of functional size measurements yield accurate results in the context of the organization under study?

The rest of the paper is organized as follows. Section 2 explores the functional size estimation methods used in our study: Use Case Points, User Story Points, COSMIC Function Points and IFPUG Function Points. Section 3 presents the related work. Section 4 describes the case study performed in the startup company. Section 5 shows the results obtained from this case study. In Section 6 we discuss and summarize the results. And section 7 presents our conclusions and future work.

2 Background

Here we describe each of the functional size estimation methods used in this study: Use Case Points, User Story Points, IFPUG Function Points and COSMIC Function Points.

2.1 Use Case Points

A *use case* details a scenario of how the software system should interact with the user –or other systems– to carry out a specific action or activity [23]. Software estimation by *use case points* is a technique to calculate and predict the size of a system for software development projects [24]. To calculate the total points, it is necessary to count the total transactions in each use case.

Use cases and its actor are categorized into simple, average and complex. For each category, a weighted point is assigned. The unadjusted use case points are the sum of all weighted points assigned.

2.2 User Story Points

User stories are the way in which requirements are captured in agile software development methodology. A *user story* is independent, negotiable, valuable, estimated, small and verifiable [25]. One method to estimate the size of a user story is through *planning poker*, which uses a Fibonacci scale. In planning poker, each team member assigns user story points for a requirement, based on its expert criteria. Then the team discusses until a single size value is agreed on, and that will be the *user story points* assigned to that requirement [26].

2.3 IFPUG Function Points

Function Point Analysis (FPA) is a proven and accepted methodology to determine the size of a software development project [27]. FPA measures software size in terms of the following attributes [27]:

- Data entering a system: external inputs (EI) as logical transaction inputs.
- Data leaving the system: external outputs (EO) or external queries (EQ) such as online screens, reports, or inputs to other systems.
- Data created and stored within the system: internal logical files (ILF) such as user-defined logical groups of data.
- Data maintained within a different system but necessary to satisfy a certain process requirement: external interfaces (EIF) as interfaces to other systems.

There are set of counting rules that assign *IFPUG Function Points* (UFP) to each EI/EO/ILF/EIF, based on the number of Data Element Types (DET) and File Type Referenced (FTR) associated with the transactional function. Such rules can be found in the work of Gandomani et al. [28].

2.4 COSMIC Function Points

System functions are modeled through functional processes, which can be divided into sub-processes [29]. Sub-processes are classified in two types: data movement and data manipulation. The data movement sub-process is the main goal for the calculation of the function point, which is categorized into four categories:

- Input (I): the movement of a user's data to a functional process.
- Output (O): the movement of data from a functional process to a user.
- Read (R): the movement of data from persistent storage to a function process. Persistent storage must be part of the system.
- Write (W): the movement of data from a functional process to persistent storage. Persistent storage must be part of the system.

In a functional process, the data movement quantity for the four categories mentioned above are presented as *COSMIC function points* (CFP), in a unit called CFSU (COSMIC functional size unit).

3 Related work

We performed a literature review and found several studies on comparing software effort estimation models, but only a few studies on convertibility of size measurements. We will first present the studies related to estimation model comparison [1, 3, 5, 9, 10, 11, 13, 15, 17, 19, 20, 22], and then the studies about convertibility between functional size measurements [7, 18].

The work by Salmanoglu et al. [17] performed three case studies that compared the effectiveness of effort estimation based on two functional size methods (CFP and USP) in an agile context. They used regression analysis to generate statistical models from software size measurements and evaluated their performance using MMRE. They concluded that CFP produced the most accurate effort estimation model.

Similarly, Ungan et al. [20] compared the effectiveness of two approaches for effort estimation in an organization that uses SCRUM. They compared USP-based effort estimation (with Planning Poker) to CFP-based effort estimation. They used regression models and artificial neural networks to develop the estimation models. They showed that COSMIC measurements are a better basis for effort estimation than User Story Points, in their context.

Paz et al. [13] applied Increment COSMIC Function Points in an agile environment, and compared its accuracy against the Rational Unified Process (RUP) method, concluding that the COSMIC-based model was better. They introduced the concept of *Incremental COSMIC Function Points* as an approach for adapting the CFP measure to agile enviroments. They proposed that the sum of all Incremental COSMIC function points for each requirement or work size unit (user story, from SCRUM standpoint), will determine the total COSMIC function points for the whole system.

Desharnais et al. [3] proposed an approach to move from COCOMO (Constructive Cost Model) to User Stories using COSMIC as the size measurement method. They showed a model that allows estimating the effort for each user story based on CFP. Sholiq et al. [19] compared UCP against UFP in an effort estimation model, concluding that UCP was slightly better. Brian et al. [1] propose an effort estimation model using external databases based on UFP and CFP, reaching the conclusion that there was no significant difference between these two software size estimation methods.

Mendes et al. [10] studied three cost estimation models applied to web hypermedia applications, using regression models to support their estimations. They compared linear and stepwise regressions, and case-based reasoning (CBR), concluding that CBR technique gave the most accurate results.

Wilkie et al. [22] explored the utility of function point software sizing techniques when applied at two levels of software requirements documentation, in a commercial software development organization. They appraised the value (cost/benefit) that functional sizing techniques can bring to the planning and management of software projects, concluding that "Estimated NESMA" is the most appropriate tool to use for size estimation in the context of the studied company.

Phannachitta [15] did a comparison of similarity measures in analogy-based software effort estimation, using a robust approach involving MMRE and some other comparison indicators. Mittas et al. [11] propose a graphical method to evaluate the performance of a cost estimation model by using an analysis of regression error characteristic. Later, Mittas et al. [12] created an algorithm to cluster and rank software cost estimation models through multiple comparisons.

Other studies [5, 9] have compared different effort estimation methods to expert-based estimates. Jørgensen and Boehm [5] debated over which effort estimation method produces better accuracy, comparing formal models against expert judgment. Elaborating on evidence that backup both approaches, they agreed there is no single *best* method, but different perspectives that benefit particular scenarios. Nonetheless, they highlight that more advanced estimation models will likely lead to significantly more accurate effort estimates. Similarly, the study by Lenarduzzi et al. [9] compared the effectiveness of an effort estimation model based on IFPUG Function Points to an expert-based estimation, in an agile environment. They showed that the accuracy of the effort estimate provided by the SCRUM team was better than the obtained through functional size measurements.

Finally, two studies [7, 18] addressed the issue of convertibility between functional size measurements. Lavazza et al. [7] presented a correlation study between IFPUG and COSMIC function points. They provide a set of models to convert counts from one software size method to the other. Santana et al. [18] examined whether function points are compatible with user story points on agile projects, and found a correlation between them. They stated that their results should respect the units of measurement and the reality of each organization.

All previously mentioned studies were performed in mid to large companies, and focused on comparing effort estimation models based on just *two* functional size measurements. Furthermore, their competing techniques consider only completed projects with a defined set of requierements and a clear scope. In contrast, our study considers effort estimation models based on *four* functional size measurements, and is performed in an agile startup company. This context poses some challenges such as unclear project scope and unstable requirements.

4 Our Case Study

We conducted a case study in a software startup company mainly dedicated to the development of mobile applications. It has four developers, who use the SCRUM methodology. The organization has been using an agile metric collection tool, hence both estimated and real effort data were available for every user requirement (use case). We obtained most of the project data from this repository. Although the requirements were developed using SCRUM, there were formal specification documents that we used to count COSMIC, IFPUG Function Points, and Use Case Points.

4.1 Goal and object selection

The goal of our case study was to accurately estimate the effort by generating models based on software functional size measurements. We scoped our work to four functional size estimation methods: Use Case Points, User Story Points, IFPUG Function Points, and COSMIC Function Points. A secondary and related goal of the study was to seek accurate convertibility models between functional size measurements. Both goals are tied to the context of the studied organization and projects, hence results of this case study are limited to this context only.

Since the organization where the study was performed used SCRUM, we selected nine epics from one project, for this case study. The epics were broken down into 32 requirements and use cases, which were in turn decomposed into 119 user stories.

4.2 Data collection procedure

We created a spreadsheet to record the functional size measurements as well as the actual effort time. To collect the functional size measurements expressed in UCP, UFP, and CFP, one of the researchers (previously trained on these size estimation methods) performed the counting corresponding to each sizing method. On the other hand, for each user story, we recorded both its actual effort, and its estimated effort obtained with planning poker.

We identified outliers by calculating the productivity index (**PI**) of each requirement under each sizing method as **PI= actual effort/size**, and then generating box-plots with this information. Outliers indicated in boxplots were then discarded.

4.3 Analysis procedure

The analysis procedure for generating the effort estimation models was based on a regression analysis. To select the regression analysis approach to follow (linear, multiple, polynomial, exponential), the dataset was analyzed with a scatterplot. Depending on the pattern revealed by the scatterplot, different regression approaches were chosen. By default, linear regression was used. In all models, the dependent variable was the estimated effort time (EFF) and the independent variables were a subset of the software functional size measurements (i.e., UCP, USP, UFP or CFP).

On the other hand, the procedure for calculating the MMRE was to apply Equation 1 to each generated model. Case study wise, the lowest MMRE would determine the best effort estimation model. Nevertheless, a model that exhibits an MMRE value less than 0.25 is considered accurate enough.

$$MMRE = \frac{100}{T} \times \sum_{i=0}^{T} \frac{|estimated\ eff\ (i) - actual\ eff\ (i)|}{actual\ effort\ (i)} \quad (1)$$

Additionally, the procedure for calculating the MBRE was as follows: first, we applied Equation 2 to obtain the Relatative Error (RY_i); then, we calculated the Balance Relative Error (R_i) by applying Equation 3; finally, we applied Equation 4 to obtain the MBRE value.

$$RY_i = \frac{estimated\ eff\ (i) - actual\ eff\ (i)}{actual\ effort\ (i)} \quad (2)$$

$$R_i = \begin{cases} \frac{estimated\ eff\ (i) - actual\ eff\ (i)}{actual\ effort\ (i)}, & estimated\ eff\ (i) - actual\ eff\ (i) \geq 0 \\ \frac{estimated\ eff\ (i) - actual\ eff\ (i)}{estimated\ eff\ (i)}, & estimated\ eff\ (i) - actual\ eff\ (i) < 0 \end{cases} \quad (3)$$

$$MBRE = \frac{1}{N} \times \sum_{i=0}^{N} R_i \quad (4)$$

In the context of the MBRE metric, a model is considered accurate enough when the MBRE value is less than 0.35. According to Miyazaki [30], 35% accurancy might be enough in the early phase of the software life cycle.

4.4 Threats to validity

We evaluated the validity of our study based on Runeson's guidelines [16], considering construct validity, internal validity, external validity, and reliability, as shown below. The threats to validity are briefly mentioned next.

Construct validity: in our case study, we created a set of effort estimation models based on functional size measurement for a specific organizational context, and evaluated their accuracy performance using MMRE and MBRE.

Internal validity: one validity threat is the small sample size used (having only 32 requirements to analyze). Additionally, a bias could have been introduced in the sample selection process. Also, some data were discarded from the analysis as they were identified as outliers. Another threat is that only one researcher performed the functional size measurement for each requirement, however, this researcher has proven experience with these counting methods. Finally, MMRE as a statistical measure to evaluate a model's performance has sometimes failed to show statistical evidence, as advised by Kitchenham et al. [6] and Lavazza et al. [8]. We tried to mitigate this threat by also comparing accurancy in combination with MBRE, which has demonstrated more effiency, according to Jørgensen [31]

External validity: the effort estimation models are applicable only to the organization described in this study. These models are not intended to be used in other contexts besides this one.

Reliability: since the organization's dataset grew with time, there is a validity threat that this case study presents non-repeatable results, as pointed out by Lavazza et al. [8]. As the organization scales up, results might vary.

5 Analysis of Results

In this section we present the results of our case study, addressing each of the research questions.

5.1 Accuracy of effort estimation models based on functional size (RQ1)

Our first research question aimed at finding the most accurate estimation model based on functional size measurements, in the context of the organization, and using MMRE and MBRE as the accuracy performance measurements.

Figure 1 describes the relationship between requirements, use cases, and user stories. For this case study, we gathered 9 Epic User Stories, which were broken down into 32 Requierements and 32 Use Cases. During the development phase, those Requirements and Use Cases were structured as 119 User Stories. These User Stories were delivered by the team, having the actual time tracked against each User Story. Requierements assets were used for UFP and CFP functional size measurements, Use Cases were used for UCP and User Story items for USP functional size measurements.

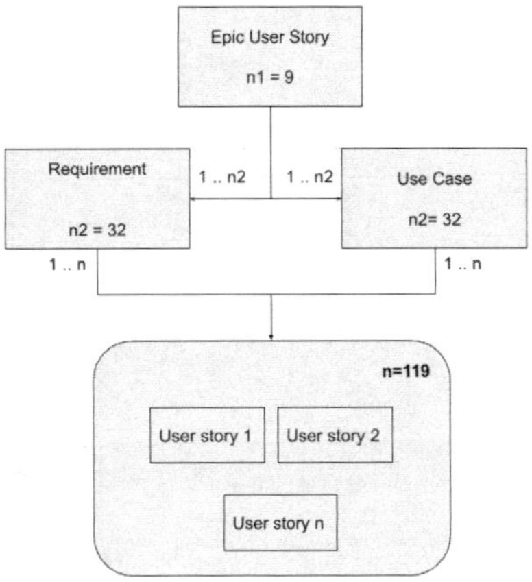

Fig. 1. Requirements detail structure.

Using regression, we developed a series of parametric statistical models to describe the relationship between size and effort. We applied different kinds of regression analyses to build the models. The model types were selected by using a visual pattern scan in the scatterplot for each functional measurement. Simple, multiple, polynomial, and exponential regression methods were applied to UCP, UFP, USP, CFP counts to render several effort estimation models. We generated scatterplots for each functional size method to decide on the type of regression to apply, based on the dataset pattern. Figure 2 shows scatterplots of actual effort vs. size for each sizing measurement: (1) UCP,

(2) UFP, (3) USP, and (4) CFP. The Y-axis represents actual effort, while the X-axis represents the functional size measurements, for each method.

In total, we developed 11 effort estimation models based on four different functional size measures. Table 1 summarizes these models, their input parameters, dependent parameters, analysis method, MMRE and MBRE

The accuracy of each effort estimation model was assessed by its Mean Magnitude of Relative Error (MMRE) and Mean Balanced Relative Error (MBRE), depicted in Equations 1 and 4. The accuracy of an estimation model increases as its MMRE gets closer to 0, thus a small MMRE value indicates that the model is a good predictor. Following [4][30], a model with an MMRE value less than 0.25 and an MBRE value less than 0.35 was deemed accurate enough to be used in the organization under study.

Model 11 from Table 1, which uses a exponential regression on COSMIC Function Points, is the most accurate effort estimation model, with an MMRE value of 0.22 and an MBRE value of 0.35. Revisiting chart (4) from Figure 2, we confirm that this dataset follows an exponential pattern, which explains why model 11 provided the lowest MMRE and MBRE of all models.

On the other hand, model 1 from Table 1 is the least accurate estimation model, and it uses a linear regression on UCP. Revisiting chart (1) from Figure 2, there is no clear pattern in this dataset, which might explain why model 1 showed a high MMRE and MBRE.

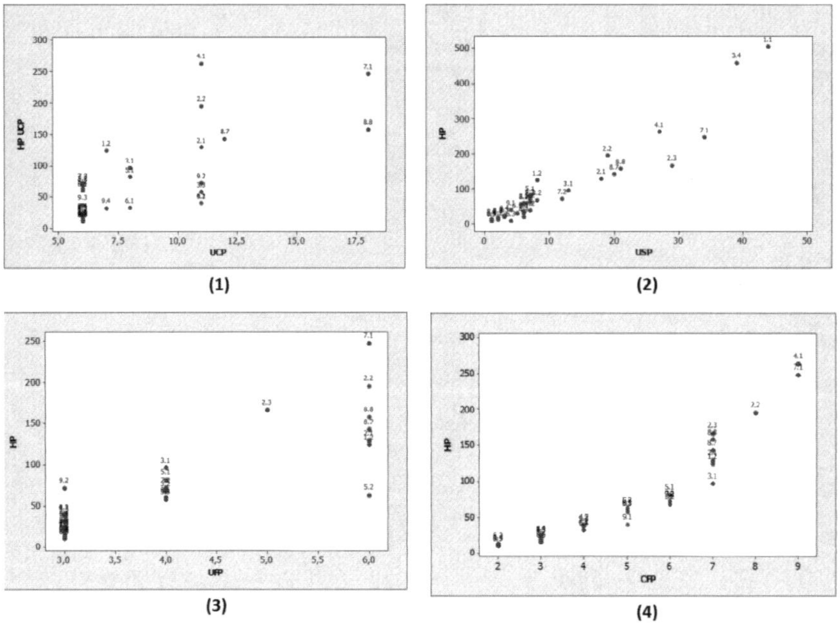

Fig. 2. Scatterplots of actual effort vs. size for (1) UCP, (2) UFP, (3) USP and (4) CFP.

Table 1. Effort estimation models based on functional size measurements.

#	Analysis Method	Parameters	Dependent Variable	Model	MMRE	**MBRE**
1	Linear	UCP	Effort	EFF = -51,0 + 14,7 UCP	0.86	0.98
2	Linear	USP	Effort	EFF = -13,1 + 9,86 USP	0.45	0.87
3	Polynomial	USP	Effort	EFF = 18,47 + 3,392 USP + 0,1650 USP^2	0.41	0.45
4	Polynomial	USP	Effort	EFF = -8,75 + 12,30 USP - 0,3977 USP^2 + 0,008921 USP^3	0.36	0.58
5	Linear	UFP	Effort	EFF = -100 + 42,9 UFP	0.48	0.53
6	Linear	DET, FTR	Effort	EFF = -46,2 + 4,51 DET + 44,0 FTR	0.36	0.54
7	Linear	DET, FTR	Effort	EFF = 1,7 + 1,47 DET + 13,9 FTR	0.31	0.45
8	Linear	DET, FTR	Effort	EFF = -86,6 + 5,93 DET + 53,3 FTR	0.23	0.36
9	Linear	CFP	Effort	EFF = -78,6 + 31,0 CFP	0.58	0.51
10	Linear	E,R,WX	Effort	EFF = -79,4 + 45,1 E + 31,4 R + 30,8 W + 15,1 X	0.47	0.79
11	Exponential	CFP	Effort	EFF = 0,789382 × CFP $^{2.63169}$	0.22	0.35

5.2 Accuracy of convertibility models for functional size measurements (RQ2)

Our second research question sought to find accurate convertibility models of functional size measurements, in the context of the organization, using MMRE and MBRE as the accuracy performance measurements.

Further analysis was done to provide a set of models that allow convertibility between different functional size measurements (e.g. from USP to CFP), without having to execute the formal counting protocol for each size estimation method. As previously stated, these convertibility models are applicable only in the context of the organization under study, and are therefore not intended to be widely used across industry.

Twelve parametric statistical models were built, one for each possible convertibility combination between funtional size measurements. We used linear regression analysis, and then we measured the accuracy by calculating the MMRE and MBRE for each model. These convertibility models are shown in Table 2, together with their analysis method, dependent variable, parameters (independent variables), MMRE and MBRE. Only models with MMRE less than 0.25 and MBRE less than 0.35 are accurate enough to be considered for common use in our company context.

Two interesting findings arise from Table 2:

1. Given the MMRE and MBRE results for models 4, 5 and 6, there is no linear model that offers an acceptable accuracy for USP convertibility from any other software size measure. Therefore, for this organization to get software size estimates in USP, they would need to perform SCRUM ceremonies (like Planning Poker) to provide them.
2. Using model 12 from Table 2, the organization would be able to convert their current USP estimates into CFP, and then use model 11 from Table 1 to estimate the effort. This approach could improve accuracy, rather than using the model 4 from Table 1.

However, this approach would lead the company to have less accuracy performance, given the probability addition rule. The MMRE must then be added to get a total MMRE of 0.45 for the whole effort estimation process. Similarly, it would lead to a total MBRE of 0.60 for the complete effort estimation process

Table 2. Convertibility models of software functional size measurements.

#	Analysis Method	Dependent Variable	Parameter	Model	MMRE	**MBRE**
1	Linear	UCP	USP	UCP = 5,57 + 0,324 USP	0.18	0.20
2	Linear	UCP	CFP	UCP = 3,09 + 1,09 CFP	0.21	0.24
3	Linear	UCP	UFP	UCP = 2,24 + 1,57 UFP	0.24	0.28
4	Linear	USP	CFP	USP = - 10,3 + 4,05 CFP	4.73	4.73
5	Linear	USP	UFP	USP = - 16,8 + 6,88 UFP	8.37	8.37
6	Linear	USP	UCP	USP = - 8,56 + 2,25 UCP	4.72	4.72
7	Linear	UFP	UCP	UFP = 2,37 + 0,195 UCP	0.21	0.24
8	Linear	UFP	USP	UFP = 2,96 + 0,113 USP	1.57	4.01
9	Linear	UFP	CFP	UFP = 1,52 + 0,506 CFP	0.14	0.15
10	Linear	CFP	UFP	CFP = - 0,435 + 1,36 UFP	0.38	0.38
11	Linear	CFP	UCP	CFP = 1,72 + 0,392 UCP	0.35	0.39
12	Linear	CFP	USP	CFP = 3,05 + 0,203 USP	0.23	0.25

6 Discussion

Regarding RQ1, we found that model 11 from Table 1 (based on COSMIC Function Points) yields the most accurate effort estimates. Comparing the accuracy of COSMIC models, we observe that the CFP-based estimation model (model 11 in Table 1) performs slightly better than the UFP-based model (model 8 in Table 1). However, model 8 is applicable only to requirements with six or more data elements (DETs). Hence, only the COSMIC-based model proved to be accurate enough and applicable to any requirement, regardless of its size or number of data elements.

These results support the findings of Salmanoglu et al. [17], who concluded that an effort estimation model based on COSMIC Function Points was more accurate than another model based on User Story Points. They also used MMRE as the performance indicator for the models, making our results quite relatable to theirs.

Our results also relate to existing evidence by Ungan et al. [20], who also found that the effort model based on COSMIC Function Points performed better than the model based on User Story Points. Besides regression analysis, they included an artificial neural networks approach to build their models, yet they obtained similar results to ours.

It is worth mentioning that our study relates to the work of Paz et al. [13] in two aspects. First, we obtained similar results, as we determined that the most accurate effort estimation model was based on COSMIC function points. Second, we followed a similar approach to estimate the software size: we both used *Incremental COSMIC Function Points*, mostly because the application was developed using a SCRUM methodology, and this approach allows to apply CFP in agile environments.

Also for RQ1, we found that model 1 from Table 1 (based on Use Case Points) yields the least accurate effort estimates. This finding differs from the results obtained by Sholiq et al. [19], as they found a slightly better performance using Use Case Points. There are, however, two main differences among the studies that could have affected the results. First, we used a regression analysis to build the effort estimation models, while they used instead a productivy factor (calculated by them) for that specific scenario. Second, they measured the size of already completed projects, whereas we measured the size of an ongoing agile project (incremental pieces of software).

Regarding RQ2, we were able to obtain accurate convertibility models for some functional size measurements, but not for every pair. The convertibility models that can be safely used in the organization context are models 1, 2, 3, 7, 9 or 12 from Table 2, given that their estimation error measured as MMRE is less than 0.25 and MBRE is less than 0.35. These results relate to the findings of Lavazza et al. [7], as both presented a model that allow convertibility from CFP to UFP (in our study, it is model 9 from Table 2). However, in the case of the convertibility from UFP to CFP, Lavazza et al. [7] showed evidence that allows it, while we were not able to find an accurate model for it (model 10 from Table 2 was not accurate enough).

7 Conclusions

In this paper, we described a case study that compares the accuracy of effort estimation models derived through regression from four functional size measurements: Story Points, Use Case Points (UCP), IFPUG Function Points (UFP), and COSMIC Function Points (CFP). Additionally, we derived a set of convertibility models between functional size measurements, which can be used to easily convert the organization's historical measurements into different software size measures.

Our results confirm findings from previous studies such as [20], [13], and [17], which concluded that effort estimation models based on CFP show better accuracy than alternative methods compared in their studies.

However, compared to counting USP, none of the convertibility models are accurate enough to estimate software size. Thus, in the organization under study, current agile ceremonies must continue to be performed in order to estimate work size.

Our convertibility models reaffirm previous evidence by Lavazza et al. [7], as they presented a scenario where UFP and CFP were correlated, and a model is proposed to convert from one software sizing method to the other. Although expert judgment is still generally preferred as the estimation method in agile environments [21], our recommendation to the organization under study is to adopt CFP as their sizing method, especially as the number of projects grows and the company scales up. There is ample evidence in the literature that using CFP could improve an organization's estimates [3], [20], [13], and [17].

As future work, we plan to replicate this study using a larger dataset with an extended sample of functional requirements. Another possible extension to our work would be to perform a statistical analysis to compare the effort estimation models, including the statistical tests suggested by Lavazza et al. [8] such as paired *t*-tests of the MRE, or paired tests of the absolute residuals.

References

1. Briand, L., & Maxwell , K. An Assessment and Comparison of Common Software Cost Estimation Modeling Techniques. *ICSE '99*, 1999, Pages: 313-323.
2. Chi-Jui , L., & Yeh, D.-M. A Software Maintenance Project Size Estimation Tool Based On Cosmic Full Function Point. *2016 International Computer Symposium (ICS)*, 2016, Pages: 555-560.
3. Desharnais, J., Buglione, L. & Kocaturk,B., Using the COSMIC Method to Estimate Agile User Stories. Proceedings of the *12th International Conference on Product Focused Software Development and Process Improvement*, 2011.
4. Foss , T., Stensrud, E., Kitchenham, B., & Myrtveit, I. A Simulation Study of the Model Evaluation Criterion MMRE. *IEEE Transactions on Software Engineering*, Volume: 29, Issue: 11, 2003, Pages: 985-995.
5. Jørgensen, M., Boehm, B., & Rifkin, S. (2009). Software development effort estimation: Formal models or expert judgment? *IEEE software*, 26(2), 14-19.
6. Barbara Kitchenham and Emilia Mendes. 2009. Why comparative effort prediction studies may be invalid. In *Proceedings of the 5th International Conference on Predictor Models in Software Engineering (PROMISE '09)*. ACM, New York, NY, USA, , Article 4 , 5 pages. DOI=http://dx.doi.org/10.1145/1540438.1540444
7. Lavazza, L., & Liu, G.. A Study of the Correlation between Functional Size Measures and Object-oriented Measures from UML Requirements Models. *IWSM Mensura 2018*, Pages:54-69
8. Lavazza, L., & Morasca, S. On the Evaluation of Effort Estimation Models. EASE'17. 2017.
9. Lenarduzzi, V, Lunesu, I., Matta, M & Taibi, D., Functional Size Measures and Effort Estimation in Agile Development: A Replicated Study. In Suomalainen, T. *Continuous Strategy Process in the context of Agile and Lean Software Development*. Springer, 2015.
10. Mendes, E., Watson, I., Triggs, C. et al. A Comparative Study of Cost Estimation Models for Web Hypermedia Applications. Empirical Software Engineering (2003) 8: 163. https://doi.org/10.1023/A:1023062629183
11. Mittas, N., & Angelis, L. Ranking and Clustering Software Cost Estimation Models through a Multiple Comparisons Algorithm. *IEEE Transactions on Software Engineering* Vol. 39, No. 4, 2013, Pages: 537- 551.
12. Nikolaos Mittas and Lefteris Angelis. 2010. Visual comparison of software cost estimation models by regression error characteristic analysis. J. Syst. Softw. 83, 4 (April 2010), 621-637. DOI=http://dx.doi.org/10.1016/j.jss.2009.10.044
13. Paz, F., Zapata, C., & Pow-Sang, J. A. An Approach for Effort Estimation in Incremental Software Development using COSMIC Function Points. *ESEM'14*, 2014.
14. Kai Petersen, Sairam Vakkalanka, Ludwik Kuzniarz, Guidelines for conducting systematic mapping studies in software engineering: An update, Information and Software Technology, Volume 64, 2015, Pages 1-18,

15. Phannachitta, P. Robust Comparison of Similarity Measures in Analogy-Based Software Effort Estimation. *11th International Conference on Software, Knowledge, Information Management and Applications (SKIMA),* 2017.
16. Runeson , P., & Höst, M. Guidelines for conducting and reporting case study research in software engineering. *Empiric Software Eng.* 2008. Pages: 131–164.
17. Salmanoglu, M., Hacaloglu, T., & Demirors, O. Effort Estimation for Agile Software Development: Comparative Case Studies Using COSMIC Functional Size Measurement and Story Points, *IWSM/Mensura '17*, 2017.
18. Santana C., Leoneo F., Vasconcelos A., Gusmão C. (2011) Using Function Points in Agile Projects. In: Sillitti A., Hazzan O., Bache E., Albaladejo X. (eds) Agile Processes in Software Engineering and Extreme Programming. XP 2011. Lecture Notes in Business Information Processing, vol 77. Springer, Berlin, Heidelberg
19. Sholiq, Renny, S., & Pribadi , A. A Comparative Study of Software Development Size Estimation Method: UCPabc vs Function Points. *4th Information Systems International Conference 2017*, Pages 470-477.
20. Ungan, E., Çizmeli, N., & Demirörs, O. Comparison of Functional Size Based Estimation and Story Points, Based on Effort Estimation Effectiveness in SCRUM Projects. *Euromicro Conference on Software Engineering and Advanced Applications*, 2014, Pages. 77-80.
21. Usman, M., Mendes, E., & Börstler, J. Effort Estimation in Agile Software Development: A Survey on the State of the Practice. *EASE'15*, 2015.
22. F.G. Wilkie, I.R. McChesney, P. Morrow, C. Tuxworth, N.G. Lester, The value of software sizing, *Information and Software Technology*, Volume 53, Issue 11, 2011, Pages 1236-1249
23. Bente , A., Hege , D., Sjøberg, D., & Magne, J. Estimating Software Development Effort Based on Use Cases - Experiences from Industry. The Unified Modeling Language. Modeling Languages, Concepts, and Tools, 2001, Pages: 487-502.
24. Karner, G. Metrics for Objectory. Diploma thesis. University of Linköping, No. LiTH-IDA-Ex-9344:21, 1993
25. Popli , R., & Chauahn , N. Managing Uncertainty of Story-Points in Agile Software. 2nd International Conference on Computing for Sustainable Global Development (INDIACom), 2015, Pages: 1357-1361.
26. Gandomani, T. J., & Mahsa Radnejad, H. F. Planning Poker in cost estimation in Agile methods: Averaging Vs. Consensus. 2019 IEEE 5th International Conference on Knowledge-Based Engineering and Innovation (KBEI), 2019, Pages: 66-71.
27. Garmus, D., & Herron, D. Function Poin Analysis: Measurement Practices for Successful Software Projects. Addison-Wesley, 2001
28. Gandomani, T. J., & Mahsa Radnejad, H. F. Planning Poker in cost estimation in Agile methods: Averaging Vs. Consensus. 2019 IEEE 5th International Conference on Knowledge-Based Engineering and Innovation (KBEI), 2019, Pages: 66-71.
29. Chi-Jui , L., & Yeh, D.-M. A Software Maintenance Project Size Estimation Tool Based On Cosmic Full Function Point. 2016 International Computer Symposium (ICS), 2016, Pages: 555-560.
30. Miyazaki, Y., et al., Robust regression for developing software estimation models. Journal of Systems and Software, 1994. 27(1): Pages. 3-16.
31. M. Jørgensen. A critique of how we measure and interpret the accuracy of software development effort estimation. Proceedings of 1st International Workshop on Software Productivity Analysis and Cost Estimation, 2007, Pages 15–22.

Ciencia de datos y Agilidad: una revisión de la literatura

Paula B. Lima [1]; Gabriel E. Giana[1]; Verónica Andrea Bollati [2]; Liliana Cuenca Pletsch[1]
[1] CInApTIC, UTN Facultad Regional Resistencia, Chaco, Argentina
[2] CONICET - CInApTIC, UTN Facultad Regional Resistencia, Chaco, Argentina
{limapaulabelen, gabrielgiana77, vbollati, liliana.cuencap}@gmail.com

Abstract. La creciente producción y recolección de los datos involucrados en proyectos de Data Science generan la necesidad de un marco de trabajo que permita el procesamiento eficiente de los mismos. A pesar de los progresos logrados en esta temática, aún se desconoce una forma de trabajo que se ajuste a estos proyectos y permita obtener mayores beneficios. Frecuentemente, se opta por la utilización de prácticas ágiles, pero los equipos se ven obligados a realizar adaptaciones sobre éstas, debido a las diferencias existentes entre los proyectos de desarrollo de software y los proyectos de Data Science. En este trabajo presentamos una revisión sistemática de la literatura con el fin de obtener el estado del arte de los enfoques de trabajo utilizados en proyectos de Data Science, sobre todo aquellos que utilizan prácticas ágiles (ya sea total o parcial), y los roles que los integrantes de los equipos desempeñan a fin de determinar puntos en común de trabajo o problemas que se evidencian en sus funciones.

Keywords: Data Science, Agilidad, Framework, Técnicas.

1 Introducción

La ciencia de datos (DS, por su denominación en inglés *Data Science*) es un concepto que no sólo sintetiza y unifica el campo de la estadística, análisis de datos y sus métodos relacionados, sino también busca comprender los resultados obtenidos [1]. Surge por la gran cantidad de datos generados sobre las personas que se encuentran disponibles en distintos medios de almacenamiento [2] y por la heterogeneidad de los elementos bajo estudio (texto, imágenes o videos) [3]. Esto genera la necesidad de incorporar herramientas de las ciencias de la computación y otras disciplinas, que permitan la integración de dos o más tipos de datos distintos [4].

A partir de la necesidad de hacer un uso eficiente y eficaz de los datos [2], se implementan herramientas de Ingeniería de Software (IS), como metodologías de desarrollo, a proyectos de esta rama. Debido a la inexactitud y al retardo de la creación de valor en las metodologías tradicionales (ej. la metodología en cascada), el enfoque predominante en proyectos de DS es el propuesto por las prácticas ágiles [5], aunque, generalmente, no son utilizadas en su totalidad, puesto que los proyectos de esta índole son muy variados, por lo que se ajustan o reemplazan algunas de sus tareas.

Entre las principales dificultades en DS se pueden mencionar, la definición de un framework de trabajo [5], los roles de los integrantes de los equipos [6] y la inexactitud de las formas de trabajo existentes de IS para este ámbito [5]. En este sentido, se considera que la utilización de prácticas ágiles, adaptadas a los proyectos de DS, pueden constituir una solución a estos problemas.

En este artículo, se presenta el análisis del estado del arte, por medio de un proceso de revisión sistemática de literatura, sobre el uso de prácticas ágiles en proyectos de DS.

El artículo se estructura de la siguiente manera: primero, se detalla el método utilizado para realizar el análisis del estado del arte (sección 2). Seguidamente, se exponen los resultados obtenidos a partir de su aplicación (sección 3). Luego, se presenta la discusión donde se da respuesta a las preguntas de investigación planteadas (sección 4). Finalmente, se presentan las conclusiones del trabajo.

2 Método

El método utilizado para la realización de este estudio es el de Revisión Sistemática de Literatura (RSL), propuesto por Kitchenham y Charters [7] y, en particular la versión propuesta por Biolchini et al. [8], cuyas fases principales son: planificación, ejecución y análisis de resultados. Paralelo a todo el proceso, se almacena la información obtenida en cada etapa, y se incorporan puntos de control para validar cada etapa. En esta sección se presentan los aspectos propuestos para la etapa de planificación.

2.1 Preguntas de investigación

En primer lugar se define el objetivo principal de la RSL, el cual es: Identificar y analizar el estado del arte de los enfoques de trabajo, procesos y equipos de DS en el contexto de la IS. A partir del mismo, se plantean las preguntas de investigación (PI):

- PI1: ¿Cuál es el enfoque de trabajo en proyectos de DS? Debido a las particularidades de los proyectos de DS (por ej., el valor entregado al cliente se relaciona con la información obtenida y no con un *Minimun Viable Product (MVP)*) y su consecuente diferencia con el desarrollo de software, interesa conocer cuál es la manera de trabajar, es decir, conocer el modo en el que se combinan las actividades científicas con las de desarrollo, identificando los diferentes frameworks que se utilizan en proyectos de DS y evaluando la efectividad de los mismos.
- PI2: ¿Cuáles son los perfiles involucrados en proyectos de DS? Debido a la naturaleza científica de los proyectos de DS participan roles propios de ciencias como estadísticas y matemáticas. Tras la necesidad de incorporar conceptos de IS para la gestión eficiente de los proyectos es importante determinar los perfiles presentes en los equipos de desarrollo, sus responsabilidades y limitaciones.
- PI3: ¿Los enfoques utilizados se aplican de manera pura o tienen adaptaciones? Es interesante conocer la forma en la que se aplican los frameworks en los proyectos de DS, para identificar las actividades que presentan mejores resultados y generan mayor beneficio, como así también identificar los problemas originados por aspectos o enfoques que no pueden aplicarse a los proyectos de DS.

2.2 Fuentes de datos y consulta

La etapa de planificación también involucra enumerar las fuentes de datos que se utilizarán para buscar estudios o trabajos previamente realizados y la definición de las consultas que se ejecutarán en dichas fuentes [7, 8].

Puesto que los frameworks aplicados a proyectos de DS son variados y en constante actualización, la búsqueda de estudios no se limitó a librerías digitales sino también se extendió a blogs técnicos. Esto no sólo permite obtener experiencias compartidas por profesionales que se desempeñan en el campo, sino también dificultades con las técnicas, a partir de vivencias de los desarrolladores. Podemos destacar las siguientes fuentes consultadas (Nombre[Acrónimo][Tipo de fuente]: website):

- IEEEXplore [IEEEX] [Librería digital]: http://ieeexplore.ieee.org/
- Google Scholar [GS] [Librería digital]: https://scholar.google.com/
- Springer Link [SPRINGER] [Librería digital]: https://link.springer.com
- Science Direct [SD] [Librería digital]: https://www.sciencedirect.com/
- ACM Digital Library [ACM] [Librería digital]: https://dl.acm.org/
- Scholar Space [SS] [Librería Digital]: https://scholarspace.manoa.hawaii.edu/
- Google [Google][Buscador generalista]: https://www.google.com

Dado que cada una de estas librerías digitales poseen su propia sintaxis, se adapto la consulta de búsqueda para ser utilizada en cada motor, como se muestra en la tabla 1.

2.3 Criterios de inclusión y exclusión

Para incrementar la precisión de la investigación, se han eliminado estudios a través de la definición de criterios de inclusión y exclusión, de acuerdo con lo recomendado por [7]. Los criterios de inclusión planteados fueron:

- El título sugiere que su contenido tiene relación con DS.
- El título sugiere que su contenido está relacionado con la gestión de proyectos de datos.
- El título posee alguna de las siguientes palabras: *Agile, Data Science, Data Teams, Data Projects, Roles*.
- El Abstract contiene alguna de las siguientes frases: *Agile Data Science, Data Teams, Data Projects, Roles*.
- El Abstract permite determinar que está relacionado con DS como así también, con su implementación en un entorno de desarrollo determinado o con la definición de perfiles asociados a este tipo de proyectos.
- Para aquellas búsquedas realizadas en los motores de búsqueda generalistas, se tendrá en cuenta si es un artículo de blog.

Tabla 1. Cadenas de texto utilizadas para las búsquedas

Fuente	Consulta utilizada	Condiciones
IEEX	(("All Metadata":data science) AND "All Metadata":agile)	Title (matches all) Filtros: 2015-2019

	((("All Metadata":data science) AND "All Metadata":software) AND "All Metadata":teams)	Filtros: 2015-2019 Conferences, Journals
Google Scholar	allintitle: agile "data science"	
	allintitle: agile "data science" teams	
Springer	agile data science	Title (matches all) AND Abstract (matches all) AND Keywords (matches all) Filtros: Entre 2016 y 2020
	agile data science teams	Title (matches all) AND Abstract (matches all) AND Keywords (matches all) Filtros: Entre 2018 y 2019
ACM	(+agile +"data science")	Any field matches all (agile "data science"
	(+agile +"data science" +teams)	Any field matches all (agile "data science" teams
SS	title:("data science")	Abstract (matches "data science" AND agile)
	title:("data science")	Abstract (matches "data science" AND agile AND teams))
Google	"agile teams OR software "data science"	
	"agile OR software OR engineer OR management "data science"	
	"software OR teams OR management "data engineer"	

Además, hemos definido criterios que permiten identificar artículos que aportan información imprecisa o irrelevante a fin de descartarlos. Es por ello que, de los artículos preseleccionados, se eliminaron aquellos que cumplían con los siguientes criterios de exclusión:

- Estudios que no estén relacionados y que no mencionen los roles asociados a proyectos de DS.
- Estudios que no proveen información detallada sobre la práctica o enfoque para abordar los proyectos de DS particularmente.
- Estudios cuyo contenido no expone información acerca de la forma de gestionar los proyectos de datos.
- Para los artículos de blog, se excluirán aquellos de los que no se pueda obtener de alguna forma, la fecha de publicación y los autores involucrados.
- Estudios que se correspondan con cursos online, foros, videos, y relacionados.
- Estudios que nos fuere imposible acceder, por motivos ajenos a los revisadores.

2.4 Extracción de datos y análisis

En la fase de extracción de datos se reunió toda la información de los estudios que permitirán dar respuesta a las preguntas de investigación [7]. Primeramente, se recolectó información fundamental para identificar cada uno de los estudios: Título y autores, Abstract, Tipo de estudio (papers, blogs, etc.), Año de publicación.

Es importante mencionar, que los artículos de blogs no tienen Abstract, por lo que se omitió este elemento. Además, para analizar con mayor profundidad los estudios seleccionados, se decidió extraer la siguiente información:

- El nombre del enfoque de trabajo adoptado.
- Las prácticas ágiles identificadas en la propuesta.
- Las adecuaciones realizadas sobre prácticas ágiles.
- Los roles involucrados en el desarrollo de proyectos de datos.
- Los problemas que surgen a partir de los roles incluidos o aquellos derivados de la ejecución de las prácticas.

Además, se conformaron Grupos de Estudio Primarios (GEP) para simplificar el análisis realizado sobre los trabajos recolectados. Se agruparon aquellos estudios que poseen líneas de investigación similares o tópicos en común. Utilizando el enfoque de GEP y las verificaciones de calidad, se pueden contestar las preguntas establecidas en la Sección 2.1.

Validaciones GEP.
En vistas de obtener un mejor análisis de los GEP con respecto al tópico de investigación, se definen 4 evaluadores de GEP (VG) y los puntajes que se tendrán en cuenta. El proceso seleccionado fue: Sí (S) = 1, Parcialmente (P) = 0,5 y No (N) = 0. Las preguntas de validación usadas en esta revisión, fueron:

- VG1: El estudio, ¿cita y describe un enfoque de trabajo para abordar los proyectos de datos? Calificación: S: Cita un enfoque de trabajo para abordar los proyectos de datos. Además, describe prácticas puntuales y/o cómo implementarlas. P: No cita un enfoque de trabajo para abordar los proyectos de datos, pero describe o indica cómo se desarrollan los proyectos. N: No cita ningún enfoque o práctica de trabajo.
- VG2: El estudio, ¿menciona los roles involucrados en la gestión del proyecto de datos? Calificación: S: Menciona todos los roles involucrados en la gestión del proyecto de datos. P: Menciona los roles asociados únicamente a la gestión de datos. N: No menciona roles asociados a la gestión de proyectos de datos.
- VG3: El estudio, ¿describe los perfiles de datos involucrados en el enfoque de trabajo adoptado? Calificación: S: Describe los perfiles de datos involucrados. P: Sólo menciona los roles relacionados a la gestión de los datos. N: No menciona roles.
- VG4: El estudio, ¿expone ventajas o beneficios de aplicar el enfoque de trabajo propuesto a partir de la experiencia? Calificación: S: Expone ventajas y beneficios de aplicar el enfoque de trabajo propuesto a los proyectos de datos a partir de casos de estudio reales. P: Expone ventajas y beneficios que podrían obtenerse del enfoque de trabajo propuesto, pero no surgen de ninguna aplicación real. N: No expone ni ventajas, ni beneficios.

2.5 Proceso que conduce la revisión

El último paso en la etapa de planificación es definir el proceso que conduce la revisión. En este caso, definimos un proceso basado en el propuesto en [9]. El primer paso en el proceso consiste en enumerar las fuentes de datos (FD) y las consultas de búsqueda usadas. Una vez identificadas las FD se debe trabajar con su motor de búsqueda. Para este propósito, el motor de búsqueda de cada FD es analizado de manera de adaptar las consultas a la sintaxis de cada motor: por lo que cada cadena de búsqueda (CB) es usada para buscar estudios en la FD correspondiente (Tabla 1). El siguiente paso consiste en almacenar y enumerar todos los estudios obtenidos de cada FD, este paso implica la extracción de algunos datos (título, autores, etc).

A continuación, la selección de estudios primarios consiste en chequear el cumplimiento de los criterios de inclusión definidos (sección 2.3). Luego, se remueven aquellos estudios duplicados que pudiera aparecer producto de la utilización de múltiples fuentes de datos; y se evalúa cada estudio no duplicado según los criterios de exclusión definidos en la sección 2.3 de manera de eliminar aquellos que no formarán parte del conjunto final, de los cuales se extraerán los datos definidos en la sección 2.4.

3 Resultados

En esta sección se presentan los resultados obtenidos en la RSL siguiendo lo detallado previamente. Nótese que el análisis fue realizado a cada estudio de forma individual.

3.1 Búsqueda y selección primaria

Se realizó la búsqueda en librerías digitales y, posteriormente, en el motor de búsqueda "Google". Los resultados se presentan agrupados.

En la Tabla 2, se muestran los resultados obtenidos, agrupados por FD. Como se puede observar, mediante la ejecución de estas búsquedas se obtuvieron 796 resultados. La segunda columna muestra los resultados de cada FD. De ellos, se seleccionaron 70, lo que representa el 8,79%, que cumplían con algún criterio de inclusión. El porcentaje se vio afectado por estudios que exponían el uso de DS para obtener métricas sobre las prácticas ágiles implementadas por algún equipo de desarrollo de software, lo cual no forma parte del objetivo de esta investigación.

La FD Google aportó 55,71% de los Estudios Relevantes (ER), siendo la de mayor peso. Sólo se tuvieron en cuenta los resultados que se encontraban hasta la segunda página (30 resultados por página). Esto se debe a la gran cantidad de elementos que el buscador obtiene, y a partir de pruebas realizadas, se concluyó que los resultados destacados se encuentran entre la primera y la segunda página.

Seguidamente, IEEEXplore aportó 22,86% de ER y la librería digital con menor porcentaje (1,43%) fue Scholar Space, aportando un único artículo.

Tabla 2. Resumen de librerías digitales

Librería digital	Resultados de la búsqueda	Estudios relevantes [E.R.]	% de resultados relevantes	% de todos los ER
IEEX	631	16	2,54	22,86
Google Scholar	14	5	35,71	7,14
Springer Link	13	3	23,08	4,29
Science Direct	28	3	10,71	4,29
ACM	13	3	23,08	4,29
Scholar Space	7	1	14,29	1,43
Google	90	39	43,33	55,71
Total	796	70	8,79	100,00

La Tabla 3 detalla las cantidades de estudios duplicados, donde el 15,71% de los estudios relevantes encontrados en esta RSL están presentes en más de una fuente de datos. A continuación, hemos removido los estudios duplicados, resultando un total de 59 estudios únicos (no duplicados). Luego, se retiraron aquellos que cumplían con algún criterio de exclusión, constituyendo un total de 26 ER descartados. Finalmente, se obtuvieron 33 ER para realizar las validaciones de calidad.

Tabla 3. Cantidad de estudios duplicados

	Cantidad	Porcentaje (%)
Estudios relevantes	70	100,00
Estudios relevantes duplicados	11	15,71
Estudios relevantes no-duplicados	59	84,29

De acuerdo con los criterios establecidos en la sección 2.4, se conformaron 6 agrupaciones GEP, que se exponen en la Tabla 4.

Tabla 4. Grupos de Estudios Primario

Nº	Tema	Autores	Título	Año
1	Roles asociados a los datos en equipos de desarrollo	M. Kim; T. Zimmermann; R. DeLine; A. Begel	Data Scientists in Software Teams: State of the Art and Challenges	2018
		M. Kim; T. Zimmermann ; R. DeLine ; A. Begel	The Emerging Role of Data Scientists on Software Development Teams [22]	2016
		J. S. Saltz; N. W. Grady	The Ambiguity of Data Science Team Roles and the Need for a Data Science Workforce Framework	2017
		I. Hukkelberg; M. Berntzen	Exploring the Challenges of Integrating Data Science Roles in Agile Autonomous Teams	2019
		J. S. Saltz; S. Yilmazel; O. Yilmazel	Not all Software Engineers can become good Data Engineers	2016
		I. Marin	Data Science and Development Team Remote Communication: the use of the Machine Learning Canvas	2019
		DJ Patil	Building data science teams	2011
		J. Anderson	Data engineers vs data scientists	2018
		O. Kharkovyna	Who is a data engineer & how to become a Data Engineer? [23]	2019
		H. Danish	The Misunderstood Role Of a Data Engineer	2019
		S. K. White	What is a data engineer? An analytics role in high demand	2018
		V. Borda	How Data Science R&D Teams Can Adapt Agile Processes [17]	2019
2	Prácticas de la IS aplicada al DS	J. S. Saltz; I. Shamshurin	Does pair programming work in data science context? An initial case study	2017
		J. S. Saltz; I. Shamshurin; K. Crowston	Comparing Data Science Project Management Methodologies via a Controlled Experiment [14]	2017
		M. Shcherbakov; N. Shcherbakova; A.	Lean Data Science Research Life Cycle: A Concept for Data Analysis Software Development	2014

		Brebels; T. Janovsky; V. Kamaev		
3	Agilidad en el DS	N. W. Grady	Agile big data analytics: AnalyticsOps for data science	2017
		J. Sauvala	Combining data science with agile software development: a case study [13]	2019
		R. Jurney	Agile Data Science 2.0	2017
		R. Jurney	A manifesto for Agile data science [10]	2017
		E. Yan	Data Science and Agile. Part - 1 [16]	2019
		E. Yan	Data Science and Agile. Parte – 2 [28]	2019
		O. Cohen	Data Science? Agile? Cycles? My method for managing data-science projects in the Hi-tech industry	2019
		B-M. Swanson	Taking an Agile Approach to Data Science	2017
		R. Dev	Applying agile to data science [25]	2018
		J. Akred	Getting Real World Results From Agile Data Science Teams [26]	2017
		N. Hotz	Is Agile a Fit for Data Science?	2019
		Ch. H. Lee	Agile in Data Science: Why my scrum doesn't work?	2019
		T. Petersen; G. Ericson; K. Sharkey; D. Mabee; C. Casey; M. Learned; J. Martens	Agile development of data science projects [27]	2019
		J. Humpherys	Why Data Science doesn't respond well to agile methodologies	2019
4	Análisis del futuro de la agilidad y los datos	D. Larson; V. Chang	A review and future direction of agile, business intelligence, analytics and data science [11]	2016
5	Problemátic as en el DS	R. DeLine	Research Opportunities for the Big Data Era of Software Engineering	2015
		N. Hotz	Lessons from 20 Data Science Teams	2019
6	Escalar hacia organizació n guiada por datos	A. Fabijan; P. Dmitriev; H. Olsson; J. Bosch	The evolution of continuous experimentation in software product development: from data to a data-driven organization at scale	2017

3.2 Resultado de los datos obtenidos

A continuación, se realizó la extracción de datos de acuerdo con lo expresado en la sección 2.4, que se expone en la Tabla 5. Es importante mencionar, que el GEP5 ha sido eliminado por no cumplir con la validación de calidad.

Tabla 5. Resumen de la extracción de datos

	Enfoque	Prácticas ágiles	Adecuaciones	Roles	Problemas
GEP1	CRISP-DM	Scrum, Kanban, Meetings, Entrega continua, equipos multifuncionales	Prototipado, se añade etapas de investigación, etc	Data Scientist Data Engineer Researcher Data Analyst	Riesgos asociados; ambigüedad de roles.

GEP2	No menciona	Scrum, Kanban, Pair programming	Rol driver-researcher para pair programming	Data Scientist	Definición de sprints. estimación, el nivel de definición de las tareas.
GEP3	Team Data Science Process; Agile Data Science	Prácticas de Scrum y Kanban; Desarrollo iterativo	Equipos de investigación; perfiles académicos; no todas las iteraciones finalizarán en un MVP	Data Scientists Project manager	Obtener mayor productividad de agilidad en DS, sin comprometer la transparencia y reproductibilidad; requerimiento no implica tener producto.
GEP4	Agile Data Warehousing Extreme Scoping	Prácticas de Scrum; Ciclos cortos	Se propone una arquitectura, visión, prototipo de los datos	Data Scientists	Proceso de convertir los datos en información; lograr la participación de stakeholders.
GEP6	No menciona	Conceptos de Lean Despliegue continuo	Experimentación continua	Data scientists Software Eng. Researcher Program manager	No menciona

Estos datos permiten obtener una aproximación de las prácticas comúnmente utilizadas en los proyectos relacionados a los datos, los roles involucrados y las problemáticas que se deben abordar.

Resultados de las validaciones de GEP

Posteriormente, se verificó la calidad de los GEP, donde se ha asignado una calificación a cada estudio dentro de un GEP por cada pregunta establecida en la sección "Validaciones GEP". Por cuestiones de espacio, el detalle de los resultados se puede consultar en frre.utn.edu.ar/cinaptic/paginas/view/item/verifcalidadgep.

La tabla 6 presenta un resumen donde se agrupan los valores obtenidos por pregunta de verificación de calidad del GEP.

La pregunta con mayor puntaje es la VG2: "El estudio, ¿menciona los roles involucrados en la gestión del proyecto de datos?". Esto sucede ya que los estudios, en su mayoría, al menos citan los roles que debería tener un proyecto relacionado al DS. Por el contrario, la que obtuvo menor puntaje es la VG3, "El estudio, ¿describe los perfiles de datos involucrados en el enfoque de trabajo adoptado?". Si bien los estudios citaban roles asociados a los proyectos de DS, no especifican para el enfoque de trabajo que describen.

Tabla 6. Puntaje de las VG

	VG1	VG2	VG3	VG4	Total
Total	2,93	3,54	2,63	2,96	12,06
%Total	24,31	29,38	21,77	24,54	100

Aunque se esperaba obtener un puntaje más alto en la VG1, los estudios no declaran un nombre para el enfoque de trabajo con el que desarrollan los proyectos de datos, sino que mencionaba las prácticas, formas de trabajar, comunicarse, herramientas utilizadas, etc., lo que disminuyó el valor de esta pregunta. Luego de las validaciones realizadas, se cuenta con 20 estudios para responder las preguntas que originan esta RSL.

4 Discusión

En esta sección se responderá a las preguntas de investigación planteadas en la sección 2.1, utilizando los principales resultados presentados en la sección anterior.

4.1 ¿Cuál es el enfoque de trabajo de proyectos de DS?

La velocidad de procesamiento es muy importante para este ambiente debido a que generalmente los datos a analizar provienen del campo de Big Data, y los modelos predictivos que se elaboran, validan y alteran en proyectos de DS, suelen desarrollarse en varios intentos. En este sentido la adopción de prácticas ágiles, y en particular el uso de iteraciones, permiten obtener resultados rápidamente, adaptarse a los cambios, eliminar pasos innecesarios en el diseño y corregir los errores en etapas tempranas [6], [10]–[13]. Esto permite disminuir los riesgos y mejorar los incrementos realizados [11].

Autores como [14]-[16] describen que el uso de Scrum en proyectos de DS permite iniciar rápidamente con las labores asociadas al desarrollo, pero presenta inconvenientes asociados a la duración de los sprints y la variabilidad de los objetivos establecidos inicialmente. Aunque menos utilizado, Kanban permite lograr mejores resultados en las tareas asociadas a la investigación [14], [15]. Además, uno de los estudios se basa en Scrumban para crear un enfoque de trabajo [17], lo cual representa una aproximación interesante.

Por otro lado, que compartir los avances frecuentemente con todo el equipo sea parte del proceso, genera un aumento en la colaboración [6]. Por lo anterior, el prototipado y la construcción de un MVP son también prácticas utilizadas en los proyectos de DS, tanto para compartir el trabajo con miembros del equipo y los Stakeholders, como para recibir feedback apropiado de los mismos [13]. Por último, existen propuestas para trabajar con agilidad en proyectos de DS en ámbitos de experimentación a gran escala [18] y en la industria [19].

Si bien en los artículos analizados se observan una gran variedad de técnicas ágiles implementadas en proyectos de DS, no están claros los beneficios que otorgan dichas técnicas.

4.2 ¿Cuáles son los perfiles en proyectos de DS?

Principalmente, se menciona el perfil del Data Scientist. Dentro de las habilidades pertinentes a este rol, se encuentran la fuerte competencia en Matemáticas, Estadísticas y Física [6], [20]–[22]. Sus actividades están relacionadas al análisis y procesamiento de los datos [5], [22], como así también, a la interacción con los clientes o miembros del negocio para la comprensión del dominio del problema en pos de obtener una mejor visión sobre los datos [20].

Otro rol frecuentemente mencionado es el Data Engineer. A diferencia del anterior, éste posee conocimientos tanto en herramientas de programación como aquellas que son de utilidad en un proyecto de desarrollo enfocado a los datos [20], [23], [24]. Las actividades que realiza están vinculadas a la construcción de los *pipelines* que los Data Scientist emplean para construir los modelos [20] y a facilitar el formato adecuado a los datos para trabajar sobre ellos [20], [24], es decir, se concentrarán en construir y mantener la infraestructura que permitirá la accesibilidad a los datos [6]. Por otro lado, se mencionan perfiles específicos a las necesidades de la organización, como el de "Investigador" [5], [22] y "Especialistas en Modelos" [22]. En cuanto a los relacionados con la IS, se mencionan al "Ingeniero de Software", "Project Manager" y "Stakeholders", entre otros.

En la mayoría de los trabajos analizados, se incorpora el rol de Data Scientist (del que se obtuvieron diversas descripciones en cuanto a tareas y responsabilidades), y se incluyen diferentes roles en función de las necesidades de los proyectos.

4.3 ¿ Los enfoques se aplican de manera pura o tienen adaptaciones?

A menudo, los equipos realizan adaptaciones para obtener más beneficios de las prácticas ágiles como, por ejemplo, mitigar riesgos relacionados a la incertidumbre que puede tener el cliente sobre las funcionalidades que solicita [17]. Se incluyen etapas asociadas a la investigación, donde se comprende el dominio del problema, se observan las demandas del producto y se piensan en posibles soluciones a las características requeridas [19], [25].

La mayoría de los estudios proponen el uso de Scrum o Kanban adaptándolas a proyectos de DS: modificando la duración de los sprints y las actividades asociadas [11], [26], [27], modificando el enfoque o los temas tratados en las reuniones de Scrum [11], [17], [19], [26] e incorporando columnas al tablero de Kanban [14], [15]. Otras de las adaptaciones que se pueden citar al implementar la técnica "*pair programming*", el rol del observador se convierte en "investigador" [12]. Además, en [28] se sugiere invertir tiempo en planificar el proyecto y escribirlo para esclarecer ideas que pueden parecer confusas.

De acuerdo con [15], la principal problemática de aplicar Scrum al DS surge de congelar el objetivo establecido para el Sprint durante 2 semanas ya que, con cada nueva información obtenida de los datos o el dominio del problema, el objetivo podría modificarse y hasta tornarse inalcanzable, y se debe interrumpir el Sprint con frecuencia.

Asimismo, existe dificultad para definir los requerimientos de acuerdo con [16], ya que no existe un camino claro hacia el objetivo del proyecto, por lo que es difícil comprometerse con necesidades al principio del sprint, ya que las mismas pueden cambiar día tras día. Esto, además, genera dificultades al realizar estimaciones. Por último, destaca la diferencia de resultados entre proyectos de desarrollo de software y proyectos de DS, donde no siempre se obtendrá un entregable para el cliente (por ejemplo, el resultado de un experimento, muy común en el ámbito de DS). Cabe destacar que en [5] se menciona la necesidad de obtener descripciones de los frameworks de trabajo, de forma tal que se pueda identificar, reclutar, entrenar, desarrollar y mantener aquellas habilidades pertinentes a través de la provisión de un lenguaje para categorizar y describir el tipo de DS que debe realizarse.

Por último, en [25] se menciona la dificultad relacionada a obtener la productividad, principal beneficio del DS Ágil, sin comprometer la transparencia y la reproductibilidad en los flujos de trabajo.

Se ha podido observar que se realizan ajustes en las técnicas ágiles de acuerdo a las particularidades de cada proyecto maximizando los beneficios obtenidos. Por lo que no se cuenta con un listado de mejoras sugeridas, sino que las mismas dependen de los proyectos y la experiencia de las personas que participan.

5 Conclusiones

Este estudio presenta un análisis del estado del arte de los enfoques de trabajo, procesos y equipos de Data Science en el contexto de la Ingeniería de Software, fundamentalmente, de la aplicación de prácticas ágiles para la gestión de proyectos y la definición de los roles involucrados.

Las conclusiones que se obtienen a partir del objetivo planteado son las que se nombran a continuación:

Se encontró una pluralidad de equipos aplican agilidad al Data Science. Sin embargo, dadas las diferencias existentes entre los proyectos de desarrollo de software y los de Data Science, las prácticas implementadas se modifican (al menos ligeramente) para obtener beneficios de su implementación y no incrementar los riesgos. Es por ello que se descubrieron propuestas de workflows para proyectos de Data Science elaboradas por profesionales a partir de sus experiencias.

A pesar de la creciente tendencia de aplicar agilidad en los proyectos de Data Science, no se dispone de descripciones de frameworks homogéneos que se implementen de forma similar en las empresas dedicadas a este tipo de trabajo, con lo que el workflow presenta considerables variaciones de organización en organización. Esto puede ser un inconveniente ya que los Data Scientists frecuentemente no poseen conocimientos en gestión de proyectos de desarrollo, con lo cual, deberán aprender cuál es el enfoque de trabajo en la organización que se insertan, pudiendo demorar más tiempo de lo usual que comiencen a producir valor.

Las responsabilidades de los distintos roles asociados a los proyectos no se encuentran claramente definidas. Esto deriva en la confusión de qué roles son los que posee la organización, las tareas que debe realizar cada miembro y qué habilidades se requieren al incorporar recursos humanos a las empresas.

Cabe destacar que la mayor cantidad de estudios se obtuvieron del motor de búsqueda "Google". Desde nuestro punto de vista, esto puede deberse a la emergente aplicación del DS, y la facilidad de publicar información, experiencias o técnicas de gestión implementadas en los proyectos de esta índole, a través de *blogs*.

Como trabajo futuro, se pretende extender está revisión para profundizar en la problemática de no disponer de descripciones de enfoques de trabajo de forma tal que se pueda corroborar si realmente los Data Scientists perciben el inconveniente de demorar tiempo entendiendo el workflow antes de comenzar a entregar resultados.

Por otro lado, se plantea realizar un análisis sobre el estado actual de los enfoques de trabajo implementados en equipos de Data Science en la República Argentina para identificar si se aplica algún framework de trabajo, cuáles son los más habituales y cuál es el nivel de implementación de agilidad en estas temáticas, con el objetivo de proponer un enfoque ágil que se ajuste a las necesidades de dichos proyectos.

Agradecimientos

Este trabajo ha sido financiado en forma conjunta por CONICET y la UTN. Se agradece el apoyo brindado por estas instituciones. Además, ha sido parcialmente financiado por el Ministerio de Economía, Industria y Competitividad del Gobierno de España, bajo el proyecto MADRID (TIN2017-88557-R)

Referencias

1. C. Hayashi, "What is Data Science? Fundamental Concepts and a Heuristic Example," pp. 40–51, 1998.
2. M. Loukides, *What ' s Data Science ?* 2011.
3. A. Liu, "Data Science and Data Scientist," p. 11, 2015.
4. B. Dhar, "Data Science and Prediction," *Commun. ACM*, vol.56, no.12, pp.64–73, 2013.
5. J. S. Saltz and N. W. Grady, "The ambiguity of data science team roles and the need for a data science workforce framework," *Proc. - 2017 IEEE Int. Conf. Big Data, Big Data 2017*, vol. 2018-Janua, pp. 2355–2361, 2017.
6. I. Hukkelberg and M. Berntzen, "Exploring the Challenges of Integrating Data Science Roles in Agile Autonomous Teams," *2019 Agil. Process. Softw. Eng. Extrem. Program. - Work.*, vol. 364, pp. 37–45, 2019.
7. B. Kitchenham, S. Charters, "*Guidelines for performing Systematic Literature Reviews in SE*," pp. 1–44, 2007.
8. P. Mian, T. Conte, A. Natali, J. Biolchini, and G. Travassos, "A Systematic Review Process for Software Engineering," *Empir. Softw. Eng.*, vol. 32, no. 3, pp. 1–6, 2007.
9. F. Pino, F. García, M. Piattini, "SW process improvement in small and medium software enterprises: A systematic review," *Softw. Qual. J.*, vol.16, no.2, pp.237–261, 2008.
10. R. Jurney, "A manifesto for Agile data science," 2017. Avail: https://www.oreilly.com/radar/a-manifesto-for-agile-data-science/. [Acces: 27-Nov-2019].
11. D. Larson and V. Chang, "A review and future direction of agile, business intelligence, analytics and data science," *Int. J. Inf. Manage.*, vol. 36, no. 5, pp. 700–710, 2016.
12. J. S. Saltz and I. Shamshurin, "Does pair programming work in a data science context? An initial case study," *Proc. - 2017 IEEE Int. Conf. Big Data, Big Data 2017*, vol. 2018-Janua, pp. 2348–2354, 2017.
13. J. Sauvala, "Combining Data Science with Agile Software Development: A Case Study," Aalto University, 2019.
14. J. S. Saltz, I. Shamshurin, and K. Crowston, "Comparing Data Science Project Management

Methodologies via a Controlled Experiment," *Proc. 50th Hawaii Int. Conf. Syst. Sci.*, pp. 1013–1022, 2017.

15. H. L. Chang, "Agile in Data Science: Why My Scrum Doesn't Work?," 2019. Avail: https://changhsinlee.com/agile-ds-scrum-kanban/. [Acces: 27-Nov-2019].
16. E. Yan, "Data Science and Agile - Part 1," 2019. Avail: https://towardsdatascience.com/agiledatascience-3b7ca65278a4. [Acces: 27-Nov-2019].
17. V. Borda, "How Data Science R&D Teams Can Adapt Agile Processes," 2019. Avail: https://blog.invoca.com/inside-engineering-adapting-agile-for-data-science-rd-teams/. [Acces: 27-Nov-2019].
18. A. Fabijan, P. Dmitriev, H. Olsson, J. Bosch, "The Evol of Continuous Experimentation in SW Product Development: From Data to a Data-Driven Organization at Scale," *Proc. - 2017 IEEE/ACM 39th Int. Conf. Softw. Eng.*, pp. 770–780, 2017.
19. O. Cohen, "Data-science? Agile? Cycles? My method for managing data-science projects in the Hi-tech industry.," 2019. Avail: https:// towardsdatascience.com/data-science-agile-cycles-my-method-for-managing-data-science-projects-in-the-hi-tech-industry-b289e8a72818. [Acces: 27-Nov-2019].
20. J. Anderson, "Data engineers vs. data scientists," 2018. Avail: https://www.oreilly.com /radar/data-engineers-vs-data-scientists/. [Acces: 27-Nov-2019].
21. M. Kim, T. Zimmermann, R. Deline, A. Begel, "Data scientists in sw teams: State of the art and challenges," *IEEE Trans. Softw. Eng.*, vol. 44, no. 11, pp. 1024–1038, 2018.
22. M. Kim, T. Zimmermann, R. DeLine, and A. Begel, "The emerging role of data scientists on software development teams," *Proc. - Int. Conf. Softw. Eng.*, vol. 14-22-May-, pp. 96–107, 2016.
23. O. Kharkovyna, "Who Is a Data Engineer & How to Become a Data Engineer?," 2019. Avail: https://towardsdatascience.com/who-is-a-data-engineer-how-to-become-a-data-engineer-1167ddc12811. [Acces: 27-Nov-2019].
24. J. S. Saltz and S. Yilmazel, "Not All Software Engineers Can Become Good Data Engineers," *2016 IEEE Int. Conf. Big Data (Big Data)*, pp. 2896–2901, 2016.
25. R. Dev, "Applying agile to data science," 2018. Avail: https://medium.com /@rahul.dev/applying-agile-to-data-science-63d482149206. [Acces: 27-Nov-2019].
26. J. Akred, "Getting Real World Results From Agile Data Science Teams," 2017. Avail: https://www.kdnuggets.com/2017/02/real-world-results-agile-data-science-teams.html. [Acces: 27-Nov-2019].
27. T. Petersen *et al.*, "Agile development of data science projects - Team Data Science Process," 2019. Avail: https://docs.microsoft.com/en-us/azure/machine-learning/team-data-science-process/agile-development. [Acces: 27-Nov-2019].
28. E. Yan, "Data Science and Agile - Part 2," 2019. Avail: https://towards datascience.com/data-science-and-agile-1cdfb1667789. [Acces: 27-Nov-2019].

Recomendações de técnicas complementares de elicitação de requisitos em um guia facetado

Nathália Liz de Brito[0000-0003-2495-3167] e Fabiane Barreto Vavassori Benitti[0000-0003-2747-9931]

Departamento de Informática e Estatística - Universidade Federal de Santa Catarina, Florianópolis, Brasil

Abstract. Requirements elicitation is a step of great importance in the development of software because if it is not well executed it can lead to the costumer's dissatisfaction with the final product. In recent research is possible to find more than 90 different techniques to carry out the requirements elicitation, which brings many options to the elicitor. To help them choose it was developed a guide that presents these techniques faceted classified, enabling facet filtering to find techniques that best fit the need of the elicitor. However, several studies claim that using only one technique is not as effective as using a combination of them. This paper presents a systematic mapping to identify complementary techniques in a requirements elicitation process. It was found 35 approaches that contemplate multiple techniques and some of them with their techniques were included in the guide so that when searching for a technique, recommendations for techniques that can be combined with it are presented.

Palavras-chave: software engineering · requirements engineering · requirements elicitation · elicitation techniques · elicitation approaches

1 Introdução

É inegável a relevância da engenharia de requisitos em um processo de desenvolvimento de um software, sendo considerada uma fase importante e vital no ciclo de vida geral da engenharia de software [11]. Uma boa parte do impacto que o processo de engenharia de requisitos tem no projeto de um software pode ser relacionado a elicitação, considerada uma atividade crucial deste processo [3], sendo reconhecida como uma das atividades mais críticas do desenvolvimento de software, a sua má execução "quase garantirá que o projeto final seja uma falha completa" [4]. A elicitação é "a atividade de desenvolvimento explicativo de ajudar os usuários a descobrirem o que querem" [8] e de forma geral ela pode ser reconhecida como "um processo complexo de solução de problemas cognitivos que ocorre em um contexto de problema não estruturado e pouco compreendido" [3].

Tendo em vista a complexidade de levantar requisitos de um software, existem diversas técnicas para elicitação. Segundo um levantamento realizado por meio de um mapeamento sistemático [5], há pelo menos 96 técnicas de elicitação de requisitos propostas na literatura. Perante tantas opções, como selecionar as técnicas mais adequadas? Estudos afirmam que "embora alguns analistas pensem que apenas uma metodologia, ou apenas uma técnica, é aplicável a todas as situações, uma metodologia ou técnica pode não ser suficiente para todas as condições" [4]. Existem outros estudos que garantem que "não há uma única abordagem de requisitos que possa articular adequadamente todos os requisitos de um sistema, tanto do ponto de vista dos desenvolvedores quanto dos usuários" [7].

Ciente que a combinação de técnicas é uma das melhores formas de elicitar requisitos de um sistema, tem-se o desafio de selecionar técnicas que são complementares, que apresentem visões diferentes do problema e levem a requisitos mais completos, com o "potencial de fornecer informações de requisitos muito mais ricas e detalhadas sobre o processo de negócio e as necessidades dos usuários" [13]. Para encontrar conjuntos de técnicas que são complementares foi realizado um mapeamento sistemático descrito na seção 3 e, posteriormente, as abordagens selecionadas foram incorporadas a um guia com técnicas e abordagens para elicitação de requisitos, descrito na seção 4.

2 Elicitação de requisitos

A elicitação de requisitos do sistema a ser desenvolvido é uma atividade central da engenharia de requisitos [9]. Autores se referem à elicitação de requisitos como levantamento de requisitos, combinando elementos de resolução de problemas, elaboração, negociação e especificação, ou seja, "os interessados trabalham juntos para identificar o problema, propor elementos da solução, negociar diferentes abordagens e especificar um conjunto preliminar de requisitos da solução" [10]. Outros autores [12] agrupam as etapas de elicitação e análise de requisitos em apenas um processo. Esse processo é dividido em quatro atividades Outros autores [12] agrupam as etapas de elicitação e análise de requisitos em apenas um processo. Esse processo é dividido em quatro atividades, como pode ser observado na figura 1.

É na atividade de descoberta de requisitos que está o foco do presente artigo. A descoberta de requisitos é "o processo de reunir informações sobre o sistema requerido e os sistemas existentes e separar dessas informações os requisitos de usuário e de sistema" [12]. Sabe-se que as informações devem ser reunidas, porém de onde elas podem ser extraídas? Algumas altenativas são [9]:

1. *Stakeholders* são pessoas ou organizações que direta ou indiretamente influenciam os requisitos de um sistema.
2. *Documentos* muitas vezes contêm informações importantes que podem fornecer requisitos.
3. *Sistemas em operação* podem ser sistemas anteriores ou legados, bem como sistemas concorrentes. Tendo a oportunidade de testar o sistema, os *stakeholders* podem formar uma ideia sobre o sistema atual e solicitar extensões ou modificações com base em suas impressões.

Fig. 1. Atividades do processo de elicitação e análise de requisitos [12]

Após a identificação de onde os requisitos podem ser extraídos e dos *stakeholders*, é necessário escolher as técnicas de elicitação de requisitos que serão utilizadas, sendo o principal objetivo de todas as técnicas de elicitação "auxiliar o engenheiro de requisitos a identificar o conhecimento e os requisitos dos *stakeholders* [...] tendo a finalidade de identificar os requisitos conscientes, inconscientes e sub-conscientes" [9]. É relevante observar a importância da escolha da melhor técnica de elicitação de requisitos para cada caso, sendo recomendável combinar diferentes técnicas, minimizando riscos inerentes ao projeto. Pontos fracos e desvantagens de uma técnica podem ser compensados pelo uso de outra técnica que apresenta pontos fortes onde a primeira técnica eventualmente seja deficitária [9].

3 Mapeamento sistemático

Uma revisão sistemática busca agregar os estudos primários em termos de seus resultados e investigar se esses resultados são consistentes ou contraditórios. Um mapeamento sistemático é focado na estruturação de uma área de pesquisa e visam classificar a literatura relevante e agregar estudos em relação a categorias definidas [6]. Desta forma, o mapeamento sistemático se mostra adequado ao presente estudo, tendo sido executado observando as etapas propostas por [6]:

- Planejamento: envolvendo a elaboração das perguntas e o desenvolvimento do protocolo de pesquisa.
- Execução: contemplando identificação da pesquisa, a seleção dos estudos, extração e síntese dos dados.
- Reporte dos resultados.

3.1 Elaboração das perguntas

Especificar as perguntas de pesquisa é a parte mais importante de qualquer revisão sistemática, sendo estruturadas basicamente a partir de três pontos: população, intervenção e resultados [6]:

- População: O mapeamento deve considerar artigos relacionados a área de elicitação de requisitos de software datados entre 01/01/2014 e 31/12/2018 para garantir que são abordagens atuais;
- Intervenção: O objetivo é estudar grupos de técnicas de elicitação de requisitos que são utilizadas de forma complementar.
- Resultados: São esperados artigos que citem grupos de técnicas de elicitação de requisitos que são utilizadas em conjunto.

Utilizando tais critérios é possível elaborar três perguntas que devem ser respondidas pela pesquisa realizada. São elas:

Q1. Quais são as abordagens para elicitação de requisitos que contemplam múltiplas técnicas?
Q2. Quais são os grupos de técnicas complementares propostos na literatura?
Q3. As abordagens e/ou técnicas complementares foram avaliadas ou aplicadas na prática?

3.2 Definição dos termos de busca

Observando a população definida para este mapeamento sistemático, é possível definir o termo "requirements elicitation" para representar a área na qual será realizada a pesquisa. É importante observar que não há um termo específico que defina combinações de técnicas de elicitação de requisitos. Durante uma breve pesquisa foi possível perceber o uso de diversos termos para definir grupos de técnicas que são usadas de forma complementar, tais como: approach, roadmaps, guidelines, methods e methodologies. Para validar os termos encontrados foi realizada uma pesquisa preliminar com cada um deles, de forma a observar os possíveis resultados obtidos caso o termo fosse utilizado na pesquisa. Foram analisados os primeiros 20 artigos retornados a partir de uma busca na base "Google scholar" e na string de busca foi incluído o termo que representa a área de pesquisa, "requirements elicitation". Os resultados foram incluídos na tabela 1.

É possível observar que o termo "approach" retorna informações sobre abordagens de técnicas específicas ou de um grupo de técnicas utilizadas em um cenário específico, o que não é o foco da pesquisa. O termo "roadmap" também retornou uma boa quantidade de resultados que não se aplicam. Como os termos "method", "guideline" e "methodolology" retornaram bons resultados, os mesmos foram incluídos na string de busca. Durante a leitura dos artigos foi possível observar que o termo "model" também representa grupos de técnicas de elicitação de requisitos e retorna bons resultados ao ser utilizado na pesquisa,

Tabela 1. Pesquisa preliminar com os termos de busca

Termo pesquisado	Resultados obtidos
"*approach*"	Retorna uma boa quantidade de abordagens de uma técnica em específico ou aplicadas em um cenário específico.
"*method*"	É amplamente utilizado como um sinônimo de técnicas, porém retornou resultados relevantes.
"*roadmap*"	Retornou muitos resultados que não se aplicam ao mapeamento.
"*guideline*"	Retornou poucos resultados porém alguns se aplicam ao mapeamento.
"*methodology*"	Retornou bons resultados, incluindo artigos já identificados anteriormente como relevantes.

portanto ele também foi incluído na string de busca. Desta forma, a string de busca foi definida de acordo com o padrão abaixo:

```
(method OR methodology OR model OR guideline) AND
("requirements elicitation")
```

3.3 Avaliar e selecionar estudos

Uma vez que os estudos primários potencialmente relevantes tenham sido obtidos, eles precisam ser reavaliados por sua real relevância [6]. Em outras palavras, após aplicar a string de busca nas bases científicas e obter os estudos retornados, eles precisarão ser selecionados. A seleção é realizada de acordo com critérios de inclusão e exclusão.

Critérios de inclusão Os critérios de seleção tem como objetivo "identificar os estudos que fornecem evidências diretas sobre a questão de pesquisa" [6]. Foram definidos os seguintes critérios de inclusão:

- Estudo que propõe a utilização de 2 ou mais técnicas de elicitação de requisitos combinadas dentro de um processo de elicitação;
- Deve ter sido publicado nos últimos 5 anos, de 01/01/2014 até 31/12/2018;

Critérios de exclusão Os critérios de exclusão definidos foram os seguintes:

- Publicações que não são revisadas por pares, como por exemplo, livros;
- Publicações como resumos, posters, tutoriais, dissertações e teses;

– Estudos publicados em um idioma diferente do inglês;
– Estudos que são pagos ou inacessíveis mesmo com a autorização da universidade;
– Estudos que estão fora da área de "Ciências da computação".

3.4 Seleção de estudos

A seleção de estudos "é um processo que ocorre em multiestágios". Os autores sugerem uma avaliação preliminar, que é realizada "interpretando os critérios de seleção inicialmente no título e no resumo" e se o trabalho avaliado não for excluído da pesquisa, "deve ser avaliado por completo" [6]. Após a execução das buscas nas bases escolhidas e a coleta dos trabalhos retornados, foram executadas então duas etapas para a seleção dos estudos:

1. **Análise preliminar**: análise do título e resumo do artigo, descartando aqueles que atendiam a pelo menos um dos critérios de exclusão definidos em 3.3, não se encaixavam no tema proposto ou ficava claro que não obedeciam nenhum dos critérios de inclusão. Quando não era possível tirar conclusões a partir do título e resumo do artigo, uma leitura superficial foi realizada pelo conteúdo do artigo para identificar se ele se encaixava nos critérios de inclusão definidos em 3.3. Como sintetizado na figura 2, na etapa de análise preliminar foram selecionados 48 artigos.
2. **Análise completa**: os artigos previamente selecionados foram analisados de forma mais aprofundada, identificando as técnicas que poderiam ser extraídas do estudo e se elas estavam sendo utilizadas em conjunto em algum processo de elicitação. Desta etapa, restaram 35 artigos dos 48 previamente selecionados.

3.5 Extração dos dados

Com a execução da pesquisa e a seleção dos artigos, se tornou possível a extração dos dados necessários para responder às perguntas definidas na seção 3.1. Para cada estudo selecionado foram extraídos os seguintes dados:

– Identificação do artigo, que contém o nome do artigo, o nome dos autores e o ano de publicação;
– O nome da abordagem de elicitação de requisitos que utiliza técnicas em conjunto, caso exista;
– A lista de técnicas utilizadas em conjunto;
– O contexto de aplicação onde tal abordagem é proposta;
– Se a abordagem foi avaliada e como foi avaliada;
– Se a abordagem foi aplicada na prática e como foi aplicada.

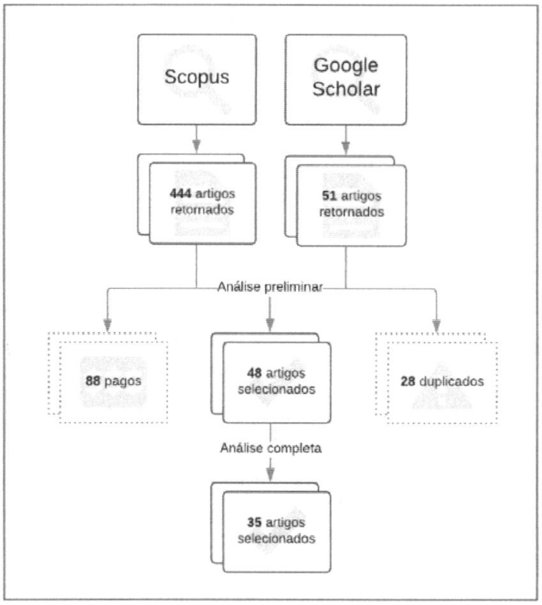

Fig. 2. Seleção de estudos

Q1 -Quais são as abordagens para elicitação de requisitos que contemplam múltiplas técnicas? Como um dos critérios de inclusão definidos em 3.3 é ser um estudo que propõe a utilização de 2 ou mais técnicas de elicitação de requisitos em um processo de elicitação, todos os 35 resultantes propõem uma abordagem para elicitação de requisitos. Na Tabela 2, observando as colunas "Nome da abordagem" e "Contexto de aplicação", é possível identificar as abordagem encontradas (14 possuem um nome que as define e outras 20 que não foram nomeadas pelos autores) além de mais de 20 contextos de aplicação diferentes para as abordagens encontradas. Entende-se por "contexto de aplicação" o contexto no qual o autor do estudo primário sugere que a abordagem pode ser aplicada ou, no caso de não haver uma generalização por parte do autor, o contexto específico no qual a abordagem foi aplicada. A referência aos estudos originários de cada abordagem pode ser encontrada em http://retraining.inf.ufsc.br/tecnicasElicitacaoComplementares.pdf.

Q2 - Quais são os grupos de técnicas complementares propostos na literatura? No grafo apresentado na figura 4 é possível observar as técnicas de elicitação de requisitos aplicadas em conjunto extraídas de cada artigo selecionado e como elas estão relacionadas. O grafo foi construído de forma que os nodos são as técnicas de elicitação de requisitos citadas e que cada técnica tenha como nodos vizinhos as técnicas que são utilizadas em conjunto com a mesma, ou seja, as arestas significam uma relação complementar entre as técnicas. Conjuntos de técnicas que foram citados somente uma vez foram agrupados em apenas um nodo.

Para a construção do grafo as técnicas foram divididas em pequenos grupos que são representados por diferentes cores. São elas:

- **Azul**: representa as técnicas que foram citadas mais de 20 vezes em abordagens de elicitação de requisitos.
- **Laranja**: representa as técnicas que foram citadas de 7 a 11 vezes em abordagens de elicitação de requisitos.
- **Amarelo**: representa as técnicas que foram citadas de 4 a 5 vezes em abordagens de elicitação de requisitos.
- **Verde**: representa as técnicas que foram citadas de 2 a 3 vezes em abordagens de elicitação de requisitos.
- **Branco**: representa as técnicas que foram citadas apenas 1 vez em abordagens de elicitação de requisitos.

Q3 - As abordagens e/ou técnicas complementares foram avaliadas ou aplicadas na prática? No diagrama de *Venn* apresentado na figura 3 é possível observar a proporção de técnicas que foram avaliadas, aplicadas na prática ou se encaixam nos dois casos. Das 35 abordagens encontradas, 19 foram avaliadas de alguma forma e 25 foram aplicadas na prática. De todas as 35 abordagens encontradas, 14 (40%) foram avaliadas e aplicadas na prática.

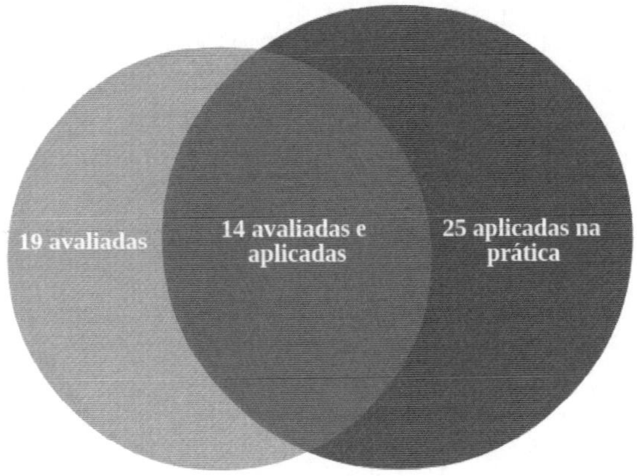

Fig. 3. Proporção de técnicas avaliadas e aplicadas na prática

Tabela 2. Dados extraídos

Nome [Referência*]	Contexto de aplicação	Técnicas relacionadas
REPES [21]	Sistemas embarcados	Domain Analysis, Define System Goals, Identification of Environmental Assumptions, Abstraction Level Definition
- [10]	Projetos de pesquisa colaborativa	Workshops: Brainstorming, Prototyping, Individual elicitation, Collective debate, Requirements grouping (KJmethod)
VBRE method [31]	Socio-political issues in RE	Interviews, Observations, Meeting, Preliminary analysis, Hunches, Taxonomy of values and motivations
RC-ASEF [2]	Context-aware systems development	Activity group, Stakeholder Diagrams, Cultural analysis, Ethical analysis (questionários ou entrevistas), Profiling guidelines
- [4]	Hospital system	Interviews, JAD, Use case, Scenarios
- [17]	Agile development	Ethnography, Interviews, Document Analysis, Meetings, Gathering tasks, Prototyping
- [8]	Information systems	Scenarios, Fundamental Goals
Design thinking [13]	Information systems	Ethnography, prototyping, Observation, meetings
- [26]	-	Observation, Interviews, Document, Questionnaire
- [29]	-	Interviews, Document review, Survey
Design thinking [20]	Design thinking for urban Solutions for Sustainable Development	Personas, Storyboards, User Journey Map, Prototyping and usability testing
Wizard-of-Oz [1]	Mobile app	Prototyping, Meetings, Client product descriptions
- [25]	Software startups	Interviews, Prototyping, Brainstorming, Questionnaires, Using social network, Feedback comments analysis, Analysis of similar products or competitors, Collaborative team invention, Involvement of model users
Bottom up approach [18]	-	Direct: Interviews, Observation, and Indirect: Document Analysis, Questioners
BORE [16]	Business Process	Semistructures and unstructured interviews, apprenticing, workshops and scrutinizing the documents
- [3]	Global Software Development	Story cards, Stories, Scenarios, Use cases
Context-based Persona Stories [30]	Agile Requirements	Personas, Storyboards
- [27]	Security Policy (domain-specific policy template derivation)	Semi-structured interview, Goal trees, Document analysis, focus group, Workshops, Questionnaire, Brainstorming on Cards, Mindmapping
- [5]	Situation-Oriented RE	Observation, Interviews
- [33]	Culturally and Technologically Diverse Settings	Customer involvement, Interviews, Engagement Scenarios
- [10]	Projetos de pesquisa colaborativa	Workshops: Brainstorming, Prototyping, Individual elicitation, Collective debate, Requirements grouping (KJmethod)
SCRAM–CK [14]	Collaborative requirements engineering	Prototypes, Scenarios, Storyboards, Design visioning, Mockups
- [11]	-	Interviews, questionnaire, brainstorming, scenarios, use cases, prototypes
- [7]	-	Domain Analysis: Scenarios, Use cases, Interviews, Information Elicitation
IEM [23]	Collaborative requirements engineering	Interviews, Workshops
- [12]	ICTD (Information and Communication Technologies and Development) Systems Development	Questionnaire, Text analysis tools, Goal analysis, Interviews
RDMod [28]	Mobile Financial Advisory Services	Expert interviews, Focus groups (FG), Literature review
- [15]	Contextual Requirements at Design Time	Interviews, scenarios, prototyping, Focus Groups
BORE [22]	Business Process	Semi-structured and unstructured interviews, apprenticing, workshops, document analysis, JAD, Use-cases
- [34]	Semantic Multimedia Content	Interviews, questionnaire, prototype
- [6]	Haptic User Interfaces	Observation, Scenarios, Document analysis
BPCRAR [16]	Collaborative Business Process	User stories, Group Storytelling, Dialogue Game, Narrative Network
- [24]	Therapist-Centered Requirements	Interviews, Observations, diary studies, user studies of a prototype
PROPRE [35]	-	Documentation analysis, meetings
- [32]	-	Structured interviews and Product Patterns, brainstorming and concepts mapping

* referências em http://retraining.inf.ufsc.br/tecnicasElicitacaoComplementares.pdf

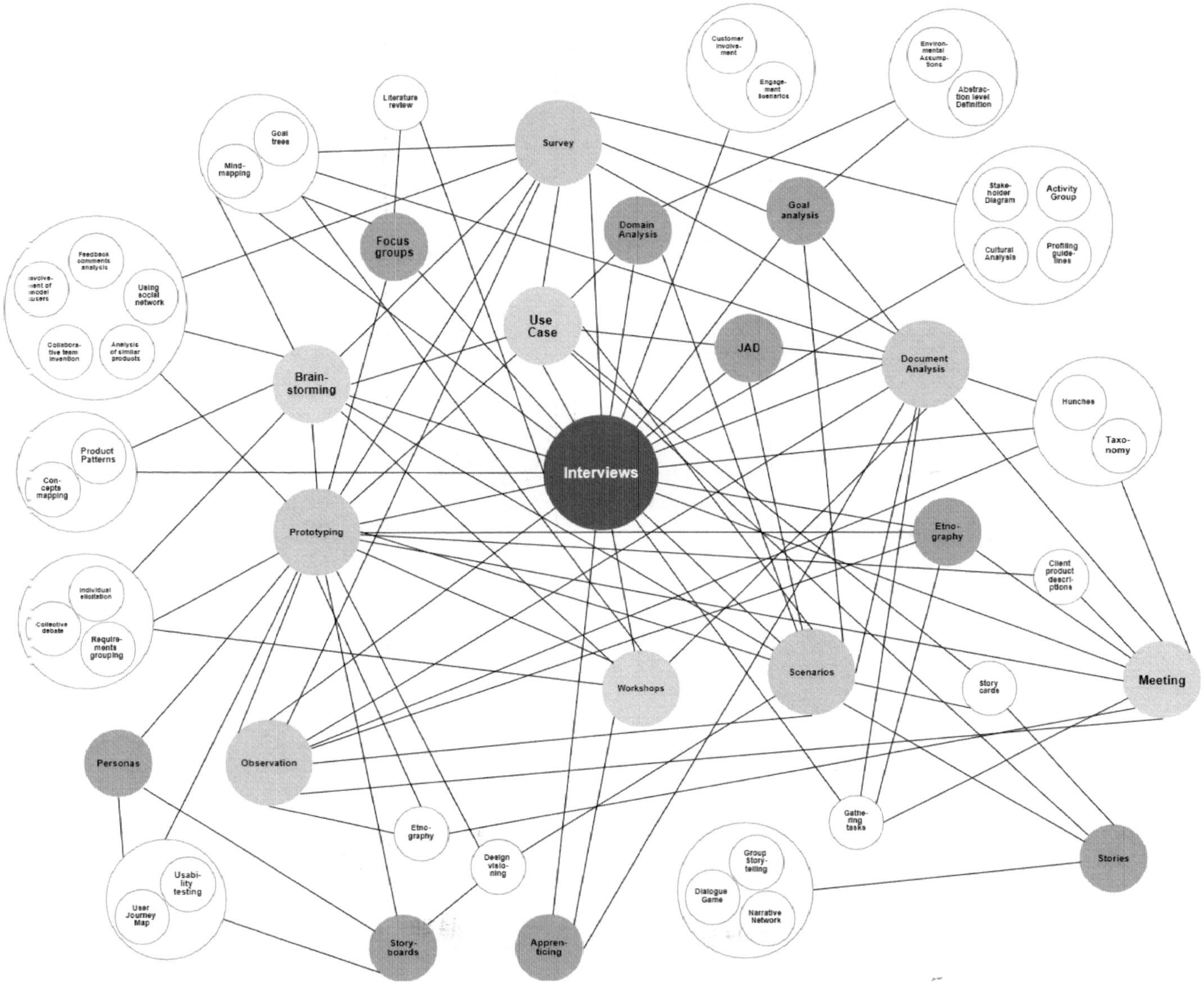

Fig. 4. Grafo de técnicas de elicitação de requisitos utilizadas em conjunto

4 Guia facetado de elicitação de requisitos *REtraining*

Em um estudo anterior [5] foi desenvolvido um guia de elicitação de requisitos, chamado *REtraining*, que tem como um de seus principais objetivos auxiliar os profissionais e alunos a ampliarem os seus conhecimentos acerca de técnicas de elicitação de requisitos. O guia, disponível em https://retraining.inf.ufsc.br/guia, apresenta as técnicas, como utilizá-las, prós e contras e exemplos de aplicação. Além disso, cada técnica contemplada no guia está facetada, ou seja, possuem um conjunto de características definidas de forma estruturada [1]. As facetas permitem que o guia apresente a funcionalidade de filtragem para que sejam apresentadas as técnicas que mais se encaixam no contexto do projeto, de acordo com os valores das facetas selecionados. A tela de filtragem do guia pode ser observada na figura 5.

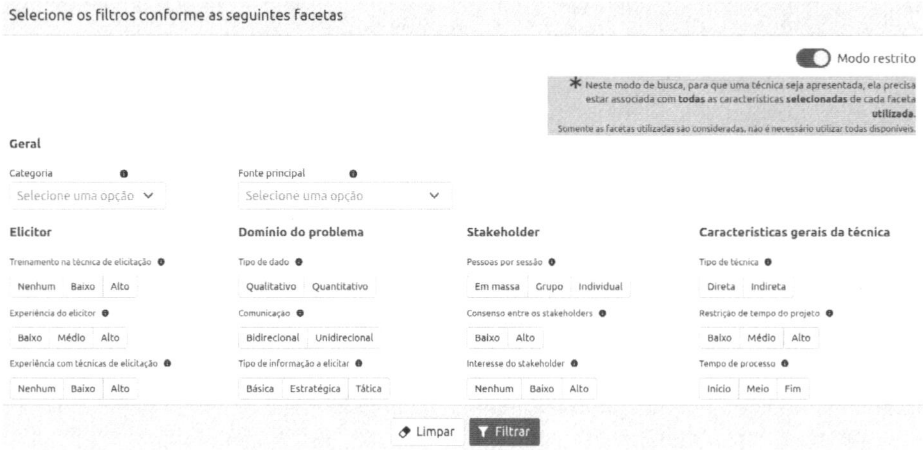

Fig. 5. Tela de filtragem de técnicas de elicitação de requisitos no guia *REtraining*

Com as informações obtidas no mapeamento sistemático descrito neste artigo, se tornou possível estruturá-las e incluí-las no guia para que os profissionais, alunos e o público em geral possam acessar o resultado da pesquisa. Desta forma, foram incluídas duas novas funcionalidades [2] no *REtraining*, (i) a listagem e visualização das abordagens de elicitação de requisitos, contemplando informações de como utilizar a abordagem e as técnicas relacionadas; e (ii) recomendação de técnicas que podem ser combinadas. A Figura 6 ilustra esta funcionalidade, quando a técnica de Storyboard foi pesquisada (Ponto A) e o guia identificou que esta técnica é utilizada na abordagem de Design Thinking (ponto B), sugerindo ver também Personas, Prototipação e Teste de Usabilidade.

O mapeamento retornou 35 abordagens, contudo, foi necessário priorizar as técnicas que seriam incluídas inicialmente no guia, através de alguns critérios:

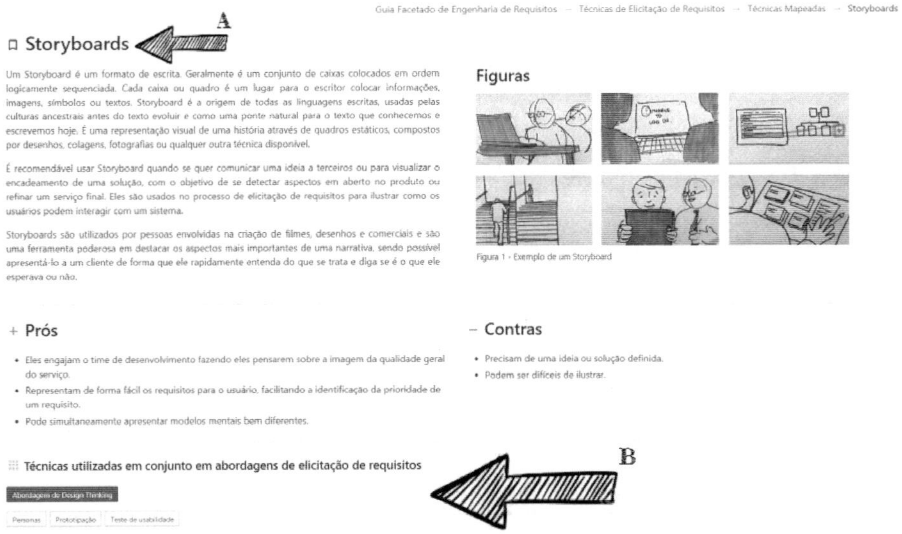

Fig. 6. Exemplo de recomendação

– **Avaliado na prática:** Como o objetivo do guia é auxiliar os profissionais e estudantes a encontrarem a técnica de elicitação de requisitos que mais se adequa ao contexto de seu projeto, buscou-se incorporar abordagens já aplicadas na prática.
– **Contexto de aplicação recorrente:** Buscou-se priorizar os contextos que são mais contemplados atualmente. Para definir o nível de relevância foi considerado o número de resultados do contexto quando realizada uma pesquisa no *Google*. Após a exclusão dos artigos não aplicados na prática, sobraram 19 abordagens que possuíam contexto de aplicação, então a pesquisa foi realizada utilizando estes 19 contextos (conforme observado na tabela 3).
– **Número de novas técnicas incluídas no guia REtraining:** Buscou-se, ainda, que ao incorporar uma abordagem ao guia esta também ampliasse o número de técnicas disponíveis.

Após aplicação destes critérios, as abordagens e as técnicas selecionadas para a inclusão no guia são as seguintes:

– **Mobile app**: *Meetings* e *Client product descriptions*;
– **Global Software Development**: *Story cards*, *Stories* e *Use cases*;
– **Design thinking**: *Personas*, *Storyboards*, *User Journey Map* e *Usability testing*;
– **Security Policy**: *Goal trees*, *Document analysis*, *Focus group*, *Workshops* e *Mindmapping*;
– **Business Process Models**: *Apprenticing*, *Workshops* e *Scrutinizing the documents*.

Tabela 3. Contexto de aplicação e números de resultados no *Google*

Contexto de aplicação	Número de resultados
Mobile app	10.520.000.000
Global Software Development	1.430.000.000
Design thinking	1.070.000.000
Security Policy Templates	991.000.000
Business Process Models	784.000.000
Hospital system	782.000.000
Business-Oriented	330.000.000
Embbeded systems	308.000.000
Collaborative requirements engineering	227.000.000
Situation-Oriented	206.000.000
Context-aware systems	199.000.000
Socio-political issues	192.000.000
Mobile Financial Advisory Services	177.000.000
Collaborative Method for Business Process	167.000.000
Software startups	102.000.000
Contextual Requirements	44.200.000
Semantic Multimedia Content	12.300.000
Culturally and Technologically Diverse Settings	4.810.000
Haptic User Interfaces	3.300.000

5 Conclusão

O presente trabalho trata de encontrar combinações de técnicas de elicitação de requisitos recomendadas à um processo de elicitação. Foi realizado um mapeamento sistemático para levantar essas combinações, que foram chamadas de abordagens, e elas foram incluídas em novas funcionalidades do guia *REtraining*.

O mapeamento sistemático descrito na seção 3 reforçou o que já é consenso na literatura, evidenciando mapeando abordagens de elicitação de requisitos compostas por múltiplas técnicas. A pesquisa resultou em 35 abordagens, sendo a maioria delas (28) criadas para um contexto específico de aplicação.

No grafo apresentado na figura 4 pode ser observado como as técnicas de elicitação de requisitos estão relacionadas entre si e como elas podem ser combinadas de acordo com a necessidade do elicitor. O mapeamento sistemático revisou a literatura, porém na prática podem existir diversas abordagens que são criadas e aplicadas todos os dias e que podem ser igualmente eficazes para os profissionais que as utilizam.

Após a pesquisa acerca das abordagens, o guia *REtraining* foi alimentado com 5 abordagens de elicitação de requisitos e 10 técnicas novas, o que o tornou mais completo e atualizado, contemplando atualmente 22 técnicas facetadas. Agora o usuário do guia poderá visualizar recomendações de técnicas que podem ser combinadas e procurar a abordagem e combinação que mais se adequam ao contexto do seu projeto.

Algumas limitações do presente estudo devem ser destacadas: (i) foram utilizadas 2 bases de dados indexadoras no mapeamento, a inclusão de novas bases pode revelar novas abordagens; (ii) a string de busca pode não contemplar todos os termos relacionados com o objetivo, embora tenha sido realizada uma pesquisa prévia para a sua definição, no momento de execução da busca as informações encontradas podem não representar todas as abordagens utilizadas no mercado; (iii) o guia apresenta atualmente 5 abordagens e 22 técnicas detalhadas, sabendo-se que existem diversas outras. Como trabalhos futuros pretende-se continuar alimentando o guia com novas abordagens e enriquecendo-o com a inclusão de outras técnicas de elicitação.

References

1. Barbosa, A.P.: Teoria e práctica dos sistemas de classificação bibliográfica. Ibbd, Rio de Janeiro (1969)
2. Brito, N.L.: Recomendações de técnicas complementares de elicitação de requisitos em um guia facetado. Tech. rep., Universidade Federal de Santa Catarina (2019), https://repositorio.ufsc.br/handle/123456789/202674
3. Franco, A., Assar, S.: Leveraging creativity techniques in requirements elicitation: A literature review. Requirements Engineering Magazine (2016-2) (2016)
4. Hickey, A.M., Davis, A.M.: A unified model of requirements elicitation. Journal of Management Information Systems **20**(4), 65–84 (2004)
5. Ignacio, R.C.: Guia facetado de técnicas de elicitação de requisitos. Tech. rep., Universidade Federal de Santa Catarina (2018), https://repositorio.ufsc.br/handle/123456789/192155
6. Kitchenham, B., Charters, S.: Guidelines for performing systematic literature reviews in software engineering. Tech. rep., Keele University (2007)
7. Kotonya, G., Sommerville, I.: Requirements engineering with viewpoints. Software Engineering Journal **11**(1), 5–18 (1996)
8. Murugesan, L.K., Hoda, R., Salcic, Z.: Identifying design features using combination of requirements elicitation techniques. In: Design and Innovation in Software Engineering (DISE), 2017 IEEE/ACM 1st International Workshop on. pp. 6–12. IEEE (2017)
9. Pohl, K.: The three dimensions of requirements engineering: a framework and its applications. Information systems **19**(3), 243–258 (1994)
10. Pressman, R.: Engenharia de software uma abordagem profissional 7ª ed (2011)
11. Rehman, N.U., Bibi, S., Asghar, S., Fong, S.: Comparative study of goal-oriented requirements engineering. In: New Trends in Information Science and Service Science (NISS), 2010 4th International Conference on. pp. 248–253. IEEE (2010)
12. Sommerville, I.: Engenharia de software. Pearson Prentice Hall, São Paulo (2011)
13. Zowghi, D., Coulin, C.: Requirements elicitation: A survey of techniques, approaches, and tools. In: Engineering and managing software requirements, pp. 19–46. Springer (2005)

Avaliando o processo de derivação de casos de uso a partir de i* e BPMN e suporte computacional

Gustavo Cesar Lopes Geraldino, Rafael Gomes da Silva and Victor Francisco Araya Santander

Universidade Estadual do Oeste do Parana, UNIOESTE Cascavel, PR, Brasil
gclgeraldino@gmail.com, rafags2005@hotmail.com and victor.santander@unioeste.br

Resumo. A engenharia de requisitos é uma fase importante da engenharia de software. A integração dos vários modelos de requisitos continua sendo um dos grandes desafios da área. Em trabalhos anteriores, apresentamos diretrizes para apoiar a geração de Casos de Uso UML a partir de modelos organizacionais i* (*istar*) e modelos BPMN (*Business Process Model and Notation*). No presente trabalho são descritos os resultados de um quase-experimento realizado em âmbito acadêmico com a finalidade de avaliar estas diretrizes, bem como a ferramenta computacional denominada JGOOSE, a qual automatiza estas diretrizes. São descritas todas as fases do quase-experimento concluindo com uma discussão visando refutar ou confirmar hipóteses sobre a derivação de casos de uso usando como base modelos gerados via i* e BPMN.

Palavras-chave: i* Framework, BPMN, Casos de Uso, Engenharia de Requisitos.

1 Introdução

O desenvolvimento de sistemas computacionais que atendam às expectativas de seus clientes tem sido o foco de esforços tanto da comunidade acadêmica quanto industrial. Neste contexto, é consenso que a engenharia de requisitos [7] [8] tem um papel fundamental no desenvolvimento de sistemas com maior qualidade. Particularmente tem sido proposto o uso de técnicas que nos permitem compreender melhor o ambiente no qual o cliente trabalha, suas necessidades, os relacionamentos e intencionalidades entre os diversos *stakeholders* envolvidos, obtendo uma visão social [8] deste ambiente. Esta visão pode ser usada para apoiar e derivar requisitos específicos em relação a sistemas computacionais pretendidos. Neste sentido, em [5] foi proposto inicialmente a obtenção de requisitos funcionais na forma de casos de uso [11] [19] a partir da técnica i* (lê-se istar) proposta em [7]. A ideia era aumentar o entendimento do ambiente organizacional via técnica i* e considerar este conhecimento para derivar casos de uso. A partir dessa proposta inicial foram também apresentadas em [1] [2] [6] [21] ferramentas de apoio para esse processo motivando também seu uso no processo de ensino e aprendizagem da engenharia de requisitos [30]. Um experimento em âmbito acadêmico foi realizado para validar essas ferramentas [24]. Mais recentemente em [26] foi proposto um novo processo de derivação de casos de uso considerando outra técnica bastante utilizada na indústria denominada de BPMN [20]. Esse processo foi definido com base em propostas de derivação já existentes e consolidadas na literatura [10] [14] [15] [16] [23]. Este novo processo foi incorporado e suportado pelo ambiente computacional que permitia derivar casos de uso a partir de modelos i*. Assim, na versão atual, o ambiente computacional citado, o qual recebe o nome de JGOOSE (*Java Goal Into Object Oriented Standard Extension*) permite derivar casos de uso UML a partir das técnicas i* e BPMN.

Considerando os trabalhos prévios já mencionados verifica-se a necessidade de avaliar como ambas as técnicas i* e BPMN podem ser integradas e/ou complementadas para derivar casos de uso UML. Isto implica em avaliar os resultados gerados pela ferramenta JGOOSE em situações reais podendo assim, comparar os casos de uso derivados a partir de i* e BPMN tanto em relação à sua corretude quanto completude. No que tange à corretude, precisamos investigar a quantidade de casos de uso corretos ou parcialmente corretos gerados em uma situação real de modelagem. No planejamento do quase-experimento definimos o que é um caso de uso correto e parcialmente correto. Da mesma forma, é importante investigar o grau de completude das descrições textuais dos casos de uso gerados. Estes aspectos são importantes para avaliar o grau de auxílio que este tipo de derivação semi-automatizada pode trazer para engenheiros de requisitos.

Cabe ressaltar que a JGOOSE foi apenas validada na sua versão inicial (i* -> casos de uso) em âmbito acadêmico [24] e carece de validação na sua versão atual. Desta forma, neste artigo apresenta-se um quase-experimento em âmbito acadêmico considerando a JGOOSE na versão atual. A realização deste experimento permitiu-nos tecer algumas considerações a respeito das hipóteses estabelecidas. Também é possível identificar modificações e melhorias necessárias na JGOOSE e processos suportados.

Este artigo, além desta seção inicial, está estruturado conforme segue. A seção 2 apresenta alguns trabalhos relacionados. A seção 3 traz um breve relato sobre as propostas de obtenção de casos de uso a partir de i* e BPMN bem como da ferramenta JGOOSE. A seção 4 apresenta uma descrição do quase-experimento [22] realizado enfatizando os resultados obtidos e uma avaliação das hipóteses previamente elaboradas. Finalmente na seção 5 são realizadas as considerações finais.

2 Trabalhos Relacionados

É importante destacar a existência de alguns trabalhos relacionados à derivação de casos de uso a partir de modelos i*. Em [19] é proposta uma metodologia para apoiar a co-evolução dos modelos i* e casos de uso. Esta metodologia considera a proposta apresentada em [5] como base e sugere diretrizes para melhorá-la definindo como as mudanças em modelos i* devem ser refletidas em modelos de casos de uso e vice-versa. Também propõe a inclusão de requisitos não funcionais à proposta apresentada em [5]. Já em [28] apresenta-se uma proposta para alinhar sistemas de informações com o negócio numa abordagem baseada em modelos. É proposto um meta-modelo para a representação unificada dos requisitos funcionais, não funcionais e de processos de negócio, acompanhado por um método personalizável para o seu levantamento conjunto, baseada em casos-de-uso, metas e regras orientadas a negócio. Também um protótipo de uma ferramenta de suporte ao método é apresentado.

Em relação à proposta de derivação de casos de uso a partir de modelo BPMN, cabe destacar alguns trabalhos relacionados. Por exemplo, a revisão sistemática realizada por [13] teve como objetivo conhecer o estado da arte no que se refere à obtenção de casos de uso a partir de modelos de processos de negócio. Como resultado final foram obtidos treze estudos para análise e extração de dados. Entre estes trabalhos podemos citar o estudo publicado em [14] o qual apresenta uma abordagem para derivação de diagrama de Casos de Uso e de descrição textual para cada caso de uso obtido a partir de modelos

BPMN. A abordagem é dividida em duas etapas, sendo a primeira responsável pela obtenção do diagrama e a segunda pela derivação das descrições textuais. Já em [16], emprega-se a *Model-driven architecture* e realiza-se a transformação de um modelo BPMN em um diagrama de Classes e diagrama de Casos de Uso. Como passo intermediário, é realizada a transformação para diagrama de Atividades UML. Em [17] é proposta a especificação de requisitos funcionais por meio do mapeamento de elementos BPMN em uma descrição textual de detalhamento. Para complementar a aplicação das diretrizes é recomendada a consulta de documentos e a realização de entrevistas com *stakeholders*. Destaca-se também o trabalho de [18], que propôs uma abordagem composta por um conjunto estruturado de diretrizes voltadas para a derivação de Casos de Uso UML a partir de modelos BPMN. Porém, a abordagem abrange um conjunto simplificado de elementos da BPMN e contempla apenas a representação diagramática de Casos de Uso. No âmbito de nossa pesquisa, os trabalhos selecionados por [13] e o proposto por [18] foram analisados e comparados, sendo constatado que o foco das iniciativas é a obtenção de representação diagramática, a qual está presente em doze dos treze trabalhos avaliados. Verificou-se que a abordagem proposta por [14] é a mais completa, contudo, o *template* adotado para representação textual possui poucos campos e carece de outras informações importantes tais como: "caso de uso pai", "casos de uso incluídos", "atores secundários" e "informação adicional", as quais, na nossa proposta, são obtidas a partir dos modelos BPMN. Assim, melhorias às propostas estudadas foram consideradas na proposta apresentada em [26], à qual é a base da nossa pesquisa sendo suportada pela JGOOSE.

Especificamente em relação à ferramenta JGOOSE, entre os trabalhos relacionados podemos destacar as várias ferramentas de modelagem i* e trabalhos publicados descritos no wiki i* [29]. Contudo, nenhuma das ferramentas disponíveis tem o foco de modelagem de derivação de Casos de Uso a partir de modelos i*. Também há vários editores [13] [20] para modelagem BPMN, mas não contemplam a derivação de Casos de Uso.

3 Obtenção de casos de uso a partir de modelos i* e BPMN com suporte da JGOOSE

A proposta de obtenção de Casos de Uso a partir de modelos i* foi inicialmente apresentada em [5]. O *framework* i* proposto por [7] descreve aspectos de intencionalidade e motivações envolvendo atores em um ambiente organizacional. Para descrever estes aspectos são propostos dois modelos: O Modelo de Dependências Estratégicas (SD) e o Modelo de Razões Estratégicas (SR). Mais detalhes sobre a técnica podem ser consultados em [7]. Por outro lado, Casos de Uso são bem conhecidos e utilizados tanto em âmbito acadêmico quanto industrial.

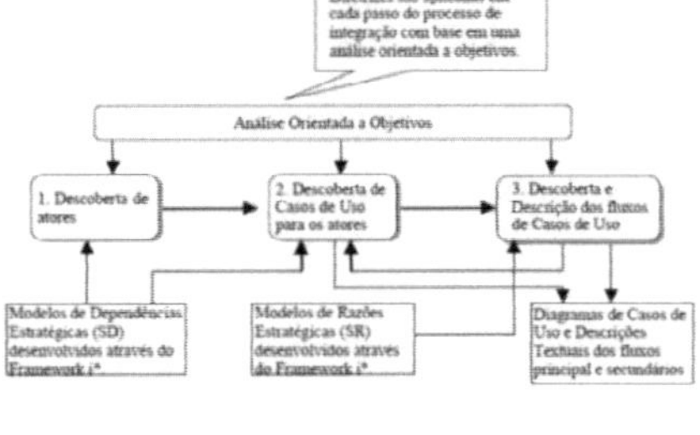

Fig. 1. Casos de uso a partir de i* [5]

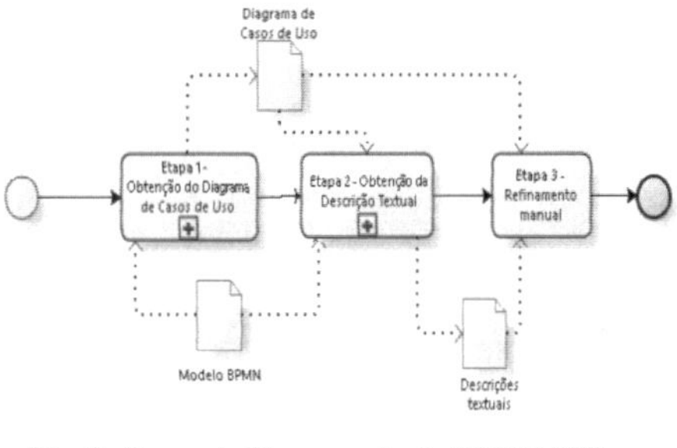

Fig. 2. Casos de Uso a partir de BPMN [26]

São utilizados para representar Requisitos Funcionais de sistemas computacionais pretendidos na forma textual [19] e diagramática [9][11]. Desta forma, a partir dos modelos SD e SR em i* são propostas diretrizes que permitem gerar os casos de uso. A fig. 1 apresenta um resumo da proposta. Os passos 1, 2 e 3 representam a descoberta de atores do sistema e seus casos de uso associados juntamente com suas descrições. A entrada para o processo de integração são os modelos SD e SR desenvolvidos através do framework i*. Nas etapas 1 e 2, a entrada é o modelo SD. A descrição de cenários para Casos de Uso, que corresponde a etapa 3, é derivada de elementos representados no modelo SR. Os resultados do processo de mapeamento são diagramas de Casos de Uso para o sistema pretendido bem como as descrições textuais de cenários para cada Caso de Uso mapeado.

Já a proposta de derivação de Casos de Uso a partir de modelos BPMN (*Business Process Model and Notation*) [20] é detalhada em [26]. BPMN é definida como padrão OMG (*Object Management Group*) e amplamente utilizada na indústria e academia. O processo de derivação de casos de uso a partir da BPMN é apresentado na fig. 2. A abordagem é dividida em três etapas, sendo a primeira responsável pela obtenção do diagrama de Casos de Uso, a segunda pela descrição textual dos Casos de Uso obtidos na etapa anterior e a terceira etapa é encarregada da revisão manual das informações obtidas nas etapas precedentes. Cada uma das etapas é composta por um conjunto de diretrizes ou recomendações. Maiores detalhes podem ser observados em [26].

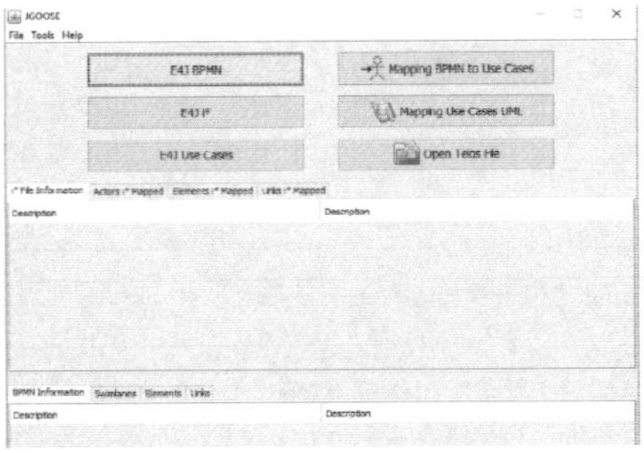

Fig. 3. Tela Principal da JGOOSE

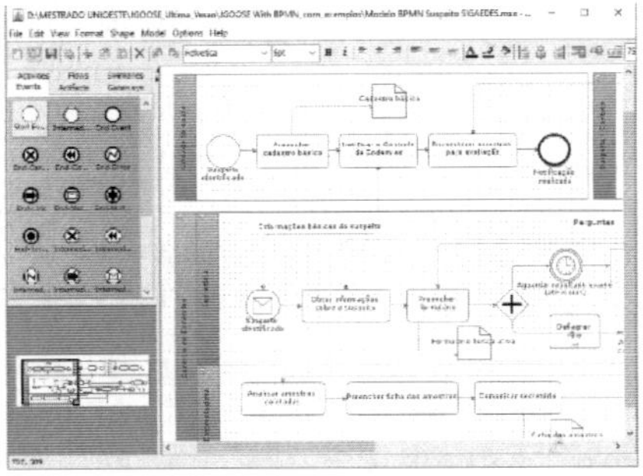

Fig. 4. Tela E4J BPMN

As duas propostas, brevemente resumidas, são suportadas pela ferramenta de apoio JGOOSE [25]. Esta ferramenta passou por várias transformações, uma evolução ao longo dos últimos 13 anos. A primeira versão foi apresentada em [1] na qual permitia-se derivar casos de uso a partir de modelos i* desenvolvidos na ferramenta OME [29]. Nesta primeira versão havia apenas um processo automatizado de transformação não permitindo-se editar os modelos i* e os casos de uso. Em seguida, foi incorporado um editor para modelos i* denominado de E4J i* [21] o qual permite criar e modificar modelos SD e SR e utilizá-los para gerar os casos de uso textuais e diagramáticos no mesmo ambiente da JGOOSE. Mais tarde, a este ambiente foi agregado um editor de casos de uso denominado de E4J Use Cases [24], o qual permite criar e modificar diagramas de casos de uso. Mais recentemente, foi adicionado o editor E4J BPMN e o módulo BP2UC (*Business Process to Use Cases*) [26]. O editor permite construir e modificar modelos BPMN e o módulo BP2UC automatiza as diretrizes propostas em [26] gerando casos de uso. A tela principal da JGOOSE é apresentada na fig. 3. Pode-se observar o acesso aos editores bem como ao mapeamento automático para casos de uso. A fig. 4 apresenta a tela principal do editor BPMN. Mais informações sobre a ferramenta podem ser consultadas em [33] [34].

4 Quase-Experimento: Derivação de Casos de Uso com a JGOOSE

O quase-experimento, estratégia de inquérito empírico similar a um experimento, no qual a atribuição de tratamentos aos sujeitos não pode ser realizada de maneira aleatória, emergindo das características dos sujeitos ou objetos em si. Com a abordagem selecionada objetivou-se avaliar a corretude e completude da derivação de Casos de Uso a partir de modelos i* e BPMN utilizando os editores E4J i* e E4J BPMN da ferramenta JGOOSE [34] e material utilizado para o quase-experimento [38].

4.1 Definição do Quase-Experimento

Como método de avaliação esse experimento foi definido por meio da obtenção de dados experimentais necessários para a realização de análise posterior, a qual permitiu obter conclusões a respeito dos resultados nos aspectos de corretude e de completude de elementos textuais e gráficos gerados. Para [22] a corretude está relacionada ao quanto um método é correto (sua extensão dos erros existentes). No que diz respeito à corretude, três parâmetros que podem envolver os casos de uso derivados:

- Caso de Uso correto: o caso de uso gerado existe e faz sentido em relação ao que se espera bem como suas relações com o ator e demais casos de uso são todas corretas;
- Caso de Uso parcialmente correto: o caso de uso gerado está correto pois existe no resultado esperado, mas nem todas as relações com o ator e demais casos de uso são corretas;
- Caso de Uso incorreto: o caso de uso gerado não existe nos resultados esperados e por consequência as suas relações não cabem a ser avaliadas.

Já sobre a completude, a mesma está relacionada à cobertura do método, se este é completo, suficiente para o experimento. No caso do nosso quase-experimento a completude dos Casos de Uso gerados foi avaliada considerando a quantidade de campos preenchidos corretamente nas descrições textuais.

O quase-experimento possui como objetivo responder à pergunta principal: Quais são as diferenças na comparação das técnicas i* e BPMN na derivação e obtenção de Casos de Uso a partir do software JGOOSE com suas respectivas ferramentas automáticas no processo de derivação (E4J i*, E4J BPMN)?

Os descritivos de situação-problema que os participantes (discentes) deverão modelar foram definidos pelos autores com base em organizações de pequeno e médio porte dos ramos de comercializada de pneus e gestão de estágios. Os participantes devem modelar os problemas utilizando i* e BPMN por meio da ferramenta JGOOSE que, posteriormente gerará automaticamente os modelos em Casos de Uso. Para comparativo de modelos, estes problemas foram previamente modelados pelos autores e gerados os casos de uso pela ferramenta. Neste quase experimento serão avaliados corretude e completude, como já mencionados, respeitando a subjetividade e singularidade dos participantes em proporem as modelagens. Este quase-experimento tem como limitação o nível de conhecimento dos participantes em relação as técnicas de modelagem (i* e BPMN). Entretanto, todos os participantes já possuíam conhecimento prévio das técnicas uma vez que as mesmas foram abordadas em disciplinas já cursadas no decorrer do curso.

4.2 Design do Quase-Experimento

Os tempos em que cada tratamento é aplicado são conhecidos como períodos. Por exemplo, na tabela 1 existem duas sequências de aplicação de tratamento: AB e BA. Além disso, também existem dois períodos: período 1, onde os sujeitos na sequência AB aplicam o tratamento A e os indivíduos na sequência BA aplicam o tratamento B; período 2, onde os sujeitos da sequência AB aplicam o tratamento B e os sujeitos na sequência BA aplicam o tratamento A.

Como entrada de cada processo será gerado um modelo (i* ou BPMN) baseado na descrição do problema apresentado para cada etapa conforme tabela 1 na seguinte sequência: Grupo I → Problema I → Tratamento A (modelagem i*) | Grupo I → Problema II → Tratamento B (modelagem BPMN) | Grupo II → Problema I → Tratamento B (modelagem BPMN) | Grupo I → Problema II → Tratamento A (modelagem i*), conforme fig. 5. O método utilizado é o *crossover* [31] [32] visando obter uma melhor representação dos dois grupos no qual os grupos experimentais apresentam-se respeitando uma ordem em que os sujeitos aplicam tratamentos.

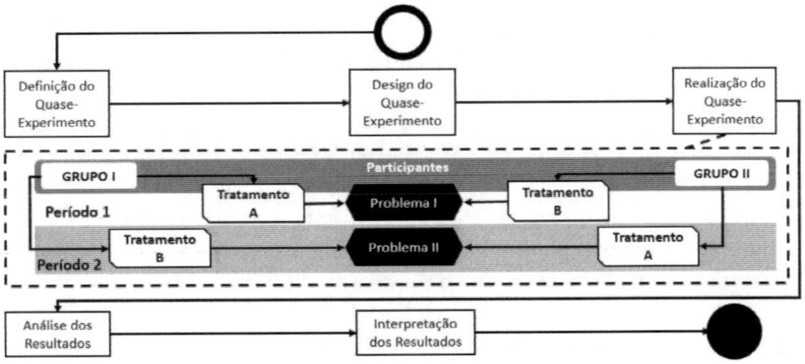

Fig. 5. Esquema do Quase-Experimento.

Tabela 1. Grupos de Controle.

Grupos	Problema I - Período I	Problema II - Período II
Grupo I Sequência AB 13 participantes	(A) Ferramenta modeladora de modelos organizacionais i* (E4J i*) e ferramenta geradora de casos de uso (Módulo do JGOOSE para derivar casos de uso)	(B) Ferramenta modeladora de modelos de processo de negócio BPMN (E4J BPMN) e ferramenta geradora de casos de uso (Módulo do JGOOSE para derivar casos de uso)
Grupo II Sequência BA 11 participantes	(B) Ferramenta modeladora de modelos de processo de negócio BPMN (E4J BPMN) e ferramenta geradora de casos de uso (Módulo do JGOOSE para derivar casos de uso)	(A) Ferramenta modeladora de modelos organizacionais i* (E4J i*) e ferramenta geradora de casos de uso (Módulo do JGOOSE para derivar casos de uso)

Os *designs* de *crossover* também têm grandes vantagens, tais como exigir menos sujeitos ou reduzir a variabilidade devido às diferenças entre os sujeitos.

Apesar das vantagens do tratamento crossover, é preciso tomar cuidado diante de tal experimento, para que os resultados não sejam impactados por problemas até mesmo invalidando o experimento. O *carryover* é um efeito que pode ocorrer quando se há sequência de tratamento onde o conhecimento prévio adquirido anteriormente pode ser utilizado de forma a influenciar um resultado de um tratamento que possa fazer de uma sequência. Consequentemente, os tratamentos administrados por último podem parecer mais eficazes do que aqueles administrados primeiro se o primeiro tratamento estiver aumentando a eficácia do segundo, ou menos eficazes se o primeiro tratamento está diminuindo a eficácia do segundo. O efeito *carryover* pode ter um grande impacto sobre o experimento e até invalidar os resultados finais de uma experiência.

Desta forma, visando reduzir os efeitos negativos no nosso experimento usando o método *crossover*, serão consideradas algumas boas práticas conforme propostas em [31]: **Defina períodos**: Decida quantas vezes os sujeitos vão repetir a tarefa experimental e estudar as implicações; **Definir sequências**: Especifique as ordens em que os tratamentos devem ser aplicados; **Lide com a transição no tempo de design**: Selecione a estratégia para ser usada para contabilizar o *carryover*; **Leve em consideração a variabilidade do assunto**: **Os dados escolhidos e a técnica de análise devem ser capazes de explicar medidas dependentes:** medidas repetidas no mesmo assunto; **Lide com o *carryover* no tempo de análise**: a maneira em que o *carryover* é contabilizado na análise deve coincidir com a decisão de design sobre o *carryover*.

- Como parte que compõe o design do experimento, algumas características foram definidas: aleatoriedade (sujeitos divididos em grupo de dois ou três participantes), bloqueio (a avaliação em grupos tende a diminuir a influência de fatores como stress), balanceamento (todos os participantes são alunos do mesmo curso e da mesma disciplina). Previamente à execução do experimento foram ministradas aulas relativas aos dois modelos (i* e BPMN), linguagem UML e ferramenta JGOOSE aos participantes. As aulas foram ministradas pelo professor da disciplina. Por fim, antes da execução do quase-experimento foram definidas as hipóteses, as quais alicerçaram a análise dos resultados:
    - Hipótese 1: a utilização dos modelos organizacionais i* juntamente da ferramenta E4J (i*) para derivação de Casos de Uso influenciou o resultado final, sendo que a quantidade de Casos de Uso corretos bem como estereótipos («include», «extend» e «generalization») e atores encontrados por quem utilizou é maior do que a quantidade encontrada por quem utilizou BPMN juntamente da ferramenta E4J (BPMN). Ou, ao contrário, sendo que a quantidade de Casos de Uso corretos bem como estereótipos e atores encontrados por quem utilizou BPMN é maior que quantidade de Casos de Uso corretos encontrados por quem utilizou i* juntamente da ferramenta E4J (i*).
    - Hipótese 2: a completude dos casos de uso corretos gerados através da derivação i* -> Casos de Uso é superior a derivação BPMN -> casos de uso ou vice e versa. Este aspecto é mensurado pela completude das descrições textuais dos casos de uso.
    - Hipótese nula: a utilização de alguma das duas técnicas assim como da ferramenta de apoio não influenciou o resultado final, sendo que não há diferença entre as abordagens em relação à quantidade de casos de uso, atores e estereótipos corretos gerados no diagrama de Casos de Uso bem como em relação à completude das descrições textuais geradas.

Com o design definido, a próxima etapa – Realização do Quase-Experimento – inicia-se com o local já definidos e os participantes, bem como o pesquisador que conduzirá o quase-experimento.

4.3 Realização do Quase-Experimento

Este experimento foi realizado no contexto de um projeto de trabalho de conclusão de curso [38], no curso de Ciência da Computação e o experimento foi realizado utilizando a infraestrutura da universidade disponibilizada para aos discentes do curso, laboratório de computação. Os participantes do experimento foram discentes do segundo ano do curso, os quais estavam cursando a disciplina de Processo de Engenharia de Software I no ano de 2019.

O quase-experimento foi realizado no dia 17 de outubro de 2019, iniciado às 8h30m e com término às 11h15m, o qual possui um intervalo de 10 minutos entre os períodos dos problemas a serem modelados. Cabe ressaltar que no planejamento inicial havia-se definido o início do experimento para as 8h e término às 11h30m. Contudo, houve atraso na chegada dos participantes (30 minutos) e a conclusão dos trabalhos ocorreu 15 minutos antes do previsto. Durante o experimento, o pesquisador [36] respondeu apenas as dúvidas frequentes referentes ao material fornecido, situação-problema a ser modelada, não influenciando o processo de modelagem/derivação. A medida a ser utilizada para análise é a diferença da quantidade de Casos de Uso corretos, parcialmente corretos e a diferença entre a completude entre os Casos de Uso obtidos pelas duas técnicas que foram coletadas em média pelos diferentes grupos.

Tabela 2. Questões e Métricas.

Questão	Métrica
Q1 Qual é a quantidade de Casos de Uso corretos gerados pela abordagem i*-> Casos de Uso?	M1 Quantidade de Casos de Uso corretos gerados.
Q2 Qual é a quantidade de Casos de Uso corretos gerados pela abordagem BPMN-> Casos de uso?	M2 Quantidade de Casos de Uso corretos gerados.
Q3 O uso dos estereótipos do tipo *include* e *extend* está correto pela abordagem i*-> Casos de uso?	M3 O uso dos estereótipos do tipo *include* e *extend* está correto.
Q4 O uso dos estereótipos do tipo *include* e *extend* está correto pela abordagem BPMN-> Casos de Uso?	M4 O uso dos estereótipos do tipo *include* e *extend* está correto.
Q5 Há diferenças entre o diagrama de Casos de Uso gerado pelo E4J Use Cases i* e o diagrama de Casos de Uso E4J Use Cases BPMN?	M5 Houve diferenças entre o diagrama de Casos de Uso gerado pelo E4J Use Cases i* e o diagrama de Casos de Uso E4J Use Cases BPMN.
Q6 Esses modelos i* e BPMN construídos para um mesmo problema da organização levam aos mesmos Casos de Uso?	M6 Os modelos i* e BPMN construídos para um mesmo problema da organização não levam aos mesmos Casos de Uso.
Q7 Qual é a quantidade de Casos de Uso parcialmente corretos gerados pela abordagem i*-> Casos de Uso?	M7 Quantidade de Casos de Uso parcialmente corretos gerados.
Q8 Qual é a quantidade de Casos de Uso parcialmente corretos gerados pela abordagem BPMN-> Casos de Uso?	M8 Quantidade de Casos de Uso parcialmente corretos gerados.
Q9 Qual é a quantidade de elementos da descrição textual de Casos de Uso preenchidos corretamente para cada Casos de Uso gerado pela abordagem BPMN?	M9 Quantidade de Casos de Uso considerando a completude dos mesmos.
Q10 Qual é a quantidade de elementos da descrição textual de Casos de Uso preenchidos corretamente para cada Casos de Uso gerado pela abordagem i*	M10 Quantidade de Casos de Uso considerando a completude dos mesmos.

O experimento foi realizado em um dos laboratórios do curso de Ciência da Computação com a utilização da ferramenta JGOOSE (editores i* e BPMN), a qual os participantes já estavam familiarizados. Entretanto, é importante ressaltar que os participantes (nas respostas do questionário aplicado [38]), a primeira e segunda pergunta se referiam à experiência dos participantes diante das técnicas utilizadas para modelar os problemas.

Todas as respostas dos 11 grupos foram direcionadas apenas à experiência adquirida durante a disciplina de Processo de Engenharia de Software I.

A métrica utilizada neste experimento foi a *Goal Question Metric (*GQM) [22][37] a qual auxilia a nortear os elementos a serem medidos no experimento definindo questões, métricas para atender os objetivos do experimento (ver tabela 2).

Para a operacionalização do experimento [22] o mesmo é dividido em três etapas distintas: preparação (fase inicial que consiste no preparo do local do experimento e recepção dos sujeitos), execução (conduzir o experimento de acordo com o que foi planejado) e validação dos dados (tomada de ações que garantam que a informação coletada seja representativa do experimento realizado).

Conforme os grupos finalizaram o primeiro problema no período 1 foram orientados a iniciar a modelagem do segundo problema no período 2.

Os participantes foram divididos em 1 grupo de 13 participantes e 1 grupo de 11 participantes, totalizando 24 alunos, os quais foram subdivididos em 11 subgrupos por meio do *design crossover* (6 subgrupos modelaram o problema 1 em i* e 5 subgrupos modelaram o problema 1 em BPMN). No período 2, houve a troca (6 subgrupos modelaram o problema 2 em BPMN e 5 subgrupos modelaram o problema 2 em i*).

Antes do início do quase-experimento foram distribuídos questionários [38] com algumas questões referentes aos problemas que foram modelados, ao conhecimento dos alunos em relação as técnicas i* e BPMN, ao uso da ferramenta JGOOSE e também com um campo para contabilizar o horário de início e término da modelagem dos problemas para ambas as técnicas, além dos problemas para a leitura dos participantes.

4.4 Análise dos Resultados

Após a preparação e realização do quase-experimento, inicia-se a fase da análise e interpretação dos dados obtidos (ver tabela 3). De acordo com [22] essa é a fase onde os dados coletados são processados e analisados, obtendo a conclusão do experimento. Os critérios de análise foram: existência de Caso de Uso correspondente ao esperado, sendo que para verificação da existência ou não da correspondência será utilizada a descrição textual do Caso de Uso; relação ao ator correto; relação aos demais Casos de Uso.

Tabela 3. Resultados Obtidos.

Grupos	Sub Grupos	Problema I			Problema II		
		Correto	Parcial	Incorreto	Correto	Parcial	Incorreto
Grupo I	Grupo 1	0	2	0	1	1	0
	Grupo 2	1	3	4	0	2	0
	Grupo 3	0	7	14	0	5	2
	Grupo 4	0	20	29	0	8	2
	Grupo 8	0	0	0	0	1	0
Grupo II	Grupo 5	1	5	4	0	5	2
	Grupo 6	0	8	3	0	1	0
	Grupo 7	0	3	1	0	0	5
	Grupo 9	0	9	7	0	6	1
	Grupo 10	0	2	5	0	20	0
	Grupo 11	0	7	12	0	2	0

Em relação a corretude, no total, foram gerados 211 Casos de Uso considerando as duas técnicas (BPMN e i*). Para a modelagem BPMN foram gerados 147 Casos de Uso, dos quais 2 foram corretos, 66 parcialmente corretos e 79 incorretos (ver figura 6). Considerando os aspectos avaliados, a técnica BPMN gerou 24 Casos de Uso parcialmente corretos que não satisfazem o segundo aspecto, que diz respeito a relação ao ator correto e 42 Casos de Uso parcialmente corretos que não satisfazem o terceiro aspecto, que é a relação do tipo <include> e <extend>. Para a modelagem i* foram gerados 64 Casos de Uso, dos quais 1 foi correto, 51 parcialmente corretos e 12 incorretos (ver fig. 5). Considerando os aspectos a serem avaliados, a técnica i* gerou 6 Casos de Uso parcialmente corretos que não satisfazem o segundo aspecto, que tem como objetivo avaliar a relação ao ator correto, também gerou 45 Casos de Uso que não satisfazem o terceiro aspecto, que avalia a presença de relações do tipo <include> e <extend>.

Em relação à compreensão de completude, foram analisados os *templates* dos Casos de Uso obtidos para cada um dos problemas propostos com as respectivas técnicas de modelagem (i* e BPMN). O *template* utilizado neste experimento é uma adaptação do template que tem o formato *fully dressed form* proposto por [19], com o objetivo de capturar um conjunto completo de informações. Assim, os *templates* dos Casos de Uso do problema 1 referentes a técnica BPMN foram comparados com os *templates* dos Casos de Uso da técnica i* e o mesmo processo foi feito para o problema 2.

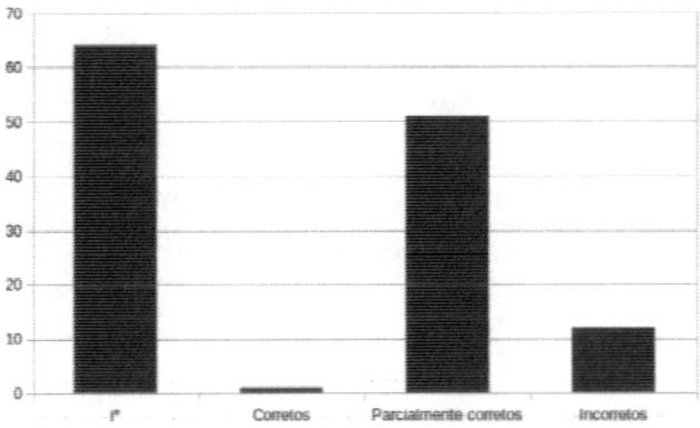

Fig. 6. UC's obtidos pela técnica i*.

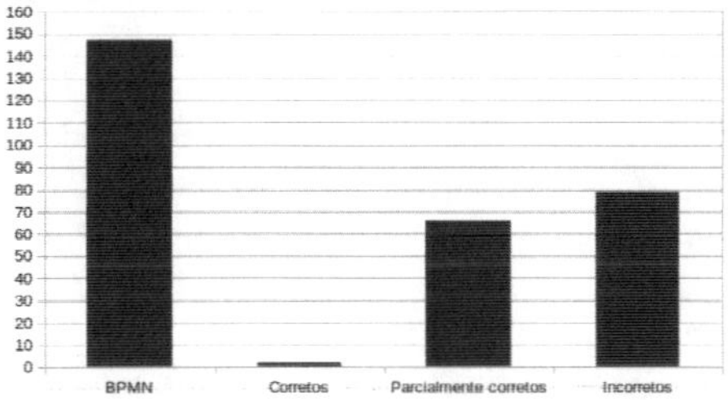

Fig. 7. UC's obtidos pela técnica BPMN.

Tabela 4. Questões e Resultados obtidos

Questão	Resultado
Q1	1
Q2	2
Q3	1
Q4	1
Q5	20 BPMN – 11 i*
Q6	Foram poucos os casos no qual os modelos levaram aos mesmos Casos de Uso
Q7	51
Q8	66
Q9	3 apenas
Q10	1 apenas

Para efetivamente obter um resultado, cada Caso de Uso correspondente à técnica BPMN, foi referenciado um Caso de Uso equivalente na técnica i*, os demais Casos de Uso que não tinham correspondências entre as técnicas foram avaliados de forma isolada, dessa forma, não interferindo no conjunto de Casos de Uso equivalentes. Logo, obteve-se um total de 6 conjuntos para os problemas I e II com Casos de Uso equivalentes, no total, 41 Casos de Uso foram equivalentes (26 do problema I, dos quais 12 Casos de Uso BPMN e 14 Casos de Uso i* e 15 do problema II foram gerados, dos quais 9 Casos de Uso BPMN e 6 da técnica i*). Cada conjunto não obteve o mesmo número de Casos de Uso, mas todos com o mesmo objetivo. Para os Casos de Uso que não tiveram correspondências entre as técnicas e foram avaliados de forma isolada aos demais Casos de Uso que tiveram correspondências, os números foram de 79 Casos de Uso no total (41 deles pertencentes ao problema I, dos quais 21 BPMN contendo 42 elementos no template e 38 pertencentes ao problema II, dos quais 20 i* contendo 20 elementos no *template*). Em percentual foram 31% de Casos de Uso (UC) gerados com a técnica i* e 69% com a técnica BPMN.

Após realizadas as duas análises, corretude e completude, pode-se responder as questões e métricas da abordagem GQM.

4.5 Interpretação dos Resultados

Como interpretação dos resultados obtidos, pode-se perceber que a técnica BPMN obteve uma ligeira vantagem na derivação dos Casos de Uso utilizando a ferramenta JGOOSE, contudo, alguns pontos importantes devem ser destacados. A técnica BPMN conseguiu derivar um número maior de Casos de Uso, porém, com muito mais Casos de Uso incorretos, que no caso eram passos ou tarefas intermediárias para chegar efetivamente no Caso de Uso esperado. Outro detalhe importante foi o conhecimento relatado pelos participantes no questionário aplicado do começo ao fim do quase-experimento, em todos os casos a experiência dos participantes sobre as técnicas foi somente a adquirida em sala de aula, portanto, o conhecimento dos participantes é o básico. No relato obtido com o preenchimento do questionário foi possível perceber que o problema I gerou mais Casos de Uso de o problema II. O tempo de execução também foi cronometrado, o tempo que os participantes utilizaram para realização do modelo em BPMN foi maior do que em i*, 65 minutos e 43 minutos consecutivos.

A partir desses resultados e informações, não é possível dizer que uma técnica se sobressai a outra, por mais que BPMN tenha gerado mais Casos de Uso corretos e parcialmente corretos também acabou gerando muito mais Casos de Uso incorretos. A técnica i* gerou um número de Casos de Uso corretos e parcialmente corretos um pouco menor, porém a eficiência da técnica se mostra na quantidade de Casos de Uso incorretos, que foi quase nula.

Em consideração as questões e métricas, respondidas por meio dos resultados obtidos, pode-se comparar esses resultados com as hipóteses utilizadas para o quase-experimento. Considerando a hipótese 1 e as questões GQM respondidas anteriormente, a utilização de modelos de processo de negócio BPMN juntamente da ferramenta E4J (BPMN) para derivação de Casos de Uso influenciou o resultado final, sendo que a quantidade de Casos de uso corretos bem como estereótipos e atores encontrados por quem utilizou modelos de processo de negócio BPMN juntamente da ferramenta E4J (BPMN) é maior à quantidade de Casos de Uso corretos encontrados por quem utilizou i* juntamente da ferramenta E4J (i*).

Considerando a hipótese 2 e as questões GQM respondidas anteriormente, a completude dos Casos de Uso gerados através da derivação BPMN -> casos de uso é superior a derivação i* -> Casos de Uso. Considerando a hipótese nula, ela pode ser refutada, pois a utilização das duas técnicas, assim como da ferramenta influenciaram o resultado final. Foi possível perceber que a técnica BPMN obteve uma vantagem nos números na derivação dos Casos de Uso utilizando a ferramenta JGOOSE. Contudo, comparando os gráficos (fig. 5 e 6) é possível verificar que a técnica BPMN conseguiu derivar um número maior de Casos de Uso corretos e parcialmente corretos, porém, com mais Casos de Uso incorretos os quais representavam passos ou tarefas intermediárias para chegar efetivamente no Caso de Uso esperado. Por outro lado, a técnica i* derivou um número menor de Casos de Uso corretos e parcialmente corretos, mas com um número menor de Casos de Uso incorretos. Em uma primeira análise, poderíamos atribuir este fato às próprias características das técnicas bem como efetividade das diretrizes em tratar essas características. Por exemplo, em relação à grande quantidade de Casos de Uso incorretos gerados pela técnica BPMN, a descrição passo a passo dos processos de negócio utilizado na técnica pode ter influenciado, já que grande parte dos Casos de Uso incorretos gerados eram passos de cenário principal e extensões de algum Caso de Uso previamente derivado. As diretrizes suportadas pelo módulo BP2UC precisam ser revistas para avaliar este aspecto. Por outro lado, a quantidade menor de Casos de Uso incorretos via técnica i* pode levar a crer que o fato da técnica i* ser parte da GORE (*Goal Oriented Requirements Engineering*) faz com que utilizadores foquem em objetivos e tarefas estratégicas, o que pode inibir a geração de Casos de Uso impróprios. Por outro lado, esta característica também pode ter tido efeito sobre a geração de menos Casos de Uso corretos e parcialmente corretos já que utilizadores de i* tendem a pensar em metas de alto nível, as quais podem incluir ou ocultar submetas típicas de Casos de Uso. As diretrizes que suportam a derivação de Casos de Uso a partir de i* também devem ser revisadas para avaliar este aspecto. Também os resultados podem ter sido influenciados pelo entendimento da descrição dos problemas adotados, tempo alocado, motivação dos estudantes. Outra possibilidade poderia ser por uma falha não crítica detectada no Editor BPMN, no qual alguns elementos como as *lanes* da *pool* e tarefas com ligações sumiam após gerar os Casos de Uso.

5 Conclusão

Neste artigo, apresentamos brevemente a ferramenta JGOOSE, bem como o quase-experimento realizado para avaliar os processos suportados pela ferramenta. Essa ferramenta é integrada pelos editores E4J i *, E4J Use Cases e E4J BPMN. Os editores integrados transformaram o JGOOSE em uma ferramenta independente, dispensando a necessidade de um software externo (ferramenta extra) para criar i *, Casos de Uso ou modelos ou diagramas BPMN.

Nos últimos anos, a JGOOSE tem sido usada para apoiar o processo de ensino e aprendizagem de alunos de graduação em cursos de engenharia de requisitos. Nossas experiências usando o JGOOSE no ensino de engenharia de requisitos estão relacionadas em [4] [30]. Como trabalhos futuros, planejamos aprimorar as funcionalidades da ferramenta JGOOSE considerando o quase-experimento realizado, bem como incorporar funcionalidades para a rastreabilidade de requisitos. A realização de novos experimentos também está prevista com maior diversificação dos participantes, bem como a utilização de novos métodos e abordagens. Outro trabalho futuro envolve o uso do JGOOSE em estudos de caso industriais. Por fim, enfatizamos que a ferramenta é um código-fonte aberto e está disponível para download (com um manual do usuário em português) em [25]. Também há um vídeo está disponível em [33].

Referências

1. Brischke, M.; Santander, V. F. A.; Castro, J. F. B., GOOSE: Uma Ferramenta para Integrar Modelagem Organizacional e Modelagem Funcional In: Jornadas Chilenas de Computación - V Workshop Chileno de Ingeniería de Software, Valdivia, Chile. (2005).
2. Brischke, M.; Santander, V. F. A.; SILVA, I. F., Melhorando a Ferramenta JGOOSE. In: 15th Workshop on Requirements Engineering, 2012, Buenos Aires, 24 a 27 de Abril. Anais do 15th Workshop on Requirements Engineering, 2012.
3. Souza, C.; Santander, V. F.; Uma Proposta de Elicitação e Análise de Requisitos no Contexto de Médias e Pequenas Empresas de Desenvolvimento de Software. 14th Workshop On Requirements Engineering. Rio de Janeiro, Brasil, 2011
4. Santander, Victor F. A. Avaliando a utilização da Técnica i* no Processo de Ensino e Aprendizagem na Engenharia de Requisitos - Um Relato de Experiência. In: IV Fórum de Educação em Engenharia de Software, XXV Simpósio Brasileiro de Engenharia de Software (SBES), São Paulo, 2011.
5. Santander, V. F., Castro, J. F. B., Deriving Use Cases from Organizational Modeling In: IEEE Joint International Requirements Engineering Conference - RE'02, p. 32-39, Essen, Germany, (2002).
6. Vicente, A. A., Santander, V. F. A., Castro, J. B., Freitas da Silva, I., Reyes Matus, F. G., JGOOSE: A Requirements Enginnering Tool to Integrate i* Organizational Modeling with Use Cases in UML. Ingeniare. Revista chilena de ingeniería., v.17, p.6 - 20,(2009).
7. Yu, E.: Modelling Strategic Relationships for Processes Reengineering. Toronto, Canadá: University of Toronto, PhD Thesis (1995).
8. Yu, E., Giorgini, P., Maiden, N., Mylopoulos, J., Social Modeling for Requirements Engineering. The MIT Press (2011).
9. Jacobson, I. Object-oriented development in an industrial environment. In: Conference Proceedings on Object-oriented Programming Systems, Languages and Applications, New York, USA: ACM, 1987.
10. Odeh, M.; Kamm, R.; Down, C. Bridging the gap between business models and system models. In: Information and Software Technology: Special Edition on Business Process Modelling. [S.l.: s.n.], 2003
11. Booch, G.; Rumbaugh, J.; Jacobson, I. Unified Modeling Language User Guide, The (2Nd Edition) (Addison-Wesley Object Technology Series). [S.l.]: Addison-Wesley Professional, 2005.
12. Shishkov, B. et al. Deriving use case from business process models developed using norm analysis. In: . Dynamics and Change in Organizations: Studies in Organizational Semiotics. Dordrecht: Springer Netherlands, 2003. p. 117–131.
13. Silva, A. L. de B. Obtendo Casos de Uso a Partir de Modelos de Processos de Negócio: Uma Revisão Sistemática. Dissertação (Monografia) — Universidade Estadual do Oeste do Paraná, Cascavel, 2015.
14. Cruz, E. F.; Machado, R. J.; Santos, M. Y. Bridging the gap between a set of interrelated business process models and software models. In: ICEIS 2015 - Proceedings of the 17th International Conference on Enterprise Information Systems, Volume 2, Barcelona, Spain, April, 2015. p. 338–345.
15. Siqueira, F. L.; Silva, P. S. M. Transforming an enterprise model into a use case model in business process systems. Journal of Systems and Software, v. 96, p. 152 – 171, 2014.
16. Rodríguez, A.; Guzman, A.; Medina, E.; Piattini, M. Semi-formal transformation of secure business processes into analysis class and use case models: An mda approach. Inf. Softw. Technol., Butterworth-Heinemann, Newton, MA, USA, v. 52, n. 9, p. 945–971, set. 2010.
17. Vara, J. L. de la; Sánchez, J. Improving requirements analysis through business process modelling: A participative approach. In: Business Information Systems: 11th International Conference, BIS 2008, Innsbruck, Austria, May 5-7, 2008. p. 165–176
18. Pessini, T.; Santander, V. F. A ; Silva, I. F. ; Andrade, S. C. ; Schemberger, E. BP2UC: De Processos de Negócio Modelados com BPMN Simplificado para Casos de Uso UML. Revista Científica Inovação e Tecnologia, v. 1, p. 2, 2017

19. Cockburn, A. Writing Effective Use Cases. 1st. ed. Boston, MA, USA: Addison-Wesley Longman Publishing Co., Inc., 2000.
20. BPMN. Business Process Model and Notation (BPMN) Version 2.0.2. [S.l.], December 2013.
21. Merlin, L. P. et al. Integrating the e4j editor to the jgoose tool. In: Anais do WER15 - Workshop em Engenharia de Requisitos, Lima, Perú, April 22, 23, and 24, 2015.
22. Wohlin, C.; Runeson, P.; Höst, M.; Ohlsson, M.C.; Regnell, B.; Wesslén, A.; Experimentation in Software Engineering; Springer; 2012.
23. Herden, A.; Farias, P. P. M.; Albuquerque,A. B. An approach based on bpmn to detail use cases. In: . New Trends in Networking,Computing, E-learning, Systems Sciences, and Engineering. Cham: Springer InternationalPublishing, 2015. p. 537–544.
24. Peliser, D. ; Santander, V. F. A ; Freitas, I. ; Andrade, S. C. ; Schemberger, E. E4J Use Cases: um editor de diagrama de casos de uso integrado à ferramenta JGOOSE. In: 35th International Conference of the Chilean Computer Science Society (SCCC 2016) held in conjuntion with the 42th Latin American Computing Conference (CLEI 2016), 2016, Valparaíso, Chile. NY 12571 USA: IEEE Catalog Number CFP16139-ART, 2016.
25. LES. Laboratório de Engenharia de Software. Disponível em: <www.inf.unioeste.br/~les>. Acessado em: 06/12/2019.
26. Girotto, A. N.; Santander, Victor F. A ; Silva, I. F. ;Toranzo, Marco. A.; Uma proposta para derivar Casos de Uso a partir de modelos BPMN com suporte computacional. In: 36th INTERNATIONAL CONFERENCE OF THE CHILEAN COMPUTER SCIENCE SOCIETY (SCCC 2017), 2017, Arica, 16 a 20 de Outubro.
27. Bhuiyan, Moshiur, et al. "Integration of organisational models and UML Use Case diagrams." *Journal of Computers*, vol. 13, no. 1, 2018, p. 1+. *Academic OneFile*, Accessed 20 Nov. 2018.
28. S. AlhajHassan, M. Odeh and S. Green, "Aligning systems of systems engineering with goal-oriented approaches using the i* framework," 2016 IEEE International Symposium on Systems Engineering (ISSE), Edinburgh, 2016, pp. 1-7.doi: 10.1109/SysEng.2016.7753125
29. iStarWiki.org. Disponível em: <http://istar.rwth-aachen.de/tiki-index.php?page=i%2A+Tools&structure=i%2A+Wiki+Home>. Acessado em: 20/11/2019.
30. Santander, Victor F. A.; SILVA, I. F. Avaliando a utilização da Ferramenta JGOOSE no Processo de Ensino e Aprendizagem na Engenharia de Requisitos: Um Relato de Experiência. In: XIX Conferência Internacional sobre Informática na Educação (TISE), 2014, Fortaleza.
31. Vegas, S.; Apa, C.; and Juristo, N.; Crossover Designs in Software Engineering Experiments: Benefits and Perils, IEEE Transaction on Software Engineering, Val. 42, No. 2, February 2016.
32. Romano, S., Scanniello, G., Fucci, D., Juristo, N. and Turhan, B. 2018. The Effect of Noise on Software Engineers' Performance. In Proceedings of ACM Conference, Washington, DC, USA, July 2017 (Conference'17), 10 pages.
33. Vídeo sobre o JGOOSE. Disponível em: <https://youtu.be/FdDaQp_XqFQ>. Acessado em: 01/12/2019.
34. Geraldino, G. C. L and Santander, V. F. A. The JGOOSE tool. In: 12th International i* Workshop. 38th International Conference on Conceptual Modeling (ER 2019), 2019. Salvador, Brasil. Vol-2490. ISSN 1613-0073.
35. Girotto, A. N.; Derivando Casos de Uso a partir de Modelos BPMN, Trabalho de Conclusão de Curso – Universidade Estadual do Oeste do Paraná, Cascavel – PR, 2016.
36. Gomes, R. S. Comparação do processo de derivação de Casos de Uso a partir de modelos BPMN e i* utilizando a ferramenta de apoio JGOOSE. Trabalho de Conclusão de Curso – Universidade Estadual do Oeste do Paraná, Cascavel – PR, 2019.
37. Pessini, T. BP2UC: Técnica para derivar Casos de Uso a partir de modelos BPMN. Trabalho de Conclusão de Curso – Universidade Estadual do Oeste do Paraná, Cascavel – PR, 2014.
38. Link para os Diagramas de Casos de Uso e questionários respondidos pelos participantes. https://drive.google.com/drive/folders/1e4aBsbjBg2SOnKgS5xpy8YrRhvy6zC3g

Avaliação de Abordagem Centrada em Modelos Conceituais em OntoUML para Apoiar a Derivação de Requisitos Funcionais

Joselaine Valaski [1[0000-0003-3319-1715]], Sheila Reinehr [1[0000-0001-9430-7713]] e Andreia Malucelli [1[0000-0002-0929-1874]]

[1] Programa de Pós-Graduação em Informática (PPGIa)
Pontifícia Universidade Católica do Paraná (PUCPR), Curitiba-PR, Brasil
joselaine.valaski@pucpr.br, sheila.reinehr@pucpr.br, malu@ppgia.pucpr.br

Abstract. A elicitação de requisitos é uma atividade orientada para o entendimento do domínio do software a ser desenvolvido e, portanto, demanda qualidade nas comunicações entre os envolvidos. Embora existam diversas técnicas para a elicitação de requisitos, algumas delas ainda são informais e dependem da experiência dos recursos humanos envolvidos. Neste sentido, um modelo conceitual pode ser um instrumento importante para apoiar a comunicação entre os envolvidos e explicitar conhecimentos de um domínio. O modelo conceitual deve ser representado em uma linguagem expressiva que potencialize os benefícios de um modelo conceitual. A OntoUML é uma linguagem ontologicamente fundamentada que possibilita maior expressividade do que outras linguagens não fundamentadas ontologicamente. No entanto, a construção de um modelo conceitual ontologicamente fundamentado não é uma tarefa trivial. Esta pesquisa tem como objetivo avaliar uma abordagem centrada em modelos conceituais OntoUML para apoiar a derivação de requisitos funcionais a partir de descrições de domínio. Os resultados apontam que é possível identificar semiautomaticamente os construtos OntoUML, bem como derivar requisitos funcionais a partir de descrições de domínios.

Palavras-chave: Elicitação de Requisitos, Modelo Conceitual, OntoUML.

1 Introdução

A elicitação de requisitos é a primeira atividade no processo de Engenharia de Requisitos de Software (ERS), e os problemas relacionados a esta atividade são os que mais afetam o sucesso dos projetos de desenvolvimento de software [1]. A falta de habilidade para discutir problemas tem sido uma das maiores deficiências da teoria e da prática em software [2]. A aquisição do conhecimento de um determinado domínio é um processo caro [3] pois necessidades mal compreendidas podem afetar negativamente etapas posteriores do desenvolvimento do software. Nas fases iniciais da ERS, nas quais ocorrem as primeiras interações com os *stakeholders*, são comuns problemas, tais como: imprecisão e deficiência na coleta de informações sobre o sistema a ser desenvolvido [4]; falta de entendimento do negócio pelos engenheiros de requisitos [5]; as comunicações entre os especialistas no negócio e da computação são deficientes e comprometem a qualidade das informações [6]; e a falta de consenso sobre o uso dos termos na organização pode levar a significados distintos [7].

Na tentativa de atender ou minimizar estas e outras necessidades decorrentes dos problemas relacionados à ERS, as ontologias têm sido um importante recurso. As possibilidades de aplicação das ontologias na ERS são diversas, tendo um papel importante nas linguagens de modelagem conceitual. Mylopoulos [8] define a modelagem conceitual como a atividade de descrever formalmente aspectos do mundo físico e social com o propósito de entendimento. Nesta abordagem trata-se da modelagem da realidade e não da modelagem do sistema computacional [9]. Henderson-Sellers et al. [10] reforçam a importância da notação da linguagem ao afirmar que bons modelos conceituais precisam de boas linguagens de modelagem. Motivado pela necessidade de uma linguagem fundamentada ontologicamente que provesse a semântica necessária para a construção de modelos conceituais e que representasse conceitos mais próximos à realidade, Guizzardi [3] propôs a linguagem OntoUML. O principal objetivo da OntoUML é atingir o comprometimento ontológico falho em outras linguagens genéricas para modelagem conceitual. A OntoUML possibilita maior expressividade nos modelos conceituais, evitando a sobrecarga e a redundância [3]. Uma das dificuldades na construção de um modelo representado em OntoUML é a identificação do construto correto para um determinado conceito a ser representado. Ainda há pouco suporte metodológico para ajudar o usuário a decidir como representar os elementos que denotam propriedades universais em um dado domínio, e, frequentemente, escolhas de modelagem são feitas de maneira ad hoc [3].

No contexto da ERS, um dos principais benefícios do modelo conceitual ontologicamente fundamentado, é a promoção do entendimento de um domínio e a melhoria da comunicação. Neste sentido, considera-se o modelo conceitual representado em OntoUML um importante instrumento para a elicitação de requisitos de software, pois pode ser aplicado para a compreensão de um domínio de conhecimento, principalmente os domínios mais complexos. Espera-se que um modelo conceitual ontologicamente fundamentado seja um instrumento facilitador na derivação dos requisitos de software. No entanto, há a necessidade de se pesquisar, avaliar e propor métodos automáticos e semiautomáticos que apoiem os envolvidos no processo de elicitação de requisitos de software a capturar os conceitos relevantes de um domínio e, por meio deles, construir o modelo conceitual ontologicamente fundamentado.

Considerando os problemas expostos anteriormente uma abordagem centrada em modelos conceituais em OntoUML para apoiar a derivação de requisitos funcionais a partir de descrições de domínio foi proposta sendo necessário avaliá-la. Este artigo tem como objetivo apresentar a avaliação da abordagem proposta. As avaliações foram realizadas em duas etapas distintas. A primeira envolvendo 10 especialistas em OntoUML, um público bem significativo, considerando o universo de especialistas disponíveis nesta área. A segunda etapa envolveu 42 profissionais da área de desenvolvimento de software e 41 estudantes de graduação da área de computação. A Seção 2 descreve a abordagem proposta, a Seção 3 apresenta o método aplicado para avaliação da abordagem, a Seção 4 apresenta e discute os resultados e, por fim, a Seção 5 finaliza o artigo com as conclusões.

2 Derivação de Requisitos Funcionais

A construção da abordagem para apoiar a derivação de requisitos funcionais a partir de descrições de domínio foi executada em quatro etapas principais descritas a seguir.

2.1 Mapeamento e Revisão Sistemática da Literatura

Nesta fase foram realizados um mapeamento [11-12] e uma revisão sistemática de literatura [13-14]. O mapeamento sistemático foi realizado com o objetivo de obter um panorama da área de Engenharia de Requisitos. A base do mapeamento foram 258 artigos publicados no Workshop em Engenharia de Requisitos (WER). Neste mapeamento foi identificado que os temas elicitação de requisitos e modelagem de requisitos são os mais discutidos na ERS ao longo de suas 15 edições. O estudo deixou evidente que ainda são necessários esforços na solução de problemas relacionados a estes temas. Já com o objetivo de compreender melhor como as ontologias estavam sendo usadas no processo da ERS foi realizada uma revisão sistemática de literatura. A revisão teve como objetivo identificar lacunas de pesquisa. A revisão iniciou com uma base de 2.407 artigos e foi concluída com a análise detalhada de 60 artigos.

Os resultados da revisão sistemática mostraram trabalhos efetivos principalmente para apoiar as atividades de análise (51,66%), elicitação (23,33%) e especificação (18,33%). As contribuições mais citadas pelas ontologias foram identificar problemas em especificação e modelos, melhorar a comunicação e construir modelos mais completos. Além disso, a revisão apontou que as ontologias têm como principal objetivo prover o entendimento de um domínio. As propostas também mostram a importância em se utilizar técnicas e linguagens de modelagem ontologicamente fundamentadas. O uso de uma linguagem com falhas de expressividade pode comprometer o entendimento dos artefatos de requisitos em fases posteriores. Uma vez que os modelos conceituais ontologicamente bem fundamentados proveem uma representação mais próxima da realidade de um domínio, alguns dos problemas recorrentes da atividade de requisitos podem ser minimizados com a intensificação do seu uso. A partir desta revisão, concluiu-se que modelos conceituais ontologicamente bem fundamentados podem ser um instrumento importante a ser utilizado na atividade de elicitação de requisitos. Detalhes sobre as abordagens propostas, referente aos 60 trabalhos identificados para o uso de ontologias em atividades pertinentes à Engenharia de Requisitos estão publicados em [14].

2.2 Avaliação da Expressividade da OntoUML

O resultado da revisão sistemática ressaltou a importância do uso de modelos conceituais ontologicamente fundamentados como instrumento para aprimorar a expressividade do conhecimento de domínio. A revisão sistemática também mostrou que a linguagem utilizada para a representação do modelo conceitual contribui para a qualidade da comunicação. Com esta motivação, a linguagem OntoUML foi a escolhida para a representação de modelos conceituais no escopo desta pesquisa. Embora Guizzardi [3] tenha ilustrado em sua tese situações em que a OntoUML possibilita melhor representação evitando sobrecarga e redundância, considerou-se importante realizar uma avaliação dentro de um contexto de sistemas de informação para verificar a expressividade da OntoUML em relação a *Unified Modeling Language* (UML).

O primeiro experimento [15] foi realizado com um grupo de oito profissionais. Considerando doze sentenças pertinentes a um domínio e a dois modelos conceituais (um em UML e o outro em OntoUML), 13% indicaram a UML como a linguagem mais expressiva, 42% indicaram a OntoUML como a linguagem mais expressiva e 46% com ambas sendo expressivas no mesmo nível. O segundo experimento [15] foi realizado com um grupo de oitenta estudantes. Considerando as mesmas sentenças e os mesmos modelos apresentados aos profissionais, 19% indicaram a UML como a linguagem mais expressiva, 42% indicaram a OntoUML como a linguagem mais expressiva e 39% com ambas sendo expressivas no mesmo nível. Apesar da falta de conhecimento da linguagem, de uma maneira geral, os participantes indicaram a OntoUML como sendo a linguagem mais expressiva. Além disso, durante a construção dos modelos pelos especialistas, o alto nível de formalidade e consistência induziu aos especialistas em OntoUML a construírem um modelo mais completo do que os especialistas em UML. O experimento mostrou que a OntoUML provoca discussões durante a construção, o que resulta em modelos mais próximos da realidade do domínio a ser representado [15]. Este resultado reforçou a motivação desta pesquisa, referente ao uso de modelos conceituais representados em OntoUML como instrumento para apoiar o processo de elicitação de requisitos.

2.3 Método para Derivação de Requisitos Funcionais

A avaliação da expressividade demonstrou diversas situações onde a OntoUML permite representações mais claras relacionados ao domínio. Este resultado reforçou a motivação desta pesquisa de que o modelo conceitual representado em OntoUML pode ser um instrumento relevante para apoiar a derivação de requisitos funcionais de domínio. Assim, um método formal para orientar a derivação de requisitos funcionais de domínio foi proposto [16]. Foram estudados nove modelos conceituais representados em OntoUML e, por meio deles, foi definida uma heurística com o objetivo de realizar a leitura e a transcrição textual destes modelos. O repositório de modelos conceituais em OntoUML, denominado *Menthor* (não está mais disponível na Web), foi utilizado como origem para a seleção de alguns modelos conceituais.

A heurística deveria percorrer todo o modelo, sem repetição e a transcrição deveria usar linguagem natural para representar possíveis requisitos funcionais de domínio. A heurística proposta foi aplicada em seis dos nove modelos inicialmente avaliados. Estes modelos foram analisados e padrões identificados. Baseados nestes padrões, uma heurística foi proposta. A Figura 1 apresenta um dos modelos conceituais selecionados e a Tabela 1 apresenta o resultado correspondente da heurística proposta.

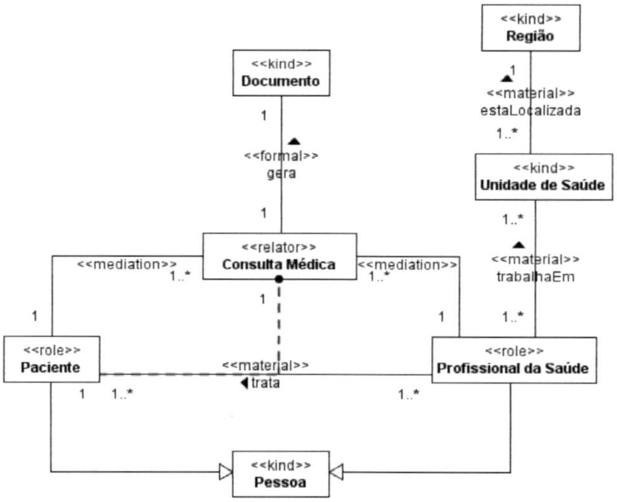

Figura 1. Modelo conceitual parcial OntoUML (Conferência Acadêmica)

Tabela 1. Resultados parciais (Conferência Acadêmica)

Id.	Descrição do requisito
RF1	O sistema deve gerenciar Consulta Médica.
RF1.1	O sistema deve prover a associação de Profissional de Saúde a Consulta Médica.
RF1.1.1	O sistema deve prover a associação de Pessoa a Profissional da Saúde.
RF1.1.1.1	O sistema deve manter os dados de Pessoa.
RF1.1.2	O sistema deve prover a associação de Unidade de Saúde a Profissional da Saúde.
RF1.1.2.1	O sistema deve manter os dados de Unidade de Saúde.
RF1.1.2.1.1	O sistema deve prover a associação de Região a Unidade de Saúde.
RF1.1.2.1.1.1	O sistema deve manter dados de Região.
RF1.2	O sistema deve prover a associação de Paciente a Consulta Médica.
RF1.2.1	O sistema deve prover a associação de Pessoa a Paciente.
RF2.1	O sistema deve gerar Documento de Consulta Médica.
RF2.1.1	O sistema deve manter os dados de Documento.
continua ...	

Considerando o resultado dos nove modelos conceituais avaliados, a heurística proposta mostrou-se viável de ser utilizada. O método foi integrado a um ambiente computacional e posteriormente avaliado [16].

2.4 Ambiente para Construção de Modelo Conceitual em OntoUML

Embora o modelo conceitual representado em OntoUML tenha se apresentado como um instrumento relevante para aprimorar a representação de um domínio do conhecimento, a sua construção não é uma tarefa trivial. Por si só, a construção de um modelo conceitual, em qualquer linguagem, requer habilidade de abstração e visão global. Estas habilidades são desenvolvidas pelos modeladores com a experiência. Além disso, a disponibilidade de um conjunto maior de construtos, que é o caso da OntoUML, aumenta a complexidade de sua construção.

Considerando estas dificuldades, Guizzardi [3] enfatiza a necessidade de desenvolver métodos e ferramentas que apoiem o processo de construção do modelo conceitual. Sendo assim, foi desenvolvido um ambiente computacional com o objetivo de apoiar a construção semiautomática do modelo conceitual em OntoUML. Para atingir este objetivo foram integrados ao ambiente: algoritmo para a identificação de termos relevantes, algoritmo para desambiguação de termos, método para a identificação do construto OntoUML [17], ferramenta para a construção do modelo conceitual em OntoUML [18] e método para a derivação de requisitos de domínio. Por meio do ambiente é possível executar seis atividades principais, as quais são: 1) identificação de termos relevantes; 2) criação de arquivo XML com os termos relevantes tagueados; 3) desambiguação e extração do *supersense* dos termos; 4) mapeamento entre os tipos semânticos e a OntoUML; 5) construção semiautomática do modelo; e 6) derivação da lista de requisitos funcionais.

Após a implementação do ambiente, um teste de viabilidade foi conduzido com o objetivo de avaliar o processo de construção semiautomática de um modelo conceitual em OntoUML. Para o teste foi selecionado um modelo conceitual, representado usando a notação Entidade-Relacionamento, e seu respectivo texto [19]. Este texto foi processado pelo ambiente, e os conceitos identificados foram comparados com os conceitos representados no modelo Entidade-Relacionamento. Os resultados do teste de viabilidade mostraram a integração e o funcionamento de diversos algoritmos e métodos que guiam o modelador na construção do modelo conceitual. Com relação ao desempenho geral do ambiente, no contexto avaliado, o ambiente conseguiu identificar automaticamente 60% dos conceituais significativos de um modelo conceitual [20-21]. Talvez seja um resultado inexpressivo para modeladores experientes, porém é útil para modeladores em fase de formação, os quais são o usuário-alvo do ambiente desenvolvido.

3 Método para Avaliação da Abordagem Proposta

Duas etapas foram executadas para avaliar a abordagem proposta, os detalhes de cada etapa são apresentados a seguir.

3.1 Avaliação da Identificação Automática dos Elementos

Na primeira etapa, seis descrições de domínio foram selecionadas a partir de publicações científicas que discutiam o uso de processamento de linguagem natural. A

Tabela 2 apresenta alguns dados dos textos selecionados, tais como, identificador do texto utilizado no instrumento, o domínio de aplicação do texto, o tamanho do texto (quantidade. de termos) e a fonte de onde o texto foi extraído.

Para o processamento dos textos foi utilizada a aplicação LEO (*Learning Ontologies System*) [27] desenvolvida no escopo da pesquisa de Leão [26]. O LEO foi utilizado por apresentar uma abordagem mais eficiente para a identificação dos termos relevantes. O LEO integra ferramentas de processamento de linguagem natural, tais como: *StanfordNLP*, *OpenNLP*, *LTH Semantic Mapper* e *WordNet* (base semântica). Este conjunto de ferramentas tem como objetivo reconhecer as unidades básicas de uma sentença. O sujeito, verbo e objeto de cada sentença são considerados os termos relevantes do domínio. Os verbos são identificados para a possibilidade de mapear as relações, porém esta funcionalidade ainda não estava implementada na ferramenta.

Tabela 2. Textos selecionados para processamento

Id. Texto Instrumento/Texto	Domínio	Qtd. Termos	Referência
1.1	Comissão de Vendas	107	[22]
1.2	Biblioteca	213	[23]
1.3	Validação Serviços	243	[24]
2.1	Editora de Livros	76	[25]
2.2	Conferência Científica	103	[26]
2.3	Roteiro de Ônibus	329	[19]

Ao final do processamento automático, para cada descrição de domínio, uma lista dos termos identificados e seus respectivos construtos foram gerados. Foram elaborados dois instrumentos, cada um deles com o resultado obtido a partir de três descrições de domínio. Cada instrumento foi enviado para dezesseis especialistas em OntoUML. A lista de especialistas foi obtida por meio da seleção de publicações científicas relacionadas a OntoUML. Para apoiar a avaliação, quatro métricas foram estabelecidas: 1) percentual de termos relevantes corretos; 2) percentual de termos desambiguados corretos; 3) percentual de termos com consenso; e 4) percentual de acerto do método.

3.2 Avaliação da Derivação Automática dos Requisitos Funcionais

A partir dos resultados obtidos na etapa anterior, os modelos conceituais em OntoUML foram construídos semiautomaticamente. Nesta etapa, cinco modelos foram utilizados, todos da Tabela 1, exceto o Id 1.3 (devido a problema de qualidade do texto). Com os modelos conceituais construídos, foi executado o método de derivação apresentado na Seção 2.3. Para cada modelo conceitual, uma lista de requisitos de domínio foi gerada. Os textos processados pelo método foram em inglês, porém eles foram posteriormente traduzidos para o português para a apresentação aos participantes da avaliação. As listas de requisitos geradas também foram traduzidas para o português.

Para esta avaliação foram elaborados três instrumentos, os instrumentos 1 e 2 com duas descrições de domínio distintos e o instrumento 3 com uma descrição de domínio. O instrumento 3 foi elaborado com apenas uma descrição por se tratar do texto mais extenso entre os selecionados. Junto com o texto foi enviada a lista de requisitos de domínio gerada automaticamente pelo método a partir do modelo conceitual OntoUML. Por meio dos instrumentos, foi possível coletar as seguintes informações: 1) perfil dos participantes; 2) qualidade dos textos; 3) percentual de requisitos funcionais não corretos gerados pelo método proposto; 4) percentual de cobertura do método; e 5) percepções gerais da avaliação. Os instrumentos foram aplicados em dois grupos distintos: o primeiro, denominado profissionais, cujos participantes eram graduados e com experiência na atividade de levantamento de requisitos, e o segundo, denominado estudantes, cujos participantes estavam cursando graduação em computação que já haviam cursado disciplinas relacionadas a atividade de levantamento de requisitos.

4 Resultado da Avaliação

Esta seção apresenta os resultados referentes à avaliação da abordagem proposta. A avaliação foi conduzida em duas etapas: a primeira para a identificação automática dos elementos em um modelo conceitual OntoUML e a segunda para a derivação automática de requisitos funcionais a partir do modelo conceitual OntoUML.

4.1 Identificação Automática dos Elementos

Entre os especialistas (trinta e dois), dez retornaram com o instrumento preenchido. Cada instrumento (total de dois) foi respondido por cinco especialistas distintos. A Tabela 3 sumariza os resultados correspondentes às métricas estabelecidas para cada um dos seis textos avaliados.

Coluna (A) "termos relevantes corretos": a média geral de acerto foi de 88% (variação de 80% a 100%). Não possível observar se o tamanho do texto interferiu no resultado, pois percentuais maiores foram obtidos tanto nos textos maiores quanto nos menores. Este resultado indicou um percentual de cobertura considerável. No instrumento, também foi solicitado que os especialistas indicassem termos relevantes não identificados pelo método. No total geral, apenas três termos foram indicados pelos especialistas como não identificados pelo método.

Coluna (B) "termos relevantes desambiguados corretos": a média geral de acerto foi de 85% (variação de 75% a 94%). Esta medida não foi obtida por meio de especialistas porque não era necessário. A avaliação ocorreu manualmente pelo pesquisador comparando o significado retornado pelo algoritmo *TargetWord* [28] e o significado correto no *WordNet*. Neste ponto do processo, houve a intervenção manual, pois em testes prévios, foram observadas situações em que a desambiguação não acontecia corretamente. Se a identificação não é feita de maneira correta, o método proposto pode fazer a indicação errada do construto. Também não foi possível encontrar relação entre o tamanho do texto e o percentual de acerto, pois percentuais maiores foram obtidos em textos maiores e menores. Talvez a qualidade e a especificidade dos termos contribuam positivamente ou negativamente com os resultados. Os termos desambiguados incorretamente não afetaram os resultados dos especialistas pois a intervenção e a correção manual aconteceram antes do envio do instrumento para os especialistas. Este resultado reforça a necessidade de que ocorra uma análise manual do usuário na etapa de desambiguação para posteriormente seguir com as próximas etapas do método.

Tabela 3. Resultado das métricas para cada texto

Id texto	Percentual termos			
	Relevantes corretos (A)	Desambiguados corretos (B)	Consenso construto OntoUML (C)	Acerto Método (D)
1.1	100%	83%	92%	100%
1.2	85%	76%	82%	86%
1.3	80%	80%	70%	93%
2.1	100%	75%	100%	100%
2.2	86%	92%	100%	75%
2.3	89%	94%	85%	90%
Total	88%	85%	86%	90%

Coluna (C) "consenso construto OntoUML": a média geral de consenso foi 86% (variação de 70% e 100%). Este resultado não avalia diretamente o método proposto, porém evidencia que mesmo em se tratando de especialistas a indicação do construto OntoUML não é uma tarefa trivial. Talvez em situações com modeladores menos experientes, o índice fosse menor, reforçando a motivação desta pesquisa de que métodos devem ser desenvolvidos para apoiar o modelador na identificação dos elementos em um modelo conceitual em OntoUML.

Coluna (D) "acerto do método": a média geral de acerto foi de 90% (variação de 75% a 100%). Certamente este percentual seria inferior se comparado com o número de termos identificados inicialmente, porém, só é possível comparar efetivamente usando os termos que em houve consenso entre os especialistas. Também foi feita uma investigação para identificar as causas da falha do método. Entre os noventa e dois termos que obtiveram consenso entre os especialistas referente ao construto OntoUML correto, apenas para nove termos o método falhou. Entre esses termos, foi possível identificar as seguintes características: sete termos compostos não foram encontrados na base WordNet, um termo com o *supersense cognition* e um termo não foi possível identificar a causa. É mais comum encontrar termos simples na base do WordNet do que termos compostos. Quando o método proposto não encontra o termo na base do WordNet, ele não consegue fazer a desambiguação e consequentemente não consegue processar as etapas seguintes do método. Uma alternativa de trabalhos futuros é fazer o processamento individual das palavras que compõem o termo composto.

4.2 Derivação Automática dos Requisitos Funcionais

Nesta etapa da avaliação, participaram 83 pessoas, sendo 42 pessoas, categorizadas como profissionais, e 41 pessoas categorizadas como estudantes. O perfil de formação dos profissionais foi: 33% com especialização, 29% apenas graduação e 26% com mestrado. Entre os profissionais 85,7% afirmaram já terem atuado em atividades de levantamento de requisitos, com uma média de 8,5 anos de experiência nesta atividade. Entre os estudantes, 36,5% afirmaram já terem atuado em atividades de levantamento de requisitos, com uma média 1,3 anos de experiência nesta atividade. A avaliação foi realizada com dois públicos diferentes (estudantes e profissionais) para avaliar se a experiência ou não poderia interferir nos resultados.

A qualidade dos textos foi analisada segundo três critérios: 1) a facilidade de entendimento do domínio, 2) a clareza do texto e a 3) utilidade do texto com fins de levantamento de requisitos. De um modo geral, tanto para os profissionais, quanto para os estudantes, foram obtidos percentuais elevados de concordância. Nos três critérios, o percentual atingido, considerando as opções concordo e concordo totalmente, foram de no mínimo 68%. O critério que alcançou maior percentual foi em relação a utilidade do texto para fins de levantamento de requisitos. Considerando as opções concordo e concordo totalmente, o resultado foi de 92% para os profissionais e 96% para os estudantes. Nenhum dos três critérios de qualidade apresentou resultado significativo que pudesse comprometer o resultado do método avaliado.

Em relação ao percentual de requisitos funcionais não corretos gerados pelo método proposto, em nenhum dos textos analisados, tanto por profissionais quanto por estudantes, se obteve percentual superior a 5%. Ou seja, os requisitos gerados pelo método, em sua maioria são corretos. A Figura 2 apresenta um recorte do Instrumento referente a lista de requisitos gerada pelo método para o texto "Comissão e Vendas". Os itens gerados a partir do constructo "Role" (ex: RF 1.1.1; RF 1.1.1.1; RF 1.1.2), após a avaliação, foram suprimidos do método proposto pois não agregam com a lista de requisitos funcionais necessárias.

ID	Descrição do RFD	NÃO é um Requisito Funcional em um SI
RF1	**O sistema deve gerenciar Pagamento**	
RF1.1	O sistema deve permitir atribuir Vendedor a Pagamento	
RF1.1.1	Vendedor é um/uma Funcionário	
RF1.1.1.1	Funcionário é um/uma Pessoa	
RF1.1.1.1.1	O sistema deve manter os dados de Pessoa	
RF1.1.2	Vendedor é um/uma Empresa	
RF1.1.2.1	O sistema deve manter os dados de Empresa	
RF1.2	O sistema deve permitir atribuir Empresa a Pagamento	
RF2	**O sistema deve gerenciar Venda**	
RF2.1	O sistema deve permitir atribuir Cliente a Venda	
RF2.1.1	Cliente é um/uma Pessoa	
RF2.2	O sistema deve permitir atribuir Vendedor a Venda	
RF2.3	O sistema deve permitir gerar Ordem de Venda	
RF2.3.1	O sistema deve manter os dados de Ordem de Venda	

Figura 2. Recorte instrumento, lista de requisitos gerada (Texto Id. 1.1)

Os resultados referentes ao percentual de cobertura dos requisitos funcionais gerados pelo método proposto são apresentados na Tabela 4. Na tabela são apresentados os resultados por categoria de participantes (profissionais ou estudantes), a escala de cobertura que poderia ser selecionada pelo participante, e os percentuais obtidos para cada texto avaliado. Analisando os resultados individualmente (Tabela 4), é possível observar que foram obtidos percentuais diferentes para cada texto. Tanto na visão dos profissionais, quanto dos estudantes, os textos 2.2 (Conferência) e 2.3 (Roteiro de ônibus) foram os textos em que o método conseguiu maior percentual de cobertura. No texto 2.2, 92% dos profissionais e 77% dos estudantes concordaram que o método lista pelo menos 75% dos requisitos, enquanto no texto 2.3, 77% dos profissionais e 87% dos estudantes concordam que o método lista pelo menos 75% dos requisitos.

Tabela 4. Cobertura do método por texto

Categoria	Escala de cobertura	Id. Texto				
		1.1	1.2	2.1	2.2	2.3
Profissional	0%	6%	0%	0%	0%	0%
	25%	0%	13%	23%	0%	0%
	50%	44%	38%	23%	8%	23%
	75%	50%	50%	54%	69%	69%
	100%	0%	0%	0%	23%	8%
	75% + 100%	50%	50%	54%	92%	77%
Estudante	0%	0%	0%	0%	0%	0%
	25%	31%	31%	8%	8%	7%
	50%	31%	23%	38%	15%	7%
	75%	38%	46%	46%	54%	73%
	100%	0%	0%	8%	23%	13%
	75% + 100%	38%	46%	54%	77%	87%

Na seção final do instrumento, foram apresentadas algumas afirmações para os participantes indicarem o percentual de concordância. Os resultados obtidos para estas afirmações foram os seguintes:

Afirmação 1: As listas geradas pelo método representaram um conjunto coerente de Requisitos Funcionais candidatos em um Sistema de Informação. Segundo os participantes, o método gera uma lista de requisitos coerente. Acumulando o percentual entre "Concordo" e "Concordo totalmente", obteve-se um percentual de 88% entre os profissionais e 76% entre os estudantes. Ou seja, a percepção geral dos participantes foi, em sua maioria, de que os resultados do método foram coerentes.

Afirmação 2: As listas geradas pelo método apresentadas de forma hierárquica podem ser úteis para apoiar a extração dos Requisitos Funcionais candidatos em um Sistema de Informação. Esta foi a afirmação que atingiu maior percentual de concordância entre os participantes. Acumulando o percentual entre "Concordo" e

"Concordo totalmente", obteve-se um percentual de 95% entre os profissionais e 98% entre os estudantes. Ou seja, a percepção geral dos participantes foi, em maioria absoluta, de que o método foi útil.

Afirmação 3: Eu utilizaria um método que gerasse a lista de Requisitos Funcionais para apoiar a identificação dos Requisitos Funcionais do Software. Acumulando o percentual entre "Concordo" e "Concordo totalmente", obteve-se um percentual de concordância de 81% para os profissionais e 83% para os estudantes. Embora esta afirmação também tenha atingido percentuais de concordância elevados, eles indicam uma maior tendência em achar o método útil, porém uma menor tendência em usar o método. Ou seja, a percepção geral dos participantes foi, em sua maioria, de que utilizaria o método para apoiar a identificação de requisitos funcionais.

Os resultados das três afirmações demonstram que os participantes tiveram uma percepção bastante positiva com relação a coerência, a utilidade e mostram pré-disposição para usar a abordagem proposta. É importante ressaltar que esta etapa da avaliação foi conduzida com participantes mais experientes e menos experientes na atividade de levantamento de requisitos. No entanto, os resultados de ambos as categorias de participantes foram muito similares. Todos os resultados, como por exemplo, avaliação da qualidade do texto, cobertura do método e percepções após o experimento, foram muito próximos. A experiência na atividade de levantamento de requisitos não interferiu nos resultados do experimento.

Como limitações desta pesquisa ressaltamos os seguintes aspectos: 1) as ferramentas de Processamento de Linguagem Natural, que produzem melhores resultados, processam textos em inglês, restringindo cenários em português; 2) os textos de domínio públicos encontrados são curtos e simples, haveria a necessidade de avaliação da proposta em textos mais longos e complexos; 3) a lista de requisitos do domínio gerada pelo método proposto é apenas uma relação em alto nível dos requisitos. Para um detalhamento destes requisitos, é necessário aprofundamento com o usuário.

5 Conclusão

A elicitação de requisitos de software é uma atividade complexa, que demanda qualidade nas comunicações entre os envolvidos para um completo entendimento do domínio do conhecimento a ser elicitado. Embora existam diversas técnicas para a elicitação de requisitos, algumas delas ainda são informais e dependem de um esforço humano considerável. A elicitação de requisitos é uma atividade que depende da experiência dos usuários envolvidos. Quando não se pode contar com esta experiência, é comum que ocorram problemas tais como: comunicação deficiente, falta de consenso sobre os termos utilizados e falta do conhecimento do domínio a ser elicitado.

Esta pesquisa apresentou a avaliação da uma abordagem baseada em modelos conceituais, representada em OntoUML, para apoiar a derivação de requisitos funcionais de domínio. Os resultados obtidos apresentam evidências mais detalhadas sobre as possibilidades e os desafios da identificação semiautomática para a construção de um modelo conceitual. A avaliação envolveu seis textos de domínios diferentes com a participação de dez especialistas em OntoUML, contexto ainda não encontrado na literatura. Os resultados também evidenciam como um modelo conceitual construído em linguagem mais expressiva pode apoiar a geração de requisitos funcionais de um software. O modelo conceitual pode contribuir para o entendimento mais próximo da realidade do domínio, antes de que artefatos tecnológicos pertinentes sejam desenvolvidos. Quanto maior o entendimento do domínio, menor serão os problemas no desenvolvimento do software decorrente da falta de compreensão. A lista de requisitos gerada pelo método proposto permite uma visão geral do escopo do domínio e também uma visão geral dos requisitos necessários, caso um Sistema de Informação seja desenvolvido. A inserção da construção do modelo conceitual em OntoUML no processo de desenvolvimento de software é uma atividade que deve aumentar o tempo alocado para o levantamento de requisitos.

Por fim, é importante ressaltar que estas conclusões foram obtidas considerando os contextos avaliados, e que para efeitos de generalização, novas avaliações em contextos distintos são necessárias.

Referências

1. Gao, US General Accounting Office. Mission Critical Systems: Defense Attempting to Address Major Software Challenges, GAO/IMTEC-93-13, December (1992).
2. Zanlorenci, E.P., Burnett, R.C. Modelo para Qualificação da Fonte de Informação do Cliente e de Requisito Funcional, In Workshop em Engenharia de Requisitos (1998).
3. Guizzardi, G. Ontological Foundations for Structural Conceptual Models, Telematica Instituut Fundamental Research Series 15, Universal Press (2005).
4. Jureta, I.J., Borgida, A., Ernst, N. A., Mylopoulos, J. TECHNE: Towards a New Generation of Requirements Modeling Languages with Goals, Preferences, and Inconsistency Handling. International Requirements Engineering Conference, p.115–124 (2010).
5. Oliveira, K.M., Zlot, F., Rocha, A.R., Travassos, G.H., Galotta, C., Menezes, C.S. Domain-oriented software development environment. Journal of Systems and Software, v.72, p.145–161 (2004).
6. de la Vara, J.L., Sánchez J. Improving Requirements Analysis through Business Process Modelling: a Participative Approach, v. 1, p. 165–176 (2008).
7. Garrido, J. L., Noguera, M., González, M., Hurtado, M. V., Rodríguez, M. L. Definition and use of Computation Independent Models in an MDA-based groupware development process". Science of Computer Programming. v. 66, p. 25–43 (2007).
8. Mylopoulos, J. Conceptual modeling and Telos, In P. Loucopoulos and R. Zicari, editors, Conceptual modeling, databases, and CASE. Wiley (1992).
9. Guizzardi, R., Franch, X., Guizzardi, G. Applying a Foundational Ontology to Analyze Means-End Links in the i* Framework. In Proceedings of the 6th International Conference on Research Challenges in Information Science, Valencia, Spain (2012).
10. Henderson-Sellers, B., Gonzalez-Perez, C., Eriksson, O., Ågerfalk, P. J. Software modeling languages: a wish list. In Seventh International Workshop on Modeling in Software Engineering, p. 72-77 (2015).
11. Valaski, J., Reinehr S., Malucelli, A. Retrospective and Trends in Requirements Engineering through the WER. In: Workshop em Engenharia de Requisitos, Montevideo (2013).

12. Valaski, J., Reinehr S., Malucelli, A. WER Overview: Retrospective, Trends and Relevance. Clei Electronic Journal, v.10, n. 3, (2013).
13. Kitchenham, B.A. Procedures for Undertaking Systematic Reviews, Joint Technical Report, Computer Science Department, Keele University (TR/SE0401) and National ICT Australia Ltda (2004).
14. Valaski, J., Reinher, S., Malucelli, A. Which Roles Ontologies play on Software Requirements Engineering? A Systematic Review". In: The 2016 International Conference on Software Engineering Research & Practice, Las Vegas. p. 24-30 (2016).
15. Valaski, J., Reinher, S. and Malucelli, A. Evaluating the Expressiveness of a Conceptual Model Represented in OntoUML and UML. In: ONTOBRAS - Brazilian Ontology Research Seminar, Curitiba. ONTOBRAS (2016).
16. Valaski, J., Reinher, S. and Malucelli, A. Deriving domain functional Requirements from Conceptual Model Represented in OntoUML. In Proceedings of the 19th International Conference on Enterprise Information Systems. v. 2, p. 263-270 (2017).
17. Leão, F., Revoredo, K., Baião, F. Learning Well-Founded Ontologies Through Word Sense Disambiguation". In Proceeding Of: 2nd Brazilian Conference On Intelligent Systems (2013).
18. OLED. https://code.google.com/p/OntoUML-lightweight-editor/, acessado em: 2014 fev 11. (2014).
19. Gemino, A., Wand, Y. Complexity and clarity in conceptual modeling: Comparison of mandatory and optional properties. Data & Knowledge Engineering v.55, p.301–326 (2005).
20. Valaski, J., Reinehr, S. and Malucelli, A. Environment for Requirements Elicitation Supported by Ontology-Based Conceptual Models: A Proposal". In Proceedings of the 2014 International Conference on Software Engineering Research and Practice (SERP'14), ISBN 1-60132-286-0, Las Vegas, USA, p.144-150 (2014).
21. Valaski, J., Reinher, S. and Malucelli, A. Computational environment to Semi-Automatically Build a Conceptual Model Represented in OntoUML. In: ONTOBRAS - Brazilian Ontology Research Seminar, 2016, Curitiba. ONTOBRAS, (2016).
22. Capuchino, A.M.; Juristo, N.; Van de Riet, R.P. Formal justification in object-oriented modelling: A linguistic approach. Data & Knowledge Engineering, v.33, i.1, p.25-47 (2000).
23. Harmain, H.M., Gaizauskas, R. CM-Builder: A Natural Language-Based CASE Tool for Object- Oriented Analysis. Automated Software Engineering., v.10(2), p.157-181 (2003).
24. Deeptimahanti D. K., Sanyal, R. Semi-automatic generation of UML models from natural language requirements. In Proceedings of the 4th India Software Engineering Conference. ACM, p.165–174 (2011).
25. Mayr, H.C., Kop, C. A user centered approach to requirements modeling. In: M.Glinz, G. Müller-Luschnat (eds.): Proc. Modellierung 2002. Lecture Noptes in Informatics P-12 (LNI), GI-Edition, p.75-86 (2002).
26. Leão, F. Expanding the Semantic Knowledge of Wordnet Through Semantic Types and UFO. Dissertação de mestrado. Universidade Federal do Estado do Rio de Janeiro (2014).
27. Leão, F. LEO - Learning Ontologies System. Acesso: 01/11/2016, disponível em: https://github.com/felipeleao/leo. (2016).
28. Pedersen, T., Kolhatkar, V. WordNet::SenseRelate::AllWords: a broad coverage word sense tagger that maximizes semantic relatedness. In Proceedings of Human Language Technologies. (2009).

Técnicas de aprendizaje automático para mejorar el rendimiento de aplicaciones web: un mapeo sistemático de literatura

Jean Carlo Zúñiga-Madrigal, Christian Quesada-López, Marcelo Jenkins, Alexandra Martínez

Universidad de Costa Rica, San Pedro, Costa Rica
{jean.zunigamadrigal, cristian.quesadalopez, marcelo.jenkins, alexandra.martinez}@ucr.ac.cr

Resumen. La proliferación de las aplicaciones web ha generado una cultura cada vez más demandante por parte de los usuarios. Se estima que un usuario promedio espera solo dos segundos antes de abandonar una aplicación web, si esta no responde dentro de ese lapso. Por esta razón, la creación de sitios web eficientes se ha convertido en una prioridad para los desarrolladores. El objetivo de este estudio es identificar las principales técnicas de aprendizaje automático utilizadas para mejorar el rendimiento de las aplicaciones web, sus indicadores de desempeño, usos, y capas de aplicación. Para esto se realizó un mapeo sistemático de literatura que identificó 37 estudios primarios. Los resultados indican que los árboles de decisión son el algoritmo más explorado para mejorar el rendimiento de las aplicaciones, seguido por las redes neuronales y las máquinas de soporte vectorial. Los indicadores más utilizados para medir el rendimiento de las aplicaciones web fueron el uso de caché, el tiempo del primer *byte* y el tiempo de carga de página. El principal uso de aprendizaje automático reportado está en la predicción efectiva de futuras acciones de un usuario durante su interacción con una aplicación web para así pre cargar recursos necesarios en memoria antes que sean requeridos. Las capas de infraestructura y *back-end* fueron las que más reportaron el uso de aprendizaje automático para mejorar el rendimiento.

Keywords: aprendizaje automático, rendimiento, aplicaciones web, mapeo sistemático

1 Introducción

El aumento exponencial de aplicaciones en Internet es evidente si analizamos las páginas indexadas por el motor de búsqueda Google: su primer índice en 1996 contenía alrededor de 50 millones de aplicaciones, mientras que en el 2011, la cantidad de aplicaciones indexadas era de alrededor de tres trillones [1]. De la mano de este crecimiento en la cantidad de sitios web, ha habido un aumento en la cantidad de usuarios que navegan en Internet diariamente. Es por esto que resulta relevante analizar alternativas para mejorar el rendimiento que ofrecen las aplicaciones web, de manera que se ajuste a las necesidades de la creciente demanda de usuarios que las frecuentan.

La motivación de este mapeo de literatura es identificar técnicas del área de aprendizaje automático que se hayan usado con el fin de mejorar el rendimiento de aplicaciones web, considerando sus indicadores de desempeño y las capas de la aplicación donde se implementaron dichas técnicas. Emplearemos este conocimiento en nuestros trabajos, actualmente muchas compañías de desarrollo de *software* se dedican a crear aplicaciones web para sus clientes. Entregar productos con buen rendimiento es importante, por lo que explorar el aprendizaje automático como medio para lograrlo es una alternativa que quisimos explorar.

Para alcanzar el objetivo planteado, se desarrolló un mapeo sistemático de literatura que buscaba responder las siguientes preguntas de investigación: ¿Cuáles técnicas de aprendizaje automático se han utilizado para mejorar el rendimiento de las aplicaciones web? (RQ1), ¿Cuáles indicadores se han usado para medir el rendimiento de aplicaciones web? (RQ2), ¿En cuáles capas de aplicación se han usado las técnicas de aprendizaje automático que mejoran el rendimiento? (RQ3).

El resto del artículo está estructurado de la siguiente manera: la sección 2 presenta el marco teórico con los conceptos que sustentan esta investigación, luego la sección 3 describe el trabajo relacionado en el área de rendimiento en sitios web, la sección 4 discute la metodología que se utilizó para desarrollar esta investigación, el análisis de los resultados se muestra en la sección 5, y finalmente, las conclusiones de esta revisión están en la sección 6.

2 Marco teórico

En esta sección se definen conceptos relacionados al aprendizaje automático y a las aplicaciones web. Estos conceptos son los que sustentan el mapeo realizado.

Aplicaciones web

Una aplicación web es un sitio en línea que puede ser accedido por usuarios a través de un navegador web [2]. Existen distintos tipos de aplicaciones web, por ejemplo, para el marco de desarrollo de Microsoft: *Web Forms*, *Web Forms* con *Asynchronous JavaScript and XML* (AJAX), *Web Forms* con controles *Silverlight*, *Model-View-Controller* (MVC) y aplicaciones *Dynamic Data* [2].

Independientemente de la arquitectura con la que se construya una aplicación web, esta debe contar con una clara división entre el cliente y el servidor [2]. En el cliente es donde se muestran las vistas de la aplicación web, las cuales son accedidas mediante navegadores web que obtienen y parsean los recursos que necesarios por la aplicación, como por ejemplo los archivos *HyperText Markup Language* (HTML) que contienen la estructura del sitio dispuestas en etiquetas, las hojas de estilo CSS (*Cascading Style Sheets*), y los archivos JavaScript que permiten introducir dinamismo en la capa del cliente para la interacción con los usuarios.

El primer paso a seguir por un navegador web es crear un árbol llamado *Domain Object Model* (DOM) para la estructura HTML y otro árbol de estilos para los archivos CSS. Durante este proceso, el JavaScript es interpretado y ejecutado según aparezca en el orden de parseo de archivos. Al ejecutar estos archivos, se introducen nuevos cambios a la estructura del DOM, dependiendo de las reglas desarrolladas en el código ejecutado.

Por otro parte, en el lado del servidor es en donde ocurre el procesamiento que resuelve las necesidades de los usuarios. Siguiendo con el caso del marco de trabajo provisto por Microsoft, un ejemplo de servidor es el *Internet Information Services* (IIS), herramienta que facilita el despliegue de aplicaciones web al proveer servicios necesarios para servir contenido web a través del protocolo de comunicación *Hypertext Transfer Protocol* (HTTP) [2].

Aprendizaje automático

El aprendizaje automático es el proceso de encontrar, de forma automática, patrones significativos en grandes conjuntos de datos [3]. Este tipo de aprendizaje se utiliza en tareas relacionadas al reconocimiento, diagnóstico, planeamiento y predicción de salidas. La aplicación de aprendizaje automático en sistema computacionales provoca cambios en su estado actual, o inclusive la creación de nuevos sistemas, a raíz de la ejecución de las tareas asociadas al aprendizaje. Shalev-Shwartz y Ben-Dav [3] mencionan distintos tipos de aprendizaje automático, se listan a continuación:

- Supervisado y no supervisado: se denomina aprendizaje supervisado al que pretende formular predicciones tomando como insumos características y etiquetas provistas por quien entrene al algoritmo. Estos insumos no son sino las preguntas y respuestas con las que trabajará el algoritmo de aprendizaje automático. Por otro lado, el aprendizaje no supervisado no cuenta con ningún insumo de entre los descritos anteriormente, la finalidad es que sea el propio algoritmo quien agrupe características comunes que encuentre en la colección de datos con la que se entrena [3].
- Activo y pasivo: la forma pasiva de aprendizaje amerita la interacción continua con el ambiente de aprendizaje, mientras que la forma pasiva se basa en la constante observación resultante de los cambios aplicados al ambiente de aprendizaje [3].
- En línea y por lotes: el aprendizaje en línea ocurre cuando un sistema toma decisiones basadas en su contexto actual, con el riesgo de cometer errores, pero que eventualmente serán cada vez menores hasta contar con un porcentaje de aciertos mayor, a raíz de la experiencia recabada. Por otro lado, el aprendizaje por lotes sucede cuando un sistema cuenta con una colección vasta de datos con los cuales trabajar para llegar al nivel de aprendizaje deseado [3].

Para este mapeo se utilizó la taxonomía creada por Shalev-Shwartz y Ben-Dav [3]. En síntesis, esta taxonomía expone las siguientes categorías: regresión, clasificación, agrupamiento, reducción de la dimensionalidad, redes neuronales, algoritmos probabilísticos, algoritmos heurísticos, y otros enfoques. A continuación se detallan estas familias de algoritmos de aprendizaje:

- Regresión: es un modelo de aprendizaje supervisado que abarca los algoritmos que buscan la relación entre variables. Dentro de los tipos de algoritmos que se listan bajo esta categoría se mencionan la Regresión lineal simple y la Regresión lineal múltiple.

- Clasificación: modelo de aprendizaje supervisado, los algoritmos que califican dentro de esta categoría son los que reciben una o más entradas e intentan predecir el valor de una o más salidas. Algunos de los algoritmos dentro de esta categoría son las Máquinas de soporte vectorial, Árboles de decisión y Naïve Bayes.
- Agrupamiento: modelo utilizado para el análisis exploratorio de datos, intenta ubicar grupos significativos de información en grandes conjuntos de datos dados puntos de información como guía para así agrupar la información que comparte características en común. Entre los algoritmos que pertenecen a esta clasificación están: *K-means* y Agrupamiento jerárquico.
- Reducción de la dimensionalidad: este modelo busca tomar datos de un espacio dimensional que está a un alto nivel y mapearlo a otro espacio cuya dimensionalidad sea más baja. Entre las razones para completar esta tarea se pueden mencionar el reducir el costo computacional de operar en un espacio dimensional alto, mejorar la generalización del algoritmo de aprendizaje automático que opera el espacio dimensional, y finalmente, dar una mejor interpretación a la información.
- Redes neuronales: se trata de un modelo computacional que se inspira en el comportamiento de las neuronas en el cerebro humano. En el contexto de la computación, una red neuronal es un grafo cuyos nodos corresponden a las neuronas, y las aristas representan las conexiones entre neuronas.
- Híbridos: se refiere a los algoritmos que combinan dos o más algoritmos para alcanzar un fin.
- Algoritmos probabilísticos: clasificación que contempla algoritmos que basan los resultados de la resolución a algún problema en cálculos probabilísticos.
- Otros enfoques: esta es una clasificación creada para los algoritmos de aprendizaje automático que no se ajustan a otras categorías de la taxonomía propuesta por Shalev-Shwartz y Ben-Dav.

3 Trabajo relacionado

No se encontraron en la literatura trabajos previos que abordaran específicamente el uso de técnicas de aprendizaje automático para mejorar el rendimiento de aplicaciones web. Sin embargo, se encontraron trabajos que han comparado y caracterizado algoritmos de aprendizaje automático, que resultan importantes de conocer para efectos de esta investigación. Estos trabajos se describen a continuación.

El estudio de Kazhmaganbetova et al. [4] evalúa técnicas de aprendizaje automático para garantizar una buena comunicación entre clientes y servidores en términos de establecimiento de protocolos seguros, tráfico inusual recibido, y cargas transportadas de un extremo a otro. El principal aporte de este estudio fue su enfoque en la predicción de anomalías en el tamaño de los paquetes de datos que se envían entre el cliente y la aplicación web, con un rendimiento de 23,5 según el valor de Error Cuadrático Medio, métrica utilizada durante la experimentación realizada.

Algunas herramientas han sido propuestas para monitorear el rendimiento de las aplicaciones web. El estudio secundario de Pradeep y Kumar [5] hace una recopilación de tales herramientas, entre ellas: *Apache Jmeter*, *Selenium*, *Cucumber* y *Web Test*. Dicho estudio presenta herramientas y código libre en general, que permita hacer entregas de productos de *software* más depurados y libres de errores. El aporte más valioso de este estudio está en la experimentación realizada con las diferentes herramientas estudiadas. El *framework Locust*, desarrollado en *Python*, es la herramienta que reportó mejores tiempos en ejecución de casos de prueba, con un promedio de 1,6966 segundos en cinco pruebas realizadas, superando a *HULK Analyzer* que promedió 1,8158 segundos, y a *Apache Jmeter* que promedió 2,1068 segundos, al realizar las mismas cinco pruebas.

También se han comparado los resultados de realizar pruebas de rendimiento automáticas *versus* manuales, este es el caso del estudio de Arslan et al. [6] donde evalúan indicadores de rendimiento, tales como consumo de recursos, latencia, utilización de memoria, entre otros más, utilizando pruebas automatizadas y manuales. Este estudio aportó importantes conclusiones sobre la ineficiencia de las pruebas manuales en comparación con las pruebas automáticas, esta conclusión se basa en características como el tiempo de ejecución de las pruebas y lo propenso de estas a fallar debido a la gran cantidad de datos necesarios para ejercitar las técnicas de aprendizaje automático.

La contribución del presente mapeo de literatura es aportar información sintetizada y relevante en un contexto novedoso como lo es el rendimiento de las aplicaciones web. La información ofrecida abarca indicadores que miden el rendimiento de las aplicaciones, así como las capas de aplicación en donde se ha utilizado aprendizaje automático.

4 Metodología

Para cumplir con el objetivo del estudio, se desarrolló un mapeo sistemático de literatura con base en las pautas de Petersen [7] y las recomendaciones de Kitchenham [8] para la conducción de este tipo de estudios secundarios. Esta sección detalla el protocolo de investigación seguido para obtener los resultados expuestos en este estudio.

El objetivo del estudio, formulado con la plantilla de objetivos *Goal Question Metric* (GQM) [9], fue analizar la mejora de rendimiento a partir de técnicas de aprendizaje automático con el propósito de caracterizarlos con respecto a indicadores y áreas de aplicación, desde el punto de vista de un investigador en el contexto de aplicaciones web.

4.1 Estrategia de búsqueda y proceso de selección de estudios

El protocolo de investigación se desarrolló durante el 2019, durante el primer semestre se ubicaron los artículos de donde se obtuvo la información para el mapeo, mientras que el segundo semestre se dedicó a la redacción del estudio.

El protocolo de investigación comenzó con una búsqueda exploratoria para encontrar artículos de investigación que sostuvieron el objetivo planteado, estos hallazgos se tomaron como artículos de control para guiar el resto de la búsqueda. Los temas que abordan los artículos de control seleccionados son la distribución de peticiones de usuario entre servidores [S02], predicción web basada en las acciones de los usuarios [S03] [S04] y la optimización de aplicaciones web en dispositivos distintos a los de escritorio [S05].

A partir del conjunto de artículos de control se concibió la cadena de búsqueda basada en el modelo PICO (Población, Intervención, Comparación, Salidas) [10], la cual buscó por términos clave en el título y resumen de estudios primarios dentro de los repositorios científicos escogidos: *Scopus*, *IEEE Xplore*, y *Web of Science*. Después de un proceso iterativo de refinamiento, esta fue la cadena de búsqueda final:

("performance" OR "optim*") AND ("web") AND ("load*" OR "render*" OR "display*") AND ("machine learning" OR "artificial Intelligence")

Tal y como se muestra en la Figura 1 La cantidad de estudios primarios recuperada para cada repositorio de búsqueda fue de 474, con la siguiente distribución: 265 estudios en *Scopus*, 44 en *IEEE Xplore* y 165 en *Web of Science*. De este conjunto se eliminaron los estudios duplicados y se aplicaron los criterios de inclusión y exclusión (E/I) para hallar el conjunto final con el que se elaboraron los resultados de la investigación.

El proceso de E/I se hizo con base en el título y el resumen de los artículos. Se incluyeron solo (I1) artículos que abordaron el rendimiento de aplicaciones web mediante técnicas de aprendizaje automático y (I2) estudios primarios. Luego, se excluyeron publicaciones que (E1) estuvieran redactados en un idioma distinto al inglés, y (E2) que no tuvieran acceso al texto completo. El conjunto final de estudios con los que se trabajó luego de terminado el protocolo de selección fue de 37 artículos primarios, la lista completa con sus respectivas referencias está disponible siguiendo este hipervínculo: https://bit.ly/36eYdgV.

4.2 Evaluación de calidad

La evaluación de la calidad refleja el nivel de detalle ofrecido por cada artículo para los aspectos estudiados. Se plantearon las siguientes preguntas de calidad: ¿hubo mejora medible en el rendimiento de la aplicación web al emplear aprendizaje automático?, ¿el artículo señaló el uso de aprendizaje automático como el principal factor de la mejora de rendimiento?, ¿el artículo detalló la metodología o estrategia seguida para aplicar el aprendizaje automático dentro de la aplicación web? y ¿se hizo alusión a indicadores de rendimiento en el estudio? La puntuación se realizó con una escala de 0 a 1, donde 0 = No cumple en lo absoluto, 0,5 = Cumple parcialmente, 1 = Cumple totalmente.

Luego de evaluada la calidad se observa que el valor más alto fue alcanzado por diez artículos [S04], [S05], [S06], [S07], [S08], [S09], [S10], [S11], [S12], [S13]. Por otro lado, hubo solo tres que obtuvieron la peor calificación [S14], [S15], [S16]. El detalle de la evaluación de calidad se encuentra disponible siguiendo este hipervínculo: https://bit.ly/352VozF, en donde se asigna el puntaje a cada estudio primario de acuerdo a los criterios de calidad contemplados.

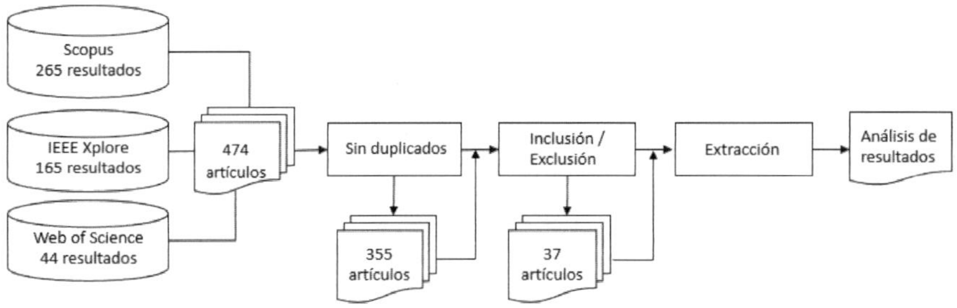

Fig. 1: Proceso para obtener los artículos del mapeo.

4.3 Amenazas a la validez

A continuación se presentan las amenazas a la validez de este mapeo de literatura, así como las estrategias para minimizarlas.

- **Construcción de la cadena de búsqueda**: la cadena de búsqueda retornó 313 estudios primarios que terminaron siendo descartados del mapeo. Aunque muchos de estos estudios abordaban temas de aprendizaje automático, sus contextos eran muy distintos al estudiado, estando la mayoría dentro del contexto de *software* para el cuidado de la salud. La estrategia seguida para mitigar esta amenaza fue hacer la lectura de todos los resúmenes de estos estudios, para así discernir si el contexto en el que se enfocaban era el de interés para este mapeo.
  El término "*artificial intelligence*" en la cadena puede crear un sesgo en los resultados hacia una tecnología en particular. Esta amenaza se mitigó al realizar varias búsquedas piloto con distintas cadenas, con esto se logró obtener un conjunto más homogéneo de tecnologías analizadas.
- **Selección de los repositorios utilizados**: elegir los repositorios de búsqueda sugiere una amenaza en la que los artículos que almacenan resulten irrelevantes en el mapeo, o que directamente no existan estudios en ellos que aporten en las respuestas de las RQs. Esta amenaza se reduce al elegir tres de los más importantes y renombrados repositorios científicos. Además, muchos de los estudios primarios seleccionados estaban en dos o tres de los repositorios, lo que sugiere su completitud de las bases de datos en cuanto al tema investigado.
- **Generalización de resultados**: si el mapeo de literatura realizado se basa en estudios que dependen de variables complejas de replicar, podría surgir la amenaza de no ser fácilmente verificable. La estrategia de mitigación radica en la elección misma de los repositorios. Al ser repositorios reconocidos y respetados se genera una alta confianza en los artículos que almacenan.
- **Inclusión y exclusión**: fueron creados criterios de Inclusión y Exclusión para apoyar en la selección de estudios primarios. Una elección inadecuada de estos criterios podría haber excluido del mapeo de literatura artículos primarios que habrían aportado en los resultados obtenidos. Se mitigó esta amenaza siguiendo un protocolo de constantes revisiones por criterios expertos de profesionales con experiencia en investigación. En particular para

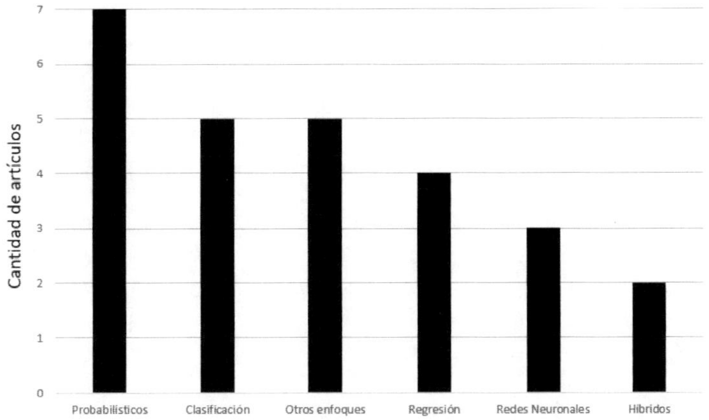

Fig. 2: Cantidad de estudios por categoría de aprendizaje automático.

el I1, se decidió ser inclusivos y también considerar estudios enfocados en rendimiento no solo en capas lógicas de las aplicaciones, sino también físicas, como la infraestructura donde estas se despliegan.

- **Repetibilidad**: crear un mapeo de literatura que sea muy similar a otros existentes lleva a que no haya aporte nuevo para el estado del arte del tema estudiado. El protocolo seguido, donde se depuró una cadena de búsqueda que se ejercitó en distintos repositorios científicos, es la forma de minimizar esta amenaza, puesto que los resultados de estas búsquedas retornaron estudios secundarios que se documentan en el trabajo relacionado, pero que no son idénticos al propuesto en este mapeo.

Tabla 1: Técnicas de aprendizaje automático más citadas.

Técnica	Estudios	Categoría	Total
Máquina de soporte vectorial	S03, S05, S11, S13, S23, S28, S36	Clasificación	7
Red neuronal	S01, S06, S10, S12, S13, S26	Red neuronal	6
Árboles de decisión	S07, S16, S21	Clasificación	3
Bosques aleatorios	S32, S34	Clasificación	2

5 Resultados

En esta sección se presentan los resultados del mapeo de literatura, basados en los 37 estudios primarios seleccionados. El detalle de estos estudios primarios se encuentra siguiendo este hipervínculo: https://bit.ly/352VozF, donde se extraen las características más importantes de cada uno respecto a lograr el objetivo de la presente investigación.

5.1 Técnicas de aprendizaje automático para mejorar el rendimiento de aplicaciones web (RQ1)

Se reportaron 26 técnicas de aprendizaje automático para mejorar el rendimiento de aplicaciones web. La Figura 2 agrupa los estudios por categoría de aprendizaje automático, según la taxonomía de Shalev-Shwartz y Ben-David [3]. Por su parte, la Tabla 1 presenta las técnicas más reportadas de aprendizaje automático, junto con su respectiva categoría de clasificación. La técnica más utilizada fue Máquina de soporte vectorial, con siete estudios, seguida de Redes neuronales, con seis estudios. Es importante notar que un total de cinco estudios utilizaron técnicas que no pudieron clasificarse dentro de la taxonomía, por lo que se agruparon en la columna "Otros enfoques" de la Figura 2. Estas técnicas fueron: *Target-driven parallelism* [S27], Doble matriz [S04], *Q-learning* [S35], *Fuzzy logic* [S21], y *Fuzzy reinforcement learning* [S17].

Las técnicas reportadas solo una vez fueron: Doble matriz [S04], *Gradient boosting* [S32], *Load estimation with pre-learning* [S02], *Particle swarm optimization* [S06], *Linear regression* [S19], Teoría Dempster-Shafer [S28], *Q-learning* [S35], *Ant colony optimization* [S09], *Honey bee algoritm* [S09], *Fuzzy reinforment learning* [S17], *Gradient descent* [S27], BayesNet [S36], NaiveBaes [S36], *Regression trees* [S34], *Regression splines* [S34], *TreeNet* [S34], *ID3* [S36], *Bayesian network* [S21], *Fuzzy logic* [S21], *Target driven parallelism* [S27], y *Multinomial logistic regression* [S01].

Fue común encontrar técnicas utilizadas para predecir las acciones que tomará un usuario mientras interactúa con una aplicación web. Al predecir las acciones antes de que estas se realicen, una aplicación web logra tomar ventaja de tiempo y preparar la respuesta a esta acción antes que el usuario la ejecute.

Se encontraron mejoras de rendimiento al utilizar SVM en problemas de predicción, por ejemplo: en peticiones almacenadas en caché tras la correcta predicción de la siguiente página que un usuario visitará durante su interacción con una aplicación web [S03]. Esto fue posible de modelar en una SVM en base al registro almacenado en archivos históricos para el caso particular de la NASA, *ClarkNet* y el departamento de Computación e Ingeniería de la Universidad de Washington.

También se emplearon SVM para el uso eficiente de los núcleos de un procesador en dispositivos móviles para renderizar sitios web. Esto se logró mediante entrenamiento *off-line* para dar con modelos predictivos a utilizarse en el proceso de renderización. Entonces, se seleccionaba el procesador adecuado de acuerdo a parámetros como el *network* en donde se estableció la conexión con la aplicación y los componentes web que se necesitaban renderizar [S13].

Las redes neuronales también se utilizaron en el proceso de renderizado de aplicaciones web [S13]. La forma en la que se aprovechó esta técnica fue, en primer lugar, predecir el tiempo de carga que tomaría a un sitio web desplegarse completamente, y por otro lado, estimar el consumo de energía que le tomaría al dispositivo este proceso de despliegue. Con esta información se toman decisiones respecto al procesador del dispositivo del cliente que debe renderizar la aplicación.

El algoritmo de doble matriz es utilizado, junto con la técnica de *pre-fetching*, para aprovechar la memoria caché de las aplicaciones web. Su objetivo es predecir la siguiente página que un usuario necesitará y pre-cargarla en caché [S04]. La doble matriz es entrenada con patrones de peticiones realizadas por los usuarios

Tabla 2: Indicadores de rendimiento para las aplicaciones web.

Indicador	Estudios	Capa	Total
Uso de caché	S03, S04, S06, S07, S08, S17, S18	*front-end*, *back-end*	7
Tiempo del primer *byte*	S07, S08, S11, S19, S20, S21	*back-end*	6
Tiempo total de carga	S01, S06, S05, S22, S23, S25	*front-end*, *back-end*	6
Latencia	S15, S18, S25, S26, S27	infraestructura	5
Carga de trabajo de la red	S05, S22, S28, S29	infraestructura, *back-end*	4
Tamaño del DOM	S01, S13	*front-end*	2
Tiempo de respuesta del servicio	S19, S30	*back-end*	2
Consumo de energía	S05, S23	infraestructura	2
Uso del CPU	S11, S31	*back-end*	2
Utilización de memoria	S11, S31	*back-end*	2
Índice de velocidad	S24, S32	*front-end*	2
Carga del servidor y ancho de banda	S26, S31	infraestructura, *back-end*	2

para que logre producir como salida la siguiente página que se visitará. Esta técnica es denominada doble matriz al contar con una matriz dedicada a almacenar la probabilidad de una página para ser elegida como siguiente página a pre-cargar, además de una segunda matriz con información sobre pesos máximos para reducir el tiempo que toma el algoritmo para ubicar la entrada más pesada por cada fila de la primer matriz.

El *target-driven parallelism* (TPC) se utilizó para corregir dinámicamente peticiones a un servidor que fueron predichas incorrectamente como peticiones de corta duración [S27]. Al corregirse dinámicamente, fue posible mover estas peticiones a una lógica de paralelismo que reduce su tiempo de completitud. Esta solución se basa en la existencia de un predictor en el servidor encargado de clasificar peticiones como de larga o corta duración. TPC corrige posibles fallas del predictor y cambia la forma en que se computan las peticiones para que tomen ventaja de la programación en paralelo.

5.2 Indicadores que permiten medir el rendimiento de las aplicaciones web (RQ2)

Se identificaron 24 indicadores para medir el rendimiento de las aplicaciones web. Este conjunto de indicadores se muestra en la Tabla 2. El indicador más citado en la literatura fue el Uso de caché, siendo citado en siete estudios, seguido por el Tiempo del primer *byte*, y el Tiempo total de carga, ambos reportados en seis estudios cada uno.

Los indicadores reportados en solo un estudio fueron: *Script size* [S06], *Average image number* [S07], *Average search response time* [S07], *Load utilization ratio* [S08], *Query to connectivity ratio* [S08], Utilización de recursos [S09], Número de conexiones por segundo [S09], Número de peticiones por segundo [S09], *Service level agreement* [S19], *Perceptual speed index* [S32], Elasticidad [S35], *Throughput* [S21], *Router roundtrip time* [S37], Tamaño de la sesión [S16].

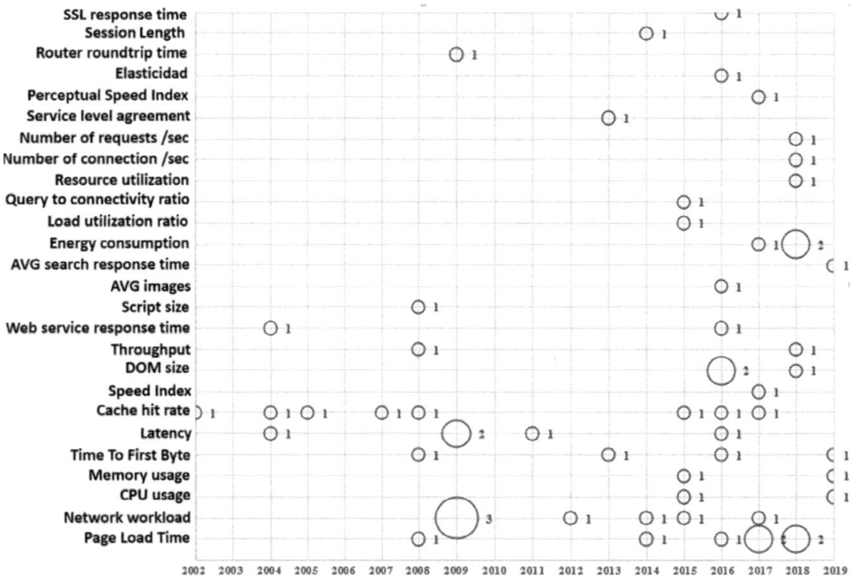

Fig. 3: Uso de diversos indicadores de rendimiento en el tiempo.

La Figura 3 muestra el uso de indicadores de rendimiento a través de los años, desde el 2002 hasta el 2019. Se puede notar que el Uso de caché ha sido reportado de forma relativamente constante a través del tiempo (con excepción del periodo 2009-2014), mientras que el Tiempo total de carga ha tenido un repunte a partir del año 2014.

Para los dos primeros lustros, que comprenden del año 2000 al 2010, el uso del caché para obtener recursos no modificados de una manera mucho más rápida fue el indicador más citado, con cinco reportes por lustro. Luego, para el lustro que comprende del año 2011 al 2015, hubo una tendencia hacia el indicador *Network workload*, con tres referencias en la literatura. Este indicador tiene que ver con la carga de trabajo de un servidor en los momentos específicos donde se toma una medición y por un periodo de tiempo dado [S22]. Finalmente, desde el año 2016 y hasta la actualidad, se reportan cinco estudios que se enfocan en mejorar el *Page load time* de los sitios en Internet. Este indicador se refiere al momento en el que transcurren dos segundos y no hay más actividad de red para cargar recursos de la aplicación [11].

5.3 Capas de aplicación web donde se ha mejorado el rendimiento con el uso de aprendizaje automático (RQ3)

Los esfuerzos para mejorar el rendimiento de aplicaciones web pueden ser clasificados según la capa de aplicación donde se utilicen: *front-end*, *back-end*, e infraestrutura de despliegue. Siguiendo esta clasificación, la Tabla 3 muestra las capas de aplicación donde se han implementado técnicas de aprendizaje automático, así como las áreas (por capa) donde se han realizado las mejoras de

Tabla 3: Capas y áreas de aplicación donde se usa aprendizaje automático.

Capa	Área	Estudios	Total
Back-end	Caché del servidor	S03, S08, S10, S17, S18, S26, S34, S36	8
	Análisis de archivos históricos	S03, S07, S16, S28	4
	Uso del CPU	S13, S27	2
Front-end	*Pre-fetching*	S04	1
	Renderizado del DOM	S05	1
Infraestructura	Balanceadores de carga	S09, S12, S14, S17, S27, S30, S36, S37	8
	Infraestructura como servicio	S11, S35	2
	Secure sockets layer	S02	1
	Procesadores de dispositivos móviles	S05	1
	Precision time protocol v2	S22	1

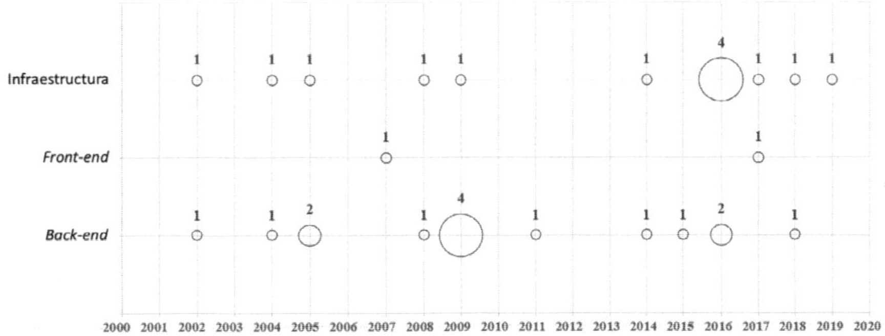

Fig. 4: Uso de aprendizaje automático por capa de aplicación, a través del tiempo.

rendimiento. A continuación se señalan las mayores incidencias por cada capa de aplicación:

- ***Front-end***: esta capa reportó mejoras al aprovechar el *pre-fetching* en los navegadores web para obtener recursos necesarios por una aplicación web antes que el usuario los requiera. Por otro lado, también se estudió un proceso de renderizado del DOM más eficiente, tomando como factor la capacidad de procesamiento en el dispositivo donde se despliega la aplicación web.
- ***Back-end***: la capa de *Back-end* tuvo un gran énfasis en el almacenamiento en caché de recursos y peticiones que los usuarios necesitan más frecuentemente. Además, reportó un gran esfuerzo en almacenar constantemente información detallada de archivos históricos sobre las incidencias de lo sucedido en los procesamientos en el servidor. Estos archivos son las principales entradas que luego se utilizan para los procesos de entrenamiento en las técnicas de aprendizaje automático. El desempeño del CPU mejoró con el uso de aprendizaje automático en características como la cantidad de ciclos de reloj ejecutadas por unidad de tiempo, los cambios de contexto necesarios para realizar una tarea y la velocidad de ejecución de procesos.

– **Infraestructura**: la capa de infraestructura reportó grandes esfuerzos por mejorar el desempeño de los balanceadores de carga. Ubicar el servidor más libre para atender una petición de usuario, un manejo de caché compartido entre servidores, y la homogeneización de peticiones de usuario para facilitar su almacenamiento en caché a través de *proxys*, son algunos de estos esfuerzos. Además, otros enfoques como el despliegue en la nube de aplicaciones web reportaron mejoras en factores como la elasticidad para encender y apagar nodos que resuelvan peticiones de usuario según sea el tráfico que recibe la aplicación en un momento dado.

Finalmente, la Figura 4 presenta la tendencia en el tiempo (del año 2000 al 2019) de los estudios realizados para mejorar el rendimiento por capa de aplicación De esta figura se observa que tanto la capa de *back-end* como la de infraestructura han tenido una cantidad constante de estudios a través del tiempo.

6 Conclusiones

Este artículo presentó un mapeo sistemático de literatura sobre el uso de aprendizaje automático para mejorar el rendimiento de las aplicaciones web. Se analizaron 37 estudios primarios, obteniendo como principales hallazgos: 26 técnicas utilizadas para la mejora del rendimiento, 24 indicadores para evaluar el rendimiento de las aplicaciones web, y 3 capas de aplicación y 10 áreas donde se aplicaron las mejoras.

Los indicadores mapeados en este estudio evalúan la actuación de una aplicación web tanto en sus tiempos del *Back-end* como del *Front-end*. El total de 24 indicadores de rendimiento ubicados abordan temas muy heterogéneos entre sí, estos van desde una efectiva utilización de caché, hasta una infraestructura óptima de servidores para recibir y responder eficientemente las peticiones que recibe una aplicación web.

Se ubicaron dos grandes conjuntos de técnicas de aprendizaje automático que se clasifican de acuerdo al tipo de problema que resuelven. Por ejemplo, problemas de clasificación son abordados primordialmente por algoritmos como las Máquinas de soporte vectorial, mientras que para problemas de decisión se prefieren algoritmos como los Arboles de decisión.

En total se ubicaron 26 algoritmos de aprendizaje atomatizado empleados para mejorar el desempeño de aplicaciones en Internet. Estos algoritmos son empleados en distintas de las capas que componen estas aplicaciones. La forma en la que se midió la mejora al emplear estos algoritmos fue mediante el uso de métricas de rendimiento, también reportadas en este estudio. La capa de infraestructura, junto con la capa del *back-end*, fueron las que recibieron más esfuerzos para la mejora de rendimiento. Es por esto que en los equipos de desarrollo de *software* siempre se debe tomar en cuenta tanto la velocidad de los procesos ejecutados, como la infraestructura donde corren estos procesos, para así obtener el máximo desempeño de una aplicación web a partir de acciones que la potencien desde el momento que esta es liberada al ambiente de producción.

Las principal limitación enfrentada fue clasificar las métricas de evaluación reportadas en los estudios primarios. La forma en la que algunos estudios reportaron las métricas no tuvo el detalle necesario para reconocerla como una métrica que aún no se reportaba, o si era la reiteración de una métrica ya contabilizada en el estudio. Por ello es que en varias oportunidades hubo un análisis más contextual alrededor de la métrica para saber cómo documentarla adecuadamente, lo cuál hizo que se demorara un poco más de tiempo para esta labor.

Como trabajo a futuro se plantea una pregunta de investigación que estudie herramientas para evaluar desempeño de las aplicaciones web. Durante este mapeo se vio la utilidad de herramientas como *Web Page Test*, *Lighthouse* o *SpeedCurve*, para el proceso de toma de métricas en una aplicación web. Sería de mucho provecho ahondar en las herramientas existentes, su respectiva comparación a nivel general, así como un análisis a detalle de cada una de ellas.

Finalmente, es grato identificar esfuerzos que se están llevando a cabo para mejorar el rendimiento en aplicaciones web, los cuales se traducen en mejores productos lanzados a Internet y mayor acogida de estos por parte de sus visitantes.

Referencias

1. A. Bleicher. (2011) A memory of webs past. [Online]. Available: https://spectrum.ieee.org/tech-history/cyberspace/a-memory-of-webs-past
2. J. Chadwick, T. Snyder, and H. Panda, *Programming ASP.NET MVC 4: Developing Real-World Web Applications with ASP.NET MVC*, 1st ed. O'Reilly Media, Inc., 2012.
3. S. Shalev-Shwartz and S. Ben-David, *Understanding Machine Learning: From Theory to Algorithms*, 2014.
4. Z. Kazhmaganbetova, S. Imangaliyev, and A. Sharipbay, "Machine learning for the communication optimization in distributed systems," *International Journal of Engineering and Technology(UAE)*, vol. 7, pp. 47–50, 09 2018.
5. S. Pradeep and Y. K. Sharma, "A pragmatic evaluation of stress and performance testing technologies for web based applications," in *2019 Amity International Conference on Artificial Intelligence (AICAI)*, Feb 2019, pp. 399–403.
6. M. Arslan, U. Qamar, S. Hassan, and S. Ayub, "Automatic performance analysis of cloud based load testing of web-application amp; its comparison with traditional load testing," in *2015 6th IEEE International Conference on Software Engineering and Service Science (ICSESS)*, Sep. 2015, pp. 140–144.
7. C. Wohlin, P. Runeson, M. Höst, M. C. Ohlsson, B. Regnell, and A. Wesslén, *Planning*. Berlin, Heidelberg: Springer Berlin Heidelberg, 2012, pp. 89–116. [Online]. Available: https://doi.org/10.1007/978-3-642-29044-2_8
8. K. BA and S. Charters, "Guidelines for performing systematic literature reviews in software engineering," vol. 2, 01 2007.
9. J. J. Marciniak, Ed., *Encyclopedia of Software Engineering*. New York, NY, USA: Wiley-Interscience, 1994.
10. M. Pai, M. McCulloch, J. D. Gorman, N. P. Pai, W. T. A. Enanoria, G. E. Kennedy, P. Tharyan, and J. M. Colford, "Systematic reviews and meta-analyses: an illustrated, step-by-step guide." *The National medical journal of India*, vol. 17 2, pp. 86–95, 2004.
11. R. Viscomi, A. Davies, and M. Duran, *Using WebPageTest: Web Performance Testing for Novices and Power Users*, 1st ed. O'Reilly Media, Inc., 2015.

Perfil Operacional do Software: investigando aplicabilidades específicas

Luiz Cavamura Júnior[1], Sandra Fabbri[1], and Auri M. R. Vincenzir[1]

Departamento de Computação, Universidade Federal de São Carlos (UFSCar)
São Carlos, Brasil
{luiz_cavamura,sfabbri,auri}@ufscar.br

Resumo O Perfil Operacional do Software (*POS*) é uma representação da maneira como os usuários usam o software, na qual as operações, executada pelo software, são associadas a uma probabilidade de ocorrência. Sendo a confiabilidade de um software dependente do contexto no qual ele é usado, o *POS* é empregado na engenharia de confiabilidade de software. Os resultados obtidos pela realização de um Mapeamento Sistemático da Literatura (*MSL*) evidenciaram que a Qualidade de Software é a área mais favorecida pelas contribuições providas pelo uso do *POS* no processo de desenvolvimento de software. Contudo, poucos foram os estudos selecionados associados à essa área, caracterizando-a, junto às demais áreas, como uma área que pode ser explorada. Esses resultados motivaram a realização de uma Revisão Sistemática da Literatura (*RSL*) que investigou o uso do *POS* como um critério de avaliação para casos de uso existentes, ou seja, sob a perspectiva de uso do software, e como um critério de priorização aplicável à artefatos e atividades inerentes ao processo de desenvolvimento de software. Como o *POS* representa a maneira como o software é operado pelos usuários e o teste de regressão é realizado quando há modificações no software, podendo ocorrer enquanto o software está em operação, o uso do *POS* em atividades de teste de regressão também foi investigado. O propósito deste artigo é prover, como contribuições, os resultados obtidos pela *RSL* realizada. Por meio dos resultados obtidos, constatou-se que, sendo um recurso adotado para determinar a confiabilidade do software, o *POS* é usado em técnicas de teste estatístico e de regressão para gerar, selecionar e priorizar os casos de teste. O uso do *POS* em outros contextos de teste e com outros propósitos não têm sido explorado. Constatou-se, também, que por ser um recurso usado em tais técnicas, informações detalhadas sobre o *POS* são escassas. Os resultados obtidos permitiram, também, caracterizar o uso do *POS* nas situações investigadas.

Keywords: Perfil Operacional · Revisão Sistemática · Qualidade de Software · Teste de Software · Perfil de Teste.

1 Introdução

A necessidade de processos eficientes faz com que as organizações estejam empenhadas na melhoria desses processos. O software é um elemento estratégico nesses processos e, assim, pode ter recursos que permitam ser parametrizado para se adaptar às diversificadas maneiras de operação, atendendo às necessidades específicas de cada organização. Nesse contexto, visando a praticidade e eficiência em suas atividades, usuários experientes conseguem adaptar a maneira como o software é operado [24]. Como a qualidade do software é dependente do seu uso operacional [8], a maneira como o software é operado torna-se relevante ao processo de desenvolvimento de software. O Perfil Operacional do Software (*POS*) corresponde a uma especificação do software que representa a maneira como o software é operado por seus usuários [8,24]. Musa [16] define o *POS* como uma caracterização quantitativa do software. Essa caracterização é baseada nas operações do software, para as quais uma distribuição probabilística é atribuída para indicar as partes do software mais usadas pelos usuários.

Dada a relevância do *POS* ao processo de desenvolvimento de software, este trabalho relata a realização de uma Revisão Sistemática da Literatura (*RSL*) que investigou o uso do *POS* sob três perspectivas (situações de uso): em atividades associadas ao teste de regressão (SU_1); como um critério de priorização aplicável a artefatos e atividades inerentes ao processo de desenvolvimento de software (SU_2); e como um critério de avaliação para casos de teste existentes (SU_3). As situações de uso investigas pela *RSL* foram definidas e estão associadas a uma pesquisa de doutoramento que investiga o *POS* em um escopo mais amplo [5]. A investigação do uso do *POS* em técnicas de teste de regressão foi motivada pela natureza do teste de regressão, o qual é executado quando modificações são feitas em um software existente [28]. No momento em que o teste de regressão é realizado, o software pode fornecer dados sobre a maneira como é operado por seus usuários. O *POS*, por representar a maneira como o software é operado pelos usuários, corresponde a um critério de priorização baseado no uso. A investigação do uso do *POS* como critério de priorização busca identificar outras atividades e recursos que podem adotar o *POS* como um critério de priorização. A investigação do uso do *POS* como um critério de avaliação dos testes existentes, gerados por outros critérios, foi definida em decorrência do possível descompasso entre as partes testadas do software e o *POS* [6]. O uso do *POS* como critério de priorização e avaliação são exemplos de uso que podem contribuir com a qualidade do software do ponto de vista dos usuários e, também, ser usado para priorizar atividades do processo de desenvolvimento do software de maior interesse do usuário, tais como manutenção, melhorias e customizações.

Este trabalho provê, como contribuições, a partir dos resultados obtidos, uma base de conhecimento sobre o uso do *POS* nos contextos investigados, fornecendo uma caracterização e entendimento quanto ao uso do *POS* nesses contextos. Este trabalho está organizado da seguinte forma: na Seção 2, os conceitos que envolvem o *POS* e a qualidade de software são abordados. A Seção 3 refere-se aos trabalhos relacionados. A Seção 4 descreve a metodologia adotada para a realização da pesquisa. As Seções 5, 6, 7, 8 e 9 descrevem a *RSL* realizada e os respectivos resultados. As ameaças à validade deste trabalho e as conclusões são apresentadas nas Seções 10 e 11 respectivamente.

2 *POS* e a Qualidade de Software

Por representar a maneira como o software será utilizado por seus usuários e sendo a confiabilidade de um software dependente do contexto em que o software é usado, o *POS* é usado em atividades relacionadas a engenharia de confiabilidade de software. Nessas atividades, o *POS* é usado para gerar dados de teste que reproduzem a maneira com a qual o software é operado pelos usuários, garantindo que os indicadores de confiabilidade do software sejam válidos para a operação do software em um ambiente de produção [17]. A confiabilidade do software é um dos atributos associados à qualidade de software e a representa a partir do ponto de vista do usuário [4,15]. Para o usuário do software, a frequência com que uma falha se torna aparente, durante a operação do software, é mais significante que as falhas remanescentes [26]. A confiabilidade do software corresponde a probabilidade de operação do software, por um determinado tempo, em um ambiente específico, sem a ocorrência de falhas [8,15]. Sendo a confiabilidade determinada pelo tempo da operação do software sem a ocorrência de falhas, e que uma falha revelada a um usuário pode não ser revelada no modo de trabalho de outro usuário, a atividade de teste está implícita à confiabilidade do software. O *POS* não garante que todos os defeitos sejam detectados, mas garante que as operações mais utilizadas do software sejam testadas.

Um Mapeamento Sistemático da Literatura (*MSL*) investigou como as contribuições providas pelos estudos que abordaram o uso do *POS* estão distribuídas nas áreas da engenharia de software correlatas ao processo de desenvolvimento de software, evidenciando que a qualidade de software é a área mais abordada pelos estudos que usaram o *POS* como um recurso nas estratégias abordadas nesses estudos. A maioria dessas estratégias estão associadas à confiabilidade de software. Embora a qualidade de software seja a área mais abordada, são poucos os estudos relacionados a essa área, situação que à caracteriza, junto às demais áreas identificadas, como uma área que pode ser explorada. A descrição detalhada do *MSL* realizado, e dos respectivos resultados, está disponível em: lcvm.com.br/artigos/anexos/cibse2020/cap-3-rs-ms.pdf.

3 Trabalhos Relacionados

Dentre os trabalhos selecionados pelo *MSL*, Smidts et al. [23] forneceram uma caracterização do modelo baseado no *POS* usado na geração de casos de teste, assemelhando-se a este trabalho dada a abordagem investigativa focada diretamente no *POS*. Os demais trabalhos usaram o *POS* como um recurso às estratégias propostas, não fornecendo, detalhadamente, informações sobre o *POS*. A caracterização, provida em [23], foi obtida por meio de mapeamentos sistemáticos e análises qualitativas. Os dados extraídos foram estruturados e classificados. A classificação desses dados forneceu uma taxonomia que diferencia e analisa os modelos baseados no *POS* sob várias perspectivas: características comuns entre os modelos, dependências necessárias à elaboração dos modelos, características do software sob teste usadas pelos modelos, dentre outros.

Constatou-se, por meio dos resultados obtidos em [23], que uma variedade de modelos baseados no *POS* podem ser construídos, sendo a definição e complexidade do modelo dependente do contexto de aplicação do software sob teste. Embora as classificações e a taxonomia desenvolvidas proveem uma compreensão e perspectivas sobre o uso do *POS* [23], por abordar especificamente os modelos de representação aplicados para a geração de casos de teste, o estudo não provê informações detalhadas sobre a obtenção do *POS*. O uso do *POS* associado a outras finalidades também não foi explorado em [23]. A *RSL* descrita neste trabalho investiga o uso do *POS* em situações de uso específicas, fornecendo, por meio da abordagem investigativa adotada, informações não providas pelo estudo realizado por Smidts et al. [23].

4 Metodologia

Foram definidas 4 questões de pesquisa cuja consecução das respostas proveem a investigação sobre o uso do *POS* nas situações descritas na seção anterior. A Tabela 1 apresenta as questões de pesquisa que foram definidas, aplicáveis às situações de uso do *POS* investigadas.

Tabela 1. Questões de pesquisa

Q_i	Descrição
Q_1	Como o *POS* foi usado nas técnicas identificadas nos estudos selecionados?
Q_2	Como o *POS* foi obtido pelas técnicas identificadas?
Q_3	Como o *POS* foi caracterizado pelas técnicas identificadas?
Q_4	Relacionado ao uso do *POS*, quais foram as dificuldades reportadas pelos estudos selecionados?

Para obter respostas às questões de pesquisa, a investigação foi feita por meio de uma *RSL* sucedida pela técnica *snowballing*(*backward* e *forward*). Para a realização dessas atividades, a metodologia de pesquisa proposta em [25] foi instanciada. A Figura 1 ilustra essa metodologia.

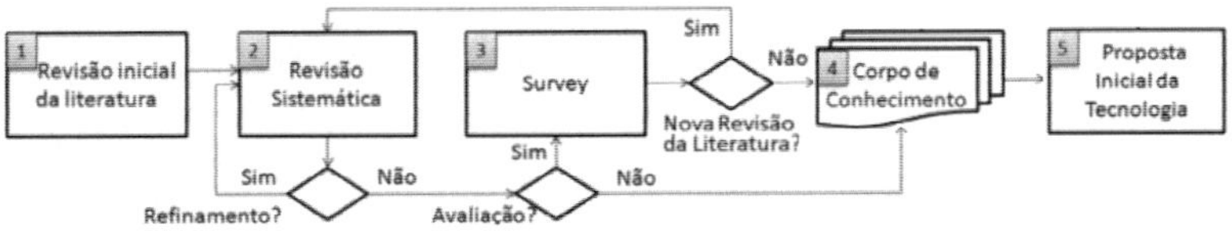

Figura 1. Representação da metodologia adotada. Adaptado de [25]

A etapa inicial (1), denominada "Revisão inicial da literatura", consiste em coletar informações básicas a respeito do tema a ser pesquisado, necessárias para a elaboração do protocolo da *RSL*. A etapa seguinte (2) compreende o planejamento e execução da *RSL* a qual, dependendo da análise dos resultados obtidos, pode ser refinada. Após a realização da *RSL*, opcionalmente, em decorrência de possíveis questionamentos que podem surgir sobre o conhecimento obtido, um *survey* (*Etapa 3*) pode ser realizado, o qual consiste em submeter o conhecimento adquirido à uma avaliação de especialistas. As duas etapas finais da metodologia (4 e 5) compreendem, respectivamente, à estruturação e consolidação do conhecimento adquirido, tornando-se a base para a idealização de novas tecnologias.

Para este trabalho, a *Etapa 1* usou os resultados do *MSL* citado na Seção 2. A *Etapa 2* refere-se à execução da *RSL* seguida pela execução da técnica *snowballing*. Referente à *Etapa 3*, o conhecimento adquirido na *Etapa 2*, realizada pelo primeiro autor, foi submetido a uma avaliação de outros pesquisadores, demais autores deste trabalho. Na *Etapa 4*, os dados obtidos pela *RSL* foram estruturados, permitindo obter respostas às questões de pesquisa e, assim, prover as contribuições esperadas para este trabalho. Essas contribuições servem como dados de entrada para a *Etapa 5*, a qual não foi abordada neste trabalho.

A *RSL* foi conduzida por um processo composto por três fases [18]: Planejamento, Condução e Publicação. O paradigma *GQM* (*Goal, Question, Metric*) foi adotado como referência para o planejamento da *RSL*. A ferramenta computacional *Start*, cuja finalidade, é prover apoio, ao pesquisador, na realização de revisões sistemáticas da literatura [9], foi usada para dar suporte à realização da *RSL*.

5 Planejamento

A *RSL* foi guiada por um protocolo no qual as diretrizes da pesquisa foram definidas. As subseções seguintes apresentam uma síntese desse protocolo.

5.1 Questões de pesquisa

O paradigma *GQM* foi adaptado para, a partir dos propósitos da pesquisa, estruturar as questões de pesquisa, identificando os dados a serem extraídos dos estudos selecionados para prover as repostas às respectivas questões. A Figura 2 ilustra, na estrutura do paradigma *GQM*, o objetivo, as questões de pesquisa e os dados a serem obtidos.

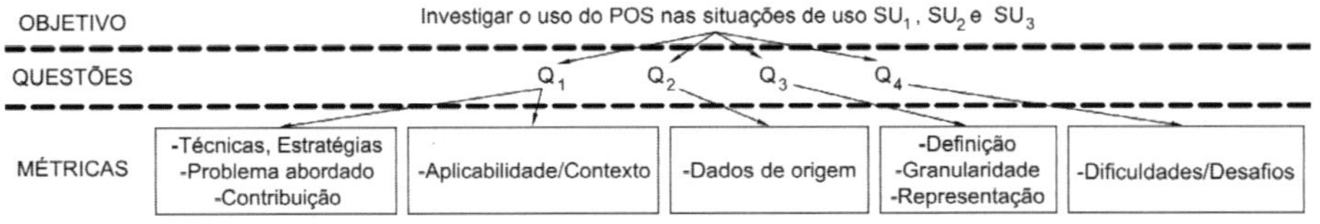

Figura 2. GQM referente ao planejamento da *RSL*

Conforme ilustrado pela Figura 2, o objetivo da *RSL* corresponde ao *Goal*, as questões de pesquisa correspondem ao *Question* e os dados a serem extraídos, dos estudos selecionados, correspondem ao *Metric*.

5.2 Grupo de controle e critérios de seleção de estudos

Foram considerados, como grupo de controle, os estudos [2] e [16]. O estudo [2] evidencia, por meio dos resultados apresentados, que informações sobre como o software é operado por seus usuários são relevantes ao processo de desenvolvimento de software. O estudo [16] refere-se a abordagem de Musa sobre o *POS*, a qual é uma das mais relevantes abordagens para a construção do *POS*. A ocorrência desses estudos, como grupo de controle, foi verificada no conjunto de estudos identificados pela *RSL* e, também, nas respectivas referências bibliográficas desses estudos. A Tabela 2 apresenta os critérios de inclusão (I) e exclusão (E) usados para a seleção dos estudos.

Tabela 2. Critérios de inclusão e exclusão

	Critério
I	O estudo usa o *POS* em teste de regressão
I	O estudo usa o *POS* como critério de priorização
I	O estudo foca no *POS* e suas características
I	O estudo usa o *POS* em técnica/estratégia para avaliar casos de teste
E	O estudo não usa o *POS* em teste de regressão
E	O estudo não aborda o teste de regressão
E	O estudo não aborda o *POS* e suas características
E	O estudo não usa o *POS* como critério de priorização
E	O estudo aborda o *POS* porém o *POS* não é usado em técnica/estratégia para avaliar casos de teste
E	O estudo aborda a avaliação de casos de teste porém não usa o *POS*

5.3 *String* de busca

As *keywords* iniciais, relacionadas ao *POS*, foram obtidas pelo *MSL* citado na Seção 2, definindo uma *string* de busca inicial. A *string* de busca inicial foi usada em um estudo piloto para identificar novas *keywords*. Os estudos, referentes ao resultado retornado pelo estudo piloto, foram registrados na ferramenta computacional *Start*. Dentre suas funcionalidades, a *Start* fornece uma lista das *keywords* detectadas nos estudos registrados, classificando-as como "usadas"ou "não usadas"na *string* de busca, e ordenando-as pela frequência com que cada uma é empregada nos estudos registrados [9]. As *keywords* consideradas relevantes foram identificadas e incorporadas à *string* de busca inicial, dando origem a uma nova versão da *string* de busca, iniciando-se, assim, uma iteratividade na execução do estudo piloto. Essa iteratividade foi processada enquanto novas *keywords* eram identificadas.

Após a definição das *keywords* relacionadas ao *POS* (S_{pos}), novas *keywords* para tratar a especificidade de cada situação de uso do *POS* investigada foram adicionadas. As *strings* de busca, relacionadas às respectivas situações de uso do *POS* a serem investigadas ($SU_{1,2,3}$), foram construídas a partir das *keywords* e do uso dos operadores lógicos "*and*" ($\wedge$) e "*or*" ($\vee$). As *strings* de busca são mostradas na Tabela 3.

Tabela 3. *Strings* de busca

String de Busca	SU
("operational profile" $\vee$ "usage model" $\vee$ "usage profile" $\vee$ "user profile" $\vee$ "users profile" $\vee$ "profile of use" $\vee$ "usage testing" $\vee$ "input distribution" $\vee$ "usage distribution" $\vee$ "operational distribution" $\vee$ "usage chain")	S_{pos}
("regression") $\wedge$ ("software") $\wedge$ ("testing" $\vee$ "test") $\wedge$ S_{pos}	SU_1
("prioritization" $\vee$ "prioritize") $\wedge$ S_{pos}	SU_2
("effectiveness" $\vee$ "efficiency" $\vee$ "evaluation") $\wedge$ S_{pos}	SU_3

6 Condução

As fontes de informação selecionadas foram *Scopus*, *ACM Digital Library*, *IEEE Xplore*, *SpringerLink*, *ScienceDirect*, *Engineering Village* e *Web of Science*. A identificação dos estudos foi feita por meio de busca automática nas fontes de informação usadas, identificando, para as situações de uso investigadas SU_1, SU_2 e SU_3, respectivamente, 130, 86 e 214 estudos. A identificação e seleção de estudos foram realizadas separadamente, não havendo dependência entre as situações de uso investigadas. Na fase de seleção, dos estudos identificados, foram selecionados os estudos em que no título, resumo ou palavras-chaves, foram identificados ao menos um dos critérios de inclusão definidos. Na fase de extração, foram mantidos os estudos que, após a leitura completa e análise desses estudos, mantiverem ao menos um dos critérios de inclusão atribuídos. Os critérios de inclusão sobrepõe os critérios de exclusão. Do total de estudos identificados, 9 estudos foram selecionados para a fase de extração de dados. Esses estudos foram submetidos a técnica *snowballing*, identificando 214 novos estudos para a situação de uso SU_1. Para as situações de uso SU_2 e SU_3, a técnica *snowballing* identificou, respectivamente 46 e 184 novos estudos. Dos 444 novos estudos identificados pela técnica *snowballing*, 2 estudos foram adicionados à fase de extração de dados, totalizando, para a extração de dados, 11 estudos. A Figura 3 mostra a quantidade de estudos processados em cada etapa da *RSL*.

7 Qualidade dos Estudos Selecionados

A cada estudo selecionado na *RSL*, um indicador, cujo valor varia entre 0 e 1, foi atribuído visando quantificar a relevância do estudo aos propósitos deste trabalho. O indicador corresponde ao valor da média aritmética dos valores atribuídos às questões de avaliação para cada estudo selecionado. Quanto maior o valor do indicador, maior é a relevância do estudo com base na avaliação da qualidade do estudo. Dada a abordagem investigativa e exploratória deste trabalho, não foi definido um valor mínimo a ser obtido pelos estudos selecionados. A Tabela 4 apresenta as questões avaliativas, a motivação que deu origem a questão e os valores que podem ser atribuídos à questão.

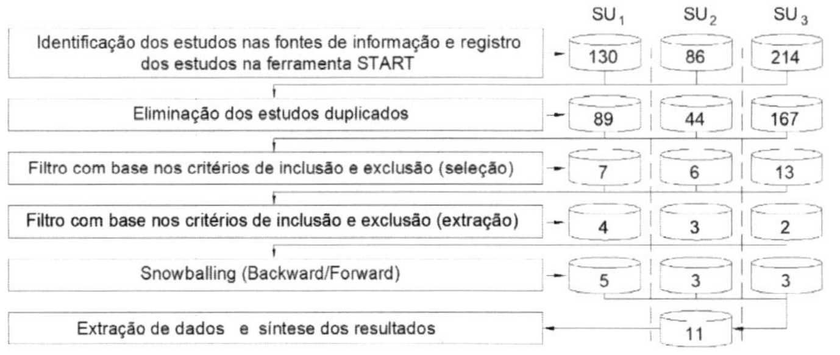

Figura 3. Quantitativo de estudos processados

Tabela 4. Questões avaliativas da qualidade dos estudos

Questão	Motivação	Valor
1-Os estudos selecionados citam estudos publicados pelos autores dos estudos de controle?	Citações de estudos publicados pelos autores dos estudos de controle são indícios de que o estudo selecionado tenha maior relevância em relação aos demais estudos	Entre 0 e 1 (conforme a quantidade de autores, dos estudos de controle, citados)
2-Qual o número de citações, em outros estudos, do estudo selecionado?	O número de citações do estudo selecionado evidencia a abrangência do estudo em contextos relacionados ao abordado neste trabalho	Entre 0 e 1 (conforme o número de citações do estudo selecionado)
3-O estudo selecionado tem o POS como foco principal da pesquisa ou relata o uso do perfil operacional?	Estudos cuja abordagem relata o uso do *POS* estão diretamente relacionados aos propósitos deste trabalho	0 ou 1 conforme a abordagem dada ao *POS* (Relata o uso do *POS*: 1; Foco nos conceitos do *POS*: 0,5)

8 Resultados Obtidos

A *RSL*, sucedida pela técnica *snowballing*, resultou em 11 estudos selecionados para a fase de extração de dados. A Tabela 5 apresenta esses estudos associados às situações de uso investigadas ($SU_{1,2,3}$).

Tabela 5. Estudos selecionados para a extração de dados

SU	Extração de dados
SU_1	Whittaker et al. [27], Takagi et al. [26], Kashyap [11], Sarwar et al. [22], Rogstad and Briand [21]
SU_2	Marijan et al. [13], Miranskyy et al. [14], Nakornburi and Suwannasart [19]
SU_3	Amrita and Yadav [1], Bertolino et al. [3], Chen et al. [7], Takagi et al. [26]

Observa-se que o estudo [26] foi identificado e selecionado nas investigações das situações de uso SU_1 e SU_3. As subseções seguintes apresentam, para cada situação de uso investigada, uma síntese desses estudos e, também, uma caracterização do uso do *POS* obtida por meio dos dados extraídos.

8.1 Uso do *POS* em técnicas de teste de regressão (SU_1)

Os estudos [22] e [21] abordam a seleção e priorização de casos de teste. Para Sarwar et al. [22], a execução de todos os planos de teste (manuais e automatizados) é uma atividade cansativa que consome tempo, custo e pode não ser efetiva na descoberta, antecipadamente, de defeitos críticos. Assim, é necessário selecionar poucos, porém relevantes, casos de teste a partir de uma massa de teste. Para isso, é proposta uma técnica para priorizar casos de teste aplicada a processos de desenvolvimento de software gerenciados pelo método organizacional *Scrum*. A técnica representa o *POS* por meio da frequência com a qual os casos de teste são executados durante o teste de regressão. Os casos de teste são priorizados por meio de um indicador quantitativo atribuído a cada caso de teste. O indicador é calculado considerando-se a frequência de execução do caso de teste, o número de falhas detectadas pelo caso de teste e a criticidade atribuída ao caso de teste.

Rogstad and Briand [21] realizaram uma investigação empírica sobre estratégias para a seleção e geração de dados de teste para técnicas de teste combinatório em nível de teste de regressão. A investigação foi realizada em um ambiente de desenvolvimento de uma aplicação persistente real e representativa. Essa investigação foi motivada pela demanda de tempo e esforço dos testadores decorrentes do uso de dados obtidos em um ambiente de produção do software (dados reais) nas atividades de teste. O uso de dados obtidos em ambiente de produção é uma estratégia comum em atividades de teste, porém, esses dados nem sempre satisfazem os requisitos do plano de teste, forçando os testadores a manipularem ou estenderem os dados de produção para torna-los adequados. O *POS* do software é usado adicionalmente em uma das técnicas de teste aplicadas na investigação, gerando um conjunto de testes alinhado com o uso do software.

Em decorrência dos problemas inerentes às tecnologias existentes, tais como a demanda de esforço e uso de técnicas *ad-hoc*, os quais geram uma alta quantidade de caminhos e cenários de teste que não refletem o uso real do software, Kashyap [11] apresenta uma abordagem para criação de modelo de comportamento que permite a geração e priorização automática dos casos de teste com base em dados de uso do software. Nessa abordagem, é criado um modelo de comportamento que permite a geração e priorização automática dos casos de teste com base em dados de uso do software.

Para Takagi et al. [26], métodos existentes baseados em teste de regressão não são apropriados para avaliar a confiabilidade do software. Takagi et al. [26] apresentam uma técnica que avalia a confiabilidade do software como parte do processo de manutenção, estimando e prevendo falhas que influenciarão na confiabilidade das próximas versões do software. A técnica gera um modelo de teste a partir do *POS*. Os resultados obtidos pela execução dos testes são mapeados no modelo de teste criado. Quando uma falha é detectada, um estado, que representa a falha, é inserido no modelo de teste e associada aos estados que representam as operações nas quais a falha foi detectada. O modelo de teste é usado para determinar o critério de parada dos testes, podendo ser determinado pela cobertura dos estados ou transições que compõe o modelo de teste, pelo número de transições incidentes nos estados de falha ou pelo número de falhas detectadas e mapeadas no modelo de teste.

Segundo Whittaker et al. [27], as estimativas de confiabilidade são obtidas por meio de modelos de probabilidade construídos a partir de dados coletados durante a realização dos testes e, assim, situações de falha são tratadas assumindo-se que obedecem uma regra de probabilidade, permitindo, a partir disso, estimar e prever futuras ocorrências de falhas. Essa abordagem fornece uma análise precisa quando a distribuição probabilística tem suporte empírico e os testes cobriram grande parte do software, porém, quando não há suporte empírico e os recursos de teste são escassos, outras abordagens são necessárias [27]. Whittaker et al. [27] propõem uma estratégia para a detecção de defeitos na manutenção do software. A estratégia proposta combina dados e resultados de testes passados com dados atuais em um único modelo de uso. Com base no modelo de uso, padrões de ocorrência de falhas são identificados para prever os resultados dos testes na próxima compilação do software.

8.2 Uso do *POS* como um critério de priorização (SU_2)

Segundo Marijan et al. [13], à medida que a complexidade de um software aumenta, a qualidade do sistema é submetida a um potencial decréscimo. Para tratar essa situação, é proposta uma metodologia para verificação automática de sistemas multimídia compreendendo a modelagem do comportamento do sistema, a geração de casos de teste baseados no modelo criado e a execução automática dos casos de teste gerados [13]. A modelagem do *POS* é baseada na especificação do sistema e em dados coletados durante a operação do sistema pelos usuários. As sequencias de transições do modelo uso dão origem aos casos de teste a serem executados. Os resultados dos testes são analisados para avaliar a confiabilidade do software.

Os dados de uso coletados dos clientes fornecem informações quantitativas valiosas sobre os padrões de uso do software. Para Miranskyy et al. [14], reunir esses perfis a partir de um grande conjunto de clientes demanda tempo e recursos. Assim, Miranskyy et al. [14] propõem uma técnica para a seleção e priorização de um conjunto mínimo de clientes a serem considerados na elaboração do *POS*, tendo, como objetivo, prover, na execução dos testes, uma cobertura para determinados conjuntos de defeitos. A técnica proposta, inicialmente, classifica e prioriza os clientes com base no histórico e tipos defeitos reportados por eles. Após a classificação e priorização dos clientes por meio de uma análise qualitativa, a técnica seleciona, para a criação do *POS*, um conjunto mínimo de clientes que tenham descoberto o maior número de defeitos. A seleção manual desse conjunto pode ser inviável. Assim, para se obter o conjunto mínimo de clientes, a priorização dos clientes, feita de maneira qualitativa, é transformada em quantitativa adotando-se o algoritmo de programação inteira binária.

Nakornburi and Suwannasart [19] relatam o desenvolvimento de uma ferramenta computacional para gerar casos de teste usando técnicas de teste combinatório e o *POS*. O *POS* é usado para priorizar e selecionar um conjunto ideal de parâmetros de entrada e os respectivos valores para os casos de teste gerados pela ferramenta proposta.

8.3 Uso do *POS* como um critério de avaliação (SU_3)

Segundo Amrita and Yadav [1], muitos pesquisadores abordam a seleção de casos de teste com base no *POS*, porém, pouco é discutido sobre as partes infrequentes. Amrita and Yadav [1] propõem um modelo que fornece a flexibilidade de alocar casos de teste conforme a prioridade definida pelo *POS* e, também, pela experiência do testador. Assim, o modelo proposto considera tanto a probabilidade de ocorrência quanto a severidade da operação. Com base nessas informações, usando lógica *fuzzy*, o modelo propõe a seleção de casos de teste. O modelo usa a criticidade atribuída às operações do software e o *POS* como variáveis de entrada para um sistema de inferências *fuzzy*. Assim, as operações do software são classificadas em: operação frequente e crítica; operação frequente e não crítica; operação infrequente e crítica; operação infrequente e não crítica. O valor da variável de saída, a ser obtido pelo sistema de inferências *fuzzy*, corresponde ao número de casos de teste a serem alocados para a operação. Fornecidas as variáveis de entrada e definidas as regras *fuzzy*, é obtido um conjunto *fuzzy* resultante que, após a geração, com base nas variações adotadas, é *desfuziado* para se obter os valores equivalentes e, consequentemente, a quantidade sugerida de casos de teste a serem alocados em cada operação.

Segundo Bertolino et al. [3], o teste baseado no *POS*, por focar nas falhas com maior probabilidade de ocorrência, pode sofrer saturação e, assim, perder eficácia na detecção de falhas. Nesse contexto, uma técnica de teste de software adaptativa e iterativa, baseada no *POS*, denominada *covrel*, é proposta por Bertolino et al. [3]. A técnica proposta é executada iterativamente. Na primeira iteração, a técnica usa o *POS* para selecionar e executar os casos de teste randomicamente, com base na probabilidade de ocorrência das partições do domínio de entrada do programa. Nas iterações seguintes, a cada iteração, a técnica calcula, para cada partição: (*i*) a quantidade de casos de teste ideal a serem selecionados; (*ii*) seleciona, prioriza e executa a quantidade de casos de teste calculada. Para determinar a quantidade ideal de casos de teste, uma probabilidade é obtida para representar o quanto o teste da partição contribui com a confiabilidade do programa. A seleção e priorização dos casos de teste é feita com base na frequência com que as partes do programa são exercitadas durante a execução dos testes nas iterações anteriores. Como o foco da abordagem é selecionar casos de teste que cobrem partes do programa que são pouco exercitadas, casos de teste associados às partes do programa pouco exercitadas têm maior prioridade.

Quando um conjunto de testes não detecta novas falhas, o uso desses testes, ou similares, pode superestimar a confiabilidade do software. Assim, quanto mais redundantes forem os casos de teste em relação ao código coberto, mais superestimada será a confiabilidade do software. Nesse contexto, Chen et al. [7] propõem uma técnica que determina uma taxa de compressão que ajusta o intervalo de tempo entre as falhas quando são detectados casos de teste redundantes durante a execução do conjunto de teste. Para obter a taxa de compressão são considerados o tempo de execução do conjunto de teste, a cobertura de código provida e, também, a detecção de casos de testes redundantes no conjunto de teste.

8.4 Caracterização do uso do *POS* nos estudos selecionados

A Tabela 6 mostra, a partir dos dados extraídos dos estudos selecionados (Tabela 5), uma caracterização do uso do *POS* nesses estudos.

Tabela 6. Questões avaliativas da qualidade dos estudos

	Granularidade adotada para o POS				Origem do POS						Representação do POS			Aplicabilidade						Atividade-fim que usou o POS					Artefato	
Referência	Dados de Entrada	Operações	Casos de teste	Clientes	Arquivos de *log*	Projetos anteriores	Histórico de uso do software	Conjunto de teste	Observação dos usuários	Não especificado	Registro de frequência de uso da granularidade adotada	Modelo de uso contendo distribuição probabilística	Não se aplica	Teste combinatório	Teste de regressão	Teste randômico	Teste baseado em modelo	Teste de confiabilidade	Não especificado	Geração	Seleção	Priorização	Estimativa	Adequação	Casos de teste	Dados do cliente
[19]	X				X						X			X						X					X	
[21]	X				X							X		X	X					X					X	
[26]		X			X							X			X	X				X					X	
[11]		X								X		X							X	X		X			X	
[22]			X					X			X				X							X			X	
[13]		X				X			X			X					X			X					X	
[27]		X					X					X			X								X		X	
[14]				X						X			X						X		X					X
[3]	X									X		X					X				X	X			X	
[1]		X								X		X					X					X			X	
[7]	X									X		X		X							X	X			X	

Por meio da Tabela 6, é possível visualizar a granularidade do *POS*, as fontes de dados usadas para obter o *POS*, a maneira como o *POS* foi representado nos estudos selecionados, a atividade na qual o *POS* foi usado e os artefatos abordados pelas atividades nas quais o *POS* foi usado. A granularidade, apresentada na Tabela 6, no contexto deste trabalho, corresponde ao nível de fragmentação, conceitual ou estrutural, com a qual o software é abordado para que uma distribuição probabilística seja atribuída aos fragmentos gerados.

9 Análise dos Resultados

A análise dos resultados obtidos permitiu responder às questões de pesquisa que foram definidas na fase de planejamento da *RSL*. As questões de pesquisa com as respectivas respostas são apresentadas seguir.

(a) **Como o *POS* foi usado nas técnicas identificadas nos estudos selecionados em cada situação de uso do *POS* investigada?**

– *Uso do POS em técnicas de teste de regressão (SU_1)*: Dado que modelos de uso do software são a base do teste estatístico, as abordagens baseadas em teste estatístico são geralmente referenciadas como teste baseado em uso [11]. Assim, verificou-se, nos estudos aceitos, que o uso do *POS* é associado, geralmente, à técnicas de teste combinatório e estatístico, as quais são empregadas nas estratégias de teste de confiabilidade e de regressão. Esse cenário é entendível dado que o teste estatístico tem, como um de seus objetivos, avaliar a confiabilidade do software e o teste de regressão tem, em sua essência, validar modificações ocorridas no software, as quais podem afetar a confiabilidade do software. Em ambas as situações, dados sobre a maneira com a qual o software é operado por seus usuários são relevantes e podem ser coletados durante a operação do software. Dos 344 estudos identificados e processados para a situação de uso do *POS* SU_1, 5 estudos foram selecionados para a fase de extração: [21,26,22,27,11]. Esses estudos abordaram o uso do *POS* em sistemáticas para gerar e priorizar casos de teste.

– *Uso POS como critério de priorização (SU_2)*: Dos 132 estudos identificados e processados para a referida categoria de uso, 3 estudos foram selecionados para a fase de extração: [19,13,14]. Desses estudos, 2 estudos usaram o *POS* em sistemáticas para geração e priorização de casos de teste. Um estudo usou o *POS* em uma sistemática para selecionar e priorizar de um conjunto mínimo de clientes para a obtenção de perfis operacionais específicos para cobrir determinados conjuntos de defeitos.

– *Uso do POS como critério de avaliação de casos de teste (SU_3)*: Dos 398 estudos identificados e processados para a referida categoria de uso, 3 estudos foram selecionados para a fase de extração: [3,1,7]. Esses estudos usaram o *POS* em técnicas para avaliar os casos de teste tendo, como propósito, selecionar e priorizar casos de teste relevantes às operações a serem testadas. Desses estudos, os estudos [3,7] avaliaram os casos de teste por meio da cobertura provida por eles, sendo que, em um desses estudos, a cobertura era avaliada em relação ao *POS* e, no outro estudo, o cobertura dos casos de teste era usada como um critério de comparação para identificar casos de teste redundantes. O estudo [1] avaliou os casos de teste por meio de critérios definidos na técnica apresentada, tais como criticidade da operação testada, frequência de execução dos casos de teste e número de falhas descobertas.

Constatou-se, assim, que as técnicas identificadas trataram a obtenção e o uso do *POS* como "atividades-meio". Entende-se por "atividade-meio" uma atividade cuja execução é necessária para que a técnica proposta pelo estudo possa ser realizada ("atividade-fim"). Por ser uma "atividade-meio", poucos detalhes foram fornecidos quanto a obtenção e representação do *POS*. Verifica-se, também, pela Tabela 6, que o uso *POS* tem maior evidência nos estudos cujas técnicas apresentadas tratam a seleção e priorização de casos de teste.

(b) **Como o *POS* foi obtido pelas técnicas identificadas?**

Dados obtidos a partir de arquivos de *log*, gerados durante a operação do software, foi a estratégia com maior evidência dentre os estudos selecionados. O uso dessa estratégia foi constato nos estudos [19,21,26,13]. Informações providas pela expectativa dos desenvolvedores, por softwares similares, pela experiência em projetos anteriores e pela observação do comportamento dos usuários podem, também, contribuir para se obter o *POS* [26,13]. [26] considera, também, na inexistência de outras fontes de informação, uma distribuição probabilística uniforme para todas as transições contidas no modelo de uso que representa o *POS*. O uso da especificação dos software para a estruturação do modelo de uso que representa o *POS* é considerado em [13].

(c) **Como o *POS* é caracterizado pelas técnicas identificadas?**

Os dados extraídos dos estudos selecionados, listados na Tabela 5, permitiram caracterizar o uso do *POS* quanto à granularidade adotada para a concepção do *POS*, origem dos dados que permitiram a concepção do *POS*, a maneira como o *POS* é representado, a estratégia e técnica de teste favorecidas pelo uso do *POS* e a relação entre o uso do *POS* e a abordagem provida pelos estudo aos casos de teste (Tabela 6). Constatou-se que a granularidade adotada para se obter o *POS* não se restringe à dados de entrada, operações e os estados que o software pode assumir. Em [26,13], além das operações do software, os estados de falha assumidos pelo software também foram considerados como um nível de granularidade para a elaboração do *POS*. O *POS*, abordado em [27], foi obtido a partir da frequência de execução e quantidade de falhas descobertas pelos casos de teste do software.

(d) **Relacionado à obtenção e uso do *POS*, quais foram as dificuldades e problemas reportados pelos estudos selecionados?**

Como foi descrito, a identificação do *POS* nas técnicas identificadas é abordada como uma "atividade-meio", não fornecendo detalhes sobre a maneira como o *POS* foi obtido. Apenas Bertolino et al. [3], por se tratar do problema abordado pela técnica apresentada, relata problemas relacionados ao uso do *POS*, porém, ressalta-se que o problema apresentado em [3] não havia sido identificado na revisão informal da literatura, a qual reportou problemas relacionados a: (*i*) demanda de esforço para se obter o *POS*[20,24];(*ii*) a dificuldade em prever o uso dos software [8]; (*iii*) modificações constantes do *POS*[12]; (*iv*) probabilidade de uso, a qual torna-se pequena quando o modelo de uso possui muitos estados que representam as operações [10].

10 Ameaças à Validade

Visando diminuir a subjetividade que poderia ocorrer na avaliação dos estudos durante a realização do *RSL*, os resultados parciais, periodicamente, obtidos por um pesquisador (primeiro autor), eram submetidos a outros pesquisadores (demais autores) para a realização de uma análise informal dos resultados obtidos. A qualidade dos estudos selecionados nessas atividades também foi avaliada, porém, dada a abordagem investigativa deste trabalho, não foi definido um valor mínimo a ser obtido pelos estudos selecionados. Os resultados apresentados fazem parte de uma tese de doutoramento com escopo mais amplo [5]. Assim, a *RSL* abordou as situações de uso do *POS* relacionadas ao escopo da tese de doutoramento citada, não abrangendo o uso do *POS* em situações diferentes das investigadas.

11 Conclusões

Este artigo apresentou os resultados obtidos por *RSL* que investigou o uso do *POS* sob três perspectivas: (*i*) em atividades associadas ao teste de regressão, (*ii*) como um critério de priorização aplicável ao processo de desenvolvimento de software e (*iii*) como um critério de avaliação para casos de teste existentes. A *RSL* está associada a uma pesquisa de doutoramento que investiga um possível descompasso entre o *POS* e o Perfil de Teste [6] e as contribuições que o *POS* pode proporcionar ao teste de software, almejando melhorar a qualidade do software do ponto de vista dos usuários. Essa pesquisa propõe, como contribuição à Engenharia de Software, especificamente à área de testes, uma estratégia que que permita (*i*) adequar, dinamicamente, um conjunto de testes existente ao *POS* e, também, (*ii*) usar o *POS* como um critério de priorização que permita, dado um conjunto de defeitos, identificar os defeitos que tem maior impacto na operação do software pelos usuários e, assim, considerar esse impacto, juntamente com outros critérios, na precificação dos defeitos.

Os resultados obtidos pela *RSL* proporcionaram respostas às questões de pesquisa que foram definidas, provendo uma base de conhecimento centralizada sobre o uso do *POS* nos contextos investigados e, assim, uma caracterização e o entendimento quanto ao *POS* nas situações de uso investigadas. Verifica-se que o uso do *POS* como um critério de priorização está associado à atividade de teste, sendo usado na priorização de casos de teste. O uso do *POS* como um critério de priorização associado à outros artefatos do processo de desenvolvimento de software não é explorado. Quanto ao uso do *POS* como um critério de avaliação, verificou-se que as técnicas identificadas abordam a geração, seleção e priorização dos casos de teste por meio da análise de cobertura. O uso do *POS* como um critério de avaliação para adequar um conjunto de teste existente, que não tenha sido criado inicialmente por meio do *POS*, também não foi explorado. Assume-se, assim, que as contribuições providas por este artigo são relevantes e fornecem informações que podem contribuir e favorecer os estudos associados à Engenharia de Software e, especificamente, à área de qualidade de software.

Referências

1. Amrita, Yadav, D.K.: A novel method for allocating software test cases. In: 3rd International Conference on Recent Trends in Computing 2015 (ICRTC-2015). vol. 57, pp. 131 – 138. Elsevier, Delhi, India (2015)
2. Begel, A., Zimmermann, T.: Analyze this! 145 questions for data scientists in software engineering. In: Proceedings of the 36th International Conference on Software Engineering. pp. 12–23. ICSE 2014, ACM, New York, NY, USA (2014)
3. Bertolino, A., Miranda, B., Pietrantuono, R., Russo, S.: Adaptive coverage and operational profile-based testing for reliability improvement. In: Proceedings of the 39th International Conference on Software Engineering. pp. 541–551. ICSE '17, IEEE, Piscataway, NJ, USA (2017)
4. Bittanti, S., Bolzern, P., Scattolini, R.: An introduction to software reliability modelling, chap. 12, pp. 43–67. Springer Berlin Heidelberg, Berlin, Heidelberg (1988)
5. Cavamura Jr, L.: Operational profile and software testing: Aligning user interest and test strategy. In: 2019 12th IEEE Conference on Software Testing, Validation and Verification (ICST). pp. 492–494 (April 2019)
6. Cavamura Jr, L., Morimotto, R., Vincenzi, A.R.M., Fabbri, S.: Operational profile vs. test profile (October 2019)
7. Chen, M.., Lyu, M.R., Wong, W.E.: Effect of code coverage on software reliability measurement. IEEE Transactions on Reliability **50**(2), 165–170 (June 2001)
8. Cukic, B., Bastani, F.B.: On reducing the sensitivity of software reliability to variations in the operational profile. pp. 45–54. IEEE, White Plains, NY, USA (1996)

9. Fabbri, S., Silva, C., Hernandes, E., Octaviano, F., Di Thommazo, A., Belgamo, A.: Improvements in the start tool to better support the systematic review process. In: Proc. of the 20th International Conference on Evaluation and Assessment in Software Engineering. EASE '16, ACM, New York, NY, USA (2016)
10. Fukutake, H., Xu, L., Takagi, T., Watanabe, R., Yaegashi, R.: The method to create test suite based on operational profiles for combination test of status. pp. 1–4. Institute of Electrical and Electronics Engineers Inc., White Plains, NY, USA (2015)
11. Kashyap, A.: A Markov Chain and Likelihood-Based Model Approach for Automated Test Case Generation, Validation and Prioritization: Theory and Application. Ph.D. thesis (2013)
12. Leung, Y.W.: Software reliability allocation under an uncertain operational profile. Journal of the Operational Research Society **48**(4), 401 – 411 (1997)
13. Marijan, D., Teslic, N., Tekcan, T., Pekovic, V.: Multimedia system verification through a usage model and a black test box. In: The 2010 International Conference on Computer Engineering Systems. pp. 178–182. IEEE, Pasadena, CA, United states (Nov 2010)
14. Miranskyy, A., Cialini, E., Godwin, D.: Selection of customers for operational and usage profiling. Providence, RI (2009)
15. Musa, J.D.: Software reliability measures applied to systems engineering. In: Managing Requirements Knowledge, International Workshop on(AFIPS). vol. 00, p. 941. IEEE, S.I. (12 1979)
16. Musa, J.: Operational profiles in software-reliability engineering. IEEE **10**(2), 14–32 (1993)
17. Musa, J.D., Ehrlich, W.: Advances in software reliability engineering. Advances in Computers, vol. 42, pp. 77 – 117. Elsevier (1996)
18. Nakagawa, E.Y., Scannavino, K.R.F., Fabbri, S., Ferrari, F.C.: Revisão Sistemática da Literatura em Engenharia de Software: Teoria e Prática. Elsevier, Rio de Janeiro, 1rd edn. (2017)
19. Nakornburi, S., Suwannasart, T.: A tool for constrained pairwise test case generation using statistical user profile based prioritization. pp. 1–6. Institute of Electrical and Electronics Engineers Inc., White Plains, NY, USA (2016)
20. Namba, Y., Akimoto, S., Takagi, T.: Overview of graphical operational profiles for generating test cases of gui software. pp. 1–3. Institute of Electrical and Electronics Engineers Inc., White Plains, NY, USA (2015)
21. Rogstad, E., Briand, L.: Cost-effective strategies for the regression testing of database applications: Case study and lessons learned. Journal of Systems and Software **113**, 257 – 274 (2016)
22. Sarwar, S., Mahmood, Y., Qayyum, Z.U., Shafi, I.: Test case prioritization for nunit based test plans in agile environment. In: Artificial Intelligence: Methodology, Systems, and Applications. pp. 246–253. AIMSA 2014, Cham (2014)
23. Smidts, C., Mutha, C., Rodríguez, M., Gerber, M.J.: Software testing with an operational profile: Op definition. ACM Comput. Surv. **46**(3), 39:1–39:39 (Feb 2014)
24. Sommerville, I.: Software Engineering. Addison-Wesley, Harlow, England, 9 edn. (2011)
25. Spínola, R.O., Dias-neto, A.C., Travassos, G.H.: Abordagem para desenvolver tecnologia de software com apoio de estudos secundários e primários. In: 5th Experimental Software Engineering Latin American Workshop. ICMC/USP, São Carlos, SP, Brasil (2008)
26. Takagi, T., Furukawa, Z., Yamasaki, T.: An overview and case study of a statistical regression testing method for software maintenance. Electronics and Communications in Japan (Part II: Electronics) **90**(12), 23–34 (2007)
27. Whittaker, J., Rekab, K., Thomason, M.: A markov chain model for predicting the reliability of multi-build software. Information and Software Technology **42**(12), 889 – 894 (2000)
28. Yoo, S., Harman, M.: Regression testing minimization, selection and prioritization: A survey. Softw. Test. Verif. Reliab. **22**(2), 67–120 (Mar 2012)

How Difficult and Effective is Writing Assertions for Observing Bugs at Runtime?

Fischer Ferreira[1], Eduardo Fernandes[2], Johnatan Oliveira[1], Maurício Souza[3], and Eduardo Figueiredo[1]

[1] Federal University of Minas Gerais (UFMG)
[2] Pontifical Catholic University of Rio de Janeiro (PUC-Rio)
[3] Federal University of Lavras (UFLA)
{fischerjf, johnatan.si, mrasouza, figueiredo}@dcc.ufmg.br, emfernandes@inf.puc-rio.br

Abstract. *Context:* Executable Assertion (EA) is a boolean expression written to assess the conformance of the program behavior with its requirements. Contrary to unit test cases, EA supports the bug detection at runtime. An advantage of adopting EA is capturing the fine-grained bug location. *Objective:* Writing EA instances can be expensive and time consuming, due to the need for understanding in depth the program structure and invariants. Unfortunately, there is no empirical evidence on how difficult and effective is writing EA instances. This paper fills this literature gap with a quasi-experiment. *Method:* We asked 22 participants to write EA instances for seven AVL Tree properties. We assessed i) the time spent to write each instance, ii) the difficultly faced by the participants, and iii) the correctness of each instance. Finally, we assessed how effective are the EA instances written by the participants in observing bugs. We relied on the analysis of 155 bugs generated via mutation testing. *Results:* Participants spent from 5.7 to 13.2 minutes in average to write each EA instance; they reported an average difficulty from 2.2 to four out of 5. In average, writing EA instances for three out of the seven AVL Tree properties was sufficient to observe 57% of the bugs. *Conclusions:* Our results suggest that writing assertions for observing bugs at runtime is feasible while quite effective, but it requires reasonable effort.

Keywords: program bug, executable assertion, runtime debugging, mutation testing, quasi-experiment.

1 Introduction

Along with the life cycle of software programs, developers may unexpectedly introduce bugs [28]. A *program bug* is a non-conformance between the expected and the observed behavior of a program [14]. The expected behavior of a program is typically characterized by the software requirements [19]. For instance, the AVL Tree is a traditional data structure designed at the binary search [25]. A major AVL Tree requirement is that inserting nodes should keep balanced the height of both left and right sub-trees for any node [25]. Thus, a bug would be observing an unbalanced height caused by a node insertion. Bugs can ultimately compromise the experience of stakeholders while using a software program [14]. Therefore, bugs should be detected, reported, and fixed as soon as possible [28].

Program debugging is the process of analyzing the occurrence of bugs [28]. Debugging has three major tasks: i) bug detection, ii) bug report, and iii) bug fixing [2]. *Bug detection* means detecting a bug instance in the source code. *Bug report* consists of reporting the location of the detected bug instance. *Bug fixing* means to fix the program behavior implemented by the bug-affected code. Debugging is far from being trivial. Particularly, tracking the exact location of a bug based on the respective bug report is challenging [28]. Through the use of traditional unit test cases, developers typically have a coarse-grained location, e.g. at the method level [28]. However, these unit test cases say little about the exact bug location in a fine-grained level, e.g. at the code statement level.

Executable Assertion (EA) [10] aims at a more fine-grained bug report [1, 10, 12]. An EA is a boolean expression written to assess the conformance of the program behavior with its requirements [12, 24]. Writing EA instances means instrumenting, i.e. equipping, the software program with a verification layer [12]. This verification layer is designed to observe the program behavior at runtime, targeting specific parts of the source code such as code statements [12]. Different of unit test cases, EA detects bugs at runtime in a fine-grained level, thereby reporting those code statements affected by bugs. The drawback of adopting EA is the need for deeply understanding the code properties and invariants, which may be expensive and time consuming [1]. Such understanding is require to write effective EA instances. Unfortunately, there is still no empirical study aimed at investigating how difficult and effective writing EA instances can be.

In this paper, we partially address the aforementioned literature gap with an empirical study. We carefully designed and performed a quasi-experiment [26] with 22 students enrolled in undergraduate and graduate courses of Computer Science and related areas. In a laboratory environment, we asked the participants to write EA instances for seven AVL Tree properties. We then assessed time spent, difficulty, and correctness of the written EA instances. Additionally, we assessed the effectiveness of these instances in detecting bugs. For this purpose, we relied on the analysis of 155 bugs automatically generated via mutation testing [14]. Mutant versions of the AVL Tree implementation were generated with MuClipse [20]. Each mutation version is affected by a bug instance, which represents a recurring bug introduced by real developers [14].

Our study results provided us with a first comprehension on how difficult and effective can be writing EA instances. Participants spent from 5.7 to 13.2 minutes in average to write each EA instance. Additionally, participants have reported an average difficulty from 2.2. to four out of five. These results regard experienced participants in AVL Tree without expertise in EA writing. Finally, in average, writing EA instances for three out of the seven AVL Tree properties was sufficient to observe 57% of the bugs. The conclusion is that, in our quasi-experiment, writing assertions for observing bugs at runtime showed feasible while quite effective. However, writing these assertions requires reasonable effort.

2 Background

2.1 AVL Tree

As discussed in Section 1, we selected the AVL Tree for supporting our quasi-experiment regarding the difficulty and effectiveness of writing EA instances. We decided to use the AVL Tree for a few reasons: i) this is a traditional data structure designed at the binary search [4, 25], ii) students are quite familiar with AVL Tree properties and implementation; iii) the AVL Tree implementation is sufficiently short and complex to be used for experimentation along a few hours. Table 1 lists seven invariant properties of the AVL Tree, which we extracted from a previous work [4] and selected for the quasi-experiment. *Invariant properties* are properties of that should always be preserved along with the use of the data structure. Due to time constraints for performing the quasi-experiment, we discarded two other properties regarding: i) the tree chaining in terms of child and father nodes and ii) the tree leaves. The AVL Tree properties are too complex to implement in a few hours.

Table 1. AVL Tree Invariant Properties Used in the Quasi-Experiemnt

ID	Property	Description
P1	Tree without elements	If the number of elements in a tree is zero then the root should be null
P2	Tree with only one element	If the root is non-null and the root height is zero then the left and right children must be null
P3	Tree with more than one element	If the root is non-null and the root height is greater than or equal to one then the left, right, or both branches should be different from null
P4	Binary search tree	For every element that belongs to the binary search tree the child on the left must be smaller than his father, and the son on the right must be bigger than your father
P5	Number of children of a node	For every element belonging to the binary search tree, you can have only one left a direct child and one right direct child
P6	Tree balancing	For every balanced tree, the height of the left node minus the height of the right node must be less than or equal to one unit
P7	Tree height	For every binary search tree, the total height must be less than $1.44 * log(n + 2) - 1.328$

2.2 AVL Tree Instrumentation

Writing EA instances implies instrumenting, i.e. equipping, the software program with a verification layer able to observe bugs at runtime [1]. In a previous work, we have introduced a systematic model for instrumenting the source code of a program aimed at incorporating EA [10]. Our model is constituted of the following steps: i) *to extend* the original class we aim at instrumenting with EA instances; ii) in the child class, *to write* each EA instance targeting an invariant property of the original class into a private method; iii) *to create* a public method called `verifier` responsible for calling all private methods that implement an EA instance; iv) *to instantiate* an object of child class for calling the `verifier` method and, therefore, triggering the written EA instances at runtime.

Aimed to support of quasi-experiment, we have provided each participant with a Java implementation of the AVL Tree program based on a previous work [25]. For the sake of simplicity, we have prepared the program to partially instrument the AVL Tree. Thus, the participant should be concerned only with the EA writing. The program was organized in two packages and seven classes. The main package, called `AVLTree`, has five classes that implement the AVL Tree data structure. The `AVLInstrumentada` class was designed for the participants to write each EA instance. Listing 1 depicts an example of a EA instance targeting the property P6 – Tree balancing (see Table 1).

```
private boolean verifyTreeBalancing(AvlNode t) {
   if (t != null) {
      verifyTreeBalancing(t.left);
      if (t.left != null && t.right != null) {
         try { if ((t.left.height - t.right.height) > 1) throw new IllegalStructureException(); }
         catch (IllegalStructureException e) e.printStackTrace(); }
      verifyTreeBalancing(t.right); }
   return true;
}
```

Listing 1. An Example of a Written EA Instance

2.3 Unit Test Cases *versus* Executable Assertions

We discuss below the practical difference between adopting unit test cases and EA. Let us assume that one method implements the node insertions into an AVL Tree. A typical unit test case would be written to assess the whole method rather than its statements. Thus, the test case could report eventual bugs at the method level, without further details on the code statement that originated the bug. Consequently, the developer in charge of fixing the bug should understand the method's source code. The bug could be related to any AVL Tree property, including the height balance. In this case, writing one EA for each AVL Tree properly could help to locate the bug. When observing the bug, an EA instance would provide the developers with the exact bug location.

Although EA is quite promising in supporting the bug detection with a fine-grained bug report, writing EA can be expensive and time consuming [1]. In the AVL Tree example, many invariant properties (Table 1) should be deeply understood by the developer. Some properties, such as the tree self-balancing, are not trivial to verify (see Listing 1). More critically, different EA instances should be written to assess each property, which is time consuming. For instance, self-balancing should be assessed for both node insertions and deletions. This study aims at exploring both time spent and difficulty in writing EA instances.

2.4 Mutation Testing

Mutation testing is an approach for enhancing the quality of test suites [2, 27]. This approach typically relies on the automatic generation of mutant versions for a given software program. Each mutant version is a similar program with punctual changes, e.g. at the code statement or method levels, applied to the original code structure. These changes represent bugs commonly introduced by real developers along with the life cycle of their programs [13]. The set of mutation versions is submitted to verification by a test suite. The higher is the percentage of bugs captured by the test suite, the higher is the test suite quality [17, 19]. A mutant version is killed whenever the test suite is able to observe the bug implemented by the mutant; otherwise, we say the mutant is alive [5].

3 Study Design

We relied on strict empirical guidelines [3, 26] for Software Engineering research in this work. We describe below our goal and research questions (Section 3.1), steps and artifacts (Section 3.2), and a participant overview (Section 3.3).

3.1 Goal and Research Questions

Based on the Goal Question Metric template [3], we systematically defined our study goal as follows: *analyze* EA instances written by participants to observe program bugs at runtime; *for the purpose of* empirically assessing how difficult and effective is writing EA instances; *with respect to* i) time spent by participants to write EA instances, ii) difficulty reported by the participants to write the EA instances, iii) correctness of these instances, and iv) effectiveness of EA instances in observing bugs; *from the viewpoint of* software developers and researchers with expertise in software testing; *in the context of* students enrolled in either undergraduate or graduate courses in Computer Science and related areas. We defined four research questions (RQs) described below.

RQ$_1$**:** *How long do participants take to complete the writing of EA instances?* –For agile development teams, time to deliver software programs is typically scarce [23]. Consequently, participants are often forced to prioritize other development tasks, e.g. the addition of new program features [6, 15], rather than testing their programs. Thus, it is desirable that bug detection techniques will not be time consuming to use. We aim at understanding how much time participants usually spent to write an EA instance. As any other lightweight formal method, EA writing can be too costly for practical recommendation. With **RQ**$_1$, we expect to acquire a first understanding on the time spent by participants experienced in AVL Tree properties but without experience in EA writing.

RQ$_2$**:** *How difficult is writing EA instances?* –Understanding the difficulty of writing EA instances is important to characterize the complexity of this task. Indeed, unit testing is quite popular in industry [22] and participants are used to write unit test cases rather than EA instances. Through **RQ**$_2$, we aim at understanding, in a Likert scale [18] from one to five, how difficult is writing EA instances. If our quasi-experiment participants are familiar with unit test cases but still find it easy to write EA instances, then adopting EA may be feasible.

RQ$_3$**:** *How often do participants write EA instances that correctly implement the AVL Tree properties?* – We designed our quasi-experiment to be performed by participants with no previous experience with writing EA instances. It may be the case that this tasks is difficult in such a way participants cannot implement correct EA instances. **RQ**$_3$ was ultimately designed to support our next RQ.

RQ$_4$**:** *How effective are the EA instances written by participants in detecting bugs?* – As important as understanding the difficulty of writing EA instances is assessing how effective these instances are in detecting bugs. Indeed, the major purpose of this technique is observing bug instances in programs. Through **RQ**$_4$, we assess the average percentage of bugs detected by the number of EA instances implemented by the participants. We expect to understand how many EA instances are necessary to detect a reasonable amount of bugs in a program.

3.2 Steps and Artifacts

The study artifacts are available in the companion research website [9].

Step 1: *Select Target Program* – As discussed in Section 2.1, we have selected an AVL Tree implementation to support our quasi-experiment. Thus, we expected to provide the participants with a program that is sufficiently short and complex for reasoning about and writing EA instances.

Step 2: *Prepare Forms* – We have defined three forms aimed at collecting all data for the quasi-experiment. *Consent Form* aims at collecting the participant consent to allow us both collecting and analyzing the quasi-experiment data. *Background Form* has six questions on the participant expertise with Software Engineering techniques, e.g. object-oriented programming and EA. *Experiment Form* describes the seven AVL Tree properties to be implemented as EA instances in up to one hour in total. For each property, we ask the participant to inform: i) start time, finish time, and EA writing difficulty in a Likert scale [18] from one, i.e. the lowest difficulty, to five, i.e., the highest difficulty or impossibility to write the EA instance. We arranged the seven AVL properties of Table 1 from the easiest to the hardest one from our opinion.

Step 3: *Run Pilot Quasi-Experiment* – We have run a pilot version of our quasi-experiment with four participants in order to shape our study design and artifacts. This pilot version helped us to refine the artifacts and the total quasi-experiment time. We carefully discarded the results provided by the pilot study participants, thereby preventing biases in our study results.

Step 4: *Recruit Quasi-Experiment Participants* – We have recruited 33 undergraduate and graduate students to participate in the quasi-experiment. These participants were enrolled in either undergraduate or graduate courses at the Federal University of Minas Gerais (UFMG). We further filtered these participants according to some important criteria described in Section 3.3.

Step 5: *Instruct Participants on the Quasi-Experiment* – All participants were accommodated in a laboratory environment. We introduced the study goal without further details that could affect the experiment with result biases. After that, we briefly instructed the participants on the basics of EA (definition and application) and the AVL Tree properties. Finally, we instructed the participants regarding the quasi-experiment procedures, especially on how to instrument the AVL Tree program to implement the EA instances (cf. Section 2.2).

Step 6: *Collect Participant Consent and Background* – We asked each participants to sign the *Consent Form*, thereby allowing us to anonymously collect and analyze the quasi-experiment data. Additionally, each participant has filled out the *Background Form*.

Step 7: *Allocate Participants to Computers* – We have allocated each participant to an individual desktop computer equipped with: the Eclipse IDE for reading and writing code; the source code of the AVL Tree program (Section 2.2) already imported into the IDE; and the formal definition of seven AVL Tree properties listed in (Table 1) for which the participants will implement the EA instances. For illustration purposes, the property P6 – Tree balancing is formalized as follows: $\forall n \in tree$: $((n \rightarrow left \mathrel{!=} null)\ \&\&\ (n \rightarrow right \mathrel{!=} null)) \Rightarrow ((n \rightarrow left \rightarrow height) - (n \rightarrow right \rightarrow height)) \leq 1$, where n is an arbitrary tree node, $\rightarrow left$ (or $\rightarrow right$) is the left (or right) child of the current node, and $\rightarrow height$ is the tree height from the current node.

Step 8: *Run the Quasi-Experiment* – All participants had up to one hour for completing the quasi-experiment while filling the *Experiment Form* (details in **Step 2**). We answered eventual questions made by the participants along with the quasi-experiment execution. Nevertheless, we carefully avoided biasing the participants' responses with our answers.

Step 9: *Compute Mutant Versions of the AVL Tree Program* – We used MuClipse[4], an Eclipse IDE plugin, to generate the mutant versions of the Java-based AVL Tree implementation (Section 2.2). MuClipse supports code changes at both class level – e.g., changes affecting the class coupling or inheritance – and method level – e.g., changes affecting the arithmetical and logical operations. We obtained 155 mutant versions that actually differ from the original program.

Step 10: *Submit Written EA Instances to Mutant Testing* – We used MuClipse to perform the mutation testing on the set of EA instances written by the quasi-experiment participants. Our goal was understanding the effectiveness of these participant-written instances in observing bugs. We set MuClipse to run with its maximal run time available. Thus, we expected to prevent that mutant versions of the program are not killed due to run time exception.

3.3 Participant Overview

A total of 11 out of the 33 participants were discarded from the study because: four participants engaged in the pilot study; four participants failed to implement EA instances to all seven AVL tree properties; one participant provided us with unreliable data; and two participants did not send us the code of the implemented EA instances by the end of the quasi-experiment. In the end, 22 participants remained for the data analysis and report. The Background Form revealed the following about the participants' expertise. The majority of participants (86.4%) have professional development experience. Additionally, 95.5% of the participants reported some experience with Java programming; the same percentage applied to object-oriented programming. Less than a half (40.9%) of the participants had previous knowledge about EA in theory or practice.

4 Results and Discussion

4.1 Time Spent to Write EA Instances (RQ_1)

Figure 1 summarizes both mean and distribution of time spent by the participants to write EA instances for each AVL Tree property. As aforementioned

[4] http://muclipse.sourceforge.net/

(Section 3.2), the time spent by participant was collected from the Experiment Form. Based on Figure 1(a), we observe that participants spent from 5.7 to 13.2 minutes to write each EA instance. Properties *P1 – Tree without elements* and *P4 – Binary search tree* required more time to be addressed with assertions: 13.2 and 11.4 minutes, respectively. This result may be partially explained by the fact that P1 was the first property presented in the Experiment Form. Indeed, participants were just starting the quasi-experiment, so that they may have spent more time in understanding the procedures and tasks. Additionally, P4 is quite time consuming to address, especially because it requires inspecting each node of the AVL Tree. Thus, it was expected that participants would spent a considerable time in drawing a strategy to navigate through the tree for inspection. For the record, P5 to P7 have a similar logic; thus, developers tend to spend less time to address these properties after P4 – which our results have confirmed.

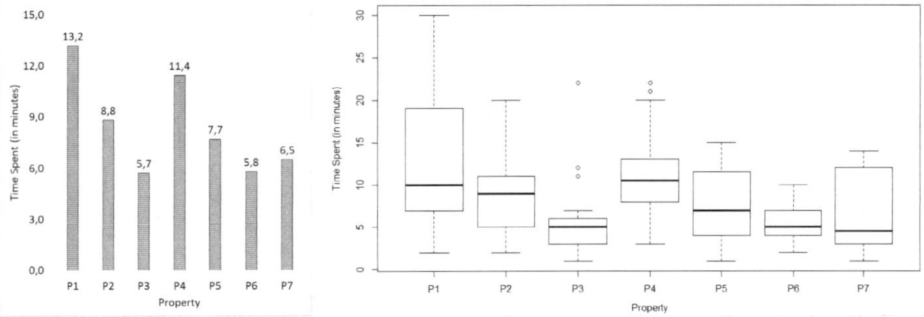

(a) Mean Time (b) Time Distribution

Fig. 1. Mean and Distribution of Time Spent by AVL Tree Property

Aimed at a detailed understanding, Figure 1(b) illustrates the time distribution for each AVL Tree property. We have grouped these results by the distribution pattern as follows. **Group 1 (P1, P2, and P4)**: P1 and P2, which are the two first properties in the Experiment Form, showed a highly spread distribution. For instance, P1 values ranged from two to 30 minutes. P4, which is a hard property to address, showed a similarly spread distribution: from three to 20 minutes besides outliers lower than 25 minutes. **Group 2 (P3, P5, P6, and P7)**: these properties showed the less spread distributions. This observation could be justified by the fact that P3 is among the easiest addressable properties, while P5, P6, and P7 have a logic quite similar to P4, which is hard rely on a similar logic of P4, which is considerably time consuming.

Summary of RQ_1: Participants took from 5.7 to 13.2 minutes in average to write EA instances for each AVL Tree property. Time distribution was highly spread for properties with a justifiable complexity according to our study design (e.g. P1 and

P4). A quite balanced distribution was found for the other properties. In summary, participants spent a reasonable time while writing EA instances.

4.2 Difficulty Faced while Writing EA Instances (RQ_2)

Figure 2 show both mean and distribution of difficulty to write EA instances for each AVL Tree property. Figure 2(a) shows an average difficulty ranging from 2.2 to four out of five. Difficulty increased along with the quasi-experiment execution, expect from P1 to P3. Indeed, *P1 – Tree without elements*, which is the first property in the Experiment Form, was when participants were introduced to EA. After that, P2 and P3 were easier to address with assertions, though these properties are more complex then P1 in our opinion. In summary, the learning factor may have facilitated the EA writing. Differently, difficulty increased from P4 on. It is worth mentioning that *P4 – Binary search tree* has a quite complex logic, but its successors (P5 to P7) share this logic. Although the participants were familiar with the AVL Tree properties (Section 3.3), they found it particularly difficult to address these more complex properties.

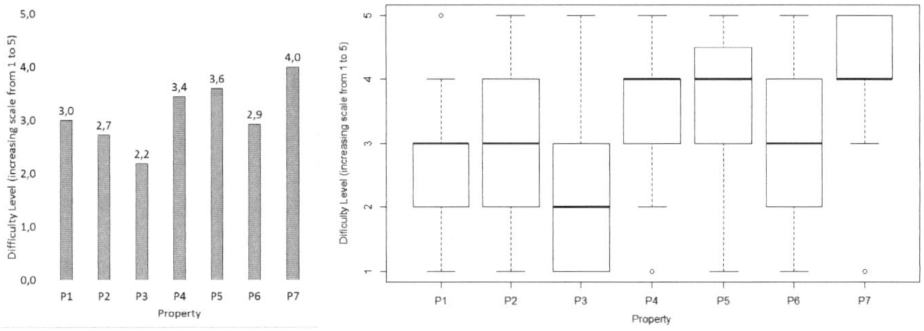

(a) Mean Difficulty (b) Difficulty Distribution

Fig. 2. Mean and Distribution of Difficulty for each AVL Tree Property

Figure 2(b) illustrates the difficulty distribution reported for each AVL Tree property. We have found two different groups of distributions described as follows. **Group 1 (P1, P2, P3, and P6)**: these properties presented the lowest distributions. This result can be partially justified by the fact that P1 to P3 have the less complicated logic. This is why we arranged these properties to be addressed first i the Experiment Form. In the case of P6, it is worth remembering that P6 reuses the logic of P4, which is quite complicated. **Group 2 (P4, P5, and P7)**: these properties showed the highest difficulty distributions. The second quantile for all three distributions is greater than three, which confirms a high effort to write EA instances for complex properties.

Summary of RQ$_2$: Participants found it considerably difficult to write EA instances. The average difficulty ranged from 2.2 to four. The most difficult properties to address with EA instances are those with a more intricate logic.

4.3 Correctness of the Participant-Written EA Instances (RQ$_3$)

Figure 3 presents the percentage of correctly written EA instances for each AVL Tree property. In this particular case, we observed three major groups of properties, which we describe as follows. **Group 1 (P2 and P3)**: only two properties presented a percentage of correctly written EA instances greater than the percentage of wrongly written instances. This result is not exactly surprising because, as discussed in Section 4.2, both P2 and P3 had a quite simple logic. Besides that, these properties succeeded P1 in the order of the Experiment Form. **Group 2 (P1 and P7)**: for these two properties, the percentages of correctly and wrongly written EA instances is practically the same. This result is partially justifiable by the fact that, as discussed in Section 4.1 and 4.2, P1 was the first property to be introduced to the participants. It is worth mentioning that only a few participants wrote EA instances for P7. Thus, the balanced rates of correctly and wrongly written EA instances is reasonable. **Group 3 (P4, P5, and P6)**: for these three properties, we observed greater rates of wrongly written EA instances when compared to correctly written ones. This result is acceptable once these properties are among the most complex ones.

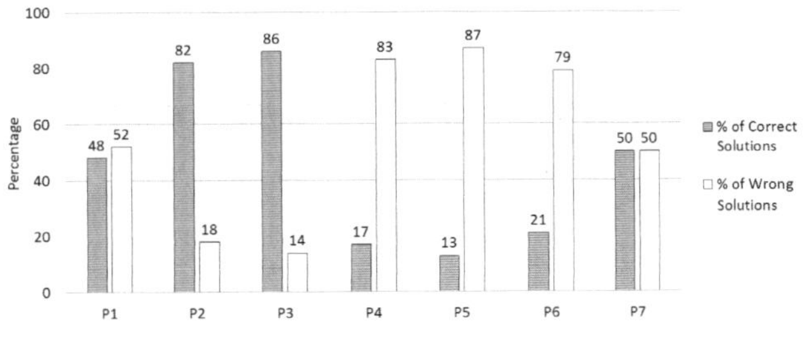

Fig. 3. Percentage of Correct EA Instances for each AVL Tree Property

Summary of RQ$_3$: Participants rarely wrote EA instances that correctly implement the AVL Tree properties. Once our participants are familiar with AVL Trees, we conclude that non-experts are quite likely to write wrong EA instances.

4.4 Effectiveness of the Participant-Written EA Instances (RQ_4)

Table 4.4 presents the percentage of participants (second column) and mean of killed mutants (third column) for different quantities of written EA instances (first column). We observed that none out of the 22 participants address all seven AVL Tree properties with EA instances. This result indicates the difficulty to perform this task in practice. Nevertheless, most participants (60%) wrote EA instances for at least tree properties. This result is particularly interesting because, with just three EA instances, an average of 57% mutants were killed. The mean percentage of killed mutants reached (70%) its peak with exactly five written EA instances. It is worth mentioning that, as discussed in Section 2.1, we have originally derived a total of nine invariant properties for the AVL Tree. Therefore, in a general analysis, addressing one third of the AVL Tree properties was sufficient to capture a half of the 155 automatically generated bugs.

Table 2. Percentage of Killed Mutants per Number of EAs

Quantity of EA Instances	Percentage	
	Participants	Mean of Killed Mutants
1	23%	46%
2	18%	52%
3	41%	57%
4	9%	65%
5	5%	70%
6	5%	66%

Summary of RQ_4: EA instances showed quite effective in detecting bugs. With only one third of the AVL Tree properties addressed with EA instances, participants were able to observe 57% of the bugs generated via mutation testing.

5 Threats to Validity

Construct Validity: We have refined our study steps and their respective artifacts through a pilot study with four participants (Section 3.2). Thus, we expected to mitigate biases regarding an insufficient data collection. Additionally, to enable the quasi-experiment execution in a feasible time, we cherry-picked the AVL Tree program for analysis and EA writing. As discussed in Section 2.1, students are familiar with AVL properties and implementation; thus, this program sounds adequate for an academic experiment. Moreover, we discarded those AVL Tree properties that we judged too hard for participants to address in an one-hour quasi-experiment. We carefully selected a laboratory environment so that participants could comfortably perform the quasi-experiment tasks. Finally, we selected a well-known tool, MuClipse, to run the mutation testing. This tool has been successfully used in both academia and industry [20].

Internal Validity: Although Internet access was available and allowed along with the quasi-experiment, we assisted the participants in performing their tasks. As discussed in Section 3.2, we addressed the participants' doubts whenever possible without biasing their responses – especially during the form filling. Thus, we expected to assure that all participants understood the study procedures and tasks. We decided to perform the quasi-experiment during a Software Engineering-related class, so that all participants are motivated to give their best to perform their tasks successfully. We asked each participant to inform both start and finish time for each EA instance implementation. This design decision, inspired by our past work [7], may represent a threat to the study validity if participants forget to compute time along with the quasi-experiment. We minimized threats of this matter by instructing the participants with examples before the quasi-experiment execution.

Conclusion Validity: We carefully filtered the quasi-experiment data before performing the data analysis. By eliminating data of participants that could compromise our study results (Section 3.3), we removed possible anomalies in the analysis of time, difficulty, and so forth. Similar to our past work [7, 8], we applied techniques of descriptive analysis focused on the data distribution. We have performed a manual analysis of the EA instances written by the participants, aimed at computing correctness (Section 4.3). Although this manual analysis could represent a threat to the study validity, we have allocated sufficient time to perform this analysis carefully. Finally, with respect to the effectiveness (Section 4.4), we carefully filtered the mutant versions of the AVL Tree program via MuClipse. Especially, we discarded all equivalent mutants, i.e., those mutant versions that are equivalent to the original program [5].

External Validity: We have performed our quasi-experiment with 22 Brazilian students. As one could expect, our participant set may not represent all Brazilian students in terms of background and professional experience. Nevertheless, this participant set allowed to achieve some preliminary insights on the difficulty and effectiveness of writing EA instances. Additionally, we restricted our quasi-experiment execution to one hour, especially because the experiment was conducted during a class. This time constraint may affect our findings, since participants may be uncomfortable to write code under time restrictions. However, according to our pilot study (Section 3.2), we observed that one hour was sufficient for participants to write at least a few EA instances correctly. Besides that, we performed the quasi-experiment in a laboratory equipped with sufficient desktop computers, aimed at a successful participation. We invite researchers to replicate our work in other academic settings and validate our study findings.

6 Related Work

Studies [1, 11, 12, 16, 21] explored the runtime bug detection via approaches similar to Executable Assertion (EA). One study [1] targeted the incorporation of Design by Contract (DbC) principles – e.g. invariants and preconditions – into concurrent Java programs. Such incorporation was enabled by runtime assertion, which verify the program conformance with those principles. Other study [16] regarding DbC introduced measures targeting i) the ability of capturing bugs at runtime and ii) the effort required to find the exact location of a program bug. Another work [11] employed EA for verifying the correctness of critical programs through their execution flow. This work, similarly to another one [21], suggested that EA instances may observed a plenty of bug types at runtime. Finally, a recent work [12] empirically validated the potential of EA instances in enhancing the maintainability of data structure invariants, such as the AVL Tree ones (Section 2.1). Nonetheless, previous studies lacked empirical evidence on how difficult and effective is writing EA instances from a developers' perspective.

7 Final Remarks

This paper discussed a quasi-experiment with 22 students on how difficult and effective is writing Executable Assertion (EA). Each participant wrote EA instances for seven invariant properties of the AVL Tree. We assessed the average time spent and difficulty of writing EA instances, plus the correctness and the effectiveness of these instances in observing 155 automatically generated bugs. We found out a considerable effectiveness of EA instances in capturing bugs (55% of the bugs observed with only a few EA instances). However, each EA instance can be costly to write, taking up to 13.2 minutes each. Our quasi-experiment provided only a few hints on the difficulty and effectiveness of adopting EA in practice. Further studies are required to: i) understand the EA adoption by developers in real-world development settings, and ii) compare the cost-benefit of adopting EA against traditional bug detection techniques, e.g. unit testing.

References

1. Araujo, W., Briand, L., Labiche, Y.: On the effectiveness of contracts as test oracles in the detection and diagnosis of functional faults in concurrent object-oriented software. IEEE Trans. Softw. Eng. (TSE) pp. 971–992 (2014)
2. Ayari, K., Bouktif, S., Antoniol, G.: Automatic mutation test input data generation via ant colony. In: 9th GECCO. pp. 1074–1081 (2007)
3. Basili, V., Rombach, H.D.: The TAME Project: Towards improvement-oriented software environments. IEEE Trans. Softw. Eng. (TSE) **14**(6), 758–773 (1988)
4. Bronson, N., Casper, J., Chafi, H., Olukotun, K.: A practical concurrent binary search tree. In: ACM SIGPLAN Notices. vol. 45, pp. 257–268 (2010)
5. DeMillo, R., Lipton, R., Sayward, F.: Hints on test data selection: Help for the practicing programmer. IEEE Computer **11**(4), 34–41 (1978)
6. Fernandes, E.: Stuck in the middle: Removing obstacles to new program features through batch refactoring. In: 41st ICSE, Doctoral Symposium. pp. 206–209 (2019)
7. Fernandes, E., Ferreira, F., Netto, J.A., Figueiredo, E.: Information systems development with pair programming: An academic quasi-experiment. In: 12th SBSI. pp. 486–493 (2016)
8. Fernandes, E., Ferreira, L.P., Figueiredo, E., Valente, M.T.: How clear is your code? An empirical study with programming challenges. In: 20th CIbSE, ESELAW Track. pp. 1–14 (2017)

9. Ferreira, F., Fernandes, E., Oliveira, J., Souza, M., Figueiredo, E.: Companion research website. https://fischerjf.github.io/assertions/ (2019)
10. Ferreira, F., von Staa, A., Figueiredo, E.: Uma análise da eficácia de assertivas executáveis como indicadoras de falhas em software. In: 9th SAST. pp. 1–10 (2015), (In Portuguese)
11. Goloubeva, O., Rebaudengo, M., Reorda, M.S., Violante, M.: Soft-error detection using control flow assertions. In: 18th DFT. pp. 581–588 (2003)
12. Gyori, A., Garg, P., Pek, E., Madhusudan, P.: Efficient incrementalized runtime checking of linear measures on lists. In: 10th ICST. pp. 310–320 (2017)
13. Jia, Y., Harman, M.: An analysis and survey of the development of mutation testing. IEEE Trans. Softw. Eng. (TSE) **37**(5), 649–678 (2010)
14. Just, R., Jalali, D., Inozemtseva, L., Ernst, M., Holmes, R., Fraser, G.: Are mutants a valid substitute for real faults in software testing? In: 22nd FSE. pp. 654–665 (2014)
15. Lavallée, M., Robillard, P.: Why good developers write bad code: An observational case study of the impacts of organizational factors on software quality. In: 37th ICSE. pp. 677–687 (2015)
16. Le Traon, Y., Baudry, B., Jézéquel, J.M.: Design by contract to improve software vigilance. IEEE Trans. Softw. Eng. (TSE) **32**, 571–586 (2006)
17. Lee, S., Bai, X., Chen, Y.: Automatic mutation testing and simulation on owl-s specified web services. In: 41st ANSS. pp. 149–156 (2008)
18. Likert, R.: A technique for the measurement of attitudes. Arch. Psychol. **140**(1), 1–55 (1932)
19. Liu, M.H., Gao, Y.F., Shan, J.H., Liu, J.H., Zhang, L., Sun, J.S.: An approach to test data generation for killing multiple mutants. In: 22nd ICSM. pp. 113–122 (2006)
20. Ma, Y.S., Offutt, J., Kwon, Y.R.: MuJava: A mutation system for Java. In: 28th ICSE. pp. 827–830 (2006)
21. Mahbub, K., Spanoudakis, G.: Run-time monitoring of requirements for systems composed of web-services: Initial implementation and evaluation experience. In: 3rd ICWS. pp. 257–265 (2005)
22. Papadakis, M., Shin, D., Yoo, S., Bae, D.H.: Are mutation scores correlated with real fault detection? A large scale empirical study on the relationship between mutants and real faults. In: 40th ICSE. pp. 537–548 (2018)
23. Poth, A., Sasabe, S., Mas, A., Mesquida, A.L.: Lean and agile software process improvement in traditional and agile environments. J. Softw.: Evol. Process pp. 1–11 (2019)
24. Venkatasubramanian, R., Hayes, J., Murray, B.: Low-cost on-line fault detection using control flow assertions. In: 9th IOLTS. pp. 137–143 (2003)
25. Weiss, M.: Data Structures and Algorithm Analysis in Java. Pearson, 3rd edn. (2011)
26. Wohlin, C., Runeson, P., Höst, M., Ohlsson, M., Regnell, B., Wesslén, A.: Experimentation in Software Engineering. Springer Science & Business Media, 1st edn. (2012)
27. Yao, X., Harman, M., Jia, Y.: A study of equivalent and stubborn mutation operators using human analysis of equivalence. In: 36th ICSE. pp. 919–930 (2014)
28. Yi, Q., Yang, Z., Liu, J., Zhao, C., Wang, C.: A synergistic analysis method for explaining failed regression tests. In: 37th ICSE. pp. 257–267 (2015)

Design Thinking in Software Requirements: What Techniques to Use? A Proposal for a Recommendation Tool

Rafael Parizi[1], Marina Moreira da Silva[1], Igor Couto[1], Kendra Trindade[1], Matheus Plautz[1], Sabrina Marczak[1], Tayana Conte[2], Heloisa Candello[3]

[1] MunDDoS Research Group – School of Technology
Pontifícia Universidade do Rio Grande do Sul (PUCRS)
Porto Alegre, Brazil
[2] USES Research Group – Institute of Computing (IComp)
Universidade Federal do Amazonas (UFAM)
Manaus, Brazil
[3] Conversation Intelligence group – IBM Research Lab
São Paulo, Brazil
{rafael.parizi,igor.couto}@edu.pucrs.br,
{marina.moreira,matheuz.plautz}@acad.pucrs.br,
kendrapavin@hotmail.com, sabrina.marczak@pucrs.br,
tayana@icomp.ufam.edu.br, heloisacandello@br.ibm.com

Abstract. Design Thinking (DT) has been incorporated into software processes by teams from startups to large companies, used in problem exploration fostering innovative solutions, and integrated into agile methods to satisfy the real stakeholders' needs. DT places the customer needs up-front and helps to empathize with users, examining their behaviors, and producing outcomes focused on users' demand. A set of techniques, like personas and user journey, can be used to support this human-centered approach. Selecting which technique to use might be challenging since factors such as the application scenario, stakeholder engagement level and previous knowledge of the problem-to-be-solved may vary from case to case. Therefore, this paper presents an ongoing research that aims to develop a collaborative tool with the purpose of providing recommendations about potential DT techniques to be used in the support of requirements engineering activities. Our tool proposal was developed from results of a DT session that identified the collaborative tool as a proposal solution, a requirements elicitation activity to define the tool scope, and an interview-based early experimental study with professionals that use DT in industry. Our preliminary results show that our proposal has the potential to contribute to professionals that apply DT in requirements engineering by suggesting the most suitable techniques according to the established context.

Keywords: Design Thinking · Technique · Recommendation System · Collaborative Tool · Experimental Study.

1 Introduction

Design Thinking is a problem-solving approach that brings human-centered design principles at its core [3]. Driven by the search for innovation, it fits the development of new products, services, or processes, from startups to large and complex environments [2], thus being used by software development teams.

As a human-centric approach [14], DT can be used in the early phases of software development process to understand and identify what the customer needs are, providing better support for downstream development activities, mainly those related to identifying a proper solution for the problem-at-hand. The multidisciplinary view offers software teams the voice for dynamic, and driven problem-based collaboration; bringing all involved parties closer together [18].

By bringing the user needs to the center of the discussion, DT also improves team communication and facilitates knowledge domain acquisition, which are well-known issues in software development [11]. Given its interactive and dynamic nature, DT is also considered an easy-in integration with and a way to boost agile development [17]. Despite the use, navigating in this new world might be challenging. Literature offers a plethora of DT tools and methods (or techniques for simplification) that form the toolkit to perform DT activities themselves. Nevertheless, there is a lack of studies mentioning strategies to support the decision process of which techniques to use and detailing which contextual factors (e.g., previous knowledge about the problem to be solved, customer engagement, etc.) affect such decision.

Therefore, considering the DT leans and how it can support the discovering of user needs and scoping of a solution [5], well-known activities of the Elicitation phase of the Requirements Engineering discipline, our long-term research goal is to support software development professionals' decision in the selection of which DT techniques to use in a certain development scenario. To achieve our goal, we adopted a long-term multi-phase research process, as follows: i) a literature review [16] to inform on the need to provide support on the DT technique selection, ii) a survey to confirm such need from industry professionals[1], and iii) a tool proposal to initially support such decision process and to later establish a community of users that can retro-feed the efficiency of the recommendations. This paper reports on our third phase–the tool definition.

We present a DT session conducted to better understand the need of a recommendation tool, a requirements elicitation activity in which we defined how the tool should work, and an early evaluation of the initial tool low-fidelity prototypes. Results show that the recommendation tool should take into account the context in which the software product will be used and project characteristics (e.g., team expertise), feedback from others using the recommendation, and

[1] We learned in this survey with 158 participants that 1/3 of them had a difficulty of 6 or up points (scale 1 to 10) in selecting a technique. We also learned that 83% of them chose techniques based on the product context, 81% on their previous experience (which includes learning from others), and 67% on the fitness of a certain technique to a certain DT working space phase (e.g, interviews to support discovering). These results support the need for a recommendation tool. Details can be found in [15]

results from the tool usage itself (e.g., the most selected techniques); and that those features would be welcomed by practitioners.

2 Background

DT is a structured approach to problem-solving by exploring the needs of users and transforming an idea into an acceptable solution via a prototype. Hiremath and Sathiyam [8] argue that DT is increasingly used in software development companies as a tool for innovation. It offers iterative learning from the beginning of the development cycle, including continuous improvement [6].

Requirements Engineering (RE) literature has also increased its interest on the topic. For instance, Hehn and colleagues' work on approaches to tailoring and integrating DT and RE [5], and Hehn, Uebernickel, and Fernandez's [7] integration of DT with software engineering processes aiming to improve the quality of requirements are examples of how RE can benefit from DT.

The approach is inherently multidisciplinary, involving professionals and participants from different domains and knowledge areas. It also uses empathy as the underlying concept to seek for what is technologically appropriate and strategically feasible to be built when proposing a solution [2].

Moreover, Brenner and Uebernickel [1] consider that DT can be conceptualized in the light of three perspectives: as a process, as a mindset, and as a toolbox. The first perspective defends that DT is a set of distinct and iterative steps (e.g., empathize, define, ideate, prototype, test) that abstract working spaces to explore the problem, propose a solution and validate it, which can be adapted and executed non-sequentially according to the necessity. Literature (e.g., [4,12,13,21]) present different process models to abstract these working spaces. The second perspective argues that DT as a mindset inspires a human-centered view, placing the user as the center of attention, seeking to understand what the problem is, among others. Finally, the third perspective supports DT as a 'toolbox', i.e., a set of techniques (e.g., persona, user journey) that support the achievement of the planned process steps. It acts as an 'operational layer' that makes it possible to obtain a solution to a problem. Our research assumes this third view as the focus of interest.

Despite the large number of studies reporting on the use of DT in software engineering [19], we still have no consolidated knowledge on how developers choose DT techniques, what criteria they consider for supporting such selection, and what sources they consult for their decisions. Initiatives such as the Luma Institute's Innovating for People Toolkit [13]–which explains the meaning of each technique and suggests related techniques for a certain purpose–, or the IDEO Toolkit [9]–which recommends techniques based on a predefined set of questions that a professional might ask about how to use DT–, are examples that demonstrate that choosing a technique is not trivial. Although highly used by practitioners, both cases fail to consider the context in which DT is being used. For instance, if the team has no previous information about the stakeholders, selecting interviews might be of more interest to learn about their profile rather than a focus group session in which people might not get along and waste effort. DTA4RE - Design Thinking Assistant for Requirements Elicitation [20] is a first step towards aiming to tailor the recommendation process. However, DTA4RE is still limited in the number of contextual factors it considers to recommend a technique and on not taking into account any kind of feedback from those who use the recommendations. Our research contributes towards filling in this gap.

3 Research Methodology

Inspired on the results of our preliminary literature review and survey, as cited in Section 1, we posed the following research question: *How can software development professionals select the most suitable Design Thinking (set of) technique to support requirements engineering?*

Figure 1 illustrates our 3-steps research methodology to answer the posed research question. First, to understand and define the problem of how to select the suitable DT techniques for supporting requirement engineering, we performed a "meta-DT" session (Step 1). We named it "meta-DT" since we conducted a 3 hours-long Design Thinking session to better understand the need to propose a recommendation system to support the selection process of DT techniques and to define how the tool should work. A total of 10 people participated in the activity–5 of them from industry and with an average of 3 years of experience working with DT, and 5 graduate students with DT as a research topic and 2 of them also with industry experience.

The session was conducted by a requirements analyst with 2.5 years of experience in DT and organized into the following activities: i) problem understanding based on the presentation of the working question; ii) problem definition which aimed to further discuss the need for a tool; iii) ideation using the Brainwriting DT technique to generate ideas; iv) convergence activity using the Affinity Diagram DT technique to find similar features; iv) prototyping the solutions (paper-based prototypes defined by two mixed groups of 5 members); and v) choice of solutions and presentation by each one of the groups through a voting activity. As a result of this session, the participants concluded that the solution would be the development of a recommendation tool associated with a community building environment through feedback, and in the future, rely on gamification mechanisms to engage tool users and promote rich feedback to maintain the community.

Step 2 focused on eliciting requirements for the elected recommendation tool solution. Carried out by the 5 graduate students, the elicitation activity step was also inspired on the use of DT techniques. Upon a 1.5 hour-long session in which each of the students suggested the use of a set of DT techniques, by unanimous decision we selected i) User Journeys[2] to represent the needed steps to a user to achieve their (business) goals, ii) Service Blueprints[3] to describe how the 'service' (tool features) may be offered to the user (touch-points), covering the

[2] User Journeys: http://bit.do/DTA4RE-user-journeys

[3] Service Blueprint: http://bit.do/DTA4RE-serviceblueprints

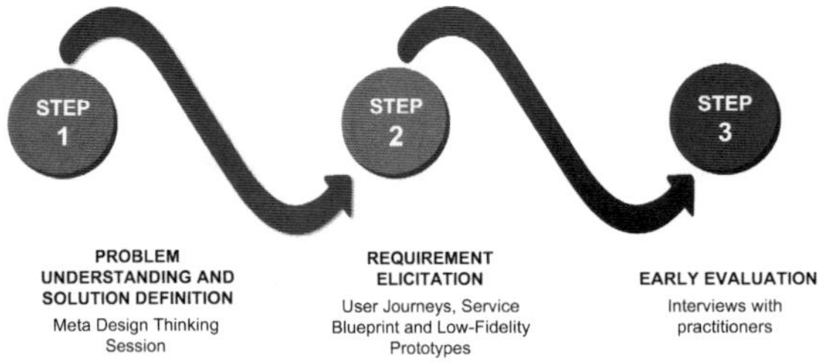

Fig. 1. Our step-wise research methodology

entire journey, identifying points for improvement and business opportunities, and iii) Low-Fidelity Prototypes[4] to define how users will interact with the tool. A sample of those are presented in Section 4.2[5]. Specifications were defined by 3 of the students and reviewed by the 2 others until a consensus was reached.

Finally, Step 3 aimed for an early evaluation of our tool specification with industry practitioners as a means to identify whether we were missing any relevant feature. We interviewed 5 practitioners (a product designer, a service designer, a product owner, a business analyst, and an IT manager) of 2 multinational IT companies, a large Brazilian TV broadcasting company, a cooperative bank and an IT provider with an average of 3.5 years of experience with DT in software development. We first openly asked them how they select the techniques they use to later present them with our recommendation tool idea and a sample of printouts of low-fidelity prototypes to discuss in details. Four of the interviews took place during coffee breaks of the DT track of an industry-based developers' conference and another one over the phone. They lasted an average of 20 min.

4 DT Techniques Recommendation Tool

This section details the activities performed to define and specify the DT techniques recommendation tool. It also presents the resulting specification, i.e., the tool proposal, and its early evaluation.

4.1 Step 1. Meta-Design Thinking Session

Our meta-DT session was guided by the the following question: *In what ways would we as Requirements Analysts/Software Engineers/Designers be able to choose the techniques to succeed in using DT to support software requirements?*

In a two-minutes time slot and using post-its, each participant described what she thought was important to provide relevant information to interested parties about the established problem. This ideation activity resulted in 24 proposed insight cards to the established problem. Then, to gain a deeper understanding

[4] Prototypes: http://bit.do/DTA4RE-prototypes
[5] The full report can be found at http://bit.do/CIBSE2020DesignThinking

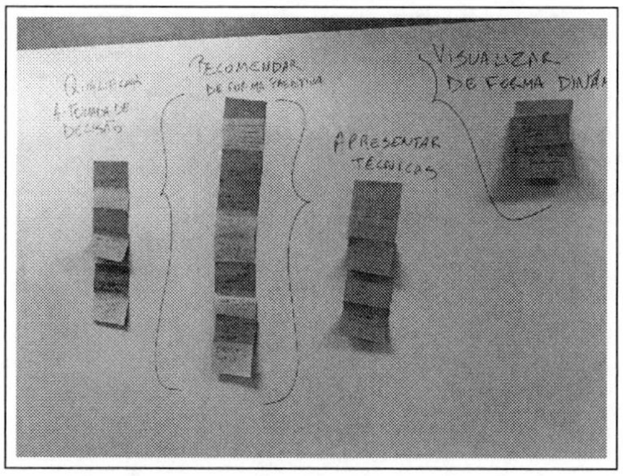

Fig. 2. Affinity Diagram identifying the DT tool macro features

Name **Joano** 	**Profile** 38 years old Single Father of a 6 years old Designer Taking a fellowship in Design Owns a car
Behaviour Hurried Studies a lot Shy Likes TV series Tries to jog Social media blogger	**Needs** Stay connected 24x7 Optimize time to complete his activities

Name **Sindi** 	**Profile** 24 years old Married Facilitator Uses transportation apps BSc in Software Engineering Travels a lot for work
Behaviour Enjoys travelling Communicative Engaged with the community Friends with lots of people Pays attention to details	**Needs** Trust people Be successful in her area of work

Fig. 3. Personas Sindi and Joano

of this scenario, an Affinity Diagram was organized (see Figure 2). This diagram allows the organization and grouping of results (insight cards) according to their similarities, dependencies, or affinities, generating a diagram that results in macro areas or features that delimit the addressed theme [22].

The four resulting identified macro features (in Portuguese, from left to right) are: i) qualified decision making; ii) prediction-based recommendation; iii) techniques presentation, and; iv) dynamic visualization of recommendations.

Next, the participants were separated into two mixed groups composed each of practitioners and graduate students to carry out a prototyping activity. These groups are named Group 1 and Group 2 from now on. The moderator introduced two personas, Joano and Sindi, presented in Figure 3 and previously created for the session. Each persona was assigned to each of the groups to work on. Group 1 was assigned to the Joano persona and Group 2 to Sindi.

Through prototyping, for about 30 minutes, each participant individually designed a first round of paper-based low-fidelity prototypes to address the 4 identified macro features. Figure 4 shows the prototypes related to the macro feature iii) present the techniques. Subsequently, each group was instructed to review the designed prototypes, group them by features and vote by posting

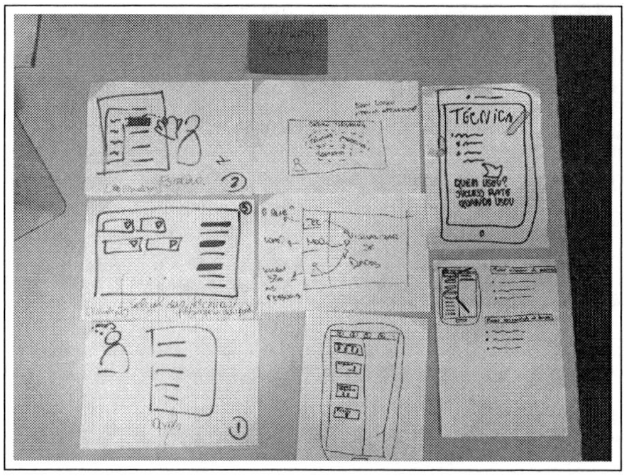

Fig. 4. First round low-fidelity prototypes for the macro feature iii)

Table 1. Identified features per persona grouped by macro feature

Macro Feature	Joano Persona (Group 1)	V_1	Sindi Persona (Group 2)	V_2
i) Qualified decision making	- Organize Techniques by Category (7a) - Qualify Decision Making (7a, 7b, 7d)	0	- Suggest Complementary Technique (7a) - Organize Techniques by Category (7a) - Qualify Decision Making (7a, 7b, 7d)	4
ii) Prediction-based recommendation	- Get to know similar cases (7b, 7c, 7d) - Consider the context of use of DT (7a, 7c) - Provide feedback (7d)	1	- Suggest tools predictively (7a) - Receive examples of the application of the technique (7b, 7c, 7d) - Consider the context of using DT (7a, 7c) - Provide feedback (7d)	2
iii) Techniques presentation	-Visualize techniques and models (7a, 7b, 7c) - Search for technique recommendations in a systematic way (7a, 7c)	3	- Visualize the techniques and models (7a, 7b, 7c)	0
iv) Dynamic visualization	- Simulate the use of combined techniques for a particular purpose (7c)	6	- Dynamic and interactive visualization (7a, 7b)	2

a yellow post-it on the grouped set of prototypes by macro feature that most represented what the tool should offer.

Table 1 summarizes the identified features per persona grouped by macro feature and the respective amount of votes attributed to them (columns (V_1) and (V_2)). The voting aimed to highlight whether certain macro features stood out and deserved priority attention or a deeper discussion. Each participant could choose between one to three features. Features with zero voting indicate that none of the participants considered it a priority. The groups differ on what they consider to be most relevant. While Group 1 considered that the visualization of techniques was the most relevant macro feature (6 out of 10 votes), Group 2 was torn among 3 of the macro features, with no predominant decision. Given the distinct persona behaviors and needs this divergent scenario was not considered an issue. The table also maps the prototyped features in round 2 as described in Section 4.2 (e.g., (7a)) to the discussed features in the meta-DT session (prototype round 1) as indicated in the referred table (e.g., Feature i)).

To conclude, each group presented their results to one another and explained their voting and motivations behind it. This discussion promoted common ground among the meta-DT session participants and made possible to the group to conclude that they have reached a tool vision.

4.2 Step 2. Requirements Elicitation

The second step includes User Journeys, Service Blueprints and Prototyping of the screen's flow. This paper presents a sample of the identified features.

User Journeys: Proceeding with the requirements gathering exercise for the tool proposed in this paper, we started with the definition of 5 User Journeys. Figure 5 shows a User Journey developed to Persona Sindi, highlighting her main actions when looking for a technique and aiming to use it in her product development. The identified functional requirements derived from this user journey are highlighted in Figure 5, described next:

- Access the system: user access the tool;
- Recommend techniques based on a self-updated visualization graph: user can receive technique recommendations and self-update the tool, collaborating with other users;
- View techniques details: user can access detailed information about a certain technique, like when, how, and why to use it;
- Attach/Add techniques from the visualization graph to a new project: user have the opportunity to choose a technique and associate it to a new project.
- Create a new project: user can create a project and manage the used techniques and previous experiences, updating the visualization graph.

Service Blueprints: As mentioned, Service Blueprints (SB's) are used to visually present the detailed specification of aspects of a service (business feature), from the user's perspective, and other relevant parts that may be involved.

Figure 6 presents a SB for the persona Sindi, related to the User Journey showed by Figure 5, aiming to get new insights and a deeper understanding of the problem. In this service blueprint, the user initially accesses system (A) and selects from the suggestion graph some technique for his DT project (B). The user can also see information about the selected technique (C) as well as linking to the running project (D). This figure also presents other expected functionalities through the relationships shown in each of the horizontal lanes physical evidence (i), customer actions (ii), contact with backstage actions (iii), and support processes (iv).

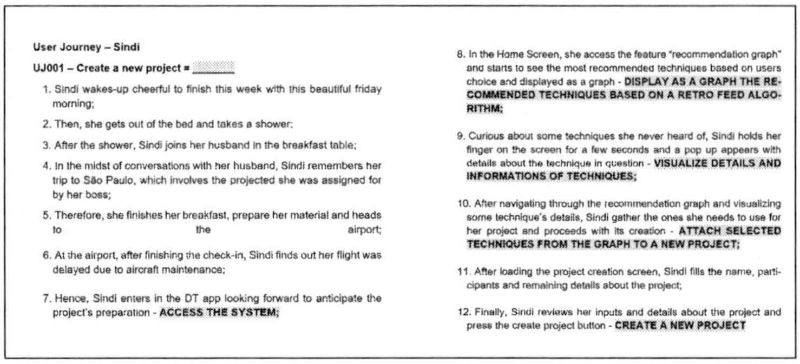

User Journey – Sindi

UJ001 – Create a new project =

1. Sindi wakes-up cheerful to finish this week with this beautiful friday morning;
2. Then, she gets out of the bed and takes a shower;
3. After the shower, Sindi joins her husband in the breakfast table;
4. In the midst of conversations with her husband, Sindi remembers her trip to São Paulo, which involves the projected she was assigned for by her boss;
5. Therefore, she finishes her breakfast, prepare her material and heads to the airport;
6. At the airport, after finishing the check-in, Sindi finds out her flight was delayed due to aircraft maintenance;
7. Hence, Sindi enters in the DT app looking forward to anticipate the project's preparation - **ACCESS THE SYSTEM;**
8. In the Home Screen, she access the feature "recommendation graph" and starts to see the most recommended techniques based on users choice and displayed as a graph - **DISPLAY AS A GRAPH THE RECOMMENDED TECHNIQUES BASED ON A RETRO FEED ALGORITHM;**
9. Curious about some techniques she never heard of, Sindi holds her finger on the screen for a few seconds and a pop up appears with details about the technique in question - **VISUALIZE DETAILS AND INFORMATIONS OF TECHNIQUES;**
10. After navigating through the recommendation graph and visualizing some technique's details, Sindi gather the ones she needs to use for her project and proceeds with its creation - **ATTACH SELECTED TECHNIQUES FROM THE GRAPH TO A NEW PROJECT;**
11. After loading the project creation screen, Sindi fills the name, participants and remaining details about the project;
12. Finally, Sindi reviews her inputs and details about the project and press the create project button - **CREATE A NEW PROJECT**

Fig. 5. User Journey – View techniques in detail – Persona Sindi

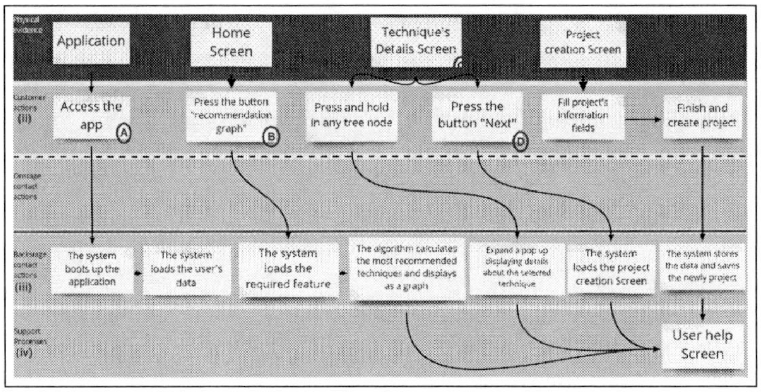

Fig. 6. Service Blueprint - Persona Sindi

Low-Fidelity Prototypes: Considering the insights gathered from the Users Journeys and the Service Blueprints, we further detailed the features through their prototypes. We designed a second round of paper-based prototypes mapping the results from the two referred elicitation techniques to consolidate our understanding as presented here.

Starting from the Techniques Recommendation Graph Screen (Figure 7-(a)), which represents one of the core value of our application, it shows the techniques within a graph according to a specific filter. Filters represent product context (e.g., scenario of use, user profile) and project characteristics (e.g., problem domain, knowledge of the stakeholders, number of participants on DT session, among others). These will be further and better defined later on as part of our future steps. By default, the graph is set to generate the vertices and edges according to the most used technique. Therefore, the starting and central node from this graph presents the most recommended technique, followed by the next most recommended nodes that relate to the first (e.g., Brainstorming followed by Journey Map and Personas). Thus, our tool presents a network of interconnected DT techniques. Yet, this Techniques Recommendation Graph should also consider other aspects, such as (i) DT models and set of techniques previously

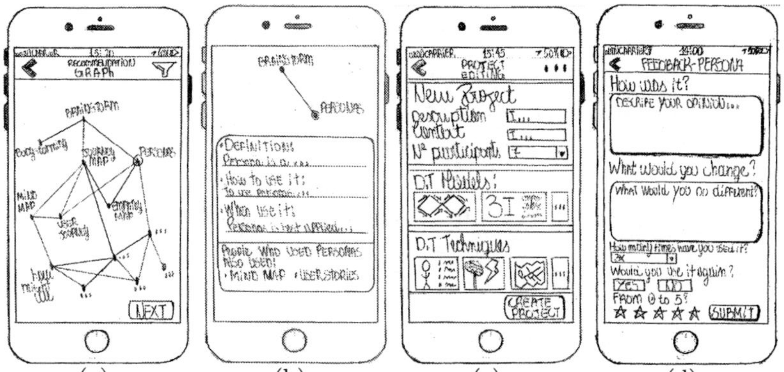

(a) (b) (c) (d)

Fig. 7. (a) Graph; (b) Technique detail; (c) Project creation; (d) Feedback

applied by the software professionals community; (ii) feedback from the users about the experience of the use of a technique or a DT model; (iii) experience from the combination of different techniques in specific scenarios of requirements engineering. These are part of our long-term research view and will be discussed only once the first tool version is made available.

In addition, if a user is not familiarized with any of the techniques, each of it contains descriptive information, e.g.: definition, case scenarios to use, and others (see Figure 7-(b)). Exactly as a haptic, when the selected technique is selected, its respective data will pop up inside a little rounded square, delivering the users dexterity and continuous use of the feature, despite having to go back and search manually about the given technique.

Figure 7 illustrates two other features. Figure 7-(c) provides the concept of a project to store related information held together, whereas having to seek them separately all the time. Therefore, the screen exhibits blank fields to be filled about the project's crucial details (e.g.: name, description, purpose and participants), and a set of available DT models to fit in their project and also a list of the previous selected techniques with the graph. This is the foundation for future use as part of the recommendation algorithm previously mentioned.

Finally, Figure 7-(d) illustrates a screen for capturing user feedback from the use of DT techniques in their software development projects, chosen through the recommendations made by the tool we are proposing in our work. In this screen, the user can inform the result of the application of a specific technique (e.g., Persona), filling in fields like what was the experience of use, if it suggested any alteration or if it was done alternatively, how many times already used, would be used again, and how to rate it (on a level of stars ranging from 1 (not suitable) to 5 (very appropriate)).

This last screen represents another core of our tool: exchange of information and experience among DT professionals, creating an effective and consolidated communication channel and establishing a community environment, especially those who apply DT in software engineering. Thus, our proposal is not limited to an information guide but defines it as an collaborative environment that enables the exchange of experiences between DT users. This feature should also be further modeled ahead as per the use of the first tool draft to be made available.

4.3 Step 3. Early Tool Evaluation

To gather the first impressions and to align our research goals in the context of this recommendation tool, we interviewed five industry practitioners. Here, to maintain the confidentiality of both the practitioners and their companies, we identify them as P1, P2, P3, P4, and P5. We asked: i) how do you select DT techniques? ii) how do you deal with changes in the technique selection during a DT session, if any?, and iii) how would you welcome a tool that recommend you techniques considering your product context and feedback from others?

Regarding the question (i) choice of DT techniques, the participants reported that they select considering the client's knowledge and feeling, according to P2; that they learn to choose from the experience gained from years of application, and that ends up creating a particular set of techniques by the results that have already been obtained in previous applications, as mentioned by P3. In addition, the techniques can be chosen and determined according to the DT working space, either for understanding the problem, for ideation or the construction of the solution. P4 unveiled it:

- *"One learn to choose techniques over time because each technique has a result. If one wants to understand the problem, one uses certain techniques. One defines ones' own toolkit overtime. Also, if one has to think about solutions, one has these (certain techniques) here that help one get there"*–P4.

On the need to looking for other techniques while conducting a DT session (question ii), interviewees responded that situations arise when users/participants are not engaged or do not understand how the technique works and need to change or adapt the technique for more meaningful results. This situation is illustrated by the answers of P3 and P4:

- *"There are situations in DT Workshops that the use of some techniques does not work, so the moderator/designer must choose another technique from their experience. There are also instances when participants find it challenging to use a particular technique, so one needs to use others".*–P3
- *"It happens that one has to change in the middle of a workshop because the customer does not respond well to a certain activity. In this situation, empathy must be used to understand what is happening and get around the situation. Changing the technique is often helpful in such situation."*–P4

Still, P5 and P2 suggest making combinations between different techniques, observing that with the applied variations, going beyond the pre-established models, one gets a more efficient result.

- *"Experiment variations between techniques (a mix of techniques), because this ensures the bias of Designer and not just replicating methods [...]"*–P5
- *"Ah, you test if this technique combines this one."*–P2

Regarding the need for a recommendation tool (question iii), the interviews showed that it will be useful and of great help to professionals who use DT. They suggested that the DT user might input some data such as: *"Do you already have the problem defined?"* to know if the person (client) already has the scope of the problem defined; *"Do you know users?"* – then suggest a particular set of tools.

For P1, the tool should be geared to the DT community by fostering information exchange (feedback, more effective techniques); should have explanations of concepts, such as whether the solution to the problem is developing an mobile app, providing useful MVP tips; and should clearly present the techniques to understanding the problem, for ideation, and for creating the solution. Also, it should establish a sense of community, with a forum for users to interact among themselves, going beyond a simple guide, and provide metrics for evaluation (number of users who accessed in a period, user satisfaction when using).

5 Discussion

The tool proposed in this paper seeks to recommend Design Thinking techniques to users who are integrating them into requirements engineering activities. To discuss our tool proposal, which results from answering our posed research question–*How can software development professionals select the most suitable Design Thinking (set of) technique to support requirement engineering activities?*, we list some relevant takeaways from this study:

- The tool seeks to provide relevant information on DT techniques, going beyond the existing user's toolkit. The tool must allow the selection of other similar techniques through its recommendation system, using a technique relationship graph that should take into account a set of items for the recommendation such as previous use of a certain technique, users feedback, product context, and project characteristics.
- The tool should be valuable and able to assist both on-boarding novice users to expert ones during their DT sessions in software development. Both profiles found the tool idea useful.
- We discussed an innovative solution presenting a recommendation tool associated with a community building environment through feedback. Thus, the industry practitioners might collaborate with their community fostering the improvement of DT in software development.

Finally, as we show in each of the three stages of tool development, it is possible to see that there is a universe not yet explored, that is, we can still consider a lot of other features and technologies to apply in this tool, such as decision support methods, recommendation systems, Artificial Intelligence, multi-platform system, and others. Thus, we seek to ensure that the software industry, from those responsible for applying DT sessions, perceive in this tool a guide of recommendations that enables effective gains in the software development process.

6 Concluding Remarks and Perspectives

This paper proposes a tool for recommendations of Design Thinking Techniques in the context of software requirements. To further the understanding of the need to propose such a tool and identify a solution, we conducted a meta-DT session (Step 1) followed of a requirements specification activity (Step 2), and an interview-based early evaluation with industry practitioners (Step 3).

As a result, we identified four macro features to be present in our recommendation tool, namely: i) qualified decision making, ii) prediction-based recommendation, iii) techniques presentation, and iv) dynamic visualization of recommendations. These macro features were broke-down into smaller features and detailed in their use (User Journeys) and functionality (Service Blueprints). In addition, they were prototyped in a second round to refine their understanding and serve as guidance for the tool early evaluation with industry practitioners.

Results of the early evaluation with 5 professionals revealed that: i) previous experience is key to select techniques, ii) new techniques might be needed during a DT session, and iii) a recommendation tool could be useful to help with the decision process and addressing changes, mainly when considering context and historical use from others.

Although our early evaluation is not generalizable, it confirms that our tool vision –also limited in the sense it was defined–is adequate and serves its purpose. We aim to broaden this evaluation within the own use of the tool. We are currently developing a working prototype that should be soon be made available for experimental use by industry practitioners. We intend to use the tool to collect data on how people are selecting the techniques and, along side with the feedback and the project context features, will retro-feed the recommendation algorithm until its stabilization. Other items might also be taken into account for defining how the recommendation should work. For instance, the work by Ignacio [10] propose a set of characteristics for recommending a requirements elicitation technique. This will complete this first phase of the tool proposal before we move to the refinement of the community building to engage users, which will both compose the tool design second phase.

Acknowledgements

This study was partially financed by the Coordenação de Aperfeiçoamento de Pessoal de Nível Superior – Brasil (CAPES) – Código de Financiamento 001.

References

1. Brenner, W., Uebernickel, F.: Design Thinking for Innovation: Research and Practice. Springer International Publishing (2016)
2. Brown, T., Katz, B.: Change by design. Journal of Product Innovation Management (3), 381–383 (2011), https://onlinelibrary.wiley.com/doi/abs/10.1111/j.1540-5885.2011.00806.x

3. Docherty, C.: Perspectives on design thinking for social innovation. Design Journal (6), 719–724 (2017)
4. Hasso-Plattner, I.: What is Design Thinking? (Accessed October 20, 2019), https://hpi-academy.de/en/design-thinking/what-is-design-thinking.html
5. Hehn, J., Mendez, D., Uebernickel, F., Brenner, W., Broy, M.: On integrating design thinking for a human-centered requirements engineering. IEEE Software pp. 25–31 (March-April, 2020)
6. Hehn, J., Uebernickel, F.: The use of design thinking for requirements engineering: An ongoing case study in the field of innovative software-intensive systems. In: Proc. of Int'l Requirements Eng. Conf. pp. 400–405. IEEE, Alberta, Canada (2018)
7. Hehn, J., Uebernickel, F., Fernandez, D.M.: Dt4re: Design thinking for requirements engineering: A tutorial on human-centered and structured requirements elicitation. In: Proceedings of International Requirements Engineering Conference. pp. 504–505. IEEE, Alberta, Canada (2018)
8. Hiremath, M., Sathiyam, V.: Fast train to dt: a practical guide to coach design thinking in software industry. In: Proceedings of Conference on Human-Computer Interaction. pp. 780–787. Springer, Las Vegas, USA (2013)
9. IDEO: IDEO Design Kit (Accessed Oct 20, 2019), https://designkit.org/methods
10. Ignacio, R.: Guia facetado de técnicas de elicitação de requisitos. Universidade Federal de Santa Catarina (11 2018)
11. Lindberg, T., Meinel, C., Wagner, R.: Design Thinking: A Fruitful Concept for IT Development?, pp. 3–18. Springer, Berlin, Heidelberg (2011)
12. Lucena, P., Braz, A., Chicoria, A., Tizzei, L.: Ibm design thinking software development framework. In: Proceedings of the Brazilian Workshop on Agile Methods. pp. 98–109. Springer, Curitiba, Brazil (2016)
13. Luma, I.: Innovating for people: Handbook of human-centered design methods. LUMA Institute, LLC (2012)
14. Plattner, H., Meinel, C., Leifer, L.: Design thinking: understand–improve–apply. Springer Science & Business Media (2010)
15. Plautz, M.: Estudo Exploratório sobre Design Thinking no Desenvolvimento de Software. Master's thesis, Escola Politécnica, Pontifícia Universidade Católica do Rio Grande do Sul, Porto Alegre, Brasil (3 2020)
16. Plautz, M., Marczak, S.: Design Thinking no Desenvolvimento de Software: Uma Revisão Sistemática da Literatura (2019) (accessed December 05, 2019)), http://bit.do/CIBSE2020DesignThinking
17. Przybilla, L., Schreieck, M., Klinker, K., Pflügler, C., Wiesche, M., Krcmar, H.: Combining design thinking and aigle development to master highly innovative it projects. Projektmanagement und Vorgehensmodelle 2018-Der Einfluss der Digitalisierung auf Projektmanagementmethoden und Entwicklungsprozesse (2018)
18. Seidel, V.P., Fixson, S.K.: Adopting design thinking in novice multidisciplinary teams: The application and limits of design methods and reflexive practices. Journal of Product Innovation Management (S1), 19–33 (2013)
19. Souza, A., Ferreira, B., Conte, T.: Aplicando design thinking em engenharia de software: um mapeamento sistemático. In: Proceedings of Ibero-American Conference on Software Engineering. Buenos Aires, Argentina (2017)
20. Souza, A.F., Ferreira, B., Valentim, N., Conte, T.: An experience report on teaching multiple design thinking techniques to software engineering students. In: Proc. of the Brazilian Symp. on Software Eng. pp. 220–229. ACM, São Carlos, Brazil (2018)
21. d.School Stanford: Design Thinking - Bootcamp Bootleg Compilation (Accessed October 20, 2019), https://dschool.stanford.edu/resources/the-bootcamp-bootleg
22. Vianna, M.: Design thinking: inovação em negócios. MJV Press (2012)

Handling Nonfunctional Requirements for Smart Cities

Isabel Sofia Brito[1[0000-0002-7556-4367]], Ana Moreira[2[0000-0003-2046-2766]]
João Araújo [3[0000-0001-5914-1631]]

[1] UNINOVA-CTS, Caparica, Polytechnic Institute of Beja, Beja, Portugal
isabel.sofia@ipbeja.pt

[2,3] NOVALINCS, Computer Science Department, Universidade NOVA de Lisboa, Portugal
[amm|joao.araujo]@fct.unl.pt

Abstract. The complexity of large-scale systems combined with their intrinsic Non-Functional Requirements (NFRs) (e.g., interoperability, scalability) constitute some of the challenges imposed by smart cities goals. Several proposals exist for eliciting and specifying NFRs, but not to deal with the smart cities core elements such as cloud-computing, physical devices and communication issues. Given the importance and complexity of NFRs, and their often conflicting nature, this research describes a Requirements Engineering approach to guide the elicitation and specification of NFRs based on a smart cities' framework. This approach to handle NFRs was developed in the context of the U Bike project.

Keywords: NFRs, smart cities framework, requirements specification.

1 Introduction

The goal of a smart city is to optimize technologies to create a sustainable and self-aware city that improves both the quality of governmental services and the citizens welfare. Thus, a city with numerous ICT (Information and Communications Technology) projects is not necessarily a smart city [1]. One of the challenges is to deal with the NFRs associated with the smart city core elements, such as cloud computing, physical devices, and communication. In the era of cloud computing, one of the challenges software providers may face is to accurately capture the real requirements from stakeholders, be them functional (e.g., software services) or non-functional (e.g., service availability). The data collected from an Internet of Things (IoT) platform, typically produced by a huge number of physical devices, can be stored and processed in a cloud environment using big data [2]. This highlights the need to support NFRs such as scalability, or interoperability to cope with the data exchanged between multiple elements. Finally, an effective communication between different network nodes (e.g., user devices, sensors, actuators) is a mandatory requirement for a smart city system.

In summary, NFRs play a significant role in a smart city system. When smart city stakeholders are looking for a service, typically they have some functional requirements in mind, as they may not be familiar with qualities and constraints. Given the importance and complexity of NFRs, and their often conflicting impact on other smart city system requirements, it is important to reason about NFRs early in the development. Some works study the different types of NFRs relevant to smart cities systems (e.g. [3] [4] [5] [6] [2]), but they do not provide a process to specify NFRs. This is why we are proposing a Requirements Engineering (RE) approach based on the smart city framework [7] to specify and reason about NFRs. This approach contributes to an understanding of a smart city system goals, by identifying stakeholder needs, specifying NFRs, and managing conflicting situations triggered by negative contributions among NFRs or between those and other system requirements. Moreover, our approach bridges the gap between NFRs analysis and design, as the framework guides the identification and specification of requirements based on the two fundamental smart city system parts, **Structure** and **Operation**. The **Structure** part describes four different components: Physical Layer, Communication Layer, User Applications, and External Services. The **Operation** part consists of three different phases used by the smart city components for interactions: collecting; transmitting; and processing, managing and utilization.

The rest of this paper is organized as follows. Section 2 describes the smart city framework used to guide our requirement approach. Section 3 presents a RE approach to identify and specify NFRs, and to identify conflicts. The process is explained using parts of the U-Bike project. This project aims to promote sustainable mobility behavior by offering electrical and conventional bikes to academic communities. Section 4 discusses related work, highlighting similarities and differences with our proposal. Finally, Section 5 concludes and suggests directions for future work.

2 The smart city framework

The smart city IoT framework guides the development of a smart city system [7] and is composed of the **Structure** and **Operation** parts. Fig. 1 summarizes the elements of the two parts of this framework.

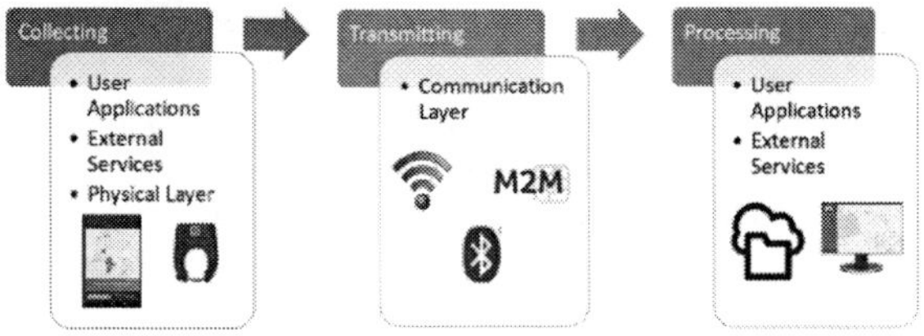

Fig. 1. Smart city framework components, from [7].

The Structure is composed by the Physical Layer, Communication Layer, User Applications, and External Services. The Physical Layer consists of many types of sensors (e.g., ultrasonic, pressure, proximity), cameras, smartphones and tablets, for example, through which the required data (e.g., environmental data) are gathered. The heterogeneity of the equipment coexisting in this layer reinforces the need for interoperability. The Communication Layer allows the transmission of data, between framework components. The User Applications component collects and manages data.

It is one of the systems' front ends, providing a range of possible applications to achieve the stakeholders' goals. Finally, the External Services are functionalities provided by external entities responsible for processing and managing the obtained data to support smart city requirements and stakeholders' goals (e.g., an interface between the Physical Layer and the User Applications, or the means to store and process large amounts of data collected by the Physical Layer and the User Applications).

The Operation consists of three phases, Collecting, Transmitting, and Processing, Managing and Utilization. Collecting senses the physical environment, collecting real-time and non-real-time data, and constructing a general perception of it. Data acquisition is performed by using different technologies and devices from the Physical Layer. The Physical Layer and the User Application component achieve the objectives of this phase. Transmitting includes mechanisms to "send" the data collected by the Physical Layer to the User Applications or the External Services, and from/to the User Applications and the External Services. Finally, the processing, managing and utilization phase uses the User Applications and the External Services components to process and analyze data/ information flows, and to provide feedback to control the applications. It is also responsible for critical tasks such as device discovery, device management, data management (filtering and aggregation).

3 The NFR RE Approach for Smart Cities

The NFR RE approach described here was created to handle NFRs in the context of the U-Bike project[1]. U-Bike provides classic and electric bicycles to the academic community (e.g., students, teachers and academic staff) in the Instituto Politécnico de Beja. U-Bike encourages a sustainable urban transportation in the city of Beja, Portugal, by fostering healthier lifestyles while reducing the CO2 footprint in the environment and saving money. The project is coordinated by the Institute of Mobility and Transport, I.P. (IMT), and is co-funded by the Portugal 2020 program, through the Operational Programme for Sustainability and Efficient Use of Resources (POSEUR). A small subset of the U-Bike requirements, used here for illustration purposes only, are:

- The bike should be used by academic users.
- The system should have the means to assess bike monitoring and maintenance (by means of bike data), in particular electric bikes.
- The system must analyze the effects of the project regarding its objectives, targets and expected results (metrics) by means of reports. These metrics are CO2 reduction, km travelled per week by each user (i.e. user and ride information), adherence rate of the academic community population to the project (by type of target audience) and the gain of healthy habits.
- The system must be available 24/7.

The approach follows an iterative and incremental process for each of the components of the Structure. It is composed of three main tasks: Elicit NFRs, Specify NFRs, and Identify conflicts.

[1] https://www.u-bike.pt/sobre/

Elicit NFRs (task 1). This task gathers NFRs from different sources, including stakeholders' opinions, to understand the system goals from different perspectives. To perform this task, we need to identify sources of domain documentation, the relevant stakeholders, and reuse information from existing catalogues and frameworks.

Identify sources (task 1.1). The smart city adoption is expected to be strongly driven by the city needs and its stakeholders. This task collects information and documentation about smart city goals, such as process models or standards, catalogues and user (or other) manuals of existing systems to help with the identification of requirements. In the U-Bike project, the main information was collected from IMT and POSEUR documentation[2].

Identify stakeholders (task 1.2). Because the RE process focuses on the stakeholders' needs, we can use the questions in [8] to identify all the persons, organizations and other systems that have a direct or indirect interest in the system under study. The U-Bike stakeholders are academic users (students and teachers), academic institution (IPBeja) who is the data owner and collects incomes (receives funds from POSEUR), and project managers (academic staff) that are involved in service monitoring, collecting incomes and managing the services. Stakeholders not belonging to the academy are project coordinator (IMT and POSEUR) who is involved in service performance measurement and funding the project, communication sector representatives and service providers or cloud service providers who sell services, and local administration (Beja municipality) who collects incomes.

Reuse knowledge from catalogues and frameworks (task 1.3). This task guides the stakeholders to identify NFRs based on existing projects, frameworks and catalogues, such as NFR catalogues [9] and the SynchroniCity technical framework [10]. Such catalogues and frameworks promote reusability. According to the U-Bike stakeholders, Interoperability, Scalability, Privacy, Security, and Availability are the NFRs this project should consider.

Specify NFRs (task 2). For each NFR, this task identifies responsibilities, contributions to other NFRs, and stakeholders' priorities.

Identify responsibilities (task 2.1). This task provides a description of the NFR intended behavior. For each framework Structure components (Physical Layer, Communication Layer, User Applications, and External Services), it is necessary to identify the required NFRs. Each NFR is described using five elements: a keyword to describe the NFR in upper case; the name of the component element; the representation of preference of the NFR ("must" for obligation, "could" for strong suggestion, "should" for suggestion without imposing or "will not" be accomplished). The action (collect, transmit, process, manage and execute, based on Operation phases of the smart city framework). Finally, the core elements handled by the system in terms of data, applications and services. The NFR description structure is:

```
<keyword> <component element> <must|could|should|will not>
<collect, transmit, processing, execute> <data, service, application>
```

Note that the elements do not follow any predefined order. The important thing is to make sure that the responsibility makes sense. Let us consider the Interoperability NFR. It needs to be *satisficed* [9] because the system consists of **heterogeneous**

[2]https://poseur.portugal2020.pt/pt/candidaturas/avisos/poseur-07-2015-31-aviso-projeto-u-bike-portugal/

devices, services and applications from different sellers and service providers using different communication technologies and formats for data exchange [11]. Using the above elements, the responsibilities are:

IntOp_Resp01: `HETEROGENEOUS smartphones (Physical Layer) must collect and transmit user bike data`

IntOp_Resp02: `HETEROGENEOUS user apps (User Applications) must collect, transmit, and process user bike data, ride data`

IntOp_Resp03: `Cloud computing (External Services) could collect, process bike data, user data`

IntOp_Resp04: `The network (Communication Layer) must transmit user bike, bike and ride data between bike, user app, project management web site, cloud computing`

Now, let's focus on Scalability, as the system must **handle a growing number of** resources and requests, due to the volume of sensor data flowing, the volume of data to be stored in databases, the number of (heterogeneous) devices handled by the management system, the amount of data processed by services and applications (cloud computing), and the number of applications and users. Therefore, scalability refers to the ability of being extensible without negatively affecting the quality of the service [11]. Some scalability responsibilities are:

Scale_Resp01: `The project management website (User Application) should HANDLE A GROWING NUMBER OF processing bike, user bike, ride data`

Scale_Resp02: `The project management website (User Application) should HANDLE A GROWING NUMBER OF execute user application`

Scale_Resp3: `The cloud computing (External Services) must HANDLE A GROWING NUMBER OF collecting, processing bike data, user data`

As a final example, let us look at Privacy, important because the platform collects, transfers, stores, and processes sensible data (e.g., personal information related to their habits and interactions with other people and services) from the city and citizens. Data **protection** and privacy issues should be addressed in several levels, from the physical layer (devices and sensors) to specific end-user applications. Some responsibilities are:

Priv_Resp01: `User app (User Applications) should PROTECT user bike personal data WHEN collect, transmit`

Priv_Resp02: `Project web site (User Applications) must PROTECT user bike personal data WHEN collecting, processing`

Priv_Resp03: `Cloud computing (External Services) must PROTECT user bike personal data WHEN collecting, transmitting, processing`

Priv_Resp04: `The network (Communication Layer) must protect user bike personal data DURING communication between User app, Project website, cloud computing`

Identify contributions between NFRs (task 2.2). NFRs impact each other. This is expressed by a contribution relationship that can be collaborative (or positive, helping the affected NFR) and represented by a "+" sign, or damaging (or negative, obstructing the affected NFR) and represented by a "-" sign. Contribution relationships maybe have different strengths (e.g. + and ++, or - and - -). Some of these relationships can be found in catalogues (e.g., [9] [12]). In the U-Bike context, Interoperability contributes negatively to Privacy.

Identify stakeholders' priorities (task 2.3). A priority expresses a stakeholder's importance to an NFR. This is relevant for conflict solving. We use a qualitative 5-values scale: Very Important (the stakeholder cannot do without it), Important (the stakeholder does not want to be without it), Medium (the stakeholder would appreciate it), Low (the stakeholder would accept its absence), Very Low (the stakeholder accepts its absence) and Don't Care (the stakeholder does not need it). In the U-Bike, the stakeholders allocated a low priority to Scalability because the number of participants is known (corresponds to the number of bikes). On the other hand, they consider Privacy to be very important to comply with the General Data Protection Regulation (GDPR), and similarly to Interoperability.

Identify conflicts (task 3). A conflict occurs any time two or more NFRs contribute negatively to each other, and are needed by the same framework component. For example, we identify a conflict between Interoperability and Privacy with respect to the user applications and external services components. To help handling this our stakeholders set a high priority to Privacy with respect to the User Applications, considering data protection, and high priority to Interoperability with respect to External Services, considering the heterogeneity of resources.

To demonstrate how these requirements were addressed, we present a brief description of the implemented system based on the framework components:

1. Physical Layer: the system has a diverse range of devices, such as iOS and Android smartphone and a SmartLock, from different sellers cooperating to achieve common goals. Therefore, the Interoperability NFR was ranked as Very Important and special care was taken to *satisfice* it (see points 3 and 4).
2. User Applications: the system has two applications for the stakeholders. The IPBeja's project managers are responsible for the system and use the U-Bike web functionalities. The academic users "own" the bike and use the mobile application (app) functionalities (see Fig. 2, right) to: start a ride by inserting her "bike number" or scanning a QR Code placed on the bike (see Fig. 2, left). This operation allows users to automatically unlock the bike; view data for each ride (bike ID, distance travelled and date) and the respective paths represented on the city map (see Fig. 2, middle). The app and web site use encryption to guarantee data privacy.

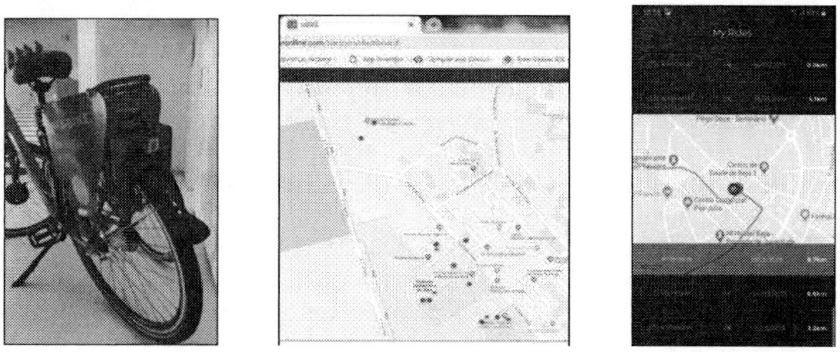

Fig. 2. (left) Bike with a SmartLock device' collects user location data and ride data; (middle) Bike monitoring system: Reservation; Tracking; Monitoring; (right) Mobile App: Unlock bike; Manage rides; Visualize rides.

3. External Services: the system uses the google API for location and AWS cloud-computing platform, which is a full management service at any scale. Interoperability and scalability are satisficed by the AWS platform.

4. Communication Layer: the system must support communications between all the components elements. Interoperability requirements are accomplished by different technologies: Wi-Fi, Bluetooth, GPRS/3G/4G, LTE and M2M. For example, the SmartLock device along with communication technologies (M2M and Bluetooth) are used to (un)lock the bike.

In summary, the NFRs can be supported in different ways for each component of a smart city system (e.g. Interoperability) and can affect design decisions. It is therefore important to have an approach that identifies, describes and reasons about NFRs early in the software development process to guide the decision process.

4 Related Work

In [5], the authors propose a template and checklist to analyze quality attributes (i.e. NFRs) for IoT based on a traffic management system. Due to the diverse set of NFRs, it is difficult to bridge the gap between requirement analysis and software design. This work inspires the identification task of our process. The works that follow helped us to identify relevant NFRs to support the specification task of our proposal. For example, the goal in [3] performed a literature review and identified 17 NFRs. Security, Scalability, Privacy are the most cited NFRs. This study also indicates that requirements are specified for different components of smart city systems such as middleware, software platforms, data solutions, and business components. Similarly, in [6] the authors present a survey to discover relevant NFRs for smart city systems. They identify that the most important NFRs are: Interoperability, Usability, Authentication and Authorization, Availability, Recoverability, Maintainability, and Confidentiality. They also propose a set of questions to identify domain stakeholders, where Municipality, Private and Public sector, Government, service provider are the most cited actors in the smart city context. These questions inspired our proposal for the stakeholders' identification. Identifying stakeholders and priorities and creating policies are one of the challenges faced in the smart cities initiatives. Jayasena et al [8] show how to identify stakeholders and their positive or negative impact to the smart cities. The authors relate them (and theirs impact) with stages of smart city development. Finally, [2] analyzes the functional requirements and NFRs extracted from the 23 software platforms for smart cities. This paper shows that NFRs for smart city systems, such as scalability, adaptation, and interoperability, are related to large, heterogeneous distributed systems. Other NFRs are related to the manipulation of critical and personal data from citizens, such as security and privacy.

The main difference between the approaches presented here and our proposal is the NFR specification task. The NFR specification is complete and consistent as it is described considering all the components of a smart city. This allows us to obtain an integrated perspective of the system.

5 Conclusions and Future Work

This paper presents an approach to handle NFRs in the smart city system context during requirements engineering. First, it proposes the use of catalogues to help the identification and specification of NFRs. The catalogues we have mainly used are the NFR framework and SynchroniCity technical framework. Second, it specifies NFRs by using a set of rules based on the smart city framework. Third, it identifies conflicting situations during the specification phase. The process described in this paper emerged from our partnership in the U-Bike project, these ideas are at an early stage of research. Therefore, we need to validate it further in other case studies. For future work, we need to define the best approach to resolve conflicts, for example how to deal with three or four NFRs simultaneously, with different contributions among them; refine NFRs to be mapped onto functional requirements; and handle sustainability issues (economic, environmental and technological) considering that one of the smart city goal is to optimize modern, useful technologies to create a sustainable and self-aware city.

Acknowledgment

This work was partially financed by Portuguese Agency "Fundação para a Ciência e a Tecnologia" (FCT), in the framework of project UID/EEA/00066/2019, and NOVA LINCS (ref. UID/CEC/04516/2019).

References

1. P. Neirotti, et al, "Current trends in Smart City initiatives: Some stylised facts", *Cities,* vol. 38, pp. 25-36, 2014.
2. E. Santana, et al, "Software Platforms for Smart Cities: Concepts, Requirements, Challenges, and a Unified Reference Architecture", *ACM Computing Surveys (CSUR),* vol. 5, pp. 1-37, 2018.
3. V. Bastidas, M. Helfert and M. Bezbradic, "A Requirements Framework for the Design of Smart City Reference Architectures", in *HICSS-51 - Hawaii International Conference on System Sciences*, Hawaii, 2018.
4. M. Maggio, et al, "SynchroniCity: Delivering an IoT enabled Digital Single Market for Europe and Beyond", 2018.
5. S. N. Mahalank, K.B. Malagund and R.M. Banakar, "Non-Functional Requirement Analysis in IoT based smart traffic management system", in *International Conference on Computing Communication Control and Automation (ICCUBEA)*, India, 2016.
6. G. Kakarontzas, et al, "A conceptual enterprise architecture framework for smart cities: A survey-based approach", *11th International Conference on e-Business (ICE-B)*, Austria, 2014.
7. I.S. Brito, et al, "Leveraging IoT Framework to Enhance Smart Mobility. The U-Bike IPBeja Project", in *Smart Systems Design, Applications, and Challenges*, IGI Global, 2020.
8. N. Jayasena, et al, "Stakeholder Analysis for Smart City Development Project: An Extensive Literature Review", *MATEC Web Conf,* p. 266 06012, 2019.
9. L. Chung, et al, Non-Functional Requirements in Software, Kluwer, 2000.
10. SynchroniCity, "Technical Framework", 2019. Available: https://synchronicity-iot.eu/tech/.
11. S. Ravidas, et al, "Access control in Internet-of-Things: A survey", *Journal of Network and Computer Applications,* vol. 144, pp. 79-101, 2019.
12. N. Nurmuliani, D. Zowghi, D. Mairiza, "Towards a Catalogue of Conflicts Among Non-functional Requirements", *Fifth International Conference on Evaluation of Novel Approaches to Software Engineering* (ENASE), pp. 20-29, 2010.

Uma Tecnologia para Apoiar a Engenharia de Requisitos de Sistemas de Software IoT

Danyllo Valente da Silva, Bruno Pedraça de Souza, Taisa Guidini Gonçalves[0000-0002-7108-1763] e Guilherme Horta Travassos[0000-0002-4258-0424]

Universidade Federal do Rio de Janeiro – PESC/COPPE, Rio de Janeiro, Brasil
{dvsilva, bpsouza, taisa, ght}@cos.ufrj.br

Abstract. Sistemas de software contemporâneos (internet das coisas, indústria 4.0, cidades inteligentes, dentre outros) incorporam novas preocupações e características em sua construção e inerentes à rede, software, hardware, sensibilidade ao contexto, e interoperabilidade. Nesse sentido, a engenharia de requisitos (ER) desempenha um papel fundamental para garantir a correta construção desses sistemas na perspectiva das necessidades do negócio e dos usuários finais. Diversas tecnologias de software para apoiar a ER estão disponíveis na literatura, porém nem todas cobrem as atividades e especificidades de sistemas de software contemporâneos, notadamente daqueles baseados em *IoT*. Nesse sentido, o presente trabalho apresenta a tecnologia RE_{IoT} (*Requirements Engineering for software systems based on IoT*), que tem como objetivo prover apoio metodológico, técnico e ferramental para a ER de sistemas de software *IoT*. A RE_{IoT} apoia a construção do documento de requisitos utilizando uma técnica de descrição de cenários *IoT*, um *checklist* para a verificação dos cenários, um processo construtivo e *templates* ajustados para sistemas de software *IoT*. As técnicas de descrição e verificação de cenários, bem como os *templates*, apresentam indicação de viabilidade de sua utilização em projetos de software *IoT*.

Keywords: Engenharia de Requisitos, Especificação de requisitos, Cenários, Verificação, Internet das Coisas, Engenharia de Software.

1 Introdução

Sistemas de software contemporâneos, tais como aqueles inerentes ao paradigma da Internet das Coisas (*IoT*), Indústria 4.0, Cidades Inteligentes, dentre outros são complexos quando comparados a sistemas de software tradicionais. Essa complexidade provém da inclusão de novas preocupações e características relacionadas à rede, software, hardware, sensibilidade ao contexto, interface, interoperabilidade [1][2].

Particularmente, os sistemas de software baseados em *IoT* buscam promover o entrelaçamento de tecnologias e dispositivos que, por meio de uma rede, são capazes de capturar e trocar dados, tomar decisões e atuar, unindo os mundos real e virtual por meio de objetos e *tags*. Devido as suas características tecnológicas específicas, construir sistemas *IoT* não é simples, exigindo tecnologias de software adaptadas e/ou inovadoras para criar e garantir a qualidade do produto construído [1].

A qualidade do desenvolvimento de sistemas de software contemporâneos depende de tecnologias de software que respondam as novas preocupações e características inerentes a esses sistemas. Como para qualquer outro produto construído com base em princípios de engenharia, uma atividade fundamental do desenvolvimento de sistemas de software *IoT* é a construção do documento de requisitos. Defeitos presentes no documento de requisitos podem ocasionar aumento do tempo, custo e esforço para o projeto; clientes e usuários finais insatisfeitos; baixa confiabilidade do sistema de software; alta quantidade de falhas; entre outros [3][4].

A engenharia de requisitos (ER) é responsável pelo ciclo de vida (concepção, elicitação, negociação, análise, especificação, verificação, validação e gestão) do documento de requisitos [4][5] e garante a construção adequada deste. A literatura técnica apresenta diversas tecnologias de software com o objetivo de apoiar a ER para sistemas de software, porém nem todas abrangem as diferentes etapas da ER e, principalmente, as especificidades de sistemas de software *IoT*.

Considerando a necessidade de tecnologias de software apropriadas para o desenvolvimento de sistemas de software *IoT*, e entendendo a importância que um documento de requisitos tem para a estabilidade, adequação, e qualidade de um projeto, este trabalho apresenta a versão inicial da RE_{IoT} (***R**equirements **E**ngineering for software systems based on **IoT***). O termo tecnologia refere-se ao apoio metodológico, técnico e ferramental oferecido pela RE_{IoT}, cujo objetivo é apoiar a construção de documentos de requisitos para sistemas de software *IoT*.

A tecnologia RE_{IoT} é composta de uma técnica de especificação de requisitos baseada na descrição de cenários *IoT* - $SCENARI_{OT}$ [6], de uma técnica de inspeção de cenários *IoT* - $SCENARI_{OT}CHECK$ [7], de um processo construtivo – versão inicial [8] e *templates* de artefatos (escopo do projeto, proposta de solução e descrição de casos de uso *IoT*) que apoiam as atividades do processo e compõem o documento de requisitos. As técnicas $SCENARI_{OT}$ e $SCENARI_{OT}CHECK$ foram avaliadas anteriormente através de estudos experimentais os quais indicaram sua viabilidade [6][9] e vêm sendo usadas nos projetos de sistemas de software *IoT* desenvolvidos pelo Grupo de Engenharia de Software Experimental (ESE) da COPPE/UFRJ.

Esse artigo tem como objetivo apresentar a tecnologia RE_{IoT} e uma prova de conceito envolvendo a comparação de seus *templates* com aqueles utilizados para apoiar a construção de documentos de requisitos de sistemas de software convencionais. Os resultados indicam que os *templates* da RE_{IoT} permitem capturar as informações necessárias para projetos *IoT* e que estão prontos para serem avaliados na construção de documentos de requisitos de sistemas de software *IoT*. Em complemento, é possível observar que a tecnologia RE_{IoT} provê cobertura para as principais fases da ER no que tange as especificidades de sistemas de software *IoT*.

Além desta introdução, este artigo apresenta outras cinco seções. A seção 2 descreve a base tecnológica da RE_{IoT}. A seção 3 apresenta a tecnologia RE_{IoT}. A seção 4 demonstra o estudo conduzido. A seção 5 apresenta alguns trabalhos relacionados encontrados na literatura. Por fim, a seção 6 apresenta os trabalhos futuros e conclui o artigo.

2 A Base Tecnológica da RE_{IOT}

Esta seção apresenta a base tecnológica da *RE_{IoT}* (**R**equirements **E**ngineering for software systems based on ***IoT***), construída para apoiar a ER de sistemas de software *IoT*. Esta tecnologia está inserida no contexto de uma abordagem de engenharia de sistemas, que contempla as grandes etapas do desenvolvimento de sistemas de software contemporâneos [1]. A base tecnológica é composta das técnicas *$SCENARI_{OT}$* [6] e *$SCENARI_{OT}CHECK$* [7] que possuem indicação experimental de viabilidade e vêm sendo utilizadas em projetos de sistemas de software *IoT* em desenvolvimento pelo Grupo ESE no DELFOS - Observatório da Engenharia do Software Contemporâneo da COPPE/UFRJ.

2.1 $SCENARI_{OT}$

$SCENARI_{OT}$ é uma técnica de especificação de cenários *IoT* [6]. A técnica adapta e desenvolve tecnologias convencionais de cenários de software para apoiar a especificação de cenários em sistemas de software *IoT*, considerando características (adaptabilidade, conectividade, privacidade, inteligência, interoperabilidade, mobilidade, dentre outras) e comportamentos (identificação, sensoriamento e atuação) específicos do paradigma *IoT* [10].

A combinação das características com os três comportamentos permitiu a criação de nove arranjos de interação *IoT* (AIIs). Esses arranjos orientam os engenheiros de software a capturar informações essenciais sobre o sistema de software que será construído, como os tipos de dados a serem coletados, identificação das "coisas" no sistema *IoT*, entre outros.

Além disso, cada AII possui um catálogo contendo as informações de todas as características a serem capturadas na descrição do cenário, conforme apresentado na Fig 1. Os AIIs (isolados ou combinados) resultam em um artefato de descrição de cenários para sistemas de software *IoT*.

O artefato de especificação de cenários produzido pela *$SCENARI_{OT}$* contém as seguintes informações: 1) Identificação dos principais elementos dos sistemas de software *IoT* que irão compor a solução, bem como a forma como estes elementos são organizados; 2) Descrição do domínio do problema, como saúde, cidades inteligentes, engenharia automotiva, entre outros; 3) Descrição do papel de cada ator dentro do cenário; e 4) Descrição das interações entre os atores e o sistema *IoT*.

2.2 $SCENARI_{OT}CHECK$

$SCENARI_{OT}CHECK$ é uma técnica de verificação de cenários para sistemas de software baseados em *IoT* [7]. Esta técnica foi criada para apoiar a verificação dos artefatos produzidos pela técnica de especificação de cenários - *$SCENARI_{OT}$* [6]. O objetivo da *$SCENARI_{OT}CHECK$* é aumentar a qualidade da especificação de cenários *IoT* realizada com a técnica de especificação *$SCENARI_{OT}$*. Ela consiste em um *checklist*, composto de duas partes, que auxilia os inspetores (com nenhum ou baixo conhecimento em sistemas de software *IoT*) a identificar defeitos na descrição dos cenários.

Fig 1. Exemplo do AII - coleta e exibição de dados e seu catálogo (baseado em [6])

A primeira parte do *checklist*, com base nos AIIs da técnica *SCENARI*$_{OT}$, visa verificar problemas gerais, capturando algumas características como domínio do problema, fluxo alternativo e de exceção, a interação e identificação entre atores, sistema e dispositivos. A segunda parte do *checklist* leva em consideração propriedades não funcionais de sistemas de software *IoT*. Essas propriedades são definidas de acordo com seis facetas: ambiente, coisas, comportamento, conectividade, interatividade e inteligência [1]. O *checklist* completo é apresentado em [9].

Após a especificação dos cenários *IoT* com a técnica *SCENARI*$_{OT}$, os inspetores aplicam a técnica *SCENARI*$_{OT}$*CHECK* para verificar a descrição dos cenários. Por fim, após a reunião de discriminação, o documento de especificação de cenários é corrigido a partir dos defeitos encontrados.

3 A Tecnologia *RE*$_{IoT}$

A tecnologia *RE*$_{IoT}$ (***R**equirements **E**ngineering for software systems based on **IoT***) é composta pela base tecnológica descrita na seção 3, de um processo construtivo (seção 3.1), e *templates* (seção 3.2) para apoiar a construção do documento de requisitos (lista de requisitos, casos de uso *IoT*, cenários *IoT*, arranjos de interação *IoT* incluindo seus respectivos catálogos) em conformidade com os princípios da ER.

3.1 Processo de Construção do Documento de Requisitos da a RE$_{IoT}$

O processo de construção do documento de requisitos da *RE*$_{IoT}$ é baseado nas principais fases da ER: concepção, elicitação, análise, especificação, verificação, validação e gerenciamento. Entretanto, a *RE*$_{IoT}$ adapta e inclui novas atividades para atender as especificidades de sistemas de software *IoT*. Uma visão geral do processo construtivo é apresentada na Fig 2. Nos próximos parágrafos um breve resumo de cada fase é apresentado.

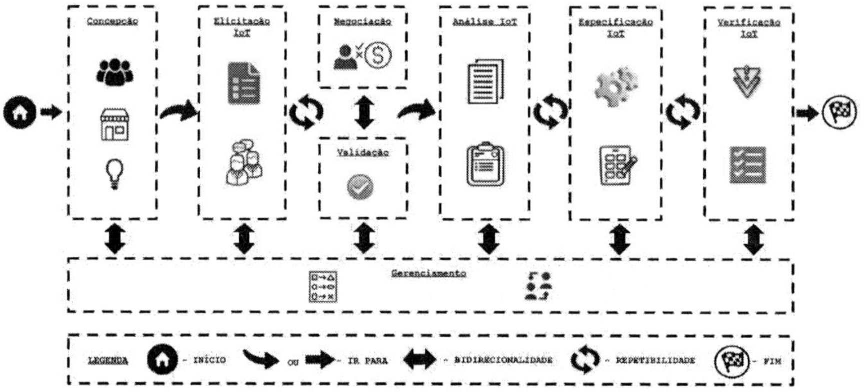

Fig 2. Visão geral da estrutura do processo de construção oferecido pela RE_{IoT}

Durante a fase de **concepção** deve-se buscar entender se o problema ou oportunidade pode ser resolvido utilizando tecnologias *IoT*. Um estudo de viabilidade também deve ser realizado para determinar se existem tecnologias disponíveis e equipe qualificada para a resolver o problema.

A fase de **elicitação *IoT*** busca refinar e transformar as necessidades de negócio e partes interessadas em requisitos. Durante essa fase é empregada a técnica $SCENARI_{OT}$ [6] para apoiar a identificação dos requisitos. Além disso, cenários *IoT* podem ser descritos para auxiliar no entendimento do comportamento do sistema. Por último, a lista de requisitos final deve organizar e classificar os requisitos em "requisitos *IoT*" e "requisitos não-*IoT*".

As fases **validação** e **negociação** ocorrem em paralelo. Durante a fase de **validação** os requisitos são validados, atestando que um entendimento comum sobre o sistema foi alcançado. Paralelamente, a fase de **negociação** busca junto as partes interessadas a priorização dos requisitos e a resolução de conflitos levando em consideração dependências e precedências entre os requisitos. A análise de custo, esforço e riscos para a construção do sistema também deve ser realizada.

Durante a fase de **análise *IoT*** são gerados modelos do sistema. Os possíveis casos de uso *IoT* e os arranjos de interação *IoT* do sistema são listados. O diagrama de casos de uso *IoT* e o preenchimento do catálogo dos arranjos de interação identificados devem ser produzidos durante essa fase. A fase de **especificação *IoT*** engloba a descrição dos casos de uso *IoT* identificados. Essa fase é executada paralelamente a fase de **análise** e fluxos iterativos entre as fases podem ocorrer.

A fase de **verificação *IoT*** engloba verificar o documento de requisitos para assegurar sua qualidade. A técnica $SCENARI_{OT}CHECK$ [7] é aplicada nessa essa fase. Na fase de **gerenciamento** a tecnologia propõe o controle de versão dos artefatos e a rastreabilidade entre requisitos, cenários *IoT*, arranjos de interação *IoT* e casos de uso *IoT*. Além disso, a RE_{IoT} oferece o gerenciamento de mudanças para que mudanças nos requisitos possam ser refletidas nos artefatos.

3.2 Templates da RE_{IoT}

Os *templates* fornecidos pela RE_{IoT} apoiam as fases de **elicitação** (ELI) (artefato "Escopo do projeto"), **análise** (ANA) (artefato "Proposta de solução") e **especificação** (ESP) (artefato "Descrição de casos de uso *IoT*"). As fases de concepção (CON), **negociação** (NEG) e **validação** (VAL) são minimamente atendidas pelo *template* "Escopo do projeto".

Os *templates* "Proposta de solução" e "Descrição de casos de uso *IoT*" apoiam a fase de **gerenciamento** (GER) mantendo a rastreabilidade entre os requisitos e os modelos de análise. Além disso, as técnicas descritas na seção 3 apoiam as fases de **elicitação** (ELI), **especificação** (ESP) e **verificação** (VER).

A subseção que segue apresenta a descrição global dos *templates* (escopo do projeto, proposta de solução e descrição de casos de uso *IoT*) definidos pela tecnologia RE_{IoT}. A Fig. 3 apresenta um extrato de cada *template* proposto pela RE_{IoT}, os quais estão disponíveis em *http://bit.ly/359uTIN*.

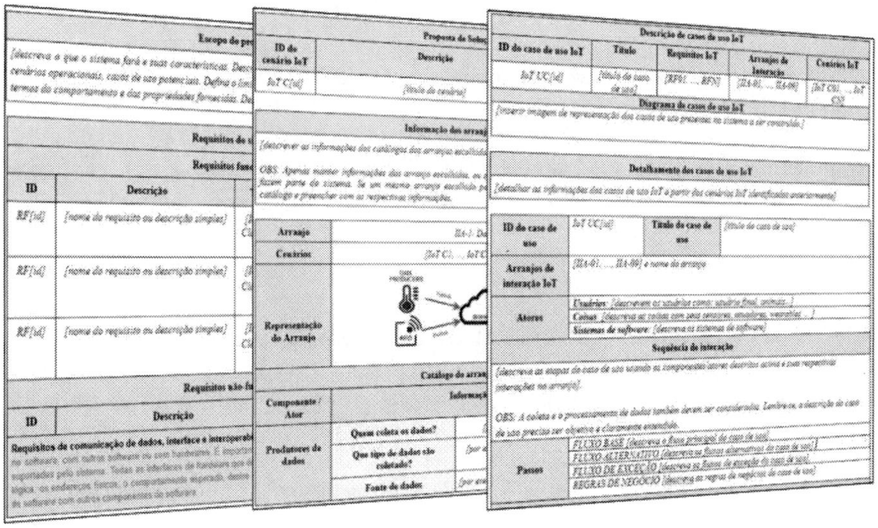

Fig. 3. Extrato dos *templates* propostos pela RE_{IoT}

3.2.1 Template "Escopo do projeto"

Este *template* apoia documentar as atividades iniciais do projeto, o problema a ser resolvido, os envolvidos no projeto, os perfis de usuários e as necessidades dos usuários que englobam as necessidades de negócio. Ele contempla a identificação e descrição de requisitos do sistema (funcionais, não funcionais, restrições, entre outros) e das regras de negócio. Além disso, a validação do documento de requisitos é viabilizada através de acordo explícito (assinatura ou cópia de e-mail). O *template* proposto é usado nas fases iniciais do projeto, ou seja, as fases de concepção (CON), elicitação (ELI), negociação (NEG) e validação (VAL).

3.2.2 Template "Proposta de solução"

Este *template* apoia documentar a descrição da solução. Nele são identificados e descritos, a partir do uso da técnica *SCENARI*$_{OT}$ [6], os cenários *IoT*, os componentes *IoT* e os arranjos de interação *IoT* (AIIs) do sistema. Além disso, fornece o detalhamento dos AIIs escolhidos para cada cenário *IoT* por meio do preenchimento dos catálogos correspondentes [6]. A rastreabilidade entre requisitos, cenários *IoT*, arranjos de interação *IoT* e seus respectivos catálogos é mantida. Este *template* deve ser utilizado nas fases de elicitação (ELI), análise (ANA), especificação (ESP) e gerenciamento (GER) visando identificar, descrever e refinar o comportamento do sistema mantendo a rastreabilidade dos requisitos.

3.2.3 Template "Descrição de casos de uso *IoT*"

Este *template* contempla a descrição dos casos de uso *IoT*. Os casos de uso são identificados e descritos fornecendo uma visão ampla do comportamento do sistema. O diagrama de casos de uso do projeto é inserido neste *template*. A rastreabilidade entre requisitos, cenários *IoT*, arranjos de interação *IoT* e casos de uso *IoT* é mantida. Este *template* deve ser usado nas fases de análise (ANA), especificação (ESP), verificação (VER) e gerenciamento (GER). A técnica *SCENARI*$_{OT}$*CHECK* [7] é aplicada durante a fase de verificação para identificar inconsistências na descrição de cenários *IoT* e seus componentes e na escolha dos AIIs.

4 Avaliando a Viabilidade dos *Templates*

A RE_{IoT} tem como objetivo apoiar engenheiros de software durante as atividades da ER. Duas das tecnologias utilizadas pela RE_{IoT} já foram avaliadas experimentalmente e têm sido utilizadas em projetos de sistemas de software *IoT*. Entretanto, a inclusão de novas facilidades para apoiar a ER com a RE_{IoT} demanda a observação inicial de viabilidade, antes da realização de estudos experimentais mais robustos. Dessa forma, esta seção apresenta uma prova de conceito da viabilidade de uso dos *templates* da RE_{IoT} em projetos de sistemas de software *IoT*.

4.1 Design

Na prova de conceito consideramos a estrutura de dois artefatos (lista de requisitos (LR) e descrição de casos de uso *IoT* (DUC1)) para sistemas convencionais que foram utilizados em projetos de sistemas software *IoT*; comparados com a estrutura dos *templates* (escopo do projeto (EP), proposta de solução (PS) e descrição de casos de uso *IoT* (DUC2)) da RE_{IoT} descritos na seção 4.

Os artefatos LR e DUC1 foram construídos a partir de *templates* convencionais em três projetos que representam problemas a serem solucionados utilizando o paradigma

IoT. São eles: i) **Projeto A** - sistema de software para apoiar a coleta de marcadores ambientais (Ex.: temperatura, umidade, particulados, nível de CO_2, e gases tóxicos); ii) **Projeto B** - sistema de software para apoiar o monitoramento de um ambiente computacional de alto desempenho (*datacentro*) envolvendo a coleta de informações de temperatura, umidade do ambiente, consumo de energia, e qualidade de fornecimento de energia; e iii) **Projeto C** - sistema de software para apoiar o monitoramento da temperatura, umidade, velocidade, e direção do vento em diferentes regiões de uma cidade.

Os artefatos LR e DUC1 foram produzidos por estudantes de graduação durante uma disciplina de Engenharia de Software na UFRJ. A disciplina contou com a participação de 21 alunos do quarto ano dos cursos de engenharia envolvendo computação. Estes alunos foram organizados em três times de desenvolvimento, com sete participantes cada um. Os times foram equilibrados e continham participantes com níveis equivalentes de conhecimento em *software* e *hardware*. Os alunos tiveram aulas expositivas sobre diferentes tópicos de engenharia de software e mentoria ao longo do projeto. Não houve intervenção dos mentores no conteúdo dos artefatos.

Os problemas tratados representavam demanda real e um *stakeholder* (totalmente externo ao curso e ao grupo de pesquisa) atuou junto com os desenvolvedores, incluindo a aceitação dos requisitos. Alguns dos tópicos ministrados na disciplina foram: engenharia de requisitos; cenários *IoT*; técnica de verificação para sistemas *IoT*, diagramas UML, entre outros. As técnicas $SCENARI_{OT}$ e $SCENARI_{OT}CHECK$ foram apresentadas aos participantes, embora não tenham sido condicionadas ao uso. Os times tinham liberdade de organizar seus projetos. O documento de requisitos representava um dos marcos de projeto. Um produto mínimo viável representa um resultado concreto a ser entregue ao final do curso.

4.2 Execução

Após a entrega do documento de requisitos pelos times, os artefatos LR e DUC1 produzidos pelos três projetos foram analisados. As estruturas dos artefatos gerados extraída com base nas informações encontradas nos mesmos foram comparadas com a estrutura de informações dos *templates* EP, PS e DUC2. Para a comparação dos *templates* foi utilizado um *checklist* que será apresentado na próxima subseção.

4.3 Resultados e Discussão da Prova de Conceito

A **Tabela 1** apresenta o *checklist* usado para comparar a estrutura de cada um dos *templates* (sistemas convencionais e tecnologia RE_{IoT}) e o resultado da análise. Analisando a **Tabela 1**, é possível observar que:

- O objetivo do projeto/sistema e o domínio do problema não são abordados pelo *template* LR. Ter conhecimento sobre o domínio do problema é uma informação essencial para sistemas *IoT* [1][2];
- O *template* LR apresenta uma descrição parcial das partes interessadas. Ele não inclui uma descrição dos perfis dos diferentes usuários que é importante para o desenvolvimento do sistema e da interface do usuário;

Tabela 1. *Checklist* de mapeamento da estrutura de informações dos *templates*

Informação do projeto/sistema	***Templates* convencionais**		***Templates* da Tecnologia RE_{IoT}**		
	LR	**DUC1**	**EP**	**PS**	**DUC2**
Nome do projeto/Responsável do projeto	T	T	T	T	T
Controle de versão	T	T	T	T	T
Acordo explícito	T		T		
Objetivo do projeto/sistema	N		T		
Domínio do problema	N		T		
Escopo do projeto	T		T		
Glossário de termos	T		T		
Descrição das partes interessadas	P		T		
Descrição das necessidades do negócio/das partes interessadas	N		T		
Requisitos funcionais	P		T		
Requisitos não-funcionais	T		T		
Negociação dos requisitos	T		T		
Regras de negócio	N	T	T		T
Análise do projeto	N		P		
Cenários *IoT*	N	P		T	T
Descrição dos componentes *IoT*		N		T	T
Arranjos *IoT*		P		T	T
Diagrama de casos de uso *IoT*		T			T
Descrição de casos de uso *IoT*		T			T
Rastreabilidade		P		T	T
Referências (outros documentos)	T		N		

* P - Coleta Parcialmente; T - Coleta Totalmente; N - Não coleta a informação; Cinza - Não se aplica

- A descrição das necessidades do negócio/das partes interessadas não é abordada pelo *template* LR. A identificação das necessidades do negócio/das partes interessadas representa a etapa inicial do projeto. Nesta etapa buscamos entender a real necessidade do cliente, que futuramente será transformada em requisitos do sistema;
- Diferentemente do *template* LR que não identifica os requisitos *IoT*, a tecnologia RE_{IoT} identifica desde o início os requisitos que direcionarão a solução *IoT*;
- O *template* DUC1 trata as informações dos cenários *IoT* e dos arranjos *IoT* parcialmente, e não trata da descrição dos componentes *IoT*. Diferentemente, a tecnologia RE_{IoT} trata estas informações totalmente nos *templates* "proposta de solução" (PS) e "descrição de casos de uso *IoT*" (DUC2);
- A rastreabilidade é tratada parcialmente pelo *template* DUC1 e tratada totalmente pela tecnologia RE_{IoT} em dois *templates*;
- O *template* LR apresenta um campo para as referências (outros documentos), o que não é abordado pela tecnologia RE_{IoT}.

Os diferentes pontos de convergência e divergência entre os *templates* (LR e DUC1) de sistemas convencionais e os *templates* da RE_{IoT} (EP, PS e DUC2), oferecem indícios de que a tecnologia RE_{IoT} é mais robusta, uma vez que trata as informações relacionadas à *IoT* desde o início do projeto.

De acordo com os resultados, foi observado que a tecnologia RE_{IoT} apresenta um potencial significativo quanto à sua utilização em sistemas de software *IoT*. Isto se deve ao fato de que ela incorpora em seus *templates* informações especificas de sistemas de software *IoT* diferentemente dos *templates* convencionais. A falta dessas informações pode ocasionar problemas na construção do documento de requisitos. No entanto, para assegurar a validade da tecnologia é necessária uma avaliação experimental para verificar, dentre outras coisas, se o encadeamento do processo construtivo bem como os *templates* são úteis, completos, corretos e intuitivos.

4.4 Ameaças à Validade e Limitações

Uma limitação é a própria prova de conceito, mesmo sendo parte da tecnologia avaliada e validada por estudos experimentais. Entretanto, os resultados apresentam indícios de que os *templates* podem capturar informação pertinentes quando comparada a uma tecnologia convencional, no que diz respeito ao uso de artefatos de projetos.

Uma **ameaça externa** diz respeito aos participantes (estudantes de graduação) que foram convidados para participar da prova de conceito. Em relação à **validade de constructo** não houve controle da criação artefatos produzidos durante a prova de conceito. Entretanto, os projetos eram equivalentes quanto ao tamanho, complexidade, e tecnologias *IoT* a serem utilizados. Pode-se destacar que os grupos receberam treinamento e mentoria em ER. Por fim, a **ameaça de conclusão** está relacionada ao estudo em si e o tamanho reduzido e homogeneidade da amostra.

5 Trabalhos Relacionados

A construção de um documento de requisitos com qualidade requer engenharia. As fases e atividades da ER podem diferir de acordo com o domínio da aplicação, pessoas envolvidas, processos, cultura organizacional, entre outros. No entanto, podemos observar algumas fases e atividades recorrentes na engenharia de requisitos como: **concepção, elicitação, negociação, análise, especificação, verificação, validação** e **gerenciamento**.

Assim sendo, esta seção apresenta um conjunto de trabalhos relacionados encontrados na literatura técnica, que abordam tecnologias para as diferentes fases da ER, citadas anteriormente. A Tabela 2 apresenta a comparação desses trabalhos em ordem cronológica).

Com relação a fase de **concepção (CON)**, as técnicas *GSEM-IoT* [11], *Ignite* [12] e a técnica de Laplante *et al.* [13] realizam a análise das partes interessadas envolvidas no sistema. Além disso, as técnicas *Ignite* e *CORE* [14] fornecem mecanismos para realizar a análise de negócio. A análise de viabilidade é parcialmente tratada pela técnica *IoT Methodology* [12].

Tabela 2. Tecnologias para requisitos x fases da ER

Tecnologia / Fase*		**CON**	**ELI**	**NEG**	**ANA**	**ESP**	**VER**	**VAL**	**GER**
Aziz *et al.* [15]					X	X			X
Mahalank *et al.* [16]						X			
Prieto-Gonzalez *et al.* [17]				X					
Takeda *et al.* [18]					X	X			
Touzani *et al.* [19]					X				
IoT-RML [20]					X	X	X		
Yamakami [21]							X		
GSEM-IoT [11]		X	X						
Carvalho *et al.* [22]							X		
Curumsing *et al.* [23]			X		X		X		X
IoT System Development Methods	*Ignite* [12]	X	X	X	X			X	
	IoT Methodology [12]	X	X					X	
Laplante *et al.* [13]		X	X		X				
Lim *et al.* [24]			X	X				X	
IoTReq [25]			X		X	X			
CORE [14]		X	X		X	X			
SCENARIoT [6]			X			X			
SCENARIoTCHECK [7]							X		
TrUStAPIS [26]			X			X			X
RETIoT		X	X	X	X	X	X	X	X

* CON – Concepção; ELI – Elicitação; NEG – Negociação; ANA – Análise; ESP – Especificação; VER – Verificação; VAL – Validação; GER – Gerenciamento

No que diz respeito à fase de **elicitação (ELI)**, Lim *et al.* [24] realizou uma revisão sistemática da literatura com o objetivo de elencar as técnicas de elicitação para sistemas *IoT*. As técnicas *SCENARIoT* [6], *Ignite* [12], *IoT Methodology* [12], Laplante *et al.* [13], *CORE* [14], Curumsing *et al.* [23], *IoTReq* [25] e *TrUStAPIS* [26] oferecem recursos para a coleta dos requisitos. *GSEM-IoT, IoTReq e IoT Methodology* propõem mecanismos para transformar as necessidades dos usuários em requisitos.

Para a fase de **negociação (NEG)**, Lim *et al.* [24] apresenta uma contribuição para a análise e resolução de conflitos. A técnica *Ignite* e a técnica de Prieto-Gonzalez *et al.* [17] abordam a análise de impacto. A análise de riscos é tratada apenas pela técnica *Ignite*.

Na fase de **análise (ANA)**, *Ignite,* a técnica de Laplante *et al.* [13], *CORE* [14], a técnica de Curumsing *et al.* [23], *IoTReq* [25], a técnica de Takeda *et al.* [18] e a técnica de Touzani *et al.* [19] usam diagramas da UML para elaborar os modelos de análise. A técnica de Aziz *et al.* [15] e a técnica *IoT-RML* [20] tratam artefatos e modelos passíveis de reuso.

Para a fase de **especificação (ESP)**, *IoTReq* [25], *CORE* [14], *TrUStAPIS* [26], a técnica de Takeda *et al.* [18] e *IoT-RML* [20] usam modelos formais (próprios) para a especificação de requisitos. A técnica de Aziz *et al.* [15] e a técnica de Mahalank *et al.* [16] fornecem *templates* para a especificação dos requisitos. A técnica *SCENARI$_{OT}$* [6] propõe a especificação de cenários *IoT* usando arranjos de interação.

Quanto à fase de **verificação (VER)**, *SCENAR$_{IOT}$CHECK* [7] e a técnica de Carvalho *et al.* [22] propõem mecanismos para verificar requisitos. A técnica de Curumsing *et al.* [23], *IoT-RML* [20], a técnica de Carvalho *et al.* [22] e a técnica de Yamakami [21], oferecem mecanismos para verificar requisitos conflitantes.

Com relação a fase de **validação (VAL)**, *Ignite* [12], *IoT Methodology* [12] *e* Lim *et al.* [24], oferecem a técnica de prototipação para garantir que o produto atenda às necessidades dos usuários.

Por último, quanto a fase de **gerenciamento (GER)**, alguns trabalhos oferecem mecanismos para viabilizar a rastreabilidade como as técnicas de Curumsing *et al.* [23] e de Aziz *et al.* [15]. A técnica *TrUStAPIS* [26] provê a rastreabilidade e o gerenciamento de mudanças dos requisitos.

A tecnologia *RE$_{IoT}$* (apresentada nas seções 3 e 4) permeia as diferentes fases da ER oferecendo apoio metodológico e técnico por meio de um processo construtivo e seus *templates*.

6 Conclusão e Trabalhos Futuros

Neste trabalho apresentamos a tecnologia *RE$_{IoT}$* (***R**equirements **E**ngineering for software systems based on **IoT***), que tem como objetivo prover apoio metodológico através de um processo construtivo (incluindo *templates* dos artefatos), técnico (técnicas de especificação e verificação de cenários *IoT*) e ferramental para a ER de sistemas de software *IoT*.

Uma prova de conceito foi realizada para comparar os *templates* (artefatos) definidos pela tecnologia *RE$_{IoT}$* com *templates* (artefatos) de sistemas convencionais (não específico para sistemas *IoT*). A comparação dos *templates* oferece indícios de que os artefatos da tecnologia *RE$_{IoT}$* podem ser mais completos do ponto de vista das informações relacionadas à *IoT*.

Alguns dos trabalhos futuros reservados para a tecnologia *RE$_{IoT}$* são: i) projeto e execução de estudos experimentais para avaliar a tecnologia *RE$_{IoT}$* em projetos de sistemas de software *IoT* nos contextos acadêmico e industrial; ii) desenvolvimento de apoio ferramental que integre o processo construtivo e os *templates* da *RE$_{IoT}$*; e iii) a partir do documento de requisitos gerado pela *RE$_{IoT}$*, apoiar a criação de casos de teste para sistemas de software *IoT*.

Referências

1. Motta, R.C., Oliveira, K.M., Travassos, G.H.: On challenges in engineering IoT software systems. J. Softw. Eng. Res. Dev. 7, 5:1-5:20 (2019). https://doi.org/10.5753/jserd.2019.15.
2. Nguyen-Duc, A., Khalid, K., Shahid Bajwa, S., Lønnestad, T.: Minimum Viable Products for Internet of Things Applications: Common Pitfalls and Practices. Future Internet. 11, Paper 50 (2019). https://doi.org/10.3390/fi11020050.
3. Arif, S., Khan, Q., Gahyyur, S.A.K.: Requirements engineering processes, tools/technologies, & methodologies. Int. J. Rev. Comput. 2, 41–56 (2009).
4. Vegendla, A., Duc, A.N., Gao, S., Sindre, G.: A Systematic Mapping Study on Requirements Engineering in Software Ecosystems: J. Inf. Technol. Res. 11, 4:1-4:21 (2018). https://doi.org/10.4018/JITR.2018010104.
5. Pandey, D., Suman, U., Ramani, A.K.: An Effective Requirement Engineering Process Model for Software Development and Requirements Management. In: International Conference on Advances in Recent Technologies in Communication and Computing. pp. 287–291. IEEE, Kottayam, India (2010). https://doi.org/10.1109/ARTCom.2010.24.
6. Silva, V.M.: SCENARIoT Support for Scenario Specification of Internet of Things-Based Software Systems, (2019).
7. Souza, B.P., Motta, R.C., Travassos, G.H.: The first version of SCENARIotCHECK: A Checklist for IoT based Scenarios. In: XXXIII Brazilian Symposium on Software Engineering. pp. 219–223. ACM Press, Salvador, Brazil (2019). https://doi.org/10.1145/3350768.3350796.
8. Silva, D., Gonçalves, T.G., Rocha, A.R.C.: A Requirements Engineering Process for IoT Systems. In: XVIII Brazilian Symposium on Software Quality. pp. 204–209. ACM Press, Fortaleza, Brazil (2019). https://doi.org/10.1145/3364641.3364664.
9. Souza, B.P., Motta, R.C., Costa, D.O., Travassos, G.H.: An IoT-based Scenario Description Inspection Technique. In: XVIII Brazilian Symposium on Software Quality. pp. 20–29. ACM Press, Fortaleza, Brazil (2019). https://doi.org/10.1145/3364641.3364644.
10. Motta, R.C., Silva, V.M., Travassos, G.H.: Towards a more in-depth understanding of the IoT Paradigm and its challenges. J. Softw. Eng. Res. Dev. 7, 3:1-3:16 (2019). https://doi.org/10.5753/jserd.2019.14.
11. Zambonelli, F.: Key Abstractions for IoT-Oriented Software Engineering. IEEE Softw. 34, 38–45 (2017). https://doi.org/10.1109/MS.2017.3.
12. Giray, G., Tekinerdogan, B., Tüzün, E.: IoT System Development Methods. In: Hassan, Q., Khan, A.R., and Madani, S.A. (eds.) Internet of Things. pp. 141–159. CRC Press/Taylor & Francis, New York (2018).
13. Laplante, N.L., Laplante, P.A., Voas, J.M.: Stakeholder Identification and Use Case Representation for Internet-of-Things Applications in Healthcare. IEEE Syst. J. 12, 1589–1597 (2018). https://doi.org/10.1109/JSYST.2016.2558449.
14. Hamdi, M.S., Ghannem, A., Loucopoulos, P., Kavakli, E., Ammar, H.: Intelligent Parking Management by Means of Capability Oriented Requirements Engineering. In: Wotawa, F., Friedrich, G., Pill, I., Koitz-Hristov, R., and Ali, M. (eds.) Advances and Trends in Artificial Intelligence. From Theory to Practice. pp. 158–172. Springer International Publishing, Cham (2019). https://doi.org/10.1007/978-3-030-22999-3_15.

15. Aziz, M.W., Sheikh, A.A., Felemban, E.A.: Requirement Engineering Technique for Smart Spaces. In: International Conference on Internet of things and Cloud Computing. pp. 54:1–54:7. ACM Press, Cambridge United Kingdom (2016). https://doi.org/10.1145/2896387.2896439.
16. Mahalank, S.N., Malagund, K.B., Banakar, R.M.: Non Functional Requirement Analysis in IoT based smart traffic management system. In: International Conference on Computing Communication Control and Automation. pp. 1–6. IEEE, Pune, India (2016). https://doi.org/10.1109/ICCUBEA.2016.7860147.
17. Prieto-Gonzalez, L., Tamm, G., Stantchev, V.: Towards a Software Engineering Approach for Cloud and IoT Services in Healthcare. In: Gervasi, O., Murgante, B., Misra, S., Rocha, A.M.A.C., Torre, C.M., Taniar, D., Apduhan, B.O., Stankova, E., and Wang, S. (eds.) Computational Science and Its Applications. pp. 439–452. Springer International Publishing, Cham (2016). https://doi.org/10.1007/978-3-319-42089-9_31.
18. Takeda, A., Hatakeyama, Y.: Conversion Method for User Experience Design Information and Software Requirement Specification. In: Marcus, A. (ed.) Design, User Experience, and Usability: Design Thinking and Methods. pp. 356–364. Springer International Publishing, Cham (2016). https://doi.org/10.1007/978-3-319-40409-7_34.
19. Touzani, M., Ponsard, C.: Towards Modelling and Analysis of Spatial and Temporal Requirements. In: 24th International Requirements Engineering Conference. pp. 389–394. IEEE, Beijing, China (2016). https://doi.org/10.1109/RE.2016.60.
20. Costa, B., Pires, P.F., Delicato, F.C.: Specifying Functional Requirements and QoS Parameters for IoT Systems. In: 15th Intl Conf on Dependable, Autonomic and Secure Computing, 15th Intl Conf on Pervasive Intelligence and Computing, 3rd Intl Conf on Big Data Intelligence and Computing and Cyber Science and Technology Congress. pp. 407–414. IEEE, Orlando, FL (2017). https://doi.org/10.1109/DASC-PICom-DataCom-CyberSciTec.2017.83.
21. Yamakami, T.: Horizontal Requirement Engineering in Integration of Multiple IoT Use Cases of City Platform as a Service. In: IEEE International Conference on Computer and Information Technology (CIT). pp. 292–296. IEEE, Helsinki, Finland (2017). https://doi.org/10.1109/CIT.2017.54.
22. Carvalho, R.M., Andrade, R.M.C., Oliveira, K.M.: Towards a catalog of conflicts for HCI quality characteristics in UbiComp and IoT applications: Process and first results. In: 12th International Conference on Research Challenges in Information Science (RCIS). pp. 1–6. IEEE, Nantes (2018). https://doi.org/10.1109/RCIS.2018.8406651.
23. Curumsing, M.K., Fernando, N., Abdelrazek, M., Vasa, R., Mouzakis, K., Grundy, J.: Emotion-oriented requirements engineering: A case study in developing a smart home system for the elderly. J. Syst. Softw. 147, 215–229 (2019). https://doi.org/10.1016/j.jss.2018.06.077.
24. Lim, T.-Y., Chua, F.-F., Tajuddin, B.B.: Elicitation Techniques for Internet of Things Applications Requirements: A Systematic Review. In: VII International Conference on Network, Communication and Computing. pp. 182–188. ACM Press, Taipei City, Taiwan (2018). https://doi.org/10.1145/3301326.3301360.
25. Reggio, G.: A UML-based proposal for IoT system requirements specification. In: 10th International Workshop on Modelling in Software Engineering. pp. 9–16. ACM Press, Gothenburg, Sweden (2018). https://doi.org/10.1145/3193954.3193956.
26. Ferraris, D., Fernandez-Gago, C.: TrUStAPIS: a trust requirements elicitation method for IoT. Int. J. Inf. Secur. 19, 111–127 (2020). https://doi.org/10.1007/s10207-019-00438-x.

Towards Supporting the Specification of Context-Aware Software System Test Cases

Andréa Cristina de Souza Doreste and Guilherme Horta Travassos

Systems Engineering and Computer Science Program
COPPE
Federal University of Rio de Janeiro, Brazil
{doreste, ght}@cos.ufrj.br

Abstract. In Software Engineering, context can be understood as the overall set of information used to characterize the situation of an entity. A software system is context-aware if it uses the context to provide relevant information or services to the user. Nowadays, different types of software systems with a profound impact on the user's life can be considered context-aware (e.g., ubiquitous and Internet of Things software systems). Therefore, it is crucial to guarantee that they behave correctly. Software Testing is the primary process for verifying system behavior. Because of the particularities of Context-Aware Software Systems (CASS), conventional testing methods are not enough to test such systems. Based on that, we propose CATS#, a technique to support software engineers with the specification of CASS test cases and capture not only the context itself but its variation as well. CATS# is an evolution of the CATS (Context-Aware Test Suite) Design technique. It introduces two relevant evolutions: test case models and a new test template. The test case models were proposed after we searched for context-aware applications through the literature and realized that the context could affect the test process in different manners. The test template was proposed to capture the variation of context by specifying which variation should occur during the test case and when it should occur. We selected one example application to apply our technique, deriving different types of test cases and showing its relevance in these initial steps.

Keywords: Context-Aware Software System; CASS; Software Testing

1 Introduction

Over the last few years, many contemporary software systems having a profound impact on society are emerging. Such systems include solutions regarding Smart Cities, the Internet of Things, Cyber-physical System (CPS), Self-driving cars, and many other modern systems susceptible to the context and its variation. Moreover, like any other software system, they must adequately behave after their deployment. A common feature among such systems is their dependency on the variation of context. Some recently reported accidents with autonomous vehicles and jet airplanes have shown the damage is enormous when the variation of context cannot be appropriately verified.

However, it is crucial to validate the behavior of context-aware software systems (CASS) regarding the variation of context before their deployment.

Software Testing is the primary process for verifying the behavior of a software system. Due to the particularities of CASS, conventional testing methods are, usually, not sufficient. There is a lack of software technologies to test CASS [1]. Despite this fact, these systems still need to be adequately tested because, like any other system, they fail [2]. Therefore, these fails must be revealed, and the defects identified and fixed before the system reaches the final users. However, a lack of testing technologies for such software systems does not contribute to mitigating their failure after deployment. That is why it is essential to propose new software technologies to support testing strategies for CASS.

The CATS (Context-Aware Test Suite) Design technique [3] resulted from the CAcTUS (Context-Aware Testing for Ubiquitous System) Project, which investigated test strategies for ubiquitous systems. CATS has the purpose of identifying the context variables and thresholds (THR) to describe the test oracle and, consequently, the test cases. The test oracle would be the combination of context variables, identified thresholds, and expected behaviors once reaching the thresholds.

CATS Design was our first step towards understanding how to test CASS. It covers most of the issues regarding the specification of test cases for CASS. However, it does not include the perception that the variation of context can affect the test cases in different ways. Therefore, we propose CATS# as an evolution of CATS Design. Based on what we observed on working in the development of and testing with CASS, we introduce two new features: the test case models and a new test template. Section 3 depicts the reasons why these features contribute to evolving the CATS Design.

Besides this introduction, there are five more parts in this article. Section 2 has the definitions; Sections 3.1 and 3.2 present the modifications we are proposing; Section 3.3 shows one example application; Section 4 shows our final considerations and next steps.

2 Basic Definitions

2.1 Context-Aware Software Systems

In our work, context is the overall set of information used to characterize the situation of an entity considered relevant to the interaction between an actor, which can be a user, and an application [4]. Furthermore, while the context is, in some way, abstract, substantial, and continuous, we can discretize it through representative context variables (CVs). Each CV represents a piece of specific information about the context [3], as can be seen in Fig 1.

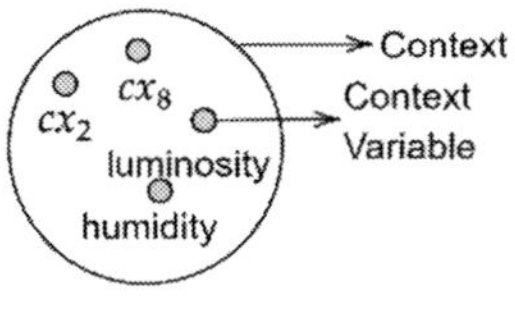

Fig 1. Context and Context Variables

A software system is context-aware, whether it makes use of context variables to provide relevant information or services to their actors. For the sake of simplicity, there are two types of CASS. The first one (T1) only uses the information regarding the context to support its behaviors (e.g., a system responsible for sensing the temperature and display it to the user). The second one (T2) has its behavior influenced by the variation of context (e.g., the same previous system using the temperature to determine, automatically, whether turning the air-conditioner ON or OFF) [4].

Nevertheless, depending on the type of the software system, being context-aware is not all. Context is something dynamic; it can change anytime, influencing the T2 system´s behaviors on the fly. Thus, the CASS must be ready to respond and adapt itself appropriately to the variation of context. As so, their testing.

2.2 Software Testing

Software testing is responsible for verifying software system behaviors and revealing failures [3]. A Test Case (TC) is composed of input values (test input), constraints under which the test item must be executed (conditions), and the expected behaviors from the software under those constraints (expected results) (Fig. 2) [5].

Test Scripts would use the Test Cases during the Test Process for the testing of a Test Item into a predefined Test Environment to produce a set of Outputs. In the end, the obtained outputs (behaviors) should be compared with the expected results specified in the test cases (Oracle) to verify the success or failure [3]. Obtained and expected results are predictable and directly comparable in this case.

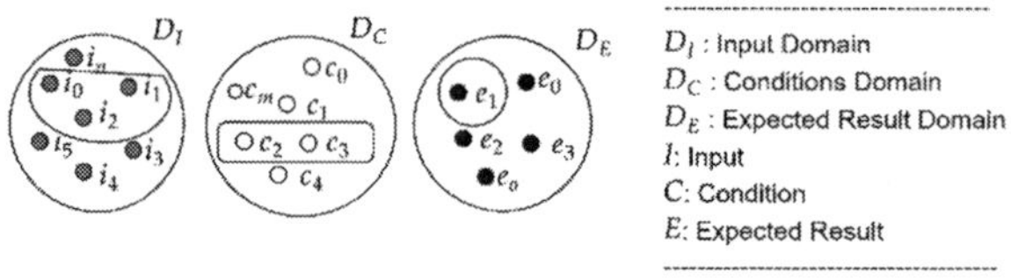

$$I = \{i_i : i_i \in D_I\},\ C = \{c_i : c_i \in D_C\},\ E = \{e_i : e_i \in D_E\}$$

$$TC = \{(I, C, E) : I \subset D_I,\ C \subset D_C,\ E \subset D_E\}$$

Fig 2. Conventional Test Model

3 Some Issues Regarding CASS Testing

The variation of context can affect the test process in two different ways: the input and/or the conditions of the test cases, which naturally affect the expected results. Consequently, sometimes, the variation of context will occur during the test execution by varying the environmental conditions. Therefore, to prepare the testing for this situation correctly, it is necessary an evolved test template. It should not just capture the variation of context (as it is in CATS) but also when such a variation should occur as well. It is not an easy task to abstract it in general scenarios, but we believe it can be done in particular cases. To support our discussions and represent these differences, we present a conceptual model in Section 3.1 and a test template in Section 3.2.

3.1 Testing Models

Section 2 illustrates a conceptual testing model for conventional software systems, but when the variation of context matters, a new set of information must be taken into consideration, as well as its influence in the test process. It has been said that the variation of context could affect the test inputs and conditions and, consequently, the expected results. Thus, when generating a model for testing CASS, it must be taken into consideration that each information on the test input and test conditions will represent and be attached to the context.

In this way, as Fig 3 shows, in CASS Testing Models, the input should be composed by a tuple (*i, cx*), where *i* is an element from the Input Domain, and *cx* is the context it represents. The same occurs with Test Conditions (*c, cx*) and with the Expected Results (*e, cx*) where *c* and *e* will be elements from the Conditions Domain and Expected Results Domain, respectively.

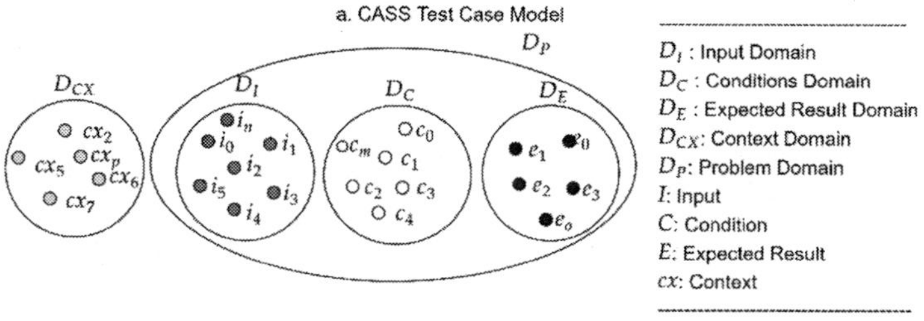

$$TC = \{(I, C, E): I \subset D_i \times D_{CX},\ C \subset D_C \times D_{CX},\ E \subset D_E \times D_{CX}\}$$

$$I = \{(i_i, cx_i): i_i \in D_I,\ cx_i \in D_{CX}\},$$
$$C = \{(c_i, cx_i): c_i \in D_C,\ cx_i \in D_{CX}\},$$
$$E = \{(e_i, cx_i): e_i \in D_E,\ cx_i \in D_{CX}\}$$

b. No Context	c. Context influences the Input
$I = \{i_i : i_i \in D_I\}$ $C = \{c_i : c_i \in D_C\}$ $E = \{e_i : e_i \in D_E\}$	$I = \{(i_i, cx_i): i_i \in D_I,\ cx_i \in D_{CX}\}$ $C = \{(c_i: c_i \in D_C\}$ $E = \{(e_i, cx_i): e_i \in D_E,\ cx_i \in D_{CX}\}$
d. Context influences the Conditions	e. Context influences the Conditions and the Input
$I = \{i_i : i_i \in D_I\}$ $C = \{(c_i, cx_i): c_i \in D_C,\ cx_i \in D_{CX}\}$ $E = \{(e_i, cx_i): e_i \in D_E,\ cx_i \in D_{CX}\}$	$I = \{(i_i, cx_i): i_i \in D_I,\ cx_i \in D_{CX}\},$ $C = \{(c_i, cx_i): c_i \in D_C,\ cx_i \in D_{CX}\},$ $E = \{(e_i, cx_i): e_i \in D_E,\ cx_i \in D_{CX}\}$

Fig 3. CASS General Test Model

It is important to note that the context element in E will always be the same one in I or C because a specific expected result would be a consequence of the context. Equations (1) and (2) demonstrate these relations:

$$I = \{i_0, i_1\},\ C = \{(c_2, cx_3), (c_4, cx_0)\},\ E = \{(e_0, cx_3), (e_2, cx_0)\} \quad (1)$$

$$TC = \{(\{i_0, i_1\}, \{(c_2, cx_3), (c_4, cx_0)\}, \{(e_0, cx_3), (e_2, cx_0)\})\} \quad (2)$$

Thus, this model can represent four situations, as summarized in Table 1:

- When there is no context ($D_{CX} = \{ \}$), the model gets back to the Conventional Test Case Model (Fig. 3.b);
- When the context influences just the input, and the conditions remain constant (Fig. 3.c), the variation of context does not happen during the execution of testing. The only consequence will be increasing the number of test cases;
- When the context influences the conditions, and the inputs remain constant (Fig. 3.d), we need a new test strategy able to capture the variation of context during the test execution, and;
- When the context influences the input and the conditions simultaneously (Fig. 3.e), we have the complete and general CASS Test Case Model. In this case, there is a need to use test environments supporting the variation of context during the test execution. As far as we are aware, there is no such environment available yet [8].

Table 1. Test Situations

	Input (I)	**Condition (C)**	**Expected Result (E)**
Conventional Test Case Model	Static Value	Static Value	Static Value
CASS Test Case Model A	Dynamic Value	Static Value	Dynamic Value
CASS Test Case Model B	Static Value	Dynamic Value	Dynamic Value
CASS Test Case Model C	Dynamic Value	Dynamic Value	Dynamic Value

3.2 Testing Template

The first column of Table 2 shows the fields of CATS Design's test template. It has the necessary information used in conventional systems and new fields specific for CASS (*in Italic*). Its objective is to specify every known threshold for each context variable related to the Test Case. Thus, if one of the specified contexts varies during the test execution, the Expected Output should be specified as well.

We intend to cause a variation of context (regarding a specific CV) during the test case execution while keeping all the other CV fixed. In doing so, some fields must be changed, and others added to the CATS template. The result is presented in the second column of Table 2. The field "Fixed Conditions" specifies which CV is static; the "Varying Conditions" field contains how the conditions must variate, crossing the previously established threshold. Finally, the CATS# template gains a structured flow similar to use cases. The tag "ci" is added to the Test Steps, indicating that conditions ci must vary just before the execution of the next test step. A filled template can be seen in Table 5.

Table 2. CATS Template X CATS# Template

CATS Template	CATS# Template
Test Case ID	Test Case ID
Test Objective	Test Objective
Precondition	Precondition
X	*Fixed Conditions*
Test Input	Test Input
Test Steps	Test Steps
Relevant Context Variables	*Varying Conditions (C)*
Known Threshold	*X*
Expected Result for each Threshold	*Expected Result (E)*
Postconditions	Postconditions

3.3 Proof of Concept

Our proposal is at its initial stage. To observe its initial feasibility, we selected an application by Afanasov, Mottola, and Ghezzi [6] to use CATS#. It is a Wildlife tracker where battery-powered nodes from a WSN (wireless sensor network) are embedded in collars and attached to animals. Each node has a GPS sensor, two low-power short-range radios working as proximity sensors, and small solar panels to prolong the node lifetime. The GPS sensor captures the pace of the animal's movement, and it may be disabled if the battery is running low. A proximity sensor is responsible for tracking an animal's encounter with other animals and logging the data. Another sensor is responsible for sending the collected data to the base-station whenever they are near. More information about the application can be found in [6]. After applying CATS#, we obtained the results presented in Table 3.

Table 3. Results after applying CATS# for Wildlife Application

Context Variable	Effect	Threshold	Test Situations
Battery Level	> threshold, GPS status = ON	Battery Level going down the threshold	CASS - Model B
	< threshold, GPS status = OFF	Battery Level going up the threshold	CASS - Model B
Animal Proximity	= YES, collect data from encounters	Getting closer to an animal	CASS - Model A
Base-Station Proximity	= YES, send data to the Base-Station	Getting closer to a Base-Station	CASS - Model A

We selected three test cases, one from each model, to show how they will differ. As Tables 3 and 4 show, in TC01, the "battery level" will be tested as a condition (CASS

Model B) related with CX0 (Bat. Level ≥ *THR*) and CX1 (Bat. Level < *THR*), and the Expected Results are "GPS Available" and "GPS Disabled," respectively.

In TC02, "BS Proximity" will be tested as an input (CASS Model A) and is related to CX0 (BS Proximity = NO) and CX3 (BS Proximity = YES). The Expected results related to CX3 is "Send Data to BS" and to CX0 is "Log in GPS information."

Finally, to show the difference, TC03 specifies a conventional test case, with no variation of context.

Table 4. Wildlife Test Cases

Id	Input	Context	Conditions	Expected Result
TC01	Animal location	CX0	Bat. Level≥ *THR*	GPS status = ON
		CX1	Bat. Level< *THR*	GPS status = OFF
TC02	BS Proximity = NO	CX0	Bat. Level ≥ *THR*	Log Data in the node
	BS Proximity = YES	CX3		Send Data to BS
TC03	Animal location	CX0	Bat. Level ≥ *THR*	Log in GPS information

As we said before, conventional strategies can be used to test the CASS Test Case Model A (see Table 1) and, consequently, TC02. Therefore, we selected TC01 to use our proposal test template (Table 5). It shows that, after the third step, the Battery Level should variate as indicated in c1, and the Expected Result for this variation is "The system disables the GPS." The template also shows that the variables Animal and BS proximity should be kept constant. Finally, the "GPS status" in Precondition and Post-condition changes because of the variation of context occurring during the test execution.

Table 5. CATS# Template for a TC from Wildlife Application

Test Id	TC01
Test Objective	Verify the variation of the CV Bat. Level
Precondition	— The BS is out of reach — Battery-Level ≥ *THR* — Solar Panel is deactivated — GPS status = ON
Fixed Conditions	— Animal proximity = NO — BS proximity = NO
Input (I)	— GPS location (lat, long)
Test Steps	1. Starts the node 2. Change the node position 3. The node starts to collect data (c1) 4. Change the node position
Varying Conditions (C)	c1. Bat. Level ≥ *THR* → Bat. Level < *THR*
Expected Result (E)	The system disables the GPS
Post condition	— GPS status = OFF — Battery-Level < *THR*

4 Final Considerations

As can be seen in [1], there is a lack of technologies to test CASS. Also, we realized that the context had been treated as someway static most of the time. Besides, the different ways of how the context affects testing are not even noticed. Thus, it cannot be captured by the test activity. CATS# is an attempt to evolve CATS adopting the learning from the literature. We propose the CASS testing models and the new test template to help software engineers understand the variation of context and adequately plan the testing for CASS. In this way, each fulfilled test template will represent a different context with its expected result and the test script necessary for the future test execution. Also, the template can be used in different levels of testing, in simple scenarios (such as varying one CV) or more complex situations (where the CVs will interact).

The application used in section 3.3 is simple. However, it intends to demonstrate the different test situations involved in the testing of CASS, as well as the influence of the variation of context in the test process.

Finally, CATS# is ongoing research. We intend to modify the entire CATS process to make it simple and easily applicable. Besides, after all the modifications, experimental studies will be conducted to adequately evaluate the behavior of CATS#, specifying test cases for different test situations and applying it in more complex scenarios. We are aware that forcing a variation of context as specified is not always an easy task when performing testing. Thus, in the future, we intend to propose a tool to control the Test Environment and, consequently, setting the context-free during testing [8].

Acknowledgments

The CNPq (Brazilian National Council for Scientific and Technological Development) and CAPES (Brazilian Coordination for the Improvement of Higher Education Personnel) support this research. Prof. Travassos is a CNPq researcher (304234/2018-4).

References

1. Amalfitano, D., Matalonga, S., Doreste, A., Fasolino, A. R., Travassos, G. H.: A Rapid Review on Testing of Context-Aware Contemporary Software System, Technical Report, UFRJ, Rio de Janeiro (2019). http://www.cos.ufrj.br/uploadfile/publicacao/2910.pdf
2. Charette, R. N.: Why software fails. IEEE Spectrum, 42(9), 42-49 (2005).
3. Silva, F. R.: CATS Design: A Context-Aware Testing Approach, Master Dissertation, UFRJ, Rio de Janeiro, (2016). http://www.cos.ufrj.br/uploadfile/publicacao/2596.pdf
4. Dey, A. K., Abowd, G. D.: Towards a better understanding of context and context-awareness, Technical Report, Georgia Institute of Technology, Atlanta (1999), https://smartech.gatech.edu/handle/1853/3389
5. Dias-Neto, A. C.: Uma infra-estrutura computacional para apoiar o planejamento e controle de testes de software, Master Dissertation, UFRJ, Rio de Janeiro (2006). http://www.cos.ufrj.br/uploadfile/publicacao/2704.pdf
6. Afanasov, M., Mottola, L., Ghezzi, C.: Software adaptation in wireless sensor networks. ACM Transactions on Autonomous and Adaptive Systems (TAAS), 12(4), 18 (2018).
7. Mirza, A. M., & Khan, M. N. A.: An Automated Functional Testing Framework for Context-aware Applications. IEEE Access, 6, 46568-46583 (2018).
8. Matalonga, S., Travassos, G.H.: Testing context-aware software systems: Unchain the context, set it free!, Proc. 31st CBSOFT/SBES. ACM (2017).

TestTDO: A Top-Domain Software Testing Ontology

Guido Tebes, Luis Olsina, Denis Peppino and Pablo Becker
GIDIS_Web, Facultad de Ingeniería, UNLPam, General Pico, LP, Argentina
guido.tebes92@gmail.com; olsinal@ing.unlpam.edu.ar;
denispeppino92@gmail.com; beckerp@ing.unlpam.edu.ar

Abstract. One of the Software Engineering (SE) areas that supports quality assurance is testing. Given that specific processes, artifacts, methods and ultimately strategies for software testing involve a large number of domain concepts, it is valuable to have a robust conceptual base, that is, a software testing ontology that defines the terms, properties, relationships and axioms in an explicit and unambiguous way. Ontologies for instance foster a clearer terminological understanding of process and method specifications for strategies, among many other benefits. After analyzing both the results of a conducted Systematic Literature Review (SLR) of primary studies on software testing ontologies and the state-of-the-art of test-related standards, we decided to develop a top-domain ontology that fits our goals. TestTDO is built in the framework of a four-layered ontological architecture, which considers foundational, core, domain and instance ontologies. In this paper, we discuss aspects of the development, evaluation, verification and validation of the TestTDO conceptualization.

Keywords: Software Testing, Top-Domain Ontology, Ontological Architecture.

1 Introduction

Companies commonly establish and reach business goals for different types of purposes. Business goals are the main goals that an organization tries to achieve. In the statement of it always lies a purpose or intentionality. The goal's purpose is the rationale to achieve it. Purposes can be classified into four categories such as evaluation, testing, development and maintenance [6]. Examples of evaluation goal purposes may include to understand, monitor, control, improve, etc. while examples of test goal purposes may entail to find defects, review, verify, validate, among others.

To achieve the purposes of business goals, strategies may be used. A strategy is a core resource of an organization that defines a specific course of action to follow. It specifies what to do and how to do it. Consequently, strategies should integrate 1) process specifications, 2) method specifications, and 3) a robust domain conceptual base – such as an ontology. This principle of integratedness promotes, therefore, knowing what activities are involved, and how to carry them out by means of methods in the framework of a common domain vocabulary. In [17], to achieve evaluation purposes, a family of strategies integrating the three-abovementioned capabilities is discussed.

Bearing in mind that already there are integrated strategies that provide support for achieving evaluation purposes, the reader can surmise that strategies that provide support for achieving test purposes are feasible to be developed as well. Given that a strategy should integrate a domain terminology, then any well-specified software testing strategy should also have this capability for the software testing domain.

Software testing is a critical process for software quality assurance. It is also a complex domain since testing has a large number of specific methods, processes and strategies. All of them involve many specific domain concepts. Hence, it is valuable to have a robust conceptual base, i.e., a conceptualized software testing ontology that explicitly and unambiguously defines the terms, properties, relationships and axioms.

A benefit of having a suitable testing ontology is to minimize the heterogeneity and ambiguity problems that we currently observe in the different concepts dealing with testing methods, processes and artifacts. On the other side, one desirable feature is if the existing testing ontologies cover concepts related to static and dynamic testing as well as their linking with Non-Functional Requirements (NFRs) and Functional Requirements (FRs) sub-ontologies. Having this feature may turn out useful for method and process specifications to our aim, i.e., for developing a family of testing strategies.

In order to adopt or adapt an existing testing ontology, or to develop a new one, we have followed the Design Science Research (DSR) [12, 22] approach. It is a rigorous research methodology, which proposes the construction of artifacts for providing useful and effective solutions to a relevant problem in a given domain. Artifacts must be innovative and useful solutions to a non-trivial problem. The artifact development implies a cycle of design-construction-evaluation activities, which should iterate as many times as necessary before the artifact (already verified and validated) is ready for its use.

To start the DSR process, the Identify the Problem/Solution (A1) activity should firstly be performed [22]. In order to find out existing solutions (i.e., conceptualized software testing ontologies) to our problem, we conducted a Systematic Literature Review (SLR) [20], from the end of May 2018 until the beginning of March 2019. We selected 12 primary studies documenting conceptualized testing ontologies, which were evaluated from the ontological quality standpoint. This includes characteristics such as structural quality, terminological coverage quality, among others [9, 21].

In general, we observed that most of them have a lack of NFRs and static testing terminological coverage. Moreover, the 12 retrieved ontologies present opportunities to improve their structural quality for different reasons such as: i) do not have all their terms, non-taxonomic relationships and properties defined as well as axioms specified; ii) do not have non-taxonomic relationships or, if they do, do not have taxonomic and non-taxonomic relationships well balanced.

As a result, we have confirmed that there exists heterogeneity, ambiguity, and incompleteness for concepts dealing with testing activities, artifacts and methods. Furthermore, they are not directly linked with NFRs and FRs concepts. So the current testing ontologies are not suitable to our aim, i.e., for terminologically nourishing specifications of methods and processes for a family of testing strategies to be developed. For this reason, after analyzing the relevancy of the problem/solution, we have developed TestTDO, a top-domain software testing ontology by performing two activities of DSR, namely: Design and Develop the Solution (A2) and Execute Verification and Validation (A3). This endeavor took us seven months, which ended by the end of Sept., 2019.

In summary, this work documents aspects of the TestTDO conceptualization and its ontological quality evaluation. In addition, by using the stated set of competency questions and a proof of concept, we illustrate aspects of its verification and validation.

It is worth mentioning that TestTDO is placed into an ontological conceptual architecture called FCD-OntoArch (*Foundational, Core, and Domain Ontological Architecture for Sciences* [6]). It is a four-layered ontological architecture that considers foundational, core, domain and instance levels. In FCD-OntoArch, ontologies at the same level can be related to each other. Also, ontologies at lower levels can be semantically enriched by ontologies at upper levels. For example, TestTDO at domain level is enriched by concepts of the ProcessCO [5] ontology placed at the core level. In turn the latter is enriched by concepts of ThingFO at the foundational level, as we see later on.

The rest of the paper is organized as follows. Section 2 provides a summary of related work on conceptualized testing ontologies. Section 3 describes where TestTDO is placed into FCD-OntoArch. Section 4 analyzes the main concepts, properties and relationships included in TestTDO. Section 5 describes how TestTDO was verified, validated and evaluated. Finally, Section 6 summarizes conclusions and future work.

2 Why is another Software Testing Ontology needed?

From the SLR performed in [20], we have selected 12 ontologies. Next, we summarize the aim of each ontology and then show aspects related to their ontological quality.

In [8], Campos *et al.* use a domain ontology named RTE-Ontology (*Regression Tests Execution*) and a provenance ontology model (PROV-O) to capture and provide regression tests data to support the continuous improvement of software testing processes. In [24, 25], Vasanthapriyan *et al.* document a software testing ontology designed to represent the necessary testing knowledge within the software testers' context. Although [24] and [25] share common terms, [25] has more terms related to static testing, while [24] adds the functional and non-functional testing terms, among others. Souza *et al.* document ROoST (*Reference Ontology on Software Testing*) [19], which aims at defining a shared vocabulary to this domain to be used in Knowledge Management initiatives. It was developed for establishing a common conceptualization about the software testing domain focusing on the testing process in order to support the communication between the stakeholders involved in such a process. In [2], Asman *et al.* present a top-domain software testing ontology that contains general software testing knowledge. They developed this ontology to serve as a basis for the development of new lower level domain ontologies.

In addition, Freitas *et al.* present PTOntology (*Performance Testing*) [11] where semantic technologies are explored to demonstrate the practical feasibility of developing ontology-based applications for assisting testers with performance test planning and management. Arnicans *et al.* [1] propose a methodology for semi-automatically obtaining a lightweight ontology to the software testing domain based on the ISTQB glossary [15]. However, they only built a taxonomy of testing techniques rather than a lightweight ontology. Sapna *et al.* [18] use a testing ontology to represent and manage use cases and scenarios and then to enumerate test scenarios in order to produce a test suite. Cai *et al.* [7] present a construction method of software testing ontologies based on SWEBOK [13] and one software testing classification ontology based on the ISO 9126 software quality model. Just like Arnicans *et al.*, the documented ontology is rather a taxonomy of testing techniques. Bai *et al.* developed TOM (*Test Ontology Model*) [3] that is compatible with the U2TP [23]. Besides, it enriches the semantics of the U2TP model with class properties and constraints using ontology information. Barbosa *et al.* built OntoTest [4], which aims at supporting acquisition, organization, reuse and sharing of knowledge on the testing domain. OntoTest has a Main Software Testing Ontology and 5 sub-ontologies that address specific concepts of it. Unfortunately, authors only documents in a graphic way the conceptualization of the Main Software Testing Ontology and the Testing Resource sub-ontology. Also, the Testing Resource sub-ontology is rather a taxonomy. Finally, Zhu *et al.* developed a system prototype for testing web-based applications that uses an ontology of software testing named STOWS [26]. It aims at facilitating the communications among agents and between agents and human developers and testers.

The abovementioned ontologies were evaluated in [20] from the ontological quality standpoint. The summarized results are shown in Table 1, while the full requirements tree (i.e., the included characteristics, sub-characteristics and attributes), and the outcomes are in http://bit.ly/OntoQualityEval. Notice that we use the metaphor of the three-colored semaphore to identify the satisfaction acceptability level achieved. The red color with values within the [0;60) range, in the percentage scale indicates an "unsatisfactory" acceptability level; yellow [60;85) indicates a "marginal" level, and green [85;100] indicates a "satisfactory" level. According to Table 1, the two best scores for the Ontological Structural Quality (1.1) sub-characteristic were obtained by ROoST [19] (79.08% ◆) followed by Asman *et al.* [2] (61.92% ◆). The remainder ontologies, none reached even the marginal level. In general, this problem is because most ontologies do not have all their terms, non-taxonomic relationships and properties defined as well as axioms specified. Only [19, 26] have fully specified axioms.

Table 1. Summary of the evaluation results of 12-selected ontologies through SLR regarding their Ontological Quality (1), which includes Ontological Structural Quality (1.1), Domain-specific Terminological Coverage Quality (1.2) and Compliance to other Vocabularies (1.3) sub-characteristics. The green color indicates "satisfactory" acceptability level (●), yellow "marginal" (◆), and red "unsatisfactory" (■). Indicators' values are expressed in [%].

	[8]	[25]	[24]	[19]	[2]	[11]	[1]	[18]	[7]	[3]	[4]	[26]
1	40.05 ■	46.62 ■	51.28 ■	79.54 ◆	66.71 ◆	36.41 ■	32.75 ■	30.95 ■	25 ■	32.79 ■	42.36 ■	39.52 ■
1.1	55 ■	33.24 ■	32.56 ■	79.08 ◆	61.92 ◆	22.81 ■	0 ■	16.40 ■	0 ■	20.08 ■	28.72 ■	59.03 ■
1.2	50 ■	75 ◆	100 ●	50 ■	100 ●	50 ■	100 ●	50 ■	50 ■	50 ■	50 ■	50 ■
1.3	8.50 ■	50 ■	50 ■	100 ●	52.50 ■	50 ■	42.50 ■	42.50 ■	50 ■	42.50 ■	60 ◆	0 ■

Looking at Table 1, only three ontologies reached 100% (●) in the Domain-specific Terminological Coverage Quality (1.2) sub-characteristic, namely: Arnicans *et al.* [1], Asman *et al.* [2], and Vasanthapriyan *et al.* [24]. This means that these ontologies have at least one term related to static testing, one related to dynamic testing, one related to functional testing and one related to non-functional testing. The remainder ontologies only achieved 50% (■) of coverage, except [25], which met 75% (◆).

Regarding the Compliance to other Vocabularies (1.3) sub-characteristic, almost all ontologies adhere their terminology to international standard glossaries. The only ones that do not specify the use of international standard glossaries are RTE-Ontology [8] and STOWS [26]. On the other hand, very few ontologies take into account the terminology of other core or domain ontologies, namely: Asman *et al.* [2], OntoTest [4],

RTE-Ontology [8] and ROoST [19]. Finally, ROoST is the only one that was built on a foundational ontology, named UFO. Therefore, ROoST is the only ontology that reached 100% (●) in Compliance to other Vocabularies (1.3) sub-characteristic.

Taking into account the above-summarized analysis, the best-ranked ontology with regard to the Ontological Quality (1) is ROoST (79.54% ◈) –although it did not achieve a satisfactory level. It has a lack of NFRs and static testing terminological coverage and there is no linking with FR and NFR terms. We need a top-domain ontology with higher coverage since we plan to develop more specific testing domain ontologies for dynamic testing such as performance testing, among others. Furthermore, although ROoST is embedded in a network of ontologies whose root is the UFO foundational ontology, we consider that the ontologies (i.e., UFO and mainly its derived process core ontology) used to enrich ROoST are a bit complex in their terminology and therefore they are hard to adopt and harmonize their terms into the architectural components that we present in Section 3. On the other side, even if Asman *et al.* [2] document a top-domain ontology, a foundational ontology as well as its specified axioms are missing.

Therefore, the existing ontologies are not suitable enough to our aim. We have built thus TestTDO taking into account many of their best-ranked features. TestTDO is a top-domain ontology for software testing, which is semantically enriched with higher-level ontologies, both core and foundational. It also serves as the basis for the development of new lower-level domain ontologies. This ultimately will permit us to build specific software testing strategies and their grouping into a family for test purposes.

3 Overview of the Four-layered Ontological Architecture

As commented in the Introduction Section, TestTDO is placed at the top-domain level into FCD-OntoArch. This is a four-layered ontological architecture, which considers foundational, core, domain and instance levels. In turn, the domain level is split down in two sub-levels, namely: Top-domain and Low-domain ontological levels. As depicted in Fig. 1, ontologies at the same level can be related to each other, except for the foundational level where there is only one ontology. In addition, ontologies at lower levels can be semantically enriched by ontologies at upper levels. For example, TestTDO placed at the top-domain level is enriched by concepts of the SituationCO and ProcessCO [5] ontologies placed at the core level. In turn, both are enriched by the concepts of ThingFO, which is at the foundational level.

ThingFO terms such as Thing, Thing Category and Assertion semantically enrich terms of components at lower levels. Thing represents a particular or individual, tangible or intangible object of a given particular world, but not a universal category –which is modeled by the term Thing Category. A Thing is not a particular object without its Properties and its Powers, therefore this triad emerge simultaneously to form a unity [10]. A Thing cannot exist or be in spatiotemporal isolation from other Things, so in a particular situation, a target Thing is always surrounded by other context Things.

Besides, we define Assertion as a "*positive and explicit statement that one or more persons make about something concerning Things, their categories, contexts or situations based on thoughts, perceptions, facts, intuitions, intentions, and/or beliefs that may be conceived with an attempt at furnishing current or ulterior evidence*". In order to be valuable, actionable and ultimately useful for any science, an Assertion should largely be verified and/or validated by theoretical and/or empirical evidence. Assertions can be represented by informal, semiformal or formal specifications. There are Assertion on Particulars for Thing, and Assertion on Universals for Thing Category. Concerning Thing, by means of assertions, we can specify aspects of its substance, relations, structure, behavior, intention, quantity and quality, among others. For example, the conceptualization of an ontology as an artifact (e.g., TestTDO in Fig. 2) represents primarily a mixture of substance-, relation-, structure- and intention-related assertions. (Notice that the axioms of an ontology can be thought as constraint-related assertions).

As commented above TestTDO is enriched mainly by concepts of the SituationCO and ProcessCO ontologies. In turn, SituationCO includes terms –some borrowed from other components- with semantic of Thing such as Person, Organization, Project and Context Entity. In addition, it includes terms with the semantic of Assertion on Particulars such as Goal and Particular Situation. Briefly, a Person/Organization conceives/establishes Goals that are operationalized by Projects. A Goal implies a Particular Situation of interest to be represented. This situation means an association between Target Entities and none or many Context Entities. Hence, a Target Entity is surrounded by context objects. Depending on the goal purpose, Target Entities can be for instance a Developable Entity (e.g., a document, a source code, etc.), an Evaluable Entity (e.g., a work product, a system, etc.), or a Testable Entity, which has the semantic of Developable or Evaluable in a given Particular Situation.

The ProcessCO ontology [5] includes terms with semantic of Thing such as Work Entity (Work Process, Activity, Task), Work Product (Artifact, Outcome), and Work Resource such as Agent, Method, Strategy, Tool, among others.

Most of the conceptual components of Fig. 1 are documented in [6] and its complementary material named "*Populating the Four-layered Ontological Conceptual Architecture*" in Research Gate. Additionally, we make available some of these ontologies as well as the whole documentation of TestTDO at http://bit.ly/TestTDO-Doc.

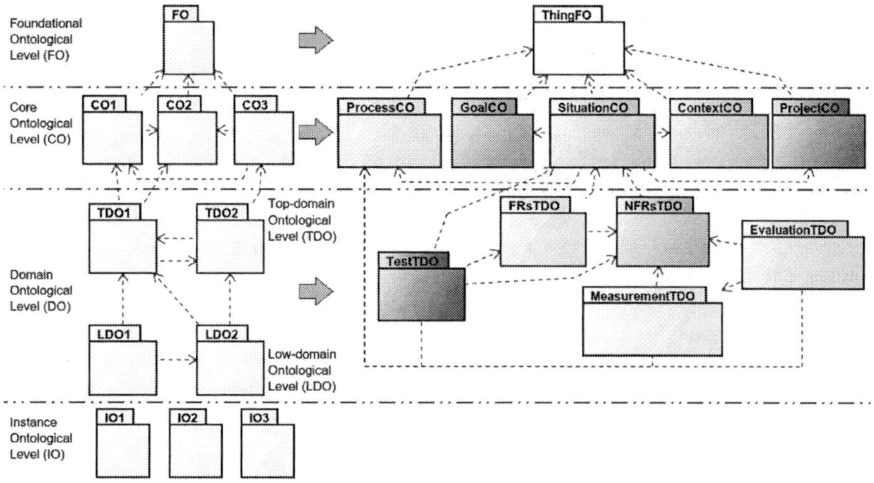

Fig. 1. Four-layered ontological architecture, which considers Foundational, Core, Domain and Instance levels. Also, some conceptual components are shown at the corresponding level. Note that NFRs stands for Non-Functional Requirements while FRs, for Functional Requirements.

4 TestTDO: A Top-Domain Ontology for Software Testing

Following the DSR process, while carrying out the Identify the Problem/Solution (A1) activity, the Artifact Requirements was produced –after performing the Specify Artifact Requirements task [22]. As part of this specification, 25 Competency Questions (CQ) to cover the TestTDO scope were agreed upon. As indicated in the Introduction Section, the artifact development implies a cycle of design-construction-evaluation activities, which must iterate as many times as necessary before the artifact is communicated and is ready for its use. Thus, we have enacted the Design and Develop the Solution (A2) and Execute Verification and Validation (A3) activities. As a result of this cycle, the developed TestTDO ontology comprises 43 defined terms, 48 defined properties, 36 defined non-taxonomic relationships as well as 14 axioms specified in first-order logic. The present section and the next one describe aspects of the CQs and the resulting artifact as well as analyze TestTDO verification, validation and evaluation respectively.

With regard to the 25 CQs, we have formulated questions related to Test Project, Goal, Requirement, Entity and Work Product aspects as well as to Testing Process, Agent, Activity and Method ones. For example, below, the CQ03 is a Work product-related question; CQ14 is a Method-related question; CQ19 is an Entity-related question; CQ24, a Test Requirement-related question; and CQ25, a Project-related question.

CQ03. What are the work products produced by a testing realization activity?
CQ14. What are the types of testing methods assigned to a testing design activity?
CQ19. In which particular situation is a testable entity considered a developable entity?
CQ24. Is a test requirement related to functional and nonfunctional requirements?
CQ25. For a test project that operationalizes a test goal, has the test project an associated testing strategy that helps to achieve the test goal purpose?

We will use these CQs for the verification matrix in Section 5. The remainder CQs can be accessed at http://bit.ly/TestTDO-CQuestions. As a result of considering the functional and non-functional requirements specified in the Artifact Requirements document, the TestTDO conceptualization was produced as depicted in Fig. 2. It represents its key terms, properties and relationships in addition to its relation with Non-Functional Requirement and Functional Requirement terms, which are included accordingly in the NFRsTDO and FRsTDO components in Fig. 1. The reader can access all definitions of terms, properties and relationships at http://bit.ly/TestTDO-Defs. Also, the 14 axioms' specifications can be accessed at http://bit.ly/TestTDO-AxiomSpecs.

In the sequel, we describe aspects of the conceptualization of TestTDO using the following convention in the text: the ontology terms begin with capital letters, the properties are italicized and relations underlined.

In order to cover project-related competency questions, TestTDO has terms such as Test Project, Testing Management, Test Plan, Testing Lyfe Cycle and Testing Strategy. These terms are semantically enriched with terms of the ProjectCO module depicted in Fig. 1. Likewise, to cover goal-related competency questions, TestTDO has terms such as Test Goal and Test Information Need, which are 'extended' from the GoalCO component (Fig. 1). In a nutshell, a Test Project (and its subTestProject, if any) operationalizes one or more Test Goals. It associates one or more Testing Strategies, which help to achieve the Test Goals' *purposes*. In addition, a Test Goal is supported by one or more Test Information Needs. Notice that the Testing Analysis activity takes into account the *statement* of a given Test Information Need goal.

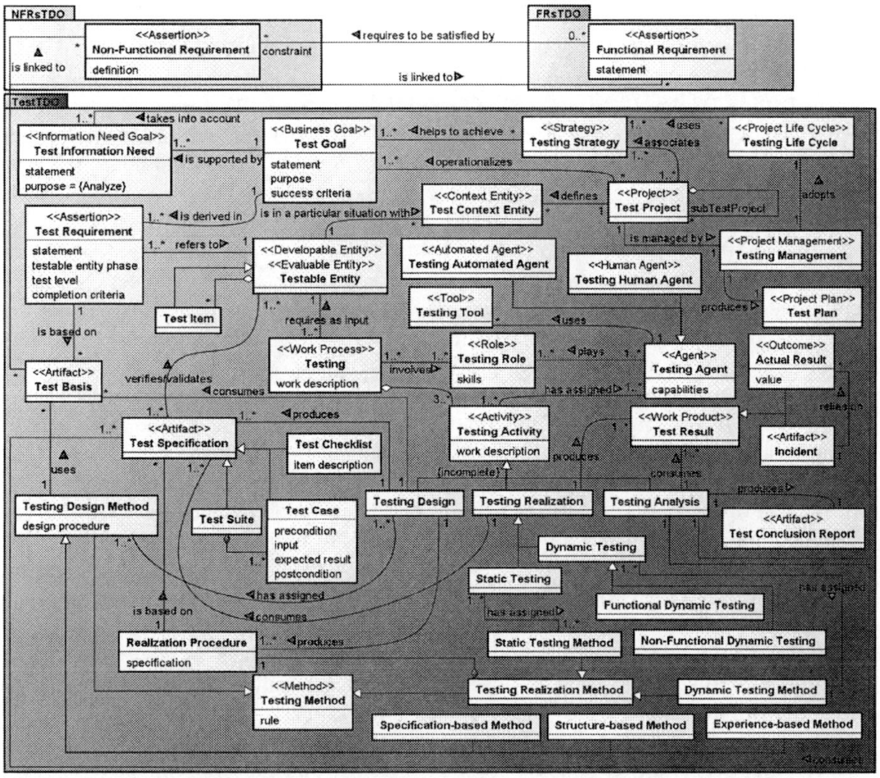

Fig. 2. Main terms, properties and relationships of the TestTDO ontology and its relation with Non-Functional Requirement and Functional Requirement terms.

In order to cover the test requirement- and entity-related scope, TestTDO has terms such as Test Requirement, Test Basis, Testable Entity, Test Item and Test Context Entity. These terms are semantically enriched with terms of ThingFO, ProcessCO, SituationCO and ContextCO modules (Fig. 1). Test Requirement "states, taking into account the Test Goal *purpose*, what must be verified/validated of a Testable Entity (and/or Test Item) based on the Test Basis, if any". Note that a Test Requirement must include the *test level* (e.g., unit, integration, system, acceptance, etc.) and the *testable entity phase* (e.g., development, operative, maintenance, etc.). While Test Basis is an "artifact used by Testing Design Methods for designing the Test Cases and Checklists". So the Test Basis represents an Artifact that may come from development and/or maintenance such as requirements specification, architectural design, documented source code, etc., which in turn could be linked to Non-Functional Requirement and/or Functional Requirement (terms with semantic of) assertions. Furthermore, Testable Entity is "a concrete object able to be tested". A Testable Entity may have none or many Test Items, which in turn are testable. Note that depending on the particular situation, Testable Entity has semantic of Developable Entity (from the FRsTDO component) or Evaluable Entity (from the NFRsTDO component). Lastly, looking at Fig. 2, we can say that Test Goal is derived in one or more Test Requirements. In turn, Test Requirement refers to a Testable Entity, which can be in a particular situation with Test Context Entities.

In order to cover the process-, activity- and agent-related scope at the top-domain level, TestTDO has terms such as Testing with semantic of Work Process, Testing Activity, Testing Design (Activity), Testing Realization, Static Testing (Realization Activity), Dynamic Testing, Functional Dynamic Testing (Realization Activity), Non-Functional Dynamic Testing, and Testing Analysis (Activity). Additionally, there are terms such as Testing Agent and Testing Role among others. These terms, their properties and relations are fully enriched with terms, properties and relations of the ProcessCO module depicted in Fig. 1. Testing "is a Work Process that is composed of at least three interrelated Testing Activities conducted to facilitate the discovery of defects and/or the assessment of Characteristics and Attributes of a Testable Entity". (Note that in this definition, the terms Characteristic and Attribute –which are kind of Non-Functional Requirement- are included in the NFRsTDO component. On the other side, notice that "...at least three..." means that we may foresee another activity such as Testing Context Set-up, knowing beforehand that the design of the context can be a sub-activity of the Testing Design activity).

In order to cover the work product-related scope, TestTDO has terms such as Test Basis, Test Specification, Test Result, and Test Conclusion Report. Particularly, Test Specification has a semantic of Artifact and there are three types of it, namely: Test Checklist, Test Case and Test Suite. On the other side, Test Result has semantic of Work Product and there are two types of it, namely: Actual Result (as Outcome) and Incident (as Artifact or document, which reports deviations –e.g. between the *expected result* and the Actual Result-, anomalies –e.g. an error or a failure- or other arisen issues during the Testing Realization). These terms, their properties and relations are fully enriched with terms, properties and relations of the ProcessCO module [5].

Regarding Test Case, it "is a Test Specification that contains the necessary information (e.g. *preconditions*, *inputs*, *expected results* and *postconditions*) to perform mainly Dynamic Testing". While Test Checklist "is a Test Specification that contains a list of *items (descriptions)* to be checked in order to perform mainly Static Testing".

We define Testing Design as a "Testing Activity aimed at designing a set of Test Specifications (i.e., Test Cases, Test Suites and/or Test Checklists) as well as Realization Procedures". This activity consumes none or more Test Basis and produces Test Specifications and Realization Procedures. Besides, we define Testing Realization as a "Testing Activity aimed at enacting a Static or Dynamic Testing". This activity consumes one or more Test Specifications and produces one or more Test Results. Lastly, we define Testing Analysis as a "Testing Activity that takes into account the specific Test Information Need in order to produce a Test Conclusion Report by consuming one or more Test Results and Test Specifications".

It is worth mentioning at this point that a Work Process or Activity primarily represents 'what' to do rather than indicate 'how' to do it by using a particular Method and Tool applied to a *work description*. Method (in ProcessCO) has two properties: procedure and rules.

To cover the method-related scope at the top-domain level, TestTDO has terms such as Testing Method with two sub-types like Testing Design Method and Testing Realization Method. For the former there are three kinds of design methods, namely: Specification-based Method (also known as black-box), Structure-based Method (white-box), and Experience-based Method. For the latter there are two kinds of realization methods, namely: Dynamic Testing Method and Static Testing Method.

We define Specification-based Method as "a Testing Design Method that always uses a Test Basis for deriving Test Specifications without referring to the internal structure of the Testable Entity". More specific types of Specification-based Methods are Boundary Value Analysis, Equivalence Partitioning, State Transition Testing, and Decision Table Testing, among others, which are not shown in Fig. 2 since TestTDO terms are a top-domain level. In addition, we define Structure-based Method as "a Testing Design Method that uses the internal structure of the Testable Entity, and sometimes also uses a Test Basis, for deriving Test Specifications". Examples of it are Branch Testing, Statement Testing, Condition Testing, and Data Flow Testing, among others.

It is important to highlight that the Testing Realization Method has a Realization Procedure, which represents the "arranged set of Testing Realization Method's instructions or operations which specifies how must be performed the Testing Realization activity using the Test Specification".

Lastly, the reader can observe that a Testing Design (Activity) has assigned one or more Testing Design Methods, while a Dynamic/Static Testing (Realization Activity) has assigned one or more Dynamic/Static Testing Methods.

Next, we first illustrate aspects of the verification of the TestTDO coverage, which embraces specified axioms as well. Then, we describe some validation and evaluation issues.

5 Verifying, Validating and Evaluating TestTDO

In order to cover the established scope in the A1 (DSR) activity, TestTDO should be able to answer all the CQs. In this direction, in the previous section we made to some extent descriptions of most of the TestTDO terms, properties and relations. In this section, in Table 2, we present an excerpt from the verification matrix with the TestTDO terms, relationships, properties and axioms that answer the five CQs listed previously, in Section 4. Note that Souza *et al.* [19] applied a similar approach for ROoST. The whole verification matrix can be accessed at http://bit.ly/TestTDO-VerMatrix.

In the cycle of DSR design-construction-evaluation activities, we continuously checked if the CQs were being answered. Consequently, when we verified that all the CQs were addressed by the terms, properties, relationships and axioms defined in the TestTDO artifact, this cycle ended. This verification matrix allowed us to check not only if the CQs were answered, but also whether there were unnecessary elements for the TestTDO scope.

On the other hand, in order to validate initially if TestTDO was able to represent concrete situations of the world, we instantiated its terms, properties and relationships using a geometrical figure application for an academic project. This proof of concept is based on the running testing example used by G. J. Myers in [16], and can be accessed at http://bit.ly/TestTDO-Val. As a result of this validation, we can conclude that TestTDO is able to represent this rather simple situation. However, we need to implement TestTDO in industrial projects that deal with more complex real-world situations. It is worth mentioning that the third co-author of this paper currently works –playing the tester role- in a company that provides software solutions mainly to abroad customers. So far, TestTDO has covered all the terminological situations he has had to tackle.

Table 2. Excerpt from the TestTDO's Verification Matrix. Note that CQ stands for Competency Question. Also note that at the bottom of this table the highlighted Axioms are specified in first-order logic.

CQ	Terms, relationships and *properties*	Axioms
CQ3	Testing Realization is-a Testing Activity Testing Realization produces Test Result Actual Result is-a Test Result Incident is-a Test Result	**A1**, A7, A11
CQ14	Testing Design is-a Testing Activity Testing Design has assigned Testing Design Method Testing Design Method is-a Testing Method Specification-based Method is-a Testing Design Method Structure-based Method is-a Testing Design Method Experience-based Method is-a Testing Design Method	**A10**, A12
CQ19	Test Requirement refers to Testable Entity Test Requirement is based on Test Basis Test Basis is linked to Functional Requirement	**A6**
CQ24	Test Requirement is based on Test Basis Test Basis is linked to Non-Functional Requirement Test Basis is linked to Functional Requirement	**A5**, **A6**
CQ25	Test Project operationalizes Test Goal Test Project associates Testing Strategy Testing Strategy helps to achieve Test Goal Test Goal has the property named *purpose*	**A8**

A1) For any Testing Realization activity that produces a Test Result, this result is therefore an Actual Result or an Incident, but not both at the same time.

$$\forall trn, \exists tr: TestingRealization(trn) \wedge TestResult(tr) \wedge produces(trn, tr) \rightarrow ActualResult(tr) \veebar Incident(tr)$$

A5) Any Testable Entity is an Evaluable Entity iff the Test Requirement that refers to this Thing is linked to a Non-Functional Requirement.

$$\forall te: TestableEntity(te) \wedge EvaluableEntity(te) \leftrightarrow \exists tr, tb, nfr: TestRequirement(tr) \wedge TestBasis(tb) \wedge NonFunctionalRequirement(nfr) \wedge refersTo(tr, te) \wedge isBasedOn(tr, tb) \wedge isLinkedTo(tb, nfr)$$

A6) Any Testable Entity is a Developable Entity iff the Test Requirement that refers to this Thing is linked to a Functional Requirement.

$$\forall te: TestableEntity(te) \wedge DevelopableEntity(te) \leftrightarrow \exists tr, tb, fr: TestRequirement(tr) \wedge TestBasis(tb) \wedge FunctionalRequirement(fr) \wedge refersTo(tr, te) \wedge isBasedOn(tr, tb) \wedge isLinkedTo(tb, fr)$$

A8) All Test Project operationalizes a Test Goal and associates a Testing Strategy iff this Testing Strategy helps to achieve the operationalized Test Goal.

$$\forall tp, \exists tg, ts: TestProject(tp) \wedge TestGoal(tg) \wedge TestStrategy(ts) \wedge operationalizes(tp, tg) \wedge associates(tp, ts) \leftrightarrow helpsToAchieve(ts, tg)$$

A10) If a Testing Design activity has assigned a Specification-based Method and produces a Test Specification, then always consumes a Test Basis, which is used by the Specification-based Method without using the internal structure of the Testable Entity.

$$\forall td, \exists spbm, ts: TestingDesign(td) \wedge Specification\_basedMethod(spbm) \wedge TestSpecification(ts) \wedge hasAssigned(td, spbm) \wedge produces(td, ts) \rightarrow \exists tb, te: TestBasis(tb) \wedge TestableEntity(te) \wedge uses(spbm, tb) \wedge consumes(td, tb) \wedge requiresAsInput(td, te) \wedge \neg uses(spbm, te)$$

Table 3. Summary of the evaluation results of the 3 best-ranked ontologies of Table 1, and their comparison with the TestTDO evaluation results. The green color indicates "satisfactory" acceptability level (●); yellow "marginal" (◆) and red "unsatisfactory" (■). Indicators' values are expressed in [%].

Characteristics / *Attributes*	**Vasant-hapriyan *et al.* [24]**	**ROoST [19]**	**Asman *et al.* [2]**	**TestTDO**
1. Ontological Quality	51.28■	79.54◆	66.71◆	98.71●
1.1 Ontological Structural Quality	32.56■	79.08◆	61.92◆	97.43●
1.1.1 Defined Terms Availability	15.60■	82.20◆	100●	100●
1.1.2 Defined Properties Availability	0■	0■	0■	100●
1.1.3 Specified Axioms Availability	50■	100●	0■	100●
1.1.4 Balanced Relations Availability	54.40■	87.32●	73.07◆	91.43●
1.1.4.1 Balanced Non-Taxonomic Relationships Availability	68◆	95.65●	66.34◆	89.29●
1.1.4.2 Defined Non-Taxonomic Relationships Availability	0■	54■	100●	100●
1.2 Domain-specific Terminological Coverage Quality	100●	50■	100●	100●
...	...	...	...	...
1.3 Compliance to other Vocabularies	50■	100●	52.50■	100●
1.3.1 Terminological Compliance to International Standard Glossaries	100●	100●	85●	100●
1.3.2 Terminological Compliance to other Domain/Core Ontologies	0■	100●	100●	100●
1.3.3 Terminological Compliance to Foundational Ontologies	0■	100●	0■	100●

Last but not least, since we have conducted the ontological quality evaluation of the 12 SLR-selected ontologies, we also planned in the DSR A3 activity to evaluate TestTDO and compare its ontological quality with them. To this end, we have used the same non-functional requirements tree (i.e., all the same sub-characteristics and attributes for the Ontological Quality characteristic), but now including the TestTDO outcomes (see http://bit.ly/OntoQualityEvalwithTestTDO). Table 3 shows a fragment of this evaluation including only the 3 best-ranked ontologies of Table 1.

For the 1.1 (Ontological Structural Quality) sub-characteristic and its 3 attributes, TestTDO has met 100% (●) since all the terms and properties are explicitly defined, and the axioms specified. The reader can see and compare this situation with the other three ontologies in Table 3.

Regarding the 1.1.4 sub-characteristic, we define it as "Degree to which an ontology has a balance between the amount of non-taxonomic and taxonomic relationships in addition to the former are defined". Note that non-taxonomic relationships are those which are not 'kind of' (is_a) or 'whole-part' (part_of). Non-taxonomic relationships should therefore be defined. We have specified in [21], for the "Balanced Non-Taxonomic Relationships Availability" (1.1.4.1) attribute, its metric that quantifies it, and its elementary indicator that interprets it. As a result of the 1.1.4 sub-characteristic, TestTDO met the satisfactory acceptability level (91.43% ●).

Looking at the Compliance to other Vocabularies (1.3) sub-characteristic, almost all ontologies adhere their terminology to one or more international standard glossaries, as commented in Section 2. TestTDO was built considering official and *de facto* international standards such as ISO 29119 [14] and ISTQB [15], which are widely adopted by professional testers. On the other hand, ROoST is the unique domain software testing ontology that was built on a foundational ontology. We have considered this attribute of ROoST as a strength to be adopted. Therefore, TestTDO was conceived at the top-domain level considering also our foundational and core ontologies in the framework of the four-layered (FCD-OntoArch) architecture depicted in Fig. 1.

6 Concluding Remarks and Future Work

As indicated in the Introduction Section, after analyzing both the results of the conducted SLR of primary studies on software testing ontologies and the state-of-the-art of test-related standards, we decided to develop a new top-domain software testing ontology that fits our aim and scope. We have confirmed that there was heterogeneity, ambiguity, and incompleteness for concepts dealing with test goals and requirements as well as with testing work products, activities and methods in the selected 12 ontologies. Furthermore, there was no software testing ontology directly linked with NFRs and FRs ontological concepts.

TestTDO was created for terminologically nourishing specifications of methods and processes to a family of testing strategies to be developed from now on. TestTDO is a top-domain level ontology in the framework of the four-layered architecture, which was designed to be extended by lower-level software testing domain ontologies.

Therefore, in the present work, we have discussed aspects of the TestTDO development, verification, validation and evaluation for its conceptualization. Depending on the research aim, a conceptualized ontology may also be implemented in a formal semantic language such as OWL. Obviously that an implemented ontology further allows it can be verified automatically by using a query language for OWL such as SQWRL for instance. Hence, CQs can be implemented in SQWRL for verification. We envision to implement TestTDO even this was not our primary aim.

Acknowledgments. This work and line of research are supported by the Science and Technology Agency of Argentina, in the PICT 2014-1224 project at UNLPam.

References

1. Arnicans G., Romans D., Straujums U.: Semi-automatic Generation of a Software Testing Lightweight Ontology from a Glossary Based on the ONTO6 Methodology, Frontiers in Artificial Intelligence and Applications, V.249, pp. 263-276 (2013)
2. Asman A., Srikanth R. M.: A Top Domain Ontology for Software Testing, Master Thesis, Jönköping University, Sweden, pp. 1-74 (2016)
3. Bai X., Lee S., Tsai W. T., Chen Y.: Ontology-Based Test Modeling and Partition Testing of Web Services, IEEE Int'l Conference on Web Services (ICWS'08), pp. 465-472 (2008)
4. Barbosa E. F., Nakagawa E. Y., Riekstin A. C., Maldonado J. C.: Ontology-based Development of Testing Related Tools, 20th International Conference on Software Engineering and Knowledge Engineering (SEKE'08), pp. 697-702 (2008)
5. Becker P., Papa F., Olsina L.: Process Ontology Specification for Enhancing the Process Compliance of a Measurement and Evaluation Strategy, CLEI eJnal., 18:(1), pp. 1-26 (2015)

6. Becker P., Tebes G., Peppino D., Olsina L.: Applying an Improving Strategy that embeds Functional and Non-Functional Requirements Concepts. Journal of Computer Science & Technology, 19:(2), pp. 153-174 (2019)
7. Cai L., Tong W., Liu Z., Zhang J.: Test Case Reuse Based on Ontology, 15th IEEE Pacific Rim International Symposium on Dependable Computing, pp. 103-108 (2009)
8. Campos H., Acácio C., Braga R., Araújo M. A. P., David J. M. N., Campos F.: Regression Tests Provenance Data in the Continuous Software Engineering Context, In 2nd Brazilian Symp. on Systematic and Automated Software Testing (SAST), Paper 10, pp. 1-6 (2017)
9. D'Aquin M., Gangemi A.: Is there beauty in ontologies? Applied Ontology, 6:(3), pp. 165-175 (2011)
10. Fleetwood S.: The ontology of things, properties and powers. Journal of Critical Realism, 8:(3), pp. 343-366, Available at http://eprints.uwe.ac.uk/15967 (2009)
11. Freitas A., Vieira R.: An Ontology for Guiding Performance Testing, IEEE/WIC/ACM International Joint Conferences on Web Intelligence (WI) and Intelligent Agent Technologies (IAT), (WI-IAT'14), V.1, pp. 400-407 (2014)
12. Hevner A. R, March S. T., Park J., Ram S.: Design Science in Information Systems Research. Management Information Systems Quarterly, 28:(1), pp. 75-105 (2004)
13. IEEE: Computer Society, SWEBOK. A Guide to the Software Engineering Body of Knowledge. Available at https://www.computer.org/education/bodies-of-knowledge/software-engineering, (2004)
14. ISO/IEC/IEEE 29119-1: Software and systems engineering - Software Testing – Part 1: Concepts and Definitons (2013)
15. ISTQB. International Software Testing Qualifications Board, Standard Glossary of Terms used in Software Testing, Version 3.2. Available at https://www.istqb.org/, (2019)
16. Myers G.J., Sandler C., Badgett T.: The Art of Software Testing (3rd ed.). Wiley Publishing, ISBN 978-1118031964 (2011)
17. Olsina L., Becker P.: Family of Strategies for different Evaluation Purposes, XX CIbSE'17, CABA, Argentina, Published by Curran Associates, pp. 221-234 (2017)
18. Sapna P. G., Mohanty H.: An Ontology Based Approach for Test Scenario Management, 5th International Conference on Information Intelligence, Systems, Technology and Management (ICISTM'2011), V.141, pp. 91-100 (2011)
19. Souza E. F., Falbo R. A., Vijaykumar N. L.: ROoST: Reference Ontology on Software Testing, Applied Ontology Journal, 12:(1), pp. 1-30 (2017)
20. Tebes, G., Peppino, D., Becker, P., Matturro, G., Solari, M., Olsina, L.: A Systematic Review on Software Testing Ontologies, 12th International Conference on the Quality of Information and Communications Technology, Springer book, CCIS V.1010, M. Piattini et al. (Eds.): QUATIC 2019, Ciudad Real, Spain, pp. 144-160 (2019)
21. Tebes, G., Peppino, D., Becker, P., Matturro, G., Solari, M., Olsina, L.: Analyzing and Documenting the Systematic Review Results of Software Testing Ontologies. Under review in an International Journal, pp. 1-34 (2020)
22. Tebes, G., Peppino, D., Rivera M.B., Becker, P., Papa, M.F., Olsina L.: Especificación del Proceso de Design Science Research: Caso Aplicado a una Ontología de Testing de Software. 7mo CoNaIISI'19, La Matanza, Argentina, Nov.14-15, pp. 1-10 (2019)
23. UML Testing Profile (U2TP), V2.0, Available at https://www.omg.org/spec/UTP2/2.0/PDF
24. Vasanthapriyan S., Tian J., Xiang J.: An Ontology-Based Knowledge Framework for Software Testing, In Comm. in Computer and Information Science, V.780, pp. 212-226 (2017)
25. Vasanthapriyan S., Tian J., Zhao D., Xiong S., Xiang J.: An Ontology-Based Knowledge Sharing Portal for Software Testing, In IEEE International Conference on Software Quality, Reliability and Security Companion (QRS-C'17), pp. 472-479 (2017)
26. Zhu H., Huo Q.: Developing A Software Testing Ontology in UML for a Software Growth Environment of Web-Based Applications, In Software Evolution with UML and XML, IDEA Group, pp. 263-295 (2005)

Specifying the Design Science Research Process: An Applied Case of Building a Software Testing Ontology

Guido Tebes, Belen Rivera, Pablo Becker, Maria Fernanda Papa, Denis Peppino, and Luis Olsina
GIDIS_Web, Facultad de Ingeniería, UNLPam, General Pico, LP, Argentina
[guido.tebes92, denispeppino92]@gmail.com
[riveramb, beckerp, pmfer, olsinal]@ing.unlpam.edu.ar;

Abstract. Design Science Research (DSR) is a rigorous investigation approach that promotes the development of artifacts to meet a useful solution to a relevant domain problem. The artifact should be an innovative solution for a non-trivial problem. After determining the relevance of a given problem/solution, the development of the artifact involves a cycle of design-development-evaluation activities, which iterates as many times as needed before the artifact is finally verified, validated and communicated for its use. The cutting-edge literature about the DSR approach permitted us to observe that, at the moment of this work, the perspectives of its process model are weakly specified. Aimed at contributing to this aspect, this work represents the DSR process specification using the SPEM language. Moreover, we illustrate its main activities by applying them in the construction process of an artifact, i.e., the software testing ontology named TestTDO. This top-domain ontology was recently developed, verified, validated and evaluated in order to afterward building strategies that help achieve diverse test goals' purposes when carrying out test projects.

Keywords: DSR, Artifact, Top-domain Testing Ontology, DSR process, SPEM

1 Introduction

A strategy is an organizational resource that defines a specific course of action to be followed for achieving goal purposes. Organizations arrange work through projects, which help operationalize goal purposes. These can be diverse and, mainly for engineering, may be classified into evaluation, testing, development, and maintenance.

So far, we have developed evaluation strategies that integrate three capabilities, namely: process specifications, method specifications, and domain conceptual bases structured in ontologies [3, 17]. Having strategies that integrate these three capabilities allows engineers to understand what to do (processes) and how to do it (methods and tools) in the context of a reliable comprehension of the key concepts for a particular domain, for example, to the measurement and evaluation domain. In [17], we discussed and illustrated a family of strategies that help achieve evaluation goal purposes.

Taking into account that integrated strategies we have developed give support for achieving evaluation goal purposes, it is possible to envision other strategies for test goal purposes using well-established testing activities and methods in the context of common terminology. Therefore, for the testing domain, we should also have a software testing ontology, which explicitly and unambiguously defines terms, properties, relationships and axioms.

Building the software testing ontological artifact is not a trivial endeavor since testing is a complex area that involves a large number of domain-specific concepts for testing activities, methods, agents, roles, as well as test goals, entities and artifacts, among others. Moreover, many of these concepts may be semantically enriched by terms of core ontologies for the process, project, goal, among others. Hence, a sound research approach may prove to be useful in the artifact development process as well.

Since Design Science Research (DSR) is a rigorous investigation approach that supports the design and construction of useful and innovative artifacts to solve non-trivial problems [11], we follow this approach to build the software testing ontology. Importantly, a non-trivial problem is a difficult problem to solve because it could be incomplete, contradictory or have changing requirements that are often hard to recognize and elicit. DSR indicates that the designed artifact must be evaluated to demonstrate that it not only solves the problem but that it does so in an effective and efficient way, giving utility to the user [11]. An artifact can be defined as an object created by a person, with the intention of later use. This definition emphasizes two key aspects of an artifact: that it does not occur naturally and that it has a certain utility [15]. According to [14] four types of artifacts can be distinguished: constructors (vocabularies), models (abstractions), methods (algorithms) and instantiations (implementations). The software testing ontology we present in this paper could be considered in both the constructor and model category.

To build any artifact, DSR proposes a set of activities that include design, construction and evaluation. These activities are repeated as many times as necessary to generate an artifact that solves the problem effectively. The literature specifies that to apply the DSR approach, it is necessary to go through a first stage of identifying the problem and its relevance. Then, the artifact that solves that problem must be designed, constructed, verified and validated to ensure that the solution constitutes an improvement for a given domain problem. Lastly, the artifact is communicated to the intended audience and the acquired knowledge should be disseminated. But so far, many authors [8, 9, 15, 16, 19, 20] agree to indicate that there are weaknesses in the current DSR process specification. To bridge this gap, it is needed to have a well-specified DSR process to allow repetitiveness and reproducibility through a set of activities with inputs and outputs, interdependencies, among other aspects.

Curtis *et al.* [5] propose four perspectives (or views) to model a process, namely: functional, informational, behavioral and organizational. The former depicts what activities are performed and which are the artifacts consumed and produced by activities and tasks. The informational view includes the structure and interrelationships among the artifacts that activities use. On the other hand, the behavioral perspective indicates in which order the activities are performed. The latter view deals with agents (in roles compliance) that perform the activities. Modeling a process taking into account these perspectives fosters to have its activities descriptions well-understood and without ambiguity, which makes it easier to communicate.

Regarding the above issues, this paper has two main contributions. On one hand, due to the weaknesses detected in the DSR process, we contribute by enhancing the DSR process specification by showing in this work just the functional and behavioral perspectives using the SPEM language [18]. On the other hand, we discuss the applicability of this process by illustrating the construction cycle of the top-domain software testing ontology named TestTDO. This ontology will serve as the conceptual basis for the development of integrated strategies that help achieve test goal purposes.

It is worth mentioning that TestTDO is integrated into the FCD-OntoArch (*Foundational, Core, and Domain Ontological Architecture for Sciences* [4]) architecture, as shown in Fig. 1. Moreover, all the previously developed ontologies [3, 4] that give terminological support to evaluation strategies are also placed into FCD-OntoArch. It is a four-layered ontological architecture that considers foundational, core, domain and instance levels. In FCD-OntoArch, ontologies at the same level can be related to each other. Ontologies at lower levels can be semantically enriched by ontologies at upper levels. For example, TestTDO, the built artifact illustrated in this paper is placed at the top-domain level. In turn, TestTDO is enriched by concepts of the ProcessCO [3] ontology placed at the core level. And ProcessCO is enriched by terms of ThingFO at the foundational level.

On the other hand, this work was initially documented in [23], in Spanish. But the present paper is a meaningful extension of [23] since we have already finished the target artifact (TestTDO), so we can now illustrate the different activities of the DSR process with all yielded artifacts during the design-build-evaluate cycle. Furthermore, in [23], we did not consider the solution requirements that TestTDO should be included in the context of the FCD-OntoArch architecture. This additional requirement had an important impact on the final version of TestTDO produced by the DSR process. Also, it helped us to exemplify issues that the DSR process must entail.

The rest of the paper is organized as follows. Section 2 shows the proposed specification for the DSR process, which is illustrated with TestTDO, the built artifact. Section 3 analyzes related work regarding DSR processes. Finally, Section 4 summarizes conclusions and future work.

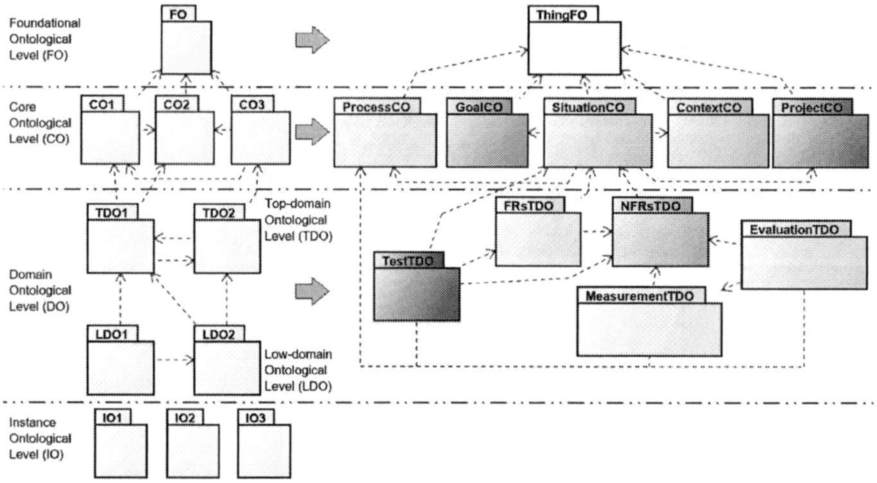

Fig. 1. Four-layered ontological architecture, which considers Foundational, Core, Domain and Instance levels. Also, some conceptual components are shown at the corresponding level. Note that NFRs stands for Non-Functional Requirements while FRs for Functional Requirements

2 Building the TestTDO Artifact using our DSR Process Model

In this Section, we deal with the two contributions stated in the Introduction Section. Thus, from the functional and behavioral perspectives, the proposed DSR process model is specified, and the illustration of each of its activities to build a software testing ontology is described.

As per [10], the DSR approach consists of three research cycles, namely: Relevance, Design and Rigor. In the Relevance cycle, state-of-the-art research is carried out to determine the relevance of the target problem to be addressed. During the Design cycle, activities to design and build the artifact (solution) are performed. This also includes selecting the design process, methods and heuristics to build the artifact, as well as determining how the design and artifact will be evaluated. Finally, in the Rigor cycle, it must be ensured that the design and construction are based on scientific theories and well-established methods stemming from the knowledge base (KB). If the artifact is useful for solving a relevant problem, it can be incorporated into the KB as a contribution.

Taking into account these three cycles in addition to related work as we analyze in Section 3, Fig. 2 shows the DSR process, which is modeled considering the functional and behavioral perspectives [5]. The activities/tasks that correspond to the Relevance cycle are included in the main activity named "A1 Identify Problem/Solution". Furthermore, the activities included in the Design cycle are considered into the main activities named "A2 Design and Develop the Solution" and "A3 Execute Verification and Validation (V&V)". Lastly, the Rigor cycle is related to the information flow from the KB to some sub-activities that belong to A1, A2 and A3. And, after knowledge dissemination ("A4 Communicate Research" activity), if the artefact is useful and adopted, KB could be fed.

Next, we describe these activities for the DSR process while illustrating its applicability through the development of a software testing ontology as an artifact.

A1 Identify Problem/Solution: as shown in Fig. 2 (light blue box), A1 is the first activity that embraces: "Define Problem/Solution", "Investigate Current Solutions" and "Specify Design Requirements" sub-activities. The former, in turn, has two tasks viz. "Define Business Goal/Problem" and "Define the Solution". To define the problem or business goal, the 'Business/Information Need Goals' artifact is required as input. That is, the organization's knowledge about the problem or objective to be achieved. To our case, we considered the following business goal: "*the GIDIS_Web research group requires an ontological conceptualization of the software testing domain to be integrated into the FCD-OntoArch architecture. This artifact must firstly be related to the FRsTDO and NFRsTDO components*". The output of this task is the artifact named 'Business Problem Definition'. In order to specify this artifact, we use the problem specification template proposed in [26]:

Obtain: a rigorous conceptualization of the testing domain.

By means of: the structuring of the domain as an ontology.

Such that: the ontology must be related to the FRsTDO and NFRsTDO components of FCD-OntoArch architecture (Fig. 1). In addition, it should be at the top-domain ontological level.

In order to achieve: support for the specification of a family of integrated testing strategies aimed at satisfying goals with test purposes.

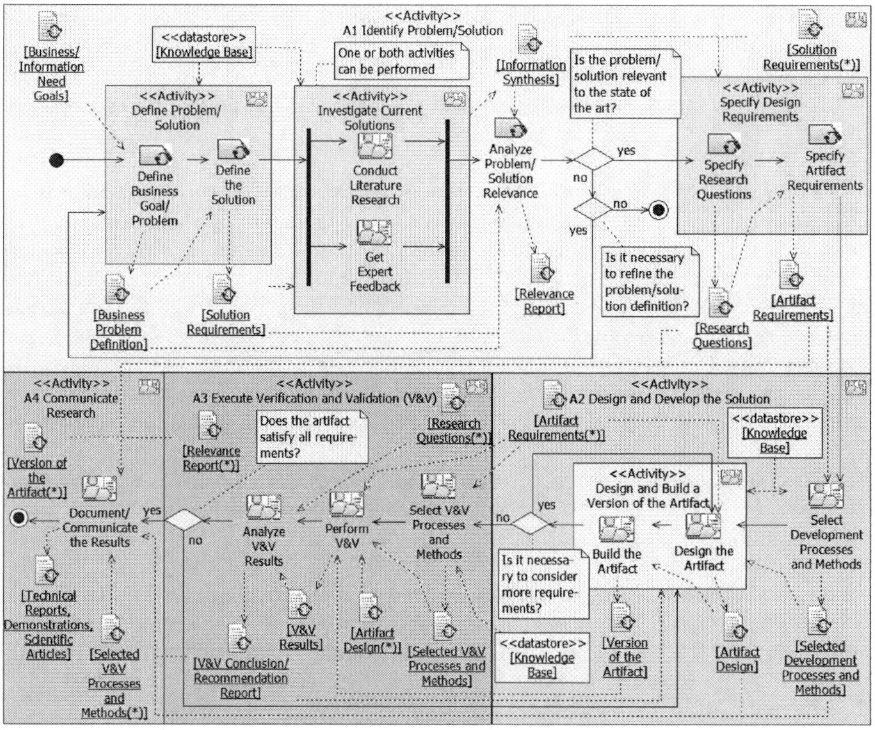

Fig. 2. Functional and behavioral perspectives for the proposed DSR process model. Note that artifacts' names tagged with (*) at the end were replicated, for readability reasons

To define the solution, first of all, it is necessary to inquire about other solutions to similar problems, as well as any other documentation that allows establishing the solution requirements. To do this, we retrieved the documents referenced in [1, 6, 12, 13, 21] from the KB. After revising these documents and considering the initial problem, we established the 'Solution Requirements'. As a result, we define 9 solution requirements (SR). For example: SR#1 *The ontology must be conceptualized but not necessarily implemented*; and SR#9 *Terms of the software testing ontology should be based on (enriched with) terms of higher-level ontologies at the core and/or foundational level.* The list of all solution requirements are at http://bit.ly/SolReqs.

The second activity of A1 is "Investigate Current Solutions", which includes 2 sub-activities: "Conduct Literature Research" and "Get Expert Feedback". Although Fig. 2 shows these activities in parallel, sometimes it is not necessary to perform both or they can be done sequentially in any order. The inputs required to perform them are the KB and the 'Solution Requirements'. We believe that it is important to make an in-depth state-of-the-art analysis of the current situation regarding the established solution requirements and, in addition, ask experts in the domain. In [2] a process that guides the main activities involved in a Systematic Literature Review (SLR) is documented. To our case, we performed the "Conduct Literature Research" activity by a SLR and obtained the 'Information Synthesis' as output. In short, we selected and evaluated 12 software testing ontologies considering also a NFRs tree for evaluation. The tree was built using the 'Solution Requirements' artifact in addition to some ontological quality practices proposed by D'Aquin *et al.* [6]. The reader can access the conducted SLR in [22], and also the NFRs tree and its evaluation results at http://bit.ly/OntoQualityEval.

According to Fig. 2, the following task to carry out is "Analyze Problem/Solution Relevance". This requires as input the 'Information Synthesis', the 'Solution Requirements' and the 'Business Problem Definition' artifacts in order to produce the 'Relevance Report'. This report describes the relevance of the problem/solution to decide whether it will be addressed by the DSR approach. Fig. 3 illustrates this document, considering the main factors that positively impacted the decision to face the building of the software testing ontology by means of the DSR approach.

Relevance Report
The following are the main reasons why to address the problem/solution through the DSR approach: i) there is no SLR-selected ontology that satisfactorily fulfils all the stated solution requirements that also meet a high level of acceptability of ontological quality, ii) to build/adapt an ontology is not a routine task, conversely, it is a complex task due to: 1) it is necessary to consider different sources of definitions of terms for the testing domain (such as international standards, other ontologies, etc.) to obtain higher coverage than the current solutions; 2) the new ontological design must allow the linkage with FRsTDO and NFRsTDO components in the context of the FCD-OntoArch architecture; and 3) the ontology should be based on (enriched with) terms of higher-level ontologies at the core and/or foundational level.

Fig. 3. 'Relevance Report' artifact for the software testing ontology case

When the problem and its solution are not relevant for the state of the art and the stakeholders, the DSR process ends or the problem/solution definition is redefined, returning to the "Define Problem/Solution" sub-activity. Otherwise, if it is relevant, the next sub-activity is "Specify Design Requirements", which includes the "Specify Research Questions" and "Specify Artifact Requirements" tasks. To perform them, the 'Information Synthesis' and 'Solution Requirements' artifacts are needed as input. As output, the 'Research Questions' and 'Artifact Requirements' are produced.

The right formulation of the RQs constitutes a paramount activity in any research study because they conduct the research and transmit its essence [24]. In our case, we have formulated three main RQs for the software testing ontology to be built:

RQ#1: What are the most appropriate requirements for the software testing ontology in order to support the testing strategies that help achieve test goals? From this, the following sub-RQs were derived:

RQ#1.1: Should the ontology to be developed be of low-domain or top-domain level?

RQ#1.2: What are the most robust and rich documented terminologies (structured as glossaries, taxonomies or ontologies) for the software testing domain?

RQ#1.3: What are the main terms that the software testing ontology should include to achieve good coverage?

RQ#1.4: Should the ontology to be developed be at the stage of conceptualization and/or implementation?

RQ#1.5: What is the suitable methodology for ontology development to be used?

RQ#2: How to integrate the testing ontology with the existing conceptual components (sub-ontologies) and levels of the FCD-OntoArch framework? From this, two sub-RQs follow:

RQ#2.1: With what FCD-OntoArch's sub-ontologies and levels should the new testing ontology be directly related?

RQ#2.2: What terms are necessary to relate and integrate the different sub-ontologies of FCD-OntoArch with the new software testing ontology?

RQ#3: How to assure the software testing ontology quality? From this, two sub-RQs follow:

RQ#3.1: What quality characteristics of the ontology should be evaluated?

RQ#3.2: What verification and validation strategies are best suited to assess the ontology?

After carrying out the "Specify Artifact Requirements" task using as input the above RQs we produced the following (software testing ontology) 'Artifact Requirements' (AR) document:

AR#1) (Related to RQ#1.1). Design and build a top-domain ontology.

AR#2) (Related to RQ#1.2). Consider mainly: i) international standard glossaries documented in ISO 29119-1 [12] and ISTQB [13]; and ii) the ROoST [21] domain ontology and the Asman *et al.* [1] top-domain ontology, which were the two-best ranked among the 12-selected and evaluated ontologies in the conducted SLR [22] (see results at http://bit.ly/OntoQualityEval).

AR#3) (Related to RQ#1.3). The terminological coverage of the top-domain ontology should be the necessary and sufficient to be extended by lower-domain ontologies. For this, it must consider terms related to static and dynamic testing, as well as functional and non-functional testing. Besides, it must consider concepts of testing work definition (work process, activity and task), test work product (artifact, result), testing method, testing agent, project, goal, requirement and entity, which should be semantically enriched with concepts from other ontologies at the core and foundational levels. For the top-domain software testing ontology, aspects related to its scope were specified in the form of Competency Questions (see the 25 resulting CQs at http://bit.ly/TestTDO-CQuestions).

AR#4) (Related to RQ#1.3). In order to favor good coverage, there must be a balance between the availability of taxonomic and non-taxonomic relationships.

AR#5) (Related to RQ#1.4). The top-domain software testing ontology must be built at the conceptualization stage without the need of implementing it in a formal language since the main goal is to use it as a common vocabulary to enrich process and method specifications for testing strategies to be developed.

AR#6) (Related to RQ#1.5). Use METHONTOLOGY [7] for the development of the ontology until its conceptualization stage. Also consider its evaluation and documentation activities.

AR#7) (Related to RQ#2.1). Link some terms of the software testing ontology with the FRsTDO and NFRsTDO sub-ontologies at the top-domain level (as highlighted in Fig. 1). Additionally, some terms should also be related to SituationCO and ProcessCO sub-ontologies at the core level. (Note that SituationCO needs terms from ProjectCO, GoalCO and ContextCO as well as from ThingFO at the foundational level).

AR#8) (Related to RQ#2.2). The necessary terms to relate and integrate the different sub-ontologies of FCD-OntoArch with the top-domain software testing ontology are mainly: i) for NFRsTDO: Non-functional Requirement and Evaluable Entity terms; ii) for FRsTDO: Functional Requirement and Developable Entity terms; iii) for GoalCO: Business Goal and Information Need Goal terms; iv) for ProjectCO: Project, Strategy and Project Plan terms; v) for ContextCO: Context Entity term; and vi) for ProcessCO: Work Process, Activity, Work Product, Artifact, Outcome, Method, Role, Tool and Agent terms. Note that SituationCO uses some terms of context, project and goal components adding some others as Particular Situation and Target Entity.

AR#9) (Related to RQ#3.1). The quality characteristics to be evaluated are the same as those used in the SLR for the 12-selected software testing ontologies, namely: Ontological Structural Quality, Balanced Relationship Availability, Domain-specific Terminological Coverage Quality, and Compliance to other Vocabularies.

AR#10) (Related to RQ#3.2). The evaluation strategy to assess the resulting ontology is GOCAME (*Goal-Oriented Context-Aware Measurement and Evaluation*) [3, 17]. Besides, the CQs should be verified with a verification matrix that includes the resulting ontology terms, properties, relations and axioms, which correspond to each CQ. The validation of the resulting ontology should be made by applying their terms to a real-world test project, in addition to being examined with other testing domain experts to get feedback.

A2 Design and Develop the Solution: looking at Fig. 2 (green box), the first sub-activity to carry out is "Select Development Processes and Methods". It has as input the 'Artifact Requirements' and the KB. In our case, according to the AR#6, we select from the KB the METHONTOLOGY approach in order to design and build the software testing ontology.

The next activity to perform is "Design and Build a Version of the Artifact". It includes: "Design the Artifact" and "Build the Artifact" sub-activities. Both activities require the 'Selected Development Processes and Methods' document, as well as the KB. Also, the 'Artifact Requirements' are needed for the "Design the Artifact" activity. As output, the 'Artifact Design' is produced, which serves as input for the "Build the Artifact" activity. For the software testing ontology artifact, the design has been made following the steps that METHONTOLOGY proposes until the conceptualization step.

Then, the "Build the Artifact" is performed to produce a version of the artifact. If it is necessary to do a re-design, e.g. because it is necessary to consider more artifact requirements, then the process has to iterate again to the "Design the Artifact" activity as depicted in Fig. 2. It is worth mentioning that if the design activity is carried out again, the 'Artifact Design' must also be an input to be able to re-design it. But we did not explicitly do so in the process diagram to avoid clutter. Otherwise, the process continues with the A3 activity.

After several iterations in this design-build cycle, we obtained a final version of the artifact, i.e., the software testing ontology, which is named TestTDO. Its conceptualization is depicted in Fig. 4. In addition, the reader can access all definitions of terms, properties and relationships of TestTDO at http://bit.ly/TestTDO-Defs, and its 14 axioms' specifications at http://bit.ly/TestTDO-AxiomSpecs.

A3 Execute Verification and Validation (V&V): looking at Fig. 2 (orange box), the first sub-activity included in A3 is "Select V&V Processes and Methods". This requires as input the 'Artifact Requirements' and the KB in order to produce the 'Selected V&V Processes and Methods' document.

On one hand, to assess TestTDO from the ontological quality standpoint (see AR#10), we selected the GOCAME evaluation strategy [3, 17] and the NFRs tree documented at http://bit.ly/OntoQualityEval. On the other hand, in order to verify that TestTDO covers the established scope in the CQs, we design a verification matrix (see Table 1). This matrix includes the resulting ontology terms, properties, relationships and axioms, which correspond to each CQ. We also decided to verify the integration of TestTDO into the FCD-OntoArch architecture. Finally, we selected validation strategies for our ontology, namely: i) applying their terms to an academic test project; and ii) getting feedback from experts in the testing domain.

Once the V&V strategies were selected, the next activity to carry out is "Perform V&V". This activity requires as input the artifact, its requirements and design, as well as the selected V&V processes and/or methods. It is important to keep in mind that both the artifact and its design can be verified against the requirements.

After performing the V&V, the 'V&V results' are produced. In our case, as above mentioned, we used the GOCAME strategy to obtain all the evaluation results (indicators' values) of TestTDO, found at http://bit.ly/TestTDO_OntoQualityEval. Additionally, we used a verification matrix to verify that TestTDO covers the established scope in the CQs.

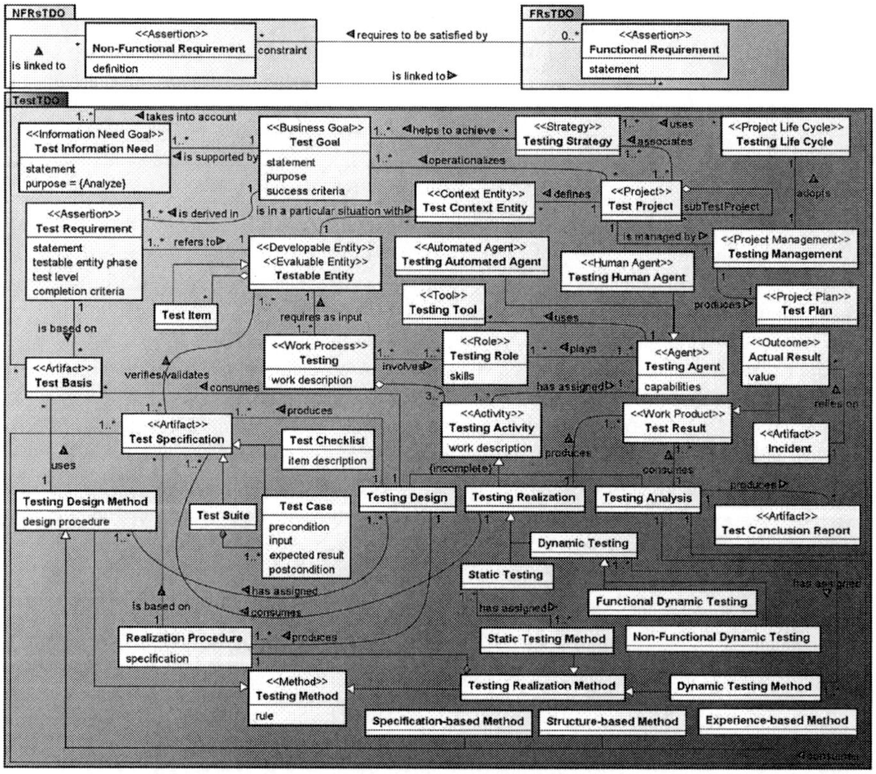

Fig. 4. Main terms, properties and relationships of the TestTDO ontology and its relation with Non-Functional Requirement and Functional Requirement terms

Table 1. Excerpt from the TestTDO's Verification Matrix. Note that at the bottom of this table the axioms are specified in first-order logic

CQ	Terms, relationships and *properties*	Axioms
CQ21	Test Goal is derived in Test Requirement	A9
CQ23	Test Requirement refers to Testable Entity Test Requirement has the property named *test level*	
CQ25	Test Project operationalizes Test Goal Test Project associates Testing Strategy Testing Strategy helps to achieve Test Goal Test Goal has the property named *purpose*	A8

A8) All Test Project operationalizes a Test Goal and associates a Testing Strategy iff this Testing Strategy helps to achieve the operationalized Test Goal.

$$\forall tp, \exists tg, ts: TestProject(tp) \land TestGoal(tg) \land TestStrategy(ts) \land operationalizes(tp, tg) \land associates(tp, ts) \leftrightarrow helpsToAchieve(ts, tg)$$

A9) For all Test Requirements derived from a Test Goal, there is at least one Test Project that operationalizes this Test Goal.

$$\forall tr, \exists tg, tr: TestRequirement(tr) \land TestGoal(tg) \land isDerivedIn(tg, tr) \rightarrow TestProject(tp) \land operationalizes(tp, tg)$$

In Table 1, we illustrate the verification matrix for the CQs #21, #23 and #25. The complete verification matrix can be accessed at http://bit.ly/TestTDO-VerMatrix. In addition, we also verify that, for terms enriched by other higher-level ontologies of FCD-OntoArch, the semantics between the enriching term and the enriched term correspond appropriately. Just to give an example, looking at Fig. 4, the term Actual Result has semantic of outcome and, therefore, is enriched with the Outcome term, and not with the Artifact term, both terms coming from ProcessCO.

In order to validate if TestTDO was able to represent concrete situations of the world, we instantiated its terms, properties and relationship using a geometrical figure application for an academic project. This running testing example can be accessed at http://bit.ly/TestTDO-Val. We are aware that TestTDO should be implemented in projects that deal with more complex real-world situations. Note that the fifth co-author of this paper currently works –playing the tester role- in a company that provides software solutions mainly to abroad customers. So far, TestTDO has covered all the terminological situations he has had to tackle.

The last activity of A3 is "Analyze V&V Results", which uses the 'V&V Results' and the RQs as input. As a result, this activity produces the "V&V Conclusion/Recommendation Report". At this point, if the artifact meets all the requirements, then the A4 activity is performed. But, if not, the "Design and Build a Version of the Artifact" sub-activity must be carried out again.

It is important to mention that all the artifacts shown in this work are the final versions yielded after several design-build-evaluation cycles. We are aware that at this point the A1 activity can be performed again to make some changes, e.g., in the RQs or in the artifact requirements. In fact, in the present case, we have done so to update the requirements. But this iteration flow is not shown in Fig. 2 to facilitate the readability of the process.

A4 Communicate Research: this last activity of the DSR process (pink box) includes only one sub-activity called "Document/Communicate the Results". It has as input most artifacts produced in the previous activities as depicted in Fig. 2. As output, it produces technical reports, demonstrations or scientific articles that allow documenting the performed research for the designed, built and evaluated artifact. This should imply being a valuable digital library resource for the interested community. In our case, the produced ontology should be interesting for the software quality assurance community. Ultimately, if in fact the artifact produces a positive impact on the scientific community, this is, it is interesting and widely adopted due to its usefulness, relevance and innovation, therefore, all documentation must be stored in the KB. This added knowledge will be available to build new artifacts.

3 Related Work

Roel Wieringa is a quoted author when referring to design science and its application in empirical software engineering. He describes design science as the design and research of artifacts in a context. Wieringa recognizes the efforts of Hevner *et al.* [9] in describing a framework for design science and proposed a similar one but containing some main differences, such as the separation of the design and the investigation. Considering this, he described a design science framework, in which two kinds of problem-solving activities are distinguished: solving practical problems through the design of an artifact, and answering RQs by scientific research [28]. The design science framework addresses the issue of building artifacts with the aim of solving practical problems in an organizational environment, thus justifies the use of DSR for investigating the properties of these artifacts. The framework presented in [27] and extended later in [26] does not formally model a design science process that details the main activities to be carried out. Instead, it indicates the relation between the design and investigation, addressing the problem context of an artifact, including for this, the social context and the knowledge context. Therefore, we cannot conclude that there is a formal proposal for a DSR process model specification that is considered similar to the one addressed in the present work.

Other papers raise concerns about DSR process and describe some process approaches to be followed. In [16], authors present a DSR process structured into three main phases: 1) problem identification, 2) solution design, and 3) evaluation, which can interact with each other. This is a relevant work, so these phases were considered when modeling our DSR process proposal. The process suggested in [16] includes the problem identification and the literature revision for determining the problem relevance. Then it takes place the design of the artifact which will give a solution to the detected problem and its subsequent evaluation to ensure its quality. Finally, results must be communicated in order to obtain feedback from the interested community. Note that our proposal is close to that described in [16]. However, they did not use a process specification language (e.g., SPEM) for the DSR process model specification. In addition, they only consider the behavioral process perspective and, therefore, did not model the produced and consumed work products in each phase as we did.

In the Hevner *et al.*'s Information System Research Framework [9, 10], 7 guidelines are presented that contain prerequisites for effectively using DSR considering the roles and techniques that can be used in information system research. In summary, these guidelines argue that DSR must produce a viable artifact that constitutes an effective solution to a relevant business problem. To determine the viability, utility, quality and efficiency, the artifact should be assessed through rigorous methods, e.g. testing, evaluation and simulation. However, as observed in the abovementioned related work, in [9, 10], a formal process model that specifies main activities and tasks to be performed is missing, as well as the produced/consumed work products by the DSR activities.

In [19, 20], the authors present a DSR process model that depicts the activities to be carried out to implement the research approach. In this way, some activities are intended to the problem identification for detecting its relevance. Then, the solution objectives are identified. The solution is an artifact to be designed and built. Finally, its effectiveness as a solution to the identified problem must be demonstrated. If it is a viable solution, the research results must be communicated to the concerned community. This proposal is also interesting and served as the basis to the construction of our DSR process. But like the other proposals, the presented process ([19, 20]) is not formally described using a process modeling language, nor does it consider different process modeling perspectives. Therefore, it does not take advantage of the benefits of process modeling, as discussed in the Introduction Section.

In [25], the authors describe a process model for applying the DSR approach with the main activities (which authors named "process steps"). As we did, they considered the behavioral and functional perspectives. Nevertheless, regarding the functional perspective, only the produced artifacts are represented while the inputs to the activities are missing.

Despite the efforts made for a common DSR process, there is still no thorough consensus on what the detailed activities are, their inputs and outputs, as well as the sequences between activities and tasks. Finally, other related work [8, 15] agrees to discuss the lack of a standardized process to implement the DSR approach.

4 Conclusions and Future Work

Computer Science/Information System adopted the DSR approach to the design and construction of artifacts. However, an analysis of the literature makes it possible to determine that the DSR process specification that establishes a flow of activities and tasks, and their corresponding inputs/outputs, is not yet formally modeled. Therefore, with the objective of contributing to this aspect, this work presents a process model specification for DSR considering the functional and behavioral modeling perspectives. The specifications were made using the SPEM language. The proposed DSR process model allows to systematically carry out the activities and tasks involved in the research approach. Having a modeled process helps to understand and communicate it to the interested community, making its application more consistent and repeatable in the execution of the activities and tasks included. On the other hand, another aim this research pursued was the illustration of the DSR process using the construction of a software testing ontology (TestTDO) as a practical case. We also show the different documents produced throughout the application of the DSR process followed.

It is worth remarking that we show a recommended flow for the DSR process since we are aware that in a process instantiation there might be some variation points, such as the parallelization of some tasks. In addition, the life cycle of a given DSR project should organize activities and tasks considering not only the prescribed DSR process but also the appropriate allocation of resources such as methods and tools, among others, for achieving the proposed goal. Therefore, there are additional activities (to those specified in Fig. 2) in which project planning must also take into accounts such as documenting artifacts in all activities and control their changes and versions. Continuous documentation and version control of artifacts are key factors to ensure consistency, repeatability and auditability of any project.

The proposed DSR process model also provides a good baseline for understanding the details and discussing alternatives or customizations to this process. In fact, the rigor provided by process modeling, where several perspectives are combined (e.g. functional, informational, organizational and behavioral), but can also be independently detached, provides a greater richness of expressiveness in sequences and decision flows, while representing different levels of granularity in the work definitions, such as activity, sub-activity and task.

TestTDO has a primary interest in our research group and may also be welcome in the software testing community. In recent years, our research efforts focused on the design and construction of integrated strategies that allow establishing a specific course of action (in addition to providing appropriate methods and conceptual bases) to achieve evaluation goal purposes. From now on, having a software testing ontology as a built artifact guided by DSR will allow us to develop integrated testing strategies that help achieve test goal purposes. Hence, as a future work, we are planning to use the DSR approach to build a family of integrated testing strategies. This future work will allow us to continue validating the specification for the presented DSR process model as well.

Acknowledgments. This work and line of research are supported by the Science and Technology Agency of Argentina, in the PICT 2014-1224 project at UNLPam.

References

1. Asman A., Srikanth R. M.: A Top Domain Ontology for Software Testing, Master Thesis, Jönköping University, Sweden, pp. 1-74 (2016)
2. Becker P., Olsina L., Peppino D., Tebes G.: Specifying the Process Model for Systematic Reviews: An Augmented Proposal, Journal of Software Engineering Research and Development (JSERD), Vol 7, pp. 1-23, (2019) https://doi.org/10.5753/jserd.2019.460
3. Becker P., Papa F., Olsina L.: Process Ontology Specification for Enhancing the Process Compliance of a Measurement and Evaluation Strategy, CLEI eJnal., 18:(1), pp. 1-26 (2015)
4. Becker P., Tebes G., Peppino D., Olsina L.: Applying an Improving Strategy that embeds Functional and Non-Functional Requirements Concepts. Journal of Computer Science & Technology, 19:(2), pp. 153-174 (2019)
5. Curtis, B., Kellner, M., Over, J.: Process Modelling, Com. of ACM, 35:(9), pp.75-90 (1992)
6. D'Aquin M., Gangemi A.: Is there beauty in ontologies? Applied Ontology, 6:(3), pp. 165-175 (2011)
7. Fernández-López M., Gómez-Pérez A., Juristo N.: METHONTOLOGY: From Ontological Art Towards Ontological Engineering, Spring Symposium on Ontological Engineering of AAAI, pp. 33–40, Stanford University, California (1997)
8. Geerts G. L.: A design science research methodology and its application to accounting information systems research, International Journal of Accounting Information Systems,

12:(2), pp. 142-151 (2011)
9. Hevner A. R., March S. T., Park J., Ram S.: Design Science in Information Systems Research, Management Information Systems Quarterly, 28:(1), pp. 75-105 (2004)
10. Hevner A. R.: A Three Cycle View of Design Science Research, Scandinavian Journal of Information Systems, 19:(2), pp. 87-92 (2007)
11. Hevner A.R., Chatterjee S.: Design Research in Information Systems: Theory and Practice, Springer Publishing Company, Incorporated, 1st Edition (2010)
12. ISO/IEC/IEEE 29119: Software and systems engineering - Software Testing. Parts 1, 2, 3 and 4 (2013)
13. ISTQB. International Software Testing Qualifications Board, Standard Glossary of Terms used in Software Testing, Version 3.2 (2019). Available at https://www.istqb.org/.
14. March S., Smith G.: Design and Natural Science Research on Information Technology, 15:(4), pp. 251-266 (1995)
15. Mckay J., Marshall P.: A Review of Design Science in Information Systems, ACIS 2005 Proceedings - 16th Australasian Conference on Information Systems (2005)
16. Offermann P., Levina O., Schönherr M., Bub U.: Outline of a design science research process, Proceedings of the 4th International Conference on Design Science Research in Information Systems and Technology, Philadelphia, Pennsylvania, pp 1-11 (2009)
17. Olsina L., Becker P.: Family of Strategies for different Evaluation Purposes, XX Conferencia Iberoamericana en Software Engineering (CIbSE'17), CABA, Argentina, Published by Curran Associates, pp. 221-234 (2017)
18. OMG. Software & Systems Process Engineering Meta-Model (SPEM) Specification, Version 2.0 (2008)
19. Peffers K., Tuunanen T., Gengler C., Rossi, M., Hui W., Virtanen V., Bragge J.: The design science research process: A model for producing and presenting information systems research, 1st International Conference on Design Science Research in Information Systems and Technology, DESRIST, pp. 83-106 (2006)
20. Peffers K., Tuunanen T., Rothenberger M., Chatterjee S.: A design science research methodology for information systems research, Journal of Management Information Systems, 24:(3), pp. 45-77 (2007)
21. Souza E. F., Falbo R. A., Vijaykumar N. L.: ROoST: Reference Ontology on Software Testing, Applied Ontology Journal, 12:(1), pp. 1-30 (2017)
22. Tebes G., Peppino D., Becker P., Matturro G., Solari M., Olsina L.: A Systematic Review on Software Testing Ontologies, International Conference on the Quality of Information and Communications Technology, Springer book, CCIS V.1010, M. Piattini *et al.* (Eds.): QUATIC 2019, Ciudad Real, Spain, pp. 144-160 (2019)
23. Tebes G., Peppino D., Rivera B., Becker P., Papa F., Olsina L.: Especificación del Proceso de Design Science Research: Caso Aplicado a una Ontología de Testing de Software, 7mo Congreso Nacional de Ingeniería Informática – Sistemas de Información (CoNaIISI'19), pp. 1-10 (2019)
24. Thuan N. H., Drechsler A., Antunes P.: Construction of Design Science Research Questions, Communications of the Association for Information Systems (2019)
25. Vaishnavi V., Kuechler B., Stacie P.: Design Research in Information Systems, Association for Inf. Sys. (2004). Available at http://desrist.org/design-research-in-information-systems
26. Wieringa, R. J.: Design science methodology for information systems and software engineering. London: Springer, https://doi.org/10.1007/978-3-662-43839-8 (2014)
27. Wieringa, R. J.: Relevance and problem choice in design science, in Global Perspectives on Design Science Research (DESRIST), 5th International Conference, St. Gallen, Lecture Notes in Computer Science, vol. 6105 (Springer, Heidelberg), pp. 61-76 (2010)
28. Wieringa, R.J.: Design science as nested problem solving, 4th International Conference on Design Science Research in Information Systems and Technology, ACM, New York, pp. 1-12 (2009)

Knowledge Management in Human-Computer Interaction Design: A Mapping Study

Murillo Vasconcelos H. B. Castro[1], Simone Dornelas Costa[1,2], Monalessa P. Barcellos[1], and Ricardo de A. Falbo[1]

[1] Ontology and Conceptual Modeling Research Group (NEMO), Computer Science Department - UFES, Vitória, Brazil
[2] Computer Department - UFES, Alegre, Brazil
murillo.castro@aluno.ufes.br simone.costa@ufes.br
{monalessa,falbo}@inf.ufes.br

Abstract. Developing interactive systems is a challenging task. It involves concerns related to the human-computer interaction (HCI), such as usability and user experience. Therefore, HCI design must be addressed when developing such systems. HCI design often involves people with different backgrounds, what makes communication and knowledge transfer a challenging issue. In this scenario, knowledge management can support understanding concepts from different knowledge areas and help learn from previous experiences. Aiming at investigating how knowledge management has supported HCI design and contributed to the development of interactive systems, we performed a mapping study and analyzed 15 studies reporting the use of knowledge management in HCI design. In this paper, we present our study and discuss its main findings.

Keywords: HCI Design · Mapping Study · Knowledge Management · Interactive Systems.

1 Introduction

The interest in interactive systems and their impact on people's life has promoted the study and practice of usability [2]. Usability is a key aspect to a successful interactive system and is related to user efficiency and satisfaction when interacting with the system. To an interactive system reach high usability levels, it is necessary to take human-computer interaction (HCI) design aspects into account during its development process [2].

HCI is concerned with usability and other aspects related to the interaction between users and computer systems, necessary to produce more usable software [2]. It involves knowledge from multiple fields, such as ergonomics, cognitive science, user experience, human factors, among others [23]. Due to the diverse body of knowledge involved when designing interactive systems, interactive system development teams are frequently multidisciplinary, joining people from different backgrounds, with their own technical language, terms and knowledge. Even the conceptualization about the product may be conflicting, what can hamper communication and knowledge transfer [2,15].

Developing software is a knowledge-intensive task. Knowledge Management (KM) principles and practices have been successfully applied to support knowledge capture, storage, use and transfer in the software development context in general [16,24]. KM can also be helpful to address challenges in the design of interactive systems, since it might provide support to capture and represent knowledge in an accessible and reusable way. As a result, the team can learn from previous experiences and share a common understanding about the system, contributing to produce better products and perform processes more efficiently.

Considering the challenges of designing interactive systems, mainly due to the diversity of knowledge and people involved, and the potential of KM to help address those challenges, we performed a mapping study to investigate the use of KM in HCI design. Before performing our study, we searched for secondary studies addressing the research topic. Since we did not find any, we decided to carry out the study addressed in this paper. A mapping study is a secondary study designed to give an overview of a research area through classification and counting contributions in relation to the categories of that classification. It makes a broad study in a topic of a specific theme and aims to identify available evidence about that topic [14]. Moreover, the panorama provided by a mapping study allows identifying issues in the researched topic that could be addressed in future research. In our study, we analyzed 12 different KM approaches used in HCI design, identified from 15 publications. In general, KM has aided in HCI design mainly by enabling replicability of knowledge and solutions, improving product quality and communication. However, difficulty to generalize knowledge, issues related to features of the system and low engagement of the team have been pointed out as challenges to implement KM in the HCI design context.

This paper is organized as follows: Section 2 provides the background for the paper, addressing HCI design and KM; Section 3 presents the research protocol used in our study; Section 4 summarizes the obtained results; Section 5 discusses the results; Section 6 presents some of the limitations of the study; and Section 7 presents our final considerations.

2 Background

2.1 HCI Design

HCI design focuses on how to design a system to support the user to achieve her goals through the interaction between her and the system [23]. It is concerned with usability and other important attributes such as user experience, accessibility and communicability. Usability is the extent to which a system, product or service can be used by specified users to achieve specified goals with effectiveness, efficiency and satisfaction in a specified context of use [10]. It addresses the effort and ease of the user during the interaction, considering her cognitive, perceptive and motor skills. User experience relates to users' emotions and feelings and is essential for interaction design because it takes into account how a product behaves and is used by people in the real world [15]. Accessibility refers to the removal of barriers that prevent interface and interaction access.

Finally, communicability concerns the ability of the interface to communicate design logic to the user [6].

HCI design is user-centered, hence it is said User-Centered Design (UCD) [3]. UCD is based on ergonomics, usability and human factors. It focuses on the use and development of interactive systems, with emphasis on making products usable and understandable. It puts human needs, capabilities and behavior first, then designs the system to accommodate them. Its main principles are user focus (its characteristics, needs and objectives), observable metrics (user performance and reactions) and iterative design (repeat as often as needed) [3,10]. The term Human Centered Design (HCD) has been adopted in place of UCD to emphasize the impact on all stakeholders and not just on those considered users [10].

In general, UCD involves: *understand and specify context of use*, which aims to study the product users and intended uses; *specify requirements*, which aims to identify user needs and specify functional and other requirements for the product; *produce design solutions*, which aims to achieve the best user experience and includes the production of artifacts such as prototypes and mock-ups that will be used in the future as a basis for developing the system; and *evaluation*, when the user evaluates the results produced in the previous activities [10].

HCI design can be understood as an intensive knowledge process, requiring effective mechanisms to collaboratively create and support a shared understanding about users, the system, its purposes, context of use and the design necessary for the user to achieve her goals. Therefore, HCI design could take advantages of KM solutions.

2.2 Knowledge Management

According to [17], knowledge is a human specialty stored in people's minds, acquired through experience and interaction with their environment. Historically, organization's knowledge was undocumented, being represented through the skills, experience and knowledge of its professionals, typically tacit knowledge [16], which made its use and access limited and difficult [13].

Knowledge Management (KM) aims to transform tacit and individual knowledge into explicit and shared knowledge. By raising individual knowledge to the organizational level, KM promotes knowledge propagation and learning, making knowledge accessible and reusable across the entire organization [13,16,17]. Knowledge helps software organizations to react faster and better, supporting more accurate and precise responses, which contributes to increase software quality and client satisfaction [17].

When an organization implements KM, its experiences and knowledge are recorded, evaluated, preserved, designed and systematically propagated to solve problems [17]. Thus, KM addresses knowledge in its evolution cycle, which consists in creating, capturing, transforming, accessing and applying knowledge [16,17].

In the software process context, KM works for explicitly and systematically managing knowledge, addressing knowledge acquisition, storage, organization, evolution, retrieval and usage. Among other aspects, KM has been applied in the software development context to support document management, competence management, experts identification, software reuse, support learning and product and project memory [16].

3 Research Protocol

Considering the challenges involving knowledge transfer and sharing in the HCI design context and the benefits of using KM in software development context, we decided to investigate the use of KM in HCI design through a mapping study. We followed the process defined in [11], which comprises: planning, when the research protocol is defined with the purpose of supporting study replicability as well as helping researchers to avoid bias when conducting the study; conducting, when the protocol is executed and data are extracted, analyzed and recorded; and reporting, when the results are recorded and made available to potential interested parties.

The study ***goal*** was to investigate the use of KM in HCI design context. For achieving this goal, we defined the research questions presented in Table 1.

Table 1: Research questions and their rationale.

ID	Research Question	Rationale
RQ1	*When and where have publications been published?*	Give an understanding on when and where (journal / conference / workshop) publications about KM in HCI design context have been published.
RQ2	*Which types of research have been done?*	Investigate which type of research is reported in each selected publication. We consider the classification defined in [27]. This question is useful to evaluate the maturity stage of the research topic.
RQ3	*Why has KM been used in the HCI design context?*	Understand the purposes and reasons of using KM in the HCI design and verify if there have been predominant motivations.
RQ4	*Which knowledge has been managed in the HCI design context?*	Investigate which knowledge items have been managed in the HCI design context, aiming to verify if some of them have been managed more frequently and if there has been more interest in certain HCI design aspects.
RQ5	*How is the managed knowledge related to the HCI design process?*	Understand, in the context of the HCI design process, from where the managed knowledge has coming from and where it has been used.
RQ6	*How has KM been implemented in the HCI design context?*	Investigate how KM has been implemented in HCI context in terms of the adopted technologies.
RQ7	*Which benefits and difficulties have been noticed when using KM in the HCI design context?*	Identify benefits and difficulties of using KM in HCI design context and analyze if there is relation between them.

The ***search string*** adopted in the study contains two groups of terms joined with the operator AND. The first group includes terms related to *HCI design*. The general term "Human-Computer Interaction" was used to provide wider search results. The second group includes terms related to *Knowledge Management*. Within the groups, we used the OR operator to allow synonyms. The following search string was used: *("human-computer interaction" OR "user interface design" OR "user interaction design" OR "user centered design" OR "human-centered design" OR "UI design" OR "HCI design") AND ("knowledge management" OR "knowledge reuse" OR "knowledge sharing").* For establishing the string, we performed tests using different terms, logical connectors, and combinations among them, and selected the string that provided better results in terms of the number of publications and their relevance. More restrictive strings excluded important publications identified during the informal literature review that preceded the study. More comprehensive strings (e.g, those including "usability") returned too many publications out of the scope of interest.

The search was performed in four ***sources***, selected based on other secondary studies recorded in the literature and on other experiences in our research group: Scopus, Science Direct, Engineering Village and Web of Science.

Publications selection was performed in five steps. In *Preliminary Selection and Cataloging (S1)*, the search string was applied in the search mechanism of each digital library used as source of publications (we limited the search scope to title, abstract and keywords metadata fields). After that, in *Duplications Removal (S2)*, publications indexed in more than one digital library were identified and duplications were removed. In *Selection of Relevant Publications - 1st filter (S3)*, the abstracts of the selected publications were analyzed considering the following inclusion (IC) and exclusion (EC) criteria: (IC1) the publication addresses KM in the HCI design context; (EC1) the publication does not have an abstract; (EC2) the paper was published only as an abstract; (EC3) the publication is not written in English; (EC4) the publication is a secondary study, a tertiary study, a summary, an editorial or a tutorial. In *Selection of Relevant Publications - 2nd filter (S4)*, the full text of the publications selected in S3 were read and analyzed considering the cited inclusion and exclusion criteria. In this step, to avoid study repetition, we considered another exclusion criterion: (EC5) the publication is an older version of an already selected publication. When the full text of a publication was not available either from the Brazilian Portal of Journals, from other Internet sources or by contacting its authors, the publication was also excluded (EC6). Finally, in *Snowballing (S5)*, as suggested in [11], the references of publications selected in S4 were analyzed by applying the first and second filters and, the ones presenting results related to the research topic were included in the study.

We used the StArt tool (`https://bit.ly/3bW3Mo6`) to support publications selection. To consolidate data, publications returned in the publication selection steps were cataloged and stored in spreadsheets. We defined an id for each publication and recorded the publication title, authors, year, and vehicle of publication. Data from publications returned in S4 and S5 were extracted and organized into a data extraction table oriented to the research questions. The spreadsheets produced during the study can be found in `https://bit.ly/36nXUAw`.

The first and second authors performed publication selection and data extraction. The third and fourth authors reviewed both. Once data has been validated, the first and the second authors carried out data interpretation and analysis, and again third and fourth authors reviewed the results. Discordances were discussed and resolved. Quantitative data were tabulated and used in graphs and statistical analysis. Finally, the four authors performed qualitative analysis considering the findings, their relation to the research questions and the study purpose.

4 Data Extraction and Synthesis

The study considered papers published until July 2019. Searches were conducted for the last time in September 2019. Figure 1 illustrates the followed process and the number of publications selected in each step.

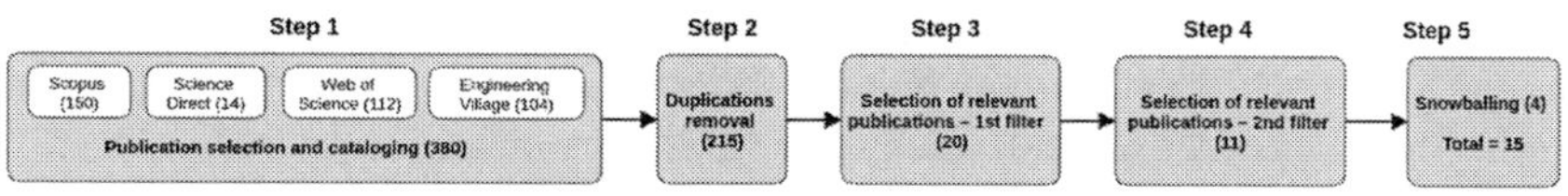

Fig. 1. Publications selection process.

In the 1st step, as a result of searching the selected sources, a total of 380 publications was returned. In the 2nd step, we eliminated duplicates, achieving 215 publications (reduction of approximately 43%). In the 3rd step, we applied the selection criteria over the abstract, resulting in 20 papers (reduction of approximately 90%). At this step, we only excluded publications that were clearly unrelated to the subject of interest. In case of doubt, the paper was taken to the next step. In the 4th step, the selection criteria were applied considering the full text, resulting in 11 publications (reduction of approximately 45%). Finally, in the 5th step, we performed snowballing technique by checking the references of the 11 selected publications and identified 4 more publications, which in total added up to 15 publications. When analyzing the publications to identify the KM approaches applied in HCI design context, we noticed that some publications addressed complementary works from a same research group. Hence, we considered complementary works as a single KM approach when extracting data about RQs 3, 4, 5, 6 and 7. Table 2 shows the list of identified KM approaches and corresponding publications. Two papers were grouped into a KM approach and three other papers were grouped in another KM approach. Thus, we considered a total of 12 different KM approaches found in 15 studies. Along this and the next section we refer to the approaches by using the id listed in the table. Detailed information about the selected publications, including a brief description and extracted data, can be found in `https://bit.ly/36nXUAw`. After Table 2, we present the data synthesis for each research question.

Table 2: Selected publications.

ID	Approach	Ref.
#01	Trading off usability and security in user interface design through mental models	[12]
#02	Knowledge management challenges in collaborative design of a Virtual Call Centre	[18]
#03	Applying knowledge management in UI design process	[22]
#04	A knowledge management tool for speech interfaces	[1]
#05	Design knowledge reuse based on visualization of relationships between claims	[25,26]
#06	Design knowledge reuse and notification systems to support design in the development process	[5,4,20]
#07	Exploring knowledge processes in user-centered design process	[21]
#08	Lessons learnt from an HCI repository	[28]
#09	A pattern language approach to usability knowledge management	[9]
#10	An expert system for usability evaluations of business-to-consumer e-commerce sites	[7]

Table 2 continued from previous page

#11	A framework for developing experience-based usability guidelines	[8]
#12	Prototype evaluation and redesign: structuring the design space through contextual techniques	[19]

Publication year and type (RQ1): Figure 2 shows the distribution of the 15 selected publications over the years and their distribution considering the publication type. Papers addressing KM in HCI design context have been published since 1995 in Journals and Conferences (no Workshop publications were found). Conferences have been the main forum, encompassing 73.3% of the publications (11 out of 15). Four papers (26.78%) were published in journals.

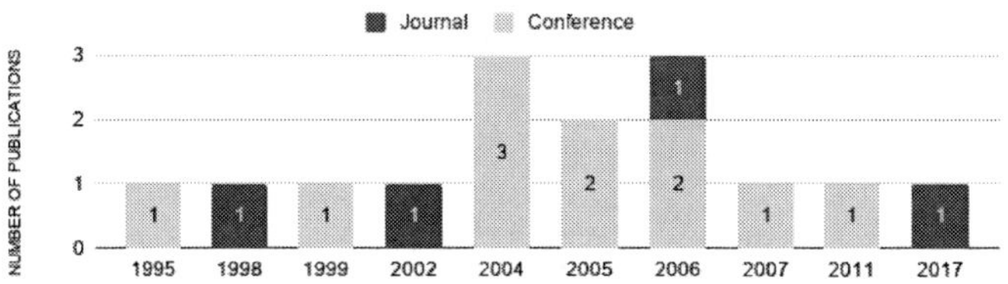

Fig. 2. Publications over the years.

Research Type (RQ2): 13 publications (86.7%) propose a solution to a problem and argue for its relevance. Thus, they were classified as *Proposal of Solution*. Five of them (33.3%) present some kind of evaluation, being one (6.7%) evaluated in practice (i.e., also classified as *Evaluation Research*), and four (26.7%) investigating the characteristics of the proposed solution not yet implemented in practice (i.e., *Validation Research*). One publication (6.7%) refers exclusively to *Evaluation Research*, discussing the evaluation of KM an industrial setting, and another is a *Personal Experience Paper*, reporting the experience of the authors in a particular project in the industry.

Motivation for using KM in HCI design (RQ3): we identified six reasons for using KM in HCI design, as shown in Table 3. Some approaches presented more than one motivation, thus the total sum is greater than 12.

Table 3: Motivations for using KM in HCI design.

Motivation	Approaches	Total
Improve product quality	#01, #02, #04, #05, #06, #07, #10, #11, #12	9
Reduce design effort	#02, #03, #08, #09, #10	5
Reduce design time	#04, #05, #08	3
Reduce design cost	#05, #10	2
Improve design team performance	#06	1
Improve HCI design learning	#06	1

Nine approaches (75%) use KM to improve product quality, most of them concerning usability. These approaches aim to provide benefits related to the quality of the interactive system in terms of its interaction with users. For example, the approach #11 is proposed to help developers to design effective, useful and usable applications. Approach #01, in turn, aims to improve alignment between design features and users' requirements. Seven approaches (58.3%) are motivated by improving one or more aspects related to the HCI design process, namely: effort, time and cost. From these, reducing effort is highlighted. 5 approaches (41.7%) use KM to reduce manpower, mainly by not depending on internal usability experts to perform HCI design activities. The approach #02, for example, applied KM to decrease the need for experts to support the design team with their knowledge and experience, due to lack of knowledge to be reused. The approaches #04, #05 and #08 were motivated by reducing HCI design time through the reuse of previous solutions implemented for similar problems. Reducing costs in the HCI design process was the motivation for the approaches #05 and #10, which focus on minimizing the involvement of external usability experts in the process and conducting usability evaluation more effectively. The approach #06 aimed to improve design team performance by providing support for team coordination and collaboration. This approach also aimed to improve HCI learning to the students involved in the project.

Managed knowledge in HCI design (RQ4): Analyzing the publications, we identified 24 different knowledge items managed by the KM approaches, as shown in Table 4. Some items are shown in the same line to safe space. The main design aspect addressed in the publications is *Usability*, being the content of all knowledge items related to it. Knowledge items managed in two approaches (#03 and #08) are also related to *Ergonomics*. Some approaches focus on particular types of design or interface. This is the case of approaches #03 and #04. The former focuses on *Task-based Design* while the latter focuses on *Speech Driven Interfaces*.

Table 4: Managed knowledge items.

Knowledge Item	Approaches	Total
Design Guidelines	#04, #08, #10, #11	4
Design Solutions	#02, #04, #07, #08	4
Test Results	#02, #04, #12	3
Claims	#05, #06	2
Design Features	#01, #12	2
Design Patterns	#09, #11	2
Lessons learned	#04, #08	2
Usability Measures	#02, #08	2
Claims Relationships	#05	1
Design Changes	#06	1
Design Feature Checklists; Design Methods; Design Processes; Design Standards; Design Templates; Interface Objects	#08	1
Interaction Model; Task Model	#03	1
Scenarios; Test Scenarios	#02	1
User Knowledge; User Needs	#07	1
User Requirements	#01	1
User Tasks	#09	1

When knowledge is captured and used (RQ5): Table 5 shows when HCI design knowledge has been captured and when it has been used along the HCI design process. Three approaches capture and use knowledge along the whole process. Eight approaches (66.7%) use knowledge when producing design solutions. A smaller number (six, 50%) capture knowledge in this activity. The behavior is the opposite in design evaluation: there are more approaches capturing (five, 41.7%) than using (three, 25%) knowledge in this activity. Only one (8.3%) approach captures knowledge during requirements specification.

Table 5: Capture and use of knowledge along the HCI design process.

Activity [10]	Knowledge Capture	Knowledge Use
Specify requirements	1 (#01)	0
Produce design solutions	6 (#02, #03, #04, #07, #10, #11)	8 (#01, #02, #03, #04, #07, #09, #11, #12)
Design Evaluation	5 (#02, #04, #09, #10, #12)	3 (#02, #09, #10)
Whole cycle	3 (#05, #06, #08)	3 (#05, #06, #08)

Technologies used in KM approaches (RQ6): Table 6 shows the technologies used in the analyzed KM approaches. The most common technologies were knowledge-based systems and knowledge repositories, followed by knowledge management systems and knowledge-based analysis. Other technologies such as ontologies, model transformation, contextual inquiry and mental models were used in only one KM approach. Details about the KM approaches can be found in the document available at `https://bit.ly/36nXUAw`.

Table 6: Technologies used in KM approaches in HCI design context.

Technology	Approaches	Total
Knowledge-based System	#02, #04, #10	3
Knowledge Repository	#05, #06, #08	3
Knowledge Management System	#09, #11	2
Knowledge-based Analysis	#03, #07	2
Ontology; Model Transformation	#03	1
Conceptual Framework	#07	1
Contextual Inquiry; Brainstorming-based Technique	#12	1
Mental Model; Internalization Awareness; Observation; Behavioral Interviews; Absorptive Capacity; Heuristic Evaluation	#01	1

Benefits and challenges of using KM in HCI design (RQ7): Table 7 summarizes the benefits and difficulties reported in the publications. As it can be noticed more benefits than difficulties were reported.

Table 7: Benefits and difficulties of using KM in HCI design context.

Benefits	Approaches	Total
Enable replicability of domain/context knowledge	#03, #06, #07, #09, #12	5
Improve product quality	#02, #05, #06, #12	4
Improve communication	#01, #03, #11	3
Increase team engagement/empowerment	#02, #06	2
Increase organizational integration	#03, #08	2
Reduce design effort	#03, #12	2
Improve design conceptualization	#03, #07	2
Promote standardization	#02	1
Increase productivity	#11	1
Promote organizational competitive advantage	#02	1
Decrease implementation and maintenance effort	#08	1
Decrease implementation and maintenance costs	#08	1
Difficulties	**Approaches**	**Total**
Knowledge is often context-specific	#02, #06, #09, #11	4
System features issues	#05, #06, #09	3
Low team engagement/empowerment	#01, #05, #08	3
User involvement	#07, #12	2

Table 7 continued from previous page.

Integration of the KM approach into the organization	#06, #11	2
Effort to implement and maintain the KM approach	#08, #09	2
Lack of consensus about HCI design conceptualization	#01, #02	2

5 Discussion

Taking the period of publications into account (RQ1), we can notice a long-term effort regarding the use of KM in HCI design, since this topic has been target of researchers for more than 20 years. However, the low average of publications per year (0.6 since 1995) shows that the topic has not been widely addressed. We can also notice that most of the publications are from the 2000s decade. The low percentage of journal publications, which generally require more mature works, can be seen as a reinforcement that the research on this topic is not mature enough yet. Besides, results about the research type (RQ2) show that only 40% of the works included some kind of evaluation, being only 13% evaluation of solutions in practice. This can be a sign of difficulty in applying the proposed approaches in industry, what reinforces that research on this topic is not mature enough yet and there seems to be a gap between theory and practice.

Concerning RQ3, we can notice that using KM in HCI design has been motivated mainly by delivering better products to users or optimizing the HCI design process in terms of effort, time and cost. Improving performance of the HCI design team was also mentioned, what is consistent with the other motivations related to the HCI design process, since increasing performance can contribute to decrease effort, time and cost. A common concern in several publications was the need for HCI design expert consultants, which can increase HCI design cost and effort. Capturing and reusing knowledge contribute to retain organizational knowledge and reduce dependence on external consultants. Another concern refers to communication problems. Smith and Dunckley [19] highlight that barriers to effective communication between designers, HCI specialists and users, due to their differing perspectives, affect product quality. KM solutions are helpful in this context.

Usability has been the focus of the KM initiatives in HCI context (RQ4). In fact, this is not a surprise, because usability has been the HCI design property more explored in the last years. Moreover, this property is quite comprehensive and includes other important aspects of HCI design, such as learnability, memorability, efficiency, safety and satisfaction [10]. However, there are other important properties not addressed in the analyzed papers, such as user experience, communicability and accessibility. The knowledge items managed by the KM approaches are quite diverse. Design solutions, guidelines, test results and design patterns are some knowledge items found in different publications. Despite the variety of knowledge items, we noticed that most of the approaches (66.7%) manage up two different knowledge items. By analyzing the coverage of the approach in terms of single or multiple projects, we found out that four approaches (#01, #03, #07 and #12) manage knowledge involved in a single project, while the other eight approaches are more extensive, accumulating knowledge from multiple projects. In order to elevate knowledge reuse to the organizational level, it is important that a KM approach comprehends multiple projects in that organization.

Concerning knowledge use and capture (RQ5), at first, we expected that knowledge was captured and used in the same activity of the HCI design process. Therefore, results showed us that the same knowledge can be produced and consumed in different parts of HCI design process. For example, there are more approaches capturing knowledge in design evaluation activity than using in it. This reinforces the iterative characteristic of HCI design, where knowledge obtained in evaluation activity in one cycle can be used to improve the design in the next cycle.

Different technologies have been used to implement KM in HCI design context (RQ6). The most common are system-based approaches that use software to support KM process and store knowledge. We expected this result because KM systems, knowledge-based systems and knowledge repositories are widely adopted technologies in KM area. Earlier steps of the development of KM solutions, such as knowledge analysis and modeling, are also addressed in some publications. Moreover, there is also concern with latter steps, like the integration of the KM system into the organization. Some approaches combine different technologies, what can be a sign that the use of different techniques is a good strategy to address a more complete KM approach in HCI design.

As for benefits and challenges of using KM in HCI design context (RQ7), when categorizing the findings, we noticed that several of them are benefits and challenges of using KM in general. However, by analyzing the context of each KM approach, we can better understand how the findings relate to HCI design. For example, regarding the benefit *improve communication*, the works highlight the use of KM to support communication among the different actors involved in the HCI design process. In #10, communication between HCI specialists, designers and users is mediated by prototypes aiming at an agreement about the system design. In #01, KM facilitates the elicitation of the user's knowledge for the designer to apply it into the design. In #03, KM reduces errors of interpretation and contextualization among the people involved in the system design.

Some of the identified challenges and benefits are opposite each other. For example, on one hand, there is the challenge *low team engagement*. On the other hand, the benefit *increase team engagement*. We kept both because they were cited in different publications, thus under different perspectives. Moreover, we can see the challenge as a difficulty that, when overcome by the use of KM, can be turned into a benefit.

By analyzing the most cited benefit and challenge, we noticed that the generality level of the knowledge is an important question in a KM approach. The most cited benefit points to knowledge replicability in a specific context/domain. The most cited challenge points to the fact that it is difficult to generalize knowledge. Looking at data from RQ5, we noticed that approaches that reported knowledge generalization challenge handle knowledge from multiple projects, while approaches handling knowledge in a single project reported easy replication of knowledge. Thus, how general will be knowledge should be determined by the context where the KM approach will be applied. When dealing with high diversity of knowledge and contexts, it becomes harder to produce general knowledge to be widely used to solve specific problems and be adopted in different contexts. One way of achieving improvements in replicability is using knowledge-based analysis methods, as reported by the approaches #03 and #07.

Based on the panorama provided by the study results, in summary, we can say that KM has not been much explored in HCI context; it has been used mainly to improve software quality and HCI design process efficiency; it has focused on usability; and the KM approaches have been based on systems and repositories. As for benefits, KM has enabled knowledge replicability, improved product quality and communication. The main difficulties have been to generalize knowledge, address issues related to features of the system and low engagement of the team.

6 Limitations of the Study

As any study, our study has some limitations that must be considered together the results. One limitation refers to the subjectivity embedded in publication selection and data extraction. They were initially performed by the first and second authors and, to reduce subjectivity, the other two authors performed these same steps. Discordances and possible biases were discussed until reaching a consensus.

Another limitation refers to the sources. We used four digital libraries selected based on other secondary studies in Software Engineering. Although this set of digital libraries represents a comprehensive source of publications, the exclusion of other sources may have left some valuable publications out of our analysis. We performed snowballing aiming to minimize this risk. There are also limitations related to the adopted search string. Even though we have used several terms, there are still synonyms that we did not use.

Another important limitation is related to the classifications we made. We defined classification schemas for categorizing data in some research questions. Some categories were based on classifications previously proposed in the literature (e.g., type of research [27]). Others were established during data extraction, based on data provided by the analyzed publications (e.g., RQ4). Classification schemas and data categorization were done by the first and second authors and reviewed by the other two authors. However, determining the categories and how publications fit them involves a lot of judgment. Thus, different results could be obtained by other researchers.

7 Conclusion

In this paper, we presented a mapping study that investigated the use of KM in the HCI design context. The results of the mapping study provide a panorama of research related to the topic. We noticed that, although HCI design is a favorable area to apply KM, there have been only few studies exploring this research topic. Due to the increasing importance of interactive systems and the diversity of interfaces that have been made available for people's use, we believe that there are many challenges and questions to be addressed in future research. For example: (i) The lack of a common conceptualization about HCI design (pointed in #01 and #02) leads to communication problems between the different actors involved in the HCI design process. We believe that the use of ontologies to establish this common conceptualization could help in this matter. (ii) The gap between theory and practice (RQ2 results) shows that it is necessary to take KM solutions to practical HCI design environments. For that, a divide and conquer strategy to reduce complexity of the conception, implementation and evaluation of a KM approach might be useful, allowing to provide results for the organizations in smaller periods of time and increasing benefits as the approach evolves. (iii) Other aspects besides usability (e.g., user experience, communicability) should be explored in KM initiatives to improve HCI design. (iv) The difficulties identified in RQ7 indicate issues that can be investigated in future research.

Concerning related works, we did not find any study investigating the use of KM in HCI context. As future work, we intend to carry out surveys with HCI design professionals aiming to identify which knowledge they consider important to manage when designing interactive systems. Thus, we intend to complement this study and provide an overview of how to use KM to aid in HCI design.

References

1. Bouwmeester, N.: A Knowledge Management Tool for Speech Interfaces. In: Proc. of the 22nd An. Int. ACM SIGIR Conf. on Research and development in Information Retrieval. pp. 293–294. ACM, NY, NY, USA (1999)
2. Carroll, J.M.: Human Computer Interaction (HCI). In: Soegaard, M., Dam, R.F. (eds.) The Ency. of Human-Computer Interaction, chap. 2, pp. 21–61. The Interaction Design Foundation, Aarhus, Denmark, 2nd edn. (2014)
3. Chammas, A., Quaresma, M., Mont'Alvão, C.: A Closer Look on the User Centred Design. Procedia Manufacturing **3**, 5397–5404 (2015)
4. Chewar, C.M., McCrickard, D.S.: Links for a human-centered science of design: Integrated design knowledge environments for a software development process. In: Proc. of the 38th An. Hawaii Int. Conf. on System Sciences. pp. 256c–256c (2005)
5. Chewar, C., Bachetti, E., McCrickard, D.S., Booker, J.E.: Automating a Design Reuse Facility with Critical Parameters. In: Jacob, R.J., Limbourg, Q., Vanderdonckt, J. (eds.) Computer-Aided Design of User Interfaces IV. pp. 235–246. Springer Netherlands, Dordrecht (2004)
6. De Souza, C.S.: The Semiotic Engineering of Human-Computer Interaction. The MIT Press, Cambridge, Massachussetts (2005)
7. Gabriel, I.J.: An expert system for usability evaluations of business-to-consumer e-commerce sites. In: Proc. of the 6th An. ISOnEworld Conf. Las Vegas, NV (2007)
8. Henninger, S., Haynes, K., Reith, M.W.: A framework for developing experience-based usability guidelines. In: Proc. of the 1st conf. on designing interactive systems: processes, practices, methods, techniques. pp. 43–53. ACM, NY, USA (1995)

9. Hughes, M.: A Pattern Language Approach to Usability Knowledge Management. Journal of Usability Studies **1**(2), 76–90 (2006)
10. ISO 9241-210: ISO 9241-210:2010(en) - Ergonomics of human-system interaction — Part 210: Human-centred design for interactive systems (2010)
11. Kitchenham, B.A., Charters, S.: Guidelines for performing Systematic Literature Reviews in Software Engineering. Tech. rep., Keele and Durham University (2007)
12. Mohamed, M.A., Chakraborty, J., Dehlinger, J.: Trading off Usability and Security in User Interface Design Through Mental Models. Behaviour & Information Technology **36**(5), 493–516 (2017)
13. O'Leary, D.E.: Enterprise Knowledge Management. Computer **31**(3), 54–61 (1998)
14. Petersen, K., Vakkalanka, S., Kuzniarz, L.: Guidelines for conducting systematic mapping studies in software engineering: An update. Information and Software Technology **64**, 1–18 (2015)
15. Rogers, Y., Sharp, H., Preece, J.: Interaction Design: Beyond Human-Computer Interaction. Wiley Publishing, Chichester, United Kingdom, 3rd edn. (2011)
16. Rus, I., Lindvall, M.: Knowledge management in software engineering. IEEE Software **19**(3), 26–38 (2002)
17. Schneider, K.: Experience and Knowledge Management in Software Engineering. Springer Publishing Company, Incorporated, Heidelberg, Berlin, 1st edn. (2009)
18. Sikorski, M., Garnik, I., Ludwiszewski, B., Wyrwiński, J.: Knowledge Management Challenges in Collaborative Design of a Virtual Call Centre. In: Knowlege-Based and Intelligent Information and Engineering Systems. pp. 657–666. Springer Berlin Heidelberg, Berlin, Heidelberg (2011)
19. Smith, A., Dunckley, L.: Prototype evaluation and redesign: structuring the design space through contextual techniques. Interacting with Computers **14**(6), 821–843 (2002)
20. Smith, J.L., Bohner, S.A., McCrickard, D.S.: Toward introducing notification technology into distributed project teams. In: 12th IEEE Int. Conf. and Workshops on the Engineering of Computer-Based Systems (ECBS'05). pp. 349–356 (2005)
21. Still, K.: Exploring Knowledge Processes in User-Centered Design Process. In: The 7th European Conf. on Knowledge Management. p. 533 (2006)
22. Suàrez, P.R., Jùnior, B.L., de Barros, M.A.: Applying Knowledge Management in UI Design Process. In: Proc. of the 3rd An. Conf. on Task Models and Diagrams. pp. 113–120. ACM, NY, USA (2004)
23. Sutcliffe, A.G.: Requirements Engineering from an HCI Perspective. In: Soegaard, M., Dam, R.F. (eds.) The Ency. of Human-Computer Interaction, chap. 13, pp. 707–760. The Interaction Design Foundation, Aarhus, Denmark, 2nd edn. (2014)
24. Valaski, J., Malucelli, A., Reinehr, S.: Review: Ontologies Application in Organizational Learning: A Literature Review. Expert Systems with Applications **39**(8), 7555–7561 (2012)
25. Wahid, S., Smith, J.L., Berry, B., Chewar, C.M., McCrickard, D.S.: Visualization of design knowledge component relationships to facilitate reuse. In: Proc. of the 2004 IEEE Int. Conf. on Information Reuse and Integration. pp. 414–419 (2004)
26. Wahid, S.: Investigating Design Knowledge Reuse for Interface Development. In: Proc. of the 6th Conf. on Designing Interactive Systems. pp. 354–356. ACM, NY, USA (2006)
27. Wieringa, R., Maiden, N., Mead, N., Rolland, C.: Requirements Engineering Paper Classification and Evaluation Criteria: A Proposal and a Discussion. Requir. Eng. **11**(1), 102–107 (2005)
28. Wilson, P., Borras, J.: Lessons learnt from an HCI repository. Int. Journal of Industrial Ergonomics **22**(4), 389–396 (1998)

Extraction of Useful Information from Unstructured Data in Software Engineering: A Systematic Mapping

Patrick R. Silva[1], Vinicius dos Santos[2], Érica F. Souza[1], Giovani V. Meinerz[1], Katia R. Felizardo[1], and Nandamudi L. Vijaykumar[3]

[1] Federal University of Technology - Paraná (UTFPR), Cornélio Procópio - Brazil
patrick.1985@alunos.utfpr.edu.br, {ericasouza, giovanimeinerz, katiascannavino}@utfpr.edu.br

[2] Universidade de São Paulo, São Carlos, São Paulo - Brazil
vinicius.dos.santos@usp.br

[3] National Institute for Space Research (INPE) and Federal University of São Paulo (Unifesp)
São José dos Campos, São Paulo - Brazil
vijay.nl@inpe.br,vijaykumar@unifesp.br

Abstract. Context: A large number of information is generated and manipulated in Software Engineering (SE) projects. The technology surrounding this domain is constantly evolving. To keep up with such evolution, developers share their knowledge and seek help from other developers by means of interactive and collaborative environments. Understanding and extracting knowledge from these environments can enable developers to identify useful information for the project. **Objective:** This work aims to identify the main textual analysis approaches to extract useful information in the SE. **Method:** To achieve the proposed objective, we conducted a Systematic Mapping (SM). **Results:** We analyzed 69 relevant primary studies addressing approaches to extract useful information in the SE. **Conclusion:** Among the main conclusions of this study, we can infer that discussion forums attracted a significantly attention in SE context and it becomes one of the main textual databases investigated to extract useful information.

Keywords: Software Engineering · Textual Analysis · Useful Information · Systematic Mapping

1 Introduction

One of the characteristics of Software Engineering (SE) projects is the large quantity of information that is generated and manipulated [22, 29]. Those involved in the project face problems such as: difficulty in systematizing the information generated throughout the software processes; difficulty in reusing the knowledge generated from one project to another; loss of intellectual capital of the organization; and the non-representation of knowledge [24]. In addition, SE is made up of a huge number of constantly evolving tools, frameworks, and APIs. Technologies that are innovative, in just over a year, may become obsolete. So, to keep up with this ever-changing pace, developers share their knowledge and seek help from other developers in areas where they have less knowledge [28].

According to Abidi et al. (2009) [1], the social web paradigm can be useful for sharing knowledge through interactive and collaborative technologies. Questions & Answers (Q&A) like Stack Overflow, control tools like Jira, Redmine and Mantis, and source code sharing platforms like GitHub, are very rich sources of information. Through these environments, the entire software development process could be discussed and documented by team members, and most are texts written in natural language. Understanding and extracting knowledge from these environments can enable developers to identify useful information such as usage trends, previously created function facilities, best practices, lessons learned and new coding methodologies [17, 28].

Manual access to the large volume of textual data generated to search for useful information becomes an arduous and complex task. Identifying relevant knowledge for reuse is difficult and requires specific approaches to handling a large volume of information [1]. For this purpose, there is a huge range of Natural Language Processing (NLP) and Text Mining tools and techniques that can be used to assist in knowledge extraction. NLP and Text Mining are both interested in processing and extracting information from texts. NLP uses different levels of linguistic analysis responsible for understanding meaning and structure of a given text [10]. On the other hand, text mining extracts hidden information inside text data through pattern recognition [6].

The demands for reduced development time and increased reliability of software need for new approaches that provide support for development and decision making process. Knowledge extraction from text data set previously collected, for example, can bring a lot of useful information related to software development. Inserted in this context, this work has an objective to identify in the literature the main textual analysis approaches to extract useful information in SE domain, such as SE activities the study focuses on (e.g. Software Requirements, Software Testing, Development), textual database considered (e.g. Forums, Wiki, Tweets), techniques, algorithms and tools that were considered. In order to achieve the proposed objective, we conducted a Systematic Mapping (SM). An SM provides a broad overview of an area of research, to determine whether there is research evidence on a particular topic [12].

We believe that results from this SM can strongly help to identify a body of knowledge to support future research, learning as much as possible from other domains related to the topic, and providing a basis for other researchers as well as students who consider learning about and contributing to this area.

The remainder of this paper is structured as follows. Section 2 presents the related publications. Section 3 introduces the method used to conduct the research. Section 4 shows the main results from studies extraction and synthesis. Section 5 reports a general discussion to highlight some research points, their implications, and limitations. Lastly, conclusions and future directions for this research are presented Section 6.

2 Related Work

We adopted concepts of a tertiary study to look for secondary studies that already investigated approaches to extract useful information in the SE considering unstructured data. Tertiary studies are reviews about other secondary studies [12]. In this study, we used the following search string: *("text mining" OR "text processing" OR "text classification" OR "knowledge extraction" OR "information extraction" OR "text cluster" OR "text data mining" OR "text association" OR "Natural Language Processing" OR "NLP") AND ("software engineering" OR "software organizations" OR "software development") AND ("systematic review" OR "literature review" OR "systematic mapping" OR "mapping study" OR "systematic map" OR "literature analysis").*

The search string was applied in the Scopus electronic database and 52 studies were returned. We analyzed each of the 52 studies and we found four studies that conducted a review on the same topic as our SM. The studies are briefly described as follows.

In Maqbool et al. [14], a Systematic Literature Review (SLR) was performed to investigate modern techniques, tools and trends for the generation of Business Process Modeling Languages (BPML) models from textual requirements by utilizing NLP techniques. Ahmad et al. [2] conducted a literature review to show how academics/practitioners can benefit from the valuable user-generated content in software repositories including the Q&A software developer community.

SLR was conducted in Ahsan et al. (2017) [3] to investigate the application of NLP techniques to generate test cases from requirements document. The main NLP techniques and tools used to extract textual information from requirements document were summarized in this study. Finally, in Shah and Pfahl [23], a mapping study was conducted to identify relevant information from the scientific literature about data sources, research contributions, and the usage of text analysis techniques for the improvement and evaluation of software quality. The authors summarized, in this study, the data sources which have been used, research contributions that have been made, text analysis techniques which have been employed and how does text analysis help in improving and evaluating software quality.

Each presented study conducted some kind of secondary study on extracting useful information in SE, but with different purposes. The main difference from the secondary studies identified with ours is that the studies found have specific scopes in SE, such as software testing, software quality or modeling languages. In our mapping study, the scope is much broader considering the various activities in SE. This gives a broader overview of where efforts for SE textual analysis research have been concentrated.

3 Systematic Mapping

SM has been used to provide a broad overview of the state of all relevant research available for a particular topic of interest. The research method in this study was defined based on Kitchenham and Charters [12]. The method involves three main phases. Firstly, a planning is elaborated. This planning refers to the pre-review activities, and establishes a protocol, defining the research questions, inclusion and exclusion criteria, sources of studies, search string, and mapping procedures. Then, in the conduction phase, search and selection activities are carried out in order to extract and synthesize data from studies included. Finally, in the final phase the results are written and disseminated to interested parties. Following, the main parts of the mapping protocol used in this work are presented.

Research Questions. This mapping study aims to answer the following Research Questions (RQs):

- RQ1. When and where were the studies published?
- RQ2. Which software engineering activities are the studies concentrated on?
- RQ3. What is the textual database considered for the study?
- RQ4. What techniques, algorithms, methods and tools were considered?
- RQ5. What are the main challenges/difficulties reported in the studies?

Inclusion and Exclusion Criteria. The selection criteria are organized in one Inclusion Criterion (IC) and eight Exclusion Criteria (EC). The inclusion criterion is: (IC1) The study must present textual analysis initiatives to extract useful information in the context of Software Engineering. The exclusion criteria are: (EC1) The study does not have a abstract; (EC2) The study is just an abstract, not having a full text; (EC3) The study is not a primary study, such as editorials, summaries of keynotes, workshops, and tutorials; (EC4) The study is not written in English; (EC5) The study is an older version (less updated) of another study already considered; (EC6) The full paper is not available; (EC7) The study must present textual analysis initiatives in the English language; and (EC8) Does not meet Inclusion Criterion (CI1).

Keywords and Search String. The search string considered two areas, Textual Analysis and Software Engineering (see Table 1), and it was applied in three metadata fields (namely, title, abstract and keywords).

Source. We chose to work with Scopus[4] database. This source is considered the largest abstract and citation database of peer-reviewed literature, with more than 60 million records. Scopus attaches papers of other international publishers, including Cambridge University Press, Institute of Electrical and Electronics Engineers (IEEE), Nature Publishing Group, Springer, Wiley-Blackwell, and Elsevier. The studies returned from Scopus database were cataloged and stored appropriately. This catalog helped us in the classification and analysis procedures.

[4] *https://www.scopus.com*

Table 1: Keywords for the search string

<table>
<tr><th>Areas</th><th>Keywords</th></tr>
<tr><td>Information Extraction</td><td>"text mining", "text processing", "text classification", "knowledge extraction", "information extraction", "text cluster", "text data mining", "text association", "Natural Language Processing", "NLP"</td></tr>
<tr><td>Software Engineering</td><td>"software engineering", "software organizations", "software development"</td></tr>
<tr><td colspan="2">Search String: ("text mining" OR "text processing" OR "text classification" OR "knowledge extraction" OR "information extraction" OR "text cluster" OR "text data mining" OR "text association" OR "Natural Language Processing" OR "NLP") AND ("software engineering" OR "software organizations" OR "software development")</td></tr>
</table>

Assessment. Before conducting the mapping study, we tested the mapping protocol in order to verify its feasibility and adequacy, based on a pre-selected set of studies considered relevant to our investigation. First, the review process was conducted by the first author of this paper, and, only then, the other authors carried out the review validation using different samples (approximately 30% each).

4 Data Extraction and Synthesis

The main steps performed in this mapping study are shown in Figure 1.

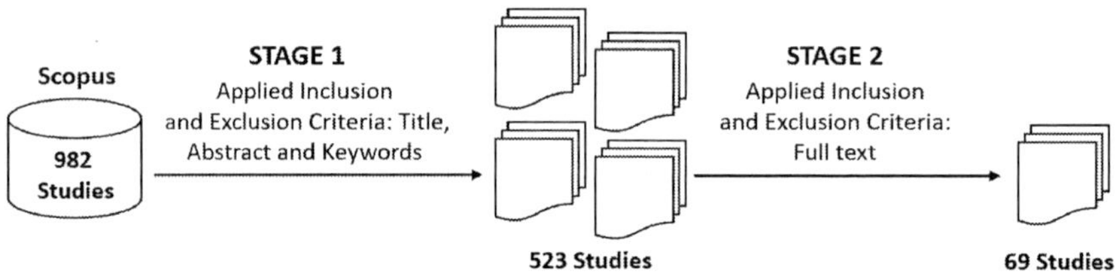

Fig. 1: Selection process

We considered the studies published in the last 10 years (2009 until April 2019). As a result, 982 publications were returned. The selection process was divided into two stages. In the 1st stage, inclusion and exclusion criteria were applied considering the title, abstract and keywords, so 459 publications (approximately 46%) were eliminated. In the 2nd stage, the exclusion criteria were applied considering the entire text, resulting in 69 studies (approximately 7% of total articles). As a result, we got a final set of 69 studies[5].

[5] Selected studies available at: *http://bit.ly/2NKq01s*

It is worth mentioning that in this SM the focus was on studies that used textual mining and NLP techniques to extract useful knowledge in order to be reused in software organizations. During the selection process, some primary studies returned, although using the same techniques for textual analysis, proposed processes to automatically generate UML diagrams from software requirements documents. The studies focus were solely in automation processes. However, that was not the scope of our focus. Studies with this objective were eliminated by the selection criteria.

We analyzed each of 69 studies in order to answer the RQs. The studies classification was made from the RQs answers. The same answers were grouped and consequently a category was defined. For some RQs in data extraction and synthesis the sum of all classifications might be greater than the total number of papers in the SM. This occurs because a given paper can answer a RQ with more than one target of our investigation. In addition, in some RQs, elements that were mentioned once were grouped into "Others" category. However, the full version of data extraction is available for consultation[6]. Next, we present the main findings from data extraction and synthesis.

RQ1. When and where have the studies been published?

A distribution of the 69 studies selected over the past ten years is shown in Figure 2. As Figure 2 demonstrates, although research on textual analysis initiatives intended to detect useful information is not recent, in SE domain the number of studies was moderate between 2010 and 2015, with a considerable increase between 2016 and 2018. Considering that the number of publications in the year 2019 is also considerable, our work, however, shows a smaller number as we consider only studies published until April 2019.

Analyzing the publication vehicle, conferences were the main communication channel, representing 72% (50 studies) of publications. The journals occupied 11% (8 studies), symposium 10% (7 studies) and workshop 6% (4 studies).

RQ2. Which software engineering activities are the studies concentrated on?

RQ2 relates to which activity of SE the study addressed. As shown in Figure 3, Software Development was the activity in which most of the studies were concentrated (54% - 37 studies). In Nembhard et al. (2018) [19], for example, text mining was used to extract knowledge from open source code in order to categorize and structure source code. By mining a subset (over 600.000 Java files) that contains over 70.000 open source projects, the authors presented that useful patterns can be extracted from source code and that these patterns can be used to create a recommends system to help programmers avoid unsafe practices.

[6] Data extraction available at: *http://bit.ly/2PiNQlC*

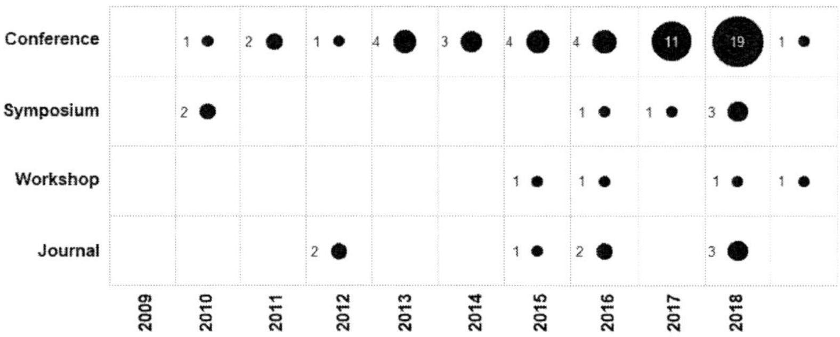

Fig. 2: Distribution of the selected studies over the years

Another example is the study conducted in Baquero et al. (2017) [5] in which, mechanisms for extracting implicit knowledge present in the Stack Overflow[7] questions were explored. In particular, the study motivation was to extract information about programming languages and their relationships. The proposed approach creates a classifier model that predicts the programming language using the content (text excerpts and source code) of a question. The method was evaluated on a set of 18.000 questions related to 18 different programming languages. The results showed that it is possible to extract non-evident information from a discussion forum, such as Stack Overflow.

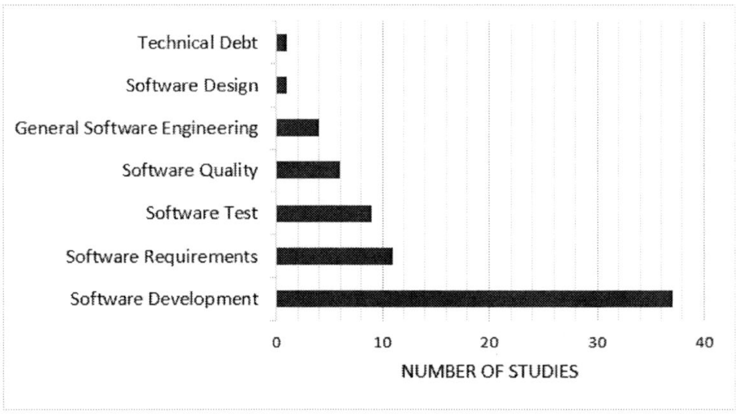

Fig. 3: Software Engineering activities analyzed

In relation to the other SE activities, software requirements occupied 16% (11 studies), software testing 13% (9 studies), software quality 9% (6 studies),

[7] *https://pt.stackoverflow.com*

general area of SE 6% (4 studies), technical debt (implied cost of rework) and software design both with 1% (1 study). Most studies proposed knowledge discovery to aid in some task involving decision making, for example, analysis of programmers comments in several project activities in order to detect behavior patterns and improve development, information reuse from old projects or identify which technology is most used [8, 9].

RQ3. What is the textual database considered for the study?

RQ3 focuses on identifying which textual database was considered in the selected studies. As shown in Figure 4, discussion forums are the most commonly used (33% - 23 studies), followed by requirements documents (14% - 10 studies), bug reports (8% - 6 studies), source code (7% - 5 studies), source code hosting platform (6% - 4 studies), code review comments (4 % - 3 studies), projects management tools (4% - 3 studies), manuals and tutorials (4% - 3).

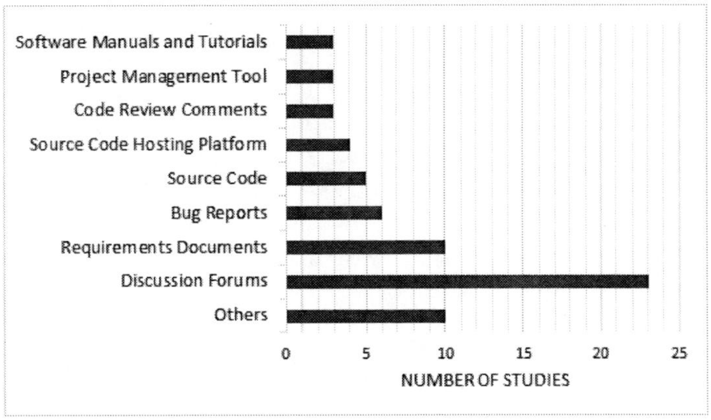

Fig. 4: Textual databases considered

Discussion forums have been the most used database for extracting useful information in SE. Out of the 23 studies that considered discussion forums, 19 used Stack Overflow as the basis for applying textual analysis techniques. Stack Overflow is a Q&A website for software development. According to Liu et al. (2018) [13], Stack Overflow's Q&A base has been increasingly used by professional software developers to get answers to their software development questions.

Stack Overflow was founded in 2008 and is the largest Q&A website for computer programming. This website currently contains a base of over 16 million questions and 24 million answers [15]. The large information data base maintained by Stack Overflow allows several searches for knowledge by researchers in SE. In the study conducted by Xu et al. (2017) [30], for example, the authors proposed a tool, called AnswerBot, that aims to help developers to quickly capture key information from various relevant posts from a technical question before reading the details of posts.

In addition to the discussion forums, another textual source presented by the selected studies was the software requirements documents. In Verma et al. (2013) [27], for example, NLP techniques were used to extract useful knowledge from requirements documents in order to represent them as a simple graph-based structure. According to the authors, this representation helps in understanding and identifying useful information from textual requirements.

Further databases identified were grouped into category "Other" (14% - 10 studies), for example, Wikis [18] and Tweets [25].

RQ4. What techniques, algorithms and tools were considered?

For RQ4, we investigated which techniques, algorithms and tools were used to support textual analysis for information extraction. Figure 5 presents the main techniques used in the selected studies. The most commonly used techniques were those used in the text preprocessing (31% - 22 studies), for example, stop word removal, tokenization, Lemmatization and Stemming. We consider this set of techniques as a single category "Text Preprocessing". Other techniques often mentioned are those related to text vectorization (13% - 9 studies), for example, Word2vec, Bag of Words (BOW) and Word Embeddings. We also consider this set of techniques in a single category "Text Vectorization Techniques". Other techniques identified were Latent Dirichlet Allocation (LDA) (5% - 4 studies), Support Vector Machine (SVM) (4% - 3 studies), Named Entity Recognition (NER) (2% - 2 studies), Naive Bayes (2% - 2 studies) and Latent Semantic Indexing (LSI) (2% - 2 studies). In the category "Others" (18% - 13 studies), techniques such as Doc2vec, ELICA and exploratory data analysis (EDA) were grouped.

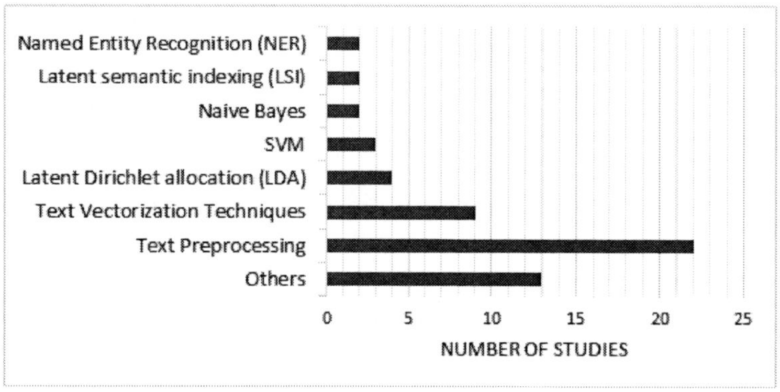

Fig. 5: Techniques used in textual analysis

Figure 6 presents the different algorithms used. The most commonly used algorithms was Term Frequency-Inverse Document Frequency (TF-IDF) with 72% (10 studies). TF-IDF algorithm maps the most relevant terms by means of their frequency, taking into consideration the frequency of this same term in a set of text analyzed [21].

We also map the tools mentioned in the selected studies. The most used tool was the Stanford CoreNLP[8] with 29% (13 studies). This tool provides a set of technologies to work with human language. For example, it gives the base forms of words, their parts of speech, normalize dates, times, and numeric quantities, mark up the structure of sentences in terms of phrases and syntactic dependencies, indicate which noun phrases refer to the same entities, indicate sentiment, extract particular or open-class relations between entity mentions.

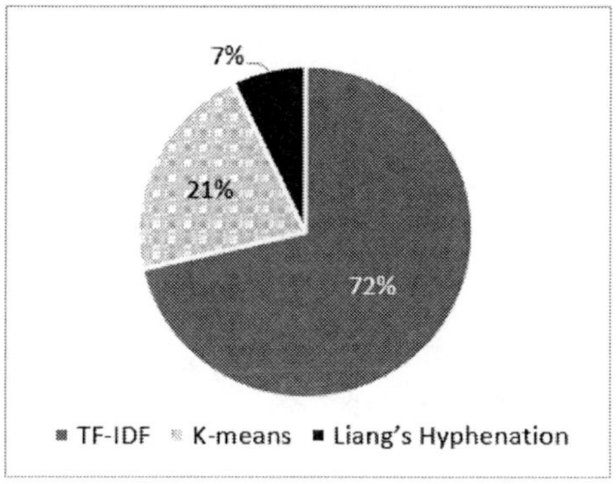

Fig. 6: Algorithms

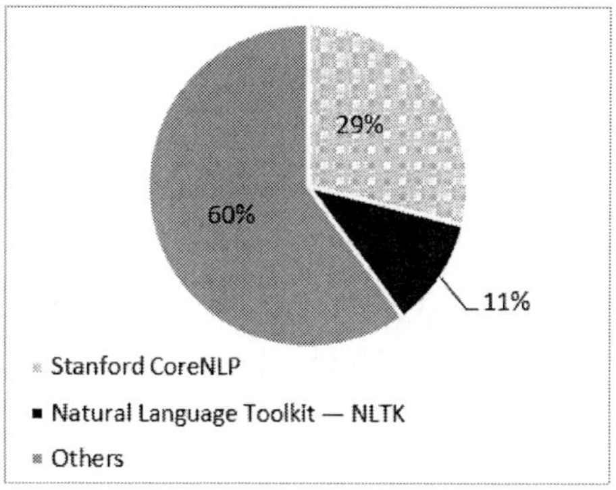

Fig. 7: Tools

Another widely used tool is the Natural Language Toolkit (NLTK)[9] (11% - 5 studies). NLTK is a tool for building Python programs to work with human language data. It provides interfaces to help to user work and a suite of text processing libraries for classification, tokenization, stemming, tagging, parsing, and semantic reasoning, wrappers for industrial-strength NLP libraries.

In "Others" category, tools such as Overlap, Gate, Scrapy, HDSKG and Sadge were mentioned.

RQ5. What are the main challenges/difficulties reported in the studies?

Although textual analysis can have several benefits in SE, some problems are also faced. The selected articles were analyzed for challenges, difficulties and problems, mentioned by the authors to identify useful information from textual

[8] *https://stanfordnlp.github.io/CoreNLP/*
[9] *https://www.nltk.org/*

databases, among the main challenges detected, we can highlight: (i) applying NLP techniques to software artifacts is complex since the artifacts have unique characteristics that not found in other natural language text [26]; (ii) software projects that are poorly documented [16]; and access to a set of industry scale domain documentations is a difficulty. Many organizations do not support the idea of publicly releasing the artifacts of their domain engineering practices. It becomes difficult to obtain real world requirement engineering documents for research purposes [4].

5 Discussion

Software engineering activities produce large amounts of unstructured data. Useful information can be extracted from such data to support SE activities, such as software development, software requirements or software test, as can be seen in RQ2. Software development activity, in particular, features many studies interested in exploring the knowledge that can be generated by considering aspects of source code, for example, language characteristics or comments in code [11].

The textual analysis in unstructured databases in SE, as presented in RQ3, is directly related to the SE activities, for example, the search for relevant information within discussion forums. Most studies that mention as purpose the use of this type of textual database are related to the software development activity. These studies look for behavioral patterns, especially in the comments from software developers. Online forums contain extensive valuable information that can aid in software development. Discussion forums are becoming rich repositories of valuable programming information that many experienced developers learn to revisit frequently [31].

Discussion forums are effective environments for facilitating the sharing of tacit knowledge among developers. Forums have become important repositories of knowledge for the following reasons: (i) useful knowledge can be generated and captured during discussions [7]; and (ii) it is considered a major challenge for knowledge management to convert tacit knowledge to explicit knowledge. Discussion forums can help in this knowledge conversion [20]. So, information extraction have been investigated to extract significant information from these unstructured data to aid in such development activities as the provision of method descriptions and the speed reading of bug reports [31].

Software developers extensively use Stack Overflow for knowledge sharing on software development. Thus, SE researchers have started mining the unstructured data present in certain software repositories including the Q&A software developer community Stack Overflow, to improve software development [2].

Extracting information for guidance of analyses is a real challenge. Those who want to follow the trends as well as predict them or even identify or detect patterns need to focus on the area of Artificial Intelligence. NLP and Text Mining, in particular, help in the forming, through unstructured data, patterns and associations useful for production of knowledge. Research conducted by EMC

Digital Universe[10], world leader of data storage, says that by 2020 there will be around 44 zettabytes (or 44 trillion GBs) of data stored. Therefore, Data Mining will become indispensable and new techniques, algorithms and tools for working with this amount of data to extract useful information are increasingly emerging.

In several areas, as in SE, researches are invested in creating techniques, algorithms or tools that are increasingly effective in extracting information from a textual database. In SE, as can be observed in RQ4, a large number of techniques can be used. With respect to tools, there are several proposals of new tools or an extension of existing ones, for example COLUA, a tool developed using python NLTK.

The research area in textual analysis has grown a lot in the last years in SE (RQ1). SE professionals have noted the benefits to the organization in identifying useful knowledge in what is textually generated by team members. In addition, the area enables researchers to focus their efforts on improving the various fronts involving this type of research, such as new techniques, tools or textual databases to be explored.

5.1 Threats to validity

Initially, our review was limited to Scopus database. Although Scopus is considered the largest abstract and citation database, it is possible that some valuable studies were left out from our analysis, since we considered papers indexed by just one database. Even so, we tried to overcome this limitation by considering papers from a control group to calibrate the search string. The categorization of papers was based on research questions. Thus, we believe that the studies discussed in this mapping provide an overview of empirical research on outcomes of existing research on textual analysis initiatives to extract useful information in unstructured databases in SE.

In addition, the study selection and data extraction were performed by the first author and some subjectivity could have been embedded. So, in order to reduce subjectivity, the other authors received different samples from the studies (about 30%) to conduct the same stages. The samples were compared to detect possible bias.

6 Conclusions

In this paper, we have reported the results of a systematic mapping on textual analysis initiatives to extract useful information in SE domain, such as the SE activities the study focuses, database, techniques, algorithms and tools that were considered.

The major contribution of this study was to summarize and highlight the main aspects associated with the search for knowledge in textual databases in

[10] https://www.emc.com/leadership/digital-universe/2014iview/executive-summary.htm

SE. The results showed in this research could be of interest to several researchers involved with the topics covered in this study. So, we believe that our summarization can help to direct researchers in their future research providing a pointer to appropriately position new activities in this research topic.

Future directions include conducting research on how the knowledge extracted from the selected studies databases has been represented/codified, for example, knowledge graph, cognitive mapping, decision trees, knowledge taxonomies, and task analysis. Knowledge representation serves the pivotal role of allowing what is collectively known to be shared and used. In addition, we intend to conduct research on the use of extracted information in SE databases and how it is represented in practice within SE organizations.

References

1. Abidi, S.S.R., Hussini, S., Sriraj, W., T.S., Finley, G.A.: Knowledge sharing for pediatric pain management via a web 2.0 framework. Health Technology and Informatics **150**, 287–291 (2009)
2. Ahmad, A., Feng, C., Ge, S., Yousif, A.: A survey on mining stack overflow: question and answering (qa) community. Data Technol. Appl. **52**, 190–247 (2018)
3. Ahsan, I., Butt, W.H., Ahmed, M.A., Anwar, M.W.: A comprehensive investigation of natural language processing techniques and tools to generate automated test cases. In: Intern. Conference on Internet of things, Data and Cloud Comp. (2017)
4. Bagheri, E., Ensan, F., Dragan, G.: Decision support for the software product line domain engineering lifecycle. Automated Software Engineering (2012)
5. Baquero, J., Camargo, J., Restrepo-Calle, F., Aponte, J., González, F.: Predicting the programming language: Extracting knowledge from stack overflow posts. In: Colombian Conference on Computing. pp. 199–210 (2017)
6. Cambria, E., White, B.: Jumping nlp curves: A review of natural language processing research. IEEE Computational Intelligence Magazine **9**, 48–57 (2014)
7. Falbo, R.A., Arantes, D.O., Natali, A.C.C.: Integrating knowledge management and groupware in a software development environment. In: International Conference on Practical Aspects of Knowledge Management. pp. 94–105. Austria (2004)
8. Flisar, J., Podgorelec, V.: Enhanced feature selection using word embeddings for self-admitted technical debt identification. In: 44th Euromicro Conference on Software Engineering and Advanced Applications (SEAA). pp. 230–233 (2018)
9. Huang, Y., Chen, C., Xing, Z., Lin, T., Liu, Y.: Tell them apart: distilling technology differences from crowd-scale comparison discussions. In: 33rd ACM/IEEE International Conference on Automated Software Engineering. pp. 214–224
10. Jurafsky, D., Martin, J.H.: Speech and language processing: an introduction to natural language processing, computational linguistics, and speech recognition. Pearson Prentice Hall, Upper Saddle River, N.J. (2009)
11. Khatiwada, S., Kelly, M., Mahmoud, A.: Stac: A tool for static textual analysis of code. In: 24th International Conference on Program Comprehension (ICPC) (2016)
12. Kitchenham, B., Charters, S.: Guidelines for performing systematic literature reviews in software engineering. Tech. Rep. EBSE 2007-001, Keele University and Durham University, UK (2007)
13. Liu, M., Peng, X., Jiang, Q., Marcus, A., Yang, J., Zhao, W.: Searching stackoverflow questions with multi-faceted categorization. In: Asia-Pacific Symposium on Internetware (2018)

14. Maqbool, B., Azam, F., Anwar, M.W., Butt, W.H., Zeb, J., Zafar, I., Nazir, A.K., Umair, Z.: A comprehensive investigation of bpmn models generation from textual requirements - techniques, tools and trends. In: International Conference on Information Science and Applications (2018)
15. May, A., Wachs, J., Hannák, A.: Gender differences in participation and reward on stack overflow. Empirical Software Engineering (2019)
16. McBurney, P.W., Liu, C., McMillan, C.: Automated feature discovery via sentence selection and source code summarization. J. Softw. Evol. Process pp. 120–145 (2016)
17. Natali, A., Rocha, A., Travassos, G., Mian, P.: Integrating verification and validation techniques knowledge into software engineering environments. In: Jornadas Ibeoamericanas de Ingeniería del Software e Ingeniería del Conocimiento. pp. 419–430. Madri, Spain (2004)
18. Nawroth, C., Schmedding, M., Brocks, H., Kaufmann, M., Fuchs, M., Hemmje, M.: Towards cloud-based knowledge capturing based on natural language processing. In: Cloud Forward (2015)
19. Nembhard, F., Carvalho, M., Eskridge, T.: Extracting knowledge from open source projects to improve program security. SoutheastCon pp. 1–7 (2018)
20. Nonaka, I., Krogh, G.: Tacit knowledge and knowledge conversion: controversy and advancement in organizational knowledge creation theory. Organization Science **30**, 635–652 (2009)
21. Robertson, S.: Understanding inverse document frequency: On theoretical arguments for idf. Journal of Documentation - J DOC **60**, 503–520 (2004)
22. Rus, I., Lindvall, M.: Knowledge management in software engineering. IEEE Software **19**(3), 26–38 (2002)
23. Shah, F., Pfahl, D.: Evaluating and improving software quality using text analysis techniques - a mapping study. In: REFSQ Workshops (2016)
24. Souza, E.F., Falbo, R.A., Vijaykumar, N.L.: Knowledge management initiatives in software testing: A mapping study. Information and Software Technology **57**, 378–391 (2015)
25. Surapat, W., Prompoon, N.: Social clues powered, personalized software engineering messages classification. In: 10th International Symposium on Communications and Information Technologies. pp. 1114–1119 (2010)
26. Treude, C., Robillard, M.P., Dagenais, B.: Extracting development tasks to navigate software documentation. IEEE Transactions on Software Engineering **41**, 565–581 (2015)
27. Verma, R.P., Beg, M.R.: Representation of knowledge from software requirements expressed in natural language. In: International Conference on Emerging Trends in Engineering and Technology. pp. 154–158 (2013)
28. Vishal, J., Bansal, S.: Identifying trends in technologies and programming languages using topic modeling. In: 12th International Conference on Semantic Computing (ICSC). pp. 391–396 (2018)
29. Vliet, H.V.: Knowledge sharing in software development. In: 10th International Conference on Quality Software (2010)
30. Xu, B., Xing, Z., Xia, X., Lo, D.: Answerbot: automated generation of answer summary to developers' technical questions. In: 32Nd IEEE/ACM International Conference on Automated Software Engineering. pp. 706–716 (2017)
31. Zhang, Y., Hou, D.: Extracting problematic api features from forum discussions. In: 21st International Conference on Program Comprehension (ICPC). pp. 142–151 (2013)

Método Multicritério Aplicado à Priorização dos Desafios da Gerência de Projetos em Desenvolvimento Distribuído de Software

Maycon Amorim dos Santos[1], Douglas Rorie Tanno[1], Renato Balancieri[2], Gislaine Camila Lapasini Leal[3] and Edwin Vladimir Cardoza Galdamez[3]

[1] Department of Computer Science, State University of Maringá, Maringá, PR, Brazil
[2] Department of Computer Science, State University of Paraná, Apucarana, PR, Brazil
[3] Department of Production Engineering, State University of Maringá, Maringá, PR, Brazil
renato.balancieri@unespar.edu.br

Abstract. Distributed Software Development (DSD) purpose is to spread software development teams in different geographic locations, seeking to expand the labor options in the market and have no worries about the increase in the physical structure of the company headquarters. With the adoption of DSD as a method of work, several challenges can occur as the project progresses and preventive measures must be taken. Thus, this paper proposes a study on DSD and its challenges, obtaining the possible causes for the event of each challenge and using the Analytic Hierarchy Process (AHP) to obtain a classification of the challenges and their causes according to the degree of importance assessed by the specialists. As a result of this work, action plans were drawn up using a 5W1H tool, designed to help managers working with DDS to mitigate one of the challenges and execute the project with quality.

Keywords: Distributed Software Development; AHP Method; 5W1H.

1 Introdução

Com o avanço da globalização e uma maior dependência em se produzir produtos de qualidade e de maneira mais rápida, a área de desenvolvimento de software adotou um método de trabalho capaz de produzir o mesmo produto, porém com seus componentes divididos entre equipes espalhadas geograficamente, denominado Desenvolvimento Distribuído de Software (DDS) [15].

No DDS surgem desafios que podem causar problemas durante o fluxo de produção, acarretando atrasos na entrega do sistema e baixa qualidade do mesmo. Pode-se destacar como desafios: a comunicação, visto que as equipes não estão no mesmo local, acarretando problemas na tomada de decisão do projeto e análise dos requisitos do cliente; cultura pessoal de cada um conforme sua região e/ou país; distância, etc [12, 15, 21].

Assim, as diversas empresas que optam por trabalhar com DDS, estão encarando desafios tais como problema na comunicação entre as equipes de desenvolvimento, diferença organizacional e de infraestrutura, diferenças culturais, entre outras, presentes nessa forma de trabalho [1]. Visando auxiliar os gerentes de projeto de empresas de desenvolvimento de software, este trabalho busca levantar os problemas mais frequentes e estudá-los, a fim de beneficiar as empresas com planos de ação para combater as causas e padronizar os processos para prevenir o reaparecimento das dificuldades impostas pela DDS.

Com foco na gerência de projetos de software com desenvolvimento distribuído, este artigo tem como objetivo coletar e analisar os desafios pertinentes em DDS e levantar soluções de melhoria, validando e estratificando os desafios mais recorrentes na literatura para desenvolver soluções de melhoria para empresas.

Foi proposta a utilização da ferramenta Diagrama de Ishikawa e o método AHP (*Analytic Hierarchy Process*), analisando os problemas mais recorrentes abordados por diversos autores na área de DDS, realizando uma estratificação dos desafios em causas menores para a análise e posteriormente priorizando na busca de soluções de melhoria por meio da ferramenta 5W1H [7].

Este artigo encontra-se estruturado em cinco seções, além desta introdutória. A Seção 2 apresenta a fundamentação teórica sobre Desenvolvimento Distribuído de Software e AHP. Na Seção 3 são descritos os procedimentos metodológicos adotados na pesquisa. A Seção 4 detalha o estudo de caso conduzido. Por fim, na Seção 5, são descritas as considerações finais.

2 Referencial Teórico

2.1 Desenvolvimento Distribuído de Software

Leal et al. [10] definem o Desenvolvimento Distribuído de Software (DDS) como sendo um desenvolvimento de software que divide sua produção em diversas localizações geográficas, envolvendo pessoas que podem ser de diferentes nacionalidades e diferentes culturas organizacionais.

Silva et al. [21] consideram que o DDS possui três categorias principais: forma de separação dos grupos (agrupamento, distância física e separação temporal); regiões envolvidas (culturas regionais, idiomas e diferenças locais); organizações participantes (culturas organizacionais, infraestrutura e relação legal). Essas categorias são cruciais para definir o funcionamento do DDS, pois durante todo o ciclo de produção elas estão presentes e acarretam problemas para o processo.

Prikladnicki e Audy [16] caracterizam o DDS pela colaboração e cooperação entre organizações e pela construção de equipes de desenvolvedores que trabalham em conjunto, localizados em cidades ou países diferentes. A busca por soluções globais se tornou frequente por conta da necessidade de vantagem competitiva de uma empresa perante as outras, o custo de desenvolvimento pode variar conforme a localidade em que o software está sendo desenvolvido, como impostos, mão de obra e recursos materiais. A escolha pelo DDS pode resultar o aparecimento de diferenças comparado com o desenvolvimento local, sendo as principais características que os diferenciam: dispersão geográfica (distância física); dispersão temporal (diferenças de fuso-horário); e diferenças culturais (idioma, tradições, costumes, normas e comportamento).

A forma como é abordado o gerenciamento de projetos de software em ambiente distribuído difere-se do modo tradicional, onde todos os envolvidos na implementação do software se encontram no mesmo local de trabalho, tendo somente o cliente como um membro fora da empresa. Essas diferenças, resultados da distância entre equipes e/ou gerente, em diversos casos se tornam desafios que devem ser superados para que o projeto seja finalizado com sucesso.

Na literatura são abordados diversos estudos [5, 9, 10, 13, 14, 17, 21] em que são abordados os desafios mais frequentes durante a execução de projetos distribuídos de desenvolvimento de software. Dentre esses trabalhos, o desenvolvido por da Silva et al. [21], merece destaque, pois utilizaram um método de pesquisa com o propósito de filtrar os trabalhos potencialmente relevantes para a pesquisa, trabalhos que passaram por uma avaliação de qualidade e pontuados como importantes para a pesquisa, sendo encontrados 1189 trabalhos e utilizados 155. Os projetos abordavam os desafios no DDS como as melhores práticas utilizadas por empresas de todo o mundo. Foram estabelecidos os seguintes desafios durante a pesquisa: D1 – Comunicação; D2 - Diferença Cultural; D3 - Coordenação; D4 - Diferença Temporal; D5 - Garantir a Cooperação/Colaboração; D6 - Confiança; D7 - Diferença Organizacional/Padrões, Processos, Metodologias e Políticas diferentes; D8 - Infraestrutura; D9 - Diferentes níveis de conhecimento/Transferência de conhecimento; D10 - Idioma/Barreira Linguísticas; D11 - Visibilidade/*Awareness* (clareza sobre quem faz o quê e onde); D12 - Distância física; D13 - Monitoramento e Controle; D14 - Gestão de Pessoas/Gestão de Conflitos; D15 - Atribuição de tarefas; D16 - Identificar papéis e responsabilidades; D17 - Manter espírito de equipe; D18 - Sincronização do trabalho entre os sites; D19 - Gestão do Escopo/Gestão de Mudança; D20 - Diferentes tecnologias; D21 - Propriedade Intelectual/Garantir Confidencialidade e Privacidade; D22 - Diferentes *Stakeholders*; D23 - Cumprimento de prazos/Gerenciar cronograma; D24 - Gestão de Riscos; D25 - Diferentes tipos de governos, leis, regras e regulamentos; D26 - Necessidade de um espaço físico; D27 - Gestão do conhecimento; D28 - Planejamento; D29 - Qualidade/Métricas; D30 - Aplicação de um processo iterativo ágil.

2.2 Analytic Hierarchy Process (AHP)

AHP é um método de apoio a tomada decisão, criado por Thomas Saaty [19], que pode incluir medidas de avaliação objetivas e/ou subjetivas. O método oferece um procedimento hierárquico para controlar a consistência das medidas de avaliação e alternativas preferidas pelo tomador de decisão, reduzindo o viés no processo decisório [19, 20]. O AHP tem como premissa a estruturação de um sistema de decisão hierarquicamente complexo em diversos níveis, definidos por afinidade. A organização do problema permite uma visão sistêmica, identificando os vários elementos, quando o problema envolve a seleção de alternativas permeadas por múltiplos critérios [4, 8].

O AHP é um dos métodos multicritérios mais utilizados, por tomadores de decisão e pesquisadores, devido à sua simplicidade [18, 22]. Emrouznejad e Marra [6] destacam que o AHP tem sido utilizado em problemas de larga escala, principalmente nas situações em que a avaliação das alternativas é subjetiva.

O AHP é desenvolvido nas seguintes etapas: i) definição do problema; ii) construção da árvore hierárquica; iii) construção das matrizes de julgamento par a par; iv) cálculo da consistência de todos os julgamentos das matrizes, para determinar a contribuição de cada critério para o objetivo global [20].

O método AHP possui como base três princípios: a estrutura hierárquica do modelo, os julgamentos comparativos das alternativas e dos critérios e a síntese das prioridades. A estrutura hierárquica ou Árvore Hierárquica, engloba todos os critérios, subcritérios e alternativas levantadas anteriormente por meio de estudos e observações. Na Árvore Hierárquica, é possível estruturar por meio de níveis qual será o foco principal da aplicação do método, quais critérios foram levantados para análise, quais subcritérios serão utilizados e quais são as alternativas disponíveis para atender o foco principal. A comparação dos critérios é realizada por meio das informações coletadas por meio de um questionário, onde é possível que o especialista faça uma avaliação minuciosa dos critérios de acordo com sua experiência e grau de importância [19].

3 Método de Pesquisa

A pesquisa foi conduzida em três etapas: Análise das Causas, Priorização das Causas e Elaboração do Plano de Ação. A etapa de Análise das Causas consistiu na realização de uma entrevista semiestruturada com o gerente de projetos mais experiente de uma empresa que atua no DDS. Nessa entrevista foram apresentados os 30 desafios elencados na seção 2.1 e solicitou-se a identificação dos 5 desafios, que na visão do gerente seriam os mais relevantes. A partir dessas informações foi utilizado o Diagrama de Ishikawa para identificar as possíveis causas dos desafios.

A etapa de Priorização das Causas envolveu a aplicação do método AHP para estabelecer um *ranking* dos desafios. Inicialmente foi elaborada a árvore hierárquica estabelecendo os desafios como critérios e as causas identificadas na etapa anterior como alternativas. Na sequência foi realizado o julgamento comparativo das alternativas por meio da aplicação de um questionário, para comparação par a par dos critérios, com seis gerentes de projetos da mesma empresa com atuação no DDS, buscando-se definir um *ranking* dos desafios. Essa etapa foi realizada envolvendo mais especialistas para minimizar o impacto da percepção individual sobre o ranqueamento dos desafios, gerando assim uma avaliação mais justa e isenta. A etapa de Elaboração do Plano de Ação consistiu na aplicação da ferramenta 5W1H para sistematizar as ações que correspondem as causas que representam 80% das dificuldades presentes no DDS.

4 Estudo de Caso

O estudo de caso foi realizado em uma empresa de desenvolvimento de software que atua com DDS. A partir dos 30 desafios apresentados na Seção 2, procedeu-se uma validação inicial por meio de uma entrevista semiestruturada, com o gerente de projetos da empresa com maior experiência na gerência de projetos distribuídos, com o intuito de identificar os desafios que mais impactam na gestão dos projetos de DDS da empresa. Os desafios identificados nessa validação foram: D1 - Comunicação; D5 - Garantir a Cooperação/Colaboração; D7 - Diferença Organizacional; D8 - Infraestrutura; e D14 - Gestão de Pessoas/Gestão de Conflitos.

4.1 Análise das Causas

As causas de cada desafio foram estabelecidas pelo gerente de projetos conforme o dia a dia de trabalho presente na vida dos profissionais dessa área.

A Comunicação é essencial em qualquer tipo de serviço prestado, visto que as empresas atuam em sistema aberto (interação com todo o ambiente), portanto todos os *stakeholders* necessitam saber sobre o andamento das atividades. Dando ênfase no desenvolvimento de software, precisam saber como está o andamento do processo, a construção dos componentes e como estão sendo desenvolvidos. A comunicação pode ser feita por meio de telefone, mensagens instantâneas, software colaborativo de comunicação, e-mail e vídeo conferência [22]. Apesar da comunicação presencial ser mais efetiva em muitos casos, o trabalho define que conversar, ouvir e discutir assuntos do projeto pode tornar o desenvolvimento melhor para todos.

A partir das informações fornecidas pelo gerente de projetos, foi elaborado o Diagrama de Ishikawa para o desafio Comunicação. As causas identificadas para esse desafio a partir do Diagrama são as seguintes: i) *Inabilidade Social:* consiste em uma equipe com baixa habilidade em se comunicar com os demais membros da equipe (gerente e demais colaboradores), associada a distância geográfica e os problemas de estabelecer uma comunicação precisa; ii) *Contexto:* causa presente durante as diferentes etapas do processo de desenvolvimento, incluindo a falta de entendimento do assunto pelos participantes, podendo gerar erros de interpretação durante a comunicação por conta da distância e dos meios em que os diálogos ocorrem; iii) *Problema de Infraestrutura:* causa relacionada à infraestrutura, onde a comunicação dificultada por problemas na ferramenta e/ou queda de rede em um dos locais.

A cooperação e colaboração entre as equipes é o ato de todos estarem unidos e organizados em busca de um objetivo comum, uma equipe unida possui maiores chances de alcançar melhores resultados no final do projeto. Casey e Richardson [3] realizaram um trabalho que estuda o planejamento de projetos com equipes geograficamente distribuídas, onde foi possível definir que coordenação, visibilidade, comunicação e cooperação entre membros e equipes são impactadas negativamente por conta da distância. Procedimentos para monitoramento de equipe precisam ser implantados para determinar o nível de cooperação entre os membros, e caso necessário, tratar problemas quando surgirem no processo.

Após a aplicação do Diagrama de Ishikawa foram levantadas as causas para o desafio Garantir a Cooperação/Colaboração. As causas para esse desafio são: i) *Perfil dos Colaboradores:* causa que envolve as pessoas, levando se em conta o perfil de cada colaborador e que está diretamente associado à diferença cultural, sendo o método individual de trabalho, costumes da região, religião, entre outros, fatores que podem dificultar o relacionamento de pessoas geograficamente separadas, porém envolvidas em um mesmo projeto; ii) *Organização do Trabalho:* causa relacionada aos processos de desenvolvimento, referindo-se à estrutura da equipe de trabalho em relação à hierarquia, divisão de tarefas, métodos de trabalho e suas respectivas relações, podendo ser diferentes quando analisadas em cada local de desenvolvimento; iii) *Clima Organizacional:* refere-se ao contexto organizacional das equipes, abrangendo o clima estabelecido no ambiente em que cada uma está situada, podendo ser diferente em cada local, gerando assim sentimentos distintos em relação ao trabalho. Cada empresa possui sua filosofia de trabalho e padrões de processo definidos, o que caracteriza a Diferença Organizacional. Empresas de software podem possuir certificações de maturidade de processo por nível e diferentes metodologias de gerenciamento de projetos, como processos ágeis, dessa forma, a diferença organizacional pode ser vista em diversos casos quando organizações são comparadas.

De acordo com a aplicação do Diagrama de Ishikawa, as causas identificadas para o desafio Diferença Organizacional são: i*) Comprometimento:* causa relacionada às pessoas envolvidas, onde o comprometimento de cada membro de cada equipe na execução das atividades ou senso de urgência não é o mesmo, gerando dificuldades no projeto; ii) *Diferença Cultural:* também relacionada às pessoas, as diferentes localizações em que cada equipe se encontra podem gerar grandes diferenças culturais entre os membros, tais como problemas no projeto por conta da jornada de trabalho, métodos aplicados, etc.; iii) *Processos Diferentes:* causa relacionada aos processos, pois cada local pode possuir processos e/ou métodos de trabalhos diferentes, acarretando divergências no decorrer do projeto; iv) *Ferramentas Diferentes*: causa relacionada ao hardware e/ou software utilizado no desenvolvimento, pois diferentes ferramentas de trabalho podem estar sendo utilizadas em cada local de trabalho, gerando incompatibilidade nos componentes; v) *Medidas de Desempenho Diferentes:* causa relacionada com o desempenho de cada equipe de desenvolvimento, pois os indicadores de produtividade podem ser diferentes em cada local, gerando estratégias de trabalho distintas.

Todas as empresas independentemente do segmento dependem de uma infraestrutura organizada e bem definida para um funcionamento contínuo. Quando se depara com o DDS, tem-se que lidar com diferentes infraestruturas dentro de um mesmo projeto, fato que pode acarretar em diversos problemas durante todo o processo.

Para o desafio Infraestrutura, por meio do Diagrama de Ishikawa, destaca-se as seguintes causas: i) *Falta de Planejamento:* causa relacionada às pessoas envolvidas, onde não ter um bom planejamento sobre a estrutura e nem planos de ação pode acarretar problemas que possam afetar todo o projeto, gerando ações reativas para resolução dos problemas, sendo assim um local propício para gerar problemas no desenvolvimento do projeto; ii) *Falta e/ou Incompatibilidade dos Indicadores:* causa relacionada ao desempenho, como a ausência de indicadores para medir a eficiência da rede interna, queda de servidores, máquinas, etc.; iii) *Disponibilidade e/ou Desempenho do Hardware:* causa relacionada às tecnologias de informação utilizadas como hardware, referindo-se aos servidores, máquinas, internet, etc. Todos os elementos necessários para um bom desenvolvimento do projeto.

A função principal de qualquer gerente em qualquer área é gerir pessoas e conflitos. Realizar atribuição de tarefas, oferecer suporte e tirar o máximo de cada membro da equipe são tarefas base para um bom gerenciamento. A liderança dentro do DDS pode ser centralizada ou não, portanto isso se torna um desafio quando há uma distância entre os membros da equipe, quando centralizada o gerente principal não tem contato com todos quando necessário e quando descentralizada o poder de decisão pode acabar sendo limitado em algumas situações.

Para o desafio Gestão de Pessoas/Gestão de Conflitos, por meio do Diagrama de Ishikawa, pode-se elencar as possíveis causas, que são relacionadas à todas as pessoas envolvidas: *i) Falta de Empatia entre Equipe e Cliente:* dificuldade em gerir conflitos existentes por parte da equipe com o cliente, pelo fato de alguns colaboradores não conhecerem o mesmo e não entender o significado de algumas demandas exigidas; *ii) Falta de Empatia entre Cliente e Equipe:* dificuldade em gerir conflitos existentes por parte do cliente com a equipe, pelo motivo do cliente investir uma alta quantia no projeto e não conhecer todos os envolvidos no desenvolvimento, principalmente quando são encontrados erros por parte do mesmo; iii) *Falta de Empatia entre as Equipes:* dificuldade em gerir os conflitos existentes entre as equipes de trabalho situadas em locais diferentes pelo fato de não se conhecerem e depender dos trabalhos desenvolvidos por cada uma delas.

4.2 Priorização das Causas

Com base nos levantamentos obtidos, foi possível definir a árvore hierárquica utilizada pelo método AHP, onde destaca-se no primeiro nível o objetivo principal (Levantar planos de ação), no segundo nível os desafios (i. Comunicação, ii. Garantir a Cooperação/Colaboração, iii. Diferença Organizacional, iv. Infraestrutura e v. Gestão de Pessoas/Gestão de Conflitos) e no terceiro nível as causas que são listadas a seguir:

- Causas do desafio Comunicação: Inabilidade Social; Contexto; e Problema de Infraestrutura.
- Causas do desafio Garantir a Cooperação/Colaboração: Perfil dos Colaboradores; Organização do Trabalho; e Clima Organizacional.
- Causas do desafio Diferença Organizacional: Comprometimento; Diferença Cultural; Processos Diferentes; Ferramentas Diferentes; Medidas de Desempenho Diferentes.
- Causas do desafio Infraestrutura: Falta de Planejamento; Falta e/ou Incompatibilidade dos Indicadores; e Disponibilidade e/ou Desempenho do Hardware.
- Causas do desafio Gestão de Pessoas/Gestão de Conflitos: Falta de Empatia entre Equipe e Cliente; Falta de Empatia entre Cliente e Equipe; Falta de Empatia entre Equipes.

Após o levantamento dos desafios do DDS e suas possíveis causas, iniciou-se a etapa de priorização. A priorização foi realizada a partir da aplicação de um questionário contendo a avaliação pareada entre os critérios (desafios) e as causas. O questionário era representado por uma matriz de 5x5, em que as linhas e colunas representavam cada um dos 5 desafios e era apresentada a escala de Saaty de nove pontos para a realização da avaliação pareada [19]. Os pontos da escala eram: 1 - igual importância; 3 – importância pequena de uma sobre a outra; 5 – importância grande ou essencial; 7 – importância muito grande; 9 – importância absoluta; 2,4,6,8 – valores intermediários [19].

A partir das avaliações par a par dos desafios, em que cada especialista atribuiu uma nota (segundo a escala de Saaty), calculou-se a média das notas e com isto, obteve-se a matriz (Tabela 1). Os valores acima da diagonal principal representam as médias (n) do grau de importância de cada desafio e abaixo da diagonal principal tem-se o inverso das médias (1/n). Os valores apresentados na Tabela 1 indicam a média dos julgamentos realizados pelos especialistas, na comparação pareada dos desafios. A diagonal principal da matriz é 1, pois representa um desafio comparado com ele mesmo, o que tem o mesmo grau de importância relativa.

Tabela 1. Matriz de julgamento dos desafios.

	Matriz de Julgamento de Critérios				
	D1	D2	D3	D4	D5
D1	1	2	6	5,5	0,6
D2	0,5	1	4,5	4,5	0,5857143
D3	0,1666667	0,2222222	1	2,2777778	0,1714286
D4	0,1818182	0,2222222	0,4390244	1	0,1714286
D5	1,6666667	1,7073171	5,8333333	5,8333333	1

D1 – Comunicação; D2 – Garantir Cooperação/Colaboração dos Colaboradores; D3 – Diferença Organizacional; D4 – Infraestrutura; D5- Gestão de Pessoas/Gestão de Conflitos.

A Tabela 2 apresenta os valores de λ_{max} que demonstra o autovalor máximo que contribui para o cálculo como sendo a medida para a consistência da aplicação do método AHP, IC (Índice de Consistência) que a1uxilia na avaliação do grau de consistência da matriz, buscando-se preferencialmente um número menor que 0,1, IR (Índice Randômico) que é uma constante utilizada nos cálculos e varia de acordo com o tamanho da amostra e RC (Razão de Consistência) que utiliza o IC e IR para avaliar a consistência do julgamento de acordo com as avaliações dos especialistas e o número de amostras, cujo os resultados também busca um valor menor que 0,1.

Tabela 2. Avaliação de consistência dos desafios e causas

	λmax	IC	IR	RC
Geral	5,1984743	0,0496186	1,12	0,0443023
Comunicação	3,1083784	0,0541892	0,58	0,0934297
Garantir Cooperação/Colaboração	3,0012647	0,0006324	0,58	0,0010903
Diferença Organizacional	5,419017	0,1047543	1,12	0,0935306
Infraestrutura	3,0913072	0,0456536	0,58	0,0787131
Gestão de Conflitos	3,0656951	0,0328476	0,58	0,0566337

Analisando a Tabela 2, tem-se que todos os RC's atentem a condição de RC $\leq$ 0,1 indicada pelo método AHP, porém os desafios Comunicação e Diferença Organizacional possuem valores próximos ao limite, visto que cada gerente avaliou os desafios conforme experiências na função, gerando uma maior inconsistência nos dados, porém sem afetar os resultados esperados neste trabalho.

A partir da aplicação dos questionários e avaliação das respostas por meio do método AHP foi possível determinar a classificação dos desafios estudados (Tabela 3).

Destacam-se Gestão de Pessoas/Conflitos (36,6%), Comunicação (30,7%) e Garantir Cooperação/Colaboração (21,1%) como os mais importantes para se resolver de imediato. É possível afirmar que ambos os desafios dependem de uma boa comunicação entre todos os envolvidos do projeto, portanto o fator distância impacta negativamente nesse aspecto, sendo necessário elaborar planos de ação para mitigar os efeitos e prover a continuidade do projeto em busca de um produto de qualidade.

Tabela 3. Classificação geral dos desafios.

Rank	Desafio	PN	Acumulado
1	Gestão de Pessoas/Conflitos	0,3668961	0,3668961
2	Comunicação	0,3070762	0,6739723
3	Garantir Cooperação/Colaboração	0,2113311	0,8853034
4	Infraestrutura	0,0667598	0,9520632
5	Diferença Organizacional	0,0479368	1

Tabela 4. Classificação geral das causas.

Rank	Causas	Peso Final	Peso Acumulado	
1	Falta de Empatia entre Equipe e Cliente	0,205574508	0,205574508	
2	Inabilidade Social	0,176973969	0,382548477	
3	Perfil dos Colaboradores	0,118341079	0,500889556	50%
4	Falta de Empatia entre Cliente e Equipe	0,113485469	0,614375026	
5	Contexto	0,102432675	0,716807701	
6	Organização do Trabalho	0,049847634	0,766655335	
7	Falta de Empatia entre as Equipes	0,047836084	0,814491419	81%
8	Clima Organizacional	0,043142382	0,857633801	
9	Falta de Planejamento	0,040887634	0,898521435	
10	Problema de Infraestrutura	0,027669605	0,92619104	
11	Comprometimento	0,022083178	0,948274218	
12	Disponibilidade e/ou Desempenho do Hardware	0,014980787	0,963255005	
13	Falta e/ou Incompatibilidade de Indicadores	0,010891338	0,974146343	
14	Processos Diferentes	0,010214273	0,984360616	
15	Diferença Cultural	0,007104607	0,991465223	
16	Medidas de Desempenho Diferentes	0,005421066	0,996886289	
17	Ferramentas Diferentes	0,003113711	1	

Em relação às causas correspondentes a cada desafio estudado, após a avaliação foi possível determinar (conforme Tabela 4) que a Falta de Empatia entre Equipe e Cliente (20,55%) referente ao desafio Gestão de Pessoas/Gestão de Conflitos, Inabilidade Social (17,69%) referente ao desafio Comunicação e Perfil dos Colaboradores (11,83%) referente ao desafio Garantir Cooperação/Colaboração dos Colaboradores representam mais de 50% de importância para os gerentes de problemas que precisam ser mitigados durante a execução de um projeto em DDS.

Para a elaboração dos planos de ação, serão trabalhadas as causas que representam 80% de importância para os seis gerentes consultados neste estudo, pelo fato deste trabalho buscar mitigar um alto volume de problemas frequentes no DDS. As demais causas (20%) poderão sem trabalhadas em futuros projetos, quando os atuais planos de ação já estiverem em execução e dando os resultados esperados.

4.3 Elaboração do Plano de Ação

A técnica utilizada para a elaboração dos planos de ação foi o 5W1H (*What:* o que; *Why:* por que; *How:* como; *Who:* quem; *Where:* onde e *When:* quando), que, segundo Baggio e Lampert [2], é uma ferramenta simples e eficaz quando for necessário detalhar como será a execução de um projeto de melhoria proposto para uma organização. O 5W1H funciona da seguinte forma: **O que**: ação proposta no plano de melhoria da empresa ou atividade a ser executada; **Por que**: justificativa ou benefícios que a organização terá pela execução da atividade; **Como:** maneiras/ações e/ou etapas que serão utilizadas para a operacionalização da atividade; **Quem:** responsável ou responsáveis pela organização e execução das ações do "como"; **Onde:** local ou locais onde serão executadas as ações previstas no "como"; **Quando:** data ou período em que serão realizadas as ações previstas no "como".

Dessa forma, foi aplicada a ferramenta 5W1H, com auxílio dos seis gerentes, para elaboração do plano de ação correspondente as causas que representam 80% das dificuldades encontradas no DDS. A causa "Perfil dos Colaboradores" será trabalhada em conjunto com as causas "Falta de Empatia entre as Equipes" e "Inabilidade Social". A seguir é apresentada a descrição do plano de ação utilizando a ferramenta 5W1H e na sequência um resumo ilustrado na Figura 1.

- **Falta de Empatia entre Equipe e Cliente:** Para que seja estabelecido um melhor relacionamento entre as equipes e o cliente, será agendada uma visita onde diversos colaboradores, preferencialmente com a participação de pelo menos um de cada local, irão visitar o local de trabalho do cliente e consequentemente coletar informações sobre como será o uso do sistema, buscando entender de forma mais precisa a realidade do cliente e o motivo da solicitação de algumas demandas durante o desenvolvimento do projeto. Este plano de ação irá estabelecer uma união mais consistente entre os envolvidos do projeto. Para medir o impacto do plano de ação, é indicada a utilização do indicador de NPS (*Net Promoter Score)* que mede "quanto" o cliente indicaria a empresa para outras pessoas interessadas em serviços semelhantes.
- **Inabilidade Social:** Em busca de uma melhor interação entre os membros das equipes que possuem inabilidade social e apresentam dificuldades em se relacionar com os demais colaboradores, serão realizadas dinâmicas em grupos para promover uma maior aproximação entre as equipes, sendo agendadas conforme a disponibilidade para encontro dos colaboradores em um mesmo local, além de treinamentos para o gerente sobre técnicas de feedback que serão úteis para o desenvolvimento das equipes. As atividades serão acompanhadas por membros capacitados, podendo ser do departamento de recursos humanos da empresa. Para medir o impacto do plano de

ação, é indicada a utilização do indicador de Índice de Satisfação Interna que mede a satisfação das pessoas em seu ambiente de trabalho.

- **Falta de Empatia entre Cliente e Equipe:** Para que seja estabelecido um melhor relacionamento entre o cliente e as equipes, será agendada uma visita onde o cliente irá visitar o local de trabalho com o maior número de colaboradores para entender a dinâmica de trabalho da equipe, obter informações de como um sistema é desenvolvido, a fim de tomar conhecimento de como os prazos para cada demanda são estabelecidos, possibilitando uma melhor compreensão durante o andamento do projeto. Será importante que seja feito um repasse para os demais locais de desenvolvimento. Para medir o impacto do plano de ação, é indicada a utilização do indicador de NPS (Net Promoter Score) que mede "quanto" o cliente indicaria a empresa para outras pessoas interessadas em serviços semelhantes.
- **Contexto:** Para que seja estabelecida uma comunicação consistente e de qualidade, será definida uma padronização dos documentos que serão utilizados para o projeto e onde será o repositório para que todos tomem conhecimento e saibam buscar quando necessário. Conforme seja necessário transmitir alguma informação pertinente para o projeto, deverão ser definidos níveis de criticidade, onde o entendimento deverá ficar o mais próximo da realidade possível, sem que ocorram problemas nos locais de trabalho. Uma ferramenta de qualidade para comunicação virtual precisa ser definida e utilizada por todas as equipes. Para medir o impacto do plano de ação, é indicada a utilização do indicador de Densidade de Erros que mede a proporção de horas gastas para corrigir erros pelas horas gastas no desenvolvimento dos componentes.
- **Organização do Trabalho:** Para resolver o problema de organização do trabalho, cada projeto terá um layout de distribuição das atividades, independente das regras de cada local de trabalho, a arquitetura será única para o projeto. As atividades serão distribuídas conforme os locais de trabalho, caso seja possível, cada componente será desenvolvido em locais diferentes, facilitando assim a comunicação e organização dos colaboradores durante as tarefas. Também será estabelecido um líder técnico em cada local de desenvolvimento, sendo ele responsável por administrar o lugar e reportar ao gerente todo o andamento do projeto. Para medir o impacto do plano de ação, é indicada a utilização do indicador de Aderência de Processo que mede se o projeto está aderente conforme os processos de produção estabelecidos pela empresa.
- **Falta de Empatia entre Equipes:** Visando um melhor relacionamento entre os membros das equipes, o gerente ficará responsável por definir momentos de integração fora do trabalho, onde todos possam se conhecer e criar um sentimento de companheirismo. É necessário que essas reuniões sejam realizadas com o maior número de colaboradores possíveis dos diversos locais de desenvolvimento. Para medir o impacto do plano de ação, é indicada a utilização do indicador de Índice de Satisfação Interna que mede a satisfação das pessoas em seu ambiente de trabalho.

O que melhorar?	Por que melhorar?	Quem irá executar?	Quando será executado?	Onde será executado?	Como será executado?
Falta de empatia entre equipe e cliente	Buscar melhor relacionamento entre os envolvidos	Gerente, equipe e cliente	Imediatamente	No local onde o sistema desenvolvido será utilizado	Agendar visita da equipe ou parte dela no local onde o sistema será utilizado para que os colaboradores percebam como será o uso e quais dificuldades podem aparecer
Inabilidade social	Falta de contato entre os coladoradores pode gerar falta de informações durante o desenvolvimento do projeto	Gerente e equipe	Imediatamente	Em todos os locais de trabalho	Serão realizadas dinâmicas em grupos para promover uma maior aproximação entre as equipes e o gerente. O gerente irá aprender técnicas de *feedback* para auxiliar no desenvolvimento da equipe
Falta de empatia entre cliente e equipe	Buscar melhor relacionamento entre os envolvidos	Gerente, equipe e cliente	Imediatamente	Na sede da empresa	Agendar visita do cliente no local com o maior número de colaboradores para que o mesmo entenda a dinâmica de desenvolvimento de acordo com as demandas solicitadas
Contexto	Erros de interpretação de informações podem acarretar problemas no desenvolvimento do projeto	Gerente e equipe	Imediatamente	Em todos os locais de trabalho	Definir documentos padrões para armazenamento de informações, especificar os locais em que os documentos se encontram, definir a criticidade do assunto e padronizar a ferramenta de comunicação
Organização do trabalho	Uma equipe mal organizada e estruturada pode gerar problemas durante o desenvolvimento do projeto, produzindo um produto final sem qualidade	Gerente e equipe	Início do próximo projeto	Em todos os locais de trabalho	Definir layout de distribuição, granularidade dos cargos e líder técnico para cada local de trabalho
Falta de empatia entre as equipes	Melhorar a união da equipe para gerar um clima tranquilo durante a execução do projeto e para todos seguirem o mesmo objetivo	Gerente e equipe	Imediatamente	Em todos os locais de trabalho	Será estabelecido pelo gerente um tempo de confraternização onde as equipes possam se conhecer melhor e gerar uma aproximação

Fig. 1. Plano de ação (5W1H).

5 Considerações Finais

Com o crescimento das empresas de desenvolvimento de software no Brasil e no mundo, a possibilidade da utilização do DDS tem se tornado cada vez mais comum, fazendo com que as organizações enfrentem os mesmos desafios presentes neste tipo de abordagem de projeto. Medidas para mitigar esses desafios precisam ser levantadas, para que problemas como comunicação, diferença cultural, cooperação entre as equipes, diferença organizacional, entre outros, não afetem o resultado final do sistema e consequentemente não gerem insatisfação para o cliente.

Dessa forma, este trabalho possibilitou o estudo de alguns desafios regularmente presentes na literatura e no cotidiano de empresas do segmento de software, para que de acordo com uma avaliação precisa de gerentes de projeto que atuam com equipes distribuídas, fosse possível levantar quais as prováveis causas que proporcionam o aparecimento de desafios tais como estabelecer uma comunicação consistente entre os locais de desenvolvimento; garantir uma cooperação/colaboração entre os colaboradores do projeto; não permitir que a diferença organizacional entre os locais de trabalho afetem o resultado final do sistema; que a infraestrutura seja de qualidade e igual em todos os lugares; e que o gerente possa gerir as pessoas e os conflitos existentes de maneira simples e eficaz.

Com os desafios e suas causas levantadas, foi possível obter uma classificação geral de acordo com o grau de importância relevante para os gerentes, podendo assim alcançar quais as causas deveriam ser priorizadas com o objetivo de mitigar em torno de 80% dos problemas mais impactantes no DDS e consequentemente levantar planos de ação de cada causa dentro da margem estabelecida e indicadores para o monitoramento das melhorias, visando auxiliar os gerentes durante a execução de um projeto.

Analisando a classificação obtida por meio da aplicação do método AHP, pode-se afirmar que gerenciar uma equipe atuando com DDS tem como principais desafios, problemas relacionados à falha de comunicação e falta de companheirismo, sendo falta de empatia entre todos os envolvidos, inabilidade social, perfil dos colaboradores, contexto das informações transmitidas, organização do trabalho, entre outros, consequências das dificuldades em se comunicar de forma efetiva, gerando um clima ruim, propício ao surgimento de problemas. O plano de ação é uma ferramenta que auxilia os gerentes de projeto a promoverem uma melhor integração entre as equipes e o cliente, diminuindo as chances de ocorrerem problemas no entendimento da demanda, sobrecarga de atividades e falta de companheirismo entre os envolvidos, durante o desenvolvimento de software. Como trabalhos futuros pode-se destacar o acompanhamento da execução do plano de ação e sua efetividade.

Referências

1. Audy, J. L. N., Prikladnicki, R.: Desenvolvimento Distribuído de Software: Desenvolvimento de Software com Equipes Distribuídas, Rio de Janeiro: Campus. 2. ed.: Elsevier (2007).
2. Baggio, A. F., Lampert, A. L.: Planejamento Organizacional. Coleção Educação a Distância. Editora Unijui. Rio Grande do Sul (2010).
3. Casey, V., Richardson, I.: Project Management within Virtual Software Teams. IEEE International Conference on Global Software Engineering (2006).
4. Cruz Junior, A. T., Carvalho, M. M.: Obtenção da Voz do Consumidor: Estudo de Caso em um Hotel Ecológico. Revista Produção, v. 13, p. 88-100 (2003).
5. Damian, D.: Global software development: growing opportunities, ongoing challenges. Software Process: Improvement and Practice, v. 8, n. 4, p. 179-182 (2004).

6. Emrouznejad, A., Marra, M.: The state of the art development of AHP (1979–2017): a literature review with a social network analysis. International Journal of Production Research, v. 55, (2017).
7. Ghinato, P.: Quality control methods: Towards modern approaches through well-established principles, Total Quality Management, v. 9, n. 6, p. 463-477 (1998).
8. Iañez, M. M., Cunha, C. B.: Uma metodologia para a seleção de um provedor de serviços logísticos, São Paulo, v. 16, n. 3, p. 394-412 (2006).
9. Jiménez, M., Piattini, M., Vizcaíno, A.: Challenges and Improvements in Distributed Software Development: A Systematic Review. Advances in Software Engineering (2009).
10. Leal, G. C. L., Chaves, A. P., Huzita, E. H. M., Delamaro, M. E.: An Integrated Approach of Software Development and Test Processes to Distributed Teams. Journal of Universal Computer Science, v. 8, n. 1, 2686 (2012).
11. Leal, G. C. L., Huzita, E. H. M., Calvi Tait, T. F.: Globalization and Socio-Technical Aspects of Information Systems Development. In Christos Kalloniatis. (Org.). Innovative Information Systems Modelling Techniques, 1. ed.: Intech, 1, p. 99-121 (2012).
12. Massago, Y., Leal, G. C. L., Balancieri, R., Galdamez, E. V. C.: Towards Classifying Sociocultural Aspects in Global Software Development. Revista de Gestão da Tecnologia e Sistemas de Informação (Online), v. 15, p. 1-19, (2018).
13. Mockus, A., Herbsleb, J.: Challenges of global software development, Proceedings Seventh International Software Metrics Symposium, p. 182-184 (2001).
14. Niazi, M., Mahmood, S., Alshayeb, M., Hroub, A.: Empirical investigation of the challenges of the existing tools used in global software development projects. IET Software, v. 9, n.5, p. 135-143 (2015).
15. Prikladnicki, R., Lopes, L., Audy, J. L. N., Evaristo, R.: Desenvolvimento distribuído de software: um modelo de classificação dos níveis de dispersão dos stakeholders. In: I Brazilian Symposium on Information Systems (SBSI 04), p. 253-262 (2004).
16. Prikladnicki, R., Audy, J. L. N.: Uma Análise Comparativa de práticas de Desenvolvimento Distribuído de Software no Brasil e no exterior. XX Simpósio Brasileiro de Engenharia de Software, Florianópolis (2006).
17. Prikladnicki, R., Audy, J. L. N, Damian, D., Oliveira, T. C.: Distributed Software Development: Practices and challenges in different business strategies of offshoring and onshoring. International Conference on Global Software Engineering, Munich, p. 262-274 (2007).
18. Russo, R. F. S. M., Camanho, R.: Criteria in AHP: A Systematic Review of Literature, Procedia Computer Science, v. 55, p. 1123-1132 (2015).
19. Saaty, T. L.: The Analytic Hierarchy Process, New York: McGraw Hill. International, Translated to Russian, Portuguese, and Chinese, Revised editions, Pittsburgh: RWS Publications (1980).
20. Saaty, T. L.: Decision Making With The analytic hierarchy process. International Journal of Services Sciences, v. 1, n. 1, p. 83-98 (2008).
21. Silva, F. Q. B., Costa, C., Franca, A. C. C., Prikladinicki, R.: Challenges and solutions in distributed software development project management: A systematic literature review, 2010 5th IEEE International Conference on Global Software Engineering, Princeton, NJ, p. 87-96 (2010).
22. Thissen, M. R., Page, J. M., Bharathi, M. C., Austin, T. L.: Communication tools for distributed software development teams (2007).
23. Vaidya, O. S., Kumar, S.: Analytic hierarchy process: An overview of applications. European Journal Of Operational Research, Issue 169, p. 1-29 (2006).

Revisiting the Bad Smell and Refactoring Relationship: A Systematic Literature Review

Cleiton Silva[1], Amanda Santana[1], Eduardo Figueiredo[1], Mariza A. S. Bigonha[1]

Department of Computer Science, Federal University of Minas Gerais, Belo Horizonte, Brazil
{cleiton.silva, amandads, figueiredo, mariza}@dcc.ufmg.br

Abstract. Bad smells are indicators of code structure problems that may be solved via refactoring. Refactoring is a process of improving the internal structure of the source code without changing the external behavior of the software system. However, the refactoring process takes effort and, so, it should be done in a disciplined manner in order to minimize the chances of introducing code errors. The goal of this paper is to present a systematic literature review with the purpose of identifying the explicit relationship between refactorings and the bad smells proposed by Fowler. This relationship is defined as the environment in which a bad smell is mentioned and a possible refactoring strategy that may be used to solve it. As a result, we have identified 20 papers that show the direct relationship between 31 different refactorings and 16 bad smells. Among the contributions of our SLR, we highlight the refactoring strategies that may be performed to eliminate bad smells; the relationship between bad smells and refactoring discussed in the literature up to now; and a contrast found between the literature and Fowler's catalog.

Keywords: Bad Smell · Code Smell · Refactoring · Literature Review

1 Introduction

Software systems must evolve to cope with new requirements from stakeholders. Hence, it requires a great effort for developers to understand and make the necessary modifications in the source code. This effort is greatly affected by aspects of the quality of the source code, such as comprehensibility, complexity, and maintainability. *Bad Smells* are indicators that there are code structure problems, which may be solved via refactoring [19]. *Refactoring* is a process of enhancing the internal structure of the source code without changing the external behavior of the software system [18].

Fowler [18] presents a catalog of bad smells and refactoring consisting of 22 bad smells and 72 refactorings, which is widely discussed in the literature [29, 33, 44]. However, in many cases, the descriptions of bad smells and their relationships with refactorings are not precise and lack a consistent level of details [4]. So, we need more studies in the area, not only in context-based evaluations of bad smells and on how to eliminate them [45], but also in research exploring the relationship between refactoring and bad smell [9].

Studies that perform analysis based on the refactoring process argue that refactoring is effective in removing bad smells in less than 10% of the time [5, 10, 11]. So, refactoring should be done in a disciplined manner to minimize the chances of introducing (i) another bad smell [10, 11, 30, 48]; (ii) other defects [6, 32, 40]; and (iii) ensure that the quality was enhanced [5, 18]. Xia et al. [53] have conducted an empirical study by surveying with developers, and they have identified the widely use of refactoring. However, participants reported that this activity is often neglected in academia, which focuses on the ability to write code from scratch. Therefore, they suggest that educators should emphasize refactoring in classes in order to identify and eliminating bad smells.

Refactor is a tricky activity since developers have to analyze the source code to (i) identify what will be refactored, (ii) the operation that will solve it, and (iii) where the refactored code will be allocated. These steps are difficult to be taught since they depend on the system context, although they may be addressed using automatic refactoring tools. Some developers do not use these tools because they do not know when and how to refactor [26]. In fact, some studies reveal that many developers prefer to refactor code manually, because they do not fully trust the tool behavior [23]. They also perform refactoring manually because existing refactoring tools may introduce new bad smells after the refactoring process [50].

To address the problems mentioned, this paper presents a systematic literature review (SLR) whose objective aims at finding direct relationship between the bad smell and the refactoring proposed in the Fowler's catalog [18]. We have identified 20 papers that show the explicit relationship between 31 different refactoring and 16 bad smells. Analyzing these papers, we have found that (1) the relationship between Move Method applied to Feature Envy appears as the most discussed one in these studies; (2) there are different refactoring strategies than those proposed by Fowler to address some bad smells. We also have found seven tools that refactor through the identification of the bad smells of Fowler. These results provide insights to researchers and developers of the existing relationships that may be used to refactor code. We also identify relationships that should be more investigated [52].

The main contributions of this SLR are four-fold. First, it shows what refactoring strategies may be performed to eliminate bad smells. Second, it reports the relationship between bad smells and refactoring discussed in the literature up to now. Third, it provides a contrast between the literature and Fowler's catalog. Finally, it help us to identify tools that refactor through the identification of Fowler's bad smells.

The remainder of this paper is organized as follows. Section 2 describes the SLR protocol we have followed. Section 3 presents the results of the conducted SLR. Section 4 discusses threats to validity. Section 5 discusses related work. Section 6 concludes this study and points directions for future work.

2 Systematic Literature Review

A Systematic Literature Review is a study that provides identification, analysis, and interpretation of evidence related to a particular research topic [52]. This work is conducted using the Kitchenham guidelines [24]. It has three stages: (i) planning, (ii) execution, and (iii) analysis [24]. The focus of this SLR is on the explicit relationship between refactoring and bad smells. Section 2.1 presents the planning phase. Section 2.2 describes the execution and the steps for the selection of primary studies. The analysis stage is presented in Section 3.

2.1 Planning

In this phase, we define: (i) the topic to be investigated; (ii) the electronic databases used to search for papers; (iii) the search string to identify relevant studies; (iv) the inclusion and exclusion criteria to obtain primary studies; and (v) timestamp in which this work has been conducted.

Research questions. To identify the relationships between refactoring and the bad smells of Fowler [18], we have defined two general Research Questions **RQ1** and **RQ2**, and two specific ones **RQ1.1** and **RQ1.2**. These RQs allow us reaching our goals, and drive all activities we have conducted within this SLR.

RQ1 Which relationships between refactoring and bad smells are explicitly discussed in the literature?

RQ1.1 Which are the most mentioned relationships between bad smells and refactoring found in the literature?

RQ1.2 Do relationships we found differ from those that Fowler presents?

RQ2 Which tools perform refactoring from bad smell detection?

Electronic databases. There are different eletronic databases to be used in literature reviews to search for primary studies. Some studies use one database [54, 55]; others use three databases [21], six databases [3, 15, 33], seven databases [1], or even eight databases [8, 29, 49]. We use seven of the most used ones [33], as exhibits Table 1. The first column in Table 1 shows the database name, while the second one presents their respective websites.

Search string. It identifies the relevant studies in the selected databases, allowing us to answer the proposed research questions. We conducted a pilot study with search strings composed of multiple different terms and applied them in each database. We evaluated their results in each database with the purpose to identify which of the search string have reached as many studies as possible in the literature. At the end, the search string was consolidated with three terms as follows.

```
(refactor OR refactoring) AND (relationship OR correlation OR
associate) AND ("code smell" OR "bad smell" OR bug OR "anti pattern")
```

Table 1. Eletronic Databases

Database	Address	Papers Returned
ACM Digital Library	http://dl.acm.org/	113
Engineering Village	https://www.engineeringvillage.com	83
IEEE Xplore	http://ieeexplore.ieee.org/	47
Science Direct	http://www.sciencedirect.com/	07
Scopus	http://scopus.com/	70
Springer	http://link.springer.com/	2,025
Web of Science	http://apps.webofknowledge.com/	44
Total		2,389

Inclusion and exclusion criteria. We have four inclusion and two exclusion criteria to select the primary studies (see Table 2). These criteria allow classifying each study under review as a candidate to be included or excluded from the SLR.

Table 2. Inclusion and Exclusion Criteria

Inclusion Criteria	Exclusion Criteria
Written in English	< 5 pages
Published in conferences, journals, workshops and book chapters*	Thesis, dissertations, tutorials, courses and magazines issues
Available in electronic format	
Present Fowler's refactoring and bad smells	

*Papers published at conferences that appear as book chapters in digital libraries

Search source. We searched all studies published up to 2018. The search process was carried out from February 6 to 9, 2019.

2.2 Execution

This phase consists of: (i) applying the search string in the selected databases, identifying primary studies, and (ii) selecting the relevant ones found through the exclusion/inclusion criteria. Figure 1 presents the resulting number of primary studies after each step, serving as input to the next step. The check symbols indicate the studies that remained in the step, while numbers near cross symbols indicate the studies excluded in the step. At the end of the process, we identified 20 papers that fit the scope of this work. These studies were analyzed and summarized in order to collect information to answer our RQs.

Search process. Table 1 presents the primary studies returned by the search in each database, with the total of 2,389 studies, including duplicates.

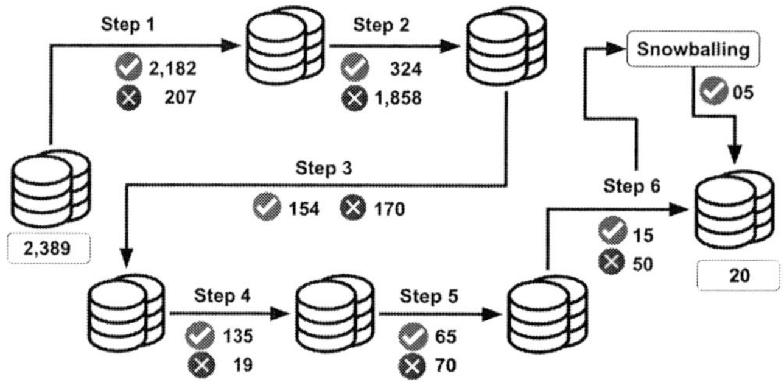

Fig. 1. Number of papers filtered in each step

Study selection process. Figure 1 presents the six steps focusing on selecting relevant papers according to its content. The result regarding each individual database is available on our website [41]. The six steps are discussed as follows.

Step 1- *Remove Duplicates.* We merge the papers returned in all databases, which cause the removal of duplicated papers. These papers were randomly eliminated, without favoring any database.

Step 2- *Reading Title.* Only those papers with excerpts of the search string used or those that could be relevant for the study are retained. In case of doubts, the papers were kept for the next filtering step.

Step 3- *Reading Abstract.* Here, we select those papers that show some evidence of being linked to the SLR context.

Step 4- *Inclusion and Exclusion Criteria.* After the application of the inclusion and exclusion criteria defined in Section 2.1, if the paper fits in at least one of the exclusion criteria, it is removed from our SLR.

Step 5- *Reading Introduction and Conclusion.* We select those papers that present evidence that they help to answer our RQs, and those that we deem relevant to the study.

Step 6- *Complete Reading of Paper.* Only those papers that are directly related to our RQs are included.

Snowballing- In our SLR, we execute the backward snowballing [51]. The process was performed with the 15 papers identified at the end of Step 6. These six steps were applied again, in order to find new candidates to be included. The snowballing has resulted in the inclusion of 5 new papers.

Data extraction. Research questions are the main drivers of what information needs to be extracted. So, the main topic of each RQ was identified and summarized in a table. For each paper found, it was documented: (i) each bad smell mentioned in the study and the refactoring operations that solve it; and (ii) each tool mentioned in the paper and their characteristics. These information allow us not only to identify the relationship that is most studied, but also to compare the Fowler suggestions against the suggestions proposed by the literature.

It also provides insights of which tools are used to study both bad smells and refactoring.

The quality assessment is an integral part of an SLR to assess the strength of the evidence, and to take it into account when synthesizing the results [2]. However, we did not perform it in this SLR. The reason is because we consider that the Study Selection Process and Data Extraction are sufficient in reaching most relevant papers to our study.

Results summarization. We found 20 studies explicitly addressing the relationship between refactoring and the bad smells proposed by Fowler [18]. It is worth noting that all selected papers were published between 2004 and 2018. This shows that the topic is still being discussed in the literature.

3 Results

This section aims to answer RQ1 and RQ2 presented in Section 2.1. Section 3.1 describes the characterization of the papers found. Sections 3.2 and 3.3 presents the analysis of the collected data to answer RQ1 and RQ2, respectively.

3.1 Overview of Primary Studies

Figure 2 shows the number of studies found per year. Observe that 2017 shows the largest number of relevant studies. The years from 2013 to 2015 show three papers each. No study discussing the explicit relationship between refactoring and bad smells was found in 2005, 2007, 2008, and 2010 to 2012. From the figure, we may argue that the topic has been recently researched.

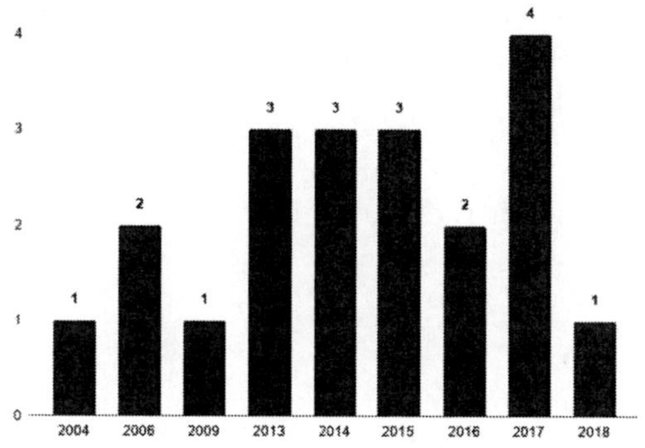

Fig. 2. Publication Year

Selected studies were mainly published in journals and conferences, with a total of 9 and 8 studies, respectively. They were published in 17 different events, most of them in the IEEE Transactions on Software Engineering and in the

International Conference on Agile Software Development (XP), with 3 and 2 papers, respectively. The remaining events presented one study each and may be found in our website [41].

3.2 Relationships between Bad Smells and Refactoring

RQ1 Which relationships between refactoring and bad smells are explicitly discussed in the literature?

Table 3 presents the relationships between refactoring and bad smells according to the analysis of the 20 papers found. Each line presents a different relationship between a bad smell and refactoring. The first column presents the bad smell, the second column shows which refactoring solves it. Columns 3 and 4 check whether the relationship is discussed by Fowler or by the literature, respectively. A bullet indicates that refactoring was discussed. It is worth noticing that a relationship may be discussed by Fowler and by the literature. The last column presents reference of the studies that discuss these relationships.

We focused on Fowler's bad smells and refactoring. But, for specific situations, we have merged different terminologies into a single bad smell, since their meaning and characteristics are similar, only changing their names. For instance, we classified Clone [27] or Code Clone [22, 28] as Duplicated Code. Parallel Inheritance [36, 40] is classified as Parallel Inheritance Hierarchies. There is a case where the authors explicitly indicated State Checking as the Switch Statements smell [12]. For the refactoring classification, we have the case where Polymorphism [12] is named for Replace Conditional with Polymorphism.

Every paper we have identified discuss more than one relationship between bad smells and refactoring. So, each relationship found is individually documented. Observe that there are cases where different refactoring may be applied to address the same bad smell. Therefore, to answer RQ1, Table 3 presents the 22 bad smells proposed by Fowler, where 16 of them (73%) are studied in the literature. This indicates concern on the part of researchers to address, as much as possible, most bad smells present in the catalog. However, the situation for refactoring is different. From a total of 72 refactoring in the catalog, only 31 (43%) of them are cited in the literature. This indicates the need to evaluate other refactoring strategies. Still, this may be an indicative that not all refactoring operations mentioned by Fowler are used in practice to remove bad smells.

RQ1.1 Which are the most mentioned relationships between bad smells and refactoring found in the literature?

Table 3 shows all relationships between refactoring and bad smells found in this SLR. To answer this RQ, we consider the relationship being discussed by the largest number of different studies. We identified that the highest number of citations is related to Move Method (refactoring) and Feature Envy (bad smell), totaling 14 different papers targeting this relationship.

According to the data presented in Table 3, the refactoring operation that solves the largest amount of bad smells is Move Method, being used to solve 11

Table 3. Relationships Between Bad Smell and Refactoring

Bad Smell	Refactoring	Fowler	Literature	References
Alternative Classes with Different Interfaces	Extract Superclass	•	•	[13]
	Move Method	•	•	[13]
	Rename Method	•	•	[13]
Comments	Extract Method	•		
	Introduce Assertion	•		
	Rename Method	•		
Data Class	Encapsulate Collection	•	•	[40, 42]
	Encapsulate Field	•	•	[13, 40, 42]
	Extract Method	•	•	[40, 42]
	Hide Method	•	•	[13, 40, 42]
	Move Method	•	•	[13, 40, 42]
	Remove Setting Method	•	•	[40]
Data Clumps	Extract Class	•		
	Introduce Parameter Object	•		
	Preserve Whole Object	•		
Divergent Change	Extract Class	•	•	[11, 36]
	Extract Method		•	[10]
	Extract Superclass		•	[11]
	Move Field		•	[11]
	Move Method		•	[11]
	Pull Up Method		•	[11]
Duplicated Code	Extract Method	•	•	[16, 22, 27, 28]
	Form Template Method		•	[16]
	Pull Up Method	•	•	[13, 16, 22]
	Replace Method with Method Object		•	[16]
	Substitute Algorithm	•		
Feature Envy	Consolidate Duplicate Conditional Frag.		•	[5]
	Extract Method	•	•	[5, 10, 40, 42, 47]
	Move Field		•	[12, 42, 47]
	Move Method	•	•	[5–7, 12, 13, 25, 28, 36–40, 42, 47]
	Pull Up Method		•	[42]
Inappropriate Intimacy	Change Bidirectional Assoc. to Unidir.	•		
	Extract Class	•		
	Hide Method	•		
	Move Field	•	•	[13]
	Move Method	•	•	[13]
Incomplete Library Class	Introduce Foreign Method	•		
	Introduce Local Extension	•		
	Move Method	•	•	[13]
Large Class	Duplicate Observed Data	•		
	Extract Class	•		
	Extract Subclass	•	•	[13]
Lazy Class	Collapse Hierarchy	•		
	Inline Class	•	•	[5]
	Move Method		•	[37]
	Push Down Method		•	[10]
Long Method	Add Parameter		•	[5]
	Consolidate Conditional Expression		•	[5, 42]
	Decompose Conditional	•	•	[42]
	Extract Method	•	•	[5, 11, 12, 20, 27, 42]
	Inline Method		•	[5]
	Introduce Explaining Variable		•	[5]
	Introduce Parameter Object	•	•	[42]
	Preserve Whole Object	•	•	[42]
	Remove Control Flag		•	[5]
	Remove Parameter		•	[5]
	Rename Method		•	[5]
	Replace Method With Method Object	•	•	[42]
	Replace Temp With Query	•	•	[42]
Long Parameter List	Replace Parameter with Explicit Methods	•		
Message Chains	Extract Method	•		
	Hide Delegate	•		
	Move Method	•	•	[13]
Middle Man	Inline Method	•		
	Remove Middle Man	•		
	Replace Delegation with Inheritance	•		
Parallel Inheritance Hierarchies	Extract Subclass		•	[36]
	Move Field	•	•	[13]
	Move Method	•	•	[13, 40]
Primitive Obsession	Extract Class	•		
	Introduce Parameter Object	•		
	Replace Data Value with Object	•		
	Replace Type Code with Class	•		
	Replace Type Code with Subclass	•		
	Replace Type Code with State/Strategy	•		
	Replace Array with Object	•		
Refused Bequest	Push Down Field	•	•	[5, 13]
	Push Down Method	•	•	[5, 10, 13]
	Replace Inheritance with Delegation	•	•	[5]
Shotgun Surgery	Move Class	•		
	Move Field		•	[11, 13, 36]
	Move Method	•	•	[11, 13, 36]
	Pull Up Method		•	[11]
Speculative Generality	Collapse Hierarchy	•	•	[5]
	Inline Class	•		
	Remove Parameter	•	•	[13]
	Rename Method		•	[13]
Switch Statement	Extract Method	•		
	Move Method	•	•	[13]
	Replace Conditional with Polymorphism		•	[12]
	Replace Type Code with State/Strategy	•		
	Replace Type Code with Subclass	•		
Temporary Field	Extract Class	•		
	Introduce Null Object	•		

types of smells. The bad smell that may be solved with the highest number of operations is the Long Method, in which 13 refactoring may solve it.

RQ1.2 Do relationships we found differ from those that Fowler presents?

To answer this question, we performed the analysis based on columns 3 and 4 of Table 3. We identified three cases: Case 1: if Column 3 is marked and Column 4 is not, this means that this relationship is discussed only by Fowler, meaning that the relationship needs to be researched, or may be not used in practice. Case 2: if the opposite situation occurs, where Column 4 is marked and Column 3 is not, it means that we found a new relationship that is not addressed in Fowler's catalog. Case 3: if columns 3 and 4 are marked, this represents that the relationship found by Fowler agrees with what the literature says.

For example, we identified for Lazy Class all refactoring operations that solve it. We found a refactoring that only Fowler presents a solution: Collapse Hierarchy (Case 1). We also found that the literature proposes two new refactoring operations to solve it: Move Method and Push Down Method (Case 2). Finally, we identify that Inline Class was found in Fowler's work and in the literature (Case 3).

From Table 3 and by the reasoning explained above, we may conclude that only Alternative Classes with Different Interfaces, Data Class, and Refused Bequest have both columns 3 and 4 being a perfect match. This indicates that there is no new refactoring strategy to solve them reported in the literature. Also, six bad smells in the catalog were not addressed by the literature. This may be due to the nature of them, since some bad smells do not impact significantly on the source quality [35]. Observe that for seven of the 22 smells, the literature has proposed more refactoring operations than Fowler. However, for these smells, Fowler has presented 18 refactorings strategies to solve them, of which only three of them were not confirmed by the literature. We identified 35 relationships in Case 1, 24 in Case 2, and 35 in Case 3.

3.3 Tools from Refactoring

RQ2 Which tools perform refactoring from bad smell detection?

It is worth noticing that not all tools that were proposed or mentioned in the literature answer the **RQ2**. The focus of this SLR is to identify studies that explicitly cite the relationship between refactoring and bad smells, and not to identify all refactoring tools. So, we documented only tools that appear in the resulting studies, which detect bad smells, and propose refactoring to solve them. Out of 20 studies, 16 have mentioned the tools used to conduct them. This list may be found on our website [41]. We observe that nine tools need more than one tool to perform the process of detecting bad smells and applying the refactoring. As the focus of our study is to tackle the refactoring and bad smell context together, we only report seven tools that target both concepts. Table 4 presents these tools and information about each tool, such as if it has an Graphical User Interface, or if it is commercial.

Table 4. Characteristics each tool supports

Tool [Ref.]	GUI	FRA	ONL	PLG	FRE	OPS	USG	SL
Extract Method Detector [27]	Yes	-	No	Yes	Yes	Yes	No	Java
JDeodorant [6, 12, 40]	Yes	-	No	Yes	Yes	Yes	Yes	Java
JMove [39]	Yes	-	-	Yes	Yes	Yes	Yes	-
Liu's Approach [25]	-	-	-	-	-	-	-	-
Methodbook [7]	-	-	-	-	-	-	-	Java
MMRUC3 [38]	-	Yes	-	-	-	-	-	Java
Tsantalis's Methodology [47]	-	-	-	-	-	-	-	Java

GUI: graphical user interface; **FRA**: framework; **ONL**: online; **PLG**: plugin; **FRE**: free for use; **OPS**: open-source; **USG**: user guide available; **SL**: supported language; "-": information not available.

4 Threats to Validity

We discuss the threats to validity listed by Wohlin et al. [52]: construct, internal, conclusion, and external.

Construct Validity: the electronic database selected might not retrieve all relevant papers. To minimize this threat, we selected seven different databases that aggregate papers from many publishers. Also, the search string used may not find all papers that are relevant to this SLR. To minimize this threat, we designed a search string that includes common terms for *"refactoring"* and *"bad smell"*. Furthermore, we performed a pilot search in each database to select a subset of the most common terms used in the research field, in order to retrieve the highest number of relevant papers. However, we may not assume that all existing related works were found by this filtering strategy.

Internal Validity: the guaranteed reproducibility of this study is due to the detailed specification of the search engines used, the search string, and the inclusion and exclusion criteria. Possible limitations of the search results were overcome by including different terms used by different authors, but that had similar concepts, staying in this SLR scope. Another threat may be related to the judgment of the information presented, which expresses only the authors point of view. To minimize this threat, the authors have carried out the selection stage, which in the initial stages made comparisons of the selected papers to avoid biasing in the selection of studies. Besides that, frequent meetings were held between all authors to discuss the relevant papers.

Conclusion Validity: the summarization of the data found in the literature and in the Fowler's catalog present the authors point of view, and may not present the actual concept conveyed by the papers. To minimize this threat, and to maintain the integrity of the information, we documented only what was explicitly presented by the papers.

External Validity: this threat is related to the representativeness of the selected papers published up to 2018 regarding the main goals of the systematic literature review. The systematic protocol was used to support a comprehensive representation of the selected papers, but some other papers may have been published after 2018 or indexed after the application of the search string in the databases. However, our findings about the relationship between refactoring and bad smells in the study period are accurate to the best of our knowledge.

5 Related Work

There are several reviews of the literature in the context of bad smells [15, 31, 34, 54] and refactoring [1, 29, 46]. However, most studies deal with these subjects individually, focusing just on one theme. Others deal with more than one theme, for instance, Sousa et al. [44] and Singh & Kaur [43].

Different from our work that focuses on the context of bad smells and refactoring, Sousa et al. [44] present a systematic literature mapping of studies that investigate the relationship between design patterns and bad smells. The authors focus on co-occurrence between design patterns and bad smells, providing a general analysis of the relationship between the GOF design patterns [14] and bad smells described by Fowler[18].

Singh & Kaur [43] perform a SLR of refactoring concerning code smells. Several data sets and tools for performing refactoring have been revealed and categorized depending on the detection approach: traditional method, visualization based technique, automatic method, semi-automatic method, empirical studies, and metric-based method. However, unlike this work, our studies treat these subjects together, arguing the explicit relationship between refactoring and bad smells discussed in the literature.

6 Conclusion

Refactoring from bad smell detection is not deeply discussed in the literature. This work presents the result of an SLR to identify the explicit relationship between refactoring and bad smells. We found 20 different papers that show the direct relationship between 31 refactoring types and 16 bad smells proposed by Fowler. We also found seven tools that apply refactoring after detecting bad smells.

We identified that the most discussed relationship in the literature is between Move Method and Feature Envy. It has also been found that: i) there are different refactoring strategies than those discussed by Fowler to address bad smells, ii) most strategies defined in the Fowler's book were addressed in the literature, and iii) most refactoring tools found may not detect bad smells.

As future work, we suggest an investigation on the feasibility of the refactoring strategies found in this SLR for the solution of bad smells proposed by Fowler, validating them and composing a more extensive and up-to-date catalog. Also, bad smells and refactorings strategies that were not proposed by Fowler and the new Fowler's catalog [17] should be investigated in comparison with the SLR findings. We also suggest an extension of RQ2, where research should be conducted focusing on identifying all refactoring tools present in the literature, that apply refactoring after detecting bad smells.

Acknowledgement

This research was partially supported by Brazilian funding agencies: CNPq (Grant 424340/2016-0), CAPES, and FAPEMIG (Grant PPM-00651-17)

References

1. Al Dallal, J.: Identifying refactoring opportunities in object-oriented code: A systematic literature review. IST **58**, 231–249 (2015)
2. bin Ali, N., Usman, M.: A critical appraisal tool for systematic literature reviews in software engineering. IST **112**, 48–50 (2019)
3. Azeem, M.I., Palomba, F., Shi, L., Wang, Q.: Machine learning techniques for code smell detection: A systematic literature review and meta-analysis. IST **108**, 115–138 (2019)
4. Basit, W., Lodhi, F., Bhatti, U.: Extending refactoring guidelines to perform client and test code adaptation. In: Int. Conf. on Agile Soft. Development. pp. 1–13 (2010)
5. Bavota, G., De Lucia, A., Di Penta, M., Oliveto, R., Palomba, F.: An experimental investigation on the innate relationship between quality and refactoring. JSS **107**, 1–14 (2015)
6. Bavota, G., De Lucia, A., Marcus, A., Oliveto, R.: Recommending refactoring operations in large software systems. In: RSSE, pp. 387–419 (2014)
7. Bavota, G., Oliveto, R., Gethers, M., Poshyvanyk, D., De Lucia, A.: Methodbook: Recommending move method refactorings via relational topic models. TSE **40**(7), 671–694 (2013)
8. Beecham, S., Baddoo, N., Hall, T., Robinson, H., Sharp, H.: Motivation in software engineering: A systematic literature review. IST **50**(9-10), 860–878 (2008)
9. Boshnakoska, D., Mišev, A.: Correlation between object-oriented metrics and refactoring. In: Int. Conf. on ICT Innovations. pp. 226–235 (2010)
10. Cedrim, D., Garcia, A., Mongiovi, M., Gheyi, R., Sousa, L., de Mello, R., Fonseca, B., Ribeiro, M., Chávez, A.: Understanding the impact of refactoring on smells: A longitudinal study of 23 software projects. In: Proc. of the 11th JointMeeting on Foundations of Soft. Engineering. pp. 465–475 (2017)
11. Cedrim, D., Sousa, L., Garcia, A., Gheyi, R.: Does refactoring improve software structural quality? a longitudinal study of 25 projects. In: Proc. of the 30th SBSE. pp. 73–82 (2016)
12. Chatzigeorgiou, A., Manakos, A.: Investigating the evolution of code smells in object-oriented systems. Innovations in Syst. and Soft. Engineering **10**(1), 3–18 (2014)
13. Counsell, S., Hassoun, Y., Loizou, G., Najjar, R.: Common refactorings, a dependency graph and some code smells: an empirical study of java oss. In: Proc. of the ISESE. pp. 288–296 (2006)
14. Erich Gamma, Richard Helm, R.J., Vlissides, J.: Design patterns: Elements of reusable object-oriented software. Addison Wesley Longman Publishing (1994)
15. Fernandes, E., Oliveira, J., Vale, G., Paiva, T., Figueiredo, E.: A review-based comparative study of bad smell detection tools. In: Proc. of the 20th EASE. pp. 1–12 (2016)

16. Fontana, F.A., Zanoni, M., Zanoni, F.: A duplicated code refactoring advisor. In: Int. Conf. on Agile Soft. Development. pp. 3–14 (2015)
17. Fowler, M.: Refactoring: Improving the Design of Existing Code. Addison-Wesley Professional (2018)
18. Fowler, M., Beck, K., Brant, J., Opdyke, W.: Refactoring: Improving the Design of Existing Code. Addison-Wesley (1999)
19. Gupta, V., Kapur, P.K., Kumar, D.: Modelling and measuring code smells in enterprise applications using tism and two-way assessment. Int. Journal of Syst. Assurance Eng. and Management **7**(3), 332–340 (2016)
20. Haas, R., Hummel, B.: Learning to rank extract method refactoring suggestions for long methods. In: Int. Conf. on Soft. Quality. pp. 45–56 (2017)
21. Hall, T., Beecham, S., Bowes, D., Gray, D., Counsell, S.: A systematic literature review on fault prediction performance in software engineering. TSE **38**(6), 1276–1304 (2011)
22. Higo, Y., Kamiya, T., Kusumoto, S., Inoue, K.: Refactoring support based on code clone analysis. In: Int. Conf. on Product Focused Soft. Proc. Improvement. pp. 220–233 (2004)
23. Kim, M., Zimmermann, T., Nagappan, N.: An empirical study of refactoring challenges and benefits at microsoft. TSE **40**(7), 633–649 (July 2014)
24. Kitchenham, B., Charters, S.: Guidelines for performing systematic literature reviews in software engineering. In Technical Report, Ver. 2.3 (EBSE) (2007)
25. Liu, H., Wu, Y., Liu, W., Liu, Q., Li, C.: Domino effect: Move more methods once a method is moved. In: 23rd SANER. vol. 1, pp. 1–12 (2016)
26. Liu, W., Hu, Z.g., Liu, H.t., Yang, L.: Automated pattern-directed refactoring for complex conditional statements. Journal of Central South University **21**(5), 1935–1945 (2014)
27. Liu, W., Liu, H.: Major motivations for extract method refactorings: analysis based on interviews and change histories. Front. of Com. Science **10**(4), 644–656 (2016)
28. Mahmoud, A., Niu, N.: Supporting requirements to code traceability through refactoring. RE **19**(3), 309–329 (2014)
29. Misbhauddin, M., Alshayeb, M.: Uml model refactoring: a systematic literature review. ESE **20**(1), 206–251 (2015)
30. Mkaouer, M.W., Kessentini, M., Bechikh, S., Cinnéide, M.Ó., Deb, K.: On the use of many quality attributes for software refactoring: a many-objective search-based software engineering approach. ESE **21**(6), 2503–2545 (2016)
31. Oliveira, J., Viggiato, M., Santos, M.F., Figueiredo, E., Marques-Neto, H.: An empirical study on the impact of android code smells on resource usage. In: SEKE. pp. 314–313 (2018)
32. Ouni, A., Kessentini, M., Sahraoui, H., Boukadoum, M.: Maintainability defects detection and correction: a multi-objective approach. ASE **20**(1), 47–79 (2013)
33. d. P. Sobrinho, E.V., De Lucia, A., d. A. Maia, M.: A systematic literature review on bad smells — 5 w's: which, when, what, who, where. TSE pp. 1–1 (2018)
34. Paiva, T., Damasceno, A., Figueiredo, E., Sant'Anna, C.: On the evaluation of code smells and detection tools. JSERD **5**(1), 7 (2017)
35. Palomba, F., Bavota, G., Di Penta, M., Fasano, F., Oliveto, R., De Lucia, A.: On the diffuseness and the impact on maintainability of code smells: A large scale empirical investigation. In: Proc. of the 40th ICSE. pp. 482–482 (2018)
36. Palomba, F., Bavota, G., Di Penta, M., Oliveto, R., Poshyvanyk, D., De Lucia, A.: Mining version histories for detecting code smells. TSE **41**(5), 462–489 (2014)

37. Pietrzak, B., Walter, B.: Leveraging code smell detection with inter-smell relations. In: Int. Conf. on Extreme Programming and Agile Proc. in Soft. Engineering. pp. 75–84 (2006)
38. Rahman, M.M., Riyadh, R.R., Khaled, S.M., Satter, A., Rahman, M.R.: Mmruc3: A recommendation approach of move method refactoring using coupling, cohesion, and contextual similarity to enhance software design. SPE **48**(9), 1560–1587 (2018)
39. Sales, V., Terra, R., Miranda, L.F., Valente, M.T.: Recommending move method refactorings using dependency sets. In: 20th WCRE. pp. 232–241 (2013)
40. Sehgal, R., Mehrotra, D., Bala, M.: Analysis of code smell to quantify the refactoring. Int. Journal of Syst. Assurance Eng. and Management **8**(2), 1750–1761 (2017)
41. Silva, C., Santana, A., Figueiredo, E., Bigonha, M.A.S.: Revisiting the bad smell and refactoring relationship - data of the study, https://cleitonsilvat.github.io/eselaw2020/, acessed December 10, 2019
42. da Silva Carvalho, L.P., Novais, R.L., do Nascimento Salvador, L., de Mendonça Neto, M.G.: An approach for semantically-enriched recommendation of refactorings based on the incidence of code smells. In: ICEIS. pp. 313–335 (2017)
43. Singh, S., Kaur, S.: A systematic literature review: Refactoring for disclosing code smells in object oriented software. Ain Shams Engineering Journal (2018)
44. Sousa, B.L., Bigonha, M.A., Ferreira, K.A.: A systematic literature mapping on the relationship between design patterns and bad smells. In: Proc. of the 33rd Annual ACM SAC. pp. 1528–1535 (2018)
45. Tahir, A., Yamashita, A., Licorish, S., Dietrich, J., Counsell, S.: Can you tell me if it smells?: A study on how developers discuss code smells and anti-patterns in stack overflow. In: Proc. of the 22nd EASE. pp. 68–78 (2018)
46. Tavares, C.S., Ferreira, F., Figueiredo, E.: A systematic mapping of literature on software refactoring tools. In: Proc. of the XIV SBSI. p. 11 (2018)
47. Tsantalis, N., Chatzigeorgiou, A.: Identification of move method refactoring opportunities. TSE **35**(3), 347–367 (2009)
48. Tufano, M., Palomba, F., Bavota, G., Oliveto, R., Di Penta, M., De Lucia, A., Poshyvanyk, D.: When and why your code starts to smell bad. In: Proc. of the 37th ICSE. pp. 403–414 (2015)
49. Vale, G., Figueiredo, E., Abílio, R., Costa, H.: Bad smells in software product lines: A systematic review. In: Eighth SBCARS. pp. 84–94. IEEE (2014)
50. Vidal, S.A., Marcos, C., Díaz-Pace, J.A.: An approach to prioritize code smells for refactoring. ASE **23**(3), 501–532 (2016)
51. Wohlin, C.: Guidelines for snowballing in systematic literature studies and a replication in software engineering. In: Proc. of the 18th EASE. p. 38 (2014)
52. Wohlin, C., Runeson, P., Höst, M., Ohlsson, M.C., Regnell, B., Wesslén, A.: Experimentation in software engineering. Springer Science & Business Media (2012)
53. Xia, X., Wan, Z., Kochhar, P.S., Lo, D.: How practitioners perceive coding proficiency. In: Proc. of the 41st ICSE. pp. 924–935 (2019)
54. Zhang, M., Hall, T., Baddoo, N.: Code bad smells: a review of current knowledge. Journal of Soft. Maint. and Evol.: Research and Practice **23**(3), 179–202 (2011)
55. Zhang, M., Hall, T., Baddoo, N., Wernick, P.: Do bad smells indicate" trouble" in code? In: Proc. of workshop on Defects in large software systems. pp. 43–44 (2008)

Predicción de Defectos Usando Métricas Estáticas y de Cambio: un caso de estudio en un Lenguaje Dinámicamente Tipado

Mauro Gullino[1] y Gabriela Robiolo[2]

[1] Facultad Regional Haedo, Universidad Tecnológica Nacional, Buenos Aires, Argentina, mgullino@frh.utn.edu.ar
[2] LIDTUA (CIC), Facultad de Ingeniería, Universidad Austral, Pilar, Argentina, grobiolo@austral.edu.ar

Abstract. La utilización de métricas para la predicción de defectos es un importante área de estudio de la Ingeniería de Software. El presente trabajo selecciona un conjunto de métricas estáticas y de cambio con el objetivo de evaluar su utilidad como predictores de defectos. Se presenta un caso de estudio sobre el proyecto de código abierto MediaWiki, que soporta a Wikipedia. Este producto cuenta con 1000 clases y 365 KLOC y está desarrollado con el lenguaje de tipado dinámico PHP, extensamente usado en la industria de desarrollo web. Luego de obtener las métricas para el historial de desarrollo del producto durante un año, lo que representó analizar 2800 commits y crear herramientas específicas, se utilizó regresión logística como método de estimación. Se verifica que la cantidad y tamaño de los cambios de tipo *"Feature Introduction"* realizados a una clase son los mejores predictores de que la misma sea defectuosa para el caso de estudio. Se comprueba que utilizando métricas de cambio es posible obtener mejores resultados en la predicción que con métricas estáticas, pero las primeras representan un mayor esfuerzo de medición.

Keywords: Métricas de Software, Métricas Estáticas, Métricas de Cambio, Predicción de Defectos, Regresión Logística

1 Introducción

Hace décadas se busca a través del estudio de las métricas de software indicios de propiedades internas de éste que resulten interesantes durante el ciclo de vida. Muchas líneas de investigación han buscado la correlación entre estas métricas y la cantidad de defectos encontrados en un artefacto. Una importante *Systematic Literature Review* realizada en 2012 [1] analizó más de 200 trabajos sobre el tema solamente en la última década, lo que pone de manifiesto la vigencia y el interés que despierta la utilidad de las métricas como predictores de defectos.

Se estima [2] que la corrección de defectos en la fase de mantenimiento abarca de un 50% a un 75% del costo total de desarrollo de sistemas. Debido a su significancia económica la búsqueda de predictores confiables de defectos se ha convertido en un importante área de trabajo dentro de la Ingeniería de Software.

Hay consenso en que no existe un juego de métricas que sea un buen predictor para absolutamente todos los proyectos, sino que debe encontrarse el conjunto adecuado a cada uno. Es decir que un conjunto de métricas puede ser un predictor de defectos válido en un proyecto y sin embargo no poder aplicarse con igual éxito en otro. [3]

El objetivo de la presente investigación es definir la o las métricas de software que mejor se comporten como predictores de defectos de una clase utilizando como caso de estudio un producto de código abierto desarrollado en un lenguaje de tipado dinámico. **Pregunta de investigación: ¿Son las métricas de cambio mejores predictores de defectos que las métricas estáticas en un lenguaje de tipado dinámico?**

Se utilizó el proyecto MediaWiki como caso de estudio debido a su característica *open source*, a la disponibilidad del historial de cambios a través del repositorio de versiones y a su innegable calidad y éxito como producto. La instalación más importante de este proyecto es la enciclopedia colaborativa Wikipedia.

MediaWiki está desarrollado con el lenguaje de programación PHP, lo que representa la oportunidad de trabajar con un sistema dinámicamente tipado. La investigación sobre métricas de software y predicción de defectos se ha centrado históricamente en lenguajes de tipado estático (principalmente Java y C++) dejando de lado, de este modo, lenguajes muy extendidos en la industria. Esto plantea la cuestión de si las métricas desarrolladas y estudiadas para lenguajes de tipado estático son útiles en lenguajes de tipado dinámico.

Se utilizó regresión logística siguiendo a los autores principales del área [4] [5] [6]. Este método de estimación permite realizar una clasificación binaria de un artefacto como defectuoso/no-defectuoso a partir de variables independientes cuantitativas que lo describen (métricas).

Este trabajo se estructura de la siguiente forma: en el punto 2 se enumeran las métricas seleccionadas para caracterizar el producto bajo estudio y su proceso de desarrollo, en el punto 3 se analiza el caso de estudio MediaWiki y se presentan los resultados de los modelos de regresión obtenidos, en el punto 4 se enumeran los trabajos relacionados más importantes y en el punto 5 se presentan las conclusiones.

2 Métricas seleccionadas

Las métricas estáticas utilizadas en este trabajo surgen del framework desarrollado por Robiolo [7] y de la suite Chidamber & Kemerer (C&K) [8], muy extendida en el área. Las métricas de cambio siguen el trabajo de Moser [5] y las definiciones de Hassan [9]. Las métricas que no tienen un nombre de uso común han sido numeradas según aparecen en el trabajo original de los autores para facilitar su tratamiento.

2.1 Métricas de sistema

Las métricas de sistema (Tabla 1) se utilizan para caracterizar al producto como un todo y no forman parte de los modelos predictivos. Para éstos se utilizan métricas de clase ya que los predictores buscados apuntan a dicha granularidad.

Tabla 1. Métricas de sistema

Métrica	Descripción	Autor
LOC	*Lines of Code* (líneas de código lógicas totales)	N/D
Rob_1	Cantidad de clases totales	Robiolo
Rob_2	Cantidad de interfaces totales	Robiolo
Rob_3	Cantidad de clases externas extendidas	Robiolo
Rob_4	Cantidad de interfaces externas extendidas	Robiolo
Rob_5	Cantidad de clases que implementan interfaces externas	Robiolo
Rob_6	Cantidad de clases raíz que poseen al menos una subclase	Robiolo
Rob_7	Cantidad de interfaces raíz que son extendidas por otra interfaz	Robiolo
Rob_8	Nivel máximo de profundidad de herencia desde las clases raíz	Robiolo
Rob_9	Nivel máximo de profundidad de herencia desde las interfaces raíz	Robiolo
Rob_10	Cantidad de clases concretas en el primer nivel de jerarquía (raíz)	Robiolo
Rob_11	Cantidad de clases concretas en el primer nivel de jerarquía (raíz) que implementan alguna interfaz	Robiolo

2.2 Métricas estáticas

Las métricas estáticas (Tabla 2) miden aspectos deducibles directamente del código fuente de cada clase. Por esta razón también son llamadas métricas de producto. Además de las métricas obtenidas de los autores de referencia se proponen métricas originales para cuantificar los aspectos de tipado dinámico del lenguaje.

Tabla 2. Definición de métricas estáticas

Métrica	Descripción	Autor
LOC	*Lines of Code* (líneas de código lógicas de la clase)	N/D
CK_WMC	*Weigthed Methods per Class* (cantidad de métodos, sin contar los heredados)	C&K
CK_CBO	*Coupling Between Object Classes* (cantidad de clases a las cuales la clase está acoplada[1])	C&K
CK_RFC	*Response For a Class* (cantidad de métodos más la cantidad de métodos que a su vez son llamados en cada uno de ellos)	C&K
Rob_12	Porcentaje de los métodos concretos que sobreescriben un método concreto heredado, sobre el total de métodos concretos	Robiolo
Rob_13	Cantidad de mensajes polimórficos enviados[2]	Robiolo
Rob_14	Promedio de sentencias que tienen los métodos de la clase	Robiolo

---

1 El acoplamiento puede deberse a varios factores, entre ellos: llamadas a métodos, instanciación, recepción como parámetro, etc.

2 Se considera "mensaje polimórfico" a una llamada a método realizada sobre objetos con tipo declarado como interfaz o clase abstracta.

Rob_15	Cantidad de métodos públicos de una clase, incluidos el constructor, los métodos abstractos y los heredados[3]	Robiolo
Rob_16	Misma métrica que Rob_15 pero aplicada en interfaces	Robiolo
Gul_1	Cantidad de métodos que no declaran un tipo de retorno ni tampoco lo documentan[4]	Gullino
Gul_2	Cantidad de métodos que no declaran un tipo de retorno pero sí lo documentan	Gullino
Gul_3	Cantidad de métodos en los que el tipo de retorno está explícitamente declarado	Gullino
Gul_4	Cantidad de parámetros de todos los métodos de la clase, incluido el constructor, que no declaran un tipo ni lo documentan	Gullino
Gul_5	Cantidad de parámetros de todos los métodos de la clase que no declaran el tipo pero sí se encuentra documentado	Gullino
Gul_6	Cantidad de parámetros de todos los métodos de la clase que declaran el tipo de manera explícita	Gullino

Se han omitido algunas métricas tanto de la suite original C&K como del framework Robiolo debido a su dificultad de medición a consecuencia del sistema de tipos del lenguaje. Dado que la declaración de tipos es opcional, por ejemplo en los parámetros de los métodos, las métricas de colaboración entre clases requerirían inspección manual o un desarrollo de inferencia de tipos que queda fuera del alcance de este trabajo. De las métricas C&K se omitieron las reportadas [4] [6] como peores predictores.

2.3 Métricas de cambio

Las métricas de cambio seleccionadas (Tabla 3) provienen de la importante investigación dentro del área realizada por Moser en 2008 [5]. A diferencia de las definiciones originales las métricas de cambio se calcularon a nivel de clase, cuando el autor las define en base a archivos. Se ha descartado la métrica Refactorings por no encontrarse un formato sistemático dentro de los mensajes de commit que pueda utilizarse para su deducción informatizada de manera confiable.

Un "cambio" se introduce a una clase por medio de un commit al sistema de control de versiones (Git). Estos se clasificaron en tres tipos, siguiendo a Hassan [9]:

- *Feature Introduction* (FI): cambio que agrega nueva funcionalidad al sistema. Abarca todo cambio que no se produce a consecuencia de un bugfix. En términos generales, es todo cambio en el código fuente que no pueda ser atribuido a las siguientes dos categorías.
- *Fault Repairing* (FR): cambio que se produce para corregir un defecto[5]. Es decir que se trata de los bugfixes que tuvo una clase.

---

[3] Es similar a CK_WMC pero considerando la herencia

[4] La documentación de un método se realiza por medio de un *docblock* o bloque de comentario, con un formato específico, que precede al código fuente del método.

[5] Se define "defecto" siguiendo a la norma IEEE 1044 [10].

- *General Maintenance* (GM): actualización de números de versión, tabulación, corrección de estilo, corrección de documentación. En general, cambio no funcional.
- Descartados: cambios que no se realizan sobre clases sino sobre archivos auxilia-res, por ejemplo archivos de configuración o de internacionalización.

Debido a que las métricas de cambio cuantifican las modificaciones hechas al código fuente en lugar del código mismo, este cálculo siempre tiene en cuenta un período de tiempo. Por esto también se llaman métricas de proceso. Las métricas estáticas, en cambio, representan una especie de "fotografía", a través de las métricas, del estado del código fuente en un punto temporal específico del repositorio.

Tabla 3. Definición de métricas de cambio

Métrica	Descripción	Autor
Revisions	Cantidad de commits de tipo FI que modificaron la clase	Moser
Bugfixes	Cantidad de commits de tipo FR que modificaron la clase	Moser
Authors	Cantidad de autores distintos que realizaron al menos un commit de tipo FI a la clase	Moser
LOC_Added	Cantidad de líneas agregadas a una clase con commits de tipo FI	Moser
Max_LOC_Added	Cantidad de líneas agregadas por el commit de tipo FI que más líneas agregó a la clase	Moser
Ave_LOC_Added	Promedio de líneas agregadas considerando todos los commits de tipo FI que modifican la clase	Moser
LOC_Deleted	Cantidad de líneas eliminadas de una clase con commits de tipo FI	Moser
Max_LOC_ Deleted	Cantidad de líneas eliminadas por el commit de tipo FI que más líneas eliminó de la clase	Moser
Ave_LOC_ Deleted	Promedio de líneas eliminadas considerando todos los commit de tipo FI que modifican la clase	Moser
CodeChurn	Es el resultado de restar LOC_Added - LOC_Deleted para una clase	Moser
Max_CodeChurn	Valor absoluto mayor que tuvo la métrica CodeChurn para todos los commits de tipo FI realizados a la clase	Moser
Ave_CodeChurn	Promedio de las líneas agregadas menos las eliminadas en los commits de tipo FI que modifican la clase	Moser
Ave_ChangeSet	En promedio, cuántas otras clases se modifican junto a ésta en el mismo commit, considerando los commits FI	Moser
Max_ChangeSet	La mayor cantidad de otras clases que se modificaron junto a cierta clase mediante el mismo commit de tipo FI	Moser
Age	Edad de la clase en semanas al momento de finalizar el período, contando desde su aparición en el repositorio	Moser
Weighted_Age	Fórmula que pondera la cantidad de líneas agregadas con la edad de la clase al momento de agregar esas líneas.	Moser

3 Caso de Estudio

MediaWiki es un sistema wiki de código abierto desarrollado por la Wikimedia Foundation cuya principal instalación, dentro de decenas de miles, es Wikipedia, posicionado dentro de los diez sitios web más visitados a nivel global[6]. El producto cuenta con 1000 clases y 365 KLOC dentro del período analizado. Se trata de un producto maduro, con un historial de 15 años desde su primera versión.

El desarrollo sigue un modelo de integración continua, donde los cambios en el código fuente se despliegan directamente en los sitios de forma regular. El código enviado al repositorio de versiones por los desarrolladores es revisado por un par (*peer review*), aprobado, y luego integrado en el producto, que a su vez se despliega en los servidores productivos rápidamente, de manera continua.

3.1 Obtención de las métricas

En la Tabla 4 se presenta una muestra de las métricas estáticas obtenidas, que totalizan 1968 filas. Las columnas seleccionadas corresponden a las métricas que forman parte del modelo de regresión que mejores resultados arrojó en la predicción posterior.

Para obtener las métricas estáticas del código fuente se construyó un programa que analiza el código fuente de cada una de las clases a considerar. Esta herramienta se realizó en lenguaje PHP aprovechando sus potentes capacidades de reflexión, esto es, la posibilidad de un programa de acceder a la propia estructura de alto nivel de sí mismo (por ejemplo: variables, clases, métodos, etc.).

Tabla 4. Selección de algunas métricas estáticas (variables independientes) y métrica Bugfixes (variable dependiente)

Semestre	Clase	LOC	CK_RFC	Rob_14	Gul_5	Bugfixes
1	Title	2644	373	5,82	60	2
1	Parser	3639	408	14,73	108	4
1	File	855	197	2,87	3	4
1	WikiPage	1887	289	8,0	54	6
2	Title	2650	377	5,6	0	2
2	Parser	3674	410	14,79	0	6

Al abrir con esta herramienta un archivo que contiene una declaración de clase se logra que el intérprete la cargue en memoria, lo que provee de una interfaz orientada a objetos para consultar, por ejemplo: si es o no una clase concreta, cuántos métodos tiene y cómo se llaman, si existe herencia, los parámetros de los métodos, etc.

Haciendo uso del análisis con expresiones regulares línea por línea de cada método de cada clase y de las características de reflexión del lenguaje se han podido obtener las métricas estáticas requeridas como datos primarios. A los efectos de calcular las

[6] Métrica disponible online en www.alexa.com/siteinfo/wikipedia.org

métricas estáticas con esta herramienta, se posicionó el repositorio de versiones en dos puntos: primer cambio realizado en enero de 2014 y primer cambio realizado en julio de 2014. Esto permite tener las métricas al inicio del primer y segundo semestre del año bajo análisis, respectivamente. Como se menciona en 2.3, la métrica Bugfixes es la cantidad de commits de tipo FR que recibió la clase en el período.

Las métricas de cambio fueron mucho más trabajosas de obtener (Tabla 5, muestra del total de 1060 filas). Esto se debe, naturalmente, a que son métricas del proceso de desarrollo y, como tales, se debieron extraer del registro del trabajo de los desarrolladores que se encuentra en el repositorio de versiones, de alguna forma "desorganizado" para su procesamiento inmediato. En este repositorio se encuentran cada uno de los commits que realizó cada programador, indicando un "mensaje de commit" redactado por él y los cambios, línea por línea, que introduce a los archivos del sistema. Cada commit puede modificar varias líneas de varios archivos, simultáneamente.

Tabla 5. Selección de algunas métricas de cambio (variables independientes) y métrica Bugfixes_prox_trim (variable dependiente)

Trimestre	Clase	Revisions	Ave_LOC_Added	Codechurn	Bugfixes_prox_trim
1	Title	13	19,7	30	0
1	Parser	8	2,5	6	4
2	Title	10	7,6	15	2
2	Parser	14	20,43	182	2
3	Title	19	6,9	-340	0
3	Parser	7	13,71	44	4

En primer lugar se obtuvo el registro total de los cambios, línea por línea, a los archivos del sistema para el período temporal bajo análisis (todo el año 2014). El archivo final conteniendo todos estos commits posee aproximadamente 500 mil líneas.

En segundo lugar se construyó un programa para realizar el *parsing* de estos cambios, de manera de organizar en una base de datos relacional todos los commits y los cambios que se realizaron a cada clase con cada uno de estos commits.

En tercer lugar se creó un programa para catalogar manualmente cada uno de los commits según las tres categorías de cambios descriptas en 2.3. En esencia, se trata de diferenciar los cambios que introducen nuevas características en el sistema (FI) de los cambios que son correcciones de defectos (FR). Debido a la ausencia de información confiable para realizar esta clasificación de manera automática, se optó por realizarla de forma manual. Para esto se construyó un programa a través del cual un operador calificado pueda examinar cada commit y decidir a qué tipo corresponde, analizando si fuera necesario los cambios en las clases involucradas línea por línea. De esta forma, un operador humano decidió a qué tipo corresponde cada commit haciendo una deducción de la intención de los cambios introducidos por ese commit y con la guía (a veces, ciertamente, escueta) del mensaje introducido por el autor. Esta tarea cognitiva sobre los 2871 commits analizados ocupó unas 60 horas reloj a lo largo de 15 días de trabajo y debe considerarse un alto costo dentro del proceso debido al conocimiento de la estructura del código fuente, la tecnología y la historia del producto que esta tarea requiere. Considerando todos los commits realizados en el proyecto durante el año 2014, se encuentran estos resultados:

- Commits descartados: 263
- Commits no descartados: 2608, de los cuales resultan
  - Feature Introduction: 1874 (72%)
  - Fault Repairing: 369 (14%)
  - General Maintenance: 365 (14%)

3.2 Método de predicción

El objetivo de los modelos de regresión logística es predecir si una clase deberá o no ser corregida (variable binaria) en función de las métricas (variables cuantitativas).

Para generar estos modelos se agregó una columna booleana "Fixed" al conjunto de datos que indica si una clase tuvo o no bugfixes, esto es, la variable dependiente a predecir. Para el análisis con métricas estáticas, realizado por semestres, una clase se considera corregida si tuvo al menos un bugfix en el semestre (cfr. Tabla 4). Para el análisis con métricas de cambio, una clase se considera corregida si tuvo al menos un bugfix en el trimestre siguiente (cfr. Tabla 5).

Los modelos de regresión logística estiman la probabilidad (entre 0 y 1) de cada clase de pertenecer a uno de los grupos (defectuosa o no-defectuosa). La asignación dicotómica final se hace en función de las probabilidades predichas. Por ejemplo, si una clase tiene un 20% de probabilidades de ser defectuosa, ¿se clasifica como defectuosa o como no-defectuosa? Luego de crear el modelo, se debe establecer un umbral de probabilidad a partir del cual se considerará que una clase es defectuosa.

		predicción	
		no-defectuosa	defectuosa
observación	no-defectuosa	811 ($n_{1,1}$)	12 ($n_{1,2}$)
	defectuosa	118 ($n_{2,1}$)	27 ($n_{2,2}$)

Fig. 1. Matriz de confusión obtenida para el modelo Fixed ~ LOC + CK_RFC + Rob_14 + Gul_5 aplicando un umbral de probabilidad de 0,5 en los datos del primer semestre

En la Tabla 6 se definen los indicadores utilizados para analizar los resultados. Estos resultados se computan a partir de la matriz de confusión obtenida con cada modelo. La Figura 1 presenta un ejemplo de matriz de confusión.

Tabla 6. Indicadores a utilizar en el análisis de los modelos de regresión

Indicador	Forma de cálculo
True Positive Rate (TP), también llamado *Recall* o *Sensitivity*	$n_{2,2} / (n_{2,2} + n_{2,1}) * 100\%$
False Positive Rate (FP)	$n_{1,2} / (n_{1,2} + n_{1,1}) * 100\%$
True Negative Rate (TN), también llamado *Specificity*	$n_{1,1} / (n_{1,2} + n_{1,1}) * 100\%$
False Negative Rate (FN)	$n_{2,1} / (n_{2,2} + n_{2,1}) * 100\%$
Porcentaje de Predicción Correcta (PC), también llamado *Accuracy*	$(n_{1,1} + n_{2,2}) / (n_{1,1} + n_{1,2} + n_{2,1} + n_{2,2}) * 100\%$
Precisión Balanceada (PB)	(TP + TN) / 2

3.3 Análisis de los resultados

Las métricas estáticas fueron calculadas sobre el código fuente correspondiente a los días 1 de enero y 1 de julio. Esto provee de dos "fotografías" del código fuente al inicio de cada semestre del año.

Todas las métricas de cambio fueron calculadas para los primeros tres trimestres del año excepto por Bugfixes (cfr. Tabla 3) que se calculó para los cuatro trimestres del año. De esta forma puede trabajarse con las métricas de un trimestre con el objetivo de predecir los bugfixes del siguiente. Por esta razón no se realizaron predicciones para el cuarto trimestre, ya que esto implica obtener los bugfixes del primer trimestre del año 2015, algo que queda fuera del alcance de este trabajo.

La Tabla 7 presenta las métricas de sistema definidas en el framework Robiolo [7] y algunos conteos relevantes, a los efectos de dimensionar el producto bajo análisis.

En líneas generales se verifica que sólo un 15% de las clases han precisado correcciones de defectos durante el período analizado. Las clases modificadas por commits de tipo FI, sin embargo, son aproximadamente el 50% y abarcan pocas líneas.

Respecto de un semestre al siguiente se evidencia un leve crecimiento en la cantidad de clases del sistema (3%) en seis meses, comparado con un cambio mínimo en las LOC (0,4 por mil). También crece en este período la cantidad de interfaces.

Tabla 7. Métricas de sistema para MediaWiki, año 2014

Métrica	Resumen	1/enero	1/julio
LOC	Líneas lógicas de código totales	364.224	365.696
Rob_1	Cantidad de clases internas	922	941
Rob_2	Cantidad de interfaces internas	24	28
---	Cantidad de clases externas	22	31
---	Cantidad de clases e interfaces totales	968	1000
Rob_3	Clases externas especializadas	1	1
Rob_4	Interfaces externas extendidas	0	0
Rob_5	Clases que implementan interfaces externas	0	0

Rob_6	Jerarquías de clase	80	82
Rob_7	Jerarquías de interfaz	0	0
Rob_8	Niveles por jerarquía de clases	5	5
Rob_9	Niveles por jerarquía de interfaces	2	2
Rob_10	Clases raíz concretas	245	245
Rob_11	Clases raíz concretas que implementan interfaces	45	46
Clases modificadas	Cantidad de clases que fueron modificadas con al menos un commit de tipo FI en el semestre	459	566
Clases no modificadas	Cantidad de clases que no fueron modificadas con ningún commit de tipo FI en el semestre	509	434
Clases sin defectos	Cantidad de clases que no fueron modificadas por ningún commit de tipo FR en el semestre	823	866
Clases con defectos	Cantidad de clases que fueron modificadas con al menos un commit de tipo FR en el semestre	145	134

A continuación se elaboran modelos de regresión utilizando las métricas obtenidas (estáticas y de cambio, para cada clase) como variables independientes.

Métricas estáticas

Se utilizaron las métricas del primer semestre para crear el modelo (datos de entrenamiento) y posteriormente se aplicó este modelo para predecir las observaciones del segundo semestre. Se construyó un modelo con las métricas LOC, CK_RFC, Rob_14 y Gul_5 ya que no están correlacionadas[7] y presentan un p-value menor a 0,05. Si se utiliza un umbral de 0,5 para la clasificación (probabilidad > 50% = clase defectuosa), se consigue la matriz de confusión de la Figura 1.

En la Tabla 8 se encuentra un resumen de los indicadores para distintos umbrales. Siguiendo a Moser [5] se considera que es más costoso corregir posteriormente en el ciclo de vida un defecto no detectado (falso negativo) que inspeccionar una clase clasificada como defectuosa cuando realmente no lo es (falso positivo). Por lo tanto, es deseable mantener bajo el indicador FN.

Como ya lo observa Moser, a medida que se modifica el modelo para reducir los falsos negativos (que resultan muy costosos) también se incrementa el esfuerzo de inspección de clases que realmente no tienen defectos, es decir, se obtendrán más falsos positivos. Esto es porque la disminución en el umbral traslada más casos “hacia la derecha” de la matriz de confusión (al clasificar más elementos como defectuosos), donde se encuentran el falso positivo y el verdadero positivo. Con otras palabras, al enviar casos hacia la columna derecha de la matriz se está reduciendo el falso negativo (en la columna izquierda de la matriz), hecho que ya se describió como deseable.

[7] Correlación de Pearson menor a 0,3

Tabla 8. Indicadores resultantes del modelo Fixed ~ LOC + CK_RFC + Rob_14 + Gul_5 para datos de entrenamiento (primer semestre) y varios umbrales de probabilidad (valores en %)

Umbral	TP	FP	TN	FN	PC	PB
0,5	19	1	99	81	87	59
0,2	48	13	87	52	82	67,5
0,15	**57**	**23**	**77**	**43**	**74**	**67**
0,1	78	45	55	22	58	66,5

En la Tabla 9 puede observarse que el desempeño del modelo con datos nuevos (segundo semestre) es prácticamente igual a los datos de entrenamiento (primer semestre). Podemos concluir que el modelo entrenado con métricas estáticas puede aplicarse a nuevos datos manteniendo su consistencia, siendo el umbral de 0,15 el más óptimo con una PB de 68,5%, TP de 55% y FN de 45%.

Tabla 9. Indicadores resultantes del modelo Fixed ~ LOC + CK_RFC + Rob_14 + Gul_5 para datos nuevos (segundo semestre) y varios umbrales de probabilidad (valores en %)

Umbral	TP	FP	TN	FN	PC	PB
0,2	40	10	90	60	84	65
0,15	**55**	**18**	**82**	**45**	**78**	**68,5**
0,1	71	40	60	29	61	65,5

Métricas de cambio

Se construyó un modelo de regresión logística con las métricas de cambio y se procedió a evaluar su desempeño de manera similar a como se hizo con las métricas estáticas. Se toman los datos del primer trimestre como entrenamiento, y se realiza la predicción para los trimestres segundo y tercero, en función de comparar su poder predictivo.

En la Tabla 10 se hallan los indicadores para un modelo de regresión construido con las métricas de cambio Revisions y Ave_LOC_Added, ya que no están correlacionadas. Puede observarse que para un umbral de 0,15 se obtiene una PB de 70%, TP de 69% y FN de 31%, lo que resulta una mejora (mayor PB, mayor TP, menor FN) sobre el modelo con métricas estáticas.

En la Tabla 11 se encuentran los indicadores para el mismo modelo, aplicado a los datos del segundo y tercer trimestre. Al igual que con las métricas estáticas, con el modelo generado con métricas de cambio se verifica un comportamiento consistente respecto de los datos de entrenamiento cuando se utiliza el modelo con datos nuevos.

Tabla 10. Indicadores resultantes del modelo Fixed ~ Revisions + Ave_LOC_Added para datos de entrenamiento (primer trimestre) y varios umbrales de probabilidad (valores en %)

Umbral	TP	FP	TN	FN	PC	PB
0,2	55	16	84	45	79	69,5
0,15	**69**	**29**	**71**	**31**	**71**	**70**
0,1	100	93	7	0	24	53,5

Tabla 11. Indicadores resultantes del modelo Fixed ~ Revisions + Ave_LOC_Added para datos nuevos (segundo y tercer trimestre) y varios umbrales (valores en %)

Datos	Umbral	TP	FP	TN	FN	PC	PB
Segundo	0,3	29	5	95	71	81	62
trimestre	0,2	43	18	82	57	74	62,5
	0,15	**57**	**31**	**69**	**43**	**66**	**63**
	0,1	99	95	5	1	24	52
Tercer	0,3	42	8	92	58	86	67
trimestre	0,2	55	18	82	45	79	68,5
	0,15	**75**	**31**	**69**	**25**	**70**	**72**
	0,1	94	89	11	6	22	52,5

Combinando métricas no correlacionadas se pueden conformar modelos con diversas variables predictoras. Sin embargo, los modelos precedentes representan las mejores combinaciones encontradas en este trabajo para métricas estáticas y de cambio.

3.4 Amenazas a la validez

Por un lado existe una amenaza a la validez interna debido a las herramientas utilizadas para la obtención de las métricas estáticas. Estas herramientas debieron ser desarrolladas para esta investigación y, si bien existe confianza suficiente en los resultados debido a las pruebas realizadas, pueden existir combinaciones sintácticas en el código fuente de rara aparición que no hayan sido observadas.

Por otro lado, el procedimiento de categorización manual necesario para calcular las métricas de cambio también puede presentar inconsistencias debido a su carga cognitiva y a la presencia de casos límite. Una decena de commits (~1%) podrían categorizarse tanto FI como FR debido a la naturaleza mixta de los cambios que introduce el desarrollador con ellos, lo que llevó a tomar una decisión que introduce un error menor.

En cuanto a la validez externa de los resultados debe observarse que, según se describió, el producto bajo estudio es de código abierto y se desarrolla mediante un proceso comunitario de integración continua, revisión de pares y testing automatizado. Esto puede limitar el alcance de los resultados si se consideran las heterogéneas metodologías utilizadas en la industria, incluso trabajando con el mismo lenguaje. Los resultados presentados corresponden a un caso de estudio individual.

4 Trabajos relacionados

Gyimothy et al. [6] analizaron las métricas C&K como predictoras de defectos. Como caso de estudio trabajaron con el código fuente del cliente de correo Mozilla, desarrollado en C++. Aplicando distintos métodos de estimación (regresión lineal, logística y árboles de decisión) logran una precisión menor a 70%, hallando en CBO y LOC los mejores predictores.

Basili [4] comparó la suite C&K con otras métricas estáticas del código fuente, encontrando que aquellas son mejores predictores (excepto LCOM). Utilizó proyectos universitarios desarrollados en C++ y aplicó regresión logística.

Moser [5], en su trabajo seminal, introduce una suite de métricas de cambio y aplica varias técnicas de estimación (regresión logística, Naive Bayes, árboles de decisión) utilizando un proyecto en lenguaje Java. Al igual que la presente investigación, encuentra que las métricas de cambio son mejores predictores que las métricas estáticas del código fuente, logrando modelos con un TP de 80%. Kamei [11], Madeyski [12] y Zhang [2] arriban a resultados similares utilizando casos de estudio comparables, con varios métodos de estimación.

Giger [13] trabajó a nivel de método y también confirmó que las métricas de cambio son mejores predictores que las métricas estáticas. Logra una precisión superior al 80% con varias técnicas de *machine learning* (Random Forest, Bayesian Network, árboles de decisión). Los casos de estudio incluyen proyectos *open source* en Java.

5 Conclusiones

La presente investigación analizó el código fuente, y las modificaciones hechas a éste, del proyecto MediaWiki durante el período de un año. Para ello se construyeron herramientas que computan las métricas y se inspeccionaron manualmente 2871 commits al repositorio de versiones. Utilizando estas métricas se construyeron modelos de regresión logística con el objetivo de obtener el mejor conjunto de métricas que predigan defectos futuros de una clase.

Los modelos definidos con métricas de cambio son los que lograron mejores resultados en la predicción. Las métricas Revisions y Ave_LOC_Added constituyen un modelo que predice una clase defectuosa con un TP del 75%, falso negativo del 25% y precisión balanceada de 72% (cfr. Tabla 11). Esto significa que la cantidad y tamaño de las modificaciones FI hechas a una clase son los mejores predictores de defectos de dicha clase.

Los modelos con métricas estáticas constituyen buenos predictores, aunque por debajo de las métricas de cambio, como ya observan otros autores (cfr. 4). Con la combinación de métricas estáticas LOC + CK_RFC + Rob_14 + Gul_5 se puede construir un modelo que predice defectos con un TP del 55%, FN 45% y PB de 69%.

Nótese que las métricas de cambio son más costosas de obtener, como se describe en 3.1.

La predicción de defectos en lenguajes de tipado dinámico es de interés para la industria si se consideran lenguajes muy extendidos como PHP, Python o JavaScript.

Referencias

1. T. Hall, S. Beecham, D. Bowes, D. Gray, y S. Counsell, «A Systematic Literature Review on Fault Prediction Performance in Software Engineering», *IEEE Transactions on Software Engineering*, vol. 38, n.º 6, pp. 1276-1304, nov. 2012.
2. F. Zhang, A. Mockus, I. Keivanloo, y Y. Zou, «Towards building a universal defect prediction model», 2014, pp. 182-191.
3. N. Nagappan, T. Ball, y A. Zeller, «Mining metrics to predict component failures», 2006, p. 452.
4. V. R. Basili, L. C. Briand, y W. L. Melo, «A validation of object-oriented design metrics as quality indicators», *IEEE Transactions on Software Engineering*, vol. 22, n.º 10, pp. 751-761, oct. 1996.
5. R. Moser, W. Pedrycz, y G. Succi, «A comparative analysis of the efficiency of change metrics and static code attributes for defect prediction», 2008, p. 181.
6. T. Gyimothy, R. Ferenc, y I. Siket, «Empirical validation of object-oriented metrics on open source software for fault prediction», *IEEE Transactions on Software Engineering*, vol. 31, n.º 10, pp. 897-910, oct. 2005.
7. Robiolo, Gabriela, «Métricas de Diseño Orientado a Objetos aplicadas en Java», tesis de Maestría, Universidad Nacional de La Plata, Argentina, 2004.
8. S. R. Chidamber y C. F. Kemerer, «A metrics suite for object oriented design», *IEEE Transactions on Software Engineering*, vol. 20, n.º 6, pp. 476-493, jun. 1994.
9. A. E. Hassan, «Predicting faults using the complexity of code changes», 2009, pp. 78-88.
10. Institute of Electrical and Electronics Engineers, IEEE Computer Society, Software Engineering Standards Committee, y IEEE-SA Standards Board, *IEEE standard classification for software anomalies*. New York: Institute of Electrical and Electronics Engineers, 2010.
11. Y. Kamei, S. Matsumoto, A. Monden, K. Matsumoto, B. Adams, y A. E. Hassan, «Revisiting common bug prediction findings using effort-aware models», 2010, pp. 1-10.
12. L. Madeyski y M. Jureczko, «Which process metrics can significantly improve defect prediction models? An empirical study», *Software Quality Journal*, vol. 23, n.º 3, pp. 393-422, sep. 2015.
13. E. Giger, M. D'Ambros, M. Pinzger, y H. C. Gall, «Method-level bug prediction», 2012, p. 171.

A survey on test practitioners' awareness of test smells

Nildo Silva Junior, Larissa Rocha, Luana Almeida Martins, and Ivan Machado

Federal University of Bahia - UFBA, Salvador - BA, Brazil
nildo.silva@ufba.br, larissars@dcc.ufba.br, martins.luana@ufba.br, ivan.machado@ufba.br

Abstract. Developing test code may be a time-consuming task that usually requires much effort and cost, especially when it is done manually. Besides, during this process, developers and testers are likely to adopt bad design choices, which may lead to the introduction of the so-called test smells in test code. Test smells are bad solutions to either implement or design test code. As the test code with test smells increases in size, these tests might become more complex, and as a consequence, much harder to understand and evolve correctly. Therefore, test smells may have a negative impact on the quality and maintenance of test code and may also harm the whole software testing activities. In this context, this study aims to understand whether test professionals non-intentionally insert test smells. We carried out an expert survey to analyze the usage frequency of a set of test smells. Sixty professionals from different companies participated in the survey. We selected 14 widely studied smells from the literature, which are also implemented in existing test smell detection tools. The yielded results indicate that experienced professionals introduce test smells during their daily programming tasks, even when they are using standardized practices from their companies, and not only for their personal assumptions. Another relevant evidence was that developers' professional experience can not be considered as a root-cause for the insertion of test smells in test code.

Keywords: Test smells · Empirical study · Expert Survey.

1 Introduction

Software projects, both commercial and open source, commonly encompass a set of automated test suites, as a crucial support to verify software quality [4]. However, creating test code may require high effort and cost [4, 20]. For example, the SCADA project used 870 hours to create a set of test scripts [19]. Automated test generation tools, such as Randoop[1], JWalk[2], and Evosuite[3], emerge as alternatives to facilitate and streamline this process. If designed with high quality,

[1] https://randoop.github.io/randoop/
[2] http://staffwww.dcs.shef.ac.uk/people/A.Simons/jwalk/
[3] http://www.evosuite.org/

automated testing offers benefits over manual testing, such as repeatability, predictability, efficient test runs, and thereby require less effort and costs [5, 20]. In this way, tests should be concise, repeatable, robust, sufficient, necessary, clear, efficient, specific, independent, maintainable, and traceable [10].

However, the development of a well-designed test code is not a straightforward task. Developers are usually under time pressure and must deal with constrained budgets, which can stimulate the use of anti-patterns in test code, leading to the occurrence of the so-called test smells. Test smells are identifiers of poor implementation solutions and problems in test code design [6]. As a consequence of introducing test smells, the produced test code would likely have reduced quality and, consequently, may not reach its expected capabilities at finding bugs while being understandable, maintainable, etc. [5, 20]. The literature reports 196 test smell types, classified in the following groups: behavior, logic, design related, issue in test steps, mock and stub-related, association in production code, code-related, and dependencies [5].

Some studies have been conducted to identify and analyze the effect of the presence of test smells in software projects in several respects [4, 6, 12, 17]. In those studies, the test smells were presented as non-functional quality attributes within the Software Test Code Engineering process, for example. Some test smell types are presented, and there is a discussion on what they may cause in the test code maintenance [4]. Metrics were defined to identify test smells on automated tools and these tools were validated by developers [6] or through a case study [17]. Some test smells were also analyzed as a way to reduce flaky tests, i.e. tests with non-deterministic behavior [12]. However, discussions about daily practices and programming styles that may contribute to inserting test smells are still lacking. Understanding the relationship between development practices and test smell insertion may support improving the test creation process.

The study aims to understand whether professionals non-intentionally insert test smells. Through an expert survey [9], we could analyze the practices adopted by developers that might introduce test smells and how frequently these practices are used during test creation and observed during test execution. The survey counted on sixty participants who work for different Brazilian companies. Our analysis may provide insights towards a better understanding of how and which practices may lead to the insertion of test smells in test code.

The following research questions were addressed in this study:

RQ1: Do professionals use test case design practices that might lead to test smell insertion? We investigate whether bad design choices may be related to test smells.

RQ2: Does the professional experience interfere with test smell insertion? We investigate whether, over time, professionals improve the test creation process.

RQ3: Which are the practices present in professionals' daily activities that lead test smells insertion? We investigate which test smells are associated with the most frequent professionals' practices.

2 Test Smells

Automated tests may yield more efficient results when compared to manually executed ones. Due to their capability of being easily repeated several times, and the lack of human interference, automated tests might lead to reductions in both time and execution effort [5, 20]. However, developing test code is not a trivial task, and once it has been poorly designed, the use of automated tools may not ensure the quality of the system [11, 18]. As aforementioned, in real-world practice, developers are likely to use anti-patterns during test creation and evolution, which may lead to mistakes in test code implementation [1, 16]. These anti-patterns may negatively impact the maintenance of the test code [17].

Several studies have investigated different types of smells. Initially, Deursen et al. [16] defined a catalog of 11 test smells and refactorings to remove test smells from test code. After that, many other authors extended this catalog and analyzed the effects of the smells on both production and test code [1, 2, 4, 6, 10–13, 16–18]. For example, Garousi and Küçük [5] found more than 190 test smells on a literature review of 166 studies.

In this study, we selected 14 types of test smells, which are frequently studied and implemented in cutting-edge test smell detection tools [10, 13, 16]. These are described next:

- **Assertion Roulette (AR)**. It occurs when tests present assertions with no explanation in test methods. If one of those assertions fails, it is not possible to identify which one caused the problem;
- **Conditional Test Logic (CTL)**. It occurs when tests present conditional logic (if-else or repeat instructions). Tests with this structure do not guarantee that the same flow is verified, besides allowing a particular piece of code not to be tested;
- **Constructor Initialization (CI)**. This smell occurs when test methods present a constructor;
- **Eager Test (ET)**. It occurs when a test method checks many object methods at the same time. This test may be hard to understand, and to execute;
- **Empty Test (EpT)**. Occurs when test methods do not contain executable assertions;
- **For Testers Only (FTO)**. Occurs when a production class has methods only used by test methods;
- **General Fixture (GF)**. It occurs when the configuration file is generic, and different tests perform tests using part of configuration data. Those files may be hard to read, understand, and they may slower test execution;
- **Indirect Testing (IT)**. It occurs when test class has methods that perform tests in different objects because there are references to those objects at the test class, for example.
- **Magic Numbers (MN)**. Occurs when tests present a literal number as a test parameter;
- **Mystery Guest (MG)**. This smell occurs when the test uses an external resource, such as a file with test data. If the external file is removed, the test results may fail;

- **Redundant Print (RP)**. Occurs when test methods contain irrelevant print statements;
- **Resource Optimism (RO)**. It occurs when the test code contains optimist assumptions about the presence or absence of external resources. The test may return a positive result once, but it may fail for the next times;
- **Test Code Duplication (TCD)**. Occurs when test code has undesired duplication;
- **Test Run War (TRW)**. It occurs when a test passes only when it is performed isolated and fails when it is performed with another test at the same time.

3 Research Methodology

3.1 Survey Design

For this study, we used the design of observation by case control. It is a descriptive design used to investigate previous situations to support the understanding of a current phenomenon [7]. We are interested in detecting the most common practices that may introduce test smells. In the questionnaire, we did not use the *test smell* term or any of its synonymous not to influence the respondents. Instead, we transcribed the rationale for each test smell and converted them into practices for both test creation and execution. Once the respondents claim they commonly adopt a given practice, and the practice is the definition of a test smell, they assume that they either insert (during test creation) or identify (during test execution) a test smell. Table 1 shows examples of those practices.

The questionnaire was split into three blocks. The first one leverages the respondents' profile. It encompasses thirteen questions, aimed to identify respondents' age, gender, degree, and testing and programming skills. The second one encompasses fourteen statements and six complementary questions: four categorical objective questions and two open-ended questions. The statements describe practices related to test smells. The respondents chose one out of five possible answers (*always, frequently, rarely, never*, and *not applicable*) for each statement, where *always* indicates the adoption of bad practice for test creation. For example, the statement *"I've already created a test to validate a feature that would not be used in the production environment"* corresponds to the `For testers only` smell. Whether the answer was *"Always"*, it meant the respondent usually uses that practice in his daily tasks, and therefore it is likely he commonly inserts this smell in the test code he develops. The six complementary questions are designed to understand how the professionals deal with the test creation process.

The third block is similar to the second one. However, there are fourteen statements taking the perspective of who executes the tests, in which a high response rate (i.e., *Always*) indicates that a respondent usually come across tests with test smells; besides, there is one complementary open-ended question, aimed to understand which problems the professionals are likely to deal with when executing the tests.

Table 1. Examples of practices related to test smells.

Test Smell	Practices for Test Creation	Practices for Test Execution
Mystery Guest	I often create test cases using some configuration file (or supplementary) as support	A test case fails due to unavailability of access to some configuration file.
Eager Test	I often create tests with a high number of parameters (number of files, database record, etc.).	I run some tests without understanding what its purpose is.
Assertion Roulette	I pack different test cases into one (i.e., put together tests that could be run separately).	Some tests fail and it is not possible to identify the failure cause.
For Testers Only	I have already created a test to validate some feature that will not be used in the production environment	I run some tests to validate features that will not be used in the production environment.
Conditional Test Logic	I have already created conditional or repeating tests.	I run tests with conditional or repeating structure.
Empty Test	I have already created an empty test, with no executable statement.	I find empty test, with no executable statement.

It is worth mentioning that we executed a pilot survey with 4 professionals to identify improvement opportunities. Based on their responses, we could improve the questionnaire prior to running the actual survey.

The questionnaire used in this survey is available online[4]. Data were gathered from April 3rd to June 3rd in 2019.

3.2 Data analysis

To answer RQ1, we analyzed the objective questions about test creation and test execution related to test smells. Each question encompassed an affirmative statement aimed to describe daily practices in software testing, such as *"I usually found empty test"* and *"I usually create test with part of external configuration file"*.

For RQ2, we compared the professional experience with the frequency of the use of test smells. We also used the same answer format as RQ1, but only considered the test creation process. During the test execution process, professionals identify test smells instead of creating them.

To answer RQ3, we grouped the practices by frequency to identify which ones are most commonly used. The practices may be associated to one or more test

[4] A copy of the questionnaire is available online at `https://bit.ly/2RQVDdc`

smells according to their characteristics, such as external file usage, conditional structure, and programming style.

The three open questions were analyzed through coding and continuous comparison [8]. Our main intention was to understand the reasons that might lead the software engineers to use practices that may insert test smells. Besides, we were also intended to understand which difficulties they come across when creating and executing tests. The coding task was performed by two researchers and validated by consensus. We also associated some of the practices with the test code characteristics defined by Meszaros et al. [10].

Since the questionnaire encompasses both close-ended and open-ended questions, after data collection, we employed open coding to identify additional reasons on why professionals use bad practices on testing activities. Codes were peer-reviewed and changed upon agreement with the authors of this paper. Considering that open questions were optional, we used coding to complement our results.

4 Results

4.1 Participants

We sent the invitation to professionals from eight Brazilian companies in a convenience sampling. We created one copy of the questionnaire for each of these companies (C1-C8) and sent them by email. The different versions of the questionnaire served to control the number of respondents from each company. Those companies have from 4 to 66 testing professionals, who perform both manual and automated tests, as Table 2 shows.

Besides, we also sent the questionnaire by direct message (D1) and posted it on a Facebook group dedicated to discussing software testing (G1). In total, 305 professionals were contacted.

As a result, we received 60 answers[5] (out of 305 potential respondents) from three different states in Brazil: BA (66.7%), SP (31.7%), and PR (1.6%). The respondents were from 22 to 41 years old, and their experience with quality assurance ranged from 0 to 13 years (5.16 on average). The experience as software developers also ranged from 0 to 13 years (average 1.67). Most of the respondents were male (65%), but results also showed female (32%) and non-binary gender (3%). Most of them hold a degree in Computer Science-related courses (83.3%), some of them hold a degree in other STEM courses (10%), and some of them hold a degree in other areas (6.7%). 90% of the respondents pursued higher education degrees, as follows: 66.7% hold a bachelor's degree, 21.7% hold a graduate degree, and 1.6% hold a postdoc.

Regarding their commonly performed software testing tasks, most of the respondents reported creating and running tests at the same rate (43.3%); but also executed tests with more frequency than they created (21.7%); and created tests with more frequency than they executed (13.3%). Moreover, some respondents only executed test cases (20%); and other respondents only created

[5] Raw data with all the answers (PT-BR) are available at `https://bit.ly/33ZOESi`

Table 2. respondents

Source	Professionals	Answers	Source	Professionals	Answers
C1	66	14	C6	4	4
C2	30	1	C7	4	4
C3	10	0	C8	4	0
C4	6	0	D1	52	35
C5	5	0	G1	124	2

them (1.7%). They performed tests over many different platforms, and most of them (53%) worked with two or more platforms: Web (65%), Android (58%), Desktop (48%), and Apple (28%) applications. Backend, microservices, API, mainframe, and cable TV had 1.67% each.

Usually, professionals tested solutions for mobile device applications (65%) and web applications (60%). We also identified the following domains they work with: embedded systems (23,33%), cloud computing (18,33%), information security (11,67%), internet of things (6,67%), big data, retail, artificial intelligence, cable tv, bioinformatics, commercial information, desktop system, and payment solutions (1,67% each one). The sources of test creation were requirements (48%); developed software (45%); source code and use cases (2% each); and 3% did not know the source.

4.2 Test creation and execution practices

Gathered data made it possible to establish a relationship between test creation and execution practices and the occurrence of test smells. Figure 1 summarizes such a relationship, by showing the frequency of test smells usage during (a) test creation and (b) test execution processes, based on the responses. We next discuss the main results.

The search for test duplication was a personal practice for most of the respondents (48%). In some cases, it was also a company practice (18%), or even both, respondent and company practices (6%). However, for 28% of respondents, this activity was not applied. Checking tests with the same objective reduces the **Test Duplication** smell.

During the test creation process, **Conditional Test Logic** and **General Fixture** were the most frequent test smells. The former obtained 47% of *Always* and *Frequently* answers, and the latter, 45% in both answers, as Figure 1(a) shows. A high rate of those responses may indicate a common use of practices related to those smells. We also analyzed why developers create tests with bad practices (one open non-mandatory question answered by 45% of respondents). The main reasons are related to company or personally employed standards, limited time, and attempt to reach better coverage and efficiency.

We also asked whether they have already changed existing test sets because they found the bad practices we presented. 12% of respondents always perform any changes in the test code, when they find test smells-related practices; 38%

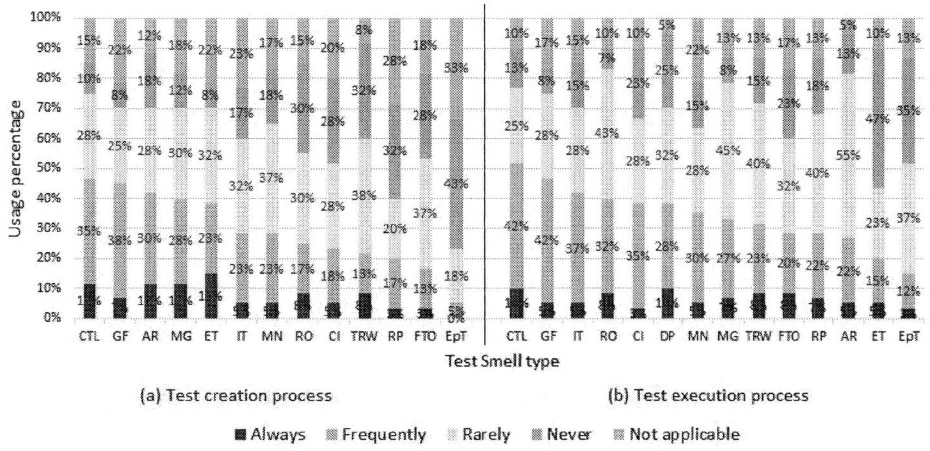

Fig. 1. Test Smells frequencies on test creation and execution.

frequently change them; 27% rarely; 12% never edit test code, and 11% answered as not applicable. Among the reasons to change the test, they informed that changing it reduces ambiguities (30%); improves execution speed (27%); they need to adequate it to company standards (23%); they change it when they do not understand the test purpose (13%); and when the corresponding production class evolves (7%).

Furthermore, the respondents had to point out which test structure problems they face. The results indicated that some tests depended on third party resources (52%); were hard to understand (48%); contained either unnecessary information or were ambiguous (40% each); depended on external files (33%); used external configuration file (10%); and presented resources limitation (2%).

Regarding difficulties in creating test cases (one open non-mandatory question answered by 38% of respondents), requirement issues were the most frequent ones (56%). Other problems were related to difficulties in performing test code reuse, lack of knowledge, issues in production code, code coverage, test environment problems, and time and resources limitation.

The questions regarding test execution also presented a sequence of statements about ordinary situations the developers usually face, in which respondents should answer according to frequency. **Conditional Test Logic** (52%) and **General Fixture** (47%) were the test smells most cited during test execution, as Figure 1(b) shows.

The most cited problem related to test execution refers to difficulties involving the test environment (34%). Some of the cited issues were related to the unavailability of the test environment, the demand for 3rd party features, or even low-performance environments. The second most common problem is associated with understanding the test purpose (28%). They informed that tests are poorly written, which allow multiple interpretations, besides lack of writing

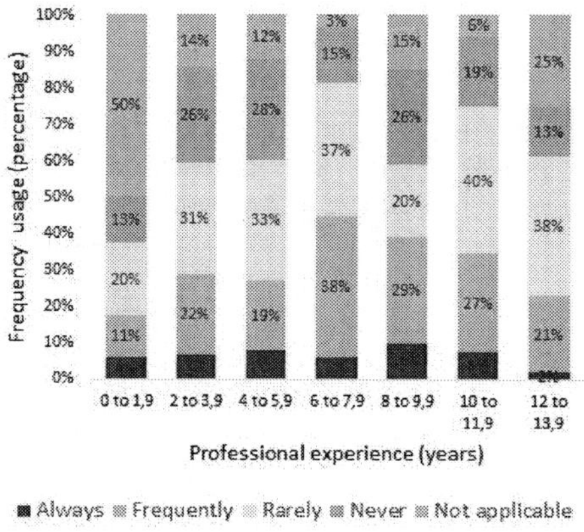

Fig. 2. Test Smells frequencies on test creation according professional experience.

standard. Lack of test maintenance was the third problem (24%), which involves outdated and incomplete tests due to the evolution of the system code.

4.3 Professional Experience

Although most respondents reported they create and execute tests at the same proportion, our investigation presents a different scenario as the tester gets more experienced. For the first two years of experience, there was a predominance of test execution. 64% only executed tests; 9% frequently executed tests and occasionally created them, and 27% created and executed them at the same proportion. Over the years, mainly after 10 years of experience, practitioners tend to create more tests than execute them. We found that the ones who only created tests had at least 12 years of professional experience. Thus, the less experienced the tester, the less number of tests they create and the more tests they execute.

We also analyzed the use of good practices to create tests as professionals become more experienced. During the creation of a test, the use of good practices tends to increase over the years, as *Rarely* and *Never* got more responses than the remainder. However, gathered data showed a slight reduction between eight and ten years, but it grows back from ten years of experience. On the other hand, the use of bad practices also increases over the years, with *Always* and *Frequently* gaining more responses, to respondents with up to eight years of experience, and decreasing thereafter, as Figure 2 shows.

5 Discussion

5.1 Test design practices that lead to test smells insertion (RQ1)

We observed that some practices might lead to the introduction of test smells in test code. Therefore, we analyzed the frequency of those practices for test creation and execution.

In the former, we observed that every test smell presented at least three out of four possible answers (*Always, Frequently, Rarely, and Never*). We then classified such gathered data into two groups: Commonly-used practices group (CPG) and the Unused practices group (UPG). CPG contains test smells that mostly present *Always* and *Frequently* as answers, and UPG that mostly present *Rarely* and *Never* as answers. We consider a test smell belonging to one of the groups when the difference between the rates of *Always* and *Frequently* versus *Rarely* and *Never* is greater than 10%. For example, `Empty Test, For testers only, Test run War, Constructor Initialization, Resource Optimism, Redundant Print, Magic Number, Indirect test` belong to the UPG group, which means professionals rarely insert those smells on testing activities. Conversely, professionals frequently adopt practices related to `General Fixture`, the only member of the CPG group. Thus, it is possible that they create many tests with that smell, which may compromise test maintenance [15]. Still, four test smells presented a similar frequency of pertinence to both groups (less than 10% of difference). For them, there was not a pattern among respondents. For instance, the `Eager Test` smell obtained 38% to CPG and 40% to UPG.

In the latter, UPG contains the following test smells: `Empty Test, Eager Test, Assertion Roulette, Redundant Print, Duplicated Test, Test Run War, For testers Only, Mystery Guest, Constructor Initialization, and Resource Optimism`, which means that professionals rarely face those smells during testing. On the other hand, professionals frequently find practices related to two test smells, which are part of CPG: `General Fixture` and `Conditional Test Logic`. Besides, other two test smells presented a similar frequency of pertinence to both groups, `Indirect Test` and `Magic Number`. Thus, there is no perceived standard among respondents for them. In general, our study identified that all test smells we analyzed appear in the testing activities. They all were cited by respondents, even rarely.

We also analyzed the reasons that lead professionals to adopt the practices presented in the survey. Since this data came from open-ended questions, we identified 16 different codes, in which the most common ones are: *company standard, personal standard, project politics, professional experience, saving time* and *improving coverage.* For example, professional #26 reported applying company standards when creating tests, and those standards may insert smells. He said he commonly applies bad practices *"to match company development standards."* Otherwise, professional #54 reported personal standard when said that *"I group tests by module so that tests can be executed sequentially without compromising effectiveness."* This behavior also indicates that participants may have misunderstood the definition of test smells. When grouping tests, it is possible to insert the `Assertion Roulette` test smell and to compromise test independence. Similar situation occurred to professionals #14, #16, #27, #50 and #59.

Table 3 summarizes the answers for each RQ.

Table 3. Summary of answers for each research question.

RQ	Answer
RQ1	We found that professionals do adopt practices for test case design, which introduce test smells. Usually, those practices come from improper personal and company standards.
RQ2	Experienced software testing professionals may not produce less test smells than inexperienced ones.
RQ3	The practices most present in the daily life of professionals that lead to test smells insertion were the use of conditional structure or repetition and the use of generic configuration data.

5.2 Professional experience and its interference on test smell insertion (RQ2)

Although we analyzed the experience of practitioners and its influence on the adoption of practices that introduce test smells, we have not identified any clear correlation. For example, the *Always* option indicates they always use bad practices. Regarding the test creation process, we cannot infer that inexperienced professionals introduce more smells on tests than the experienced ones. We found the following rates (from less experienced to the most experienced professionals): 6% of professionals from 0-2 work years answered *Always*, 7% to 2-4 work years, 8% to 4-6, 6% to 6-8, 10% to 8-10, 8% 10-12 and 2% for over 10 years.

When testers are inexperienced programmers, they may write lower quality tests, but when they are more experienced, they can carry programming biases that may also contain bad practices. The absence of a tendency indicates a non-behavioral change between less and more experienced software testing professionals.

5.3 Professional practices that might lead to introducing test smells (RQ3)

Tests can be performed either manually or automatically. Although there are specific tools to support test automation [3, 14], 62% of respondents perform more manual than automated tests. In addition, they are also inexperienced in software development; 55% have no experience with software development (less than 2 years of experience on average). Lack of experience with software development in general may contribute to the use of bad practices.

According to the practices explored in this study, we identified that two development activities are very present in professionals' daily life: *(ii) the use of generic configuration data*, which produces `General Fixture`. This smell is the most frequent on test creation and execution processes for CPG; and *(i) the use of conditional structure or repetition*, which is directly associated to

`Conditional Test logic` smell. It was the second most detected smell on test execution (CPG group).

Professionals indicated they commonly face several problems with tests, such as poorly written tests and outdated and incomplete test procedures. According to them, when tests are associated with generic configuration data, test case gets hard to understand and also may cause incorrect results due to the lack of maintenance. Moreover, the presence of conditional logic on tests does not make it clear which structure of the production code is being covered. Understanding which practices are most prevalent in the professionals' activities supports improving test quality. Other problems are related to incomplete, outdated, or lack of documentation, which make difficult to reach traceability, evolution, and maintenance testing tasks.

6 Threats to validity

Internal validity. Although there are more than 100 test smells, this study only considered 14 of them. However, we selected the most frequently smells discussed in the literature. In addition, the smells were presented in the survey as practices. To mitigate ambiguities and text comprehension, we applied a pilot with 4 testers from different companies.

External validity. We sent the survey to 305 professionals, but only received 60 answers. Although our results may not generalize, they provide an initial view of the practices adopted by testers. Despite the limitations, we performed the survey procedure and data was made available to allow further replications of this study.

Construct validity. During the survey, it was not informed that the questions referred to test smells to do not influence the results. For open questions, a peer-reviewed coding process was performed to avoid bias. The survey and answers were written in Portuguese and translated into English by one author, but reviewed by all others.

Conclusion validity. Since this is a qualitative study, we cannot use a statistical argument to generalize the results. We mitigated this threat by sending the questionnaire to different companies and states of Brazil.

7 Related work

Bavota et al. [2] presented a case study to investigate the impact of test smells on maintenance activities. In that study, developers and students analyzed testing code to compare whether their experience would make a difference in identifying test smells. As a result, they identified that test smells have a significantly negative impact on maintenance activities. Conversely, our study identified for the professionals that we surveyed, the experience does not interfere in the test smell introduction during the creation and execution of a test.

Palomba and Zaidman [12] conducted a study to analyze the relationship between test smells and flaky tests. They analyzed test smells identified in a multivocal review and detected five flakiness-inducing test smell types [5]. After that, a semi-structured interview was conducted with 10 developers with more than 10 years of experience. As a result, no new test smell was found as a flakiness-inducing, and the five previously identified test smells were ratified. In our study, we were careful not to use the expression test smell as a means to prevent any influence on the respondents' answers. Besides, professionals with different backgrounds participated in the survey.

Tufano et al. [15] proposed a study with 19 participants to investigate developers' perception of test smells. They performed an empirical investigation to analyze where test smells occur at source code. The results showed that developers generally do not recognize test smells, and they are usually introduced since the first commit at the repository. Our study found that most of the professionals frequently adopt practices that lead to smells. However, we use the term *practices* instead of *test smells*. We did not find any study investigating how professional practices affect the introduction of test smells.

8 Concluding Remarks

Test smells may decrease the quality and maintenance of the testing code. Our study aimed at identifying whether professionals know that they introduce smells during test activities, besides understanding whether professional experience influences the adoption of test smells. Our initial results showed that they commit bad practices out of habit or because they follow company standards. We also found that no bad practice was utterly unknown, and all 14 are adopted, even if rarely.

Furthermore, we found that experienced professionals do not insert a few smells than inexperienced ones. As future work, we intend to extend this study to understand better how the industry deals with test smells. We also intend to investigate which techniques companies and professionals could adopt to reduce vices that may lead to test smells.

Acknowledgments. This research was partially funded by INES 2.0; CNPq grants 465614/2014-0 and 408356/2018-9 and FAPESB grant JCB0060/2016.

References

1. Bavota, G., Qusef, A., Oliveto, R., Lucia, A., Binkley, D.: An empirical analysis of the distribution of unit test smells and their impact on software maintenance. In: 28th IEEE International Conference on Software Maintenance (ICSM) (2012)
2. Bavota, G., Qusef, A., Oliveto, R., Lucia, A., Binkley, D.: Are test smells really harmful? An empirical study. Empirical Software Engineering **20**(4) (2015)
3. Fraser, G., Arcuri, A.: Evosuite: Automatic test suite generation for object-oriented software. In: 13th European Conference on Foundations of Software Engineering. ESEC/FSE, ACM, New York, NY, USA (2011)

4. Garousi, V., Felderer, M.: Developing, verifying, and maintaining high-quality automated test scripts. IEEE Software **33**(3) (2016)
5. Garousi, V., Küçük, B.: Smells in software test code: A survey of knowledge in industry and academia. Journal of systems and software **138** (2018)
6. Greiler, M., van Deursen, A., Storey, M.: Automated detection of test fixture strategies and smells. In: 2013 IEEE Sixth International Conference on Software Testing, Verification and Validation (2013)
7. Kitchenham, B.A., Pfleeger, S.L.: Principles of survey research part 2: designing a survey. ACM SIGSOFT Software Engineering Notes **27**(1) (2002)
8. Kitchenham, B.A., Budgen, D., Brereton, P.: Evidence-based software engineering and systematic reviews, vol. 4. CRC press (2015)
9. Linåker, J., Sulaman, S.M., Maiani de Mello, R., Höst, M.: Guidelines for conducting surveys in software engineering. Tech. rep., [Publisher information missing] (2015), `https://lup.lub.lu.se/search/ws/files/6062997/5463412.pdf`
10. Meszaros, G., Smith, S.M., Andrea, J.: The test automation manifesto. In: Maurer, F., Wells, D. (eds.) Extreme Programming and Agile Methods - XP/Agile Universe 2003. Springer Berlin Heidelberg (2003)
11. Palomba, F., Di Nucci, D., Panichella, A., Oliveto, R., De Lucia, A.: On the diffusion of test smells in automatically generated test code: An empirical study. In: 9th International Workshop on Search-based Software Testing. ACM (2016)
12. Palomba, F., Zaidman, A.: The smell of fear: On the relation between test smells and flaky tests. Empirical Software Engineering (2019)
13. Peruma, A.S.A.: What the Smell? An Empirical Investigation on the Distribution and Severity of Test Smells in Open Source Android Applications. PhD Thesis, Rochester Institute of Technology (2018)
14. Smeets, N., Simons, A.J.: Automated unit testing with Randoop, JWalk and μJava versus manual JUnit testing. Research report, Department of Computer Science, University of Sheffield/University of Antwerp, Sheffield, Antwerp (2011)
15. Tufano, M., Palomba, F., Bavota, G., Di Penta, M., Oliveto, R., De Lucia, A., Poshyvanyk, D.: An empirical investigation into the nature of test smells. In: 31st International Conference on Automated Software Engineering. IEEE (2016)
16. Van Deursen, A., Moonen, L., Van Den Bergh, A., Kok, G.: Refactoring test code. In: Proceedings of the 2nd international conference on extreme programming and flexible processes in software engineering (XP) (2001)
17. Van Rompaey, B., Du Bois, B., Demeyer, S.: Characterizing the relative significance of a test smell. In: 22nd International Conference on Software Maintenance (2006)
18. Virgínio, T., Santana, R., Martins, L.A., Soares, L.R., Costa, H., Machado, I.: On the influence of test smells on test coverage. In: Proceedings of the XXXIII Brazilian Symposium on Software Engineering. ACM (2019)
19. Wiederseiner, C., Jolly, S.A., Garousi, V., Eskandar, M.M.: An open-source tool for automated generation of black-box xunit test code and its industrial evaluation. In: Bottaci, L., Fraser, G. (eds.) Testing – Practice and Research Techniques. Springer Berlin Heidelberg (2010)
20. Yusifoğlu, V.G., Amannejad, Y., Can, A.B.: Software test-code engineering: A systematic mapping. Information and Software Technology **58** (2015)

Technical knowledge and soft skills in the founding teams of software startups

Gerardo Matturro[1], Martín Solari[1], Angélica Buffa[1] and Diego Febbles[1]

[1] Universidad ORT Uruguay, Montevideo, Uruguay
matturro@uni.ort.edu.uy, martin.solari@ort.edu.uy,
buffa.angelica@gmail.com, diegofebles@gmail.com

Abstract. A software technology startup is an emerging company focused on the creation and development of an innovative software-intensive product or service as the basis for creating business value. Essential elements for the success of the venture are, among others, the technical knowledge, experience, and skills that the members of the team of founders have in relation to the needs and challenges of the venture. This paper presents the results of a field study whose purpose was to identify the most valued technical and soft skills in the founding team of software startups. Based on semi-structured interviews with founders of 10 software ventures, the technical knowledge to perform market analysis, define the business model, and develop the business plan appear as the most necessary, while motivation, leadership, and ability to learn from experience appear as the most important soft skills. On the other hand, as the startup grows, other knowledge and skills become more valued, such as financial knowledge, due to the need to sell the product or service, or to find investment, and soft skills like opportunity recognition, and resilience.

Keywords: software startups, technical knowledge, soft skills.

1 Introducción

Un emprendimiento (startup) tecnológico de software es una empresa de reciente creación con escaso o nulo historial operativo, enfocada en la creación y desarrollo de un producto o servicio innovador intensivo en software como base para la creación de valor de negocio [1], [2]. Entre los principales desafíos de los emprendimientos de software es frecuente que se mencionen su escasez de recursos, ser altamente reactivas, estar formadas por pequeños equipos con poca experiencia, confiar en un solo producto, y comenzar a operar en condiciones de incertidumbre, de rápida evolución, con presión del tiempo, altos riesgos y dependencia [2].

Según Unterkalmsteiner y colegas [1], estas condiciones ameritan la realización de estudios empíricos orientados a identificar qué conocimientos y habilidades de desarrollo de software son necesarios para superar esos desafíos, así como para conocer cómo cambian las necesidades de conocimientos y habilidades a lo largo de la evolución de las nuevas empresas de software y de qué manera se gestiona ese cambio.

Según mencionan Hallam y Flannary, diversos estudios han demostrado que la probabilidad de éxito de una nueva empresa en una industria dinámica aumenta si el emprendimiento incluye profesionales capacitados en las diversas disciplinas esenciales para competir en una economía global compleja. Otros estudios han demostrado que el equipo original de fundadores puede no tener la capacidad de guiar al emprendimiento desde la etapa inicial a través de un rápido crecimiento [3].

Por su parte, Tanner considera que el éxito o el fracaso de un emprendimiento empresarial se relaciona con la calidad de las personas que componen el equipo inicial de fundadores, y la nueva compañía florecerá o fracasará dependiendo de lo bien que reclute, construya y retenga al equipo [4], así como de los conocimientos, habilidades técnicas y destrezas que los miembros de ese equipo tengan en relación con las necesidades y desafíos del emprendimiento. Similar opinión presentan Seppänen y colegas, para quienes es crucial que un emprendimiento pueda obtener y disponer de los conocimientos, habilidades y capacidades necesarios para crear un producto basado en la innovación [5].

El propósito de este artículo es reportar los resultados de un trabajo de campo orientado a identificar cuáles son los conocimientos técnicos y las habilidades blandas más valorados en el equipo fundador al inicio de un emprendimiento de software, y cómo evolucionan estas necesidades a medida que el emprendimiento crece.

El resto de este artículo está organizado de la siguiente manera. En la sección 2 se presenta una breve revisión de la literatura general sobre los conceptos de conocimientos técnicos y habilidades blandas, así como de los conocimientos y habilidades específicamente considerados para este trabajo. La sección 3 explican el diseño metodológico del estudio donde se exponen las preguntas de investigación, la selección de los emprendimientos de software a estudiar y los informantes claves, así como los procedimientos de recolección, preparación, y análisis de datos. En la sección 4 se presentan los principales resultados obtenidos, mientras que en la sección 5 se discuten estos resultados. La sección 6 aborda las amenazas a la validez de este estudio y en la sección 7 se presentan las conclusiones y se esbozan los trabajos futuros.

2 Antecedentes

En esta sección presentamos una breve revisión de la literatura general (no limitada al área de ingeniería de software) sobre los conceptos de conocimientos técnicas y habilidades blandas, así como de los conocimientos y habilidades consideradas para este estudio.

2.1 Los conceptos de conocimientos técnicos y de habilidades blandas

El concepto de "conocimientos técnicos" refiere a la capacidad técnica y el conocimiento factual necesario para hacer el trabajo, y son las competencias técnicas que posee un individuo, adquiridas a través del aprendizaje educativo y su aplicación práctica [6], que generalmente se asocian con el conocimiento necesario para la comprensión y ejecución de tareas y procesos [7].

Por su parte, las denominadas "habilidades blandas" se definen como la combinación de las habilidades, actitudes, hábitos y rasgos de personalidad que permiten a las personas desempeñarse mejor en el lugar de trabajo, complementando los conocimientos técnicos necesarios para hacer su trabajo e influyendo en la forma en que se comportan e interactúan con los demás [8].

Ha habido un reconocimiento creciente por parte de los investigadores; gerentes, representantes de la industria, y formuladores de políticas educativas que las habilidades blandas son cruciales para promover el crecimiento personal y colectivo para crear nuevas prácticas en contextos profesionales, vocacionales y educativos. Hoy en día, las habilidades blandas se reconocen como competencias transversales que existen en una relación recíproca con los conocimientos técnicos complementando cualquier esfera de la vida humana (personal, social o profesional). Por esta razón, los conocimientos técnicos y las habilidades blandas no están destinados a competir entre sí, sino a ser complementarios, y no pueden considerarse a unos más relevantes que a las otras [9].

2.2 Conocimientos y habilidades del equipo emprendedor

Para Shane y colegas, los emprendedores deben tener "algo de conocimiento" sobre la industria y los mercados en los que están involucrados y la tecnología que es relevante para el éxito proyectado de las actividades empresariales. Además, los emprendedores deben tener ciertas habilidades, cuyo rango depende de las circunstancias, a las que se puede recurrir durante las diversas etapas del proceso empresarial, y mencionan a modo de ejemplo venta y negociación, liderazgo, planificación, toma de decisiones, resolución de problemas, trabajo en equipo, comunicación y gestión de conflictos. Estos autores sostienen que los emprendedores pueden contratar personas para llenar los vacíos en su propio "conjunto de habilidades"; sin embargo, consideran que no pueden confiar en otros para el conocimiento sobre la industria y la tecnología que es crucial para establecer el curso correcto durante el proceso empresarial [10].

2.3 Conocimientos y habilidades consideradas para este estudio

En relación con los conocimientos técnicos, en la literatura se hace énfasis en que para iniciar y evolucionar un emprendimiento es necesario que el equipo fundador tenga ciertas categorías de conocimientos y habilidades, tales como capacidad de gestión [11], [12], competencias de negocio [11], capacidad de producción [11], y competencias financieras [11], [12].

Los conocimientos técnicos de gestión, de negocios, y financieros considerados para este estudio fueron seleccionados de los artículos referidos en el párrafo anterior.

En relación con los conocimientos de "producción", éstos refieren a la capacidad de procesar productos, desde materias primas hasta productos terminados, e incluye las capacidades técnicas requeridas para desarrollar el proceso de producción. Para el caso particular de los emprendimientos tecnológicos de software, esta "capacidad de producción" corresponde a los conocimientos necesarios para la "creación y desarrollo de un producto o servicio innovador intensivo en software como base para la creación de valor de negocio", según la definición dada al comienzo de este artículo. Con esta definición, los conocimientos técnicos de esta categoría considerados para este estudio fueron seleccionados de [13], [14], y [15].

El conjunto de conocimientos técnicos de las categorías anteriores considerados para este estudio se muestra en la Tabla 1.

Table 1. Categorías de conocimientos técnicos de este estudio

Categorías	Conocimientos técnicos
Producción	Ingeniería de requisitos, Prototipación, Modelado de sistemas, Diseño de experiencia de usuario, Diseño arquitectónico, Codificación, Testing, Procesos de software, Infraestructura
Gestión	Metodologías ágiles, Planificación y gestión de proyecto, Gestión de calidad, Gestión del cambio
Habilidades de negocio	Análisis FODA, Análisis de mercado, Análisis del entorno, Definir un modelo de negocio, Definir un plan de negocio, Marketing
Habilidades financieras	Conocimientos contables básicos, Planificación y presupuestación, Confección y análisis de flujos de caja, Análisis de inversiones

Con respecto a las "habilidades blandas", diversos autores han tratado de definir y caracterizar este término, pero el entendimiento general es que es una tarea difícil de realizar, porque es un concepto amplio, que abarca muchas dimensiones del desarrollo de la esfera personal, y que involucra una combinación de componentes emocionales, conductuales y cognitivos; debido a esto, es arduo determinar qué incluir o excluir en su definición. Como forma de ampliar la base del estudio de campo, las habilidades blandas consideradas para este estudio fueron tomadas de diversas fuentes [16], [17], [18], y aparecen listadas en la Tabla 5.

2.4 Trabajos relacionados

Si bien el estudio de las competencias emprendedoras en general es extenso, son relativamente muy pocos los trabajos encontrados en la literatura referidos específicamente a los conocimientos técnicos y habilidades blandas más valoradas para los emprendimientos tecnológicos de software.

En este ámbito en particular, Santisteban y Mauricio identificaron, a partir de una revisión sistemática de literatura sobre factores de éxito en emprendimientos en tecnologías de la información, las siguientes categorías de conocimientos y habilidades en el equipo fundador: experiencia en el sector industrial, formación académica, conocimientos tecnológicos y de negocio, habilidades de comunicación y de negociación, y liderazgo [19].

Seppänen y colegas, por su parte, centraron su estudio en los conocimientos técnicos y mencionan las categorías de desarrollo de software y conocimientos del dominio de aplicación como las más relevantes [5].

3 Diseño metodológico

El diseño metodológico consistió en la definición de las preguntas de investigación, la selección de los informantes claves, la elaboración del instrumento de recolección de datos, su aplicación en entrevistas personales semi-estructuradas, la lectura crítica y codificación de las respuestas obtenidas, y el análisis y la interpretación de los resultados obtenidos.

3.1 Preguntas de investigación

- RQ1: ¿Cuáles son los conocimientos técnicos más valorados en el equipo fundador de un emprendimiento de software?
- RQ2: ¿Cuáles son las habilidades blandas más valoradas en el equipo fundador de un emprendimiento de software?
- RQ3: ¿Cómo evolucionan las necesidades de nuevos conocimientos y habilidades requeridas por el equipo fundador cuando el emprendimiento crece?

3.2 Informantes claves

Según Hernández Sampieri y colegas [20] el muestreo cualitativo (como es el caso de este estudio) es propositivo, y las primeras acciones para elegir la muestra ocurren desde el planteamiento mismo del problema de investigación y cuando se selecciona el contexto en el cual se esperan encontrar los casos que interesan. Para estos autores, en los estudios cualitativos el tamaño de la muestra no es importante desde una perspectiva probabilística pues lo que se busca en la indagación cualitativa es profundidad. Lo que interesa son casos o unidades (participantes, organizaciones, eventos, etc.) que ayuden a entender el fenómeno de estudio y a responder a las preguntas de investigación.

Los diez emprendimientos participantes de este estudio son empresas emergentes incubadas o en proceso de incubación en el Centro de Innovación y Emprendimientos (CIE)[1], incubadora universitaria de la Universidad ORT Uruguay.

[1] https://cie.ort.edu.uy/

3.3 Recolección de datos

La recolección de datos fue realizada mediante entrevistas semi-estructuradas a los informantes claves, siguiendo las pautas establecidas en un cuestionario elaborado a tales efectos, y utilizado como guion para desarrollar cada entrevista.

El proceso de recolección de los datos fue el siguiente:

- Coordinar entrevistas a los informantes claves de las empresas participantes, poniendo especial cuidado en que cumplan con el criterio de **pertenecer al equipo fundador del emprendimiento**.
- Durante cada entrevista se utilizó el cuestionario mencionado arriba para ir preguntando sobre los aspectos de interés para la investigación, y se solicita aclaración o ampliación en caso necesario.
- Cada entrevista fue grabada, con la autorización del entrevistado, de modo de tener una referencia posterior para extraer las respuestas a las preguntas formuladas.

Las preguntas formuladas durante las entrevistas estuvieron directamente vinculadas a la obtención de información para dar respuesta a las preguntas de investigación planteadas. En particular, para la identificación de los conocimientos técnicos y las habilidades blandas más valoradas, se le presentó a cada entrevistado una lista de conocimientos y otra de habilidades, seleccionadas según se indicó en la sección 2.3. Cada elemento de las listas podía ser valorado según una escala de Likert con una de las siguientes opciones: "No necesaria", "Poco necesaria", "Neutral", "Muy necesaria", "Imprescindible".

El guión para las entrevistas y las transcripciones de las respuestas pueden obtenerse del primer autor.

4 Resultados obtenidos

En esta sección se muestran datos demográficos relevantes de los emprendimientos participantes de este estudio y se presentan las respuestas a las preguntas de investigación planteadas.

4.1 Sobre los emprendimientos de software participantes y sus fundadores

Se realizaron entrevistas a fundadores de diez emprendimientos de software, con diferente grado de desarrollo, según se muestra en la Tabla 2.

Table 2. Grado de desarrollo de los emprendimientos

Grado de desarrollo	Cantidad
Egresadas	5
En incubación	3
Abandonaron	2

En la tabla, "Egresadas" significa que los emprendimientos finalizaron con éxito el proceso de incubación, mientras que "Abandonaron" significa que no completaron ese proceso de incubación.

De los diez emprendimientos considerados en este estudio, la Tabla 3 muestra las cantidades de emprendimientos en función de la formación de grado de al menos uno de los fundadores.

Table 3. Formación de grado de fundadores de los emprendimientos

Formación de grado	Cantidad
Ingeniería y desarrollo de software	7
Administración y Negocios	3
Otras disciplinas	1

En particular, uno de los emprendimientos tiene un fundador con formación en Administración y negocios, y sus otros dos fundadores con formación en Ingeniería y desarrollo de software (contado dos veces en la tabla). El emprendimiento que aparece con formación de grado "Otras disciplinas" tiene un fundador con formación en Gestión agropecuaria y el otro fundador es Dr. en Ciencias Veterinarias.

4.2 Conocimientos técnicos más valorados en el equipo fundador (RQ1)

En cada entrevista se presentó una lista de conocimientos técnicos a los entrevistados, con la posibilidad de agregar elementos. En la Tabla 4 se presentan los diez tipos de conocimientos técnicos más valorados por parte de los informantes claves entrevistados. En todos los casos, los entrevistados marcaron las diferentes opciones como "Muy necesaria" o "Imprescindible". Por este motivo, para distinguir y ponderar la importancia relativa asignada a cada conocimiento, el método de ponderación consistió en asignarle a cada respuesta "Muy Necesaria" 1 punto, y a cada respuesta "Imprescindible" 2 puntos. Para cada habilidad incluida en el cuestionario se suma el total de respuestas ponderadas (Muy necesaria e Imprescindible). Para armar el ranking, se ordena la tabla de mayor a menor por cantidad de respuestas ponderadas. Al no haber respuestas del tipo "No necesaria" y "Poco necesaria", estos valores no afectan el resultado de la ponderación

Table 4. Conocimientos técnicos más valorados en el equipo fundador

Conocimientos técnicos	Importancia
Análisis de mercado	18
Definir un modelo de negocio	16
Definir un plan de negocio	14

Diseño de experiencia de usuario	13
Infraestructura	13
Testing	12
Gestión de calidad	12
Codificación	12
Prototipación	12
Planificación y presupuestación	12

4.3 Habilidades blandas más valoradas en el equipo fundador (RQ2)

En relación con las habilidades blandas necesarias en el equipo de fundadores, la Tabla 5 lista el ranking de las diez habilidades blandas mencionadas como más necesarias. Se presentan ordenadas descendentemente, según la importancia asignada por los entrevistados, ponderada de la misma manera que la utilizada en 4.2.

Table 5. Habilidades blandas más valoradas en el equipo fundador

Habilidad blanda	Importancia
Motivación y perseverancia	19
Adaptabilidad	18
Aprender a través de la experiencia	18
Liderazgo	18
Resiliencia	18
Creación de valor	17
Aprovechamiento de recursos	16
Comunicación	15
Reconocimiento de oportunidades	15
Transmitir una visión convincente	15

4.4 Evolución de los conocimientos y las habilidades requeridas (RQ3)

En relación con los conocimientos técnicos adquiridos durante el desarrollo del emprendimiento, siete entrevistados mencionan haber adquirido fundamentalmente conocimientos de negocio, de los cuales destacan: análisis del mercado, análisis del entorno, definir un modelo de negocio, definir un plan de negocio, y marketing. De los conocimientos financieros, tres indican haber adquirido conocimientos contables básicos, y análisis de inversión. En menor medida, se mencionan los conocimientos de las categorías de gestión y de producción: gestión de la calidad, gestión del cambio, planificación de proyectos, codificación, prototipación, diseño gráfico, infraestructura. Esto último debido a que la mayoría de los fundadores entrevistados tienen formación de grado en ingeniería y desarrollo de software y, en consecuencia, ya tenían estos conocimientos en forma previa al inicio del emprendimiento.

Respecto a la evolución de los conocimientos técnicos, cinco entrevistados coinciden en que los conocimientos necesarios van cambiando a medida que el emprendimiento crece. Según dos fundadores, al inicio del emprendimiento es relevante tener los conocimientos técnicos para implementar un Producto Mínimo Viable, principalmente codificación y negocios; pero a medida que el emprendimiento evoluciona, estas habilidades pueden perder importancia en pos de otras que permiten hacer frente a nuevos desafíos asociados a la evolución del emprendimiento. Por ejemplo, los conocimientos financieros y de gestión de proyectos se tornan más necesarios en etapas más tardías, en detrimento de la codificación. Uno de los emprendedores entrevistados destaca que las habilidades de negocio son necesarias cíclicamente. También se pone de manifiesto que, frente a la escasez de recursos característica de los emprendimientos, los fundadores deben adquirir sobre la marcha los conocimientos técnicos necesarios para resolver los desafíos que surgen. Otro de los entrevistados manifiesta que los conocimientos técnicos se van adquiriendo en "forma escalonada", y propone que a medida que el emprendimiento evoluciona, los fundadores dejan de hacer ciertas cosas para hacer otras a modo de no perder de vista el objetivo que se quiere alcanzar.

En cuanto a las habilidades blandas, los resultados indican que las habilidades de adaptabilidad, aprovechamiento de recursos, creación de valor, gestión y mitigación de riesgos, resolución creativa de problemas / imaginación, motivación y perseverancia, y resiliencia están desarrolladas en la mayoría de los fundadores desde antes de comenzar con el emprendimiento. Estos datos se pueden correlacionar con el marco teórico ya que estas habilidades se mencionan como características de la personalidad emprendedora. Cabe destacar que cinco de estas habilidades (adaptabilidad, aprovechamiento de recursos, creación de valor, motivación y perseverancia, resiliencia) forman parte a su vez del ranking de las 10 habilidades blandas más necesarias en el equipo fundador de un emprendimiento de software según los entrevistados (Tabla 5). Otras habilidades blandas tales como aprender a través de la experiencia, comunicación, creación y uso de redes, y evaluación de oportunidades son desarrolladas por la mayoría de los fundadores a medida que el emprendimiento evoluciona. En cuanto a liderazgo, organización y ejecución, y reconocimiento de oportunidades, la mitad de los entrevistados que la consideraron indicaron que las tenían desarrolladas desde antes, mientras que la otra mitad indicó que la adquirió durante el transcurso del emprendimiento.

Respecto a si las habilidades blandas varían al evolucionar el emprendimiento, cinco emprendedores coinciden en que sí varían, y brindan las mimas razones que para el caso de los conocimientos técnicos: hay habilidades como la adaptabilidad, motivación y perseverancia, que son más necesarias al comienzo, y otras como el liderazgo, gestión y la mitigación de riesgos que se vuelven necesarias al crecer el emprendimiento. Cabe destacar que tres emprendedores manifiestan que ciertas habilidades tales como reconocimiento de oportunidades, resolución creativa de problemas, tener una visión convincente, trabajo en equipo, comunicación y pensamiento emprendedor, tienen que estar presentes en todas las etapas del emprendimiento. Para dos emprendedores, el peso de las habilidades blandas varía de acuerdo con las situaciones que se enfrenten y a la evolución del emprendimiento.

5 Discusión

5.1 Conocimientos técnicos en el equipo fundador

Los emprendimientos se caracterizan por tener recursos limitados (tiempo, dinero y/o personal). Por esta razón, y en especial durante las primeras etapas, los fundadores son quienes desempeñan la mayor cantidad de tareas, lo cual hace necesario poseer y dominar ciertos conocimientos técnicos. A partir de la lista de conocimientos técnicos discutida con los entrevistados, se identificó que los cinco más relevantes y valorados son:

- **Análisis de mercado.** De los conocimientos técnicas que forman parte de esta investigación, éste es el único que todos consideran necesario. Este resultado es esperable porque el análisis de mercado aporta información que permite analizar la viabilidad comercial del emprendimiento, y no saber hacerlo puede significar invertir esfuerzo en una idea sin potencial de negocio.
- **Definir un modelo de negocio.** La definición del modelo de negocio puede condicionar el éxito del emprendimiento, porque éste permite visualizar cuál es la propuesta de valor del producto o servicio, cuál es el mercado objetivo, de qué forma se va a comercializar, y cómo se generan ingresos. Además, es información que debe presentarse si se desea acceder a financiación.
- **Definir un plan de negocio.** Esta habilidad complementa las dos primeras porque permite definir los objetivos y plan de trabajo para poner en práctica el modelo de negocio definido, en el contexto identificado.
- **Diseño de experiencia de usuario.** A medida que los usuarios adoptan el uso de soluciones de software en su rutina diaria, se hace crítico ofrecerles una experiencia de usuario fluida y sencilla que se alinee con su estilo de vida. Los usuarios esperan una experiencia de usuario optimizada como requisito básico, lo que hace fundamental la incorporación de habilidades de diseño con el propósito de crear una experiencia de usuario agradable que fomente la adopción del producto o servicio ofrecido.
- **Infraestructura.** Esta habilidad es necesaria porque se parte de la base que, al desarrollar un producto o servicio de software, la infraestructura juega un papel determinante en el funcionamiento óptimo de una solución tecnológica porque puede representar una ventaja competitiva al optimizar el funcionamiento del negocio.

Los conocimientos de negocio ocupan las tres primeras posiciones del ranking de los conocimientos técnicos necesarios porque, en general, las habilidades emprendedoras están fuertemente relacionadas con las competencias vinculadas al proceso de identificación y/o creación de oportunidades; la capacidad de capitalizar las oportunidades identificadas; y una gama de habilidades asociadas con la validación, el desarrollo e implementación de planes de negocios viables que permitan concretar dichas oportunidades. Respecto a los conocimientos sobre diseño de experiencia de usuario e infraestructura, en el entorno empresarial digital moderno, las empresas tienen que competir por la atención del usuario como nunca antes, y una forma de captarla es a través una buena experiencia de usuario y funcionamiento optimizado del negocio que se logran a través de un diseño e infraestructura adecuados.

5.2 Habilidades blandas en el equipo fundador

Hoy se ha extendido el concepto que las habilidades blandas complementan a las técnicas y ayudan al éxito en varias esferas. Por eso es importante determinar qué habilidades blandas debe tener el equipo fundador de un emprendimiento de software. A continuación, se listan dichas habilidades:

- **Motivación y perseverancia.** Comenzar un emprendimiento es difícil, y la motivación juega un papel determinante ya que es la razón o razones que obligan a alguien a seguir esforzándose y trabajando. Proporciona esperanza y claridad cuando las circunstancias se vuelven difíciles y desalentadoras. La motivación, entonces, es fundamental a la hora de decidir emprender, no solo porque los emprendedores necesitan comprender, aprovechar y mantener su propia motivación para iniciar un negocio, sino porque deben ser capaces de motivar a otros para que acepten su idea.
- **Adaptabilidad.** Es importante estar preparado para afrontar los cambios asociados al contexto inestable e impredecible de un emprendimiento. Como emprendedor, se debe tener claro que el cambio ocurre con frecuencia y rapidez, especialmente durante las etapas de planificación a medida que surgen nuevas oportunidades e ideas, y que probablemente la idea original no sea la definitiva.
- **Aprender a través de la experiencia.** Con frecuencia, los emprendedores se enfrentan a situaciones para las cuales no están preparados. Entonces, esta habilidad es fundamental para incorporar y hacer uso del conocimiento aprendido durante el transcurso del emprendimiento.
- **Liderazgo.** El liderazgo es un factor que hace que todo funcione en conjunto porque proporciona inspiración, visión, organización y motivación. En etapas tempranas, al menos uno de los fundadores debe poseer esta característica para llevar adelante el proyecto. Más adelante, y en especial cuando se tienen personal a cargo, cobra mayor relevancia porque hay que alinear una mayor cantidad de personas con los objetivos.
- **Resiliencia.** El fundador de un emprendimiento vive por naturaleza en entornos hostiles. Sin resiliencia se hace difícil emprender, porque no sólo se trata de soportar el fracaso o situaciones adversas, sino de salir fortalecido y seguir adelante.

Estos resultados coinciden con lo que la literatura afirma sobre la esencia de los emprendimientos de software. La adaptabilidad permite sobrellevar los cambios constantes. La resiliencia y motivación son clave porque por cada éxito se tienen muchos fracasos, y permite salir fortalecido de situaciones adversas. Aprender a través de la experiencia ayuda a resolver situaciones para las cuales muchas veces no se cuenta con preparación (académica o profesional), el aprender rápido y aplicar ese conocimiento permite seguir adelante. A través del liderazgo, se puede organizar, planificar, definir y transmitir una visión y lograr que las personas se involucren.

5.3 Evolución de los conocimientos y las habilidades adquiridas en el equipo

Podemos concluir que el conjunto de conocimientos técnicos y habilidades blandas necesarios durante el transcurso del emprendimiento varía, de acuerdo con las situaciones que se van presentando y a medida que la empresa madura. Esta conclusión respalda la opinión de [3], para quien las habilidades y capacidades del equipo fundador probablemente cambiarán a medida que la empresa evolucione. Durante la etapa inicial, los conocimientos técnicos que tienen mayor relevancia son los de negocio y de producción porque son necesarias para definir y validar la idea (recopilar requerimientos, realizar análisis de mercado, definir un plan de negocios), o para implementar el producto o servicio de software (codificación, prototipado). A medida que se avanza, surge la necesidad de comercializar el producto y/o buscar financiación, y en ese momento los conocimientos financieros cobran más importancia. Con las habilidades blandas pasa algo similar, con la salvedad que ciertas habilidades (reconocimiento de oportunidades, comunicación, entre otras) son siempre necesarias porque hacen a la naturaleza emprendedora y siempre deben estar presentes.

6 Amenazas a la validez

Según Merriam y Tisdell [21], los estándares para el rigor en la investigación cualitativa difieren necesariamente de los de la investigación cuantitativa. Así, en [20] se menciona una serie de criterios para establecer cierto "paralelo" con la confiabilidad, validez (interna y externa) y objetividad cuantitativa, que han sido aceptados por la mayoría de los investigadores (aunque reconocen que son rechazados por otros). Estos criterios sustitutivos se denominan dependencia, credibilidad, y transferencia.

El criterio de dependencia se define como el grado en que diferentes investigadores que recolecten datos similares en el campo y efectúen los mismos análisis generen resultados equivalentes. Hernández Sampieri y colegas, citando a Franklin y Ballau, mencionan dos clases de dependencia: a) interna (grado en el cual distintos investigadores, al menos dos, generan categorías similares con los mismos datos) y b) externa (grado en que diferentes investigadores generan categorías similares en el mismo ambiente y período, pero cada uno recaba sus propios datos) [20].

Para cumplir con el criterio de dependencia interna, el análisis de los datos recolectados se hizo en forma independiente por pares de autores de modo de identificar y discutir las diferencias que pudieran surgir y arribar a resultados unificados.

El criterio de dependencia externa no se pudo verificar pues no hay otros investigadores (más allá de los de este estudio) que hayan recolectado datos de los mismos entrevistados y en circunstancias similares (mismo ambiente y período).

El criterio de credibilidad refiere a si el investigador ha captado el significado completo y profundo de las experiencias de los participantes, particularmente de aquellas vinculadas con el planteamiento del problema. En este sentido, el haber grabado las entrevistas y disponer de los audios ha permitido volver a escuchar lo declarado por cada entrevistado, de modo de asegurar no haber omitido nada importante. Además, se procuró evitar los sesgos del investigador en cuanto a ignorar o minimizar datos que no apoyen sus creencias y conclusiones.

Finalmente, en cuanto al criterio de transferencia o aplicabilidad de los resultados a otros contextos, si bien los informantes claves entrevistados son fundadores de emprendimientos de software, todos sus emprendimientos fueron incubados en la misma incubadora de empresas (CIE, mencionado arriba). La transferencia de los resultados podrá establecerse, al menos parcialmente, incorporando al estudio nuevos emprendimientos de software incubados en otras incubadoras, aspecto que se menciona como uno de los trabajos futuros.

7 Conclusiones y trabajos futuros

Uno de los focos de la serie de entrevistas fue recoger la percepción del equipo fundador de emprendimientos de software respecto a la importancia relativa de los dos tipos de habilidades. Hay una clara tendencia a destacar la relevancia de las habilidades blandas en un contexto de emprendimiento porque: a) algunas habilidades blandas no son fáciles de adquirir porque se las define como una combinación de componentes emocionales, conductuales y cognitivos que forman parte de la personalidad de cada individuo, b) los conocimientos técnicos son contratables, mientras que no todas las habilidades blandas lo son (por ejemplo, no se puede contratar resiliencia), y c) hay ciertas habilidades que hacen a la personalidad emprendedora que si no se tienen no te conducen a comenzar un emprendimiento (motivación, resiliencia). Los resultados obtenidos apoyan la opinión de [11] que las habilidades blandas han tenido un reconocimiento creciente, pero contradice su postura respecto a que las habilidades blandas y los conocimientos técnicos son complementarios.

Existe una correlación entre la importancia que tienen las habilidades y la dificultad para adquirirlas. Con respecto a esto concluimos que las habilidades blandas son más difíciles de adquirir porque: a) no se adquieren asistiendo a cursos, sino a través de la experiencia; b) al estar ligadas a la personalidad, su aprendizaje se hace trabajoso porque requiere modificar elementos de la personalidad, y modificar la personalidad no se logra de inmediato; y c) hay que tener cierta predisposición natural para desarrollarlas.

Con respecto a los conocimientos técnicos, el énfasis de los entrevistados está en los relativos a aspectos de negocio: análisis de mercado, y definición del modelo de negocio y del plan de negocio.

Como trabajos futuros se plantea la replicación de este estudio incorporando emprendimientos de software incubados en otras incubadoras de empresas, así como indagar qué tipo de apoyo brindan las incubadoras para la adquisición de conocimientos técnicos y el desarrollo de las habilidades blandas más valoradas en el equipo fundador.

Referencias

1. M. Unterkalmsteiner, P. Abrahamsson, X. Wang, y A. Nguyen-Duc, «Software Startups: A Research Agenda», *e-Informatica Software Engineering Journal*, vol. 10, n.º 1, pp. 89-123, 2016.
2. C. Giardino, M. Unterkalmsteiner, N. Paternoster, T. Gorschek, y P. Abrahamsson, «What Do We Know about Software Development in Startups?», *IEEE Software*, vol. 31, n.º 5, pp. 28-32, 2014.
3. C. Hallam y W. Flannery, *Engineering the High Tech Start Up: Fundamentals and Theory. Vol. 1*. New York: Momentum Press, 2018.
4. K. Tanner, *The entrepreneur's guide to hiring and building the team*. Westport: Praeger Publishers, 2008.
5. P. Seppänen, K. Liukkunen, y M. Oivo, «Little Big Team: Acquiring Human Capital in Software Startups», en *18th International Conference on Product-Focused Software Process Improvement (PROFES 2017)*, 2017, pp. 280–296.
6. N. Bhatnaga, *Effective communication and soft skills*. New Delhi: Dorling Kindersley, 2012.
7. E. S. Prince, *The advantage. The 7 soft skills you need to stay one step ahead*. Financial Times Press, 2013.
8. G. Matturro, F. Raschetti, y C. Fontán, «A Systematic Mapping Study on Soft Skills in Software Engineering», *Journal of Universal Computer Science*, vol. 25, n.º 1, pp. 16-41, 2019.
9. E. Dell'Aquila, D. Marocco, M. Ponticorvo, A. di Ferdinando, S. M., y O.: Miglino, *Educational Games for Soft-Skills Training in Digital Environments*. Springer, 2017.
10. S. Shane, E. Locke, y Ch. Collins, «Entrepreneurial motivation», *Human Resource Management Review*, vol. 13, n.º 2, pp. 257-279, 2003.
11. B. Riyanti, C. Sandroto, y M. Warmiyati, «Soft Skill Competencies, Hard Skill Competencies, and Intention to Become Enterpreneur of Vocational Graduates», *International research journal of business studies*, vol. 9, n.º 2, pp. 119-132, 2016.
12. G. Gianesini, S. Cubico, G. Favretto, y J. Leitão, «Entrepreneurial Competences: Comparing and Contrasting Models and Taxonomies», en *Entrepreneurship and the Industry Life Cycle. Studies on Entrepreneurship*, S. Cubico, G. Favretto, J. Leitão, y U. Cantner, Eds. Berlin: Springer, 2018.
13. B. Cavalcante, G. Lapasini, R. Balancieri, y I. de Farias, «Technical Aspects of Software Development in Startups: A Systematic Mapping», en *XLIV Latin American Computing Conference (CLEI 2018)*, 2018.

Análise Comparativa das Características e Impactos de Conflitos Interpessoais no Contexto da Engenharia de Requisitos

Gustavo Dias Alexandre[1[0000-0003-4715-9361]]
Maria Lencastre[1[0000-0002-8032-8801]]

Escola Politécnica de Pernambuco, Universidade de Pernambuco, Recife, Brasil
gfda@ecomp.poli.br
mlpm@ecomp.poli.br

Abstract. Interpersonal conflicts in software projects impact success, product quality, team performance, and health. However, in Requirements Engineering (RE), previous research has focused in conflicts among requirements; there are few studies on interpersonal conflicts in RE that address the issue of characteristics (like severity and activities in which they occur) and the impact of conflicts on project parameters (such as risks and costs). We identified only two studies, in the context of interpersonal conflicts in the RE; they include an exploratory case study in a single project in the industry, and a survey applied in the industry, for eliciting and classifying conflict scenarios from different professionals and companies. This paper makes a complementary analysis based on both works, aiming to help to consolidate and deepen the results obtained, such as recurring conflict types, stakeholders, management styles adopted for conflict resolution, and impacts on project risks. As a result, it was also possible to form a new base of real conflict scenarios, classified in a homogeneous and detailed way, which can be applied to further studies of the area.

Keywords: Interpersonal Conflitcs · Requirements Engineering · Real Conflicts Scenarios.

1 Introdução

Em projetos de desenvolvimento de software um fator importante, para o seu sucesso ou fracasso, são os recursos humanos. Artigos e relatos de experiência na área mostram que, nas organizações, estes recursos incentivam e fortalecem a inovação, além de motivar tomadas de decisão, liderança, comunicação e gerenciamento dos negócios. Neste contexto, um dos problemas que tem se tornado cada vez mais comum é o impacto dos conflitos interpessoais na realização do trabalho.

Especificamente, a subárea da Engenharia de Software (ES), a Engenharia de Requisitos (ER) - que envolve elicitar, analisar, estruturar e gerenciar os requisitos - requer do analista um domínio sólido da linguagem, que saiba ouvir, compreender e consolidar de forma clara as necessidades das partes interessadas (*stakeholders*) [1]. Por se tratar de uma área de constante interação humana, onde falhas de comunicação e de entendimento são geralmente inevitáveis entre os *stakeholders*, surgem frequentemente conflitos interpessoais [2]. Entre as principais causas desses conflitos destacam-se: males entendidos, rivalidade e competição entre indivíduos, diferentes percepções acerca de responsabilidades, valores ou normas acerca do desenvolvimento de software, ataques pessoais e descumprimento de regras da organização [3, 4].

Estudos sobre conflitos na ER são importantes para que se criem estratégias de mitigação e prevenção dos danos causados por estes no desenvolvimento do software. Conflitos interpessoais em projetos de software têm impacto no sucesso, qualidade do produto, saúde e desempenho da equipe. Segundo [5], as correções tardias nos erros de requisitos podem custar até 200 vezes mais do que as correções realizadas durante a fase de ER.

No âmbito mais genérico das organizações, existem vários estudos que buscam dar suporte às questões relacionadas à resolução de conflitos interpessoais. Trabalhos como [6] utilizam um Método de Estruturação de Problemas (PSM) com o objetivo de que cada parte compreenda as posições da outra. Já os autores de [7], analisam como equipes líderes negociam e atingem um consenso num ambiente de crise. [8] investiga, ainda, a influência de mapas causais sobre a eficiência do trabalho. Outros trabalhos se baseiam no uso do *Group Support System* (GSS), evidenciando a sua importância na redução de conflitos interpessoais [4, 9]. No entanto, na ER, há escassez de pesquisas sobre esse tópico, tanto em relação à prevenção quanto à mitigação; estudos anteriores se concentraram amplamente em ferramentas e *frameworks* para identificar e resolver conflitos entre requisitos [10].

São raros os trabalhos, sobre conflitos interpessoais na ER, que abordam o tema relativo a características (por exemplo, gravidade dos conflitos, atividades onde foram encontrados) e o impacto dos conflitos interpessoais na ER em parâmetros do projeto, como riscos, custos, e qualidade. Foram encontrados, na literatura, apenas dois trabalhos no contexto de ER: Walia [10] e Barbosa [11]. [10] analisa as características e os impactos dos conflitos em um projeto de software sob o contexto da ER, tomando como base uma Revisão Sistemática da Literatura (RSL) sobre o assunto. Já [11] utiliza entrevistas semiestruturadas, com diversos profissionais da área de Tecnologia da Informação, para relatar situações reais de conflito em seu cotidiano, levantando e classificando-as.

Buscando contribuir com mais trabalhos que abordam questões de conflitos na ER, nesta pesquisa são analisados cenários de conflitos, os impactos e riscos, ao projeto de software, causados pelas discordâncias interpessoais ocorridas nas atividades da ER e as estratégias de gerenciamento aplicadas. Para isso, foram feitos levantamentos e análises complementares, aos dois trabalhos encontrados [10] e [11] sobre o tema, visando aprofundar o conhecimento referente à análise de cenários reais de conflito.

Este artigo está organizado da seguinte maneira. A seção 2 apresenta o *background*. A seção 3 descreve a metodologia utilizada. A seção 4 compara e apresenta os resultados obtidos. Por fim, a seção 5 traz as conclusões, ameaças à validade e considerações para trabalhos futuros.

2 Background

Nesta seção, inicialmente, são detalhados conceitos sobre conflitos; em seguida são analisados os conflitos na ER, e são então apresentados os dois trabalhos relacionados, que serviram de base para o desenvolvimento deste artigo.

2.1 Conflitos

O termo conflito tem sua raiz etimológica no latim – conflictos - que significa desacordo, choque. O vocábulo, na língua portuguesa, expressa "profunda falta de entendimento entre duas ou mais partes" [12]. O conflito é um processo inerente às relações humanas, especialmente em ambientes de trabalho. As pessoas têm diferentes experiências, valores, opiniões e maneiras de realizar tarefas, as quais provavelmente levam a discordâncias [13]. Em projetos de desenvolvimento de software, conflitos são inevitáveis. [14] define conflito como "um processo que tem início quando uma das partes percebe que a outra parte afeta, ou pode afetar, negativamente, alguma coisa que a primeira considera importante".

Pesquisas sugerem a existência de três principais tipos de conflitos interpessoais em ambientes de trabalho. Para [15], **Conflitos de Relacionamento** são desacordos e incompatibilidades entre os membros do grupo em relação a questões pessoais, que não são relacionados a tarefas. Os conflitos de relacionamento, mais frequentemente relatados, são sobre eventos sociais, valores, crenças, atitudes, opiniões políticas e *hobbies*. Os **Conflitos de Tarefas** consistem em divergências relacionadas a ideias e opiniões sobre a tarefa que está sendo executada, como executar tarefas específicas, particularmente em relação a discrepâncias sobre procedimentos ou a distribuição dos recursos disponíveis, discordâncias sobre as estratégias de contratação atuais de uma organização. Já os **Conflitos de Processo** são definidos como divergências sobre os meios para realizar as tarefas, não sobre o conteúdo ou a substância da tarefa em si, mas sobre estratégias para executá-las.

2.2 Conflitos na Engenharia de Requisitos

São poucos os estudos científicos conduzidos sob os aspectos de conflitos interpessoais na ER. Um exemplo de conflito interpessoal, inerente à ER, é o desacordo entre clientes e desenvolvedores sobre a seleção ou priorização dos requisitos para a próxima *release* [10]. Determinar os tipos de riscos associados aos requisitos afetados pelos conflitos de ER podem ajudar os profissionais a iniciar o processo de gerenciamento de riscos na própria fase de ER, geralmente considerada a partir da fase de projeto [16]. [16] relatam que 24% dos riscos gerais do projeto que são "riscos de alto nível" ocorrem nas fases iniciais do desenvolvimento do software. Além disso, tanto a falta de gerenciamento de conflitos quanto à gestão de riscos foram declaradas independentemente como fatores principais que levam a falhas no projeto [17,18].

Estudo de Caso sobre conflitos em uma Empresa Foi conduzido um estudo exploratório em um projeto de software de uma empresa de desenvolvimento de pequeno porte, para investigar as questões da pesquisa relacionadas a conflitos de relacionamentos. Pontos importantes foram utilizados para a elaboração das entrevistas e questionários aplicados no estudo [10].

Durante o estudo de caso realizado foram identificados os tipos de conflitos ER (ver Tabela 1). As principais atividades da ER, utilizadas pra identificar presença de conflitos, foram: Elicitação; Negociação; Especificação; Priorização; Análise; Validação [19]. Quanto à severidade, foi utilizada uma escala ordinal, proposta por [20], ordenada de '1' (representando o menor grau de severidade) até '6' (representando o maior grau) com o objetivo de representar os níveis de gravidade dos conflitos na ER (ver Tabela 2).

Para levantar as características dos conflitos interpessoais, foram elaboradas questões sobre os tipos, atividades da ER nas quais os conflitos foram encontrados, *stakeholders* envolvidos, severidade, grau de resolução e estratégias de gerenciamento adotadas; sobre os impactos, foram elaboradas questões tratando dos riscos ao projeto associados aos requisitos.

Cenários Reais de Conflitos em Diferentes Empresas No trabalho de [11] foram selecionados 9 profissionais de diferentes empresas para realização das entrevistas, com pelo menos 10 anos de experiência, para garantir maturidade em termos profissionais e conflitos potencialmente interessantes. Após contatados, foram realizadas entrevistas individuais, semiestruturadas, com esses profissionais. Por fim, os cenários foram transcritos e classificados, de acordo com as estratégias usadas para resolver os conflitos (acomodação, competição, colaboração) e o tipo de conflito (processo, tarefa, relacionamento). Por fim, um desses cenários serviu como base para a criação de um jogo baseado em fatos reais. Como resultados da análise dos cenários teve-se a identificação dos:

- Efeitos dos conflitos: equipe desestabilizada, cliente inseguro, equipe insegura, estresse da equipe, desgaste nas relações pessoais, sobrecarga na equipe, perda de foco, expectativas não atendidas, contratação de novos desenvolvedores;
- Reflexos dos conflitos para o projeto: atraso na entrega, custo, mudança de escopo, qualidade do produto, reestruturação das atividades, entre outros.

3 Metodologia

A Figura 1 ilustra todo o processo utilizado para a construção desta pesquisa. Inicialmente, foi realizada a leitura e revisão de artigos sobre conflitos interpessoais no contexto da ER e seus impactos nos riscos de requisitos, para a geração de uma base teórica para o trabalho. Em seguida, foram extraídos de [10], para serem tomados como base, os tipos de conflitos (ver Tabela 1), suas definições e seu grau de severidade dentro do processo de desenvolvimento de software (ver Tabela 2), as partes envolvidas nestes conflitos interpessoais e em que etapas das atividades de ER ocorrem com maior frequência, as soluções adotadas para gerenciamento dos conflitos (ver Tabela 3), e os impactos nos riscos de projeto (ver Tabela 4). Junto a estas informações, foi possível obter questionários que foram previamente validados por especialistas e utilizados como base para condução da pesquisa em um ambiente real.

Tabela 1. Tipos de conflito e sua descrição. Fonte: Traduzido de Walia [10].

Tipos de Conflitos ER	Descrição
Conflitos sobre prioridades do projeto.	Desacordos entre *stakeholders* sobre priorizações /sequenciamento em relação aos requisitos, módulos, tarefas e etc.
Conflitos sobre procedimentos administrativos.	Desacordos entre *stakeholders* sobre questões administrativas, como definir os prazos do projeto (*deadline*), alocação de recursos e etc.
Conflitos sobre assuntos técnicos.	Desacordos / divergências entre *stakeholders* sobre assuntos técnicos como linguagem de programação adotada para o desenvolvimento, seleção do modelo de desenvolvimento de software, etc.
Conflitos sobre custos.	Divergências entre *stakeholders* sobre custos e budget do (para o) projeto.
Conflitos sobre cronogramas.	Desacordos/divergências entre *stakeholders* sobre o cronograma/planejamento, como definir os cronogramas de reuniões.

Tabela 2. Escala dos níveis de severidade dos conflitos. Fonte: Traduzido de Walia [10].

ID	Descrição
1	Premissa aceita sem críticas, sem interação entre os membros da equipe.
2	Lidou com suavidade e harmonia após uma breve discussão.
3	Longo período de debate construtivo, discutindo as virtudes de um problema.
4	Causou uma pequena interrupção ao forçar as pessoas a resolver problemas relevantes.
5	Longo período de debates destrutivos, resultando em perda de muito tempo para voltar aos trilhos.
6	Causou interrupção completa no trabalho da equipe.

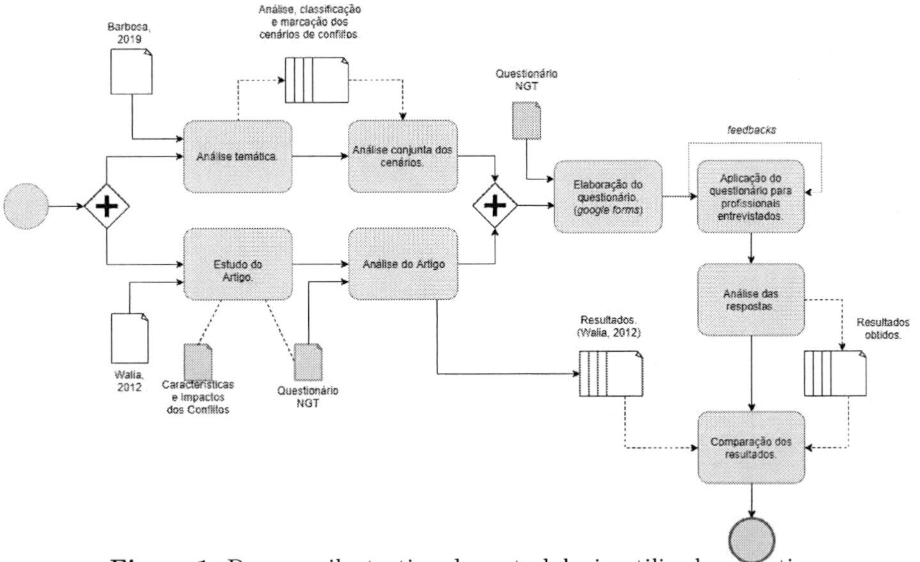

Figura 1. Processo ilustrativo da metodologia utilizada no artigo.

De [11] foram extraídas as transcrições de entrevistas que foram realizadas com profissionais de TI, com pelo menos 10 anos de experiência, de diferentes empresas que contribuiu com uma base de cenários reais de conflitos. Em seguida foi realizada uma análise temática sobre o trabalho de [11], para familiarização com os dados, as transcrições foram lidas várias vezes, resumos e anotações também foram feitas, uma vez que esta etapa é considerada parte fundamental da análise temática; na etapa seguinte, foram feitas marcações com o intuito de codificar unicamente cada conflito identificado, as estratégias de solução e os riscos causados aos projetos.

Após as demarcações, cada conjunto de cenários foi avaliado e debatido junto com outros pesquisadores com experiência em requisitos e conflitos interpessoais, visando uma definição precisa sobre as características e impactos dos conflitos encontrados, para responder o questionário elaborado sob a Técnica Nominal de Grupo (NGT - *nominal group technique*) utilizado por [10]. Após esta fase, o questionário foi enviado para as pessoas entrevistadas em [11] via plataforma de formulários do Google (*google forms*) [21] para que as respostas obtidas fossem comparadas com as respostas da avaliação com os pesquisadores.

Finalizado o processo de obtenção das respostas, o passo seguinte consistiu em comparar os resultados obtidos em [11] com os resultados deste artigo, para observar os efeitos da generalização da pesquisa, visto que em [10] o questionário foi aplicado em um projeto de software de uma empresa de desenvolvimento de pequeno porte, além de propor mudanças no questionário baseado nos *feedbacks* enviados pelas pessoas que foram entrevistadas.

Por fim, no que diz respeito às características dos conflitos interpessoais, são exploradas as estratégias ou estilos de gerenciamento adotados para resolução dos conflitos. Sobre a importância do gerenciamento de conflitos, existe uma abundância de pesquisas relacionadas na área de Engenharia de Software, mas não é tão explorado na ER. A Tabela 3 apresenta uma lista de estratégias de gerenciamento de conflitos e uma breve descrição baseados em [22].

Sobre os impactos causados por conflitos interpessoais na ER, são apresentados os sete maiores riscos ao projeto de software e suas 6 dimensões: usuário, requisito, complexidade do projeto, planejamento e controle, equipe e ambiente organizacional (ver Tabela 4).

Tabela 3. Estratégias de gerenciamento de conflitos. Fonte: Traduzido de Walia [10].

Estilo	Descrição
Retirada/Evitação	Retirar-se de uma atual ou potencial situação de conflito.
Suavização / Acomodação	Enfatizar as áreas de acordo em vez das áreas de diferença.
Comprometimento	Procurar e negociar soluções que tragam algum grau de satisfação a todas as partes.
Forçar	Impulsionar o ponto de vista de alguém em detrimento de outros; oferece apenas situações de ganha-perde.
Colaboração	Incorpora vários pontos de vista e ideias de diferentes perspectivas; leva ao consenso e compromisso.
Confrontação	Trata o conflito como um problema a ser resolvido examinando alternativas; Requer atitude de troca e diálogo aberto.

Tabela 4. Riscos de projetos de software. Fonte: Traduzido de Walia [10].

Riscos	Dimensão
Incompreensão dos requisitos.	Requisito
Falta de comprometimento e suporte da alta gerência.	Ambiente organizacional
Falta de envolvimento adequado do usuário.	Usuário
Falha em obter o envolvimento do usuário.	Usuário
Falha ao gerenciar a expectativa do usuário final.	Usuário
Mudanças no requisito.	Requisito
Falta de uma metodologia eficaz de gerenciamento de projetos.	Controle e Planejamento

4 Resultados

Nesta seção são exibidos e analisados os resultados obtidos em um estudo de caso, analisando as características e os impactos aos riscos de requisitos em um projeto de desenvolvimento de software, causados por conflitos interpessoais [10]. Em seguida são exibidos também os resultados e interpretações deste estudo, baseado nas respostas dos profissionais de T.I, obtidas por meio da aplicação do questionário NGT. Por fim, é feita uma comparação entre ambos os resultados.

4.1 Resultados do Estudo de Walia

Por meio de questionários fechados, entrevistas semiestruturadas e questionários NGT [10] obteve os resultados do seu estudo. Tais métodos foram validados realizando as entrevistas apenas a cargos específicos, que foram Gerente de Projetos (PM) e Analistas de Requisitos (RA), em seguida, em grupos, validaram os cenários de conflitos.

Na análise dos resultados, [10] mostra que dos tipos identificados, os conflitos sobre procedimentos administrativos (47%) tiveram a maior ocorrência no projeto, sendo os conflitos sobre cronogramas (8%) com menor número de ocorrências, apenas uma em um total de treze identificações. Baseado nisto, associados da indústria e especialistas no campo da ER e ES, envolvidos no trabalho, interpretam que uma razão plausível para tais resultados é que durante a realização do estudo de caso, clientes e desenvolvedores não haviam trabalhado em conjunto e, portanto, não tinham conhecimento dos processos administrativos uns dos outros.

Sobre as ocorrências durante as atividades da ER, o estudo mostrou que as maiores proporções dos conflitos, ocorreram durante as fases de Elicitação (46%) e Negociação (31%). Os números apresentados estão diretamente relacionados com o fato de que durante os processos de negociação e elicitação, ocorre maior interação entre *stakeholders* para questões como: Compreensão do problema, necessidade de chegar a um acordo entre as partes, negociação de custos, domínio da aplicação, necessidades e restrições do sistema, entre outros.

Na escala de severidade, aproximadamente metade das incidências ocorridas (em uma escala que vai de 1 a 6, sendo 6 o nível de severidade mais alto) tiveram nível de gravidade 6 (38%) e 5 (8%), enquanto no nível mais baixo 1 (0%) não foram identificados nenhum caso. Estes números impactaram diretamente na satisfação dos membros da equipe e, consequentemente, pelo excesso de conflitos não resolvidos a pessoa responsável pela gerência (PM) decidiu abandonar o projeto.

Dos questionários NGT aplicados à Analistas de Requisitos (RA) e Gerentes de Projeto (PM), foi possível extrair informações sobre os estilos de gerenciamento adotados para resolver os conflitos identificados na ER. As estratégias de Forçar (39%) e Acomodação (30%) foram as mais utilizadas para a solução, enquanto a Colaboração (0%) não foi adotada em nenhum momento. Neste contexto, a maior adoção por forçar e nenhuma aplicação da colaboração, foi interpretado como fator negativo para o sucesso do projeto já que afeta diretamente o relacionamento entre clientes e time de desenvolvimento.

Por fim, tratando-se dos impactos dos conflitos aos riscos do projeto associados aos requisitos, os resultados mostraram que os riscos de mudanças contínuas dos requisitos, requisitos mal compreendidos, e mudanças tardias nos requisitos

(80% cada), foram os mais afetados pelos conflitos da ER. Em contrapartida, alguns riscos, como requisitos redundantes, requisitos não testáveis, requisitos não conformes os padrões de negócios e requisitos desnecessários não foram de todo afetados pelos conflitos.

4.2 Resultados do Estudo Realizado

Após a aplicação do questionário NGT, o mesmo utilizado no estudo de caso de [10], foram obtidas as respostas dos profissionais baseadas em suas experiências, de pelo menos 10 anos, na área de T.I e em contato de alguma forma com análise de requisitos. Foi possível contabilizar nos cenários de conflitos relatados, no que diz respeito às características, tipos de Conflito da ER (ver Tabela 1), atividades da ER onde foram encontrados, nível de severidade dos conflitos da ER (ver Tabela 2) e as estratégias de gerenciamento aplicadas para solucionar os conflitos (ver Tabela 3). Sobre os impactos ao projeto de software, foram contabilizados os principais riscos associados aos requisitos causados pelos conflitos interpessoais (ver Tabela 4).

Os tipos de conflitos da ER identificados na pesquisa; a maior parte ocorre sobre as prioridades do projeto (25%) e procedimentos administrativos (19%) (ver Figura 2).

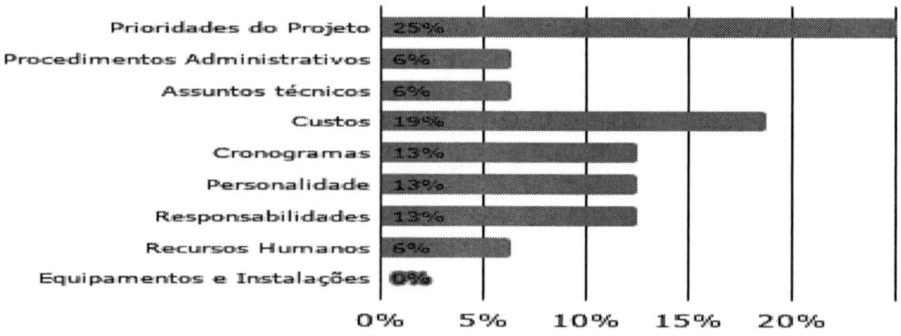

Figura 2. Resultados tipos de Conflitos da ER.

As atividades da ER onde os conflitos foram encontrados são apresentadas na Figura 3. Em alguns casos específicos, os conflitos foram observados em mais de uma atividade da ER. Portanto, as porcentagens da Figura 3 não somam 100. A contagem dos níveis de severidade dos conflitos ocorridos é mostrada na Figura 4.

Em uma resposta do questionário, a questão dos níveis de severidade não ficou clara para a pessoa que respondeu e a seguinte observação foi feita: *"Não entendi como poderei classificar o nível de severidade com base nesse formato de pergunta. "*, a resposta foi computada com o marcador (*). Não houveram ocorrências dos níveis mais baixos, 1 e 2 (0%). A Figura 5 mostra as estratégias de gerenciamento adotadas para resolver os conflitos. Por fim, é apresentada

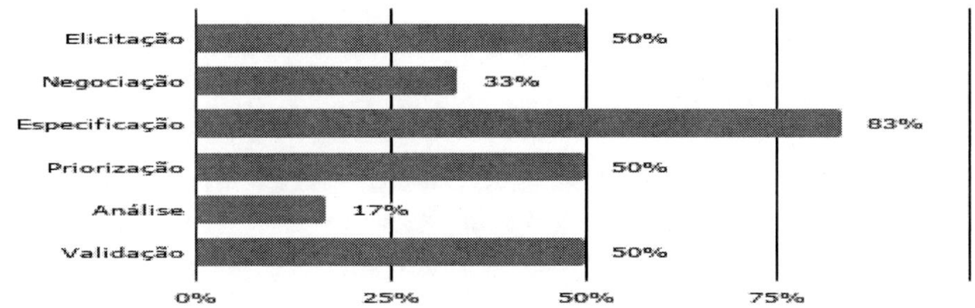

Figura 3. Resultados atividades ER onde os conflitos foram encontrados.

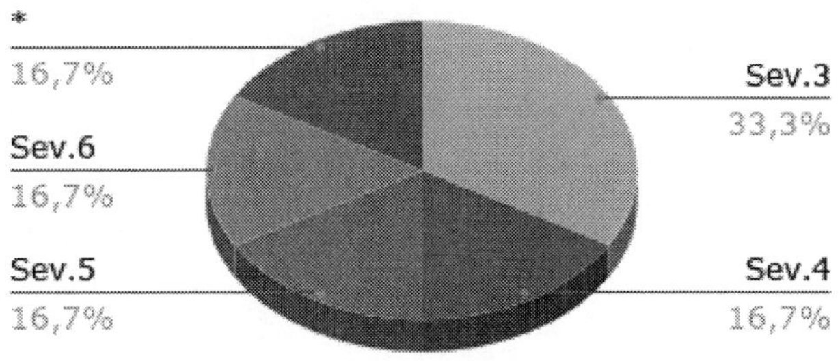

Figura 4. Resultados níveis de severidade dos conflitos da ER.

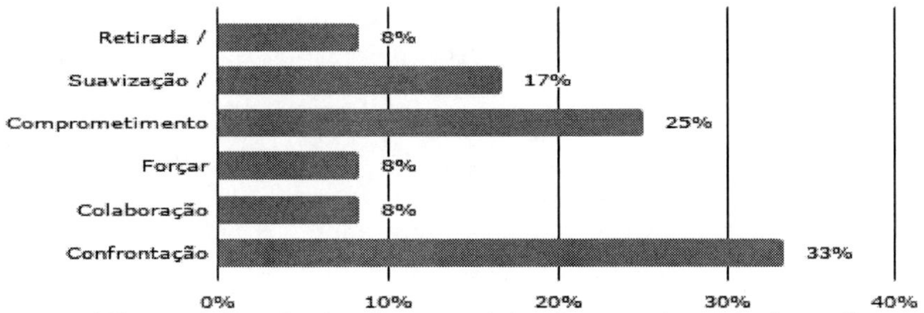

Figura 5. Resultados das estratégias de gerenciamento de conflitos.

a contagem dos riscos ao projeto associados aos requisitos impactados pelos conflitos (ver Figura 6).

4.3 Análise Comparativa

Os resultados obtidos no estudo de caso de [10] são apresentados e comparados com os resultados desta pesquisa. De forma percentual, os tipos de conflitos encontrados (ver Figura 7), as atividades da ER (ver Figura 8), a severidade dos conflitos (ver Figura 9). As estratégias de gerenciamento aplicadas para solução são apresentadas de maneira comparativa (ver Figura 10).

Os resultados mostraram que os conflitos sobre prioridades do projeto (25%) e procedimentos administrativos (19%) tiveram maior ocorrência, enquanto os

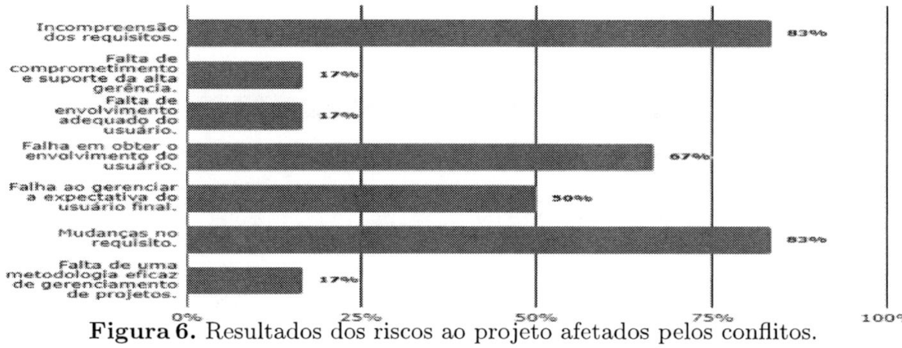

Figura 6. Resultados dos riscos ao projeto afetados pelos conflitos.

conflitos sobre equipamentos e instalações (0%) não ocorreram nos cenários analisados, mostrando que divergências sobre o uso de equipamentos compartilhados não são tão frequentes quanto divergências sobre sequenciamento de tarefas ou questões administrativas. Por ter sido analisada as incidências pontuais de conflitos em diferentes projetos ao invés de uma análise aprofundada no mesmo projeto, o resultado sobre equipamentos e instalações pode ter sido impactado.

Durante as atividades de especificação (83%) dos requisitos, foi detectada a maior incidência de conflitos, observa-se, porém, que os mesmos conflitos podem ocorrer em uma ou mais atividades na fase da ER. Não houveram conflitos classificados nos níveis de severidade mais baixos, a porcentagem foi distribuída a partir do nível 3 (33.3%), deixando claro que em todos os casos houve um longo período de debate, sendo ele construtivo ou não para tentar solucionar as divergências. Especificamente, um dos respondentes não entendeu como classificar a severidade no formato que a questão foi proposta, o que mostra que o questionário tem espaço para possíveis revisões.

Dos estilos ou estratégias de gerenciamento adotados para solucionar uma incidência de conflito, Confrontação (33%) e Comprometimento (25%) foram as mais aplicadas, provando que nos cenários analisados a opção por negociar, analisar alternativas e dialogar abertamente buscando comum acordo solucionaram maior parte dos conflitos.

Os impactos causados aos projetos foram bastante graves, tendo em vista que o mesmo conflito pode afetar em mais de um risco ao projeto, a incompreensão (83%) e mudanças nos requisitos (83%) tiveram maiores porcentagens, junto com a falha em obter o envolvimento do usuário (67%) e a falha ao gerenciar expectativa do usuário final (50%) também ocorreram com grande frequência.

Neste trabalho alguns pontos limitam, dificultam a comparação e ameaçam a pesquisa:

- O questionário foi aplicado com participantes de diferentes empresas; por não ter sido aprofundado em um único projeto, os resultados podem ter sido superficiais; porém, a quantidade de casos coletados durante a pesquisa foi razoável para garantir uma diversidade de cenários no contexto da ER;

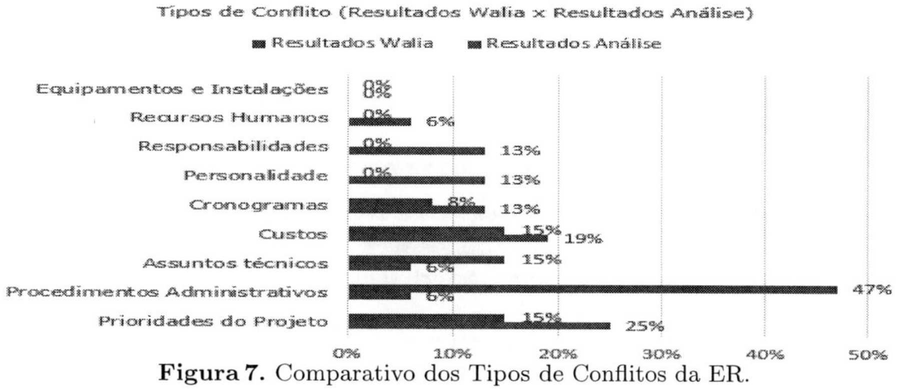

Figura 7. Comparativo dos Tipos de Conflitos da ER.

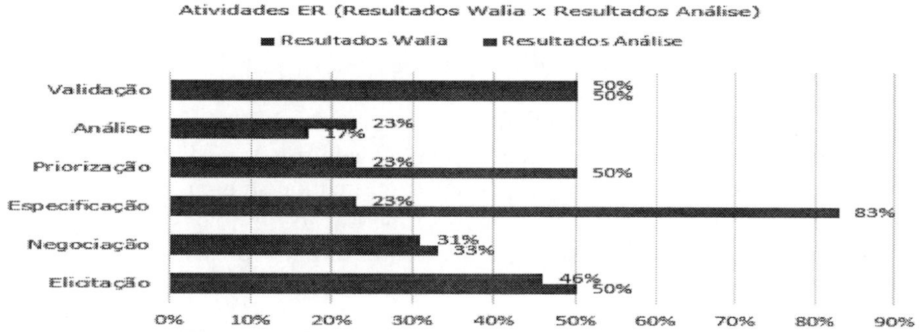

Figura 8. Percentual comparativo Atividades da ER.

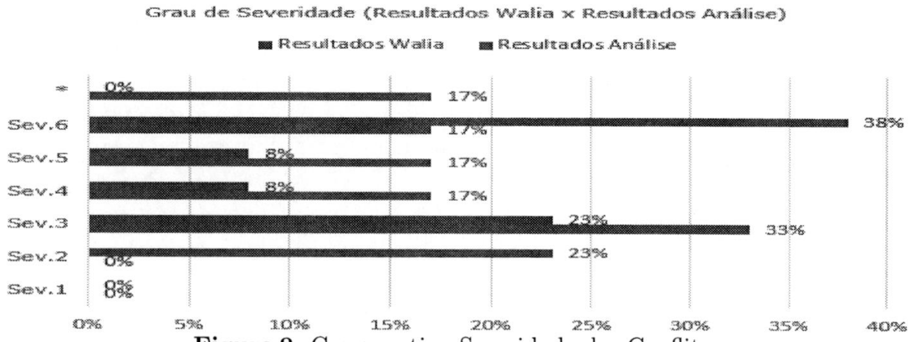

Figura 9. Comparativo Severidade dos Conflitos.

- O método utilizado para coletar os dados de resposta foi um questionário via *google forms*, enquanto [10] utilizou entrevistas semiestruturadas; além de questionários;
- A maneira como o questionário foi elaborado e aplicado gerou dúvidas, alguns participantes não souberam responder ou não conseguiram identificar, dentre as opções, aquela que contemplasse a situação de conflito descrita.

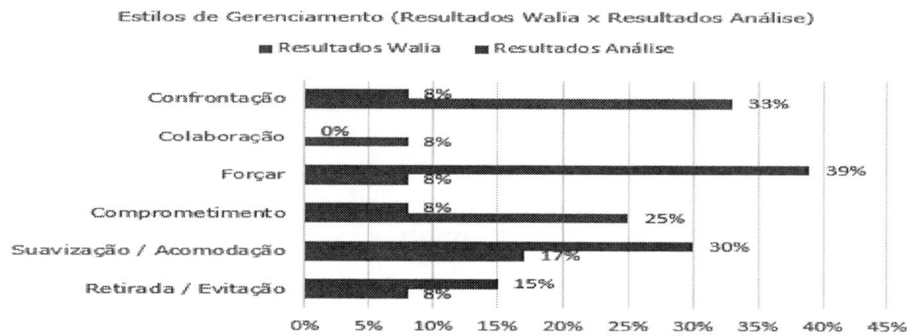

Figura 10. Percentual comparativo Estratégias de Gerenciamento.

5 Conclusões e Trabalhos Futuros

Observando que no campo da ER existem poucos estudos que relacionam os conflitos interpessoais e seus impactos em questões dos projetos, este trabalho busca contribuir comparando os resultados de dois estudos existentes para observar comportamentos, padrões de ocorrência dos conflitos da ER e as estratégias mais adequadas para mitigar ou solucionar cada incidência com maior eficiência.

Este estudo poderá ser usado para o aumento de pesquisas sobre o ensino através do método PBL, *Problem-based Learning*, que representa a Aprendizagem Baseada em Problemas, que estimula a busca por solução e a construção do conhecimento a partir de discussões em grupo de um problema, incentivando a comunicação e a importância do trabalho em equipe.

Como trabalhos futuros, baseando-se nos *feedbacks* dos participantes, este trabalho abre possibilidades de revisões dos questionários e roteiros para as entrevistas, incorporando melhorias, novas perspectivas e buscando tornar os métodos de coleta de informações cada vez mais abrangente, de modo que se tornem aplicável aos mais variados ambientes. Com relação à resolução de conflitos pode ser explorado o GSS com o apoio de mapas causais como apresentado em [4].

Referências

1. Pohl, K., Rupp, C.: Fundamentos da Engenharia de Requisitos, 1 ed., vol. 3, CA, (2011)
2. Camacho, C.: Gerenciando conflitos em reuniões: uma estratégia para a elicitação de requisitos de software. Dissertação de Mestrado-Departamento de Informática, Pontifícia Universidade Católica do Rio de Janeiro, 168 páginas, (2005)
3. Gren, L.; Lenberg, P.: The Importance of Conflict Resolution Techniques in Autonomous Agile Teams. A-TEAMS'18, Porto, Portugal. (2018)
4. Ackermann, F.; Eden, C.; Pyrko, I.: Accelerated Multi-Organization Conflict Resolution. Group Decis Negot. 25:901–922, (2016)
5. Boehm, B. W.: Software engineering economics. Englewood Cliffs, N.J, Prentice-Hall, (1981)

6. Cronin, K.; Midgley, G.; Jackson, LS.: Issues mapping: a problem structuring method for addressing. science and technology conflicts. Eur J Oper Res 233:145–158. doi:10.1016/j.ejor.2013.08.012, (2014)
7. Combe, IA.; Carrington, DJ.: Leaders' sensemaking under crises: emerging cognitive consensus over time within management teams. Leadersh, Q. doi:10.1016/j.leaqua.2015.02.002, (2015)
8. Paroutis, S.; Franco, LA.; Papadopoulos, T.: Visual interactions with strategy tools: producing strategic knowledge in workshops. Br J Manag, 26:S48–S66. doi:10.1111/1467-8551.12081, (2015)
9. Ackermann, F.; Franco, LA.; Gallupe, B.; Parent, M.: GSS for multi-organizational collaboration: reflections on process and content. Group Decis Negot 14:307–331. doi:10.1007/s10726-005-0317-4, (2005)
10. Walia, A.: Characteristics and Impact of Interpersonal Conflicts on Requirements Risks. Electronic Thesis and Dissertation Repository. 1034, (2012)
11. Barbosa, A. F.: Artefatos instrucionais para a análise de conflitos na Engenharia de Requisitos com base na CNV. Dissertação de Mestrado-Programa de Pós-Graduação em Engenharia de Computação, Escola Politécnica de Pernambuco - Universidade de Pernambuco, pp. 126 , (2019)
12. Dicionário Houaiss da Língua Portuguesa. Rio Janeiro, Ed. Objetiva, (2001)
13. Martínez-Corts, I.: Coping with Interpersonal Conflict at Work in Small Business: The Moderating Role of Supervisor and Co-Worker Support. Revista de Psicología del Trabajo y de las Organizaciones; Vol. 27, no. 2. (2011)
14. Robbins, H; Finley, M.: Por que as equipes não funcionam. Rio de Janeiro: Campus, (1997)
15. Jehn, K. A.: A qualitative analysis of conflict types and dimensions in organizational groups. Adm Sci Q 42, pp. 530–557. (1997)
16. Amber, S., Shawoo, N., Begum, S.: Determination of Risk During Requirement Engineering Process. Journal of Emerging Trends in Computing and Information Sciences, **3** (3), pp. 358-364. (2012)
17. Gobeli, D.H., Koenig,H.F., Bechinger, I.: Managing conflict in software development teams: a multilevel analysis. The Journal of Product Innovation Management,**15** (5), pp. 423-435. (1998)
18. Sherif, K., Zmud, R.W., Browne, G.J.: Managing Peer-to-Peer Conflicts in Disruptive Information Technology Innovations: The Case of Software Reuse. MIS Quarterly, **30** (2), pp. 339-356. (2006)
19. Kotonya, G., Sommerville, I.: Requirements engineering: processes and techniques. John Wiley, Chichester. (1998)
20. Karn, J. An ethnographic study of conflict in software engineering teams. Journal of Information, Information Technology, and Organizations, 3, pp. 105, (2008)
21. Google. Formulários Google: crie e analise pesquisas gratuitamente, https://www.google.com/forms/about/. Último Acesso 21 Nov 2019
22. Verma, V. K.: Conflict Management. From The Project Management Institute Project Management Handbook. Ed: Jeffrey Pinto. (1998)

Mapeamento de Critérios de Aceitação de Transparência de Software para Testes Automatizados

Bruno Luiz Gonçalves, Ernani César Dos Santos, Patrícia Vilain

Universidade Federal de Santa Catarina, Florianópolis SC, Brasil
brunolg9@gmail.com
ernani.santos@posgrad.ufsc.br
patricia.vilain@ufsc.br

Abstract. Quality requirements include software transparency, which defines how information should be presented and how the software should run and be developed. In order to ensure compliance with these requirements in the Brazilian Public Sector, the Law on Access to Information (LAI) was proposed, which establishes rules for the disclosure of information, demonstrating the need for transparency of processes and information in public organizations. In this context, we propose the creation of abstract acceptance test case templates in order to evaluate the fulfillment of requirements on public organizations' websites. To validate the work, automated tests were developed using Cucumber and Selenium tools. These tests were defined from the abstract templates and addressed sites that meet and do not meet the requirements being tested. The results show that the proposed templates can serve as acceptance tests to be used during the design of government websites

Keywords: Software Transparency, Acceptance Tests, Non-Functional Requirements, Test Case Templates.

1 Introdução

O crescimento do armazenamento de dados e o acesso direto às informações de várias fontes, por usuários internos e externos de organizações, têm ampliado a necessidade por informações de alta qualidade [1]. Nas organizações públicas, a sociedade, que é afetada pelas ações do estado, tem o direito de acesso às informações que forem necessárias para monitorar a implementação das políticas públicas e da qualidade do serviço público. Quanto maior a transparência pública, maior o conhecimento sobre o andamento da gestão e maior a eficiência dos gastos públicos [2].

De acordo com [3], para uma informação ser considerada transparente, as seguintes premissas devem ser cumpridas: *ser completa*, *objetiva*, *confiável*, *relevante*, *acessível* e de *fácil compreensão*. No Brasil, para garantir o acesso e a transparência das informações à população, foi sancionada a Lei de Acesso à Informação (LAI - Lei nº 12.527/2011). Esta lei regulamenta o direito constitucional de acesso às informações públicas. A LAI abrange os três Poderes da União, Estados, Distrito Federal e Municípios. O objetivo é que essas instituições implementem gestões transparentes, disponibilizando as informações para todos através da Internet [4].

Em [6] são apresentados vários requisitos não-funcionais de qualidade, associados à transparência de software, através de um *checklist* denominado *checkTrans*, voltado para organizações públicas. Todavia, apesar do *checkTrans* definir os requisitos não-funcionais associados à transparência de software, essa definição não assegura que um software atenda a esses requisitos.

Para tanto, neste trabalho propõe-se que estes requisitos não-funcionais de qualidade sejam identificados e descritos através de cenários de teste de aceitação. Foram selecionados alguns requisitos definidos no *checkTrans* e para estes requisitos, foram definidos cenários de testes de aceitação abstratos, isto é, *templates* de cenários de teste. Desta forma, outras organizações poderão utilizar estes *templates* para avaliar a transparência de seus produtos de software ou, ainda nos casos de terceirização do desenvolvimento do produto de software, estes *templates* de testes de aceitação poderão compor a descrição do objeto no instrumento convocatório (edital de licitação ou carta convite).

Este trabalho está organizado da seguinte forma, a Seção 2 aborda uma visão geral de alguns conceitos utilizados neste trabalho. Na Seção 3 são apresentados os requisitos de transparência de software que foram selecionados para serem mapeados para *templates* de testes de aceitação. A Seção 4 detalha os *templates* de testes de aceitação e na Seção 5 é discutida a validade dos *templates* definidos. Na Seção 6 são apresentados os trabalhos relacionados. Finalmente, as conclusões e trabalhos futuros são apresentados na Seção 7.

2 Visão Geral

2.1 Transparência de Software e *CheckTrans*

Um software é considerado transparente não apenas se as informações apresentadas aos usuários são transparentes, mas, também, se todo seu processo de engenharia de requisitos é transparente. Neste contexto, entende-se que a transparência de software deve ser considerada como um requisito não-funcional, que, por sua vez é representado por um conjunto de requisitos associados à qualidade do software [5].

A transparência de software é realizada através de 5 atributos: (i) *acessibilidade*, (ii) *usabilidade*, (iii) qualidade da informação – o software é *informativo*? – , (iv) *entendimento,* (v) *auditabilidade.* Com o intuito de definir os requisitos de transparência de software, [3] associou a estes 5 atributos de transparência um conjunto de 33 requisitos não-funcionais.

O *checkTrans* é um conjunto de ações organizado em formato de *checklist.* O objetivo deste *checklist* é apresentar as ações e exemplos para realização dos requisitos não-funcionais de qualidade associados à transparência de software e definidos por [3]. A seleção das ações foi baseada no Catálogo de Transparência do Grupo ER - PUC-RIO [6].

Para cada ação sugerida no *checkTrans*, são associados exemplos com o intuito de auxiliar no entendimento do que deve ser feito para atingi-la [6]. Na Tabela 1 são apresentadas duas ações e exemplos do requisito de *Publicidade* do atributo de *Acessibilidade*. A tabela completa do *checkTrans* está disponível na URL http://leb.inf.ufsc.br/index.php/home/cibse2020/tabela1.

Tabela 1. Ações e Exemplos para o requisitos de Publicidade do atributo de Acessibilidade

Ações	Exemplos
Fornecer informações sobre o conjunto de dados do sistema.	Catálogo de Dados.
Definir as facilidades de navegação, inclusive, para pessoas com deficiência.	Acesso ao computador sem mouse. Padrões de acessibilidade (e-MAG).

2.2 Testes de Aceitação e BDD

Os testes de aceitação fazem parte do processo de validação do software. Estes testes são realizados pelo cliente para que ele decida se o software é bom o suficiente para ser implantado e usado em seu ambiente operacional [7]. Os testes de aceitação são definidos a partir das necessidades dos usuários identificadas durante o processo de elicitação e documentação dos requisitos. Eles podem ser especificados no início do processo de desenvolvimento de um software ou no final, na etapa de validação. Na entrega do produto, os testes são executados para que o cliente decida se o sistema é aceitável ou não [7]. Existem diversas técnicas para o desenvolvimento e execução de testes de aceitação. O *Behavior-driven development* (BDD) é um exemplo de técnicas de teste de aceitação amplamente utilizadas na indústria e academia [8]. No processo de análise do software, o BDD utiliza *templates* predefinidos para a criação de histórias de usuário e cenários de teste. Entre as ferramentas mais populares que utilizam BDD está o *Cucumber* [9].

2.3 Testes Automatizados

Testes automatizados são trechos de código-fonte que exercitam as funcionalidades de um software e realizam asserções automáticas com o resultado do processamento do sistema em teste (*System Under Test – SUT*). Ao contrário dos testes manuais, a execução dos testes automatizados, por ter pouca ou nenhuma dependência da intervenção humana, é mais efetiva tanto na verificação quanto na validação do software. Entretanto, os testes automatizados requerem implementação, manutenção e gerenciamento da execução [10]. Dentre as diversas ferramentas existentes utilizadas para o desenvolvimento de testes automatizados está o Selenium, uma ferramenta para criação e execução de testes automatizados para aplicações Web.

3 Requisitos de Transparência de Software Selecionados

Nem todos os requisitos modelados no *checkTrans* conseguem ser mapeados para testes de aceitação automatizados. As seguintes restrições foram consideradas na seleção de atributos do *checkTrans*: (1) os testes devem ser executados sob a perspectiva do usuário, pois do contrário, os próprios testes não seriam transparentes. Sendo assim, serão definidos *templates* de teste somente para ações e exemplos de atributos que podem ser testados a partir da máquina do usuário; (2) embora não seja desejável que testes de aceitação sejam realizados sobre a GUI, para evitar o acoplamento e dependência, esta é a interface mais disponível para realização de testes sob a perspectiva do usuário e de forma transparente. Portanto, os testes devem ser executados através de um navegador Web em um software disponível na Internet com interface baseada em elementos DOM; (3) ações e exemplos que buscam validar atributos de transparência relacionados a ações do processo de desenvolvimento de software serão desconsiderados; (4) os *templates* de teste para as ações e exemplos de um atributo devem ser automatizáveis. A partir destas restrições foram extraídos do *checkTrans* os atributos, junto com suas respectivas ações e exemplos, que podem ter seus *templates* de teste de aceitação especificados. A Tabela 2 lista todas as ações dos atributos identificados como adequados para serem mapeados para *templates* de testes de aceitação automatizados.

Tabela 2. Atributos selecionados do *checkTrans*

Atributos (Requisitos)	**Ação sugerida**	**Exemplos**
Portabilidade	Especificar as diferentes tecnologias onde o software poderá ser utilizado.	(i) Navegadores Internet Explorer e Chrome; (ii) Padrões de desenvolvimento W3C.
Publicidade	Definir as facilidades de navegação, inclusive, para pessoas com deficiência.	(i) Acesso ao computador sem mouse; (ii) Padrões de acessibilidade (e-MAG).
	Definir e fornecer alternativas para disponibilização da informação.	Informações em figuras, vídeos e áudios.
Amigabilidade	Definir os elementos de informação que são apresentados em cada contexto.	Ferramenta de busca presente em todas as páginas, mapa do sítio ou sistema, índice de palavras.
Simplicidade	Especificar os elementos que ajudam a simplificar a interação do usuário.	Formulários simplificados, disponibilizar ajuda dentro do próprio sistema.
	Definir como serão destacados os elementos essenciais.	(i) Conteúdos mais importantes, páginas, seções ou serviços mais utilizados no início da página; (ii) Campos obrigatórios ou opcionais indicados.

4 Mapeamento dos Critérios de Aceitação

Para mapear os critérios de aceitação de requisitos não-funcionais de qualidade para testes de aceitação foi utilizado como artefato cenários escritos na linguagem *Gherkin,* linguagem utilizada pelo BDD. A linguagem *Gherkin* foi escolhida por ser muito próxima de uma linguagem natural, o que facilita sua compreensão por até mesmo usuários não-técnicos [8]. Além disso, os cenários de teste escritos em *Gherkin* são compatíveis com uma séria de *frameworks* que os integram com outras ferramentas de testes automatizados.

4.1 *Templates* dos Cenários de Testes

Nesta seção serão apresentados alguns *templates* de testes de aceitação para validação do atributo de Portabilidade. Os *templates* dos demais atributos selecionados estão disponíveis em http://leb.inf.ufsc.br/index.php/home/cibse2020/templates.

Atributo Portabilidade. Validar se a página Web mostra as mesmas informações em diferentes navegadores e se foi implementada de acordo com os padrões da W3C.

Feature. *Portabilidade*

Eu, como usuário do Website <site governamental>

Quero ter acesso a informações transparentes de qualquer lugar

Então poderei acessar ao Website <site governamental> de diversas plataformas, sistemas operacionais ou navegadores de Internet.

Cenário 1. Acessar <site governamental> através de diferentes navegadores de Internet no sistema operacional <sistema operacional>

Dado que estou utilizando um computador <sistema operacional>

Quando eu acesso a página <página> do Website <site governamental> utilizando o navegador de Internet <navegador A>

E acesso esta mesma página utilizando o navegador de Internet <navegador B>.

Então as informações contidas na página são disponibilizadas da mesma forma tanto com <navegador A> quanto no <navegador B>.

Cenário 2. Acessar Website <site governamental> através de uma mesmo navegador em diferentes plataformas

Dado que estou acessando a página <página> do Website <site governamental> utilizando o navegador de Internet <navegador> em um <dispositivo A> <sistema operacional A>

Quando eu acesso esta mesma página utilizando o mesmo navegador em um <dispositivo B> <sistema operacional B>

Então as informações contidas na página são disponibilizadas da mesma forma tanto no <dispositivo A> quanto no <dispositivo B>.

5 Validação dos Testes de Aceitação

Para avaliar a validade dos *templates* de testes definidos na subseção 4.1, foram executados em sites do governo casos de teste criados a partir destes *templates*. Todavia, antes da execução automatizada de cada um dos casos de teste, foram identificados, através de uma validação manual, sites governamentais que atendem e que não atendem aos atributos de transparência associados aos *templates* criados. Através deste procedimento foi possível avaliar se os *templates* cumprem com o esperado, isto é, não apontam falhas em sites cujo atributo de transparência testado é satisfeito e apontam falhas quando o atributo não é satisfeito.

5.1 Especificação dos Testes de Aceitação Concretos

Os cenários de teste foram adaptados para a linguagem *Gherkin*, substituindo as *tags* do *template* por valores reais, assim como no exemplo a seguir, aonde o cenário é definido a partir do *template*.

Template. *Template* de cenário de teste para validação do atributo de Publicidade. Permitir a navegação no site <site governamental> sem utilizar o mouse

Dado que eu estou utilizando um computador <sistema operacional> sem mouse

Quando eu acesso a página <página> do Website <site governamental> utilizando o navegador de Internet <navegador de internet>

E eu interajo utilizando apenas as teclas TAB e ENTER do teclado

Então eu consigo acessar a página <pagina> do site

Cenário. Navegação no site "https://www.fernao.sp.gov.br" sem utilizar o mouse

Dado que eu estou utilizando um computador Linux sem mouse

Quando eu acesso a página "/" do Website "https://www.fernao.sp.gov.br" utilizando o navegador de Internet Firefox

E eu interajo utilizando apenas as teclas TAB e ENTER do teclado

Então eu consigo acessar a página de contato do site

Com as *tags* dos *templates* devidamente substituídas por valores reais, para executar os testes de aceitação dos atributos de transparência é necessário conectar os testes ao site governamental a ser testado (SUT). Esta conexão é realizada através do código de cola.

O código de cola é uma classe *Java* denominada *Feature* gerada automaticamente pela próprio *Cucumber*. Para cada passo do teste é gerado um método nesta classe. Então, para fazer o teste funcionar, é necessário implementar este método. A seguir é apresentado um exemplo de método escrito em *Java* que liga um passo do teste de aceitação ao SUT.

```
@Quando("^eu acesso a pagina \"([^\"]*)\" do site \"([^\"]*)\" utilizando o navegador web Firefox$")
public void eu_acesso_a_pagina_do_site_utilizado_o_navegador_web_Firefox(String pagina, String site) {
        this.firefoxDriver = DriverFactory.getDriver("firefox");
        this.firefoxDriver.get(site + pagina);}
```

5.2 Resultados

Para os 4 atributos de transparência foram mapeados 8 *templates* de testes de aceitação. Todos estes *templates* foram automatizados para sites que cumpriam os requisitos de transparência de software e também para sites que não cumpriam estes requisitos, totalizando 16 cenários de teste automatizados. É importante ressaltar que cada página possui um DOM diferente e é através deste documento que o *Selenium* encontra os componentes HTML utilizados para executar os testes. Apesar de ser possível a generalização de cenários para diferentes páginas Web, a implementação de cada teste automatizado é diferente. Por este motivo, cada cenário foi avaliado em apenas uma página que atendia ao requisito e uma página que não atendia.

A Tabela 3 apresenta um resumo do resultado da execução dos testes.

Tabela 3. Ações e Exemplos para o requisitos de Publicidade do atributo de Acessibilidade

Atributo	Cenário	Site	Resultado esperado	Resultado obtido
Portabilidade	Acessar site através de diferentes navegadores Web	A	Sucesso	Sucesso
		B	Fracasso	Fracasso
Publicidade	Navegar no *site* sem utilizar o *mouse*	C	Sucesso	Sucesso
		D	Fracasso	Fracasso
	Alternativas para imagens ou vídeos	E	Sucesso	Sucesso
		F	Fracasso	Fracasso
Amigabilidade	Ferramenta de busca presente em todas as páginas	G	Sucesso	Sucesso
		H	Fracasso	Fracasso
	Existência do mapa do site	I	Sucesso	Sucesso
		J	Fracasso	Fracasso
Simplicidade	Informações que orientem no preenchimento de formulários	K	Sucesso	Sucesso
		L	Fracasso	Fracasso
	Elemento essencial destacado na página inicial do site	M	Sucesso	Sucesso
		N	Fracasso	Fracasso
	Indicação de campos obrigatórios ou opcionais	O	Sucesso	Sucesso
		P	Fracasso	Fracasso

(A) estrutura.ufsc.br/servicos-gratuitos/ (B) sectur.ma.gov.br/ (C) http://ufsc.br/mapa-do-site/ (D) http://fernao.sp.gov.br/ (E) http://noticias.ufsc.br/2019/10/pesquisa-da-ufsc-revela-nova-perspectiva-para-diagnostico-e-tratamento-da- http://tuberculose/ (F) desterrodeentrerios.mg.gov.br/noticias/?noticia=25 (G) prae.ufsc.br/ (H) alterosa.mg.gov.br/ (I) consulta.tesouro.fazenda.gov.br/gru_novosite/gru_simples.asp (J) contas.tcu.gov.br/debito/Web/Debito/CalculoDeDebito.faces (K) ufsc.br/ (L) trabiju.sp.gov.br/ (M) tjsc.jus.br/ (N) tjrs.jus.br (O) otrs.setic.ufsc.br/otrs/public.pl?Action=NewTicketWizardPublic (P) contas.tcu.gov.br/debito/Web/Debito/CalculoDeDebito.faces

Os resultados obtidos mostram que os casos de testes automatizados derivados dos *templates* definidos não apresentaram falsos positivos ou falsos negativos. Acredita-se, que as organizações públicas possam fazer uso desses *templates* para validar, de forma automatizada, que os produtos de software, desenvolvidos *in company* ou por empresas terceirizadas, atendem aos requisitos de transparência selecionados.

6 Conclusão

A proposta deste trabalho foi mapear critérios de aceitação de 4 atributos de transparência de software por meio de testes de aceitação abstratos (*templates*). A definição dos critérios de aceitação foi realizada com base nas ações e exemplos propostos no *checkTrans*. Os *templates* definidos foram especificados como cenários de testes de aceitação concretos e executados em sites do governo. Não foram detectados falsos positos ou negativos durante a validação dos *templates*, o que aponta que estão prontos para serem utilizados em ambiente produtivo.

Em [11], os autores adaptaram o *checkTrans* em um novo *checklist*, selecionando ações que podem ser aplicadas em sites existentes, entretanto as ações não são mapeadas para testes de aceitação automatizados. Outros dois trabalhos propuseram o uso de testes de aceitação automatizados para requisitos não-funcionais, porém, o foco não é a transparência de software. Em [12], os autores desenvolveram testes de aceitação para garantir acessibilidade, simulando a navegação em aplicações web utilizando o teclado. Em [13], os autores implementaram testes automatizados para avaliar um software de controle de qualidade através da injeção de código de testes no código em produção, o que a diferencia da proposta do presente trabalho.

O código fonte da implementação dos testes automatizados está disponível no endereço https://github.com/brunolg6/testesTransparencia/.

Referências

1. LEE, Y. W. et al. AIMQ: a methodology for information quality assessment. Information & management, v. 40, n. 2, p. 133-146, 2002.
2. MELO, D. A.. Transparência da informação pública: uma avaliação de sítios eletrônicos de universidades federais brasileiras. Dissertação (Pós-Graduação em Administração Pública) - Universidade Federal de Goiás, Goiânia, 2019.
3. CAPPELLI, C. Uma Abordagem para Transparência em Processos Organizacionais Utilizando Aspectos. 2009. 328p. Tese de doutorado (Pós-Graduação em Informática), Pontifícia Universidade Católica do Rio de Janeiro, Rio de Janeiro, 2009.
4. BRASIL. Acesso federal à informação. Disponível em: http://www.acessoainformacao.gov.br. Último acesso em: 06/12/2019.
5. CAPPELLI, C., LEITE, J. C. S. P. Transparência de Processos Organizacionais. Universidade Federal Fluminense. II Simpósio Internacional de Transparência nos Negócios. 2008.
6. MACEDO, F. F. de.. Transparência de software como apoio à publicidade da administração pública. Dissertação (Pós-Graduação em Ciência da Computação) - Universidade Federal de Santa Catarina, Florianópolis, 2014.
7. SOMMERVILLE, I.. Software Engineering. Pearson, 9ª Edição, São Paulo, 2011.
8. DOS SANTOS, E. C., VILAIN, P. Automated Acceptance Tests as Software Requirements: An Experiment to Compare the Applicability of Fit Tables and Gherkin Language. In International Conference on Agile Software Development (pp. 104-119).
9. SOLIS, C.; WANG, X.. A study of the characteristics of behaviour driven development. In: 2011 37th EUROMICRO Conference on Software Engineering and Advanced Applications. p. 383-387, IEEE, 2011.
10. CHEQUE, P.. Padrões de testes automatizados. Dissertação (Mestrado em Ciência da Computação) - Universidade de São Paulo, São Paulo, 2011.
11. FORTE, F. B., VILAIN, P., MACEDO, F. F. Adaptação de um Checklist para Análise de Transparência de Software em Sites. Anais do XI Simpósio Brasileiro de Sistemas de Informação (SBSI 2015), 2015. p.355-362.
12. WATANABE, W. M.; FORTES, R. P. M.; DIAS, A. L.. Using acceptance tests to validate accessibility requirements in RIA. In: Proceedings of the International Cross-Disciplinary Conference on Web Accessibility. ACM, p. 15, 2012.
13. METSA et al.. Testing Non-Functional Requirements with Aspects: An Industrial Case Study. In: Seventh International Conference on Quality Software (QSIC 2007). 2007.

Systematic mapping on the use of games for software engineering education

Diego Castro[1], Diogo Matheus Costa[1], and Cláudia Maria Lima Werner[1]
{diegocbcastro, dmc, werner}@cos.ufrj.br

COPPE/Computer Systems Engineering Program, Federal University of Rio de Janeiro, Rio de Janeiro, Brazil

Abstract. Games appeal to all kinds of people and are used for a wide range of purposes, from pure entertainment to educational research. Software Engineering is an area of computing that has much content to explore, distributed in different knowledge areas. Thus, there are many theoretical classes that make learning tiresome. In this scenario, educators and researchers are looking for new methods to engage students in order to facilitate the learning process. Many studies have already been produced using games as a teaching method. However, a recurring mistake when using games as a teaching method is the application of the wrong approach to a context that often hinders student learning. This paper presents a systematic mapping that aims to identify the main ways that games are being used as a teaching method focused on Software Engineering. The results highlight five ways of using games as a teaching method, where Game-based Learning, Digital Game-based Learning and Gamification are the most used ones.

Keywords: Serious Games, Software Engineering, Systematic Mapping.

1 Introduction

Going to college and entering a classroom to study a particular subject becomes a routine in a student's daily life. Over time, this can become a tedious situation where students end up losing interest in the matter. In this scenario, educators are increasingly exploring innovative learning strategies that combine pleasure with education [1]. Trying to make learning something enjoyable can be a great help to students who need to study a subject. It is worth remembering that according to Wolfman [2], people remember 15% of what they hear, 25% of what they see and 60% with which they interact. Since games are mostly interactive, this becomes an excellent opportunity to make students remember what has been taught. Based on this, the use of games in education seeks to make the teaching of a subject something more interactive and more pleasurable [3].

The idea of games was introduced into the academic world, creating a new vocabulary: "serious games", where this instrument provides a framework of entertainment, in which content is incorporated [1]. Squire [4] states that recent studies show that when playing a particular game, people are involved in more complex and challenging learning activities than most college tasks. Keeping in mind that games can be used to develop new skills and engage in more complex operations than those presented in the classroom, it is intended to use the full potential of games to facilitate the learning of Software Engineering (SE).

This paper presents a systematic mapping focused on the use of games as a teaching method in SE, identifying the main ways that games are being used for this purpose. The remainder of this paper is presented as follows: Section 2 presents a brief background on the use of games as a teaching method; Section 3 describes the research method used in the systematic mapping; Section 4 shows the results that were found; and Section 5 concludes with the final remarks.

2 Background

SE is an area of computing that seeks to create the specifications of a project and assist in the development and maintenance of systems [5]. SE is related to all stages of a software product and, therefore, it is necessary to have a good knowledge of the process that it addresses. However, it has many concepts and subdivisions related to it (i.e., knowledge areas), such as requirements, software quality, project management, among others [6].

To be able to have competent professionals in the future, they must have a good understanding of the concepts that are taught at the university. Connolly, Stansfield, and Hainey [7] claim that SE has been described as a "perverse problem", where different points make it difficult to be taught, such as few questions with clear answers, among others. In addition, Navarro and Van Der Hoek [8] affirm that there is a large gap in traditional SE education techniques, where "students are exposed to various concepts and theories of SE in lectures but have few opportunities to put these ideas into practice". Claypool and Claypool [9] argue that, currently, many SE projects lack the fun factor to engage students in learning. To reduce this teaching difficulty, different concepts have been employed to try to teach it otherwise. One is the use of games.

Caillois [10] define a game as an activity that is fun for the user and has an unpredictable result that is inside something fictitious and does not generate anything productive. According to Salen, Tekinbaş, and Zimmerman [11], a game is a system in which players participate in an artificial, rule-defined conflict that concludes a quantifiable result. Therefore, in general, games can be defined as activities that use an abstract world through decisions, actions, and rules, which aim at a recreational activity, in the form of distraction or amusement [12].

Games that have functions beyond entertainment, such as teaching, training, informing, or assisting in something, are called serious games. According to Adams and Dormans [13], the term serious game was designed in recognition that games can be used for purposes other than entertainment. Although there is no standard definition for serious games, this work adopts the following description: serious game is a game developed with a purpose beyond entertainment, offering opportunities for the user to try new approaches with safety, low cost, and without consequences [13].

3 Research Method

Systematic mapping is a method that makes aggregation of information based on studies related to a specific research topic [14], based on a structured and repeatable protocol that explores and categorizes studies and provides an overview [15]. The mapping to be presented was carried out in the period from 2018-12-15 to 2019-03-02 and followed the protocol proposed by Kitchenham [16], covering the articles published until the end of 2018.

The **protocol implementation** procedure followed three well-defined phases: Execute the search string in Scopus as recommended by other studies [17, 18]; apply the inclusion/exclusion criteria based on the title, abstract and full text; and perform the tasks from the previous phase for the articles found in the snowball procedure that will be described in detail in the next section. The **inclusion criteria** selected for this study were: the article must be in the context of using games for ES teaching; the article must provide data to answer at least one of the research questions; and the article should be written in English. The **exclusion criteria** were: Book chapters, conference call; and studies that can not be fully accessed.

3.1 Research Questions

- **Q1:** What game definition was used?
- **Q2:** What is the main advantage / motivation of the use of games to teaching software engineering?
- **Q3:** What is the disadvantage of the use of games to teaching software engineering?
- **Q4:** What are the research areas that the game intends to teach?
- **Q5:** What is the main characteristic of the game used?

3.2 Search String

The definition of the search keywords was made based on the PICO strategy [19], using three of the four levels.

The search string was defined by grouping keywords of the same domain with the logical operator "OR" and grouping the three domains with the logical operator "AND". In the first instance, the search string formed by the three PICO levels returned a result of 4,428 articles. Since the number of papers returned was relatively large, it was decided to use a date filter, searching only for documents that were published within the last five years, as performed by Jiang, Zhang, Gao, Shao, and Rong [20]. The keywords, PICO structure and the search string can be seen in Table 1.

To validated the search string, an ad-hoc literature review was performed by selecting two knowledge control articles that can be seen in Table 1. Using this kind of control, the validation is performed by executing the search string and it should return the selected control articles.

Table 1. Descriptive table with search string and keywords.

Pico	Synonyms
Population	Software engineering
Intervention	Tutoring, teach*, instruction, discipline, schooling, education*, mentoring, course, learn*, train*, syllabus
Comparison	Not applicable
Outcome	Game*, gami*, play*, "serious games", edutainment, "game based learning", simulation
Search String	
Control Article	(1) Software engineering education and games: A systematic literature review; (2) SimulES-W: A collaborative game to improve software engineering teaching
Filter	(LIMIT-TO (PUBYEAR , 2018) OR LIMIT-TO (PUBYEAR , 2017) OR LIMIT-TO (PUBYEAR , 2016) OR LIMIT-TO (PUBYEAR , 2015) OR LIMIT-TO (PUBYEAR , 2014))
TITLE-ABS-KEY (("Software engineering") AND (tutoring OR teach* OR instruction OR discipline OR schooling OR educat* OR mentoring OR course OR learn* OR train* OR syllabus) AND (game* OR gami* OR play* OR "serious games" OR edutainment OR "game based learning" OR simulation) AND (LIMIT-TO (PUBYEAR , 2018) OR LIMIT-TO (PUBYEAR , 2017) OR LIMIT-TO (PUBYEAR , 2016) OR LIMIT-TO (PUBYEAR , 2015) OR LIMIT-TO (PUBYEAR , 2014)))	

4 Results

The search string returned a total of 1,229 papers. Applying the inclusion and exclusion filters, this number dropped to 37 papers. As there is no perfect search string, and the work was only performed at Scopus, the snowball procedure was used to minimize the lack of other search bases [17]. This procedure aims to find new references based on the articles that were cited in the papers that were read (backward snowballing) and in relation to the papers that referred to the article read (forward snowballing) [17]. In the backward snowballing process, 382 articles were identified; applying the filters, this number dropped to only 2. In forward snowballing, 311 articles were identified, and 5 more articles were included. After all the search process, 44 papers were included. Table 2 shows the detailed analysis of the articles and Table 3 lists all articles that were included in the review, demonstrating which questions each article was able to answer.

Table 2. Analysis of the articles

	Main study		Snowballing backward		Snowballing forward	
Activity	**Result**	**Number of papers**	**Result**	**Number of papers**	**Result**	**Number of papers**
First Execution	1229 added	1229	382 added	382	311 added	311
Repeated Papers	32 withdraw	1197	36 withdraw	346	78 withdraw	233
Papers in another language	12 withdraw	1185	17 withdraw	329	51 withdraw	182
Remove conference / workshops	57 withdraw	1128	0 withdraw	329	0 withdraw	182
Remove books	43 withdraw	1085	21 withdraw	308	4 withdraw	178
Remove by title	638 withdraw	447	236 withdraw	72	112 withdraw	66
Remove by abstract	379 withdraw	68	64 withdraw	8	51 withdraw	15
Papers not found	0 withdraw	68	1 withdraw	7	2 withdraw	13
Remove by full paper	31 withdraw	37	5 withdraw	2	8 withdraw	5
Total papers included	**37 documents**		**2 documents**		**5 documents**	
Extracted Papers	**44 documents**					

4.1 Findings' Summary

Q1: What game definition was used? Video games have been in our lives for over 50 years, quickly becoming one of the most important, lucrative, and

Table 3. Traceability matrix.

Title	Year	Q1	Q2	Q3	Q4	Q5
A serious game to support the ISO 21500 standard education in the context of software project management	2018	X	X		X	X
What can go wrong in a software project? Have fun solving it	2018	X	X	X	X	X
Games for Requirements Engineers: Analysis and Directions	2018	X	X		X	X
How to design gamification? A method for engineering gamified software	2018	X	X	X		X
Classutopia: A serious game for conceptual modeling design	2018	X	X		X	X
SimulES-W: A collaborative game to improve software engineering teaching	2018	X	X		X	X
Experiences of using a game for improving learning in software requirements elicitation	2018	X	X	X	X	X
Gamification Applied in the Teaching of Agile Scrum Methodology	2018	X	X		X	X
Gamification in Software Testing: A Characterization Study	2018	X	X		X	X
Gamification in Software Engineering Education: An Empirical Study	2017	X	X			X
Teaching ISO/IEC 12207 software lifecycle processes: A serious game approach	2017	X	X	X	X	X
Integrating serious games as learning resources in a software project management course: The case of ProDec	2017	X	X		X	X
Game elements in a software engineering study group: A case study	2017	X	X		X	X
Teaching software testing concepts using a mutation testing game	2017	X	X	X	X	X
A case study of software engineering methods education supported by digital game-based learning: Applying the SEMAT Essence kernel in games and course projects	2017	X	X		X	X
Developing and implementation of decision-making games for business education of engineering students	2017	X	X	X	X	X
Simkan: Training kanban practices through stochastic simulation	2017	X	X		X	X
Deploying a gamification framework for software process improvement: Preliminary results	2017	X	X	X		X
Coverage of ISO/IEC 29110 project management process of basic profile by a serious game	2017	X	X		X	X
Coverage of the ISO 21500 Standard in the Context of Software Project Management by a Simulation-Based Serious Game	2017	X	X	X	X	X
Gamification of software testing	2017	X	X		X	X
An agile software engineering process improvement game	2016	X	X		X	X
GSDgame: A serious game for the acquisition of the competencies needed in GSD	2016	X	X	X		X
The effects of students' motivation, cognitive load and learning anxiety in gamification software engineering education: a structural equation modeling study	2016	X	X	X		X
A serious game to promote object oriented programming and software engineering basic concepts learning	2016	X	X		X	X
Methodology to construct educational video games in software engineering	2016	X	X			X
Improving programming education through gameful, formative feedback	2016	X	X	X		X
Coverage of ISO/IEC 12207 software lifecycle process by a simulation-based serious game	2016	X	X		X	X
Ace that game: Educating students to gamified design thinking	2016	X	X	X	X	X
SCRUM-X: An interactive and experiential learning platform for teaching scrum	2016	X	X		X	X
Proposal to Teach Software Development Using Gaming Technique	2016	X	X		X	X
Project management game 2D (PMG-2D): A serious game to assist software project managers training	2015	X	X	X	X	X
The issues of adopting simulation games in software engineering classes	2015	X	X			X
Experimental evaluation of a serious game for teaching software process modeling	2015	X	X		X	X
Gamification of software engineering curriculum	2015	X	X	X		X
Gamification proposal for a software engineering risk management course	2015	X	X		X	X
Examining the effectiveness of 2D and 3D online environment in enhancing students' learning of software engineering	2015	X	X			X
Anukarna: A software engineering simulation game for teaching practical decision making in peer code review	2015		X		X	X
Implementing gamification techniques into university study path - A case study	2015	X	X			X
InspectorX: A game for software inspection training and learning	2014	X	X		X	X
Research on teaching gamification of software engineering	2014	X	X	X		X
Evaluating GameDevTycoon for teaching Software Engineering	2014	X	X		X	X
A general framework for software project management simulation games	2014	X	X		X	X
StrateJect: An Interactive Game for Project Management Experiential Learning	2014		X		X	X

influential ways to entertain [21]. A game is an activity between two or more independent decision-makers trying to achieve their goals in some limited context. A more conventional definition would say that a game is a context with rules between opponents trying to achieve goals [22]. According to Laskowski [23], a game is a non-serious and voluntary activity, intentionally separated from the real world. An activity that absorbs the player fully and intensely and is not related to any benefit. A game requires the player to play at a specific time and place and to do so under the established order and rules [23].

One of the first serious games to be developed was Army Battlezone, a project developed by Atari in the early 1980s that was created to train soldiers on a battlefield [24]. However, for Gannod, Burge, and Helmick [25], the term serious game was first used only in 2002 in a release of a military training simulator called "America's Army", created by the US Army and distributed for free over the Internet.

Serious games are designed in such a way that the primary purpose is not to entertain the user but to train him/her in a particular area. This does not mean that the game cannot be fun, but the entertainment derived from the game is designed to educate so that the player's learning experience becomes fun [26]. Serious games are designed for a different purpose than just entertaining the user [22, 27]. The adjective "serious" indicates that their goal is more than just fun and that they are designed to educate, train, or inform users [28]. For Maxim, Kaur, Apzynski, Edwards, and Evans [29], serious games make use of the artistic means of games to convey a message, teach a lesson, or provide an experience.

According to Ramírez-Rosales, Vázquez-Reyes, Villa-Cisneros, and De León-Sigg [21], a serious game with a didactic purpose is one in which some kind of knowledge is obtained through playing, facilitating the teaching and learning process.

In this scenario, this question was added to find out the game definitions that were used, aiming to identify the main ways (i.e., approaches) that games are being used as a teaching method focused on Software Engineering. In general, five ways of using games as a teaching method were found: Game-based Learning; Digital Game-based Learning; Game Development Based Learning; Simulation; and Gamification. Based on the collected data, Game-based Learning, Digital Game-based Learning and Gamification are the most used ones.

Garcia, Pacheco, León, and Calvo-Manzano [30] use the term Game-based Learning (GBL) to represent the application of games for educational purposes. For them, GBL can be defined as applying the principles of traditional games in real-life situations, to get students' attention and encourage knowledge creation. Thus, the concept of GBL mostly refers to the use of games to support teaching and learning [30, 31]. GBL can be understood as any use of a game for educational purposes. However, it has a branch called Digital Game-based Learning (DGBL) that comprises games in their digital versions [32].

One more approach is Game Development Based Learning, that represents the activity of developing games as a practical learning experience. Games represent an eminent domain of students, thus facilitating the understanding of requirements. Games are attractive, motivating, and involve students in their creative process. Finally, the varied complexity of games can provide educators with a wide range of options for classroom tasks and projects [33].

Another approach that has been found as a method that can improve the current way of teaching is the use of Simulation, that can be understood as attractive approaches within a risk-free environment [34]. Simulation games mimic a given situation and bring a more realistic experience [35]. Nassal [36] believes that simulation games are an alternative tool to gain experience in a controlled and risk-free manner. Simulation games also let users try out various strategies at once.

Finally, another approach related to enriching training and teaching through games is the phenomenon of Gamification, which, according to Calderón, Ruiz, and O'Connor [22] can be understood as the use of game elements and game design techniques in non-playful contexts. Unkelos-Shpigel [37] adds by saying that this technique is defined as integrating game mechanics into non-playful environments to increase engagement, loyalty, fun, and can even stimulate user participation and contribution. For Herranz, Colomo-Palacios, and Al-Barakati [38] gamification is the use of game elements in other contexts to alter and inspire people's behavior. The intention is to inject fun, play, and passion into tasks and processes [38, 39]. Gamification has attracted the attention of practitioners and researchers as a way to use game-based mechanics, aesthetics, and thinking to motivate people, promoting learning to increase end-user engagement and change behaviors in many contexts, such as teaching [22].

Q2: What is the main advantage / motivation of the use of games to teaching software engineering? Using games as a reinforcement tool to teach skills can be a very beneficial strategy for students. They have proven to be a useful tool to complement conventional learning methods. Games allow visualizing concepts that could be perceived as too abstract. They also help to familiarize the students with the knowledge and techniques that may be tedious to study, offering a cycle of challenges and rewards that drives the learning experience [26, 40, 41].

Many benefits are linked to the use of games in education, such as increased collaboration and competition, immediate feedback, the possibility of reflecting on the results achieved, and the transfer of content so that learning is an integral part of education [42]. Another advantage attributed to serious games is the ability of the user to assume real roles [43]. As training tools, serious games increase students' conceptual knowledge, increase task completion, student's confidence, and improve knowledge retention [44].

SE education lacks practical experience, which is essential for understanding problems and especially their solutions [36]. It is crucial that these experiences are based on real scenarios so that the student can make a good use of the content. Many areas of higher education are difficult to practice due to their long duration and the potential for severe damage. However, games represent an alternative tool for gaining experience in a controlled and risk-free manner [36]. Playing does not take as much time and care as in a real project, and in case of failure, the game can be restarted. Games have a significant advantage for teaching; that is their repeatability. They can be reset at any time, allowing students to learn through their failures [45].

A game is a visible and physical representation of a problematic space, a captured mental model that can be repeated. As such, they are places to test new ideas and experiment with established theories; repeat the activities as many times as necessary; areas where time and space can be contracted or expanded; places where it is only acceptable to try different things and where it is possible to learn more by failure than by success [36].

Simulation increases the opportunity to learn from failure without any loss in reality, but in a very timely manner, and can bring engagement and motivation on the part of students. One of the main advantages that simulation can bring is feedback, in which, the student knows if he/she is doing a particular task right or wrong, seriously influencing the learning effects. Also, simulation games promote numerous cognitive benefits for students, such as motivation, visual effects, experimentation, self-efficacy, self-monitoring, problem-solving, and critical thinking skills [46].

Finally, the gamification approach can have a positive impact on increasing user motivation and engagement concerning a particular behavior [32].

Q3: What is the disadvantage of the use of games to teaching software engineering? Few papers have reported problems. In this scenario, only 7 of 44 studies mentioned disadvantages.

The limited use of serious games in formal education may be related to the issues surrounding the use of leisure games, such as a view where games can be addictive, unproductive and may teach misconceptions [26]. Another very relevant point about not using games as a teaching method is that players usually learn through repetition, patterns, and exploration, which contrasts with learning discrete amounts of information, as in college.

To create an educational game is not enough to use a game that performs an activity to teach something. To effectively teach and retain practice, students need to be more active and being provided with better instructional methods in which they participate in higher-level cognitive tasks [24]. Another problem with using games is that they are just a representation of how the real world works. Therefore, it is potentially dangerous to the players leave the game environment with the belief that the effective strategies employed in the game are directly transferable to the real world [47].

Gamification explores different game elements. However, some of these elements may cause problems if not used correctly. Herranz, Colomo-Palacios, and Al-Barakati [38] stated that it is not easy to manage and that there is a danger of misinterpreting the conceptualization and improper implementation of game elements, and, finally, they stated that gamification is not easy to manage because there is a risk of misinterpretation through users, which occurs in unexpected results, such as the introduction of unfair competitiveness, demotivation generated by scoreboards, among other problems. Morschheuser, Hassan, Werder, and Hamari [48] complement by saying that games in education are challenging to design different reasons, such as games are complex, multifaceted and therefore difficult to create; they aim to affect behavior and not just entertain, which implies understanding a range of (motivational) psychology and requires appropriate skills in the development team.

Q4: What are the research areas that the game intends to teach? As already mentioned in Section 1, SE has many subdivisions (i.e., knowledge areas) to be taught, such as requirements, software quality, project management and more. In this scenario, this question was added to find out which SE area are most explored through games.

To answer this question, the identified studies were classified. However, some studies did not have a well-defined SE area. Therefore, this kind of study was classified as others. Although the work references only 44 papers (i.e., selected documents), different studies addressed more than one SE area. The frequency of each area is presented as follows: Project Management (13 out of 44); Software Engineering (11 out of 44); Software Testing and Software Quality (5 out of 44); Software Development, Software Process and Agile Methodology (4 out of 44); Software Requirement (3 out of 44); Software Modeling (2 out of 44); Risk Management and Software Inspection (1 out of 44). Based on the collected data, the mostly addressed SE area was Project Management (13 studies).

Q5: What is the main characteristic of the game used? Different games and ways to use them as a teaching method have been analyzed, each one has its characteristics, which give "life" to the game and make it productive or not. Among the main features observed, the ones that stand out most are a real-world representation, levels or phases, constant feedback, and the use of graphs that catch the user's eye.

When building an education game, some contextual characteristics should be taken into account. Games must represent the real world complexity, emphasizing authentic tasks and encouraging experiences and reflections through collaboration, competition, social negotiation, simulations and feedback [42]. Another essential information that must be taken into account is the creation of dependent phases, where the player can gradually learn and build up his/her knowledge [49].

There are also features that reference the game's interface and gameplay. Among these characteristics stand out mainly the narratives and graphics that can bring the right motivation. An attractive game must have a minimalistic graphic, displaying easy-to-interpret buttons, lists, and menus. Similarly, game elements should be natural to interpret using some familiar game components such as life bars, dialog windows, score, avatars, scoreboard, leaderboard, checkpoints, sprites, boss fights, missions, badges, and rewards in general [27].

One of the most common concepts in games is the idea of levels. In educational games, they are used to divide content that should be presented in a sequential manner, which can be aggregated with the concept of time [21, 22]. Another important feature that was applied in games was the use of the level map and a help session, where the player can go back to the part that he/she had the most difficulty in solving, but now having extra help [21].

In this scenario, the Gamification approach can provide several features to non-playful context, such as levels, points, badges, avatars, leaderboard, progress bar, title changes, and status changes [29, 39]. In this scenario, the use of online plataforms was observed, such as Moodle to manage content [37].

Finally, it was also identified the main languages used to develop educational games, which were Java, JavaScript, C++ and C Sharp. In addition, the use of the Unity 3D game engine was explored when related to 3D programming because of the ease of exporting to multiple platforms (e.g., PC, Mac, web and mobile) [8, 21, 24, 28, 41].

Summary Result. This study identified different games and characteristics that sought to increase motivation and engagement through fun. In most studies, games are used by participants with minimal or no knowledge in the subject to be taught. In this case, it is expected that these games have resources to introduce certain concepts in a way that the player feels more engaged to continue learning the subject, as well as to help in the practical training.

In general, five ways of using games as a teaching method were found. In this scenario, Figure 1 shows a table summarizing the collected data to facilitate the reader to be able to choose the method that best suits his/her teaching purpose. Based on it, the reader can see the purpose of each approach and its main characteristics, and from that, make his/her interpretations and find out which one to use.

	Game-based learning	Digital Game-Based Learning	Game Development Based Learning	Simulation	Gamification
Definition	Use of games for learning purposes	Use of digital games for learning purposes	Use of the game development activity for learning purposes	Real-world imitation for learning purposes	Use of games' elements in non-playful contexts
Purpose	Learning			Learning, training, etc	Increase engagement
Fun	✓	✓	✓	✓	✓
Gameplay	✓	✓			
Advantage / Motivation	The use of games entertainment as a reinforcement tool		Practical training	Experimentation through a simulated environment	Increased user motivation and engagement through the use of game elements
Virtual world		✓		✓	
Learning by failure	✓	✓		✓	
Digital Resources		✓	✓	✓	✓
Observations	Mainly used as a complementary method			Just a representation of the real world, not necessarily an absolute truth	Something new, be careful to not lose the original application concept

Fig. 1. Findings' summary

5 Final Remarks

The presented work aimed to identify the main ways that games are being used as a teaching method in SE. To achieve this goal, a systematic mapping was performed based on five questions. These questions sought to find out which methods were most used based on their advantages, disadvantages, elements and characteristics.

Based on the collected data, it was possible to observe that the most used methods are Game-based Learning, Digital Game-based Learning and Gamification, but there are other ways to use games in education, such as Simulation and Game Development Based Learning.

Some limitations can be identified by performing a critical analysis of the work. The used search filters represent a scope limitation. In addition, the ad-hoc categorization of the SE knowledge areas also limit the work. In this scenario, the SWEBOK knowledge areas could be used.

The present work is part of a more extensive research focused on the use of games as a teaching method for Software Reuse (SR). Initially, a research focused on the use of games for teaching SR was conducted. However, no results were found. Since SR is one of the SE knowledge areas, it was decided to generalize the research by searching the use of games for teaching SE. Thus, it is expected that it will be possible to use the collected data to support the creation of a game to teach SR.

Acknowledgment. The authors would like to thank CAPES and CNPq for their financial support.

References

1. Ritterfeld U, Cody M, and Vorderer P. Serious games: Mechanisms and effects. Routledge, 2009.
2. Wolfman DE. Criando em multimídia. Rio de Janeiro: Campus 1994 (in portuguese).
3. Ludens H. A Study of the Play Element in Culture. Trans. by RFC Hull.(London, 1949) 1955:168.
4. Squire K. Changing the game: What happens when video games enter the classroom? Innovate: Journal of online education 2005;1.
5. Pressman RS. Software engineering: a practitioner's approach. Palgrave Macmillan, 2005.
6. Sommerville I, Arakaki R, and Melnikoff SSS. Engenharia de software. Pearson Prentice Hall, 2008.
7. Connolly TM, Stansfield M, and Hainey T. An application of games-based learning within software engineering. British Journal of Educational Technology 2007;38:416–28.
8. Navarro EO and Van Der Hoek A. Software process modeling for an educational software engineering simulation game. Software Process: Improvement and Practice 2005;10:311–25.

9. Claypool K and Claypool M. Teaching software engineering through game design. In: *ACM SIGCSE Bulletin.* Vol. 37. 3. ACM. 2005:123–7.
10. Caillois R. Les jeux et les hommes. Le masque et le vertige. Editions Gallimard, 2015 (in french).
11. Salen K, Tekinbaş KS, and Zimmerman E. Rules of play: Game design fundamentals. MIT press, 2004.
12. Xexéo G, Carmo A, Acioli A, et al. O Que São Jogos? 2017 (in portuguese).
13. Adams E and Dormans J. Game mechanics: advanced game design. New Riders, 2012.
14. Keele S et al. Guidelines for performing systematic literature reviews in software engineering. Tech. rep. Technical report, Ver. 2.3 EBSE Technical Report. EBSE, 2007.
15. Steinmacher I, Chaves AP, and Gerosa MA. Awareness support in distributed software development: A systematic review and mapping of the literature. Computer Supported Cooperative Work (CSCW) 2013;22:113–58.
16. Kitchenham B. Procedures for performing systematic reviews. Keele, UK, Keele University 2004;33:1–26.
17. Matalonga S, Rodrigues F, and Travassos GH. Characterizing testing methods for context-aware software systems: Results from a quasi-systematic literature review. Journal of Systems and Software 2017;131:1–21.
18. Motta RC, Oliveira KM de, and Travassos GH. Characterizing Interoperability in Context-aware Software Systems. In: *2016 VI Brazilian Symposium on Computing Systems Engineering (SBESC).* IEEE. 2016:203–8.
19. Petticrew M and Roberts H. Systematic reviews in the social sciences: A practical guide. John Wiley & Sons, 2008.
20. Jiang S, Zhang H, Gao C, Shao D, and Rong G. Process simulation for software engineering education. In: *Proceedings of the 2015 International Conference on Software and System Process.* ACM. 2015:147–56.
21. Ramírez-Rosales S, Vázquez-Reyes S, Villa-Cisneros JL, and De León-Sigg M. A serious game to promote object oriented programming and software engineering basic concepts learning. In: *2016 4th International Conference in Software Engineering Research and Innovation (CONISOFT).* IEEE. 2016:97–103.
22. Calderón A, Ruiz M, and O'Connor RV. A serious game to support the ISO 21500 standard education in the context of software project management. Computer Standards & Interfaces 2018;60:80–92.
23. Laskowski M. Implementing gamification techniques into university study path-A case study. In: *2015 IEEE Global Engineering Education Conference (EDUCON).* IEEE. 2015:582–6.
24. Lino JEN, Paludo MA, Binder FV, Reinehr S, and Malucelli A. Project management game 2D (PMG-2D): A serious game to assist software project managers training. In: *2015 IEEE Frontiers in Education Conference (FIE).* IEEE. 2015:1–8.

25. Gannod G, Burge J, and Helmick M. Using the inverted classroom to teach software engineering. In: *2008 ACM/IEEE 30th International Conference on Software Engineering*. IEEE. 2008:777–86.
26. Valencia D, Vizcaino A, Garcia-Mundo L, Piattini M, and Soto JP. GSDgame: A serious game for the acquisition of the competencies needed in GSD. In: *2016 IEEE 11th International Conference on Global Software Engineering Workshops (ICGSEW)*. IEEE. 2016:19–24.
27. Larenas F, Marín B, and Giachetti G. Classutopia: A Serious Game for Conceptual Modeling Design. In: *SEKE*. 2018:116–5.
28. Calderón A and Ruiz M. Coverage of ISO/IEC 12207 software lifecycle process by a simulation-based serious game. In: *International Conference on Software Process Improvement and Capability Determination*. Springer. 2016:59–70.
29. Maxim BR, Kaur R, Apzynski C, Edwards D, and Evans E. An agile software engineering process improvement game. In: *2016 IEEE Frontiers in Education Conference (FIE)*. IEEE. 2016:1–4.
30. Garcia I, Pacheco C, León A, and Calvo-Manzano JA. Experiences of using a game for improving learning in software requirements elicitation. Computer Applications in Engineering Education 2019;27:249–65.
31. Su CH. The effects of students' motivation, cognitive load and learning anxiety in gamification software engineering education: a structural equation modeling study. Multimedia Tools and Applications 2016;75:10013–36.
32. Uskov V and Sekar B. Gamification of software engineering curriculum. In: *2014 IEEE Frontiers in Education Conference (FIE) Proceedings*. IEEE. 2014:1–8.
33. Souza MR, Veado L, Moreira RT, Figueiredo E, and Costa H. Games for learning: bridging game-related education methods to software enginering knowledge areas. In: *Proceedings of the 39th International Conference on Software Engineering: Software Engineering and Education Track*. IEEE Press. 2017:170–9.
34. Morales-Trujillo ME, García-Mireles GA, and Maslova P. What can go wrong in a software project? Have fun solving it. In: *2018 Federated Conference on Computer Science and Information Systems (FedCSIS)*. IEEE. 2018:995–1004.
35. Peixoto DC, Resende RF, and Pádua CIP. The issues of adopting simulation games in software engineering classes. In: *2015 IEEE Frontiers in Education Conference (FIE)*. IEEE. 2015:1–8.
36. Nassal A. A general framework for software project management simulation games. In: *2014 9th Iberian Conference on Information Systems and Technologies (CISTI)*. IEEE. 2014:1–5.
37. Unkelos-Shpigel N. Ace That Game: Educating Students to Gamified Design Thinking. In: *STPIS@ CAiSE*. 2016:75–82.
38. Herranz E, Colomo-Palacios R, and Al-Barakati A. Deploying a Gamification Framework for Software Process Improvement: Preliminary Re-

sults. In: *European Conference on Software Process Improvement.* Springer. 2017:231–40.

39. Jesus GM de, Ferrari FC, Paula Porto D de, and Fabbri SCPF. Gamification in Software Testing: A Characterization Study. In: *Proceedings of the III Brazilian Symposium on Systematic and Automated Software Testing.* ACM. 2018:39–48.
40. Qu WQ, Zhao YF, Wang M, and Liu BQ. Research on teaching gamification of software engineering. In: *2014 9th International Conference on Computer Science & Education.* IEEE. 2014:855–60.
41. Jiménez-Hernández EM, Oktaba H, Piattini M, Arceo FDB, Revillagigedo-Tulais AM, and Flores-Zarco SV. Methodology to construct educational video games in software engineering. In: *2016 4th International Conference in Software Engineering Research and Innovation (CONISOFT).* IEEE. 2016:110–4.
42. Pieper J, Lueth O, Goedicke M, and Forbrig P. A case study of software engineering methods education supported by digital game-based learning: Applying the SEMAT Essence kernel in games and course projects. In: *2017 IEEE Global Engineering Education Conference (EDUCON).* IEEE. 2017:1689–99.
43. Lopes FJR and Petrillo F. SimKan: Training Kanban Practices Through Stochastic Simulation. In: *Brazilian Workshop on Agile Methods.* Springer. 2016:110–21.
44. Pötter H, Schots M, Duboc L, and Werneck V. InspectorX: A game for software inspection training and learning. In: *2014 IEEE 27th Conference on Software Engineering Education and Training (CSEE&T).* IEEE. 2014:55–64.
45. Szabo C. Evaluating GameDevTycoon for teaching software engineering. In: *Proceedings of the 45th ACM technical symposium on Computer science education.* ACM. 2014:403–8.
46. Calderón A, Ruiz M, and Orta E. Integrating serious games as learning resources in a software project management course: the case of ProDec. In: *Proceedings of the 1st International Workshop on Software Engineering Curricula for Millennials.* IEEE Press. 2017:21–7.
47. Caulfield C, Xia JC, Veal D, and Maj S. A systematic survey of games used for software engineering education. Modern Applied Science 2011;5:28–43.
48. Morschheuser B, Hassan L, Werder K, and Hamari J. How to design gamification? A method for engineering gamified software. Information and Software Technology 2018;95:219–37.
49. Dlamini RS. Examining the effectiveness of 2D and 3D online environment in enhancing students' learning of software engineering. International Journal of Innovation and Learning 2015;17:425–52.

Evaluating the Students' Experience with a requirements elicitation and communication game

Jéssyka Vilela[1] and Jonas Lopes[2]

[1] Centro de Informática, Universidade Federal de Pernambuco, Brasil
jffv@cin.ufpe.br
[2] Universidade Federal do Ceará, Brasil
jonaslopes2011@gmail.com

Abstract. Context: Group dynamics and games are used to provide practical support to theoretical concepts. Many of them are proposed in the literature, however, they do not receive an evaluation of their efficiency in teaching. Objective: to present an evaluation of the game "Translation Loss" whose goal is to be an immersible educational game to teach requirements elicitation and communication abilities. Method: we evaluated the students' experience in two classes from two different universities. In the first execution, we planned and executed the game with the participation of 40 students. Then, the students evaluated the game, considering the Model for the Evaluation of Educational GAmes (MEEGA). In the second execution, we relied on the participation of 27 students. Results: All aspects covered by the MEEGA model were approved by the students, concluding that the game had a good acceptance. Conclusions: We obtained empirical evidence that the Translation Loss contributes to improving requirements elicitation and communication skills in the students, and it could be a great educational material to simulate real tasks during the RE process.

Keywords: Requirements Engineering Education · Requirements Communication · Requirements Elicitation · Software Quality.

1 Introduction

Failures in software development projects are mainly caused by problems in the Requirements Engineering process [15][16]. Regardless of the process model adopted, the focus of every software project should be on quality at every step. The exit condition for every process activity, action, and task should focus on the quality of the work product that has been produced [7].

Fernandes et al. [5] state that 85% of software problems originate from the requirement elicitation activity. Projects fail because important information falls into the cracks and/or stakeholders fail to coordinate their efforts to create a successful product [7].

Effective communication (among technical peers, with the customer and other stakeholders, and with project managers, for example) is among the most challenging activities faced in the software development process [19][7]. The communication of requirements among stakeholders is critical for system quality [19]. The critically derives from the fact that requirements should be understood in the same way by different roles in the development.

Communication problems in software development were investigated by some authors such as Brady et al. [1], Pernstal [10], Rasmussen and Lundell [11], Wang et al. [18] and Vilela et al. [19][17]. RE focuses on good specification practices but has yet to find working solutions for effective requirements communication [19] considering its potential in supporting the improvement of software processes and the quality of the final product.

One of the main causes of the failures and deficiencies of software systems is the lack of appropriate skills and knowledge of those engaged in RE activities. Requirements related problems, as well as communication and coordination, is an essential undertaking in software engineering education if the field is to have professionals who are capable of accomplishing software projects.

In this context, educational games can bring benefits to the teaching and learning processes, and several games have already been developed and are used in different levels of teaching and disciplines [12]. However, there is a surprising lack of empirical evidence on its utility. Moreover, simulating real scenarios of projects in the classroom and providing experiences in decision making and problem-solving for the students is a challenge activity. Another important fact is that in many areas of technology games are used as a teaching tool, but this is rare in the field of Requirements Engineering.

This paper presents an experience report of the application of a game called "Translation Loss" [2] in two undergraduate classes of different universities. The first class was composed of 40 students from the second semester of the Software Engineering course at Universidade Federal do Ceará (UFC) - Campus Quixadá. The second class consisted of 27 students from the first semester of the Information Systems course at Universidade Federal de Pernambuco (UFPE). The game aims to support the requirements engineering teaching, focusing on the activities of requirements elicitation and communication with the client. The target audience is undergraduate students of courses in the area of computing, which have in their grid, disciplines that involve requirements engineering.

In this game, the participants must carry out the requirements elicitation from a client. To perform such task, participants must collect information about the system and separate system and user requirements [14] in two stages with the absence/presence of the client to simulate a traditional software process and an agile one.

This study is indicated to requirements engineering professors who want to make their classes more dynamic and fun, using a game that was empirically assessed in relation to students learning and experience through the MEEGA model for educational games [12]. In overall, the students positively evaluated the game since all MEEGA model aspects were well scored by the students.

Therefore, we conclude that the game can be considered as an effective learning approach that allows practical experience on requirements communication.

This article is structured as follows: in the Second section, we define the theoretical foundation, and discuss related works; in the Third, we explain the rules of Translation Loss game; In Fourth section, we describe the methodology used; in Fifth section, we report the results, and finally, in Sixth section, we present conclusions and future work.

2 Background and Related Work

In this section, we describe the main concepts involved in this work, and we discuss related works.

2.1 Evaluation Model for educational games quality (MEEGA)

The MEEGA model was proposed by Savi et al. [12] to assess the quality of educational games. The model aims to evaluate if a game: i) can motivate students to use it as learning material; (ii) provides good user experience (e.g., if it is fun); and (iii) it generates a perception of educational utility among its users (i.e., whether students think they are learning the topic). The MEEGA model defines three components: motivation, user experience, and learning that are evaluated by attributes as illustrated in Figure 1.

Fig. 1. The MEEGA model (adapted from [12]).

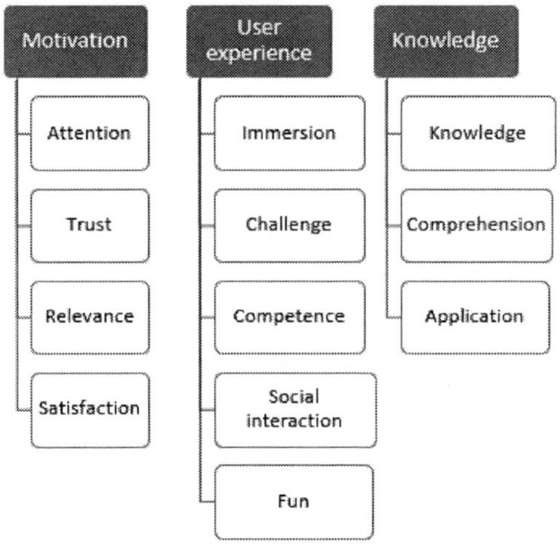

Motivation is divided into attention, trust, relevance and satisfaction [12]. Attention refers to students' cognitive responses to instructional stimuli, and Trust is related to creating positive expectations in the students. Relevance evaluates whether the game allows the student to connect the content of learning with their professional or academic future. Satisfaction is concerned with providing positive feelings in the students about the experience of learning.

User experience is divided into immersion, challenge, competence, social interaction, and fun [12]. Immersion distorts the notion of time, leading the player to have an experience of deep involvement in the game. Challenge evaluates whether the level of difficulty changes and gradually increases to maintain the player's interest as he develops his skills. Competence assesses the perception of skills, control, and use of these skills to explore the game and progress. Social interaction is related to the feeling of sharing an environment with other people and of having an active role in it. Finally, fun is concerned with the game providing feelings of fun, pleasure, relaxation, distraction, and satisfaction.

Knowledge is divided into learning questions [12]. Knowledge is the ability to remember information about facts, dates, words, theories, methods, classifications, places, rules, criteria, procedures, etc. Comprehension is to understand the information or the fact, grasping its meaning, using it in different contexts. Furthermore, Application is to apply knowledge in concrete situations.

2.2 Related Works

In the literature, some games and dynamics contribute to teaching requirements engineering. For instance, we found games to teach agile methodologies [8][9], Requirements Elicitation [13], Requirements modeling [3].

The Scrum Card Game [8] allows players to experience the execution of agile software development project activities and dealing with different issues that occur in day-to-day agile teams working with Scrum. Another approach to student teams learn the Scrum roles, events, and concepts in practice is by simulating several development Sprints incrementally planning and building a product of LEGO blocks [9].

Silva et al. [13] present an experiment with the game ELEMENT, which is a software solution that allows elicitation techniques teaching. The game provides support for a variety of problems and training scenarios in some key elicitation techniques, i.e., brainstorming and interviewing.

The Modeling game [3] aims to provide support for teaching engineering requirements. Its objective refers to the elaboration of a conceptual model of software development based on a given scenario. During the game, participants perform a series of activities called "Plays", sequentially arranged: (1) the Start Play, (2) the Play of Actions (which is a set of activities), and (3) the Validation Play. Nevertheless, the management effort and the amount of assumptions this game requires makes the complexity of its application higher compared to the ELEMENT game. We explain the Translation Loss game in the next section.

3 The "Translation Loss" Game

The goal of the game is to understand the difficulties related to verbal communication between clients and the development team. Another objective is to understand the advantages of client presence practice and prototyping in requirements development. The estimated duration time to execute the game is 2 hours (but it can be reduced according to the time available for the class), and the material needed is pens, papers, stopwatch, and a picture collection. Figure 2 presents the flow followed during the game execution. This process was designed from the steps produced by Carvalho [2].

Fig. 2. Steps to execute the translation loss game.

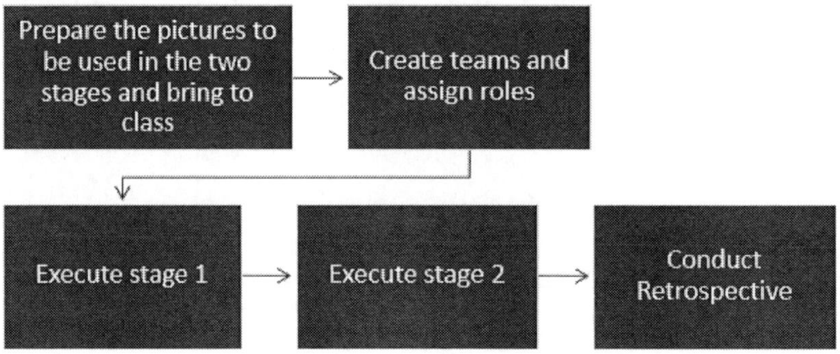

The class is divided into groups of 4 (minimum) and 6 (maximum) people. The groups nominate one customer, one requirements analyst, and the other members play the role of developer. The game is divided into two stages. Each stage has 4 distinct phases that are: (1) analysis, (2) interview, (3) development, and (4) delivery.

In stage 1, in the analysis phase (1):

- The client of each group leaves the room and receives a picture from the instructor.
- He analyzes the picture for 5 minutes and returns it to the instructor.

The Translation Loss is a non-digital game. Hence, we can use pictures such as Figure 3 and Figure 4, whose requirements should be elicited by the teams from the client.

After the analysis of the picture by the client, he returns to the room to start the interview phase (2).

- The developers leave the room.

Fig. 3. Example of a picture to be developed by the team in the first stage [2].

Fig. 4. Example of a picture to be developed by the team in the second stage [2].

- The requirements analyst interviews the client in a predefined time (we adopted 7 minutes) to elicit the requirements.
- The client describes the figure to the analyst (without drawing).
- The analyst takes note of "requirements", and he can ask whatever he wants to the client in the time available.
- Another rule is that the analyst cannot draw, only write the requirements in natural language.

In the development phase (3):

- The developers return, and the client leaves the room.
- The analyst provides the written specifications to developers.
- Analyst can talk freely with developers that are the only ones allowed to draw the picture on a predefined time (we adopted 10 minutes). improved.

In the delivery phase:

- The client returns to the room.
- He analyzes what was designed by the team.
- He compares with the picture given to him at the beginning.
- At this point, feedback is provided in 10 minutes on what went right or wrong, as well as what could be improved.

In stage 2, the same procedure of the four stages is conducted but with a different picture, for example Figure 4. However, in this stage:

- The analysis lasts 3 minutes, and the client is interviewed by the team (not only the requirements analyst) by 15 minutes.
- The client participates actively in the development, and he explains at any moment how he wants the final product.

At the end of the game, a retrospective (around 10 minutes) is conducted to discuss questions like [2]:

1) What problems occurred in Stage 1, how do they relate to traditional methods of development?

2) What elicitation technique was used in Stage 2, what benefits did it bring to development?

3) Indicate at least two fundamental competencies that can be related to the challenges experienced in the game;

4) Explain why competency would facilitate or enable the execution of requirements engineering activities?

We define the research methodology adopted in this work in the following section.

4 Methodology

In this paper, we intend to answer the following research questions:

RQ1: What was the students' reactions to the Translation Loss game?

RQ2: Did the students consider that they improve their requirements communication and elicitation skills by participating in the game?

The methodology used in this work to assess the learning results from teaching the importance of requirements elicitation and communication using the Translation Loss game consisted of two steps: (1) game planning and application; (2) game evaluation by the students.

4.1 Step 1: game planning and application

In Step 1, we executed the game following its rules described in Section 3. The game was applied in two undergraduate classes. The first class was composed of 40 students from the second semester of the Software Engineering course at Universidade Federal do Ceará (UFC) - Campus Quixadá. The second class consisted of 27 students from the first semester of the Information Systems course at Universidade Federal de Pernambuco (UFPE). During the activity, the game facilitator could answer questions from the students about the game itself.

4.2 Step 2: game evaluation by the students

We used a mixed-method approach combining qualitative and quantitative methods in Step 2. The assessment is based on the student's opinion about the game considering the model developed by Savi et al. [12] that proposes a model for the evaluation of educational game quality. The model defines three components: motivation, user experience, and knowledge, as described in Section 2.1.

The evaluation was performed considering students' perceptions measured by the MEEGA model and its assessment questionnaire. Some questions have been modified to suit the scope of our application. The questionnaire is composed of three parts where each one evaluates a component of the MEEGA model. The questions are presented in Table 1, Table 2, Table 3.

Table 1. Questionnaire to evaluate the Motivation component of "Translation Loss" game.

Aspect	Question	Answer
Attention	Q1: There was something interesting at the beginning of the game that captured my attention.	( )( )( )( )( )
	Q2: The form, content, information, and excitement helped me to maintain attention to the game.	( )( )( )( )( )
Relevance	Q3: It became clear to me how the content of the game is related with concepts I already knew.	( )( )( )( )( )
	Q4: You considered the content of the game relevant to teaching requirements development.	( )( )( )( )( )
	Q5: You believe that the operation of the game is suitable for learning through a game.	( )( )( )( )( )
Trust	Q6: In the course of the game, I felt confident that I was learning.	( )( )( )( )( )
	Q7: The activities of the game were easy to understand and I could accomplish them.	( )( )( )( )( )
Satisfaction	Q8: Completing the stages of the game gave me a sense of accomplishment.	( )( )( )( )( )
	Q9: I am satisfied because I know that I will have the opportunity to use in practice the lessons I have learned from the game.	( )( )( )( )( )
Legend: ( )( )( )( )( ) Totally Agree/ Agree/Neutral/ Disagree/Totally Disagree		

We changed the format of the responses from a 7-point to 5-point Likert scale, in the ranges of Strongly disagree to Strongly Agree. We made this choice considering the difficulty people have in choosing from a 7-point scale.

In the next section, we present and discuss the results obtained from the selected studies.

5 Results

The evaluation of the students' experience was generally positive in all aspects. When there was an indication of disagreement by the students, this percentage was low, lower than 5.97%. However, for some statements there was an indication

Table 2. Questionnaire to evaluate the User Experience component of "Translation Loss" game.

Aspect	Question	Answer
Immersion	Q10: I did not notice the time passing while I participated, when I realize, it was over.	( )( )( )( )( )
	Q11: I felt stimulated to learn from the game.	( )( )( )( )( )
Challenge	Q12: My skills have gradually improved by overcoming the challenges in the stages of the game.	( )( )( )( )( )
Skill/Competence	Q13: I had positive feelings of progress during the course game.	( )( )( )( )( )
Social Interaction	Q14: I felt that I was collaborating with other colleagues.	( )( )( )( )( )
	Q15: The game supports social interaction between players. ( )( )( )( )( )	
Fun	Q16: I was able to fit in and feel good during the game.	( )( )( )( )( )
	Q17: I would play this game again.	( )( )( )( )( )
Legend: ( )( )( )( )( ) Totally Agree/Agree/Neutral/ Disagree/Totally Disagree		

Table 3. Questionnaire to evaluate the Knowledge component of "Translation Loss" game.

Question	Answer
Q18: The game was efficient for my learning as compared to other discipline activities.	( )( )( )( )( )
Q19: The game contribute to my learning in the discipline.	( )( )( )( )( )
Q20: After the game I feel that I can better apply the themes related to the game.	( )( )( )( )( )
Legend: ( )( )( )( )( ) Totally Agree/Agree/Neutral/Disagree/Totally Disagree	

of neutrality by students. In this section, we present and discuss the answers of our research questions.

5.1 RQ1: What was the students' reactions to the Translation Loss game?

After the game application, we asked the students to answer the questionnaire described in Table 1 to 3 using a Google Form. We received 40 answers from the first application in University 1 (U1) and 27 from University 2 (U2) that we analyzed considering the components and aspects of the games evaluation methodology of Savi et al. [12].

The percentages of all questions are presented in Tables 4 and 5. We observed that all components were well evaluated by the students. The *Motivation* was evaluated considering its four aspects: Attention (Q1 and Q2), Relevance (Q3, Q4, and Q5), Trust (Q6 and Q7), and Satisfaction (Q8 and Q9); the *User experience* is divided into Immersion (Q10 and Q11), Challenge (Q12), Competence (Q13), Social interaction (Q14 and (Q15), and Fun (Q16 and Q17); and the Knowledge was evaluated by questions Q18, Q19 and Q20.

Table 4. Results of students evaluation of "Translation Loss" game (part 1).

	Q1	Q2	Q3	Q4	Q5	Q6	Q7	Q8	Q9	Q10
TA	58.21	61.19	56.72	64.18	65.67	37.31	46.27	37.31	46.27	56.72
A	38.81	37.31	23.88	28.36	26.87	43.28	41.79	38.81	38.81	31.34
N	2.99	1.49	19.40	7.46	5.97	19.40	5.97	23.88	10.45	5.97
D	0	0.00	0.00	0.00	1.49	0.00	4.48	0.00	4.48	5.97
TD	0.00	0.00	0.00	0.00	0.00	0.00	1.49	0.00	0.00	0.00

Table 5. Results of students evaluation of "Translation Loss" game (part 2).

	Q11	Q12	Q13	Q14	Q15	Q16	Q17	Q18	Q19	Q20
TA	47.76	31.34	31.34	50.75	62.69	61.19	65.67	43.28	52.24	41.79
A	43.28	46.27	46.27	43.28	31.34	29.85	20.90	37.31	41.79	41.79
N	7.46	16.42	19.40	5.97	5.97	8.96	8.96	14.93	4.48	16.42
D	1.49	5.97	2.99	0.00	0.00	0.00	2.99	2.99	0.00	0.00
TD	0.00	0.00	0.00	0.00	0.00	0.00	1.49	1.49	1.49	0.00

Due to space constraints, the pictures and tables of each aspect per university can be found at our website `www.cin.ufpe.br/~jffv/papers/cibse2020`.

5.2 RQ2: Did the students consider that they improve their requirements communication and elicitation skills by participating in the game?

We present the results about the Knowledge (Learning) aspect in questions Q18, Q19 and Q20 in Table 5. 80.60% of the students agree or totally agree that *The game was efficient for my learning as compared to other discipline activities (Q18)*; 94.03% agree that *The dynamics contribute to my learning in the discipline (Q19)*; and 83.58% agree that *After the game I feel that I can better apply the themes related to the game (Q20)*.

We observed that the results obtained in the second stage were generally higher than the first. This can be compared to the difference of the contact that the client has in the traditional methodologies and agile methodologies. In the second execution of the dynamic at UFPE, we asked open questions regarding the game whose subjects' answers are presented below.

What problems occurred in both rounds? Regarding the problems faced, we received answers such as (Student 1): *"At first it was taking things from text to draw, and in the second trying to understand what the client was talking about, since the developers had not seen the image"*.

(Student 2): *"In the first round the analyst in my group did not quite understand the client's description of perspective in which the image was being viewed. Already on Monday, the analyst was unable to pass to developers the proper proportion of certain parts of the image that the customer described."*

(Student 3): "In the first the difficulty of understanding completely without the help of the client and in the second, there was a lack of interaction between the developers and the analyst, given the client's presence."

Is there any relationship between the rounds and the development methods discussed previously in the class? *(Student 4): "Yes, everything that was presented in the classroom dynamics had already been cited by the teacher."*

(Student 5): *"Yes, but the approach was more external to the content, giving us the basic insight into how requirements-building works in practice."*

(Student 6): *"Yes, the study of methodologies behind software design, both traditional methodology, and agile methodologies."*

What was the biggest challenge you faced? *(Student 7): "Try to do what the customer really asked for."*

(Student 8): *"To be able to pass the details of the figure without being able to draw."*

(Student 9): *"The deadline for delivery of the final drawing."*

(Student 10): *"At first the communication. Already in the second moment, I believe that by being with the customer from the moment of conception until the end of the process, the number of details and the billing increased."*

Did you enjoy the performance of your team? Why? The majority of students liked the experience of learning from the game with comments such as: *(Student 11): "Yes, we were too excited.*

(Student 12): *"I liked it. It stimulated our imagination, and our communication in the second round improved a lot."*

(Student 13): *"Yes, although we were unable to achieve the customer's wishes perfectly, the group interacted and had a great time."*

(Student 14): *"Yes, I believe a good team relationship helps in a more satisfying final work."*

However, some subjects got disappointed for not being able to finish the task: *(Student 15): "No. Because they did more than I said and took longer."*

(Student 16): *"no, because we did not get close to what the client wanted."*

(Student 17): *"no, we could have done better."*

(Student 18): *"No, because the first round did not go as the customer wanted."*

List at least two key competencies that can be related to the challenges experienced in the game. The competences related to the "Translation Loss" game that the students state as fundamental to requirements engineering are listed in Table 6.

Table 6. Competences related to the "Translation Loss" game the students listed as fundamental.

Good communication / Dialogue	14
Agility / Time Management / Deadline	10
Team spirit / Teamwork / sociability	8
Attention/Concentration	7
Understanding / Similarity / Interpretation of the idea requested by the client	4
Details identification	3
Drawing skills	2
Imagination	1
Organization	1
Commitment	1
Analysis skills	1
Client feedback	1
Logical reasoning	1

5.3 Threats of the validity

As the study subjects are undergraduate students with none experience in requirements elicitation and without previous contact with the game, we can consider them representative for the evaluation of learning from the game as also pointed out by related work [8]. Although the two executions of the game were well-evaluated by the students considering it an interesting game, we can point our some threats to validity [19].

The use of pictures instead of technical requirements artifacts, such as requirements models or software specification may affect in some manner the study results. However, we claim the approach presented in this work is a good start to teach RE since one of the main problems in RE is communication and coordination that happens in both traditional and agile methodologies [6]. We claim that first the students should be aware how important communication among stakeholders, specially with the client is, then we move towards teaching technical content. This is a good awareness exercise with students in the beginning of the course (first and second semesters) as in our executions. A follow-up approach would be explaining the differences of requirements types (functional, non-functional, business rules) and move to requirements specification documents or models which are the RE skills required for software development.

A related point is one can consider the game a general teaching methodology where the communication among different team roles is relevant rather than a specific approach for requirements elicitation. We disagree with the affirmation as previous discussed since the process of requirements elicitation involves communication skills with the team and the client. Finally, aiming to avoid the crossing influence among the different groups, we provide an incentive of determining a winner team that came closest of the figures, i.e the requirements of the client. The winner team graded some extra point as motivation.

6 Conclusions

The aim of agile methodologies is always to have the customer actively parting of the team. Constant contact with the customer enables rapid feedback and facilitates communication. Greater communication allows us to identify and solve problems more quickly [4]. The evaluation of educational material is an activity recognized as essential in the teaching and learning process because it is necessary to evaluate if an educational product can fulfill what was planned for it [12].

In this paper, we present an experience report of the application of a game conducted in two undergraduate classes of different universities. Our goal was to improve requirements elicitation and communication skills in those students by showing how risk management and system quality are positively affected by good customer collaboration.

From the student's feedback, we concluded that the objectives were successfully achieved. The challenge and satisfaction aspects of the game received scores above average. Nevertheless, the scores were lower than the other aspects. On the other hand, students learning received a high percentage of agreement.

The learning was effective; however, it is necessary to make some adjustments, as, for example, the definition of milestones of the game and to provide a more focused explanation on the common points, the agile methodologies and the game Loss in Translation.

As future works, it is expected to carry out further experiments with larger samples of students from disciplines that involve requirements engineering to improve further the application of this group game and understanding of the concepts involved. Another future work would be investigating the game application in industrial scenarios. An open question is *Could it be possible to teach improved requirements elicitation in already established companies?* We observe that there differences in instructing students and professionals, and the road to teaching requirements elicitation in the industry has not been paved yet, and it may be a very promising research niche.

Acknowledgments

We would like to thank the professor Rainara Carvalho to make available to us the game description and the students who participated in the game.

References

1. Brady, A., Seigel, M., Vosecky, T., Wallace, C.: Addressing communication issues in software development: A case study approach. In: Software Engineering Education & Training, 2007. CSEET'07. 20th Conference on. pp. 301–308. IEEE (2007)
2. Carvalho, R.M.: es4fun (2018), `https://sites.google.com/view/es4fun/praticas/requisitos-de-software?authuser=0`
3. Da Silva, J.C., Sousa, S., Kulesza, R., Brito, A.V.: Uma avaliação do emprego do jogo modelando como apoio ao ensino de engenharia de requisitos (2012)

4. Fadel, A.C., Silveira, H.d.M.: Metodologias ágeis no contexto de desenvolvimento de software: Xp, scrum e lean. Monografia do Curso de Mestrado FT-027-Gestão de Projetos e Qualidade da Faculdade de Tecnologia–UNICAMP **98**, 101 (2010)
5. Fernandes, J.M., Machado, R.J., Seidman, S.B.: A requirements engineering and management training course for software development professionals. In: 2009 22nd Conference on Software Engineering Education and Training. pp. 20–25. IEEE (2009)
6. Fernández, D.M., Wagner, S., Kalinowski, M., Felderer, M., Mafra, P., Vetrò, A., Conte, T., Christiansson, M.T., Greer, D., Lassenius, C., et al.: Naming the pain in requirements engineering. Empirical software engineering **22**(5), 2298–2338 (2017)
7. Leveson, N.: Engineering a safer world: Systems thinking applied to safety. MIT press (2011)
8. Moreira, G.G., dos Santos Marques, A.B.: Evaluating the students' experience with the scrum card game: an experience report in a software engineering course. In: Proceedings of the 17th Brazilian Symposium on Software Quality. pp. 344–353. ACM (2018)
9. Paasivaara, M., Heikkilä, V., Lassenius, C., Toivola, T.: Teaching students scrum using lego blocks. In: Companion Proceedings of the 36th International Conference on Software Engineering. pp. 382–391. ACM (2014)
10. Pernstal, J.: Towards Managing the Interaction between Manufacturing and Development Organizations in Automotive Software Development. Ph.D. thesis, Department of Computer Science and Engineering, CHALMERS UNIVERSITY OF TECHNOLOGY (2015)
11. Rasmussen, J., Lundell, Å.K.: Understanding "communication gaps" among personnel in high-risk workplaces from a dialogical perspective. Safety science **50**(1), 39–47 (2012)
12. Savi, R., Von Wangenheim, C.G., Ulbricht, V., Vanzin, T.: Proposta de um modelo de avaliação de jogos educacionais. Renote **8**(3) (2010)
13. Silva, M.V., Barbosa, M.W.: Desenvolvimento e avaliação de jogo de treinamento para ensino de técnicas de elicitação de requisitos de software. Belo Horizonte, MG (2008)
14. Sommerville, I.: Software engineering. Addison-Wesley/Pearson (2011)
15. Thiry, M., Zoucas, A., Gonçalves, R.Q.: Promovendo a aprendizagem de engenharia de requisitos de software através de um jogo educativo. In: Brazilian Symposium on Computers in Education (Simpósio Brasileiro de Informática na Educação-SBIE). vol. 1 (2010)
16. Vilela, J., Castro, J., Martins, L.E.G., Gorschek, T.: Integration between requirements engineering and safety analysis: A systematic literature review. Journal of Systems and Software **125**, 68–92 (2017)
17. Vilela, J., Castro, J., Martins, L.E.G., Gorschek, T., Almendra, C.: Requirements communication in safety-critical systems. In: Workshop on Requirements Engineering (WER) (2019)
18. Wang, Y., Graziotin, D., Kriso, S., Wagner, S.: Communication channels in safety analysis: An industrial exploratory case study. arXiv preprint arXiv:1804.08909 (2018)
19. Wohlin, C., et al.: Experimentation in software engineering: An introduction (2000)

Teaching Scrum Practices with the Support of Brazilian Startups: an Initiative in Software Engineering Course

Leo Natan Paschoal and Simone R. S. Souza

Institute of Mathematics and Computer Sciences – University of São Paulo
paschoalln@usp.br, srocio@icmc.usp.br

Resumo For a long period, software engineering education had been about the transfer of knowledge related to the software development life cycle through the traditional approaches to teaching and learning. In recent years, with the emergence of some pedagogical models, the software engineering community has begun to invest efforts in promoting initiatives that emphasize not only the transfer of knowledge in the classroom but conducting activities and projects that promote effective learning. Therefore, different approaches were incorporated into the teaching of this course. Despite many examples of reports, few initiatives promote practical experiences together with the "real world". Promote experiences of the "real world" is a challenge highlighted by recent work in this area. We believe that for the context of software engineering, the application of practical approaches must be accompanied by industry partners, who promote a real world view for the application of concepts seen during the course. This paper reports an experience of Software Engineering Education using real projects and industry partnerships, developed using the Scrum. This experience has provided real scenarios to the students, aiming for the learning of agile practices related to the development and management of a software project. The paper reports the students' feedback on the learning of software engineering in practice, showing the student perspective of this learning experience.

Keywords: Scrum · Startups · Software Engineering Education.

1 Introdução

Ao longo dos anos, a ideologia por trás do desenvolvimento de software passou por um processo de transição, em que a comunidade de desenvolvimento de software passou a valorizar os indivíduos e interações mais que processos e ferramentas, colaboração com cliente mais que negociação de contratos e responder à mudanças mais que seguir um plano [2]. Ao passo que a Engenharia de Software foi reconhecendo as transformações e o surgimento de diferentes técnicas, métodos e ferramentas, ela foi sendo incorporada aos currículos de referência e às diretrizes de desenvolvimento de cursos de graduação e pós-graduação. Assim, tornou-se um componente curricular obrigatório nos cursos de graduação [11].

De modo geral, a disciplina de Engenharia de Software busca oferecer aos alunos a capacidade de compreender o desenvolvimento do software desde a fase inicial até a implantação do produto. Apesar de ser uma disciplina essencial para o aluno obter o entendimento necessário para produção de um software com qualidade, os alunos gastam uma quantidade significativa de tempo estudando processos de desenvolvimento de software, a fim de compreender e decidir se um determinado processo pode funcionar para um determinado projeto ou não [4].

Ainda que o ensino de Engenharia de Software deva enfatizar princípios e reconhecer os conceitos estáveis e duradouros da disciplina, os aspectos do estado de prática (*i.e.*, tecnologia, ferramentas e métodos) não podem ser ignorados [8]. Outra questão que deve ser levada em conta é a dissociação entre teoria e prática [5]. Conforme Fox e Patterson [6], a articulação entre teoria e prática é essencial para que iniciantes sejam capazes de compreender a natureza e as inter-relações entre as diversas atividades do desenvolvimento de software. Estudar princípios sobre livros didáticos e até mesmo fazer exercícios não é um "aprendizado real" sem uma experiência prática [8]. No entanto, a prática de Engenharia de Software em um segmento da indústria não é bem suportada pelas disciplinas de cursos de graduação [1].

Estudos recentes descrevem que a maioria dos recém-formados em Engenharia de Software muitas vezes enfrenta dificuldades ao iniciar suas carreiras profissionais, em decorrência do desalinhamento das habilidades aprendidas em sua formação universitária com o que é necessário na indústria [7]. Em virtude disso, nos últimos anos alguns esforços realizados por professores de Engenharia de Software foram sendo reportados, de modo que o aluno tenha uma formação sólida tanto do ponto de vista conceitual quanto prático.

Para apoiar o aprendizado prático de Engenharia de Software, algumas abordagens de ensino têm sido utilizadas, como *capstone projects*, *flipped classroom*, *game based learning*, *problem based learning*, *project based learning*, dentre outras. Ainda que algumas iniciativas tenham sido estimuladas e realizadas, estudos descrevem que é difícil reproduzir em sala de aula, ambientes muito próximos àqueles que os alunos enfrentarão ao adentrarem na indústria de software [8]. Dentre as dificuldades que são reportadas, Ghezzi e Mandrioli [8] mencionam que os projetos de software precisam ter um escopo reduzido, porque os alunos precisam conciliar com atividades de outras disciplinas. Outro aspecto a ser considerado é o conhecimento técnico dos alunos sobre programação, redes de computadores e ferramentas de apoio ao desenvolvimento de software [16]. De fato, construir uma iniciativa educacional que reflita e acompanhe a prática industrial não é trivial, mas precisa ser realizada [3].

Para contornar os desafios imbricados ao ensino de práticas de Engenharia de Software, um grupo de professores da Universidade de São Paulo vem incluindo estratégias de ensino diferentes do tradicional nessa disciplina, que envolvem a participação de clientes reais, projetos do "mundo real" e a execução de práticas do Scrum, dado que o Scrum é provavelmente um dos métodos de desenvolvimento mais prestigiados pela atual indústria de software. Neste artigo é reportada uma iniciativa realizada durante o ensino de Engenharia de Software no Instituto de Ciências Matemáticas e de Computação da Universidade de São Paulo – ICMC/USP. Esta iniciativa buscou oferecer experiências práticas aos alunos do curso de bacharelado em ciências de computação, a partir do aprendizado do conteúdo por meio de uma metodologia teórico-prática conduzida através de um parceria estabelecida com um grupo de *startups* da cidade de São Carlos – SP, Brasil. Essa metodologia envolve o aprendizado teórico do conteúdo e a realização de práticas de desenvolvimento de projetos de software por meio de práticas utilizadas por essas *startups* para produção de sistemas de software. Para o desenvolvimento dos projetos, os alunos receberam treinamento das *startups* sobre práticas do método Scrum, foram supervisionados por representantes dessas *startups* e tiveram que propor soluções de software reais.

Para apresentar o relato de experiência, este artigo foi organizado da seguinte forma: a Seção 2 apresenta uma visão geral sobre o Scrum e suas práticas. A iniciativa é apresentada na Seção 3. Um *feedback* emitido pelos alunos sobre a experiência é descrito na Seção 4. Por fim, as conclusões e algumas perspectivas de estudos futuros são discutidos na Seção 5.

2 O Método Scrum

O desenvolvimento de software passou por diversas transações, movendo-se de um período em que não existiam mecanismos de apoio ao estabelecimento sistemático de software, chegando ao ponto em que modelos de processos são produzidos para atender o desenvolvimento de sistemas com características específicas, como os jogos eletrônicos [10]. Apesar de modelos de desenvolvimento de software estarem sendo produzidos até hoje para atender às necessidades de uma indústria do software cada vez mais heterogênea, muitos dos sistemas de software vêm sendo produzidos através de metodologias ágeis, como o Scrum.

De acordo com Schwaber [15] o Scrum é um processo de desenvolvimento que tem foco no gerenciamento do desenvolvimento iterativo. Ele vai ao encontro do manifesto ágil e é adequado para ambientes complexos em que as equipes precisam reagir e se adaptar rapidamente a novas situações no sistema (*e.g.*, mudanças de requisitos e/ou de tecnologia) [9]. Pode ser visto como um modelo ou método de desenvolvimento de software que foi estabelecido para lidar com problemas complexos, ajudando a fornecer produtos de maneira produtiva e criativa [17].

O modelo é constituído basicamente por três fases: **(i) planejamento geral**, em que são estabelecidos os objetivos do projeto, é feito a conceituação e análise para definição de um *backlog*[1], assim como, a estimação de seu custo; **(ii) ciclos de *sprint***, em que são desenvolvidos artefatos que incrementam o sistema e geram valores ao cliente; **(iii) fase de encerramento do projeto** [15]. Vale salientar que um ciclo de *sprint* envolve a seleção de um item do *backlog*, o desenvolvimento da funcionalidade pela equipe de Scrum, a revisão e o teste dessa funcionalidade.

[1] Conjunto de funcionalidade que precisam ser implementadas.

Em relação à equipe de Scrum, ela é composta por um número definido de membros, preferencialmente inferior a dez [13]. Apesar do número limite de membros, um projeto pode ser desenvolvido por várias equipes. Os membros de uma equipe podem desempenhar determinados papéis - a saber: *product owners*, *scrum master* e *development team* [17].

- *Product owner*: O *product owner* é responsável por gerenciar o *backlog* do projeto, identificar e priorizar corretamente os itens do *backlog* para atingir as metas definidas, garantir que o *backlog* do projeto esteja claro e transparente para todos os membros da equipe [9].
- *Scrum master*: O *scrum master* é o líder da equipe de Scrum e tem a responsabilidade de garantir que sua equipe tenha compreendido as atividades necessárias que precisam ser realizadas e a competência de assegurar que essas atividades estejam sendo executadas/realizadas [9]. Além disso, o *scrum master* é responsável pela aderência dos membros do time aos valores do Scrum e princípios ágeis.
- *Development team*: A equipe de desenvolvimento (*development team*), por sua vez, é representada pelos profissionais que são responsáveis por implementar e avaliar as funcionalidades implementadas [9]. Esses papéis foram definidos com o propósito de facilitar o gerenciamento das *sprints*[2] [14].

Uma *sprint* tem um tempo de duração que pode variar, apesar de existirem recomendações para que ela dure entre duas até quatro semanas. Durante a realização de uma *sprint*, alguns eventos são previstos: reunião de planejamento da *sprint* (*sprint planning*), reunião diária (*daily Scrum*), reunião de revisão da *sprint* (*sprint review*) e retrospectiva da *sprint* (*sprint retrospective*). Cada um desses eventos será descrito a seguir:

- *Sprint planning*: Essa reunião é realizada para decidir o que será implementado em uma *sprint* e como o trabalho será realizado pela equipe. Durante a reunião, o cliente deve mostrar à equipe o *backlog* do produto com os itens classificados de acordo com sua prioridade, explicando o que deve ser feito em cada item de trabalho. A equipe precisa estimar o esforço necessário para implementar os itens e fazer um acordo com cliente sobre o que será entregue no final da *sprint*, considerando a ordem de prioridade estabelecida pelo proprietário do produto. Essa reunião envolve a decisão de tarefas que serão realizadas pelos membros da equipe, em que cada membro da equipe seleciona a quantidade de trabalho que cada um se compromete a desenvolver e entregar no final da *sprint* e o tempo (em horas) necessário para concluí-la é estimado.
- *Daily Scrum*: Todos os membros da equipe devem realizar uma reunião diária para obter uma visão geral do projeto, descobrir novas dependências, atender às necessidades individuais dos membros da equipe e ajustar o plano de trabalho em tempo real à necessidade do dia a dia. Na reunião diária, os membros da equipe são convidados a responder três perguntas fundamentais: (I) O que foi realizado no dia anterior à reunião? (II) O que será realizado hoje? (III) Existe algum obstáculo para realizar o trabalho?. Idealmente, essas reuniões devem ser realizadas pela manhã, permitindo o estabelecimento de prioridades de trabalho para o dia.

[2] É um período delimitado de um mês ou menos, durante o qual uma versão potencialmente utilizável do produto é criada.

– *Sprint review*: Essa reunião é realizada no final de cada *sprint* para demonstrar o trabalho realizado durante o período. Nesse sentido, a equipe deve demonstrar os recursos implementados para o cliente. O cliente deve verificar se os recursos estão de acordo com o que ele espera e, quando necessário, sugerir modificações.
– *Sprint retrospective*: Essa reunião é realizada imediatamente após a revisão da *sprint*. Nesse momento, a equipe de Scrum deve discutir o que está funcionando e o que não está funcionando no projeto e chegar a um acordo sobre as mudanças necessárias para a próximo *sprint*.

Esses eventos são reconhecidos na pesquisa de Qumer e Henderson-Sellers [13] como práticas ágeis do Scrum. As práticas ágeis são sugeridas pelos métodos de desenvolvimento para atingir seus objetivos específicos [12]. Cada modelo de desenvolvimento de software tem suas próprias práticas, apesar de alguns complementarem suas práticas com práticas oriundas de outros métodos. No método XP, por exemplo, a programação por pares é uma prática necessária para atingir o objetivo do método [13]. Em razão dos modelos possuírem suas próprias práticas, quando eles são ensinados para alunos e ou profissionais que estão recebendo treinamento, as práticas precisam ser exteriorizadas.

3 Iniciativa

Após o estudo sobre a execução de projetos similares ao reportado neste artigo, em particular por meio dos relatos compartilhados por Fioravanti *et al.* [5] e Souza *et al.* [16], decidiu-se por incluir na disciplina a participação de *startups* e definiu-se um projeto guarda-chuva, a partir do qual cada equipe de alunos iria propor uma solução de software. Dessa maneira, os alunos tiveram a oportunidade de desenvolver seu potencial criativo, definindo quais seriam suas soluções e, com o apoio das *startups*, definindo o escopo de seus projetos. De maneira simplificada, o projeto guarda-chuva envolve a construção de uma plataforma de apoio para estudantes que chegam a São Carlos, com aplicativos de apoio para auxílio a encontrar moradia, para conhecer a cidade, conhecer a universidade, entre outras ideias que partiram dos próprios alunos.

3.1 Abordagem de Ensino

A disciplina foi ministrada para os alunos do curso de Ciências de Computação, no 1º semestre de 2018, para 57 estudantes. Essa disciplina é obrigatória, possui quatro créditos-aula (60 horas-aula no semestre, divididas em duas aulas semanais). O objetivo dela é oferecer uma visão geral dos processos de desenvolvimento de software e as técnicas e/ou práticas que podem ser utilizadas em cada fase do ciclo de vida do software.

A metodologia foi definida de modo que todo o conteúdo teórico da disciplina fosse ministrada antes do início do desenvolvimento dos projetos. Buscou-se fazer com que o aluno tivesse uma visão geral e abrangente da Engenharia de Software e de seus processos, métodos e ferramentas antes da aplicação prática. Assim, a disciplina foi fracionada em duas partes:

- **Aulas tradicionais:** compreende a primeira etapa da disciplina, em que os alunos assistiam as aulas teóricas, realizavam exercícios (durante a aula e fora da sala de aula) e participavam de discussões sobre o conteúdo.
- **Aulas em parceria com a indústria:** compreende a segunda etapa da disciplina, em que os alunos desenvolviam o projeto prático: recebiam treinamento por um grupo de *startups*, planejavam *backlog* do produto com os clientes, interagiram com clientes reais em cada início e final de uma *sprint*, apresentavam funcionalidades desenvolvidas para seus clientes, realizavam reuniões e (re) planejavam entregas.

3.2 Projetos do "Mundo Real"

Após o aprendizado teórico na disciplina, os alunos foram apresentados aos projetos que deveriam ser realizados. Nesse sentido, a professora da disciplina optou por estabelecer uma parceria com a Arquivei[3], uma *startup* da cidade de São Carlos. Os sócios dessa organização aceitaram colaborar com o ensino prático da disciplina e propuseram o envolvimento de outras *startups* da cidade de São Carlos, em especial aquelas que estão incubadas no ONOVOLAB[4]. Assim, estabeleceu-se a parceria com a Liber[5].

Para o contexto desta disciplina, uma reunião com um grupo de *startups* interessadas foi realizada, visando apresentar a proposta de promover um ambiente facilitador aos alunos de Engenharia de Software, de modo que eles pudessem conviver com a prática de desenvolvimento de projetos de software. Para tanto, inicialmente foi definido que os alunos iriam se envolver com práticas do Scrum. Na sequência foi definido o problema que seria considerado nos projetos desenvolvidos, optando-se pela geração de aplicativos e sistemas de apoio para os alunos que chegam para estudar na cidade. Esse tema foi escolhido porque a maioria dos estudantes de São Carlos vem de outros locais do país e precisam de material de apoio para conhecer a cidade e as universidades que possuem sede na cidade.

Com base nessa ideia, os alunos tiveram um tempo para definirem seus projetos. Um total de nove propostas foram feitas pelos estudantes (descritas na Tabela 1). Todos os projetos possuem um caráter social e seriam desenvolvidos tendo como base a filosofia de software livre. Desse modo, os projetos não visam retorno financeiro.

Após definidos os projetos, foram estabelecidos quem seriam os clientes de cada um, com base nas *startups* envolvidas. No período, os alunos tiveram a possibilidade de visitar as *startups*, solicitar treinamento de alguma tecnologia necessária para o desenvolvimento dos seus projetos e utilizar a infraestrutura necessária dessas organizações para hospedagem das plataformas. Além disso,

[3] Mais informações disponíveis em: <https://arquivei.com.br/>.

[4] Um campus de inovação que busca oferecer um ambiente para o desenvolvimento de projetos inovadores, apoiando pessoas, empresas e o Brasil. Mais informações pode ser obtidas em: <https://www.onovolab.com/>.

[5] Mais informações disponíveis em <https://www.libercapital.com.br/>.

os clientes colaboraram com a delimitação dos projetos e estabelecimento do escopo, de modo que fossem viáveis de serem desenvolvidos no tempo disponível (2 meses).

Tabela 1. Descrição dos projetos

#	Projeto	Descrição do projeto	Tipo de aplicação
1	#deSCubra	Uma plataforma com o objetivo de apresentar aos usuários a cidade de São Carlos em um escopo histórico, cultural e informativo.	Web
2	Entretenibit	Uma plataforma para que usuários conheçam eventos culturais de São Carlos e recebem e-mails sobre esses eventos.	Web
3	BusCarlos	Uma plataforma que permite que usuários de transporte circular de São Carlos consigam fazer busca por linhas do transporte e pontos de paradas.	Web
4	SanConnect	Uma plataforma de divulgação de micro-eventos de modo a integrar pessoas, ajudar a fazer novas amizades, com interesses em comum.	Web
5	Roomates	Uma plataforma que visa facilitar a divisão de contas em um grupo de amigos, que possivelmente dividem uma moradia, permitindo o gerenciamento de contas e gastos.	Web/ Mobile
6	SddsR$	A plataforma tem por objetivo auxiliar um novo estudante de São Carlos a gerenciar seu dinheiro, tendo conhecimento das bolsas de projetos (de iniciação científica, de extensão, de cultura ou de ensino) disponíveis nas instituições públicas de ensino da cidade.	Web
7	House Trinder	A plataforma tem o objetivo de auxiliar novos alunos na busca de moradia em São Carlos assim como, ajudar a encontrar potenciais colegas de quarto que possuam interesses em comum, de maneira similar ao Tinder.	Mobile
8	Morar, Morei	A plataforma tem a finalidade de facilitar a busca por informações relacionadas à moradia (repúblicas, room mate e apartamentos) e as respectivas regiões da cidade, unificando anúncios de moradia de mobiliarias da cidade, similar ao Buscapé.	Web
9	SancaServ	Um site que reúne anúncios de empregadas domésticas, permitindo que um usuário logado ao site possa filtrar parâmetros de seu interesse, obtendo assim o contato que mais se adéque às suas necessidades.	Web

3.3 Desenvolvimento dos Projetos

O desenvolvimento seguiu as práticas que caracterizam o Scrum, definindo-se: *scrum master, scrum teams, product backlog, sprint backlog, sprint planning meeting, daily Scrum meeting e sprint review.* Para que os alunos conseguissem adotar com precisão essas práticas, um treinamento foi proposto pelas *startups.* Nesse treinamento, os alunos tiveram oportunidade de conhecer como as *startups* trabalhavam na prática. Eles também puderam solucionar dúvidas com os profissionais que ministravam o treinamento. O treinamento foi no ICMC e os alunos foram convidados a visitar as *startups* para acompanhar como as equipes trabalhavam nos projetos reais e executavam na prática o Scrum.

Foram necessárias algumas adaptações nas práticas, pois os alunos não tinham dedicação exclusiva ao projeto da disciplina. Assim, decidiu-se que as reuniões diárias, nos dias que não havia aula, seria feito da maneira que fosse mais conveniente para a equipe, podendo ser por meio de aplicativo de mensagens, por exemplo. As reuniões de retrospectiva foram realizadas sempre em sala de aula. As reuniões de iteração com clientes, em sua maioria, foram feitas fora do ICMC (*i.e.*, nas *startups* ou por videoconferência). O papel do *scrum master* e da equipe de desenvolvimento permaneceu o mesmo que é descrito na literatura (mencionados na Seção 2). Em relação às *sprints*, foi definido que elas teriam duração de uma semana.

Como os alunos já haviam aprendido os conceitos teóricos, o tempo em sala de aula foi dedicado para solução de dúvidas, realização de reuniões, implementação e acompanhamento dos projetos. Salienta-se que para acompanhar o desenvolvimento dos projetos, a professora da disciplina solicitou a entrega de alguns artefatos que eram produzidos pelos alunos nas *sprints*. A Tabela 2 contém detalhes dos artefatos que eram utilizados para acompanhar o andamento dos projetos.

Tabela 2. Artefatos a serem entregues pelas equipes de cada projeto. Adaptado de Souza *et al.* [16].

Artefato	Descrição
Planejamento da entrevista	Documento com a descrição do roteiro a ser seguido durante a entrevista com o cliente.
Plano de projeto	Documento contendo descrição do escopo e objetivos do projeto, matriz de riscos, organização da equipe para o desenvolvimento, cronograma, recursos utilizados, resultados esperados e recursos para monitoramento e acompanhamento do projeto.
Plano de teste	Documento contendo uma descrição sobre o que e como vai ser testado, os testes a serem aplicados, prazos e os recursos alocados.
Backlog do produto	Construção da lista contendo todas as funcionalidades desejadas para o produto e descrição das funcionalidades na forma de histórias de usuário.
Detalhamento de cada *sprint*	Construção da lista de funcionalidades do *sprint*, em ordem de prioridade.
Relatório de execução dos testes	Resultados da execução dos testes, com histórico de defeitos encontrados e corrigidos.

4 Percepção dos Alunos

Para ter uma visão geral sobre a percepção dos alunos a respeito da metodologia teórico-prática adotada na disciplina, um questionário foi preparado, contendo sete itens no total, sendo que seis eram obrigatórios. Os itens são apresentadas na Tabela 3. O formulário foi construído na ferramenta Google Forms[6] e foi encaminhado para envio ao final do semestre, não contabilizando como atividade avaliativa da disciplina. Um total de 36 estudantes responderam ao questionário.

Em relação ao primeiro item, observa-se que a maioria dos respondentes avaliou como adequado o Scrum para os projetos adotados na disciplina (Figura 1). Cinco participantes declararam que ficaram indecisos. Por último, três alunos acreditaram que o modelo não foi adequado para os projetos. As respostas desses três alunos também não proveem de participantes de um mesmo grupo.

[6] Mais informações disponíveis em <https://www.google.com/forms/about/>.

Tabela 3. Questionário de coleta de feedback

Itens	Opções de resposta
(1) O Scrum foi adequado ao desenvolvimento do projeto?	Escala Likert
(2) Quais foram as maiores dificuldades? (o aluno pode selecionar diversas opções)	☐ Entender o Scrum e aplicá-lo ao mesmo tempo; ☐ Não conhecer as tecnologias necessárias para o desenvolvimento do projeto; ☐ O cliente (pouco colaborativo, pouco presente); ☐ Conciliar o projeto com as outras atividades do semestre; ☐ A equipe não colaborou para a aplicação do Scrum; ☐ Trabalhar em equipe; ☐ Fazer um projeto prático não me agrada; ☐ Outro (detalhar):
(3) Você sente que aprendeu melhor Engenharia de Software com a prática?	○ Sim ○ Não ○ Não sei opinar
(4) Quais foram suas expectativas em participar de um projeto envolvendo *startups*?	Resposta aberta
(5) Descreva sobre a sua percepção em relação a participação dos sócios das *startups*	Resposta aberta
(6) Apresente sugestões para melhorar a abordagem usada em sala de aula	Resposta aberta
(7) Se desejar, comente outros aspectos sobre a sua experiência ao desenvolver o projeto e forneça sugestões adicionais	Resposta aberta

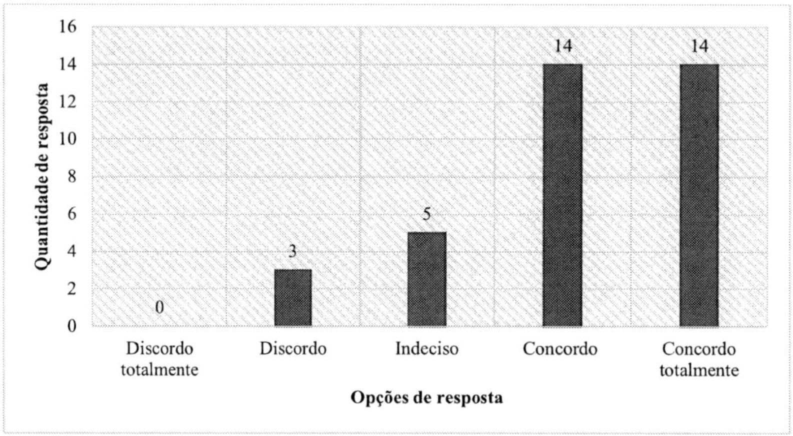

Figura 1. Percepção sobre adequação do Scrum aos projetos

Os alunos puderam selecionar e indicar as maiores dificuldades que eles tiveram ao longo da realização do projetos. Foi possível observar que a maior dificuldade foi conciliar as atividades do projeto com as demais atividades que eles faziam ao longo do semestre. Outro item que recebeu mais de 50% das respostas dos participantes se refere à falta de conhecimento sobre as tecnologias necessárias para realização do projeto (Figura 2). Salienta-se que durante o planejamento da iniciativa já se tinha imaginado que os alunos teriam dificuldades em se organizar com as demais disciplinas em que eles estavam matriculados e com a tecnologia utilizada. Por conta disso, quando a parceria foi estabelecida foi necessário definir projetos que não seriam tão complexo e, para os mitigar problemas associados às tecnologias, as *startups* ficaram disponíveis para oferecer apoio e treinamento.

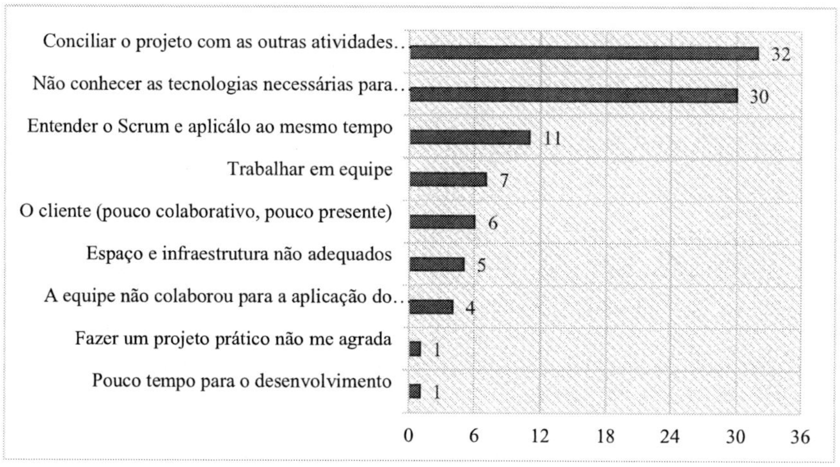

Figura 2. Principais dificuldades dos alunos

O terceiro item buscou compreender se os alunos ao final da disciplina acreditaram que conseguiram aprender melhor o conteúdo com a prática de projetos. A Figura 3 representa as respostas emitidas pelos respondentes. Foi possível observar que a maioria dos estudantes indicou que acredita que conseguiu aprender o conteúdo com precisão.

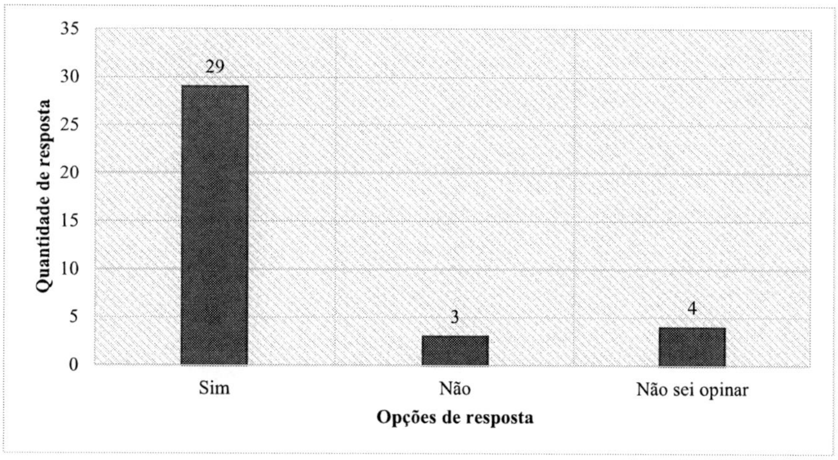

Figura 3. Visão geral sobre a sensação de aprendizado

No quarto item, os alunos relataram suas expectativas em participar do projeto. Uma sumarização das respostas é apresenta na Tabela 4. Conforme é possível observar, a maioria das respostas sobre as expectativas dos alunos estão concentradas na oportunidade criada para eles se aproximarem da realidade do mercado de trabalho e aplicarem conhecimento para solucionar problemas reais.

Tabela 4. Expectativas dos estudantes

Feedback dos alunos	**Número de ocorrência**
Aproximar-se mais da realidade do mercado de trabalho e entender como funciona o trabalho nessas *startups*	11
A possibilidade de aplicar nosso conhecimento para resolver problemas reais	10
Nada a declarar	6
Tive boas expectativas em aprender com profissionais que já possuem experiência	5
Não criei grandes expectativas com a iniciativa	4

Os alunos também foram questionados sobre suas percepções quanto ao apoio oferecido pelos profissionais das *startups* (item 5). Conforme é possível observar na Tabela 5, os alunos indicaram que gostaram. Alguns alunos acreditaram que foi significativa para realização do projeto até o final, outros indicaram que foi importante para apoiar na atividade de teste. Apesar disso, alguns alunos acreditaram que a participação deles não foi importante. É possível que esses alunos não tenham tido tanta dificuldade ao compreender o que precisavam fazer e/ou até mesmo não tenho gostado de ter que sair em determinados momentos do ICMC para solucionar suas dúvidas nas sedes das *startups*.

Tabela 5. Percepção em relação à participação dos profissionais das *startups*

Feedback dos alunos	**Número de ocorrência**
Eles foram muito prestativos, sempre dedicando boa parte de seu tempo a ajudar nos projetos	14
A participação deles no projeto não foi muito significativa	5
Gostei da iniciativa deles e das aulas que eles foram falar, porém senti uma distância durante o período de desenvolvimento do projeto	5
Eles ajuda muito em relação a dar dicas, ideias e solucionar os defeitos no código	4
Foram de grande auxílio e contribuíram bastante para o produto final	4
Não tenho nada a declarar	4

Os alunos foram convidados a apresentar sugestões de melhorias para a iniciativa realizada. Um resumo das sugestões foi realizado e está disponível na Tabela 6. De modo geral, alguns alunos relataram que o projeto poderia começar no início do semestre e ser executado em paralelo às aulas teóricas. Alguns alunos também indicaram que seria interessante realizar o projeto em parceria com outras disciplina.

Tabela 6. Um resumo das sugestões de melhoria

Feedback dos alunos	Número de ocorrência
Não tem sugestões de melhoria.	13
O projeto poderia começar no início da disciplina, uma vez que o tempo é pouco para realizar atividades do projeto e conciliar atividades de outras disciplinas.	10
O projeto poderia ser realizado em conjunto com outras disciplinas como desenvolvimento *web*.	3
Focar em projetos de escopos menores e mais simples.	3
Adotar um conjunto padrão de ferramentas (de desenvolvimento) e gestão de projetos.	2
A temática do projeto poderia ser outra.	2
Os projetos deveriam ser definidos para desenvolvermos soluções que temos conhecimento para desenvolver. Nestes projetos, a maioria dos alunos teve que aprender outras linguagem de programação.	1
Eu acho que a participação das *startups* poderia ter sido reduzida. Sinto que eles focaram muito em coisas técnicas.	1
A professora da disciplina poderia ter ensinado as tecnologias necessárias para realização do trabalho e/ou indicado materiais sobre o assunto.	1

Por fim, no último item do questionário, os alunos puderam fazer comentários e emitir depoimentos. Os comentários estão listadas na Tabela 7. Conforme é possível perceber, os alunos que aceitaram responder apresentaram elogios e algumas críticas. Em relação às críticas, observa-se que elas têm relação com a necessidade dos alunos terem tido que aprender a trabalhar com tecnologias que eles ainda não tinham estudado. Apesar das críticas, a maioria dos alunos consideraram proveitosa a experiência.

Tabela 7. Comentários emitidos pelos alunos

Feedback dos alunos
(1) As reuniões realizadas em sala de aula foram muito interessante para discutirmos avanços em relação aos *sprints* e fornecer feedbacks necessários para se discutir possíveis pontos de melhoria de cada integrante da equipe.
(2) A proposta do trabalho me interessou, e também os integrantes do meu grupo. No entanto, a maneira como o projeto foi abordado dificultou a conciliação com outras atividades da disciplina.
(3) Eu queria deixar um elogio para a ideia do projeto final. Acredito que a experiência da prática oferece um aprendizado que nunca teria obtido se não fosse por esse projeto (ainda mais Engenharia de Software, que todo mundo fala que é a disciplina mais "chata"). Eu gostei bastante de trabalhar nesse projeto com meu grupo, e pôr a mão na massa! Acho que aprendi muito não só sobre Engenharia de Software, mas também sobre como é uma rotina de desenvolvimento de um produto. Então espero que os próximos oferecimentos dessa disciplina continuem com esse diferencial também!
(4) O escopo definido como um projeto *web* dinâmico não foi uma boa escolha visto que a maioria dos alunos ainda não tinha feito a disciplina de *web*. Logo, além desenvolver o projeto junto com todos os problemas já normais da graduação, tínhamos que correr atrás de aprender programação *web* e banco de dados. Eu acho que a disciplina de Engenharia de Software acabou ficando em segundo plano quando o grupo teve que aprender tantas outras coisas.
(5) Foi um projeto que o resultado ficou tão legal que é até válido como portfólio. Eu acho que seria interessante se a disciplina fosse ensinada após desenvolvimento *web*.
(6) Acredito que o projeto foi uma ótima forma de aprender Engenharia de Software na prática, porém senti, especialmente no final de semestre, um enorme peso. Tal fato se deve pelo tamanho do projeto em concomitância com atividades de outras disciplinas e a dificuldade de se aprender diversas tecnologias em curto espaço de tempo, que levou na frustração de não conseguir terminar como queríamos o projeto.

5 Conclusões

Este artigo descreve um relato sobre uma experiência realizada na disciplina de Engenharia de Software. A experiência foi conduzida em parceria com um grupo de *startups* da cidade de São Carlos. As *startups* ofereceram treinamento aos alunos sobre práticas ágeis utilizadas no estabelecimento de soluções de software, bem como sobre tecnologias que os alunos ainda não haviam tido contato anteriormente. O propósito do projeto foi estabelecer um cenário em que os alunos teriam que praticar o Scrum e interagir com clientes reais.

Por meio do artigo, tentou-se demonstrar que é possível criar oportunidades mais próximas do "mundo real" para que os alunos tenham uma visão não apenas teórica ou simulada da Engenharia de Software. Em particular, pôde-se capacitar os alunos a utilizarem o Scrum. Apesar do cenário proposto ter sido de grande serventia para estimular a prática da Engenharia de Software, durante o desenvolvimento dos projetos notou-se que os alunos tiveram que enfrentar alguns desafios, como o aprendizado de tecnologias que não estavam acostumados a utilizar. Além disso, muitos dos participantes não tinham aprendido programação *web*, outros estudantes estavam matriculados em muitas disciplinas no semestre e alegaram sobrecarga de trabalho. Embora alguns problemas tenham surgido, foi possível contorná-lo pela flexibilidade do Scrum e auxílio das *startups* que apoiaram a iniciativa. O aprendizado de novas tecnologias normalmente ocorre por meio de oportunidades em conhecê-las e aplicá-las em novos projetos. Assim, acreditamos que os projetos oportunizaram esse aprendizado aos estudantes, apesar dos desafios e dificuldades.

Ainda que a iniciativa adotada nesta experiência tenha sido inspirada nas experiências da professora que ministra a disciplina, problemas diferentes foram observados e reportados pelos alunos. Assim, acredita-se que melhorias precisam ser feitas na forma como a experiência foi conduzida. Portanto, como continuidade deste trabalho, pretende-se evoluir a iniciativa de modo que seja possível evitar problemas como sobrecarga de trabalho nos alunos e dificuldades associadas às tecnologias necessárias para o desenvolvimento dos projetos.

Agradecimentos

Os autores gostariam de agradecer a CAPES - Código de Financiamento 001, a FAPESP (Processos 2018/26636-2, 2017/10941-8 e 2013/07375-0) e ao CNPq (Processo 312922/2018-3) pelo apoio financeiro.

Referências

1. Bass, M.: Software engineering education in the new world: What needs to change? In: International Conference on Software Engineering Education and Training. pp. 213–221 (2016)
2. Beck, K., Beedle, M., Van Bennekum, A., Cockburn, A., Cunningham, W., Fowler, M., Grenning, J., Highsmith, J., Hunt, A., Jeffries, R., et al.: Manifesto for agile software development (2001)
3. Chatley, R., Field, T.: Lean learning - applying lean techniques to improve software engineering education. In: International Conference on Software Engineering. pp. 117–126 (2017)
4. Devadiga, N.M.: Software engineering education: Converging with the startup industry. In: Conference on Software Engineering Education and Training. pp. 192–196 (2017)
5. Fioravanti, M.L., Sena, B., Paschoal, L.N., Silva, L.R., Allian, A.P., Nakagawa, E.Y., Souza, S.R., Isotani, S., Barbosa, E.F.: Integrating project based learning and project management for software engineering teaching: An experience report. In: ACM Technical Symposium on Computer Science Education. pp. 806–811 (2018)
6. Fox, A., Patterson, D.: Crossing the software education chasm. Communications of the ACM **55**(5), 44–49 (2012)
7. Garousi, V., Giray, G., Tuzun, E., Catal, C., Felderer, M.: Closing the gap between software engineering education and industrial needs. IEEE Software pp. 1–11 (2019)
8. Ghezzi, C., Mandrioli, D.: The challenges of software engineering education. In: Inverardi, P., Jazayeri, M. (eds.) Software Engineering Education in the Modern Age. pp. 115–127. Springer Berlin Heidelberg, Berlin, Heidelberg (2006)
9. Gonçalves, L.: Scrum. Controlling & Management Review **62**(4), 40–42 (2018)
10. Liu, J.W., Ho, C.Y., Chang, J.Y., Tsai, J.C.A.: The role of sprint planning and feedback in game development projects: Implications for game quality. Journal of Systems and Software **154**, 79 – 91 (2019)
11. Mead, N.R., Garlan, D., Shaw, M.: Half a century of software engineering education: The cmu exemplar. IEEE Software **35**(5), 25–31 (2018)
12. Nafchi, M.Z., Zulzalil, H., Gandomani, T.J.: On the current agile assessment methods and approaches. In: Malaysian Software Engineering Conference. pp. 251–254 (2014)
13. Qumer, A., Henderson-Sellers, B.: An evaluation of the degree of agility in six agile methods and its applicability for method engineering. Information and Software Technology **50**(4), 280 – 295 (2008)
14. Rubin, K.S.: Essential Scrum: A practical guide to the most popular Agile process. Addison-Wesley (2012)
15. Schwaber, K.: Agile project management with Scrum. Microsoft press (2004)
16. Souza, S.R.S., Oliveira, B.H., Grillo, F., Cico, C.: Construção de plataformas digitais durante o ensino de engenharia de software: um relato de experiência. In: Fórum de Educação em Engenharia de Software. pp. 13–22 (2016)
17. Sutherland, J., Viktorov, A., Blount, J., Puntikov, N.: Distributed scrum: Agile project management with outsourced development teams. In: Annual Hawaii International Conference on System Sciences. pp. 274–274 (2007)

Combining Design Thinking and Scrum to enhance Test Suite during innovative software development*

Flávia Lobato de Morais[1 [0000-0003-4981-0250]], Awdren Fontão[2 [0000-0002-2988-9646]], and Sergio Cleger Tamayo[1 [0000-0002-2025-1638]]

[1] SIDIA - Institute of Science and Technology, Manaus, Brazil
{flavia.morais, sergio.tamayo}@sidia.com
http://www.sidia.com/
[2] FACOM - Federal University of Mato Grosso do Sul
awdren@facom.ufms.br

Abstract. Design Thinking (DT) is a human-centered methodology that has been used in generating and testing innovative ideas. It supports on how to understand user needs in order to derive solutions. Some of these solutions involve innovative functionalities. However, DT applies a test level (acceptance testing) only at the end of the cycle. When using an agile methodology such as Scrum, it is necessary to anticipate everything that might interfere with a Sprint Release. The innovative functionality must be delivered quickly due to competitiveness and time-to-market with the fewest possible defects in the hands of users. From the Software Testing perspective as a way of optimizing the testing process, it is interesting to anticipate all inputs that will allow the improvement of the Test Suite. Our goal is to explore how DT with Scrum can anticipate a set of inputs for Test Suite enhancement in innovative functionalities development. In this study, the DT method was applied within a Scrum setting in a case study that was conducted within the Brazilian Institute of Science and Technology. It involves a partner retail company that requested a user system with face authentication and recognition functionalities.

Keywords: Software Testing · Test Suite · Design Thinking · Scrum.

1 Introduction

The industry around software projects has moved to an agile paradigm that needs to prioritize high quality. This quality is an embracing theme in Software Engineering, and, can be quantified through software functionality and user acceptance. Design Thinking (DT) can be characterized as an attempt and error-based learning iterative process through prototyping and user testing [4]. This iterative feature is the essence of agile methodologies, such as Scrum. Scrum has been used in projects where you need to add value in the software for the

* Supported by organization Sidia.

customer in a short time, which includes innovative projects. Like DT, agile product development is characterized by iteration and experimentation with a clear focus on user requirements [2]. When it comes to requirements, software testing is an essential activity for Software Engineering, which is observing software execution to validate whether it behaves as expected [16].

A problem within Scrum is the gap of communication and constant cooperation between the Scrum team and its customers [14], but there is a bridge that exists between the two, that is the PO (*Product Owner*). This problem can be supported by using DT, since there are team interactions with the user (through testing) to get usage perceptions [15]. In any case, DT may not favor team negotiations and engagement, this is a point that Scrum can support by increasing change capacity and collaborating to continually exchange experience and knowledge [14]. The DT only considers the acceptance test level, ie the final user determines if the software is working according to what the user expects [17], and these many interactions can result in interface and interaction paths modifications. This can propagate changes to alternate flows, and also, new functional test cases [20]. Variations in interaction flow sets, however related to user perceptions, can lead to changes in functional requirements and, consequently, an increase in the suite of test cases.

Due to the presented scenario, and as indicated by Micheli et al. [15], it is important to explore the synergies between DT and other processes during software development. Bertolino in [3] also mentions that there is a need to cohesively test the interconnection with other disciplines (in the case of this study: DT and Scrum) to explore the functional and non-functional properties of the software; even within emerging development paradigms, such as those involving innovative functionality, thus facilitating rapid feedback throughout the development cycle. And this development paradigm that requires fast/frequent changes integration, has driven the need for improvement of the test suite [11].

Thus, the purpose of this paper is to investigate the use of DT to improve the test case suite in a Scrum environment for software development with innovative features. For this, an exploratory case study is described that helps to identify existing benefits and challenges in the project. This project involves the development of software with innovative features such as authentication and facial recognition on retail mobile devices. Findings from our study indicated that, for example: (1) Analyzing the testing requirements at the same time as the functional and non-functional software requirements proved to be the most efficient approach; (2) Identifying the high importance interaction flows around the innovative feature; (3) Mapping a set of models and architectures as a way to refine the parameter that can be used on input set to test cases.

This paper is organized as follows. The next section presents the concepts related to DT, Scrum and Software Testing. Following, Section 3 presents related work. The DT + Scrum + Test approach is presented in 3.1 subsection. The case study, including planning, execution, and results analysis are described in 4 section. And, lastly, the conclusion and future works are presented.

2 Background

2.1 Design Thinking (DT)

According to [5] design thinking (DT) is a collaborative and user-centered approach for problem resolution, that drives innovation through iteration, idea generation, and creative practices. DT permeates human-focused innovation activities through a detailed understanding process (through direct observation) to extract the wants and needs of people not described in traditional research, such as an interview [6]. DT consists of six stages [6]:

- Empathise: consists in imagining and observing scenarios from different users' perspectives in order to capture the context, understand the problems that will be the focus of the project and develop solutions;
- Define: analysis and synthesis, where user information is analyzed and insights obtained to propose new solutions;
- Ideate: innovative solutions are created from the insights gained in the previous step. That's when the big brainstorming occurs. Stakeholders are encouraged to think and propose solutions that are in accordance with the observed context;
- Prototype: can occur in parallel with the definition and ideation stages and allows the construction of solutions;
- Test: tests are applied to users in order to validate ideas generated through prototypes. UX assessment techniques (*User eXperience*) can be applied as a way to evaluate proposed solutions.;
- Implementation: after testing the prototype with users, where feedback and improvements are obtained, the time has come for the idea to be implemented and marketed.

2.2 Scrum

Schwaber [18] defines Scrum as "an Agile process or framework for Agile project management. It's a project management process, certainly not a methodology, because that would be too heavy". The methodology focus is to find a way for team members to produce software flexibly and in a changing environment. The Scrum framework is a framework where you can address and solve complex and adaptive problems while developing products that are productive and creative and have the highest possible value-added [18].

The Scrum framework is constituted in the following way: the product backlog is done through the so-called user stories (list of requirements necessary for the development of the product). The product backlog is transformed into a sprint backlog, these tasks will be developed during each sprint. It can be from 2 to 4 weeks, and each sprint backlog item corresponds to one working day, then, for each sprint the product increments.

2.3 Software Testing

As said by [3]: "Software testing is a broad term encompassing a wide spectrum of different activities, from the testing of a small piece of code by the developer (unit testing), to the customer validation of a large information system (acceptance testing), to the monitoring at run-time of a network-centric service-oriented application."

3 Related Work

Häger et al. [10] describe an approach that integrates DT with Scrum (DT @Scrum) with the propose of inserting DT during software development. The authors highlighted the potential for developing innovative solutions that are allowed when integrating DT with Scrum. However, they do not address the perspective of Software Testing and, more specifically, the improvement of the test case suite.

Hehn and Uebernickel [12] investigate the use of DT to support requirements engineering for projects that involve intensive and innovative software systems. The authors further indicate that investigating the integration between DT and other Software Engineering disciplines is important to understand the benefits and challenges. The authors, while addressing requirements engineering, did not analyze integration from the perspective of test case improvement.

Dobrigkeit et al. [7] propose a methodology that integrates DT, Scrum, and Lean Startup. The study does not evaluate the proposed methodology nor analyze it in the software testing scenario. In this same research line, Sohaib et al. [19] share an experience report about a framework that unifies DT with XP (eXtreme Programming). The framework has not been applied to real software projects. The authors indicate the opportunity to research DT together with Scrum.

Among existing mapping or systematic reviews of DTs there is motivation to: (1) study how DT improves software development strategies [8]; (2) articulate DT with other disciplines [13]; (3) experimentally investigate approaches involving DT in innovation processes [15]. From a Software Testing perspective, the research agenda leads to: (1) exploring the advantages and disadvantages of black-box testing aligned with other processes [1]; (2) proposing appropriate testing approaches to the required objectives (in this case, innovative features) [13]; (3) even if multiple techniques have been applied together to enhance software testing, it is necessary to explore the practicality of these [9] method combinations.

As a way to explore the practicality of combining DT, Scrum and Software Testing to improve the test suite, we planned and executed a case study.

3.1 Approach based on a mix of Scrum, Design Thinking and Software Testing

The purpose of this case study is exploratory, that is, an investigation of a particular case in various scenarios. The case study analyzed in this paper refers to the combination of DT, Scrum, and Software Testing to improve the test case suite. All this in the context of a software project with innovative features. The idea of this paper is to anticipate all inputs that will allow improving the test case suite, as a way of optimizing the testing process. For this purpose, we explore the combination of DT stages and Scrum in the testing for a biometric authentication system to retail.

4 Case Study in a biometric authentication system

This project developed a face recognition system for a large retail company. This company needed to improve its service to its customers/users by facilitating the identification in auto self totems spread across its 20 stores in four Brazilian states. This project was designed, implemented and tested in six sprints in three months.

The case analysis perspective is from the viewpoint of software testers, who want to use the combination of DT + Scrum + Software Testing to improve the test case set (test suite). Table 1 below describes each of the proposed activities, while Fig. 1 shows which activities were applied to the project.

Table 1. Activities Project

ID	Activity Name
ID01	Conducting client interviews
ID02	Investigating the features used by users in the self-service system
ID03	Researching in blog sites
	Researching papers on face recognition studies
ID04	Investigating existing face recognition architectures
ID05	Elaborating interface flow, navigation, and iteration between system screens
ID06	Creating paper usability testing and prototyping
ID07	Creating interactive prototyping
ID08	Performing paper usability testing and prototyping
ID09	Performing functional registration and facial recognition tests
ID10	Reporting defects and defect reporting system improvements
	Supporting developers and designers with possible questions about the registration process done by testers
ID11	Validating the new screen flows of the system through interactive prototyping
ID12	Modifying interface and interaction flow between system screens
ID13	Performing exploratory registration and face recognition tests
ID14	Performing guerrilla tests using the observation technique
ID15	Validating the new system screen flow by applying exploratory and guerrilla tests

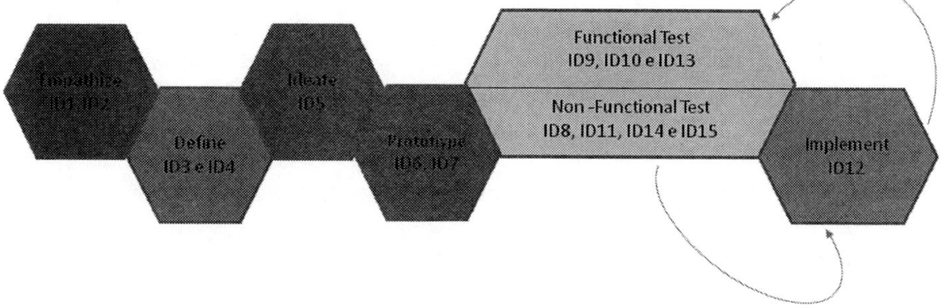

Fig. 1. Design Thinking applied to face recognition

- Empathize: this phase groups the activities ID01 and ID02. Where it is proposed to interview with the client to understand their needs and expectations. And more specifically, understanding what is expected of innovative functionality. In this phase, it is also proposed to investigate which features are most and least used in similar characteristics systems. This phase is conducted by the design team;
- Define: activities ID03 and ID04 are associated with this phase. In activity ID03, Design, Development and Validation teams propose research on websites, blogs, and journals on existing studies around innovative functionality. The activity ID04 is performed by the Development team and proposes the research of architectures related to innovative functionality;
- Ideate: phase involving activity ID05. This is an activity performed by the Design team that elaborates interface flow, navigation, and iteration between system screens;
- Prototype: phase applied by the Design team and involving activities ID06 and ID07 that are related, respectively: Creation and conducting usability testing in paper prototyping; and Prototyping and creating interactive prototyping;
- Test: this phase is characterized by grouping various activities and interaction with the implementation phase. It is performed by the design and validation teams. For a better understanding of the activities involved, it was divided into two sub-phases: Functional and Non-functional (originally present in the DT phases).
    - Functional sub-phase, being represented by ID09, ID10 and ID13 activities. In these activities, functional and exploratory tests are performed around innovative functionality. The activity ID09 produces the defect report and improvements, to the defect reporting system. Activity ID10

supports developers and design teams for any doubts or questions about applied test records. Activity ID13 produces performing exploratory registration and face recognition tests;

- Non-Functional sub-phase, being represented by ID08, ID11, ID14 and ID15 activities. The activity ID08 produces performing paper usability testing and prototyping. Activity ID11 validates the new system screen flow through interactive prototyping. Activity ID14 covers the implementation of the guerrilla test using the observation technique. In Activity ID15 the validation of the new flow system interfaces takes place, applying exploratory and guerrilla tests.

– Implement: Activity ID12 is found in this phase, being the responsibility of the Design team. Its main activities are modifications, interfaces and interaction flows between system screens.

4.1 Execution

For the execution of this study, we considered a self-service project, consisting of a mobile application for the Android platform and the face recognition customer authentication service. For this, the project was developed in five sprints (Sprint 0 to Sprint 4). Next, principal activities during the project are shown by specific sprints, the participating teams, and the inputs generated to improve the test suite. For each sprint, there is a table that allows you to understand the inputs generated from the integration of DT, Scrum and Software Tests.

– **Sprint 0 held from 10/23/2018 to 11/07/2018.** In this sprint are present the Empathize and Define phases. The Empathize phase consisted, as in its definition, of the participation of the Design team. In the first activity (ID01) retail store employees who use the system or know the existing self-service system were interviewed. The goal was to learn about the need to offer its users the face recognition system and what they expected to improve with this new service. As an artifact, this activity receives information from the customer and has helped to generate knowledge about the customer's needs and expectations regarding the innovative functionality of the system, in this case, face recognition. Information on customers that the system should eliminate/mitigate for possible purchase fraud was acquired for the improvement of the test suite, as well as to speed up the use of the self-service system. Then, it was possible to identify what should be included and prioritized in the test cases focused on system security.
In the activity ID02, which seeks to investigate which features are most and least used, we use the observation and interview technique. These were carried out with retail store staff and with customers. It was possible to identify which features of the self-service system were most used and which were the least used. In addition, we identify difficulties, ease of use and existing problems. As an artifact, this activity receives which features are most used and least used by the various users in the self-service system. And it generates

Table 2. Sprint 0 - From 10/23/2018 to 11/07/2018.

Sprint 0	**Empathize** – Customer information was acquired in order to meet their expectations of providing their users with a face recognition system for self-attendant.	**Testing Description** – We obtained knowledge from the customers due to their interest in the self-service system and in reducing fraud. – New usability features and improvements to existing features.
	Team(s) – Design	**Inputs generated** – Knowledge body about features to offer with the new product. It aims to support an early test requirement identification. – A set of existing features in the current self-attendant system and their related issues.
	Define – Research was conducted on facial recognition studies, self-attendant services and technical studies on face recognition.	**Testing Description** – Planning and specification of test cases based on the most common face recognition characteristics and identification parameters to be used for face recognition.
	Team(s) – Design – Development – Validation	**Inputs generated** – Existing models on face recognition. – Self-attendant services. – Registration and face recognition processes.

knowledge about the features existing in the system, and its ease of use.
The purchase and payment features pf the self-service systems were identified for the improvement of the test suite. Thus, test cases should faithfully cover the main and alternative purchase and payment flows.
This Sprint also comprises the "Define" phase, specifically in the third and fourth activity with the participation of the Design, Development and Validation teams.
For activity ID03 we highlight the research in information sources, focusing on face recognition functionality, indicated in this activity. Technical studies on face recognition were performed and, with this, it was possible to analyze contents about facial recognition and self-services. This provided knowledge of facial recognition, as well as self-service.
As an input for the improvement of the test suite were generated existing types and models of training for easy registration and recognition, as well as self-service services. This allowed us to start specifying test cases based on the most common features of facial recognition. In activity ID04 the ex-

Table 3. Sprint 1 - From 11/07/2018 to 11/14/2018.

Sprint 1	**Define** – Continuity of research on facial recognition studies initiated in sprint 0 but focusing on the difficulties detected in registering and recognizing users. – We researched on existing types of face recognition architectures (**Activity developed until Sprint 3**).	**Testing Description** – Specification of new test cases from the difficulty scenarios detected while registering images for the face recognition system. – We have obtained knowledge of existing architectures for face recognition.
	Team(s) – Design – Development – Validation	**Inputs generated** – Knowledge and analysis of the difficulties detected during the face recognition stages. – Knowledge of existing architectures for face recognition. – Parameters configuration for testing planning.
	Ideate – Elaboration of interface flows, navigation and iteration between system flows from interviews and meeting with retail store employees and self-service users.	**Testing Description** – We received the UX and UI documents. – We analyzed the exception flows.
	Team(s) – Design	**Inputs generated** – New interface and navigation flow to be developed and specified on features.

isting architecture survey of facial recognition was performed. This activity was characterized by planning and specifying the tests after identifying the parameters to be used for face recognition. As an artifact, this activity receives several existing and applied architectures and, therefore, it is possible to generate the implementation of registration and facial recognition.

- **Sprint 1 held from 11/07/2018 to 11/14/2018.** In this sprint are present the Define and Ideate phases. Specifically, in the Define phase, the focus is on activities ID03 and ID04. For these activities, we continue to analyze and improve the knowledge database on innovative functionality. These activities further extended this sprint as a way of establishing a common vocabulary shared with the teams involved. As far as testers are concerned,

Table 4. Sprint 3- From 12/05/2018 to 12/19/2018.

	Prototype	**Testing Description**
Sprint 3	– Paper prototype usability tests were created to simulate the use of the self-service system with real users, in order to gauge the understanding of the system flow.	– We got knowledge of the prototype that would be applied. – We received updates the UI and UX documents.
	Team(s)	**Inputs generated**
	– Design	– Review test case and new specification.

Table 5. Sprint 4- From 12/20/2018 to 01/08/2019.

	Test	**Testing Description**
Sprint 4	– We performed usability tests with real users (**Activity developed until Sprint 5**).	– We obtained knowledge of the feedbacks presented by users from the usability tests applied. – Execution of functional test cases with real users to validate registration and face recognition functionalities. – We performed defect reporting and enhancements to the defect reporting system. In addition to supporting developers and designers in the possible existing doubts of the registers performed, functional test, exploratory and guerrilla tests. – We performed exploratory tests of registration and face recognition.
	Team(s)	**Inputs generated**
	– Design – Validation	– New test case specifications and changes to existing cases were generated. – Knowledge of the defects and improvements that were evidenced for later registration. – Estimated effort to run the test suite.

this vocabulary served as input for terms to be adopted in the test cases. Since vocabulary was common, this further helped developers and designers to find it difficult to replicate test cases.

In the Ideate phase, activity ID05, from the results of previous activities, consisted of the elaboration of the interface flow, navigation, and interaction between system screens for face recognition. From interviews with retail store employees and self-service users, it was possible to identify the need to

Table 6. Sprint 5 - From 01/09/2019 to 01/22/2019.

Sprint 5	**Prototype** – Creation of interactive prototyping in order to validate interface and flow modifications suggested by real users. **Team(s)** – Design	**Testing Description** – Interactive prototyping was created to validate the feedback given by users during functional and exploratory tests. **Inputs generated** – -
	Test – Validation of new system screen flows was performed through interactive prototyping. – The guerrilla test was applied using real users. We used the observation technique. – Exploratory tests were applied along with guerrilla tests using real users. **Team(s)** – Design. – Validation.	**Testing Description** – We obtained user feedback from the new flow showed. – We obtained feedback on the usability seeking to improve user interaction with existing face recognition functionalities. – We obtained feedback on existing face recognition bugs, enhancements and improvements to existing flows. **Inputs generated** – Test cases update. – Participation and interaction of validation and designer teams for the improvement of flow and screen interface. – Feedback from valid users who have led change flows and updates in test cases. – New defect and improvement records were generated to describe the continuous improvement of software quality.
	Implement – We performed modification of interface and interaction flow between the system screens, according to the feedback obtained in the tests. **Team(s)** – Design.	**Testing Description** – Review of test cases based on modifications implemented for FR. **Inputs generated** – Knowledge of changes made to new screen flows and revision of test case specifications.

create new screen flows and navigation between them. In this activity it was evident the need to balance the expectations of the customer (the retailer) and potential users of the system. The documents generated by the designers that contained the flows of user interaction and navigation between screens was used as input for the improvement of the test suite. This facilitated the description of expected flows in the test cases and the gestures with which it would be possible to interact with the software. These inputs were also used as criteria for defining the set of inputs from the perspective of interaction gestures for the test cases.
Sprint 2 (11/15/2018 - 12/4/2018) involves activities developed and described in Sprints 1 and 3.

- **Sprint 3 held from 12/05/2018 to 12/19/2018.** In this Sprint the Prototype phase is applied through activities ID06 and ID07. Activity ID06 consists of creating paper prototypes that allow an initial usability test. The prototypes focused on the screens and flow of innovative functionality: customer recognition and facial identification. In activity ID07, interactive prototypes to be used in the Test phase (Sprint 4) were obtained from feedback gathered using the paper prototype. This Sprint was focused on prototyping so that screen and interaction flows could be validated by users. Thus, this sprint was not focused on generating any input for the improvement of test cases. However, with the usability tests applied it was possible to verify the proposed flows in the previous Sprints. This allowed the refinement of the flows described in the test cases.

- **Sprint 4 held from 12/20/2018 to 01/08/2019.** In this sprint, the focus is on the Test non-functional phase, which is the nature of the DT through the ID08, ID11, ID14 and ID15 activities. These cycles don't test the other non-functional related activities, as these involve other flows.
  Considering the non-functional part of the Test phase, during these activities, both the paper prototype and the interactive prototype, generated in the previous sprint, were presented to internal employees as a way of evaluating whether the defined flow would meet the actual interaction flow with the face recognition system. With this, it was possible to update the knowledge database around the perceptions about the system use. The prototypes also made it easier to exercise the previously defined test suites. In this case, we generate a sets of defect reports related to the system represented in the prototypes.
  As new defects and flow improvements were identified, it was necessary to rerun the activity ID07 in order to update the interactive prototype and apply new interactive usability tests until the registration and facial recognition was showing a correct and clear flow to the user.
  Once the prototype was defined, the functionalities and flows defined were implemented, a release for the validation team was generated and cycles of functional, exploratory and guerrilla tests were carried out.

Thus, there is a set of inputs generated in this sprint: (1) new test case specifications and refinements in existing ones; (2) reporting defects and improvements, and; (3) estimated effort to run the test suite.

- **Sprint 5 held from 01/09/2019 to 01/22/2019.** This sprint focuses on the Test and Implement phases. In the Test phase we exercised both the non-functional form through the activities (ID08, ID11, ID14 and ID15) performed in the previous sprint, as well as the functional form with the activities (ID09, ID10 and ID13) performed in the current sprint. This sprint also covers the implement phase that is exercised by activity ID12. It is important to highlight that activities related to functional testing can only be performed after activity ID12, as it involves the implementation of functionalities in the software. For each Test Phase activity we then performed activity ID12 for the Implement Phase. This activity generated input for the review of test cases based on the modifications focused on registration and facial recognition. All other functional test activities (ID09, ID10 and ID13) were performed after cycle releases.

5 Conclusion and Future Work

Findings from our study indicated that combining DT, Scrum and Software Testing supported in: (1) Analyzing testing requirements at the same time as functional and non-functional software requirements including user feedback as a validation strategy; (2) Identifying the high importance interaction flows around the innovative feature, specifically, features related to the innovative aspect; (3) Mapping a set of models and architectures as a way to refine the parameter that can be used on input set and expected results in a Test Suite; (4) Establishing a common vocabulary among the team members. This helped in understanding and replication of the Test Suite; (5) Refining the input set (gestures) on Test Suite description; (6) Validating and enhancing the test case flows; (7) Early prototyping in interactive mode, more than paper prototype, helped the testers to perform functional tests; (8) Introducing innovation features into software development helped to discover how cultural, physical and demographic characteristics can be important to enhance the test suite.
As future work we are applying the approach in other projects with innovative features. It can help to refine the approach and list other gaps and benefits from combining DT+Scrum+Software Testing. We also plan to apply a set of interviews with team members in order to obtain a qualitative perspective from the approach used.

References

1. Ahmad, J., ul Hassan, A., Naqv, T., Mubeen, T.: A review on software testing and its methodology. i-Manager's Journal on Software Engineering **13**(3), 32 (2019)

2. Beck, K., Beedle, M., Bennekum, A.v., Cockburn, A., Cunningham, W., Fowler, M., Grenning, J., Highsmith, J., Hunt, A., Jeffries, R., et al.: Manifesto para desenvolvimento ágil de software. Retirado em **20** (2001)
3. Bertolino, A.: Software testing research: Achievements, challenges, dreams. In: 2007 Future of Software Engineering. pp. 85–103. IEEE Computer Society (2007)
4. Beverland, M.B., Wilner, S.J., Micheli, P.: Reconciling the tension between consistency and relevance: design thinking as a mechanism for brand ambidexterity. Journal of the Academy of Marketing Science **43**(5), 589–609 (2015)
5. Bonini, L.A., Sbragia, R.: O modelo de design thinking como indutor da inovação nas empresas: um estudo empírico. Revista de Gestão e Projetos-GeP **2**(1), 03–25 (2011)
6. Brown, T., et al.: Design thinking. Harvard business review **86**(6), 84 (2008)
7. Dobrigkeit, F., de Paula, D., Uflacker, M.: Innodev: A software development methodology integrating design thinking, scrum and lean startup. In: Design Thinking Research, pp. 199–227. Springer (2019)
8. Elsbach, K.D., Stigliani, I.: Design thinking and organizational culture: A review and framework for future research. Journal of Management **44**(6), 2274–2306 (2018)
9. Garousi, V., Mäntylä, M.V.: A systematic literature review of literature reviews in software testing. Information and Software Technology **80**, 195–216 (2016)
10. Häger, F., Kowark, T., Krüger, J., Vetterli, C., Übernickel, F., Uflacker, M.: Dt@ scrum: integrating design thinking with software development processes. In: Design thinking research, pp. 263–289. Springer (2015)
11. Haghighatkhah, A., Mäntylä, M., Oivo, M., Kuvaja, P.: Test prioritization in continuous integration environments. Journal of Systems and Software **146**, 80–98 (2018)
12. Hehn, J., Uebernickel, F.: The use of design thinking for requirements engineering: An ongoing case study in the field of innovative software-intensive systems. In: 2018 IEEE 26th International Requirements Engineering Conference (RE). pp. 400–405. IEEE (2018)
13. Hrabovská, K., Rossi, B., Pitner, T.: Software testing process models benefits & drawbacks: a systematic literature review. arXiv preprint arXiv:1901.01450 (2019)
14. López-Martínez, J., Juárez-Ramírez, R., Huertas, C., Jiménez, S., Guerra-García, C.: Problems in the adoption of agile-scrum methodologies: A systematic literature review. In: 2016 4th International Conference in Software Engineering Research and Innovation (CONISOFT). pp. 141–148. IEEE (2016)
15. Micheli, P., Wilner, S.J., Bhatti, S.H., Mura, M., Beverland, M.B.: Doing design thinking: Conceptual review, synthesis, and research agenda. Journal of Product Innovation Management **36**(2), 124–148 (2019)
16. Myers, G.J., Sandler, C., Badgett, T.: The art of software testing. John Wiley & Sons (2011)
17. Pugh, K.: Lean-Agile Acceptance Test-Driven-Development: Better Software Through Collaboration. Pearson Education (2010)
18. Schwaber, K., Sutherland, J.: Guia do scrum-um guia definitivo para o scrum: As regras do jogo. Obtido em **16** (2013)
19. Sohaib, O., Solanki, H., Dhaliwa, N., Hussain, W., Asif, M.: Integrating design thinking into extreme programming. Journal of Ambient Intelligence and Humanized Computing **10**(6), 2485–2492 (2019)
20. Tahera, K., Wynn, D.C., Earl, C., Eckert, C.M.: Testing in the incremental design and development of complex products. Research in Engineering Design **30**(2), 291–316 (2019)

Model-Based Testing in Agile Projects: An Approach Based on Domain-Specific Languages*

Aline Zanin[1], Avelino Fracisco Zorzo[1], and Henry Cabral Nunes[1]

PUCRS - Porto Alegre, Brazil
aline.zanin@edu.pucrs.br, henry.numes@edu.pucrs.br and avelino.zorzo@pucrs.br

Abstract. Model-Based Testing (MBT) can bring several benefits to software quality. However, generally, MBT is applied in traditional software development lifecycle models, with few studies exploring its application in agile software development context. Hence, usually, agile development teams (AT) do not benefit from the advantages that the MBT technique provides, for example, reuse of artifacts and traceability between requirements and test artifacts. Thus, this article presents an approach for applying MBT in agile software development teams. This approach is based on the use of a semi-natural language to write scenarios for the automatic generation of models and test scripts. To exemplify the application of this approach, we also present a Domain-Specific Language (DSL) called Aquila, in which new functional test related keywords are added to the Gherkin DSL. We also present, based on a literature review, the majors challenges and difficulties of applying MBT in AT. To validate the proposed approach a Focus Group study was used.

Keywords: Software Testing, Agile, DSL, MBT

1 Introduction

The increasing search for quality improvement in software products induces companies to innovate and to optimize their processes, techniques and tools. Model-based Testing (MBT) is one of the techniques that helps such improvement in the context of software testing. MBT focuses on creating test artifacts and on reusing models designed by development teams. In general, these teams create models to perform activities such as requirements and systems analysis. So, MBT uses these artifacts to facilitate the generation and maintenance of test artifacts to improve traceability of system requirements and software testing [5].

MBT is widely used in traditional lifecycle software development, *e.g.* Waterfall lifecycle. However, although the benefits of MBT are already known and disseminated, few studies present the application of this technique in an agile software development context, since applying MBT in an agile context brings

* This study was financed in part by Coordenação de Aperfeiçoamento de Pessoal de Nivel Superior – Brazil (CAPES) – Finance Code 001

new challenges. Those challenges are related to time management and human effort required to create models. Since the teams work with short cycles of continuous delivery, the time available for creating models, executing tests, and correcting possible failures is reduced [11] [10] [9].

Furthermore, according to the Agile Manifest [1], it is very important that Agile Teams (AT) use simple and efficient documentation. One way of doing that could be to use software requirements specifications using a Domain-Specific Language (DSL), for example Gherkin [4]. One the other hand, through the scenarios written in Gherkin and using Behavior Driven Development (BDD) [18], it is possible to generate methods (just skeletons) that will structure the test automation for a specific functionality.

On the other hand, BDD does not completely automate the creation of scripts for test automation, BDD only structures it. Therefore, it is still necessary for the test analyst to code the test scripts, and this is a time-consuming activity that could be used for other activities related to system development. MBT can provide the complete automation of this process, optimizing the human effort and time efficiency.

In this context, the research question of this study is: **How can MBT support the automated generation of test scripts in the agile software development context?**

In order to provide answers to the above question: 1) we analyzed the difficulties and challenges to apply MBT in AT reported by researchers in the literature; 2) based on the difficulties and challenges identified by these studies, we propose an approach for adopting MBT in AT; 3) taking into consideration Steps 1 and 2, we designed a new DSL, called Aquila; and, 4) to provide an evaluation of this approach and language, we conducted a survey in which participants had the opportunity to experiment Aquila, create a test scenario, and generate test scripts. To confirm this evaluation we conducted a Focus Group study where we discuss the applicability of Aquila.

This paper is organized as follows. Section 2 describes related work. Section 3 presents the challenges and difficulties to apply MBT in AT and also a set of practices to facilitate the adoption of MBT in AT. Section 4 presents a DSL that allows the use of MBT in AT. Section 5 describes the validation of our approach with AT members. Finally, Section 7 presents the conclusion of this study.

2 Related Work

This section describes some of the papers that were analyzed in a systematic literature review (SLR). We analyzed papers that present some discussion on MBT and AT, and also describe some challenges and difficulties faced by AT when applying MBT. The literature analysis is based on a previous SLR [2]. That SLR mapped all the studies that present approaches, strategies, techniques, methods and methodologies for MBT adoption and were published up to 2016. We analyzed the papers selected for that study [2], and by reading the titles and abstracts, we extracted the papers that present MBT specifically applied to agile context [10] [17] [8] [13]. Later, based on the related work of these selected papers, other papers were identified. The main papers directly related to this work are mentioned next.

Törsel [22] presents a study that uses Domain-Specific Language (DSL) to create models for test scripts generation. This study is different from ours, because the DSL used for creating models is not semi-natural language, it is similar to a programming language.

Yue *et al.* [19] present an approach to perform MBT based on DSL. The major difference between our approach and the one proposed by Yue *et al.* is that we use an extension to Gherkin to design scenarios and automatically generate models. Besides that, using our approach it is easier to understand how the mapping from the scenario to the model is performed, allowing to implement graphics extension for visual display of this model. In Yue's work, a behavioral model is not generated, and it is difficult to analyze the flows generated by the MBT technique.

Entin *et al.* [8] introduce an approach to use semi-natural language and Gherkin to generate models to apply MBT. However, the scenarios must be exclusively written using Gherkin, which does not have enough details to generate a complete model that allows the generation of test scripts. For this reason, human interference is required to create the model, and no strategy is proposed to automate the generation of test scripts from these models.

Li *et al.* [12] present an approach to generate Gherkin scenarios from models. This approach is similar to ours because both use Gherkin. However, our approach generates models from scenarios and test scripts from models. So, it is possible to create models and generate test scripts only using semi-natural language in our approach.

Dwarakanath *et al.* [6] and Thummalapenta *et al.* [21] propose approaches where DSLs are used to automatically generate test scripts. The DSLs used in those works are similar to the one proposed in our approach, since all of them use semi-natural language based on English. However, Dwarakanath and Thummalapenta do not use the MBT technique. Thus, those works do not benefit from the advantages provided by MBT. For example, in our approach, it is possible to combine alternative system flows to generate test scripts that validate all possible flows of the System Under Test (SUT).

3 Applying MBT in AT: Using a DSL

The main difficulties and challenges for using MBT in AT that we identified through our systematic literature review, mentioned in Section 2, are summarized as: 1) Models created by AT rarely contain enough details to apply MBT [11] [10] [13]; 2) It is difficult to guarantee that all requirements are covered by the generated tests artifacts [17] [11]; 3) AT, in general, prefer easy to use testing tools [11]; 4) Agile process often works with short development cycles [7] [8]; 5) Lack of time to create models [7] [8]; 6) Continuous requirements changes [7] [9] [17] [8]; 7) Difficult test artifact maintenance [9] [8]; and, 8) Professionals do not have enough expertise in software modeling languages such as Unified Modeling Language (UML) [9] [8] [13].

Based on the difficulties and challenges mentioned above, we can point out to the following improvements in the MBT process to make it applicable by AT:

1. Supporting automatic creation of models, based on the requirements documents usually adopted by AT, such as user stories or scenarios. This is important for reducing the learning curve and simplify the adaptability of the teams to the technique.
2. Supporting requirements changes by modeling adaptation.
3. Supporting automation of script generation, avoiding the generation of manual test cases.
4. Avoiding the generation of excessive documentation.

Based on these suggestions, we propose, in this work, a solution focused on the automation of model creation. To this end, the idea is that the software testers write requirements in a semi-natural language, and from this language, models could be generated automatically.

One example of semi-natural language used to write scenarios in AT is Gherkin [4]. However, in order to make possible to generate models to apply MBT in AT, the language used to write scenarios, should also provide a simple way of describing, also, functional testing requirements, which currently is not supported by Gherkin, and, therefore, an extended version of Gherkin is needed (see Section 4). Gherkin scenarios are written basically using the keywords GIVEN, WHEN, THEN and AND. GIVEN represents the actual state of the system, WHEN represents one action performed in the system and THEN represents the result of this action. The AND keyword can be used with GIVEN and THEN keywords to complement the information.

Therefore, in order to apply a DSL in MBT and AT, the following guidelines should be observed when designing a new DSL:

1. All scenarios must have, in addition to the status information and expected result, details of actions that must be performed by the tester in the system.
2. Scenarios should not contain too much information, for example, they should not explicitly contain the step-by-step test case describing each of the fields in a form. This is because in this case the improvement in productivity, through automation, would be negatively affected.
3. Scenarios should be complemented with keywords that represent generic behaviors (which often happens in several functionality), for example, filling in all fields in a form with valid information.
4. Scenarios should be complemented with generic result verification information, for example, validating a value in a form.
5. Each scenario should the converted to a model, in order to be able to apply MBT.
6. From the generated model, it should be possible to create test artifacts for any system platform.

7. From the generated model, it should be possible to create test artifacts for any functional testing tool.

From the above mentioned guidelines, a new Domain-Specific Language, called **Aquila**, was created. This new language includes each of the above-mentioned guidelines to Gherkin scenarios. This new DSL is described in Section 4.

4 Aquila - a DSL for Agile Functional Testing

Aquila is a Domain-Specific Language for agile functional testing. Hence, one of the major requirements of Aquila design is that Aquila can be used to write test documentation, *e.g.*, test scenarios. In this context, Aquila was designed as an extension of Gherkin, thus, the main characteristic of Aquila is the insertion of test information in Gherkin scenarios. This test information is represented by adding new keywords in test scenarios. These new keywords are related to the user interaction with the system, for example: input values and click buttons. This test information will allow one to automatically generate a model that will later be translated into test scripts to execute the test automatically. For the definition of these keywords, we performed a mapping of the main actions that a user can perform in a system. This mapping is performed initially through the W3C [23] documentation[1]. We also address some aspects of user interaction based on our experience performing software testing in industry [15] [3] [14].

Each Aquila keyword is associated to a Gherkin keyword. The association between Aquila keywords and Gherkin keywords follows the following pattern: Aquila keywords that represent actions are associated to the Gherkin keyword WHEN; Aquila keywords representing results are associated to the THEN keyword; and, symbols “{ }” and “< >” are used with the GIVEN keyword.

Table 1 shows the selected keywords, the behavior represented by each of the keywords and the associated Gherkin keyword. These keywords are used in the mapping between the scenarios and the models, in which each keyword has a specific representation in the generated models.

Some Aquila scenarios can require input or selection of values, *i.e.*, scenarios that use keywords: put, use-valid-data, checked, choose, and select-data. For this purpose, input tables are created and in these tables the name of the fields and their respective input values are specified. For example, for a scenario that requires input data for the fields “Country” and “State”, the following piece of Aquila code would represent the tables that contains field names and their respective values. This example can be seen in Figure 1

For the use-valid-data keyword, it is possible to create a table with all fields, and respective values, as shown in the next piece of Aquila code. This example cam be see in Figure 2.

[1] https://www.w3.org/Consortium/

Table 1. Aquila DSL Keywords

Aquila keyword	Definition	Gherkin keyword
< >	Used to enter a URL	GIVEN
{ }	Used to reference a scenario in another scenario	GIVEN
click[field]	Represents the action of clicking on a specific field	WHEN
click-link[field]	Represents the action of clicking on a link	WHEN
put[field]	Represents the action of inserting values in a specific field	WHEN
use-valid-data	Represents that all fields present on the feature under test and listed in the input table will receive valid values	WHEN
dont-fill-out[field]	Represents that no values will be entered in a specific field	WHEN
checked[field]	Represents the selection of an option in a checkbox	WHEN
choose[field]	Represents the selection of an option in a radio button	WHEN
select-data[field]	Represents the selection of an option in a list	WHEN
mouse-over[field]	Represents the placement of the mouse over a given field	WHEN
enable[field]	Represents verification if a field is active	THEN
disable[field]	Represents verification if a field is not active	THEN
showed[field]	Represents checking for the presence of a particular word or phrase on the SUT	THEN
opened[url]	Represents checking the correct opening of a page	THEN
showed-title[word]	Represents page title verification	THEN

```
When I select-data[Country]
| Country |
| USA     |
And I select-data[State]
| State  |
| Nevada |
| Texas  |
```

Fig. 1. Select-data keyword example

```
When I use-valid-data:
| Country | State | Email          | FirstName |
| France  | Loire | alice@test.com | Alice     |
```

Fig. 2. use-valid-data keyword example

4.1 Aquila DSL Usage

In this section, we describe how a DSL, *i.e.*, Aquila, is used in order to generate and execute test scripts in the context of AT. The complete flow of Aquila utilization is formed by six steps (see Figure 3), in which, two require human interaction (Writing Aquila scenarios and Test Script Improvements), three are automatically executed by Aquila tool (Model Generation, Test Sequence Generation and Test Script Generation) and one is executed by a testing automation tool, for example, Selenium Webdriver. The Aquila tool is available for downloading at: https://github.com/alinnezanin/Aquila/

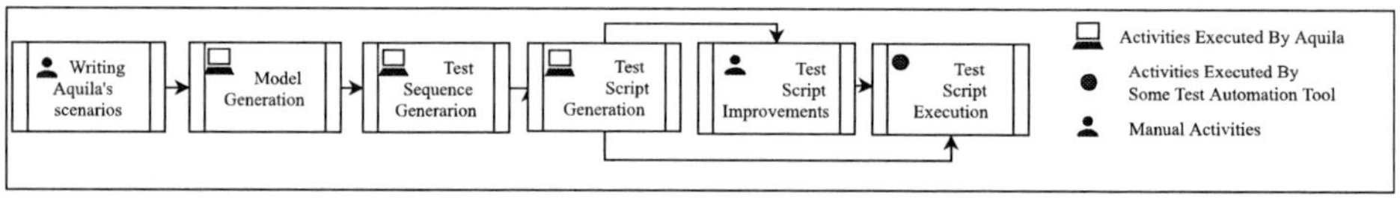

Fig. 3. Aquila steps

1) Writing Aquila's scenarios: This is one of the majors steps of the Aquila usage process. In this step, the scenarios are created. To exemplify each step, we use an online web store, *i.e.*, http://demo.cs-cart.com/. For example, to test this web store we chose the scenario that validates the registering of a new customer and the insertion of a new product into the shopping cart. Figure 4 shows an Aquila code that represents this scenario. In the code, it is possible to see the use of the following tags: click-link, click, use-valid-data, put and showed.

2) Model Generation. The model chosen for MBT application, in this work, is the Directed Acyclic Graph (DAG). In the model generation process, each DAG node represents an Aquila keyword used in the scenario. The exception to this rule is the use-valid-data keyword that generates not only one node, but one node for each field present on the system and specified in the input table. For the scenario in Figure 4, the respective model is represented in Figure 5. In this model, it is possible to realize that there is some alternative flows. These flows represent the second input option for the use-valid-data and put keywords specified in the input table (lines 7,8,13 and 14 of the scenario in Figure 4). It is important to highlight that the number in the DAG nodes is the line number in the scenario code.

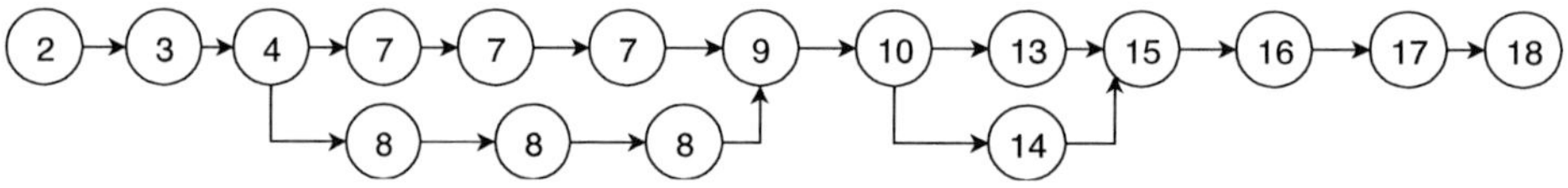

Fig. 5. New User Registration Model

1. **Scenario:**Register Customer and Add Product
2. **Given** <https://demo.cs-cart.com >
3. **When I click-link**[my account]
4. **And I click**[register]
5. **And I use-valid-data:**
6. |**email**| **password**| **news**|
7. |custo@mer.com | c123@ |news|
8. |tes@te.com | a143@ |news|
9. **And I click**[register]
10. **And I click**[search-performed]
11. **And I put**[search-performed]
12. |**search-performed**|
13. |bike|
14. |game|
15. **And I click**[search]
16. **And I click-link**[Catania]
17. **And I click**[addToCard]
18. **Then showed**[The product was added to your cart]

Fig. 4. Register a new customer and add a product to the customer cart

3) Test Sequence Generation. A test sequence is generated before the test script creation and describes the path traversed between the initial node and the last node in the graph. To generate a test sequence, we use the Depth-First Search algorithm (DFS) [20]. Using this algorithm, test sequences that combine the inputs used in each field of the system are generated. This ensures that if there are peculiar behaviors related to the combination of two or more inputs, these behaviors are tested.

The sequences are formed by the numbers that represent lines of a scenario and their respective nodes in the DAG. For a scenario line that contains the use-valid-data keyword, this line will be repeated several times in the sequence, because this keyword generates multiple nodes in the DAG, one for each field that will be filled.

For the model in Figure 5, four test sequences are generated. This is because there are two alternative flows in the model, and Aquila combines these flows. The following test sequences are generated:
1) 2 - 3 - 4 - 7- 7- 7 - 9 - 10 - 13 - 15 - 16 - 17 - 18
2) 2 - 3 - 4 - 7- 7- 7 - 9 - 10 - 14 - 15 - 16 - 17 - 18
3) 2 - 3 - 4 - 8- 8- 8 - 9 - 10 - 13 - 15 - 16 - 17 - 18
4) 2 - 3 - 4 - 8- 8- 8 - 9 - 10 - 14 - 15 - 16 - 17 - 18

4) Test Script Generation. The test script is based on the previously generated models and test sequences. For each model, one or more test scripts can be generated according to the number of generated test sequences. Figure 6 shows a snippet of a code generated for the Selenium Webdriver tool. This tool was chosen because it is widely used within IT companies. However, the same

Aquila scenario can be used to generate scripts for different tools or languages. Figure 6 shows the code for the "Register Customer and Add Product" scenario.

```
@Test
public void newCustomerRegistration() {
  Webdriver driver = new FirefoxDriver();
  driver.get("https://demo.cs-cart.com");
  WebElement linkText = driver.findElement(By.linkText("my account"));
  linkText.click();
  WebElement register = driver.findElement(By.name("register"));
  register.click();
  WebElement email = driver.findElement(By.name("email"));
  email.sendKeys("cuso@mer.com");
  WebElement password = driver.findElement(By.name("password"));
  password.sendKeys("c123@.com");
  WebElement register2 = driver.findElement(By.name("register"));
  register2.click();
 (...)
}
```

Fig. 6. Generated code for "Register Customer and Add Product" scenario

5)Test Script Improvements. These improvements might be necessary when a test engineer uses some field name different from the one used in the application, to correct some mistake in the scenarios, or to create a script for an action that is not completely covered by Aquila. In these cases a partial script is generated, and the test engineer will have to complete the generated script. The partial script is generated into a library and can be edited at any time. This allows the test engineer to customize their tests for peculiar situations not covered by Aquila tags.

6) Test Script Execution. To execute the test scripts, it is necessary to use a traditional testing automation tool, for example: Seleniun Webdriver. This tool should be compatible with the syntax of the generated script.

5 Aquila Validation: a Focus Group Study

In order to validate the applicability of Aquila, we used a Focus Group method. Hence, we established two research questions (RQ) that we wanted to answer by the end of the Focus Group study: *RQ1*) What is the specialists perception on the productivity that can be achieved when using Aquila, compared to manual test scripts creation for test automation? *RQ2*) What are the experts' perceptions regarding the learning curve on the use of Aquila, when compared to the learning curve for the manual test scripts creation for test automation?

Once the research questions were defined, we set the profile and the number of specialists that would participate in the Focus Group execution. There were eight people participating in this Focus Group session. Table 2 presents an overview on the subjects profile. The Focus Group session was performed based on following questions:

Table 2. Individual Subjects Profile

S1	Professional with more than 2 years of programming experience, initial knowledge in test automation, business and Gherkin and no management knowledge.
S2	Professional with up to 2 years of Gherkin test automation experience and more than 2 years of programming, business and management experience.
S3	Professional who has up to 2 years of Gherkin experience, initial knowledge in test and business automation and no programming knowledge and agile project management.
S4	Professional with initial knowledge in test automation, business, management and Gherkin and no programming knowledge.
S5	Professional who has more than 5 (five) years of testing experience and business experience, has up to 2 (two) years of Gherkin experience and has initial knowledge in programming and agile project management.
S6	Professional with up to 2 (two) years of experience in test automation and programming, with more than 2 (two) years of business and management experience and with more than 5 (five) years of experience with Gherkin.
S7	Professional with more than 5 (five) years of programming experience, up to 2 (two) years of experience in test automation and initial knowledge in business, management and Gherkin.
S8	Professional with up to 2 (two) years experience with Gherkin test automation and more than 5 (five) years experience with programming, business and management.

1. Do you believe that using Aquila can improve team productivity? If yes, how?
   - *Discussion analysis*: For this topic it can be said that the group considered that Aquila influences positively the team productivity, provided that some conditions are respected: the tester must have a minimum knowledge on test automation; the business person needs to be involved with the creation of the scenarios; and, the project must be organized for this framework of scenario utilization and test automation. These conclusions are reinforced by the following statements:

     "I have a feeling that if the tester is a beginner on test automation, it is a lot easier, but it is a feeling [S4]."

     "If we take this to the business area, for them to write the test scenarios, and someone else just complement them, it is much faster for them to type keywords than it is to write Java code [S2]."

2. Compared to the manual creation of scripts for test automation, would you consider Aquila more productive, less productive or indifferent? Justify.
   - *Discussion analysis*: In this topic, there was a consensus among participants that Aquila could present an improvement in productivity when compared to the manual creation of scripts for test automation. However, some limits were pointed out by the participants that should be the focus of the researchers in the development of future work related to Aquila. These conclusions are reinforced by the following statements:

     "But compared to manual test scripts creation I believe it would increase productivity for the reasons already mentioned [S4]."

     "It could be productive to some extent depending on what would have to be changed manually [S7]."
3. What is your perception regarding the learning curve of the use of Aquila in relation to the learning curve for manual creation of scripts for test automation?
   - *Discussion analysis*: Analyzing the participants comments, we can conclude that Aquila could easily be learned and used by professionals. Like any innovative tool, Aquila requires a learning curve and a period of adaptation, but the discussions indicate that the curve is smaller than the curve that usually exists for learning, for example, a programming language and that Aquila can easily be used in conjunction with any other automation tool. Furthermore, Aquila will generate the code that represents actions, and a beginner programmer could see this code generated, being able to analyze, understand and memorize it. These findings are reinforced by the following statements from the participants.

     "In my opinion Selenium (manual creation) is more complex, Aquila does not have many commands like Selenium, so it is easier [S6]."; "I think it is simpler because it is closer to a natural language [S8]."

     "I think the Aquila learning curve is less steep, but a person needs to know how to write tests manually to be able to edit them [S5]."
4. Would you apply Aquila on a test project that is working with agile software development? Why?
   - *Discussion analysis*: In this topic several opinions were expressed by the participating subjects. No participating subject stated that they would not use Aquila, however, several points were raised that would be considered by professionals when deciding to use Aquila or not. The main point, which was quoted by several participants, is that Aquila application is better recommended in projects that are already using the BDD technique or writing requirements using Gherkin. Another factor considered to be determinant in the choice of whether or not to use Aquila is the amount of changes that need to be made to the Aquila generated scripts, and this amount of changes is highly related to system complexity and type of features that the system contains. Analyzing the subjects comments, we can say that Aquila can be applied to the context that it was proposed to. It was designed for AT that use Gherkin for writing requirements, or AT that are looking for using this approach. As for the

amount of scripts changes needed, Aquila is prepared to automate most of the actions that can be performed on the system for the domain to which it was proposed to.

It is important to emphasize that the participants already had previous contact with these questions. After reading, and answering the questions individually, they discussed the same questions as a group. The conclusions mentioned above are related to the group discussion.

6 Aquila Validation: a Survey with professionals

This study aimed to understand the interference of DSL Aquila on productivity and test automation learning curve, considering the opinion of testing engineers. For this study we brought together a group of professionals who work with software testing on agile teams. These professionals used the Aquila DSL, and based on this usage, they provided feedback about Aquila.

Thirteen professionals participated in this study. All of them work in agile teams (their profile is detailed in Table 3). The profile considers the professionals self-assessment about their previous knowledge according to the following following criteria: Beginner: I have knowledge, I can perform basic tasks; Intermediate: I have knowledge and can perform complex tasks; Advanced: I have knowledge and can perform all kinds of tasks including management; I am not aware: Professional without knowledge on the subject.

Table 3. Profile of the subjects

Knowledge area	Knowledge level			
	Beginner	**Intermediate**	**Advanced**	**Not aware**
Test Automation	9	4	0	0
Gherkin	6	4	0	3
Agile Methods	4	7	2	0
Software Test	3	4	0	3

The participants took one hour to write the scenarios and to generate the scripts. After completing the challenge, participants answered questions on: 1) Learning difficulty of DSL Aquila; 2) Possibility to write scenarios and generate scripts using Aquila in a sprint of an agile project; 3) Advantages and disadvantages of using Aquila in an agile project. They were also asked to suggest improvements on the language and tool.

The first question is related to the difficulties encountered in learning to use Aquila. In this sense, ten participants answered that they consider it was easy to learn; two participants considered that the level of difficulty was average, and one participant considered it difficult.

In the second question, a comparison is made between the easiness to learn Aquila against the easiness to learn other testing tools. For this question, seven participants found it was easier to learn Aquila, four mentioned the learning curve was similar, and two said it was harder. The two participants, who believed it was more difficult to learn Aquila than another testing tool, had never seen Gherkin before, and, therefore, either way, previously knowledge on using a DSL (for example, Gherkin) may have influenced the participants perception.

The third question aimed to understand if it would be possible to complete the DSL Aquila utilization cycle in an agile project sprint. For this question, only one participant said he did not believe using Aquila would help in an agile project sprint. Regarding the advantages, disadvantages and improvements of Aquila, several professionals have pointed out as advantages the easiness of use and the fact that the tool generates scripts. Regarding disadvantages, one participant mentioned that the code generated by the tool presented some faults (this has already been reviewed and the faults corrected). Some of the participants also pointed out that tool usability should be improved.

7 Conclusion

In this paper we presented an approach to use MBT in Agile projects. This approach was validated through a survey in which participants had the opportunity to experiment Aquila, and its tool. In the experiment, all participants were able to complete the full scenario creation and test scripts generation. This produced an excellent view from the participants in the sense that Aquila can positively influence productivity and facilitate the learning of test automation. This result confirms the result that we had already obtained through a focus group study, before the tool was ready to be used. Some improvements are still necessary, as mentioned before, in order to the full adoption of our language and tool in actual agile environments. For example, a framework such as Usa_DSL[16] may be used to help improving Aquila usability.

References

1. Beck, K., Beedle, M., Van Bennekum, A., Cockburn, A., Cunningham, W., Fowler, M., Grenning, J., Highsmith, J., Hunt, A., Jeffries, R., et al.: Manifesto for agile software development. http://www.agilemanifesto.org (2001), access in 03/07/2019
2. Bernardino, M., Rodrigues, E.M., Zorzo, A.F., Marchezan, L.: Systematic mapping study on mbt: tools and models. IET Software **11**(4) (2017)
3. Bernardino, M., Zorzo, A.F., de M. Rodrigues, E.: Canopus: A domain-specific language for modeling performance testing. In: 9th IEEE International Conference on Software Testing, Verification and Validation (ICST) (2016)
4. Cucumber: Gherkin. https://docs.cucumber.io/gherkin/ (2019), access in 03/07/2019
5. Dalal, S.R., Jain, A., Karunanithi, N., Leaton, J., Lott, C.M., Patton, G.C., Horowitz, B.M.: Model-based testing in practice. In: International Conference on Software Engineering (ICSE) (1999)
6. Dwarakanath, A., Era, D., Priyadarshi, A., Dubash, N., Podder, S.: Accelerating test automation through a domain specific language. In: 10th International Conference on Software Testing, Verification and Validation (ICST) (2017)

7. Entin, V., Winder, M., Zhang, B., Christmann, S.: Combining model-based and capture-replay testing techniques of graphical user interfaces: An industrial approach. In: 4th International Conference on Software Testing, Verification and Validation Workshops (ICSTW) (2011)
8. Entin, V., Winder, M., Zhang, B., Claus, A.: A process to increase the model quality in the context of model-based testing. In: 8th International Conference on Software Testing, Verification and Validation Workshops (ICSTW) (2015)
9. Entin, V., Winder, M., Zhang, B., Christmann, S.: Introducing model-based testing in an industrial Scrum project. In: 7th International Workshop on Automation of Software Test (AST) (2012)
10. Jalalinasab, D., Ramsin, R.: Towards model-based testing patterns for enhancing agile methodologies. In: 14th International Conference on Intelligent Software Methodologies, Tools, and Techniques (SoMeT) (2012)
11. Katara, M., Kervinen, A.: Making model-based testing more agile: a use case driven approach. In: 11th Haifa Verification Conference (HVC) (2006)
12. Li, N., Escalona, A., Kamal, T.: Skyfire: Model-based testing with cucumber. In: 9th International Conference on Software Testing, Verification and Validation (ICST) (2016)
13. Li, N., Escalona, A., Kamal, T.: Skyfire: Model-based testing with cucumber. In: 9th International Conference onSoftware Testing, Verification and Validation (ICST) (2016)
14. de M. Rodrigues, E., Bernardino, M., Costa, L.T., Zorzo, A.F., de Oliveira, F.M.: Pletsperf - A model-based performance testing tool. In: 8th IEEE International Conference on Software Testing, Verification and Validation (ICST) (2015)
15. Rodrigues, E.M., de Oliveira, F.M., Costa, L.T., Bernardino, M., Zorzo, A.F., do Rocio Senger de Souza, S., Saad, R.S.: An empirical comparison of model-based and capture and replay approaches for performance testing. Empirical Software Engineering **20**(6), 1831–1860 (2015)
16. Rodrigues, I.P., Zorzo, A.F., Bernardino, M., de Borba Campos, M.: Usa-DSL: usability evaluation framework for domain-specific languages. In: 33rd Annual ACM Symposium on Applied Computing. pp. 2013–2021 (2018)
17. Sivanandan, S., B, Y.C.: Agile development cycle: Approach to design an effective model based testing with behaviour driven automation framework. In: 20th Annual International Conference on Advanced Computing and Communications (ADCOM) (2014)
18. Smart, J.: BDD in Action: Behavior-Driven Development for the Whole Software Lifecycle
19. Tao, Y., Shaukat, A., Zhang, M.: Rtcm: A natural language based, automated, and practical test case generation framework. In: International Symposium on Software Testing and Analysis (ISSTA) (2015)
20. Tarjan, R.: Depth-first search and linear graph algorithms. SIAM journal on computing **1**(2), 146–160 (1972)
21. Thummalapenta, S., Sinha, S., Singhania, N., Chandra, S.: Automating test automation. In: 34th International Conference on Software Engineering (ICSE) (2012)
22. Törsel, A.: A testing tool for web applications using a domain-specific modelling language and the nusmv model checker. In: 6th International Conference on Software Testing, Verification and Validation (ICST) (2013)
23. W3C: Html input types. https://www.w3schools.com/ (2018), access in 03/07/2019

iStar4G: Estendendo a linguagem *iStar 2.0* para modelagem de jogos digitais

Sanderson de Paula Barbosa e André Luiz de Castro Leal

Departamento de Computação, UFRRJ
Núcleo de Práticas de Engenharia de Software Aplicadas a Games (NuESGames)
Seropédica, Rio de Janeiro

sandersonbarbosa36@gmail.com, andrecastr@gmail.com

Abstract. Digital games, if considered software products, can and should be built with technical criteria and supported by Software Engineering practices to properly achieve desired qualities. Goal oriented modeling presents itself as an applicable approach to the initial stages of software prospection and development, being able to make explicit stakeholders' intentions and objectives. Applying the iStar 2.0 language to digital game modeling, through a process of reverse engineering, revealed limitations to original elements' usage in actor/agent and resource modeling within the scope of the analyzed games. From such limitations, we propose extending the traditional iStar 2.0 language into *iStar for Games* (*iStar4G*), seeking to achieve desired representations to support digital game definition and development.

Keywords: Game Development Process, Game Modeling, , istar, Requirements Engineering, Goal-Oriented Model, GORE.

Resumo. Jogos digitais, se considerados como produtos de software, podem e devem ser construídos com critérios técnicos e suporte da Engenharia de Software para que alcancem as qualidades desejadas. A modelagem orientada a objetivos se apresenta como uma possibilidade aplicável aos estágios iniciais de prospecção do desenvolvimento de softwares, permitindo explicitar intencionalidades e objetivos de *stakeholders* do produto. A aplicação da linguagem *iStar 2.0* na modelagem de jogos, por meio de engenharia reversa, revelou limitações ao uso de seus elementos originais para se modelar atores/agentes e especificação de recursos dos personagens dentro do escopo dos jogos analisados. A partir dessas limitações, propomos a extensão da linguagem *iStar 2.0* tradicional para a linguagem *iStar For Games* (*iStar4G*), com o objetivo de atingirmos as representações desejadas para dar suporte à definição e desenvolvimento de jogos digitais.

Palavras-chave: Processo de Desenvolvimento de Jogos, Modelagem de Jogos, istar, Engenharia de Requisitos, Modelagem Orientada a Objetivos.

1 Introdução

Na Engenharia de Software (ES), o processo de construção de software de qualidade consiste em trabalhar diversas etapas, cada uma com sua complexidade específica e possíveis variações de metodologia com uso de procedimentos, técnicas e métodos adequados [1][2]. Elicitar e especificar necessidades do software em termos de requisitos funcionais, tomado como uma das etapas de construção, requer o uso de linguagens e métodos para se entender e documentar os diversos tipos de requisitos que comporão o software [3]. Como exemplo de linguagem para se modelar software pode-se citar a linguagem iStar [4][5], que apresenta-se como uma abordagem que leva em consideração aspectos sociais e interativos que influenciam a estrutura de requisitos funcionais e não-funcionais [4].

Os jogos digitais podem ser compreendidos como produtos de software se considerarmos algumas intercessões entre eles e os softwares tradicionais, como a necessidade de utilização de recursos computacionais, definições de escopo, prazo e critérios de qualidade [6]. O clássico *Super Mario World*[1], lançado em 1990 para o *Super Nintendo Entertainment System* (SNES), pode ser visto como um título influente no mercado de jogos, e um marco em termos de evolução da jogabilidade, requisito de qualidade, já estabelecida pelos seus predecessores. Por esse motivo, foi o jogo escolhido para esta análise.

O presente trabalho apresenta a modelagem do clássico jogo *Super Mario World* com o uso da linguagem *iStar 2.0* e discute possibilidades iniciais para uma extensão da linguagem, para o que é denominado nesse estudo como *iStar4G* (*iStar for Games*), proposta para a modelagem de jogos digitais. Tendo como base as limitações percebidas na aplicação do *iStar* ao jogo analisado, o *iStar4G* se propõe a dar suporte à definição e especificação dos elementos que compreenderão o produto final. O objetivo central com a aplicação da linguagem na construção de jogos digitais é poder proporcionar uma ferramenta que faça que construtores de jogos digitais a pensem em termos de requisitos e projeto antes de se codificar o jogo.

Para a apresentação do trabalho, o presente documento encontra-se distribuído da seguinte forma: na seção 2 encontra-se a fundamentação teórica; na seção 3 está descrito o método de avaliação; na seção 4, os resultados e discussão; na seção 5, a proposta da linguagem *iStar4G*; e na seção 6, a conclusão.

2 Fundamentação Teórica

O *iStar* é uma linguagem de modelagem orientada a objetivos e agentes [7]. Essa abordagem tem como foco evidenciar interações e compensações de requisitos dentro de um contexto. O *iStar 2.0* foi selecionado para utilização por se tratar de uma evolução do já estabelecido i* [4] que, por sua vez, tem sido a linguagem predominante na modelagem orientada a objetivos [8].

A proposta dessa abordagem é apresentar os objetivos (*goals*) e atores, com intenções e objetivos distintos, como forma abstrata de expor as características que são interessantes aos *stakeholders* [9][10], além de apresentar os *stakeholders* atuantes no

---

[1] Super Mario World, 1990, https://www.mariowiki.com/Super_Mario_World.

processo, suas intencionalidades, interações e interdependências. [11][12]. Para Yu [13], essa abordagem deve ser utilizada quando se pretende compreender as correlações entre os envolvidos, de acordo com os diversos atores do sistema; compreender as razões dos processos de decisões ou quando se pretende ilustrar modelos para compreensão dos requisitos.

3 Quanto aos Métodos

O estudo consiste em uma análise qualitativa, com estudo da literatura e com a engenharia reversa de jogos digitais tais como: *Sonic the Hedgehog*[2], *Orcs Must Die*[3], e *Pokémon*[4], porém com maior foco no uso e nas características do jogo *Super Mario World*, possível a partir do ato de jogar o jogo e analisar os componentes envolvidos. Com base em estudos realizados a respeito dos conceitos e aplicações da modelagem orientada a objetivos, tal como dos elementos associados à linguagem *iStar 2.0*, foi realizada uma análise adicional dos diferentes formatos de interação entre os personagens do jogo *Super Mario World* nos sistemas que compreendem o ambiente virtual.

Foram identificados dois principais formatos distintos dentro do jogo, onde as interações de jogabilidade se mostraram drasticamente diferentes entre si. Estes formatos foram mapeados isoladamente, desconsiderando o papel do jogador como agente responsável por realizar as interações, tal como seus objetivos individuais. Deste modo, a aplicação da linguagem se restringe à proposta que o jogo tem como produto e abstrai os objetivos individuais de diferentes jogadores, que podem interagir com o jogo de maneiras distintas.

Os dois grandes formatos entendidos como parte do sistema são o mapa (Figura 2) e as fases (Figura 3). Por mapa, denominado daqui em diante como *off-stage*, entendem-se os momentos em que o personagem interage com os obstáculos (fases a serem vencidas) estáticos que bloqueiam seu caminho. Neste estado do jogo, as interações são extremamente reduzidas, não existem inimigos e nem estado de falha.

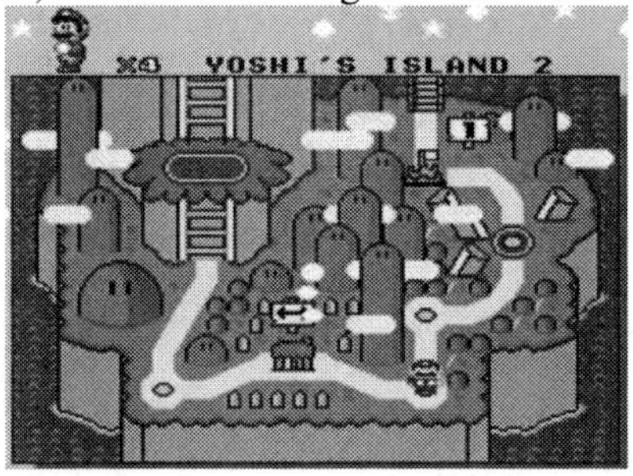

Fig. 1. Super *Mario World*: Mapa do Mundo (*off-stage*)

[2] Sonic the Hedgehog, 1991, https://pt.wikipedia.org/wiki/Sonic_the_Hedgehog_(personagem), Sega Games Co., Ltd.

[3] Orcs Must Die, Robot Entertainment, https://robotentertainment.com/omd3

[4] Pokémon, 1996, https://www.pokemon.com/br/, Game Freak Inc.

Ao selecionar uma fase, '*Yoshi's Island 2*' (Figura 1), inicia-se outro formato de interação, chamado daqui em diante de *on-stage*. Neste estado, as interações são mais dinâmicas. Existem inimigos e outros objetos interativos; estes auxiliam ou atrapalham o personagem a concluir a fase. Na figura 2, podemos identificar alguns destes objetos e personagens: o protagonista Mario, ao centro, e à sua direita um item do tipo casco de tartaruga; e inimigos do tipo *Koopa Troopa* (tartarugas de casco vermelho, na plataforma superior); além dos elementos da interface, na parte superior.

Fig. 2. Super *Mario World: 'Yoshi's Island 2' (on-stage)*

4 Resultados e Discussão

Considerando os formatos estabelecidos na seção 3, foram analisadas as intencionalidades dos personagens autônomos dentro do jogo. Foram obtidos três modelos SR em *iStar 2.0*. Os modelos referem-se, respectivamente, aos dois estados de interação: *off-stage* (Figura 3) e *on-stage* (Figuras 4 e 5).

No estado *off-stage*, o objetivo principal do Herói é ter a 'princesa em segurança'. Para atingi-lo, tarefas derivativas precisam ser executadas, consistindo em 'derrotar o chefão' e 'abrir o caminho' até ele, e para isso há necessidade de que fases sejam concluídas. O único processo de decisão delegado ao jogador nesse estado é escolher quais fases tentar.

Extraordinariamente, o modelo foi desenvolvido considerando apenas a intencionalidade do Herói, uma vez que não existe interação entre outros personagens neste formato.

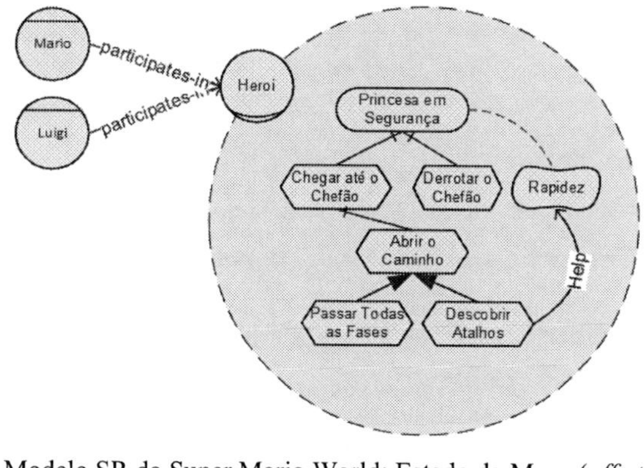

Fig. 3. Modelo SR do Super Mario World: Estado do Mapa (*off-stage*)

Ao optar por entrar em uma determinada fase, o dinamismo das entre 'Inimigo' e 'Herói' deve ser considerado. Inimigos foram assim considerados por terem a capacidade de interromper o progresso dos heróis. Durante a elaboração do modelo, porém, não foi encontrado um método de associar ambos os papéis diretamente. Segundo a sintaxe de *iStar*, as associações por relações de dependência implicam na colaboração entre os agentes envolvidos [7]. Por este motivo, foram feitos dois modelos SR, referentes ao estado *on-stage*: um do Inimigo e um do Herói, e a repetição da qualidade 'longevidade' nos dois modelos é usada para representar que o objetivo do Inimigo impede que essa qualidade, associada ao objetivo do Herói, seja atingida.

Entende-se por 'longevidade' neste modelo a qualidade de se cumprir o objetivo especificado, de concluir a fase, sem perder vidas extras (*1-ups*)[5]. 'Derrotar inimigos' é uma tarefa opcional, que se executada auxilia na busca pela qualidade 'longevidade', custando, porém, tempo. Adicionalmente, mecânicas de interação, como o 'Pulo', foram consideradas como recursos, que permitem que o Herói cumpra suas tarefas.

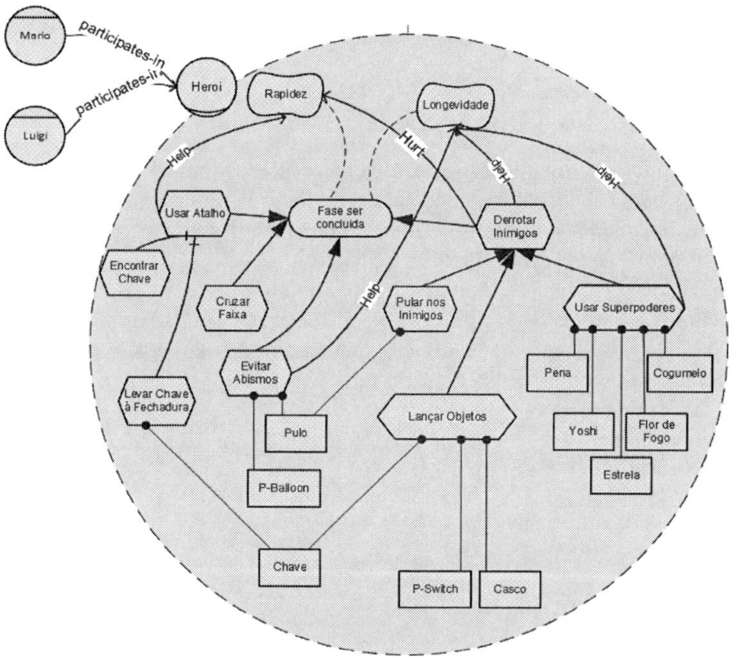

Fig. 4. Modelo SR do SMW: Estado das Fases (*on-stage*): Heróis

---

[5] *1-ups* referem-se às vidas extras no Super Mario World. São itens específicos que, quando adquiridos, dão ao personagem uma chance a mais de entrar em uma fase.

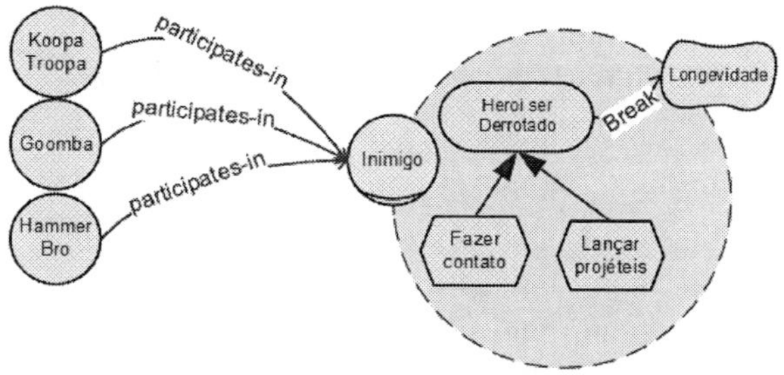

Fig. 5. Modelo SR do SMW: Estado das Fases (*on-stage*): Inimigos

5 Adaptação da Linguagem: o *iStar4G*

Considerando que o *iStar 2.0* não foi elaborado para o contexto de jogos digitais, a tentativa de aplicá-lo nesse estudo evidencia algumas limitações. Houve a necessidade da inclusão de atores sem relações entre si, separando-os em modelos diferentes; e a utilização dos recursos não evidencia com clareza as significativas diferenças que eles têm entre si em termos de comportamento e influência no mundo do jogo.

Os estudos realizados irão evoluir para a proposição de adaptações sintáticas e criação de novos elementos para que se possa representar com maior clareza interações e especificações que precisaram ser explicitadas textualmente. O estudo aqui presente, apesar de incipiente, já é um primeiro esforço dos pesquisadores para propor uma linguagem orientada a objetivos adaptada e com suporte em *iStar 2.0* para ser utilizada na modelagem de requisitos de jogos, o *iStar4G*.

5.1 Novos elementos no iStar4G

No cenário do jogo, há uma diferenciação considerável entre recursos mecânicos de interação entre personagem e mundo; objetos manuseáveis pelo personagem; objetos não manuseáveis que modificam os métodos de interação com o mundo, dando ou restringindo capacidades; e objetos, manuseáveis ou não, que modificam o comportamento ou configuração do cenário em que o personagem se encontra.

Com base nesses quatro tipos de recurso diferentes e suas funções dentro do sistema, propomos especifica-los visualmente dentro do recurso original. Na figura 6 estão os ícones de especificação propostos (lado esquerdo) e sua aplicação (lado direito).

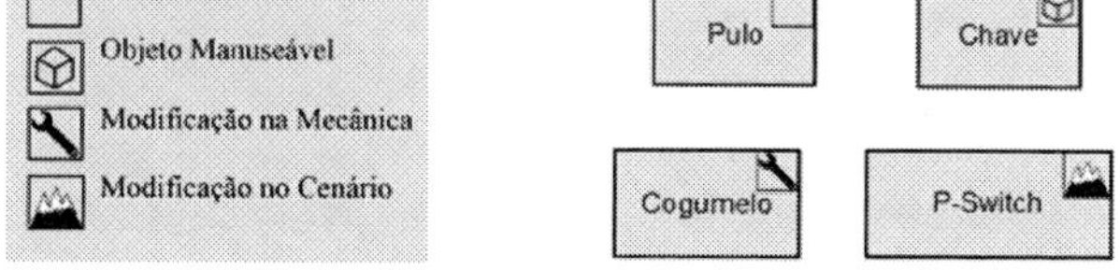

Fig. 6. Ícone, descrição e exemplo dos novos elementos.

Adicionalmente, entendemos que a representação de relações de antagonismo entre diferentes atores pode ser uma limitação significativa à modelagem em jogos, onde relações de inimizade são comuns. Por isso, propomos novos links de qualificação, baseados nas pré-existentes *Help*, *Hurt*, *Make* e *Break*. Com isso, passa a ser possível uma relação de antagonismo entre diferentes atores. Na figura 7, representamos visualmente essas novas relações e sua equivalência, em intensidade, às já existentes.

Fig. 7. Proposta de novas qualificações, entre atores diferentes.

5.2 Modelo *Strategic Rationale* em *iStar4G*

Na Figura 8, podemos encontrar um modelo SR alternativo ao das figuras 4 e 5, levando em consideração as alterações propostas na sessão 5.1. Nesta nova linguagem, torna-se possível incluir ambos os atores na mesma figura, adotando as novas qualificações; além de especificar com maior clareza os diferentes recursos do jogo.

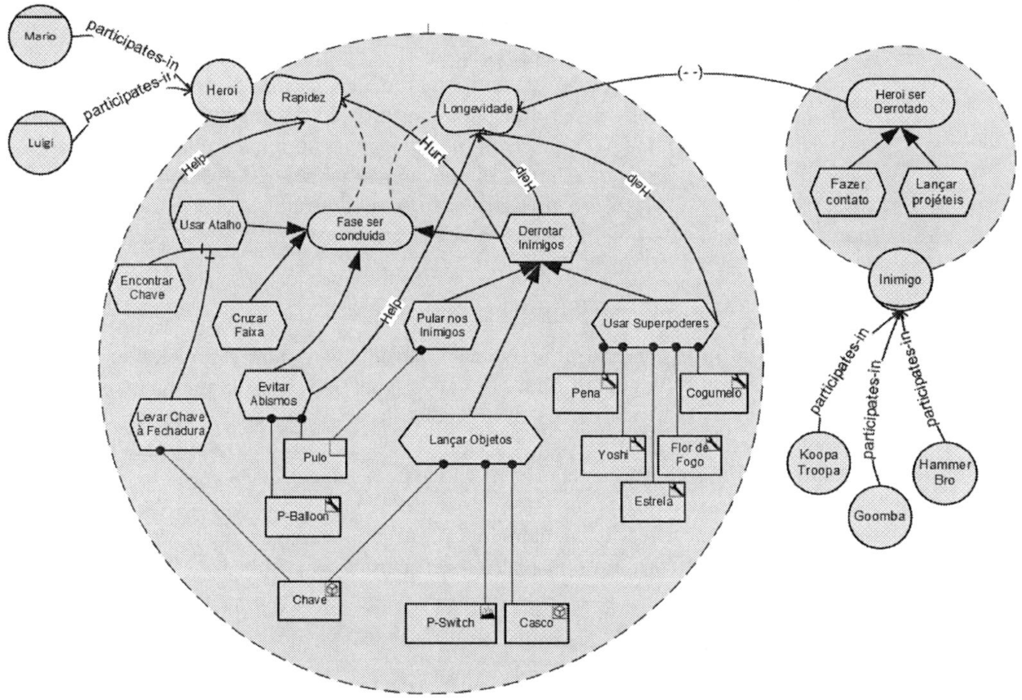

Fig. 8. Modelo SR em iStar4G: *Super Mario World* (*on-stage*)

6 Conclusão

Utilizando a linguagem iStar 2.0, verificamos que é possível modelar aspectos da interação entre personagens de jogos digitais em alto nível de abstração, referente aos estágios iniciais de sua prospecção e construção. Acreditamos que a utilização desta abordagem pode dar suporte ao desenvolvimento do já utilizado *Game Design Document* na especificação de requisitos funcionais e não funcionais para jogos digitais.

Para a posteridade, consideramos: uma melhor estruturação do *iStar4G* tendo como base o estado da arte na pesquisa sobre desenvolvimento de jogos e extensões do *iStar;* validar do uso do *iStar4G* por meio de novos casos e a elaboração de mais arquétipos e relações a partir das limitações encontradas, como no estudo aqui presente; aplicar o *iStar4G* na modelagem de um jogo ainda não existente, averiguando também sua integração com processos já estabelecidos de desenvolvimento de jogos; ou o desenvolvimento de ferramentas que permitam a modelagem em e adoção de *iStar4G* pela comunidade de engenheiros e desenvolvedores.

Agradecimentos

Os pesquisadores envolvidos no estudo agradecem à Universidade Federal Rural do Rio de Janeiro pela bolsa PIBIC 2019.

Referências

1. PRESSMAN, R. S. (2016). Engenharia de software. São Paulo: Makron Books.
2. SOMMERVILLE, I. (2019). Software Engineering, Global Edition. Addison Wesley, 2019.
3. BOURQUE, P. and FAIRLEY, R.E., eds. (2014), Guide to the Software Engineering Body of Knowledge, Version 3.0, IEEE Computer Society, 2014; www.swebok.org. – Acessado em 30 de Setembro de 2019.
4. YU, E. S. K. (1995). Modelling Strategic Relationships For Process Reengineering. Ph. D. dissertation. Dept. of Computer Science, University of Toronto, 1995.
5. iStar Wiki (2019). <Disponível em: http://istar.rwth-aachen.de/tiki-index.php> <Acessado em: 30 de setembro de 2019>.
6. RUCKER, R. (2002) Software Engineering and Computer Games, Addison-Wesley, New Jersey.
7. DALPIAZ, F.; FRANCH, X.; and HORKOFF, J.. (2016). iStar 2.0 Language Guide.
8. HORKOFF, J. et al., "Goal-Oriented Requirements Engineering: A Systematic Literature Map," 2016 IEEE 24th International Requirements Engineering Conference (RE), Beijing, 2016, pp. 106-115
9. ALI, R., DALPIAZ, F. and GIORGINI, P. (2010). A goal-based framework for contextual re-quirements modeling and analysis. Requirements Engineering, 15(4), pp.439-458.
10. YU E., MYLOPOLOUS J, (1998) Why goal-oriented requirements engineering. In: Dubois E, Opdahl AL, Pohl K (eds) Proceedings of the 4th international workshop on requirements engineering: foundation for software quality (RESFQ 1998). Presses Universitaires de Namur, Namur
11. LAPOUCHNIAN, A. (2005). Goal-oriented requirements engineering: An overview of the cur-rent research. University Of Toronto, 32. Retrieved from http://www.cs.toronto.edu/~alexei/pub/Lapouchnian-Depth.pdf
12. FRANCH, X., LÓPEZ, L., CARES, C., & COLOMER, D. (2016). The i* Framework for Goal-Oriented Modeling. Domain-Specific Conceptual Modeling. Springer, Cham. Retrieved from https://link.springer.com/chapter/10.1007/978-3-319-39417-6_22
13. YU, E. (2002). Agent-Oriented Modelling: Software Versus World, In: Proceedings of the Agent-Oriented Software Engineering, Edited by Wooldridge, M., Weiss, G. and Ciancarini, P., LNAI, 2222, Springer-Verlag, p. 206 – 225

Quality-based Methodology for Assessing the Applicability of Microservices Architecture

Andrés Nebel y Laura González

Instituto de Computación, Facultad de Ingeniería
Universidad de la República
J. H. y Reissig 565, Montevideo, Uruguay
{andres.nebel, lauragon}@fing.edu.uy

Resumen Microservices architecture is an approach for developing a system as a set of «small» independent services. Although this architecture has advantages (e.g. in terms of scalability, maintainability), it is not a general solution applicable to all scenarios. This paper proposes a quality-based methodology for assessing the applicability of a microservice architecture to build a system. The methodology includes an impact analisys of microservices on quality attributes that, together with the quality objectives of the system to be developed, constitute the basis for the assessment. The methodology is applied in a real-world case study for a middleware platform in the area of e-government, which provides an example of its use, as well as a first validation of the proposal.

Keywords: Microservices architecture · Quality attributes · e-government.

1. Introducción

La arquitectura de microservicios es un enfoque para construir sistemas que está ganando popularidad [22], y que proporciona ventajas en cuanto a escalabilidad y mantenibilidad, que resultan interesantes en varios escenarios. Aun así, sus propias características hacen que no sea aplicable a todos los contextos [3].

Por otro lado, reportes de la industria muestran que en ocasiones se decide utilizar microservicios sin un análisis adecuado [3,12,14], en particular, respecto al impacto sobre la calidad del sistema y a las consecuencias sobre los objetivos del negocio. Esto puede ocasionar que se adopte este enfoque incluso cuando no se adecua a las necesidades. Es de interés entonces contar con una forma sistemática de evaluar la aplicabilidad de microservicios para un contexto determinado.

Este artículo propone una metodología basada en atributos de calidad para evaluar la aplicabilidad de una arquitectura de microservicios para construir un sistema. La metodología se apoya en un estudio del impacto sobre atributos de calidad, elaborado también en este trabajo, que se contrasta con los objetivos de calidad del sistema a desarrollar. La metodología se aplica en un caso de estudio para una plataforma de middleware en el área de gobierno electrónico, permitiendo ejemplificar su uso y brindar una primera validación de la propuesta.

Nuestra propuesta se diferencia de trabajo existente por su metodología enfocada en atributos de calidad para evaluar la aplicabilidad de microservicios, así como por el número de atributos de calidad sobre los cuales se analiza el impacto de esta arquitectura. En [7] se utiliza ATAM (*Architecture Trade-off Analysis Method*) para evaluar la aplicabilidad y guiar las decisiones de migración hacia microservicios. Dicho trabajo reporta un esfuerzo considerable de costo y tiempo, mientras que nuestra propuesta acota el esfuerzo a identificar los objetivos de calidad y contrastarlos con los resultados de la Sección 3. En [23] el SEI (*Software Engineering Institute*) presenta un análisis donde clasifica el grado de satisfacción que provee SOA (*Service-oriented Architecture*) y tecnologías relacionadas sobre los atributos de calidad. En contraste, nuestra propuesta se orienta a microservicios, basándose en el concepto de preocupaciones de calidad y el impacto sobre éstas. Por otro lado, si bien existen trabajos [9,16] que realizan un análisis de impacto de microservicios sobre atributos de calidad, estos no abordan la misma cantidad de atributos y no consideran algunos trabajos relevantes en materia de desempeño [2,10,15,19,20,25] y testabilidad [9,17,26]. Otros trabajos [5] se enfocan en el impacto percibido y no en el real, como nuestra propuesta.

El resto del artículo se organiza de la siguiente manera. La Sección 2 presenta la metodología propuesta. La Sección 3 analiza el impacto de microservicios sobre la calidad de un sistema. La Sección 4 describe la aplicación de la metodología en un caso de estudio. La Sección 5 presenta conclusiones y trabajo a futuro.

2. Metodología de Evaluación de Aplicabilidad

Esta sección describe la metodología propuesta, la cual permite evaluar la aplicabilidad de una arquitectura de microservicios para construir un sistema. Para este trabajo se considera que dicha arquitectura es aplicable, cuando los beneficios sobre los objetivos de calidad del sistema resultan favorables aún considerando los posibles desafíos implicados.

La idea general de la metodología consiste en obtener los objetivos de calidad del sistema a construir, y analizar cómo son afectados por la utilización de microservicios. Dichos objetivos, se especifican como preocupaciones sobre atributos de calidad del estándar ISO/IEC 25010:2011. Un subatributo constituye una «preocupación» cuando es de interés particular de los *stakeholders*, o si se requieren consideraciones especiales para satisfacerlo.

Notar que el análisis requiere conocer cuál es el impacto de aplicar microservicios sobre los atributos de calidad. Dicho estudio constituye parte de los aportes de este trabajo y se describe en la Sección 3.

La metodología consiste de cuatro actividades principales:

1. Identificar Preocupaciones: En esta actividad, se deben realizar reuniones con los *stakeholders*, para identificar las preocupaciones de calidad en base a los objetivos de calidad del sistema a construir. El resultado es un listado de los subatributos de calidad que constituyen una preocupación para el sistema.

2. Determinar Impacto de Microservicios sobre Atributos de Calidad: En esta actividad se debe determinar el impacto de aplicar una arquitectura

Tabla 1: Impacto de microservicios sobre calidad del sistema

Atributos de Calidad del sistema		**Arq. de Microservicios**	**Referencias consultadas**	**Preocupación Caso Estudio**
Atributo	**Subatributo**			
Eficiencia de Desempeño	Comportamiento del Tiempo	??	[2,10,15,17,19,20,25,27,28,29]	P
	Uso de Recursos	A+(*)	[11,15,27]	P
	Capacidad	A+(*)	[11]	P
Compatibilidad	Interoperabilidad	A+	[6,8,11,22]	P
Mantenibilidad	Modularidad	A+	[6,8,11,22]	P
	Reusabilidad	A+	[6,8,11,22]	P
	Evaluabilidad	P	[6,8,11,22]	P
	Modificabilidad	A+	[6,8,11,22]	P
	Testabilidad	P	[9,11,17,26]	P
Portabilidad	Adaptabilidad	A+	[6,8,11,22]	P
	Instalabilidad	—	[4,6,8,11,22]	P
	Reemplazabilidad	A+	[6,8,11,22]	P
Confiabilidad	Madurez	—	[6,8,11,22]	P
	Disponibilidad	A+	[6,8,11,22,24]	P
	Tolerancia a Fallas	A+	[6,8,11,18,22,24]	P
	Recuperabilidad	A+	[6,8,18,24]	P

A+: Afecta positivamente. P: Implica una preocupación —: No afectado ??: No determinado (*): Solo si se cumplen ciertas condiciones

de microservicios sobre los atributos de calidad. El resultado de esta actividad constituye parte de los aportes de este trabajo y se describe en la Sección 3, indicando qué impacto tiene la arquitectura sobre cada subatributo de calidad.

3. Analizar Impacto de Microservicios sobre Preocupaciones: En esta actividad se toman los resultados anteriores para analizar si la arquitectura de microservicios beneficia o no a las preocupaciones de calidad planteadas. El resultado de esta actividad es un listado que combina y contrasta los resultados de las dos primeras actividades, mostrando para cada preocupación, si el subatributo es afectado positivamente o no al aplicar la arquitectura.

4. Determinar Aplicabilidad de Microservicios: En esta actividad se debe determinar la aplicabilidad de una arquitectura de microservicios para construir el sistema, en base al resultado de la tercera actividad. El resultado de esta actividad muestra en qué medida esta arquitectura es aplicable para el sistema.

3. Impacto de Microservicios sobre Atributos de Calidad

En esta sección se analiza el impacto teórico en base al estado del arte actual, de una arquitectura de microservicios sobre los atributos de calidad de un sistema, extendiendo lo presentado en [21]. La Tabla 1 resume los resultados del análisis, brindando referencias a trabajos consultados.

El análisis se basa en los atributos del estándar ISO/IEC 25010:2011, de los cuales algunos como *Usabilidad* se omiten, por no ser afectados por microservicios, y *Seguridad* no se incluye por cuestiones de alcance. Los subatributos pueden: i) no ser afectados, ii) ser afectados positivamente o iii) ser una preocupación, y iv) ser afectados si cierta condición se cumple.

Por otro lado, el impacto de microservicios se estudia como un conjunto de enfoques que incluye: i) el uso de contenedores, ii) la aplicación de DevOps y iii) el despliegue en una plataforma de orquestación de contenedores (p. ej. *Openshift*).

El motivo es que microservicios no se aplica generalmente en forma aislada, sino como una serie de enfoques que abordan problemáticas relacionadas.

3.1. Eficiencia de Desempeño

Comportamiento del tiempo: Se observa que en teoría podría ser una preocupación debido a: i) la redundancia introducida por la virtualización de los contenedores y redes superpuestas [19,20] (aunque contradiciendo [10] y [27]), y ii) debido a las implicancias de los sistemas distribuidos, ocasionadas entre otros por el aumento de las comunicaciones de red [17]. En [2,28,29] se presentan pruebas de rendimiento similares, que comparan aplicaciones análogas de microservicios y monolíticas, donde se muestran tiempos de respuesta levemente mejores para la arquitectura monolítica. Sin embargo, dichos resultados no coinciden con los de [15] y [25] donde se obtienen mejores tiempos de respuesta con microservicios en pruebas similares. En resumen, los resultados de trabajos actuales no permiten concluir que este subatributo sea una preocupación.

Uso de recursos: Es afectado positivamente cuando se requiere escalamiento, ya que se escalan solo los microservicios requeridos, y no todo el sistema [11]. El impacto es mejor al utilizar patrones de diseño de microservicios [15] y al usar contenedores [27] y plataformas de orquestación de contenedores, que proporcionan escalamiento elástico. Si no se requiere escalamiento, la arquitectura de microservicios podría utilizar más recursos que la monolítica, debido a la redundancia de desplegar dependencias compartidas y componentes usados en sistemas distribuidos (p. ej. balanceadores). Esta redundancia se compensa al escalar, dado que los sistemas monolíticos escalan todo el sistema.

Capacidad: Tiene un impacto análogo al de Uso de Recursos, ya que si éste se beneficia se podrá satisfacer de mejor forma los requerimientos de capacidad.

3.2. Compatibilidad y Mantenibilidad

Interoperabilidad, Modularidad, Reusabilidad, Modificabilidad: Se afectan positivamente por las características que definen a microservicios [6,8,11,22].

Evaluabilidad: Constituye una preocupación. Si la cantidad de microservicios es alta, puede ser complejo determinar el impacto de una modificación, por la dificultad para determinar qué microservicios son afectados por el cambio. Existen herramientas como *DeployHub* que disminuyen en parte la complejidad al permitir visualizar las interacciones entre servicios y sus versiones.

Testabilidad: Constituye una preocupación. Si bien se simplifican las pruebas unitarias por la modularidad (y usualmente por automatización), las pruebas integrales son más complejas por haber varias partes involucradas [9]. Además, la distribución dificulta identificar dónde se originan errores no triviales. En [26] se muestran informes de la industria que reportan el testing como una preocupación de los desarrolladores respecto al enfoque, lo cual es consistente con lo anteriormente mencionado. Fowler advierte que el testing es más complejo [11], aunque alega que existen algunos enfoques para satisfacer el atributo [17].

3.3. Portabilidad

Adaptabilidad: Es afectada positivamente. Los contenedores aíslan las problemáticas de dependencias, temas de *hardware* y sistemas operativos, mejorando la adaptabilidad. Además, en el estándar ISO/IEC 25010:2011 el subatributo incluye la escalabilidad, la cual es beneficiada [11]. El impacto se puede mejorar si el sistema se despliega en una plataforma de orquestación de contenedores, donde el escalamiento elástico es manejado automáticamente.

Instalabilidad: Si bien la separación de un sistema en varias partes agrega complejidad operacional, existen enfoques y herramientas para satisfacer el subatributo, por lo cual no se lo considera una preocupación de calidad. Aún así, no puede afirmarse que la instalabilidad sea afectada positivamente.

Por un lado, *DevOps* beneficia este subatributo, uniendo responsabilidades sobre las mismas personas, y apoyándose en herramientas de entrega continua. Por otro lado, las plataformas de orquestación de contenedores mejoran la instalabilidad, al automatizar despliegues y gestión de componentes utilitarios.

Reemplazabilidad: Es afectada positivamente. Los microservicios son fáciles de sustituir, permitiendo el reemplazo sin desplegar el sistema entero [11].

3.4. Confiabilidad

Tolerancia a Fallas: Es afectada positivamente. Si bien los sistemas distribuidos agregan problemas de arrastre de fallas y más comunicaciones de red que pueden fallar, existe una amplia cobertura sobre el tema [6,8,24] y soluciones varias que permiten satisfacer el subatributo.

Los sistemas basados en microservicios no poseen un único punto de falla, lo cual permite aislar y controlar mejor las mismas al usarse patrones como *Circuit Breaker* y *Bulkhead*, los cuales suelen complementarse con políticas de expiración de pedidos (i.e. *timeouts*) y de reintentos, beneficiando el subatributo [18]. En el aspecto tecnológico bibliotecas como *Netflix Hystrix* y *Polly* aportan funcionalidades para tolerancia a fallas y latencia en sistemas distribuidos.

Recuperabilidad: Análogo al subatributo anterior, es afectada positivamente, ya que existen enfoques y tecnología para satisfacerla. Los enfoques ya mencionados en tolerancia a fallas, aportan también a la recuperabilidad: i) el patrón *Circuit Breaker* permite recuperar la operatividad normal, ii) el uso de *timeouts* y reintentos brinda recuperabilidad frente a fallas de latencia o de red.

Por otro lado, el patrón *health check* puede usarse para detectar si los servicios están disponibles [24] y abortar en caso necesario la operación; también para medir si el servicio está operativo, reiniciando en caso contrario su contenedor. Esto es posible debido a que: i) los microservicios no suelen poseer estado [18] y ii) el tiempo de inicio de los microservicios y contenedores es rápido [18].

Disponibilidad: Por las razones vistas para los dos subatributos anteriores, la disponibilidad es afectada positivamente. Además, el patrón *health check* contribuye a mantener la alta disponibilidad (i.e. durante el despliegue permite saber cuándo la nueva instancia está disponible, para no remover la versión anterior hasta ese momento y no tener tiempos de baja). Esto es usado por plataformas de orquestación de contenedores, como *OpenShift*.

4. Caso de Estudio: Plataforma Middleware e-Gobierno

La Plataforma de Interoperabilidad (PDI) apunta a facilitar y promover la implementación de servicios de gobierno electrónico en Uruguay y fue puesta en marcha por la agencia de gobierno electrónico de este país (AGESIC). Uno de sus componentes es la Plataforma de Middleware (PM) [13], que se utiliza por los organismos para publicar y consumir servicios. La PM se implementó inicialmente con un *Enterprise Service Bus* (ESB) [13] con arquitectura monolítica y se migró recientemente a microservicios, lo cual resultó beneficioso [1].

La aplicación de la metodología para la PM consistió en (cf. Sección 2):

1. Identificar Preocupaciones. Se elaboró un listado inicial de atributos de calidad que se entendió constituyen preocupaciones para la PM, en base a: i) las características de la PM, ii) el conocimiento de los autores sobre la PM, y iii) documentación [13]. El listado se presentó y enriqueció con referentes de la PM, dando como resultado lo presentado en la última columna de la Tabla 1.

Por ejemplo, el Comportamiento del Tiempo y la Disponibilidad constituyen preocupaciones dado el tipo de sistemas que se apoyan en la PM (p. ej. Historia Clínica Electrónica Nacional). La Capacidad y Adaptabilidad (que incluye escalabilidad) también se identificaron como preocupaciones, dado que la PM procesa todas las interacciones entre servicios de los organismos, los cuales pueden tener picos de utilización. La Modularidad e Interoperabilidad también se identificaron como preocupaciones, dado que la PM incluye componentes (p. ej. servicio de ruteo) que pueden ser implementados por distintos proveedores así como con distintas tecnologías y pueden tener que interactuar entre sí.

2. Determinar Impacto de Microservicios. Se utiliza el resultado del estudio descripto en la Sección 3 (cf. tercera columna de Tabla 1).

3. Analizar Impacto de Microservicios sobre Preocupaciones. Para esta actividad se contrastan la tercer y última columna de la Tabla 1, con el fin de conocer el impacto que tiene la arquitectura de microservicios sobre las preocupaciones de calidad de la PM. Se observa que microservicios tiene un impacto positivo para la mayoría (once de dieciseis) de las preocupaciones de calidad de la PM. Además para dos de las preocupaciones (Madurez e Instalabilidad) el atributo no se ve afectado y para una de ellas (Comportamiento del Tiempo) el impacto no está determinado. Sólo dos de las preocupaciones de la PM son también una preocupación al utilizar una arquitectura de microservicios.

4. Determinar Aplicabilidad de Microservicios. Si bien existen dos preocupaciones de la PM que son también preocupaciones para microservicios, se entiende que los beneficios a la calidad de la PM son ampliamente favorables. En particular, la arquitectura de microservicios afecta positivamente once de las preocupaciones de la PM, varias de las cuales son de alta prioridad. En base a esto, se determina que la arquitectura de microservicios es aplicable para la PM.

Resumen de la Aplicación de la Metodología en el Caso de Estudio. La aplicación de la metodología permitió ejemplificar su uso y determinar que la arquitectura de microservicios es aplicable para la PM. También permitió comprobar que para el caso de estudio los resultados concuerdan con lo reportado por la AGESIC [1], y con lo reportado en las reuniones con referentes de la PM.

El caso de estudio también identificó que el impacto teórico de microservicios (cf. Sección 2), se corresponde con el impacto real que la arquitectura tuvo sobre varios de los atributos de calidad de la PM. En particular, en base a la reunión con referentes de la PM se supo que microservicios afectó positivamente el Uso de Recursos, la Modularidad y la Adaptabilidad (en particular, la escalabilidad).

5. Conclusiones y Trabajo Futuro

Este artículo propone una metodología basada en calidad, que permite evaluar la aplicabilidad de una arquitectura de microservicios para un sistema. La metodología define actividades, que buscan contrastar las preocupaciones de calidad de los *stakeholders* con el impacto de microservicios. La metodología se utiliza en un caso de estudio real, lo cual permite ejemplificar su aplicación y brindar una primera validación de la propuesta.

Los principales aportes de este trabajo son la metodología y su aplicación a un caso de estudio real, el estudio del impacto de microservicios sobre los atributos de calidad, y la presentación unificada de trabajos en esta área.

Como conclusiones generales, percibimos interés en metodologías para evaluar la aplicabilidad de microservicios y en su impacto sobre la calidad. El caso de estudio permitió comprobar la adecuación de la propuesta a contextos reales y contar con una primera validación.

Como trabajo a futuro se plantea incorporar el atributo de seguridad, soportar la priorización y ponderación de preocupaciones en el análisis de impacto, e incorporar aspectos económicos. Se apunta también a aplicar la metodología en otros contextos reales y a generalizarla para otro tipo de evaluaciones.

Agradecimientos. Los autores agradecen a AGESIC por las reuniones mantenidas, las cuales permitieron el desarrollo del caso de estudio.

Referencias

1. Actualización tecnológica de la plataforma de interoperabilidad. https://centroderecursos.agesic.gub.uy/web/arquitectura-de-gobierno/noticia-actualizacion-tecnologica-de-la-plataforma-de-interoperabilidad-publico.
2. Al-Debagy, O., Martinek, P.: A comparative review of microservices and monolithic architectures. CoRR **abs/1905.07997** (2019)
3. Balalaie, A., Heydarnoori, A., Jamshidi, P.: Migrating to cloud-native architectures using microservices: An experience report (2015)
4. Balalaie, A., Heydarnoori, A., Jamshidi, P.: Microservices architecture enables devops: Migration to a cloud-native architecture. IEEE Software **33**(3), 42–52 (2016)
5. Bogner, Fritzsch, et al.: Microservices in industry: Insights into technologies, characteristics, and software quality. In: IEEE ICSA-C (Mar 2019)
6. Carneiro, C., Schmelmer, T.: Microservices From Day One : Build Robust and Scalable Software From the Start. Apress (2016)
7. Cruz, Astudillo, Hilliard, Collado: Assessing migration of a 20-year-old system to a micro-service platform using atam. In: IEEE ICSA-C (Mar 2019)

8. Daya, Duy, V., et al.: Microservices from Theory to Practice: Creating Applications in IBM Bluemix Using the Microservices Approach. IBM Redbooks (2016)
9. Dragoni, Giallorenzo, et al.: Microservices: yesterday, today, and tomorrow. CoRR (2016)
10. Felter, W., Ferreira, A., et al.: An updated performance comparison of virtual machines and linux containers. In: IEEE ISPASS (Mar 2015)
11. Fowler, M., Lewis, J.: Microservices. 2014
12. Fritzsch, Bogner, et al.: Microservices migration in industry: Intentions, strategies, and challenges. CoRR **abs/1906.04702** (2019)
13. González, Ruggia, et al.: A service-oriented integration platform to support a joined-up e-government approach: The uruguayan experience. In: EGOVIS/EDEM. Lecture Notes in Computer Science, vol. 7452, pp. 140–154. Springer Berlin Heidelberg (2012)
14. Gouigoux, J., Tamzalit, D.: From monolith to microservices: Lessons learned on an industrial migration to a web oriented architecture. In: 2017 IEEE International Conference on Software Architecture Workshops (ICSAW). pp. 62–65 (Abr 2017)
15. Guaman, D., Yaguachi, L., et al.: Performance evaluation in the migration process from a monolithic application to microservices. In: 13th Iberian Conference on Information Systems and Technologies (Jun 2018)
16. H. Zhang, S. Li, J.S.Z.J.Z.L.: Understanding quality attributes in microservice architecture. Tech. rep., Nanjing University, Nanjing, China (Ene 2018)
17. Hassan, S., Bahsoon, R.: Microservices and their design trade-offs: A self-adaptive roadmap. IEEE International Conference on Services Computing (SCC) **00** (2016)
18. Indrasiri, K., Siriwardena, P.: Microservices for the Enterprise : Designing, Developing, and Deploying. Apress (2018)
19. Kratzke, N.: About microservices, containers and their underestimated impact on network performance. CoRR **abs/1710.04049** (2017)
20. Lloyd, W., Ramesh, S., et al.: Serverless computing: An investigation of factors influencing microservice performance. In: 2018 IEEE International Conference on Cloud Engineering (IC2E) (Abr 2018)
21. Nebel, A.: Arquitectura de microservicios para plataformas de integración (Dic 2018), tesis de Maestría en Ingeniería de Software
22. Newman, S.: Building Microservices: Designing Fine-Grained Systems. O'Reilly Media (2015)
23. O'Brien, Bass, Merson: Quality attributes and service-oriented architectures. Tech. Rep. SEI-2005-TN-014, SEI, Carnegie Mellon University, Pittsburgh, USA (2005)
24. Richardson, C.: Pattern: Microservice Architecture. [En línea] Disponible en: http://microservices.io/patterns/microservices.html [Accedido: 01-06-2017]
25. Singh, V., Peddoju, S.K.: Container-based microservice architecture for cloud applications. In: 2017 ICCCA (May 2017)
26. Soldani, J., Tamburri, D., Heuvel, W.J.: The pains and gains of microservices: A systematic grey literature review. Journal of Systems and Software **146** (Sep 2018)
27. Soltesz, Pötzl, et al.: Container-based operating system virtualization: A scalable, high-performance alternative to hypervisors. SIGOPS Oper. Syst. Rev. **41**(3) (Mar 2007)
28. Ueda, T., Nakaike, T., Ohara, M.: Workload characterization for microservices. In: IEEE International Symposium on Workload Characterization (Sep 2016)
29. Villamizar, Garces, et al.: Evaluating the monolithic and the microservice architecture pattern to deploy web applications in the cloud. In: 10th Colombian Computing Conference. UNIANDES (2015)

Uso de experimentação contínua para a instrumentação e o empacotamento do coorte PIPA UFRJ

Luciana Nascimento[1][0000-0002-0129-4042], Cecilia Apa[2][0000-0003-1588-709X], Diego Cerqueira [1][0000-0003-4861-3394], Michael Rassu[4][0000-0002-2857-2671], Vladimir Erthal[1][0000-0002-0637-3479], Vitor Maia[1][0000-0001-9999-0195], Thatiana Fernandes[3][0000-0001-5447-7531], Guilherme Horta Travassos[1][0000-0002-4258-0424]

[1] PESC/COPPE-UFRJ, Brasil
{lmnascimento,dc,vladimirerthal,ght}@cos.ufrj.br,vcm@ufrj.br

[2] Fing/UdelaR, Uruguay
ceapa@fing.edu.uy

[3] IESC-UFRJ, Brasil
thatianafernandes@iesc.ufrj.br

[4] Avignon Université, França
michael.rassu@alumni.univ-avignon.fr

Abstract. A experimentação contínua permite apoiar a tomada de decisão no desenvolvimento de sistemas de software contemporâneos. Seu uso aparenta trazer vantagens quando a presença dos clientes e a definição de requisitos não ocorre de forma direta. Atualmente, diferentes tipos de sistemas de software representam desafios em sua construção, considerando a necessidade de encapsulamento de conhecimento, integração com dispositivos no ambiente e o acompanhamento dos eventos ocorridos durante sua utilização. Esse é o caso de software para apoiar estudos de coorte (um tipo de estudo longitudinal), os quais evoluem continuamente ao longo de seu ciclo de vida. Este artigo apresenta os resultados preliminares e reflexões sobre o uso de experimentação contínua na instrumentação e empacotamento de um estudo de coorte, o PIPA UFRJ, na área de saúde ambiental coletiva. Os desafios que observamos, relacionados com aspectos importantes no desenho experimental, ainda não têm sido tratados de forma mais detalhada na literatura. Acreditamos que tais desafios representam oportunidades de pesquisa e de contribuição para a utilização dos princípios de experimentação contínua em projetos de software para domínios de problema não convencionais.

Keywords: Continuous Experimentation, Longitudinal Study, Cohort, Laboratory Package, Environmental Health, Experimental Software Engineering.

1 Introdução

A experimentação contínua consiste no uso do método científico para a avaliação sistemática de ideias e opções de solução em projetos de software. Tais opções podem ser vistas como hipóteses que precisam ser avaliadas com os usuários finais para inferir qual delas provoca o efeito esperado na aceitação do produto de software [1]. Encontramos abordagens genéricas, como o *Lean Startup* [2], difundindo estes princípios para a prática, principalmente em contextos de desenvolvimento onde é necessário continuamente evoluir o software para aumentar sua percepção de valor para os usuários. Assim, sistemas contemporâneos e intensivos em software são desenvolvidos de forma incremental e evolutiva, tendo as suas características definidas pelo conhecimento obtido do retorno dos usuários e/ou pela observação do software em uso [3].

A construção de software com o uso de experimentação contínua exige a disponibilidade de infraestrutura computacional adequada, que permita apoiar a inserção e entrega dos tratamentos previstos para a coleta de dados dos eventuais efeitos de uma ou outra opção. Propostas para organização de ambientes e atividades estão disponíveis para apoiar a experimentação contínua em engenharia de software [4] [5], sendo possível observar que existe grande cooperação entre a indústria e academia na investigação desta prática [1]. Notadamente, o uso de práticas e tecnologias associadas à experimentação contínua tem ocorrido, majoritariamente, em situações onde o uso do software envolve um volume considerável de usuários em testes A/B. Porém, diferentes contextos de desenvolvimento de software com alta incerteza podem se beneficiar de experimentação contínua mesmo sem ter usuários em larga escala, demandando que outros métodos de experimentação sejam aplicados.

Nesse artigo descrevemos as experiências iniciais e lições aprendidas com a utilização de experimentação contínua em um projeto de software contemporâneo e não convencional, a infraestrutura computacional para apoiar o estudo de coorte PIPA UFRJ. Buscamos aplicar o conhecimento de instrumentação e empacotamento previamente aplicados por nosso Grupo de Engenharia de Software Experimental da COPPE/UFRJ em estudos experimentais, combinados com práticas de experimentação contínua, a fim de criar uma solução para o PIPA UFRJ.

Esse artigo é composto de mais quatro seções além desta introdução. A próxima seção apresenta o conceito de estudo de coorte e descreve o projeto PIPA UFRJ. Na seção três é fornecida uma visão geral da solução projetada e as características do projeto que motivam a utilização de experimentação contínua. Um caso é descrito na seção quatro e os nossos primeiros resultados de pesquisa, que são os desafios observados para o uso de experimentação contínua, são descritos na seção cinco.

2 Domínio do Problema: O Estudo de Coorte PIPA UFRJ

Estudos de coorte são estudos de observação que segmentam os participantes da pesquisa no decorrer do tempo, potencializando as evidências. São mais comumente utilizados em estudos no domínio da saúde, em que os indivíduos possuem uma condição em comum e são classificados em expostos e não expostos à um tratamento cujo efeito é observado em sua saúde. Durante o tempo do estudo de coorte, que pode ser prospectivo ou retrospectivo, periodicamente são coletados dados dos participantes da pesquisa de forma a apoiar a análise da frequência de ocorrência dos supostos efeitos do tratamento nos participantes [6]. Em engenharia de software o seu uso ainda é incipiente, embora algumas experiências iniciais tenham sido realizadas por pesquisadores da área [7]. Como limitação para a execução de um estudo de coorte temos seu alto custo financeiro e o risco da perda de participantes ao longo do seguimento.

O Projeto Infância e Poluentes Ambientais (PIPA UFRJ) é uma iniciativa pioneira no Brasil para a execução de um estudo de coorte de nascimentos de base hospitalar com o objetivo de avaliar a exposição de mães e crianças aos poluentes ambientais, sendo elegíveis para participação todas as crianças nascidas na Maternidade Escola da Universidade Federal do Rio de Janeiro (ME/UFRJ). Estudos científicos apontam para evidências de que exposições ambientais nos estágios iniciais do desenvolvimento humano (da concepção até a primeira infância) são determinantes para as condições de saúde e na influência para a ocorrência de doenças na vida adulta [8] [9]. Em várias partes do mundo são conduzidos este tipo de estudo, dentre os quais podemos exemplificar: o estudo The Norwegian Mother and Child Cohort Study (MoBa) [10] e o estudo The Maternal-Infant Research on Environmental Chemicals Study (MIREC)/Canada [11]. No projeto PIPA UFRJ, a avaliação da exposição ambiental será realizada pela análise de material biológico (metais/agrotóxicos/plastificantes) e monitoramento de marcadores ambientais.

O início do coorte de nascimentos do PIPA UFRJ está previsto para 2020, devendo ter a duração total de quatro anos durante os quais os participantes serão acompanhados por um grupo de pesquisadores em dez marcos de coleta de dados. O primeiro marco do estudo é o de abordagem de gestantes elegíveis da maternidade da UFRJ. As que aceitarem participar no projeto devem responder ao questionário de pré-nascimento e realizar a coleta de material biológico. O segundo marco é o de nascimento e compreende tanto a condução de um segundo questionário quanto a realização de coleta de materiais biológicos da mãe e da criança. A mãe ainda deve realizar exames referentes ao leite materno nos três próximos marcos: 1º mês, 3º mês e 6º mês de vida da criança. A partir do quinto marco a mãe será responsável apenas por responder aos questionários de acompanhamento. As coletas de material biológico e de dados antropométricos da criança ocorrerão até o final do quarto ano do projeto, nos seguintes marcos: nascimento, 1º, 3º, 6º, 12º, 18º, 24º, 36º e 48º mês de vida.

3 Uma solução para o PIPA UFRJ

Um piloto do coorte PIPA UFRJ foi realizado de setembro de 2017 até agosto de 2018, sem o uso de apoio computacional e tendo como foco o primeiro marco de coleta de dados. Os resultados do piloto têm sido usados como fonte de informação para o projeto de uma solução computacional semiautomatizada para o coorte PIPA UFRJ (apresentada na seção 3.1 a seguir). As incertezas decorrentes da aplicação de processos tradicionais de desenvolvimento aliados a experiência dos desenvolvedores com experimentação em engenharia de software direcionaram ao uso de experimentação contínua para o desenvolvimento da solução (discutido na seção 3.2).

3.1 Visão Geral de uma Solução para o PIPA UFRJ

O planejamento da solução, no primeiro momento, buscou compreender e estabelecer o fluxo de trabalho que pudesse ser automatizado (Figura 1), fornecendo ferramentas e instrumentos para captação das participantes elegíveis, aplicação dos instrumentos de pesquisa (questionários), coleta de dados biológicos, medição de dados antropométricos da criança e coleta de dados dos marcadores ambientais, organização dos dados do estudo em repositórios apropriados para sua análise, observação de requisitos de anonimidade e estruturação de dados, e integração e/ou exportação com ferramentas de análise estatística e de visualização de dados externas.

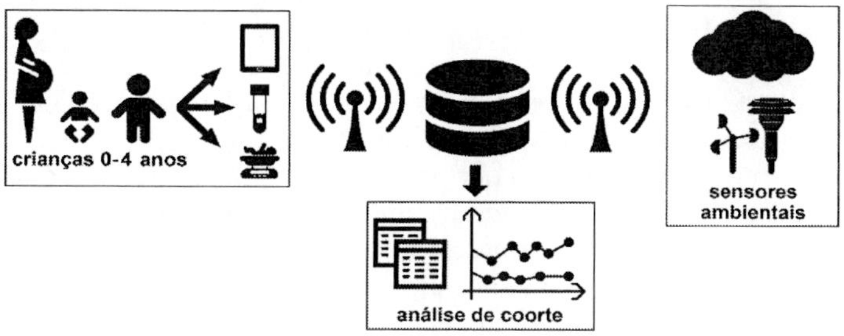

Fig. 1. Visão Geral de uma estratégia de solução para o PIPA UFRJ.

A solução proposta busca respeitar o direito à privacidade, como dispõe a Lei Geral de Proteção de Dados (LGPD) brasileira [12], que entra em vigor em agosto de 2020. Para garantir o direito à anonimização dos dados dos participantes, estes serão armazenados em bases de dados distintas, nomeadas como Controle Coorte e Dados Coorte. Na primeira base serão armazenados dados pessoais sensíveis e a segunda armazenará os dados coletados de forma anônima, constituindo a base longitudinal. O consentimento do armazenamento dos dados pelo participante, previsto em lei, é obtido através da assinatura de um Termo de Consentimento Livre e Esclarecido (TCLE).

3.2 Motivações para o uso da experimentação contínua no PIPA UFRJ

A solução proposta para o PIPA UFRJ, construída em processo de experimentação contínua, se apresenta como mais complexa que a construção de um sistema de gerenciamento de dados convencional. A principal característica do PIPA UFRJ que motiva o uso de experimentação contínua é a indisponibilidade de requisitos bem definidos para o software de apoio à instrumentação e ao empacotamento dos dados.

O coorte PIPA UFRJ é conduzido por diferentes pesquisadores em parceria com a Maternidade Escola da UFRJ, que recebe grávidas encaminhadas de diferentes unidades de saúde do município do Rio de Janeiro, fonte inicial de dados. Como resultado do piloto conduzido, os pesquisadores do PIPA UFRJ observaram a complexidade de estabelecer e orquestrar procedimentos e instrumentos de coleta e empacotamento de dados, preservando os dados para não perder participantes da coorte, e considerando os diferentes marcos do projeto que ocorrem para cada participante de forma paralela.

Assim, o processo de desenvolvimento para a solução PIPA UFRJ deve ser incremental e evolutivo, com algumas características de software a serem evoluídas conforme evidências da adequação de alternativas em uso e outras como resultado das futuras definições dos pesquisadores, visto que os mesmos também estarão em processo de aprendizagem durante a execução do estudo de coorte.

Observou-se também que o desconhecimento acerca do impacto que a eficiência de comunicação entre os diferentes atores do projeto (pesquisadores, técnicos de saúde, genitoras atendidas) é um risco ao estudo de coorte do PIPA UFRJ. Para evitar desistências de participação e garantir a qualidade das informações obtidas, é importante que os instrumentos dos questionários sejam fáceis de manusear e de entender e tenham tempo médio de execução razoável (inferior a 40 minutos) para a expectativa dos entrevistadores e das genitoras, considerando ainda que o grupo de entrevistadores pode mudar. O tempo de consumo e a qualidade da interpretação dos materiais coletados em exames ou dados antropométricos devem também ser avaliados.

Com isso, dentre os vários pontos que possibilitam a introdução da experimentação contínua ao longo do desenvolvimento da solução, envolvendo a instrumentação da coleta de dados dos participantes, temos decisões a serem tomadas sobre: (1) a lista de gestantes elegíveis, (2) o questionário de pré-nascimento, (3) o questionário de nascimento, e (4) o questionário de acompanhamento. A Figura 2 apresenta os materiais que serão obtidos em cada um dos marcos do coorte PIPA UFRJ e oportunidades de avaliação de características destes materiais. É importante notar que vários marcos podem ocorrer em paralelo no decorrer do projeto. Por exemplo, ainda no primeiro mês é possível que hajam casos dos marcos Gestação e Nascimento. Para cada ponto de experimentação existem diferentes opções de procedimentos e ferramentas a adotar para realizar o empacotamento dos materiais utilizados (objetos de estudo). A decisão sobre qual é a melhor combinação a utilizar depende das diferentes características de qualidade a serem observadas na experimentação, devido as múltiplas características de qualidade de um objeto de estudo.

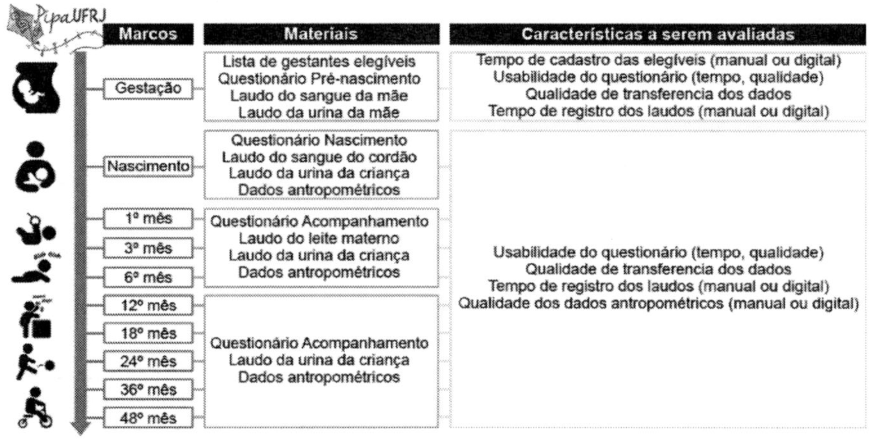

Fig. 2. Materiais e características a serem avaliadas a cada marco do Coorte PIPA UFRJ.

4 Caso de experimentação no PIPA UFRJ

Uma das possibilidades observadas para experimentação contínua foi o desenho de suporte ferramental para o questionário de pré-nascimento (Q1), que compõe a lista de materiais do primeiro marco. O Q1 é aplicado na primeira fase do coorte e coleta dados sobre o terceiro trimestre de gestação. Estrutura-se em 15 blocos, que contemplam dados da gestante (identificação, dados socioeconômicos, dados da gestação, hábitos, saúde), dados sobre o pai biológico e dados sobre a moradia.

O questionário foi modelado para permitir sua aplicação com as mães através do uso de *Tablets* pelos pesquisadores, visando facilitar a coleta dos dados e diminuir o tempo de abordagem do entrevistador com a gestante. A experimentação pode ser aplicada neste cenário, por exemplo, através da modelagem de diferentes formatos do questionário, para observar qual melhor se adapta ao tamanho e utilização dos *Tablets* e resultam em tempo de preenchimento em conformidade com o requisito do projeto (< 40 min). Para a primeira execução de experimentos, o instrumento foi desenvolvido utilizando a ferramenta *LimeSurvey*[1].

Diferentes alternativas de experimentação devem ser propostas visando melhorar as características de qualidade mais importantes. Para determinar as possibilidades de experimentação do Q1 (primeiro objeto de estudo) foi necessário entender quais características de qualidade deveriam ser avaliadas para o PIPA UFRJ, quais as prioridades de tais características e quais alternativas de instrumentação viabilizam a melhoria dessas características. Sob o ponto de vista do pesquisador do estudo de coorte, essas características são: tempo, qualidade do preenchimento do questionário, percepção da usabilidade, entendimento do questionário pela participante e capacidade de capturar mais e melhor informação. Também é preciso tratar outras características relacionadas à integração da solução, tais como a compatibilidade de migração dos dados coletados pelos questionários para um sistema de banco de dados (minimizar a perda de informação e semântica dos dados) e a integração da solução computacional com dispositivos construídos para coleta de dados com base no paradigma da Internet das Coisas (balança infantil, sensores ambientais, dentre outras).

Nesta etapa de planejamento da experimentação contínua, surgem questionamentos cuja discussão não foi encontrada nos relatos da literatura técnica que reportam experiências da utilização de experimentação contínua. Eles são relacionados a:

1. Quantidade de alternativas viáveis para avaliar: No estudo de coorte PIPA UFRJ é prevista a participação de 2000 gestantes (com base na execução do piloto) que serão abordadas nos primeiros cinco meses do projeto. Em média, 100 gestantes serão captadas por mês (assumindo uma distribuição normal). Do ponto de vista experimental, na execução de um experimento em um período de uma semana não é possível avaliar mais do que três alternativas em arranjo fatorial, já que a quantidade de observações por alternativa (25) não seria suficiente para garantir confiança nos resultados. É importante avaliar as alternativas propostas num período de tempo adequado para que a informação obtida permita a tomada de decisão e agregue valor ao coorte.

---

[1] *LimeSurvey* é uma plataforma de para aplicação de questionários online.

2. Definição das hipóteses e métricas associadas: As hipóteses do experimento precisam estar associadas com as características de qualidade a avaliar (variáveis independentes), tendo métricas e processos de medição para coletar a medida na condução do estudo. Algumas variáveis não apresentam complexidade nesse sentido (i.e., tempo de preenchimento), mas outras variáveis apresentam desafios em relação a definição da métrica e a coleta da medida (i.e., entendimento do questionário pela participante), sendo mais complexos os dados qualitativos. Outro desafio é como combinar as diferentes hipóteses para a tomada de decisão.

3. Arranjo experimental: Um aspecto a ser determinado é como as alternativas serão administradas entre os pesquisadores. No caso do PIPA UFRJ, a caracterização do pesquisador (quem aplica o questionário) é um aspecto importante a ser considerado. Por exemplo: existem pesquisadores que participaram do piloto e outros que não participaram? A experiência dos pesquisadores difere entre eles? Se alguma das respostas for sim, os resultados do experimento devem ser tratados de forma diferenciada (bloqueio) ou as alternativas devem ser administradas num grupo de pesquisadores com essas características balanceadas (balanço). Também é importante identificar outras causas que possam ter influência no resultado do experimento, como por exemplo, o perfil socioeconômico da mãe (pode influenciar no entendimento do questionário). Esses tipos de influências são "fatores de confusão" e é preciso identificá-los com o objetivo de minimizar ameaças à validade do experimento.

5 Considerações Finais: Desafios e Oportunidades de Pesquisa

A aplicação da experimentação contínua em domínios de problemas não convencionais não tem sido relatada na literatura técnica. Entretanto, acreditamos que é importante incluir essa discussão. Tomando o estudo de coorte PIPA UFRJ como um caso não convencional, no contexto de sistemas com usuários em pequena/média escala, ainda em desenvolvimento, e com tempo de avaliação de alternativas muito limitado, nos defrontamos com vários desafios ainda não considerados e/ou relatados pela comunidade científica. Interessante observar que, mesmo no contexto de grande quantidade de usuários, a coleta de dados quantitativos através de testes A/B não garante que os mesmos contribuam para o direcionamento das decisões da organização de software. Um dos motivos é a falta de contextualização dos dados [13], que demandam a utilização de métodos para a coleta de dados qualitativos para entender a resposta dos usuários em relação as mudanças no software que lhe são propostas.

Os aspectos da aplicação da experimentação contínua com os quais lidamos, que não têm sido tratados na literatura técnica, e que acreditamos em sua importância são:

1. Determinação da quantidade de alternativas a avaliar tendo em vista a quantidade de observações por alternativa, o tempo máximo de execução do experimento, e o nível mínimo de confiança aceitável;
2. Adequação da definição das medidas a serem coletadas durante a execução dos experimentos com o processo de coleta e sua fidedignidade de representação em relação ao comportamento a ser observado;
3. Adequação na definição das hipóteses e viabilidade de sua combinação no momento da tomada de decisão; e

4. Utilização da caracterização do participante para identificação de fatores de confusão no planejamento do arranjo experimental.

Acreditamos que o aprofundamento e extensão das discussões dessas questões contribuem com o objetivo de apoiar, viabilizar, e encorajar a aplicação dos princípios de experimentação em engenharia de software e de práticas de experimentação contínua na construção de soluções para distintos domínios de problema.

Referências

1. Auer, F., Felderer, M.: Current state of research on continuous experimentation: a systematic mapping study. In : 44th Euromicro SEAA., pp.335-344 (2018)
2. Ries, E.: The Lean Startup: How Today's Entrepreneurs Use Continuous Innovation to Create Radically Successful Businesses. Crown Business (2011)
3. Fagerholm, F. et al : Building blocks for continuous experimentation. In ACM : Proceedings of the 1st international workshop on rapid continuous software engineering., pp.26-35 (2014)
4. Fagerholm, F. et al .: The RIGHT model for continuous experimentation., 292-305 (2017)
5. Fabijan, A. et al.: The evolution of continuous experimentation in software product development: from data to a data-driven organization at scale. In IEEE-Press: Proceedings of the 39th ICSE, pp.770-780 (2017)
6. Blumenthal, U. J. et al.: Epidemiology - a tool for the assessment of risk.. In : Water quality: guidelines, standards & health. IWA publishing. (2001)
7. Fucci, D. et al.: A longitudinal cohort study on the retainment of test-driven development. In ACM, ed. : Proceedings of the 12th ACM/IEEE ESEM., p.p.18 (2018)
8. Barker, D. et al.: Fetal origins of adult disease: strength of effects and biological basis. International journal of epidemiology. 31(6), 1235-1239 (2002)
9. Gluckman, P. et al.: The fetal, neonatal, and infant environments - the long-term consequences for disease risk. Early human development 81(1), 51-59 (2002)
10. OLSEN, S. et al.: Possibilities and considerations when merging dietary data from the world's two largest pregnancy cohorts: the Danish National Birth Cohort and the Norwegian Mother and Child Cohort Study. Acta obstetricia et gynecologica Scandinavica. 93(11), 1131-1140 (2014)
11. Haines DA, A. et al.: Reporting results of human biomonitoring of environmental chemicals to study participants: a comparison of approaches followed in two Canadian studies. Journal of Epidemiology & Community Health, 191-198 (2011)
12. Instituto de Tecnologia e Sociedade: LEI GERAL DE PROTEÇÃO DE DADOS PESSOAIS (LGPD) E SETOR PÚBLICO. (Acessado em 2019) Disponível em: https://itsrio.org/wp-content/uploads/2019/05/LGPD-vf-1.pdf.
13. Fabijan, A. et al.: Experimentation growth: Evolving trustworthy A/B testing capabilities in online software companies. Journal of Software: Evolution and Process. 30(12), e2113 (2018)

SmartMoving: una aplicación para peatones con movilidad reducida *

Mónica Fatecha[1], Patricia Fauvety[1], Nathalie Aquino[1], Magalí González[1], Daniel Romero[1], Luca Cernuzzi[1], Javier Paniagua[2], and Ronald Chenú-Abente[2]

[1] Universidad Católica "Nuestra Señora de la Asunción"
monica.fatecha@uc.edu.py, patyfauvety@gmail.com,
nathalie.aquino@uc.edu.py, mgonzalez@uc.edu.py, lcernuzz@uc.edu.py
[2] Universidad de Trento
jpaniagualaconich@gmail.com, chenu@disi.unitn.it

Abstract. En la ciudad de Asunción existen problemas de movilidad urbana. Uno de los problemas es el estado de las veredas, por falta de rampas, existencia de desniveles, obstrucciones, entre otros. En este trabajo presentamos la herramienta SmartMoving, que recolecta información sobre el estado de las veredas, con ayuda de la ciudadanía, y recomienda caminos peatonales con menos obstáculos. SmartMoving es una aplicación móvil que puede ser especialmente útil para personas con movilidad reducida. En ese sentido, la aplicación fue probada por personas que usan sillas de ruedas. La evaluación de usabilidad que realizaron arrojó resultados preliminares positivos.

Keywords: Movilidad peatonal, movilidad reducida, reporte ciudadano, visualización en mapa, recomendación de caminos.

1 Introducción y motivación

Caminar por las calles de Asunción implica encontrar veredas deterioradas, desperdicios, obras de construcción y actividades comerciales que bloquean el tránsito libre y seguro. Todo esto implica que, muchas veces, los peatones se ven obligados a transitar por la calzada vehicular, con la incomodidad y los peligros que ello conlleva. Según datos facilitados en una entrevista con actores de la Municipalidad de Asunción, en el año 2018 se recibieron un total de 1836 denuncias relacionadas a problemas en las veredas (749 por obstrucción y ocupación, 686 relacionadas a construcción y reparación, 213 por falta de rampas y 188 por desniveles). Cabe señalar que el trabajo de controlar el estado de las veredas está a cargo de solo seis funcionarios municipales, a quienes les lleva tiempo verificar las denuncias y notificar a los respectivos responsables.

* Este trabajo es cofinanciado por el Consejo Nacional de Ciencia y Tecnología (CONACYT) con recursos del FEEI, en el marco del proyecto "SmartTraffic: sistemas colectivos adaptativos para una ciudad inteligente" (PINV15-166).

Por otra parte, según una encuesta realizada en Paraguay en el año 2017, el 94% de los encuestados posee un smartphone y el 86% lo tiene conectado a Internet [7]. Por ende, aprovechando la disponibilidad local de smartphones conectados a Internet, este trabajo propone la utilización de dicha tecnología para recolectar datos relacionados al estado de las veredas para mejorar la movilidad peatonal en la ciudad de Asunción. Es así que proponemos la herramienta SmartMoving, una aplicación que utiliza tecnología para paliar la dificultad de circular por veredas en mal estado, con la ayuda de los mismos peatones que proporcionan información sobre el estado de las veredas. Cabe mencionar que SmartMoving no apunta a la reparación de las veredas en sí, sino en ayudar al peatón en el uso de las mismas, proporcionando información sobre caminos alternativos con menos dificultades para transitar por las calles. Este tipo de soluciones puede ser particularmente útil para personas con movilidad reducida (por ejemplo, personas que utilizan sillas de ruedas o bastones). Además, la información sobre el estado de las veredas puede ser útil para los funcionarios del sector de intervención en el dominio público de la municipalidad.

SmartMoving fue desarrollada siguiendo una metodología de diseño centrado en el usuario [2]. Sus principales funcionalidades permiten que los usuarios reporten problemas u obstáculos en las veredas y consulten caminos peatonales con menos dificultades. Este artículo se enfoca en presentar la herramienta SmartMoving, sus funcionalidades principales y algunas estrategias de la implementación. Se presenta también una validación de la usabilidad de la herramienta. Dicha validación fue llevada a cabo con la participación de usuarios con movilidad reducida.

El resto del documento tiene la siguiente estructura: en la sección 2 se presentan trabajos académicos y aplicaciones móviles relacionadas a SmartMoving; en la sección 3 se presenta la herramienta SmartMoving, incluyendo la descripción de sus características, la implementación y la evaluación de la misma; por último, en la sección 4 se presenta la conclusión del trabajo.

2 Trabajos relacionados

Entre los trabajos relacionados a SmartMoving, se identifican los siguientes trabajos académicos que ofrecen la posibilidad de identificar obstáculos en las veredas y/o de elegir caminos alternativos:

- *mPASS* [5,6] es un prototipo de un sistema que indica rutas personalizadas accesibles. Tiene tres tipos de reportes: de sensores, de usuarios y de autoridades. Para evaluar el prototipo en una primera fase involucraron a 60 usuarios con algún tipo de discapacidad, se utilizó un cuestionario y la presentación de la interfaz de *mPASS* a través de mockups. Luego desarrollaron la solución y, en la segunda fase, hicieron test del prototipo con 10 usuarios con algún tipo de discapacidad. La evaluación consistía en utilizar la funcionalidad de recomendación de camino, aplicando la técnica *thinking aloud*. A pesar de que actualmente la aplicación no está disponible para la descarga, este proyecto muestra diversos aspectos positivos y en particular, en la primera etapa de validación ha contado con la participación de un importante número de usuarios. Sin embargo, las funcionalidades que implementaron y los tipos de incidentes que un usuario puede reportar, son distintos a los de SmartMoving.

- *CrowdWatch* [8] ayuda a peatones distraídos alertando acerca de obstáculos temporales (por ejemplo, auto, basura, etc.) de manera automática mediante los sensores de GPS, aceleración y orientación del dispositivo smartphone, y recomendando de qué lado de la vereda deben pasar. Al no tener forma de reconocer qué tipo de obstáculo está detectando, para confirmarlo se recurre a un segundo usuario que pasa por el mismo lugar y se le habilita la cámara del dispositivo para que tome una foto del obstáculo. Para evaluar las prestaciones de *CrowdWatch* se realizó un experimento con 30 voluntarios. La evaluación se enfocaba en la prueba de las funcionalidades, no en la respuesta y comportamiento que el usuario tenía al utilizar la aplicación.
- *ParticipAct* [1] es una plataforma que permite visualizar un mapa de una ciudad incluyendo información sobre puntos de interés y barreras arquitectónicas (por ejemplo, escaleras, andamios). Evaluaron la plataforma con respecto al consumo de recursos (memoria y CPU) de los dispositivos de los usuarios.

Por otra parte, también hemos explorado aplicaciones móviles, comerciales o no, relacionadas a SmartMoving. Hemos partido del objetivo de descargar, instalar y probar las aplicaciones, en especial lo relacionado a los reportes que puede hacer un usuario y la funcionalidad de recomendación de caminos peatonales, pero algunas aplicaciones no estaban disponibles en Paraguay, y las que sí lo estaban, no tenían usuarios ni datos cargados sobre las veredas de Paraguay.

- *CIT2ADM For Pedestrians* [3] permite al usuario reportar cualquier problema que encuentra cuando está caminando por la vereda (iluminación de las aceras, obstáculos, paso de cebra, etc.). Esta herramienta ayuda al municipio a simplificar y optimizar los procesos y filtrar toda urgencia en tiempo real. El uso de la misma, requiere de un pago por parte de la municipalidad.
- *Accessibility Plus* [4] permite consultar puntos de interés libres de barreras de accesibilidad (baños, gasolineras, etc.). El usuario puede reportar puntos de interés accesibles, incidencias, y programar viajes y rutas libres de barreras. La aplicación está disponible en España.
- *GoogleMaps* [5] es una aplicación de uso general. Uno de los servicios específicos que ofrece es la navegación para personas que utilizan silla de ruedas, en donde recomienda rutas que sean accesibles y libres de barreras. Sin embargo, este servicio específico está disponible solo en algunas ciudades del mundo.

[3] https://www.cit2adm.com/p/cit2adm-for-pedestrians
[4] https://play.google.com/store/apps/details?id=es.sdos.accesibility&hl=en
[5] https://play.google.com/store/apps/details?id=com.google.android.apps.maps&hl=en

– *WheelMap* [6] muestra en un mapa los lugares (bares, baños, supermercados, etc.) accesibles y el usuario puede contribuir reportando si es completamente, parcialmente o no accesible. La aplicación está disponible en Paraguay.

SmartMoving ofrece servicios que no están disponibles en Paraguay: información sobre el estado de las veredas y navegación peatonal reduciendo la cantidad de obstáculos. Además, destacamos que el diseño y el desarrollo de la solución se ha basado en un proceso de participación continua de los usuarios, siguiendo la metodología de diseño centrado en el usuario.

3 La solución SmartMoving

Como ya se ha mencionado, SmartMoving tiene como objetivo proporcionar al usuario información sobre el estado de las veredas cerca de su ubicación actual y recomendar caminos peatonales con menos obstáculos hasta un destino. Los mismos usuarios serán los encargados de aportar información a SmartMoving sobre inconvenientes detectados en las veredas.

En ese contexto, sus funcionalidades principales son: 1) visualizar caminos peatonales con reportes de obstáculos; 2) crear y reubicar reportes de obstáculos; 3) recomendar caminos con menos obstáculos; y 4) configurar niveles de gravedad de obstáculos.

A la izquierda en la Figura 1 se presenta la pantalla principal de SmartMoving. En la misma se visualiza un mapa de los alrededores de la ubicación del usuario y los reportes POI (*Point Of Interest*) que ya fueron reportados previamente por distintos usuarios. Los reportes POI están representados con *markers* o marcadores de distintos colores y formas. Conforme la metáfora del semáforo, el marcador verde circular representa un reporte positivo, el amarillo triangular representa un reporte negativo leve y el rojo triangular representa un reporte negativo grave.

[6] https://play.google.com/store/apps/details?id=org.wheelmap.android.online&hl=en

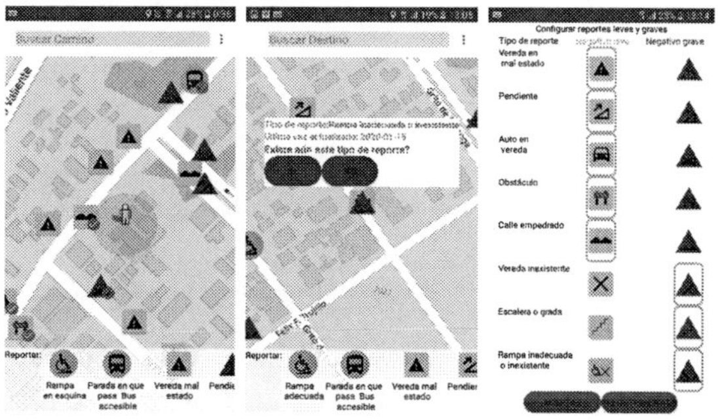

Fig. 1. Capturas de pantallas de la herramienta SmartMoving

Los diferentes tipos de reportes POI son incidencias comunes que un ciudadano puede encontrar al caminar por las veredas: rampa en esquina, parada en que pasa bus accesible, vereda en mal estado, vereda inexistente, pendiente, escalera o grada, vehículo en vereda, obstáculo, calle empedrada, sin rampa en esquina. Los íconos de algunos de estos tipos de reporte se visualizan tanto en el mapa como en la parte inferior de la primera pantalla de la Figura 1. Los de la parte inferior, permiten al usuario crear un nuevo reporte del tipo seleccionado.

Si el usuario presiona alguno de los reportes POI que se visualizan en el mapa de la primera pantalla de la Figura 1, pasará a visualizar la segunda pantalla, en la que se presentan más detalles sobre el reporte POI seleccionado. Además, el usuario podrá contribuir a la información de SmartMoving confirmando la existencia y persistencia del reporte POI (por ejemplo, un vehículo que sigue estacionado en una vereda) o bien, indicando que ese reporte POI ya está solucionado y ha dejado de ser un obstáculo (por ejemplo, el vehículo ya fue retirado de la vereda). Para estos fines, se presentan dos botones, uno para confirmar la existencia del incidente/evento y el otro para marcarlo como solucionado.

Por su parte, la pantalla de la derecha de la Figura 1 permite al usuario categorizar los reportes negativos como leves o graves, según su parecer.

En la Figura 2 se encuentra la secuencia de pantallas relacionada a la funcionalidad de recomendación de camino. Si el usuario presiona la barra que dice "Buscar Camino" que se encuentra en la parte superior de la primera pantalla, se habilitará el teclado para ingresar el destino deseado. Una vez escrito el nombre de la calle destino, aparecerá una lista de direcciones donde puede seleccionar una de ellas, como se puede visualizar en la segunda pantalla. Al seleccionar una dirección, pasará a la tercera pantalla, donde se visualiza el marcador de color rojo en el mapa, ubicado en la dirección que se haya seleccionado. En esta pantalla se le da la opción al usuario para reubicar el destino. Una vez que seleccione el botón "Iniciar", pasará a visualizar la cuarta pantalla, donde se presenta el camino recomendado a través de lineas de color azul pintadas desde la ubicación del usuario hasta el destino. Durante el recorrido, el usuario puede crear y contribuir reportes POI. Cuando llega al destino, pasará a la quinta pantalla, donde se visualiza una ventana que indica que ha llegado al destino y se le pide una valoración sobre el camino recomendado, de 1 a 5 estrellas. Cuando el usuario presiona el botón "Aceptar", pasa a la primera pantalla de la Figura 2.

3.1 Estrategias utilizadas en la implementación

En esta sección describimos un par de estrategias que definimos para la implementación de la aplicación SmartMoving.

Verificación de reportes POI: Para verificar los datos que obtenemos con la ayuda de los usuarios, creamos un sistema de puntuación de reportes POI con el objetivo de evitar la generación de datos falsos. Cada reporte POI recibe contribuciones de los usuarios, y definimos dos tipos de contribuciones: la primera es la confirmación de existencia o persistencia; y la segunda es de contribuciones

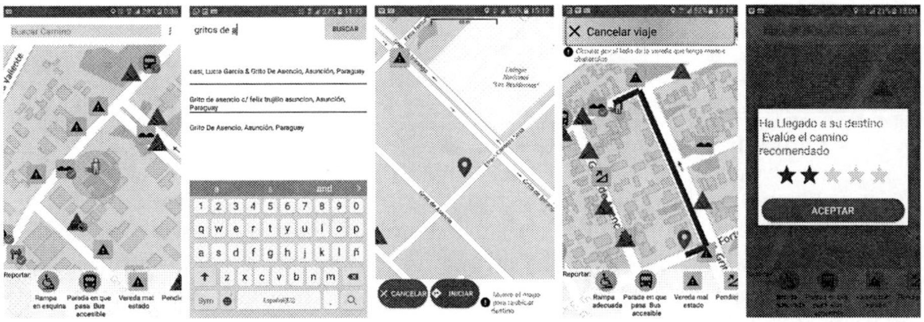

Fig. 2. Secuencia de pantallas para recomendación de camino

de inexistencia o ausencia de una incidencia. Cada reporte POI tiene un estado y definimos tres tipos de estados: *desconocido*, cuando la cantidad de contribuciones de existencia e inexistencia es menor a 3; *confirmado*, cuando tres o más usuarios hayan contribuido la existencia o persistencia del reporte POI; *resuelto*, cuando tres o más usuarios hayan contribuido la inexistencia o ausencia del reporte POI. Cuando un usuario crea un nuevo reporte POI, se le asigna el estado *desconocido*. Por un lado, los reportes POI que tienen estado desconocido y confirmado serán visibles en el mapa y por el otro lado, los que tengan estado resuelto no serán visibles en el mapa de la aplicación.

Recomendación de caminos: La herramienta SmartMoving utiliza los datos y varias de las herramientas ofrecidas por OpenStreetMap [7]. Para la funcionalidad de recomendación de caminos utilizamos la extensión *PgRouting*, que es un servicio que provee la funcionalidad geospacial de ruteo. Utilizamos el algoritmo *K-Shortest Path* que está basado en el algoritmo de Yen, donde "K" es el número de caminos más cortos deseados. En SmartMoving, la recomendación de caminos consiste en buscar tres rutas alternativas de un origen a un destino, donde se toma en cuenta los reportes POI que hay en la zona. Cada ruta posee un costo, que está definido por *PgRouting*, y al que le agregamos un costo adicional relacionado a los reportes POI que están en cada ruta. El costo adicional que definimos por cada reporte POI depende de cómo el usuario configuró los reportes POI en negativos leves y graves. Los reportes negativos leves tienen un costo adicional de 0.0001 y los reportes negativos graves tienen un costo adicional de 0.002. Definimos estos costos adicionales de tal manera que al calcular un nuevo camino, tome la ruta que contienen la menor cantidad de reporte negativos. Una vez que se obtienen los nuevos costos, se ordenan las 3 rutas alternativas según el nuevo costo. En la aplicación se visualizará la ruta con el menor costo.

SmartMoving ha sido implementado para el sistema operativo Android. El código fuente del servidor se encuentra en https://github.com/SmartTrafficPY/

[7] https://www.openstreetmap.org/about

smartcity-asuncion. El código fuente del cliente se encuentra en https://github.com/SmartTrafficPY/smartmoving.

3.2 Evaluación de usabilidad

Se ha realizado una evaluación preliminar de SmartMoving, con el objetivo de obtener una percepción acerca de su utilidad, calidad de información y de interfaz, y usabilidad general, utilizando el cuestionario CSUQ (Computer System Usability Questionnaire) [3,4]). Para ello, se contó con la participación de tres usuarios de género masculino, dos de ellos se movilizan en silla de ruedas y uno se moviliza en una patineta. Los usuarios, acompañados por un evaluador, utilizaron SmartMoving en las veredas, para ir hasta un destino cercano (unos 400 metros). Cada usuario utilizó la aplicación SmartMoving emulada en un smartphone de sistema operativo Android (versión 23). Previamente, el evaluador había cargado la información acerca del estado de las veredas en la zona donde se realizó la evaluación. Una vez terminado el recorrido, el evaluador le entregó al usuario el cuestionario de usabilidad CSUQ. El cuestionario tiene un total de 16 preguntas (las mismas se pueden ver en https://drive.google.com/file/d/1xB5XBb45ZH1BjfQfcAwB39Dbslqa8Zqw/view?usp=sharing). Las preguntas se contestan usando una escala Likert de 7 puntos, siendo el 1 el mejor puntaje de conformidad del usuario (fuertemente de acuerdo) y el 7 el peor puntaje (fuertemente en desacuerdo).

Las preguntas del 1 al 6 se orientan a medir la percepción de utilidad del sistema, y obtuvimos un promedio de 1.55. Las preguntas del 7 al 12 fueron definidas para medir la percepción de la calidad de información, y obtuvimos un promedio de 1.61. En ambos casos, el puntaje obtenido implica que los tres usuarios están de acuerdo con una percepción positiva acerca de la utilidad del sistema y la calidad de la información. Las preguntas del 13 al 15 son para evaluar la calidad de las interfaces. En este caso obtuvimos un promedio de 1.16, lo que implica que los usuarios están fuertemente de acuerdo con una percepción positiva acerca de la calidad de las interfaces. Finalmente, al considerar en conjunto las preguntas de la 1 a la 16 se obtiene una percepción acerca de la usabilidad general de la aplicación. En este caso, obtuvimos un promedio de 1.47, lo que corresponde a estar de acuerdo con una percepción positiva acerca de la usabilidad general de SmartMoving.

Si bien esta evaluación ha involucrado a un número pequeño de usuarios, los resultados positivos que hemos obtenido nos alientan a realizar posteriormente otras evaluaciones de mayor envergadura. Cabe también señalar que el retorno de los usuarios acerca de la aplicación ha sido positivo.

4 Conclusión

En este trabajo presentamos la solución SmartMoving como una herramienta de ayuda para los peatones para moverse en las vías públicas, en especial para aquellos que tienen movilidad reducida. Como no hay una base de datos que contenga información sobre el estado de las veredas en Asunción, esta solución será la primera en generar estos datos con la ayuda de la contribución de los usuarios.

En la evaluación de la herramienta se obtuvieron resultados favorables y comentarios positivos de parte de los usuarios, quienes afirmaron que SmartMoving les será de gran ayuda. Esta solución puede también servir a la municipalidad para gestionar denuncias sobre las veredas que no cumplen con el reglamento vigente, y a los encargados de recorrer las zonas para hacer el seguimiento de cada denuncia. Al obtener información sobre el estado de las veredas, se podrá analizar la dimensión de la gravedad del problema y proponer soluciones necesarias. También se podría incorporar otra información útil para otro perfil de usuarios (por ejemplo, ciclistas, turistas, entre otros), y así ampliar el alcance de la aplicación.

References

1. Cortellazzi, J., Foschini, L., Rolt, C.R.D., Corradi, A., Neto, C.A.A., Alperstedt, G.D.: Crowdsensing and proximity services for impaired mobility. In: 2016 IEEE Symposium on Computers and Communication (ISCC). pp. 44–49 (June 2016). https://doi.org/10.1109/ISCC.2016.7543712
2. Garreta Domingo, M., Mor Pera, E.: Diseño centrado en el usuario. Universitat Oberta de Catalunya (2010)
3. Lewis, J.R.: IBM computer usability satisfaction questionnaires: Psychometric evaluation and instructions for use. International Journal of Human-Computer Interaction **7**(1), 57–78 (1995). https://doi.org/10.1080/10447319509526110, https://doi.org/10.1080/10447319509526110
4. Lewis, J.R.: Measuring perceived usability: The csuq, sus, and UMUX. International Journal of Human-Computer Interaction **34**(12), 1148–1156 (2018). https://doi.org/10.1080/10447318.2017.1418805, https://doi.org/10.1080/10447318.2017.1418805
5. Mirri, S., Prandi, C., Salomoni, P.: Personalizing pedestrian accessible way-finding with mpass. In: 2016 13th IEEE Annual Consumer Communications Networking Conference (CCNC). pp. 1119–1124 (Jan 2016). https://doi.org/10.1109/CCNC.2016.7444946
6. Prandi, C., Salomoni, P., Mirri, S.: mpass: Integrating people sensing and crowdsourcing to map urban accessibility. In: 2014 IEEE 11th Consumer Communications and Networking Conference (CCNC). pp. 591–595 (Jan 2014). https://doi.org/10.1109/CCNC.2014.6940491
7. Secretaría Nacional de Tecnologías de la Información y Comunicación: Encuesta sobre acceso y uso de internet en paraguay. http://gestordocumental.senatics.gov.py/share/s/ntjnuNLeT8u3gbAHC6WeVw (2017)
8. Wang, Q., Guo, B., Wang, L., Xin, T., Du, H., Chen, H., Yu, Z.: Crowdwatch: Dynamic sidewalk obstacle detection using mobile crowd sensing. IEEE Internet of Things Journal **4**(6), 2159–2171 (Dec 2017). https://doi.org/10.1109/JIOT.2017.2750324

Descripción de *code smells*: Enfoque ontológico

Ivian Laobel Castellano Betancourt[1[0000-0001-6459-0263]], Nemury Silega Martínez[1[0000-0002-8436-5650]], Katya Martha Faggioni Colombo[2[0000-0001-6577-5761]], Gilberto F. Castro[2, 3[0000-0001-9050-8550]]

[1]Universidad de las Ciencias Informáticas, Habana, Cuba
{ilcastellano,nsilega}@uci.cu
[2] Universidad de Guayaquil, Guayaquil, Ecuador
{katya.faggionic, gilberto.castro}@ug.edu.ec
[3] Universidad de Católica Santiago de Guayaquil, Guayaquil, Ecuador
gilberto.castro@ucsg.edu.ec

Abstract. Los *code smells* son problemas asociados a fragmentos del código fuente de un software que, aunque no impiden que este funcione correctamente, deben ser reestructurados pues generan un impacto negativo en su calidad. Estas anomalías son comunes durante el desarrollo de software y generalmente suceden por la incorrecta aplicación de buenas prácticas en la programación, por parte de los desarrolladores y arquitectos de software con insuficiente conocimiento. Afectan las características de calidad del software como la mantenibilidad degradando la reusabilidad y la comprensibilidad. La coexistencia de estos errores en el código fuente provoca problemas de arquitectura que dificultan el proceso de mantenimiento y evolución del software aumentando los fallos en el futuro. Para abordar el problema descrito, en este artículo se presenta una ontología que permite describir los *code smells* como base de conocimiento. Para el desarrollo de la misma se utilizó la herramienta Protégé y se siguió una metodología para el desarrollo de ontologías, también se utilizó el razonador Pellet para inferir el conocimiento. Finalmente, la ontología podrá ser utilizada para capacitar a desarrolladores y arquitectos de software mediante una base de conocimiento que permitirá compartir y comunicar el conocimiento generado, así como la descripción de la información relacionada con los *code smells*.

Keywords: Descripción, *Code smells*, Ontología.

1 Introducción

En la actualidad, la industria del software se ha desarrollado a medida que evolucionan las tecnologías de la información. De igual manera, han surgido nuevos modelos y propuestas para obtener productos de software con calidad, cumpliendo las expectativas del cliente y ciertos requisitos de calidad [1].

La norma ISO/IEC 25010 determina las características de calidad de un software que se pueden evaluar, entre ellas se encuentra la mantenibilidad [2]. Esta se define como la capacidad del producto de software para ser modificado efectiva y eficientemente, por necesidades evolutivas, correctivas, perfectivas o adaptativas [2]. La evolución y mantenimiento de un software son tareas costosas en el desarrollo de software. Estos costos crecen mientras que los sistemas sean más grandes y complejos [3].

Una preocupación común que dificulta este proceso es la existencia de problemas de diseño estructural, que no fueron atendidos en etapas tempranas de desarrollo. Estos problemas se describen como *code smell* (CS). Este concepto fue atribuido a Kent Beck en el año 1999 [4] y luego, su marco conceptual se complementó con anomalías o malos "síntomas" a nivel de diseño de software.

Los CS son problemas estructurales en el código fuente de un software. Están asociados a fragmentos de código que deben reestructurarse para mejorar la calidad. Surgen por la incorrecta aplicación de buenas prácticas, lo que demuestra que el código esté pobremente escrito, tenga mala calidad y esté mal organizado o estructurado. En consecuencia, generan un impacto negativo en la calidad, sea difícil de extender, modificar y que dificulte el mantenimiento en etapas maduras del software. Además, ralentizan el desarrollo de software y aumentan el riesgo de errores o fallos en el futuro. Estas anomalías generalmente ocurren por el insuficiente conocimiento de los programadores y arquitectos con poca experiencia en el desarrollo de software [5].

Con el fin de conocer el comportamiento de los CS, la importancia que se le atribuyen y el estado actual de este tema en el desarrollo de software, se realizó un estudio empírico a partir de una encuesta. Esta se aplicó a programadores y arquitectos, en dos empresas de desarrollo de software en Cuba. Para la aplicación del instrumento se tuvo en cuenta los tipos de CS definidos por Fowler [4] y Lanza [6]. El cuestionario consta de dos partes. La primera parte recopila información de los encuestados acerca de antecedentes sobre las respuestas, como años de experiencia en la producción de software, lenguajes de programación conocidos y utilizados, proyectos en los que han participado y roles desempeñados. La segunda parte proporciona información referente a los CS y el seguimiento que se les realiza.

La encuesta demostró que solo el 47 % de los encuestados refieren poseer conocimientos básicos sobre los CS, aunque reconocen que en los proyectos que han participado se le atribuye poca importancia y se aborda poco sobre el tema. Esto demuestra que no se realiza un seguimiento adecuado a los CS por falta de preparación de los roles involucrados. Así mismo, se listan los tipos de CS más comunes en los proyectos mencionados. Además, el 100 % de los encuestados afirma que no se aplican buenas prácticas o alternativas para disminuir la ocurrencia de los CS en los proyectos que han participado. Se demostró la baja tasa de explotación de herramientas que apoyen la detección de CS, solo el 44 % afirman que se emplea la herramienta *SonarQube*, además se pudo comprobar que no se cuenta con especialistas capacitados para la correcta gestión de los CS. El resultado de la encuesta demuestra la necesidad de alternativas para capacitar a especialistas involucrados en la gestión de los CS.

Por otro lado, las ontologías sirven como instrumento útil para compartir y comunicar el conocimiento [7]. En la literatura se han documentado sus beneficios en diferentes áreas de la ingeniería del software [8]. Para explotar sus potencialidades, el objetivo de este trabajo es desarrollar una ontología que permita describir los CS como base de conocimiento. La ontología describirá los distintos tipos de CS, sus clasificaciones, además de las características de calidad y elementos o principios de diseño de software que afectan. Describirá los problemas de arquitectura que provocan ante la presencia de aglomeraciones de código. También, posibilitará compartir y comunicar el conocimiento explícito acerca del tema representado en la bibliografía científica. Tiene como propósito de brindar apoyo a los profesionales del desarrollo de software permitiendo capacitar a programadores y arquitectos.

Este artículo se enfoca en la creación de una ontología que permite describir los CS teniendo en cuenta las metodologías para el proceso de creación de ontologías. Se ha estructurado la información de la siguiente forma: la Sección 2 se presentan los conceptos básicos de la investigación y se describen los trabajos relacionados y en la Sección 3 se desarrolla la ontología para la descripción de CS. Finalmente, se presentan las conclusiones y trabajos futuros.

2 Trabajos relacionados

2.1 *Code smell*

Un CS es una estructura o "anomalía" en el código fuente que puede degradar diferentes aspectos de la calidad del código fuente de un sistema informático, como la reusabilidad, comprensibilidad y mantenibilidad. A pesar de que no impide el funcionamiento del software podría ralentizar su desarrollo, aumentar el riesgo de errores o llevar a la introducción de fallas en etapas maduras del producto informático [9-11].

Mäntylä [12] describe diferentes problemas comunes durante el desarrollo de software que pudieran ser causantes de que existan problemas de diseño y arquitectura [13]; se plantea que existen clases con una considerable cantidad de líneas de código debido a diferentes razones las cuales se destacan: innecesario código repetido, variables que no se utilizan y temporales, lo que lleva consigo bajos niveles de abstracción, diseño y reutilización. Se aborda la existencia de métodos con una lista excesiva de parámetros siendo difíciles de comprender e incrementan el acoplamiento.

En ocasiones es necesario realizar cambios en una clase, con lo cual se deben realizar varias modificaciones adicionales en diversos lugares para compatibilizar el cambio realizado, debido a esto, se pierde en tiempo de desarrollo. A su vez, se encuentran diferentes funcionalidades dentro de un sistema que dan solución a un mismo problema, teniendo como resultado que no se cumpla la reutilización de código, lo que conduce a que surjan problemas de rendimiento.

Teniendo en cuenta lo anterior y la importancia que se le atribuye al conocimiento de los CS por parte de los programadores y arquitectos de software se realizó una revisión de la literatura [4-6, 11, 14, 15], la cual permitió identificar un conjunto de catálogos de CS y clasificaciones de estos en cuanto a granularidad y similitud. Como resultado de la búsqueda se evidenció que entre los CS más abordados se encuentran los presentados por Fowler [4] y Lanza [6].

Varias investigaciones han demostrado el impacto de la identificación de CS en etapas tempranas del desarrollo de software y el análisis de estos para poder adoptar decisiones. Por ejemplo, Bastias [16] y López [2] hacen referencia a la herramienta *SonarQube*, siendo útil para el análisis de diferentes elementos de calidad y determina la deuda técnica de un software en cuanto a CS. Tiene como desventaja que los CS identificados contienen un alto número de falsos positivos y además esta herramienta tiene dificultades para analizar código que no se encuentra compilado [17].

Masson [15] realiza un análisis acerca de las herramientas *inCode* e *iPlasma*; donde se deduce que una de las mayores limitantes de estas es que usualmente identifican una cantidad considerable de CS; lo que podría volverse un problema en el desarrollo de software por las siguientes razones.

- El desarrollador pudiera verse abrumado por la cantidad de información a analizar; este sería quien decide en cada caso si se le debe dar tratamiento a los CS señalados, pues no todos indican un problema de diseño.
- Cada síntoma encontrado requiere de un análisis particular y teniendo en cuenta su entendimiento del sistema poder identificar aquellos que necesitan ser reparados.

Una vez analizados los resultados del estudio de estas herramientas, se constata que son aplicadas para la identificación de anomalías en el código fuente. Aunque, se abordan un conjunto reducido de CS. También, la precisión de detección varía entre cada una de las herramientas. En los ejemplos anteriores se evidencia que existe inestabilidad para priorizar y realizar análisis de detección de CS. Esto depende en gran medida de la importancia que se le atribuye al seguimiento de los CS durante el desarrollo de software, además de la experiencia y el conocimiento que tengan los programadores y arquitectos.

2.2 Ontología

La ontología es una disciplina de la filosofía que trata con lo que es, con los tipos y estructuras de objetos, propiedades y otros aspectos de la realidad [18]. En la rama de la informática se define una ontología como: *"Una descripción formal y explícita de los conceptos en un dominio de discurso, las propiedades de cada concepto que describen los rasgos y atributos del concepto y las restricciones de los slots"*[7]. Una ontología con un conjunto de instancias individuales de clases constituye una base de conocimiento [7]. En la literatura científica existen estudios de soluciones basadas en ontologías, adecuados para compartir y comunicar el conocimiento en diferentes dominios [7]. Motivado por estos resultados se determinó que el desarrollo de una ontología constituye una solución interesante para abordar los problemas analizados referente a la descripción y análisis de los CS.

Partiendo de la exploración efectuada en la literatura científica acerca de la conceptualización de los CS y sus diferentes comportamientos durante el desarrollo de software, se elabora una ontología basada en la gestión de conocimiento. Tiene como principal utilidad la descripción de los CS en sus diferentes escenarios. La solución propuesta permite describir y compartir su base de conocimiento, la cual es útil para los programadores y arquitectos de software, dado que ayuda a conocer y comprender a mayor escala los CS, facilitando su identificación y análisis en etapas tempranas de desarrollo, así como determinar que tratamientos aplicarles.

3 Ontología para la descripción de *code smells*

Entre los lenguajes más populares para especificar ontologías se distingue OWL por las facilidades que brinda. Está basado en un modelo lógico que le permite definir los conceptos tal y como son descritos. Utiliza razonadores que permite chequear automáticamente la consistencia de los modelos representados. Para elaborar la ontología se utiliza la herramienta Protégé 5.0 para representar el conocimiento, la cual posee una arquitectura flexible y extensible [19]. Se utiliza el razonador Pellet pues permite realizar las inferencias en el Protégé sobre las instancias y comprobar las propiedades lógico-formales validando la consistencia de la ontología.

Para alcanzar resultados satisfactorios en el desarrollo de la ontología, se debe utilizar una metodología que guíe el proceso de su construcción. En este trabajo se adopta la metodología propuesta por Alvarado [20], creada a partir de los principios y buenas prácticas de las metodologías: *Methontology* [21] y *Desarrollo de ontologías-101* [7]. La metodología propone cinco actividades: 1) determinación de los requerimientos de la ontología, 2) reutilización de ontologías, 3) elaboración del modelo conceptual, 4) implementación y 5) evaluación de las ontologías.

A partir de los conceptos identificados y explicados en los requerimientos de la ontología se elaboró el modelo conceptual haciendo uso de estos conceptos, así como las relaciones entre ellos. En la Tabla 1 se muestran estos conceptos y describen los principales conceptos utilizados. En la Tabla 2 sus relaciones con otros conceptos.

Tabla 1. Términos representativos del dominio. Fuente: elaboración propia

Nombre	**Descripción**
Tipo de *code smell*	Problemas estructurales en el código fuente de un software. Están asociados a fragmentos de código que deben reestructurarse para mejorar la calidad. Surgen por la incorrecta aplicación de buenas práctica [6, 7].
Clasificación de *code smell*	Términos que agrupan a los CS en cuanto a la similitud que podrían tener entre ellos.
Aglomeración de código	Grupo de CS que están relacionadas entre sí por alguna razón. La relación entre dos CS puede establecerse, por ejemplo, a través de llamadas a métodos o herencia [22].
Anomalía de arquitectura	Síntoma de degradación de la arquitectura de un software en su implementación a través de la introducción progresiva de CS [22].
Norma de calidad	Normas internacionales de calidad [2].
Caracteríctica de calidad	Características de calidad que establecen las normas de calidad para un producto de software [2].
Subcaracterística de calidad	Subcaracterísticas de calidad contenidas dentro de las características de calidad [2].
Elemento de diseño	Principios, buenas prácticas o patrones de diseño.
Herramienta	Herramientas que son utilizadas para la identificación de CS.
Métrica	Métricas utilizadas en las herramientas para la identificación de los CS.
Sistema	Producto de software que pudiera tener problemas de arquitectura debido a la ocurrencia de CS.
Componente	Pieza de código preelaborado que encapsula alguna funcionalidad expuesta a través de interfaces estándar en un sistema.
Clase	Plantilla para la creación de objetos de datos según un modelo predefinido.
Método	Subrutina cuyo código es definido en una clase y puede pertenecer tanto a una clase, como a un objeto, como es el caso de los métodos de instancia.
Lenguaje de programación	Lenguaje formal que proporciona instrucciones que permiten al programador escribir secuencias a modo de controlar el comportamiento físico y lógico de una computadora con el objetivo de que produzca diversas clases de datos.

Tabla 2. Conceptos de la ontología y sus relaciones. Fuente: elaboración propia

Concepto	Relación	Concepto
Tipo de *code smell*	Afecta	Elemento de diseño
		Caracteríctica de calidad
Clasificación de *code smell*	Clasifica a	Tipo de *code smell*
Aglomeración de código	Compuesta por	Tipo de *code smell*
	Está presente en	Componente
	Provoca	Anomalía de arquitectura
Norma de calidad	Contiene	Caracteríctica de calidad
Caracteríctica de calidad	Contiene	Subcaracteríctica de calidad
Herramienta	Identifica	Tipo de *code smell*
		Anomalía de arquitectura
	Soporta	Lenguaje de programación
	Utiliza	Métrica
Métrica	Puede identificar	Tipo de *code smell*
Componente	Tiene	Método
		Clase
Sistema	Tiene	Componente
	Utiliza como tegnología	Lenguaje de programación
Clase	Tiene	Método

Las clases, propiedades, restricciones e instancias son los componentes más importantes de una ontología. Una vez detallados los conceptos relacionados con los CS se realizó un análisis para identificar cada uno de los elementos de la ontología a desarrollar. La Fig. 1 muestra un fragmento de las 22 clases identificadas.

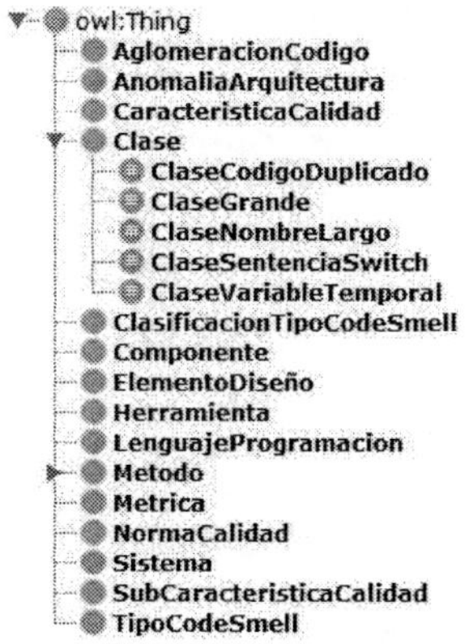

Fig. 1. Clases de la ontología para describir los CS. Fuente: elaboración propia

Una vez identificadas cada una de las clases de la ontología y modeladas en la herramienta, se establecieron las propiedades de cada una de ellas. Las propiedades pueden ser de dos tipos: propiedad de objeto (*object property*) o de dato (*data property*). Las propiedades de objetos permiten restringir las relaciones de un individuo.

En la Fig. 2 se muestra un fragmento de las 36 propiedades de objetos representadas en la ontología desarrollada mediante una representación de relaciones binarias entre estas propiedades.

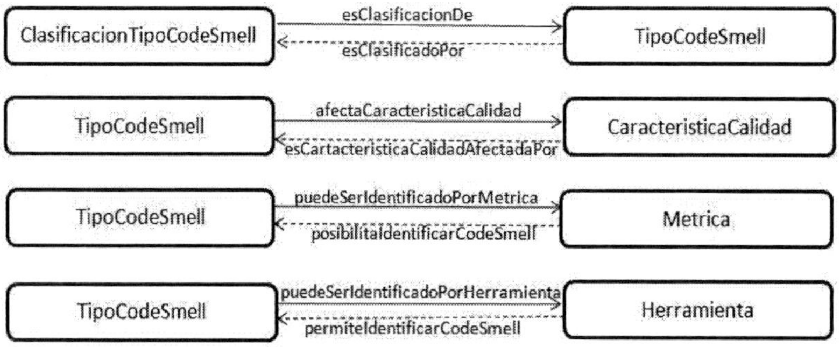

Fig. 2. Propiedades de objeto de la ontología. Fuente: elaboración propia

Con el objetivo de describir los conceptos se definieron en la ontología los atributos de las clases. En la Fig. 3 se muestran las propiedades de dato de la ontología.

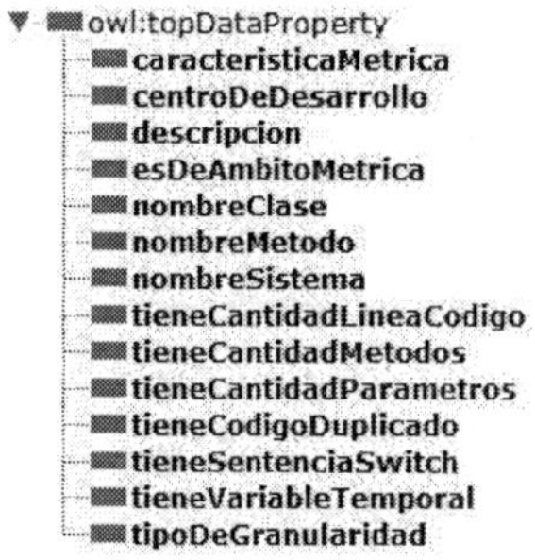

Fig. 3. Propiedades de dato de la ontología. Fuente: elaboración propia

4 Conclusiones y trabajo futuro

La revisión de la literatura permitió analizar los tipos de CS y su relación con otros conceptos. La aplicación de una encuesta en proyectos de desarrollo de software teniendo en cuenta la experiencia de los encuestados, permitió conocer los tipos de CS que a menudo inciden en el código fuente de los proyectos, la baja tasa de explotación de herramientas que apoyen la detección de CS, así como la necesidad de aplicar alternativas como soporte para la capacitación de programadores y arquitectos en aras de realizar una adecuada gestión de los CS. Con el uso de la herramienta Protégé y el lenguaje OWL se elaboró una ontología que permite representar el conocimiento. La utilización de una metodología para el desarrollo de ontologías permitió guiar el proceso de construcción teniendo en cuenta las actividades propuestas.

Como trabajo futuro se pretende elaborar un método que incluya secuencias de actividades para el proceso de utilización, mantenimiento y evolución de la ontología. También, se validará la solución mediante la evaluación de la ontología en proyectos de desarrollo de software y la aplicación de un estudio de caso como método de investigación científica. Se pretende que la ontología creada se utilice en proyectos de desarrollo de software y pueda ser empleada para capacitar a programadores y arquitectos.

Referencias

1. González, L.A.E., N.J. Acosta, and J.L.G. Tovar, *Estándares para la calidad de software.* Tecnología Investigación y Academia, 2017. **5**(1): p. 75-84.
2. López, J.V., *AUDITORÍA MANTENIBILIDAD APLICACIONES SEGÚN LA ISO/IEC 25000.* 2015.
3. April, A. and A. Abran, *Software maintenance management: evaluation and continuous improvement.* Vol. 67. 2012: John Wiley & Sons.
4. Fowler, M., et al., *Refactoring: improving the design of existing code.* 1999: Addison-Wesley Professional.
5. Malavolta, A., *Análisis de detección de Code Smells para el lenguaje JavaScript.* 2018.
6. Lanza, M. and R. Marinescu, *Object-oriented metrics in practice: using software metrics to characterize, evaluate, and improve the design of object-oriented systems.* 2007: Springer Science & Business Media.
7. Noy, N.F. and D.L. McGuinness, *Ontology development 101: A guide to creating your first ontology.* 2001, Stanford knowledge systems laboratory technical report KSL-01-05 and ....
8. Garzás, J. and M. Piattini, *An ontology for microarchitectural design knowledge.* IEEE software, 2005. **22**(2): p. 28-33.
9. Yamashita, A. and L. Moonen. *Do code smells reflect important maintainability aspects?* in *2012 28th IEEE international conference on software maintenance (ICSM).* 2012. IEEE.
10. Di Nucci, D., et al. *Detecting code smells using machine learning techniques: are we there yet?* in *2018 IEEE 25th International Conference on Software Analysis, Evolution and Reengineering (SANER).* 2018. IEEE.
11. Alonso, M. and F.H. Klaver, *Aplicación de un Proceso de Refactoring guiado por Escenarios de Modificabilidad y Code Smells.* 2016.
12. Mäntylä, M.V. and C. Lassenius, *Subjective evaluation of software evolvability using code smells: An empirical study.* Empirical Software Engineering, 2006. **11**(3): p. 395-431.
13. Aniche, M., et al., *Code smells for model-view-controller architectures.* Empirical Software Engineering, 2018. **23**(4): p. 2121-2157.
14. AlKharabsheh, K., et al. *Comparación de herramientas de Detección de Design Smells.* 2016. JISBD.
15. Masson, I. and R. Pastore, *Análisis y mejoras de usabilidad y performance sobre una herramienta de asistencia en el refactoring de aplicaciones.* 2016.
16. Bastias, O.A., *Código con"mal olor": un mapeo sistemático.* Revista Cubana de Ciencias Informáticas, 2018. **12**(4): p. 156-176.
17. Ospina Delgado, J.P., *Análisis de seguridad y calidad de aplicaciones (Sonarqube).*
18. Welty, C. and N. Guarino, *Supporting ontological analysis of taxonomic relationships.* Data & Knowledge Engineering, 2001. **39**(1): p. 51-74.
19. Fernández Hernández, A., *Modelo ontológico de recuperación de información para la toma de decisiones en gestión de proyectos.* 2016.
20. Alvarado, R. *Metodología para el desarrollo de ontologías. 2010.* 28 noviembre 2018]; Available from: https://es.slideshare.net/Iceman1976/metodologia-para-ontologias.
21. Fernández-López, M., A. Gómez-Pérez, and N. Juristo, *Methontology: from ontological art towards ontological engineering.* 1997.
22. Oizumi, W.N., et al., *On the relationship of code-anomaly agglomerations and architectural problems.* Journal of Software Engineering Research and Development, 2015. **3**(1): p. 11.

A Framework to support the Experimental Evaluation Process of the Pedagogical Conversational Systems*

Leo Natan Paschoal

Institute of Mathematics and Computer Sciences – University of São Paulo
paschoalln@usp.br

Abstract. Conversational systems are applications whose main characteristic is interaction with humans through spoken or written natural language. Initially, they have been established for educational purposes, dedicated to supporting students while learning new subjects, motivating them while carrying out activities, solving their questions, indicating new learning materials, among others. Several studies show the benefits of using conversational systems how a support tool, promoting the application of active learning methodologies. However, recent studies have mentioned that these systems are not being adequately evaluated since it is not possible to observe systematization in the evaluations, the selection of variables is not standardized, and there is no replicated study yet. Experimental Software Engineering presents robust procedures for experimentation. It can indicate better strategies to evaluate this type of system and offer subsidies to improve the visibility of the potential of these systems as a learning support mechanism. In this project, we intend to collaborate whit the evaluation process of the conversational systems, proposing a framework to support the planning, execution, and reporting of the experimental studies. The area lacks adequate methodologies for reliable experimental studies and, therefore, this project can contribute to improving the quality of conversational systems.

Keywords: Chatbots · Experimentation · Dialogue Systems.

1 Introdução

Sistemas conversacionais representam aplicações que são capazes de processar e emitir a linguagem humana, por meio de texto ou voz [1]. Exemplos comuns dessas aplicações são os assistentes virtuais *Siri, Google Assistant e Cortana* [12]. Além de serem reconhecidos como assistentes virtuais, na literatura acadêmica, é possível identificá-los como agentes conversacionais, *chatbots*, *chatterbots*, sistemas de diálogo, dentre outros [13]. Devido às habilidades do processamento de linguagem natural, essas aplicações têm sido estabelecidas para contextos

* This work is funding by the University of São Paulo and by CAPES - Coordenação de Aperfeiçoamento de Pessoal de Nível Superior - Brazil - Finance Code 001.

de uso específicos, em diferentes áreas do conhecimento humano. Também são definidos para serem usados em conjunto com outros sistemas. Um exemplo é sua integração com sistemas de informação do tipo CRM (*Customer Relationship Management*), para prestar atendimento aos usuários [24].

Sem dúvida, o maior interesse para o uso desses sistemas é no domínio da educação. Isso pode ser observado em recentes estudos secundários que buscam definir um panorama sobre os sistemas conversacionais produzidos para fins educacionais (*e.g.*, [7,8]). Por intermédio dessas pesquisas, é possível observar que os sistemas conversacionais educacionais/pedagógicos estão sendo produzidos para apoiar temáticas específicas, como o ensino de física, matemática, ciência da computação, engenharias e saúde. Além disso, eles são definidos com propósitos diferentes, na medida em que podem ser usados para solucionar dúvidas de alunos que não compreenderam um assunto, repassar informações que sejam relevantes, fornecer *feedback* para as ações realizadas pelos estudantes, usar discurso motivacional para estimular os estudantes, contribuir com a aquisição de conhecimento do aluno, contribuir com o desenvolvimento de competências sociais, dentre outros. Ainda, eles podem ser definidos para se comportarem como tutores, professores ou estudantes.

A exploração do uso de sistemas conversacionais pedagógicos em cursos de plataformas MOOCs (*Massive Open Online Courses*) tem se intensificado [2], uma vez que esses cursos possuem uma ampla quantidade e diversidade de estudantes, e nem sempre há um professor disponível para atender aos questionamentos elaborados pelos alunos. Em trabalhos anteriores, o autor explorou o uso desses sistemas como apoio a práticas de ensino baseadas em metodologias ativas, como *Flipped Classroom* [16]. Apesar de serem estimulados para uso em práticas ativas, esses sistemas também podem ser explorados no ensino tradicional (presencial ou a distância) [11]. Nesse sentido, podem ser usados em conjunto com outros recursos educacionais, tais como ambientes virtuais de aprendizagem, redes sociais, mundos virtuais e jogos educacionais.

Dado a versatilidade e aplicabilidade desses sistemas, era esperado que existissem mais estudos na literatura sobre a implantação dos mesmos em práticas educacionais. Todavia, observa-se que a comunidade não tem apresentado relatos sobre a implantação efetiva desses sistemas em cenários de ensino, pois a maioria dos trabalhos tem focado em descrever o desenvolvimento do sistema conversacional pedagógico e tem se distanciado em explorar sua implantação. Foram identificados estudos dedicados a avaliar, por exemplo, a usabilidade de sistemas conversacionais pedagógicos [15]. Também foram encontrados estudos que descrevem o *feedback* dos alunos ou do professor sobre o benefício do agente conversacional [8,22]. No entanto, esses estudos também são feitos pelos autores para comprovar alguma funcionalidade ou conferir se ele atende a algum objetivo específico [7]. Portanto, relatos de experiência da implantação dos sistemas conversacionais pedagógicos não são comuns em fóruns de divulgação científica ou em artigos científicos.

Devido a falta de relatórios ou artigos científicos sobre as experiências em implantações desses sistemas, não existem lições a serem aprendidas. Por outro lado, isso pode levar a alguns questionamentos associados à viabilidade das aplicações que estão sendo desenvolvidas. A viabilidade dos sistemas conversacionais poderia ser comprovada por meio de estudos experimentais, como é feito por pesquisadores de engenharia de software quando buscam compreender a viabilidade de técnicas, procedimentos e novas ferramentas [23]. No entanto, trabalhos recentes apontam a falta de sistematização nos estudos que estão sendo produzidos no contexto de sistemas conversacionais [22]. Sabe-se que isso dificulta o entendimento dos procedimentos e resultados apresentados e a sua replicação [6]. Além disso, cada estudo avalia um aspecto do sistema conversacional, portanto, não há padronização no que é considerado durante a avaliação [7]. Por exemplo, enquanto alguns pesquisadores avaliam somente aspectos técnicos dos sistemas conversacionais pedagógicos, outros consideram somente as percepções dos estudantes e não observam questões técnicas, como a qualidade da conversa.

Essa falta de pesquisas sobre avaliações no contexto de sistemas conversacionais pedagógicos pode ter relação com a falta de procedimentos de apoio à sistematização, como também a falta de conhecimento sobre a necessidade dessa sistematização [8]. Como a área é constituída por pesquisadores com formações em diferentes domínios, é possível que as avaliações que estão sendo realizadas tenham relação direta com o que o pesquisador está acostumado a utilizar em trabalhos de sua área. Por exemplo, um pesquisador da área de física pode não conhecer os procedimentos que apoiam a avaliação experimental utilizados por pesquisadores da área da computação.

Neste panorama e considerando que os sistemas conversacionais se diferem dos sistemas de software tradicionais, o desafio desta pesquisa de doutorado é caracterizar os tipos de avaliação que são necessários neste contexto, propondo mecanismos para apoiar a sistematização de avaliações desses sistemas. Espera-se propor um framework de apoio para avaliações experimentais de sistemas conversacionais pedagógicos de modo que a viabilidade, qualidade e outros requisitos de interesse possam ser avaliados com maior confiabilidade. O objetivo é padronizar as avaliações experimentais de modo que os resultados possam ser melhor comparados. Para tanto, acredita-se que os procedimentos da engenharia de software experimental possam ser estendidos para o contexto dos sistemas conversacionais pedagógicos. Assim, o objetivo da pesquisa é promover direcionamento para apoiar pesquisadores a definir avaliações sistemáticas de sistemas conversacionais pedagógicos, concentrando nos diferentes estágios de uma avaliação sistemática – a saber: planejamento, operação, execução e divulgação.

2 Justificativa

Os sistemas conversacionais emergem como sistemas de software com potencial para solucionar ou minimizar problemas associados ao ensino e a aprendizagem, uma vez que flexibilizam a interação entre homem-máquina e podem estar disponíveis para uso a todo momento, isto é, 24 horas por dia e 7 dias por semana [9]. Com base nessa premissa, muitos pesquisadores vêm tirando proveito desses sistemas para propor soluções às problemáticas que permeiam o âmbito educacional. Apenas a proposta e o desenvolvimento desses sistemas, no entanto, não garante que os problemas estão sendo solucionados.

De acordo com Shull *et al.* [18] e Travassos *et al.* [20], os produtos de software não deveriam ser apenas propostos, desenvolvidos ou apresentados para venda sem experimentação e validação. Na visão de Basili *et al.* [3], só é possível verificar se o entendimento atual sobre a temática está correto por meio de estudos experimentais. Desse modo, acredita-se que só é possível averiguar se sistemas conversacionais pedagógicos conseguem solucionar os problemas para os quais são propostos por meio da condução de avaliações/estudos experimentais.

O paradigma experimental tem sido adotado e adaptado por diversas linhas de investigação dentro da Ciência da Computação, tais como sistemas operacionais [5] e engenharia de software [23]. No âmbito da engenharia de software existem algumas definições para os propósitos da experimentação. Conradi *et al.* [4] descrevem que a experimentação auxilia a construir uma base de conhecimento confiável, permitindo reduzir as incertezas sobre quais as teorias, ferramentas e metodologias são adequadas. Adicionalmente, a experimentação elimina suposições errôneas e oferece suporte para orientar a teoria nas direções promissoras de pesquisa [4].

Apesar da experimentação estar bem estabelecida na área da engenharia de software, a condução de experimentos em outras áreas ainda não é uma prática habitual. De acordo com Kitchenham *et al.* [10], algumas áreas de pesquisa têm dificuldade em realizar estudos experimentais. Em virtude disso, existem estudos que discutem sobre a necessidade de adaptar os modelos já estabelecidos e consolidados em outras áreas ou desenvolver modelos específicos para o domínio de investigação. Considerando as necessidades intrínsecas da área e tipos de aplicações, muitas áreas têm concentrado esforços para o estabelecimento de diretrizes, processos e *frameworks* de apoio a experimentação. Na pesquisa de Sheard *et al.* [17], por exemplo, os autores mencionam sobre a necessidade de adequação de um modelo de experimentação para ambientes de apoio ao ensino de programação.

Em decorrência do atual estado da arte sobre os sistemas conversacionais pedagógicos, acredita-se que é necessário oferecer apoio metodológico, visando estimular a condução de estudos experimentais na área. Supõe-se que o apoio metodológico aumentará o rigor da pesquisa na área e contribuirá com a adesão de procedimentos sistemáticos durante a condução desses estudos. Adicionalmente, é necessário apoiar a replicação dos experimentos, estimulando a geração de pacotes de dados experimentais com conjunto de informações importantes para a replicação, buscando facilitar o compartilhamento e reúso de materiais produzidos, adotados e gerados durante a condução de experimentos.

3 Solução proposta

Considerando que o projeto de pesquisa conduzido no contexto do doutorado envolve a investigação e o estabelecimento de um *framework* para apoiar o planejamento, operação, condução e relato de estudos experimentais sobre sistemas conversacionais pedagógicos, busca-se:

(i) Estabelecer um vocabulário de experimentação para que pesquisadores conduzam e reportem seus estudos utilizando conceitos e terminologias comuns. O vocabulário é importante porque a comunidade de pesquisa que trabalha com sistemas conversacionais pedagógicos provêm de diferentes áreas do conhecimento humano e precisa conseguir utilizar a mesma linguagem para compartilhar os resultados de suas avaliações.

(ii) Definir um corpo de conhecimento sobre variáveis e métricas. O corpo de conhecimento possibilitará ao usuário final do *framework* reconhecer quais as variáveis que podem ser controladas e não podem ser controladas na condução de experimentos sobre sistemas conversacionais pedagógicos, dando ênfase às variáveis dependentes e variáveis independentes. Nessa etapa, serão investigadas e classificadas as variáveis dependentes que são de interesse para estes sistemas (*e.g.*, eficácia, desempenho, qualidade das respostas, qualidade da interface, funcionalidade, percepção e contribuição para o que se propõe). Adicionalmente, será definido, com base na literatura, um conjunto de possíveis métricas para essas variáveis.

(iii) Produzir diretrizes para que os pesquisadores ao projetarem as avaliações experimentais possam identificar as possíveis ameças à validade do estudo. Essas diretrizes devem apresentar recomendações para evitá-las.

(iv) Propor um guia de experimentação para o condução de experimentos sobre sistemas conversacionais pedagógicos. Nessa perspectiva, o guia indicará atividades que devem ser planejadas e realizadas durante a condução do experimento. O guia tem o propósito de orientar o usuário final do *framework* na realização das atividades para o planejamento e realização do experimento. Adicionalmente, o guia deverá indicar quais são as informações relevantes que devem compor o relatório do experimento.

(v) Desenvolver um ambiente de apoio a experimentação. Um ambiente que apoia a experimentação é necessário, uma vez que a condução de estudos experimentais consome tempo do investigador e produz um grande volume de informações e conhecimento [19]. Assim, buscando facilitar a condução desse tipo de experimento, uma infraestrutura informatizada deverá ser desenvolvida.

4 Procedimentos metodológicos

Para o desenvolvimento deste projeto, estão previstas oito atividades. Elas constituirão artefatos que compõem o *framework* de pesquisa:

- **Mapeamento das avaliações existentes:** inicialmente, serão localizados estudos que reportam a avaliação de sistemas conversacionais pedagógicos. Apesar desses não apresentarem avaliação sistemática, por meio deles é possível começar a identificar variáveis e métricas que poderão fazer parte do *framework*. Para mapeá-los será replicado o mapeamento sistemático feito pelo autor e descrito em [14], incluindo critérios que permitem a seleção de estudos primários sobre sistemas conversacionais que abordem algum tipo de avaliação.

- **Definição de um vocabulário:** a replicação do mapeamento permitirá ter um entendimento mais detalhado sobre o estado real de uso de conceitos e terminologias. Assim, considerando os estudos de Wohlin *et al.* [23] e Shull *et al.* [18], será definido um vocabulário para experimentação de sistemas conversacionais pedagógicos.
- **Agrupamento de métodos e abordagens de avaliação:** um mapeamento sistemático sobre métodos e abordagens que são definidos para apoiar a avaliação de sistemas conversacionais está previsto. Espera-se que esse mapeamento possibilite a identificação de métricas, medidas e instrumentos que possam apoiar a definição do corpo de conhecimento sobre variáveis e métricas.
- **Construção do corpo de conhecimento:** Após a realização dos estudos secundários, as informações extraídas nos estudos selecionados devem ser reunidas, organizadas e disponibilizadas para acesso público como base de pesquisa e consulta. O corpo de conhecimento será definido considerando uma instanciação da abordagem de Vos *et al.* [21].
- **Reconhecimento e escrita das ameças à validade:** a definição das diretrizes para os pesquisadores reportarem ameaças à validade será inspirada em procedimentos adotados no estudo de França e Travassos [6].
- **Proposta de um guia de apoio à experimentação:** o guia para apoiar a experimentação de sistemas conversacionais pedagógicos será planejado considerando o processo experimental de Wohlin *et al.* [23]. Esse guia ilustrará procedimentos e apresentará exemplos de planejamentos de experimentos.
- **Concepção do ambiente de apoio à experimentação:** um ambiente será estabelecido buscando apoiar o gerenciamento do conhecimento científico durante todo o processo de experimentação. O ambiente será desenvolvido tomando como base o ambiente de apoio a experimentação de larga escala em engenharia de software relatado no estudo de Travassos *et al.* [19]. Adicionalmente, esse ambiente também conterá elementos que auxiliarão o pesquisador na tomada de decisão, auxiliando-o a identificar as variáveis experimentais e métricas.
- **Avaliação do framework:** após a definição dos artefatos, o *framework* de pesquisa proposto será avaliado. A avaliação será realizado por meio de um estudo experimental conduzido com pesquisadores que trabalham com sistemas conversacionais pedagógicos.

5 Resultados esperados

Com o desenvolvimento deste projeto de doutorado espera-se obter as seguintes contribuições:

1. Fortalecer o entendimento que a comunidade vinculada aos sistemas conversacionais pedagógico tem sobre avaliações sistemáticas.
2. Aprimorar a condução de estudos experimentais por intermédio de um corpo de conhecimento, um guia de experimentação e um ambiente para apoiar a automatização do processo de experimentação.
3. Possibilitar o desenvolvimento de sistemas conversacionais com mais qualidade, uma vez que a partir dos estudos experimentais é possível analisar adequadamente a viabilidade das soluções propostas.
4. Ampliar a credibilidade dos sistemas conversacionais como mecanismo de apoio ao ensino.

6 Estado atual da pesquisa

O projeto ainda está em fase inicial. Apesar disso, alguns resultados já foram obtido. Foi feito um mapeamento sistemático das pesquisas brasileiras, na tentativa de compreender como conceitos de experimentação estão sendo utilizado na avaliação dos sistemas conversacionais pedagógicos. Ao final, foram selecionados 13 estudos. Observou-se que a maioria dos estudos não define adequadamente as informações sobre os experimentos (*e.g.*, quais as variáveis investigadas). Isso gerou algumas dificuldades para reconhecer as variáveis e métricas relatadas nos estudos primários. Apesar disso, foi possível localizar uma diversidade de variáveis e métricas. O autor fez uma classificação preliminar dessas variáveis e métricas. Essa organização ainda precisa ser revisada. No próximo passo, será feita uma análise no âmbito da literatura internacional.

References

1. Abdul-Kader, S.A., Woods, J.: Survey on chatbot design techniques in speech conversation systems. International Journal of Advanced Computer Science and Applications **6**(7), 72–80 (2015)
2. Aguirre, C.C., Kloos, C.D., Alario-Hoyos, C., Muñoz-Merino, P.J.: Supporting a MOOC through a conversational agent. In: International Symposium on Computers in Education. pp. 1–6 (2018)
3. Basili, V.R., Shull, F., Lanubile, F.: Building knowledge through families of experiments. IEEE Transactions on Software Engineering **25**(4), 456–473 (1999)
4. Conradi, R., Basili, V.R., Carver, J., Shull, F., Travassos, G.H.: A pragmatic documents standard for an experience library: Roles,documen, contents and structure. Tech. rep., University of Maryland (2001)
5. Fortier, P.J., Michel, H.E.: System performance evaluation tool selection and use. In: Fortier, P.J., Michel, H.E. (eds.) Computer Systems Performance Evaluation and Prediction, pp. 331 – 344. Digital Press, Burlington (2003)
6. França, B.B.N., Travassos, G.H.: Experimentation with dynamic simulation models in software engineering: planning and reporting guidelines. Empirical Software Engineering **21**(3), 1302–1345 (2016)
7. Hobert, S.: How are you, chatbot? evaluating chatbots in educational settings–results of a literature review. In: Lecture Notes in Informatics, pp. 259–270 (2019)

8. Io, H., Lee, C.: Chatbots and conversational agents: A bibliometric analysis. In: International Conference on Industrial Engineering and Engineering Management. pp. 215–219 (2017)
9. Jain, M., Kumar, P., Kota, R., Patel, S.N.: Evaluating and informing the design of chatbots. In: Designing Interactive Systems Conference. pp. 895–906 (2018)
10. Kitchenham, B.A., Pfleeger, S.L., Pickard, L.M., Jones, P.W., Hoaglin, D.C., Emam, K.E., Rosenberg, J.: Preliminary guidelines for empirical research in software engineering. IEEE Transactions on Software Engineering **28**(8), 721–734 (2002)
11. Krassmann, A.L., Paz, F.J., Silveira, C., Tarouco, L.M.R., Bercht, M.: Conversational agents in distance education: comparing mood states with students' perception. Creative Education **9**(11), 1726–1742 (2018)
12. Laranjo, L., Dunn, A.G., Tong, H.L., Kocaballi, A.B., Chen, J., Bashir, R., Surian, D., Gallego, B., Magrabi, F., Lau, A.Y., et al.: Conversational agents in healthcare: a systematic review. Journal of the American Medical Informatics Association **25**(9), 1248–1258 (2018)
13. Montenegro, J.L.Z., da Costa, C.A., da Rosa Righi, R.: Survey of conversational agents in health. Expert Systems with Applications **129**, 56 – 67 (2019)
14. Paschoal, L.N.: Contribuições ao ensino de teste de software com o modelo flipped classroom e um agente conversacional. Master's thesis, USP (2019)
15. Paschoal, L.N., de Oliveira, M.M., Chicon, P.M.M.: A chatterbot sensitive to student's context to help on software engineering education. In: Latin American Computer Conference (CLEI). pp. 839–848 (2018)
16. Paschoal, L.N., Turci, L.F., Conte, T.U., Souza, S.R.S.: Towards a conversational agent to support the software testing education. In: Brazilian Symposium on Software Engineering. pp. 57–66 (2019)
17. Sheard, J., Simon, S., Hamilton, M., Lönnberg, J.: Analysis of research into the teaching and learning of programming. In: International workshop on Computing education research. pp. 93–104 (2009)
18. Shull, F., Carver, J., Travassos, G.H.: An empirical methodology for introducing software processes. In: International symposium on Foundations of software engineering. pp. 288–296 (2001)
19. Travassos, G.H., d. Santos, P.S.M., Mian, P.G., Neto, A.C.D., Biolchini, J.: An environment to support large scale experimentation in software engineering. In: International Conference on Engineering of Complex Computer Systems. pp. 193–202 (2008)
20. Travassos, G.H., Gurov, D., Amaral, E.A.G.: Introdução à engenharia de software experimental. Tech. rep., Rio de Janeiro (2002)
21. Vos, T.E.J., Marín, B., Escalona, M.J., Marchetto, A.: A methodological framework for evaluating software testing techniques and tools. In: ICQS. pp. 230–239 (2012)
22. Winkler, R., Söllner, M.: Unleashing the potential of chatbots in education: A state-of-the-art analysis. In: Academy of Management Annual Meeting. pp. 1–40 (2018)
23. Wohlin, C., Runeson, P., Höst, M., Ohlsson, M.C., Regnell, B., Wesslén, A.: Experimentation in software engineering. Springer Science & Business Media (2012)
24. Xu, A., Liu, Z., Guo, Y., Sinha, V., Akkiraju, R.: A new chatbot for customer service on social media. In: Conference on Human Factors in Computing Systems. pp. 3506–3510 (2017)

Software Deployment and Self-adaptation of IoT Systems

Iván Alfonso[1][0000-0003-3940-0629]

Department of Systems and Computing Engineering, Universidad de los Andes, Bogotá, Colombia
id.alfonso@uniandes.edu.co

Abstract. Traditional software engineering methods bring challenges to the construction of IoT systems. In particular, software deployment in distributed systems is not trivial. Resource limitations at the edge/fog layer nodes and heterogeneity of technologies and communication protocols are some of the challenges that can generate failures in deployment and operation. It is necessary to make intelligent decisions on the location of the deployed software in the system infrastructure to favor the quality of service (QoS). Additionally, the operation of IoT systems with distributed architectures becomes complicated due to the dynamic environment and the events produced that can impact QoS. We present Ph.D. Thesis proposal for intelligent decision making of software redeployments in the edge/fog layer devices of a distributed IoT system, and a method for self-adapting the system architecture.

Keywords: Internet of Things · Software deployment · Self-adaptive architecture · Edge computing · Fog computing.

1 Introduction

About twenty years ago the term Internet of Things (IoT) was publicly used by Professor Kevin Ashton [2]. From that moment, the interest around IoT has been growing and a lot of startups and companies working in this area have emerged. Gartner Inc. envisions that by 2020, about 20 billion IoT endpoints will be in use [4]. However, this growth in the use of IoT introduces challenges in software development and systems operation. Designing IoT systems using traditional architectures and software development methodologies present problems such as slow upgrades, security issues, increased costs, low performance, and reduced platform reliability [10].

Traditionally, software engineering has addressed these issues by introducing new architectures, techniques, and development methodologies that have been adopted by vendors and software development teams. For example, DevOps methodology promises to improve the performance of work teams and streamline the tasks of software development and operation of the system. DevOps combines development and operation in a single process consisting of several stages in a loop. In the literature, the use of DevOps predominates in web development mainly in SaaS applications, but there are few advances in the use of this methodology in the domain of IoT. Furthermore, there are some problems to adopt DevOps for IoT systems. For example, the complexity and limitations of creating test environments due to heterogeneity of device hardware [7]. Also, the complexity to remotely deploy software on tiny devices that do not support containerization or have no Internet connection [11], and the complexity to deploying and orchestrating software on systems with distributed architecture. Additionally, in the operation state the dynamic environment in an IoT system induce changes that impacts quality of service (QoS). In this research, we propose an approach to deploying and orchestrating software on IoT systems with distributed architectures, as well as a strategy for self-adapting the architecture to dynamic events that affect QoS.

The conventional IoT architecture consists of three main layers: (1) the cloud layer, which has unlimited processing and storage resources, hosts the application logic and perform the processing tasks; (2) the device layer which contains the system devices such as sensors and actuators; (3) and the network layer –composed of several types of communication technologies– which enables communication between physical layer devices and cloud layer servers. This centralized architecture reduces maintenance costs and application development efforts, but it has limitations such as low latency response, security risks, and high bandwidth consumption [5]. Distributed IoT architectures have emerged to address these problems. Edge and fog computing are technologies introduced as layers in a decentralized IoT architecture. Both technologies offer advantages in terms of latency, security and bandwidth usage. Because these allow move computation, storage, communication, control, and decision making closer to the network edge where data is being generated. This research addresses distributed architectures for IoT systems, to take advantage of edge and fog computing.

2 Related Work

In order to identify and to analyze relevant studies, we conducted a Systematic Literature Review (SLR). The SLR helped us systematically reach a comprehensive and fair assessment of the topic. The main goal of the SLR was to identify the dynamic environmental events in the physical and edge/fog layers of an IoT system that could impact its QoS. In addition, we classified the strategies to achieve this self-adaptation and we identified weaknesses.

After the screening and study quality assessment stages, we obtained 20 relevant studies to the research. We found six dynamic events that impact the QoS of the IoT system: (1) mobility client, (2) dynamic data transfer rate, (3) dynamic network connectivity, (4) attacks from the traffic sensor, (5) failures and software aging, and (6) important event detected by sensors. Some of the least explored events by the community are 5 and 6 (failures and software aging and important event detected by sensors). For example, studies that addressed *important event detected by sensors* –as [16]– proposed an IoT architecture that detects a physical event (e.g., when it starts raining) and changes the priority of the sensor data that is sent for analysis in the cloud. This dynamic architecture was designed using Flow-Based Programming (FBP), and the adaptive decisions were made by analyzing the data in an edge layer device. [14] proposed an architecture for a Video Surveillance System that horizontally scales virtual machines deployed in fog layer nodes when emergency surveillance was detected by the cameras. This architecture was implemented in an OpenStack based virtualization environment using Network Functions Virtualization (NFV) and Software-Defined Networking (SDN). Studies that addressed the issue of *failures and software aging* –as [15] and [9]– propose strategies for software deployment in the edge and fog layers of the architecture. For instance, [15] proposed Foggy, a framework used to automate application deployment in Fog Computing architectures. Foggy was based on the use of Docker containers and deployment rules to facilitate dynamic resource provisioning.

We found four techniques or strategies used to address these dynamic events: (1) data flow reconfiguration, (2) auto-scaling of services and applications, (3) software deployment and upgrade, and (4) task prioritization in edge/fog nodes. Some of these strategies require tasks of deploying, updating, or moving software artifacts on the edge/fog layer nodes and devices. Most of the analyzed studies semi-automate these tasks but the allocation decisions in the nodes are taken by DevOps engineer. Intelligent deployment and location decisions must be made by analyzing the current and historical metrics information about nodes resources consumption and QoS.

We propose an approach for smart re-deployment in distributed architecture IoT and to self-adapt the system to two dynamic events that impact the QoS (failures and software aging and important event detected by sensors). In contrast to these studies, we are interested in a method of monitoring and logging metrics about the node resources consumption and QoS. One of the components of our proposed solution analyzes this information to take intelligent re-deployment decisions.

3 Problem Statement

Most of the strategies we found in the literature to adapt the architecture IoT systems require deploying, updating, or moving software artifacts between nodes of the three layers: physics, edge/fog, and cloud. However, managing software deployments on IoT systems poses challenges due to the heterogeneity of communication devices and protocols. Unlike the cloud layer, at the edge/fog layer resources are not centralized and the network environment is heterogeneous, making it difficult to manage resources to balance the load and dynamically scale [3]. In addition, edge nodes have limited computational resources unlike cloud servers. Because of these reasons, the orchestration strategies and tools currently used in the cloud must be adapted to work together between the edge/fog and cloud layers.

We address two dynamic events mentioned in the SLR chapter 2:

Failures and software aging IoT systems require frequent software deployments, software updates, or movement of software artifacts, either to solve problems, improve performance, improve system security, or expose new services to the end-user. However, automating software deployment in IoT systems is a challenge given the heterogeneity and the large number of devices that must be handled. Intelligent allocation decisions are crucial to efficiently deploy software at the edge/fog layer of the system [13]. Kubernetes[1] (an open-source tool for automating the management of containerized applications) has provisioning capabilities, but these only consider the number of requested resources (CPU, RAM) on each node. Other factors such as time, energy consumption, network latency, reliability, bandwidth usage, and mobility should be taken into account when choosing the nodes or the best location to deploy.

In addition, the update process may fail, or the software displayed may have errors. One of the basic solutions, when an upgrade error occurs, is to roll back to an earlier stable software version. However, there are deployment patterns primarily used in web development to improve reliability and reduce the probability of failure in a production environment (e.g., rolling deployment, blue-green, or canary) [1]. These patterns must be explored to facilitate the process of deployment and to give reliability to software deployments on IoT systems.

Important event detected by sensors There are changes that can be detected by system sensors that force the reaction or adaptation of the IoT system architecture. For example, when the cameras of a video surveillance system detect motion, the video is transferred to fog nodes or cloud servers in real-time to be processed. Data sent from devices to application servers increases, therefore the bandwidth consumption and response latency also increase, and the QoS of the system will be affected. The IoT system should detect and adapt the architecture to support these events, e.g. scaling the application containers to meet the increased load.

According to the identified problems, we propose a general research objective: to propose and develop an approach for smart software re-deployments in IoT systems and the self-adaptation of the system architecture in response to dynamic events detected by system sensors. We propose four sub-objectives: i) to provide a mechanism to smart redeploy and orchestrate software in a distributed architecture IoT systems; ii) to provide a mechanism to monitor and log metrics in IoT systems; iii) to design (or reuse if existing) strategies to self-adapt the IoT system architecture when a deployment failure or event is detected by system sensors; and iv) to validate our approach by simulating a realistic case study and evaluating the response to the dynamic events addressed.

In order to achieve these goals, we define three research questions and two sub-questions: (1) How to take intelligent allocation decisions to redeploy and orchestrate software containers in distributed architecture IoT systems? (1.a) Which metrics should be analyzed to make intelligent allocation to software re-deployment? (1.b) How to implement deployment patterns in a distributed architecture IoT systems? (2) How to adapt the architecture of an IoT system

[1] https://kubernetes.io

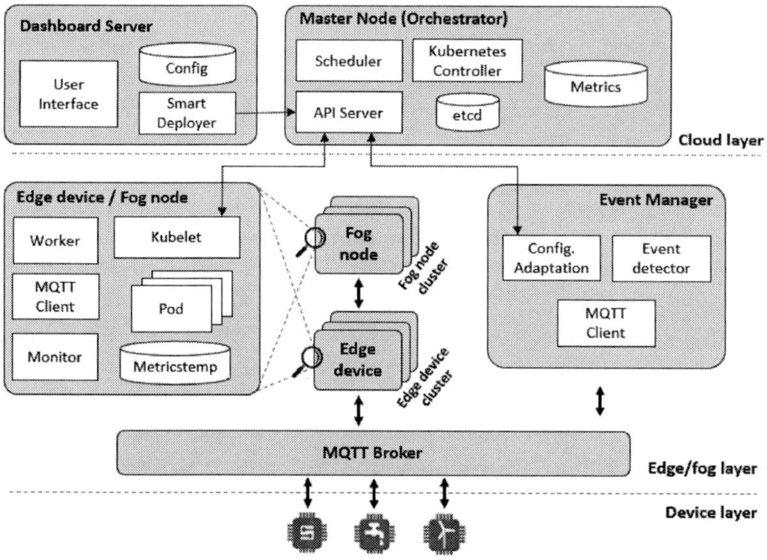

Fig. 1. High level architecture

to ensure QoS in response to dynamic events detected by system sensors? and (3) How to monitor and log service quality metrics for an IoT system?

4 Proposed Solution

We propose an approach that has three main contributions: (1) it allows developers to deploy, manage, and monitor software version deployments on edge/fog layer; (2) suggests intelligent re-deployment decisions after analyzing metrics about node resources consumption and QoS; and (3), analyzes the sensor data to detect dynamic events that induce adaptations in the architecture.

We designed a Kubernetes-based approach to the deployment and orchestration of edge/fog layer devices and nodes. We chose Kubernetes because it is infrastructure-agnostic and allows developers to simplify their DevOps practices by reducing the time spent at integrating with heterogeneous operating environments. The basic control and management unit of Kubernetes is the Pod, which represents the collection of containers and storage (volumes). Figure 1 shows the proposed high-level architecture which is composed of three layers: the device layer contains the sensors and actuators of the system, the edge/fog layer contains devices and nodes to perform tasks on the edge, and the cloud layer contains the deployment orchestrator and the user interface. The main components of the architecture are described in detail below.

Dashboard Server: the *Dasboard Server* provides the user interface and enables the developer or DevOps engineers to perform the following tasks: (1) configure and deploy software versions on the system's edge devices and fog nodes; (2) configure the adaptation rules composed of a stimulus and an action; (3) visualize in real-time the status of the Pods deployed on the nodes. The *Config database* stores the deployment configuration information and the adaptation rules created by the user. When the DevOps engineer configures and runs a new software deployment, *Smart Deployer* component sends the information to the master node to start the deployment. **Master Node (Orchestrator):** the Orchestrator is responsible for the software deployment and the management of resources (nodes). The *Master Node* has the following components: *etcd* is a lightweight, distributed key-value data store that reliably stores cluster configuration data; the *Scheduler* is a component that checks the available infrastructure resources to locate the pods. the *Kubernetes Controller* is a daemon responsible to ensure the desired state of the cluster; the *API Server* is the gateway to the Fog/edge node clusters (this component implements a RESTful API over HTTP); and finally, the *Metrics* component is a time series database responsible for storing the metrics about nodes resources consumption and QoS. We store this information to make an analysis of this data, give valuable feedback to DevOps engineers, and suggest smart re-deployment decisions in future releases.

Edge Device and Fog Node: edge devices and fog nodes make up the node clusters that are managed by the *Master Node*. Each *Edge/fog* node has the following components: The*Kubelet* which connects to the *APIServer* to synchronize information and execute instructions sent from the *MasterNode*; the *Kubelet* ensures that the containers described by the *MarterNode* are functioning and healthy on each node; the *Monitor* component is responsible for collecting and storing the resource consumption metrics of each Pod in a *Metrics temp* database (a lightweight key-value database to temporarily store the metrics); the *Worker* component periodically stores the metric information from the temp database in the Metrics database of the cloud layer; and the *MQTTClient* component is a client capable of interacting with MQTT servers through the publish/subscribe pattern.

MQTT Broker: the *MQTT Broker* is the communication bridge between the device layer devices and the edge/fog layer nodes. The MQTT communication protocol is highly used in IoT systems due to the advantages of the publish/subscribe pattern regarding scalability, asynchronism, decoupling between clients, low bandwidth, and power consumption.

Event Manager: the controller component is responsible for applying the adaptation rules defined by the DevOps engineer. An adaptation rule consists of a stimulus and an action. The stimulus can be detected by analyzing sensor data, for example when a temperature sensor exceeds a limit or when a surveillance camera detects movement. The action is the adaptation of the system in response to the stimulus, such as scaling containers on edge devices, stopping the execution of containers, or moving pods from one node to another. The *Event Detector* component analyzes the sensors data to detect dynamic events. When a dynamic event is detected, the *Config Adaptation* component makes the necessary adaptations to the architecture according to the configured adaptation rule.

5 Methodology and Preliminary Results

Our research began with an exploratory stage, in which we conducted a systematic literature review to understand the needs and challenges in the operation of IoT systems. The SLR is based on the methodology proposed by Kitcheham et al. [6], and it consists of six main steps (planing, search process, inclusion and exclusion criteria, study quality assessment, data collection, and data analysis). For the development stage, we use the Design Science Research methodology (DSR) [8] which has as a fundamental block the design, construction, and evaluation of artifacts. Following the DSR methodology, we designed an initial approach for semi-automating deployment, monitoring and visualization of the impact of software updates on edge devices of the IoT system. We used Docker as the containerization technology and designed an orchestrator to manage software version deployments. We monitored the availability and consumption of computer resources of the edge devices and stored the information in a time-series database. The historical information monitored is presented to the user through metric-centered visualizations. Finally, we experimentally validated our first development using a prototype of an IoT temperature monitoring system and presented the work at MODELS Conference 2019 [12]. After analyzing the results obtained with the first approach, we redesigned the architecture proposed to use Kubernetes because of the advantages in automating the deployment of software, orchestration, and management of distributed systems. We added the components needed to monitor the system, analyze the monitoring data to suggest re-deployment decisions, and make self-adaptations to the architecture. Currently, we are in the construction stage of the software components of the architecture. Shortly, we plan to evaluate the artifacts by making a case study that experimentally validates the built prototypes. After analyzing these results, we will make the necessary adjustments and improvements incrementally until obtaining the expected results.

6 Conclusion and Future Work

We presented an approach for software deployments on IoT systems with a distributed architecture that monitors operation and self-adapts the system architecture. We propose the use of Kubernetes as a tool for deployment and orchestration in edge/fog layer devices and nodes. Pods and containers are periodically monitored and its metrics are logged to analyze them and make intelligent software re-deployment decisions. Our approach allows configuring adaptive rules to support dynamic events detected by system sensors.

Future work is devoted to the development and validation of the architecture components. In particular, the *Config Adaptation* and *Smart deployer* are the components that make the adaptations in the architecture to maintain or improve the QoS of the system. Additionally, we will perform the validation using the test scenarios for the identified case study.

References

1. Ahmadighohandizi, F., Systä, K.: Application development and deployment for iot devices. In: European Conference on Service-Oriented and Cloud Computing. pp. 74–85. Springer (2016)
2. Ashton, K., et al.: That 'internet of things' thing. RFID journal **22**(7), 97–114 (2009)
3. Giang, N.K., Lea, R., Blackstock, M., Leung, V.C.: Fog at the edge: Experiences building an edge computing platform. In: 2018 IEEE International Conference on Edge Computing (EDGE). pp. 9–16. IEEE (2018)
4. Hung, M.: Leading the iot, gartner insights on how to lead in a connected world. Gartner Research pp. 1–29 (2017)
5. Jiang, Y., Huang, Z., Tsang, D.H.: Challenges and solutions in fog computing orchestration. IEEE Network **32**(3), 122–129 (2017)
6. Kitchenham, B., Brereton, O.P., Budgen, D., Turner, M., Bailey, J., Linkman, S.: Systematic literature reviews in software engineering–a systematic literature review. Information and software technology **51**(1), 7–15 (2009)
7. Lwakatare, L.E., Karvonen, T., Sauvola, T., Kuvaja, P., Olsson, H.H., Bosch, J., Oivo, M.: Towards devops in the embedded systems domain: Why is it so hard? In: 2016 49th hawaii international conference on system sciences (hicss). pp. 5437–5446. IEEE (2016)
8. March, S.T., Smith, G.F.: Design and natural science research on information technology. Decision support systems **15**(4), 251–266 (1995)
9. Morabito, R., Beijar, N.: A framework based on sdn and containers for dynamic service chains on iot gateways. In: Proceedings of the Workshop on Hot Topics in Container Networking and Networked Systems. pp. 42–47. ACM (2017)
10. Motta, R.C., de Oliveira, K.M., Travassos, G.H.: On challenges in engineering iot software systems. In: Proceedings of the XXXII Brazilian Symposium on Software Engineering. pp. 42–51 (2018)
11. Nguyen, P., Ferry, N., Erdogan, G., Song, H., Lavirotte, S., Tigli, J.Y., Solberg, A.: Advances in deployment and orchestration approaches for iot-a systematic review. In: 2019 IEEE International Congress on Internet of Things (ICIOT). pp. 53–60. IEEE (2019)
12. Prens, D., Alfonso, I., Garcés, K., Guerra-Gomez, J.: Continuous delivery of software on iot devices. In: 2019 ACM/IEEE 22nd International Conference on Model Driven Engineering Languages and Systems Companion (MODELS-C). pp. 734–735. IEEE (2019)
13. Santos, J., Wauters, T., Volckaert, B., De Turck, F.: Resource provisioning in fog computing: From theory to practice. Sensors **19**(10), 2238 (2019)
14. Wang, J., Pan, J., Esposito, F.: Elastic urban video surveillance system using edge computing. In: Proceedings of the Workshop on Smart Internet of Things. p. 7. ACM (2017)
15. Yigitoglu, E., Mohamed, M., Liu, L., Ludwig, H.: Foggy: a framework for continuous automated iot application deployment in fog computing. In: 2017 IEEE International Conference on AI & Mobile Services (AIMS). pp. 38–45. IEEE (2017)
16. Young, R., Fallon, S., Jacob, P.: A governance architecture for self-adaption & control in iot applications. In: 2018 5th International Conference on Control, Decision and Information Technologies (CoDIT). pp. 241–246. IEEE (2018)

A Test Strategy for Configurable Software Systems Using Machine Learning

Fischer Ferreira

Federal University of Minas Gerais
Belo Horizonte, Minas Gerais, Brazil
fischerjf@dcc.ufmg.br

Abstract. Configurable software systems are software systems that can be adapted or configured according to a set of features to increase reuse and productivity. The testing process is essential because configurations that fail may potentially hurt user experience and degrade the reputation of a project. However, testing configurable systems is very challenging due to the number of configurations to run with each test, leading to a combinatorial explosion in the number of configurations and tests. Currently, several testing techniques and tools have been proposed to deal with this challenge, but their potential practical application remains largely unexplored. Our main goal is to investigate test strategies for configurable systems and provide a method to improve the approaches presented in the literature. To achieve this goal, we divided our work into seven steps. We conducted a systematic mapping study for understanding the state-of-the-art testing approaches for configurable systems. We are also proposing a dataset with 30 configurable software systems, an extensive test suite, failures found, and source code metrics. Furthermore, we performed a comparative study with test tools from different strategies. Finally, we introduce a new test strategy for configurable systems. At the moment, we have a prototype tool to support our test strategy for configurable systems. In future purposes, we want to evaluate the efficacy and efficiency of our approach to observing known failures. The preliminary results of the work indicate that testing configurable software systems is an interesting research topic with many opportunities and gaps in the literature. A method that benefits from metrics extracted from the source code of the configurable system could be a promising approach. We believe that our approach can better the efficiency and efficiencies of the state-of-the-art testing tools for configurable systems.

Keywords: Testing Configurable Systems · Machine Learning

1 Introduction

Configurable systems are software systems that can be adapted or configured according to a set of features (configuration options). Configurable systems offer numerous options to fit specific customer needs [18], and developers may activate or deactivate options to address a diversity of deployment contexts and usages.

To ensure that all configurations correctly compile, build, and run, developers usually spend considerable effort testing their systems because configurations that fail may hurt potential users, and degrade the reputation of a project [8].

Software testing is a key component for ensuring that all configurations work properly. However, testing configurable systems is more challenging than testing monolithic systems. While in monolithic software systems there is only one configuration, for configurable systems we need to run all tests in several different configurations, which leads to a combinatorial explosion of configurations and tests. Therefore, testing thoroughly, against all configurations, is a cost practice. Alternatively, a popular strategy used in industry is to run the tests for a default configuration. This approach is efficient, but it can miss bugs [7, 14].

Besides those two cases (testing only the default configuration or exhaustively testing all configurations), several approaches for testing configurable systems have been proposed [13, 15, 17]. Some of them consider only the Feature Model (FM)[1] [10–12] in order to generate products to be tested (Combinatorial Interaction Testing). However, they may explore configurations not reached by tests. Other approaches [17] take the code (test or app) into account in addition to FM, and dynamically explore all reachable configurations from a given test. However, such dynamic techniques only explore configurations related to testing. Even with a large number of testing techniques and tools for configurable systems [15, 17], their potential practical application remains mostly unexplored. We still lack a deeper understanding of the effectiveness of test strategies for configurations systems for finding failures in the configurable system with a test suite.

This paper presents a proposal for a Ph.D. thesis in Computer Science. Our main goal is to provide more effective strategies for testing configurable software systems. For this purpose, we designed seven study steps including systematic mapping study on detection of test strategies for configurable software systems, empirical investigation of detection strategies, proposing a dataset with 30 configurable software systems, a comparative study with test tools from different approaches, the definition of a new test strategy and implementation of this strategy. Finally, in future purposes, we want to evaluate the efficacy and efficiency of our approach to observing known failures. Additionally, we report the main results achieved with the study.

2 Background

2.1 Variability Encoding Overview

Configurable systems have long been studied by the software product line engineering community [16] and represent a configurable set of systems that share a common, managed set of options (or features) to address specific needs. Among the strategies to introduce variability in software systems, variability encoding has drawn practitioners' attention since developers only need to *annotate*

[1] The *Feature Model* defines valid feature combinations or configurations.

variation points on their existing systems. Thus, developers simply activate or deactivate features to address different deployment contexts. For short, while annotating variation points, developers should create a configuration file where they determine options that are going to be active in a target variation.

Listing 1 presents a fragment of source code in a configurable systems named Companies. In this example, the method *getTotal* returns a string containing a calculated value. If the feature TOTAL_WALKER is active, the method returns the value calculated by the TotalWalker class. If the feature TOTAL_REDUCER is active, the method returns the value calculated by the TotalReducer class. On the other hand, if the features TOTAL_WALKER and TOTAL_REDUCER are not active, no value will be calculated.

```
public String getTotal() {
    String value = "";
    if (Configuration.TOTAL_WALKER) {
        TotalWalker walker = new TotalWalker();
        walker.postorder(currentValue);
        value = Double.toString(walker.getTotal());
    } else if (Configuration.TOTAL_REDUCER) {
        TotalReducer total = new TotalReducer();
        double valueDouble = total.reduce(currentValue);
        value = Double.toString(valueDouble);
    }
    return value;
}
```

Listing 1.1. Variability Encoding Example

2.2 Testing Configurable Systems

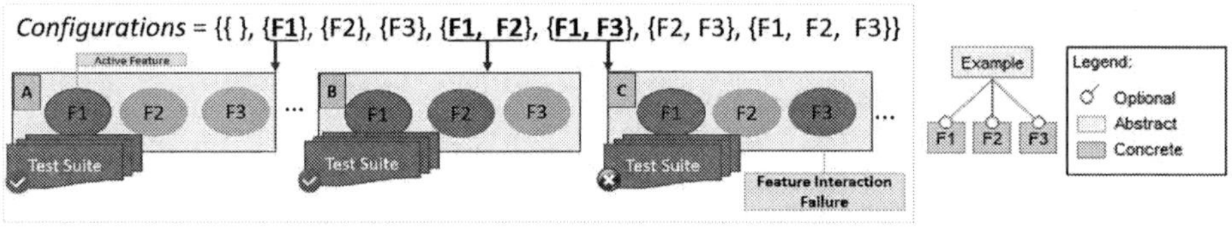

Fig. 1. Feature Interaction Failure

A major challenge for developers of configurable systems is to ensure that all configurations correctly compile, build, and run. Even when each feature performs well individually, interactions among them are prone to happen and introduce unexpected behavior to the system [2]. Feature interaction is a well-known problem for configurable systems and enforces the need for test suites covering all potential feature interactions. Figure 1 presents an example of 3 features of an illustrative configurable system and all the possibilities of combining the three features. In addition, Figure 1 shows the A, B, and C configurations submitted to the test suite. We see that both F1 and F3 features are active in the C configuration and that the test suite reports failure. However, the test suite does not find failures for configurations A and B. The interaction between the F1 and F3 features causes the feature interaction failure. Above a certain amount of features, it is infeasible to test all possible feature combinations. This way, researchers and practitioners have to choose somehow the configurations they want to test. However, it is not trivial to know which priority configuration.

3 The Proposed Approach

This Ph.D. project aims to provide more effective strategies for testing configurable software systems. Therefore, the goal of this research is:

To evaluate testing strategies in the context of testing configurable systems in the perception of software developers and researchers with expertise in software testing to propose a new test strategy for configurable systems.

To achieve this goal, we propose a seven step research design (Figure 2). We discuss each study step as follows.

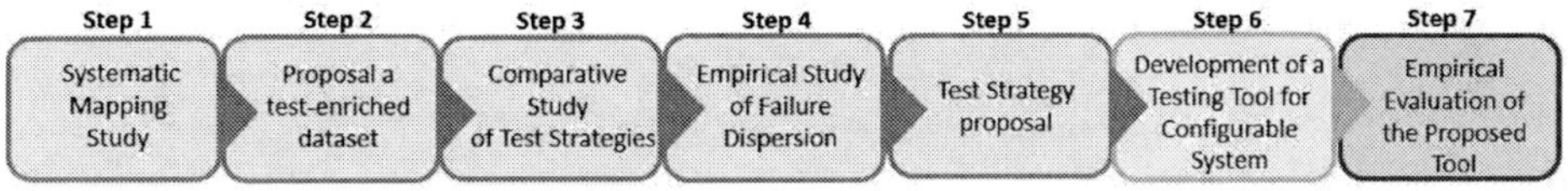

Fig. 2. Study Steps

Step 1: We performed a Systematic Mapping Study [5] to survey the literature on test strategies for configurable systems. Our goal was to identify and analyze tools reported and used in the literature for testing configurable software systems. This step provided state-of-the-art testing tools for configurable systems.

Step 2: We designed a dataset composed of 30 configurable systems with extensive test suite [6]. The goal was to establish a standardized dataset for executing and comparing test strategies for configurable systems. As a contribution, we provided the research community with the first dataset for configurable systems with an extensive test suite and reported feature interaction failures.

Step 3: We evaluated testing tools in two comparative studies. In the first study [5], we conducted a comparative study to evaluate two testing tools found (VarexJ and SPLat). We decided to focus our research on tools that implements dynamic testing techniques, that is, to test all possible configurations of the configurable software systems. In the second study, we designed and performed a comparative empirical study of four state-of-the-art combinatorial interaction testing tools (IncLing [1], ICPL [11], Chvatal [10], and Random [4]). This strategy uses techniques to test only a representative subset of all possible configurations.

Step 4: We investigated the dispersion of failures found by the test suites over the dataset subjects. To support our analysis, we identified classes and features in each system with at least one failure.

Step 5: We are working on a machine learning algorithm to support the identification of priority configurations for testing. Based on software metrics, a machine learning based strategy provides the capability of understanding the properties present on the configurable systems (CS), and based on them, it performs failure detection. Figure 3 presents the steps in the proposed method divided into two main parts Model Building and Model Application.

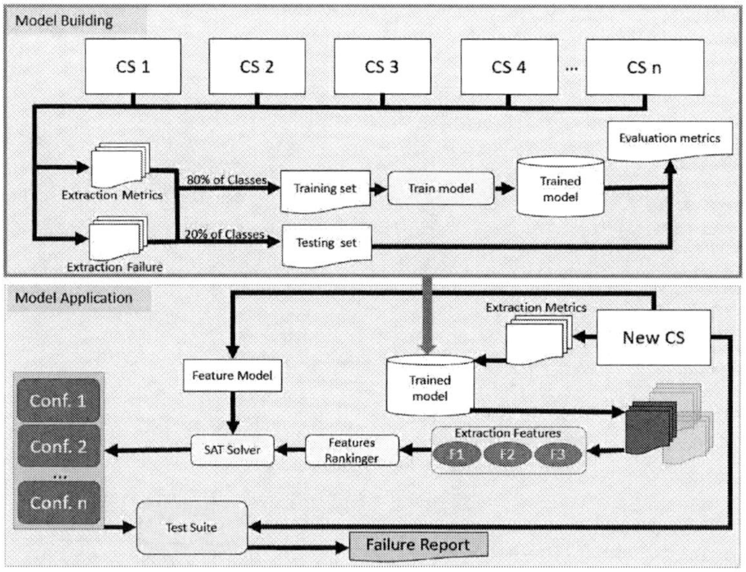

Fig. 3. Proposed Strategy

Model Building: The model building demonstrates the training part of our model using a machine learning algorithm (classifier). Each instance is formed by a set of metrics (Extraction Metrics) and a label (Extraction Failure) to be predicted 1 or 0 indicating the occurrence or not of the failure, respectively.
Model Application: Using the trained model, it is possible to discover the classes of the configurable system source code that are prone to failures. Once we discover these parts of the source code, it is possible to determine the related active features. Using a SAT Solver, we will assemble all the configurations in which the features are present. Finally, for these configurations found, we submit the test suite.

Step 6: We plan to integrate our tool with FeatureIDE. FeatureIDE is an Eclipse-based IDE that supports all phases of the development of configurable systems [19].

Step 7: After the development of our testing strategies in Step 6, we can conduct experiments to evaluate the effectiveness and efficiency of our approach to finding failure in configurable systems.

The steps 1 to 5 (colored in green in Figure 2) have been completed. We are currently executing step 6, the development of a testing tool for configurable systems (colored in yellow in Figure 2). Step 7 (colored in red in Figure 2) is related to the evaluation of the proposed test strategy and tool. Therefore, this final step is scheduled to be executed after step 6 is complete.

4 Preliminary Results

In Step 1, we conducted a Systematic Mapping Study [5] on testing tools for configurable systems. We obtained a set of 34 tools. We defined these characteristics based on previous studies: graphical user interface, prototype, online, plugin, free for use, open-source, user guide available, solution examples available, supported language, tested, code level test, feature model check, feature interaction, and tool Web site. We also compared tools in terms of test strategies. We found the following test strategies for configurable systems in the analyzed papers. Sound Testing Techniques is used to test all possible configurations of the configurable software systems. Combinatorial Interaction Testing uses techniques to test only a representative subset of all possible configurations.

In Step 2, we first proposed a test-enriched dataset with 30 configurable software systems. This dataset was created based on a literature review and further implementation of test suites to improve code coverage. We created 727 test cases for 20 configurable systems and further 90 tests for the three systems that we extended. Our dataset has a total of 3 182 tests. As means for quality assurance, we created tests until the have a coverage of 70% and kill at least 40% of mutants. The final dataset has 30 systems varying in domains, size, variability, and test suite size. We are confident that this dataset will benefit practitioners and also be useful for researchers comparing testing approaches and methods.

In Step 3, we observed that VarexJ and SPLat presented distinct results for efficiency while testing the target systems. VarexJ found more errors than SPLat for the majority of the target systems. In the second part of our study, we also conducted a comparative study of tools (IncLing [4], ICPL [11], Chvatal [10], and Random [4]) to compute recall, precision, and F-measure.

In Step 4, our failure report shows that 254 failures occurred in 151 different configurations, and that 70 test cases failed. All failures that we found involve more than one feature, so, we call them feature interaction failures. In addition, 14 out of the 30 systems of our test-enriched dataset have failures. Our analysis of the dispersion of failures shows that in 11 of the 14 systems that failed, all failures are in the same class. In other words, feature interaction failures are normally concentrated in one (or few) class(es) of configurable systems. We hope that this failure report and these preliminary analyses support practitioners on understanding the failures that happen in their systems.

5 Related Work

Many approaches have been proposed in the literature to test configurable systems [15, 17]. Some approaches generate configurations for testing, considering only the feature model [15]. Other strategies implement a dynamic technique that explores all reachable configurations from a given test [17]. Our method ranks software components identified priority configurations for testing. Some approaches in the literature that use machine learning techniques to prioritize configurations for testing configurable systems consider only the Feature Model [3]. However, the main difference regarding our approach is that through our machine learning, we can find the priority points in the source code for testing, and we discover configurable that manipulate these components of the source code. Other strategies use software metrics and machine learning to identify failures in monolithic systems [9]. We propose to use the technique to detect failures in configurable systems. We expect that this approach is useful for testing configuration systems with greater efficiency and efficiency than state-of-the-art.

6 Conclusion and Future Work

This paper presents a proposal for a Ph.D. thesis in Computer Science that focuses on the test strategy for configurable systems. We aim to introduce new test strategies with machine learning algorithms to support the identification of priority configurations for testing, in the expectation of proposing a test strategy with greater effectiveness and efficiency than the tools present in the literature. We present an overview of the thesis and also discuss some preliminary results of previous studies. As future work, we intend to conclude the last study steps, publish the study results as papers for the community, complete the study in parallel with Step 6 and Step 7, and finish this Ph.D.'s in March 2021 with the thesis defense.

References

1. Al-Hajjaji, M., Krieter, S., Thüm, T., Lochau, M., Saake, G.: Incling: Efficient product-line testing using incremental pairwise sampling. In: Proceedings of the 2016 ACM SIGPLAN International Conference on Generative Programming: Concepts and Experiences. pp. 144–155. GPCE 2016, ACM, New York, NY, USA (2016). https://doi.org/10.1145/2993236.2993253, http://doi.acm.org/10.1145/2993236.2993253
2. Apel, S., Kolesnikov, S., Siegmund, N., Kästner, C., Garvin, B.: Exploring feature interactions in the wild: The new feature-interaction challenge. In: In 5th International Workshop on Feature-Oriented Software Development (FOSD). pp. 1–8 (2013)
3. Devroey, X., Perrouin, G., Cordy, M., Samih, H., Legay, A., Schobbens, P., Heymans, P.: Statistical prioritization for software product line testing: an experience report. Software & Systems Modeling (SSM) pp. 153–171 (2017)
4. FeatureIDE: featureide tool, https://featureide.github.io/, Accessed 15-nov-2019
5. Ferreira, F., Diniz, J.P., Silva, C., Figueiredo, E.: Testing tools for configurable software systems: A review-based empirical study. In: Proceedings of the 13th International Workshop on Variability Modelling of Software-Intensive Systems. pp. 1–10 (2019)
6. Ferreira, F., Vale, G., Figueiredo, E., Diniz, J.P.: On the proposal and evaluation of a test-enriched dataset for configurable systems. In: Proceedings of the 14th

International Working Conference on Variability Modelling of Software-Intensive Systems. pp. 1–10. VAMOS '20 (2020)
7. Greiler, M., Deursen, A.v., Storey, M.A.: Test confessions: A study of testing practices for plug-in systems. In: Proceedings of the International Conference on Software Engineering. pp. 244–254. IEEE (2012)
8. Halin, A., Nuttinck, A., Acher, M., Devroey, X., Perrouin, G., Baudry, B.: Test them all, is it worth it? assessing configuration sampling on the jhipster web development stack. Empirical Software Engineering (ESE) pp. 674–717 (2019)
9. Jiang, Y., Cuki, B., Menzies, T., Bartlow, N.: Comparing design and code metrics for software quality prediction. In: Proceedings of the 4th international workshop on Predictor models in software engineering. pp. 11–18 (2008)
10. Johansen, M.F., Haugen, Ø., Fleurey, F.: Properties of realistic feature models make combinatorial testing of product lines feasible. In: 14th International Conference on Model Driven Engineering Languages and Systems (MODELS). pp. 638–652 (2011)
11. Johansen, M.F., Haugen, Ø., Fleurey, F., Eldegard, A.G., Syversen, T.: Generating better partial covering arrays by modeling weights on sub-product lines. In: International Conference on Model Driven Engineering Languages and Systems. pp. 269–284. Springer (2012)
12. Krieter, M., T., S.T., Saake, L.M., Al-Hajjaji, G.: Incling: efficient product-line testing using incremental pairwise sampling. In: 15th Proceedings of the ACM SIGPLAN International Conference on Generative Programming: Concepts and Experiences (GPCE). pp. 144–155 (2016)
13. Liebig, J., von Rhein, A., Kästner, C., Apel, S., Dörre, J., Lengauer, C.: Scalable analysis of variable software. In: Proceedings of the Foundations of Software Engineering. pp. 81–91. ACM (2013)
14. Machado, I., McGregor, J., Cavalcanti, Y., Almeida, E.: On strategies for testing software product lines: A systematic literature review. Information and Software Technology (IST) pp. 1183 – 1199 (2014)
15. Medeiros, F., Kästner, C., Ribeiro, M., Gheyi, R., Apel, S.: A comparison of 10 sampling algorithms for configurable systems. In: Proceedings of the International Conference on Software Engineering. pp. 643–654. ACM (2016)
16. Pohl, K., Metzger, A.: Software product line testing. Information and Software Technology (IST) pp. 78–81 (2006)
17. Souto, S., d'Amorim, M., Gheyi, R.: Balancing soundness and efficiency for practical testing of configurable systems. In: In 39th Proceedings of the International Conference on Software Engineering (ICSE). pp. 632–642 (2017)
18. Svahnberg, M., Van Gurp, J., Bosch, J.: A taxonomy of variability realization techniques. Software: Practice and experience (SPE) pp. 705–754 (2005)
19. Thüm, T., Kästner, C., Benduhn, F., Meinicke, J., Saake, G., Leich, T.: Featureide: An extensible framework for feature-oriented software development. Science of Computer Programming (SCP) pp. 70–85 (2014)